THE OXFORD HANDI

THE HISTORY OF
INTERNATIONAL LAW

THE OXFORD HANDBOOK OF

THE HISTORY OF INTERNATIONAL LAW

Edited by

BARDO FASSBENDER

and

ANNE PETERS

Assistant Editors

SIMONE PETER
DANIEL HÖGGER

OXFORD
UNIVERSITY PRESS

OXFORD
UNIVERSITY PRESS

Great Clarendon Street, Oxford, OX2 6DP,
United Kingdom

Oxford University Press is a department of the University of Oxford.
It furthers the University's objective of excellence in research, scholarship,
and education by publishing worldwide. Oxford is a registered trade mark of
Oxford University Press in the UK and in certain other countries

© Oxford University Press 2012

The moral rights of the authors have been asserted

First Edition published in 2012
First published in paperback 2014

Published in the United States of America by Oxford University Press
198 Madison Avenue, New York, NY 10016, United States of America

British Library Cataloguing in Publication Data
Data available

Library of Congress Cataloging in Publication Data
Data available

ISBN 978-0-19-872522-0

PREFACE

....

On 17 October 1724, Ahmed III, Sultan of the Ottoman Empire, granted an audience to the French Ambassador Vicomte d'Andrezel whom he received in the Topkapı Palace in Constantinople. A French contemporary painter, Jean Baptiste van Mour (1671–1737), depicted the meeting in a beautifully carpeted and decorated red room, showing the sultan on his throne surrounded by a large group of officials which almost encircle the foreigners who appear rather small besides the Ottomans with their high hats. This sumptuous scene, reproduced on the jacket of the hardback edition of this Handbook, might not be visible to all readers of the book in public or university libraries. The original oil painting *Réception de l'Ambassadeur de France, le vicomte d'Andrezel, par le Sultan Ahmed III, le 17 octobre 1724, à Constantinople* can be seen in the Musée des Beaux-Arts (Museum of Fine Arts) of Bordeaux.

We chose this picture for the jacket because it illustrates one of the objectives of this Handbook, namely to explore the history of encounters between political and economic actors rooted in different legal cultures which gave rise to the emergence of what we now call 'international law'. Vicomte d'Andrezel was by far not the first French ambassador in Constantinople. Diplomatic relations between the Sultan and the French King had been entertained since 1536, and at the time of our scene the 'union of the lily and the crescent' was firmly established.[1] A historian commented that such meetings between Sultans or Grand Viziers and foreign ambassadors 'appeared to be a collision between two worlds; they wore different costumes, spoke different languages and followed different religions. In reality, through their respective interpreters they spoke a common language of power, profit and monarchy.'[2] One of the central questions of this Handbook is whether they also spoke a common legal language.

Sadly, three authors are no longer with us to see their contribution in print. Peter Krüger (1935–2011) was professor of modern history at the University of Marburg. His research focused on the history of international relations, the history of ideas, and constitutional history. A leading expert in the history of the interwar period, he wrote the chapter 'From the Paris Peace Treaties to the End of the Second World War'. Despite illness, he participated actively in our Interlaken workshop in January 2011 where first drafts of the contributions were discussed among the authors and editors.

Antonio Cassese (1937–2011) was an outstanding international lawyer who combined a career as a university professor with membership in important UN bodies and work as an international judge. From 1993 to 2000, he was the first President (1993–97) and a presiding judge (1998–2000) of the International Criminal Tribunal for the former Yugoslavia. In

---

[1] P Mansel 'Art and Diplomacy in Ottoman Constantinople' (1996) 46(8) History Today 43–49, at 44.
[2] Ibid at 45.

2004, he chaired the UN International Commission of Enquiry into Violations of Human Rights and Humanitarian Law in Darfur. From 2009 to 2011, he was President of the Special Tribunal for Lebanon. Notwithstanding his immense workload, he did not hesitate a minute when we asked him to write the chapter 'States: Rise and Decline of the Primary Subjects of the International Community' for this Handbook.

David J Bederman (1961–2011) was the K H Gyr Professor in Private International Law at Emory University, Atlanta. Prior to coming to Emory, he practised law in Washington, DC, and worked as a legal adviser at the Iran/United States Claims Tribunal at The Hague. Professor Bederman published extensively on diverse legal topics, including legal history, constitutional law, international legal theory and practice, and the law of the sea. His chapter 'The Sea' in this Handbook combines a number of his areas of expertise.

We mourn the passing of our friends and colleagues. We are grateful for their important contributions to this work and will remember them as superb legal scholars and wonderful human beings.

This project would have been impossible without the generous funding by several institutions: the *Schweizerische Nationalfonds* (Swiss National Science Foundation), the Swiss Federal Department of Foreign Affairs, the *Freiwillige Akademische Gesellschaft* (Basel), the *Gerda Henkel Stiftung* (Düsseldorf), the Jacobs Foundation (Zurich), and the *Stiftung zur Förderung der rechtlichen und wirtschaftlichen Forschung an der Universität Basel*.

We could not have handled the great number of manuscripts published in the present work, could not have kept track of virtually hundreds of emails which we exchanged with our authors, and could not have organized the very fruitful Interlaken workshop without the diligent work of the assistant editors Simone Peter and Daniel Högger: Thank you very much! Simone also lent invaluable assistance to the development of the concept of the Handbook, in particular its global history approach.

It was a difficult task to make the manuscripts, and especially the footnotes, conform to the editorial rules of the publisher. This task has been skillfully accomplished by our student research assistants Lilian Buchmann and Madeleine Schreiner in Basel, and Konstantin Seliverstov in Munich. Further, our special thanks go to the senior research assistants Anja Kiessling, Carolin König und Iris Ludwig in Munich, who contributed to the editorial work and to Claudia Jeker in Basel for her unwawering support and dedication in all respects. John Louth and Merel Alstein from Oxford University Press gave advice and support to the project right from the start.

We finally most sincerely wish to thank, once more, our authors: It is a banal but nevertheless true statement that without you the present volume could not have come into existence. We are grateful for your hard work, your enthusiasm and your patience. We hope that you are satisfied with what we achieved together.

Munich and Basel, July 2012
Bardo Fassbender and Anne Peters

Contents

PART I: ACTORS

PART II: THEMES

PART III: REGIONS

PART IV: INTERACTION OR IMPOSITION

PART V: METHODOLOGY AND THEORY

PART VI: PEOPLE IN PORTRAIT

Table of Instruments

International Jurisdictions

International Arbitrations

League of Nations Council

Permanent Court of International Justice

International Court of Justice

International Criminal Tribunal for the former Yugoslavia

UN Human Rights Committee

NATIONAL AND REGIONAL JURISDICTIONS

European Court of Human Rights

India

United Kingdom

United States of America

TABLE OF INSTRUMENTS

Treaties

UN SECONDARY SOURCES

NATIONAL LEGISLATION

Canada

France

Germany

Haiti

Netherlands

New Zealand

Russia

Spain

Switzerland

United Kingdom

United States of America

Notes on the Contributors

Kinji Akashi is Professor of International Law at Keio University, Japan. He holds a PhD from the University of Utrecht (1996).

Joaquín Alcaide Fernández is Professor of Public International Law and International Relations at University of Seville (Spain). He has published extensively on terrorism, human rights and humanitarian law, State and criminal responsibility, peace and security, law of the sea and environment.

Antony Anghie is the Samuel D Thurman Professor of Law at the University of Utah, where he teaches various subjects in the international law curriculum including public international law, international business transactions, and international environmental law. His research interests include the history and theory of international law, globalization, human rights, law and development, and Third World approaches to international law.

Mashood A Baderin, LLB (Hons) (Shari'ah and common law), BL (Barrister and Solicitor of the Supreme Court of Nigeria), LLM (public international law), PhD (international human rights and Islamic law), is Professor of Law and head of the School of Law, School of Oriental and African Studies (SOAS), University of London.

Upendra Baxi is Emeritus Professor of Law University of Warwick and Delhi; he served as the Vice Chancellor of Delhi University. He has written extensively on comparative constitutionalism, social theory of human rights, the emergent 'post-human', and approaches to global justice.

Arnulf Becker Lorca is a visiting faculty member at the International Relations Program, Brown University. His research examines the history of international law from the point of view of the non-Western regions of the world.

David J Bederman (1961–2011) was the K H Gyr Professor in Private International Law at Emory University, Atlanta. He wrote extensively on the substantive doctrines of the law of the sea and the management of international common resources, as well as the theory and history of international law. Prior to coming to Emory, he practised law in Washington, DC, and worked as a legal adviser at the Iran/United States Claims Tribunal at The Hague.

David S Berry is the Dean of the Faculty of Law of the University of the West Indies, Cave Hill Campus (Barbados), and teaches and practises in the areas of public international law and Caribbean regional integration law.

Armin von Bogdandy is Director at the Max Planck Institute for Comparative Public Law and International Law (MPIL), Heidelberg, and Professor of Law at the Goethe University, Frankfurt.

Annabel Brett is Senior Lecturer in History at the University of Cambridge and Fellow of Gonville & Caius College, Cambridge. She has published extensively in the history of natural law and natural rights in the early modern period.

Anthony Carty holds the Sir Y K Pao Chair of Public Law at the Faculty of Law of the University of Hong Kong. He took his PhD in Cambridge under the supervision of Clive Parry from 1969 to 1972. He was a Lecturer and Senior Lecturer at the Universities of Edinburgh and Glasgow before going on to hold chairs in Derby, Westminster, Aberdeen, and Hong Kong.

Antonio Cassese (1937–2011) was Professor of International Law at the University of Florence and a member of the *Institut de Droit International*. He was the first President of the Council of Europe Committee for the Prevention of Torture, the first President (1993–97) and presiding judge (1998–2000) of the International Criminal Tribunal for the former Yugoslavia, the Chairperson of the UN International Commission of Enquiry into Violations of Human Rights and Humanitarian Law in Darfur (2004), and the President of the Special Tribunal for Lebanon (2009–11).

Georg Cavallar, *Universitätsdozent* of Modern History at the Department of History, University of Vienna, Austria, has published on Kant's political philosophy, the history of international law, and the philosophy of cosmopolitanism.

Ken Coates is Professor of History at the University of Waterloo. He has studied Indigenous legal history and contemporary Aboriginal rights in the former British colonies.

Matthew Craven is Professor of International Law and Director of the Centre for the Study of Colonialism, Empire and International Law at the School of Oriental and African Studies, University of London. His current research interests lie in the field of international legal history and legal theory, focusing in particular on the themes of imperialism, colonialism, and decolonization.

Sergio Dellavalle is Professor of State Theory at the University of Turin.

Oliver Diggelmann is Professor of Public International Law and Constitutional Law at the University of Zurich, Switzerland. His areas of focus include theory and history of international law, legal philosophy, and comparative constitutional law.

Seymour Drescher is a scholar of slavery and abolition. He is Distinguished University Professor of History at the University of Pittsburgh.

Heinz Duchhardt studied in Mainz, Bonn, and Vienna, took his PhD (Dr. phil.) in 1968 and finished his habilitation in 1974. He was full Professor of Early Modern and Modern History, respectively, at Bayreuth and Munster Universities, and Director of the Institute of European History Mainz from 1994 to 2011.

Abdelmalek El Ouazzani is University Professor and Doctor of Political Sciences at the University Caddi Ayyad, Faculty of Law, Marrakech, Morocco, as well as co-Director of the *Laboratoire de Recherche sur la Coopération Internationale pour le Développement*

(Laboratory of Research in the Development of International Cooperation) and the research unit connected to the National Centre for Scientific Research (URAC59).

Jorge L Esquirol is Professor of Law at Florida International University in Miami. He writes in the areas of comparative law, legal theory, and law and development in Latin America. He has a JD (1989) and an SJD (2001) from Harvard Law School, and a BSBA (1986) in finance from Georgetown University.

Arthur Eyffinger is classicist and legal historian. He published extensively on the life and works of Hugo Grotius, on the history of The Hague tradition of international law, and The Hague international courts and institutions.

Bardo Fassbender is Professor of International Law, European Law and Public Law at the University of St. Gallen, Switzerland. He holds an LLM from Yale Law School and a Doctor iuris from the Humboldt University in Berlin. His principal fields of research are international law, United Nations law, comparative constitutional law and theory, and the history of international and constitutional law. He is co-editor of the series *Studien zur Geschichte des Völkerrechts* (Studies in the History of International Law).

Paul Finkelman is a historian of slavery, American constitutional history, and the history of American law. He is currently the John Hope Franklin Visiting Professor of American Legal History at Duke Law School; he is also the President William McKinley Distinguished Professor of Law and Public Policy at Albany Law School.

Jörg Fisch is Professor of History at the University of Zurich. His research focuses on the history of international law and international relations.

Andrew Fitzmaurice is Associate Professor of History at the University of Sydney. His research focuses on the intellectual history of European empires.

James Thuo Gathii holds the Wing-Tat Lee Chair in International Law at Loyola Chicago Law School. Previously, he was the Associate Dean for Research and Scholarship and the Governor George E Pataki Professor of International Commercial Law at Albany Law School in New York. His main areas of research, in which he has published widely, are public international law, and international trade and economic law.

Dominique Gaurier is Assistant Professor at the School of Law in Nantes and lectures on the history of international public law. He wrote a handbook on the history of public international law and translated authors of the 16th–18th centuries such as Conrad Braun, Alberico Gentili, Richard Zouche, and Cornelis van Bijnkershoek, from Latin into French.

Knud Haakonssen is Professor Emeritus of Intellectual History at the University of Sussex, and Honorary Professor of History, University College, London. He has published extensively on Enlightenment moral, political, and legal thought.

Peter Haggenmacher is Honorary Professor of the Graduate Institute of International and Development Studies, Geneva, where he taught international law during three decades with special emphasis on its historical and philosophical aspects.

Daniel Högger is PhD candidate and works as Research and Teaching Assistant to the Chair of International Law at the University of Basel. He holds a degree (lic phil/MA) in political science, international law, and history from the University of Zurich, and a degree (MA with distinction) in international studies from the University of Birmingham, UK.

Mark W Janis is William F Starr Professor of Law, University of Connecticut, and Visiting Fellow and Formerly Reader in Law, University of Oxford.

Emmanuelle Jouannet is Professor of International Law at the Sorbonne Law School (University Paris I) where she manages the research programme 'International Law and Justice in a Global World'. Her research focuses on human rights, law of development, theory and history of international law.

Shin Kawashima is Associate Professor of History of International Relations in East Asia at the University of Tokyo.

Daniel-Erasmus Khan is Professor of International Law and European Law at the Bundeswehr University in Munich. His main focus of research is on the international law of territory and a historically oriented analysis of other issues of general international law.

Martin Kintzinger is Professor of Medieval History at the University of Munster, Germany. His main focus of research is on the history of schooling and universities, of international relations and foreign policies, and the history of France in the late Middle Ages.

Pauline Kleingeld is Professor of Philosophy at the University of Groningen, The Netherlands.

Robert Kolb is Professor of Public International Law at the University of Geneva.

Martti Koskenniemi is Academy Professor of International Law at the University of Helsinki and Director of the Erik Castrén Institute of International Law and Human Rights. His present research focuses on the history of international legal thought.

Peter Krüger (1935–2011) was Professor of Modern History at the University of Marburg. His research focused on the history of international relations, the history of ideas, and constitutional history. He was a leading expert in the history of the Paris Peace Treaties of 1919 and the era of the League of Nations.

Randall Lesaffer is Professor of Legal History at Tilburg Law School and part-time Professor of International and European Legal History at Leuven. Since 2008, he serves as the Dean of Tilburg Law School.

Lydia H Liu is the Wun Tsun Tam Professor in the Humanities at Columbia University. She has published extensively on translation theory, media technology, Chinese history and literature, and on the circulation of legal texts among China, Japan, and the West.

Cecelia Lynch is Professor of Political Science at the University of California, Irvine.

Lauri Mälksoo is Professor of International Law at the University of Tartu, Estonia. He has degrees from Tartu (LLB), Georgetown (LLM) and Berlin's Humboldt University (Dr iur). His research focuses on the history and theory of international law and comparative aspects of international law, especially in Eastern Europe.

Janne Nijman is Associate Professor of Public International Law and Senior Research Fellow of the Amsterdam Center for International Law, University of Amsterdam.

Liliana Obregón is Associate Professor of Law at the Universidad de Los Andes, Bogotá, Colombia and was a Postdoctoral Researcher for the 'Research Project Europe 1815–1914' at the University of Helsinki, Finland. She holds a doctoral degree in law (SJD) from Harvard University, a master's degree (MA) in international relations from the School of Advanced International Studies of the Johns Hopkins University, and a law degree from the Universidad de Los Andes.

Mary Ellen O'Connell holds the Robert and Marion Short Chair in Law and is Research Professor of International Dispute Resolution at the Kroc Institute for Peace Studies, University of Notre Dame. Her research areas are international legal theory, international law on the use of force, and dispute resolution.

Umut Özsu is an Assistant Professor at the University of Manitoba, Faculty of Law. His principal research interests lie in public international law, and the history and theory of international law.

Bimal N Patel is Professor and Director (Vice-Chancellor) at the Gujarat National Law University, Gandhinagar, India. He is author and editor of various books, reports, and articles on international law, state practice of India and international law, the International Court of Justice, and law of the Sea.

Simone Peter holds a doctoral degree in law (Dr iur) and a degree in general history and German language (lic phil/MA). She worked as a Research Assistant to the Chair of International Law at the University of Basel from 2006 to 2012. Her research covered the field of general public international law and the history of international law. She currently works as a lawyer in the public administration of Basel-Stadt.

Anne Peters is a Director at the Max-Planck-Institute for Comparative Public Law and Public International Law, Heidelberg (Germany), professor at the universities of Heidelberg and Basel (Switzerland). Her current research covers public international law, especially its constitutionalization, governance, and human rights, and global animal law. She is a co-editor of the *Journal of the History of International Law*.

Cornelis G Roelofsen holds an MA in History from the University of Groningen (1967). He taught public international law and its history at the Utrecht Law Faculty (1967–2010), received his PhD in 1991, and is recipient of the Sarton Medal of Gent University (1998). Since 1991, he is member of the editorial board of Grotiana. Among his main interests are the law of maritime warfare and self-determination.

Fatiha Sahli is University Professor and Doctor of Public Law at the University Caddi Ayyad, Faculty of Law, Marrakech, Morocco as well as Director of the *Laboratoire de Recherche sur la Coopération Internationale pour le Développement* (Laboratory of Research in the Development of International Cooperation) and the research unit connected to the National Centre for Scientific Research (URAC59).

Merio Scattola teaches history of political ideas at the University of Padua. He published monographs and articles on natural law, political theology, and history of political doctrines.

Mathias Schmoeckel is Professor of Civil Law and Legal History at Bonn University. His main research is on the impact of theology on law. He also publishes on the history of international law and changes in law due to the industrial revolution.

Iain Scobbie LLB (Hons) (Edin), LLB (Cantab), GDIL (ANU), PhD (Cantab) is the Sir Joseph Hotung Research Professor in Law, Human Rights and Peace Building in the Middle East at the School of Oriental and African Studies, University of London.

Koen Stapelbroek is an Associate Professor in the History of Political and Administrative Thought at Erasmus University Rotterdam. He received his PhD from Cambridge University and published a monograph (Toronto 2008) and several edited volumes on 18th-century intellectual history.

Chi-hua Tang is Professor of History at National Cheng-chi University in Taipei. He received his PhD from London School of Economics and Political Science (LSE).

Kaius Tuori is a legal historian at the University of Helsinki with research interests in Roman legal history, legal anthropology, and classical archaeology.

Antje von Ungern-Sternberg, a lawyer and historian, is a Senior Research Fellow at the Chair of Public Law and Public International Law, Ludwigs-Maximilian University in Munich. She works on comparative constitutional law, public international law, and law and religion.

Miloš Vec is a jurist (habilitation 2005). He works at the Max Planck Institute for European Legal History in Frankfurt am Main, Germany and teaches at Goethe University. He is co-editor of the series *Studien zur Geschichte des Völkerrechts* (Studies in the History of International Law).

Silja Vöneky is Professor of Public International Law at the University of Freiburg, Germany. Her areas of focus include international humanitarian and environmental law, legal philosophy, and German as well as foreign public law.

Masaharu Yanagihara is Professor of Public International Law at the Kyushu University, Japan. He received his PhD (University of Tokyo) in 1981. He was Visiting Professor at Ludwig-Maximilians University Munich from 2000 to 2001, and at the Catholic University of Leuven in 2002.

INTRODUCTION: TOWARDS A GLOBAL HISTORY OF INTERNATIONAL LAW

BARDO FASSBENDER AND ANNE PETERS

1. 'THE ROAD LESS TRAVELED BY'

WITH this Handbook, we, the editors and authors, tried to depart from what has been aptly described as the 'well-worn paths'[1] of how the history of international law has been written so far—that is, as a history of rules developed in the European state system since the 16th century which then were spread to other continents and eventually the entire globe.[2] It has also been written as a progressive history that in the end would lead to a

---

[1] See the contribution by M Koskenniemi 'A History of International Law Histories' in this volume at 970.

[2] See only F Amerasinghe 'The Historical Development of International Law—Universal Aspects' (2001) 39 Archiv des Völkerrechts 367–93 at 368: '[M]odern international law is linearly derived from earlier developments in the European world and adjacent areas and earlier international relations in other parts of the world, such as China and South Asia had little influence in shaping this law'. Amerasinghe nevertheless pleads for also studying the history of international law outside the European sphere 'as an addendum' (ibid 388).

world governed by the ideals of the Enlightenment, and the American and French Revo-lutions.[3] That history of progress in the name of humanity certainly has its beauty. It provides the history of international law with a clear underlying purpose and direction, and thus gives it a comprehensible structure. But unfortunately, this beauty is false.

The Eurocentric story of international law has proven wrong because it is incom-plete. Not only does it generally ignore the violence, ruthlessness, and arrogance which accompanied the dissemination of Western rules, and the destruction of other legal cultures in which that dissemination resulted. Like most other histories, this history of international law was a history of conquerors and victors, not of the vic-tims. Furthermore, the conventional story ignores too many other experiences and forms of legal relations between autonomous communities developed in the course of history. It even discards such extra-European experiences and forms which were discontinued as a result of domination and colonization by European Powers as irrelevant to a (continuing) history of international law.

To leave a well-worn path is exciting but always risky. It is an adventure as well as an experiment. Leaving the trodden path means meeting unforeseen obstacles. And if one wants to shed light on developments which so far remained in darkness, one better be prepared to encounter the unexpected and not so easily understood. In this sense, the present Handbook is a beginning only. It represents a first step towards a global history of international law. In the words of Robert Frost's wonderful poem, we tried to take the road 'less traveled by',[4] but we appreciate that we have only come so far.

The difficulties in writing a truly global history of international law begin (but do not end) with determining the time to be covered. In that respect, we did not succeed in completely avoiding a Eurocentric perspective as we started out from the notion of 'modern international law' as established in the Western historiography of international law. In other words, as far as Europe and the Western world are concerned, we wanted to exclude pre- and early history as well as Greco-Roman antiquity, although there is a fairly rich literature on the latter.[5] Furthermore, we decided to include European medieval history only in the light of a 'fluent passage' from the Middle Ages to modernity. The reason for this limitation was first practical (not everything can be achieved at a time, or in a single book), and secondly, the idea of focusing on that international law which has had a bearing on the contemporary international legal order in the sense that there is a 'living bond' between the past and the present. As Antonio Cassese remarked, '[t]he origin of the international commu-nity in its present structure and configuration is usually traced back to the sixteenth century'.[6] However, that does not mean that the law of antiquity, or of the early Middle

---

[3] Cf T Skouteris *The Notion of Progress in International Law Discourse* (Asser The Hague 2010).

[4] See R Frost 'The Road Not Taken' in *Mountain Interval* (Henry Holt and Co. New York 1916) at 9.

[5] See DJ Bederman *International Law in Antiquity* (CUP Cambridge 2007) (with a bibliography at 290 ff).

[6] A Cassese *International Law* (2nd edn OUP Oxford 2005) at 22.

Ages,[7] is completely absent from the pages of this Handbook. It is in fact discussed whenever it played a role, especially by way of its reception and transformation, in the construction of modern international law.[8]

Less Eurocentric is, we think, our decision to ask authors to end their respective accounts in 1945 because the end of the Second World War and the founding of the United Nations mark a caesura not only in Western but in world history.[9] Of course it is possible to write a history of international law of the 1950s or 1960s, but in a larger perspective the international law in force is still the law of the era of the United Nations founded in 1945.

For the history of the non-European regions, the beginning of the European modern era in the 16th century is not a meaningful divide. Accordingly, each author (writing, for example, about Africa, China, or India) had to decide where to start the respective history—a history which at some point of time converged with Western history.

Looking over the table of contents of this book, the reader will easily distinguish chapters with more conventional themes from those with which we tried to present something new. Examining the chapters more carefully, the reader will also see that many authors were assigned particularly difficult tasks. They were asked to write about subjects covered by very little literature, so that they had to start from scratch. The reader will also find that this Handbook is pluralist in many senses, something we see as an advantage but which again does not come without risk. The authors have different academic backgrounds; they are lawyers, historians, and political scientists. They come from, and work in, different regions of the world. They have chosen different historiographical methods. The result is, in some way, a Handbook not of *the* history, but of many histories of international law.

But enough of that *captatio benevolentiae*. Instead, we want to say a bit more about what we had in mind when devising this book, and of where in our view future historical research in international law should be heading.

---

[7] For a recent admirable study of that period, see H Steiger *Die Ordnung der Welt: Eine Völkerrechtsgeschichte des karolingischen Zeitalters (741 bis 840)* (Böhlau Köln 2010).

[8] See the contributions by M Kintzinger 'From the Late Middle Ages to the Peace of Westphalia' and by K Tuori 'The Reception of Ancient Legal Thought in Early Modern International Law' in this volume.

[9] In contrast, many authors consider the First World War as *the* watershed in the modern history of international law. See eg R Lesaffer 'The Grotian Tradition Revisited: Change and Continuity in the History of International Law' (2002) 73 British Yearbook of International Law 103–39 at 106 n 14 with numerous references. See also W Preiser *Die Völkerrechtsgeschichte, ihre Aufgaben und ihre Methode* (Sitzungsberichte der Wissenschaftlichen Gesellschaft an der Johann Wolfgang Goethe-Universität Frankfurt/Main (1963) Nr. 2, 31–66, repr Franz Steiner Wiesbaden 1964) at 62. M-H Renaut *Histoire du droit international public* (Ellipses Paris 2007) ends her historical acount with the Treaty of Versailles which in her view, 'esquisse une nouvelle metamorphose du droit international qu'il convient de réserver aux spécialistes du droit international public contemporain.'

2. Overcoming Eurocentrism

Traditional history writing in international law focused on the modern European system of states, its origins and precursors in antiquity and the Middle Ages, and the expansion of that system to the other continents. Non-European political entities appeared mainly as passive objects of European domination.[10]

Accounts of the history of international law, written from a non-European perspective, are still rare. Important examples are the works of Taslim Olawale Elias, Slim Laghmani, and Ram Prakash Anand.[11] More recently, critical scholarship has addressed 'international law's dark past',[12] the use of brutal power against, and the exploitation of, the colonized and dominated peoples which was an integral part of the imposition of European rule.[13] Guided by the best intentions, this scholarship, however, is also in a sense Eurocentric. As Emmanuelle Jouannet recently argued, the current historiographical strand which conceives of international law as being built on and imbued by the distinction between Europeans and Others, a distinction allegedly specifically designed to facilitate European hegemony over the rest of the world, corresponds neither to the intentions of the 17th- and 18th-century authors, nor—more importantly—to the objectives of the European sovereigns of the time. Jouannet, in our view correctly, points out that the 'counter-narrative' in fact perpetuates what it seeks to condemn, and basically reproduces the conservative effects of 'classical conservative historiography'. In reality, international law is and was neither 'good' nor 'bad'. It can be used for different and contradictory ends: for oppression and hegemony, but also for emancipation and stability.[14]

---

[10] But see for important examples of a more balanced historiography CH Alexandrowicz *An Introduction to the Law of Nations in the East Indies (16th, 17th, and 18th Centuries)* (Clarendon Press Oxford 1967); J Fisch *Die europäische Expansion und das Völkerrecht: Die Auseinandersetzungen um den Status der überseeischen Gebiete vom 15. Jahrhundert bis zur Gegenwart* (Franz Steiner Stuttgart 1984); G Gong *The Standard of 'Civilization' in International Society* (OUP New York 1984); N Berman *Passion and Ambivalence: Colonialism, Nationalism, and International Law* (Brill Leiden 2011).

[11] TO Elias *Africa and the Development of International Law* (R Akinjide ed) (Martinus Nijhoff Dordrecht 1988); S Laghmani *Histoire du droit des gens—du* jus gentium *impérial au* jus publicum europaeum (Pedone Paris 2004); RP Anand *Studies in International Law and History: An Asian Perspective* (Martinus Nijhoff Leiden 2004).

[12] See the contribution by A Becker Lorca 'Eurocentrism in the History of International Law' in this volume at 1054.

[13] See eg B Rajagopal *International Law from Below* (CUP Cambridge 2003); RP Anand *Development of Modern International Law and India* (Nomos Baden-Baden 2005); A Anghie *Imperialism, Sovereignty and the Making of International Law* (CUP Cambridge 2005); JT Gathii 'Imperialism, Colonialism, and International Law' (2007) 54 Buffalo Law Review 1013–66; A Becker Lorca 'Universal International Law: Nineteenth-Century Histories of Imposition and Appropriation' (2010) 51 Harvard International Law Journal 475–552; A Orford *International Authority and the Responsibility to Protect* (CUP Cambridge 2011).

[14] E Jouannet 'Des origines coloniales du droit international: A propos du droit des gens moderne au XVIIème siècle' in V Chetail and P-M Dupuy (eds) *Mélanges Peter Haggenmacher* (Brill Leiden 2012 forthcoming).

Arnulf Becker Lorca highlighted that the Eurocentric historical narrative is polit-ically relevant to the extent that is has often performed an ideological function, namely to universalize and legitimize the particular Western standpoint. He argues, in this Handbook, that international lawyers should therefore 'devote energy to pro-duce a divergent narrative and reveal a Eurocentric distortion'.[15] Indeed, we tried to pay particular attention to the non-European influences on the history of interna-tional law. Part III on 'Regions' includes sections on Africa and Arabia, Asia, and the Americas (including the Caribbean). Authors here often focus on the period before the arrival of the Europeans and 'their' international law. In a section called 'Encoun-ters', we reflect on the situations and ways in which China, Japan, India, Russia, and the indigenous peoples of the Americas, respectively, opened themselves to European influences, knowledge, and law, and experienced European repression and domina-tion. Not all of these encounters resulted in violent conflicts; some also led to creative forms of cooperation. They brought about 'altered forms and new mixtures,...and not just hegemony or homogeneity'.[16] In a more general way, many of the issues appearing in these encounters are dealt with in Part IV on 'Interaction or Imposition'.

The 'Encounters' section takes up the study of 'cultural encounters' by the pioneers of global historiography[17] who understand 'the self' and 'the other' as shifting con-structions so that 'the West' (or 'Europe') can be seen as an invention responding to a global experience.[18] Of particular interest is the question whether there was not only a reception of European concepts and standards by the non-European states and peoples but also an influence in the other direction. In other words, we specifically asked what the contributions of a specific country or region to the development of international law were. As one might expect, the findings differ. The most 'acknow-ledged' regional contributions are probably the Latin American ones. Jorge Esquirol in his chapter on Latin America mentions in this context non-intervention by third-party States, compulsory international arbitration for State-to-State disputes, terri-torial limits based on *uti possidetis iuris,* third-party right to recognition of internal belligerents, the right of diplomatic asylum, the principle of *ius soli* in nationality laws, freedom of national rivers navigation, coastal security jurisdiction, and free-dom of neutral trade in times of war.[19] Esquirol abstains from taking sides in the controversy whether a *separate* American international law existed or not. Instead, he argues that international law has been normally 'idiosyncratically adapted to local

---

[15] See the contribution by A Becker Lorca 'Eurocentrism in the History of International Law' in this volume at 1035.

[16] R Grew 'On the Prospect of Global History' in B Mazlish and R Buultjens (eds) *Conceptualizing Global History* (Westview Press Boulder Colorado 1993) 227–49 at 244.

[17] Seminally JH Bentley *Old World Encounters: Cross-Cultural Contacts and Exchanges in Pre-Modern Times* (OUP New York 1993).

[18] 'On the Prospect of Global History' (n 16) 242.

[19] See the contribution by J Esquirol 'Latin America' in this volume at 465.

circumstances' everywhere, whether this local adaptation is acknowledged or not, and that 'both approaches mobilize the identity of international law in support of *different* constructions of legal authority'.[20] In substance, Esquirol finds that the fleshing out of the topic of foreign interference in the affairs of relatively weak States was a particularly important contribution of international law in Latin America to international law as a whole, actually to its core concepts of modern sovereignty and statehood.

As regards Africa north of the Sahara and Arab countries, Fatiha Sahli and Abdelmalek El Ouazzani conclude that '[i]f there is a contribution of Islam to international law, it is in the field of the protection of the laws of the persons, particularly in the laws of the *Dhimmi*, and more precisely in the laws of the religious minorities and the humane treatment of the war prisoners'.[21] Bimal Patel in his chapter on India rejects explicitly the conceived wisdom that the earlier legal system of India was confined to its own civilizations, and has 'left no trace of continuity of history'. Instead, Patel opines that the rules of warfare observed by Indian kings and princely States prior to 1500 and even during 1500–1945 'were unique to the Indian civilization and have made a significant contribution to modern international humanitarian law'.[22]

As far as an Asian influence is concerned, Yasuaki Onuma had in a seminal article opined that there were only *coincidental practices* in Asia (for example, on the treatment of foreigners, on the law of the sea), but that it has so far not been demonstrated that these Asian practices brought about or influenced the formation and development of these rules in European international law.[23] This finding is resonated by Kinshi Akashi who, in his chapter on the Japanese–European encounter, gives our question a short shrift: 'if it is asked whether the original Japanese ideas on "international relations" and "international legal order" had "any influence and impact" on the body of international law as it emerged from the "encounter", the answer should be negative'.[24] Nevertheless, Akashi concludes that while the Japanese–European encounter did not result in a transfer of Japanese institutions to global international law (in the style of a 'micro-transferral' of single instruments and institutions), it did demonstrate the 'universal applicability of the concept and logic of international law' in a dynamic process of universalization.[25]

It is well known that non-Europeans appropriated 'European' international law and used it to further their political objectives (in part against European domination). For example, the North American Deskaheh and the Council of the Iroquis Confederacy addressed themselves to the League of Nations.[26] China, to give another

---

[20] ibid at 566 (emphasis added).

[21] See the contribution by F Sahli and A El Ouazzani 'Africa North of the Sahara and Arab Countries' in this volume at 405.

[22] See the contribution by BN Patel 'India' in this volume at 514.

[23] Y Onuma 'When was the Law of International Society Born?' (2000) 2 Journal of the History of International Law 1–64 at 61 fn 170 (with a reference to Alexandrowicz's work).

[24] See the contribution by K Akashi 'Japan–Europe' in this volume at 741.

[25] ibid at 742.

[26] See the contribution by K Coates 'North American Indigenous Peoples' Encounters' in this volume.

example, made international law arguments to get rid of the unequal treaties—for instance at the Paris Peace Conference of 1919 and the Washington Naval Conference of 1921.[27] But, arguably, Europeans inversely delved into regional systems and adapted themselves, too. For example, it is currently debated whether the European trading nations 'Westernized' the traditional China-centered East Asia trading system, or whether the Europeans—on the contrary—joined it themselves.[28] In the latter case, the conclusion would be that the Chinese system was never broken, even under European pressure, and has recovered quite well.[29]

Cases in which the encounter resembled more a 'one-way street' than a mutual give-and-take might be assessed in ethical terms. The judgment depends, *inter alia*, on whether this reception was (at least to some extent) voluntary and a result of reflection, also on the side of the receiver, or only brought about by force, intimidation, and economic coercion. Often both persuasion *and* imposition will have played a decisive role.

What can be learned is that genealogy does not determine identity. 'The transistor in Japan is no more American than the paper in Europe is Chinese. Like rubber, maize, or the potato, elections or political parties or corporate hierarchies may carry names that reflect a foreign origin, but they have been woven into diverse societies'.[30] This 'domestication' is not limited to technical or cultural products but also includes legal institutions, among them rules and standards of international law. Cherished examples are human rights, the rule of law, and democracy. But there are also less liked cases of 'domestication', such the Japanese theory of 'Great East Asian International Law', arguably a modified version of the national socialist German '*Grossraum*' or '*Lebensraum*' theory.[31] Unsurprisingly, these processes of creative appropriation and hybridization have recently been highlighted both by global historians[32] and by international and comparative lawyers.[33]

---

[27] See the contribution by S Kawashima 'China' in this volume.

[28] The Europeans and the Chinese sides may have had differing views on this already at the time. In Qing's official documents, the Netherlands and other European states were recorded as tributaries without those states necessarily being aware of that status. One of the reasons for the diverging views were translations: The European mission's official letters to the Qing emeperor did not follow the Chinese formalities for tribute in their original lanaguage, but the Chinese versions, actually submitted to the court, were considerably modified by the Chinese authorities so as to conform with the tribute formalities (S Hamamoto 'International Law, Regional Developments: East Asia' in *Max Planck Encyclopedia of Public International Law* (OUP Oxford 2012) para 14).

[29] See the contribution by C-H Tang 'China–Europe' in this volume, with further references.

[30] 'On the Prospect of Global History' (n 16) at 234.

[31] See the contribution by K Akashi 'Japan–Europe' in this volume at 741.

[32] Seminally, Jerry Bentley sought 'to identify and understand the patterns of cross-cultural conversion, conflict and compromise that came about when peoples of different civilizations and cultural traditions interacted with each other over long periods of time'. Bentley concluded that 'syncretism represented an avenue leading to cultural compromise' (*Old World Encounters* (n 17) at vii–viii). See also EW Said *Orientalism* (Penguin Books London 2003) at xxii: 'Rather than the manufactured clash of civilizations, we need to concentrate on the slow working together of cultures that overlap, borrow from each other, and live together in far more interesting ways than any abridged or inauthentic mode of understanding can allow.'

[33] See in legal scholarship notably M Delmas-Marty 'Comparative Law and International Law: Methods for Ordering Pluralism' (2006) 3 University of Tokyo Journal of Law and Politics 43–59.

3. GLOBAL HISTORY AND THE CONTRIBUTION OF THE HISTORY OF INTERNATIONAL LAW

This Handbook is inspired by a global history approach.[34] A related concept is that of a world history.[35] In simplified terms, these schools are the answer of (Western) historians to globalization. Both global and world history reject the 18th- and 19th-century essentialist concepts of a 'universal history'. The protagonists neither seek to establish a 'master narrative' (as, for example, Immanuel Wallerstein did),[36] nor wish to give a sweeping account of the course of the world's history, from a quasi celestial perspective (in the style of Oswald Spengler, Arnold Toynbee, or William McNeill[37]).

'Global history' is not produced by simply assembling all the events of world history. It rather needs to be conceptualized. This was done by one of its pioneers, Bruce Mazlish, in the following way: global history 'focuses on new actors of various kinds; it is dramatically concerned with the dialectic of the global and the local (recognizing, for example, that the global helps to create increased localism as a response); it embraces methods of both narrative and analysis as befitting the specific phenomena under investigation; and it necessarily relies a good deal on interdisciplinary and team research'.[38] Jürgen Osterhammel on his part defined global history ('in a narrow sense') as 'the history of continuous, but not linear intensification of interactions across vast spaces and of the crystallization of these interactions into extended networks or, sometimes, institutions which usually possess their own hierarchical structure. The tension between the global and the local is crucial for this approach'.[39]

---

[34] See seminally B Mazlish and R Buultjens (eds) *Conceptualizing Global History* (Westview Press Boulder Colorado 1993); also D Reynolds *One World Divisible: A Global History since 1945* (Allen Lane London 2000). For surveys, see P Manning *Navigating World History: Historians Create a Global Past* (Palgrave Macmillan Basingstoke 2003); further P Vries 'Editorial: Global History' (2009) 20 Global History 5–21. For the meta-level of history writing, see GG Iggers and QE Wang with the assistance of S Mukherjee *Global History of Modern Historiography* (Pearson Longman Harlow 2008); R Blänkner 'Historische Kulturwissenschaften im Zeichen der Globalisierung' (2008) 16 Historische Anthropologie 341–72.

[35] J Osterhammel (ed) *Weltgeschichte: Basistexte* (Franz Steiner Stuttgart 2008). Three journals have been founded as platforms for these approaches: The Journal of World History, founded in 1990; the Journal of Global History founded in 2006 (see WG Clarence-Smith, K Pomeranz, and P Vries 'Editorial' (2006) vol 1, 1–2); and the e-journal World History Connected, <http://worldhistoryconnected. press.illinois.edu> (accessed 5 May 2012).

[36] I Wallerstein *Modern World System* (4 vols Academic Press New York, Academic Press San Diego, University of California Press Berkeley 1974, 1980, 1989, 2011).

[37] O Spengler *The Decline of the West* (CF Atkinson trans) (2 vols Alfred A Knopf New York 1922); A Toynbee *A Study of History* (12 vols OUP Oxford 1934–61); WH McNeill, *The Rise of the West: A History of Human Community* (University of Chicago Press Chicago 1963).

[38] B Mazlish 'An Introduction to Global History' in *Conceptualizing Global History* (n 34) 1–24 at 6.

[39] J Osterhammel 'Global History in a National Context: The Case of Germany' (2009) 20 Global History 40–58 at 44.

Concomitantly, the same author defined 'world history' as 'a de-centered, and certainly not Eurocentric, perspective, detached, as far as possible, from the concrete circumstances and the national identity of the observer'. . . . 'World history considers interaction between peoples, but does not privilege it at the expense of internal developments. It only deserves its name when it is more than the addition of regional histories. In other words: World history is meaningless without some kind of comparative approach'.[40] Global history thus focuses on transfers, networks, connections, and cooperation between different actors and regions, while trying to avoid the temptation to draw straight lines from one time and place to another.[41] Another theme is 'transformation', highlighting processes rather than outcomes.[42]

Global history no longer takes the nation-state as the traditional object of historical analysis.[43] Instead, to global historians, the major actors or subjects of a global history are movements (such as the peace movement, or the women's suffrage movement), and business (such as chartered companies). Interestingly, current international legal scholarship also focuses on non-state actors as emerging subjects of international law.

Another objective of global history is to overcome the (primarily European) heritage of national history.[44] Therefore, attention is directed to non-European societies and regions. Their modern history is understood as an autonomous development, and not as a mere reaction to European conquest. This move is aptly captured in Dipesh Chakrabarty's quest for 'provincializing Europe'.[45] In legal scholarship, a parallel endeavour has been undertaken in a 'peripheries series' in the Leiden Journal of International Law which seeks to explore international law and international lawyers of the 'peripheries' (of Europe), with 'periphery' being understood 'geographically,

---

[40] ibid 43.

[41] cf *Navigating World History* (n 34) 3 and 7: '[W]orld history is the story of connctions within the global human community. The world historian's work is to portray the crossing of boundaries and the linking of systems in the human past. . . . I define world history as a field of study focusing on the historical connections among entities and systems often thought to be distinct.' See also E Vanhaute 'Who is Afraid of Global History?' (2009) 20 Zeitschrift für Geschichtswissenschaft 22–39 at 25, who propagates a threefold trajectory ('trinity') consisting in comparative analysis, a focus on connections and interactions, and a systems-analysis.

[42] Cf J Osterhammel, *Die Verwandlung der Welt: Eine Geschichte des 19. Jahrhunderts* (CH Beck München 2008), Engl transl *The Transformation of the World: A History of the 19th Century* (Princeton University Press 2011).

[43] 'An Introduction to Global History' (n 38) 5. 'On the Prospect of Global History' (n 16) 245: Global history should be 'substituting multicultural, global analysis for the heroic, national narratives on which our discipline was founded.' See also N Zemon Davis 'Global History, Many Stories' in J Osterhammel (ed) *Weltgeschichte: Basistexte* (Franz Steiner Stuttgart 2008) 91–100 at 92.

[44] B Mazlish, *The New Global History* (Routledge New York 2006) at 104.

[45] D Chakrabarty *Provincializing Europe: Postcolonial Thought and Historical Difference* (Princeton University Press 2000). See also A Dirlik 'History without a Center? Reflections on Eurocentrism' in E Fuchs and B Stuchtey (eds) *Across Cultural Borders: Historiography in Global Perspective* (Rowman & Littlefield Lanham 2002) 247–84.

politically, economically, and discursively'.[46] The objective of the series is 'to foster engagement with the discursive function of centre-periphery oppositions in public international law in their various iterations, and through this to confront questions of resource allocation, dependency, geography, and power'.[47] However, that perspectival shift will only be completed once Europe itself is understood as 'a series of assembled peripheries'.[48]

Along this line, Bruce Mazlish called '[p]erhaps the single most distinguishing feature' of global historiography 'that of perspective, awareness, or consciousness'.[49] 'The challenge of global history is to construct global perspectives'.[50] It is not denied that any writer, be it a lawyer or a historian, inevitably analyses the past and its legal institutions from his or her own perspective which is necessarily rooted in the present, and often uses categories and logics developed in a 'Western' system of thinking. But globally oriented historiographers are conscious of this very fact. They try to avoid the narrow perspective of traditional epistemic Eurocentrism which constructed and reified periods, regions, and cultures.[51] This attitude is shared by international lawyers who seek to overcome the epistemic nationalism of their discipline.[52] The approach not only 'challenges the often too readily accepted notion that the Western model remains at the centre of historical studies and radiates its influence all over the world', but more radically it challenges 'the Western/non-West dichotomy underpinning many well intentioned comparative studies'.[53] The crucial endeavour seems to be to shift perspectives, and to allow for a multipolar perspective, acknowledging that the dynamics for developing these perspectives have been generated by various sources and emerged from all parts of the world. Accordingly, there is no single global history, no universal law to be discovered resulting in a unidirectional evolution of the world.[54] Instead, there have been and will be many global experiences.

Even if this multiperspectival ideal can never be fully realized, it is our hope that a collective work such as this Handbook can at least come close to it. Global (or world)

---

[46]   F Johns, T Skouteris and W Wouter 'The League of Nations and the Construction of the Periphery: Introduction' (2011) 24 Leiden Journal of International Law 797–8 at 797.

[47]   F Johns, T Skouteris and W Wouter 'Editors' Introduction: India and International Law in the Peripheries Series' (2010) 23 Leiden Journal of International Law 1–3 at 3.

[48]   E Balibar 'Europe as Borderland' The Alexander von Humboldt Lecture in Human Geography, University of Nijmegen (24 November 2004) at <http://socgeo.ruhosting.nl/colloquium/Europe%20as%20Borderland.pdf>, at 12 (with reference to Edward Said who used that term for European literature in a posthumously published interview ('An interview with Edward Said' (2003) 21 Society and Space 635–51 at 647)).

[49]   'An Introduction to Global History' (n 38) 6.

[50]   'On the Prospect of Global History' (n 16) 237.

[51]   R Sieder and E Langthaler 'Was heißt Globalgeschichte?' in R Sieder and E Langthaler (eds) Globalgeschichte 1800–2010 (Böhlau Wien 2010) 9–36 at 12.

[52]   A Peters 'Die Zukunft der Völkerrechtswissenschaft: Wider den epistemischen Nationalismus' (2007) 67 Zeitschrift für ausländisches öffentliches Recht und Völkerrecht 721–76.

[53]   Global History of Modern Historiography (n 34) 394.

[54]   'An Introduction to Global History' (n 38) 4.

history is already now an interdisciplinary endeavour to which many disciplines contribute—economics, sociology, anthropology, demography, archaeology, geography, the history of music, art history, historical linguistics, geology, biology, and medicine.[55] It is therefore not far-fetched that legal studies can also make a meaningful contribution to that effort of a comprehensive *Welterfassung*, or recognition and understanding of the world.

4. EVENTS, CONCEPTS, PEOPLE: THREE MODES OF WRITING HISTORY

History can be written in many modes or forms. Simply put, three such modes can be distinguished—the history of events, the history of concepts, and the history of individual people. All three approaches have also been used in the historiography of international law.[56] There is the tradition of a doctrinal history which analyses the teachings of important theorists of international law, their development, and interaction.[57] There is further the tradition of a diplomatic history which focuses on events which had a bearing on international law. Thirdly, international legal historiography has occasionally also used the biographical method by recounting in detail the life and work of an important scholar, statesman, or diplomat.[58] Many chapters of this Handbook try to combine these three approaches, realizing, for instance, that a

---

[55] *Navigating World History* (n 34) 121–36.

[56] See for (older) surveys of the historiography of international law F Stier-Somlo 'Völkerrechts-Literaturgeschichte' in K Strupp (ed) *Wörterbuch des Völkerrechts und der Diplomatie* (de Gruyter Berlin 1929) vol 3, 212–27; A Nussbaum *A Concise History of the Law of Nations* (1st edn Macmillan New York 1947) 293 ff (Appendix: 'Survey of the historiography of international law').

[57] The classic work (though not using modern historiographical methods) is DHL von Ompteda *Literatur des gesamten natürlichen als positiven Völkerrechts* (2 vols Montags Regensburg 1785, repr Scientia Aalen 1963). Its first part is a history of international legal scholarship, starting with the Roman authors (at 139 ff). See further eg C von Kaltenborn *Die Vorläufer des Hugo Grotius auf dem Gebiete des ius naturae et gentium sowie der Politik im Reformationszeitalter* (2 vols Mayer Leipzig 1848); A Rivier *Note sur la littérature du droit des gens: Avant la publication du Jus Belli Ac Pacis de Grotius (1625)* (F Hayez Bruxelles 1883); A de la Pradelle *Maîtres et doctrines du droit des gens* (Les Editions internationales Paris 1939, 2nd edn 1950). For a modern classic, see R Tuck *The Rights of War and Peace: Political Thought and the International Order from Grotius to Kant* (OUP Oxford 1999).

[58] Fine modern examples are provided by the series 'The European Tradition in International Law' in the European Journal of International Law, beginning in 1990, featuring Georges Scelle, Dionisio Anzilotti, Alfred Verdross, Hersch Lauterpacht, Hans Kelsen, Charles de Visscher, Alf Ross, Max Huber, and—most recently—Walther Schücking (2011). The Leiden Journal of International Law reacted with its series on non-European international legal scholars, so far featuring Alejandro Alvarez (2006) and Taslim Olawale Elias (2008).

history of a certain concept, idea, or notion were incomplete without enquiring into the people who invented them, or saying something about the historical events which occasioned that invention.

To turn to the history of events or facts first, international legal historiography treated wars and treaties as the most significant 'events'. The treaties attracting particular interest were treaties of alliance, seeking to forestall war, on the one hand, and peace treaties, ending wars in a legal sense, on the other hand. As a third group, treaties of commerce can be mentioned. In this mode, history is told as a matter-of-fact story, concentrating on states, power, war, trade, and diplomacy. It is therefore often called 'diplomatic history'.

This type of historiography treats law as a dependent variable of political and military events. However, the degree of impact or importance ascribed to international law varies greatly. Law might be considered as completely ancillary to political power or on the contrary as a normative power shaping the events. A more critical and more distanced way of writing history in this factual mode is to problematize the respective role of international law, and to ask whether and why this role was 'small'[59] or 'great', and which factors account for that result. In his influential book *The Epochs of International Law*, about we shall say more later in this introduction,[60] Wilhelm Grewe defended his emphasis on state practice as follows:

Numerous authors examining the history of the law of nations adopted a peculiar and methodologically questionable separation of theory and state practice. In doing so they were placing themselves at a disadvantage, as such a separation does not concern two divided branches of the history of the law of nations, but rather only two sides of the same process. On the one hand, they lost themselves in an abstract history of the theory, which could not acknowledge the concrete intellectual historical position of a Vitoria, a Gentili or a Grotius, nor the concrete political and sociological background to their theories. On the other hand, inter-State relations were regarded as a bare array of facts to be grasped and systematised by way of a theoretically-derived, abstract intellectual method.[61]

The structure of his own book, Grewe said, was 'based on the conviction that it is important to recognise and demarcate the close connection between legal theory and State practice, and to comprehend that both are forms of expression of the same power, which characterise the political style of an epoch just as much as its principles of social, economic and legal organisation'.[62]

---

[59] See SC Neff 'A Short History of International Law' in MD Evans (ed) *International Law* (3rd edn OUP Oxford 2010) 3–31 at 27: 'If there is one lesson that the history of international law teaches, it is that the world at large—the "outside world" if you will—has done far more to mould international law than *vice versa*.'

[60] See Section 7 'About the Handbook's Place in the Historiography of International Law' below.

[61] WG Grewe *The Epochs of International Law* (Michael Byers trans) (Walter de Gruyter Berlin 2000) at 2.

[62] ibid 6. See for a seminal methodological critique along this line already *Die Völkerrechtsgeschichte, ihre Aufgaben und ihre Methode* (n 9) *passim*, esp at 39, 46, 48, 50.

After the cultural turn in historiography, many historians have denounced the history of power politics and diplomacy as *demodé*. However, as much as it is important to study cultural and social history, power and competing state interests have not become irrelevant. The legal historian should still take them into account.[63] Furthermore, the empirical study of events should complement any account of the history of legal ideas and doctrines, as developed by scholars or practitioners. It does matter in which particular (political or military) context an idea or doctrine was brought up, and it is of course crucial whether and how ideas were implemented in practice.

For these reasons, the authors of this Handbook were asked to give, *inter alia*, an account of the practice of international law. It is, for example, important to know not only which treaties were concluded, but also whether and for which reasons they were complied with or not. A difficulty in this respect is that for many issues historical research has so far not compiled sufficient empirical data. And the further into the past we look, the more difficult it will be to establish both categories and facts, especially on compliance.

In German historical scholarship, the history of events (*'Ereignisgeschichte'*) has traditionally been contrasted with the history of ideas (*'Ideengeschichte'*). A subfield of the latter is conceptual history (*'Begriffsgeschichte'*) as developed by Otto Brunner and Reinhart Koselleck.[64] In this Handbook, contributions in Parts II and IV (on 'themes' and 'interaction or imposition', respectively), but also in other sections, deal with such concepts or notions as 'territory', 'domination', or 'the civilized'. Concep-tional history is particularly relevant to legal history because legal rules consist of, and are based on, concepts.

Concepts change over time. They are no more solid than the period or context in which they originated. Therefore, the analysis of a legal concept should include a reflection about the social and political context of the concept, and the political agenda behind it, about the 'speakers' and the 'addressees', and about the shifting meaning of a concept in the course of time. Surely a legal historian should not limit him- or herself to concepts found in legal documents. Other concepts too can be of legal relevance. Conversely, notions used in legal texts may have turned out not to

---

[63] J Osterhammel 'Internationale Geschichte, Globalisierung und die Pluralität der Kulturen' in W Loth and J Osterhammel (eds) *Internationale Geschichte, Themen, Ergebnisse, Aussichten* (Oldenburg München 2000) 387–408 at 398. See also Stephen Neff's approach to his very 'short history of interna-tional law' which covers 'both ideas and State practice', with the author pointing out that 'it was the two in combination—if not always in close harmony—that made international law what it became', 'A Short History,' (n 59) 3–4.

[64] R Koselleck 'Einleitung' in O Brunner, W Conze and R Koselleck (eds) *Geschichtliche Grundbegriffe: Historisches Lexikon zur politisch-sozialen Sprache in Deutschland* (Klett Cotta Stuttgart 1972) xiii–xxvii; R Koselleck *Vergangene Zukunft: Zur Semantik geschichtlicher Zeiten* (Suhrkamp Frankfurt aM 1979), translation: *Futures Past: On the Semantics of Historical Time* (Keith Tribe trans) (Columbia University Press 1985).

affect the practice of international law. Such a distinction can help to identify blind spots in the law, or illustrate the blurred boundary between the spheres of law and politics.

In the biographical mode of history writing, the persons studied may be politicians, legal practitioners, or scholars. Biographical history need not tell a story of heroes, and it need not overstate the role individuals have in 'making history'. The context in which the person described lived and worked can be featured. Or he (rarely she) can on the contrary be presented as a representative of an epoch. The persons' ideas and acts can be 'keyholes' through which we can see an entire 'room' or historical space. In this Handbook, the biographical mode of history writing is used in Part VI, 'People in Portrait', but also in other chapters.

As already mentioned, all three historiographical approaches need 'contextualization',[65] in order to avoid history 'lite', or what David Bederman called 'Foreign Office International Legal History'.[66] The relevant context must be established according to the chosen approach and the historical problem to be solved. For a conceptual historian, for instance, the textual context of a legal text matters greatly. But beyond that, the contextualization of a legal idea or doctrine requires, in our view, an analysis of the *Leitmotive* and academic styles of the time.[67] With regard to events, contextualization means looking also at processes, and not only at outcomes. Often, the relevant process is determined by the domestic political situation of a state. For example, a main reason for Japan's swift adaptation to European legal standards was the Japanese revolution ('Restoration'), and the new government's desire to change the entire legal and political system.[68] Ideally, contextualization should also bear in mind the *Zeitgeist* shaping or influencing certain developments. It is, for example, noteworthy that the delegates of the two international peace conferences in The Hague in 1899 and 1907 met in 'Japanese' and 'Chinese' rooms which were fashionable at the time. Furthermore, the contextualization of events and ideas means to look at long-term developments and trends. That perspective may lead to a relativization of what usually is considered a historical caesura or break. The First World War, for instance, was on the one hand a rupture, but on the other hand a bridge to the international law of the League of Nations period.

[65]   Q Skinner *Visions of Politics*, vol 1: *Regarding Method* (CUP Cambridge 2002); Q Skinner 'Surveying the Foundations: A Retrospect and Reassessment' in A Brett, J Tully and H Hamilton-Bleakley (eds) *Rethinking the Foundations of Modern Political Thought* (CUP Cambridge 2006) 236–61.

[66]   By this, Bederman understood picking and choosing facts and primary sources ripped out of context to serve purposes of a lawyer's brief, 'in order to make some point that has no basis in reality' (D Bederman 'Foreign Office International Legal History' in M Craven, M Fitzmaurice and M Vogiatzi (eds) *Time, History and International Law* (Martinus Nijhoff Leiden 2007) 43–63 at 46).

[67]   For a good example, see JE Nijman *The Concept of International Legal Personality: An Inquiry into the History and Theory of International Law* (TMC Asser Press The Hague 2004).

[68]   See the contribution by M Yanagihara 'Japan' in this volume.

5. THE LINGUISTIC TURN AND BEYOND

In all three modes of historiography (the history of events, of concepts, and of people) the writer is, to our mind, free to choose whether to write about events, texts, or persons, or about *narratives (or pictures) about* events, texts, and persons. Behind this distinction lurks a fundamental epistemological problem, not limited to historiography but also present whenever we study contemporary events or texts. In fact, the problem arises in any scientific research, and relates to all kinds of the acquisition and transmittal (or communication) of knowledge: can we 'really' 'know' anything of, and make true statements about, events, texts, and persons? The answer to that problem depends on what we mean by 'knowledge' and 'truth'.

Some historians believe that there are no 'objective' facts or texts, or that, if they exist, observers (such as historians and lawyers) never can get access to them.[69] From that perspective, it is only possible to write *about narratives about* facts, texts and people. This also means, crucially, that there is no clear-cut difference between historiography and fiction.

In contrast to this stance, we believe that an intersubjective consensus (if only a very narrow one) can be established among historiographers about the meaning and significance of past events, texts, and of the conduct and actions of individual people. In that limited sense, there do exist 'objective' historical facts, and there is a distinction between description and fiction, and between writing and making history. We deem three insights crucial for modern history writing, as follows:

Perspectives: The first insight is that history cannot be written from an external omniscient point of view. As Hilary Putnam said, '[t]here is no God's Eye point of view that we can know or usefully imagine; there are only the various points of view of actual persons reflecting various interests and purposes that their descriptions and theories subserve'.[70] Every author writes from an individual perspective. As lawyers, we inevitably use our own legal experience as a tool for understanding the past, and if we do so we tend only to see what we already know or believe to know.[71] The writing as well as the reading of history takes place within the writers' and the readers' horizons. When both writers and readers are conscious of the inevitability of a subjective perspective, it is not unscholarly to approach an issue (such as colonialism) with ethical considerations or preferences.

Selectivity: Writing history on a given subject depends on making innumerable choices. The historian constantly must decide which facts, developments, documents, persons, and so on, he or she considers significant to his or her research question. What is important is that authors consciously reflect about the choices they make, and are explicit and transparent about them.

---

[69] See M Stolleis *Rechtsgeschichte schreiben: Rekonstruktion, Erzählung, Fiktion?* (Schwabe Basel 2008).

[70] H Putnam *Reason, Truth and History* (CUP Cambridge 1997, orig 1981) at 50.

[71] *Rechtsgeschichte schreiben* (n 69) 27.

The multiplicity of histories: There is a temptation to tell one, and only one, story. Some fifty years ago, the Dutch historian of international law, Johan Verzijl, had posed the question, with regard to the (ancient) laws of Egypt, Asia Minor, the Far East, and India: 'have not all those individual roads of the law of nations appeared to be blind alleys?...Is it therefore not necessary, instead of descending from antiquity to the present, rather to start as a matter of principle from the contemporary law of nations as the object of historical research and to attempt to retrace the origins of that law by moving from the present to the past until we reach the point where no traces are any longer discernible?'[72] Verzijl had thus basically asked for writing legal history 'backwards', taking the current law as point of departure. In contrast, this Handbook's methodological guideline was to avoid 'cutting alleys through history'. Former legal ideas, concepts, and rules are not necessarily 'precursors' of the law (including international law) as it stands now.[73] There are lines of evolution, but there is also discontinuity, conceptual fragmentation, contradiction, modification, and rearrangement.[74] In many chapters of this Handbook these phenomena are highlighted.

6. Lost in Translation?

Historiography comprises (even if only implicitly) a *diachronic comparison* (of the past international law with the present law). In order to describe, as a present-day author to a present-day readership old international legal institutions, both writer

---

[72] JHW Verzijl, *International Law in Historical Perspective* (AW Sijthoff Leyden 1968) vol 1, at 403–4.

[73] In other words, the idea is to avoid what Randall Lesaffer scathingly called 'evolutionary history of the worst kind' ie 'genealogic histories from present to past', a history writing which 'leads to anachronistic interpretations of historical phenomena, clouds historical realities that bear no fruit in their own times and gives no information about the historical context of the phenomenon one claims to recognise. It describes history in terms of similarities with or differences from the present, and not in terms of what it was. It tries to understand the past for what it brought about and not for what it meant to the people living in it.' (R Lesaffer 'International Law and its History: The Story of an Unrequited Love' in *Time, History and International Law* (n 66) 27–41 at 34–5).

[74] See for an attempt to make sense of international law through a history of its 'finalités' E Jouannet *Le droit international libéral-providence: Une histoire du droit international* (Bruylant Bruxelles 2011), translation: *The Liberal-Welfarist Law of Nations: A History of International Law* (C Sutcliffe trans) (CUP Cambridge 2012). Jouannet seeks to seize international law's 'logiques originaires' and diagnoses its 'double fin', namely liberalism and welfarism. She describes her approach as not being 'une histoire historienne' but as a type of history writing which seeks to open 'des pistes de réflexion' for comprehending our current international law by furnishing a new angle of reflexion, a strategy to acquire the means to rethink the significance of contemporary international law (at 1 and 9).

and reader inevitably rely on and relate the historical account to the contemporary understanding of concepts and legal institutions.

The difference between the diachronical comparison (of the past and present law) and the synchronological comparison (of different contemporary legal systems) seems to be twofold. First, history is inevitably within us (like in Wittgenstein's fibre metaphor),[75] whereas the 'other' legal system or culture does not necessarily form part of our own identity. Second, in contrast to an at least potentially dialogical transnational legal comparison, no dialogue can be entertained with the past.

But despite these two important differences, the comparative method (be it diachronic or synchronic) is in its basic structure similar. Just as in comparative legal scholarship, the diachronic comparison needs a *tertium comparationis* to compare (or only to relate) another epoch's and region's legal institutions to the present ones. The choice of the *tertium comparationis* depends on the research question and on values. Depending on that choice, the outcome of the comparison will differ. So the point is that we need not only to compare, but to actively *translate*.[76] Such a translation is a creative, and not a mechanical act. The translation is even more complex if it does not only involve the temporal dimension (translating from past to present meanings) but additionally a regional dimension (for example, translating Asian to European meanings).[77]

Let us give some examples of translations undertaken in this Handbook. A writer might compare the Japanese *Iiki*[78] to the (historical) European concept of *hinterland* by pointing out that both concepts sought to establish and justify control over territory. Or, Fatiha Sahli and Abdelmalek El Ouazzani, in their chapter 'Africa North of the Sahara and Arab Countries', find that the Muslim international law principles applied after a conquest of non-Muslim countries (*Futuhat*) can be 'compared to the spirit of colonization of a civilization because the Muslims intended to bring to the conquered population the "divine" message that was Islam'.[79] Ken Coates, in his chapter on the encounters of North American Indigenous peoples with Europeans,[80] traces how the

---

[75] 'Our concept of, let us say, peace, has grown like in the making of a thread by drilling fibres with other fibres. The strength of the thread does not lie in the fact that one fibre runs through its entire length, but in the interlinkages of so many fibres.' (L Wittgenstein 'Philosophische Untersuchungen No 67' in L Wittgenstein *Werkausgabe* (Suhrkamp Frankfurt 1984) vol 1, at 278).

[76] In a somewhat different sense, Baltic lawyers have historically been translators from Russian to (Western) European international law, and have thereby also shaped the history of international law; cf L Mälksoo 'Russia–Europe' in this volume.

[77] Seminally LH Liu *The Clash of Empires: The Invention of China in Modern World Making* (Harvard University Press Cambridge Mass 2006). See also LH Liu 'Henry Wheaton' in this volume.

[78] cf the contribution by M Yanagihara 'Japan' in this volume.

[79] See the contribution by F Sahli and A El Ouazzani 'Africa North of the Sahara and Arab Countries' in this volume at 395.

[80] See the contribution by K Coates 'North American Indigenous Peoples' Encounters' in this volume.

first partnerships between Aboriginals and Europeans were, due to their formality, the annual payments, and rituals of alliance, conceived by both sides as 'nation-to-nation' relationships with considerable authority. It could be further asked whether the North American Aboriginal peoples had prior concepts of boundedness akin to treaties, and to what extent the alliances with the Europeans mirrored these pre-existing concepts. In any case, writes Coates, these arrangements gave 'Aboriginal people the clear expectation that they had a permanent role in the emerging societies of North America', and that they had a formally equal status to the newcomers, which however did not survive the 19th century.[81]

An additional difficulty of any translation is that the understanding of traditional legal concepts, even within their own 'culture', has been and continues to be in flux. For example, Muslim legal consultants have in the past strongly disagreed and continue to disagree about the meaning of *Jihad*.[82] Or think of the Ottoman capitulations. Umut Özsu, in his chapter on the Ottoman empire, retraces their qualification in their own time. Capitulations had been issued unilaterally by Ottoman sultans, but many European and American jurists sought to endow them with greater legal force and therefore presented them as treaties imposing binding legal obligations upon both parties, not only on the non-Muslim power but also on the Ottoman sultans themselves. Such jurists cast the capitulation not as a temporary and unilateral concession, but as an enduring and bilateral treaty. In contrast, the Ottoman lawyers generally insisted that the capitulations were not to be confused with treaties in the European sense. It was exactly this 'interpretational fluidity' which characterized the capitulations.[83] An example for a retrospective re-interpretation is the quality of the traditional Chinese trading scheme(s). It has now become controversial which parts constituted a tributary system and which were mutual trade.[84]

Most often, we rely—for the comparison, or translation—on the lead categories of our historical, legal (and social and cultural) research, such as the state, politics, law, and justice, and use those as a *tertium comparationis* (of diachronical or synchronical comparison). But these lead categories have not in every part of the world and in any time corresponded to the same phenomena. The categories are not merely cloaked differently while being 'functionally' identical.[85] Despite their abstract quality, the

---

[81] 'First Nations passed from military and political allies to wards of the State in less than two generations', ibid at 792.

[82] See the contribution by F Sahli and A El Ouazzani 'Africa North of the Sahara and Arab Countries' in this volume. See also M Fadel 'International Law, Regional Developments: Islam' in *Max Planck Encyclopedia of Public International Law* (OUP Oxford 2012) paras 58–59.

[83] See the contribution by U Özsu 'Ottoman Empire' in this volume at 432.

[84] See the contribution by C-H Tang 'China–Europe' in this volume, with further references. In parallel, the merit of the influential description of the tributary system by the US-American historian John Fairbank and its possibly 'hegemonial' impact on the academic dicourse is being challenged (ibid).

[85] But see H Steiger 'Universality and Continuity in International Public Law?' in T Marauhn and H Steiger (eds) *Universality and Continuity in International Law* (Eleven International Publishing The Hague 2011) 13–43, esp at 30–2, 40, 42.

categories are never historically empty, but are impregnated by the respective ideational, cultural, and social context. Along this line, Shin Kawashima, in his chapter on
China, argues that China's understanding of the *Wanguo Gongfa* in a Chinese context
in the second half of the 19th century did not necessarily dovetail with the international community's understanding of international law by the first half of the 20th
century. He hypothesizes that 'China's own view of the international order and
understanding of international law continued to exist in the first half of the 20th
century, like overlapping layers of low-pitched sounds.'[86]

Additionally, the problem of perspective comes in. Even if *we* realize the experience,
ideologies, myths, and values inscribed in the said lead categories, we inevitably do this
within an aura which is itself saturated with meaning, and in which we as scholars have
been socialized and trained.[87] So ultimately, in historiography as in comparative law,
the question of commensurability or incommensurability arises. Although new psychological research has demonstrated that not only value-judgments, but more generally the subject's way of intellectually grasping and structuring the world seems to be
contingent upon culture,[88] these modes of thought and judgement are not fix and
determined (just as cultures do not have sharp boundaries or fixed identities). Writers
of international history can, upon self-consciousness and self-reflection, espouse also
the Others' perspective, and overcome their epistemological and moral 'paradigm'—
they are not trapped in it.[89] To conclude, because of all these complexities, something
might get lost in translation. But something might also be gained.

7. ABOUT THE HANDBOOK'S PLACE IN THE HISTORIOGRAPHY OF INTERNATIONAL LAW

We wish briefly to situate the Handbook in the historiographical landscape of international law, and to acknowledge the previous work on which it builds. In a modern
sense, the history of international law has been academically treated since the first
half of the 19th century. However, much of that history writing was either based on
an assumption of linear progress which strikes contemporary observers as almost

---

[86] See the contribution by S Kawashima 'China' in this volume, at 473.

[87] 'Was heißt Globalgeschichte?' (n 51) 13.

[88] RE Nisbett *The Geography of Thought: How Asians and Westerners Think Differently…and Why*
(Free Press New York 2003).

[89] A Peters and H Schwenke 'Comparative Law Beyond Post-modernism' (2000) 48 International and
Comparative Law Quarterly 800–34.

naïve,[90] or it was essentialist, assuming that international law was eternal and immutable, 'un droit qui a existé de tout temps et au sein de toutes les civilisations'.[91] The concept of a critical historiography, which relies on sources (in particular written documents) and on a critical analysis of those sources, which dismisses the idea of a grand narrative of progress, and which recognizes as inescapable the particular perspective of an individual historian, was accepted in the historiography of international law only belatedly.[92]

The number of scholars seriously studying the history of international law in the 19th and 20th centuries was so small that the lack of exploration of the issue has been called an 'intellectual scandal'.[93] Several reasons account for this scandal, one of them being that historians, not trained in legal science, often felt they were not sufficiently competent to analyse complex legal issues of the past. Lawyers, on their part, were generally not very much interested in legal history, and if they were, that history was usually the history of their own law (for instance, *Deutsche Rechtsgeschichte*), of Roman law, or of canon law. Even today no single chair or university institute is—to

[90] See eg H Wheaton *Histoire de progrès de droit des gens depuis la Paix de Westphalie jusqu'au Congrès de Vienne* (Brockhaus Leipzig 1841). Wheaton wrote his treatise in response to a call for papers issued by the *Académie des Sciences morales et politiques de l'Institut de France* in 1839. The (arguably suggestive) question of the Academy was as follows: 'Quels sont les progrès qu'a faits le droit des gens en Europe depuis la paix de Westphalie?' Wheaton concluded that 'le droit international s'est perfectionné, comme système des lois positives, ou d'usages servant à régler les relations mutuelles des nations, par le progrès de la civilisation générale, dont ce système est un des plus beaux résultats' (ibid v and 440). See also the 17 volumes F Laurent *Histoire du droit des gens et des relations internationales* (Gand Paris 1850–70). From the fourth volume on, Laurent had added a new sub-title: *Etudes sur l'histoire de l'humanité*. The object of the enterprise was, as Laurent defined it in his preface to the second edition of the first volume: '*suivre les progrès du genre humain vers l'unité*' (2nd edn 1861, vol 1, at v, emphasis added). See also C Calvo *Le droit international théorique et pratique précédé d'un exposé historique des progrès de la science du droit des gens* (6 vols Rousseau Paris 1887–96). But see alreadyR Redslob *Histoire des grands principes du droit des gens depuis l'Antiquité jusqu'à la veille de la grande guerre* (Rousseau Paris 1923) at 547: 'L'histoire du droit des gens n'est pas l'histoire d'un progrès continu, méthodique et toujours grandissant.'
[91] O Nippold 'Le Développement Historique du Droit International depuis le Congrès de Vienne' (1924-I) 2 Recueil des Cours de l'Académie de la Haye 5–124 at 5.
[92] See F Stier-Somlo who opined that, until the end of the 19th century, 'the history of international law or what was taken to be such did not possess sufficient sources' ('Völkerrechts-Literaturgeschichte' (n 56) 214, trans by the authors). The book FC von Moser *Beyträge zu dem Staats- und Völker-Recht und der Geschichte* (4 vols JC Gebhard Franckfurt 1764, 1765, 1772), is, despite its promising title, basically a compendium of legal acts and a description of practices of the German territories. A 'pre-modern' historiography of international law was R Ward *An Enquiry into the Foundation and History of the Law of Nations in Europe, from the Time of the Greeks and Romans to the Age of Grotius* (2 vols Wogan Dublin 1795). According to Arthur Nussbaum, who mentioned this work right at the beginning of his survey of the literature on the history of international law, that 'was the first literary enterprise of its author (born 1765), who later won some renown as a novelist. Its core consists of a stupendous if sometimes diffuse compilation of historical data and anecdotes, preceded by a lengthy theoretical 'Introduction' (Concise History (n 56) 293).
[93] 'A Short History' (n 59) 3–31 at 3.

the best of our knowledge—exclusively devoted to the study of the history of international law anywhere.

If the number of scholars turning to historical questions of international law has been small, the circle of scholars who did not only write about particular events (such as peace conferences and diplomatic summits, or the creation of a new state) but who tried to give a systematic account of the (modern) history of international law is even smaller.[94] In 1947, Arthur Nussbaum's *A Concise History of the Law of Nations* was published in New York; a second, enlarged edition followed in 1954 and was translated into German.[95] Nussbaum, born in Berlin in 1877, had practised law and taught trade law, banking law, and stock exchange law at Berlin University before he was forced to emigrate to the United States in 1934.[96] He taught at the Columbia Law School as a Research Professor of Public Law from 1934 until his retirement in 1951, and died in 1964 in New York.

By far more influential was Wilhelm Grewe's book *Epochen der Völkerrechtsgeschichte*,[97] translated into English by Michael Byers (*The Epochs of International Law*).[98] The work was soon acknowledged as a standard text on the history of modern international law.[99] It interpreted that history as a sequence of particular epochs defined in each case by the then-dominant power in the system of states. The modern history of international law, according to the author, began at the time of the French invasion of Italy under Charles VIII of France in 1494. Since then, there has been a modern system of states characterized by the principle of the balance of power and the 'infrastructure' of a permanent diplomacy. The author divided the succeeding periods according to the politically dominant power which in his view substantially influenced, or even created, the respective legal order. Grewe distinguished a Spanish age (1494–1648), a French age (1648–1815), and a British age (1815–1919). This periodization

[94] In addition to the works of Arthur Nussbaum, Wilhelm Grewe, and Martti Koskenniemi which we discuss in greater detail below, we would like to mention G Butler and S Maccoby *The Development of International Law* (Longmans London 1923); A Wegner *Geschichte des Völkerrechts* (Kohlhammer Stuttgart 1936); A Truyol y Serra *Histoire du droit international public* (Economica Paris 1995) (in Spanish under the title *Historia del derecho internacional publico* (Tecnos Editorial Madrid 1998)); C Focarelli *Lezioni di Storia del Diritto Internazionale* (Morlacchi Editore Peruggia 2002); D Gaurier *Histoire du droit international: Auteurs, doctrines et développement de l'Antiquitié à l'aube de la période contemporaine* (Presses Universitaires de Rennes 2005); DM Johnston, *The Historical Foundations of World Order: The Tower and the Arena* (Martinus Nijhoff Leiden 2007).

[95] A Nussbaum *A Concise History of the Law of Nations* (2nd edn Macmillan New York 1954); ibid *Geschichte des Völkerrechts in gedrängter Darstellung* (H Thiele-Fredersdorf trans) (CH Beck München 1960).

[96] See EC Stiefel and F Mecklenburg *Deutsche Juristen im amerikanischen Exil (1933–1950)* (JCB Mohr Tübingen 1991) at 62–4.

[97] WG Grewe *Epochen der Völkerrechtsgeschichte* (Nomos Baden-Baden 1984, 2nd unchanged edn 1988).

[98] *The Epochs of International Law* (n 61).

[99] The following is taken from B Fassbender 'Stories of War and Peace: On Writing the History of International Law in the "Third Reich" and After' (2002) 13 European Journal of International Law 479–512.

was recognized by other authors[100] and by the editors of the *Encyclopedia of Public International Law* at the Max Planck Institute in Heidelberg[101] which in turn led to a universal dissemination of Grewe's ideas.[102] While Grewe was strongly influenced by the ideas of Carl Schmitt, his periodization followed that suggested by the historian Wolfgang Windelband.[103]

A first manuscript of the *Epochen* was already completed in late 1944, but in the conditions prevailing in Germany in the last months of the war the book could not be printed. However, in a long article published a year earlier Grewe had summarized the principal findings of his as yet unpublished book.[104] He turned to the manuscript again after his retirement from the German diplomatic service. He revised and expanded the text, taking into consideration the literature that had appeared since the 1940s; he continued the account beyond the year 1939 (where the original text had ended), and added a new chapter dealing with the period since 1945 under the title 'United Nations: International Law in the Age of American-Soviet Rivalry and the Rise of the Third World'. In this form, the book was published in 1984.

While Grewe's resolute view of the history of international law as a function of great power politics was new, he continued a tradition of writing the history of international law begun in the 19th century. The founders of that tradition had taken the State as they experienced it in their times as a starting point for their historical reflections, and had looked back on the past with that particular form of State in mind. Grewe revitalized that tradition and even carried it over the edge of a new century. He certainly reinvigorated the study of historical issues in international law, and drew the attention of a new generation of scholars to the discipline.

Very differently from Grewe's work, Martti Koskenniemi's *The Gentle Civilizer of Nations* of 2002,[105] a series of essays covering the period from 1870 to 1960, combined

---

[100] KH Ziegler *Völkerrechtsgeschichte: Ein Studienbuch* (CH Beck München 1994, 2nd edn 2007). Alternative periodizations have been proposed by Heinhard Steiger and Douglas M Johnston. See H Steiger 'Vom Völkerrecht der Christenheit zum Weltbürgerrecht: Überlegungen zur Epochenbildung in der Völkerrechtsgeschichte' in P-J Heinig et al (eds) *Reich, Regionen und Europa in Mittelalter und Neuzeit: Festschrift für Peter Moraw* (Duncker & Humblot Berlin 2000) 171–87, repr H Steiger *Von der Staatengesellschaft zur Weltrepublik? Aufsätze zur Geschichte des Völkerrechts aus vierzig Jahren* (Nomos Baden-Baden 2009) 51–66; Engl version H Steiger 'From the International Law of Christianity to the International Law of the World Citizen' (2001) 3 Journal of the History of International Law 180–93; and *The Historical Foundations of World Order* (n 94).

[101] See the articles by W Preiser et al in R Bernhardt (ed) *Encyclopedia of Public International Law* (North-Holland Publ Co Amsterdam 1984) Instalment 7, at 126–273, and vol II of the 'Library Edition' (North-Holland Publ Co Amsterdam 1995) at 716–861.

[102] See the contribution by O Diggelmann 'The Periodization of the History of International Law' in this volume.

[103] W Windelband *Die auswärtige Politik der Grossmächte in der Neuzeit* (1494–1919) (Deutsche Verlags-Anstalt Stuttgart 1922, 5th edn 1942). See 'Stories of War and Peace', (n 99) 505–7.

[104] WG Grewe 'Die Epochen der modernen Völkerrechtsgeschichte' (1943) 103 Zeitschrift für die gesamte Staatswissenschaft 38–66 and 260–94.

[105] M Koskenniemi *The Gentle Civilizer of Nations: The Rise and Fall of International Law 1870–1960* (CUP Cambridge 2002).

legal analysis with (postmodern) historical and political critique, drawing in part on the biographical method with a study of key figures (including Hans Kelsen, Hersch Lauterpacht, Carl Schmitt, and Hans Morgenthau). Koskenniemi challenged the metanarrative of progressive legal development, and emphasized concealed anti-nomies in international law and the problem of interests and values protected and promoted by international law. He unveiled 'the radical character of the break that took place in the field between the first half of the nineteenth century and the emergence of a new professional self-awareness and enthusiasm between 1869 and 1885'.[106] In the author's own words, the book constitutes 'an experiment in departing from the constraints of the structural method in order to infuse the study of international law with a sense of historical motion and political, even personal, struggle.... [N]o assumption about history as a monolithic or linear progress narrative is involved'.[107] By analysing the ideas and arguments of some of the most influential international lawyers of the 19th and 20th centuries, Koskenniemi sought to describe 'a particular sensibility, or set of attitudes and preconceptions about matters international', and the 'rise' and 'fall' of that professional sensibility.[108] However, despite the difference of approach, Koskenniemi, like Grewe, emphasized the dependence of the development of international law on power and politics.

The translation of Grewe's work into English and the *Gentle Civilizer* have triggered a 'historiographical turn' in the discipline of international law.[109] Not only the history of international law, but also its methods and the objectives of studying this history have found heightened scholarly attention. It is therefore unsurprising that, quite recently some new collective works on the history of international law have been published.[110] However, histories written from a non-European perspective are still the exception.

---

[106] ibid 3–4.   [107] ibid 2.   [108] ibid.

[109] See GR Bandeira Galindo 'Martti Koskenniemi and the Historiographical Turn in International Law' (2005) 16 European Journal of International Law 539–59. Already some years before, the Journal of the History of International Law had been launched. In its first editorial, Ronald Macdonald described the journal's objective as 'to contribute to the effort to make intelligible the international legal past, however varied and eccentric it may be, to stimulate interest in the whys, the whats and the wheres of international legal development, without projecting present relationships upon the past, and to promote the application of a sense of proportion to the study of modern international legal problems.' (R St J Macdonald 'Editorial' (1999) 1 Journal of the History of International Law 1). See also IJ Hueck 'The Discipline of the History of International Law' (2001) 3 Journal of the History of International Law 194–217; A Kemmerer 'The Turning Aside: On International Law and its History' in RM Bratspies and RA Miller (eds) *Progress in International Law* (Martinus Nijhoff Leiden 2008) 71–93.

[110] *Time, History and International Law* (n 66); T Marauhn and H Steiger (eds) *Universality and Continuity in International Law* (Eleven The Hague 2011); A Orakhelashvili (ed) *Research Handbook on the Theory and History of International Law* (Edward Elgar Cheltenham 2011). See also International Law (n 6) 22–45 ('The historical evolution of the international community') and 'A Short History' (n 59) 3–31.

An eminent historian of international law remarked that 'one cannot learn any-thing from the histories of international law, at least nothing in concrete terms'.[111] We respectfully disagree. It is true that it is difficult to 'learn' from history in the sense that one could avoid making the same mistakes as in the past because situations and con-stellations always change so that experience can hardly be carried over from one time to another. But, we believe, studying the history of international law can help better to understand the character of that particular legal order, its promise and its limits. If we are not mistaken, we live right now in a period of fundamental change of interna-tional relations, a process instigated by the collapse of the Soviet Union and the com-munist bloc of states, and the end of the Cold War. If the history of international law since the 16th century has been characterized by a global expansion of Western ideas, and with it of Western domination, many signs today suggest that this history is drawing to a close. To know, in this situation, a bit of the law of nations of the past can help us to see the larger picture, and incite informed curiosity about how the histories of international law will continue.

---

[111] H Steiger 'Was heisst und zu welchem Ende studiert man Völkerrechtsgeschichte?' in I Appel, G Hermes and C Schönberger (eds) *Öffentliches Recht im offenen Staat: Festschrift für Rainer Wahl zum 70. Geburtstag* (Duncker & Humblot Berlin 2011) 211–23 at 222 (trans by the authors).

PART I

ACTORS

CHAPTER I

....

PEOPLES AND NATIONS

....

JÖRG FISCH

1. INTRODUCTION: PEOPLES' LAW AND STATES' LAW

....

INTERNATIONAL law is, and always has been, law between States and thus between political entities, not law between nations, peoples, or other groups of human beings. This holds at least for international law in the Greco-Roman tradition which has become the foundation of the worldwide international law, and which has also provided most of its terminology. States have never been the only subjects of international law, but they have always been the most essential ones.

While it seems uncontested that international law is first and above all law between States, 'States' law' plays an insignificant role in the history of the concept of international law. At least in European languages, the terms for international law used today do not refer to the State but to concepts with different backgrounds: to nations, from which 'international law', *droit international,* etc. comes, or to peoples (*gentes*), from which *droit des gens, derecho de gentes, diritto delle genti, Völkerrecht,* etc. are derived. This is no coincidence. The history of the concept of international law itself shows a clear insistence on this terminology. While 'States' law' or *Staatenrecht,* etc. as a term has been used occasionally, it has always remained an exception.[1] It seems that those involved did not want to use it as long as they could avoid it. This means that the terminology of international law is dominated by the idea of persons as actors. They form peoples and nations, not institutions and organizations.

2. The Terminology of 'Peoples' and 'Nations'[2]

In classical Greek, no term exists for what is now called 'international law'. The words from which derivations might come, such as 'demos' or 'polis', never seem to have lent themselves to such meanings. This does not necessarily mean that there was no equivalent of international law in ancient Greece, but there seems to have been no systematic reflection on it. The terms used today go back to Latin *ius gentium*. There is no *ius civitatum*, or *ius rerum publicarum*, or any other term derived from 'state' and its equivalents. Instead, the subject is a *gens*. This is a term with a very broad meaning. Yet it never encompasses the State, but rather a community of common descent. Thus at the origins of the terminology of international law, the emphasis is on a (real or invented) group or community and not on an organization; it is not law between states but instead between groups of human beings.

Gens was used for relations between states and political entities only after a kind of incubatory phase. First, *ius gentium* meant, instead of law between *gentes*, law common to all *gentes*. *Ius gentium* was natural law, in contrast to *ius civile*, the domestic law of Rome. International law maintained this dual character of (natural) law common to all mankind (not necessarily to states), and law for the relations between different *gentes*, although in reality it regulated relations between states or other political organizations. Thus international law seems or claims to differ from states' law. Linguistically, it represents itself as law between peoples and/or nations. The State is a phenomenon which in the first place reflects power relations, while peoples and nations are the products of the will of the human beings involved.

---

[1] Eg I Kant 'Die Metaphysik der Sitten' in *Gesammelte Schriften* (Akademie-Ausgabe) (Königlich Preußische Akademie der Wissenschaften Berlin 1902-; repr de Gruyter Berlin 1968) vol 6, 343 ff ('Staatenrecht'); for further distinctions see KHL Pölitz *Natur- und Völkerrecht; Staats- und Staatenrecht, und Staatskunst* (Hinrich'sche Buchhandlung Leipzig 1823) at 301–4.

[2] For the history of the terminology cf especially E Reibstein *Völkerrecht: Eine Geschichte seiner Ideen in Lehre und Praxis* (2 vols Karl Alber Freiburg 1957); H Steiger 'Völkerrecht' in O Brunner, W Conze, and R Koselleck (eds) *Geschichtliche Grundbegriffe* (Klett-Cotta Stuttgart 1992) vol 7, 97–140; R Koselleck et al 'Volk, Nation' in *Geschichtliche Grundbegriffe* (Klett-Cotta Stuttgart 1992) vol 7, 141–431; M Canovan *The People* (CUP Cambridge 2005).

The formative period of the modern terminology of international law was during the 16th and especially the 17th and 18th centuries, when the hitherto dominating Latin concepts were translated into the vernaculars. Translation led to a diversification of the terminology, which however, strictly kept to groups of people, not to political entities, especially states. But first, there was a kind of *translatio* within Latin: instead of *gens*, or rather beside it, *populus* and *natio* were used. Strictly speaking, these terms were not used in Latin but only in the Romance languages. First, *ius gentium* was translated without difficulties into, for example, *droit des gens, derecho de gentes, diritto delle genti,* or *direito das gentes.* Germanic languages stretched this conceptual translation further: *gens* became *Volk*, leading to *Völkerrecht* in German, *volkenrecht* in Dutch, *folkeret* in Danish, or *folkrätt* in Swedish. Strangely enough, the one language which is more a mixture of Romance and Germanic languages than any other—English—did not accept this translation: there was no significant use of the terms 'law of peoples' or 'peoples' law'.

The importance of the new concept is indirectly emphasized by the fact that a second terminological tradition developed. Both *Volk* and *gens* referred to *populus*, which became a competitor for *gens*. But the use of *populus* had a disadvantage: it also, and sometimes exclusively, meant the ordinary people, the low people, and even the rabble. This meaning was more pronounced in the Romance than in the Germanic languages and thus probably led to a tendency to avoid the use of 'people' altogether. Thus there was no 'peoples' law' or *droit des peuples*, while *Völkerrecht* became quite frequently used.

Perhaps due to these difficulties a further competitor for a translation from Latin arose: *natio*. It had a partly similar etymology, referring mainly to communities of common descent, but it lacked the pejorative component of *populus*. Hitherto it had differentiated between relatively coincidental groups, especially in universities, while now a nation became a human group definitely distinguished from other groups which tended to form a state. The Romance languages spoke of *droit international, derecho internacional, direito internacional,* etc., while the Germanic languages used *internationales Recht, volkenrecht,* etc. Thus there were two sets of terms for international law, one going back to *populus* and the other to *natio*. The question was which would gain precedence in the long run. Until the 20th century, the competition between them was open. In the end, *natio* won the day, possibly for mainly linguistic reasons. While English had, for unknown reasons, not coined 'people's right', it had used 'law of nations' as early as in the 16th century.

This linguistic particularity, in connection with the rapid and global spread of English in the 20th and 21st centuries, contributed to the victory of the English terminology, which can perhaps best be seen in encyclopedias. While the first and the second editions of the German standard reference work on international law, published in 1925 and 1962 respectively, were entitled *Wörterbuch des Völkerrechts (und der Diplomatie)*, the following editions were published in English only, under the title *Encyclopedia of Public International Law* (1992–2003; now online as *Max Planck Encyclopedia of Public International Law*, <http://www.mpepil.com/>). Whether in the end the terminology of international law will be reduced to the derivations of *natio*, completely eclipsing *populus* and *gens*, remains to be seen. It is undeniable, however, that in international law, the terminology referring to persons (in the plural) and not to institutions has won. This emphasizes not the reality but the ideal of international law, by deliberately avoiding every word that might convey the idea of a law of or between states, while the terms actually used transport the idea of an informal set of relations between groups.

3. State Power and the Will of the People

As far as history can show, most existing and former states were not the products of democratic processes but of their own power. This is particularly clear in former colonies. These were lands conquered by European powers which became independent within the borders drawn by these powers. Only in rare cases were new states founded, fully or in part, by real democratic processes. And even then, there often was little choice for the individuals concerned to choose not to become part of the new state.

The actual territorial distribution of the world thus reflects and is the result of the worldwide distribution of power, and there seems to be little chance that this pattern will be replaced by determining the will of the people. The existing terminology conveys the idea that, ideally, those whose lives are determined by existing borders should have the right to decide the questions connected with their place within international law. To what extent has this postulate been realized? If such wishes are to be taken seriously, it must be possible to revise borders from time to time, which means that the possibility must exist that any new wishes of the people can be expressed by redrawing the boundaries of the state.

4. Borders

Most existing international borders are the result of fighting, or at least of power relations. Of course, this is not an automatic mechanism. A state may become more powerful than its neighbour in the course of centuries without a single change of borders or an armed conflict. But once there is a conflict, its resolution of border disputes will usually reflect not the preferences of the people on both sides (or of the two nations) but their respective strength at any given moment. If one takes a worldwide survey of borders of independent states, by far the greatest number of them are the result of colonialism, but in a very specific sense. Borders outside Europe are, by and large, not the result of European conquest overseas and thus of delimitations between European and local powers, but either of conflicts and compromises between European powers both within and outside Europe, or of administrative acts of colonial powers. This holds for most borders in the Americas and in Africa, in the Pacific and in the Caribbean, and for many in Asia. By far the greatest number of them have been imposed upon the independent states which were the result of decolonization between 1783 (recognition of American independence) and the late 20th century. This was the so-called principle of *uti possidetis* which had been developed in Latin America to adopt the borders drawn by the colonial powers irrespective of the wishes of the peoples concerned, not only of the conquered peoples and the slaves, but also of the settlers who became the ruling groups of the new states.[3]

This is not new. There may be a few states in the world which owe their existence, and especially their borders, to plebiscites, but there is not one single state which in its actual territorial shape is the exclusive result of the wishes of the people living in it.

5. PEOPLES AND NATIONS IN THE HISTORY OF INTERNATIONAL LAW

5.1. 16th–18th Centuries

Little is known about the role of peoples and nations in pre-modern international legal relationships both in theory and in practice. We know that part of the people had a say in Greek democracies and, to a lesser extent, in republican institutions in Rome. But with regard to the central focus of this chapter, states were constituted, annihilated, extended, or reduced mainly by force, not by discussions or plebiscites. This view found its clearest expression in Thucydides' dialogue between the Athenians and the Melians: it is not the majority but the most powerful who decide.[4] This

---

[3] O Corten et al (eds) *Démembrements d'états et délimitations territoriales: L'uti possidetis en question(s)* (Bruylant Brussels 1999).

[4] Thucydides, *History of the Peloponnesian War* (MI Finley ed, R Warner trans) (Penguin London 1972) 5.84–5.116.

holds even more true for the Middle Ages, as there were few democratic institutions (while there were many forms of participation by estates).

Somewhat more is known about the early modern period, with regard to both theory and practice. There were three sets of theories which, if rendered into practice, would have abolished unilateral decisions.

First, there was the theory of the original contract.[5] According to this view, the state was not the result of conquest or of the use of force in general, but of a contract made between all members of a newly founded state and thus of the wishes of those involved. Ideally, the whole people participated, and the state was the result of their wishes.

The second theoretical aspect had an even greater impact on international law, especially from the 18th century on, with Rousseau as its most influential protagonist. It dealt with the international legal consequences of sovereignty which had been discussed since Bodin had published his *Les six livres de la république* in 1576. There were two very different relevant aspects. The theory (or rather the postulate) of popular sovereignty displaced sovereignty from the hands of a monarch or an aristocracy into those of the people. A possible consequence was the spread of democracy. This, however, did not mean that subjects of international law (states) were no longer constituted by force. The emphasis on popular sovereignty was a precondition for a more important position of the people, but this position was not its necessary consequence.[6]

The third theoretical position which had the potential to improve the position of the people, and even of nations, was the right to resistance, which had its roots in the Middle Ages, and which gained strength since the 16th century.[7] It presupposed a right to resist unjust laws and government. It went even further than the other two theoretical positions by allowing victims to reject the power of those who treated them unjustly and, in very serious cases, even to take their lives. It was a right of the entire people, not just, as other rights, of a single ruler or of a few aristocrats. In the same way as with popular sovereignty, this right did not exclude the use of force—it even tended to increase it, by inciting resistance. But it allowed the building of new states based not on force but on the wishes of the people.

Up until the late 18th century, however, these three elements remained largely hypothetical. There were no treaties between rulers and subjects, 'the people' did not really exercise sovereignty, and, although there might be resistance, the right to resist was fiercely resisted by the rulers and did not really become constitutional law.

Nevertheless, other rights of the people were gradually conceded in international law. They still depended on power relations, but in a different manner. They were not the rights the victors usually gained in the ordinary fashion, but rights of the

---

[5] Cf N Southwood *Contractualism and the Foundations of Morality* (OUP Oxford 2010); D Boucher and P Kelly (eds) *The Social Contract from Hobbes to Rawls* (Routledge New York 1994).

[6] Cf R Prokhovnik *Sovereignty: History and Theory* (Imprint Academic Exeter 2008).

[7] Cf R von Friedeburg *Widerstandsrecht in der frühen Neuzeit* (Duncker & Humblot Berlin 2001).

vanquished. And they were not rights of the defeated ruling groups only. Rather, they were rights of the vanquished people as a whole. Of course there had even before been in international law certain rules in favour of the weak, especially in warfare. But the new rights went further, in connection with the conclusion of peace treaties. It was a kind of individualization. If territory was ceded after a war, those who did not want to remain and lose their citizenship were allowed to emigrate, maintaining their previous citizenship. They had a *ius emigrandi*, limited first to those who wanted to maintain their religion. Later on, this right, usually called 'option', was generalized.[8] It was a very limited right, but it was a right in favour of the people, to mitigate the hardships of the vanquished. It was not a right to choose one's status freely, as it was not allowed simply to maintain the majority citizenship and/or religion while remaining in the ceded territory. Nevertheless it was a very valuable right if compared with the position of civilians in the 20th century who, after the loss of a war, frequently were either expelled from their land, or prevented from leaving it, or even killed.

5.2. The American Revolution, Decolonization, *Uti Possidetis*, and Secession

Measured with the yardstick of the three theoretical postulates of contract theory, people's sovereignty, and the right to resist, these were limited rights indeed. But theory now gradually influenced practice. The first and most important step to its realization was the American Revolution. Admittedly even here the decisive factor was power. Independence was, in the last analysis, the result of victory. War was not abolished, either in theory or in practice. But new rights were derived from the theoretical postulates. 'The people' claimed sovereignty for themselves. This meant that they claimed rights which hitherto had been the prerogative of the ruler or of the ruling group. According to the insurgents, these rights had been infringed, thus conveying a right to resistance. Consequently, at least two of the three postulates were put into practice. Most important, because most concrete, was the right to resist. In time, revolutionaries did not only claim to recover their particular rights which according to them had been violated; rather, the infringement of so many and important rights by the King of Great Britain gave them in their own view a more general right to reject all claims made on themselves by the King, which meant they could claim independence. Independence was not just a reward for victory (although, of course, without victory there would have been no independence), but a natural right that—although with some restrictions—had belonged to the insurgents even before the War of Independence.

[8] Cf H Wehberg *Plebiszit und Optionsklausel* (Volksverein-Verlag Mönchengladbach 1915).

The independence of the United states was one of the great victories of a people in world history. In the War, a new right had been vindicated: the right of a suffering and exploited, unjustly treated people to independence. As important as it was, if it was examined more closely, this was only a partial victory. The Americans claimed for themselves only a conditional right: if they were unjustly treated, they had a right to break all ties with their previous masters. It is easy to imagine instead an unconditional right: in this case, a people, although it might be treated on a footing of perfect equality or even on a preferential basis, nevertheless would prefer independence.

This would be an immense step forward in the position of the people in international law. A people and, *a fortiori*, a nation (which, from this time onward, came to mean the population of a state, and sometimes even the state itself) would have the right to independence, to build a sovereign state, and not just to be granted some autonomy. The insurgents had made it clear in the Declaration of Independence: they claimed equal rights with Britain, and they called themselves, in the Constitution of 1787, 'We the people', and not 'We, part of the people'.

The Founding Fathers themselves probably at first did not fully realize how far-reaching the step they had taken had been. Even if the natural right to independence was restricted to a conditional right, dependent upon the violation of rights of the settlers by the King, it was easy to imagine that other groups which considered themselves peoples or nations would also claim such a right. And this process could go on indefinitely: a state could separate from the United States, and a county could separate from a state. Indeed, the first century of American history was shaped to a great extent by the effort not to concede a right of independence (first conditional, then unconditional) to parts of the Union. The climax of these events was the Civil War (1861–65), when the southern states, claiming a right to secede from the Union, declared themselves, following the example of the Union, free and independent, but were forced back into the Union in the bloodiest war in the history of the United States.

The precedent contained in the Declaration of Independence of the United States had unforeseen consequences. After 1776, the Union was mainly occupied with preventing secessions, not with conveying rights to peoples. Three instruments were developed to prevent secessions or at least limit them to the most extreme cases, which at the same time meant that the rights of peoples were gradually restricted.

Such limitations were not easy to enforce once a right to independence, even though only a confined, conditional, or remedial one (for injustices suffered), had been granted, at least in principle. Basically, each group or collective which considered itself a people, and even more a nation, could claim independence. In order to avoid this disruptive consequence, it became the aim of the foreign policy of the United States not to encourage secessions. The US tried to maintain the status quo in the distribution of America among European claimants. The following instruments and principles were developed.

5.2.1. *Decolonization*

The principal category was decolonization. This process was only named in the 20th century, but the principle could be derived from the history of the independence of the United States. There was no general right to independence, but only such a right for colonies. At first, as long as it was conditional, it was not even a right for all colonies but only for colonies which had been suffering from serious and frequent injustices. This restriction, however, was abandoned in Latin America and later in all other colonies, although the United States continued to maintain it in a limited manner, expressed especially in the Monroe Doctrine of 1823: it did not urge an immediate end of colonialism, but it rejected any kind of new colonialism by European powers in America.[9] Once a colony had declared its independence, whether for good or for dubious reasons, it was not to be forced back under colonial rule. This was a doctrine of the status quo which, if it was impossible to maintain, could be changed in one way only: by granting independence to the colonies concerned. In theory, this held for the whole world; in practice, it was restricted to the Americas, as illustrated by the US conquest of the Philippines (1899–1902), which demonstrated a flat denial of independence.

Decolonization thus meant the limitation of the right to independence to areas that were ruled by states situated at a distance, usually overseas, but sometimes separated by huge stretches of land constituting third states. Decolonization did not mean, at least in principle, secession of contiguous territory.

The interest the United States and other states, which were the result of decolonization, had in preventing a right to independence of contiguous territories is fairly self-evident. Without such a guarantee they ran the risk of losing parts of their territory.

The rule of contiguity prohibiting, except in special cases, secession, and especially decolonization, is one of the most widely accepted rules in international law—but it has never unambiguously and explicitly been formulated. Decolonization of contiguous territory is not really prohibited but it is, due to its feared consequences, heavily discouraged. Looked at from the point of view of peoples and nations, it is a rather strange and even unjust rule. If a population that lives far from the centre of the state have a right to found a state of their own, why should a group living in an area contiguous to the centre not have the same right?

5.2.2. Uti Possidetis

The second principle was originally developed not by the United States but in Latin America. It was built upon the first principle, but it was more restricted and at the same time more precise: the principle of *uti possidetis*. It said that administrative borders within, and national borders between, newly founded states were not to be freshly drawn during the decolonization process. Instead, the colonial borders had to

---

[9] The text is in HS Commager (ed) *Documents of American History* (7th edn Appleton-Century-Crofts New York 1963) at 235–7.

be confirmed, both between colonies of different colonial powers (mainly between Spain and Portugal, which decided the eventual borders of Brazil), and between different Spanish (or Spanish-claimed) administrative units. The message not just to America but to the whole world was clear: once decolonization was over, the new American states wanted at least as much stability as their European counterparts. In fact, they became even more stable because they were less plagued by the centuries-old border conflicts which were so frequent in Europe. *Uti possidetis* meant that borders from now on should be immutable. This again meant, as in the case of decolonization, reducing, and even abolishing, the role of native American peoples and nations. The colonial borders everywhere in the Americas were the result of power struggles between the respective colonial powers (and thus, states), not of the wishes of the interested peoples and nations. So a whole continent, later to be followed by other parts of the world, fell back on the principle of power deciding instead of democratic processes. What remained was the doctrine of people's sovereignty as justification for decolonization.

Uti possidetis gradually determined the borders of the whole world, right up to the dissolution of Yugoslavia and the Soviet Union. Once there was no longer any formal discrimination between the inhabitants of different continents or other areas, it was the most convenient means to maintain international stability—provided it was possible to discard the wishes of those peoples whose claims to statehood did not coincide with the traditional, internationally recognized borders. It meant that states had priority over peoples and nations, and this priority was gathering momentum more or less continuously.

5.2.3. *Prohibition of Secession*

The third principle was contained in the first and in the second, but its emphasis was different. In a sense it was obvious, but it gained much more gravitas once it had been vigorously demonstrated. It was the rigorous prohibition of any kind of secession unless it could be described as decolonization. It was rather risky to proclaim this rule, as it defied all groups that wanted to found a state of their own. So it is not surprising that it had to be enforced in one of the bloodiest wars of modern history, in the American Civil War, whose central contentious issue was not slavery, at least not in the beginning, but secession. The Confederates in 1861 claimed for themselves the same right the Thirteen Colonies had claimed in 1776. They had the better argument—but the Union was stronger and succeeded in prohibiting secession. Strictly speaking, this was valid for the United States only. What began as a rule of US constitutional law, however, soon was welcomed as a worldwide rule. France, for example, declared in all its constitutions since 1791 that the kingdom (or republic) was 'un(e) et indivisible'.[10] But the principle never became formal law. This was prevented mainly

---

[10] J Godechot *Les constitutions de la France depuis 1789* (Garnier-Flammarion Paris 1970).

by the United States: one of the most blatant secessions in the 19th and 20th centuries was the breaking away of Panama from Colombia in 1903 which never could have been realized without US support.

Looking back at the role of the American Revolution in the development of an independent position of peoples and nations in international law, all this involved one step forward and three steps back. The step forward was the emphasis on peoples' sovereignty, the steps back involved the limitation to decolonization, *uti possidetis*, and the prohibition of secession. But the advance was still more important than the retreat. Nevertheless it was obvious that strong fetters were limiting any progress in the role of peoples and nations in international law. They saved states from being continuously partitioned.

There is no doubt that the leading position in this early development of an independent position for peoples and nations in international law belonged to the United States of America. But this development soon became an inter-American and finally a worldwide matter which, however, maintained important regional differences.

5.3. Plebiscites in the 19th Century

The immediate successors to the American Revolution were the Latin American revolutions between around 1808 and 1826, mainly concerning Spanish territories.[11] They not only developed the principle of *uti possidetis*, they claimed what in the North prior to 1776 not even a radical like Thomas Paine had dared to ask: an unconditional right to independence for all colonies, regardless of their status and of how they had been treated by their mother country. This was the beginning of the end of colonialism long before the European colonial empires had achieved their greatest reach.

It was an ambivalent legacy. *Uti possidetis* meant that the partition of the American continent had to be effected as a consequence of administrative acts of European states in earlier centuries, while the right to independence left it to the people whether they wanted a state of their own, whatever the consequences in practice might be. Both rights, or principles, were formulated without restrictions, but in practice both were, for the moment at least, limited to colonies in America. There was no right to independence for other continents, but in the long run it would be difficult to maintain such a distinction.

In 1789, between the American revolutions in the North and in the South, the first successful great and radical European revolution occurred in France. There were important differences between America and Europe. Certainly there was

---

[11] For the sources see J Malagón (ed) *Las actas de independencia de América* (Organización de los Estados Americanos Washington 1973); a concise overview is J Lynch *The Spanish American Revolutions 1808–1826* (Weidenfeld & Nicolson London 1973).

unrest in the French colonies overseas, and Saint-Domingue/Haiti even won its independence, but on the whole, the French Revolution was not a colonial but a domestic revolution. There could thus be no right to independence, although an emphasis on peoples' sovereignty suggested itself strongly. But who were 'the people'? Those living in the same state? According to the formula of peoples' sovereignty, the people were to decide who was to build a state. Hitherto, the distribution of territories and their population among states had been the mirror or the consequence of the distribution of power. If the people were really sovereign, they had to decide themselves not between colonies and mother countries, as this was a distinction that could not be made within Europe, but according to their real wishes. The result could be a new state.

The solution was easy, at least in principle: it was the plebiscite, which indeed was developed in France shortly after the outbreak of the French Revolution, from 1791.[12] If it was taken seriously, the plebiscite was a revolution in itself. What had hitherto made up the strength of the state—its population—could lose its importance altogether if the people did not want to participate. Power would no longer convey any title to territory—it was replaced by the people's will. It was difficult to imagine that previously powerful states would accept such methods and sacrifice themselves as victims to be torn to pieces by plebiscites. This was too radical a revolution. Until the First World War, it was never fully and unconditionally accepted by strong states, while to weak states and strong peoples it suggested an opportunity to increase their own strength. The result was a very limited success: up until the time of the First World War, there was not one case in which a European border was determined (and not just moved from one state to another) by plebiscite.

Plebiscites in territorial questions were first used by France, between 1791 and 1860, in connection with the annexation of neighbouring territories. The results claimed were that usually between 99 and 99.9 per cent of the votes cast were in favour of joining France, a rather unlikely proportion of support.[13]

The second important round of plebiscites was held in 1859/1860 in Italy, in order to support unification, with even more one-sided results.[14] In the smaller Italian states, the votes were in favour of joining the newly founded kingdom of Italy, while in Savoy and Nice plebiscites were used to give the Italian people's blessing to the cession of territory to France, as a reward for French support in the war against Austria. It was difficult to imagine a plebiscite that resulted in favour of Italy, with France losing the reward it had been promised by Sardinia-Piemont (and paid by winning the

---

[12] The best works on the history of the plebiscite are still those by S Wambaugh *A Monograph on Plebiscites* (OUP New York 1920) and *Plebiscites Since the World War* (2 vols Carnegie Endowment for International Peace Washington 1933); for recent developments see A Peters *Das Gebietsreferendum im Völkerrecht: Seine Bedeutung im Lichte der Staatenpraxis nach 1989* (Nomos Baden-Baden 1995).

[13] *Monograph on Plebiscites* (n 12).

[14] Ibid 83 and 86; PL Ballini *Le elezioni nella storia d'Italia dall'unità al fascismo* (Il Mulino Bologna 1988) at 243 f.

war against Austria). So it was quite obvious that plebiscites were not used to assess the wishes of the people but instead to confirm the results previously reached by diplomacy and/or war. If there was uncertainty about the outcome, voters had to be influenced and results rigged.

This background shows that the plebiscite was not an instrument used to assess the wishes of the people. But the fact that plebiscites, however manipulated, were held, was an indicator of the growing importance of democracy. Once a plebiscite had been admitted, it was difficult to refuse it next time, and there was a growing likelihood that it would gradually become the expression of the people's will.

It would be wrong to presume a general tendency to more democracy and, especially, to more plebiscites in the 19th century. This is confirmed in the context of the German unification. There was—in contrast to the unification of Italy—no single plebiscite in the course of the German unification. Yet it is difficult to maintain that what happened in Italy was more democratic, that people had a greater say in its unification than was the case in Germany. It is often emphasized that the fact that the Germans refused to hold a plebiscite was one of the main reasons for the long conflict about Alsace-Lorraine. This is an unlikely thesis. Holding a plebiscite had not become, by 1870, a condition for territorial change. France in 1870, before its defeat, had claimed German territories to improve its Eastern border without giving a thought to a plebiscite. To expect, on the other hand, Germany to organize a fair plebiscite in Alsace-Lorraine at the risk of losing the contested territory after a brilliant military victory would have been such a humiliation for a loser, and more so for a winner, that it is simply impossible to imagine. Of course, it might have been wise for the Germans to renounce territorial acquisitions all the same. But this would have been something completely different. A real plebiscite would have been a revolution. It would have meant a change from a decision as a result of power to a decision as a consequence of the people's wishes.

In the meantime, around 1850, the principle had finally found its linguistic expression. While in America there had never been a generally accepted term for the right to independence of a people or a nation, the Europeans now coined the term 'right of self-determination of peoples', or 'national self-determination'.[15] Again it was a matter of the people or the nation, not of the state, and it would remain so until today. But the terms continued to be used only with reference to Europe, not to America.

The use of the plebiscite did not become more frequent; rather, it almost became phased out after the 1860s. Peoples and nations lost importance in favour of states, and the right of self-determination was not much discussed in international law. The only exception were the Marxist-Socialist parties in Central and Eastern Europe, as a

---

[15] The Hungarian politician Lajos Kossuth spoke on 3 November 1851 in London of a 'sovereign right of every nation to dispose of itself'. L Kossuth *Selected Speeches of Kossuth: Condensed and Abridged With Kossuth's Express Sanction* (FW Newman ed) (CS Francis New York 1854) at 15.

result of intensifying conflicts among nationalities which could threaten the unity of the workers in these areas.

5.4. The First World War: Lenin and Wilson

The First World War began as a traditional power conflict between states. The wishes of the peoples involved were irrelevant. Each belligerent had territorial aims which were usually not legitimized with a purported right of self-determination of the nations, nationalities, peoples, minorities, or groups involved. One of the most glaring examples was Italy, which was promised important territories, some Italian-speaking and some not, in a treaty of 1915 with the allied powers. It seemed too dangerous to demand new borders according to the principle of nationalities—such an act would have threatened the very existence or at least the unity of states on both sides: on the side of the Central Powers it might have disrupted the multinational Habsburg and Ottoman empires, while the Allies might have lost their huge colonial empires and Russia would have opted out. Whoever used the principle of self-determination ran the risk of being destroyed or at least weakened.

The first big state threatened by a crushing defeat was Russia, in the Revolution of 1917. The new regime at first undertook to keep pledges made to its allies, despite the disastrous situation. The consequence was that it threatened to fall apart. In this situation Lenin, in October 1917, proclaimed the right to self-determination as principle for the conclusion of a lasting peace. He had urged it since at least 1903, but only on behalf of his party. Now it became official policy of revolutionary Russia. Under the threat of losing his position altogether, Lenin was consistent, and proclaimed self-determination not only for his enemies, endangering them and their colonial empires, but also and foremost for Russia itself, declaring himself prepared to grant independence to all peoples living within the borders of Russia, with a right to secede, which meant the right to form an independent state.

This was a serious threat both for the other Allies and for the Central Powers, all the more so as Lenin did not only recognize a theoretical right to independence but accepted it in practice (which meant secession), especially in Finland and in the Baltic states.

Lenin's enemies attempted to avoid the subject. This, however, was not easy as the demand for self-determination became more and more popular. President Woodrow Wilson undertook to offer an answer. His thoughts on a general peace greatly differed from Lenin's. He did not urge a right to independence for all (and especially colonial) peoples, but he proclaimed self-government and autonomy, which basically meant democracy, but not necessarily independence. This was a popular, but an insufficient demand. Democracy and autonomy were truly attractive for a people as a people only if they were already independent. Wilson found himself in a difficult situation. If he proclaimed 'self-government', he proclaimed a prestigious but not terribly inspiring message. If, instead, he used 'self-determination', he relied on a formula which was extremely successful and popular but which did not express what he really meant. He had no real choice. If he wanted to succeed, he had to adopt Lenin's slogan. He did so, still meaning 'self-government' while he spoke of 'self-determination'. But he was understood in the sense of Lenin, whether he wanted this or not. When he proclaimed self-determination, a term which he used but seldom, he might define it as he liked, people still understood the term in the sense that Lenin had used it.

While Lenin had offered self-determination first and foremost to his own country and its nationalities, Wilson did not recommend it to his own allies. He did not proclaim a right to self-determination of colonial peoples. No colonies with a non-white population gained real independence in the peace treaties of 1918–23, regardless of their contribution to the war.

While, at least for the moment, self-determination did not become an object for colonial powers, it had more influence in Europe, especially among its many minorities. But it still competed and collided with the age-old principle that borders were drawn not according to the wishes of the people (and peoples) concerned but according to the strength of the parties involved. A supposed right to self-determination might have had contradictory consequences. It could strengthen the victor by confirming his claims to territory by a popular vote, and at the same time further weaken the claims of the vanquished. But it could also weaken the victor by a popular vote against him and thus strengthen the conquered. From the standpoint of international stability, this was the most destabilizing consequence possible. If fighting had shown the actual distribution of power, the wishes of the people might indicate a different direction that might be taken. Whoever wanted a full correspondence between the results of the fighting and the distribution of territories had to avoid plebiscites.

It was quite out of the question to find a real and lasting solution for all these problems, even though they might be restricted to Europe. Most famous and most difficult became the dissolution of Austria-Hungary. This was done largely on the basis of historical borders, some of which were more or less accepted by the populations concerned. But this acceptance was only presumed and not really expressed by the people. In other cases there was outright opposition against some new international borders; for example, between Italy and Austria. A union of Austria and Germany, which would probably have been popular with a great majority of the population in both countries, was prohibited without a plebiscite.[16] Wherever the distribution of power was obviously in their favour, the victors did not want to run the risk of losing a plebiscite. The growing weight of the opinion of the people showed itself in cases in which the victors were not terribly interested because they were not important for the

---

[16] Treaty of Peace Between the Allied and Associated Powers and Austria (signed 10 September 1919, entered into force 16 July 1920) 2501 LNTS art 88.

balance of power. Here some plebiscites were held, especially between Poland and Germany.[17] They showed that it was possible to draw state borders that were accepted by a reasonable and sometimes even a huge majority of the populations. Although this method was unsuited to solve all conflicts, it at least permitted the confirmation (or rejection) by popular vote of a border that previously had been imposed by force. Popular sovereignty was no longer just a formal principle. Instead it influenced the distribution of power. But the basic decisions about this distribution remained the result of power, not of the wishes of the peoples (or of nations).

5.5. The Period between the World Wars: Hitler's Long Shadow

Outside Europe the principle of self-determination did not play an important role once peace had been restored in Europe. This does not mean that there were no conflicts between colonial powers and colonial peoples, the foremost struggle being that of the Indian national movement against the British. This was a question of decolonization, comparable with the first decolonization in the Americas. There was, however, an important difference between the first and the second waves of decolonization. Most American revolutions had been led by European settlers or their descendants. Now, anti-colonial liberation movements all over the world were led by natives or at least non-whites. Thus, while there was little change in the terminology of self-determination, the groups behind such movements were radically different; they were no longer almost exclusively European but were largely from a mainly non-European background. But on the whole, between the two World Wars, anti-colonial movements with claims for self-determination remained rather muted. Instead, the slogan 'self-determination' in the sense that each people and perhaps even each minority had a right to a state of their own, had strong ramifications in Europe. It was, as the American Secretary of state Robert Lansing had noted as early as in 1918, a question 'simply loaded with dynamite',[18] for two reasons. First, it was in itself a problem that could not really be solved to the satisfaction of all interested groups and even less to the satisfaction of all interested individuals. Second, even if a solution had been possible, the peace treaties after the Great War had, partly inadvertently and partly deliberately, confirmed or redrawn thousands of kilometres of borders which were bound to generate discontent. These peace treaties drew many borders which were less contested and which did respect the wishes of the people better than previous borders had, as was the case with some parts of Poland. But they

---

[17] See *Plebiscites Since the World War* (n 12).

[18] R Lansing *The Peace Negotiations: A Personal Narrative* (Houghton Mifflin Company Boston 1921) at 97.

also produced new minorities. It was easy to understand that the victors did not want to change borders in order to satisfy people's aspirations if they risked being weakened themselves.

Thus Europe became a continent plagued by revisionisms, with dissatisfied majorities and minorities of nationalities which were refused what to them seemed just claims. But it was difficult to speak of justice in a situation in which legitimate wishes of one group excluded the legitimate wishes of others.

Such clashes were particularly serious and had particularly far-reaching consequences in the fully or partly German-speaking areas of Central Europe. As a result of the peace treaties, there was a fairly compact German-speaking bloc distributed over several states. In some of these, German speakers were in the majority, in others they were minorities. If nationality (or language) had been taken as criterion for drawing borders, a strong German national bloc would have been the result and thus exactly what the victors had fought to prevent. From a political point of view, it would have been absurd thus to lose all fruits of victory. But once self-determination had become one of the decisive criteria for drawing borders it was difficult to reject it.

This situation allowed Hitler to implement his expansionist programme in the traditional military manner, but seemingly also as a realization of a right of self-determination. As a rule, the victors of 1918 would reject any kind of revisionism, as it would weaken their position. But if it concerned self-determination, they were bound to have a bad conscience, as they had, in defence against Lenin, proclaimed the principle but not kept their promises. As long as Hitler was able to use self-determination as a basis for his plans, he had a good chance of fooling the world by appearing to be an innocent sufferer.

It began in 1935, when, pursuant to the Versailles Treaty, there was a plebiscite in the Saarland.[19] More than 90 per cent of the population voted for a return to Germany. It was a small territory, but it was a great victory for Hitler. He gained two greater ones. In March 1938 he annexed Austria, without a prior plebiscite. It was not a contested fact that the great majority of Austrians were in favour of a union. It was difficult for the victors of the Great War to reject an act which could be considered as self-determination. In the end, Mexico was the only country which voiced any real protest against the *Anschluss*. Afterwards, Hitler held a plebiscite which had about the same legitimacy as the Italian plebiscites in the 1860s: everybody knew that the people at large were in favour of union, but they also knew that the result (99.02 per cent for union in Germany, 99.73 per cent in Austria) was bound to be rigged.[20] Respect for the wishes of the people had not advanced very far since 1860.

[19] cf J Fisch 'Adolf Hitler und das Selbstbestimmungsrecht der Völker' (2010) 290 Historische Zeitschrift 93–118.

[20] O Jung *Plebiszit und Diktatur: Die Volksabstimmungen der Nationalsozialisten* (JCB Mohr (Paul Siebeck) Tübingen 1995) at 119–22.

Hitler's next great victory, this time without even a plebiscite ex post, was the annexation of the German-speaking Sudetenland of Czechoslovakia in September 1938, as a consequence of the Munich Conference. In 1918/19 most of its inhabitants wanted to join Germany, but their land was adjudicated to Czechoslovakia in the peace treaties, for strategic reasons. Again, it was difficult to justify this rejection once self-determination had been declared an important principle of the peace. So Britain, France, and Italy capitulated in Munich. By now it had become clear that Hitler was a virtuoso of self-determination. He was able to be so just because he was not interested in self-determination. He had a far-reaching programme of annexations, as he showed when he occupied the remaining Czech-speaking territories of Bohemia-Moravia in March 1939, and conquered Poland in September 1939. It was impossible to pretend that the majority of these people wanted to join Germany. The principle of self-determination had been led *ad absurdum*, but it had enabled Hitler to realize an annexationist programme. That it had not been a victory for the sovereignty of peoples or nations had been clear from the beginning, and it became clearer as Hitler's war unfolded. It was a traditional war of conquest that had nothing to do with the wishes of a people, not even with the wishes of the German people, and much less, of course, of the subjugated and exploited peoples. Instead of being consulted for their wishes, peoples simply became objects of Hitler's politics of *Lebensraum*, being dominated, expelled, deported, and even killed in great numbers in order to consolidate German power throughout Europe. They became objects of Himmler's murderous politics of race.

5.6. The Second World War

How would the victims—individuals and collectives, peoples, nations, and states—react to this new situation which, from the point of view of the position of peoples and nations in international law, was a clear step backward, as power and not the wishes of those concerned was more influential than ever? Basically, the Wilsonian view of self-determination as self-government was maintained, as exemplified in the Atlantic Charter of August 1941 between the United States and Britain and afterwards signed by most Allied Powers. The Charter only promised restoration of the conquered territories; it did not cite 'self-determination'.[21] Much more typical of the attitude of the victors was the insistence on unconditional surrender, which meant that the decision was not by the peoples' wishes but by the sword.

If there were any doubts about the words, the deeds were obvious. The victors did not adopt traditional self-determination. Instead, they shifted around whole

---

[21] 'Joint Statement by President Roosevelt and Prime Minister Churchill, 14 August 1941' in *Foreign Relations of the United States 1941* (US Government Printing Office Washington 1958), vol 1, 355.

populations. First, they decided—from the point of view of states, not of peoples—which state was to get which territory, and then people were moved according to the new borders. This was not a step back behind the first decolonization, but it was a new policy. Instead of adapting borders to peoples, peoples were adapted to borders.

This was a bad omen for the future of self-determination. It seemed as if it had vanished completely; as if, after all, Hitler's spirit had won. So it was quite astonishing that in the end, self-determination—and with it, the role of peoples and nations—did not just gain a new lease of life but became one of the most popular slogans of international law and politics. But this was not the result of the politics of the traditional great powers. The colonial powers, with the exception of the United States, tried to restore their empires and were prepared to fight for them. So for them decolonization was still reserved, as it had been in the 18th and 19th centuries, to European settlers and their descendants.

5.7. Cold War and Third World

This was unacceptable to the national movements in the colonies. The colonial peoples had fought in the War and contributed heavily to the economic war effort. To deny them independence and perhaps even autonomy was to treat them not as partners but as vanquished peoples. It was hardly imaginable that they would accept such a role without attempts at resistance. Nevertheless, regardless of their wishes, they probably would have been silenced if the main victorious powers, especially the Big Four, had stood together and promoted the view that native peoples did not have a right to self-determination, in contrast to Europeans and their descendants.

The Cold War brought decisive changes. The conflict among the principal victors turned self-determination into a weapon. Basically, both sides could use it. But as long as decolonization was considered mainly as the dissolution of colonial empires overseas, and not of contiguous territories, the Soviet Union was in much less danger than Britain, France, the Netherlands, or Belgium. The Soviets had a good chance of weakening their Cold War adversaries by adopting the call of self-determination of the national movements in the colonies. They did it very successfully. The first attempt, however, failed. The Soviets and some of the new states wanted to include an article on self-determination in the *Universal Declaration of Human Rights* in December 1948, which was rejected. This defeat later led to a coalition between the Soviet bloc and the rapidly growing number of Third World countries, which were former colonies. The Third World won a great victory when in 1966 self-determination was not just recognized as a human right among others, but became the first and foremost of all human rights: the identical first articles of the *International Covenant on Civil and Political Rights* and of the *International Covenant on Economic, Social, and Cultural Rights* stated that 'all peoples have the right to self-determination. By virtue of that right they freely determine their political status and freely pursue their economic, social and cultural development'.

This was a tremendous victory, especially from the ideological point of view. The covenants were accepted on 10 December 1966 without a single negative vote and without abstentions.

The victory had been prepared on 14 December 1960 by UNGA Resolution 1514 (XV), the *Declaration on the Granting of Independence to Colonial Countries and Peoples*. In contrast to 1948, the Western States in 1960 no longer dared to reject self-determination for the colonial peoples. Eighty-nine States were in favour of the declaration, without any votes against, and with nine abstentions.

Was it a real and lasting victory, or only a Pyrrhic one? It was undeniably real, especially if one read the Declaration of 1960 together with the pacts of 1966. It had become impossible to reject decolonization—its main thrust had indeed been between 1960 and 1966. Most colonies gained independence without loss of blood, while wars usually ended with a victory of the colonies.

At first glance this was an almost total victory. There were important limits, however. The three limiting factors were again introduced: independence and self-determination were restricted to cases of decolonization, which usually occurred in areas overseas; the principle of *uti possidetis* supported international and administrative borders; and secession was strictly prohibited. In addition, the international community has consistently refused to define the word 'people', which meant that it could decide each case on its own merits. Nobody was much interested in terminological questions. Since the 19th century, both 'peoples' and 'nations' have been used in the context of self-determination, especially in the formulas 'self-determination of peoples' (and/or nations), and 'national self-determination'. In the course of the elaboration of the *International Covenants on Human Rights* in the 1950s, 'nations' was dropped without much discussion. The main reason probably was that 'nation' was more closely linked to 'state' than 'people'.

Within these confines a second process of decolonization continued. It began soon after the War, with the independence of the Philippines in 1946, reached a first climax in 1947 with the dissolution of British India, and a second in the 1960s, when a great number of new states were formed, and it ebbed out in the 1970s and 1980s when all, or at least the greatest part of the territories that might have been called colonies, had become independent. By the turn of the century it could reasonably be argued that decolonization was a phenomenon of the past.

Such a conclusion, however, was wrong. The decision of 1966 to convey self-determination to all peoples and not just to colonial territories (although most states accepted the three restrictions) kept the door open for new claims for independence. Strictly speaking, such claims were incompatible with custom and had to be rejected. But it was difficult to maintain that a collective showing the usually accepted attributes of a people had no right to independence, while some chance products of colonialism, like East Timor or the Western Sahara, could opt for full independence. It was clear that there would be strong opposition against a general rule granting independence to any group whatsoever, but it was also very likely that in cases in which a general promise of independence weakened some states by dismantling them it would be accepted by those who benefited from a secession. This occurred after 1989 when the Soviet Union and Yugoslavia were dissolved. Both states of course had the right to dissolve themselves, provided all groups concerned accepted. But this would open the door for a continuous process of secession. To prevent such an outcome, the principle of *uti possidetis* was adopted. This meant a serious restriction of self-determination. The dissolution of the Soviet Union and Yugoslavia offered chances for conveying self-determination to all groups who claimed it for themselves. Plebiscites were indeed held. But they were not plebiscites to assess the wishes of the peoples. Instead, they had the traditional function of reflecting and confirming the existing power structure. The federations were dissolved along the existing administrative borders, into the constituent republics, which became independent states. But not a single metre of new borders was drawn.

6. Conclusion

The history of international law concerning its subjects cannot be written as a story of continuous progress. The principle of self-determination of all peoples, which later became even the right to self-determination of all peoples, has been able to survive against all odds. At least twice it survived in a very unpromising environment: when the Nazis tried to destroy it, and after decolonization had, for all practical purposes, been achieved. Thus, self-determination has shown itself resistant against all attempts at its dissolution. But it has shown itself incapable to develop into an instrument of assessing the wishes of the people. The drawing of borders has not become a matter of peoples and nations, but it is still the result of the distribution of power. Thus international law will remain to a great extent state law. It would be a loss to abandon self-determination, but it would be an illusion to imagine that international law might bring about the actual division of the world to be replaced by self-determination instead of power. As long as a right to self-determination of peoples will be spoken of, there will be objects for it. Despite its basically anarchic character, it remains irreplaceable as one of the few elements of change international law has to offer: while decolonization, *uti possidetis,* and the prohibition of secession prevent territorial change, the right of all peoples to self-determination allows and maybe even provokes it.

Recommended Reading

Buchanan, Allen E *Secession: The Morality of Political Divorce From Fort Sumter to Lithuania and Quebec* (Westview Press Boulder Colorado 1991).

Canovan, Margaret *Nationhood and Political Theory* (Polity Press Aldershot 1996).

Cobban, Alfred *The Nation State and National Self-determination* (Collins London 1969).

Crawford, James *The Creation of States in International Law* (OUP Oxford 1979).

Elsner, Bernd R *Die Bedeutung des Volkes im Völkerrecht* (Dunker & Humblot Berlin 2000).

Fisch, Jörg 'Das Volk im Völkerrecht: Staat, Volk und Individuum im internationalen Recht am Ende des Ersten Weltkrieges' in Manfred Hettling (ed) *Volksgeschichten im Europa der Zwischenkriegszeit* (Vandenhoeck & Ruprecht Göttingen 2003) at 38–64.

Fisch, Jörg *Das Selbstbestimmungsrecht der Völker: Die Domestizierung einer Illusion* (CH Beck München 2010).

Koselleck, Reinhart et al 'Volk, Nation' in Otto Brunner, Werner Conze, and Reinhart Koselleck (eds) *Geschichtliche Grundbegriffe* (Klett-Cotta Stuttgart 1992) vol 7, 141–431.

Manela, Erez *The Wilsonian Moment: Self-determination and the International Origins of Anticolonial Nationalism* (OUP Oxford 2007).

Morgan, Edmund Sears *Inventing the People: The Rise of Popular Sovereignty in England and America* (WW Norton New York 1988).

Peters, Anne *Das Gebietsreferendum im Völkerrecht: Seine Bedeutung im Lichte der Staatenpraxis nach 1989* (Nomos Baden-Baden 1995).

Summers, James *Peoples and International Law: How Nationalism and Self-determination Shape a Contemporary Law of Nations* (Martinus Nijhoff Publishers Leiden 2007).

Wambaugh, Sarah *A Monograph on Plebiscites* (Oxford University Press New York 1920).

Wambaugh, Sarah *Plebiscites Since the World War* (2 vols Carnegie Endowment for International Peace Washington 1933).

CHAPTER 2

STATES: RISE AND DECLINE OF THE PRIMARY SUBJECTS OF THE INTERNATIONAL COMMUNITY

ANTONIO CASSESE

1. THE EMERGENCE OF MODERN STATES

THE international community in its modern shape is contemporaneous with the consolidation of States. States gradually evolved in Europe between the 12th and the 16th centuries. Modern States arose in England, France, Spain, and Portugal, consisting mainly of centralized power structures wielding exclusive political and moral authority as well as a monopoly of force over a population living in a more or less vast territory. According to the historian JR Strayer, what characterizes the modern State and differentiates it both from the 'great, imperfectly integrated empires' of the past and the 'small, but highly cohesive units, such as the Greek city state' are a few notable characteristics: 'the appearance of political units persisting in time and fixed in space, the development of permanent, impersonal institutions, agreement on the need for an authority which can give final judgment, and acceptance of the idea that this authority should receive the basic loyalty of its subjects'.[1] At that time, States were monarchies exercising a few prerogatives: making laws, commanding an army, setting up courts of justice, levying taxes, and ensuring law and order in the country through the use of centralized enforcement agents. These States were few in number, the overwhelming space of the world community—particularly outside Europe—being made up of hundreds of communities subject to local overlords.[2] The power of these emerging States was to some extent overshadowed by the two central potentates: the emperor, at the head of the Holy Roman Empire, and the Pope, at the head of the Catholic Church.

2. Sovereign States are Coeval with the Birth of the International Society

It is only around the peace of Westphalia (1648), which put an end to the sanguinary Thirty Years War, that the modern State emerged as an international subject and the international society took its current shape.[3] States now show the following commonalities. First, they are all 'sovereign', in that they do not accept nor are they prepared to bow to any superior authority (*superiorem non recognoscentes*); in 1836, Wheaton would term them 'separate political societies of men living independently of each other',[4] adding that '[a]s independent communities acknowledge no common

---

[1] JR Strayer *On the Medieval Origins of the Modern State* (Princeton University Press Princeton 1970) at 9–10; on the formation of States in Europe, see also C Tilly 'Reflections on the History of European State-Making' in C Tilly (ed) *The Formation of National States in Western Europe* (Princeton University Press Princeton 1975) 25–46; M Merle *Les acteurs dans les relations internationales* (Economica Paris 1986) at 30–1.

[2] According to Strayer, 'it should be remembered that the structure of European states, imperfect though it was, was considerably stronger than that of most of the overseas political communities with which Europeans had to deal. There was nothing in the Americas, nothing in India or the East Indies, and nothing in most of Africa that had the cohesion and the endurance of a European state. And if the broad belt of Asian empires, stretching from Turkey through Persia to China and Japan could rival European states in organization and power up to the end of the eighteenth century, still the European states were improving their apparatus of government while the structures of the Asian empires were beginning to weaken.' *On the Medieval Origins* (n 1) 105.

[3] In the 17th century, the central authorities are assisted by a modern bureaucracy, which by now constitutes the central core of the State, although one must wait until the adoption, on 25 May 1791, of the French *décret* establishing the various ministries for 'the principle of division of labour to be completely carried through in the public administration, and for ministers in the sense of administrative law [ie as heads of departments] to side by the monarch'. G Jellinek 'Die Entwicklung des Ministeriums in der Konstitutionellen Monarchie (1833)' in G Jellinek *Ausgewählte Schriften und Reden* (O Häring Berlin 1911) vol 2, 89–139 at 98; see also W Fischer and P Lundgreen 'The Recruitment and Training of Administrative and Technical Personnel' in *The Formation of National States* (n 1) 475–527.

[4] H Wheaton *Elements of International Law, with a Sketch of the History of the Science* (B Fellowes Ludgate Street London 1836) vol 1, at 62; see also FF Martens *Traité de droit international* (A Léo trans) (Librairie Maresco Aîné Paris 1883) vol 1, at 273.

superior, they [the States] may be considered as living in a state of nature with respect to each other'.[5] Sovereignty had been defined and theorized in 1576 by Jean Bodin[6] and was identified as the major feature of modern States by Hobbes (for whom it was a necessary condition for the existence of States, for it is 'an artificial soul, as giving life and motion to the whole body').[7] The quintessence of sovereignty resided in the exclusive authority to impose and enforce commands on any individual living in a territory belonging to the sovereign. As the leading Italian publicist and politician Vittorio Emanuele Orlando (1860–1952) stated in 1923, the famous Cartesian dictum, if applied to States, should sound as follows: *iubeo, ergo sum* (I command, hence I exist).[8]

Second, States, although they may be and indeed often are markedly different in size, population, economic, and military power, are all 'equal' in the legal sense: as Vattel would later comment (in 1758), 'a dwarf is as much a man as a giant; similarly, a small republic is no less a sovereign state than the most powerful kingdom'.[9]

Third, strikingly, each of these States pursues its own political, economic, and military interests and does not share any interest with other States, except for momentary alliances dictated by transient political or military motivations. Each State is a monad living by itself and ready to link up with another State only to the extent that this serves its own interests. In this respect, Nietzsche's proposition that States are 'the coldest of all cold monsters' (*das kälteste aller kalten Ungeheuer*),[10] is apposite. The international community in most of the modern era, then, has not been a community proper, but rather a cluster of entities, separate and unconnected, which have been compelled by historical reasons to somehow live together in an uneasy cohabitation. This disjointed community reminds me of the figures of some paintings by El Greco (1541–1614) or, even more, by the Italian Alessandro Magnasco (1667–1749) where each character lives by himself in his own abstract solitude. Perhaps the only common concern was that of fighting piracy. This concern, however, only gave rise to the general authorization to capture and try pirates, whatever their nationality, and whoever their previous victim. In this respect, the position of the international community can be compared to a densely wooded area inhabited by groups of families, in which fires frequently break out: no coordinating authority is established, no common action is envisaged, let alone a fire brigade with commonly owned fire-extinguishing appliances; rather, each inhabitant puts out by himself and with his own means any fire licking his house and does not care about fires threatening other houses; when progress over the years is made, it only consists of the spontaneous

---

[5] *Elements of International Law* (n 4) 35.

[6] See J Bodin *Les six livres de la république* (1576) book I, ch 8.

[7] T Hobbes *Leviathan* (CB Macpherson ed) (Penguin Harmondsworth 1983) at 81.

[8] VE Orlando 'Francesco Crispi' in VE Orlando *Scritti varii di diritto pubblico e scienza politica* (Giuffré Milano 1940) 395–417 at 400.

[9] E de Vattel *Le droits des gens, ou principes de la loi naturelle* (Aillaud Paris 1830) vol 1, at 47 (*Préliminaires* para 18).

[10] F Nietzsche *Sämtliche Werke* (Kröner Stuttgart 1964) vol 6 (*Also sprach Zarathustra*), at 51.

formation of charitable groups, which succour the old, the weak, and the handi-capped, to help them extinguish the fires menacing their life and assets.[11]

It should nevertheless not be surprising that in that period, the State was regarded as the only and the best-suited subject of the international community. As the leading Italian jurist and politician Terenzio Mamiani (1799–1885) wrote in 1860, 'the state is the perfect individual of the universal city or republic' (*l'individuo perfetto della città o repubblica universale*).[12]

3. EUROPEAN STATES AS THE SPINE OF THE INTERNATIONAL SOCIETY IN ITS EARLY STAGES

How many States made up the international community in the early period? Few: most of them were European (England, Spain, France, the Netherlands, Sweden). Powerful States outside Europe were the Mogul Empire in India, the Ottoman Empire, Persia, and China. The European States were, however, much stronger and moulded the international standards of behaviour. Initially, they distinguished themselves from non-Christian States, and often used for those States the term 'barbarian', whereas for themselves they used the term 'civilized'. European States had a common religious matrix (they were all Christian nations), a common economic mould (they were all the outgrowth of capitalism), and a common political structure (they embraced absolutism, to be replaced in subsequent centuries by parliamentary democracy).[13] Thanks to the early progress of their economic and social develop-ment and to the consequent formation of a strong middle class, European States set the tone of the international community for many centuries. Paraphrasing what Hegel wrote with regard to southern Europe, one could say that Europe was the 'the-atre of world history' (*das Theater der Weltgeschichte*) and that there, the 'world spirit' (*Weltgeist*) found its home.[14]

---

[11] I am elaborating upon the metaphor of the fire and the ways to fight it propounded by A Ross *Constitution of the United Nations: Analysis of Structure and Function* (Rinehart and Company New York 1950) at 137–9.

[12] T Mamiani *D'un nuovo diritto Europeo* (Gerolamo Marzorati Torino 1860) at 48.

[13] L Oppenheim wrote that '[t]he modern law of nations is a product of Christian civilisation'. L Oppen-heim *International Law* (H Lauterpacht ed) (6th edn Longmans London 1947) vol 1, at 45. Contemporary scholars and politicians were aware of and laid much stress on the two different classes of States. In 1837, for example, Wheaton distinguished between 'Turkey and the Barbary states on the one hand and the Christian nations of Europe and America on the other'. *Elements of International Law* (n 4) 52.

[14] GWF Hegel *Sämtliche Werke* (G Lasson ed) (Felix Meiner Leipzig 1920) vol 8 (*Vorlesungen über die Philosophie der Weltgeschichte*), at 230.

European States also engaged in strong expansionism, which would fundamentally shape the structure of international relations. They developed two distinct classes of relations with the outside world. With states proper (the Ottoman Empire, Persia, Thailand, China, Japan, etc.), they based their relations on the 'capitulation system', a blatantly unequal legal regime. Capitulations were agreements that tended to grant European countries non-reciprocal privileges (among other things, Europeans could not be expelled from a country without the consent of their consul; had the right to practise worship and build churches; enjoyed freedom of trade and commerce, and were exempted from certain import and export duties; could not be the object of reprisals, especially in case of insolvency; and were not subjected to the territorial courts in the event of disputes between Europeans, but to the jurisdiction of the consul of the defendant or the victim). The other class of foreign countries, namely those that did not even possess the legal trappings of states proper (as recognized by the European States), were considered by the European countries to be mere objects of conquest and appropriation, and were consequently turned into what were later regarded as colonial territories.

Sovereign States (and most notably European States) also classified other States within categories that denoted their minor status. Thus, they first spoke of 'vassal States' and 'tributary States'. According to the prevailing opinion, there was a relationship of 'suzerainty' between a sovereign State and a tributary vassal State, in that the latter only enjoyed a limited control over domestic affairs, while foreign affairs were run by the sovereign State.[15]

More significant was the later contrast between sovereign States and 'colonial nations' or 'colonial countries', or simply 'colonies'. These terms designated those populations which had been subjected to the political and military domination and economic exploitation of European States. These countries, with the passage of time and the changing historical conditions, then became 'dominions' or 'States under protectorate', then 'dependent' countries, or 'trust territories'. These variations in terminology were meant to indicate gradations in the dependency of those countries on the authority of the dominant Western States. The fact remains that from the inception of the world community until the end of the decolonization process (1970s) there have existed two categories of States, those endowed with full sovereignty (European countries, plus the United States, and later on China, Japan, the Soviet Union, and so on),

---

[15] A different view was suggested by Wheaton: '[T]ributary states, and states having a feudal relation to each other, are still considered as sovereign so far as their sovereignty is not affected by this relation. Thus it is evident that the tribute formerly paid by the principal maritime powers of Europe to the Barbary states did not at all affect the sovereignty and independence of the former. ... So also the king of Naples has been a nominal vassal of the Papal See ever since the eleventh century: but this feudal dependence, now abolished, was never considered as impairing the sovereignty of the kingdom of Naples.' *Elements of International Law* (n 4) 64. FF De Martens suggested that one should distinguish between sovereign and half-sovereign States (*souverains* and *mi-souverains*), such as Egypt, Syria, and so on; *Traité de droit international* (n 4) vol 1, at 330–3.

and those that were subjected to European countries. It is a victory of the modern international community that different categories of States no longer exist in law. Today, the distinction between industrialized and developing countries only refers to their economic structure and output, not to any differentiation in legal status.

4. DISTINCTIVE FEATURES OF EARLY INTERNATIONAL SOCIETY

What characterized the first centuries of development of the international community was the sole presence of States as actors on the international scene. Peoples and individuals had no say, and individuals were only objects of state power, either as nationals, or as foreigners, or as pirates (emphatically designated with the expression of *hostes humani generis*).

Another striking feature of the world community in this initial stage (and until the 19th century) was the paucity of legal rules regulating international intercourse. States were both unable and uninterested in agreeing upon common standards of behaviour. There only existed a core of rules: those on the conclusion of treaties; the exchange of, and the rights and privileges accruing to diplomats; the free use of the high seas; the capture of pirates; and the resort to force (admissible both to protect one's own interests and to vindicate one's rights); as well as some rudimentary rules of warfare. The major powers were content with this modicum of norms, for the paucity of rules reserved for States maximum discretion. Small States, which would have been interested in the protection of law, were unable to impose any rule, since at that stage international legal standards were posited either by treaty (and no major power would have ever concluded a treaty limiting its 'privileges') or by custom, which in that period was conceived of as tacit agreement (*pactum tacitum*), hence not susceptible to evolve if major powers opposed it. What is even more striking is that there was no mechanism for law enforcement, except for war (by powerful States against other powerful countries or smaller States).[16]

---

[16] In 1832, Austin wrote: 'The rule regarding the conduct of sovereign states, considered as related to each other, is termed *law* by its analogy to positive law, being imposed upon nations or sovereigns, not by the positive command of a superior authority, but by opinions generally current among nations. The duties which it imposes are enforced by moral sanctions: by fear on the part of nations, or by fear on the part of sovereigns, of provoking general hostility, and incurring its probable evils, in case they should violate maxims generally received and respected.' J Austin *The Province of Jurisprudence Determined* (W Rumble ed) (CUP Cambridge 1995) at 147–8 and 207; see also ibid iv. If in 1860 Mamiani wrote that 'states do not have above them other power than the moral and invisible power of law, common to whole mankind and imposed by nature', he was clearly referring to natural law, more than to positive rules of law. *D'un nuovo diritto Europeo* (n 12) 15.

It is also unique to this period that States emphasized three fundamental rights: the right to self-preservation, the right to self-defence, and the right of intervention,[17] to which one should also add the right of independence (as Mamiani wrote, 'every real state is free and inviolable vis-à-vis all peoples and all states').[18] Since these rights were regarded as 'absolute', their proclamation boiled down to the assertion of an unfettered use of force any time a State found it expedient to attack another State and appropriate its territory. The law of that period was pithily epitomized by Montesquieu in 1748, when he wrote that '[t]he object of war is victory; that of victory is conquest; and that of conquest preservation. From this and the preceding principles all those rules are derived which constitute the law of nations.'[19]

5. THE LOATHED EVIL: REBELS

What was common to all nation-states was the threat of civil wars. Hobbes aptly epitomized the tension between the sovereign State and insurgency by contrasting the Leviathan to Behemoth:[20] two Molochs, one symbolizing the State, and the other what Kant later called 'an internal illness of the state',[21] namely civil war, or the attempt to break up the structure of sovereign States.[22] It is indeed no coincidence that no international rule evolved on civil wars while States dominated the structure of the international community, the matter being generally regarded as exclusively domestic and to be dealt with only by internal methods (rebels being seditious criminals to be killed or hanged). Under this State-centric perspective of international law, third States must keep aloof from civil wars in other States: as noted by Wheaton, '[u]ntil the revolution is consummated, whilst the civil war involving a contest for the government continues, other states may remain indifferent spectators of the controversy'.[23]

---

[17] See eg *Elements of International Law* (n 4) 108–92.

[18] *D'un nuovo diritto Europeo* (n 12) 95; see also *Elements of International Law* (n 4) 131.

[19] CL Montesquieu *De l'esprit des lois* (Flammarion Paris 1979) vol 1, at 127.

[20] I am referring of course to *Leviathan* (n 7) and T Hobbes *Behemoth or the Long Parliament* (F Tönnies ed) (2nd edn Barnes and Nobles New York 1969). In *Leviathan* (n 7) 81, Hobbes defined 'sedition' as a sickness and 'civil war' as 'death'.

[21] Kant speaks of a State in civil war being 'a people independent of others, which only struggles with an internal illness'. I Kant *Zum Ewigen Frieden* (F Nicolovius Königsberg 1795) at 12.

[22] However, for Hobbes, the Leviathan was an entity *indispensable* for modern society and in order to combat what for him was the really dangerous monster, namely civil strife.

[23] *Elements of International Law* (n 4) 92. Wheaton adds, however, that third States may then espouse the cause of one of the contestants, with the consequence that 'it becomes of course, the enemy of the party against whom it declares itself, and the ally of the other'; ibid 93.

6. Evolution of the Domestic Structure of States and of National Doctrines: their Ramifications for the International Society

The substantially authoritarian structure of European States did not change until the 19th century. Thus the architecture of the international society remained largely static until the upheaval in the internal State structures or the emergence of new political doctrines, starting in the late 1700s.

The first major impact of domestic changes on international relations was the French Revolution (1789). The violent removal of aristocracy, the proclamation of the ideals enshrined in the Declaration of the Rights of Man and of the Citizen, and the formation of the new middle classes keen on economic development free from any traditional trammels meant that France propounded new ideals as a participant in international relations as well: sovereign equality among States, self-determination of peoples as a concept guiding any transfer of territory, the prohibition of interference in internal affairs of other States, the ban on wars of aggression or conquest, the prohibition of slavery, as well as the principle of armed intervention in favour of oppressed peoples.[24] For all the talk, the reality of France's actual conduct did not change dramatically. For instance, full implementation of the new values would have entailed the end of French colonialism and slavery. However, when it turned out that those principles clashed with the interests of French planters in the colony of San Domingo, the French Assembly in March 1790 passed a resolution stating that the constitution framed for France was not intended to embrace the internal government of French colonies. A liberal decree passed on 15 May 1791 was also repealed on 24 September of that year because the Paris Assembly feared it would lose the colony. In short, the ideals proclaimed by the French Revolution did not have an immediate bearing on the French attitude to other States or on its dealings with other international subjects. Those ideals instead primarily constituted a leaven destined to transform international dealings in the long run, changing the general ethos and the outlook on the State and the international society. It is no coincidence that Kant wrote in 1795, shortly after the Revolution, that 'a state is not, like the ground on which it has its seat, a piece of property (*patrimonium*). It is a society of men which no one but itself is called upon to command or to dispose of.'[25]

---

[24] See A Cassese 'The Diffusion of Revolutionary Ideas and the Evolution of International Law' in A Cassese (ed) *The Human Dimension of International Law: Selected Papers* (OUP Oxford 2008) 72–92.
[25] *Zum Ewigen Frieden* (n 21) 7.

Second, the doctrine of nationalities propounded by the Italian politician and lawyer Pasquale Stanislao Mancini (1817–88) in 1851 considered the nation rather than the State as the real linchpin of international relations. In his view,[26] a nation, if it does not manage to achieve unity and independence by acquiring statehood, remains a lifeless body, a mere natural reality which, although ineradicable, is devoid of any vitality. This doctrine essentially asserted that any nation should be able to become a State, with a twofold consequence: (i) nations scattered among multiple States (such as Italy before its unification in 1860) should be united in one State only, whereas (ii) States embracing more nations (such as the Ottoman or the Austro-Hungarian Empires) should break apart so that each nation would constitute a separate and distinct State. This doctrine did have a considerable impact on the redistribution of power in the world community, in that it led to the formation of new States by either the merger of existing scattered States (this was the case of Italy and Germany) or the break-up of multinational States (as was the case with the Ottoman and the Austro-Hungarian Empires). Thus, the doctrine influenced the internal structure of some States (states became real nation-states), but this development did not affect the attitude of the new States towards the international community.

A third doctrine was destined to have a considerable influence on the structure of international relations, more than on the domestic structure of States. This is the doctrine of self-determination proclaimed by the leading Russian politician Vladimir I Lenin (in 1916–17) on the one hand, and by the US President Woodrow Wilson (in 1917–18) on the other.[27] This doctrine, which Georges Scelle termed 'a formula of collective freedom and human progress',[28] was conceived of quite differently by the two political leaders. For Wilson, it meant democracy at home and the need to take into account the aspirations and claims of colonial peoples,[29] whereas for Lenin, self-determination meant the break-up of multination empires and the end of colonialism. These were two markedly different views: one moderate, chiefly

---

[26] See PS Mancini *Della nazionalità come fondamento del diritto delle genti* (Eredi Botta Torino 1851); *La vita de' popoli nell'umanità* (G Via Roma 1872); *Diritto internazionale: prelezioni. Con un saggio sul Machiavelli* (Giuseppe Marghieri Napoli 1873); *Della vocazione del nostro secolo per la riforma e la codificazione del diritto delle genti e per l'ordinamento di una giustizia internazionale* (Civelli Roma 1874).

[27] For references, see A Cassese *Self-Determination of Peoples: A Legal Reappraisal* (CUP Cambridge 1995) at 14–23.

[28] G Scelle *Précis de droit des gens* (Recueil Sirey Paris 1934) vol 2, at 257.

[29] The fifth of the famous Fourteen Points proclaimed by Wilson in his address delivered on 8 January 1918 before a Joint Session of the US Congress requested '[a] free, open-minded, and absolutely impartial adjustment of all colonial claims, based upon a strict observance of the principle that in determining all such questions of sovereignty the interest of the populations concerned must have equal weight with the equitable claims of the government whose title is to be determined.' W Wilson 'Address to Congress, Stating the War Aims and Peace Terms of the United States (Delivered in Joint Session, 8 January 1918)' in A Shaw (ed) *State Papers and Addresses by Woodrow Wilson* (George H Doran Company New York) 464–72 at 468.

hinging on internal self-determination (democracy), the other instead radical, primarily addressing the issue of external self-determination. While Wilson's views were aimed at spreading democracy and self-government within the various States, Lenin's postulates were intended to subvert the existing interstate relations. It should not be surprising that the US Secretary of State Robert Lansing wrote that Lenin's programme threatened 'the stability of the future world by applying the self-determination principle to the colonial world', and went on to note that 'however justified may be the principle of local self-government, the necessities of preserving an orderly world require that there should be a national authority with sovereign rights to defend and control the communities within the national boundaries'.[30]

Which of the two doctrines had a greater impact on the domestic structure of States and the attitude of States towards the international community? Both doctrines exercised a significant influence, but only in the long run. Lenin's principles eventually contributed to the gradual decline of colonialism (1950–70), while Wilson's principle of self-government helped spread the notion of internal self-determination as the free and genuine choice of government by the whole people (see common article 1 of the UN Covenants on Human Rights of 1966).

Another radical domestic change that might have had a great bearing on the structure of States and international relations was the Russian Revolution (1917). This revolution created a striking cleavage in the international society. Although some members of that society (such as the Ottoman Empire, Japan, Persia, Siam, China) had a different economic and ideological outlook to that of European States, they had actually yielded to the Christian bloc's market economy. The Russian Revolution broke this trend, by proclaiming an ideology and a political philosophy radically at odds with those upheld by the other nations. At the international level, the Soviet Union propounded three principles: (i) self-determination of people, chiefly as anti-colonialism; (ii) the substantive equality of all States (hence the repudiation of unequal treaties or of treaties imposing onerous economic conditions or commercial terms on small countries); and (iii) the partial rejection of international law, chiefly treaty law unacceptable to the Soviet ideology and interests.

It was only in the long run that the Russian Revolution would bear its fruits at the domestic level (when, after the Second World War some Eastern European countries turned to communism under Soviet pressure or threat), as well as at the international level (with the demise of colonialism after that war, and the gradual insistence of developing countries on the need for real and effective equality between States).

---

[30] R Lansing *Papers Relating to the Foreign Relations of the United States* (US Government Printing Office Washington DC 1939–40) vol 2, at 247.

7. ATTEMPTS BY SMALL STATES TO RESTRAIN THE HEGEMONY OF ECONOMICALLY AND MILITARILY STRONG STATES

In the 19th century, two distinguished representatives of a Latin American state, Argentina, tried to set limits to great powers' dominance. Both attempts ended in failure.

The first effort was instigated by the Argentine jurist and politician Carlos Calvo (1822–1906) in the middle of the 19th century.[31] Many Latin American States began to insert into concession contracts with foreign nationals a clause (called a Calvo clause after the Argentine statesman), which stipulated that, in the event of a dispute arising out of a contract, foreigners relinquished the right to request the diplomatic and judicial protection of their own national State and agreed to have the dispute settled by local courts. The clear intent was to limit the legal and political intervention of Western capital-exporting countries, which often used the right to enforce contracts with Western nationals as a pretext or occasion for political pressure or even armed intervention in Latin American countries. The attempt was ill-fated. Numerous international courts and claims commissions ruled that the Calvo clause was legally invalid or ineffective, since States could not be deprived by virtue of a contract between a State and a foreigner of their international right—deriving from an international customary rule—to protect their nationals. Hence, the clause was set aside or downgraded to a superfluous proviso requiring exhaustion of local remedies before the initiation of international action.

Another attempt was made by the Argentine Foreign Minister Luis María Drago (1859–1921) in the early 20th century. States, having an unfettered right to resort to force either to vindicate their rights or to protect their own interests, often used military power to forcibly recover payments due by foreign States to their nationals who had invested money in those foreign countries. Indeed, in 1902, Great Britain, Germany, and Italy used force against Venezuela on the basis of compensation due for damage caused to nationals of the three European countries during the civil war which had raged from 1898 to 1900, and for Venezuela's seizure of fishing boats and other commercial ships, as well as to repay loans made to Venezuela for the building of its railway. The three European countries, considering the settlement proposed by Venezuela unacceptable, sank three Venezuelan ships, bombarded the locality of Puerto Cabello, and instituted a naval blockade of the coasts of Venezuela. Venezuela caved in. However, on 29 December 1902, Foreign Minister Drago sent a note to the United States on behalf of the Argentine government, in which he claimed that the Europeans' armed intervention, in addition to running counter to the Monroe Doctrine,

---

[31] The doctrine was set out in C Calvos *Derecho internacional teórico y práctico de Europa y América* (2 vols Amyot Durand et Pedone-Lauriel Paris 1868).

could not be justified, since 'the collection of loans by military means requires territorial occupation to make them effective, and territorial occupation signifies the suppression or subordination of the governments of the countries on which it is imposed'.[32] The US Secretary of State John M Hay responded with a lukewarm note of 17 February 1903, substantially dismissing the Drago Doctrine and siding with the European countries. Thus that Doctrine fell into oblivion for a few years. Then, at the 1907 Hague Peace Conference, when Drago resuscitated the doctrine, the US delegate Horace Porter watered it down by convincing the conference to adopt a convention which allowed resort to force, but only upon non-acceptance by the debtor State of international arbitration, or by its failure to carry out an arbitral award. Significantly, no European State ratified the convention, thereby conveying the notion that even given this emasculated form of the doctrine, those States were not prepared to restrain their own powers.

Thus, initial attempts to restrain the hegemony of great powers ended up in total failure.

8. The Gradual Self-Limitation of Sovereign States

I have noted above that, until the 19th century, international law constituted a core of legal standards that attributed great latitude to States in the conduct of their foreign affairs, and substantially refrained from regulating most matters relating to international intercourse. Since the end of the 19th century, however, States have become aware of the need for a detailed regulation of at least some major aspects of their international relations, and they set in motion normative processes to achieve this purpose. Two different paths were taken: drafting or promoting collective treaties on some major matters, and soliciting a contribution to the clarification and development of customary law through arbitral courts and tribunals.

First of all, States pushed for international diplomatic conferences aimed at agreeing upon some set of rules applicable to all participant States. One of the major problems in need of extensive legal regulation was war. The Brussels Conference of 1874 on the laws of warfare (attended by fifteen States, including all the European powers and Turkey, but not China, Japan, and the United States) ended in failure, for the final text did not become a binding treaty. The 1899 Hague Peace Conference (attended by

---

[32] See the text LM Drago 'Argentine Republic: Ministry of Foreign Relations and Worship' (1907) 1 American Journal of International Law Supplement 1–6.

27 States, including the European countries plus China, Iran, Japan, Mexico, Thailand, Turkey, and the United States) was instead successful, and managed to bring about leading texts not only on war, but also on the peaceful settlement of disputes. The subsequent Hague Conference of 1907 (attended by 44 States, including all the States that had been at The Hague in 1899, plus Argentina, Bolivia, Brazil, Chile, Colombia, Cuba, Dominican Republic, Ecuador, El Salvador, Guatemala, Haiti, Nicaragua, Panama, Paraguay, Peru, Uruguay, Venezuela) revised, ameliorated, and broadened the scope of those treaties.

It should be added that a major impulse to the codification of existing customary law or to the development of new rules came from an academic institution that in the 19th and early 20th centuries played a conspicuous normative role: the *Institut de droit international* (founded in Ghent, Belgium, in 1873), which adopted important resolutions on many crucial matters in need of regulation. Thus almost every year, one or more aspects of war and neutrality were touched upon, culminating in the Oxford Session of 1880, when the *Institut* adopted the famous Oxford Manual on the War on Land. Other matters included the international arbitral procedure (1875 and 1879), the admission and expulsion of foreigners (1888 and 1892), State immunity (1891), extradition (1892 and 1894), the territorial sea (1894), diplomatic immunities (1895), consular immunities (1896), the responsibility of States for damages to foreigners caused by a civil war (1900), and the rights and duties of States towards the incumbent government in the event of insurrection (1900). All these resolutions, followed by many others in the following years, suggested new ideas or propounded constructive and forward-looking interpretations of existing principles or rules so as to prompt States to at least clarify and update the law, but more often to fill gaping lacunae in the existing law.

Another major contribution to filling gaps came from case law. In this respect some cases stand out for their particular relevance to the development of international law: the *Alabama Arbitration* (1872), the *Tinoco Case* (1923), the *Lotus Case* (1927), the *Island of Palmas Arbitration* (1928), and the *Naulilaa Case* (1928). In each of these cases the arbitrator(s) either clarified existing principles, or incrementally developed the law by enunciating rules or principles previously never articulated in so many words. In the *Alabama Arbitration*, the United States had put forward a string of claims for damages against Great Britain for the assistance given, in breach of neutrality, to the cause of the Confederacy during the American Civil War (1861–65).[33] The Arbitral Court upheld the US claims in 1872, applying the three rules on neutrality laid down in the arbitration treaty and pronouncing on the law of neutrality.[34] The *Tinoco Case* (*Costa Rica v Great Britain*) is important because the arbitrator (the US statesman William H Taft) clarified the law concerning the identity and

---

[33] JB Moore *History and Digest of the International Arbitrations to Which the United States Has Been a Party* (US Government Printing Office Washington DC 1898) vol 1, 495–682.

[34] See A Cook *The Alabama Claims* (Cornell University Press Ithaca NY 1975).

continuity of governments and the value of recognition of governments.[35] The *Lotus Case* (*France v Turkey*) made an important contribution to the notion of sovereignty and the extension of criminal jurisdiction of States.[36] The arbitral award by Judge Max Huber in the *Island of Palmas Case* (*United States v The Netherlands*) concerned the sovereignty over a tiny island, of scant value, located within the Dutch East Indies. The question was whether a territory belongs to the first discoverer, even if he does not exercise authority over it, or rather to the State which actually exercises sovereignty there. The award is a major contribution to the determination of the notion of territorial sovereignty, its nature, its content, and the ways sovereignty can be acquired.[37] Finally, the *Naulilaa Case* (*Portugal v Germany*) determined the conditions to be fulfilled for lawfully resorting to armed reprisals in time of peace.[38]

9. STATES' ATTEMPTS TO SET UP COLLECTIVE BODIES DESIGNED TO MANAGE JOINT INTERESTS

Although, as noted above, sovereign States have always constituted monads eager to look after their own interests and unmindful of collective needs, let alone universal values, some attempts have been made by them to set up some form of collective arrangement for protecting joint or common interests. There are four such endeavours. Most of them have ended up in failure, or at least in very minor success.

The first move to devise a collective system designed to restrain the powers of sovereign countries and enforce the law was made at the very outset of the international community, namely in 1648, with the Treaties of Westphalia. Article 123 of the Treaty of Münster provided that, faced with a threat to peace or any other serious violation of the law, the victim State must not resort to war but should 'exhort the offender not

---

[35] See *Tinoco Arbitration (Great Britain v Costa Rica)* (1923) 1 Rep Intl Arbitral Awards 369.

[36] See *The Case of the SS 'Lotus' (France v Turkey)* PC IJ Rep Series A No 10.

[37] See *Island of Palmas Case (Netherlands v United States of America)* 2 Rep Intl Arbitral Awards 831.

[38] *Responsabilité de l'Allemagne à raison des dommages causés dans les colonies portugaises du Sud de l'Afrique (Germany v Portugal)* 2 Rep Intl Arbitral Awards 1019. The Special Arbitral Tribunal held that reprisal, first, comprises acts which would normally be illegal but are rendered lawful by the fact that they constitute a reaction to an international delinquency; second, they must be 'limited by considerations of humanity (*les expériences de l'humanité*) and the rules of good faith applicable in the relations between States'; third, they must not be excessive, although they need not be strictly proportionate to the offence; fourth, they must be preceded by a request for peaceful settlement (they must 'have remained unredressed after a demand for amends'); fifth, they must 'seek to impose on the offending State reparation for the offence, the return to legality and the avoidance of new offences'.

to come to any hostility, submitting the cause to a friendly composition or to the ordinary proceedings of justice'. Article 124 envisaged a cooling-off period, lasting as long as three years; if at its expiry no settlement had been reached, the injured State was entitled to wage war, and all the other contracting States were to assist it by the use of force. In addition, pursuant to article 3, States were duty-bound to refrain from giving military assistance to the offender, nor were they permitted to allow its troops to pass through or stay in their territories. In short, this 'collective security system' hinged on three main elements, which with modern terminology can be defined as follows: (i) a sweeping ban on the use of force; (ii) the prohibition of individual self-defence, except after the expiry of a long period; and (iii) the duty of all States to support the victim of a wrong in collective self-defence.

This scheme, which strongly resembles the later system of the League of Nations (1919), was too far ahead of its time and too much at odds with the real interests of the sovereign States that had appeared on the international scene. It goes without saying that it was never put into effect and remained a grand illusion.

A second attempt, which to some extent was less unsuccessful for it was more realistic, was made in 1815, after the defeat of Napoleon: the Concert of Europe. Napoleon had shattered deep-rooted principles and upset the existing order. The victors felt that they had to protect the interests of European monarchies against the seeds of revolution. They thus devised a system capable of putting a straitjacket on the new forces of progress which were urging the dismantling of aristocratic privileges and the abolition of old practices. The new system, put in place by virtue of a series of treaties in 1815, rested on three essential elements: a declaration of principle, a military alliance, and a new procedure for the settlement of political questions. The declaration of principles was embodied in the Treaty of Paris of 26 September 1815, instituting the Holy Alliance between Austria, Russia, and Prussia, to which all European states adhered (except for England, the Papal States, and the Ottoman Empire).[39] The declaration proclaimed that all States would take as their standards of behaviour the precepts of Christian religion and considered themselves as members of the same 'Christian family'.[40]

The military alliance (in which Austria, Prussia, Russia, England, and subsequently France, participated) envisaged a system of collective security designed to forestall or stifle any recurrence of Bonapartism in Europe as well as any revolutionary movement likely to overthrow European monarchies. Three measures were provided for in the Treaty of 1820:[41] (i) the State where a revolution would break out ceased to be a member of the Concert of Europe; (ii) the new government resulting from a revolution

---

[39] Holy Alliance between Austria, Prussia, and Russia (signed 11 [26] September 1815) (1815–16) 65 CTS 199.

[40] The principles laid down in the treaties mentioned above were aptly summarized in *D'un nuovo diritto europeo* (n 12) 275–6. The author opposed to them a set of democratic principles of 'a new European law'; ibid 277–9.

[41] 'Troppau Protocol' (signed 19 November 1820) in *Fontes Historiae Iuris Gentium* (WG Grewe ed) (de Gruyter Berlin 1988–95) vol 3(1), at 110–12.

would not be recognized; (iii) the States directly concerned, or otherwise the Holy Alliance, would intervene with their troops to put an end to the revolution. This repressive system proved effective in practice: in 1821 Austrian troops were sent to Naples and Turin to suppress liberal insurgents; in 1823 French troops were dispatched to Spain, again to thwart a liberal attempt at independence.

The third element of the Concert of Europe was a new procedure for the settlement of political disputes: in short, it was envisaged that all the sovereigns concerned should meet to discuss political matters and try to settle them. Thus, multilateral diplomacy, based on periodical summit meetings, was for the first time contemplated and practised.

This system was realistic, because it was based on the common interest of some major powers. However, it was short-lived, because in a matter of a few years, nationalist movements became so powerful and widespread in Europe that monarchies had to bow to them and take on board many of their ideals. Thus, the traditional policy of balance of power soon replaced the collective system inaugurated in 1815.

In contrast, a return to idealistic and illusionary principles inspired the League of Nations, set up in 1919 as a reaction to the dreadful First World War. Unlike the Concert of Europe, the League aspired to be worldwide: it had an original membership of 42 States, including five British Dominions (India, New Zealand, Canada, Australia, and South Africa). The main traits of the League very much resembled those of the settlement of Westphalia: (i) resort to war was banned (except for a limited number of cases); (ii) when nevertheless admissible, recourse to war was subjected to a cooling-off period of three months; and (iii) if a dispute was submitted to the League Council, to the Permanent Court of International Justice, or to an arbitral tribunal, war could only be resorted to three months after the decision of one of these bodies. The system was flawed in many respects: first, there was no ban on resort to force short of war; second, war was not banned altogether, but only subjected to a cooling-off period; third, no collective system proper was set up for enforcing the law against a State breaking the prohibitions laid down in the Covenant; it was only provided that all member States were to provide assistance to the victim State, but no collective action by the League organs was envisaged. In short, any reaction to aggression hinged on the voluntary action of other members of the League. The system was too unrealistic to prove successful. It is no surprise that it failed in a matter of a few years.

The fourth and most recent collective security system is that established in 1945 by the UN Charter. It hinges on a ban on the use of force, the collective enforcement action of the Security Council, and right of individual or collective self-defence in case of armed attacks. The system combines elements of realism (the veto power of the five permanent members of the Security Council; the right of self-defence) with lofty—perhaps too high-flying—illusions (such as that of a UN armed force made up of military contingents of member States and under the command of a Military Staff Committee). Sovereignty has not been dislodged, but only slightly restrained.

This accounts for the relative failure of the security system. In summary, and to return to the metaphor of the fire likely to break out in a densely wooded area, in none of these cases was there a fire brigade set up or were there any common fire-extinguishing appliances put together and made available to the collective. The inhabitants of the area only attempted (or managed) to establish a sort of 'fire council' tasked to determine when there arose the need to put out a fire and to recommend or to authorize the dispatching of one or members of the community to extinguish it, regardless of whether or not it was necessary to pass through the land of one of the inhabitants of the area. Sovereignty has remained the major stumbling block to any real progress towards an international community proper.

10. THE GRADUAL DETHRONEMENT OF STATES IN MODERN INTERNATIONAL SOCIETY

At the beginning of the international community and for many centuries, sovereign States have been the overlords in that community and have run the show. The emergence of the nation-state has been a fundamental stage in the development of modern international society. Various merits can be attributed to States. At the *domestic* level, they have somehow amalgamated communities and established, through a centralized monopoly of force, a minimum of law and order, thereby preventing excessive violence from disrupting social intercourse. At the *international* level, States have constituted interlocutors responsible for the actions of their own nationals and capable of entertaining relations with other international subjects. In addition, they have made it possible for the various areas of the inhabited world to be represented in international fora. They also have tried somehow to introduce a remedy to the factual inequality and heterogeneity of international subjects by providing a general legal framework for international dealings and the coexistence of all international entities.[42] However, their unbound authority began to creak at the beginning of the 20th century, and they are increasingly losing their central and dominant place in the world community. The gradual but inexorable dwindling of their authority is principally due to the slow emergence of new actors on the international scene.

The first non-state subjects that emerged were creatures of the States themselves: intergovernmental organizations. They were organized entities charged with fulfilling tasks on behalf of the member States. The first ones were essentially technical: the

---

[42] On these last three points, see *Les acteurs dans les relations internationales* (n 1) 58–61.

Universal Postal Union, set up in 1875; the Union of the Protection of Industrial property, established in 1883; the International Institute for Agriculture, created in 1905; as well as the various River Commissions (for the Rhine, the Danube, etc.). They were merely collective instrumentalities for the joint performance of actions which each member State would otherwise have had to undertake by itself. They were deprived of international legal personality, being considered as organs common to all member States. After the First World War, two important organizations were set up: the League of Nations and the International Labour Organization (both in 1919). In spite of their political importance, they too were conceived by member States as structures hardly possessing any independent existence or autonomous role in relation to the member States. It is only after the Second World War, both with the establishment of the United Nations and the proliferation of other intergovernmental organizations (the Council of Europe, the Organization of American States, the Arab League, the Organization of African Unity, NATO, and the various specialized agencies of the UN) and with the Advisory Opinion of the ICJ on *Reparation for Injuries* (1949)[43] that intergovernmental organizations came to occupy the centre stage and be regarded as autonomous entities endowed with rights and obligations distinct from those of the member States—in a word, as international legal subjects.

Undoubtedly, formally speaking, all these organizations may be undone by legal fiat, through a treaty or a decision of all member States repealing the founding treaty. In fact, however, like other political and bureaucratic institutions at every level, these organizations tend to consolidate their authority once they come into operation. One contributing factor to this gradual growth of autonomy is that the organizations rest on the consent of a number of States which are politically neither homogeneous nor united. Thanks to divisions and conflicts among member States, international organizations gain strength and effectiveness which would otherwise be beyond their grasp. It follows that even powerful members are unable to influence organizations decisively or to make them take a path different from that agreed upon by the majority of states. Great powers are faced with institutions which, although formally dependent on States, eventually wield authority over individual member States.

This de facto authority expands when organizations are given by the member states powers that substantially imply a transfer of aspects of sovereignty. This holds true for the European Union, an organization vested with strong economic powers in some specific areas (powers that entail the making of binding decisions), as well as with the authority to legislate in some fields. Here the erosion of sovereignty has already taken giant steps and might lead in time to the evolution of an entity that replaces sovereign powers, at least in a number of areas.

Another set of entities that to some extent have made a dent in the States' authority are *peoples* as a collective. However, here States have been extremely cautious in order

---

[43] See *Reparation for Injuries Suffered in the Service of the United Nations (Advisory Opinion)* [1949] ICJ Rep 174.

to limit any attempt by peoples to replace States or even to have a say on the international scene. Only three categories of peoples were admitted as possible interlocutors: (i) colonial peoples, (ii) peoples subjected to belligerent occupation or foreign domination and represented by an organization (a national liberation movement), and (iii) peoples subjected to extreme racial discrimination and denied access to government (as well as endowed with a representative organization). Peoples constituting ethnic or religious groups or minorities have otherwise generally been denied any access to the world community. In addition, peoples living in sovereign States have been granted a right to self-determination in the form of free and peaceful choice of representative government, but not, however, the right to overturn the government or to secede. To these conspicuous limitations, one should add that the emergence of organized peoples was a phenomenon limited in time: it coincided with the decline of colonialism (the first liberation movement was the FLN, or *Front de Libération Nationale*, set up in Algeria in 1954; by the 1980s, almost all liberation movements had disappeared). Furthermore, the fight of the peoples referred to above is aimed at establishing new sovereign States, not to create centres of power restraining States' authority. Hence the impact of peoples on sovereign States has been limited in time and scope.

Much stronger and indisputably durable has been the impact of the emergence of individuals as world actors. For centuries they have been non-existent on the international scene. Then, after the Second World War they gushed out on that scene thanks to two distinct but concurrent developments. First, the world community realized that it was individuals who had committed horrendous crimes during the war and who must therefore be brought to trial and punished, rather than (or in addition to) the States on whose behalf they had acted (hence the celebrated proposition of the Nuremberg International Military Tribunal that international law is also concerned with the acts of individuals, and that individuals, and not the states for which they act, bear responsibility for any gross violation of international law amounting to international crime).[44] The second development was the diffusion of the human rights doctrine (prompted by the horrors of the war and President Roosevelt's famous 'Four Freedoms' Speech in 1941): the clear implication of the doctrine was that individuals were entitled to claim respect for their human rights; hence they could challenge their own governments as well as foreign governments for breaching their human rights. This doctrine entailed among other things that States could no

---

[44] The Tribunal said the following: 'It was submitted that international law is concerned with the action of sovereign States, and provides no punishment for individuals; and further, that where the act in question is an act of state, those who carry it out are not personally responsible, but are protected by the doctrine of the sovereignty of the State. In the opinion of the Tribunal, both these submissions must be rejected.... [I]ndividuals can be punished for violations of international law. Crimes against international law are committed by men, not by abstract entities, and only by punishing individuals who commit such crimes can the provisions of international law be enforced.' *Trial of the Major War Criminals before the International Military Tribunal* (Nuremberg 1947) vol 1, at 222–3.

longer legitimately claim immunity from prosecution for their officials accused of international crimes (a manifest inroad into state sovereignty), and that they had to accept being challenged before international bodies for the conduct they had taken within their domestic legal order towards nationals or foreigners (another major indentation of their sovereign authority). In short, States are no longer free to behave as they please vis-à-vis individuals, but must respect their fundamental rights, and can even be called to account for their possible misbehaviour.

Another development that is restraining state authority is the mushrooming of rebellion in sovereign States. Admittedly this is not a new phenomenon. What is, however, new is the multiplication of instances where ethnic groups, minorities, or political organizations take up arms against the central authorities, and promote insurgency and even secession. This trend is linked to the structure of many African and Asian countries whose borders had been arbitrarily shaped by colonial countries without attention to tribes, groups, nationalities, religion, and so on. It is also linked to the end of the Cold War and the demise of two blocs of States, which has released forces and scattered authority over the planet. What is also new is that in protracted civil wars, rebels often manage to acquire a State-like structure, with a functioning administration and courts of law that pass judgment on crimes by the government forces and even by rebels.[45]

A totally novel phenomenon is the formation of non-state entities (other than rebels) over the territory of sovereign States or on the territories occupied by foreign belligerents: it suffices to think of Hezbollah in Lebanon or of Hamas in Gaza. These developments are the consequence of States' (or recognized entities such as the Palestinian Authority's) loss of actual control and contribute in turn to further weakening the central organs of States (or recognized authorities). This is a danger-ous phenomenon, for it testifies to the further fragmentation of the international society.

Finally, a new force that heavily conditions the conduct of States is public opinion, especially in democratic countries. In the past, it did not play a major role; at present, the media may have a deterrent effect as well as the effect of pointing to grave breaches of law by sovereign States. As early as 1931, JL Brierly stressed the importance of public opinion as a sanction in international relations, noting that

it is intrinsically a weaker force than opinion in the domestic sphere, yet it is in a sense more effective as a sanction of law. For whereas an individual law-breaker may often hope to escape detection, a State knows that a breach of international law rarely fails to be notorious; and whereas again there are individuals so constituted that they are indifferent to the mere disapproval, unattended by pains and penalties, every State is extraordinarily sensitive to the mere suspicion of illegal action.[46]

---

[45] See S Sivakumaran 'Courts of Armed Opposition Groups: Fair Trials or Summary Justice?' (2009) 7 Journal of International Criminal Justice 489–513.

[46] JL Brierly 'Sanctions' in JL Brierly *The Basis of Obligation in International Law and Other Papers* (H Lauterpacht and CHM Waldock eds) (Clarendon Press Oxford 1958) 201–11 at 203.

11. CONCLUSION

Sovereign States have been the backbone of the international community since its inception. They have been the primary actors on the international scene. Without them that community would not have existed. They have always been polarized, though, and their actions have essentially been based on self-interest. However, they also needed social intercourse with other States in order to survive and flourish. Clive Parry is right when he points to the paradox of 'the simultaneous power and impotence of the individual state';[47] namely its omnipotence, within its own borders, over all human beings living there, and its relative helplessness outside its own frontiers, with respect to other States—except when it intends to conquer and appropriate other States. Nevertheless, the 'sociability' of States has not led them to create a community proper, the *societas generis humani* (society of mankind) dreamed by Grotius,[48] or what Terenzio Mamiani, in his footsteps, termed 'the great universal city of humankind' (*la gran città universale del genere umano*).[49] To return to the metaphor of fires and their extinguishing, no fire brigade has yet been established in the international community, let alone a set of tools to put out the fire, jointly owned by all members. Each sovereign State continues to pursue its own interest, although now, much more than in the past, it has to take into account pressures, incentives, and exhortations of other subjects.[50] In 1929, Sigmund Freud, speaking of the progress of men, said that 'the substitution of the power of the community for that of the single individual has marked the decisive step towards civilization'.[51] One may well wonder when this step will be taken at the international level, that is, when the individual State's authority will be replaced by the power of the community.

RECOMMENDED READING

Antonowicz, Lech 'Definition of State in International Law Doctrine' (1966–67) 1 Polish Yearbook of International Law 195–207.

[47] C Parry 'The Function of Law in the International Community' in T Sørensen (ed) *Manual of Public International Law* (Macmillan London 1968) 5–6.

[48] See H Grotius *De jure belli ac pacis libri tres* (Nicolaus Byon Paris 1625) at 439 (book II, ch XX, s XLIV) where Grotius confines himself to citing Cicero. More developments can be found in Grotius *Mare liberum* (Ex Officina Elzeviriana Leiden 1633) in the 'Introduction' and at 2 (ch 1) and 74 (ch XII).

[49] *D'un nuovo diritto Europeo* (n 12) 10.

[50] See A Cassese 'Soliloquy' in A Cassese *The Human Dimension of International Law: Selected Papers* (OUP Oxford 2008) lviv–lxxxi at lxxvi–lxxx; L Condorelli and A Cassese 'Is Leviathan Still Holding Sway over International Dealings?' in A Cassese (ed) *Realizing Utopia: The Future of International Law* (OUP Oxford 2012) 14–25.

[51] S Freud 'Das Unbehagen in der Kultur' in S Freud *Das Unbewusste: Schriften zur Psychoanalyse* (A Mitscherlich ed) (Fischer Frankfurt aM 1969) 386–7.

Arangio-Ruiz, Gaetano 'L'état dans le sens du droit des gens et la notion du droit international' (1976) 26 Österreichische Zeitschrift für öffentliches Recht 3–63 and 265–406.

Cassese, Antonio *International Law in a Divided World* (Clarendon Press Oxford 1986).

Cassese, Antonio *International Law* (2nd edn OUP Oxford 2004).

Crawford, James *The Creation of States in International Law* (2nd edn Clarendon Press Oxford 2006).

Detter Delupis, Ingrid *International Law and the Independent State* (2nd edn Aldershot Gower 1987).

Doehring, Karl 'State' in R Bernhardt (ed) *The Max Planck Encyclopedia of Public International Law* (North-Holland Elsevier 2000) vol 4, 600–5.

Grant, Thomas D *The Recognition of States: Law and Practice in Debate and Evolution* (Praeger Westport 1999).

Hinsley, Francis H *Sovereignty* (2nd edn CUP Cambridge 1986).

Maiolo, Francesco *Medieval Sovereignty: Marsilius of Padua and Bartolus of Saxoferrato* (Eburon Academic Publishers Delft 2007).

Merle, Marcel *Les acteurs dans les relations internationales* (Economica Paris 1986) at 30–1.

Societé française pour le droit international *L'état souverain à l'aube du XXIème siècle* (Pedone Paris 1994).

Strayer, Joseph R *On the Medieval Origins of the Modern State* (Princeton University Press Princeton 1970).

Tilly, Charles (ed) *The Formation of National States in Western Europe* (Princeton University Press Princeton 1975).

Vitzthum, Wolfgang G *Der Staat der Staatengemeinschaft: Zur internationalen Verflechtung als Wirkungsbedingung moderner Staatlichkeit* (Schöningh Paderborn 2006).

Warbrick, Colin 'States and Recognition in International Law' in Malcolm Evans (ed) *International Law* (2nd edn OUP Oxford 2006).

CHAPTER 3

PEACE TREATIES AND THE FORMATION OF INTERNATIONAL LAW

RANDALL LESAFFER

1. INTRODUCTION

EVER since pre-classical antiquity, peace treaties have been important instruments for ending wars as well as for the political and legal organization of international communities. Peace treaties were of particular importance to Europe and the West between 1500 and 1920. The relative number of wars which were ended through peace treaties steadily rose from less than half in the 16th century to almost 90 per cent at the beginning of the 20th century.[1] Peace treaties played a primary role in the formation of Europe's classical law of nations (1500–1815) and the West's modern international law (1815–1920). Historians have long since acknowledged that the string of peace treaties that runs from Westphalia (1648) to Versailles (1919) formed the backbone of Europe's international constitution. These and other peace treaties laid down some foundational principles of international order, such as religious neutrality, the common responsibility of states for upholding peace and stability, the special role of

---

[1] Q Wright *A Study of War* (5 vols Chicago University Press Chicago 1942); Q Wright 'How Hostilities Have Ended: Peace Treaties and Alternatives' (1970) 392 Annals of the American Academy of Political and Social Science 51–61.

great powers therein and the balance of power.[2] But peace treaties are also an inform-ative and constitutive source of two essential, specific branches of international law, the law of treaties and the *ius post bellum*. To these two aspects of the contribution peace treaties made to international law, scholars have devoted far less attention than they deserve. Particularly the latter is of great importance for the study of interna-tional law and for understanding its impact on people's lives. The *ius post bellum* forms the third logical part, next to the *ius ad bellum* (use of force law) and the *ius in bello* (the laws of war) of what was historically known as the *ius belli ac pacis* (laws of war and peace).[3] Between the 16th and the 20th centuries, a large body of law on the ending of war and the restoration of peace was articulated in peace treaties.

2. Classical and Medieval Peace Treaties

The Roman usage and customs of peace treaty-making were informed by Greek practices, which in turn drew on those of the pre-classical civilizations of the Middle East. By consequence, ancient peace treaty practice shows a remarkable continuity.[4]

All through antiquity, peace treaties were primarily oral agreements. The constitu-tive element of their binding character was the mutual oath undertaken by treaty partners. Typically, the oath would include an invocation to the gods to act as wit-nesses and guarantors of the treaty. Already in pre-classical times, there are examples of treaties negotiated by ambassadors, which were later ratified by oath by the rulers. The Romans distinguished between *foedera* and *sponsiones*. A *foedus* was the tradi-tional form of a treaty whereby the Roman people bound themselves. Initially, it was sworn to by fetial priests through an elaborate ritual, committing Jupiter, the supreme deity, to the treaty. The fetials would only act after a positive decision of the Senate. Later, they were replaced by magistrates, and ultimately by the emperor. A *sponsio* was an agreement entered into by Roman magistrates, often commanders in the field, at their own initiative. It had to be ratified by the Senate and people of Rome. The

---

[2] A Osiander *The States System of Europe, 1640–1990: Peacemaking and the Conditions of International Stability* (OUP Oxford 1994).

[3] Cicero (106–43 BC) *Pro Balbo* 6.15.

[4] C Baldus 'Vestigia pacis. The Roman Peace Treaty: Structure or Event?' in R Lesaffer (ed) *Peace Treaties and International Law in European History: From the Late Middle Ages to World War One* (CUP Cambridge 2004) 103–46; DJ Bederman *International Law in Antiquity* (CUP Cambridge 2001) 137–206; H Bengtson *Die Staatsverträge des griechisch-römischen Welt von 700 bis 338 v. Chr* (Die Staatsverträge des Altertums) (CH Beck Munich 1962) vol 2; HH Schmitt *Die Verträge der griechisch-römischen Welt von 338 bis 200 v. Chr* (Die Staatsverträge des Altertums) (CH Beck Munich 1969) vol 3; KH Ziegler 'Conclusion and Publication of International Treaties in Antiquity' (1995) 29 Israel Law Review 233–49; KH Ziegler 'Friedensverträge im römischen Altertum' (1989) 27 Archiv des Völkerrechts 45–62.

Romans reserved the right not to ratify these engagements, under the condition that they surrendered the magistrate who made the *sponsio*. In antiquity, peace treaties were commonly written down and published on pillars or tablets. Its recording was not constitutive to the treaty but served as proof for the treaty text and was a way of making it known. The Greeks, and through their influence, the Romans, also developed the concept of faith (πίστις, *fides*) to the given word as a foundation for the binding character and the strict upholding of a treaty.

Ancient peoples distinguished between peace treaties and armistices. Greek peace treaties were almost always made for a limited time. The Romans reserved the term *pax* (peace) for the state of peace, to be distinguished from the state of war. The peace treaty itself they would refer to as *foedus pacis*.[5] *Indutiae* was the term used for armistices. Until the early 3rd century BC, the Romans would use *indutiae* for peace treaties limited in time, which restored the state of peace for a long period. After that, the term *indutiae* gained its meaning as a treaty suspending hostilities but not ending the state of war or restoring the state of peace.[6] The glossator Accursius († 1263) distinguished between *indutiae*, armistices only suspending hostilities during war, and *treugae*, truces temporarily ending war and temporarily restoring peace.[7]

Ancient peace treaties were brief and, with the Greeks and the Roman, clauses were standardized. In ancient peace treaties, the three main categories of clauses that could later be found in (early-)modern peace treaties can already be distinguished: first, clauses dealing with the issues underlying the war; second, clauses ending the state of war, thus reflecting upon the past; and third, clauses restoring and safeguarding the state of peace, thus referring to the future. Just like early-modern peace treaties, ancient peace treaties often included stipulations on prisoners of war. In this context, the Roman *ius postliminii* should be mentioned. The *ius postliminii* implied that Roman citizens, who were taken captive by the enemy and lost their citizenship and all their property, regained their rights upon their return. The Greeks introduced general peace treaties, which did not only involve the actual belligerents but extended to third powers. These treaties included the provision that all powers involved would commonly act against the perpetrator of a breach of treaty.

The Roman practices of peacemaking did not disappear with the fall of the Roman Empire in the West (476 AD). They lived on through the early Middle Ages, in the practices of the Byzantine Empire, the Germanic successor kingdoms, and the Islamic

---

[5] Isidorus of Seville (*c* 560–636) *Etymologiae* 5.6.

[6] See Aulus Gellius (2nd century BC) *Noctes Atticae* 1.25.4: 'neque pax est indutiae—bellum enim manet, pugna cessat' ('and an armistice is neither peace—for the state of war endures; fighting stops') (trans by the author); KH Ziegler 'Kriegsverträge im antiken römischen Recht' (1985) 100 Savigny Zeitschrift für Rechtsgeschichte Romanistische Abteilung 40–90.

[7] *Glossa Pasciscuntur* ad D. 2.14.5: 'ut treugas, quae sunt in longum tempus. Item inducias, quae sunt in breve' ('such as truces, which are made for a long time. Further armistices, which are made for a short time') and *Glossa Lacessant* ad 49.15.19.1: '... Sed treugae in longum, et dicuntur foedera, ('But truces are for a long time, and they are called treaties'). See also *Glossa Foederati* ad D. 49.15.7.

world.[8] All through the Middle Ages, ratification by oath remained the foundational stone of the binding character of treaties. In the Latin West, oaths were taken in church whereby the Holy Gospel, the Holy Cross, the Eucharist, or relics were touched. Under canon law, the enforcement of treaties fell under the jurisdiction of ecclesiastical courts, as the breaking of a promise was a sin. This was all the more true for treaties confirmed by oath, as perjury was considered an even more grave sin.[9] In the 15th and 16th centuries, princes would often expressly subject themselves to ecclesiastical or papal jurisdiction and sanctions, up to excommunication.[10] In some peace treaties, princes renounced the possibility of denouncing their oath as invalid and requesting the pope for dispensation from their oath.[11]

The learned *ius commune* of Roman and canon law contributed to the development of a doctrine of peacemaking from the late 11th century onwards. The laws of war and peace did not form an autonomous body of law with its own literature. Roman and canon lawyers would comment upon issues relating to war and peace at appropriate places in their general writings. Only in the 14th and 15th centuries, self-standing treatises on matters of war and peace would appear. Treatises on peace treaties were few and far in between.[12] Justinian's (527–65) collection of Roman law held scant evidence of Roman peace treaty practice. Most relevant was title D. 49.15 *De captivis et postliminio et redemptis ab hostibus* from the Digest which informed about the distinction between *foedera* and *indutiae* and about *postliminium*. Therefore, Roman jurisprudence could add little knowledge to what had remained from Roman peace treaty practice all over the Middle Ages, but the inclusion of this information in the *Digest* allowed the civilians to elaborate on these subjects. The presence of the *Pax Constantiae* of 1183, a treaty between Emperor Frederick I Barbarossa (1158–91) and the Lombard League, in the medieval collection of the Justinian codification spurred off some writings on peace treaties.[13] But by far the most significant contribution of the medieval civilians to the development of a doctrine of the law of peacemaking came through the application of Roman private law to peace treaties. To the medieval mind, this was not a 'transplant' but a self-evident application of the law at

---

[8] B Paradisi 'L'organisation de la paix au IVe et Ve siècles' in B Paradisi *Civitas maxima. Studi di storia del diritto internazionale* (Olschki Florence 1974) vol 1, 236–95.

[9] Decretal *Novit Ille* by Innocent III (1198–1216) in *Liber Extra* (1234) X. 2.1.13.

[10] Eg Traité de Paix entre Charles VIII, Roi de France et Henri VII, Roi d'Angleterre, fait à Etaples (3 November 1492) in J Dumont *Corps universel diplomatique du droit des gens* (Brunel Amsterdam 1726) (hereinafter CUD) vol 3:2, 291–7, art 28.

[11] Eg Traité, ou Trêves Marchandes faites pour neuf ans entre Louis XI, Roi de France et Charles, dernier Duc Bourgogne, fait à Soleuvre (13 September 1475) in CUD (n 10) vol 3:2, 508, *in fine*.

[12] Most significant is MG Laudensis 'De confoederatione, pace et conventionibus principum' (15th century) (A Wijffels ed) in Peace Treaties and International Law (n 4) 412–47.

[13] Baldus de Ubaldis (1327–1400), see B de Ubaldis *Super usibus feudorum et commentum super pace Constantiae* (F Patavinus ed) (in domo Antonii et Raphaelis de Vulterris Rome 1474); G Dolezalek 'I commentari di Odofredo e Baldo alla pace di Constanza' in *La pace di Costanza 1183* (Cappelli Bologna 1984) 59–75.

large on what was just another category of contracts. During the Middle Ages, sovereignty—*superiorem non recognoscens* or the non-recognition of a superior— was a relative concept and extended to a variety of rulers and communities including kings, feudal lords, and vassals, clerical institutions, towns, and even rural communities. The right to use force and make peace was not restricted to supreme princes such as the pope, emperor, or kings. Consequently, there was no strict distinction between public and private peacemaking. Among the contributions of medieval civilian doctrine to (peace) treaty making should be mentioned the use of the Roman contract of *mandatum* in the context of diplomatic practice.[14] The contribution of canon law to the development of a doctrine of peacemaking was if anything more significant than that of Roman law. From late antiquity onwards, the Church had deferred to Roman law for its own legal organization. Isidorus' definition of *ius gentium* (law of nations) with its reference to *foedera pacis* and *indutiae* had found its way into Gratian's *Decretum* (*c* 1140) and thus into classical canon law. The *Liber Extra* (1234) contained a title *De treuga et pace*,[15] inducing canon lawyers to write commentaries and later, in the 15th and 16th centuries, treatises on the subject.[16] The reference to 'truce and peace' actually stemmed from the Church's attempts from the 10th and 11th centuries to limit violence through the protection of certain persons and places (*pax Dei*), and the prohibition to fight at certain times (*treuga Dei*). Undoubtedly the most crucial contribution of medieval canon law to the doctrine of treaty law in general and peace treaty making in particular is the articulation of the principle *pacta sunt servanda*, of the binding character of all contracts and pacts.[17] Another significant contribution from canon law and late-medieval theology is the doctrine of *clausula rebus sic stantibus*. The Middle Ages saw the emergence of what has been the normal method of the negotiation of peace treaties ever since. Under this method, three different sets of documents were produced: the mandates which rulers bestowed upon the representatives who negotiated with their counterparts; the treaty text as arrested by these representatives; documents attesting the ratification by oath by the rulers themselves. During the late Middle Ages, these documents were commonly made by public notaries and were signed and sealed. It was also common for the diplomats to swear an oath to the treaty text, engaging their principals to ratify the treaty with their own, subsequent oath. By the 13th century, the ratification documents came to serve two purposes. They rendered proof of the actual oath taking by the ruler, which remained the main constitutive underpinning of the treaty, making it binding and enforceable

---

[14] KH Ziegler 'The Influence of Medieval Roman Law on Peace Treaties' in Peace Treaties and International Law (n 4) 147–61.

[15] Liber Extra (n 9) X. 1.34.

[16] See *Tractatus universi juris* (F Ziletti Venice 1583–86) vol 11.

[17] Liber Extra (n 9) X. 1.35.1; R Lesaffer 'The Medieval Canon Law of Contract and Early Modern Treaty Law' (2000) 2 Journal of the History of International Law 178–98; KH Ziegler 'Biblische Grundlagen des europäischen Völkerrechts' (2000) Savigny Zeitschrift für Rechtsgeschichte Kanonistische Abteilung 1–32.

under canon law. But the signing and sealing of the documents had also become a constitutive act, binding the signatories under the law in general.[18]

3. PEACEMAKING FROM 1500 TO 1920

Between the 15th and the 18th centuries, peace treaties grew into far more extensive documents than they were before, containing a manifold of legal stipulations relating to the ending of war and the restoration of peace. This change was consequential to a change in the realities and concept of war after 1500. The rise of the modern State and the gradual monopolization of war by sovereign rulers transformed wars from a contest between princes and their allies and adherents to an all-out war between territorial States, making them more encompassing and more disruptive of normal relations between rulers and their respective subjects. This change of the reality of war was mirrored in doctrine. Under the medieval just war theory, war was perceived as an instrument of justice. It was the forcible self-help of a wronged party against the perpetrator of a prior injury. As such, the war was limited in its scope and goals to retribution for the wrong committed and compensation for the costs and damages of the war. It was also perceived as a set of separate acts of war rather than an all-encompassing state.[19] Whereas the medieval concept of just war proved resilient, the 16th and 17th centuries saw the rise of a second concept of war: that of legal war (*bellum legale*) or formal war (*bellum solemne*). The concept, which was clearly spelled out by 16th- and early 17th-century writers such as Baltasar de Ayala (1548–84), Alberico Gentili (1552–1608), and Hugo Grotius (1583–1645), had antecedents in medieval civilian jurisprudence.[20] For a war to be legal, it had to be waged by a sovereign and to be formally

[18] L Bittner *Die Lehre von den völkerrechtlichen Vertragsurkunden* (Deutsche Verlags-Anstalt Stuttgart 1924); A Hertz 'Medieval Treaty Obligation' (1991) 6 Connecticut Journal of International Law 425–43; A Nussbaum 'Forms and Observance of Treaties in the Middle Ages and the Early Sixteenth Century' in GA Lipsky (ed) *Law and Politics in the World Community: Essays on Hans Kelsen's Pure Theory and Related Issues in International Law* (University of California Press Berkeley 1953) 191–6;, 'Influence of Medieval Roman Law' (n 14) at 152–4. On signed and sealed documents, see R Lesaffer 'Peace Treaties from Lodi to Westphalia' in *Peace Treaties and International Law* (n 4) 9–44 at 25–7; H Steiger 'Bemerkungen zum Friedensvertrag von Crépy en Laonnais vom 18. September 1544 zwischen Karl V. und Franz I.' in U Beyerlin et al (eds) *Recht zwischen Umbruch und Bewahrhung: Völkerrecht—Europarecht—Staatsrecht. Festschrift für Rudolf Bernhardt* (Springer Berlin 1995) vol 2, 249–65 at 256–60.

[19] J Barnes 'The Just War' in N Kretzman et al (eds) *The Cambridge History of Later Medieval Philosophy* (CUP Cambridge 1982) 750–84; P Haggenmacher *Grotius et la doctrine de la guerre juste* (Presses Universitaires de France Paris 1983); FH Russell *The Just War in the Middle Ages* (CUP Cambridge 1975).

[20] See the contributions by M Scattola 'Alberico Gentili (1552–1608)' and by P Haggenmacher 'Hugo Grotius (1583–1645)' in this volume.

declared. In the latter condition lay the *ratio existendi* of the concept. From the 16th century onwards, formal declarations of war grew into substantial documents. The declaration of war indicated that from now on a legal state of war reigned between the belligerents and their subjects.[21] By consequence, the laws of peace were superseded by the laws of war. Often, the declarations spelled out the consequences of the state of war, announcing a series of measures such as the arrest or eviction of enemy subjects, the confiscation of their property, the prohibition to pay debts to enemy subjects or their confiscation, the prohibition of trade with the enemy and of travel towards enemy territory, the eviction of diplomats, and the revocation of passports. By consequence, peace treaties had to include elaborate regulations to end the state of war and restore the state of peace.[22] As declarations of war marked the beginning of the legal state of war and regulated the consequences thereof, peace treaties marked the beginning of the state of peace and regulated the consequences thereof. Early-modern and modern peace treaties had a similar structure as treaties had held before. First, there was a pre-amble, in which reference was made to past events and in which the treaty partners expressed their desire to restore peace and stated their main goals in doing so. Second came the material clauses and stipulations. As mentioned before, these can be classi-fied under three headings: clauses dealing with the outstanding issues between the parties, clauses making an end to the state of war and dealing with its consequences, and clauses which pertained to the restoration and safeguarding of the state of peace for the future. Third, the treaty ended with stipulations about ratification and publica-tion. Regarding the state of war, peace treaties would commonly have a general clause about the ending of hostilities, an amnesty clause, and include stipulations about the withdrawal of troops, occupied territory and fortresses, confiscated and sequestered enemy property and assets, pre-war debts, and wartime procedures between enemy subjects, prisoners of war, general and particular reprisals, seized documents. Regard-ing the state of peace, peace treaties would have a general clause about the restoration of peace and friendship, including the prohibition to harm one another or condone one's subjects to do so, and would further entail stipulations on free movement of persons, commerce, navigation, the rights of people living in ceded territories, access to justice, and protection against arrest and confiscation in case of new war. There was another reason why it was necessary to articulate the legal implications of war and peace in detail in declarations of war and peace treaties. The 16th and early

---

[21] Eg H Grotius *De jure belli ac pacis libri tres* (1625) at 1.2.1.1: 'But Custom had so prevailed, that not the Act of Hostility, but the State and Situation of the Contending Parties, now goes by the Name; so that War is the State or Situation of those (considered in that Respect) who dispute by Force of Arms.' H Grotius *The Rights of War and Peace* (R Tuck ed, J Morrice trans) (3 vols Natural Law and Enlightenment Classics Liberty Fund Indianapolis 2005).

[22] S Whatley (ed) *A General Collection of Treatys, Declarations of War, Manifestos, and other Publick Papers, Relating to Peace and War, Among the Potentates of Europe, from 1648 to the Present Time* (4 vols Knapton etc London 1710–32); R Lesaffer 'Defensive Warfare, Prevention and Hegemony. The Justifications for the Franco-Spanish War of 1635' (2006) 8 Journal of the History of International Law 91–123 and 141–79 at 111–23; SC Neff *War and the Law of Nations: A Historical Survey* (CUP Cambridge 2005) at 54–68 and 96–119.

17th centuries were marked by a crisis of the international order of Europe. The Reformation and the emergence of the sovereign State destroyed the religious unity of the
Latin West and struck hard at the last remnants of the universal authority of the
emperor and the pope. The Reformation caused half of Europe to reject the authority
of canon law and the jurisdiction of pope and Church. Where canon law once had
been the foundational stone of the legal unity of the West and the authority on which
the *ius gentium* rested, it now became a cause of contention. Moreover, the rise of the
sovereign states devalued the role of Roman law as a common source of authority for
international relations. By the mid-16th century, the authority on which the medieval
ius gentium as part of the *ius commune* rested had collapsed. The kings and princes of
Europe, who had achieved complete external sovereignty, were thrown upon their
own devices, and their mutual agreements, to organize their relations. Nevertheless,
many of the concepts and rules that came out of medieval jurisprudence were sustained in early-modern treaty practice and recycled—often through the mediating
role of natural law—in early-modern doctrine. During the later 18th and 19th centuries,
peace treaties became less extensive again. For this, several explanations can be forwarded. First, common clauses were standardized, simplified, and abridged. Second,
over the 17th and 18th centuries, new or renewed general laws about the state of war
and of peace were developed under the newly emerging law of nations, both in practice and doctrine. As a consequence, it became less necessary to spell them out in particular treaties. Moreover, for some clauses—such as the amnesty clause—it became
generally accepted that it was automatically implied. Third, important aspects of the
peaceful relations between States became the subject of separate treaties. From the late
17th century onwards, a separate treaty of friendship, commerce, and navigation was
often made. In the 18th and particularly the 19th century, it became common to revive
pre-war treaties on trade, navigation, and other aspects of peaceful relations which
had been abrogated by the state of war, instead of negotiating new settlements in or
outside the peace treaty.[23] From the mid-19th century onwards, large tracks of general
international law were codified in multilateral conventions. In this, the peace treaties
ending the Napoleon Wars acted as trailblazers. The Congress of Vienna (14–1815)
introduced or codified general international law regarding the slave trade, the status of
international rivers, and diplomats. Later, peace treaties were only rarely used in this
way for the formation or codification of general international law outside the *ius post
bellum*. However, the inclusion into the Versailles Peace Treaty[24] and the other Parisian
Peace Treaties at the end of the First World War (1919/20) of the Covenant of the League
of Nations, which among others laid out a new *ius ad bellum*, should be mentioned.

---

[23] SC Neff 'Peace and Prosperity: Commercial Aspects of Peacemaking' in *Peace Treaties and International Law* (n 4) 365–81; H Steiger 'Peace Treaties from Paris to Versailles' in *Peace Treaties and International Law* (n 4) 59–99 at 94–6.
[24] Treaty of Peace between the Allied and Associated Powers and Germany (signed 28 June 1919) (1919)
225 CTS 188 ('Treaty of Versailles').

Early-modern peace treaty practice built on the inheritance of classical antiquity and the Middle Ages. Renaissance humanism (15th–17th centuries) enhanced knowledge about Biblical, Greek, and particular Roman practice through the humanists' study of ancient historical (for example, Livy) and rhetorical texts (for example, Cicero).[25] But the significance of this humanist rediscovery of Antiquity should not be overstated and certainly does not compare with the mediating role of late-medieval civilian and canon jurisprudence in the formation of the law of nations in general and the law of peacemaking in particular. The writers of the law of nations of the humanist period used ancient practices as *exempla* to illustrate their opinions rather than that those had a fundamental role in the formation thereof.

Between the 16th and the 18th centuries, the law of peacemaking through treaties found its place in doctrinal writings. The number of self-standing treatises on peace treaties remained very limited.[26] Many of the general treatises on the laws of war and peace, such as those of Gentili and Grotius, or the law of nations (and of nature) of the 16th to 18th centuries contained reflections on peacemaking and peace treaties. In general, these were not all that elaborate or systematic. Until the 17th century, many of the old topical issues which had dominated civilian and canon doctrine were still discussed, often beyond the point of their being relevant for contemporary practice. For the writers of the 17th and 18th centuries, it can be said that, with the exception of some doctrinal discussions such as the one on the exception of duress in case of peace treaties and the *clausula rebus sic stantibus*, doctrine was reflective of rather than constitutive for peace treaty practice. Among the classics of international law, the treatment of the law of peace treaties by Gentili as well as Christian Wolff (1679–1754) and Emer de Vattel (1714–67) stands out for length, depth, and systematization.[27] With Wolff and Vattel, the doctrine of peace treaties had been largely laid out and relatively little was added during the 19th century.[28]

---

[25] KH Ziegler 'Römische Grundlagen des europäischen Völkerrechts' (1971) 4 Ius commune 1–27 at 16–27.

[26] Exceptions include P Gudelinus *De jure pacis commentarius* (Dormalius Leuven 1620); see R Lesaffer 'An Early Treatise on Peace Treaties: Petrus Gudelinus between Roman Law and Modern Practice' (2002) 23 Journal of Legal History 223–52.

[27] See the contributions by K Haakonssen 'Christian Wolff (1679–1754)' and by E Jouannet 'Emer de Vattel (1714–1767)' in this volume.

[28] A Gentili *De jure belli libri tres* in JB Scott (ed) *Classics of International Law* (2 vols OUP Oxford 1933) book 3, ch 1; C Wolff *Jus gentium methodo scientifica pertractatum* in JB Scott (ed) *Classics of International Law* (2 vols Clarendon Oxford 1934); E de Vattel *Le droit des gens ou principes de la loi naturelle* in JB Scott (ed) *Classics of International Law* (3 vols Carnegie Washington 1916); R Phillimore *Commentaries upon International Law* (3rd edn Buttersworths London 1879–89) vol 3, at 770–811; P Fauchille *Traité de droit international public* (Rousseau Paris 1921–23) vol 2, at 1030–59; see R Lesaffer 'Alberico Gentili's *ius post bellum* and Early Modern Peace Treaties' in B Kingsbury and B Straumann (eds) *The Roman Foundations of the Law of Nations: Alberico Gentili and the Justice of Empire* (OUP Oxford 2010) 210–40; R Lesaffer 'A Schoolmaster Abolishing Homework? Vattel on peacemaking and peace treaties' in V Chetail and P Haggenmacher (eds) *Vattel's International Law in XXIst Century Perspective/Le droit international de Vattel vu du XXIe siècle* (Brill Leyden 2011) 353–84.

The main source of peace treaties were peace treaties themselves. Diplomats and jurists based themselves on previous peace treaties and copied many of the clauses found therein. Peace treaties themselves formed the *usus* and rendered proof of the *opinio iuris* of the customary body of *ius post bellum* that emerged after 1500. One can distinguish several traditions of peace treaty practice according to the powers involved. Two traditions from before 1500 are foundational to subsequent peace treaty practice: the Italian practice and the practices of France, England, and the Burgundian Nether-lands. Through their wars in Italy after 1494 and through the personal union between the Burgundian Netherlands and Spain under the Habsburgs (1516), the two leading powers of the 16th century, France and Spain, fell heir to these traditions. The major peace treaties of the 16th century between these powers—Madrid (1526), Cambrai (1529), Crépy (1544), Câteau-Cambrésis (1559), and Vervins (1598)—further developed the laws and customs of peace treaties and laid the basis for the general European practice of later times. To these need to be added the contribution from treaties involv-ing England and the Republic to matters of navigation and trade and as well as that from the treaties of the Eighty Years War (1567–1648) between Spain and the Republic—in particular the Twelve Years Truce of 9 April 1609, and the Peace Treaty of Münster of 30 January 1648[29] that was largely copied from the Truce—to matters of private prop-erty. The peace treaties that came out of the general peace conferences of the 17th and 18th centuries—Westphalia (1648),[30] Nijmegen (1678/79),[31] Ryswick (1697),[32] Utrecht/ Rastatt (1713/14),[33] Aix-la-Chapelle (1748),[34] Paris/Hubertusburg (1763)[35]—drew on these traditions and developed the general law and lore of European peacemaking.[36]

---

[29] Treaty of Peace between Spain and the Netherlands (signed 30 January 1648) (1648) 1 CTS 1, art 21.

[30] The Peace of Münster: Treaty of Peace between Spain and the Netherlands (n 29). The Treaties of Münster: Treaty of Peace between the Holy Roman Empire and France (signed 24 October 1648) (1648) 1 CTS 271; and Osnabrück: Treaty of Peace between the Holy Roman Empire and Sweden (signed 24 October 1648) (1648) 1 CTS 198. Together these treaties form the Peace of Westphalia.

[31] H Bots (ed) *The Peace of Nijmegen 1676–1678/79/La paix de Nimègue 1676–1678/79* (Holland Univer-siteits Pers Amsterdam 1980) (proceedings of the conference marking the tricentennial anniversary of the Treaties of Nijmegen, Nijmegen, 14–16 September 1978).

[32] Treaty of Peace Between France and The Netherlands (signed 20 September 1697) (1697) 21 CTS 347.

[33] Treaty of Peace and Friendship Between France and Great Britain (signed 11 April 1713) (1713) 27 CTS 477 ('Treaty of Utrecht'); Treaty of Peace Between the Emperor and Spain, and France (signed 7 March 1714) (1714) 29 CTS 1 ('Treaty of Rastatt').

[34] Treaty of Aix-la-Chapelle (signed 18 October 1748) (1748) 38 CTS 297.

[35] Definitive Treaty of Peace and Friendship between France, Great Britain and Spain (signed 10 Feb-ruary 1763) (1763) 42 CTS 279; Treaty of Peace between Austria and Prussia (signed 15 February 1765) 42 CTS 347.

[36] J Fisch *Krieg und Frieden im Friedensvertrag: Eine universalgeschichtliche Studie über die Grundlagen und Formelemente des Friedensschlusses* (Klett-Cotta Stuttgart 1979) at 536–7; R Lesaffer 'Charles V, *mon-archia universalis* and the Law of Nations (1515–30)' (2003) 71 Legal History Review 79–123; 'Gentili's *ius post bellum*' (n 28) 212–13; R Lesaffer and EJ Broers 'Private Property in the Dutch-Spanish Peace Treaty of Münster (30 January 1648)' in M Jucker et al (eds) *Rechtsformen Internationaler Politik: Theorie, Norm und Praxis vom 12. bis 18. Jahrhundert* (Zeitschrift für Historische Forschung Beihefte Duncker & Hum-blot Berlin 2011); 'Friedensvertrag von Crépy' (n 18).

4. Parties, Forms, and Safeguards

4.1. Treaty Parties

The emergence of the sovereign State after 1500 had a deep impact on peace treaties. By the 17th century, in all major States, the right to make war and peace had become the monopoly of the sovereign to the exclusion of all subject powers, the exceptions being the Estates of the German Empire and the Northern Italian States, which fell under the feudal suzerainty of the emperor. For the late 15th century, some examples can be quoted of peace treaties between French kings and their rebellious subjects.[37] But the peace agreements made between the French kings and their subjects in the context of the French Wars of Religion (1562–98) were styled as unilateral concessions by the king and were laid down in the form of royal edicts.[38] After that, no regular peace treaties between princes and rebels can be found, except those ending in the successful secession of the rebels.

From the Middle Ages to the early 20th century, the preambles of the peace treaties mentioned the princes and not their realms as contracting parties. The main articles in which the state of peace was restored stated that the peace would apply between the princes, their heirs and successors, lands and subjects.[39] Until deep into the 18th century, princes were mentioned by name and title; afterwards by title only.[40] This was to some extent even paralleled in the case of Republics. The peace treaties entered by the Republic of the United Provinces mentioned the Estates-General, the highest sovereign body, as treaty partner and not the Republic itself.[41] This would only change with the French Revolution (1789–99).[42] Under this remarkable stability of form lurked an important change. After 1500, peace treaties gradually transformed from compacts between princes to public treaties between States. At the end of the 15th century, peace treaties were still personal contracts which princes made in their own name. It was the princes, and not their realms or subjects, who were bound to the treaties. The latter were only indirectly bound through the mediation of their prince and his promise to impose the treaty upon them. As princes claimed the monopoly of war

---

[37] Traité de Paix entre Louis XI, Roi de France d'une part, Charles Comte de Charlois et les Princes Liguez, sous le nom du Bien d'autre part, fait à Conflans (5 October 1465) in CUD (n 10) vol 3:1, 335–7.

[38] Edit de Henri IV, Roi de France par la Pacification des Troubles de son Royaume, fait à Nantes (April 1598) in CUD (n 10) vol 5–1, 545–58, Preamble.

[39] Still in Treaty of Peace between Bulgaria, Greece, Montenegro, Serbia and Turkey (signed 30 May 1913) (1913) 218 CTS 159 and Treaty of Peace between Bulgaria, Greece, Montenegro, Romania and Serbia (signed 19 August 1913) (1913) 218 CTS 322. The first peace treaty mentioning States is the Treaty of Peace between France and Germany (signed 10 May 1871) (1871) 143 CTS 163.

[40] J Ray 'La communauté internationale d'après les traités du XVIe siècle à nos jours' (1938) 3 Annales Sociologiques, series C, 14–49 at 19.

[41] Treaty of Peace between Spain and the Netherlands (n 29) Preamble.

[42] Treaty of Campo Formio (signed 17 October 1797) (1797) 54 CTS 157 at 158, Preamble.

and peace and of representing their realms on the international scene, they started to act as representatives of their realms, making their commitment sufficient to bind their realms and subjects directly. By the mid-17th century, this transformation was already well under way; peace treaty practice made this apparent in several ways. First, there was a subtle if significant change in the preambles. Until the end of the 15th century, the preambles of peace treaties expressly stated that princes entered the compact 'for' themselves, their vassals, and subjects.[43] After 1500, these wordings disappeared and vassals and subjects were not mentioned anymore. This indicated that it was more readily accepted that the partaking of the prince to the treaty implied the allegiance of his subjects. Second, there is the question whether peace treaties were binding upon the successors of the signatories. It was generally accepted that a prince 'could' bind his successors to a treaty, but it was not evidently implied that they did so. Some 15th- and 16th-century peace treaties stipulated that they would remain valid for a certain period of time after the death of one of the signatories, during which his successor could ratify the treaty.[44] These clauses disappeared by the 1530s. Others prescribed that the heir to the throne would co-ratify the treaty. This was largely restricted to treaties involving the cession of territories or rights.[45] Third, there was co-ratification. In treaties from the 14th to the mid-16th century, it was customary for treaty partners to agree that the peace treaty would be co-ratified by certain nobles, clerics, and towns subject to the signatory princes. This had a double function: it bound the notables more directly to the treaty; often, they also promised to act as guarantors for the execution of the treaty by their prince.[46] Over the 16th century, these clauses disappeared. In a limited number of peace treaties, they were first accompanied and later substituted by the promise to have the treaties registered by the highest courts, the exchequers or, exceptionally, the Estates, of the realm.[47] This started as a form of institutionalized co-ratification, strengthening the allegiance of the realm to the treaty beyond the mere engagement of the prince. Although these clauses have certainly acted as precedents to constitutional rules on the ratification of treaties by legislative assemblies which appeared at the end of the 18th century, they are also fundamentally

---

[43] Appunctuamenta amicitiae perpetuae inter Carolum Audacem, Ducem Burgundiae et Eduardem IV, Regem Anglicae (25 July 1474) in CUD (n 10) vol 3:1, 485–6, Preamble.

[44] Etaples (n 10) art 1.

[45] Traité de Paix entre Henri II, Roi de France et Filippe II, Roi d'Espagne, fait à Câteau-Cambrésis (3 April 1559) CUD (n 10) vol 5:1, 34–44 at 41, art 47.

[46] Traité de Paix entre Louis XI, Roi de France, le Dauphin et le Royaume d'une part et Maximilien, Duc d'Autriche, Mr le Duc Philippe et Mademoiselle Marguerite d'Autriche d'autre part: Contenant entr'autres, un Accord de Mariage entre ledit Prince Dauphin et ladite Princesse Marguerite (23 December 1482) CUD (n 10) vol 3:2, 100–10 at 107, art 88. Divergent view, K Neitmann *Die Staatsverträge des deutschen Ordens in Preussen 1230–1449: Studien zur Diplomatie eines spätmittelalterlichen deutschen Territorialstaates* (Neue Forschungen zur brandenburg-preussischen Geschichte 6) (Böhlau Cologne 1986) at 276–81.

[47] Traité de Paix entre Henri IV, Roi de France, Philippe II, Roi d'Espagne et Charles-Emanuel, Duc de Savoie, fait à Vervin (2 May 1598) in CUD (n 10) vol 5:1, 561–9 at 564, *in fine*.

different. Whereas modern ratification by parliaments is an institution of national constitutional law, the early-modern involvement of representative and judicial organs was a matter of treaty law to strengthen the direct binding of a prince's subjects to a treaty. The introduction of parliamentary ratification moreover marked a final step in the transformation of treaties from compacts between princes to treaties between States.

4.2. Forms, Ratification and Safeguards

The Reformation did not put an end to the ratification of treaties by oath. Until deep into the 17th century, the custom persisted. The Reformation, however, wrought an important change. By 1550, express references to jurisdiction and sanctions had disappeared from peace treaties, even among Catholics. The Reformation destroyed the common authority under the binding character of treaties—that of canon law. The law of nations that began to emerge as an autonomous body of law had to provide a new one: *pacta sunt servanda* and *bona fides* to one's own consent. Under the new law of nations, ratification by oath was just another form of expressing the consent which bound a ruler to a treaty. Gradually, it was superseded and then totally replaced as the main constitutive element of the treaty by the exchange of signed and sealed documents. Between the 15th and 20th centuries, the mechanisms used to safeguard the peace evolved. Until the end of the 17th century, most peace treaties expressly stipulated that a violation of the treaty by a subject would not lead to a breach of the peace, but that the perpetrator would be punished and restitution would be done.[48] Peace treaties of the 16th and 17th centuries often provided for the appointment of special commissioners or arbitrators to resolve conflicts about the interpretation and execution of the treaty, as well as work out some outstanding issues.[49] Before the Reformation, ecclesiastical jurisdiction and sanctions had been the strongest and most general mechanism to enforce the peace upon the treaty parties. The use of hostages was fairly uncommon and it was mainly used to guarantee the execution of particular clauses in peace treaties, such as the surrender of territories, towns, or fortresses or money payments. Sometimes, princes pledged all their goods to the treaty, thus giving the treaty partner a claim to lawfully seize these goods in case of a breach of treaty and the resulting new war. By the mid-17th century, these practices had largely fallen into disuse. Between the mid-17th and the mid-18th centuries, treaty partners frequently made use of guarantors. A guarantee implied that a power would enforce the treaty upon the treaty partners, if necessary through the use of force. A distinction can be made between guarantees from treaty partners and guarantees from third

---

[48] Treaty of Peace between England and the Netherlands (5 April 1654) (1654) 3 CTS 225 at 234–5, art 24.

[49] Treaty of Peace between Spain and the Netherlands (n 29) art 21.

powers. The first form only makes sense for multilateral peace treaties, which were very uncommon until the mid-18th century. The main exceptions are—seemingly— the two Peace Treaties of Westphalia (24 October 1648)—that of Münster between the empire and France, and of Osnabrück between the empire and Sweden—to which not only the emperor and the king of France, respectively the queen of Sweden, but also a great number of imperial Estates acceded.[50] More frequent were guarantees by third powers. Some of the peace treaties coming out of the great peace conferences from the late 17th and 18th centuries invited the powers which had acted as mediators to become guarantors.[51] Guarantees in peace treaties fell into disuse during the second half of the 18th century. Special treaties of guarantee whereby powers promised their support for the upholding of certain rights became more common over the 19th century. That century also saw the emergence of new enforcement means for peace treaties, which would survive into the 20th century. These were mostly of a military nature such as the (temporary) occupation of part of the territory or the imposition of military restrictions.[52]

5. Perpetual and General Peace

5.1. Perpetual Peace

Most peace treaties from the 16th to the early 19th century expressly stated that peace would be perpetual. This was not the—seemingly stubborn and naïve—expression of a legal commitment never to resort to war again, but held more specific implications under the law of nations. Already the medieval civilians had acknowledged that if a new war broke out between treaty partners for a new cause, other than the one underlying the previous war which had been settled in the peace treaty, this did not constitute a breach of the treaty.[53] From this, one can deduce *e contrario* that a peace treaty exhausted the right of the former belligerents to resort to armed force over the disputes settled in the peace treaty. But it would take Samuel Pufendorf (1632–94),[54]

---

[50] Treaty of Peace between France and the Empire (signed 24 October 1648) (1648) 1 CTS 271 at 354, para 124 and Treaty of Peace between Sweden and the Empire (signed 24 October 1648) (1648) 1 CTS 198, art 17(4).

[51] Treaty of Peace of Nijmegen (signed 10 August 1678) (1678) 14 CTS 365 at 374, art 20. H Duchhardt 'Peace Treaties from Westphalia to the Revolutionary Era' in *Peace Treaties and International Law* (n 4) 45–58 at 55.

[52] 'Peace Treaties from Paris to Versailles' (n 23) 91–2.

[53] Baldus de Ubaldis *Consilium* 2.195. See 'Gentili's *ius post bellum*' (n 28) 227.

[54] See the contribution by K Haakonssen 'Samuel Pufendorf (1632–1694)' in this volume.

Wolff, and Vattel to state it so straightforwardly.[55] The perpetual character of a peace distinguished it from a truce. A truce could, as much as a peace treaty, put an end to all measures that had been taken at the inception of the war, and thus for all practical purposes suspend the state of war and restore the state of peace, but parties had the right to resort to war for the same issues once the truce had lapsed.

5.2. General Peace

Before the Peace of Aachen (1748), peace treaties were almost always bilateral.[56] This was as true for peace treaties made at general, multilateral peace conferences. The Peace Treaties of Münster and Osnabrück (24 October 1648) were not truly exceptions to the rule. Their multilateral character was consequential to their hybrid nature: they were at once international peace pacts between the empire and France or Sweden respectively as well as internal peace compacts between the emperor and the Estates of the Holy Roman Empire. As international peace compacts, they were not different from regular, bilateral peace treaties, both in form as in substance. Their much-acclaimed contribution to the development of the law of nations and the constitution of Europe stems from the fact that their hybrid nature caused constitutional settlements which pertained to the Empire to seep into international treaties and thus find their way into the law of nations.[57]

Some peace treaties of the early-modern age, particularly those coming out of multilateral peace conferences, were expressly said to inaugurate a 'universal' peace, under which term Christian Europe was meant.[58] These claims to universality seem to be corroborated by the custom to 'include' numerous third powers into the treaties. But one should be careful not to overstate the implications of these inclusions. Inclusion clauses were very common in peace treaties between the 15th and 18th centuries and were certainly not limited to so-called universal peace treaties or peace treaties from multilateral conferences. With these clauses, treaty partners associated their allies and auxiliaries to the peace treaty. In some of the important peace treaties, almost all important powers were included. An in-depth study of diplomatic practice would have to show what the exact legal implications of inclusion were, but it is clear that it did not amount to full accession. The main effect of

---

[55] S Pufendorf *De jure naturae et gentium libri octo* (CH and WA Oldfather trans) (2 vols Classics of International Law Clarendon Oxford 1934) 8.7.4; *Jus gentium* (n 28) 8.987; *Droit des gens* (n 28) 4.2.19.

[56] K Marek 'Contribution à l'étude de l'histoire du traité multilatéral' in E Diez et al (eds) *Festschrift für Rudolf Bindschedler* (Stämpfli Bern 1980) 17–39.

[57] R Lesaffer 'The Westphalia Peace Treaties and the Development of the Tradition of Great European Peace Settlements prior to 1648' (1997) 18 Grotiana NS 71–95; H Steiger 'Der westfälische Frieden—Grundgesetz für Europa?' in H Duchhardt (ed) *Der westfälische Friede: Diplomatie, politische Zäsur, kulturelles Umfeld, Rezeptionsgeschichte* (Oldenbourg Munich 1998) 33–80.

[58] Treaty of Peace between France and the Empire (n 50) 321–2, para 1.

inclusion was that it committed the treaty partner not to enact retribution against the allies of its former enemy. In the 17th and 18th centuries, inclusion had most relevance in relation to auxiliary powers. Inclusion protected States which had supported a certain side in the war—with money or troops—without being openly at war. Inclusion did not make the whole treaty applicable to the included power nor granted it the same rights and imposed the same obligations—which would be impractical without particular negotiations—but extended the general clause of peace and amity to the included power. Inclusion did not suffice to restore peace between powers that were actually at war with one another. For this, a separate peace treaty or full accession to a peace treaty was necessary.[59] Some peace treaties of the 17th and 18th centuries referred back to older peace treaties. This has been indicated in modern scholarship as proof for their constitutional role in the European States system. Until the end of the 17th century, references to previous peace treaties as 'base and foundation' of a new treaty were restricted to the Holy Roman Empire. The first treaties to be mentioned thus way were the Westphalian Treaties.[60] This was in fact a consequence of these Treaties having been declared imperial law.[61] However, the practice took hold in international relations and became general in the 18th century. The Peace Treaty of Paris of 10 February 1763 named the Treaties of Westphalia, Nijmegen, Ryswick, Utrecht, Baden (1714), Vienna (1738), Aachen (1748), as well as the Triple and Quadruple Alliances (1717/18), and some particular treaties between Great Britain and Spain and Portugal and Spain as 'base and foundation'.[62] These treaties can indeed be considered 'constitutional' to the order of Europe to the extent that they settled major dynastic and territorial disputes and reflected some of the leading principles of European order. But, formally speaking, they were just regular treaties without any superior authority. In fact, in most cases, it was expressly stated that these treaties were renewed and were to be held applicable as if they were inserted 'word for word' in the new treaty, at least inasmuch as it did not derogate from it.[63] These older treaties were not paramount law in relation to the new treaty, as any special position they had derived from the new treaty.

The notion of 'universal peace' was relevant in yet another way. The preambles of peace treaties often indicate which ulterior purposes the treaty partners had in making peace. From the vast majority of peace treaties from the 15th to the 20th centuries, it appears that the powers of Europe considered a general peace within Christianity

---

[59] *Jus gentium* (n 26) 8.1009; *Droit des gens* (n 28) 4.2.15; R Lesaffer 'Amicitia in Renaissance Peace and Alliance Treaties' (2002) Journal of the History of International Law 4 77–99; 'Westfälischer Frieden' (n 57) at 45–8.

[60] Of the Peace Treaties made at Ryswick the one between the Empire and France was the only one to mention Westphalia and Nijmegen (30 October 1697) (1697) 22 CTS 5, art 3.

[61] Treaty of Peace between France and the Empire (n 50) 353, para 120 and Treaty of Peace between Sweden and the Empire (n 50) art 17(2).

[62] Definitive Treaty of Peace between France, Great Britain and Spain (n 35) art 2.

[63] Treaty of Aix-la-Chapelle (n 34) art 3.

(15th–18th centuries) or Europe (17th–20th centuries) the ultimate purpose of their endeavours and their common responsibility. To this, the particular, generally bilateral peace treaty was said to contribute, and treaty parties implicitly explained their willingness to grant concessions in these terms. The goal of general peace was associated with other goals or principles which evolved over time. In the 15th and early 16th centuries, it was linked to the need for unity of the Christian world in the face of the Turkish threat. In the late 17th and 18th centuries, mention was made of the 'tranquility and security of Europe'. This referred to the need to uphold the dynastic and territorial status quo as laid down in great peace compacts. Although express references to the balance of power were rare, it was considered a necessary precondition for the tranquility and security of Europe.[64] During the 18th and 19th centuries, it became accepted that the great powers held a particular responsibility, and therefore special rights, to uphold the peace and security of Europe. The Triple and Quadruple Alliances of 1717–18 and some treaties of guarantee of the 18th century offer early expressions thereof. In the 19th century, the great powers assumed their role through the Congress of Europe, whereby regular multilateral conferences were convened to decide about major issues of peace and security and wherein the great power took a dominant role. This 'great power principle' was later institutionalized in the Council of the League of Nations (1919) and the Security Council of the United Nations Organisation (1945).[65]

6. JUST AND FORMAL WAR, JUST AND FORMAL PEACE

Under a consequential application of the just war doctrine, a just war needed to end in a just peace. Wolff and Vattel spelled out the multiple, far-reaching consequences thereof. First, it meant that the unjust belligerent lost his claim to the object over which the war was fought. Second, he was liable for all the damages and costs suffered by the just belligerent because of the war. Under the just war doctrine, the

---

[64] H Duchhardt 'The Missing Balance' (2000) 2 Journal of the History of International Law 67–72; R Lesaffer 'Paix et guerre dans les grands traités du XVIIIe siècle' (2005) Journal of the History of International Law 7 25–41 at 37–40.

[65] R Lesaffer 'The Grotian Tradition Revisited: Change and Continuity in the History of International Law' (2002) 73 British Yearbook of International Law 103–39 at 133–5; *States System of Europe* (n 2) 321–30; G Simpson *Great Powers and Outlaw States: Unequal Sovereigns in the International Legal Order* (CUP Cambridge 2004) at 91–131.

unjust belligerent could not benefit from the full protection of the *ius in bello*; all hostile actions by the unjust belligerent were unjust actions for which he was liable. Third, the just belligerent was also liable for his unjust wartime actions—that is, actions that went against the laws of war.[66] But Wolff and Vattel found this totally impractical as in most cases it was impossible to discern who held just cause, and it could not be expected that sovereigns would subject themselves to the judgment of their peers. As most writers had done since Grotius, Wolff and Vattel banished the justice of war into the sphere of natural law, which was only enforceable in con-science. The externally enforceable law of nations only dealt with the question of the legality of the war. The peace that answered to such a formal or legal war would not have to deal with the question of justice but would be a compromise reached through negotiation and sanctioned by the consent of the parties. By applying the distinction between natural and positive law to just and legal war, Grotius—who built on the ideas of the Spanish neo-scholastics—and his successors gave both medieval tradi-tions of the *ius ad bellum,* the canonical theologian tradition of just war and the civilian tradition of legal war, a place in early-modern doctrine. But more to the point, this duality reflected the duplicity of reality. On the one hand, the doctrine of just war still held sway among the sovereign princes of early-modern Europe, as they continued to justify their wars in terms of the justice of their cause. Declarations and manifestos of war as well as alliance treaties clearly drew on the traditions of just war. Some hostile measures against the enemy, such as the seizure of private prop-erty, were at least implicitly justified by the acclaimed justice of the war. But on the other hand, during war, belligerents applied the laws of war to all belligerents with-out any discrimination for the justice or injustice of their respective positions. Nei-ther did claims to the justice of the war play any role in the making of peace, at least not among European sovereigns.[67] In other words, the sovereign powers of Europe went to just war, fought a formal war, and made a formal peace. Some examples of peace treaties which can be considered 'just' can be quoted from antiquity and the Middle Ages. Generally but not exclusively, such peace treaties were only made after a clear victory or in the context of a hierarchical relation.[68] Typically, such treaties contained an express judgment on the justice of the war and attributed the respon-sibility for the war to one of the belligerents. The concessions the 'unjust' side had to make came as a result of the injustice of his cause or actions during the war. Com-pensations for the mere act of having fought an unjust war and/or for the damages and costs of the war were often imposed, mostly in the form of a tribute. In some cases, restrictions on the military capacity of the unjust belligerent were provided, in order to prevent him from resorting to war again. None of the peace treaties between European sovereigns of the 16th to early 20th centuries was of that type. In

---

[66] *Jus gentium* (n 28) 8.986; *Droit des gens* (n 28) 4.2.18.
[67] 'Gentili's *ius post bellum*' (n 28) 237–40; 'A Schoolmaster Abolishing Homework' (n 28).
[68] *Krieg und Frieden* (n 36) 69–70 and 81–8.

not a single peace treaty was judgment rendered on the justice of the war, nor did a single treaty contain an attribution of guilt to one of the belligerents. In the preambles to peace treaties, the signatories most often limited themselves to deploring the war and the hardship it had brought in the most general terms. This was different for part of the peace treaties made between European and non-European rulers. Particularly in the Americas, the European powers styled peace treaties as unilateral grants of peace. The treaties laid the blame for the war, which was often labelled a rebellion, at the doorstep of the indigenous peoples. Amnesty was a unilateral act of mercy, which had to be paid for through cessions and tributes.[69] The absence of any judgment on the justice of war meant that concessions could not be explained in terms of the injustice of a belligerent's cause for war or the underlying claims about conceded rights and territories. Neither were express references made to a right of conquest—although this was often implied and the right of conquest was *a contrario* upheld in some peace treaties.[70] Hardly the only justifications which were ever offered, and very rarely so, were general references to the interest of a stable and enduring peace and friendship.[71] The basis for treaty concessions was ultimately nothing but the consent of the parties. The refusal to judge was not restricted to the level of the *ius ad bellum*, but extended to the *ius in bello*. From the late 15th century onwards, it became customary for the signatories to include a clause of amnesty and oblivion in the treaty. This implied that the signatories waived all claims for damages and costs because of the war, for themselves as well as for their subjects.[72] By the beginning of the 19th century, these clauses disappeared, but by then it had become accepted that they were automatically implied.[73] The amnesty clause was tied in with another common stipulation, relating to the restitution of private property. During the early-modern age, it was customary for the belligerents to seize the property of enemy subjects found on their territory. Under the just war doctrine, this was done to safeguard the future payment of the damages and the costs of war caused by the unjust belligerent. As peace treaties did not render judgment on the justice of war, the legal basis for their seizure collapsed. Therefore, most peace treaties included a general clause of automatic restitution. To this standard provision, treaties also made a standard exception for movables.[74]

---

[69] *Krieg und Frieden* (n 36) 139–204.

[70] Treaty of Berlin between Hungary and Prussia (signed 28 July 1742) (1742) 36 CTS 409 at 414–16, art 5; Definitive Treaty of Peace between France, Great Britain and Spain (n 62) art 23. S Korman *The Right of Conquest: The Acquisition of Territory by Force in International Law and Practice* (OUP Oxford 1996) at 67–73.

[71] Definitive Treaty of Peace between France, Great Britain and Spain (n 35) art 7.

[72] *Krieg und Frieden* (n 36) 92–123.

[73] *De jure belli ac pacis* (n 21) 3.20.15; *Jus gentium* (n 28) 8.990; *Droit des gens* (n 28) 4.2.20.

[74] H Neufeld *The International Protection of Private Creditors from the Treaties of Westphalia to the Congress of Vienna: A contribution to the history of the law of nations* (Sijthoff Leyden 1971).

7. The Expansion of European Peace Treaty Practice

Until the 19th century, the European law of nations with its practices and laws of peacemaking was but one of several regional systems. Other civilizations developed their own regional systems of peacemaking and peace treaties.

Since the 8th century, the Latin West and the Islamic world had been in constant contact. The discoveries and the early empire-building by Europeans from the late 15th century onwards expanded the scope of Europe's international relation to America, sub-Saharan Africa and Asia. But for a long time, this did not lead to the expansion of the European legal order to other parts of the world. Instead, we can discern two different patterns of behaviour. First, in some cases, contacts and wars between Europeans and non-Europeans led to the articulation of a peace treaty practice which built on the practices and laws of the two civilizations involved, forming a kind of supra-regional system particular to their mutual relations. This was the outcome when Europeans had to deal with powerful contenders, such as the Arab rulers in the Middle Ages, the Ottoman Empire, or the princes and empires of India and East and South-East Asia. Second, when European powers were in a position to impose their will, as was often the case in the Americas or Africa, they imposed a particular design of treaties which was different from that used among European sovereigns. These often included attributions of guilt for the war as well as total subjection or the imposition of harsh conditions on the basis of the indigenous people's one-sided responsibility for the conflict.[75]

The achievement of independence by the white settler colonies of America around 1800 expanded the European law of nations and its system of peacemaking over the Atlantic. The Peace of Paris (1856)[76] expressly stipulated that the Ottoman Empire would enjoy the advantages of the public law and the Concert of Europe. In the middle of the 19th century, the European power and the United States forced China and Japan into their systems of international law and forced Western peace treaty practices upon them. The decolonization of the 20th century made Western international law and its peace treaty practices truly global.

---

[75] CH Alexandrowicz 'Treaty and Diplomatic Relations Between European and South Asian Powers in the Seventeenth and Eighteenth Centuries' (1960) 100 *Recueil des Cours de l'Académie de Droit International* 207–320; CH Alexandrowicz *An Introduction to the Law of Nations in the East Indies 16th, 17th and 18th Centuries* (Clarendon Oxford 1967); CH Alexandrowicz *The European–Africa Confrontation: A Study in Treaty Making* (Sijthoff Leyden 1973); J Fisch *Die europäische Expansion und das Völkerrecht. Die Auseinandersetzungen um den Status der überseeischen Gebiete vom 15. Jahrhundert bis zur Gegenwart* (Steiner Stuttgart 1984); FP Prucha *American Indian Treaties: The History of a Political Anomaly* (University of California Press Berkeley 1994); KH Ziegler 'The Peace Treaties of the Ottoman Empire with European Christian Powers' in *Peace Treaties and International Law* (n 4) 338–64.

[76] General Treaty for the Re-Establishment of Peace between Austria, France, Great Britain, Prussia, Sardinia, Turkey and Russia (signed 30 March 1856) (1856) 114 CTS 409, art 7.

8. The Transformation of Peace Treaty Practice and Law after the First World War

Versailles and the other Parisian peace treaties at the end of the First World War (1919–20) mark a sudden break in European peace treaty practice. To some extent, they constitute a return to a concept of just peace. Article 231 of the Versailles Treaty put the blame for the war on Germany because of its acts of aggression. Article 232 imposed upon Germany the obligation to pay compensation for all damage done to civilians and their property, as well as compensate for the debts of Belgium to its allies for its war costs. In itself, the imposition of compensation for the costs and damages of war by the victor upon a defeated power were not new. They had been introduced during the Napoleonic Wars and had been provided for in important peace treaties such as those of Paris (1814–15) and Frankfurt (1871).[77] These compensations had in no way been related to an attribution of guilt for the war but were merely consequential to the defeat. The return to a concept of 'just peace' went even further in the Versailles Peace Treaty. In the Treaty, the German Emperor was made liable to criminal prosecution for his 'supreme offence against international morality and the sanctity of treaties' through his aggression (article 227). The Treaty also provided for the criminal prosecution by the Allied and Associated Powers of Germans for violations against the laws and customs of war (article 228). Furthermore, it imposed severe military restrictions on Germany.[78]

The return to just peace was not followed through after Versailles. Throughout the 20th century, most interstate peace treaties were still formal peace treaties without attributions of guilt. But the peace treaties with the European allies of Germany (Paris 1947) after the Second World War applied a sort of concept of just peace. The same goes for the conditions for ending the hostilities imposed upon Iraq by the United Nations Security Council (Resolution 687)[79] at the end of the First Gulf War (1991).[80]

Twentieth-century peace practice saw more fundamental changes than this partial revival of just peace. First, the relative number of interstate armed conflicts ended by peace treaties seriously declined after 1945. In some cases, as that of Germany after the Second World War, this was due to political circumstances. But more generally, this decline was consequential to a change in the concept of war. The outlawing of war—in the Kellogg–Briand Pact (1928)[81] and the UN Charter—has caused a sharp decline in

---

[77] Treaty of Frankfurt between France and Prussia (signed 10 May 1871) (1871) 143 CTS 166, art 7.

[78] Treaty of Versailles (n 24).

[79] UNSC Res 687 (3 April 1991) UN Doc S/Res/687.

[80] G Fitzmaurice 'The Juridical Clauses of the Peace Treaties' (1948) 73 *Recueil des cours* 259–367 at 262–8; R Lesaffer *Europa: een zoektocht naar vrede? (1453–1763 en 1945–99)* (Europe: A Quest for Peace? (1453–1763 and 1945–99)) (Universitaire Pers Leuven Leuven 1999) at 562–7; M Weller *Iraq and the Use of Force in International Law* (OUP Oxford 2010) at 49–54.

[81] General Treaty for the Renunciation of War as an Instrument of National Policy (signed 27 August 1928, entered into force 25 July 1929) 94 LNTS 57.

the number of formally declared 'legal wars'. Under the post-Charter *ius ad bellum*, the distinction between the state of war and a state of peace has become more relative and 'wars' are again perceived in terms of separate acts of war or hostility rather than as an all-encompassing legal state. For this reason, the traditional peace treaty has fallen into relative disuse. But whereas this is often seen as the demise of peace treaty practice, it can as readily be considered part of a process of its transformation. Formal peace treaties marking the transit from state of war to state of peace may have become relatively rare but have not disappeared altogether.[82] As legal forms and concepts of interstate armed conflict became more varied, legal forms and contents of agreements to end them likewise became more varied. Some conflicts ended with an armistice and/or a preliminary agreement whereby relations quickly or gradually regained a level of normalcy. In other cases, treaties of friendship organizing aspects of the relations between belligerents were used without a formal end to the war being expressly declared.[83]

Second, the years since 1945 have been marked by a proliferation of intra-state armed conflicts, in which third powers were often involved. In this context, hundreds of peace agreements were made. These agreements often take the form of international treaties but are mostly hybrid in nature, because they span inter- and intra-state affairs. More than being instruments of conflict resolution, current peace agreements are as much instruments of constitutional formation that break through the confines of domestic and international order. They include detailed regulations of constitutional (re-)formation.[84]

Third, next to State building, another important issue has come to expand the concern of peacemaking—or peace building as it is now called—and widened the domain of the *ius post bellum*: the protection of human rights. This has started with the inclusion of stipulations on minority rights in the late 19th century.[85] By the late 20th century, this has come to include stipulations on general human rights, including political and economic rights as well as on the prosecution of violations against international humanitarian law.[86]

Fourth, peacemaking turned into a drawn-out process of peace building, implying a series of agreements and documents. This is not completely new as also in the early-modern age use was made of armistices and preliminary peace treaties in preparation

---

[82] Treaty of Peace between the State of Israel and the Hashemite Kingdom of Jordan (signed 26 October 1994) (1995) 34 ILM 46, art 1.

[83] See eg WG Grewe 'Peace Treaties' in R Bernhardt (ed) *Max Planck Encyclopedia of Public International Law* (2nd edn Elsevier Amsterdam 1992–95) vol 3, 938–46 at 943.

[84] C Bell *On the Law of Peace: Peace Agreements and the Lex Pacificatoria* (OUP Oxford 2008).

[85] Eg Preliminary Treaty of Peace between Russia and Turkey (signed 19 February 1878) (1878) 152 CTS 395; Treaty between Austria-Hungary, France, Germany, Great Britain, Italy, Russia and Turkey for the Settlement of Affairs in the East (signed 13 July 1878) (1878) 153 CTS 171.

[86] C Bell *Peace Agreements and Human Rights* (OUP Oxford 2000); *On the Law of Peace* (n 84) 218–58.

of the peace treaty as well as particular treaties following up on different aspects of peacemaking. But then, there had always been a formal peace treaty at the centre which marked the momentary transition from war to peace. As war and peace have become relative concepts, so the notion of a sudden transition has made place for that of a transition process.

9. Conclusion

Early-modern Europe developed a particular kind of peace treaty practice and law which was premised on the sovereign State in three ways. First, the sovereign State monopolized the right to make peace treaties. Second, a formal concept of war was introduced which excluded all notions of justice and discrimination on the basis of justice in the waging of war (*ius in bello*) and the making of peace (*ius post bellum*). Third, the collapse of supra-state authorities gave consent through treaty a central role in the articulation of general as well as particular law of nations. Peace treaties naturally were most relevant to the development of the *ius post bellum*. The 20th century saw the relative demise of the sovereign state in international law, and changed the law and practice of peacemaking. The traditional formal interstate peace treaty lost its quasi-monopoly as legal instrument of peacemaking. Instead a variety of peace agreements emerged. Moreover, the boundaries between inter- and intra-state peacemaking became transparent again and the *ius post bellum* expanded into a *ius post bellum* encompassing the protection of human rights and state building.

Recommended Reading

Baldus, Christian *Regelhafte Vertragsauslegung nach Parteilrollen im klassischen römischen Recht und in der modernen Völkerrechtswissenschaft: zur Rezeptionsfähigkeit römischen Rechtsdenkens* (2 vols Lang Frankfurt 1998).

Bell, Christine *Peace Agreements and Human Rights* (OUP Oxford 2000).

Bell, Christine *On the Law of Peace: Peace Agreements and the Lex Pacificatoria* (OUP Oxford 2008).

Boemeke, Manfred F (ed) *The Treaty of Versailles: A Reassessment after 75 Years* (CUP Cambridge 1998).

Croxton, Derek and Anuschka Tischer (eds) *The Peace of Westphalia: A Historical Dictionary* (Greenwood Westport/London 2002).

Davenport, Francis G (ed) *European Treaties Bearing on the History of the United States and its Dependencies* (4 vols Carnegie Washington 1917).

Fisch, Jörg *Krieg und Frieden im Friedensvertrag: Eine universalgeschichtliche Studie über die Grundlagen und Formelemente des Friedensschlusses* (Klett-Cotta Stuttgart 1979).

Frey, Linda and Marsha Frey *The Treaties of the War of the Spanish Succession: An Historical and Critical Dictionary* (Greenwood Westport/London 1995).

Lesaffer, Randall 'The Westphalia Peace Treaties and the Development of the Tradition of Great European Peace Settlements prior to 1648' (1997) 18 Grotiana NS 71–95.

Lesaffer, Randall 'The Grotian Tradition Revisited: Change and Continuity in the History of International Law' (2002) 73 British Yearbook of International Law 103–39.

Lesaffer, Randall (ed) *Peace Treaties and International Law in European History: From the end of the Middle Ages to World War One* (CUP Cambridge 2004).

Lesaffer, Randall 'Alberico Gentili's ius post bellum and Early Modern Peace Treaties' in Benedict Kingsbury and Benjamin Straumann (eds) *The Roman Foundations of the Law of Nations: Alberico Gentili and the Justice of Empire* (OUP Oxford 2010) 210–40.

Neitmann, Klaus *Die Staatsverträge des deutschen Ordens in Preussen 1230–1449: Studien zur Diplomatie eines spätmittelalterlichen deutschen Territorialstaates* (Neue Forschungen zur brandenburg-preussischen Geschichte 6) (Böhlau Cologne 1986).

Neufeld, Hans *The International Protection of Private Creditors from the Treaties of Westphalia to the Congress of Vienna: A Contribution to the History of the Law of Nations* (Sijthoff Leyden 1971).

Osiander, Andreas *The States System of Europe, 1640–1990: Peacemaking and the Conditions of International Stability* (OUP Oxford 1994).

Steiger, Heinhard 'Der westfälischen Frieden—Grundgesetz für Europa?' in Heinz Duchhardt (ed) *Der westfälische Friede: Diplomatie, politische Zäsur, kulturelles Umfeld, Rezeptionsgeschichte* (Oldenbourg Munich 1998) 33–80.

Steiger, Heinhard 'Friede in der Rechtsgeschichte' in W Augustyn (ed) *PAX. Beiträge zu Idee und Darstellung des Friedens* (Scaneg Munich 2003) 11–62.

Steiger, Heinhard 'Vorsprüche zu und in Friedensverträgen der Vormoderne' in Heinz Duchhardt und Martin Peters (eds) *Kalkül—Transfer—Symbol. Europäische Friedensverträge der Vormoderne* (Veröffentlichungen des Instituts für Europäisches Geschichte Beihefte Online 1 Mainz 2006) 6–40 <www.ieg-mainz.de/vieg-online-beihefte/01-2006.html> (30 March 2012).

Ziegler, Karl-Heinz 'Friedensverträge im römischen Altertum' (1989) 27 Archiv des Völkerrechts 45–62.

CHAPTER 4

MINORITIES AND MAJORITIES

JANNE E NIJMAN

1. INTRODUCTION: INTERNATIONAL LAW AND THE TREATMENT OF THE OTHER

FEAR and intolerance of 'the other' represent some of the darkest sides of global human history, responsible for grave crimes and mistreatment. But the Other has also received protection and respect. International law has been concerned with the (ill-)treatment of the Other, or more specifically, with the question of minorities. This chapter examines the relationship between minorities and international law. Arguably this relationship is as old as international law itself. As Inis Claude observes in the opening lines of his seminal work *National Minorities: An International Problem* (1955), '[t]he relationship between majorities and minorities is a perennial problem of politics'.[1] The term 'minority' may only have been used in international treaty law since 1919,[2] but the relationship between minorities and majorities

---

[1] IL Claude *National Minorities: An International Problem* (Greenwood Press New York 1955) at 1; also, on the origins of the (national) minorities problem, CA Macartney *National States and National Minorities* (OUP London 1934) at 21–9.

[2] See eg Minorities Treaty between the Principal Allied and Associated Powers and Poland (signed 28 June 1919) (1919) 225 CTS 412, art 8; also called 'Little Versailles' (hereinafter 'the Polish Minorities Treaty'). In the arts 86 and 93 of the Treaty of Versailles, on the Czecho-Slovak and Polish State respectively, the Parties avoid using 'minority' by using the following description 'inhabitants of that State who differ from the majority of the population in race, language, or religion'.

emerges in international politics and international law from the time 'differences of one sort or another—religious, racial, or ethnic—have been so seriously regarded as to give rise to politically significant minority problems'.[3] What sort of 'difference' or 'otherness' is politically significant so as to cause (international) 'problems' is, of course, subject to the sociopolitical context of time and place, and to the claims minorities make. Hence, the question of religious minorities exerted a significant influence on pre-18th-century international law, while the question of national minorities, which only emerged as an international problem with the late 18th-century rise of European nationalism, left a mark on 19th- and early 20th-century international law.

A global history of the relationship between minorities and international law is predominantly a history of minorities as victims of massacres, persecution, and discrimination, and of the way in which international law was used to respond to these crimes; for example, international law was used as a defence mechanism against external scrutiny by the perpetrating political rulers, or as a protective instrument of the international community to command non-discriminatory treatment of a minority population within a society. This chapter recounts the history of minorities as the object of international concern within the context of the question how international law—in particular the notion of sovereignty—was conceptualized and implemented with respect to minorities and majorities. It tells the history of minorities as beneficiaries of international rights guaranteed by various protectors throughout history. The history of the enforcement of these (generally treaty-based) rights then quickly turns into a history of intervention and just war, and subsequently into a political history of the 'abuse'[4] of the role of protector of minorities as a pretext for intervention. Intervention (religious and otherwise) and just war are, however, treated elsewhere in this book.

This chapter addresses the history of international law's relation with minorities at three levels. First, as minorities have always been the Other in international law because they did not wield the power of the State, the relationship between minorities and majorities is 'one of the oldest concerns of international law'.[5] They are, so to speak, the Other within the international legal system. How does international law deal with minorities? What are the international obligations for dealing with minority questions? What does article V § 28 of the Treaty of Osnabrück or article 12 of 'Little Versailles' stipulate on minority rights? To give an overview of all international law concerned with minorities throughout the ages is impossible, thus this chapter is necessarily incomplete. It focuses on two episodes in the history of international law and minorities. These are minorities in relation to the 1648 Westphalian Peace Treaties

---

[3] *National Minorities* (n 1) 1.
[4] ibid 7–9 on the League on Nations system and its 'susceptibility to abuse'.
[5] P Thornberry *International Law and the Rights of Minorities* (Clarendon Press Oxford 1991) at 1.

(Section 4), and minorities in the Peace of Versailles (1919) and the related international legal instruments (Section 5).

We also seek to analyse international law, not so much in terms of specific rights and obligations, but as a 'system' on which minority questions have had a notable effect. While in classic doctrine, minorities were not the addressees of international law, they have constituted a significant factor in the development of international law, with the concept of sovereignty as a notable example. Here minorities appear as a so-called 'constitutive Other' to a traditionally 'inter-sovereign' legal system. This aspect surfaces especially in Sections 4 and 5.

The third level of analysis is concerned with the historical account of the position of minorities in international law. Section 3 of this chapter explains how over the last two centuries minorities feature merely in the margins of general histories of international law. This is mainly due to the state-centrist orientation of these histories.

On the basis of initial findings at these three levels of analysis, this chapter concludes by arguing for a timely revision of the traditional position of minorities in the history of international law. The remainder of this chapter addresses some questions of scope and terminology (Section 2) and, by way of background, sketches the position traditionally occupied by minorities in international legal history (Section 3).

2. Terminology and Scope

Before 1945, a global and uniform body of international minority law did not exist. Even inter-war international minority protection was not a general regime established by the Covenant of the League of Nations. Instead, it was a complex of specific provisions incorporated in minority treaties, peace treaties, and unilateral declarations negotiated on the occasion of—or in the years immediately after—the Paris Peace conference. The treaties may have used the word 'minority', but they did not include 'minority' in the abstract as a relevant legal category nor did they establish a generally accepted definition of the term—resulting in much confusion and much debate.

The Permanent Court of International Justice (PCIJ) had to bring terminological clarity to the debate on the formal legal meaning of 'minority' within the Versailles system. In its advisory opinion on the *Greco-Bulgarian 'Communities'* case, the Court opined on the possible liquidation of property of Greco-Bulgarian 'communities' (*inter alia* churches, convents, schools) and their dissolution when members voluntarily emigrated. In doing so, it defined 'community' and therewith 'minority'.[6] In this, the Court addressed both the subjective and objective conceptions of 'minority', which represent the two positions in the debate.[7]

Even now, there is no generally agreed definition for the purposes of international law, but the legal definition of 'minority' most commonly used builds on the 1930 definition of the PCIJ. It was proposed by Special Rapporteur Capotorti in his 1979 study for the UN Sub-Commission on Prevention of Discrimination and Protection of Minorities,[8] and includes the element which also defines 'minority' in the sociological tradition: that is, non-dominance. In both the legal and sociological tradition, scholars go so far as to understand also oppressed majorities as 'minorities'.[9] This chapter follows the definitions of 'minority' which hinge on inferiority in terms of number as well as power in relation to majority populations, and consequently does not discuss 'dominant' minorities such as the Dutch, English, or Spanish minorities in the New World during the so-called Age of Discovery. Nor does this chapter include European minority rule in States in Africa and Asia during the Age of Colonialism. Also outside the scope of this chapter is an analysis of how minorities as non-state actors have influenced actively international politics and international law making throughout the centuries.[10]

---

[6] Cf eg J Jackson Preece *National Minorities and the European Nation-States System* (Clarendon Press Oxford 1998) at 17. See eg Redslob who argues the subjective position that the nation is not a given but based on will and choice, hence action. R Redslob *Histoire des grands principes du droit des gens depuis l'Antiquité jusqu'à la veille de la grande guerre* (Rousseau Paris 1923) at 31–2.

[7] *Greco-Bulgarian 'Communities' (Advisory Opinion)* PCIJ Rep Series B No 17, at 21. Herein, the Court interprets the Convention Between Greece and Bulgaria Respecting Reciprocal Emigration and in doing so equates 'communities' with 'minorities' and defines 'community': 'By tradition . . . the "community" is a group of persons living in a given country or locality, having a race, religion, language and traditions of their own and united by this identity of race, religion, language and traditions in a sentiment of solidarity, with a view to preserving their traditions, maintaining their form of worship, ensuring the instruction and upbringing of their children in accordance with the spirit and traditions of their race and rendering mutual assistance to each other. . . . [T]he aim and object of the Convention, its connection with the measures relating to minorities, the desire of the signatory Powers, to which the whole Convention bears witness, that the individuals forming the communities should respectively make their homes permanently among their own race, the very mentality of the population concerned—everything leads to the conclusion that the Convention regards the conception of a "community" from the point of view of this exclusively minority character. . . ." See also N Berman '"But the Alternative Is Despair": European Nationalism and the Modernist Renewal of International Law' (1993) 106 Harvard Law Review 1792–903.

[8] 'A group numerically inferior to the rest of the population of a state, in a non-dominant position, whose members—being nationals of the state—possess ethnic, religious or linguistic characteristics differing from those of the rest of the population and show, if only implicitly, a sense of solidarity, directed towards preserving their culture, traditions, religion or language.' *Study on the Rights of Persons Belonging to Ethnic, Religious and Linguistic Minorities* (1979) UN Doc E/CN.4/Sub.2/384/Rev.1, at 96.

[9] Eg F Ermacora 'The Protection of Minorities before the United Nations' (1983) 182 Recueil des cours 247–370 at 319.

[10] See C Fink *Defending the Rights of Others: The Great Powers, the Jews, and International Minority Protection, 1878–1938* (CUP Cambridge 2004); DH Nexon *The Struggle for Power in Early Modern Europe: religious conflict, dynastic empires, and international change* (Princeton University Press Princeton 2009).

A major question in minority politics was whether international concern for minority protection has been animated by considerations of morality and justice, or by considerations of national and international stability, or by both. On the one hand, one finds the realists who explain historic international minority protection merely in terms of the balance of power principle, state interests, and the search for stability at the domestic and international level.[11] On the other, there are the constructivist scholars who rather draw on principles of justice and morality to explain the phenomenon of international minority rights and protection.[12] A clear example of the latter—some would say 'idealistic'—view is found in the work of the prominent inter-war author on national minorities, CA Macartney. He explains historic international minority protection as that which has been animated by a general assumption of 'the existence of a higher law: the right of the individual to practise a certain religion not that authorized by the sovereign'. The interest of the 17th-century religious interveners, he argues, 'was founded solely in the community of religious belief between himself and the persons whom he desired to protect'.[13] This chapter concentrates on the formation of international law as brought about by the recurring confrontation with minority questions, with additional attention given to the politics of international minority protection where possible.

3. THE TRADITIONAL POSITION OF MINORITIES IN INTERNATIONAL LEGAL HISTORY

The position of minorities in international legal history is traditionally rather marginal.[14] Two narratives which dominate the literature on the history of international law and on minority rights and minority protection, respectively, largely explain the scant attention given to the relationship between minorities and international law: the 'myth of 1648' and the narrative of progress.

---

[11] B de Carvalho 'Keeping the State: Religious Toleration in Early Modern France and the Role of the State in Minority Conflicts' (2001–2) 1 European Yearbook of Minority Issues 5–27; also L Henkin *International Law: Politics and Values* (Martinus Nijhoff Dordrecht 1995) at 170–1.

[12] Cf eg R Jennings and A Watts (eds) *Oppenheim's International Law* (9th edn Longman London 1992) at 972, motivated by 'human dignity'.

[13] National States (n 1) 158.

[14] Grewe's realist account of international law history refers to the international protection of minorities merely to illustrate the epochal or 'hegemonic' shifts in the development of international law. WG Grewe *The Epochs of International Law* (Walter de Gruyter Berlin 2000) at 290.

First, since the 19th century,[15] general histories of international law take the 1648 Westphalian Peace Treaties to mark the foundation of modern international law. The historiography of international law consequently focuses on (the emergence of) the modern sovereign State and on the consolidation of the 'Westphalian Order', that is, an international legal order among absolute sovereign States which separates their internal life from their international life by a firm inside/outside distinction. General international law history is dominated by this state-centric paradigm, which prevents minority rights and protection from being anything but an 'anomaly' of the Westphalian order.[16] The history of minorities and majorities in international law, however, has clear roots in periods before 1648, for example, in 4th–6th-century Asia Minor. The exception that proves the rule is *Histoire des grands principes du droit des gens* (1923) of the Strasbourg professor, Robert Redslob. Redslob also cites 1648 as the starting point, but deals extensively with how 'nationality' has influenced the history of international law.[17] His account is contrary to other histories of international law. Arthur Nussbaum, for example, observed in passing that the provisions which 'accorded protection to the religious affiliations of the individual' made the Peace of Westphalia 'a landmark in the development of international law'.[18] Verzijl concluded that international minority protection 'fairly frequent[ly] ... limit[ed] ... national sovereignty'.[19] And Macartney has stated that the right to intervene based on 'a higher law' in order to protect a religious minority was in fact 'a denial of the claim of absolute sovereignty'.[20] And yet, neither Nussbaum nor Verzijl nor Macartney drew fundamental conclusions on Westphalian sovereignty or the system of international law. In short, the Westphalian paradigm has shaped traditional thinking about the history of minorities and international law in two ways. On a factual level, the Westphalian Peace Treaties are generally presented as the starting point of the development of international law, thus allowing for historical myopia and Eurocentrism. On a

---

[15] In 1841, the American jurist Henry Wheaton published a fully state-centric history of the modern law of nations starting in 1648. While writing after the 1815 Congress of Vienna, he uses the notion of the 'national' frequently, but always in relation to the nation as State and never to the (abstract notion of) national minority. In concrete terms, however, the question of the Polish nation and the issue of treating the Poles 'as Poles' by the host-states is discussed. H Wheaton *History of the Law of Nations in Europe and America from the Earliest Times to the Treaty of Washington* (Gould, Banks & Co New York 1845) at 69, 432, and eg 561.

[16] *National Minorities and the European Nation-States System* (n 6) 10.

[17] *Histoire des grands principes* (n 6) 28, 31, and 415–16; see for an excellent discussion, 'Alternative Is Despair' (n 7).

[18] A Nussbaum *A concise history of the law of nations* (The Macmillan Company New York 1954) at 115–16.

[19] JHW Verzijl *International Law in Historical Perspective* (1969) vol 2, at 467; see also, S Verosta 'History of International Law, 1648 to 1815' in R Wolfrum (ed) *The Max Planck Encyclopedia of Public International Law* (Oxford University Press Oxford 2008) at <www.mpepil.com>. Verosta mentions minorities once: 'Even during the period of absolutism, the new ruler recognized the rights and privileges of the various estates. In special provisions in the treaties he committed himself to the protection of religious minorities.'

[20] *National States* (n 1) 158.

conceptual level, the myth of 1648 has contributed to the general absence of minorities from histories of the formation of international law, and tends to marginalize the formative contribution of minorities.

The second narrative which has informed the historiography on minorities is the narrative of 'progress'. The concise chapters in the minority and human-rights literature describe minority rights as part of a teleological story which starts in 1648,[21] then discuss the major European treaties (1815, 1878, 1919) and the increasing minority rights,[22] leading eventually to the universal international human rights instruments of the late 20th century.[23] According to this story, the protective clauses of the Westphalian Peace Treaties are the original model on which subsequent protective provisions are based.[24] Nussbaum, for example, points to the minority arrangements of the Treaty of Berlin (1878) as 'a progressive step in the protection of human rights by imposing upon Turkey and the Balkan countries the obligation not to discriminate against religious minorities'.[25] Generally, three main stages are identified in pre-1945 developments.[26] First, the early modern age (1648–1815), with a focus on religious minorities. Second, the period of rapid emergence of nationalism in Europe (1815–1919), which contributed to the shift of protective clauses from religious to national minorities, and to the emergence of the nationality principle in international law, and third, the era of the first international 'system' of minority protection supported by the monitoring role of the League of Nations and the jurisdiction of the

[21] See eg L Gross 'The Peace of Westphalia, 1648–1948' (1948) 42 American Journal of International Law 20–41 at 22; A Balogh *Der internationale Schutz der Minderheiten* (Südost-Verlag Adolf Dresler München 1928); *National Minorities and the European Nation-States System* (n 6) 55–6; *National States* (n 1) 157; *A concise history* (n 18) 126 and 115–16; The Epochs of International Law (n 14) 290; C Walter 'Religion or Belief, Freedom of, International Protection' in *The Max Planck Encyclopedia of Public International Law* (n 18).

[22] See eg *National States* (n 1) 161 and 157; see also, A de Lapradelle 'Préface' in J Fouques-Duparc *La protection des minorités de race, de langue et de religion. Étude de droit des gens* (Librairie Dalloz Paris 1922) i–iv at ii: '*les progrès accomplis*'.

[23] Cf eg AWB Simpson *Human rights and the end of empire: Britain and the genesis of the European Convention* (OUP New York 2001) at 107; *International Law and the Rights of Minorities* (n 5). Thornberry points to how the development of treaty protection included the broadening of 'guarantees beyond freedom of worship to encompass the range of civil and political rights'. Also, JHW Verzijl *International Law in Historical Perspective* (AW Sijthoff Leyden 1972) vol 5, at 178.

[24] *National States* (n 1) 5.

[25] A Nussbaum *A concise history of the law of nations* (The Macmillan Company New York 1947) at 188. And yet, when he deals with minorities a second time, in the context of the League of Nations, he does not deal with minority questions when examining PCIJ cases. ibid 250.

[26] See eg H Wintgens *Der völkerrechtliche Schutz der nationalen, sprachlichen und religiösen Minderheiten* (W Kohlhammer Stuttgart 1930); E Ruiz Vieytez, 'The History of Legal Protection of Minorities in Europe' (1999) University of Derby Working Papers in International Relations No 1, also, H Hannum 'The Concept and Definition of Minorities' in M Weller *Universal Minority Rights* (OUP Oxford 2007) 49–73 at 52–3; less explicitly, *International Law and the Rights of Minorities* (n 5) 25–54, and N Lerner 'The Evolution of Minority Rights in International Law' in CM Brölmann et al *Peoples and Minorities in International Law* (Martinus Nijhoff Publishers Dordrecht 1993) 77–101 at 81–2.

PCIJ on the interpretation of the relevant treaty provisions (1919–45). The tendency to present minority rights as long-time precursors of emerging human rights exists also in the scholarship of the inter-war period itself,[27] which includes serious and extensive historical studies on the issue.[28] The newly established international minority system was a rewarding subject to investigate at a time in which progressive international legal scholars looked for renewal and revision of international law.[29] Frequently such teleological accounts turned into conceptual questions related to self-determination, state sovereignty, and the nature of the real international legal person.[30]

4. Minorities and Westphalia

4.1. Pre-Westphalian Minority Protection

The protection of minorities by way of international law is understood to have its origins in the development of religious liberties.[31] The story, however, does not start with the 17th-century treaties between Roman Catholic and Protestant rulers. As early as in the 4th century the East Roman or 'Byzantine' empire and the Sassanid empire of Persia included minority protection clauses in their treaties. After the rise of Islam in the 7th century, relations between the Byzantine empire and the Muslim Caliphs and subsequently the Sultan of the Ottoman empire continued as per the old, regional practice. These vast empires in Asia Minor 'had to come to terms with the question of dissenting minorities' within their own territory, as well as within the territories of their rivals.[32] To this end, they developed internal and external minority laws, which apparently comprised notions of legal status and subjective rights. Byzantine emperor Justinian I (527–565) and Sassanid emperor Khusrau I (531–579), for

---

[27] Cf AN Mandelstam 'La protection des minorités' (1923) 1 Recueil des cours 369–82. The interwar sensitivity to minority questions speaks from the many interwar Hague Academy courses that touch upon minorities. See for a full account 'The Protection of Minorities before the United Nations' (n 9) 260–1.

[28] *La protection des minorités de race* (n 22); D Krstitch *Les minorités, l'état et la communauté internationale* (Rousseau Paris 1924); *National States* (n 1); *Der völkerrechtliche Schutz* (n 26).

[29] JE Nijman *The Concept of International Legal Personality: An Inquiry into the History and Theory of International Law* (Asser Press The Hague 2004).

[30] See eg 'La Protection des Minorités' (n 27) 367–517.

[31] See eg MD Evans *Religious Liberty and International Law in Europe* (CUP Cambridge 1997).

[32] CE Bosworth 'The Concept of Dhimma in Early Islam' in B Braude and B Lewis (eds) *Christians and Jews in the Ottoman Empire: The Functioning of a Plural Society* (Holmes and Meier New York 1982) vol 1 (The Central Lands), 37–50 at 37.

example, annexed to their 562 peace agreement a specific treaty on 'the status of the Christians in Persia'[33] which held clauses geared to protect Christian minorities in Persia against persecution.[34] Minority protection and regulation was already part and parcel of (international) law and politics in Asia Minor in the period of Roman–Persian relations—a fact which defies the narrative in which it was merely 'imposed' by Western European powers in their relations with the Ottoman Empire later on.

In pre-Reformation Europe's *republica Christiana*, religious minorities had been not so much a concern of 'the law of nations and nature'. The 16th-century reformations created religious minorities in Europe and made religious liberty and liberty of conscience an international concern. This is not to say that there were no religious or ethnic minorities in Europe before the Reformation, or that there was no reason for concern. On the contrary, in medieval Europe tolerant practices did exist here and there, but (legal) discrimination and persecution of minorities—the *Zigeuner*, or Sinti, and the Jews—dominated.[35]

Since the beginnings of the Reformations (1517),[36] religious minorities were, however, one of 'the' issues at stake in the world of politics, domestic as well as European, and in the world of ideas. How tightly the two realms were interrelated is shown beautifully by Stephen Toulmin's careful reconstruction of the background and effect of a major crime committed against a religious minority: the massacre of St Bartholomew's Day (1572). [37] Toulmin shows how the mass murder of members of the Huguenot minority affected not just French and European politics, but European intellectual life as well as the course of Western philosophy. Descartes' quest for certainty, which would prevail over Montaigne's tolerance of uncertainty and diversity, was in a way a response to this Massacre. In the same vein, Quentin Skinner understands the episode as one of the foundational events in the history of European political thought. This was because it inspired the formulation of a radical Calvinist

---

[33] Menander Protector *History of Menander the Guardsman* (RC Blockley ed and trans) (F Cairns Liverpool 1985) at 76. An extract of the treaty text survived in the work of this East Roman Greek, known as Menander Protector.

[34] S Verosta 'International Law in Europe and Western Asia between 100 and 650 A.D.' (1964) 113 Recueil des cours 491–613 at 608–10.

[35] See eg D Nirenberg *Communities of Violence: Persecution of Minorities in the Middle Ages* (Princeton University Press Princeton NJ 1996). See on medieval toleration JC Laursen and CJ Nederman (eds) *Beyond the Persecuting Society: Religious Toleration Before the Enlightenment* (University of Pennsylvania Press Philadelphia 1998); PC Hartmann *Das Heilige Römische Reich deutscher Nation in der Neuzeit 1486–1806* (Reclam Stuttgard 2005) at 107–8. For the Jewish minorities in the German Empire, 1350–1650 is described as '*eine lange Krise*', A Herzig *Jüdische Geschichte in Deutschland: Von den Anfängen bis zur Gegenwart* (2nd edn CH Beck München 2002) at 52. See for the change in the situation of the European Jewry around 1570 and their impact on the European world from 1650–1713, JI Israel *European Jewry in the Age of Mercantilism, 1550–1750* (OUP Oxford 1985).

[36] See eg M Boegner 'L'influence de la réforme sur le développement du droit international' (1925) 6 Recueil des cours 241–324. Also PH Kooijmans 'Protestantism and the development of international law' (1976) 152 Recueil des cours 79–118 at 91–109.

[37] S Toulmin *Cosmopolis: The Hidden Agenda of Modernity* (University of Chicago Press Chicago 1992).

theory on the right to resistance, on the one hand,[38] and the so-called 'Divine Rights of Kings' theory of Jean Bodin, on the other. The latter's 'public doctrine always took the form of claiming that there can never be any question of accepting the natural right of minority relations to be tolerated'.[39]

Hugo Grotius took a different approach to religious diversity in Europe. In early modern European jurisprudence, the position of minorities is largely treated within the context of just war theory.[40] In 1621, Grotius, a Protestant with remonstrant sympathies, escaped from the Dutch Republic, which was torn by religiously tainted civil war, and taken refuge in Catholic France.[41] In the early 1620s, he wrote and published his monumental *De iure belli ac pacis* (1625) in which he also contributed to the debate on religious tolerance. Grotius warns that waging war 'against those who err in the interpretation of the Divine law' is unjust, and 'likewise those who oppress with punishment persons that accept the law of Christ as true but who are in doubt or error on some points [of interpretation] act most wickedly'.[42] In this context, Grotius also refers to *Menander Protector* to draw on Persian–Byzantine relations for an example of circumstances amounting to 'tyrann[y] over subjects'. In his opinion, the oppression and 'persecuti[on]' of Christian minorities by Persian Emperors had been a 'just cause for war' for the Roman Emperors, protectors of Christianity, under the natural law of nations (the Law or 'Right of Human Society').[43] Those who persecute Christians 'do make themselves justly obnoxious to Punishment'.[44] War against the Persians therefore was just, it was punishment for oppression of the Christian minorities, according to Grotius. His theory supports liberty of conscience and 'freedom of judgment' in religious matters,[45] supremacy of the State in religious affairs to secure freedom for and tolerance of religious sects, and a general responsibility of sovereigns for the society in their care as well as for universal human society at large.[46] The tolerant, neutral position on which his rationalist theory of the law of nations and nature was built, was unacceptable

---

[38] Q Skinner *The Foundations of Modern Political Thought* (CUP Cambridge 1978) vol 2 (The Age of Reformation) at 239–54. See also D Parker 'The Huguenots in Seventeenth-Century France' in AC Hepburn (ed) *Minorities in History* (Edward Arnold London 1978) 11–30 at 16–17.

[39] *The Foundations of Modern Political Thought* (n 38) vol 2, at 253.

[40] See eg Gentili's call for religious toleration within and among States, A Gentili *De iure belli* book I, ch X, s 69–72; see also 'La protection des minorités' (n 27) 57–63.

[41] He never developed close relations with the Paris Huguenot community. Nellen situates this in the context of the 'categorical...rejection' by the French Calvinists of Arminianism in 1620 and the policy of repression of Protestantism by the French government, which started in 1621 and eventually led to the revocation of the Edict of Nantes (1598) in 1685. HJM Nellen 'Grotius' Relations with the Huguenot Community of Charenton (1621–1635)' (1985) 12 Lias 147–77 at 149–50.

[42] H Grotius *De iure belli ac pacis* (J Brown Scott ed) (OUP Oxford 1925) book II, ch XX, s 50, at 518–19.

[43] H Grotius *The Rights of War and Peace* (R Tuck ed) (Liberty Fund Indianapolis 2005) book II, ch XXV, s 8, at 1161.

[44] ibid book II, ch XLIX, s 1, at 1044–5.

[45] ibid book II, ch XX, s 48–50, at 1041–50.   [46] ibid 1028.

to the orthodox, dogmatic Calvinists as well as to the Jesuits. The impact of the early modern debate on (religious) tolerance[47] on the position and protection of religious minorities cannot be denied.[48]

4.2. Responsibility for Minorities as a Characteristic of Westphalian Sovereignty

This section shows how the Westphalian Peace Treaties, notably the Peace of Osnabrück, deal with religious minorities. Close reading of the 1648 treaties purport moreover that the old concept of reified Westphalian sovereignty is in need of reconstruction. The Peace of 1648 built on the Peace of Augsburg (1555). The latter had attributed the *ius reformandi* (the right to decide to which denomination their subjects would adhere) to both Lutheran and Catholic rulers, and established the principle of *cuius regio, eius religio* for the Holy Roman Empire—with the exception of free and imperial cities where religious diversity was maintained. Hence, the 1555 Peace—in an attempt to mitigate imperial politics—'territorialized' religious identity and linked it to the territorial sovereign. The ruler's sovereign rights were not unlimited, the *ius emigrandi* of individual subjects gained new prominence around the same time.[49] Together—the Sovereign's right to decide which religion is adhered to within the territory, and the subject's right to emigrate if he adhered to a different religion—these rights had a destabilizing effect.

In order to end the Thirty Years War and introduce a 'Christian and Universal Peace',[50] the Westphalian Peace Treaties included a more comprehensive arrangement to protect religious minorities in Europe than the Augsburg Peace. The obligations to respect and protect religious minorities were addressed to the various sovereign rulers and cities of the Empire. The Reformed or Calvinists were newly recognized in 1648, and accorded the same rights in religion and other matters as Lutherans (and Catholics). Religious tolerance did not, however, extend beyond these three denominations.[51]

Although with some reticence, religious diversity was accepted, and both 'liberty of conscience' and the 'free Exercise of . . . Religion', privately and publicly, was

[47] See eg CJ Nederman and JC Laursen (eds) *Difference and Dissent: Theories of Tolerance in Medieval and Early Modern Europe* (Rowman & Littlefield London 1996). See also *The Foundations of Modern Political Thought* (n 38).

[48] Nor can the political necessity of religious toleration for domestic and international peace be denied either. See 'Keeping the State' (n 11).

[49] Peace of Augsburg (signed 25 September 1555) §24.

[50] Treaty of Peace between France and the Empire (signed 24 October 1648) (1648) 1 CTS 271 at 321, art I.

[51] Treaty of Peace between Sweden and the Empire (signed 24 October 1648) (1648) 1 CTS 119 at 239–40, art VII.

recognized.[52] The churches were returned to 'those of the Confession of Augsburg' (that is, the Lutherans), if these 'were in the possession of Churches' on 1 January 1624.[53] In some cases, they were allowed to build new churches. The Peace also stipulated equality before the law for both Catholics and Lutherans in, for example, Bohemia.[54] Apart from several provisions in both treaties which establish religious freedom for Protestant or Catholic minorities in specific German cities or States, the most notable provision of the Westphalian peace in the context of this chapter is the comprehensive article V of the Treaty of Osnabrück, which reads *inter alia*:

It has moreover been found good, that those of the Confession of *Augsburg*, who are Subjects of the Catholicks, and the Catholick Subjects of the States of the Confession of *Augsburg*, who had not the publick or private Exercise of their Religion in any time of the year 1624. and who after the Publication of the Peace shall profess and embrace a Religion different from that of the Lord of the Territory, shall in consequence of the said Peace be patiently suffer'd and tolerated..., without any Hindrance or Impediment to attend their Devotions in their Houses and in private, with all Liberty of Conscience, and without any Inquisition or Trouble, and even to assist in their Neighbourhood, as often as they have a mind, at the publick Exercise of their Religion, or send their children to foreign Schools of their Religion, or have them instructed in their Families by private Masters; provided the said Vassals and Subjects do their Duty in all other things, and hold themselves in due Obedience and Subjection, without giving occasion to any Disturbance or Commotion. In like manner Subjects, whether they be Catholicks, or of the Confession of Augsburg, shall not be despis'd any where upon account of their Religion, nor excluded from the Community of Merchants, Artizans or Companies, nor depriv'd of Successions, Legacies, Hospitals, Lazar-Houses, or Alms-Houses, and other Priviliges or Rights, and far less of Church-yards, and the Honour of Burial; nor shall any more be exacted of them for the Expence of their Funerals, than the Dues usually paid for Burying-Places in Parish-Churches: so that in these and all other the like things they shall be treated in the same manner as Brether and Sister, with equal Justice and Protection.[55]

At least on paper, deviation from the state religion came to be accepted, subjects no longer had to follow their sovereign when he converted, and social or civic exclusion on the basis of religious deviation was not allowed (with the exception of the Protestant minorities in the territories of the House of Austria, to whom no religious freedom was granted by the 1648 peace). Moreover, if an individual subject who had had no public or private religious freedom before 1624, now wanted to move or was ordered to do so by the territorial sovereign, 'he [was] at liberty to do it'.[56] '[T]he Lord of the Territory shall allow a space and time, not less than five years, for his subjects to

[52] Treaty of Peace between France and the Empire (n 50) 327, 331 and 332, arts XXVIII, XLIII, and XLIX.

[53] Treaty of Peace between Sweden and the Empire (n 51) 205, art IV, §17.

[54] Treaty of Peace between France and the Empire (n 50) 332, art XLVI. See also Treaty of Peace between Sweden and the Empire (n 51) 213, art IV, §53.

[55] Treaty of Peace between Sweden and the Empire (n 51) 228–9, art V, §28.

[56] ibid art V, §29 (*ius emigrandi*).

remove . . .' .[57] This is an example of the notion of responsibility accompanying territorial sovereignty in the Westphalian peace. Another paragraph stipulates as a condition of the continuous free exercise of the religion of the Lutheran princes and towns of Silesia, 'that in other things they do not disturb the publick Peace and Tranquility, and behave themselves as they [the minorities] ought towards their Sovereign Prince'.[58] Such 'public order' restrictions on religious dissent became part of national and international law with a view to managing religious pluralism and accommodating religious minorities.[59] Tyrannical behaviour of the lord of the territory towards religious minorities was judged illegal, not only by Grotius but now also by treaty law. The principle of religious tolerance of minorities had to replace the practice of religious wars, and the responsibility to protect co-religionists outside the sovereign's territory was replaced—that is, on paper—by an emerging responsibility to guarantee religious liberties and just and equal treatment of minorities and majorities within the sovereign's territory. The Westphalian principles of religious tolerance and equal treatment ended neither persecution nor (religious) intervention. Tyrannical treatment of religious minorities continued to be a cause for punitive war against the perpetrator.

The Westphalian Peace Treaties of 1648 have been revisited in a recent debate in international relations on 'Westphalia' and the concepts reified on the basis of the traditional interpretation of 1648. Stéphane Beaulac,[60] Stephan Krasner,[61] Andreas Osiander,[62] and Daniel Philpott[63] all attribute defining importance to the arrangements for minority protection included in the 1648 Peace Treaties, when addressing the 'constitutive foundation myth' that that date signified in international relations and international law.[64] Recently, Luke Glanville has given a short account of this debate which is not repeated here. It suffices to concur with the conclusion that is also supported by the close reading above: 'in reality, the idea that sovereignty entails

---

[57] ibid art V, §30.   [58] ibid art V, §31.

[59] Treaty of Peace between Great Britain and France (signed 11 April 1713) (1713) 27 CTS 475 at 475, art 14. Also the Definitive Treaty of Peace between France, Great Britain and Spain (signed 10 February 1763) (1763) 42 CTS 279, art 4. See on the national level, CH Parker 'Paying for the Privilege: The Management of Public Order and Religious Pluralism in Two Early Modern Societies' (2006) 17 Journal of World History 267–96.

[60] S Beaulac 'The Westphalian Legal Orthodoxy—Myth or Reality?' (2000) 2 Journal of the History of International Law 148–77.

[61] SD Krasner and DT Froats 'Minority Rights and the Westphalian Model' in DA Lake and DS Rothchild (eds) The International Spread of Ethnic Conflict: Fear, Diffusion, and Escalation (Princeton University Press Princeton NJ 1998).

[62] A Osiander 'Sovereignty, International Relations, and the Westphalian Myth' (2001) 55 International Organization 251–87; A Osiander The States System of Europe 1640–1990: Peacemaking and the Conditions of International Stability (Clarendon Press Oxford 1994).

[63] D Philpott 'The Religious Roots of Modern International Relations' (2000) 52 World Politics 206–45.

[64] B Teschke The Myth of 1648: Class, Geopolitics and the Making of Modern International Relations (Verso London 2003).

responsibilities has deep historical roots'.[65] Krasner has examined the relation between minority rights and Westphalian sovereignty extensively. He contests recent calls that minority—and human rights are 'a revolutionary development'; such calls are seriously 'myopic' if they ignore 'the long history of external involvement in the treatment of minorities within states'.[66] From a legal-theory perspective, however, the international practice that becoming the lord of the territory, that is becoming sovereign, included becoming legally obliged to respect religious liberties and equal treatment of minorities, requires the reconstruction of Westphalian sovereignty as inclusive of responsibility.

4.3. Minority Protection Treaties in the 17th and 18th Centuries

The Peace of Westphalia set the trend for provisions arranging protection of religious minorities in major 17th and 18th-century peace treaties between Christian sovereigns. Treaties, such as the those of Oliva (1660),[67] Nijmegen (1678), Rijswijk (1697), Utrecht (1713), Breslau (1742), Dresden (1745), Paris (1763), and Warsaw (1772), dealt with the position of Catholic minorities in Protestant states, or vice versa, in particular in the context of cession of territory.[68] Gradually, the guaranteed liberties expanded and came to include 'civil' rights, liberties, and privileges as well as ecclesiastical and religious ones. In the 17th-century practice of cession of territory features a concept of sovereignty that underscores the reconstruction of Westphalian sovereignty suggested above. When territory was ceded, the new lord of the territory had to swear an oath 'to preserve intact the existing institutions and liberties'—among which the religious liberties of the inhabitants of the ceded territory.[69] Hence, cession—when arranged by peace treaty—involved the recognition of responsibilities towards the new minorities that came with the ceded territory. The practice of including the recognition of the sovereign's responsibilities towards minority subjects living in ceded territory may be feudal in origin, but early modern practice points in any case to a concept of sovereignty as responsibility operating in international law, and the legitimacy of enforcement by intervention when a Sovereign failed to secure minority rights.

[65] L Glanville 'The Antecedents of "Sovereignty as Responsibility"' (2011) 17 European Journal of International Relations 233–55 at 234.

[66] 'Minority Rights' (n 61) 226.

[67] Treaty between Poland, the Empire and Brandenburg, and Sweden (signed 23 April 1660) (1660) 6 CTS 9 at 60–92.

[68] See eg A Nussbaum *A Concise History of the Law of Nations* (Macmillan New York 1962) at 126; *La protection des minorités de race* (n 22) 75–7.

[69] *National States* (n 1) 158.

In the late 18th century, when Enlightenment and the ideals of the French Revolution brought a new perspective on man and society, the focus of politics and law shifted way from communities, or groups, to the individual and his rights. Religion and religious communal life became private matters to be met with religious tolerance.[70] Emer de Vattel favoured this development as beneficiary for international peace.[71] Every person would be first of all a 'citizen'—individual bearer of religious, civil, and political rights—and the social boundaries between religious minority and majority groups would fade into the background.[72] In real life, however, the minority problem did not disappear. Soon, the logic of nationalism would emerge, leading to the construction of minorities on the basis of a new attribute.

5. Minorities After Paris 1919

5.1. National States and National Minorities (1815–1919)

During the 19th century, European international politics were shaped to a significant degree by nationalism. This century saw the demise of the Napoleonic and Ottoman empires, while nationalist aspirations became omnipresent, and the number of national or nation-states in Central and Eastern Europe grew steadily. The political principle of nationality—that is, the idea that the nation is the legitimate basis of sovereign statehood—was problematic to say the least. On the one hand, it was respected as an organizing principle of international society, thus new national States were welcomed into the family of nations, provided they arranged for minority protection. On the other hand, 'nationality' became a rationale for policies of (forced) assimilation, persecution, and expulsion of national minorities. Weitz observes: 'deportations and [minority] protection ran together—they emerged chronologically at roughly the same point in time, the 1860s, and were both often legitimized by bilateral and multilateral treaties that the Great Powers either signed or blessed'.[73] International protection arrangements shifted from religious to national minorities.

---

[70] JB Muldoon 'The Development of Group Rights' in JA Sigler (ed) *Minority Rights: A Comparative Analysis* (Greenwood Press London 1982) 31–66 at 61–2.

[71] E de Vattel *Droit des gens* in JB Scott *The Classics of International Law* (Carnegie Institution Washington 1916) vol 1, ch 12, para 135, at 125–6.

[72] V Van Dyke 'The Individual, the State, and Ethnic Communities in Political Theory' (1977) 29 World Politics 343–69.

[73] Cf ED Weitz, 'From the Vienna to the Paris System: International Politics and the Entangled Histories of Human Rights, Forced Deportations, and Civilizing Missions' (2008) 113 The American Historical Review 1313–43 at 1313.

While people's nationalist aspirations were accepted as a legitimate basis for independence, the legitimacy of the ensuing new 'national sovereignty' was conditional upon the new State's protection of minority rights within its borders.[74] The Final Acts of the three major 19th-century European Congresses—Vienna (1815), Paris (1856), and Berlin (1878)—all include minority protection provisions.

After the 1878 defeat of the Ottoman empire, some States—such as Montenegro, Serbia, and Roumania—gained independence, while others obtained an extension of territory.[75] The Congress of Berlin (1878) stipulated as a condition of recognition to these new and/or extended state obligations to protect minorities and their rights.[76] Likewise, the Ottoman sultan accepted minority obligations.[77] Minority-rights protection as a yardstick for the 'standard of civilization' required to enter the European Family of Nations was thus established. In the words of Claude:

> The protection of minorities became, at least in theory, an act of European public policy, rather than an arbitrary act of interested states, when plenipotentiaries of the great powers at the Congress of Berlin in 1878 declared that prospective members of the European family of states should affirm the principle of religious liberty as one indication of their general acceptance of the principles which are the basis of social organization in all States of Europe.[78]

As such, the Treaty of Berlin was, according to De Visscher, 'a landmark in the history of minorities' because of the influence of the treaty's 'underlying idea':

> [w]hen new states are called into being, Europe, represented by the concert of the great powers, is under a moral responsibility to establish this new international order [of equal treatment]. It therefore has the right to impose upon these new states to which it has accorded recognition, certain principles of government in the superior interests of humanity, because it has the corresponding duty to see that these new sovereignties which have been called into existence do not become instruments of oppression of the most sacred rights of man.[79]

The Berlin minority-protection provisions for the new Balkan were, however, 'ineffective'.[80] The imposition of 'conditions on the internal governance of four new

---

[74]   Eg the case of Greece, Protocol of Conference Relative to the Independence of Greece (signed 3 February 1830) (1830) 80 CTS 327 at 327–34 and 81 CTS 48 at 48–52.

[75]   Bulgaria became 'an autonomous and tributary Principality under the suzerainty' of the Sultan'. Treaty for the Settlement of Affairs in the East (signed 13 July 1878) (1878) 153 CTS 171, art 1 (hereinafter 'Treaty of Berlin'). The 1878 Treaty of San Stefano was revised.

[76]   Eg Treaty of Berlin (n 75) art XXXV: 'In Serbia the difference of religious creeds and confessions shall not be alleged against any person as a ground for exclusion or incapacity in matters relating to the enjoyment of civil or political rights, admission to public employments, functions, and honors, or the exercise of the various professions and industries, in any locality whatsoever. The freedom and outward exercise of all forms of worship shall be assured to all persons belonging to Serbia, as well as to foreigners, and no hindrance shall be offered either to the hierarchical organization of the different communions, or to their relations with their spiritual chiefs'. Art XLIV is a similar article for Romania.

[77]   ibid art LXII.   [78]   National Minorities (n 1) 6.

[79]   Ch De Visscher The Stabilization of Europe (University of Chicago Press Chicago 1924) at 34–5. (One recognizes the progress narrative.)

[80]   ibid 35.

states...[b]y expanding the principle of internationally dictated, nonreciprocal minority rights...created an onerous legacy of resentment, defiance, and frustration'.[81] The Treaty of Berlin was an important influence on the Paris Peace deal of 1919, but the legacy of 1878 was an ambivalent one. The Berlin Treaty had covered both aspects of sovereignty—the responsibility to respect 'the sacred rights of man' and the 'sovereign equality' of States as a formal principle. But it had also established a practice in which the latter principle could be applied selectively.

5.2. Minorities and the League System

Like the provisions in 1648 and 1878 discussed above, *interbellum* minority protection obligations have been constitutively significant to the concept of sovereignty. It is worth noting that the significance of 'minorities' for the development of international law after 1919 reached beyond concrete cases. The new concept of sovereignty, which comprised responsibility for minority subjects, challenged the sovereignty of 'all' States. At the end of the Great War, minority issues were among the most complex, grave, and fundamental problems threatening European peace and stability.[82] They contributed to many of the legal and institutional innovations which characterize post-Versailles international law and to animated debates in inter-war scholarship.

In Paris, the peacemakers responded to the destabilizing forces of European nationalism by creating new and enlarged national States to succeed the four multinational empires and by laying down an international system to protect national minorities living within these States. The rights of these minorities were (in the case of Austria, Bulgaria, Hungary, and Turkey) enshrined in the Peace Treaties, or (in the case of Czechoslovakia, Greece, Poland, Romania, and the Serb-Croat-Slovene State) in the Minority Protection Treaties concluded with the new national States, or (in the case of Albania, Estonia, Lithuania, Latvia, and Finland) in unilateral declarations made by States before the League Council.[83] The specific provisions in these legal instruments were in substance virtually identical since all were modelled on the first minority treaty that had been concluded, the 'Little Versailles'. Together with the Versailles Treaty, the latter re-established Poland as a sovereign State under the condition that the new State accept to protect its minorities: 'the stipulations...so far as they affect persons belonging to racial, linguistic or religious minorities, constitute

---

[81] Defending the Rights of Others (n 10) 37–8. Also, National Minorities and the European Nation-States System (n 6) 62.

[82] Cf The Stabilization of Europe (n 79) vii–viii.

[83] See for a full list eg A Meijknecht 'Minority Protection System between World War I and World War II' in *The Max Planck Encyclopedia of Public International Law* (n 18).

obligations of international concern and shall be placed under the guarantee of the League of Nations'.[84] In effect, the totality of these specific provisions constituted a new international minority protection system under the guarantee of the League of Nations.

The responsibility of the League of Nations in this respect was twofold.[85] First, it entailed supervision over the implementation by States of the 1919–21 minority obligations in their domestic legal orders. National law and policy had to be brought into conformity with the treaty clauses, whether these would be turned into fundamental laws of the minority States,[86] or would become binding on the States as an international obligation. The minorities were protected against loss of nationality and in some cases obtained the right of option. All persons, including persons belonging to minorities, were granted full and complete protection of life and liberty, freedom of religion and religious practices, and civil and political rights.[87] Questions of equality between minorities and majorities soon reached the PCIJ, whose notion of 'equality in law and in fact' proved to be a standard-setting interpretation.[88] The requirement of equal treatment, for example, obliged States not to hinder minorities in the establishment of schools or other religious or social institutions, nor to restrict the use of the mother tongue in primary school and in private and community life, and to provide an equitable share of public funds for education, religious, or charitable purposes. In 1923, the PCIJ confirmed that the international minority obligations were binding even if the (new) State in question no longer consented to these obligations or gave them a reading different from that of the majority of state parties.[89]

---

[84] Polish Minorities Treaty (n 2) art 12(1). This article was copied into the treaties with Czechoslovakia, Yugoslavia, Romania, Greece, Austria, Bulgaria, and Hungary.

[85] The League's minority protection system is discussed extensively at numerous places. See eg *National Minorities* (n 1); *National Minorities and the European Nation-States System* (n 6) 67–94; *International Law and the Rights of Minorities* (n 5) 38–52; 'Minority Protection System' (n 83).

[86] Cf eg Polish Minorities Treaty (n 2) art 1.

[87] Cf eg ibid art 2.

[88] Cf eg *Settlers of German Origin in Poland (Advisory Opinion)* PCIJ Rep Series B No 6 at 23–5 and 36–7; see also *Minority Schools in Albania (Greece v Albania) (Advisory Opinion)* PCIJ Rep Series A/B No 64 at 17 and 19: 'there would be no true equality between a majority and a minority if the latter were deprived of its own institutions, and were consequently compelled to renounce that which constitutes the very essence of its being as a minority' and '[e]quality in law precludes discrimination of any kind; whereas equality in fact may involve the necessity of different treatment in order to attain a result which establishes an equilibrium between different situations.' See, in general, CM Brölmann 'The PCIJ and International Rights of Individuals and Groups' in M Fitzmaurice, C Tams, and P Merkouris (eds) *The Permanent Court and Modern International Law: Reflections on the PCIJ's Lasting Legacy* (Martinus Nijhoff Leiden 2012).

[89] *Acquisition of Polish Nationality (Advisory Opinion)* PCIJ Rep Series B No 7 at 13–17. Herein, the PCIJ found that international law determines who is a minority according to the Polish Minorities Treaty and the Versailles Peace Treaties, not the Polish State unilaterally. See also 'Alternative Is Despair' (n 7).

The second aspect of the League's responsibility was that in case of (imminent) violation of international minority obligations, the League Council may 'take such action and give such direction as it may deem proper and effective in the circumstances'.[90] Only members of the non-plenary Council had a 'right'—that is, a duty when international peace was under threat—'to bring to the attention of the Council any infraction, or any danger of infraction, of any of these obligations'.[91] To this end, another novelty was introduced: minorities themselves as well as third parties (in order to stop the kin-states' interventionist practices of the past) were given the right to bring a petition to the League's Secretariat.[92] Only after due consideration—first by the Secretariat, then (if admissible)[93] by the Council's 'Committee of Three'—the host State would be asked for a response. If that response was unsatisfactory, the complaint would be brought by the Secretariat before the Council. Minorities did not have the right to bring their complaint to the Council nor did they have *locus standi* before the PCIJ, even if after a failed conciliation between the State and its minority, the dispute qualified as a 'dispute of international character', and thus fell within the jurisdiction of the Court.[94]

5.3. The Failure of a Global Minority Regime

The international minority protection system under the League's guarantee in the formal sense was not a global legal regime, part of the League Covenant, binding upon 'all' League members. The initial proposal to that end by US president Woodrow Wilson had hit a wall of resistance on the part of *inter alia* Great Britain for 'assail[ing] the holy principle of "full internal sovereignty".[95] 'Wilson's desire for a global solution to the minorities question through the new League of Nations' had been a late insight.[96] Charles de Visscher, an eyewitness to the Paris Peace Conference,[97] observed that initially Wilson had not foreseen the possible implications when he asserted the right to self-determination in his 1918 Fourteen Points. Only while in Paris in 1919, he realized how explosive the combination of self-determination and the principle of nationality really was: 'When I gave utterance to these

---

[90] Cf eg Polish Minorities Treaty (n 2) art 12(2).   [91] ibid.

[92] See on the right to petition eg J Robinson (ed) *Were the Minorities Treaties a Failure?* (Antin Press New York 1943) at 128.

[93] Claims which sought political secession or independence were not admissible.

[94] See eg art 12 Polish Minorities Treaty in conjunction with art 14 of the Covenant of the League of Nations.

[95] Cf *Defending the Rights of Others* (n 10) at 152–4, and *International Law and the Rights of Minorities* (n 5) at 38–40.

[96] *Defending the Rights of Others* (n 10) 153.

[97] *The Stabilization of Europe* (n 79) 19.

words, I said them without the knowledge that nationalities existed. . . . You do not know and cannot appreciate the anxieties that I have experienced as the result of these many millions having their hopes raised by what I have said.'[98] These anxieties troubled Wilson while he was negotiating a global international legal protection of minorities. Ultimately, 'it [his "grand project"] failed because all the victors of 1919, large and small, were reluctant to assume even the most abstract collective burdens. The minority clause, limiting every League's member's power over its citizens, was potentially as grave an encroachment on national sovereignty as the collective security obligation in article 10.'[99]

5.4. Minority Protection and Sovereign Equality

Without the global minorities regime binding upon all League's members, Versailles accepted the 'inequality' of sovereign States. On the one hand, the sovereignty of new, expanded, or defeated States continued the tradition developed in response to cession: no recognition without minority protection guarantees. On the other hand, the old and established European States refused to subject to this international legal standard. That outcome stirred debate. Ultimately, as Fouques-Duparc explained, the discussion boiled down to the question as to whether international minority protection was an institution of justice and thus applicable to all, or on the other hand a political institution, which then raised the question 'de quel droit nous a-t-elle été imposée?'[100] Fouques-Duparc, among others, discerned 'un acheminement vers un statut général des minorités' in the Versailles system.[101] This debate on the general normative (in contemporary terms: 'law-making') character of the Versailles minority regime challenged in a fundamental way the inequality in sovereignty accommodated by the 1919 Peace scheme.

Public and scholarly opinion on the League in general and on its system of minorities protection in particular changed in the course of the 1920s. Initially, there had been excitement and hope;[102] for example, of fostering political democracy and economic liberalism in Central and Eastern Europe. From the 1930s on, however, it became commonplace to refer to the League's minorities protection system as a failure.[103] Be that as it may, the system has had a lasting impact on the

---

[98] ibid at 18.

[99] *Defending the Rights of Others* (n 10) 160.

[100] J Fouques-Duparc 'Le développement de la protection des minorités' (1926) Revue de droit international et de législation comparée 509–24 at 519–21.

[101] ibid 520; also on the 'generalization' of the Treaties, National States (n 1) 487–94.

[102] See eg The Stabilization of Europe (n 79) viii.

[103] *Were the Minorities Treaties a Failure* (n 92) v; see also eg National Minorities (n 1) 31–50; *National Minorities and the European Nation-States System* (n 6).

development of international law as such and of the notion of sovereignty in particular. The system of minority protection under the League of Nations may have been an 'experiment'[104] but it cannot be set aside as merely a 'historical experiment'[105] without a lasting legacy.

It is not possible to discuss all inter-war international legal innovations, but the 'experiments in internationalisation'[106] in Saarland, the Free City of Danzig, and Upper Silesia cannot be left unmentioned, since these were animated partly by minority questions. In these cases, the Versailles agreement established international administration by the League over these territorial units, and agreed to a plebiscite to determine the long-term fate of the people and the territory.[107] The many plebiscites and the interpretation and implementation of their outcome by international authorities challenged the traditional concepts of sovereignty and international law. As is also argued by Berman, the empowerment of international authority through the organization and interpretation of these plebiscites 'worked a profound transformation of sovereignty'.[108]

Hence, during 'Versailles' and its aftermath, minority questions can be said to have had constitutive significance for the development of international law and legal doctrine and the legal conceptualization of sovereignty, continuing the (historical) Westphalian construction discussed above. Meanwhile, post-Versailles minority protection also bears the marks of what Koskenniemi and Anghie have identified as the 'civilizing mission' inherent in international law.[109] This mission explains the maintained distinction between old, civilized Europe and new, aspiring civilized States. The former rejected a global minority protection regime, and created minority obligations on a case by case basis for the new States only. This leads to the second element of the reconstitution of sovereignty, by accommodating unequal obligations of States regarding minority protection, Versailles contributed to a new international legal system based on sovereign inequality. Arguably, minority rights protection was not only part of the justification for the granting of sovereignty to a State (which guaranteed minority rights), but it was also an inherent element of old Europe's power politics. Minority rights thus played a justificatory role in the constitution of the post-Versailles international legal system. The politics of Versaillesian minority protection, in other words, was ambiguous. While minority issues impacted the legal construction of sovereignty and the international

[104] *Were the Minorities Treaties a Failure* (n 92) v.
[105] *National Minorities and the European Nation-States System* (n 6) 94.
[106] 'Alternative Is Despair' (n 7) 1874.
[107] See Part III of the Treaty of Versailles (signed 28 June 1919) (1919) 225 CTS 188.
[108] 'Alternative Is Despair' (n 7) 1873.
[109] See M Koskenniemi *The Gentle Civilizer of Nations. The Rise and Fall of International Law 1870–1960* (CUP Cambridge 2002); A Anghie *Imperialism, Sovereignty and the Making of International Law* (CUP Cambridge 2005).

legal system based thereon, the system then failed to protect the minorities partly due to the built-in inequality.[110]

5.5. Minorities and the Inter-war Debate on International Legal Personality

After the First World War, international legal scholars debated the 'shortcomings' of international law and sought remedies to 'rehabilitate' and renew it.[111] Nathaniel Berman and Marti Koskenniemi have established that the quest for renewal in inter-war scholarship should also be read as attempts to reconcile nationalism and internationalism.[112] Berman examines how the reconciliation of nationalism and internationalism played out in theory—that is, in Redslob's international legal theory, since it provides, according to Berman, 'a general framework for understanding interwar texts dealing with nationalism'[113]—and in practice—that is in the institutions of international minority protection, plebiscites, and international administration of Danzig, Saar, and Upper Silesia. Berman presents nationalism and national minorities as the issue at stake for inter-war international jurists, consequently, 'new'—or in his words 'modernist'—international law is the international law of Versailles that has taken up the nationalist challenge. Modernist international legal theory and practice is shaped by its 'ambivalent' relationship with nationalism, which is rooted in the perception of nationalism as both a destructive and a rejuvenating energy. Nationalism is a source of hope and fear at the same time when called upon to redefine key concepts such as 'the State' or 'international law' as such. On the basis of a careful study of inter-war texts, Berman shows how (national) minority questions have determined international law to the extent that today—for example, in the case of Bosnia or Palestine—both scholars and the international community reproduce inter-war thinking, policy proposals, and institutions when confronted with questions of nationalism and national minorities.[114] In addition to Berman's conclusion

---

[110] See for a similar argument, which supports the general claim of this chapter, 'Alternative Is Despair' (n 7). Berman shows how the inter-war minority protection system has 'effected the permanent embroidering of the sovereign into the fabric of the international legal community'. Berman points out that 'minority protection made the creation of national states possible, for only by providing for the protection of the new minorities could international law sanction the creation of national states' (ibid 1872–73 and 1825).

[111] JL Brierly 'The Shortcomings of International Law' in JL Brierly, H Lauterpacht, and CHM Waldock (eds) *The Basis of Obligation in International Law* (Clarendon Press Oxford 1958) 68–80; see also D Kennedy 'The Move to Institutions' (1987) 8 Cardozo Law Review 841–988; *The Concept of International Legal Personality* (n 29) ch 3.

[112] 'Alternative Is Despair' (n 7), and *The Gentle Civilizer of Nations* (n 109).

[113] 'Alternative Is Despair' (n 7) 1820.

[114] ibid (n 7) 1799.

on how contemporary international law has been shaped fundamentally by the 'modernist' project of redefining international law to meet the nationalist challenge, a brief pause at the inter-war debate on the concept of international legal personality supports this chapter's claim that minorities have been significant to the (inter-war) constitution of international law. Inter-war scholarship offers two schools of response to the Great War and to the failure of 'old' international law to prevent war: those who wanted to restore and improve the old order, and those who wanted to revise international law and establish a new order.[115]

Within this universe of discourse, the debate on the position of minorities after Versailles shows a division between progressive and conservative scholars. Conservative scholarship argued that only States had and should have international legal personality; individuals or minority groups were object not subject of law.[116] This division becomes visible in the discussion on whether minority rights were national or international rights,[117] or in the discussion on the position of minorities within the League's system and the legal meaning of their right to petition.[118] Another intense debate concerned the question of whether minority rights were group rights or individual rights, and what this meant for international legal personality.[119] Generally, scholars agreed that in the majority of minority protection provisions, the suggestion of a 'group right' was avoided by referring to 'persons belonging to racial, religious, or linguistic minorities' in the same way as the present-day article 27 of the ICCPR. The PCIJ case law is inconclusive on this point.[120] More progressive scholars like Fouques-Duparc, Kelsen, Scelle, or Mandelstam were generally inclined to see minorities and/or the persons belonging to minorities as an international legal person or as in the process of rising to that status.[121] Fouques-Duparc articulated the issue at stake: how to reconcile a degree of international legal personality for minorities with the fundamental international law concept of State sovereignty.[122] As such, the discussion was part of a bigger debate on sovereignty, the individual, and the system of international law. This discussion did not end in agreement but by the outbreak of another war.

---

[115] This is addressed extensively in *The Concept of International Legal Personality* (n 29).

[116] Cf D Anzilotti *Cours de Droit International* (Recueil Sirey Paris 1929) at 127–31 and 135; P Heilborn 'Les Sources du Droit International' (1926-I) 11 Recueil des cours 1–63 at 5–11; E Kaufmann 'Règles générales du droit de la paix' (1935-I) 54 Recueil des cours 309–620; H Triepel 'Les rapports entre le droit interne et le droit international' (1923) 1 Recueil des cours 77–121 at 81.

[117] Cf eg L Oppenheim *International Law: A Treatise* (RF Roxburgh ed) (3rd edn Longmans, Green & Co London 1920) at 457–61: where it is denied that minority rights as included in the Minorities Treaties are international rights and so minorities are denied international legal personality.

[118] See eg H Lauterpacht *International Law and Human Rights* (Archon Books Hamden 1968) at 54.

[119] See eg *The Stabilization of Europe* (n 79) 28.

[120] See eg on the one hand *Jurisdiction of the Courts of Danzig Case* PCIJ Rep Series B No 15 17–18 and on the other hand *Greco-Bulgarian 'Communities'* (n 7).

[121] Cf eg 'Le Développement' (n 100); G Scelle *Précis de droit des gens, principes et systématique* (Sirey Paris 1932) vol 1, at 48: Scelle sees a 'mouvement d'extention de la personnalité juridique des individus'. Also, La protection des minorités (n 27) 472.

[122] 'Le développement' (n 100) 519.

Nonetheless it goes to show how minorities function as the constitutive Other of international law. They are excluded as an Other and then included by the discourse as a possible new, emerging, international legal person.

6. Conclusion

This chapter demonstrates the paradox of minorities as a constitutive Other of international law. While throughout centuries minorities have been viewed as outside the international legal system, minorities have at the same time made a significant and fundamental contribution to precisely that system, as they are among the oldest challenges of international (legal) relations between empires, cities, and States. This chapter addresses the arrangements for minority protection in two very different periods in history: 17th-century Westphalian system and 20th-century *interbellum*. In doing so, we have moved between different levels of analysis: histories of international law and the position of minorities therein; instances of positive international law regarding minorities; and, on a more general level, the contribution of minorities as outsiders to the 'system' of international law. As this chapter aims to show, the exclusion of minorities from the inter-state international system coupled with their inclusion as an Other in need of protection has contributed significantly to the development of international law in theory and practice. An examination of international minority rights and their international protection casts doubt on the traditional conceptualization and subsequent reification of 'Westphalian sovereignty' as unlimited and unconditional authority. Westphalian sovereignty is better conceived as comprising not only supreme authority but also responsibility. Minority protection was also part of a legitimating discourse on the sovereignty claim of a new or newly enlarged State. This link is also found in the political processes of 1919 as well as today; for example, in the Opinions of the Badinter Committee.[123] In short, minority rights and obligations are not an invention of late modernity. Rather, minority rights and the State's duty to protect these seem to be an integral part of the definition of 'sovereignty'. The politics of international minority protection deserves more research as well. This will arguably lay bare the dark side of the relation between international law and minorities.

---

[123] Cf Opinion No 2 para 4 of the Arbitration Committee, in A Pellet 'The Opinions of the Badinter Arbitration Committee—A Second Breath for the Self-Determination of Peoples' (1992) 3 European Journal of International Law 178–85 at 184.

Recommended Reading

Berman, Nathaniel '"But the Alternative Is Despair": European Nationalism and the Modernist Renewal of International Law' (1993) 106 Harvard Law Review 1792–903.

Braude, Benjamin and Bernard Lewis (eds) *Christians and Jews in the Ottoman Empire: The Functioning of a Plural Society* (Holmes and Meier New York 1982).

Claude, Inis L *National Minorities: An International Problem* (Greenwood Press New York 1955).

Fink, Carole *Defending the Rights of Others: The Great Powers, the Jews, and International Minority Protection, 1878–1938* (CUP Cambridge 2004).

Fouques-Duparc, Jaques *La protection des minorités de race, de langue et de religion: Étude de droit des gens* (Librairie Dalloz Paris 1922).

Jackson Preece, Jennifer *National Minorities and the European Nation-States System* (Clarendon Press Oxford 1998).

Krasner, Stephen D and Daniel T Froats 'Minority Rights and the Westphalian Model' in David A Lake and Donald S Rothchild (eds) *The International Spread of Ethnic Conflict: Fear, Diffusion, and Escalation* (Princeton University Press Princeton NJ 1998).

Macartney, Carlile A *National States and National Minorities* (OUP London 1934).

Meijknecht, Anna 'Minority Protection System between World War I and World War II' in R Wolfrum (ed) *The Max Planck Encyclopedia of Public International Law* (Oxford University Press Oxford 2008) at <www.mpepil.com>.

Thornberry, Patrick *International Law and the Rights of Minorities* (Clarendon Press Oxford 1991).

Verosta, Stephan 'International Law in Europe and Western Asia between 100 and 650 A.D.' (1964) 113 Recueil des cours 485–651.

Wintgens, Hugo *Der völkerrechtliche Schutz der nationalen, sprachlichen und religiösen Minderheiten* (W Kohlhammer Stuttgart 1930).

CHAPTER 5

HOSTES HUMANI GENERIS: PIRATES, SLAVERS, AND OTHER CRIMINALS

JOAQUÍN ALCAIDE FERNÁNDEZ

1. INTRODUCTION

DESPITE Cicero's celebrated definition of pirates as *hostes humani generis*,[1] there is no trace of the expression in (positive) international law. The 'criminals against humanity'—which included enslavers and sexual slavers,[2] but not (yet) pirates or terrorists—come the closest today to those 'enemies of all humanity'. There being no mention on international treaties, what is it that scholars have meant when they referred to *hostes humani generis* in treatises on international law? The meaning was generally twofold:

---

[1] Cicero used the phrase '*communis hostis omnium*' in his *De Officiis* III, 29 and in *Contra Verres* II, iv, 21 (cf AP Rubin *The Law of Piracy* (2nd edn Transnational Publishers Irvington-on-Hudson NY 1998) at 5 fn 19 and 17 fn 61).

[2] Rome Statute of the International Criminal Court (adopted 17 July 1998, entered into force 1 July 2002) 2187 UNTS 90, art 7.

pirates were worthy of punishment; and, to put it plainly as did Grotius, any pirate 'is justiciable by any State anywhere'.[3]

Concerning the historical legal foundations in accordance with which pirates, slavers, and others might be considered as (international) criminals, there are several questions. Since when can it be affirmed that they were such criminals? Was prohibition equal to criminalization? Provided that legality is a principle of international law—it might not have been so before 1945,[4] although the principle *nullum crimen, nulla poena sine lege* was soon recognized afterwards in human rights law—even 'any' generally accepted definition does not satisfy the requirement of specificity. Perhaps the Nuremberg trials were not the only exception aiming for substantive justice at the expense of strict legality. Further questions which may be posed include: were these criminals subject to universal jurisdiction? And last but not least, was every State eventually bound to prosecute?

The responses always depend upon the theory ('positivist' or 'naturalist') one adheres to relating to the foundation, nature, and scope of (criminal) international law. As the international law of piracy has not been universally codified (or progressively developed) until 1958, it is necessary to rely on practice and to identify the 'proper' law under consideration, be it municipal or international law. States and their mentioned municipal courts whose findings were supposedly based on 'the law of nations' have frequently used anti-piracy municipal laws as international law; municipal assertions of law have been received as persuasive statements of true international law.

For a long time, there had been no 'international' means of capturing, trying, or punishing criminals. Not a single proposal—either governmental or non-governmental—to create a criminal international court was successful before 1945. Although international law might have defined the elements of the crime (*mens rea, actus reus,* and *locus*), the recognition of the acts as constituting crimes, and the trial and punishment, were left by international customs or treaties to the municipal law and courts. Some scholars state that while piracy[5] or slave trade, or enslavement,[6] for instance, might have been crimes under municipal law, they were not crimes against international law, but only constituted a special basis of States' jurisdiction, otherwise restricted to crimes committed on its territory or by its nationals. States were then not obliged to prosecute and punish these criminals. It has

---

[3] H Grotius *De jure belli ac pacis* (1625) vol 2, ch 20, para 40.

[4] A Cassese *International Criminal Law* (OUP Oxford 2003) at 72.

[5] 'Draft Convention on the Competence of Courts in Regard to Foreign States: Part IV—Piracy' (1932) 26 American Journal of International Law Supplement: Research in International Law 739–885 at 754; *The Law of Piracy* (n 1) 335–45 and 360.

[6] J Allain *The Slavery Conventions. The* Travaux Préparatoires *of the 1926 League of Nations Convention and the 1956 United Nations Convention* (Martinus Nijhoff Publishers Leiden 2008) at 129.

been mainly since 1945—especially after the Cold War—when international law admitted individual criminal responsibility, both at the municipal and at the international level. This led to the International Criminal Court (ICC). Scholars still debate whether or not the duties set forth to bring criminals to justice at the municipal level fall within the realm of what is today criminal international law. Most criminals will usually be prosecuted and punished according to international law by any State which happens to seize them, as even the ICC is only complementary to national criminal jurisdiction.

The interrelationships between the criminal acts and the legal responses should be highlighted. Firstly, war crimes and crimes against humanity might encompass otherwise discrete crimes (enslavement, terrorism, torture, etc.). Pirates did not renounce 'man stealing', and even privateers did not merely take captives, but sold them as slaves and interfered with the slave trade.[7] Pirates/privateers became slavers, and vice versa.

Secondly, willing to establish criminalization and universal jurisdiction, some States—namely the United Kingdom and the United States—were prone to equate slave trade at sea to piracy (the 'piracy analogy'). British attempts go back to the 1822 Congress of Verona and only reached a conclusion with the codification of the law of the sea.[8] By 1882, a network of more than fifty bilateral agreements permitted the search of suspected slave vessels on the high seas, without regard to their flag. Precisely in connection to British arrests of foreign vessels engaged in the slave-trade, the freedom of the (high) sea(s) gained general acceptance as it was formulated by English and American courts early in the 19th century,[9] once piracy had declined. Even a treaty for the abolition of the slave trade was held not to justify the arrest of a vessel of the other party, unless the treaty specifically conferred that right upon the contracting States.[10] And the treaty can be interpreted as an acceptance of limits to the exercise of jurisdiction whose extension had been previously generally accepted.[11] Some treaties also compared the violation of the laws of war to piracy (with the clause 'as if for an act of piracy').[12] The same comparison has been used decades later when acts against the security of (civil) aviation have been called 'aerial piracy' in legal literature and municipal law,[13] and recently, acts against the

[7] WR Riddell 'Observations on Slavery and Privateering' (1930) 15 The Journal of Negro History 337–71.

[8] WG Grewe The Epochs of International Law (M Byers trans) (de Gruyter Berlin 2000) at 554–69.

[9] Le Louis (1817) 12 Dods 210, 165 ER 1464; and The Antelope 23 US 66, 10 Wheat 66 (1825).

[10] JL Brierly The Law of Nations (CHM Waldock ed) (6th edn Clarendon Press Oxford 1963) at 307.

[11] 'Articles of the Draft Code of Crimes against the Peace and Security of Mankind' (1996-II) Yearbook of the International Law Commission 17–42 at 29.

[12] See Section 2.1.3.

[13] For instance, E McWhinney Aerial Piracy and International Terrorism (Martinus Nijhoff Publishers Dordrecht 1971); Air Piracy 49 USC App § 1472(n)(1988); and United States v Fawaz Yunis 681 F Supp 896 (DDC 1988) and 924 F 2d 1086 (DC Cir 1991).

safety of maritime navigation or the taking of hostages at sea have been treated as piracy.[14]

2. PIRACY

Piracy is much older than maritime navigation, although its rise in modern times was connected to the increase of trade with the Indies and of privateering—that is, private vessels acting under a commission ('letter of marque and reprisal') issued by a State to capture vessels of an enemy State, and neutral States trading with it, giving to the privateer the prizes taken, with the exception of a percentage to the Crown, and providing for the speedy adjudication of claims.[15]

The legal recognition of pirates as criminals emerged from centuries of intermittent cooperation and conflict between States and privateers, involved in piracy-like acts, as the difference between privateering and piracy was usually blurred in practice. Furthermore, it has been said that many States, by not inserting in their municipal law provisions for prosecuting and punishing piracy in all circumstances even when committed by foreigners outside the State's ordinary jurisdiction, simply assumed piracy to constitute a special basis of State's jurisdiction. It is certainly difficult to find cases of an exercise of jurisdiction over piracy which could not be supported on one or more of the usual grounds.

2.1. Towards an Absolute Prohibition of Piracy

Modern international law did not outlaw piracy absolutely (privateering included) at least until the second half of the 19th century.[16] Even then, this can be determined only by indirect references to piracy in international negotiations and treaties.

---

[14] I Shearer 'Piracy' in R Wolfrum (ed) *The Max Planck Encyclopedia of Public International Law* (OUP Oxford 2008) at <www.mpepil.com>.

[15] JL de Azcárraga y de Bustamante *El corso marítimo* (CSIC-Instituto 'Francisco de Vitoria' Madrid 1950).

[16] Because proposals to define piracy referred to '[a]ny "illegal" act ...', AP Rubin still wondered in 1976 whether piracy was illegal. AP Rubin 'Is Piracy Illegal?' (1976) 70 American Journal of International Law 92–5.

2.1.1. *Cooperation and Conflict between States and Private Vessels: Privateers versus Pirates*

States began the prohibition of piracy long ago. There were a number of piracy trials before municipal courts. The trial *R v Joseph Dawson* before the High Court of Admiralty, and the charge that Sir Charles Hedges submitted to the grand jury in 1696,[17] or the case *United States v Smith* in 1820,[18] are all examples. It might follow from that, that piracy may be considered as a violation of international law, and perhaps subject to the (criminal)[19] jurisdiction of all States.

Notwithstanding, modern States soon discovered the benefits of using privateers as adjuncts of the State's armed forces (even preceding royal navies) and, as a sign of the building of modern States, accepted licensing privateers as a prerogative of recognized States—and only of States, as was the case with resorting to war. As early as the end of the 13th century, municipal laws often authorized privateering; amongst other municipal or international legal criteria (such as validity of the commission, nationality of the captured vessel or its cargo, bonds furnished, respect of the temporal and material constraints of the commission, having no commissions from more than one sovereign, etc.), the commission was necessary to prevent the privateers from being treated as pirates (who, at best, governed themselves by the so-called pirate articles, mainly based on terror, fear, etc.). These regulations can be traced from the Pisa (1298) and Geneva (1313–16) laws, Pedro IV of Aragon's Ordinance of 1356, the Laws of the Hanseatic League (1362–64), Charles V of France's Ordinance of 1373, the seminal prize court regulation in English Parliamentary Act of 1414, etc., to the French Ordinance of 1778 or the Spanish Ordinance of 1801, and additions.

But differentiation between pirates and privateers was subtle in practice. From the 16th century onwards, cooperation and conflict between States and privateers were dependent upon the (un)friendly relationships between old European States; namely, England, France, and Spain, but also the Netherlands, hence the centrality of privateering in Grotius' or Bynkershoek's writings. The perceptions about the status of the private vessels differed, so piracy was not the same for each and every State everywhere and every time. History and the romantic imagination have been filled with heroes and villains (the Vikings, Barbary pirates and privateers, Sir Francis Drake, Edward Teach called 'Blackbeard', etc.), somehow anticipating the political exemption problem in the fight against terrorism in the 20th century, which permitted States not to extradite terrorists because their actions were considered political offences rather than common offences.

English and Spanish legislative practices are examples of this cooperation and conflict. For instance, Henry VIII (English Offences at Sea Act 1536) and Elizabeth I

---

[17] *R v Joseph Dawson* (1696) 13 Howell's St Tr 451.

[18] *United States v Smith* 18 US 153, 5 Wheat 153 (1820) at 161. See also *The Magellan Pirates* (1853) 1 Sp Ecc & Ad 81, 164 ER 47, cited in *The Law of Nations* (n 10) 307 and fn 3.

[19] Notwithstanding *The Law of Piracy* (n 1) 61–70.

(Proclamations of 1569 or 1575) outlawed pirates while authorizing privateers against Spanish trade. After the accession of James I and the end of the Spanish wars (1604), new anti-piracy acts were declared and commissions revoked. At the end of the wars between England and Spain (1692) and 'King William's War' (Treaty of Ryswick), England revoked the licences of its privateers (Piracy Acts of 1698). But during the War of the Spanish Succession (1702–13) England attacked the Spanish monopoly of commerce in the 'South Sea', where Spain had made it piracy for any but a Spanish vessel to trade there (English Act of 1707).

After the Peace of Utrecht (1713), the so-called 'Golden Age of Piracy' declined due to one essential factor: piracy was the victim of its own success. Excess of trained sailors without employment or rebels against the established order—many of them former privateers—had become pirates who damaged and threatened all trade everywhere, and without distinction amongst nations. More than ever before, piracy was considered an act of savagery by Western States (for instance, English acts of 1717, 1721, 1744, and 1837), so it was only accepted as 'reasonable' if committed by 'savages'— even though sponsored by Western States. The next step forward was to recover the definition of pirates as 'enemies of all humanity', while tolerance for privateers was wearing thin by all nations.

2.1.2. *The 1856 Declaration: The Abolition of Privateering*

When some municipal laws were eventually adopted to prohibit privateering, and when commissions were revoked (for example, by the Royal Pragmatic issued in 1498 by Fernando 'the Catholic', King of Aragon), several international treaties and practices prohibited privateering as well. England and France did so many times, starting with the diplomatic overtures of Edward III in 1324, and a number of unilateral and bilateral declarations limiting privateering between 1785 and 1823, but none remained in force after a war broke out between the parties involved.

From a French proposal, the Declaration (actually a treaty) Respecting Maritime Law was signed in Paris, in 1856.[20] According to the Declaration, '[p]rivateering is, and remains, abolished'. None of the States parties could authorize as privateering the acts which otherwise would be considered piracy; however, once captured, privateers commissioned by third States were still to be treated as prisoners of war. Other States acceded later to the Declaration (for example, Spain in 1908, but not the United States).[21] Privateering begun to fall into disuse, and its abolition began to gain 'objective' authority. For example, a number of resolutions of the Institute of International Law affirmed that privateering was forbidden: if not the 'Rules of Washington' (1875), at least the Resolutions of Zurich (1877), Turin (1882), and Oxford (1913).

---

[20] Declaration Respecting Maritime Law (signed 16 April 1856) (1856) 115 CTS 1.
[21] While the Declaration (ibid) advocated protecting all civilian property on the high seas, the US Constitution lists issuing letters of marque as a power of the Congress (art 1, s 8, cl 10).

Only under exceptional conditions could a private vessel converted into a warship have the rights and duties accruing to such vessels. The 1907 VII Convention[22] codified, and resolutions of the Institute of International Law reaffirmed,[23] the State practice (Prussia in 1870, Russia in 1877, the United Kingdom in 1887, France, Germany, United States, etc.) which indicated that those vessels should be placed under the direct authority, immediate control, and responsibility of the power whose flag they flew.

2.1.3. *The Clause 'As if for an Act of Piracy'*

Piracy and privateering also formed the background to other treaties. Although never entered into force because France failed to ratify, it is worth noting that signatory powers of the 1922 Treaty of Washington relating to the Use of Submarines and Noxious Gases in Warfare[24] stated that

> any person in the service of any Power who shall violate any of [the rules set forth in article 1]...shall be deemed to have violated the laws of war and shall be liable to trial and punishment as if for an act of piracy and may be brought to trial before the civil or military authorities of any Power within the jurisdiction of which he may be found.

Furthermore, on 14 September 1937, during the Spanish civil war, representatives of several States signed at Nyon an accord for the purpose of denouncing the attacks by submarines against merchant ships not belonging to either of the conflicting Spanish parties[25] as violations of 'the established rules of international law'. Even though neither the clause 'as if for an act of piracy', nor the term 'piracy', are used in either of those 'established rules', the 'anti-piracy agreements' of 1937 declared that the said attacks are 'contrary to the most elementary dictates of humanity, which should be justly treated as acts of piracy'. The parties to the accord agreed as well to special collective measures 'against piratical acts by submarines' (or surface vessels or aircraft, according to a supplementary agreement signed three days later at Geneva, 17 September, by the same powers).[26] These agreements contained no provisions for the punishment of the officers and crews of offending vessels or craft as pirates who were caught committing 'piratical acts'. The legal basis for declaring those attacks in the Mediterranean to be acts of piracy seems to be the lack of recognition of belligerency

---

[22] Hague Convention (IV) Concerning the Laws and Customs of War on Land (opened for signature 18 October 1907, entered into force 26 January 1910) (1907) 205 CTS 277.
[23] 'The Oxford Manual of Naval War' in JB Scott (ed) *Resolutions of the Institute of International Law* (OUP New York 1916) 174–201.
[24] 'A Treaty between the Same Powers, in Relation to the Use of Submarines and Noxious Gases in Warfare' (1922) 16 American Journal of International Law Supplement: Official Documents 57–60, art 3.
[25] The Nyon Arrangement, with Annexes and Map (signed 14 September 1937) 181 LNTS 137.
[26] ibid.

of the (thus simply insurgent) parties to the conflict in Spain.[27] In its protests to Germany during the World Wars, the United States applied also the term 'piracy' to the acts of German submarines against merchant vessels.

2.1.4. *Piracy and the League of Nations*

During the era of the League of Nations (LoN), an attempt was made to provide a general agreement on piracy. Following the Assembly resolution of 1924, the League appointed a sub-committee of its Committee of Experts for the Progressive Codification of International Law. In the 'Matsuda report', the sub-committee stated that 'according to international law, piracy consists in sailing the seas for private ends without authorization from the government of any State with the object of committing depredations upon property or acts of violence against persons'. The definition did not deal with an armed rising of the crew or passengers with the object of seizing the ship on the high sea.[28] The so-called questionnaire on piracy (consisting of the 'Matsuda report' and Matsuda's draft provisions for the suppression of piracy) was submitted to a number of States,[29] but some of them did not acknowledge the desirability/possibility of a convention on the question. Some commentators criticized the report itself and even the transmission of the report to States because of 'the present immature stage' not of the subject in itself, but of the report.[30]

The League's efforts fizzled out, and the subject was dropped from any conference for two reasons: piracy seemed not to be an urgent problem, and it was not likely that an agreement would be reached.

2.2. The Anti-piracy International Legal Regime around 1945: A Brief Overview

A sort of syllogism may help to overcome the confusion regarding the international law of piracy. There is no doubt that the provisions enshrined in the 1958

---

[27] GA Finch 'Piracy in the Mediterranean' (1937) 31 American Journal of International Law 659–65; R Genet 'The Charge of Piracy in the Spanish Civil War' (1938) 30 American Journal of International Law 253–63.

[28] See proceedings in LN Doc C/196/M/70/1927/V, at 116.

[29] The 'questionnaire' is reproduced in 'Questionnaire No. 6: Piracy' (1926) 20 American Journal of International Law Supplement 222–9; the analysis of the States' replies in 'Legal Status of Government Ships Employed in Commerce' (1926) 20 American Journal of International Law Supplement 260–78 at 273. The reply of Romania was written by V Pella, who took the opportunity to give the course 'La répression de la piraterie' (1926) 15 Recueil des Cours de l'Académie de Droit International de La Haye 145–268.

[30] ED Dickinson 'The Questionnaire on Piracy' (1926) 20 American Journal of International Law 750–2.

Convention on the High Seas[31] were based on the ILC's draft convention and later inserted in the 1982 UNCLOS.[32] For its part, apparently the ILC closely followed the research carried out at the Harvard Law School which had culminated in a draft convention prepared in 1932 (indeed, all provisions contained in the rapporteur François' draft, adopted as the ILC draft, were a French translation of the Harvard Draft Convention on Piracy).[33] Finally, although it is not unanimously accepted that the 1958 Convention strictly 'codified' the traditional international law of piracy, there is widespread agreement that, although it still raised difficulties, the piracy rules contained in the UNCLOS reflect customary international law. The Harvard Draft Convention has been used by some scholars to discuss the history and development of that international law of piracy 'as it developed over many centuries'.[34] I will refer briefly to the definition of piracy and the jurisdiction over pirates, leaving aside matters such as property rights ('*pirata non mutat dominium*', etc.).

2.2.1. *The Definition of Piracy: International Law and Municipal Law*

Over the centuries, there was no authoritative definition of piracy in general international law. Acts that are piratical under municipal law[35] may not be so under international law (for example, in English criminal law it has been piracy to engage in slave trading). Although the lack of adjudication and of pertinent instances of State practice occasioned some confusion among experts as to what international law includes, or should include, in the definition of piracy, it seemed to be accepted that it was 'of the essence of a pirate act to be an act of violence, committed at sea or at any rate closely connected with the sea, by persons not acting under proper authority'.[36] There has been and there still is debate about other elements—other than the choate or inchoate criminality[37]—such as the purpose (robbery or private ends versus

---

[31] Convention on the High Seas (signed 29 April 1958, entered into force 30 September 1962) 450 UNTS 82, arts 14–21.

[32] United Nations Convention on the Law of the Sea (signed 10 December 1982, entered into force 16 November 1994) 1833 UNTS 397, arts 100–7.

[33] 'Report of the International Law Commission Covering the Work of its Eighth Session, 23 April–4 July 1956' (1956-II) Yearbook of the International Law Commission 253–302 at 282.

[34] BH Dubner *The Law of International Sea Piracy* (Martinus Nijhoff Publishers The Hague 1980) at 37–102.

[35] See the appendix (pt V) to the Harvard Draft Convention: S Morrison (ed) 'Part V: A Collection of Piracy Laws of Various Countries' (1932) 26 American Journal of International Law Supplement: Research in International Law 887–1013.

[36] The Law of Nations (n 10) 154. The definition of piracy in the sixth edition of Brierly's *Law of Nations*, of 1963, was rewritten (by Waldock) to accommodate to the definition contained in the 1958 Convention.

[37] It has been adjudicated that a frustrated attempt to commit a piratical robbery is equally piracy according to international law (*In re Piracy jure gentium* [1934] AC 586 (LR PC)).

political ends)[38] and the place (acts committed outside all territorial jurisdiction, but not on the high seas).[39]

After the 1856 Declaration, it was generally accepted that the proposition according to which pirates may be lawfully captured on the (high) seas by armed vessels of any State and brought within its territorial jurisdiction for trial before its municipal courts, should 'be confined to piracy as defined by the law of nations, and [could not] be extended to offences which [were] made piracy by municipal legislation'.[40]

2.2.2. *Universal Jurisdiction*

Because piracy had to occur outside the municipal jurisdiction of any nation, it has been considered as a, if not the, quintessential crime subject to universal jurisdiction. Although this conclusion has been contested,[41] it appears, for instance, from the published records of the conference where the provision 'punishment as if for an act of piracy' was inserted in the 1922 Treaty of Washington. The representatives assented to the following proposition as one of the core provisions of the treaty: under that provision, the offender would not be subject to the limitations of territorial jurisdiction, the peculiarity about the punishment for piracy being that, although the act is done on the high seas and not within the jurisdiction of any country, nevertheless it can be punished in any country where the offender is found.[42]

Accordingly, every State might (or must)[43] seize a pirate ship (later a pirate aircraft as well), or a ship taken by piracy and under the control of pirates, and arrest the persons and seize the property on board, pending the seizing State's court decision upon the penalties and the action to be taken with regard to the ships (or aircraft) and property.[44] The seizure should only be carried out by warships (or, afterwards, by military aircraft), or other ships (or aircraft) on government service authorized to that effect[45] (for instance, a French law enacted in 1825 authorized the merchant vessels to carry out the seizure).

It was generally (but not unanimously) accepted that the right of hot pursuit did not cease when the pirate ship pursued entered the territorial waters of a State other than the pursuing State, unless prohibited by the coastal State,[46] the courts of which

---

[38] See H Lauterpacht 'Insurrection et piraterie' (1939) 46 Revue Générale de Droit International Public 513–49; and the debate in the ILC (Report of the International Law Commission (n 33)).

[39] For instance, Dickinson's critique of 'Matsuda report': The Questionnaire on Piracy (n 30).

[40] WB Lawrence *Wheaton's Elements of International Law* (6th edn Little, Brown and Company Boston MA 1857) 184–6. See also The Law of Nations (n 10) 154.

[41] *The Law of Piracy* (n 1) 343.

[42] CP Anderson 'As if for an Act of Piracy' (1922) 16 American Journal of International Law 260–1.

[43] Report of the International Law Commission (n 33).

[44] Draft Convention on Piracy (n 5) arts 2 and 6 and the respective comments.

[45] ibid art 12 and the comment.

[46] ibid art 7 and the comment; see also El corso marítimo (n 15) 130.

have, however, jurisdictional priority. There was also a provision on the liability of the pursuers or seizing State against damages to non-pirate ships or to other States,[47] and a statement of the rights of persons accused of the crime.[48]

3. SLAVERS

Throughout the ages, different societies and civilizations have considered slavery as a 'natural' state or a fair penalty, but almost always some thought of it as morally reprehensible.[49] The method of enslavement was sometimes considered legal, in other times illegal. From the 16th century onwards, when the numbers alone exceeded any past practice, the native Africans ('Negroes') were the main victims, but in earlier times no race was exempt or 'unenslavable'. Both enslavement and slave trade were very profitable branches of commerce, offering widespread economic benefit, and— in contrast to piracy—slavery was legal in most countries of the world.

At dawn of the 19th century, when European empires were trafficking with 'Negroes', technical and economic circumstances changed—because the decline of the relevance of manpower—as moral and religious circumstances did, mainly under the direction of the Church of England, followed by the Pope's instructions, and the abolitionist movement, which gained strength after the famous case of James Somerset (1772),[50] and drew moral and intellectual inspiration from the general proclamations of human rights. Even Haiti became independent in 1804 after a slave revolt. These were the days when Britain wanted rival colonial and maritime powers to join its 'crusade' against the slave trade so as to prevent trade and manpower— power itself—from passing to rivals hands.[51]

International cooperation began openly in 1814–15, mainly occupied with African slave trade, but the abolition of the slave trade did not entail immediately the prohibition of ownership of slaves. The British Slavery Abolition Act was passed in 1833, and emancipation spread throughout most new independent Latin American States, to France in 1848 and to the United States in 1863. Firstly the enslavement and slavery-related practices were prohibited in the laws and customs of war, yet the different legal status of the slave trade and slavery is still evident in article 2 of the 1926 Slavery

---

[47] Draft Convention on Piracy (n 5) arts 8–11 and the respective comments.
[48] ibid arts 14 and 15 and the respective comments.
[49] See the contribution by S Drescher and P Finkelman 'Slavery' in this volume.
[50] *Somerset v Stewart* (1772) Lofft 1, 98 ER 499.
[51] For a background, AM Trebilcock 'Slavery' in R Bernhardt (ed) *Encyclopedia of Public International Law* (North-Holland Elsevier 2000) vol 4, 422–6.

Convention.[52] Furthermore, as piracy provisions, the prohibition of the slave trade transformed the law of the sea in itself—the 1958 Convention on the High Seas (article 13) and the 1982 UNCLOS (article 99). However, as opposed to the anti-piracy regime, here there is no recognition of universal jurisdiction. The 1926 Convention was supplemented in 1956, when other main steps forward had been, or were about to be, taken (articles 1.3, 55 and 56 of the UN Charter; articles 1, 3, 4, 5, and 6 of the UDHR; articles 8 and 15 of the 1966 ICCPR; *obiter dictum* in the 1970 judgment of the ICJ; etc.). It should be noted however that it is difficult not only to determine when the slave trade and enslavement became a violation of customary international law,[53] but also to find anyone tried before criminal courts for slave-trading or enslaving before 1945.

3.1. The Abolition of African Slave Trade and the Woman and Children Traffic

In 1807, US Congress passed the Act to Prohibit the Importation of Slaves, renewed between 1818 and 1820, as the British Parliament adopted the Act for the Abolition of the Slave-Trade, revised in 1824, 1843, and 1873. A number of declarations and international treaties were then designed to abolish first the African slave trade (once the Atlantic trade had declined in the last third of 19th century, there was still an active trade from Africa to the Muslim World), then the white-slave trade, trade in women, and child trafficking.

3.1.1. *The Congress of Vienna (1815) and the Treaty of London (1841)*

The first international instrument to deal specifically with the slave trade in general was the 1815 Declaration Relative to the Universal Abolition of the Slave-Trade (the 'Eight Power Declaration'), signed in Vienna on 8 February 1815.[54] The Declaration acknowledged that the slave trade was 'repugnant to the principles of humanity and universal morality', but did not contain provisions to enforce a duty

---

[52] Slavery Convention (signed 25 September 1926, entered into force 9 March 1927) 60 LNTS 253.

[53] Confronting enslavement and sexual slavery during Second World War accusations, Japan has argued that there was no customary law against slavery then; UN Commission on Human Rights (Sub-Commission) 'Systematic Rape, Sexual Slavery and Slavery-like Practices during Armed Conflict: Final Report Submitted by Gay J. McDougall, Special Rapporteur' (22 June 1998) UN Doc. E/CN.4/Sub.2/1998/13, para 4.

[54] Declaration of the Eight Powers relative to the Universal Abolition of Slave Trade, annexed as Act XV to the 1815 General Treaty of the Vienna Congress (signed 8 February 1815) (1815) 63 CTS 473. The signatory States were Austria, France, Great Britain, Portugal, Prussia, Russia, Spain, and Sweden; all of them, except Spain, secretly signed the Treaty of Paris of 30 May 1814, where France and Great Britain pledged to abolish the slave-trade.

to prohibit, less criminalize, it. Elsewhere it was declared to be condemned by 'the laws of religion and nature' (treaty signed on 20 November 1815 among Austria, France, Great Britain, Prussia, and Russia), whereas the Treaty of Peace and Amity, signed in Ghent, 18 February 1815 by United States and Great Britain, had declared that the slave trade was 'irreconcilable with the principles of humanity and justice'.[55]

Most of the signatories of the 1815 Declaration—which a few years later reaffirmed their opposition to the slave trade and their intention to its abolition in the Declaration Respecting the Abolition of the Slave Trade, 28 November 1822[56]—signed in London, on 20 December 1841, the Treaty for the Suppression of the African Slave-Trade.[57] The object and purpose were to give full and complete effect to the principles of the 1815 Declaration, deeming the slave trade equal to piracy and enshrining not just duties to prohibit, prevent, prosecute, and punish,[58] and establish a criminal jurisdictional basis,[59] but also to cooperate, including through judicial assistance.[60]

3.1.2. *The General Acts of Berlin (1885) and Brussels (1890) Conferences and their 1919 Revision*

The Declaration Concerning the Slave Trade and the Operations Which on Land or Sea Furnish Slaves to the Trade, discussed and adopted during the Conference of Berlin, and attached to the General Act signed on 26 February 1885, joined new States to those which were parties to the 1815 Declaration, including the United States.[61] This Declaration recognized that the slave trade was prohibited in accordance with 'the principles of the law of nations', and the Powers exercising sovereignty or influence in the Congo Basin engaged 'to use all means at its disposal to put an end to this trade and to punish those engaging in it'.[62] Another declaration contained the engagement of these Powers to strive for the suppression of slavery and especially of the slave trade.[63]

Five years later, during the 1889–90 Brussels Conference, a comprehensive international treaty against the slave trade in Africa was adopted.[64] The parties to the General Act signed on 2 July declared to be inspired by 'the firm intention of putting an end to the crimes and devastations engendered by the traffic in African slaves', and the wish

---

[55] Treaty of Peace and Amity (signed 18 February 1815) (1815) 12 TIAS 47.

[56] Portugal, Spain and Sweden were absent in the Congress of Verona (1822).

[57] Treaty for the Suppression of the African Slave-Trade (signed 20 December 1841) (1841) 73 CTS 32.

[58] ibid arts I, III, and X.

[59] ibid arts VI, VII, X, and annex B.

[60] ibid art XV.

[61] The act is reproduced in 'General Act of the Conference of Berlin Concerning the Congo' (1909) 3 American Journal of International Law Supplement: Official Documents 7–25.

[62] ibid art 9.

[63] Declaration Relative to the Liberty of Commerce in the Basin of the Congo, its Embouchures and Neighbouring Country, and Dispositions Connected Therewith, attached to the General Act (art 6).

[64] General Act of the Brussels Conference Relating to the African Slave Trade (signed 2 July 1890, entered into force 31 August 1891) (1890) 173 CTS 293.

to give fresh sanction to the decisions already adopted in the same sense and at different times by the powers, to complete the results secured by them, and to draw up a body of measures guaranteeing the accomplishment of the work which is the object of their common solicitude.

Yet the General Act also served the powers' territorial and commercial ambitions. It enshrined humanitarian provisions such as measures to be taken in the places of origin; provisions concerning caravan routes and transportation of slaves by land; the repression of the slave trade at sea (including a right to visit, search and detain vessels, and the provision according to which any slave who takes refuge on board any vessel of a State signatory shall be immediately and definitively set free); or duties of countries to which slaves are sent. Therefore, signatory States established obligations to repress the slave trade on land and sea. For the first time in history, a treaty-monitoring body was established, the International Maritime Office, based in Brussels and Zanzibar, for the exchange of information on slave-trade and anti-slavery municipal laws.

However, because of the commercial restrictions posed by the Brussels General Act, the colonial powers had no desire to renew it after the First World War and substituted it by a clause inserted into the Convention Revising the Berlin and Brussels Acts, signed on 10 September 1919, at Saint-Germain-en-Laye,[65] which in fact abrogated those acts concerning the slave trade for those States that ratified it. Yet according with the 1919 Convention, the Powers exercising sovereignty in African territories affirmed their intention to 'endeavour to secure the complete suppression of slavery in all its forms and of the slave trade by land and sea'.[66]

3.1.3. *White Slave Trade and Traffic in Women and Children:*
The 1904, 1910, 1921, and 1933 International Conventions

The suppression of the white-slave trade was the object and purpose of both the 18 May 1904 International Agreement,[67] and of the 4 May 1910 International Convention and Final Protocol,[68] signed in Paris. The first established the cooperation in the prosecution and punishment of that traffic, including judicial assistance;[69] the second contained 'minimum' provisions to prohibit, prevent, prosecute, and punish the proscribed practice—including cooperation through judicial assistance concerning the transmission of Letters of Request and the communication of records of

---

[65] Convention Revising the Berlin and Brussels Acts (signed 10 September 1919) (1919) 225 CTS 500. The United States never ratified the 1919 Convention.

[66] ibid art 11.

[67] International Agreement for the Suppression of the White Slave Traffic (signed 18 May 1904) 1 LNTS 83; 195 CTS 326.

[68] International Convention for the Suppression of White Slave Traffic (signed 4 May 1910, entered into force 14 August 1951) (1910) 211 CTS 45.

[69] ibid arts 1–3.

convictions[70]—to extradite the (presumably) responsible, and to establish a criminal jurisdictional basis.[71]

Furthermore, the parties to the International Convention for the Suppression of the Traffic in Women and Children, signed in Geneva on 30 September 1921,[72] agreed to take all measures to discover and prosecute, and secure the punishment of, or to extradite, persons who are engaged in the traffic in children of both sexes and who committed offences within the meaning of the 1910 Convention.[73] This Convention was followed by the International Convention for the Suppression of the Traffic in Women of Full Age, signed in Geneva on 11 October 1933,[74] which enshrined the duties to prohibit, prosecute, punish, and to cooperate therein.[75]

All these conventions were amended in 1947[76] or 1949[77] to enable the UN to perform all duties in place of the LoN, and the 1950 Convention for the Suppression of Traffic in Persons and of the Exploitation of the Prostitution of Others[78] supersedes them in the relations between parties thereto.

3.2. The 1926 League of Nations' Slavery Convention and Subsequent Developments

By appointing in 1924 a Temporary Slavery Commission (TSC)—with Albrecht Gohr as Chairman—the LoN ended up shifting from monitoring to making the international law on the suppression of the slave trade and slavery, devising a general convention—beyond article 23 of the Covenant and against all predictions, because there was no enthusiasm from any State, not even from Britain, and some

---

[70] ibid arts 6 and 7.

[71] ibid arts 1–3, art 5 and the Final Protocol.

[72] International Convention for the Suppression of the Traffic in Women and Children (signed 30 September 1921) 9 LNTS 415.

[73] ibid arts 2–4.

[74] International Convention for the Suppression of the Traffic in Women of Full Age (signed 11 October 1933) 150 LNTS 431.

[75] arts 1–3.

[76] The 1921 and 1933 Conventions: Protocol to Amend the Convention for the Suppression of the Traffic in Women and Children and the Convention for the Suppression of the Traffic in Women of Full Age (signed 12 November 1947) 53 UNTS 13; International Convention for the Suppression of the Traffic in Women and Children Amended by the Protocol (signed 12 November 1947) 59 UNTS 39; and International Convention for the Suppression of the Traffic in Women of Full Age Amended by the Protocol (signed 12 November 1947) 53 UNTS 49.

[77] The 1904 and 1910 Conventions: International Agreement for the Suppression of the White Slave Traffic Amended by the Protocol (signed 4 May 1949) 92 UNTS 19; International Convention for the Suppression of the White Slave Traffic Amended by the Protocol (signed 4 May 1949) 98 UNTS 101.

[78] Approved by General Assembly resolution 317 (IV) of 2 December 1949: Convention for the Suppression of Traffic in Persons and of the Exploitation of the Prostitution of Others (entered into force 25 July 1951) 96 UNTS 271.

open reluctance, for example from the Portuguese delegate. The International Convention with the Object of Securing the Abolition of Slavery and the Slave Trade, signed in Geneva, on 25 September 1926,[79] was ultimately inspired by Sir Frederick Lugard, British member of the TSC, through the provisions officially proposed by the United Kingdom. The LoN Assembly's resolution recommending for approval the annexed draft convention was adopted on the proposal of Viscount Cecil of Chelwood, the British delegate to the League.

The parties to the 1926 Convention went on to differentiate two international legal regimes, one on the slave trade, the other on slavery, as they undertake 'to prevent and suppress the slave trade', and 'to bring about, progressively and as soon as possible, the complete abolition of slavery in all its forms'.[80] The formulation of the duty relating to slavery composed in 1926 had many positive elements: it must be a 'complete abolition' and 'in all its forms'. But, despite the duty to secure the complete suppression of slavery in all its forms seemingly set out at Saint-Germain-en-Laye in 1919, there were also negative elements: the abolition might be brought about only 'progressively and as soon as possible'. The drafters within the LoN were too cautious in seeking to gain the acceptance of provisions on penalizing violations of the proposed Convention. Notwithstanding, the parties undertook to give one another every assistance with the object of securing both the abolition of slavery and the slave trade;[81] when necessary, to adopt the necessary measures so that severe penalties may be imposed in respect of infractions of laws and regulations enacted both to prevent and suppress slave trade and to abolish slavery;[82] and to communicate any these laws and regulations. The Convention contains no other mechanism of enforcement, although the LoN would establish a Committee of Experts on Slavery, later Advisory Committee on Slavery.[83]

The Convention enshrined the definitions of both slavery and the slave trade.[84] It also referred to an apparently different but related practice: forced or compulsory labour.[85] Being the most debated provision during the drafting process, article 5 on forced labour when used for private ends was rather limited in 1926. On 28 June 1930, the General Conference of the ILO adopted the Convention Concerning Forced and Compulsory Labour.[86]

---

[79] International Convention for the Abolition of Slavery and the Slave Trade (signed 25 September 1926, entered into force 9 March 1927) 60 LNTS 253. The 1953 Protocol brought the Convention into the UN system (Protocol Amending the Slavery Convention (entered into force 7 December 1953) 182 UNTS 51); yet there are States which have consented to the 1926 Slavery Convention but not to the 1953 Protocol.

[80] Convention for the Abolition of Slavery and the Slave Trade (n 79) arts 2 and 3.

[81] ibid art 4. This general obligation was never concretize in specific bilateral or multilateral agreements.

[82] ibid art 6.   [83] ibid art 7.   [84] ibid art 1.   [85] ibid Preamble and art 5.

[86] Convention Concerning Forced or Compulsory Labour (ILO No 29) (adopted 28 June 1930, entered into force 1 May 1932) 39 UNTS 55. The 1930 Convention—which gathers many of the principles and limitations announced in the '1928 Bellot Rules', adopted by the ILA in Warsaw—was modified in 1946 and complemented in 1957.

Later, according to the 1956 UN Supplementary Convention on the Abolition of Slavery, the Slave Trade, and Institutions and Practices Similar to Slavery[87], the States parties reinforced the criminalization of the slave trade, enslaving, and related practices,[88] and undertook to adopt measures to abolish debt bondage, serfdom, forced marriage, and child exploitation.[89] The status of these is not necessarily 'slavery', but defined as 'servile',[90] and other institutions and practices similar to slavery and the slave trade have been identified.[91] Although the definition of slavery has not evolved since 1926 (1956 Convention[92] and 1998 ICC Statute),[93] its interpretation is contested. Furthermore, as new forms of slavery and slave-related, or similar practices have appeared, perhaps the definition might have proven too limited to cover all these new forms. The political and emotional significance of the 'label' slavery, and the legal force of the prohibition of slavery nowadays explain that some legal scholars propose to extend this definition to institutions and practices similar to slavery.[94]

The 1926 Convention continued with the 'civilizing mission', yet Western or mandatory powers sought to ensure that the Convention did not apply to their colonial or mandated territories.[95] And twice during the drafting process, the United Kingdom sought to have the slave trade at sea assimilated to piracy. The other delegations did not agree—even though Britain would have been satisfied with a right to visit and search, and not to seize. According to the resulting article 3, the parties undertook to adopt all appropriate measures with a view to preventing and suppressing the embarkation, disembarkation, and transport of slaves simply 'in their territorial waters and upon vessels flying their respective flags'. The complementary general convention or special agreements due to be negotiated have never been negotiated or concluded,

---

[87] Supplementary Convention on the Abolition of Slavery, the Slave Trade, and Institutions and Practices Similar to Slavery (signed 7 September 1956, entered into force 30 April 1957) 226 UNTS 3.

[88] ibid arts 3, 5, and 6.

[89] ibid art 1.

[90] If not covered by the 1926 Convention (n 79), the 1956 Convention (n 87) considers the victim as a 'person of servile status' (art 7(b)), but not a 'slave' (art 7(a)).

[91] Such as, *inter alia*, the traffic in persons and the exploitation of the prostitution of others, 1949 UN Convention (n 78); or trafficking in persons, especially women and children, and the smuggling of migrants, Protocols Supplementary to the Convention against Transnational Organized Crime (adopted 15 November 2000, entered into force 29 September 2003) 2225 UNTS 209.

[92] However, the definition of 'slave-trade' (art 7(c)) differs in an insignificant manner from the definition found in the 1926 Convention (n 79).

[93] The definition of 'enslavement' (not of 'slavery') contained in the art 7.2(c) is identical to that of slavery in the 1926 Convention (n 79), but includes the exercise of the powers attaching to the right of ownership 'in the course of trafficking in persons, in particular women and children'.

[94] See J Hathaway 'The Human Rights Quagmire of "Human Trafficking"' (2008) 49 Virginia Journal of International Law 1–59; and AT Gallagher 'Human Rights and Human Trafficking: Quagmire or Firm Ground? A Response to James Hathaway' (2008) 49 Virginia Journal of International Law 789–848.

[95] Namely, the 'colonial clause' (art 9); it is noticeable the different wording of art 12 of the 1956 Convention (n 87).

and the United Kingdom made a last attempt (again unsuccessfully) during the negotiations of the 1956 Convention.[96]

3.3. The Enslavement and other Slavery–related Crimes in the Laws and Customs of War

The regulation of the use of prisoners of war (POWs) for labour and the prohibition
of any compulsion of the population of occupied territory to take part in military
operations against its own country are dealt with in the 1899 Hague Convention (II)
on the Law and Customs of War on Land and the Regulations annexed, adopted on
29 July,[97] and the 1907 Hague Convention (IV) and the Regulations annexed, adopted
on 18 October, which replaced the 1899 Hague Convention (II) and Regulations
between States parties.[98] There we find incorporated some protections for both
civilians and belligerents from enslavement and forced labour in (international)
armed conflict or in the situation of occupation.[99] The respective chapter II of the
1899 and 1907 Regulations was complemented by the Geneva Convention Relating
to the Treatment of Prisoners of War, adopted on 27 July 1929.[100] Sometimes the
protection offered to POWs was unilaterally extended to civilian enemy aliens in the
territory of the belligerent.[101]

Besides the Charter of the [Nuremberg] International Military Tribunal,[102] the
1899 and 1907 Regulations or the 1929 Convention were the legal foundation of the
Nuremberg indictments on slave labour and enslavement as war crimes or crimes
against humanity counts, although the laws and customs of war contained no rules
regarding criminal responsibility (apart from the somewhat weak provision in article
30 of the Geneva Convention and other circumstantial evidence).[103]

---

[96] The proposal of 1956 Drafting Committee of the ILC concerning the regime of the high seas influenced the drafting of the 1956 Convention (n 87).

[97] Hague Convention Concerning the Laws and Customs of War on Land (adopted 29 July 1899,
entered into force 4 September 1900) (1899) 187 CTS 429.

[98] Hague Convention (IV) Concerning the Laws and Customs of War on Land (n 22).

[99] arts 6, 44, and 52 of the 1899 Hague Convention (n 97), and arts 1, 6, 46, and 52 of the 1907 Hague
Convention (IV) (n 22).

[100] Convention Relative to the Treatment of Prisoners of War (adopted 27 July 1929, entered into force
19 June 1931) 118 LNTS 343; arts 30–1 deal with forced labour from POWs.

[101] This is the meaning of the Declaration of the US State Department in 1941 concerning the Japanese-
Americans interned in the US; CH Rosenberg 'International Law Concerning Accidents to War Prisoners
Employed in Private Enterprises' (1942) 36 American Journal of International Law 294–8 at 298.

[102] art 6 of the Charter of the [Nuremberg] International Military Tribunal (signed and entered into
force 8 August 1945) 82 UNTS 279; see also art 5 of the Charter of the International Military Tribunal for
the Far East (signed and entered into force 19 January 1946) 4 Bevans 20.

[103] The circumstantial evidence were the propositions in which art 3 of the 1922 Treaty of Washington
(n 24) was based.

Later on, the prohibition of slavery and the identification of slavery-related crimes were reaffirmed in subsequent codification and progressive developments on war crimes and crimes against humanity: the four 1949 Geneva Conventions and the two 1977 Protocols;[104] the recognition that no statutory of limitation shall apply to slavery and related crimes;[105] and the ICC Statute.[106] In 1950, the ILC stated that those violations of the laws or customs of war constitute 'war crimes' or 'crimes against humanity'.[107]

Remarkably, in addition to the focus on human rights, the determination of slave-trading and enslaving as (international) crimes adds the perspective of individual criminal responsibility. Therefore the interpretation of the slave trade, slavery, and enslavement may differ from (a human rights) court to (a criminal) court.[108]

4. OTHER CRIMINALS

There is some evidence that, according to international law up to 1945, war criminals and other war-related criminals, and perhaps terrorists (but, surprisingly, not torturers as such), might be defined as criminals.

---

[104] Geneva Convention for the Amelioration of the Condition of the Wounded and Sick in Armed Forces in the Field (signed 12 August 1949, entered into force 21 October 1950) 75 UNTS 31; Geneva Convention for the Amelioration of the Condition of the Wounded, Sick and Shipwrecked Members of Armed Forces at Sea (signed 12 August 1949, entered into force 21 October 1950) 75 UNTS 85; Geneva Convention Relative to the Treatment of Prisoners of War (signed 12 August 1949, entered into force 21 October 1950) 75 UNTS 135; Geneva Convention Relative to the Protection of Civilian Persons in Time of War (signed 12 August 1949, entered into force 21 October 1950) 75 UNTS 287; Protocol Additional to the Geneva Conventions of 12 August 1949, and Relating to the Protection of Victims of International Armed Conflicts (Protocol I) (adopted 8 June 1977, entered into force 7 December 1978) 1125 UNTS 3; and Protocol Additional to the Geneva Conventions of 12 August 1949, and Relating to the Protection of Victims of Non-international Armed Conflicts (Protocol II) (adopted 8 June 1977, entered into force 7 December 1978) 1125 UNTS 609.

[105] Convention on the Non-Applicability of Statutory Limitations to War Crimes and Crimes against Humanity (adopted 26 November 1968, entered into force 11 November 1970) 754 UNTS 73.

[106] arts 7 and 8.

[107] 'Formulation of the Nürnberg Principles' (1950-II) Yearbook of the International Law Commission 374–8.

[108] For example, the ECHR (Judgment of 26 July 2005, *Siliadin v France* (2006) 43 EHRR 16, para 122) and the ICTY (*Prosecutor v Dragoljub Kunarac, Radomir Kovac and Zoran Vukovic (Judgment)* ICTY-96-23-T & ICTY-96-23/1-T (22 February 2001) para 539 and *passim*; and *Prosecutor v Dragoljub Kunarac, Radomir Kovac and Zoran Vukovic (Judgment)* ICTY-96-23-T & ICTY-96-23/1-A (12 June 2002) paras 117–19; also *Prosecutor v Milorad Krnojelac (Judgment)* IT-97-25-T (15 March 2001) at 353 and fns 955–7).

4.1. War Criminals and Other War-related Criminals

The rules defining acceptable behaviour in war are as old as war itself, and the trial of Peter von Hagenbach by an ad hoc tribunal of the Holy Roman Empire in Breisach (Germany), 1474, might be the first 'international' war crime (or crime against humanity) trial.[109] Until recently, municipal laws of war addressed interstate wars (the Lieber Code during the US Civil War being a notable exception). International law followed this pattern when several instruments adopted in Geneva and Hague paved the way to modern war crimes (and crimes against humanity): the 1864 Geneva Convention for the Amelioration of the Condition of the Wounded in Armies in the Field,[110] updated in 1906 and 1929,[111] but never complemented by the permanent international court proposed by Gustave Moynier in 1872;[112] the 1899 and 1907 Hague Conventions, which embodied the 'Martens clause' and the principles of necessity, distinction, and proportionality;[113] and the 1929 Geneva Convention on POWs.[114]

War crimes and war-related crimes against humanity and crimes against peace were not new in 1939–45. The Commission on the Responsibility of the Authors of the War and the Enforcement of Penalties, established in 1919, worked on three legal determinations: the responsibility of Kaiser Wilhelm II and his senior ministers for initiating a war of aggression in Europe; the violations of the laws and customs of war by Germany and its allies; and the prosecution of some Ottoman Empire officials for the deportation and massacre of its Armenian population—which had prompted the Allied governments of France, Great Britain, and Russia to issue on 24 May 1915 a joint declaration denouncing these acts as 'crimes against humanity and civilization'.[115] In a rather enigmatic manner, articles 227 to 330 of the Treaty of Versailles, signed on 28 June 1919,[116] were drawn up for the arrest and trial of German officials defined by the Allied governments as war criminals before an international court or

---

[109] G Schwarzenberger *International Law as Applied By International Courts and Tribunals* (Stevens & Sons London 1968) vol 2 (*The Law Of Armed Conflict*), at 462–6; E Greppi 'The Evolution of Individual Criminal Responsibility under International Law' (1999) 81 International Review of the Red Cross 531–53.

[110] Geneva Convention for the Amelioration of the Treatment of Wounded in the Field (adopted 22 August 1864, entered into force 22 June 1865) (1864) 129 CTS 361.

[111] Convention for the Amelioration of the Condition of the Wounded and Sick in Armies in the Field (entered into force 9 August 1907, no longer in force) 11 LNTS 440; and Convention for the Amelioration of the Condition of the Wounded and Sick in Armies in the Field (entered into force 19 June 1931) 118 LNTS 303.

[112] CK Hall 'The First Proposal for a Permanent International Criminal Court' (1998) 38 International Review of the Red Cross 57–74.

[113] These principles found still expression in art 3 of the ICTY Statute.

[114] Convention Relative to the Treatment of Prisoners of War (n 100).

[115] France, Great Britain and Russia Joint Declaration of 24 May 1915 (Record Group, US National Archives, Papers relating to the Foreign Relations of the US, No 59, 867.4016/67).

[116] Treaty of Peace at Versailles (adopted 28 June 1919, entered into force 10 January 1920) (1919) 225 CTS 188.

Allied domestic courts. The Dutch government never handed over the former Kaiser; and, with Allied acceptance, several German military commanders were—reluctantly—tried from in 1921 by the German Supreme Court ('Leipzig War Crimes Trial').

New developments were to come before the outbreak of Second World War not only in the laws and customs of war (including, it may be recalled again, the circumstantial evidence offered by article 3 of the 1922 Treaty of Washington),[117] but with the prohibition of aggressive war itself: the Preamble to the 1924 Geneva Protocol (not entered in force)[118] had stated that 'a war of aggression constitutes a violation of [the international] solidarity and is an international crime'. On 24 September 1927, the Assembly of the League had declared that 'all wars of aggression are, and shall always be prohibited'. The 1928 'Briand–Kellogg Pact'[119] tried to fill the gap in the LoN Covenant and to translate into law the St Augustine's and St Thomas Aquinas' doctrines on (un)just wars.

Clearly, there was a need to develop law against atrocities, as there was need for a name to qualify the Nazi 'final solution' and other previous massacres (the 'Armenian genocide'). The term 'genocide' was coined in 1944 by Raphaël Lemkin—who advocated for the adoption of UN General Assembly Resolution 96 (I) and the 1948 Convention—and it was employed in the indictment of Hermann Göring and others on 8 October 1945.

The post-Second World War evolution was announced through the 1943 Moscow Declaration, the 1945 Potsdam Declaration and international instruments of surrender or armistices and declarations regarding these instruments, or treaties of peace.[120] Articles 6 (and 1946 Protocol) and 5, respectively, of the Nuremberg[121] and Tokyo[122] Charters empowered the tribunals to try and punish individuals charged with war crimes, crimes against humanity, and crimes against peace. The trials before international courts and victorious powers' domestic courts in their zones of occupation in Germany—the vast majority of prosecutions, under Allied Control Council Law No 10, adopted in Berlin on 20 December 1945[123]—took place, and the general principles

---

[117] See the Treaty of Washington (n 24); also J-M Henckaerts and L Doswald-Beck (eds) *Customary International Humanitarian Law* (CUP Cambridge 2005) vol 1 (*Rules*), rule 151.

[118] Reprinted in 'Protocol for the Pacific Settlement of International Disputes' (1925) 19 American Journal of International Law Supplement: Official Documents 9–17 at 9.

[119] General Treaty for the Renunciation of War or the World Peace Act (signed 27 August 1928, entered into force 24 July 1929) 94 LNTS 57.

[120] All reprinted in (1948) 42 American Journal of International Law Supplement: Official Documents: 'Allied and Associated Powers and Italy: Treaty of Peace' 47–177; 'Treaty of Peace with Roumania' 252–77; 'Treaty of Peace with Hungary' 225–51; 'Treaty of Peace with Bulgaria' 179–202; and 'Treaty of Peace with Finland' 203–23.

[121] Charter of the [Nuremberg] International Military Tribunal (n 102).

[122] Charter of the International Military Tribunal for the Far East (n 102).

[123] Allied Control Council Law No 10: Punishment of Persons Guilty of War Crimes, Crimes Against Peace and Against Humanity (20 December 1945) 3 Official Gazette of the Control Council for Germany (31 January 1946) 50–5.

of international law recognized were affirmed by UN General Assembly's resolution 95 (I)[124] and the ILC.[125]

4.2. Terrorists

Despite the widespread occurrence of terrorist acts since the 19th century, States dealt with terrorism through municipal law; the first attempt to approach it as a discrete subject matter of (criminal) international law was only in the mid-1930s.

Yet the laws and customs of war had prohibited afflicting terror on a civilian population and the Commission on Responsibilities established in 1919 reported that Germany and its allies had planned and executed a 'system of terrorism'.[126] Recently, it has been determined that the acts of violence the primary purpose of which is to spread terror among the civilian population are a war crime.[127]

But it was the LoN which attempted to define and codify terrorism as an international crime following the assassination in Marseille, on 9 October 1934, of King Alexander I of Yugoslavia and French Foreign Affairs Minister, Louis Barthou. Not all States were convinced of the need for, or the utility of, a convention, and the LoN attempt prefigured many of the legal, political, ideological, and rhetorical disputes which would be exacerbated after the Second World War.[128] Noting that 'the rules of international law concerning the repression of terrorist activity are not at present sufficiently precise to guarantee efficiently international cooperation', a resolution adopted by the Council of the LoN in 1934 established an intergovernmental expert Committee for the International Repression of Terrorism. The Committee was mandated by the Council to draft a convention to repress 'conspiracies or crimes committed with a political and terrorist purpose'[129] and later, in a resolution adopted in 1936, the Assembly of the LoN stated that the convention should have 'as its principle objects', amongst others, the prohibition of any form of preparation or execution of terrorist outrages upon the life or liberty of persons taking part in the work of foreign public authorities and services and to punish terrorist outrages which 'have an

---

[124] UNGA Res 95 (I) (11 December 1946) UN Doc A/RES/1/95.

[125] UN ILC 'Principles of International Law Recognized in the Charter of the Nürnberg Tribunal and in the Judgment of the Tribunal, with Commentaries' (1950-II) Yearbook of the International Law Commission 274–8.

[126] 'Commission on the Responsibility of the Authors of the War and on Enforcement of Penalties' (January–April 1920) 14 American Journal of International Law 95–154 at 113.

[127] *Prosecutor v Stanislav Galić (Judgment)* ICTY-98-29-T (5 December 2003) para 70.

[128] B Saul 'The Legal Response of the League of Nations to Terrorism' (2006) 4 Journal of International Criminal Justice 78–102.

[129] Sixth Meeting (Public) of the Eighty-Third Session of the Council (1934) 15 League of Nations Official Journal 1758–60 at 1760.

international character'. Neither Council nor Assembly defined terrorism in their resolutions.

Based on the draft submitted by the Committee, two conventions were adopted at Geneva in 1937:[130] the Convention for the Prevention and Punishment of Terrorism (requiring States to prosecute or extradite international terrorist offences, although it did not exclude the offences from the political offence exception to extradition), and the Convention for the Creation of an International Criminal Court (as an alternative to domestic courts). Although States could become parties to either convention separately, neither of them ever entered into force.

Terrorism would not reappear in international law until the 1970s.[131] It is nowadays still pending a universally accepted definition, seemingly due to a reluctance by some to criminalize (any) political resistance against forcible action which deprives peoples of their right to self-determination and freedom and independence, and by others for fear of impairing the right of asylum and refugee status.

5. CONCLUSION

Legal literature and States have built upon Cicero's legacy on pirates as *hostes humani generis*, extending to other acts the legal consequences attached to them (criminalization and universal jurisdiction): the slave trade or enslavement, war crimes, crimes against peace, crimes against humanity, terrorism, etc. Concepts, persons (diplomats, scholars, activists, etc.), and organizations (both intergovernmental and NGOs), and a quite 'relative normativity' (practices, treaties entered and not entered into force, public and private drafts, resolutions, declarations, etc.) are involved in the assertions of the criminal character of certain acts and the establishment of universal jurisdiction. However, international legal foundations (ranging from principles of humanity, universal morality, justice, to the laws of religion and nature, etc.) posed several questions by 1945 because of the confusion regarding the law-making and law enforcement, the lack of judicial practice, etc., even after the ICRC had managed to convince States to invert Cicero's maxim *silent enim leges inter arma*.

---

[130] Reproduced in LN International Conference Proceedings on the Repression of Terrorism, Geneva (1–16 November 1937) LN Doc C/94/M/47/1938/V (LN Archives Geneva: Council Members Docs) vol 1103, Annex I, at 5 and 19.

[131] There was a soviet tentative to introduce terrorism in the Nuremberg Charter (n 102), and terrorism was incorporated in the 1954 ILC's 'Draft Code of Offences against the Peace and Security of Mankind' (1954-II) Yearbook of the International Law Commission 112–22; later in the draft art 5 of the 'Report of the Preparatory Committee on the Establishment of an International Criminal Court' UN Diplomatic Conference of Plenipotentiaries on the Establishment of an International Criminal Court (Rome 15 June–17 July 1998) (14 April 1998) UN Doc A/CONF.183/2/Add.1.

Piracy, slavery, and other acts or activities which are nowadays considered criminal were not necessarily considered so in other times. The theoretical distinction between piracy and privateering blurred in practice, and the interaction and confusion between municipal laws and the law of nations were commonplace where States' contradictory interests and perceptions of reality met. Hence, to find a clear internationally relevant practice—in the absence of an international treaty—turned out anything but easy.

There have been a number of 'positive' international data endorsing the prohibition of the slave trade and enslavement or the laws and customs of war. Yet it is difficult—if not impossible—to find judicial practice before 1945. Curiously, the resort to the 'piracy analogy' and the clause 'as if for an act of piracy' gives rise to two remarks. First, being included in international treaties, those provisions are some of the clearest and more explicit (although indirect) historical recognition by States of piracy as an international crime subject to universal jurisdiction. Second, prohibiting acts did not always mean criminalizing them, extending States' jurisdiction, and punishing perpetrators. The 'piracy analogy' proved the willingness of States to accept (regarding violations of laws and customs of war at sea) or to reject (regarding slave-trade at sea, as concerned the right to seize) subjecting the suppression of these acts to universal jurisdiction.

Whether one adheres to a 'positivist' or a 'naturalist' understanding of international law conditions the determinations concerning the existence and definition of an international crime, and the title or basis of State's jurisdiction to prosecute and punish criminals; namely, bearing in mind a necessary balance between substantive justice and legality. No less important than determination on the matter, mainly from a historical perspective, is the 'critical date' from when one may assert that there has been an international crime, and eventually a crime subject to universal jurisdiction. Regarding the law of piracy, it has been said that

[a]s a practical matter…a competent lawyer can construct a model of reality using legal words that will seem to justify whatever a statesmen thinks is in the political interest of his state. But under 'naturalist' theory, that justification is merely an argument with which others, believing themselves more attune to the eternal rules of morality and 'true law', can disagree. Under 'positivist' theory, no state has the legal power to determine rules of international law, but only the power to interpret those rules for itself and try to convince others that that interpretation is correct.…The arguments among lawyers and policy-makers about these matters are endless…[but] the 'victory' for the most articulate naturalist model builders resulted in a meaningless codification of no law.[132]

International law provided arguments and legal foundations to address the repression of pirates, slavers, and other criminals before 1945, yet law-enforcement practice also offered arguments to prevent their criminal prosecution on a universal jurisdiction basis. Law as usual.

---

[132] *The Law of Piracy* (n 1) 310–11.

Recommended Reading

Allain, Jean *The Slavery Conventions. The* Travaux Préparatoires *of the 1926 League of Nations Convention and the 1956 United Nations Convention* (Martinus Nijhoff Publishers Leiden 2008).

Azcárraga y Bustamante, José Luis de *El corso marítimo* (CSIC Instituto 'Francisco de Vitoria' Madrid 1950).

Bush, Jonathan A '"The Supreme…Crime" and Its Origins: The Lost Legislative History of the Crime of Aggressive War' (2002) 102 Columbia Law Review 2324–69.

Dubner, Barry H *The Law of International Sea Piracy* (Martinus Nijhoff Publishers The Hague 1980).

Graven, Jean 'Le crimes contre l'humanité' (1950) 76 Recueil des cours 427–608.

Greppi, Edoardo 'The Evolution of Individual Criminal Responsibility under International Law' (1999) 81 International Review of the Red Cross 531–3.

Piggott, Francis Taylor *The Declaration of Paris 1856: A Study* (University of London Press London 1919).

Rubin, Alfred P *The Law of Piracy* (2nd edn Transnational Publishers Irvington-on-Hudson NY 1998).

Schwelb, Egon 'Crimes Against Humanity' (1946) 23 British Yearbook of International Law 178–226.

Sottile, Antoine 'Le terrorisme international' (1938) 65 Recueil des cours 87–184.

Vabres, H Donnedieu de 'La répression internationale du terrorisme: Les Conventions de Genève (16 novembre 1937)' (1938) 62 Revue de droit international et législation comparée 37–74.

CHAPTER 6

....

INTERNATIONAL ARBITRATION AND COURTS

....

CORNELIS G ROELOFSEN

1. INTRODUCTION

....

THE title of this chapter promises an account of the role of arbitration and adjudication in international relations. That is indeed what the reader will find here but it is fair to add a warning that this is not a straightforward tale, such as is to be found in Jan HW Verzijl's and Wilhelm G Grewe's grand histories.[1] Verzijl rather stresses continuity as does Karl-Heinz Ziegler. They present arbitration/adjudication as an institution linking medieval, early modern, and modern/contemporary times. This is often done in popular presentations of the subject too. Grewe, on the other hand, rejects continuity between antiquity, Middle Ages, and the modern period (19th and 20th centuries) in rather absolute terms. I will take another position, maintaining a greater degree of continuity than Grewe admits. However, there are important discontinuities, and concepts no doubt have been changing.[2] To clarify my position,

---

[1] WG Grewe *The Epochs of International Law* (M Byers trans) (De Gruyter Berlin 2000) at 104; JHW Verzijl *International Law in Historical Perspective* (12 vols Sijthoff Leiden 1968–98); K-H Ziegler *Völkerrechtsgeschichte* (2nd edn CH Beck München 1994).

[2] H Steiger 'Probleme der Völkerrechtsgeschichte' (1987) 26 Der Staat: Zeitschrift für Staatslehre, öffentliches Recht und Verfassungsgeschichte 103–26.

I will use two examples from doctrine and state practice, both taken from the period before the First World War. I begin with the German/Swiss publicist Otfried Nippold, the author of a book on the prospects of arbitration, published at the eve of the second Hague Peace Conference.[3]

Nippold (1864–1938), the son of a Swiss theologian established in Germany, made his academic career in Germany as an expert in international law. He was a prominent member of this emerging profession, *inter alia* serving as advisor to the Japanese government (1889–92). Nippold may be considered a typical member of what Jenks has called 'the earlier generation...whose thinking largely guided...the master craftsmen who drafted the Statute of 1920'.[4] He concentrated his argument on what he correctly considered would become a major issue at The Hague: obligatory arbitration of international disputes. This had been emphatically rejected by Germany at the first Hague Conference, but the question would certainly arise again. The discussion in German official and academic circles was mainly concerned with the alleged infraction of German sovereignty that would result from the restriction of German freedom of action in future disputes.

Nippold would have none of this. Quoting traditional views on absolute state sovereignty, in his opinion mistaken and misleading, he contrasted these with the 19th-century growth of international cooperation. This had led to the development of 'new areas of public international law, which are quite independent of politics, or could be, because in themselves they have nothing to do with politics'.[5] In proof he pointed to the general progress of arbitration in state practice in the past years, which admittedly contrasted with German restraint in concluding bilateral arbitration agreements.[6] German colleagues like Philipp Zorn and Heinrich Triepel who feared the erosion of German sovereignty misunderstood the character of public international law. To quote Nippold,

[t]he subjection to an arbitral court absolutely depends on the free will of states. This is of course also the case as regards so-called obligatory arbitration....Subjection to the arbitral court always rests, even if it has a quite general character, on the *sovereign* will of the contracting partners; it is in all circumstances the result of this sovereign will and as such can never be considered a contradiction to state sovereignty.[7]

The argument harmonizes with Nippold's reference to the age-old principles of arbitration, 'whose efficiency has been indicated by their historical origins'.[8] The logical development of these principles, viz the step from voluntary to mandatory

---

[3] O Nippold *Die Fortbildung des Verfahrens in völkerrechtlichen Streitigkeiten* (Duncker und Humblot Leipzig 1907).

[4] CW Jenks *The Prospects of International Adjudication* (Stevens and Sons London 1964) at 2.

[5] Fortbildung des Verfahrens (n 3) 31.

[6] ibid 274 fn 55.

[7] ibid 246 (my translation).

[8] ibid 152 'Das beweist schon das Alter dieser Institute, schon ihr historisches Werden deutet auf ihre prinzipielle Zweckmässigkeit hin.'

arbitration, could not have caused serious objections to a government in step with the present time. This important question should not be treated as a hobby-horse by politicians, as the German delegation did in 1899.[9]

These quotations offer an insight into Nippold's mind. They are also selective. In their context, they are part of an elaborate argument, mainly consisting of a description of state practice, quotes from contemporary authors, particularly German colleagues, and resolutions of representative institutions like the *Institut de Droit International* and the Inter-Parliamentary Union.[10] Nippold's book was obviously addressed to an academic public. Clearly, it was an attempt to convince his German colleagues to join him in his criticism of the German Empire's opposition to international cooperation. But he stressed also that he did not wish to 'abandon the firm base of healthy national realist policy'. He merely wanted 'to overcome the present unhealthy political situation, viz the incompleteness of public international law'.[11] At the second Hague Peace Conference the logical follow-up to the 1899 conference would be a treaty founding an 'arbitration union'. The states parties would accept the general obligation to submit disputes to arbitration, according to a procedure established by the convention. An international secretariat should be established to oversee procedure. The obligation to arbitrate disputes would be subject to the traditional reservation of 'the honour and essential interests of states'.[12] Even if Nippold expressed hopes for a further extension of the field of arbitration, his suggestions appear thoroughly 'realistic' and offer an interesting prediction of what was going to happen at The Hague. He is studiously moderate. But this should not deceive us. Time and again he demonstrated the unrealistic background to his propositions. At the very end of the book, he exclaimed: '[i]f European politicians do not themselves arrive at the conviction that more intensive international cooperation is necessary, Asian and American states will teach them!'[13]

His later career is also highly instructive. The great public was to know him particularly for his castigation in 1913 of the German press's warmongering. After the outbreak of the war, he left Germany and established himself in Switzerland to become a well-known critic of German policy and of Germany's conduct of the war.[14]

We may conclude, then, that to Nippold, the step towards at least a token universal system of adjudication of disputes had a high symbolic effect. Even if he did not overrate its immediate practical value, it would be an important signal in the

---

[9] ibid 253 and note 'blosse Prinzipienreiterei'.

[10] A periodic meeting of members of European parliaments. A Eyffinger *The 1899 Hague Peace Conference* (Kluwer Law International The Hague 1999) at 366.

[11] Fortbildung des Verfahrens (n 3) 607.

[12] ibid.

[13] ibid 606.

[14] O Nippold *The Awakening of the German People* (A Gray trans) (George Allen and Unwin London 1918) and O Nippold *Le chauvinisme allemand* (Payot and Cie Paris 1921) (translation of the German editions 1913 and 1917); see also O Nippold *The Development of International Law after the World War* (AS Hershey trans) (Clarendon Press Oxford 1923).

progress of public international law and a victory over 'old politics'. Interestingly, a dyed-in-the-wool conservative like Karl von Stengel, a member of the German delegation to the First Hague Peace Conference, in 1909 still maintained as a question of principle his opposition to compulsory arbitration even though the German government in 1907 had agreed to a compromise.[15] But Stengel was exceptional. Nippold's belief in the progressive development of international adjudication was far more representative. 'Belief' is a term we use deliberately. To Nippold, as we have seen, it was an article of faith that the march of progress of international law would go on, not to be stopped by the frivolous actions of politicians. International law, notably international adjudication, was to be if not the main instrument, at least an important one in creating—in the long term—a peaceful and just international order. In the 19th and 20th centuries, such views exercised a great influence on the writing of the history of international law, a subject that acquired a certain vogue from the 1850s on. François Laurent's massive *History of International Law and International Relations* was extreme in its frankly avowed ideological position of tracing the progress of humanity to the influence of liberalism and Protestantism, but the idea of looking at history for progress and continuity was fairly common.[16] The age-old institution of arbitration having its sources in antiquity had passed the test of history and carried great promise for the future.[17] This explains the particular attention to arbitration in historical legal research. The overriding purpose here was to prove the continuity of arbitration throughout European history. This discourse of progress and development is still very much with us.[18] The 19th–20th century surge of international adjudication particularly lent itself to this, as we have seen in Nippold. However, at the same time another attitude towards international law and its functions was demonstrated, not as a rule to the general public but highly influential all the same. This discourse that we may call pragmatic, indeed, at times sceptical, is to be found among practising lawyers and their political masters.

For a case in point we will turn to the German–Dutch dispute of 1912–14 regarding the sovereignty over the Ems. It allows us to meet with that great pragmatist Tobias MC Asser, at that time the dominating, indeed domineering, legal adviser to the Dutch Minister of Foreign Affairs.[19] We have first to deal with the rather

---

[15] M Koskenniemi *The Gentle Civilizer of Nations: The Rise and Fall of International Law 1870–1960* (CUP Cambridge 2001) at 211.

[16] F Laurent *Histoire du droit des gens et des relations internationales* (Lacroix Verboeckhoven et Cie Brussels 1861/62).

[17] Compare n 8.

[18] T Skouteris *The Notion of Progress in International Law Discourse* (TMC Asser Press The Hague 2010) at 2.

[19] A Eyffinger *T.M.C. Asser [1838–1913] Founder of the Hague Tradition* (TMC Asser Press The Hague 2011); also CCA Voskuil 'Tobias Michael Carel Asser—1838–1913' in CCA Voskuil et al (eds) *The Moulding of International Law: Ten Dutch Proponents* (TMC Asser Instituut 1995) 1–25. Asser was the Nobel Prize Laureate of 1911 (shared with the Austrian Alfred Fried).

complicated case. In 1912, the German government made a deliberate attempt to solve a historical dispute that had been pending for some three centuries: the questioned sovereignty over the tidal mouth of the Ems River. The Dutch favoured a *thalweg* frontier that would have given them about half the river. The German Reich as successor to the historical rights assumed by the counts of Eastern Frisia claimed the whole of the stream except a tiny strip of water along the Dutch coast. In 1912, Germany had a particular reason to want a quick solution to this legal conflict. In wartime, the Germans planned to close the mouth of the Ems by a mine barrage against enemy attacks. The Dutch pretensions to the Western half of the Ems would complicate this, since the Dutch, as presumable neutrals in a forthcoming armed conflict, could not assist Germany in the closure of the Ems. The Dutch government was very much alive to the complications that the territorial dispute might cause to their position and would at that time gladly have recognized the German claims to the whole of the Ems. However, an outright cession to Germany was out of the question since the North Sea Convention of 1908, to which all States bordering on the North Sea were parties, guaranteed the territorial status quo. Britain, for instance, could have accused the Netherlands of breaching their policy of impartiality between the Great Powers and their obligations under the North Sea Convention if the Dutch were considered voluntarily to have changed the status of the Western Ems.[20] The Germans thought they had found a way out of this quandary. An impressive historical and legal memorandum was handed over by the German special envoy Johannes Kriege.[21] If the Dutch government was not only convinced of the indisputable strength of the German case but also could be persuaded that they could represent to Parliament their acquiescence in the German claim as inevitable, Germany and the Netherlands would together have solved what the Germans considered 'a common problem', not really a dispute between the two countries. We have to add here that Germany was prepared to guarantee the free navigation of the Ems to Dutch shipping. Indeed, for practical purposes the situation would be unchanged in peacetime. Officials of the Dutch Foreign Office were much impressed by the Kriege memorandum. The Dutch government was indeed ready to yield to the German arguments, but considered that it could only do so if Dutch experts agreed with the German position.

Consequently, on 7 July 1912 the Dutch Minister of Foreign Affairs discussed the situation in two separate conversations with the head of the National Record Office,

---

[20] C Smit (ed) *Bescheiden betreffende de Buitenlandse Politiek van Nederland 1907–1914* (Documents concerning Dutch Foreign Policy 1907–1914) (Dutch Department of Education The Hague 1963). Accounts of the discussions between Dutch officials and the Dutch ministers of Foreign officers and of the Dutch–German negotiations under 'Eems'.

[21] A member of the German delegation to the second Hague Peace Conference. A *bête noire* of Nippold.

Robert Fruin, and the legal adviser to the minister, Tobias MC Asser. Both had read the German memorandum and taken note of the government's point of view. We have only the lapidary notes of minister René de Marees van Swinderen, not the brightest of Dutch diplomats, to reconstruct the conversations of the experts with the minister. To Asser, the overriding consideration was apparently the serious risk to Dutch neutrality in a European conflict. The embarrassing Dutch territorial title to the Western Ems rested on a highly arguable interpretation of the legal position in the 16th century and subsequent practice. Even if the German title was debatable as well, it could be considered the stronger one. In an aside Asser had already a month earlier remarked to Swinderen '[i]f it comes to an arbitration we will lose'. But in the July conversation he was to shock the minister by his answer to Swinderen's question about the legal position. As Swinderen recorded, Asser answered: '[o]h come, you can fashion International Law as you wish'. Swinderen added a few exclamation marks. Clearly, it was not what he had expected as the spontaneous reaction from a Nobel Prize winner. He failed to appreciate that Asser took political expediency into account in the interpretation of the legal situation. In view of the ambiguity of the historical titles involved and the considerable interests at stake, he was ready to present a—sustainable—legal interpretation in accordance with the government's wishes. Fruin took another position: this highly respected legal historian refuted the German memorandum and maintained Dutch rights to sovereignty over the Western Ems. He declared that he must excuse himself from giving another opinion for expediency's sake. This changed the situation. Asser conceded that the government could not credibly accept the German position in the face of Fruin's expert opinion. Even if the Dutch legal position in the opinion of a commission of experts installed after Assser's demise in 1913 was weaker than that of Germany, it was not that weak as to be unsustainable. The Dutch government could not compromise itself by a unilateral concession to Germany. There was a stalemate. In the final stage of negotiations, a new Dutch government in 1914 suggested arbitration by a neutral expert. This was clearly intended as a practical way out of a diplomatic impasse. Third states parties to the North Sea Convention would have to respect the verdict of an independent arbitrator. The Dutch Parliament, very much in favour of international arbitration, would approve of this solution to the German and Dutch conflict as setting an example to the world at large. The Germans, however, hesitated before the risk that an independent arbitrator might reject the German claim. After they finally agreed to invite a Norwegian international lawyer, the First World War intervened. The Ems question dragged on until the 1963 Dutch–German territorial treaty. Even though to all intents and purposes this introduced a final division of the Wester Ems between the two countries, the abstract question of the sovereign title to the contested territory was left pending.

The affair illustrates the predicament inherent in the position of a legal adviser. It is his task to find legal arguments for a policy that may be debatable in legal terms, and/or at odds with previous obligations.[22] Adjudication here appears simply as an instrument of diplomacy. But the suggestion of arbitration had interesting repercussions. The Dutch in fact turned the tables on the Germans, who did not like the thought of a truly independent arbitrator and tried in vain to fix the outcome beforehand. The story gives the lie to the optimistic, high-minded discourse of the progress of arbitration at the epoch of the Hague Peace Conferences.

These two tales may stand for the two strands in this chapter. I will attempt to deal with high-minded theory and public statements of governments as well as with the pedestrian tale of international adjudication as considered, practised, and developed by lawyers and diplomats. I do not pretend to be exhaustive in my treatment, however. I will adhere to the more or less agreed epochs adopted in European general history, a personal choice, at variance with Grewe and Ziegler. It seems to me that this serves best the combination of theory and practice.

2. Late Middle Ages and the Early Modern Period (15th and 16th Centuries)

2.1. The Popularity of Arbitration and the Quasi-international Functions of Courts

'Arbitration' means the submission of a dispute to 'the decision of a person (or persons), other than a court of competent jurisdiction'. 'Adjudication' is 'the judgment or decision of a court'.[23] Referring to these elementary definitions, after I have used the two terms somewhat loosely in the introduction, we find ourselves in the middle of one of the major problems that I will deal with here. In the epoch now under consideration it is an anachronism to start from the modern dichotomy of 'national jurisdiction' as opposed to 'international arbitration and adjudication'. Medieval Christendom, the *respublica Christiana*, was still very much alive as a legal unit in the 15th century. Western and Central Europe recognized the common Roman Catholic faith and the authority of the Roman Catholic Church. They also shared the Roman

---

[22] A Carty and RA Smith *Sir Gerald Fitzmaurice and the World Crisis: A Legal Adviser in the Foreign Office 1932–1945* (Kluwer Law International The Hague 2000).

[23] DM Walker *The Oxford Companion to Law* (Clarendon Press Oxford 1980) at 24 and 73.

legal heritage, accepting the *ius commune* as the overarching common legal system.[24] Political subdivisions were not fault-lines within the legal continuum of Christendom. On the other hand, under these overarching recognized formal and general structures there was a bewildering variety of jurisdictions and local custom. Local rulers and distant overlords, enjoyed a de facto independence, as did many towns and a number of rural communities. They had the right to wage war, or to engage in feuds, which might be serious armed conflicts or degenerate in what later generations would consider 'legalized' local robbery. In summary, a bewildering variety of situations could and did lead to arbitration, confusingly often including, according to our sources, mediation, interposition, and amicable composition. Many a medieval (or early modern) 'arbitration' should in modern terms have been called a mediation.[25] We cannot cling to 'adjudication' as the definition of the normal function of a court exercising its regular competence. The situation is complicated by the creation of supreme courts, such as the Parliament of Paris (1345), the Burgundian Grand Council at Mechlin (1473), the Imperial Chamber (1495). Lords protesting their right to exercise sovereign justice had gradually been forced to recognize the jurisdiction of these courts.[26] In conflicts between subjects which had before been solved by arbiters of their own choice, they were now urged to accept judgment by the royal court. Often, honour was saved on all sides by presenting subjection to the court as a non-prejudicial submission to arbitration. Between German territorial rulers, imperial decrees established, or rather confirmed, a system of arbitral dispute settlement capped by the right of appeal to the Imperial Chamber.[27] In the Swiss and Hanseatic confederations, arbitration was a political instrument to reinforce the cohesion of the members of these confederated organizations. Arbitration clauses, establishing the obligation to subject future disputes to arbitration, were common in such contexts.

Arbitration then in the late Middle Ages was quite popular, though its incidence was regionally diverse. For various reasons it was not as prominent in the 16th century. The cause was no doubt the rise of monarchical authority in Western Europe as manifested *inter alia* by the increasing role of state organs and the establishment of territorial jurisdiction by the royal courts. The decline was, however, not as steep and radical as Grewe suggests.[28] That much of late medieval arbitration might be rather called 'quasi-international' than 'international' should be stressed. Of course this is hardly surprising. Procrustean attempts like Verzijl's of putting medieval arbitration into the frame of modern categorization provide us with a useful warning against a

---

[24] F Wieacker *Privatrechtsgeschichte der Neuzeit* (Van den Hoeck und Rupprecht Göttingen 1967).

[25] The distinction was of course well known to medieval lawyers. Practice was, however, confused. *The Epochs of International Law* (n 1) 100.

[26] JH Shennan *The Parlement of Paris* (2nd edn Sutton Publishing Ltd Thrupp 1998) at 78.

[27] *International Law in Historical Perspective* (n 1) vol 2, 277–80.

[28] *The Epochs of International Law* (n 1) 104.

forced quest for modern analogies.[29] For instance, the custom of having peace treaties guaranteed by third parties, notably high nobles of the realm and the parties' allies, smacks of constitutional and international guaranties. Such agreements did indeed at times lead to legal procedures. However, we should rather look at them in the context of war being waged as a feud undertaken by the king with his lieges and allies as 'feud-helpers'. These people were personally involved in the conflict and had a personal interest in the upholding of the peace. Nussbaum's curt dismissal of medieval patterns of thought and practice as 'barriers to international law' represent the other extreme.[30] I can do no more than touch briefly on this discussion.[31] An analysis of the influence of Spanish scholastic doctrine upon the idea of arbitration would carry us too far from our subject.

2.2. Two Substantive Regimes: The Law of Arms and Prize Law—The Persistent Ideal of the European Arbiter

What we may call the medieval and early modern inheritance of modern international law, in particular as regards arbitration and adjudication, is important both in substance and in ideological terms. I begin by discussing the law of arms, the medieval technical term for the modern law of war, at least in its *ius in bello* aspect, regarding conduct permitted in wartime. This was a generally recognized regime within Christendom. It rested on custom, but also to a certain extent on canon law, the law of the church, enforced by ecclesiastical courts throughout Europe, and traditionally also upon the Code of Chivalry, binding knights to standards of conduct. Conventions between belligerents, the so-called cartels, apparently did not play a significant role. We find the law of arms administered by the ordinary courts. Notably, the Parliament of Paris recognized the claims of English captors for ransoms due to them by their French captives.[32] An exceptional 15th-century criminal case is the condemnation to death of the knight Peter Hagenbach for alleged violations of the Code of Chivalry in the service of Charles the Bold, Duke of Burgundy. The ad hoc tribunal was composed of delegates from the victors and hardly offered an impartial forum.[33] All the same, the verdict has been considered a significant prec-

---

[29] *International Law in Historical Perspective* (n 1) vol 8.

[30] A Nussbaum *A Concise History of the Law of Nations* (The Macmillan Company New York 1954) at 17.

[31] 'Probleme der Völkerrechtsgeschichte' (n 2) 105.

[32] MH Keen *The Laws of War in the Late Middle Ages* (Routledge and Kegan Paul London 1965); P-C Timbal *La guerre de cent ans vue à travers les registres du parlement (1337–1369)* (Centre national de la recherche scientifique Paris 1961) at 349.

[33] G Schwarzenberger 'Breisach Revisited. The Hagenbach Trial of 1474' in CH Alexandrowicz (ed) *Grotian Society Papers, 1968: Studies in the History of the Law of Nations* (Martinus Nijhoff The Hague 1968) 46–51.

edent for the Nuremberg Trials since the court at Breisach rejected the defence of superior orders.

In contrast to the law of arms, prize law had a rather firm conventional base. Maritime commerce had of necessity been a subject of treaties between European powers and indeed of Muslim-Christian capitulations as well. Piracy, the status of neutral shipping, and neutral merchandise at sea during an armed conflict, and redress for injuries were subjects that simply had to be dealt with. Clauses in maritime treaties soon acquired a standard character, slowly evolving as they were renewed time and again.[34] Prize law also generated an impressive amount of jurisprudence. Both specialized admiralty jurisdictions and courts of appeal like the Parliament of Paris and the Burgundian Grand Council dealt with prize cases. Here one can find a body of international law specialists, a prime example being offered by Alberico Gentili's (1552–1608) career at the English Admiralty Court.[35] Western European Prize Courts resembled each other. They followed a Roman law procedure. Substantive rules were much alike, but showed some significant differences for example as regards the enemy provenance of goods. Even though advocates sometimes invoked a general 'maritime law', admiralty courts were of course national courts, administering the law of the land. Admiralty judges were bound by domestic legislation, such as the French maritime ordinances. In practice, their attitude might depend on political considerations. Local interests often were much in evidence as well.

In such a situation it comes as no surprise that some attempts were made to have disputes settled by cooperation between the states parties. But this hardly amounted to a joint legal procedure. Political pressure under threat of reprisals for revision of lower courts' verdicts was common and at times successful. We may detect here a semi-internationalized procedure in which legal arguments played a significant role. Jurisdiction, however, remained with the state responsible for the capture.[36] The age of effective mixed commissions was yet to come.

Last but not least, we have to deal here with an important element in the ideological prestige of arbitration: the conception of a 'European arbiter', a hegemonic ruler imposing peace in Christendom. This role in the high Middle Ages had been

---

[34] A prime example is offered by the Anglo-Flemish treaties of intercourse concluding with the *Magnus Intercursus* of 1496. International Law in Historical Perspective (n 1) vol 11 offers an impressive collection of materials. Cf DJ Bederman 'The Feigned Demise of Prize' (1995) 9 Emory International Law Review 31–69.

[35] See the contribution by M Scattola 'Alberico Gentili (1552–1608)' in this volume.

[36] A Dumas *Étude sur le jugement des prises maritimes en France jusqu'à la suppression de l'office d'Amiral (1627)* (Émile Larose Paris 1908); KES Roscoe *A History of the English Prize Court* (Lloyd's London 1924); KH Böhringer *Das Recht der Prise gegen Neutrale in der Praxis des Spätmittelalters dargestellt anhand Hansischer Urkunden* (thesis Frankfurt 1970); CG Roelofsen *Studies in the History of International Law, Practice and Doctrine in Particular with Regard to the Law of Naval Warfare in the Low Countries from circa 1450 until the Early 17th Century* (thesis Utrecht 1991).

claimed by the papacy. In the 15th century, in spite of the decline of the power of the church, it was still at times effectively exercised. A triumph of ecclesiastical diplomacy is no doubt its role at the Congress of Arras (1435). The two cardinals respectively representing Pope Eugenius IV and the Council of Basle acted as mediators in the Franco-Burgundian negotiations but assumed the position of judges when the treaty had been concluded. They rendered a verdict, declaring the prior Anglo-Burgundian alliance null and void and imposing ecclesiastical sanctions on the Duke of Burgundy and the French King if they violated their agreement. In the words of Dickinson: 'the cardinals ceased to be mediators,... they became judges pronouncing sentence'.[37] The papacy having lost much of its prestige, both Charles V and Francis I competed in the 16th century for the role of 'Arbiter of Europe'. As Kampmann described, the ideal of the *arbitre de paix*, prominently present in Bodin, remained an important theme in European public discussion throughout the 17th century. Arguably, it was in the 16th century that arbitration as a mechanism for the guarantee of peace entered the European agenda.[38] Grotius quoting Saint Louis in the appendix to his famous book alluded to a tradition.[39]

3. EARLY MODERN PERIOD AND 18TH CENTURY (1600–1815)

3.1. 17th Century: The Age of Diplomacy—Continuity and Change

The generally accepted view considers the 17th century as the period of the waning of arbitration. In the 18th-century arbitration and adjudication are said to have totally disappeared, only to re-emerge with the Jay Treaty arbitrations of 1794.[40] In our opinion Lingens convincingly attacked this *idée fixe*. However, as he remarked, only a number of studies of regional practice can give us a more definite view of the

---

[37] JG Dickinson *The Congress of Arras 1435* (Clarendon Press Oxford 1955) at 174.

[38] C Kampmann *Arbiter und Friedensstiftung: Die Auseinandersetzung um den politischen Schiedsrichter im Europa der Frühen Neuzeit* (Ferdinand Schöningh Paderborn 2001).

[39] H Grotius 'De iure belli ac pacis libri tres' (1625) in JB Scott (ed) *The Classics of International Law* (Clarendon Press Oxford 1913–25).

[40] Treaty of Amity, Commerce and Navigation between Great Britain and the United States (signed 19 November 1794) (1793–95) 52 CTS 243 ('Jay Treaty').

importance of arbitration and adjudication in this period.[41] A general acquaintance with the diplomatic history of this epoch and some special interest in certain aspects of international relations will have to serve us here. The striking change is the intense development of diplomacy. The European state system became more closely knit. Diplomats had a rich toolbox at their disposal. It contained *inter alia* mediation, decision by a mixed commission, decision by a court, and the arbitration clause sometimes provided with a deadline leading to arbitration or mediation coupled with arbitration. Negotiators were expected to be fertile in their suggestion of expedients.[42] Supplementing Lingens' and Verzijl's catalogues of cases I will here offer a few illustrations.

In 1609, a case arose between the Dutch Republic and the Duke of Pomerania, putting in a claim on behalf of his subjects, merchants of Stettin. They had in 1606 freighted a ship destined for Spain. The ship and its cargo had been taken by a privateer commissioned by the admiralty at Amsterdam, a Dutch state organ. This privateer turned pirate, and the Pomeranian merchants who could obtain no redress of grievances at the Amsterdam Admiralty Board found their ruler readily disposed to take up their case. In his letter to the States General, the Duke of Pomerania hinted at the possibility of reprisals if his subjects were denied justice in the Netherlands, Dutch shipping in Pomeranian harbours offering an easy target for arrest.[43] The situation is typical of numerous international disputes about the application of the law of prize which turned upon issues of state responsibility. Characteristic of German practice at the time was the Duke's suggestion to have the case decided by an 'impartial law faculty'. The States' General reply was more innovative. Instead of upholding exclusive admiralty jurisdiction, they proposed to have the dispute adjudicated by the Supreme Court of Holland and Zealand. This tribunal, the court of final appeal in the two maritime provinces, decided in favour of the defendant in 1617. The case has an added interest, because the plea formally presented by the Advocat Fiscal of the admiralty was in fact produced by Grotius.[44]

Should we call the case an instance of international adjudication? That would seem appropriate. Even if the applicants, the Pomeranian merchants, were obviously private persons, they appeared before the tribunal at the direction of the Duke. The defendant, the Amsterdam admiralty, acted on behalf of the States General who had assumed responsibility. The Supreme Court would have lacked jurisdiction if it had

---

[41] KH Lingens *Internationale Schiedsgerichtbarkeit und Jus publicum europaeum 1648–1794* (Duncker and Humblot Berlin 1988) at 21.

[42] MS Anderson *The Rise of Modern Diplomacy* (Longman London 1993); L Bély *Espions et ambassadeurs au temps de Louis XIV* (Fayard Paris 1990).

[43] CG Roelofsen 'State Responsibility and Jurisdiction: Grotius and an Early 17th Century Case' in TD Gill and WP Heere (eds) *Reflections on Principles and Practice of International Law: Essays in honour of LJ Bouchez* (Marinus Nijhoff The Hague 2000) 175–89.

[44] J Naeranus (ed) *Hollandse Consultatiën* (Rotterdam 1664) at 1–8. I thank Robert Feenstra (Leiden University) for this correction of my original text.

not been for the parties' submission. In fact, the informal agreement between two sovereign entities, the Dutch Republic and the Duke of Pomerania, may be considered a compromise, laying the base of the proceedings. That the case was indeed one of international law was stressed in the admiralty's plea. It was not, as the defendant argued, a matter of liability in Dutch law, to be argued in terms of the *ius civile*, but a case of maritime prize law to be decided according to *ius gentium*, international law, as demonstrated by precedents in Dutch and French practice. This issue—the European *ius commune* against emerging international law—was familiar in prize cases.[45] Since the affair was briefly resumed in Grotius' *De iure belli ac pacis*, it played some role as a precedent, case law becoming of increasing importance in the creation of international law.

Grotius' best-known legal work, *Mare liberum* deserves to be quoted here as well. This booklet, published in April 1609 at the end of The Hague Peace Congress of 1608–9 largely comprises chapter 12 of a manuscript composed by Grotius in 1602–6, *De jure praedae commentarius*.[46] For the 1609 publication he added a foreword consisting of a rousing vindication of the Dutch right to navigation to the East Indies against the Portuguese assumed monopoly. On this issue the arbitration of the 'Rulers and the Free Nations of the World' was invoked.[47] Such a rhetorical exercise, deliberately adopted by Grotius, only made sense if he considered arbitration to enjoy a certain popularity with the informed European public he was addressing. Happily, he ignored that at least the head of French delegation in March 1608 had been considering a joint Anglo-French 'mediation', to be accepted by both Spain and the Dutch Republic, as a means of imposing on the Dutch the surrender of the East Indies trade.[48] Things had however gone in a different direction, and the two kings found themselves in 1609 guaranteeing the Spanish-Dutch Twelve Years Truce and the right of the Dutch to trade with the Indies. Continuing our selection of Dutch precedents, at the Münster Peace Treaty of 1648 Spain and the Dutch republic agreed on the creation of a mixed tribunal, the so-called *chambre mi-partie*.[49] This was an arbitral tribunal equally divided between the two parties. Its tasks, procedure, and competence were carefully laid down in the peace treaty and subsequent treaties. They were among others to control the execution of the commercial clauses of the treaty and in general to ensure its observation.

[45] A Wijffels *Consilium facultatis juridicae tubingensis* (Ius Deco Publications Leiden 1993).

[46] MJ van Ittersum (ed) *Commentary on the Law of Prize and Booty* (Liberty Fund Indianapolis 2006).

[47] H Grotius *Mare Liberum 1609–2009* (R Feenstra ed) (Brill Leiden 2009) at 21; H Grotius *The Free Sea* (D Armitage ed, R Hakluyt trans) (Liberty Fund Indianapolis 2004) at 8.

[48] MJ van Ittersum 'Preparing *Mare liberum* for the Press: Hugo Grotius' Rewriting of Chapter 12 of *De iure praedae* in November–December 1608' (2007) 26 Grotiana 246–80; MJ van Ittersum *Profit and Principle: Hugo Grotius, Natural Rights Theories and the Rise of Dutch Power in the East Indies 1595–1615* (Brill Leiden 2006) at 246; P Jeannin *Les négociations de Monsieur le Président Jeannin* (André de Hoogenhuysen Amsterdam 1695) vol 2, at 147.

[49] The Peace of Münster: Treaty of Peace between Spain and the Netherlands (signed 30 January 1648) (1648) 1 CTS 1 art III.

The numerous territorial disputes left pending in 1648, though on principle included in its jurisdiction, were at the initiative of the Dutch solved bilaterally between the parties. This considerably reduced the scope of the *chambre*'s jurisdiction. The Dutch indeed seem soon to have lost interest in the institution. It did not correspond to the new important issues in Dutch foreign policy, notably Anglo-Dutch maritime rivalry and the threat of French domination. The *chambre* functioned from 1653 until about 1675. A number of judgments were passed, long believed to have been lost but recovered some twenty-five years ago.[50] The institution seems to have faded away after a not too notable existence.

A far more lasting impression was made by the Anglo-Dutch peace of 1674 and its separate maritime treaty. This laid down the rules of prize law between the parties as well as establishing the right to appeal in prize jurisdiction. Since the appellate bodies functioned at The Hague and London respectively, diplomats could effectively assist their nationals in cases where leading principles were at stake. This may be considered a contributory element in the high standards reached by British prize jurisdiction in the 18th century.[51]

Dutch commercial and colonial expansion in Asia was at the heart of important political and legal debates between European powers. In the inter-European discussion, the relations between Europeans and Asian rulers, such as privileged trading agreements, were represented in European legal terms.[52] It is a tantalizing question whether in fact Europeans effectively exported European legal concepts, notably arbitration and adjudication. A Dutch scholar attempted to answer this from the Dutch records.[53] There are indeed a number of quotes in the company's records from which it appears that the Dutch East India Company imposed itself as the mediating and at times deciding body in disputes between Indonesian rulers. However, the author has not recorded any formal or semi-formal procedure. We would need more detailed research for a final answer. From the facts in our possession it seems rather that the Dutch company as the hegemonic power simply interfered at will in the affairs of some Indonesian powers.[54]

A spectacular arbitration during this epoch is the affair of the Palatinate succession between the Duchess of Orléans and the Elector Palatine. The two arbiters appointed by the King of France and the emperor respectively, acting as independent judges,

---

[50] International Law in Historical Perspective (n 1) 8, 114–16; C Streefkerk 'Cedant Arma Togae. De sententiën van de Chambre mi-partie' (The Judgments of the Chambre mi-partie) (1987) 5 Verslagen en Mededelingen Stichting tot uitgaaf der bronnen van het oud-vaderlands recht (Accounts and Communications of the Foundation for the Edition of the Sources of Ancient National Law) 103–16.

[51] HJ Bourguignon *Sir William Scott: Lord Stowell Judge of the High Court of Admiralty, 1798–1828* (CUP Cambridge 1987) at 27.

[52] Studies in the History of International Law (n 36) 40–72.

[53] LW Alders *Internationale Rechtspraak tussen Indonesische Rijken en de V.O.C. tot 1700* (International Adjudication between Indonesian Principalities and the Dutch East India Company until 1700) (Centrale Drukkerij Nijmegen 1955).

[54] See the contribution by K Stapelbroek 'Trade, Chartered Companies, and Mercantile Associations' in this volume.

disagreed. The decision then was taken, according to the compromise transferred to the Pope as 'superior arbiter'. Six papal delegates decided in favour of the Elector. Such arbitrations by sovereign rulers were not uncommon, republics enjoying according to Lingens an unexpected popularity.[55]

3.2. *Ancien Régime* and Revolution: Decline of International Arbitration in Practice—An Ideological Base for International Adjudication

In the 18th century, the idea of arbitration enjoyed a certain popularity but its actual practice was in decline. Even though there was no total eclipse of arbitration in diplomatic practice, the number of actual cases of arbitration from the 1730s on recorded in treaty practice is small. Lingens ascribes this to the increasing popularity of European congress diplomacy.[56] Vattel's remark that 'they [sovereigns] sometimes confide the decision of the matter in dispute to arbitrators chosen by mutual consent'[57] does not indicate that it had fallen into total desuetude. All the same, his ensuing praise for the Swiss traditional practice of including arbitration clauses in their alliances, the only example quoted, has a suspiciously parochial character.[58] Georg Friedrich von Martens in the first and second edition of his manual refers for actual practice only to arbitral clauses in the early 18th century. He remarks that actual arbitrations have become increasingly rare, and interestingly, also that the difficulty of having decisions executed must be blamed for the reduction in their number.[59]

As against the realists Vattel and Martens, one can point to Abbé Saint-Pierre's utopian project of 1713 for the guarantee of perpetual peace by the creation of a European union.[60] A cornerstone of this institution was to be the obligatory adjudication of disputes between its members by the supreme organ of the union. Saint-Pierre derived this concept from the example of the standing adjudication of disputes between member states of the empire by the Imperial Chamber. As Marc

[55] *Internationale Schiedsgerichtbarkeit* (n 41) 74–8.

[56] ibid 144.

[57] E de Vattel 'Le droit des gens ou principes de la loi naturelle' (1758) in JB Scott (ed) *The Classics of International Law* (Carnegie Institution Washington DC 1916) vol 3, at 223.

[58] E de Vattel 'Le droit des gens ou principes de la loi naturelle' (1758) in JB Scott (ed) *The Classics of International Law* (Carnegie Institution Washington DC 1916) vol 1, 515–41; CG Roelofsen 'The Jay Treaty and All That' in AHA Soons (ed) *International Arbitration: Past and Prospects* (Kluwer Dordrecht 1990) 201–10 at 202.

[59] GF de Martens *Précis du droit des gens moderne de l'Europe fondé sur les traités et l'usage* (2nd edn Diettrich Göttingen 1801) at 270; see also the contribution by D Gaurier 'Cosmopolis and Utopia' in this volume.

[60] C-I de Castel de Saint-Pierre *Projet pour rendre la paix perpétuelle en Europe* (S Goyard-Fabre ed) (Fayard Paris 1986); H Houwens Post *La société des nations de l'abbé de Saint-Pierre* (De Spieghel Amsterdam 1932).

Belissa puts it: '[h]e is supported by well-tried models and expresses the aspirations to peace of his generation in the then current terms of diplomacy'.[61] This sounds too realist a note. I would suggest that Saint-Pierre first established the close association between institutional arbitration and pacifism that was to be an important element in the popularity of arbitration in the 19th century. At the end of the 18th century Jeremy Bentham, certainly not a linear ideological descendant of Saint-Pierre's, nevertheless echoes the Abbé's criticism of the old aristocratic and bellicose European order.

This leaves us here to deal with the Jay arbitrations and their alleged importance as a revolutionary new juridical resurgence of arbitration. Lingens dismisses this with the remark that in 1794 there was a simple continuation of practice of 1730.[62] It was only in 1877, according to Lingens, that the Jay arbitrations were considered a new starting point for arbitration. In an admittedly somewhat cursory search we found no traces of particular attention being paid to them by American authors in early 19th-century manuals.[63] This is surprising, since Jay's mission to London created quite a stir in American politics, and the ensuing treaty was bitterly unpopular. One would expect the ensuing arbitrations to have caught the attention of the American public. However, as late as 1900, John Watson Foster briefly dismissed the arbitration clauses of the Jay Treaty, which he presumably included among the 'valuable features' of a treaty marking 'a distinct advance in international practice'.[64]

The Jay Treaty[65] became a landmark of the renaissance of arbitration only in the last quarter of the 19th century, after the emergence of a particular interest in international arbitration and its history. Yet a brief discussion of two of the three Jay arbitrations is called for, since they illustrate some basic problems of arbitration at the threshold of the 19th century. The disputes assigned to the decision of the two mixed commissions were both typical of the kind of questions bedevilling international relations at the time. Article 6 dealt with some unfinished business from the American War of Independence. In the peace negotiations the British government had brought up against the US the losses British subjects had suffered from the hostilities. These were losses from the freezing of debts owed to English merchants by American retailers and from the confiscation of property owned by loyalists, who had fled the US and established themselves in British territories. These private claims had been settled in articles 4 and 5 of the Paris Peace Treaty (1783).[66] Such clauses, to be

---

[61] M Belissa *Fraternité universelle et intérêt national (1713–1795): Les cosmopolitiques du droit des gens* (Kimé Paris 1998) at 44.

[62] *Internationale Schiedsgerichtbarkeit* (n 41) 153.

[63] 'The Jay Treaty' (n 58) 204, fn 16.

[64] JW Foster *A Century of American Diplomacy* (Houghton Mifflin and Company Cambridge MA 1900) at 165.

[65] Jay Treaty (n 40).

[66] Definitive Treaty of Peace and Friendship (signed 3 September 1783) (1783) 48 CTS 487 ('Paris Peace Treaty').

implemented by the courts of the parties, were a standard element of peace treaties.[67] The US judicial system, however, proved incapable of a bona fide application. State governments interfered with the settlement of British claims, not considering themselves bound by the treaty concluded by Congress. Only after the adoption of the US Constitution could the Supreme Court impose the respect of treaties. John Jay, the first Chief Justice of the US Supreme Court, was well aware of the problem. His consent to allowing 'divers British merchants and others His Majesty's subjects' to have their claims decided by a mixed commission 'according to justice and equity' represented a real concession. The sensitive question of dealing with the aftermath of the American Revolution was withdrawn from American domestic jurisdiction. There is to my knowledge no detailed record of the negotiations between Jay and Foreign Secretary William Grenville.[68] Articles 6 and 7 may have to be considered as reciprocal concessions. Article 7's mixed commission for prize cases at London appears the counterpart to the article 6 commission at Philadelphia, the then American capital.

Exclusive belligerent prize jurisdiction in maritime conflicts was a fundamental principle of British policy, upheld throughout the 18th century. The British position was that British Admiralty Courts administered international law and were indeed international courts.[69] The unanimous opinion of the US Supreme Court as pronounced by Jay in *The Betsey* (1794) also held that prize law was basically international law.[70] Practice, particularly in the British West-Indian Vice-Admiralty Courts, hardly corresponded to this high standard. American merchants trading in the West-Indies considered themselves victimized by partial judges favouring the local privateer interest and keen on upholding British trade regulations under cover of prize jurisdiction. On the other hand, in 1793, there had been some cases of French privateers using American ports, a violation of American neutrality protested by Great Britain. The solution adopted in article 7 of the Jay Treaty[71] respected British and American susceptibilities. There would be no formal revision of verdicts. Titles to prize goods granted to captors would not be invalidated. Compensations due for claims brought by American and British parties before a mixed commission sitting in London would be paid by the State responsible.

The composition and the rules of procedure of the mixed commissions obviously represented a careful compromise solution. Great Britain and the US were to appoint two arbiters each. The fifth, the presiding member, would be a national of one of the parties as well, to be chosen by agreement between the four appointed members or, if

---

[67] R Lesaffer *Europa: Een Zoektocht naar Vrede? 1453–1783 en 1945–1997* (Europe: A Quest for Peace? 1453–1763 and 1945–1997) at 472; cf n 50.

[68] AM Stuyt *Survey of International Arbitrations* (3rd edn Martinus Nijhoff Dordrecht 1990) nos 2 and 3; SF Bemis *Jay's Treaty: A Study in Commerce and Diplomacy* (Yale University Press New Haven 1962).

[69] R Pares *Colonial Blockade and Neutral Rights 1739–1763* (Porcupine Press Philadelphia 1975) at 149.

[70] JB Scott (ed) *Prize Cases Decided in the United States Supreme Court 1789–1918* (Clarendon Press Oxford 1923) 9–19 at 19.

[71] 'The Jay Treaty' (n 58).

necessary, by lot. The participation of the president and of at least one member from both sides was necessary for taking a decision. These rules were obviously aimed at preventing both a stalemate and an absolute preponderance of the national majority of a commission. The institutions created by the agreement presumably corresponded to the common purpose of Jay and Grenville. The two autonomous common judicial institutions exonerated both governments from granting concessions to the other party, yet the two mixed commissions remained ultimately under national control. Their fates were to diverge. In London, where an American majority emerged, the commission evidently functioned to the satisfaction of both parties. The article 6 commission, however, was not so fortunate. The British majority that emerged here raised the delicate subject of the claims of pro-British former inhabitants of the American colonies who had had to flee the US because of their opposition to the American Revolution. The American minority seceded after the commission declared these 'loyalist' claims admissible. Proceedings came to a standstill. Diplomatic negotiations lead to an agreement (1802) on a lump sum to be shared by the British creditors, and a repeated reference to article 4 of the Treaty of Paris.[72] In view of the subsequent history of British–American arbitrations we may assume that at least in the Foreign Office and the Department of State the Jay Treaty had been registered as a useful precedent.

4. 19TH AND 20TH CENTURIES (1815–1945): THE RISE OF ARBITRATION AND THE CREATION OF INSTITUTIONAL ADJUDICATION—HIGH HOPES AND DISAPPOINTMENT

4.1. 1815–1914: General Appreciation of Arbitration as an Instrument of Diplomacy—Hesitatant Institutionalization

There is a startling increase in the number of international arbitrations after 1815. Arguably, this reflects a fundamental change in the relations between the members of the European states system. After the shocks of the French Revolution and the

---

[72] *International Law in Historical Perspective* (n 1) vol 8, at 277; JB Moore *History and Digest of the International Arbitrations to Which the United States Has Been a Party* (Government Printing Office Washington 1898).

Napoleonic hegemony, the return to the old system of the balance of power was also a restoration of legalism. Intricate legal systems were created at Vienna, such as the German Confederation and the Central Commission for the Navigation of the Rhine. The American-British Peace Treaty of Ghent (1814)[73] created four mixed commissions. The Jay Treaty provision for a president chosen by lot was not included. Another guarantee was provided for: recourse to 'a friendly sovereign'. After the failure to agree on the commissioners under article 5 (the definition of the frontier between Maine and Canada) this led to the submission of the dispute to 'a friendly sovereign', King William I of the Netherlands.[74] Arbitration by a foreign sovereign was to enjoy considerable vogue in the 19th century.[75]

Evolving state practice led to an increasing volume of arbitrations on familiar issues, territorial disputes and claims for damages suffered by subjects. New ground was broken by the British crusade against the Atlantic slave trade.[76] This policy was the result of what may be called the first international humanitarian mass action: the anti-slavery movement originating in Great Britain. The dominating maritime power, Britain, more or less coerced the minor States involved on the slave trade, the Netherlands, Brazil, Spain, and Portugal to agree to the prohibition of the slave trade, to be guaranteed by mixed courts. British-Dutch, British-Spanish, British-Portuguese, and British-Brazilian mixed commissions were established.[77] In 1839–41, a number of South-American States also agreed to establish mixed commissions in Sierra Leone.[78] Although France and the US (until 1862) remained outside this system, it substantially added to the effective exercise of British sea-power against slavers. Ships under non-British flags were in fact subjected to British jurisdiction. In the African seats of these tribunals (Sierra Leone and Cape Town) they functioned fairly well, the legality of captures only marginally being contested by non-British judges. Implementation in Cuba and Brazil was another matter. As Jennifer S Martinez concludes: 'the treaties seemed to embody strong international enforcement mechanisms' even though 'naval enforcement alone was unlikely to end the slave trade'.[79]

In a material sense, the coolie trade was a continuation of the slave trade. Here also, one can find international law invoked. The *Maria Luz* case (1873) demonstrated that Japan was not under an obligation to restore coolies, victims of irregular recruitment, who had escaped from a Peruvian ship in a Japanese harbour. Peru's appeal to her

---

[73] Treaty of Ghent (signed 24 December 1814) (1814) 63 CTS 421.

[74] *Survey of International Arbitrations* (n 68) nos 12 and 27.

[75] *International Law in Historical Perspective* (n 1) vol 8, 264–9.

[76] See the contribution by S Drescher and P Finkelman 'Slavery' in this volume.

[77] *Survey of International Arbitrations* (n 68) nos 23 and 26; only the British–Portuguese agreement is included in the survey.

[78] JS Martinez 'Antislavery Courts and the Dawn of International Human Rights Law' (2008) 118 Yale Law Journal 550–641 at 595.

[79] Ibid 615.

extra-territorial rights in Japan was rejected by the arbiter, Tsar Alexander II, or rather by his adviser, the Russian internationalist Friedrich de Martens.[80] It was a clear success for Japan, slowly emerging as an equal member of the international community of 'civilized States'. British assistance probably played a role in the Japanese action, but this does not detract from the case's symbolical value.[81]

As the European system took on global dimensions, international law was increasingly invoked in the colonial and semi-colonial practice of European powers. British representatives 'suggested' and no doubt in fact imposed arbitrations on Arab and African parties.[82] Consent in such cases may have been doubtful and hardly well-informed. Yet such arbitrations demonstrated a considerable technical progress from 17th-century Dutch informal colonial practice.[83] Documentation of international relations also vastly increased. Diplomatic correspondence was published for parliamentary information. International case law was systematically published by interested experts. International law grew into a recognized branch of jurisprudence, a development reflected as well as fostered by the foundation of the *Institut de Droit international* (1873).[84] The keen interest in international affairs of a significant part of public opinion, as illustrated by the anti-slavery campaign, also played a major role. Pacifist tendencies grew and increased the interest in peaceful settlement of international disputes. Arbitration became popular with the liberal public and with progressive international lawyers, such as Nippold.[85]

The great example here was no doubt the *Alabama* arbitration.[86] Here the danger of an armed conflict between the US and Great Britain was to the apparent public. The US brought claims not only for the direct damage due to the British partisan behaviour which had enabled Confederate privateers to start their successful campaign against American shipping, but also for the 'indirect damages' caused by the prolongation of the Civil War. The dramatic, but eventually successful history of the arbitration itself, with the British arbitrator refusing to sign the verdict, confirmed the impression of 'the most august and impressive...arbitration' ever held.[87] The three neutral arbitrators declared the indirect claims inadmissible, as Secretary of State Hamilton Fish firmly expected. In bringing these claims nevertheless, he silenced his critics who had insisted on them.[88] John Westlake's perceptive comments of 1896 on 'the famous Alabama affair' deserve to be quoted. The American–British conflict, he argued, could not have been subjected to arbitration as long as the parties did not

---

[80] *Survey of International Arbitrations* (n 68) no 104.
[81] I thank Prof Kinji Akashi (Keio University) for his assistance.
[82] *Survey of International Arbitrations* (n 68) no 62 and 92.
[83] Cf n 53.
[84] JB Scott (ed) *Resolutions of the Institute of International Law* (OUP New York 1916) at vi.
[85] Cf n 3.
[86] *Survey of International Arbitrations* (n 68) no 94.
[87] *A Century of American Diplomacy* (n 64) 424.
[88] H Lauterpacht *Private Law Sources and Analogies of International Law* (Longmans, Green and Co London 1927) at 216–23 and 227 fn 1.

agree on the law applicable. The situation had fundamentally changed because Britain consented in the Treaty of Washington (1871)[89] to the strict definition of neutral duties held by the US and agreed to a retroactive application of this definition. But, if there is no agreement on the law applicable, should the arbiter act as legislator? Progressive internationalists certainly argued that arbitration should be—at least in the long term (as Nippold held in 1907)—universally applied. Arbiters then, Westlake developed that position, would act as mediators and legislators as well. Such a solution, Westlake concluded, might be acceptable in affairs of secondary importance but 'one cannot imagine a nation to abandon by a general agreement the control of its destiny to such a jurisdiction'. In prophetic terms Westlake here anticipated the outcome of a long discussion to which we will now briefly return.[90]

It was a natural choice to include arbitration among the chief topics of the Hague Peace Conferences of 1899 and 1907. We have already viewed through Nippold's eyes the debate on a general obligation to accept arbitration. Notwithstanding Germany's negative position in 1899, rather more radically formulated than would have been necessary, the creation of the Permanent Court of Arbitration was a substantive practical result.[91] That body, although in the words of the American delegate John B Scott in 1907 'neither a court nor permanent'[92] but indeed merely a rudimentary organization which on request would facilitate and regulate arbitrations, was after all the first global legal institution. At the second Peace Conference, the 1899 Convention for the Pacific Settlement of Disputes[93] was amplified. The main subject of discussion, however, was the American proposition for a Court of Arbitral Justice, a real permanent court to which States parties would agree to submit their disputes. After long and heated debate, the convention foundered on disagreement over the appointment of judges to such a court. It was merely adopted as a recommendation (*voeu*). Essentially, we may regard these discussions of 1907 as part of the *travaux préparatoires* to the Statute of the Permanent Court of International Justice (1920).[94] A long-standing issue, the status of national prize courts as courts administering international law seemed about to be solved by the adoption of the Convention Relative to the Creation of an International Prize Court.[95]

[89] Treaty for the Amicable Settlement of All Causes of Difference Between the Two Countries (signed 8 May 1871) (1871) 143 CTS 145 ('Treaty of Washington').

[90] J Westlake 'Appendice: L'arbitrage international' in J Westlake *Traité de droit international* (AG de Lapradelle trans) (OUP Oxford 1924) 367–84 (article originally published as 'International Arbitration' (1896) 7 The International Journal of Ethics 1–20).

[91] WL Langer *The Diplomacy of Imperialism 1890–1902* (2nd edn Alfred A Knopf New York 1965) at 591.

[92] JB Scott (ed) *The Proceedings of the Hague Peace Conference* (repr William S Hein and Co Buffalo 2000) vol 3, at 319.

[93] Pacific Settlement of International Disputes (concluded 29 July 1899, entered into force 4 September 1900) 1 Bevans 230.

[94] Statute of the Permanent Court of International Justice (concluded 16 December 1920, entered into force 20 August 1921) 6 LNTS 379.

[95] *The 1899 Hague Peace Conference* (n 10); *Proceedings of the Hague Peace Conference* (n 92) vol 4, at 599–615.

This, however, did not materialize as the subsequent definition of the laws of maritime warfare (blockade and contraband) was not ratified by the British Parliament.

4.2. Versailles, the World Court, and the League of Nations: Arbitration and Adjudication as Alternatives—Progress and Disappointment

The victorious Allied and Associated Powers tried at Versailles, among other things, to fulfil the aspirations to a new global order, outlined at the Hague Peace Conferences. Germany, it was held, had been guilty of starting the war and of atrocities in its conduct. Articles 227–230 of the Versailles Treaty[96] laid down the Allies' intention to prosecute the former German emperor as well as some 900 members of the German armed forces. The outcome on this part of their programme was disappointing. The German emperor Wilhelm was not extradited by the Netherlands. To prevent the demand for extradition of the Germans inculpated, the German government offered to try them before the Imperial Court at Leipzig. The Allies accepted the offer, but found these 'Leipzig Trials' highly disappointing. British and French public opinion considered the trials after numerous acquittals and disproportionately moderate punishments, 'a mockery of justice'. This unsuccessful first modern experiment with international criminal jurisdiction was therefore a not unimportant precedent for adjudication by the victors themselves in 1945.[97] A 'High Court of International Justice' for international crimes was briefly discussed by the League Assembly.[98]

A far more impressive fate lay in store for article 14 of the famous treaty, the projected establishment of a Permanent Court of International Justice. The problem on which the Hague project of 1907 had foundered was solved by the structure of the League 'reconciling the "democratic" principle of the juridical equality of States … and their political inequality'. By the cooperation of the Assembly and the Council of the League, a 'really permanent court' was constituted. 'The ideal … of so many centuries and so many eminent minds' was at last realized. Verzijl here describes in laudatory terms the creation of a delicate relationship between the court and the League's principal organs.[99]

From a quite different perspective, the American sociologist Frances Kellor voiced severe criticisms. She points to the Council's refusal to admit the court's obligatory

---

[96] Treaty of Peace Between the Allied and Associated Powers and Germany (signed 28 June 1919, entered into force 10 January 1920) (1919) 225 CTS 188 ('Versailles Peace Treaty').

[97] H Wiggenhorn *Verliererjustiz: Die Leipziger Kriegsverbrecherprozesse nach dem Ersten Weltkrieg* (Nomos Verlag Baden-Baden 2005).

[98] Cf League of Nations *Records of the First Assembly, Committees* (League of Nations Geneva 1920) vol I, at 494 and 505.

[99] *International Law in Historical Perspective* (n 1) vol 8, at 327.

jurisdiction in legal disputes and refers in disparaging terms to the results of the optional clause, a compromise solution proposed by the Brazilian representative. All in all, she was disappointed by the outcome of the 1920 debates of the Permanent Court's Statute, which in her opinion reflects the Great Powers' refusal to admit the court to a significant role in the preservation of peace. In her opinion, there was a sad retreat from the positions taken in 1907 at The Hague.[100] She had a point.

Indeed, the debate over the Permanent Court's jurisdiction demonstrated that it was not only German opposition which had frustrated the attempts of 1907.[101] States proved hesitant to subject disputes to an untried body on whose composition they had scant influence. The Permanent Court had a slow start. From 1922 to 1926, it functioned mainly as an advisory organ to the League, rendering twelve advisory opinions against four contentious cases.[102] Arbitration remained popular.[103] As a quasi-diplomatic instrument, it had a confidential character and was to a certain extent regulated by the parties. Max Huber as single arbiter in the American-Dutch dispute regarding the sovereignty over the Island of Palmas (Pulau Miangas)[104] rendered a verdict that is still the classical text on the acquisition of sovereignty. It solved an issue that was later to be of great importance in stabilizing post-colonial frontiers but was at the time of slight practical interest to the governments concerned. The disagreeable aspects of state control over arbitration were experienced by Jan HW Verzijl, as president of the French-Mexican mixed commission.[105] In spite of the guarantees offered by the Hague Rules, Mexico effectively blocked the arbitral proceedings by withdrawing the Mexican delegate from the commission. Finally, the French claims were settled by agreement. Mexico could hardly have acted in this fashion in a litigation at The Hague.

Another and by no means unimportant reason for the hesitant attitude of states towards the Permanent Court was the uncertainty over important parts of public international law. How would the new court interpret the law? Crucial in establishing confidence was in this respect the famous verdict in the *Lotus Case* (1927). The casting vote of President Huber 'anchored the general principles of international law in customary law' according to Verzijl's contemporary comment.[106] This points to one of the major merits of the Permanent Court, its authoritative contribution in defining the law. The 1946 International Court of Justice essentially continued this tradition of the Permanent Court.

[100] F Kellor and A Hatvany *Security Against War* (The MacMillan Company New York 1924) vol 2 (*Arbitration, Disarmament Outlawry*), 454–519.
   [101] ibid 367, Ms Kellor quoting the Dutch delegate B Loder.
   [102] JHW Verzijl *The Jurisprudence of the World Court* (Sijthoff Leiden 1965) vol I (*The Permnanent Court of International Justice (1922–1940)*).
   [103] An overview of the situation 1920–40 with a discussion of the impact of the General Act of 1928, see *International Law in Historical Perspective* (n 1) vol 8, at 240–9.
   [104] *Island of Palmas (Netherlands v United States of America)* (1928) 2 RIAA 829 at 839.
   [105] *Survey of International Arbitrations* (n 68) nos 366 and 363.
   [106] *The Jurisprudence of the World Court* (n 102) 85.

5. CONCLUSION

Ending this tale in 1945 has a certain logic, as new institutions, the UN and the International Court of Justice, succeeded to those created at Versailles. A global order replaced an essentially European dispensation. However, we may doubt whether we would really regard 1945 as the essential end of an epoch. Would we now perhaps not rather consider the start of the 'century of Asia' about the year 2000 as the real ending of an era of European international law and of the prominent role of such an old-world court like the Hague International Court of Justice? What we certainly do not feel is the self-confidence of an earlier generation which wrote legal history backwards. Time and again they demonstrate the conviction that present-day international law represents an advanced stage of progress, prepared by earlier, less perfect, attempts. This leads to a lack of empathy with earlier systems of dispute resolution and a drawing of analogies with modern situations which can lead to serious distortions in the presentation of the past. The history of arbitration offers one of the prime examples. Modern authors are often so much preoccupied with demonstrating the links between various epochs of arbitration that they lose sight of the function of arbitration in a particular context. We have tried to escape from this pitfall by adopting a somewhat different chronological framework and trying to analyse various epochs on their own merits, rather than merely as steps in a development towards the present. We could of course in this chapter give indications rather than elaborate them. The 'quantum leap' of arbitration from about 1850 and the change in its character should certainly not have escaped the reader.

Institutions for the peaceful settlement of disputes developed considerably since the hesitant start at the Hague Peace Conferences. Yet as Clarence W Jenks warned, quoting Huber, 'the willingness of governments to bind themselves to the judicial settlement of a dispute is decisive'.[107] This may stand as the epitome of international arbitration and international adjudication in the period discussed. By definition, the submission of sovereign powers to an international judiciary process is a voluntary one, even if considerable outside pressure has been used to obtain that submission. Sophisticated judiciary systems for dispute settlement were, however, useless when States refused to submit to them as Japan, Italy, and Germany did in the 1930s.

RECOMMENDED READING

Grewe, Wilhelm G *The Epochs of International Law* (M Byers trans) (De Gruyter Berlin 2000).
Jenks, Clarence W *The Prospects of International Adjudication* (Stevens and Sons London 1964).

[107] *The Prospects of International Adjudication* (n 4) 16.

Lingens, Karl-Heinz *Internationale Schiedsgerichtbarkeit und Jus Publicum Europaeum 1648–1794* (Duncker und Humblot Berlin 1988).

Nippold, Otfried *Die Fortbildung des Verfahrens in völkerrechtlichen Streitigkeiten* (Duncker und Humblot Leipzig 1907).

Politis, Nicolas and Albert G de Lapradelle *Recueil des arbitrages internationaux* (5 vols A Pedone Paris 1905–54).

Ralston, Jackson H *The Law and Procedure of International Tribunals* (revised edn Stanford University Press Stanford 1926).

Soons, Alfred HA (ed) *International Arbitration: Past and Prospects* (Kluwer Dordrecht 1990).

Stuyt, Alexander M *Survey of International Arbitrations 1794–1989* (3rd edn Martinus Nijhoff Publishers Dordrecht 1990).

Verzijl, Jan HW *The Jurisprudence of the World Court* (Sijthoff Leiden 1965) vol 1 (*The Permanent Court of International Justice*).

Verzijl, Jan HW *International Law in Historical Perspective* (Sijthoff Leiden 1976) vol 8 (*Inter-State Disputes and Their Settlement*).

CHAPTER 7

INTERNATIONAL ORGANIZATIONS: BETWEEN TECHNOCRACY AND DEMOCRACY

ANNE PETERS AND SIMONE PETER

1. INTRODUCTION

INTERNATIONAL organization in the singular is a slightly older idea than the use of the term 'international organizations' in the plural. It can be traced back to the Scottish lawyer James Lorimer.[1] The expression 'organization' to designate an inter-governmental institution was first used in the peace treaties after the First World War. Article 23(a) of the League of Nations Covenant, which was Part I of all three peace treaties, mentioned 'organizations' in the plural, with regard to the issue of labour.[2] Part XIII of the

---

[1] J Lorimer *The Institutes of the Law of Nations* (W Blackwood and Sons Edinburgh 1883) vol 1, at 11.
[2] The term was also used for the bodies of the Assembly of the League of Nations, for what we would now call committees.

Treaty of Versailles[3] established an 'Organization of Labour' (ILO). Article 67 of the revised Statute of the Permanent Court of International Justice (PCIJ) in 1929 mentioned 'international organizations',[4] apparently in order to avoid a reference to the ILO. Dionisio Anzilotti, then president of the PCIJ, found it a *malheureuse expression*.[5]

Before the word, unfortunate or not, came into general use, international organizations existed, albeit under different labels. 1865 has been called the *annus mirabilis*[6] of international organizations, because then the International Telegraph Union,[7] and the Light-House of Cape Spartel in Tangier,[8] the first inter-state institution with the membership of the US, were both established. In 1900, there were around thirty inter-governmental organizations compared to around forty States.[9] By 2010, UN membership comprised 192 States, and estimated 250 intergovernmental organizations existed.[10]

2. HISTORICAL OVERVIEW UNTIL THE FIRST WORLD WAR

2.1. Congresses as Precursors

International organizations emerged from the congresses of statesmen and plenipotentiaries of the 18th and early 19th centuries.[11] These congresses, at first mainly or exclusively convened after a war, were dominated by the Great Powers. These assumed

---

[3] The Constitution of the ILO was Part XIII of the Treaty of Versailles (Treaty of Peace with Germany (signed 28 June 1919) (1919) 13 American Journal of International Law Supplement 151–386, as amended 20 April 1948, 15 UNTS 40), see art 387.

[4] *Revised Statute of the Permanent Court of International Justice* PCIJ Rep Series D No 1 13–28.

[5] Dionisio Anzilotti, in his observations on the project of revision of the rules of the PCIJ in 1924 in PCIJ Rep Series D, Add No 2 (1926) at 290.

[6] M Herren-Oesch *Internationale Organisationen seit 1865: Eine Globalgeschichte der internationalen Ordnung* (Wissenschaftliche Buchgesellschaft Darmstadt 2009) at 18.

[7] Convention télégraphique internationale de Paris (1865) et Règlement de service international (1865) in *Documents diplomatiques de la conférence télégraphique internationale de Paris* (Imprimerie impériale Paris 1865) 1–67 ('Telegraph Convention 1865'). All historic documents and treaties are available on the homepage of the ITU, at <http://www.itu.int/en/history/plenipotentiaryconferences/Pages/1865Paris.aspx> (accessed 9 July 2012).

[8] Convention Concerning the Administration and Upholding of the Light-House at Cape Spartel of 31 May 1865, 14 Stat 679; 18 Stat (2) 525.

[9] WJ Feld and RS Jordan *International Organizations* (2nd edn Praeger New York 1988) at 14.

[10] Union of International Associations (ed) *Yearbook of International Organizations* (46th edn Saur München 2009/2010) vol 5, at 33.

[11] NL Hill *The Public International Conference* (Stanford University Press Stanford 1929).

law-making functions and regulated matters of transnational interest, with effects for non-parties, notably for small and weak States.

The Final Act of the Congress of Vienna of 9 June 1815,[12] to which Austria, France, Portugal, Prussia, Russia, Sweden, and the United Kingdom were parties, established the principle of free navigation on European rivers,[13] and declared the abolition of the slave trade.[14] In several identical bilateral alliance and friendship treaties,[15] the Great Powers affirmed their

duty to redouble their watchfulnes for the tranquillity and interests of their People, engage, in case so unfortunate an event should again occur, to concert amongst themselves … the measures which they may judge necessary to be pursued for the safety of their respective States, and for the general Tranquillity of Europe.[16]

Regular consultations of the Great Powers were the instrument to secure 'the happiness of world'.[17] To that end, the Powers 'agreed to renew their meetings at fixed periods'.[18] These regular meetings became the 'congress system' in which the Great Powers met in Aix-la-Chapelle (1818), Carlsbad (1819), Verona (1822), and later in London (1832) and Berlin (1878). A parallel strand of development was the arbitration movement with its quest for settling inter-state disputes through arbitral bodies which required some degree of institutionalization.

2.2. Confederations

In North America, representatives of thirteen British colonies gathered in their second congress to adopt the declaration of independence in 1776. The articles of Confederation and Perpetual Union of 1777 then established a 'confederacy' of American States whose members retained their 'sovereignty, freedom and independence' (article 2).[19] The American Confederacy or Confederation lasted from 1777 to 1787. The German Confederation (*Deutscher Bund*) counted forty-one

---

[12] 'Acte du Congrès de Vienne' (signed 9 June 1815) in GF de Martens (ed) *Supplément au Recueil des Principaux Traités d'Alliance, de Paix, de Trêves, de Neutralité, de Commerce, de Limites, d'échange etc* (Dieterich Goettingen 1818) vol 6, 379–450.

[13] ibid art 108.

[14] 'Annexe XV de l'Acte final de Vienne: Déclaration des Puissances sur l'abolitions de la traité des Nègres du 8 fevrier 1815' in Supplément au Recueil des Principaux Traités d'Alliance (n 12) vol 6, 432–4.

[15] One of them was the Treaty of Alliance and Friendship between His Britannic Majesty and the Emperor of Austria (signed 20 November 1815) in TC Hansard (ed) *The Parliamentary Debates from the Year 1803 to the Present Time* (Hansard London 1816) vol 32, 269–73.

[16] ibid art II.   [17] ibid art VI.   [18] Identical art VI of the bilateral treaties.

[19] Articles of Confederation and Perpetual Union between the States of New Hampshire, Massachusetts Bay, Rhode Island, and Providence plantations, Connecticut, New York, New Jersey, Pennsylvania, Delaware, Maryland, Virginia, North Carolina, South Carolina, and Georgia of 15 November 1777 (William Purdie Williamsburg 1777).

States and lasted from 1815–66.[20] The Swiss Confederation existed from 1815 to 1848 and comprised twenty-two States.[21] All three confederations ended up in federal States based on a State constitution. This finality is often highlighted as a distinguishing factor to the administrative unions.

2.3. River Commissions

The most important river commissions were the Rhine Commission, installed with the Act of Vienna of 1815,[22] and—even more powerful—the European Commission of the Danube, established by the Paris Treaty of 1856.[23] Referring to the Final Vienna Act, the 1856 Treaty applied the principles governing European rivers to the Danube, and stated that this rule 'henceforth forms a part of the public law of Europe'.[24]

The mandate of the river commissions basically was to supervise and enforce the regime of free navigation of the rivers, including the physical works in the river bed and the banks needed to maintain the navigability, and to raise levy tonnage dues. To that end, the commissions were granted rule-making, executive, and judicial powers. The European Danube Commission could also call at need upon warships stationed by the mouth of the Danube by the member States. It thus had the option to resort to military sanctions.[25] Both commissions have been frequently reformed, were set on new treaty bases, and their powers were extended.[26]

---

[20] 'Deutsche Bundesakte of 8 June 1815' in D Gosewinkel and J Masing (eds) *Die Verfassungen in Europa 1789–1949* (CH Beck München 2006) 740–7.

[21] For the period from 1803 to 1815 it is disputed whether Switzerland was a confederation or a federation, see JF Aubert *Traité de droit constitutionnel suisse* (Dalloz Paris 1967) vol 1, at 13–14.

[22] 'Acte du Congrès de Vienne' (signed 9 June 1815) in Supplément au Recueil des Principaux Traités d'Alliance (n 12) vol 6, acte principal 379–432; 'Annexe XVI: Règlements pour la libre navigation des rivières' in Supplément au Recueil des Principaux Traités d'Alliance (n 12) vol 6, 434–50; see WJM van Eysinga *Die Zentralkommission für die Rheinschiffahrt: Geschichtliche Darstellung* (W Sijthoff Leiden 1936) with the most important documents reprinted at 139 ff.

[23] 'Traité général de paix entre l'Autriche, la France, la Grande-Bretagne, la Prusse, la Russie, la Sardaigne et la Porte Ottomane' (signed 30 March 1856) in C Samwer (ed) *Martens Nouveau Recueil Général (MNRG) de traités, conventions et autres transactions remarquables, servant à la connaissance des relations étrangères des puissances et états dans leurs rapports mutuels* (Dieterich Goettingen 1857) series 1 vol 15, 770–81.

[24] Paris Treaty 1856 (n 23) art 15.

[25] 'Acte public, relatif à la navigation des embouchures du Danube' (signed 2 November 1865) in C Samwer and J Hopf (eds) *MNRG* (Dieterich Goettingen 1873) series 1 vol 18, 144–53 at 149, art 11.

[26] For example, the European Commission of the Danube was given the power to decide definitely the disputed question regarding the choice amongst the three branches of the Danube delta to become the definitive channel. See art 2 and art 3 'Acte public' (n 25); in scholarship E Krehbiel 'The European Commission of the Danube: An Experiment in International Administration' (1918) 33 Political Science Quarterly 38–553 at 45–7.

Their headquarters have moved to different cities. The Rhine Commission moved from Mayence to Mannheim and is now (since the Treaty of Versailles) located in Strasbourg.[27] The Danube Commission had its original seat at Galatz, since 1954 it has been located in Budapest.[28] Both commissions still exist today.[29]

In 1927, the Permanent Court of International Justice issued an advisory opinion on the Danube Commission in which it formulated the principle of speciality. An international 'institution' as the Court said (it did not yet use the word 'organization') possesses only the powers which have been conferred upon it by the member States through the foundational document.[30] The Court distinguished 'territorial' and 'functional' powers and held that the 'powers of regulation and jurisdiction belong to the territorial authorities; the right of supervision with a view to ensuring freedom of navigation and equal treatment of all flags, belongs to the European Commission'.[31] The Danube Commission has been qualified as 'a distinct international entity possessing sovereignty over the broad waters of the Danube'.[32]

2.4. International Unions

The 19th-century international unions were in French called *unions administratives*,[33] *unions internationales*,[34] or *unions universelles*,[35] in German *internationale Verbind-*

---

[27]   The Rhine Commission was reformed with the Convention of Mayence in 1831: 'Convention entre les Gouvernements des Etats riverains du Rhin et règlement relatif à la navigation du dit fleuve conclue à Mayence' (signed 31 March 1831) in F Saalfeld (ed) *Martens Nouveau Recueil (MNR) des Traités d'Alliance, de Paix, de Trève, de Neutralité etc* (Dieterich Goettingen 1833) series 1 vol 9, 252–312; the headquarter was transferred to Mannheim by the 1868 Act of Mannheim: 'Convention révisée pour la navigation du Rhin entre la France, la Prussie, les Pays-Bas, la Bavière et les Grands-Duchés de Bade et de Hesse, suivie de deux modèles et d'un protocole de clôture' (signed 17 October 1868) in C Samwer and J Hopf (eds) *MNRG* (Dieterich Goettingen 1875) series 1 vol 20, 355–74. Finally, the headquarters were moved to Strasbourg (art 355 Treaty of Versailles (n 3)).

[28]   The Danube Commission was reformed with the 1865 'Acte public' (n 25) which was affirmed by art 53 of the 1878 Berlin Treaty: 'Traité de Berlin' (signed 18 July 1878) in C Samwer and J Hopf (eds) *MNRG* (Dieterich Goettingen 1878–79) series 2 vol 3, 449–65. The powers of the European Commission were prolongated for twenty-one years by art 2 of the 1883 London Treaty concerning the navigation of the Danube: 'Traité de Londres' (signed 10 March 1883) in J Hopf (ed) *MNRG* (Dieterich Goettingen 1884) series 2 vol 9, 392–413.

[29]   See on the Rhine commission <http://www.ccr-zkr.org/> accessed 15 November 2011; on the Danube commission <http://www.danubecommission.org/index.php/de_DE/index> accessed 15 November 2011.

[30]   PCIJ *Jurisdiction of the European Commission of the Danube between Glatz and Braila (Advisory Opinion)* PCIJ Rep Series B No 14, at 64.

[31]   ibid 67.

[32]   GA Blackburn 'International Control of the River Danube' (1930) 32 Current History 1154–9 at 1154.

[33]   G Scelle *Précis de droit des gens : Principes et systématique* (Sirey Paris 1932) at 207.

[34]   L Renault 'Les unions internationales : Leurs avantages et leurs inconvénients' (1896) 3 Revue général de droit international public 14–26.

[35]   G Moynier *Les bureaux internationaux des Unions universelles* (Cherbuliez Genève 1892) at 8.

ungen,[36] *internationale Verwaltungsvereine,*[37] *Verwaltungsunionen,*[38] *Vereinigungen zu Verwaltungszwecken,*[39] or *Verwaltungsgemeinschaften.*[40]

Most of the general international legal literature of the time did not pay any special attention to those unions. At best the books mentioned the founding treaties without pointing out that these had installed stable institutions.[41] Standard English-language treatises such as Phillimore,[42] Hall,[43] and Westlake[44] did not discuss the unions.

It was Georg Jellinek who clearly perceived the *Verwaltungsbündnisse,* as he called them, as something new and important, and who suggested a clear systematization of the new phenomenon. In *Die Lehre von den Staatenverbindungen,* published in 1882, Jellinek spoke of the beginning of a new epoch of international administrative unions which would characterize the future intercourse among the civilized world.[45] Probably the German writers were more sensitive towards the new unions because of their preoccupation with State building. The result was their keen scholarly interest in the legal construct of a confederation (such as the *Deutscher Bund*), and hence also in the administrative unions.

The International Telegraph Union (ITU) is today considered a 'prototype'[46] of an administrative union. It was founded with the Treaty of Paris of 17 May 1865, signed by then twenty States, among them numerous German small kingdoms, the free city of Hamburg, Switzerland, Russia, and the Ottoman empire.[47] In 1906, a separate organization for wireless telegraphy was founded, the International Radiotelegraph Union. The Telegraph Union merged with that Radio Union in 1934, and since then carries the name International Telecommunication Union (also abbreviated as ITU). It still exists today.[48]

The qualitative leap in terms of institutionalization took place with the first revision of the treaty on the Telegraph Union in Vienna in 1868,[49] three years after its foundation.

---

[36] AW Heffter *Das europäische Völkerrecht der Gegenwart auf den bisherigen Grundlagen* (7th edn Schroeder Berlin 1881) para 241, at 467.

[37] G Jellinek *Die Lehre von den Staatenverbindungen* [1882] (Scientia Aalen 1969) at 159.

[38] K Strupp *Grundzüge des positiven Völkerrechts* (Röhrscheid Bonn 1921) at 40; JL Kunz *Die Staatenverbindungen* (Kohlhammer Stuttgart 1929) at 374.

[39] E Ullmann *Völkerrecht* (Mohr Tübingen 1898) para 13 fn 4, at 46.

[40] Strupp employs both terms as closely related: 'Verwaltungsgemeinschaften, im engeren Sinne auch Unionen genannt...' (*Grundzüge des positiven Völkerrechts* (n 38) 92).

[41] For example T Funck Brentano and A Sorel *Précis du droit des gens* (3rd edn Plon Paris 1900) at 185–202.

[42] R Phillimore *Commentaries Upon International Law* (3 vols Butterworths London 1854–57).

[43] WE Hall *A Treatise of International Law* (Clarendon Press Oxford 1895).

[44] J Westlake *International Law* (2 vols 2nd edn Cambridge University Press Cambridge 1910–13).

[45] 'Auf jeden Fall stehen wir am Beginne einer Epoche internationaler Verwaltungsbündnisse, welche dem Verkehrsleben der civilisirten Welt ein neues Gepräge aufdrückt.' (*Die Lehre von den Staatenverbindungen* (n 37) 111).

[46] *Internationale Organisationen seit 1865* (n 6) 21.

[47] Telegraph Convention 1865 (n 7).

[48] International Telecommunication Convention, with annexes (adopted 9 December 1932) 151 LNTS 4.

[49] 'Convention télégraphique internationale de Paris, révisée à Vienne (1868) et Règlement de service international (1868)' in *Documents de la conférence télégraphique internationale de Vienne* (Imprimerie impériale et royale de la Cour et de l'Etat Vienna 1868) 1–86 ('Telegraph Convention 1868').

The original 1865 treaty had not foreseen a permanent office, but had left all administrative measures to that State in which the periodic conference took place (article 55 of the 1865 treaty). The 1868 treaty introduced a completely new provision which set up a 'telegraphic administration, designated by the Conference' (article 61 of the 1868 treaty). The task of this new administration was to take all proper measures, to facilitate, 'in the common interest', the execution and application of the Telegraphic Convention. The conference was to organize, under the heading *Bureau international des Administrations télégraphiques* 'a special service which would function under its [the conference's] direction'.[50]

The competences of the bureau were enumerated as follows. The bureau was to 'centralize all information concerning international telegraphy, fix the tariff, write a general statistic, proceed to studies of common usefulness (*d'utilité commune*) of which it is seized, and edit a telegraphic journal in French language'.[51] This was the first permanent secretariat, established by an international treaty, and entrusted to 'apply and execute'[52] that treaty—to manage it, as we would today say.

The Universal Postal Union[53] was modelled along the lines of the Telegraphic Union in 1874. The 'Treaty concerning the formation of a Postal Union' fixed a general union's rate of postage; for example, 25 centimes for a single prepaid letter in 1874 (article 3). In 1878, the name was changed from 'General Postal Union' into 'Universal Postal Union' (UPU).[54] The UPU was reformed various times, and is now—since 1948—a specialized agency of the United Nations. The UPU, like the Telegraphic Union, had three organs. Regular 'congresses' (of governments), regular 'conferences' of administrative officers of the member States, and a 'Bureau' or 'Office',[55] in both cases situated in Berne.

The administrative unions, viewed at large as treaty regimes, must be distinguished from the international offices they set up. States were reluctant to equip those offices with proper authority. They were not intended to be 'authoritative but simply as auxiliary'[56] as the Belgian delegate Vinchent put it at the Paris Postal Congress in 1874.

---

[50] ibid art 61.

[51] ibid art 61 sec 2 (trans by the authors). The journal appeared from 1869 on as 'Journal Télégraphique', available online on the sites of the French National Archives (<http://gallica.bnf.fr/>).

[52] ibid art 61.

[53] 'Traité concernant la création d'une Union générale des postes (signed 9 October 1874) suivi d'un protocol final en date du même jour, et du protocol d'échange des ratifications (signed 8 Mai 1875)' in C Samwer and J Hopf (eds) *MNRG* (Dieterich Goettingen 1876) series 2 vol 1, 651–9 ('GPU Convention').

[54] 'Convention d'une union postale universelle suivie d'un Protocole final' (signed 1 June 1878) in C Samwer and J Hopf (eds) *MNRG* (Dieterich Goettingen 1878–79) series 2 vol 3, 699–708 ('UPU Convention').

[55] See for the competences of the Office of the Postal Union art 15 of the GPU Convention (n 53) (English Text provided by <http://avalon.law.yale.edu/19th_century/usmu010.asp> accessed on 15 November 2011).

[56] '[L]e bureau international ne serait pas une *autorité*, mais simplement un *aide*'. Statement in 'Congrès international des Postes, Procès-verbaux des séances du Congrès tenu à Berne' (1875) 15 Archives diplomatiques vol 4, 143–263, protocol of the 5th session of 23 September 1874, at 191 (emphasis added).

2.5. The Inter-war Period: The ILO and the League of Nations

In the aftermath of the First World War, two organizations were established directly by the peace treaties. These were the League of Nations and the International Labour Organization.[57] Both founding documents were not only formally part of the Versailles peace treaties, but explicitly referred to each other, and to the immediately preceding war as their material *raison d'être*. Thus, the Preamble of Part XIII of the Treaty of Versailles, which was the ILO Constitution, stated:

Whereas the League of Nations has for its object the establishment of universal peace, and such a peace can be established only if it is based upon social justice; And whereas conditions of labour exist involving such injustice, hardship, and privation to large numbers of people as to produce unrest so great that the peace and harmony of the world are imperilled; ... The High Contracting Parties, moved by sentiments of justice and humanity as well as by the desire to secure the permanent peace of the world, agree to the following. ...

The League of Nations' Covenant's preamble did not mention the past war, but highlighted that the High Contracting Parties agreed to this Covenant '[i]n order to promote international co-operation and to achieve international peace and security'. The Council of the League, its most powerful organ, was to 'consist of the representatives of the Principal Allied and Associated Powers' as permanent members, hence of the victors of the war. That link to the Great War and the institutional set-up that resulted was one of the reasons for the lack of trust in the organization, and undermined its authority.

3. CAUSES AND MOTIVES

This section explores the factors contributing to the emergence of the international organizations in the second half of the 19th century.

3.1. Material Factors

A first crucial factor was the enormous growth of international trade and the parallel free-trade ideology. Second, technical progress was rapid in the field of traffic and communication. Traffic and communication were in turn two enabling factors

---

[57] The Covenant of the League of Nations was Part I of the Treaty of Versailles (n 3), the ILO Constitution was Part XIII ('Labour').

for international trade. The—already mentioned—commissions and administrative unions were founded exactly in these two fields. A third enabling factor for international trade was the harmonization of measures, terms, and standards. In 1875, the *Bureau International de Poids et Mesures* (BIPM) was established in Sèvres by the Metric Convention.[58] Fourth, technical innovation and international trade increased the demand for the protection of intellectual property. Two unions in this field were founded in the 1880s.[59] Fifth, the business sector was interested in the regulation of the use of natural resources. An important administrative union in this field was the International Sugar Union, which existed from 1902 to 1920.[60] A final global problem that had to be dealt with as a consequence of increased international trade, traffic, and the concomitant mobility of persons, was health. Already in 1838, the *Conseil Supérieur de Santé* was established in Constantinople[61] to deal with diseases such as the Cholera that had been imported from Near Asia to Europe.[62]

3.2. Ideational Factors

The ideas and ideologies accompanying the economic growth and the technological progress were both realist and idealist. Around the turn of the 19th to the 20th centuries, there was a clear perception that the international organizations and international cooperation were a product of the *force des choses*. In 1882, Georg Jellinek observed a kind of 'compelling force' towards international organization which would not be founded on the 'will and power of the single State, but on those of a community'.[63] James Brierly wrote in 1928:

[58] 'Convention concernant la création et l'entretien d'un bureau international des poids et mesures, suivie d'un règlement et de dispositions transitoires' (signed 20 May 1875) in C Samwer and J Hopf (eds) *MNRG* (Dieterich Goettingen 1876) series 2 vol 1, 663–72.

[59] See on these unions below nn 109–110 and accompanying text.

[60] 'Convention relative au régime des sucres' (signed 5 March 1902) in F Stoerk (ed) *MNRG* (Dieterich Leipzig 1904) series 2 vol 31, 272–90 ('Sugar Convention').

[61] The Council was established by the 'Règlement organique du Conseil de santé à Constantinople pour les provencances de mer' (signed 10 June 1839) in F Murhard (ed) *MNR* (Dieterich Goettingen 1842) vol 16, part 2, 920–6. According to its art 19, the *règlement* was the fundamental and organisational act of the Council (*fera foi comme acte organique et fondamental*).

[62] See for the history of the Council JD Mizrahi, 'Politique sanitaire et impérialisme à l'heure de la revolution pastorienne: Le Conseil sanitaire de Constantinople 1838–1923' in: W Arbid et al (eds) *Méditerranée, Moyen-Orient: Deux siècles de relations internationales: Recherche en hommage à Jacques Thobie* (Paris L'Harmattan 2003) 221–42.

[63] The full quote is: 'Hier auf dem Gebiete der Verwaltung entwickelt sich in Folge der immer steigenden Solidarität der Staaten *mit zwingender Kraft eine Organisation*, welche nicht mehr auf dem Willen und der Kraft des Einzelstaates, sondern auf dem der Gemeinschaft beruht. Die internationalen Organe der Schifffahrts-, Post-, Telegraphen-, Meterconventionen bezeichnen den Anfang eines neuen zwischenstaatlichen Lebens. Die immer zahlreicher werdenden internationalen Congresse, sei es staatlicher Delegirter, sei es Privater zum Zwecke der Berathung oder Anregung internationaler Massregeln, die internationalen Ausstellungen zeugen von der steigenden Bedeutung des weit über den Einzelstaat

[I]n the nineteenth century, a rudimentary international administrative system came into existence. The motive was not any idealistic theory of international relations, but the *compelling force of circumstances;* in one department of administration after another experience showed that government *could not be even reasonably efficient* if it continued to be organized on a purely national basis.[64]

An important theme was the necessity to cooperate in order to satisfy the common interest of the civilized nations.[65] For example, the provision of the Telegraphic Union Agreement establishing the International Telegraphic Office stated that the office should apply and execute the agreement in a common interest, *dans un intérêt commun.*[66]

The insufficient problem-solving capacity of individual States (for satisfying public interests) was especially highlighted by Ernst Ullmann. He wrote that it was established 'today' (in 1898) that in the most areas of governance, the material and formal means at the disposal of government must fail, and 'what the single State in the field of national administration could no longer perform could be achieved by the collective function of States'.[67]

Besides, nationalism and imperialism were driving forces for international organization. In 1902, John Hobson wrote that '[n]ationalism is a plain highway to internationalism, and if it manifests a divergence we may well suspect a perversion of its nature and its purpose'.[68] The postal service has been called a 'civilian technique of colonisation'.[69] Even after the recognition of Turkey as a sovereign State, and with Turkey being a signatory of the Postal Union Agreement in 1874, other States reserved for themselves the right to install postal offices in the Turkish territory.[70] Similarly, the health *Conseil*

---

hinausragenden Culturlebens, welches, wie alles Leben, *mit unwiderstehlicher, wenn auch langsam wirkender Gewalt, eine Organisation aus sich hervortreibt.' Die Lehre von den Staatenverbindungen* (n 37) 110 (emphasis added).

[64] JL Brierly *The Law of Nations: An Introduction to the International Law of Peace* (Clarendon Press Oxford 1928) at 199 (emphasis added).

[65] See eg *Die Lehre von den Staatenverbindungen* (n 37) 109 ('Aber die moderne Weltcultur hat gemeinsame Interessen aller civilisirten Völker sowohl, als auch einer grösseren oder geringeren Anzahl unter ihnen geschaffen, und diese gemeinsamen Interessen, welche auf der gemeinsamen Cultur beruhen und daher bleibend sind, gewähren eine sichere und dauernde Basis sowohl für Verträge, welche die ganze Zeit ihres stipulirten Bestandes hindurch eingehalten werden, als auch für bleibende internationale Institutionen'); *Völkerrecht* (n 39) para 104, at 252–3 ('Die meisten Interessen, welche den Gegenstand staatlicher Verwaltung bilden, haben sich innerhalb der Gemeinschaft civilisirter Staaten geradezu zu solidarischen und sohin zu internationalen Interessen ausgebildet'); see also W Schücking *Der Staatenverband der Haager Konferenzen* (Duncker & Humblot München 1912) at 18, who argued that the principle of international solidarity was the nucleus for later evolution of international organizations.

[66] Telegraph Convention 1868 (n 49) art 61.

[67] *Völkerrecht* (n 39) para 104, at 252 (trans by the authors).

[68] JA Hobson *Imperialism: A Study* [1902] (Cosimo Classics New York 2005) at 11.

[69] O Simons 'Heinrich von Stephan und die Idee der Weltpost' in A Honold and KR Scherpe (eds) *Mit Deutschland um die Welt: Eine Kulturgeschichte des Fremden in der Kolonialzeit* (Metzler Stuttgart 2004) 24–35.

[70] F von Liszt *Das Völkerrecht* (5th edn Haering Berlin 1907) at 244.

supérieur de Constantinople[71] was an attempt of the European Great Powers to remove from the Turkish sultan the authority to impose quarantine measures on their ships.[72]

Furthermore, international organizations were conceived as civilizing power. The League of Nations' commentator Jean Ray compared the League to the papacy because both claimed to exercise a moral power over the world.[73] Besides, diverse ideals such as solidarity, international social action, pacifism, Europeanism, and democracy constituted ideational factors supporting the establishment of international organizations.[74]

3.3. Strategic Factors

A third type of factors might be called the strategic ones. The international organizations served, first, as a back door to power.[75]

3.3.1. *Power Gain for some States*

Some types of States sought to enter stage through this door. The French Second Empire for example, which suffered from legitimacy deficits, arguably tried to cover these through international action.[76] More importantly, the small neutral States (Switzerland and Belgium in particular) competed for hosting the international administrative unions. Being a seat of an administrative union not only offered the seat State a political platform, but also, initially, some income from taxes, and a measure of control over the administrative union. Switzerland hosted the international offices of the Telegraph Union and of the Postal Union. Both offices were part of the Swiss administration, and annual reporting was included in the annual report of the Swiss Federal Council to the Swiss Parliament.[77]

Bringing a problem to the international agenda was also a means for governments to detract from domestic problems. This was especially visible in the field of labour. The Swiss canton of Glarus was one of the leading cantons of early modernization in textile industries; already in 1855, its government called for international agreements among all

---

[71] 'Règlement organique du Conseil de santé à Constantinople pour les provenances de mer' (n 61).

[72] B von Stoll *Der oberste Gesundheitsrat von Konstantinopel in seiner völkerrechtlichen Bedeutung, 1838–1914* (Piloty & Loehle München 1922) at 5.

[73] J Ray *Commentaire du Pacte de la Société des Nations selon la politique et la jurisprudence des organes de la Société* (Sirey Paris 1930) Preamble, at 68: 'la Société des Nations est faite pour avoir . . . un pouvoir d'ordre moral sur le monde entier.'

[74] See quotes given in n 65.

[75] *Internationale Organisationen seit 1865* (n 6) 10–11 and 34.

[76] M Herren-Oesch in this context refers to two World Expositions in Paris (in 1855 und 1867) and to the Latin Monetary Union (concluded between France, Belgium, Switzerland, and Italy in 1865), *Internationale Organisationen seit 1865* (n 6) 17.

[77] See for example 'Bericht des Bundesrathes an die hohe Bundesversammlung über seine Geschäftsführung im Jahre 1876' in *Schweizerisches Bundesblatt* (1877) 437–82.

European industrialized States on uniform labour standards. This was to prevent unfair competition by States with low labour standards.[78] After the harmonization of Swiss labour laws by a federal statute in 1877,[79] the Swiss government sought to initiate international action. However, the Swiss plans for an international conference were rendered moot by the German emperor William II, who convened the first intergovernmental conference on labour issues in Berlin in 1890, also mainly for internal reasons. However, William's public announcement in the *Reichsanzeiger* of 4 February 1890 provoked a diplomatic incident with the Swiss Federal Council who had been preparing such a conference for years.[80] This minor episode shows that initiating an international conference had become a prestigious matter by the end of the century.

3.3.2. *Power Gain for Non-State Actors and Non-State Entities*

Social groups which on the domestic plane did not wield any political power, such as women and workers, or those which had lost their political role, such as the nobility, tried to gain influence on the international plane. In the domestic context, participation in politics was conditioned on citizenship and formal voting rights. By contrast, the international sphere was much less rigid and thus open for informal political activity of disenfranchised groups. In the inter-war period, 'the very lack of democratic accountability which critics have identified as a weakness of international politics thus worked to the advantage of previously marginalized political actors'.[81]

This was especially true for women. The League of Nations Covenant contained a hard-fought-for equality article for the staff, stating that '[a]ll positions under or in connection with the League, including the Secretariat, shall be open equally to men and women'.[82] In fact, the number of women in the League of Nations committees was relatively high.

As for workers, the notion 'international' apparently entered the dictionaries in 1864 with the establishment of the International Workingmen's Association (IWA) in London, also called the 'First International'.[83] The statutes of the association held that the

---

[78] 'Bericht des Bundesrathes an die Bundesversammlung, betreffend die Frage internationaler Regelung des Arbeiterschutzes und die Berliner Konferenz vom 9. Juni 1890' in *Schweizerisches Bundesblatt* (1890) 46–781 at 692.

[79] 'Bundesgesetz betreffend die Arbeit in den Fabriken' (as of 23 March 1877) in *Schweizerisches Bundesblatt* (1877) 483–94.

[80] See for all details and a reprint of the emperor's public announcement 'Bericht des Bundesrathes an die Bundesversammlung, betreffend die Frage internationaler Regelung des Arbeiterschutzes und die Berliner Konferenz vom 9. Juni 1890' in *Schweizerisches Bundesblatt* (1890) 46–781; Diplomatic material relating the incident is reprinted in Commission pour la publication de documents diplomatiques suisses (ed) *Documents diplomatiques suisses* (Benteli Bern 1994) vol 4, 14–16 and 25–6.

[81] D Gorman 'Empire, Internationalism, and the Campaign against the Traffic in Women and Children in the 1920s' (2008) 19 Twentieth Century British History 186–216 at 215.

[82] art 7(3) of the Covenant (n 57).

[83] W Eichhoff *Die Internationale Arbeiterassociation: Ihre Gründung, Organisation, politisch-sociale Thätigkeit und Ausbreitung* (Albert Eichhoff Berlin 1868).

'emancipation of labour is neither a local, nor a national, but a social problem, embracing all countries in which modern society exists'.[84] The idea was that the worker's movement should be based on international solidarity—'workers of all nations, unite!'[85]

Finally, the international plane offered opportunities for non-sovereign entities. Egypt, for example, although still subject to the suzerainty of the Ottoman empire (or Turkish empire),[86] was a founding member of the Postal Union in 1874. Also British India and French, Danish Dutch, and Portuguese colonies became members of the Universal Postal Union.

4. Aspects of Technicality, Technocracy, and Functionalism

4.1. Territorial versus Functional Entities?

Current political-science integration theories typically contrast the territorial with the functional logic of integration.[87] Applying this grid to the entities of the 19th century, we might distinguish the territorial entities (the confederations) from the functional ones (the administrative unions). But this distinction is elusive, as shall be demonstrated with three examples.

First, the Postal Union, a prime example for an ostensibly 'functional' union, was—above all—a territory. Article 1 of the treaty stated that 'the countries between which the present treaty is concluded shall form, under the title of General [later Universal] Postal Union, a single postal territory'.[88]

Second, (territorial) nation States also emerged from initially 'functional' cooperation. The founding of the *Deutsches Reich* in 1871 was mainly the result of the strong Prussian-led ('functional') *Deutscher Zollverein* (1834–71),[89] and not a political consequence of the weak ('territorial') German Confederation (*Deutscher Bund* of 1815–66).[90]

---

[84] K Marx 'Provisional Rules of the Working Men's International Association' in Internationales Institut für Sozialgeschichte Amsterdam (ed) *K Marx and F Engels Gesamtausgabe MEGA* (Dietz Berlin 1992) vol 20:1, 13–15 at 13.

[85] Karl Marx in his opening speech to the IWA (reprinted in *Die Internationale Arbeiterassociation* (n 83) 5–15).

[86] See eg *Das Völkerrecht* (n 70) 55–6.

[87] See only D Mitrany 'The Prospect of Integration: Federal or Functional' (1965) 4 Journal of Common Market Studies 119–49.

[88] art 1 of the GPU Convention (n 53): 'Les pays ... formeront ... un seul territoire postal ...'.

[89] B Reinalda *Routledge History of International Organizations: From 1815 to the Present Day* (Routledge London 2009) at 32.

[90] N Weiss *Kompetenzlehre internationaler Organisationen* (Springer Dordrecht 2009) at 88–91.

Third, the river commissions were in a way also linked to territory, namely to the river. Some authors called them 'river States' (*Flussstaaten*).[91] The reason might have been that those authors could not think of any other way to conceptualize the far-reaching and 'quasi-sovereign' power of these commissions than by analogy to States.

4.2. Administrative Unions: Functional and Technical?

In the view of the time, the administrative unions with their international offices were merely functional and technical, and therefore non-political. In 1912, the title of Oppenheim's respective chapter was 'Unions concerning common non-political interests'.[92] Karl Strupp in 1921 defined administrative unions as 'treaty-based relations between independent States designed to pursue common non-political aims'.[93]

But the perception of administrative unions as being 'non-political' is contradicted by the set-up of these unions. They were in themselves constructed so as to espouse both the 'technical' and the 'political' dimension. Their legal basis was a dual one. It consisted in a convention and a *règlement* (regulation). The convention was the 'political' document, the regulation was the 'technical' one which specified the technical details (*mesures d'ordre* and *règles de détails*) of the respective service (for example, telegraphic or postal), and thus complemented the convention.[94]

The duality of the regime was reflected in the plenary organ, which was split up into two parts.[95] The political part was the 'congress' (of the plenipotentiaries), and the merely technical part of the plenary organ was the 'conference' of representatives

---

[91] *Das Völkerrecht* (n 70) 45. Von Liszt refers to authors such as Engelhardt, Geffcken, von Holtzendorff and Heilborn—however, the term *Flussstaat* seems to be his own invention. Engelhardt spoke of a 'state within the state' (*Etat dans l'Etat*), E Engelhardt 'Les embouchures du Danube et la Commission instituée par le Congrès de Paris' (1870) 40 Revue des deux mondes 93–117 at 117.

[92] L Oppenheim *International Law: A Treatise* (2nd edn Longmans Green London 1912) at 612–26.

[93] *Grundzüge des positiven Völkerrechts* (n 38) 40: 'völkerrechtliche Vertragsverhältnisse unabhängiger Staaten zur gemeinsamen Verfolgung gemeinsamer *unpolitischer* Ziele' (emphasis added).

[94] The Telegraph Union of 1865 was based on two texts entitled Convention et Règlement 1865 (n 7). The *Convention* referred to the *règlement* in art 54: 'Les dispositions de la présente Convention seront complétées, *en ce qui concerne les règles de détail* du service international, par un règlement commun qui sera arrêté de concert entre les administrations télégraphiques des Etats contractants.' (This provision became art 59 (1868), and later art 13 (1875)) Art 15 of the 1875 Convention explained the normative equal rank of Convention, Regulation (and tariff): 'Le tarif et le règlement... *ont la même valeur* et entrent en viguer en même temps qu'elle [the Convention].' The founding document of the GPU Convention (n 53) mentioned the *règlement* in art 13 (which became later art 14 of the UPU Convention (n 54)).

[95] See PS Reinsch 'International Unions and Their Administration' (1907) 1 American Journal of International Law 579–623 at 583 on the ITU: 'The double nature of the conference [1868], composed as it was of diplomatic and technical representatives, was preserved on this as well as on subsequent occasions.'

of the member States' administrations.[96] In both early administrative unions (the Postal Union and the Telegraph Union), the 'administrative' plenary organ was only created after the first years of functioning of the union through a subsequent revision of the founding treaty.

Both plenary bodies assumed the law-making functions, that is, the task to develop and to adapt the regime, 'with a view of perfecting the system of the Union', as the Postal Convention formulated it.[97] The political organ, the congress, was in charge of (periodically) revising the convention.[98] The technical organ, the conference, was competent to amend the regulation through a 'common agreement of the administrations'.[99] However, these amendments of the regulations could only enter into force (become *exécutoires*) after the approval (*approbation*) of all governments'.[100]

Besides, the activities such as telecommunications or postal services were directly related to national interests, and hence to politics, even 'high' politics. Communication, just like transport, had security aspects, and both were important for the national economy. Therefore, it is misleading to label the respective unions 'non-political'.

4.3. The League of Nations and its Technicality

The League of Nations was, in contrast to the preceding administrative unions, perceived to be the first 'political' organization. According to the preamble of the Covenant, it had a dual mandate: 'to promote international co-operation and to achieve international peace and security'.

The first limb, international cooperation, related to economic and social fields. The issues were enumerated in article 23 of the Covenant: 'fair and humane conditions of labour' (lit a); 'just treatment of the native inhabitants of territories under their control' (lit b); 'traffic in women and children' and 'traffic in opium' (lit c); 'free-

---

[96] Art 19 of the revised UPU Convention (n 54) introduced this duality four years after the foundation of the Union; arts 15–16 of the Telegraphic Convention of 1875 (ten years after the foundation of the Telegraph Union), foresaw *'conférences administratives', 'composées des délégués représentant les Administrations des Etats contractants'*.

[97] GPU Convention (n 53) art 18.

[98] Telegraph Convention 1865 (n 7) art 56: 'La présente Convention sera soumise à de révisions périodiques, où toutes les Puissances qui y ont pris part seront représentées.' In art 18 GPU Convention (n 53), the power of the congress to amend the Treaty was only implicit. The subsequent GPU Convention (n 54) did not mention revisions.

[99] Under art 20 UPU Convention (n 54), the administrations were allowed to make *'propositions concernant le régime de l'Union'*. Art 54 Telegraph Convention 1865 (n 7) stipulated: 'Les dispositions de ce règlement entreront en vigueur en même temps que la présente Convention: *elles pourront être, à toute époque, modifiées d'un commun accord par les dites administrations'* (emphasis added); the provision later became art 59 of the 1868 Convention. Arts 15–16 of the Telegraph Convention in the Petersburg version of 5/17 May 1875 foresaw that the *règlement* and the tariffs could be revised by the administrative conferences.

[100] Telegraph Convention 1875 (n 99 and n 7) art 16.

dom of communications and of transit and equitable treatment for the commerce of all Members of the League' (lit e); and finally the 'prevention and control of disease' (lit f). The League created three so-called 'organizations' in line with article 23, the Economic and Financial Organization, the Organization for Communications and Transit, and the Health Organization, as well as numerous committees.

In the first years of the League, its economic and social sphere of activity was qualified as 'technical', and sharply distinguished from the 'political' matters relating to peace and security.[101] With regard to this distinction, three points can be made. First, on the one hand, the social and economic work of the League was debased by critics of the League by calling it technical, whereas—according to the critics—the League should concentrate on its political mission to foster international peace and security.[102]

Second and inversely, the 'technicality' of the League was used as a disguise and as a defence against the reproach formulated by the statist camp that the League was a 'super-State'. A recent historical analysis of the League's 'Economic and Financial Organization' came to the conclusion that

[t]he key to understanding the often seemingly abstruse functioning and structure of the League was that its rules and procedures were deliberately kept ambiguous in order to provide the flexibility to pursue *political* negotiations by a variety of means, *frequently under the guise of 'technical' or functional discussions.*[103]

In the 1920s, the phrase '*La Société n'est pas un super-Etat*' (the League of Nations is not a super-State) pervaded the debate on the League. According to the Covenant's commentator Jean Ray, that phrase had the dual function of securing both acceptance of the League and preventing it from acquiring a greater (political) significance.[104]

Third, the League came to recognize the importance of the 'technical' cooperation in the 1930s, probably to make up for its failure in the field of peace and security.[105] More than 50 per cent of the League's budget was spent on the 'technical' work.[106] Present-day historians agree that the 'technical' work of the League was, in contrast to its failure in the 'political' domain, a lasting success. It brought about tangible progress (for example through the conclusion of more than a hundred conventions),

---

[101] C Tams 'League of Nations' in R Wolfrum (ed) *The Max Planck Encyclopedia of Public International Law* (OUP Oxford 2008) at <www.mpepil.com> MN 36, criticizing this distinction as simplistic from the outset on.

[102] See S Pedersen 'Back to the League of Nations' (2007) 112 The American Historical Review 1091–117 at 1108, referring to Secretary-General Drummond who complained about the intensifying activities of the League in allegedly non-political affairs.

[103] P Clavin and JW Wessel 'Transnationalism and the League of Nations: Understanding the Work of its Economic and Financial Organisation' (2005) 14 Contemporary European History 465–92 at 491 (emphasis added).

[104] *Commentaire du Pacte de la Société des Nations* (n 73) 61.

[105] 'League of Nations' (n 101) MN 39.

[106] 'Back to the League of Nations' (n 102) 1108.

and constituted a positive (not only negative) blueprint for the institutional design of the UN, for example for the ECOSOC.[107]

5. DEMOCRATIC ASPECTS

5.1. International Organizations and Non-State Actors: Civil Society and Business

Civil society, including business, has, since the 19th century, played an important role for the formation of international organizations.[108] This pattern is visible in the field of the protection of intellectual property. Inventors were reluctant to display their inventions at the world exhibitions which took place since 1851, if visitors were free to copy them. Therefore, in 1858 the first international congress on authors' copyrights was organized in Brussels. It was attended by private individuals, delegates from learned societies, and some government representatives, and led to the adoption of the 1883 Paris convention for the protection of industrial property, with a seat (*bureau*) in Berne,[109] and in 1886 to the creation of the International Union for the Protection of Literary and Artistic Property, likewise with a bureau in Berne.[110]

Private initiative in some instances led to the establishment of a public union in that field of activity. For example, the Metric Union which was founded in 1875[111] had been prepared by several international congresses sponsored by various scientific organizations.[112]

---

[107] I Claude *Swords into Plowshares: The Problems and Progress of International Organization* (University Press London 1965) at 357.

[108] S Charnovitz 'Two Centuries of Participation: NGOs and International Governance' (1997) 18 Michigan Journal of International Law 183–286.

[109] 'Convention pour la protection de la propriété industrielle, suivie d'un Protocole de clôture' (signed 20 March 1883) in J Hopf (ed) *MNRG* (Dieterich Goettingen 1885–86) series 2 vol 10, 133–9. The *travaux préparatoires* of the Convention, reprinted in that volume (ibid 1–132), frequently refer to the Brussels congress.

[110] 'Convention concernant la création d'une Union internationale pour la protection des œuvres littéraires et artistiques suivie d'un article additionnel d'un protocole de clôture et d'un procès-verbal de signature' (signed 9 September 1886) in F Stoerk (ed) *MNRG* (Dieterich Goettingen 1887) series 2 vol 12, 173–92.

[111] 'Convention concernant la création et l'entretien d'un bureau international des poids et mesures' (n 58).

[112] See for the history of the Metric Union M Vec *Recht und Norminierung in der Industriellen Revolution: Neue Strukturen der Normsetzung in Völkerrecht, staatlicher Gesetzgebung und gesellschaftlicher Selbstnormierung* (Vittorio Klostermann Frankfurt 2006).

Industry branches founded international industrial federations. The International Federation of Cotton Spinners, founded in 1904,[113] became a model for the 20th-century industrial federations. In 1919, the International Chamber of Commerce was founded in Atlantic City, NJ, and held its constituent congress in 1920 in Paris.[114]

Also, business was confronted with the Socialist International and feared that a revolution like the Russian one would happen in Western Europe. With the objective to forestall such events, entrepreneurs promoted the adoption of labour conventions, and the foundation of the International Labour Organization in 1919. The governments 'bought off' the revolutionaries by inserting Part XIII ('Labour') in the Treaty of Versailles.[115]

The world exhibitions were a matter of prestige and a source of expected income for governments, and an ideal meeting place and publicity for businessmen. They were often a platform for the foundation of new international organizations and associations.[116]

Perceptions about providing telegraphic and other means of communication as a public function, as a *service public*, shifted. American telegraphic companies were partly in private hands, and therefore the US (which became an ITU member only in 1908) had requested that private parties should be allowed to take a full part in the ITU proceedings. In 1871, the ITU admitted important private telegraph companies to its conference in Rome; they could officially make proposals. The organization since then had a 'mixed character'.[117] Since the 1990s, with the liberalization and privatization of the telecommunications sector, the ITU is, under the influence of the World Bank policies, being 'privatized' again.[118]

We witness here a temporal evolution from private trans-national associations to inter-governmental organizations and back again. This oscillation, just as with the activities of the societal and economic actors within international organizations, and the resulting hybridity of institutions, all manifest a blurriness of the 'private' and the 'public' sphere.

Probably until the establishment of the UN-ECOSOC's modus of cooperation with NGOs in 1968,[119] a clear-cut distinction between inter-governmental and non-governmental organizations was missing in practice. In compilations and statistics on international organizations of the 19th and early 20th centuries,

---

[113] CW Macara *Internationaler Verband der Baumwollspinner- und Weber-Vereinigungen—Erste Anfänge und Entwicklung* (Taylor Garnett Evans Manchester 1911).

[114] 'Business Men Go Abroad' *New York Times* (New York 6 June 1920).

[115] *Routledge History of International Organizations* (n 89) 226.

[116] GP Speeckaert 'Un siècle d'Expositions Universelles: Leur influence sur les Congrès internationaux' (1951) Bulletin NGO ONG 265–70.

[117] *Routledge History of International Organizations* (n 89) 86.

[118] J Støvring '"The Washington Consensus" in Relation to the Telecommunication Sector in African Developing Countries' (2004) 21 Telematics and Informatics 11–24.

[119] ECOSOC Res 1296 (XLIV) of 23 May 1968.

private associations were listed as well.[120] This means that inter-governmental and non-governmental organizations have in reality never been fully closed categories. The phenomenon of mixed membership is not a new trend but has been present from the very beginning of international organization. In conclusion, even if the mentioned private-public interactions do not constitute 'democracy' in a formal sense, they at least demonstrate some input by society to international governance.

5.2. The League of Nations and Democracy

Also '[t]he League of Nations owes its existence…to private initiative', wrote Oppenheim.[121] Already during the First World War, two liberal internationalists, John Hobson and Leonard Woolf, sketched out an international peace organization. In both their works, democracy and democratic lawmaking occupied a prominent space.[122] Similarly, the 'Hague Congress of Women', which in 1915 gathered more than 1000 women, adopted several resolutions which called for the democratic control of foreign policy.[123] The link between peace and democracy was also emphasized by President Wilson in his declaration of war on Germany: '[T]he world must be made safe for democracy'.[124] By distinguishing the belligerent German government from the 'German people', Wilson implied that 'self-governed nations' were more peaceful. He envisaged a 'partnership of democratic nations' which would henceforth secure peace. Also, the League should provide a forum for what Wilson termed the 'organised opinion of mankind'.[125]

[120] M Wallace and D Singer 'International Organization in the Global System 1815–1964: A Quantitative Description' (1970) 24 International Organization 239–87 at 244.

[121] L Oppenheim *International Law: A Treatise* (H Lauterpacht ed) (5th edn Longmans Green London 1937) vol 1 para 137, at 300. In 1915, a group of Englishmen under the chairmanship of Viscount Bryce published 'Proposals for the Avoidance of War' which foresaw the creation of a league. The movement installed the so-called Bryce-committee which led to the foundation of 'The League of Nations Society' whose programme was that a treaty should be made to establish a league of nations. A similar movement arose in the US, where in June 1915 'The League to Enforce Peace' was founded under the chairmanship of ex-President William Taft.

[122] JA Hobson *Towards International Government* (Allen & Unwin London 1915) ch 12, at 198–212; LS Woolf *International Government* (2nd edn Allen & Unwin London 1916) pt 2, ch 4, at 266–310.

[123] Resolution 8 of the Congress on 'Democratic Control of Foreign Policy' held: 'Since war is commonly brought about not by the mass of the people, who do not desire it, but by groups representing particular interests, this International Congress of Women urges that Foreign Politics shall be subject to democratic Control; and declares that it can only recognise as democratic a system which includes the equal representation of men and women', repr in J Addams, EG Balch and A Hamilton *Women at The Hague: The International Congress of Women and its Results* (University of Illinois Press Urbana 2003) appendix 3, at 74.

[124] President Wilson's Declaration of War, Message to Congress (2 April 1917); Records of the United States Senate; Record Group 46; National Archives (reprint available on <http://www.ourdocuments.gov/doc.php?doc=61> accessed 15 November 2011).

[125] 'President Wilson's Four Points, from his address at Mount Vernon, 4 July 1918' in RS Baker (ed) *Woodrow Wilson and World Settlement* (Doubleday, Page & Company New York 1922) vol 3, 45–6 at 46.

In line with these Wilsonian ideas, George Scelle described the League as a federation of liberal and democratic States, as a 'league of the free peoples'.[126] But exactly this exclusivity made the League suspect in the eyes of some. Notably Germany found that this organization was unfairly designed by the victorious States to their advantage, and was a part of the 'dictate of Versailles'.[127] By contrast, the fact that the League's Council and Assembly were composed by representatives of governments and not of peoples was perceived as undemocratic by other observers.[128]

5.3. Participation of 'Stakeholders'

A next feature of international organizations which might be qualified as constituting a form of participatory democracy is the participation of stakeholders in the decision-making processes of the organizations. Here the ILO *tripartisme* stands out.[129] It is the thus far purest example of 'functional', and not national, representation in the working of an international institution. This *tripartisme* is of course profoundly political. The fact that it is not national does not make it non-political.

Although no formal relationships between NGOs and the League of Nations were established, there was room for authentic private influence in the League. Their representatives spoke in commissions, produced reports, started discussions, and even proposed resolutions and amendments. In 1932, NGOs were allowed to address the delegates to the League's disarmament conference in a plenary session.[130] The intense campaign against trafficking in women and children, conducted by several voluntary humanitarian associations, finally led to the establishment of the League's Advisory Committee on the Traffic in Women and Children in 1922. The work of this Committee was then closely followed by those associations, and they continued to furnish knowledge and information.[131]

In the course of the years, however, the relationship between the League and the NGOs deteriorated. Formally, the League organs interpreted article 24 of the Covenant which allowed to place 'under the direction of the League all international bureaux

---

[126] G Scelle *Précis de droit des gens: Principes et systématique* (Sirey Paris 1932) at 247 and 249. Scelle justified the closed circle of membership of the League by pointing out that the League should be open only to political collectives which govern themselves freely. 'Democracy... and the right of peoples to dispose of themselves... were at the base of this conception', at 247 (trans by the authors).

[127] BW von Bülow *Der Versailler Völkerbund: eine vorläufige Bilanz* (Kohlhammer Berlin 1923).

[128] *International Law: A Treatise* (n 121) para 167r, at 339.

[129] cf arts 3 and 7 ILO Constitution (n 3).

[130] K Hüfner 'Non-Governmental Organizations' in R Wolfrum (ed) *United Nations: Law, Policies and Practice* (Beck München 1995) vol 2, para 6, 927–35 at 928.

[131] See D Gorman 'Empire, Internationalism, and the Campaign against the Traffic in Women and Children in the 1920s' (2008) 19 Twentieth Century British History 186–216.

already established by general treaties of the parties' narrowly, so as to exclude NGOs from the scope of the provision.[132] This allowed the League to gradually curtail NGO participation and privileges.

5.4. State Equality, Unanimity, and Majority Rule in International Organizations

Another manifestation of democracy in the work of international organizations seems to be the voting rule 'one state, one vote'.[133] (But note that the Covenant assigned a privileged status to the permanent Council members.[134] Contemporaries perceived this as a reflection of the 'Concert of Europe'[135]). However, this is at best a kind of inter-state democracy. Once it is accepted that the starting point of democratic governance should be the individual human being, State's equal votes obtain a different flavour. The scheme grossly misrepresents individuals. The equal voting power of States within international organizations could therefore even be called anti-democratic.

Already before 1945, the second voting rule, the principle of unanimity, was considered a reflection of sovereign equality[136] (a principle codified only later in article 2(1) UN Charter). Unanimity was the principal rule for the voting procedures of early international organizations.[137] Unanimity was enshrined in article 5 of the Covenant of the League of Nations for decisions of the Assembly and the Council. The requirement of unanimity was deemed self-evident, especially for political bodies. The PCIJ held in 1925 that 'Article 5 states a general principle ... [which] may be regarded as the rule natural to a body such as the Council of the League of Nations'.[138] In line with that, unanimity in voting or an explicit subsequent consent of States to decisions taken by international institutions was the rule for all

---

[132] *Commentaire du Pacte de la Société des Nations* (n 73) art 24, at 670.

[133] For the Rhine Commission art 94 of the Convention of Mayence (1831) (n 27); art 18 UPU Convention (1874) (n 54); art 16 Telegraph Convention (n 94); art 7 Sugar Convention (n 60).

[134] The Council (art 4 of the Covenant) had four (later five) permanent members: France, Italy, Japan, and the UK. The US failed to take its allotted place. From 1926 to 1933, Germany was a permanent member, and from 1934–39 the Soviet Union.

[135] *International Law: A Treatise* (n 121) vol 1, at 316.

[136] ibid vol 1 para 116a, at 226.

[137] See PS Reinsch *Public International Unions: Their Work and Organization: A Study in International Administrative Law* (Athenaeum Boston 1911) at 152; W Koo *Voting Procedures in International Political Organizations* (Columbia University Press New York 1947) at 8.

[138] PCIJ, *Article 3, Paragraph 2, of the Treaty of Lausanne (Frontier between Turkey and Iraq) (Advisory Opinion)* PCIJ Rep Series B No 12 at 30.

decisions which had a high political impact or imposed new duties upon the members.[139] Decisions by the majority without subsequent State consent[140] were in most cases limited to decisions with a merely internal effect.[141] Despite the limited significance of majority voting rules in practice, they have always been highly symbolic and important for the theory of international law. The mere possibility of binding a State to a rule to which it did not explicitly consent brings up the question of State sovereignty and of the corresponding authority of the international organization. One early and often discussed example was the International Sugar Union established in 1902.[142] Its article 7 installed a permanent commission which, by majority vote, could impose decisions with immediate effect on its members. In article 10, the commission was granted a decisive role in the process of admission of new member States. The Sugar Union thus developed a 'veritable international authority',[143] which was qualified as a 'remarkable abandonment of sovereignty'.[144]

Strict unanimity tends to be ineffective. Therefore, the organs of the League of Nations developed ways of circumventing the strict wording of article 5 of the Covenant. For example, the Council and the Assembly agreed to the principle that abstentions were disregarded, qualifying abstaining states as non-present states.[145]

The unanimity principle has been heralded by many as democratic. Unanimity guarantees a chain of legitimacy because the decision of the international organization may ultimately be traced back to the will of the people of the individual member States. States defend unanimous decision making particularly for matters which might affect important national interests.[146]

[139] For the Rhine Commission see art 20 of the Convention of Mayence 1831 (n 27) and later art 46 of the Act of Mannheim (1868) (n 27); for the Universal Postal Union see art 20 UPU Convention (n 54).

[140] For the Rhine Commission art 94 of the Convention of Mayence 1831 (n 27); for the ITU see art 16 (1875) (n 94).

[141] For example, majority voting was foreseen in the 'comité international' of the Metric Union in art 12 of the *règlement* (n 58); however, the Comité had no law-making functions at all.

[142] Sugar Convention (n 60).

[143] N Politis 'L'organisation de l'union internationale des sucres' (1904) 2 Revue de Science et de Législation Financières 1–27, at 1 (trans by the authors).

[144] DW Bowett *The Law of International Institutions* (Stevens and Sons London 1963) at 8.

[145] *Commentaire du Pacte de la Société des Nations* (n 73) art 5, at 228.

[146] This was famously enshrined in the so-called 'Luxembourg Compromise' of 29 January 1966 which put an end to an institutional crisis of the European Community. While the States formally adhered to a majority voting rule in the Council, they decided that unanimity should apply when important national interests were at stake. Moreover, France stated that in any case the 'discussion must continue until an unanimous agreement is reached'. See W Nicoll 'The Luxembourg Compromise' (1984) 23 Journal of Common Market Studies 35–43.

5.5. The Autonomy of International Organizations and Democratic Deficits

The increasing autonomy of international organizations created a tension to the ideal of democracy. The early administrative unions' bureaux were still part of the national administration. The host States had the powers to regulate the administration and procedures of the international offices. An example was the International Union of Railway Freight Transportation whose central office was foreseen by article 57 of the Convention of 1890.[147] The *règlement* entrusted the Swiss Federal Council with the organization of that central office.[148] Finally, the office was established in 1892 by enactment of the Swiss Federal Council.[149] The Swiss Federal Council was even empowered to regulate the arbitral procedure foreseen by article 57(3) of the Railway Freight Convention of 1890.[150] These provisions show that the secretariats or bureaux of the unions were initially fully dependent on the government of the host State which in turn was accountable to its national parliament.

Initial lack of autonomy was exacerbated by the fact that civil servants of administrative unions and river commissions did not enjoy immunity. Provisions which granted 'neutrality'[151] or 'inviolability'[152] to those institutions or their personnel were precursors of immunity. The immunity of international organizations and their staff historically then evolved through an extension of the diplomatic immunities of state diplomats in foreign countries to the immunity of member state representatives in international organizations, and then to the organizations and their officials themselves.[153] The analogy to diplomats was still present in the wording of the League Covenant which granted 'diplomatic privileges and immunity' to the League officials 'when engaged on the business of the League'.[154] Gradually, the insight gained ground

---

[147] 'Convention internationale sur le transport de marchandises par chemins de fer du 14 Octobre 1890' in F Stoerk (ed) *MNRG* (Dieterich Goettingen 1894) series 2 vol 19, 289–366.

[148] 'Règlement relatif à l'institution d'un Office central' in F Stoerk (ed) *MNRG* (Dieterich Goettingen 1894) series 2 vol 19, 327–30.

[149] The executive order is reprinted in G Eger *Die Einführung eines internationalen Eisenbahnfrachtrechts* (Kern Breslau 1877) at 765.

[150] 'Verordnung des Bundesrates betreffend das schiedsrichterliche Verfahren in den vor das Centralamt für den internationalen Transport gebrachten Streitfällen vom 29 November 1892' in *Schweizerisches Bundesblatt* (1892) 554–5.

[151] For the staff of the Rhine Commission 'neutrality' was granted in art 131 of the French-German treaty of 1804, called 'Octroi du Rhin' ('Convention relative à l'octroi de la navigation du Rhin' (signed 15 August 1804) in M de Clercq (ed) *Recueil des traités de la France* (Amyot Paris 1864) vol 2, 91–115); then 'neutrality' was guaranteed in art 108 of the 1831 Mayence Convention (n 27).

[152] art 18 of the 'Acte Générale de la Conférence de Berlin' of 26 February 1885 in J Hopf (ed) *MNRG* (Dieterich Goettingen 1885–86) series 2 vol 10, 414–27 at 422. It was surely no coincidence that the privilege of inviolability was conferred to an international body which was expected to take up work outside Europe. However, the Congo Commission never came into being.

[153] J Kunz 'Privileges and Immunitites of International Organizations' (1947) 41 American Journal of International Law 828–62.

[154] art 7 of the Covenant (n 57).

that the immunity of international organizations and of the international function-aries was a novel issue, distinct from diplomatic immunity.[155]

Overall, the governance activities of autonomous international organizations with genuine international functionaries who are not accountable to any nation state, and in which member states' representatives can sometimes be outvoted by majority decisions, may hardly be qualified as democratic by their link to the (potentially democratic) member states, because that link is loosened or even severed. On the normative premise that international organizations should be 'democratic' or at least somehow accountable, new types of democratic procedures need to be developed.

6. Conclusions: the Imbrications of Technicality and Democracy

6.1. Technicality as a Factor of the Legitimacy of International Organizations

At the turn of the 19th to the 20th century, the compatibility of membership in interna-tional organizations with State sovereignty was as vividly discussed a topic as it is today. Sovereigntists warned against too far reaching transfers of sovereignty. In 1896, Louis Renault demanded that States must reserve for themselves the supervision of the inter-national conventions which united them (and which constituted the foundational docu-ments of the administrative unions). States must not leave this 'to an authority which would superimpose itself in some way to the States with regard to the respective matter. That would be an abdication of sovereignty.'[156] Renault went on to say that the desirable governmental supervision over the unions had so far been indeed respected by the exist-ing international bureaux. They did 'not have a proper authority of their own.'[157]

More internationalist-minded lawyers, such as Ernst Ullmann, pleaded for an extension of international cooperation (*inter alia* through administrative unions). Ullmann considered this possible without 'damage to sovereignty.'[158]

---

[155] 'Privileges and Immunitites of International Organizations' (n 153) 841.
[156] 'Les unions internationales' (n 34) 25 (trans by the authors).
[157] ibid.
[158] *Völkerrecht* (n 39) para 104, at 253: 'Die Gemeinschaft dieser Staaten würde nur unvollständig ihre historische Mission erfüllen, wenn die Einzelstaaten einem nüchternen Formalismus folgend ihre ver-waltende Thätigkeit auf die formellen Konsequenzen der Einzelsouveränetät beschränken wollten. Wir sehen vielmehr in unserer Zeit, wie ohne Schädigung der Einzelsouveränetät die Kräfte der civilisirten Staaten in ihren kollektiven Leistungen sich auf so vielen Gebieten ruhmreich entfalten.'

The gist now is that both camps considered the 'technical character' of the admin-istrative unions, and later even of the League of Nations, to be a saviour of the sover-eignty of the member States. The 'technicality'-*topos* was used as a pacifier against critics. If the autonomy of the international organization related only to technical matters, then the 'real' sovereignty of the member States was preserved.

The modern version of this old theme is that purely 'functional' or 'technical' international cooperation does not affect popular sovereignty, in other words, democracy. A merely 'technical' organization does not need a democratic basis, because the matters are both too unimportant and too difficult for the people to decide on them. Defenders of the unions (and of present-day organizations) argued and still argue: it's only technical! Any autonomy which the organization might enjoy is limited to these 'technicalities', and therefore democrats need not worry about losses of democratic self-determination through the transfer of powers to organizations.

6.2. Technicality as a Factor of Efficacy of the International Organizations

In present-day political science, 'functionalism' is employed both as an explanation of the phenomenon of integration,[159] and as a recipe for the success of an integra-tion project. Similarly, in the 19th century, the technicality of the international organizations was regarded not only as a factor of their legitimacy, but—equally important—as a factor of their efficacy. In 1896, Louis Renault cautioned that international unions should be established only in those domains whose ('techni-cal') nature would permit the expectation that States would have the will and the power to comply with the treaty.[160] Otfried Nippold in his Hague Lecture of 1924 on the history of international law was convinced that the institutionalization of inter-state cooperation by administrative unions constituted an 'unimagined progress in the development of international law which was completely different' from all those 'political principles' which had been attributed to international law in the 19th century.[161]

---

[159] KW Abbott and D Snidal 'Why States Act Through Formal International Organizations' (1988) 42 Journal of Conflict Resolution 3–32. See for functionalist versus inter-governmentalist explanations of the processes leading to the establishment of the League of Nations MD Dubin 'Transgovernmental Processes in the League of Nations' (1983) 37 International Organization 469–93.

[160] 'Les unions internationales' (n 34) 22.

[161] O Nippold 'Le Développement Historique du Droit International depuis le Congrès de Vienne' (1924-I) 2 Recueil des Cours de l'Académie de la Haye 5–124 at 77 (trans by the authors).

6.3. The Politics of Technocracy

Due to the explosion of technical innovation, industrialization, and science, and the concomitant increasing complexity of societal life in the 19th century, governments felt the need to rely on 'technical' expertise in order to be able to run a country and to fulfill public functions. This might be called the beginning of 'technocracy' in the proper sense of a government of experts.

Both the States and the new public international unions relied on new intellectual disciplines that had emerged only in the last decades of the 19th century, ranging from sociology to statistics and engineering. It was therefore natural that experts had to be integrated into the political machinery.

The politics of technocracy were visible in the fact that the directors of the administrative unions which were based in Switzerland were leading politicians, and not administrative specialists for postal or telegraphic issues.[162] For example, the director of the International Telegraph Union was (from 1897 to 1921) the former Swiss Federal Council (a member of the collective government), Emil Frey.

The politics of technocracy also show in the staffing of the Economic and Financial Organization in the League of Nations with its powerful Economic Committee and Financial Committee. Those bodies had an exclusive mandate to advise the Assembly and the Council. The committees were composed of experts who were mostly high-ranking civil servants from national ministries of finance, directors of central banks, and specialists in areas such as trade and monetary affairs.[163] The technical institutions of the League were open to non-members of the League and thus 'mitigated the organization's transparent Eurocentrism'.[164] Overall, the reliance on experts was in various ways a part of politics.

6.4. From Techniques to Politics?

The ultimate question is whether there has been and whether there can be an evolution from techniques to politics. It is obvious that the 'technical' administrative unions were in some respects the path-clearers for the (more 'political') League of Nations. The economic and social matters, listed in article 23 of the Covenant, were, with the exception of the treatment of native inhabitants, all matters that had been on the agenda of the administrative unions of the 19th century.

But has such an evolution in a deeper sense taken place? An evolution from economic and technical cooperation to political cooperation, with a concomitant

---

[162] *Internationale Organisationen seit 1865* (n 6) 47.

[163] P Clavin and JW Wessel 'Transnationalism and the League of Nations: Understanding the Work of its Economic and Financial Organisation' (2005) 14 Contemporary European History 465–92 at 473.

[164] 'Back to the League of Nations' (n 102) 1110.

evolution of the status of the individual from a global bourgeois to a global citizen? Such a 'progress' was perceived by Franz von Holtzendorff in 1873. He diagnosed the arrival of 'a new era, in which the most important demands of modern world trade' were satisfied. 'But thereby the ... task of international law, namely to safeguard the highest and most perfect development of human culture and the personal rights of the individuals is coming to completion'. Holtzendorff found the significance of international law confirmed by the parallel trends of accepting both 'the basic ideas of the cosmopolitan citizenship of man *and* of the formation of nation-States by those people who were capable of independent culture work'.[165] Von Holtzendorff opined that, despite the absence of democratic government in most States, global economic and financial interdependence had created a 'new cosmopolitan factor', consisting in the material community (*Gütergemeinschaft*) among the nations.[166] This is a perfect statement of the idea of a spillover from technical and economic cooperation and integration to political cooperation and integration, which was only fifty years later fleshed out as a political science theory,[167] and which in the EU context has to some extent been confirmed by the facts.

Another way of explaining or predicting such a spillover lies in the argument that technical cooperation renders wars impossible, for two reasons. First, technical cooperation is rational and dispassionate and can therefore not be exploited to incite passions and obsessions which may end up in hatred and killings. The second reason is that the technical cooperation will bring peoples together and make them get used to each other, that technical cooperation has a socializing effect. Taken together both aspects of technical cooperation promote peace among nations. As Paul Reinsch wrote in 1911: 'War becomes criminal, a perversion of humanity in such cases. *There is no high ideal which can be appealed to for the killing of those with whom we cooperate in the work of making the world a better place'.*[168]

---

[165] F von Holtzendorff 'Das europäische Völkerrecht' in F von Holtzendorff (ed) *Encyclopädie der Rechtswissenschaft* (Duncker & Humblot Leipzig 1870) 747–823 at 762 (trans by the authors).

[166] ibid 760: '*Obschon politisch niedergehalten*, enfalten während eines langen Friedens die Völker ihre wirthschaftlichen Kräfte im Zusammenhang mit einer unermesslichen Entwickelung der Verkehrsmittel, durch welche die räumlichen Entfernungen auf ein mindestes Zeitmass verkürzt, die *handelspolitischen Interessen der Nationen unlösbar mit einander verknüpft* werden.... In den kostspieligen Eisenbahnlinien der Continentalstaaten, in den industriellen Anlagen der minder reichen Länder, in den Staatsanleihen verknüpfen sich die Capitalinteressen der europäischen Geldmäkler, die Speculation der Börse. Auf diesen Grundlagen erwächst ein *neuer kosmopolitischer Factor* der materiellen Gütergemeinschaft unter den Völkern, durch welchen die Oekonomie der Nationen sich langsam zu einer Weltwirthschaft umgestaltet' (emphases added).

[167] D Mitrany *The Progress of International Government* (Allen & Unwin London 1933); D Mitrany *A Working Peace System* (Royal Institute of International Affairs London 1943); EB Haas *Beyond the Nation State: Functionalism and International Organization* (Stanford University Press Stanford 1964). The theory of spill-over has been developed by Mitrany, but the term was coined by Haas (ibid at 111).

[168] *Public International Unions* (n 137) 7 (emphasis added).

The rise of cosmopolitanism through 'technical' cooperation in administrative unions was also predicted by Simeon Baldwin in 1907. He highlighted that the Universal Postal Union was so important because

it touches every man's daily life…Every man who sends a letter from New York to Tokio with quick dispatch, and for a fee of only five cents, knows that he owes this privilege to an international agreement, *and feels himself by virtue of it a citizen of the world.*[169]

Baldwin foresaw that acceptance by the population, what we now call social legitimacy, is a crucial factor of success of international organization.

What Baldwin did not foresee was that international organizations can also become a victim of their own success. Today's man or woman in New York takes the possibility of writing a letter to Tokyo for granted, and does not realize that he or she owes this privilege to an international organization. Just as our children in Europe do not realize that they owe the possibility of travelling from Germany to France without having to change money, and without having a passport, to the European Union.

This might be one reason why the existence and the functioning of international organizations have remained precarious until today. They have to be regained every day anew.

Recommended Reading

Bowett, Derek W *The Law of International Institutions* (Stevens & Sons London 1963).

Charnovitz, Steve 'Two Centuries of Participation: NGOs and International Governance' (1997) 18 Michigan Journal of International Law 183–286.

Claude, Inis L *Swords Into Plowshares: The Problems and Progress of International Organization* (University Press London 1965).

Herren, Madeleine *Internationale Organisationen seit 1865: Eine Globalgeschichte der internationalen Ordnung* (Wissenschaftliche Buchgesellschaft Darmstadt 2009).

Hobson, John A *Towards International Government* (Allen & Unwin London 1915).

Lyons, Francis SL *Internationalism in Europe 1815–1914* (Sijthoff Leiden 1963).

Murphy, Craig N *International Organization and Industrial Change: Global Governance since 1850* (Polity Press Cambridge 1994).

Reinalda, Bob *The Routledge History of International Organizations from 1815 to the Present Day* (Routledge London 2009).

Reinsch, Paul S *Public International Unions: Their Work and Organization, a Study in International Administrative Law* (Athenaeum Press Boston 1911).

---

[169] SE Baldwin 'The International Congresses and Conferences of the Last Century as Forces Working Toward the Solidarity of the World' (1907) 2 American Journal of International Law 565–78 at 567–8 (emphasis added).

CHAPTER 8

PEACE MOVEMENTS, CIVIL SOCIETY, AND THE DEVELOPMENT OF INTERNATIONAL LAW

CECELIA LYNCH

1. INTRODUCTION

THE impact of peace movements on the development of international law over the course of the 19th and early 20th centuries was significant, especially in advancing norms of equality of status and in advocating for and legitimizing international organization. This chapter relates the impact of peace movements and other civil society actors on the development of international law beginning in the early 19th century and culminating with the creation of the United Nations in 1945. During this period, civil society actors, including peace movements, had considerable success influencing international legal norms, the development of institutions, and the negotiation of treaties regarding arbitration, humanitarianism, and arms control. The establishment wing of peace movements linked with the movement for the development and codification of international law, which developed and strengthened enormously, especially in the US and Europe, during the 19th century. More grassroots and radical peace movement groups linked peace to anti-imperialism and abolitionism. Both of these movement trends had memberships that extended beyond the growing numbers of legal experts to include a variety of civil society groups, religious and secular, and these expanded exponentially in the period before, during, and after the First World War.

While the primary focus of this chapter of necessity concerns 'Western' and especially Anglo-American peace activists from the 'Global North', it also incorporates wherever possible actors from other parts of the world, including Asia, Latin America, and Africa. Much of Asia and Africa remained colonized by Westerners until after the Second World War, but activists such as Mahatma Gandhi influenced other groups and individuals around the world during the period. Because most Latin American and many Caribbean nations were liberated from colonialism in the 19th century (after the Haitian Revolution), their representatives often collaborated with peace-movement activists from other parts of the world to place measures for disarmament and arbitration on the agendas of international organizations, including the League of Nations. African activists and intellectuals also articulated cosmopolitan norms of democracy and independence, which intersected with developing human rights law and justifications for decolonization. Finally, Japan developed a peace movement in the early part of the 20th century, which also linked to activists from Western States through transnational peace networks.

The story of the intersection between these civil society actors and international law is, therefore, one of efforts to achieve several intertwining and sometimes contradictory goals: taming sovereign States and reducing their ability to wage war, democratizing foreign policy, expanding free trade, but also challenging great-power imperialism. Kantian universalist, Whig-progressivist, critical-Marxist, and religious politics informed each other, and sometimes clashed, as the following narrative demonstrates.

Legal norms promoted by these actors included constraints on States' rights to wage war and the requirement that States attempt to resolve conflict peacefully before using force. Over time, these norms were embodied in treaties and agreements such as the Hague Conventions (1899 and 1907), the Covenant of the League of Nations (1919), the Pact of Paris (1928) (also known as the Kellogg–Briand Pact),[1] and the Charter of the United Nations (1945). Additional norms promoted by peace movements include the constitutive principles of universalism (the notion that all

---

[1] Kellogg–Briand Pact (concluded 27 August 1928, entered into force 24 July 1929) 94 LNTS 57.

political actors should participate in decisions about peace, security, and the improvement of international life), and equality of status (the notion that they should do so on an equal basis and that rights should be granted to and obligations binding upon all) that provide the foundation for 20th-century universal international organizations such as the League of Nations and the United Nations. But while all groups promoted equality of status, they differed on whether to advocate immediate or more gradual abolition in the 19th, and decolonization in the 20th century. As a result, ideas about how to achieve peace could conflict with demands for independence or liberation, highlighting the different dimensions of the question of equality of status. Finally, and as a partial outgrowth of these earlier movements, civil society actors during the period were at the forefront of articulating norms underpinning the post-1945 development of international human rights and humanitarian law.

2. CIVIL SOCIETY ACTORS AND THE PHILOSOPHICAL BASES OF INTERNATIONAL LAW

Despite the ethical and programmatic differences among civil society actors, they were similar in that they all attempted to achieve particular moral goods, for some partially and for others entirely, through new international legal norms, treaties, and codes. This use of international law, for better or worse, differs from its use merely to achieve a 'practical association' of States; for example, to guide behaviour without any assumption of a more overarching common purpose.[2] Indeed, some might argue that such a practical association always embeds purposeful norms that cannot evade moral connotations. In this view, the content of the moral code becomes extremely important. These actors created a space for ethical debate by providing reasons to legitimize certain types of action and delegitimize others.[3] These reasons were contested within peace movement and other civil society groups as well as between these groups and government officials. The new legal procedures and institutions created over the course of this period demonstrates the constitutive nature of modern international law, that is, the role of social agents along with State representatives in articulating, legitimizing, and implementing it.

---

[2] T Nardin *Law, Morality, and the Relations of States* (Princeton University Press Princeton 1983).
[3] F Kratochwil *Rules, Norms, and Decisions: On the Conditions of Practical and Legal Reasoning in Domestic Politics and International Affairs* (CUP Cambridge 1989); C Lynch *Beyond Appeasement: Interpreting Interwar Peace Movements in World Politics* (Cornell University Press Ithaca 1999).

Immanuel Kant is frequently invoked to describe the relationship between civil society and international law, especially regarding how the development of cosmopolitan ethics can foster peaceful legal norms. Kant's understanding of the institutionalization of a republican peace and its relationship to 'perpetual peace' relies on the combination of political and moral action. Coming from a long tradition that understands human nature as inherently flawed, and writing during the period of Enlightenment thinking that espoused human reason as able to overcome moral and political flaws to engender human progress, Kant saw the creation of republics (which allowed participation and the use of reason at the domestic level) leading to the creation of an international law of nations to solidify peace at the global level. Both would be made possible by the use of ethical reason by enlightened peoples, who would connect with each other in a zone of peace that would gradually enlarge as others saw its benefits until it encompassed the world.[4] This type of Kantian 'cosmopolitanism' is often viewed as the basis for civil society attempts to create a League of Nations in the early 20th century.[5] The primary criticism of Kantian cosmopolitanism is that it is based on deontological ethics that reject consequentialist arguments for 'doing good' and promoting international law in favour of principled ones. Deontological ethics formed the basis of Kant's moral reasoning, which he called the categorical imperative, asserting both that one must act according to principles that can be universalized, and that human beings, having the power to reason, must be respected as 'law-giving beings' in and of themselves. According to proponents of cosmopolitanism, therefore, respecting others and acting according to principles capable of being universal can lay the foundations for peaceful relations among peoples.

In the early 20th century, Edward H Carr was the principle critic of this type of cosmopolitanism, arguing that it promoted a false harmony of interests based on liberal assumptions that what was good for some was good for all. In particular, Carr criticized the civil society groups that promoted the League of Nations and international law as being unrealistic 'utopians'.[6] But a more sophisticated critique of Kantian cosmopolitanism was offered by West African thinkers in the 1940s, who coupled

---

[4] A classic collection of Kant's political essays is found in L White Beck (ed) *Kant on History* (L White Beck, R E Anchor, and EL Fackenheim trans) (Macmillan New York 1963); other sources include I Kant *The Metaphysics of Morals* (M Gregor intr and trans) (CUP New York 1991) and I Kant *The Moral Law: Groundwork of the Metaphysics of Morals* (HJ Paton intr and trans) (Routledge London 1991). Michael Doyle is the primary exponent of Kant's political writings in international relations, beginning with M Doyle 'Kant, Liberal Legacies, and Foreign Affairs, Part I', (1983) 12 Philosophy and Public Affairs 205–35; 'Kant, Liberal Legacies, and Foreign Affairs, Part 2' (1983) 12 Philosophy and Public Affairs 323–53. My own interpretation of Kant and the democratic peace literature is in C Lynch 'Kant, the Republican Peace, and Moral Guidance in International Law' (1994) 8 Ethics & International Affairs 39–58.

[5] For a more expansive understanding of Kant's ethics for international law see the contribution by P Kleingeld 'Immanuel Kant (1724–1804)' in this volume.

[6] EH Carr *The Twenty Years' Crisis 1919–1939: An Introduction to the Study of International Relations* (2nd edn Harper & Row New York 1964); *Beyond Appeasement* (n 3).

the promotion of humanism and democracy with an unbending adherence to equality of status between individuals of every race as well as between colonial powers and colonies.[7]

In the narrative that follows, I demonstrate the complexity of the currents of thought and action that made up 19th and early 20th century civil society activities in favour of international legal norms and institutions. I suggest that the content of norms promoted during these periods emanates from constitutive processes that contain significant moral tensions and contradictions for the movements and actors involved. This narrative highlights not only the moral agency of these actors, but also the constitutive processes at play in which States (government officials), and historical trends (material and ideational) shaped their group identities, programmatic goals, and successes and failures.[8]

As a result, I argue that the non-state actors who promoted international legal norms and institutions 'cannot be easily classified within either the ideal-typical Kantian moral paradigm that keeps them in a deontological straightjacket', or the utopian nomenclature of liberal harmony.[9] Instead, these actors formed an integral part of the struggle for norms and mechanisms for peace-through-law that also embraced and reflected often contradictory tendencies as well as bargaining with States.

3. PEACE MOVEMENTS AND INTERNATIONAL LAW IN THE 19TH CENTURY[10]

From the 19th century to 1945, peace activism moved from origins in Anglo-American non-conformist Protestantism to a broader demographic that split into working-class versus free-trade activism in the 1930s and 1940s, to the beginnings of a non-sectarian humanitarianism during the Crimean and US Civil Wars, to a renewed

---

[7] SN Grovogui *Beyond Eurocentrism and Anarchy* (Palgrave New York 2006); Comité de coordination du RDQ *Au service de l'Afrique noire. Le Rassemblement démocratique africain dans la lutte anti-impérialiste* (Les Impressions rapides Comité de coordination Paris 1949); Albert M'Paka *Félix Eboué: 1884–1944. Gouverneur général de l'Afrique équatoriale française. Premier résistant de l'Empire* (L'Harmattan Paris 2008).

[8] A Klotz and C Lynch *Strategies for Research in Constructivist International Relations* (ME Sharpe Armonk NY 2007).

[9] C Lynch 'Debating Moral Agency and International Law in an NGO World' in O Kessler et al (eds) *On Rules, Politics and Knowledge: Friedrich Kratochwil, International Relations, and Domestic Affairs* (Palgrave New York 2010) 145–57.

[10] Much of the discussion of US and British peace activity in sections 3 and 4 is taken or revised from C Lynch 'Political Activism and the Social Origins of International Legal Norms' in C Lynch and M Loriaux (eds) *Law and Moral Action in World Politics* (University of Minnesota Press 2000) 140–74. The permission granted by University of Minnesota Press to reprint the respective parts is gratefully acknowledged.

push for peace through law (in the Hague Peace Conferences), social justice (through progressivism), and socialism (through the trade-union movement) in the late 19th and early 20th centuries, to the movements for universal international organization, arbitration, and disarmament from the League to the UN. Consistent with the constitutive framework outlined above, it is important to emphasize that the origins and development of peace movements occurred in conjunction with varying national and international events and trends. Peace movements were affected by sociological developments in each period and their consequent interaction with other types of domestic issues and movements; their goals and composition were often transformed by wars and international economic rivalries, and they were spurred on by nascent attempts at institutionalized international cooperation. All of these, in turn, influenced the content of movements' efforts to shape international law and organization. Movements broadened in their sociological composition throughout the 19th century, gradually expanding from origins in Anglo-American Protestant nonconformism to include secular, radical, and internationalist elements. National and international security concerns also affected the movements in both countries, influencing their growth, decline, ability, and desire to promote specific kinds of normative standards and institutional mechanisms for the maintenance of peace. From the late 19th century on, and especially during the inter-war period, civil society actors interacted (through demonstrations as well as bargaining) with government officials to promote legal norms and institutions.

The centre of transnational peace activity was located in Britain and the US, with additional links to other parts of Europe (Germany, France, Russia, Switzerland), Japan and elsewhere in Asia, parts of Latin America, and parts of Africa and the Middle East. Much more needs to be written about local-transnational interactions on peace in the 'non-Western' parts of the world. While non-party organizations were typical of the US and Great Britain, peace affiliations with political parties occurred for a time in France. Russian peace activism was best exemplified by Tolstoy, who influenced Gandhi and many activists in Europe and the US.[11] Women's activism produced transnational peace links between the West, Japan, and abolitionist. Later, pan-African groups demanding decolonization intersected with peace organizations and brought together activists from the Caribbean, the US, and the African continent.

3.1. Movement Foundations and Growth in the First Half of the 19th Century

In the United States, three peace societies were founded separately in New York, Massachusetts, and Ohio between August and December 1815. All three fused into the

---

[11] L Tolstoy 'A Letter to a Hindu' in L Tolstoy *Recollections & Essays* (Aylmer Maude intr and trans) (OUP London 1937) 433–9.

American Peace Society under the leadership of William Ladd in 1827. In Britain, William Allen founded the London Peace Society in June 1816. These societies organized in the aftermath of significant transnational events: the American Revolution and War of 1812 (with Britain), the French Revolution and the attempted French hegemony in Europe led by Napoleon, and the Haitian Revolution and the rise of anti-slavery activism by slaves, former slaves, and white sympathizers.

These first peace societies, however, represented primarily a nonconformist Christian attempt to enter the political realm. Although technically non-sectarian, they included traditional Christian pacifists, primarily Quakers, and thus employed Christian arguments in favour of peace. Historically, they are important because they moved anti-war sentiment into public debate. According to Peter Brock, this new Christian activism in the form of peace societies (instead of rejecting participation in the political realm) represented a new phase for Nonconformists and other Protestant churches in the 19th century.[12] These societies eventually learned of each other's existence. They were 'surprised and delighted' by this knowledge, and after a time began to initiate mutual contacts.[13]

The efforts of the British and American peace societies between 1814 and 1816 represented, then, an organized but non-institutionalized expression of anti-war sentiment that was not replicated on the European continent until 1830.[14] The primary questions debated by early 19th-century movements included whether opposition to all war was required by Christian ethics. This debate brought into the open a fundamental division that would plague all Anglo-American peace movements thereafter. Pacifist opposition to war took the form of ethical opposition to all killing, while many who opposed war on a more selective basis, later to be called pacifists and some to become internationalists, promoted a Whiggish-functionalist belief in international progress and reform.[15]

The London peace group attempted to spread its ideas on the continent, but the US society concentrated on proselytizing and disseminating tracts to religious congregations at home. However, despite the fact that movements tended not to target political institutions, they did begin discussing and debating methods of reversing and transcending the 'custom of war'.[16] Both pacifists and other antiwar society members agreed even at this stage on the need to renounce wars of aggression; their joint call of opposition to the customary character of war represented a nascent, vaguely formulated aspiration, and the beginnings of action to influence international legal

---

[12] P Brock *Pacifism in Europe to 1914* (Princeton University Press Princeton 1968) at 345 and 383; ACF Beales *A History of Peace* (Dial Press New York 1931) at 45.

[13] SN Cooper *Internationalism in Nineteenth Century Europe: The Crisis of Ideas and Purpose* (Garland New York 1976) at 21; *A History of Peace* (n 12) 45.

[14] *Internationalism in Nineteenth Century Europe* (n 13) 16–19.

[15] M Ceadel *Pacifism in Britain: 1914–1945* (OUP New York 1980) at 1–8.

[16] P Brock *Freedom from War: Nonsectarian Pacifism, 1814–1914* (University of Toronto Press Toronto 1991) at 37–44.

norms. They acted primarily for themselves and not to influence governments; neither governments nor the Concert of Europe took much notice of the peace societies.[17]

Both 'radicals' and 'free traders' challenged the religious nature of peace societies, and the broader composition of civil society activity for peace also gave rise to a series of international peace conferences in the 1840s. These congresses provided a forum for the articulation and debate of a wide range of normative projects (including the idea of a congress of nations), some of which would endure to become the precursors to 20th-century plans for global international organization.

The radical movement for peace arose as part of new forms of social activism in the 1830s. In particular, attention to issues of social and economic 'justice' came from the abolitionist movement in the US and labour organizing in Britain. William Lloyd Garrison's New England Non-Resistance Society, founded in 1838, sent emissaries to Britain to recruit working-class Chartists to the methods of non-resistance, although with only limited success.[18] Likewise, labour activism for peace began to spread to the United States: in 1846 Elihu Burritt founded the League of Human Brotherhood, an international organization that attempted to attract a working-class membership.[19] The league experienced considerable organizing success on both sides of the Atlantic. However, the older groups' leadership was more conservative and less inclined to challenge political structures, which limited cooperation between them and the Garrisonians, who embraced a radical rejection of government, and the British worker's movement, who engaged in overt political organizing.[20] These attempts to merge issues of human rights, social justice, and peace continued throughout the 19th and 20th centuries, but their effects on the development of international law tended to be piecemeal rather than united.

In addition to differences in methods and influence on international norms and conventions, civil society groups also engaged in vociferous debates over free trade during this period. The Quaker John Bright became the first persuasive proponent within the movement of the liberal belief in free trade that was taken up by Richard Cobden. This belief rested on three assumptions: that peace and prosperity were indissolubly linked, that both were possible to attain for all levels of the citizenry, and that both could only be attained by eliminating barriers to transnational (especially commercial) exchange.[21] Working-class radicals lost additional ground vis-à-vis

---

[17] *Internationalism in Nineteenth Century Europe* (n 13) 14.

[18] *Pacifism in Europe to 1914* (n 12) 396–7; *Freedom from War* (n 16) 30–1.

[19] *Pacifism in Europe to 1914* (n 12) 104–13.

[20] CF Howlett and G Zeitzer *The American Peace Movement: History and Historiography* (American Historical Association Washington DC 1985); RG Walters *American Reformers: 1815–1860* (Hill and Wang New York 1978) at 115–17; *Pacifism in Europe to 1914* (n 12) 347.

[21] AL Wolfers and L Martin 'Richard Cobden' in A Wolfers and L Martin (eds) *The Anglo-American Tradition in Foreign Affairs* (Yale University Press New Haven 1956) 196–205.

free-traders because of the changing economics of agriculture reflected in the domestic legal landscape in Britain. After repeal of the Corn Laws in 1846, which had previously protected domestic agricultural producers against foreign exports, it was clear that the free traders had won.[22] This explicit linking of free trade and peace characterized the dominant peace activity of the 1840s in Britain. It also resulted in the co-optation of British working-class radicalism by the middle-class concern with prosperity through tariff reduction, which in turn affected the course of peace activity by diverting demands for peace based on economic equality to peace based on the promise of future prosperity.[23] After 1840, Cobden himself began to speak of free trade and peace as one and the same cause.

The coalition of mid-century peace forces on both sides of the Atlantic, however, also began to organize international peace congresses in the 1840s. These congresses were designed to spread the faith more widely and, in particular, to encourage continental Europeans to engage more actively in the discussion of how to attain a pacific world. In effect, their significance lies in the fact that they debated and articulated, over a six-year period, plans for international institutions that embodied norms of arbitration, adjudication, and, to a lesser extent, universalism.

At the first International Peace Congress, held in London in 1843, delegates agreed on resolutions advocating arbitration clauses as a means of settling international disputes and a 'high court of nations' to keep the peace in Europe.[24] The Brussels Congress of 1848 and the Paris Congress of 1849 emphasized the need for international arbitration mechanisms and the creation of some type of international court. Other proposals, however, such as the arguments for a congress of nations (a project continually pushed by Elihu Burritt, who was originally inspired by William Ladd's writings of the 1820s), could not overcome the opposition of Europeans.[25] Likewise, delegates easily agreed upon the need for disarmament and reductions of weapons expenditures at the 1843 congress, but by 1848 and 1849 disarmament held different meanings for Anglo-Americans, revolutionary sympathizers, and advocates of the European status quo. Although the majority of British and US delegates could not sanction attempts to change oppressive domestic regimes through (violent) revolution, they registered 'ringing denunciations' of British and French foreign policy in Tahiti, China, and Afghanistan for engaging in bloody repressions of non-European peoples.[26]

---

[22] The Corn Laws were enacted in 1815 to preserve the profits of British landowners. See E Hobsbawm *Industry and Empire: The Birth of the Industrial Revolution* (The New Press New York 1999) at 175.

[23] G Claeys 'Mazzini, Kossuth, and British Radicalism, 1848–1854' (1989) 28 Journal of British Studies 225–61; *Pacifism in Europe to 1914* (n 12) 396; A Briggs *The Making of Modern England, 1783–1867* (Harper & Row New York 1965) at 321; EP Thompson *The Making of the English Working Class* (Vintage Books New York 1966) at 807–30.

[24] *Internationalism in Nineteenth Century Europe* (n 13) 22–7; *A History of Peace* (n 12) 67.

[25] *Internationalism in Nineteenth Century Europe* (n 13) 23–5, C Northend, *Elihu Burritt: A Memorial Volume* (D Appleton & Co New York 1879).

[26] *Internationalism in Nineteenth Century Europe* (n 13) 22.

The peace congresses did not receive much, if any, official notice, and their proceedings and plans were ridiculed by those segments of the press who did pay attention.[27] Still, they represented the first public discussions and agreement by various movement factions (religious pacifists, members of Burritt's League, and centrist peace society members) to institutionalize the international legal norms of conflict resolution through arbitration. In addition, the discussion (without agreement) of disarmament obligations attendant upon all States and the condemnation of the control and repression of territories and peoples outside of Europe represented a further step toward the recognition of the responsibility of all States in ensuring peace (an aspect of the norm of universalism) and the rights of peoples to determine their own fate in international society (an aspect of the norm of equality of status).

Yet the belief that peace and harmony could be attained by prosperity brought about by liberal economic policies gained the upper hand with those newly called internationalists, who convinced many pacifists in both countries of their logic. Richard Cobden attended the second International Peace Congress, which promoted a liberal political-economic agenda. Free-trade rhetoric increasingly suffused the British movement, particularly after 1846, and Cobden strengthened the explicit link between notions of liberal harmony and peace activism by publicly crediting the nonconformist peace testimony with influencing the broader repudiation of war that he himself did much to popularize.[28]

As a result, peace groups increasingly tended to support the international status quo against revolutionary movements of the late 1840s. Cobden and other liberals in the movement, for example, 'had little sympathy . . . with the contemporary movements for national liberation on the continent', because they feared that the breakup of States into smaller political units would worsen nationalism and hamper free trade.[29] However, neither strict pacifism nor Cobden's brand of free-trade liberalism were able to survive the mid-century wars fought by Britain and the United States. These tendencies would be supplemented by yet new sociological-intellectual currents in the latter part of the century that nonetheless continued to provoke discussion and debate of international legal and institutional mechanisms to ensure peace. These new currents would demonstrate that agreement on norms of arbitration and the observance of legally sanctioned rules of State conduct did not automatically go hand in hand with free-trade notions of harmony. Moreover, the increasing critique of imperialism and colonization in the late 19th century would also challenge both economic liberalism (in the form of free trade and 'free' access to raw materials) and lay the foundation for legal moves in favour of self-determination and equality of status.

---

[27] ibid 23–4; *A History of Peace* (n 12) 68.
[28] *Pacifism in Europe to 1914* (n 12) 406.
[29] ibid 389.

3.2. Mid-century Transformations and Competing Norms

The mid-century wars shattered the fragile unity among the original religious peace groups, the small radical components, and the then dominant free-trade leadership. For Britons, the Crimean War, which broke out in 1854 and involved Britain in a major European war for the first time in forty years, roused patriotic fervour, while some peace activists' attempts to stop the war once it had begun discredited the movement.[30] After 1857, with nationalism and imperialism on the rise, both Cobden and the Quaker liberal John Bright, the leaders of the then more-or-less fused free-trade and peace movements, lost their seats in Parliament.[31]

In the United States, the war with Mexico seemed to improve the peace movement's status during the 1840s, but the Civil War fifteen years later, like the Crimean War for the British, had the effect of seriously curtailing peace activism and decimating the membership of peace societies. The American Peace Society, fearful of losing its *raison d'être*, refused to take a position for or against slavery, while the conflict itself made many who had previously believed war to be an unmitigated evil conclude that force provided the best means of eliminating slavery and the danger of breaking apart the union. Moreover, in addition to the negative effects that involvement in war produced for the individual movements in each country, the Civil War caused a breach of the heretofore amicable communications between the British and the American peace societies: the British could not approve of the majority of the US peace workers' endorsement of the war.[32]

This mid-century peace activity occurred in the US in the midst of strong social justice and human rights moves in favour of abolition. Abolitionists also created strong cross-Atlantic ties (the British had banned the slave trade half a century earlier), but the work of William Lloyd Garrison, Frederick Douglass, and numerous other anti-slavery advocates in the US brought the tension between peace and social justice into the open. In addition, the 'crucial role of African-Americans in the abolitionist movement', which is often overlooked,[33] needs to be recognized to understand both the tensions between peace and social justice and the relationships between activists across continents on both issues.

This period 'cleansed', in a sense, the movements of their early faith in the power of Christian values and public opinion to achieve national and international peace. It forced many, in the United States especially, to rethink the boundaries of what they had previously considered to be absolute pacifism, a dilemma

---

[30] *A History of Peace* (n 12) 132.

[31] *The Making of Modern England* (n 23).

[32] *Pacifism in Europe to 1914* (n 12) 390; *The American Peace Movement* (n 20); DS Patterson *Towards a Warless World: The Travail of the American Peace Movement, 1887–1914* (Indiana University Press Bloomington 1976) at 2.

[33] A Klotz 'Transnational Activism and Global Transformations: The Anti-Apartheid and Abolitionist Experiences' (2002) 8 European Journal of International Relations 49–76 at 60.

that would arise anew during the 1930s. The experience of devastating wars also compelled movement activists who began to reorganize peace efforts in the latter part of the century to replace their faith in the power of public opinion and free trade with more insistent demands for legal and institutional supports for peace.

At the same time as strictly 'peace' movements were in decline, civil society humanitarian efforts to relieve suffering in wartime took off. Nicholas Onuf traces the composition and constitutive nature of 19th-century humanitarianism in 'Humanitarian Intervention: The Early Years'. As Onuf explains, 19th-century humanitarianism resulted from the intersection of state and non-state agency, intersecting with the ideological trends and external events that shaped the peace activity (and its decline) discussed above.

[H]umanitarian sentiments drew their sustenance from a potent combination of evangelical and utilitarian beliefs and practices—a Protestant ethic, as it were. They also combined with Romantic tendencies so much in evidence at that time to reinforce imperialist, nationalist and orientalist beliefs and practices. In turn, all of these beliefs fed a sense that humanitarian concerns demanded action, whether by governments or against them.[34]

Nevertheless, these reformist sensibilities gave way in the latter part of the century to yet another ideological development in social Darwinism. According to Onuf, it was in this context of 'an international relations increasingly conducted on Darwinist premises', that modern humanitarianism in the form of the Red Cross was born.

Inspired by the example of the International Committee of the Red Cross (ICRC), national red cross societies and many other organizations throughout the liberal world join governments in treating natural disasters as humanitarian emergencies warranting concerted intervention.[35]

Onuf also points out that this type of 'emergency intervention' required a legal framework, first outlined by Henri Dunant's successful efforts to bring governments together to negotiate a treaty in 1864.[36]

Thus, in Onuf's narrative, mid-19th century humanitarian intervention was a product of the fusion of romanticism, utilitarianism, religious and secular movements, and Darwinism, which soon intersected with the growing Progressivism of the late 19th century: 'Progressive movements in liberal society learned how to construct longstanding but despised social conditions into humanitarian emergencies warranting intervention within the law.'[37]

---

[34] N Onuf 'Humanitarian Intervention: The Early Years' (2004) 16 Florida Journal of International Law 753–87 at 778–9.

[35] ibid 781.

[36] ibid 782.

[37] ibid 757.

4. Late 19th- and Early 20th-Century Activism, the World Court, and Universal International Organization

The last decade of the 1800s and the first two decades of the 1900s are often referred to as the progressive era, one characterized by a 'search for order',[38] when 'the gospel of expertise and efficiency merged with economic regulation, social control, and humanitarian reform to become a conspicuous part of the public life of both countries'.[39] Many progressive reformers joined forces with older, bourgeois peace groups to work for arbitration, and increasingly added disarmament and the development of international organization to their peace programmes.[40] The most significant new push during the late 19th century, however, was the move by international legal specialists in favour of the codification of international law. During this period, movements began to have a more direct impact on State policies regarding accepting and institutionalizing two legal norms: conflict resolution through arbitration, as demonstrated by the establishment in 1900 of the Permanent Court of Arbitration (PCA) and later in 1920 of the Permanent Court of International Justice,[41] and universal participation in and responsibility for decisions about peace and security, as demonstrated by debates over plans for a league of nations.

In the last decades of the century, peace activism first appeared to take up where it had left off in the 1850s: the decline of the quasi-pacifist and radical wings of the two movements (begun in the 1840s with their co-optation into free-trade liberalism), combined with the fact that both Britain and the United States were major players on the world stage, gave a greater voice to the growing number of establishment internationalists who emerged as leaders of the movement, especially in the United States.[42] This revival of peace activism also appears at first glance to confirm the hold that liberal economic norms, including free trade, held over peace groups. Yet both Britain and the United States were also caught up in a new competition that affected security relations. The imperialist rivalries of the late 19th and early 20th centuries, attested to by Britain's leading role in the scramble for Africa and the Boer War, and the Spanish–American War waged by the United

---

[38] R Wiebe *The Search for Order, 1877–1920* (Hill and Wang New York 1967).

[39] M Keller 'Anglo-American Politics, 1900–1930, in Anglo-American Perspective: A Case Study in Comparative History' (1980) 22 Comparative Studies in Society and History 458–77 at 463.

[40] *Internationalism in Nineteenth Century Europe* (n 13) 13–14.

[41] Statute of the Permanent Court of International Justice (concluded 16 December 1920, entered into force 20 August 1921) 6 LNTS 379, 390 (often also referred to as 'World Court').

[42] R Osgood *Ideals and Interests in American Foreign Relations* (University of Chicago Press Chicago 1953) at 86–7; *Towards a Warless World* (n 33) 126 and 131.

States again reinforced the complexity of efforts for peace. Peace groups co-existed uneasily with nationalist claims, although a number of internationalists in both countries resolved the dilemma by justifying their own country's imperialism in the name of a 'civilizing mission' of spreading liberalism and democracy to 'backward peoples'.[43] These sentiments were reinforced by some elite internationalist leaders such as General Jan Smuts of South Africa as the peace movement became more transnationalized.

Consequently, renewed imperialist policies during the late 19th and early 20th centuries, accomplished with the collaboration of governments and militaries (as well as corporations and missionaries) caused rifts in the peace movement and encouraged the Left in many European countries to cultivate an increasingly antiwar stance, which it would maintain during the lead-up to the First World War as the Anglo-German naval race heated up and hostilities on the European continent became more pronounced.

Renewed imperialism also occurred in the midst of the rise of progressivist notions of progress and rationalist models of problem-solving. Progressivism and its impact on politics, including foreign affairs, is open to a wide variety of assessments and interpretations.[44] David S Patterson, for example, points out that for elite leaders of the movements in this era, the equation of peace with free trade was at its apex.[45] The trends towards professionalization of many occupations (for example, teaching, medicine, law, and social work) did little at first to negate the growing elite establishment influence on the movements—indeed, well-connected spokespersons were most often seen as a boon to the cause. In Britain, establishment activists who felt that the traditional peace societies were 'too closely identified with Nonconformist pressure groups' joined the American-led International Law Association to further projects for international arbitration among elite classes of lawyers and public officials.[46] Nevertheless, many progressive reformers made new connections between peace and economic and social needs, both at home and abroad, connections that engendered a distinct unease with liberal notions of harmony. Many progressives, who worked to reform domestic economic and political practices, extended their concerns about the exclusionary aspects of turn-of-the-century liberal society (the concern with the unemployed and marginalized by the settlement house movement imported into the United States from Britain by Jane Addams; suffragists' efforts to end the exclusion of women from political participation in both countries)

---

[43] M Swartz *The Union of Democratic Control in British Politics during the First World War* (Clarendon Press Oxford 1971); T Richard and N Young (eds) *Campaigns for Peace: British Peace Movements in the Twentieth Century* (Manchester University Press Manchester 1987); *The Search for Order* (n 38).

[44] DT Rodgers 'In Search of Progressivism' (1982) 10 Reviews in American History 113–32.

[45] *Towards a Warless World* (n 32) 12–13 and 126–9.

[46] K Robbins *The Abolition of War: The 'Peace Movement' in Britain, 1914–1919* (University of Wales Press Cardiff 1976) at 8.

into their peace activities on the international level. The Women's International League for Peace and Freedom (WILPF), for example, was suspicious of laissez-faire economic policies, and also worked to democratize decision-making on security issues.[47]

Moreover, a left-wing critique of war was also, once again, growing in influence during the progressive era. Although socialists were not consistently concerned with foreign policy issues during the latter half of the 19th century, the birth of the Labour Party in Britain and the activism of the Independent Labour Party (ILP) engendered a more developed critique of war in the UK,[48] while socialists in Europe refined their critique of war and US union organizers and radical pacifists did the same across the Atlantic. Despite the differences in the analysis of economic practices on the part of establishment liberals, progressive reformers, and the socialist Left, all movement components, however different their analyses of the causes of war, worked to legitimize norms that constrained States' right to wage war and institutionalize mechanisms for engendering inter-state cooperation.

Through the course of the 19th and early 20th centuries, peace groups and civil society activists reflected contemporary events and ideological struggles in their attempts to influence international legal norms. They broadened their sociological base as other domestic social movements grew and found common ground in the goal of promoting peace through arbitration, although they differed on support of workers' rights and abolition. In the 1840s and 1850s, the dominant theme in peace-group activism encouraged the notion of a harmony of interests between the promotion of individual prosperity and international peace and the concomitant promotion of both civic rights among States and rights to private property, with trade on the international level occurring among property owners according to a free-market regulation of supply and demand. The link between free trade and peace also encouraged a status quo conception of international order with movement leaders arguing against intervention in support of revolutionary movements on the continent. The decimation of the mid-century movements, however, was accompanied by the rise of the humanitarian in the Crimean and US Civil Wars, with a new motive for making the conduct of war more humane and less debilitating for non-combatants through agreement on international legal standards and codes. At the turn of the century, progressive reformers merged with peace, social justice, and international humanitarian groups. This reintegrated, albeit problematically, radicals, reformers, and liberal internationalists into increasingly transnational collaborations for peace.

---

[47] C DeBenedetti *Origins of the Modern American Peace Movement, 1915–1978* (KTO Press Millwood NY 1978); C Chatfield *For Peace and Justice: Pacifism in America, 1914–1941* (University of Tennessee Press Knoxville 1971).

[48] J Hinton *Protests and Visions: Peace Politics in Twentieth-Century Britain* (Hutchinson Press London 1989) at 32.

Thus, as a result of the changing sociological composition of groups interested in peace, the developing concern with humanitarianism both on the domestic and transnational levels, and the new competition between States for colonies and prestige, the mix of norms and institutions that civil society activists attempted to internationalize evolved. As new actors struggling for additional rights on the domestic level became interested in the peace issue (including abolitionists, labour unions, settlement house workers, and suffragists), civil society actors increasingly reflected a concern with 'humanizing' international relations and with ensuring the participation of all peoples and political entities in decisions affecting their welfare. Because of these concerns, civil society actors were also influential in the period just before the First World War in bringing about the creation of the World Court. At the turn of the century, the Darwinian struggle among the Great Powers for colonies and influence left a great number of new civil society activists uneasy with, and many openly critical of, founding international legal norms on rights to ownership and control of resources, people, and territory. As a result, some began to question the 'civilizing effects' of empire, and most concentrated their peace efforts on promoting international order through universalist civic rights and creating an international judiciary and legislature for discussing and resolving disputes. Many saw the two international congresses at The Hague in 1899 and 1907, which resulted in the creation of the Permanent Court of Arbitration (PCA), as the first tangible institutional fruits of their efforts; some new critics of old notions of harmony also saw in these mechanisms the means by which imperialism might be delegitimized, subject peoples granted rights as participants in international society, and peaceful change made possible. The role of civil society activists in the eventual creation in 1920 of the World Court was significant: some argue that the Second Hague Conference of 1907, at which the idea of such a court was discussed (although not yet realized), was 'a meeting that the powers would not have spontaneously convoked without considerable pressure exerted on them'.[49]

At the same time, movements for peace increasingly became transnationalized, a trend that would continue before and especially after the First World War. Internationalists, peace and non-violence activists from South Africa, Japan, and India, for example, broadened the movement's base, sometimes reinforcing Western legal norms of paternalism and other times introducing new models of action and challenges for international law. General Jan Smuts, South African diplomat and proponent of global international organization through both the League and the United Nations, was in the first category. In addition to his work in favour of arbitration, Smuts was an important figure in the design of article 22 of the

---

[49] *Internationalism in Nineteenth Century Europe* (n 13) 17–18; W Kuehl *Seeking World Order: The United States and International Organization to 1920* (Vanderbilt University Press Nashville 1969).

League Covenant and the Mandate system. This system assigned designations of 'A',
'B', and 'C' to different territories, allegedly according to their level of development
(Smuts was instrumental in placing South West Africa in the 'C' or 'least-developed'
category).[50] The Mandate system remained a difficult issue for peace groups
throughout the inter-war period, with some groups criticizing its imperialist
assumptions and others arguing that it was a necessary step in the cause of self-
determination.

Other areas of the world also exhibited peace activism. The Women's International
League strove to create ties across Europe, including German, Austrian, and Swiss as
well as Japanese activists after the First World War. In Japan, peace activism had also
taken root in the late 19th century, although on a smaller scale than in Europe and the
US. Japan's first peace group, *Nihon heiwa-kai*, was founded in 1889, and the writer
Uchimura Kanzō, who became a pacifist after the 1894–95 war against China (which
he had originally supported), 'is often considered Japan's most distinguished pre-
World War II pacificist', who 'spoke out consistently against war and militarism until
his death in 1930'.[51] First in South Africa and later in India, Mahatma Gandhi practised and refined his method of non-violence, known as *satyagraha*, in order to
achieve rights of representation, economic justice, and eventually total sovereign
independence. Gandhi's actions had a significant impact on peace activists in the
'Global North', who debated whether and how they could be implemented in Europe.
Gandhi's nonviolent actions in favour of Indian independence from Britain also
ignited debates among peace activists regarding the limits of self-determination in
legal norms of equality of status.

4.1. From the League of Nations to the United Nations

Civil society actors are now given credit for creating plans for global international
organization that became influential vis-à-vis governments. For example, the Wom-
en's International League for Peace and Freedom and other groups' proposals appear
to have influenced Wilson's 14 Points as well as the content of the Charter of the
League.[52] These actors during and after the First World War played a significant role
in ensuring that the normative foundations of their projects would provide new
standards of diplomacy and guides for State foreign policy practice, in the form of

---

[50] SN Grovogui *Sovereigns, Quasi-Sovereigns, and Africans* (University of Minnesota Press Minneapolis 1996) at 134–5.

[51] D Cortright *Peace: A History of Movements and Ideas* (CUP Cambridge 2008) at 29.

[52] MD Dubin 'Toward the Concept of Collective Security: The Bryce Group's "Proposals for the
Avoidance of War," 1914–1917' (1970) 24 International Organization 288–318 at 299; *Seeking World Order*
(n 49); P Yearwood, '"On the Safe and Right Lines": The Lloyd George Government and the Origins of
the League of Nations, 1916–1918' (1989) 32 Historical Journal 131–55.

mechanisms for arbitration, arms control treaties, and the development of international courts.

More specifically, inter-war movements differed from their 19th- and early 20th-century predecessors in their direct experience of worldwide, cataclysmic war, conducted with enormously destructive weapons such as submarines, poison gas, and aeroplanes that for the first time directly targeted civilians. After the First World War, faith in State security practices and traditional forms of diplomacy was at a low never before seen, resulting in a widespread willingness to criticize government policies and put forth detailed alternatives that were based on principles of international law and organization. Consequently, inter-war movements no longer expressed qualms about disarmament: arms reduction, either unilateral or multilateral, became the primary focus of many civil society actors for more than a decade. Disarmament supplanted even the progressive-era push for codification of international law in the eyes of many activists, because they believed that merely codifying existing practices in international law—particularly the foundational respect for States' sovereign rights and the concomitant disregard for the 'self-determination of peoples'—would assist in perpetuating an unjust status quo. These movements, therefore, promoted the League, international law, and principles of universal participation and equality of status to restrain Britain, France, the United States, and other powers. Inter-war peace movements and their supporters by and large believed that international legal norms and institutions had to possess the capacity to control, in addition to reform, States' war-prone tendencies. Both the experience of imperialism and that of the pre-First World War alliance system had convinced many peace activists that Great Power concordats needed to be replaced with universal responsibility for maintaining peace and equality of treatment at the international level.

Peace movements promoted international legal norms and mechanisms for disarmament and arbitration, through the principle of equality of status, in a number of ways. First, peace activists expected the newly created League of Nations to represent all States, and if possible all peoples, and toward this end worked for self-determination and in some cases independence of colonies as well as the inclusion of both the Soviet Union and Germany in the League. Second, they differed from pre-First World War activists in their concentrated and relatively unified stance in favour of the principles that all States should disarm, and that trade in arms should be controlled, even though they argued among themselves about unilateral versus multilateral disarmament. Arbitrating conflict had been the leitmotif of the 19th-century peace movements, and although peace groups in the immediate pre-First World War era agitated against the Anglo-German arms race, disarmament as a movement goal finally gained an equal footing with arbitration in the aftermath of the Great War. The continuing development of weapons of mass destruction during the inter-war period, particularly the bomber and various chemical weapons, encouraged the perception that civilization could not survive another war and fuelled the fire for disarmament.

These developments each had important implications for movement activism. 19th-century activism can be seen as a struggle among those who would prioritize universalist legal norms and their institutionalization, those who would stress founding peace on rights to private property and free trade, and those who believed that peace could only be attained through social justice and equality of individuals, groups, and nations. By the end of the First World War, the focus had coalesced around plans to internationalize participatory institutions (and their concomitant rights) in the belief that peace required universal participation and equality of status—norms that, it was believed, would allow for peaceful change rather than legitimize an unjust status quo. Peace and other civil society actors believed that these norms, when institutionalized through a league of nations, would also replace the management of conflict by either unstable alliances or Great Power machinations. By the inter-war period, agreement on the use of liberal economic institutions to foster peace had disintegrated, but accord on what might be called the republican compromise—institutionalizing norms of universalism, both in terms of rights to participation and in terms of obligations—was quite strong. Thus, in addition to working for recognition of the rights of Germany and the Soviet Union to full membership in the League of Nations and the principle of equality of status in armaments, inter-war movements promoted the recognition of parity in the naval arms race between the United States and Britain (with something less than parity for Japan), and obligatory arbitration of conflict on a basis of juridical equality. In place of liberal mechanisms such as free trade, then, was a stronger push for building on the creation of the League to institutionalize arbitration and arms control in multilateral form.[53]

Peace movements made an impact during the period because many groups could legitimately claim to represent thousands and in the case of the League of Nations societies, hundreds of thousands of adherents, which increased their chances of being heard in the press, parliaments, congress, and League organizations.[54] Peace groups engaged in transnational collaboration to promote the Geneva Protocol of 1925,[55] and after its failure, French and US groups decided to push for the Pact of Paris of 1928[56] as a second-best option to a more comprehensive League of Nations ban against aggressive war. Nevertheless, civil society actors compromized and agonized over legal norms and principles throughout the period. The Pact of Paris of 1928, for

---

[53] 'Debating Moral Agency' (n 10) 162.

[54] D Birn *The League of Nations Union, 1918–1945* (OUP Oxford 1981) at 80–1; R Taylor and N Young (eds) *Campaigns for Peace: British Peace Movements in the Twentieth Century* (Manchester University Press Manchester 1987); L Wittner *Rebels Against War: The American Peace Movement, 1933–1983* (Temple University Press Philadelphia 1984) at 13–15; C Chatfield (ed) *Peace Movements in America* (Schocken Books New York 1973) at 95–101.

[55] Protocol for the Prohibition of the Use in War of Asphyxiating, Poisonous or Other Gases, and of Bacteriological Methods of Warfare (concluded 17 June 1925, entered into force 8 February 1928) 94 LNTS 65.

[56] Kellogg–Briand Pact (n 1).

example, outlawed 'aggressive war', but was a product of compromise between activists who did not want to go outside of the League of Nations machinery and States that insisted on so doing. It is interesting that this pact, which has been vilified as naïve and inconsequential, remains one of the major pillars of international legal controls on States' war-making prerogatives.

From the London Naval Conference of 1930 to the World Disarmament Conference several years later, campaigns grew in numbers and in transnational representation. Women's peace groups spearheaded the collection of millions of signatures to pressure governments to reduce armaments at the London Naval Conference, the third of three conferences (after Washington in 1922 and the Coolidge Conference in 1926) to attempt to control the weaponry of the three major naval powers of the time.

The series of naval disarmament conferences between the US, Britain, and Japan achieved only limited movement objectives. As a result, peace activists worked still harder to demonstrate a transnational show of support for the World Disarmament Conference of 1932–1934, which took place at the League of Nations in Geneva. However, the World Disarmament Conference, which was to be the culmination of peace movement work to get rid of the most destructive forms of weapons, ended in failure (due in part to the rise of Hitler in Germany). As successive aggressions by Japan, Italy, and Germany succeeded each other in the 1930s and peace movement fissures deepened, it appeared that movements' efforts to institutionalize legal controls on war had failed. The failures of the World Disarmament Conference, followed by the Italian invasion of Abyssinia, the Spanish Civil War, the Anschluss, and eventually Munich, split the movements in most countries.

In retrospect, however, one of the major achievements of inter-war civil society activism was laying the normative foundations for the continuation of international organization in the form of the United Nations.[57] The peace movement was also becoming increasingly transnational in the 1930s, not only in women's groups and the League of Nations societies, but also in transnational faith-based peace activism. Mary Church Terrell, a long-time member of the Women's International League for Peace and Freedom (WILPF) in the US, who worked for racial inclusion in the WILPF and other organizations, described the International Assembly of the World Fellowship of Faiths in 1937 in London. In addition to Emperor Haile Selassie of Ethiopia, the assembly included delegates from the East Indies, Ceylon, Germany, the Netherlands, Hungary, India, and Mexico, as well as the US and Britain.[58] All of these groups continued to advocate for universal international organization as war loomed, and also after it broke out in 1939–41. This push by peace activists across most of the political spectrum in favour of a continuation of global international organization

---

[57] *Beyond Appeasement* (n 3).
[58] MC Terrell *A Colored Woman in a White World* (Arno Press New York 1980) at 403.

also resulted in representation at the San Francisco Conference of June 1945. Civil society groups were included in many of the forums of the League, but their organizational work in favour of a United Nations (although they tended to oppose granting veto power to the new Security Council, disagreed on Mandates, and wanted stronger measures against military and economic conflict), and their efforts resulted in the creation of new official channels for civil society input as consultative organizations to the UN Economic and Social Council (a status that has continued in greatly expanded form to this day).

Moreover, post-First World War civil society groups increasingly included transnational humanitarian concerns such as the 'traffic in women and children', the opium trade, the effects of reparations, and the blockade of formerly enemy countries, at the forefront of their work. Equality of status continued to be an international norm promoted on the individual and group as well as national levels: anti-slavery activists realized the coming into force of the Slavery Convention (1926),[59] US and Latin American activists worked to delegitimize American actions in occupying and controlling Haiti (from 1915 to 1934) and peace movements as a whole continued to debate the merits of the Mandate system versus self-determination and independence of colonies.

Regarding imperialism and colonization, while the more establishment wing of the Western peace movement favoured eventual 'self-determination', others inspired by Mahatma Gandhi began to experiment with nonviolent activism; others inspired by pan-Africanist writers and activists such as William Edward Burghardt DuBois as well as African intellectuals demanded decolonization and the overturning of imperialist policies towards what would eventually become 'the Third World'.

5. CONCLUSION

The examples of 19th- and early 20th-century non-State moral action discussed above emanated first from civil society organizations in Britain and the US, but soon had transnational components that increased in strength particularly in the 20th century. Their projects for international law were shaped primarily by liberal principles and legal norms, in both the democratic theory and economic senses of the term liberalism. Yet struggles over the meaning of justice and equality of status infused these movements as well, intersecting with 19th-century workers' rights and

---

[59] Slavery Convention (concluded 25 September 1926, entered into force 9 March 1927) 60 LNTS 253.

abolitionist organizations and 20th-century socialist and (to a lesser extent) communist parties and self-determination efforts. Non-state actors have gradually become adept at using legal norms to push for a variety of actions, including an expansion of legal institutions, mechanisms, and procedures (the League of Nations, the Permanent Court of International Justice, the UN, the International Court of Justice, the ICC) and the extension of norms, charters, and treaties to cover new areas from human rights to humanitarian relief, from just war principles to war crimes and charges of genocide.[60]

This narrative of civil society activism to promote international legal norms and institutions cannot, I assert, be analysed as static or as fitting into a single ideological paradigm. For example, if we label such activism as simply liberal or utopian, as Edward H Carr did, then we miss the constitutive nature of law, historical developments, and both state and non-state activism. Rather, as I have argued elsewhere, Kantian ethics—in their conceptual, deontological form rather than the practical form described by Kant in 'Perpetual Peace'[61]—provide an extremely limited understanding of constitutive processes of civil society influence on the development of international law. The result of this narrative of civil society influence is not deontological moral action, but contextualized ethical contestation and normative development.[62]

Of course, some groups and individuals, in hindsight, negotiated their goals better than others within this context of rapidly evolving political circumstances. But moral and pragmatic struggles over content, procedure, law, and policy merged together during the 19th and 20th centuries. This history of peace movement and civil society activism is significant for understanding the resulting legal principles and norms, such as the equality of sovereign States, the reduction of arms, and the peaceful resolution of disputes, and institutions such as the PCIJ, the ICJ, the League, and the UN. It is also significant because these norms and institutions, particularly the meaning of equality of status and further developments in international law, continue to be negotiated by civil society actors and governments today.

Recommended Reading

Birn, David *The League of Nations Union, 1918–1945* (OUP Oxford 1981).
Brock, Peter *Pacifism in Europe to 1914* (Princeton University Press Princeton 1968).
Carr, Edward H *The Twenty Years' Crisis* (2nd edn Harper and Row New York 1964).
Ceadel, Martin *Pacifism in Britain, 1914–1945* (OUP New York 1980).

[60] 'Debating Moral Agency' (n 9).
[61] 'Kant, the Republican Peace, and Moral Guidance in International Law' (n 4).
[62] 'Debating Moral Agency' (n 9).

Chatfield, Charles *For Peace and Justice: Pacifism in America, 1914–1941* (University of Tennessee Press Knoxville 1981).

Comité de coordination du RDQ *Au service de l'Afrique noire. Le Rassemblement démocratique africain dans la lutte anti-impérialiste* (Les Impressions rapides Comité de coordination Paris 1949).

Cooper, Sandi E (ed) *Internationalism in Nineteenth-Century Europe: The Crisis of Ideas and Purpose* (Garland New York 1976).

Cortright, David *Peace: A History of Movements and Ideas* (CUP Cambridge 2008).

DeBenedetti, Charles *Origins of the Modern American Peace Movement, 1915–1978* (KTO Press Millwood NY 1978).

Doyle, Michael 'Kant, Liberal Legacies, and Foreign Affairs, Part I' (1983) 12 Philosophy and Public Affairs 205–35.

Doyle, Michael 'Kant, Liberal Legacies, and Foreign Affairs, Part II' (1983) 12 Philosophy and Public Affairs 323–53.

Hinton, James *Protests and Visions: Peace Politics in Twentieth-Century Britain* (Hutchinson Press London 1989).

Hobsbawm, Eric *Industry and Empire: The Birth of the Industrial Revolution* (The New Press New York 1999).

Kant, Immanuel *The Metaphysics of Morals* (M Gregor intr and trans) (CUP New York 1991).

Kant, Immanuel *The Moral Law: Groundwork of the Metaphysics of Morals* (HJ Paton intr and trans) (Routledge London 1991)

Kuehl, Warren *Seeking World Order: The United States and International Organization to 1920* (Vanderbilt University Press Nashville 1969).

Lynch, Cecelia 'Kant, the Republican Peace, and Moral Guidance in International Law' (1994) 8 Ethics & International Affairs 39–58.

Lynch, Cecelia *Beyond Appeasement: Interpreting Interwar Peace Movements in World Politics* (Cornell University Press Ithaca 1999).

Lynch, Cecelia 'Political Activism and the Social Origins of International Legal Norms' in Cecelia Lynch and Michael Loriaux (eds) *Law and Moral Action in World Politics* (University of Minnesota Press Minneapolis 2000) 140–74.

Lynch, Cecelia 'Debating Moral Agency and International Law in an NGO World' in Oliver Kessler et al (eds) *On Rules, Politics, and Knowledge: Friedrich Kratochwil, International Relations and Domestic Affairs* (Palgrave-MacMillan New York 2010).

M'Paka, Albert *Félix Eboué: 1884–1944. Gouverneur général de l'Afrique équatoriale française. Premier résistant de l'Empire* (L'Harmattan Paris 2008).

Northend, Charles *Elihu Burritt: A Memorial Volume* (D Appleton & Co New York 1879).

Onuf, Nicholas 'Humanitarian Intervention: The Early Years' (2004) 16 Florida Journal of International Law 753–87.

Patterson, David S *Towards a Warless World: The Travail of the American Peace Movement, 1887–1914* (University Press Bloomington 1976).

Robbins, Keith *The Abolition of War: The 'Peace Movement' in Britain, 1914–1919* (University of Wales Press Cardiff 1976).

Taylor, Richard and Nigel Young (eds) *Campaigns for Peace: British Peace Movements in the Twentieth Century* (Manchester University Press Manchester 1987).

Tolstoy, Leo 'A Letter to a Hindu' in Leo Tolstoy *Recollections & Essays* (Aylmer Maude intr and trans) (OUP London 1937) 433–9.

White Beck, Lewis (ed) *Kant on History* (L White Beck, R E Anchor, and EL Fackenheim trans) (Macmillan New York 1963).

Wiebe, Robert *The Search for Order, 1877–1920* (Hill and Wang New York 1967).

Wittner, Lawrence S *Rebels Against War: The American Peace Movement, 1933–1983* (Temple University Press Philadelphia 1984).

PART II

THEMES

CHAPTER 9

TERRITORY AND BOUNDARIES

DANIEL-ERASMUS KHAN

1. INTRODUCTION

1.1. Man, Space, and Borders

In 1966, Robert Ardrey put a surprisingly simple question on the world's intellectual map: 'Is *Homo sapiens* a territorial species?'[1] For the self-made anthropologist the answer was unambiguously clear: 'Man . . . is as much a territorial animal as is a mockingbird singing in the clear Californian night.'[2] Even if we are not ready to share the somewhat disquieting view that 'certain laws of territorial behaviour apply as rigorously in the affairs of men as in the affairs of chipmunks',[3] and despite a number of important objections to any kind of (excessive) 'biological reductionism',[4] it is

---

[1] *The Territorial Imperative. A Personal Inquiry into the Animal Origins of Property and Nations* (Atheneum New York 1966) at 4.

[2] ibid 5; for a critical assessment of Ardrey's thesis (territory as a genetically determined form of behaviour and the single most influential force in driving human action) V Reynolds 'Open Groups in Hominid Evolution' (1966) 1 Man 441–52; and A Tildwell *Conflict Resolved? A Critical Assessment of Conflict Resolution* (Continuum London 1998) at 45 ff.

[3] *The Territorial Imperative* (n 1) 4.

[4] In recent years anti-reductionist views have gained some ground: D Ruben *The Metaphysics of the Social World* (Routledge London 1985); and the seminal paper by J Fodor 'Special Sciences (or: The Disu-

probably correct to assume that unanimity prevails in the various branches of today's social science community that 'territoriality' does indeed constitute one of the key imperatives of human behaviour. This comes hardly as a surprise for two reasons. First, territory provides an undeniable (survival) value to all human beings—as a living space, as a repository for resources of vital importance, and finally as a *conditio sine qua non* for a vast array of world systems, such as the production of oxygen, the purification and storage of water, and others.[5] And, second, controlling people and things territorially simply saves effort[6] and thus provides the 'territory owner' with a clear 'evolutionary advantage'. It is certainly easier to supervise one's livestock by fencing it in than to follow each head of cattle around, and the most efficient way to control and protect human and natural resources of a given area is probably to patrol its outer margins.

With respect to his intellectual perception, man is also inextricably bound to spatiality:[7]

Space…is a necessary representation a priori, which serves for the foundation of all external intuitions. We never can imagine or make a representation to ourselves of the non-existence of space.[8]…[I]f we take away by degrees from our conceptions of a body all that can be referred to mere sensuous experience…the space which it occupied still remains, and this it is utterly impossible to annihilate in thought.[9]

No doubt, territory, space, boundaries, and borders are inescapable companions of every human being, both regarding his physical and intellectual existence.

1.2. Communities, Territory, and Boundaries

There is strong evidence that long before the transition of mankind to a sedentary lifestyle, 'territoriality' as a type of intraspecific competition was already a distinctive

nity of Science as a Working Hypothesis)' (1974) 28 Synthese 97–115; more recently E Svertlov 'Is Biological Reductionism Losing Ground? What is Next?'(2006) 76 Herald of the Russian Academy of Sciences 339–51; multidisciplinary debate in D Charles and K Lennon (eds) *Reduction, Explanation and Realism* (OUP Oxford 1992).

  [5] A Kolers *Land, Conflict, and Justice. A Political Theory of Territory* (CUP Cambridge 2009) at 8.
  [6] R Sack *Human Territoriality. Its Theory and History* (CUP Cambridge 1986) at 22.
  [7] In-depth discussion G Hatfield *The Natural and the Normative: Theories of Spatial Perception from Kant to Helmholtz* (MIT Press Cambridge 1990); F Dolins and R Mitchell (eds) *Spatial Cognition, Spatial Perception. Mapping the Self and Space* (CUP Cambridge 2010); whether or not spatial conception is pivotal to cognition in general, is again open to debate: S Levinson 'Studying Spatial Conceptualization across Cultures: Anthropology and Cognitive Science' (1998) 26 Ethos 7–24.
  [8] I Kant *The Critique of Pure Reason* (MD Meiklejohn trans) pt 1, ss 2, no 2.
  [9] ibid ('Preface' 2nd edn 1787); the 'a priori' function attributed to space in Kant's transcendental aesthetics bears a striking similarity to the role territory is playing with respect to the conception of modern statehood.

feature of most (semi-)nomadic hunter-gatherer societies.[10] For prehistoric groups, claims to a certain territory to the exclusion of others ('*raumgebundene Intoleranz*'[11]) aimed in particular at monopolizing food resources, but also other essentials for individual and group survival, including sexual partners. However, domination over space did in general not only serve such basic physiological needs, but satisfied higher levels on the hierarchy of needs as well.[12] This is in particular true for the pyramid's top level: the need to connect to something beyond the ego ('self-transcendence'). From the dawn of civilization up to the present day, spiritual needs are indeed satisfied not least by mythical or sacred places.[13] Ever since, and almost everywhere in the world, places with special significance for a specific group of people have been made an almost indispensable accompaniment of the life of organized communities. Hence, as a rule, for human societies a bordered territory has always served a double function: It constitutes a basic prerequisite for survival and a means of identification ('*raumbezogene Identität*').[14] Sociological research supports the assumption of a quasi-necessary correlation between limitations and identification: 'An individual system can observe and describe itself [only] if it can organize difference and limitation for this purpose.'[15]

No wonder, therefore, that the origin of the distribution of space among men was not only traced back to mythical ages—in the words of Ovid (recalling the bygone golden and silver ages of Saturn and Jupiter): 'The ground, too, hitherto common as the light of the sun and the breezes, the cautious measurer marked out with his lengthened boundary.'[16] Territory and boundary-making have also been always intimately associated with religious and ethical concepts:[17] 'And sing your praises, sacred

---

[10] From the rich anthropological literature G King 'Society and Territory in Human Evolution' (1976) 5 Journal of Human Evolution 323–31; J Stevenson *Dictionary of Concepts in Physical Anthropology*—'*Territory*' (Greenwood Press New York 1991) 395–401; for a vigorously interdisciplinary approach *Human Territoriality* (n 6); D Delaney 'Territory and Territoriality' in R Kitchin and N Thrift (eds) *International Encyclopedia of Human Geography* (Elsevier Amsterdam 2009) 196–208.

[11] A Gehlen 'Philosophische Anthropologie und Verhaltensforschung (1968)' in KS Rehberg (ed) *Arnold Gehlen. Gesamtausgabe* (Klostermann Frankfurt 1983) vol 4, 216–21 at 217.

[12] Obviously, reference is made here to A Maslow's pyramid of needs, one of the most cognitively contagious ideas in the behavioural sciences: 'A Theory of Human Motivation' (1943) 50 Psychological Review 370–96; fully developed in A Maslow *Motivation and Personality* (Harper New York 1954).

[13] From the overwhelming literature see eg S Hashmi 'Political Boundaries and Moral Communities: Islamic Perspectives' in A Buchanan and M Moore (eds) *States, Nations, and Borders. The Ethics of Making Boundaries* (CUP Cambridge 2003) 181–213 at 186ff (sacred space in the Qur'an and Sunna); for creative perspectives on the spatiality of nature, culture, and religion, which aim at demonstrating that the self and its surroundings are ontologically part of each other: S Bergmann et al (eds) *Nature, Space and the Sacred. Transdisciplinary Perspectives* (Ashgate Farnham 2009).

[14] P Weichhart *Raumbezogene Identität. Bausteine zu einer Theorie räumlich-sozialer Kognition und Identifikation* (Franz Steiner Verlag Stuttgart 1990).

[15] N Luhmann *Social Systems* (Stanford University Press Stanford 1995) at 266.

[16] Ovid *Metamorphosis* (H Riley trans) book I, MNs 135 and 136.

[17] See the most inspiring contributions in *States, Nations, and Borders* (n 13).

Terminus: "You set bounds to peoples, cities, great kingdoms: Without you every field would be disputed…".[18] Ovid's conception is paradigmatic of a widespread ambivalence towards the phenomenon of bordered territory: On the one hand, it is tagged with a clearly negative connotation by setting it into a sharp contrast to the Arcadian world (Ovid) or, some 1800 years later, branding it as the work of an impostor, who wants one to 'forget that the Fruits of the Earth belong equally to us all, and the Earth itself to nobody'.[19] On the other hand, a carefully bonded territory has always been viewed as a guarantee of peaceful relations between neighbouring individuals, social or political entities, and was even vested with metaphysical or supernatural legitimacy[20]—even where religious doctrine actually raises a claim for universality.[21] As the psalmist said to God, 'It was you who set all the boundaries of the earth' (Psalm 74: 17) and, in order to reconfirm a long-established territorial status quo, the Pentateuch commands, 'Do not move your neighbor's boundary stone set up by your predecessors in the inheritance you receive in the land the LORD your God is giving you to possess' (Deuteronomy 19: 14). The land thus promised to the Jewish people is further specified in Deuteronomy 34: 1–3[22]—with far-reaching consequences, as we experience painfully, down to the present day.[23] The deeply rooted sanctification of boundaries by words and deeds, which can actually be traced back to royal inscriptions of early Mesopotamian civilizations and thus to the very first 'inter-state' treaty relations ever,[24] still resonates in the modern concept of the 'sanctity of boundaries'.[25]

[18] Ovid *Fasti* (A Kline trans) book II, MN 658–60.

[19] JJ Rousseau *Discourse upon the Origin and Foundation of the Inequality among Mankind* (R and J Donsley London 1761) at 97.

[20] HW Nicklis 'Von der "Grenitze" zur Grenze. Die Grenzidee des lateinischen Mittelalters (6–15. Jhdt.)' (1992) 128 Blätter für deutsche Landesgeschichte 1–29 at 3.

[21] On the Islamic tradition: K Abou El Fadl 'The Unbounded Law of God and Territorial Boundaries' in *States, Nations, and Borders* (n 13) 214–27.

[22] For an unconventional approach see M Weinfeld *The Promise of the Land: The Inheritance of the Land of Canaan by the Israelites* (University of California Press Berkeley 1993).

[23] See, however, for two remarkably different views on the Biblical perception of the land of Israel: M Lorberbaum 'Making and Unmaking the Boundaries of Holy Land' in *States, Nations, and Borders* (n 13) 19–40; and D Statman 'Man-Made Boundaries and Man-Made-Holiness in the Jewish tradition' in *States, Nations, and Borders* (n 13) 41–53.

[24] J Cooper 'International Law in the Third Millennium' in R Westbrook (ed) *A History of Ancient Near Eastern Law* (Brill Leiden 2003) vol 1, 241–51. Two and a half millennia later, the *gromaticus* (land surveyor) Siculus Flaccus records in detail how Roman boundary stones (*termini*) were sanctified. S Flaccus *De Condicionibus Agrorum* (1st/2nd century AD) at 11; Nilklas, 'Von der "Grenitze" zur Grenze' (n 20) 6, reports of the medieval use of carrying precious relics all around a parcel of land in order to provide its limits with divine force. With special emphasis on the involvement of the Germanic pantheon in boundary-making: J Grimm *Kleinere Schriften* (Dümmlers Verlagsbuchhandlung Berlin 1865) vol 2, ch 2 ('Deutsche Grenzalterthümer'), 30–74 at 53 ff.

[25] A status-quo promoting norm meant to ensure stability of international relations even and in particular in case of fundamental political changes, such as revolutions and decolonization (embodied eg in arts 3 of the 1963 Organization for African Unity Charter).

The time-honoured German words *'umfrieden/Umfriedung'* (fencing/fence) still bear witness to the once inseparable unity of the concepts of 'peace' (*'Frieden'*) and 'boundaries'—an etymological bridge which got lost in most other languages. It is indeed one of the great tragedies of the phenomenon of bounded territory that, designed to avoid strife among individuals and peoples, territory and boundaries have instead—in the long course of history—evolved into the prime cause for belligerent unrest in the world.[26]

2. EARLY RECORDS OF TERRITORY AND BOUNDARY-MAKING

The exercise of authority over land has been an indispensable prerequisite for politico-economic organizations of almost all times, at almost all places, and under almost all circumstances. A geographically defined territorial base was essential for small city-states (Greece) as much as for empires (Rome), and all forms of political organization in between these two extremes. No wonder, therefore, that when in the dim, dark past, two neighbouring political entities agreed to formalize their relations, issues regarding the designation of territory and its delimitation soon became a matter of primordial importance.

With the invention of scripture emerging from the mist of prehistory, the ancient kings of Mesopotamia are the first to provide us with relevant records.[27] The exciting account of a boundary dispute in the Presargonic period (approximately 2700–2350 BC)[28] commences as follows:

The god Enlil, king of the lands, father of all the gods, by his authoritative command, demarcated the border between the gods Ningirsu [Lagaš] and Šara [Umma]. Mesilim, king of Kiš, at the command of the god Ištaran, stretched the measuring rope on the field and erected a monument there.[29]

---

[26] See also N Hill *Claims to Territory in International Law and Relations* (OUP London 1945) at 3: 'The relations between modern states reach their most critical stage in the form of problems relating to territory.'

[27] Meticulous edition of royal inscriptions D Frayne *The Royal Inscriptions of Mesopotamia: Early Periods, Volume 1: Pre-Sargonic Period (2700–2350 BC)* (University of Toronto Press Toronto 2008).

[28] Detailed analysis A Altman 'Tracing the Earliest Recorded Concepts of International Law. The Early Dynastic Period in Southern Mesopotamia' (2004) 6 Journal of the History of International Law 153–72 at 158 ff; JS Cooper *Reconstructing History from Ancient Inscriptions: The Lagash-Umma Border Conflict* (Undena Publications Malibu 1981).

[29] Royal Inscriptions (n 27) 195. It is noteworthy that the Sumerian godfather Enlil bears the title 'king of all lands', which does not only provide his particular reign with a distinctively spatial dimension, but also constitutes a reflection of the territory-based political organization in the mortal world as such.

In blatant disregard of king Mesilim's 'arbitral award', the rulers of Umma later 'smashed that monument and marched on the Eden district of Lagaš',[30] thus triggering an epic confrontation between the two Southern Mesopotamian city-states. Possession and agricultural usufruct of fertile lands (Guendena region), irrigation rights, and the quest for the drawing of a boundary-line to the greatest possible strategic and economic advantage were at the heart of the conflict, which did even not shy away from destroying 'the dedicated [?] chapels of the gods that were built on the [boundary-levee called] Namnunda-kigara'.[31] Brief détente periods witnessed the conclusion of a parity boundary treaty (the earliest recorded example of an 'inter-state' agreement at all, in approximately 2470 BC), joint demarcation-works, and even the setting up of some sort of buffer zone (no man's land) in order to prevent future conflict.[32]

Once again for the sake of peace, some 2500 years later (approximately 20 BC–23 AC) the Greek geographer Strabo, repudiating earlier views, strongly advocated a most accurate delimitation and demarcation of boundaries:

Where there are no precise boundary marks, columns, or walls … it is easy for us to say such a place is Colyttus, and such another Melitè, but not so easy to show the exact limits: thus disputes have frequently arisen concerning certain districts. … The reasoning of Eratosthenes, however, is still more absurd, when he declares that he sees no advantage in being acquainted with the exact boundaries of countries, and then cites the example of Colyttus and Melitè, which prove just the contrary of his assertion. Surely if a want of certainty respecting the boundaries gave rise to war [as in the case of Thyrea and Orpus], a knowledge of the limits of different districts must be of practical importance.[33]

It seems in fact that the ingredients of a conflict over territory or boundaries, the desire to overcome it by the most accurate drawing of lines, and, finally, the means to achieve this end have not changed much in the course of the last four and a half millennia.

[30] ibid 195.

[31] ibid 196.

[32] For details G Steiner 'Der Grenzvertrag zwischen Lagaš and Umma' (1986) 8 Acta Sumerologica 219–300; A Altman 'How Many Treaty Traditions Existed in the Ancient Near East?' in Y Cohen, A Gilan and JL Miller (eds) *Pax Hethitica. Studies on the Hittites and their Neighbours in Honour of Itamar Singer* (Harrassowitz Verlag Wiesbaden 2010) 17–36.

[33] *Geography* (Loeb Classical Library ed and HL Jones trans) (William Heinemann & Co. London 1917) book I, ch IV, ss 7 and 8. Interesting insight on the significance of territory in the ancient Greek world: I Malkin 'Land Ownership, Territorial Possession, Hero Cults, and Scholarly Theory' in RM Rosen and J Farrell (eds) *Nomodeiktes. Greek Studies in Honor of Martin Oswald* (University of Michigan Press Ann Arbor 1993) 225–34.

3. DISAMBIGUATION: TERRITORY, BOUNDARIES, FRONTIERS

Land as such is no territory. A desert, a swamp, or an impenetrable forest do not make up for a frontier, and a natural barrier, such as a river or a mountain chain, does not constitute a boundary. Rather what is needed for a mere geographical feature to become 'territory' or 'boundary' is its reference to a man-made political structure: The twofold etymological root of the Latin word 'territorium' aptly demonstrates this intrinsic correlation: 'terra' (earth, land), and the suffix '-orium' denoting place.[34] And indeed, when first appearing in late Medieval Europe, the term 'territory' was to denominate a 'land under the jurisdiction of a city or town'. Alternative theories suggest derivation from the Latin word 'terrere' (to frighten, see also 'terrible'—thus territorium would mean 'a place from which people are warned off'); or consider 'torium' as the root from which derived words such as 'tower', 'tour', and 'torre', which conveyed in Medieval English, Old French, Italian, and Spanish the meaning of both 'a well-rounded building' and 'a position of strength'.[35] These various etymological hypotheses, however, are not contradictory but rather complementary. Control over a geographic area provides a community with a position of (economic) strength, which needs to be maintained by constant vigilance with a view to deter potential intruders. And it is finally not by chance that in its original usage, the concept of territory was assigned to smaller political entities alone, such as cities and towns, whereas the position of power of larger kingly or princely entities in Europe, deeply rooted in the Christian-Medieval theological-political cosmos, was still considered to rest primarily on allegiance of individuals and organizations, not territory.

It was only in the late 15th century that, seconded and driven by the Renaissance critique of hierarchy,[36] the dominant model of juridico-political power of a vertical, highly complex, and heterogeneous hierarchical character was superseded by the concept that political spaces are to be ordered along a horizontal plane, something which placed 'territory' centre stage in political thought.[37] Exclusive control over a

---

[34] WW Skeat *The Concise Dictionary of English Etymology* (Wordsworth Hertfordshire 1993) at 499. According to others, the correct reference would be to the suffix –'torium', which seems to have meant 'belong to' or 'surrounding' (J Gottmann *The Significance of Territory* (The University Press of Virginia Charlottesville 1973) at 15), a proposition, however, which could not be confirmed.

[35] *The Significance of Territory* (n 34) 15.

[36] Illuminative explanations by J Larkins *From Hierarchy to Anarchy. Territory and Politics Before Westphalia* (Palgrave Macmillan New York 2010) at 101 ff.

[37] Territory and its limitations have of course already been important elements in the tool-box of political actors in the European Middle Ages and the most powerful of them aspired indeed to some status of 'final authority'. However, these aspirations were not essentially territorial in character (for a detailed discussion: S Sassen *Territory, Authority, Rights. From Medieval to Global Assemblages* (Princeton University Press Princeton 2006) at 31 ff).

distinct geographical area soon became not only an indispensable, but probably the most distinctive feature of the new ideal of exercising political authority: 'Lo Stato'.[38] With lasting effect, Machiavelli in his seminal work *Il principe*,[39] along with other participants in Renaissance legal discourse, added to the Latin word 'dominium' with its firmly established Roman private law connotation a second, public law meaning; territory over which single and superior authority is exercised, thus heralding the modern concept of sovereign territoriality. Quite literally dismissing 'the ancient [Augustinian] doctrine by which the ruler...existed for the realization of...a superior moral purpose',[40] Machiavelli limited politics to the terrestrial world. However, it was still a long way to go to achieve complete congruency between the concepts of 'territory' and 'sovereignty' and thus to entirely eliminate from this domain of international law the Roman private law antecedents, remnants of which can still be found today—in particular regarding the modes of acquiring and loosing territory. Regardless of the vast scholarly discussion on the exact legal relationship between a State and 'its' territory,[41] the latter's pivotal role within the identity kit of modern statehood has never since seriously been challenged.[42] 'It is because the State is a territorial organization that violation of its frontiers is inseparable from the idea of aggression against the State itself.'[43]

Unanimity has always prevailed that all what is needed for a State to come into or to remain in existence is some sort of undisputed 'core territory'.[44] The nature and character of the outer margins of the physical substratum of statehood, however, has not only witnessed a considerable factual evolution (from boundary zones or borderlands to boundary lines), but is also characterized by certain conceptual as well as terminological ambiguities. The most important of these ambiguities concerns the use of the term 'frontier'. Deriving from the classical Latin root *'frons'* (front or forepart)—in later medieval usage developing into *'fronteria'*, meaning front line of an army or line of battle[45]—in European usage the term became virtually synonym-

---

[38] ibid 123 ff.

[39] Published posthumous (1532); unpublished Latin version (*De principatibus*) 1513.

[40] FH Hinsley *Sovereignty* (2nd edn CUP Cambridge 1986) at 110.

[41] It is somewhat symptomatic that this rather abstract discussion with very limited practical value was almost exclusively a domain of German and, in particular, Austrian scholars, complemented by some significant—albeit rather isolated—French (L Delbez 'Le territoire dans ses rapports avec l'état' (1932) 39 Revue Générale de Droit International Public 705–38) and Italian (D Donati *Stato e territorio* (Athenaeum Roma 1924)) contributions; W Schoenborn 'La nature juridique du territoire' (1929) 30 Recueil des cours de droit international de La Haye 81–190 at 85 ff (with complete references).

[42] A distinct and very specific US sense as 'organized self-governing region not yet a state' was first attributed to the term in 1799.

[43] C de Visscher *Theory and Reality in Public international Law* (Princeton University Press Princeton 1957) at 197 f.

[44] *Deutsche Continental Gas-Gesellschaft v Polish State* (1929) 5 Annual Digest Public Intl L 11 at 15.

[45] JT Juricek 'American Usage of the Word "Frontier" from Colonial Times to Frederick Jackson Turner' (1966) 110 Proceedings of the American Philosophical Society 10–34.

ous with the term 'boundary'.[46] However, triggered by a seminal essay by Frederick Jackson Turner (1893),[47] a significantly different American approach ('frontier thesis') acquired considerable prominence in the New World and beyond. Turner held that the very idea behind the American frontier was less the European one of a fixed boundary[48] than rather that of a moving line of military and cultural advance and retreat, which he called 'the outer edge of the wave—the meeting point between savagery and civilization'.[49] With this reinterpretation for expansionist purposes of a rather settled concept, Turner became one of the pioneers of the worldwide geopolitics movement,[50] which has succinctly been labelled as 'nothing but the ideology of imperialist expansion'.[51] Although today no longer considered a 'serious starting point for historical inquiry',[52] the 'frontier thesis' marks the intellectual antipode to the established, but everything but self-evident idea of the boundary or frontier as an immobile and, ideally, linear concept.

4. TERRITORY AND THE STATE

Unanimity prevails that territoriality is a defining attribute of the Westphalian State and it is probably even correct to assume that a 'territory owner ethos' constitutes the most distinctive feature of traditional international law.[53] However, it

---

[46] Derived from the Medieval Latin words 'bodina, butina'.

[47] 'The Significance of the Frontier in American History' (1893) paper read at the meeting of the American Historical Association in Chicago 12 July 1893.

[48] 'The American frontier is sharply distinguished from the European frontier' see FJ Turner *The Frontier in American History* (Henry Holt New York 1921) at 3.

[49] ibid.

[50] The term itself was coined in 1899 by R Kjellén (Sweden); major protagonists include F Ratzel, K Haushofer (Germany), H Mackinder (UK), and NJ Spykman (US).

[51] F Neumann *Behemoth: The Structure and Practice of National Socialism* (OUP New York 1942) at 147; see also R Strausz-Hupé *Geopolitics: The Struggle for Space and Power* (GP Putnam's Sons New York 1942). With striking openness, Turner later admitted to his 'imperial philosophy': 'For nearly three centuries the dominant fact in American life has been expansion. With the settlement of the Pacific coast and the occupation of the free lands, this movement has come to a check. That these energies of expansion will no longer operate would be a rash prediction; and the demands for a vigorous foreign policy, for an interoceanic canal, for a revival of our power upon the seas, and for the extension of American influence to outlying islands and adjoining countries, are indications that the movement will continue' ('The Problem of the West' in The Frontier in American History (n 48) 219 (first published (1896) 78 The Atlantic Monthly 289–97)).

[52] GH Nobles 'Breaking into the Backcountry: New Approaches to the Early American Frontier, 1750–1800' (1989) 46 The William and Mary Quarterly 641–70.

[53] International law serves 'to enable state-societies to act as closed systems internally and to act as territory-owners in relation to each other': P Allot *Eunomia. New Order for a New World* (OUP Oxford 1990) at 324.

must be recalled that it was only in the late 19th century that the existence of a territorial basis took centre stage in the perception of statehood. Indeed, as far as the spatial element as a *conditio sine qua non* for statehood is concerned, Georg Jellinek's seminal 'three-element theory' (territory, population, ultimate ruling power)[54] and other similar definitions from that period[55] find no equivalent in 17th- and 18th-century post-Westphalian writings. Still very much obliged to a social contract theory approach, both Grotius ('a perfect society of free men, united for the promotion of right and the common advantage')[56] and Vattel ('political bodies, societies of men who have united together and combined their forces, in order to procure their mutual welfare and security')[57] laid emphasis rather on population, collective will, and government than on territory. Although both authors and their contemporaries did of course not abstain from treating various territorial and boundary issues, the fixation on territory as the main guiding and organizing principle of policy making is thus a rather recent phenomenon. The new perception of the existence of some sort of intrinsic and inextricable bond between the State and its territory may be illustrated by the fact that the second half of the 19th century witnessed the rather sudden end of the hitherto widespread and quasi-commercial practice of selling and purchase of State territory—the last important example probably being the United States 1867 Alaska purchase. Hence, regarding the 'upgrading' of territory, too, Westphalia did certainly not constitute a cataclysm but one, albeit important installment in the ongoing and century-long transitional process from medieval to modern statehood.

5. Territory and the Others

To claim territory is to deny it to others. However, as a rule, in inter-state relations claims of kind do not call into question the right as such of the competitor to dispose of a recognized territorial setting for the exercise of its sovereign powers. Hence, in a more categorical sense, the 'denial' referred to here is what one may describe as an essential ingredient of the predator competition launched by the State society against all Others who lay claim for title to territory. The delegitimization of all other forms of the exercise of supreme political authority in and over territory has indeed been a

---

[54] *Die Lehre von den Staatenverbindungen* (Alfred Hölder Wien 1882) at 22.
[55] Eg A Rivier *Principes du Droit des Gens* (A Rousseau Paris 1896) vol 1, at 45–51.
[56] H Grotius *De jure belli ac pacis* (1625) book 1, ch 1, para XIV.
[57] E de Vattel *Le droit des gens* (1758) Preliminaries, para 1.

continuous feature of the evolution of the very distinct 'Westphalian' model of the symbiosis between a people and its territory. Colonialism in Africa is but one example, the removal of American Indians and the Māori from their historic lands others.

The history of the seizure of the African continent by European colonial powers—in the aftermath of the Berlin Africa Conference 1884 culminating in the so-called scramble for Africa[58]—is a complex and multifaceted story of the delegitimation of pre-colonial political powers over territory and people. The status of the so-called Kings and Chiefs of Old Calabar, recently a key issue in a territorial dispute before the International Court of Justice,[59] may serve as just one significant example in this respect. In face of Nigeria's assertion to the contrary, the court assumed that a treaty eventually concluded in 1884 between these indigenous rulers and Great Britain was not 'governed by international law', since it was an 'agreement not between equals', 'not with States, but rather with important indigenous rulers exercising local rule over identifiable areas of territory'.[60] Probably perfectly sound from a Westphalian perspective, the inevitable consequence of this legal assessment, however, was simple. There is no room for the recognition on the international plane of any different form of title to territory. 'At the international level the Kings and Chiefs of Old Calabar' thus 'disappeared from view',[61] as did claims to 'their' territory. The law at the time, as confirmed by the court, conferred on Great Britain a full territorial title which it could eventually transfer to Germany some three decades later.

The long history of how Anglo-Americans justified the dispossession of Native Americans—somewhat obfuscated behind the broad smokescreen of a complex and contradictory controversy on the legal nature, contents, and limits of aboriginal and other (territorial) title of American Indians in the United States—cannot be even sketched here.[62] However, the gist of one crucial element of the entire issue was probably best captured in the US Supreme Court's 1831 landmark decision in the case *Cherokee Nation v Georgia*.[63] After an extended discussion of the nature of Indian tribal sovereignty,

---

[58] For an overview see J Lonsdale 'The European Scramble and Conquest in African History' in R Oliver and GN Sanderson (eds) *The Cambridge History of Africa* (CUP Cambridge 1985) vol 6, 680–766 and HL Wesseling *Divide and Rule: The Partition of Africa, 1880–1914* (Praeger London 1996).

[59] *Case Concerning the Land and Maritime Boundary between Cameroon and Nigeria (Cameroon v Nigeria: Equatorial Guinea intervening) (Jurisdiction)* [2002] ICJ Rep 303. On this particular aspect of the judgment: M Craven 'International Law and its Histories' in M Craven, M Fitzmaurice and M Vogiatzi (eds) *Time, History and International Law* (Martinus Nijhoff Leiden 2007) 1–25 at 19 ff; E Milano *Unlawful Territorial Situations in International Law. Reconciling Effectiveness, Legality and Legitimacy* (Martinus Nijhoff Leiden 2006) at 74 ff.

[60] *Cameroon v Nigeria* (n 59) para 205.

[61] J Crawford *The Creation of States in International Law* (2nd edn OUP Oxford 2005) at 314.

[62] Recently (although not uncontroversial) S Banner *How the Indians Lost Their Land. Law and Power on the Frontier* (Belknap Cambridge MS 2005).

[63] *Cherokee Nation v Georgia* 30 US 1, 5 Pet 1 (1831).

the majority held that Indian tribes had no standing to bring suit directly to the Supreme Court (against State legislation aiming at the removal of the Cherokee people from their historic lands), since they were neither a foreign nor an American State:

They may more correctly, perhaps, be denominated domestic dependent nations. They occupy a territory to which we assert a title independent of their will, which must take effect in point of possession when their right of possession ceases; meanwhile, they are in a state of pupilage. Their relations to the United States resemble that of a ward to his guardian.[64]

Although directly concerned only with a very limited procedural issue, the (highly disputed)[65] denial of sovereign statehood of Indian Nations by the court had far-reaching consequences. Deprived of the umbrella of sovereign statehood, the 'unquestionable, and, heretofore, unquestioned right to the lands they occupy'[66] proved of little value for the effective protection of the Cherokee Nation's title to their territory.

The encounter of the European concept of territorial sovereignty with a very different perception of governance (over land and people) has probably become most obvious in the 1840 treaty of Waitangi between the British Crown and the Māori, the indigenous population of what today is called New Zealand.[67] In the English text of article 1 of the treaty, Māori ceded 'sovereignty', whereas in the Māori text, the Māori gave the British merely a right of governance (*kawanatanga*).[68] As a result, Māori believed—and still do so—that they ceded to the Queen a limited right of governance only in return for the promise of protection, while retaining the authority they always had to manage their own affairs. However, not surprisingly, the European conception prevailed and although the 1975 Treaty of Waitangi Act paved the way for an investigation by individuals on their own behalf or on behalf of a group of Māori of treaty-based claims dating back to 1849,[69] the issue of (the legitimacy of the acquisition of) territorial sovereignty was obviously never seriously at stake.

---

[64] ibid 17 (Chief Justice Marshall delivering the Court's opinion).

[65] ibid 53 (Justice Thomson, dissenting): 'Testing the character and condition of the Cherokee Indians by these rules [reference is made to Emer de Vattel's notion of statehood], it is not perceived how it is possible to escape the conclusion, that they form a sovereign state.'

[66] ibid 17.

[67] For an in-depth historical analysis: C Orange *An Illustrated History of the Treaty of Waitangi* (2nd edn Bridget Williams Books Wellington 2004); with a wider (legal) perspective M Belgrave, M Kawharu and D Williams *Waitangi Revisited: Perspectives on The Treaty of Waitangi* (2nd edn OUP Oxford 2005).

[68] (Local) chiefs (*Rangatira*) exercising autonomy and authority over their own domains only (*rangatiratanga*), the Māori were simply unfamiliar with the concept of a supreme ruler of the whole country. The somewhat unfortunate (while artificial) recurrence to the term *kawanatanga* made reference to the role of the *Kawana* (Governor of New South Wales), whose jurisdiction then extended and was confined to British subjects in New Zealand.

[69] Public Act 1975 No 114; amended in 1985, 1988 (twice), 1993, 2006, and on 16 December 2010, the Act established the Waitangi Tribunal and, for the first time ever, gave the 1840 treaty recognition in New Zealand domestic law.

6. Title to Territory

6.1. General Aspects

The existence of distinct territorial entities, each with one single power to exercise supreme authority to the exclusion of all others, is not only the brand mark of the post-Westphalian idea of sovereign statehood.[70] To establish territory as the pivotal sounding board for the exercise of sovereign powers was in fact the very idea behind the paradigm shift away from the (medieval) concept of governance (personal jurisdiction). No wonder, therefore, that the disentanglement of spatially overlapping spheres of jurisdictional competences and activities soon became a matter of major concern for all States affected. In the, at best slightly exaggerated, words of Sir Robert Yennings: 'The mission and purpose of traditional international law has been the delimitation of the exercise of sovereign power on a territorial basis.'[71] The objective of the newborn territorial State to exercise its sovereign powers both with the highest possible degree of effectiveness and autonomy was also a major reason for a remarkable reshaping of the highly fragmented political map inherited from medieval times. The creation of a contingent territory being considered a suitable means to further reduce mutual dependencies between adjacent political entities (transit rights and other servitudes), once omnipresent enclaves and exclaves, that is territories legally attached to a State with which it is not physically contiguous,[72] were one by one erased from the political map. The formerly quite ordinary option for a joint exercise of sovereignty, too, became increasingly rare in practice and 'Condominia'[73] have now been reduced to somewhat quaint remnants of a distant past.[74]

However, in order to translate into reality the absolutist dream of undivided exercise of sovereign power within clearly defined limits, it was first of all necessary to be aware of the exact scope and extent of territory claimed. Hardly astonishing, it was the Absolutist State par excellence, the France of Louis XIV, which in the 1670s

---

[70] For details, see B Fassbender 'Sovereignty and Constitutionalism in International Law' in N Walker (ed) *Sovereignty in Transition* (OUP Oxford 2003) 115–143.

[71] *The Acquisition of Territory in International Law* (Manchester University Press Manchester 1963) at 2.

[72] P Delsalle and A Ferrer (eds) *Les Enclaves Territoriales aux Temps Modernes (XVIe–XVIIIe siècles): Actes du Colloque de Besançon* (Presses Universitaires Franc-Comtoises Besançon 2000).

[73] For details: A Coret *Le condominium* (Pichon & Durand-Auzias Paris 1960).

[74] Established by art XXV para 4 s 2 of the General Treaty of the Final Act of the Congress of Vienna (signed 9 June 1815) (1815) 64 CTS 453: '...the rivers themselves, in so far as they form the frontier, shall belong in common to the two powers', concretized the following year and reconfirmed in 1984 (see art 1 para 2 of the Treaty between the Federal Republic of Germany and the Grand Duchy of Luxembourg concerning the course of their common border of 11 July 1959 (BGBL 1960 II, 2077)), the Moselle River and its tributaries still constitute a condominium between Luxembourg and Germany (for details see DE Khan *Die deutschen Staatsgrenzen* (Mohr Siebeck Tübingen 2004) at 476 ff).

pioneered in an arduous and meticulous surveying and mapping of its territory.[75] Using Gemma Frisius' technique of triangulation,[76] almost a century later the venture was crowned with the finalization of the first ever topographical map of an entire country.[77]

6.2. Modes of Acquisition of Territory

Given the dynastic and feudal structure of medieval governance, it is hardly surprising that in the formative stages of rules governing title to territory private law analogies prevailed. Based on Roman law principles, classical international law thus knew of five modes of acquisition of territory. Occupation of *terra nullius*, prescription, cession, accretion, and subjugation (conquest).[78] However, while in principle doctrinally neat, the borderlines between these classical modes have always been blurred,[79] in particular regarding occupation and prescription. The Age of Discovery with its exponential growth of potential conflicts between European 'conquistadores' imperatively called for a new legal framework acceptable to all relevant actors of the time.[80] No wonder therefore that initial attempts of authoritatively distributing vast portions of the globe among two States only (Portugal and Spain) by sole virtue of Papal Bulls (*Romanus Pontifex* 1455, *Inter Caetera Divinae* 1493) were doomed to failure due to the resistance of powerful competitors, such as England, France, and the Netherlands. Alternative approaches, such as in particular the 'first come, first served principle' (discovery) always remained controversial too, due to the sweeping and often enough dubious character of many claims based on this title. It seems that as early as 1506, the Pope himself carefully shied away from his earlier pretensions, when explicitly confirming Spanish and Portuguese title to 'discovered

---

[75] Conducted by four generations of the Cassini family: Jacques Dominique (1625–1712), Jacques (1677–1756), César François (1714–84), and another Jacques Dominique (1748–1845).

[76] In his *Libellus de locurum*, included in the enlarged 1533 edition of his ground-breaking 'On the Principles of Astronomy and Cosmography...' (*De principiis astronomiae cosmographicae*), Frisius (1508–55) not only described the theory of trigonometric surveying but also proposed to use it as a method of accurately locating places (ND Haasbroek *Gemma Frisius, Tycho Brahe and Snellius and their Triangulations* (Netherlands Geodetic Commission Delft 1968) at 16ff.

[77] At the rather precise scale of 1:86,400. Increased access and familiarity with maps and mapping did not only enhance military, local and state administration (A Godlewska *Geography Unbound: French Geographic Science from Cassini to Humboldt* (University of Chicago Press Chicago 1999) at 129), but has also made a significant contribution to change the way in which the State was conceptualized as such.

[78] M Shaw 'Territory in International Law' (1982) 13 Netherlands Yearbook of International Law 61–91 at 79.

[79] G Schwarzenberger 'Title to Territory: Response to a Challenge' (1957) 51 American Journal of International Law 308–24 at 310.

[80] For details, see the contribution by A Fitzmaurice, 'Discovery, Conquest, and Occupation of Territory', in this volume.

and occupied islands' only.[81] Effective occupation as a *conditio sine qua non* for legitimate title to territory—eventually becoming the leitmotif in acquisition-related discourse and practice—was indeed by no means an innovative idea: Bartolus de Saxoferrato in his early 14th-century *Tractatus de Insula* already vigorously maintained with respect to earlier papal donations: 'But what is the law if he to whom the right is awarded neglects to occupy? The question is whether he loses that right? I answer: Yes; he loses his right of occupation if he defers it without due reason....'.[82] Some 600 years later, this dictum resonates in Max Huber's seminal award in the *Island of Palmas Case* (1928), where the arbitrator underlined that discovery as such gives only an inchoate title, which, in order to become opposable to others on the international plane, must be followed by effective occupation.[83] Although it was always recognized that the necessary amount of *effectivité* may vary according to geographical and other circumstances,[84] in the past 200 years, state practice, international jurisprudence, and doctrine have never seriously called into question that the 'continuous and peaceful display of territorial sovereignty' is an indispensable prerequisite for a valid title arising from occupation and prescription alike.[85] Although a complex and multifaceted legal concept, the core idea underlying the *uti possidetis* doctrine ('as you possess, so may you possess'),[86] which gained particular prominence in the struggle for independence of Latin American (19th century) and African (20th century) States, is also obliged to this very idea. The gist of the *raison d'être* for the existence of an inextricable bond between 'possession' and 'sovereignty' was again aptly articulated by Max Huber:

Territorial sovereignty cannot limit itself to its negative side, i.e., to excluding the activities of other states; for it serves to divide between nations the space upon which human activities are employed, in order to assure them at all points the minimum of protection of which international law is the guardian.... International law ... cannot be presumed to reduce a right such as territorial sovereignty, with which almost all international relations are bound up, to the category of an abstract right, without concrete manifestations.[87]

---

[81] '*Ea quae*' Bull of Pope Julius II (with respect to the Antilles Islands).

[82] *Consilia, quaestiones et tractatus* (Venice 1585) at 137 ff; translation by FA von der Heydte 'Discovery, Symbolic Annexation and Virtual Effectiveness in International Law' (1935) 29 American Journal of International Law 448–71 at 450 f.

[83] *Island of Palmas Case (Netherlands v United States of America)* 2 Rep Intl Arbitral Awards 829 at 846; DE Khan 'Max Huber as Arbitrator: The Palmas (Miangas) Case and Other Arbitrations' (2007) 18 The European Journal of International Law 145–70 at 158 ff.

[84] For references from the rich jurisprudence: Territory in International Law (n 78) 83.

[85] Possessionless claims, such as the so-called Hinterland theory, have indeed never been recognized as a viable title. For just one example from State practice: 'Letter of Count Hatzfeld to Baron von Marschall of 14th May 1890' in ETS Dugdale (ed) *German Diplomatic Documents 1871–1914* (Methuen London 1929) vol 2, 32–4 at 32 f: 'Lord Salisbury ... observed that the Hinterland theory, which had been invented by us ... had not been accepted in International Law.'

[86] For details S Rattner 'Drawing a Better Line: *Uti Possidetis* and the Borders of New States' (1996) 90 American Journal of International Law 590–624.

[87] *Island of Palmas Case* (n 83) 838 ff.

7. THE CHANGING CHARACTER OF BOUNDARIES AND FRONTIERS

The paradigmatic shift from the personalized nature of sovereign power to political spaces ordered along a horizontal plane had far-reaching consequences for the perception and construction of the outer margins of these spaces, too. When territory became the physical and legal embodiment of the legitimate exercise of highest-ranking political power,[88] boundary-making was suddenly placed centre stage in the thinking and acting of politicians and lawyers alike. 'Frontiers are indeed the razor's edge on which hang suspended the modern issues of war and peace, of life or death of nations', as Lord Curzon still put it in his influential 1907 Romanes lecture,[89] tying in with a 150-year old Vattelian proposition: 'Since the least encroachment upon the territory of another is an act of injustice, in order to avoid being guilty of it, and to remove all occasion of strife and dispute, the boundary lines of territories should be clearly and precisely determined.'[90] This unequivocal 'invitation' stimulated the gradual replacement of the widespread phenomenon of frontier zones of various type (march or mark, buffer zone, no-man's land, *Grenzsaum*, and others) by the (modern) concept of linear boundaries,[91] 'that is to say to draw the exact line...where the extension in space of the sovereign powers and rights...meet'.[92]

The comprehensive process of a linearization of boundaries also extended to rivers and mountain ranges, established natural boundary features since time immemorial. No longer considered of sufficient precision, watercourse boundaries have since been made concrete by either the middle line or the Thalweg principle (centre of the main navigable channel), and in high mountain regions, the watershed principle gained prominence in order to draw a virtually invisible line separating with precision the respective spheres of sovereignty of neighbouring States: '[O]ne of the essential elements of sovereignty is that it is to be exercised within territorial limits,

[88] It is, however, important to recall that territory and its limitations have of course already been important elements in the tool-box of political actors in the European Middle Ages and the most powerful of them aspired indeed to some status of 'final authority'. However, these aspirations were not essentially territorial in character (in-depth discussion Territory, Authority, Rights (n 37) 31 ff; D Willoweit *Rechtsgrundlagen der Territorialgewalt* (Böhlau Köln 1975) at 276).

[89] Lord Curzon of Kedleston 'Frontiers' in *Oxford Lectures on History, 1904–1923* (Clarendon Press Oxford 1924) vol 1, 1–58 at 7.

[90] *Le droit des gens* (n 57) book II, ch VII, para 92.

[91] For a classical, albeit not uncontroversial analysis of the entire process regarding *Mitteleuropa* still H Helmolt 'Die Entwickelung der Grenzlinie aus dem Grenzsaume im alten Deutschland' (1896) 17 Historisches Jahrbuch 235–64.

[92] *Aegean Sea Continental Shelf Case (Greece v Turkey) (Judgment)* [1978] ICJ Rep 35 MN 85.

and that, failing proof to the contrary, the territory is co-terminous with the sovereignty....'.[93]

8. Dominion Over the Sea and its Seaward Limits[94]

8.1. The Sea: Godly Domain or Legitimate Object of Human Aspirations?

From time immemorial, the open sea has inspired fear and respect as well as the curiosity of the restless, questing mind of courageous men and women. For millennia, a similar ambiguity has prevailed with respect to claims by littoral States to a maritime *Aquitorium*.[95] In ancient history, disapproval of a *dominium maris* was not only based on the sea's very nature—unlike the *terra ferma* resisting possession in the proper sense. Reluctance in this respect was also intrinsically tied to one of the grand themes of mankind, the encounter of man with the other, godly world: 'The Sea is His' as the Psalmist sings (Psalm 95: 5). And the unique 'Report of Wenamon' from the late 20th dynasty of Ancient Egypt (approximately 1086 BC) is unmistakable in its branding the sea as forbidden terrain for appropriation by earthly authority: 'The sea is his... don't wish for yourself anything belonging to Amon-Re, [king of] the gods'.[96] A similar attitude prevailed among Roman writers, who at times went even so far as to consider mere navigation as an offence against the gods: 'The race of man... through forbidden wickedness [disregards that] God in his wisdom divided the countries of the earth by the separating ocean'.[97] However, divine warnings in this vein against the 'transgressional' hubris of men to reach out for domination of the sea served perfectly the Mediterranean community's more profane interest in free communication for commercial and, occasionally, also military purposes. No wonder therefore that

---

[93] *The North Atlantic Coast Fisheries Case (Great Britain v United States of America)* 11 Rep Intl Arbitral Awards 167 at 180.

[94] For details see the contribution by D Bederman 'The Sea', in this volume.

[95] Term coined by W Graf Vitzthum *Handbuch des Seerechts* (Beck München 2006) at 69.

[96] JH Breasted *Ancient Records of Egypt* (The University of Chicago Press Chicago 1906) vol 4, at 274 ff (paras 557 ff). To be sure, Wenamon (ab)used the alleged godly prerogatives to corroborate Egyptian hegemonic aspirations in the Eastern Mediterranean.

[97] Horace *Odes/Carmina* book 1, ch 3, 21–6; C Phillipson *The International Law and Custom of Ancient Greece and Rome* (Macmillan London 1911) vol 2, at 369 f: 'the Romans regarded the sea with horror...and so, to navigate it has usually thought to be an offence against the gods...'.

the Antique world hardly knew of any jurisdictional claims over parts of the sea, and sea-related sets of legal rules, such as the *Lex Rhodia* (2nd century BC),[98] were strictly confined to regulations indispensable for maritime trade, including the fight against probably the most serious challenge for seafaring nations: the scourge of piracy. Even if, for security and economic reasons, claims may occasionally have been laid on certain very limited offshore waters,[99] and irrespective of the Roman Empire's merely political and military, but certainly not legal, *mare nostrum* claim with respect to the Mediterranean as a whole, the overall picture that the Antique world, in Europe and elsewhere,[100] treated the sea as something clearly beyond the jurisdictional reach of States, remains unclouded. This maxim was so generally accepted that for the city of Byzantinum, trying to impose tolls on shipping passing through the Bosporus (220 BC), the immediate declaration of war by the Republic of Rhodes in response must have come hardly as a surprise. It was only the city's complete drawback from this audacious assault on the freedom of the seas which eventually prevented a full-size military confrontation: 'The Byzantines engage not to levy toll on ships bound for the Pontus, and on this condition the Rhodians and their allies shall be at peace with the Byzantines.'[101]

8.2. *Mare liberum* contra *mare clausum*

More than 1800 years later, the antique conception that no one has dominion or supreme control over the sea resonates in Hugo Grotius' seminal work *The Freedom of the Seas* (1608): 'The sea is a thing so clearly common to all, that it cannot be the property of any one save God alone.'[102] However, at the time of writing, this principle had not only become increasingly strained in the real world. It was also subject of probably the first great doctrinal dispute in the history of international law:[103] Do States dispose of a jurisdictional prerogative in waters adjacent to their coast, and if this were so, to what extent? Whereas the first question was soon answered in the affirmative, the second remained on the international agenda up to the very recent

---

[98] For details W Ashburner *Nomos Rhodion Nautikos. The Rhodian Sea-Law* (Clarendon Press Oxford 1909).

[99] Treaties among Greek City States (5th century BC): Thucydides *The History of the Peloponnesian War* (431 BC) ch V.

[100] RP Anand arrives at virtually the same conclusion for the Asian world (*Origin and Development of the Law of the Sea* (Martinus Nijhoff The Hague 1982) at 10 ff).

[101] Polybios (*c* 200–120 BC) provides a full account of this episode: *Historiai* (WR Paton trans) (Loeb Classical Library 1922) book 4, at 52.

[102] H Grotius *The Freedom of the Seas* (1608) at 34.

[103] The so-called battle of books: Expression ('*bataille de livres*') coined by E Nys *Les origines du droit international* (Castaigne, Thorin & Fils Bruxelles 1894) at 262; see also, E Nys 'Une bataille de livres: Episode de l'histoire litteraire du droit international' in E Nys *Etudes de droit international et de politique* (Castaigne, Fontemoigne Bruxelles 1901) vol 2, 260–72.

past. The intellectual dispute was triggered by hard facts. At the turn of the 17th century, many seas in Europe had become economic areas of competition, in particular with regard to fishing. No wonder, therefore, that not only did a number of States lay—sometimes merely symbolic—claims on certain maritime areas;[104] some seas had actually become more or less effectively appropriated, notably the Baltic Sea (Sweden) and the British Sea (England and Scotland).[105] The question of control *vel* liberty of sea lanes, too, had grown into an issue of vital importance for the prosperity of entire nations. The egregious claims for exclusivity by Portugal and Spain regarding the use of major sea lanes vital for trade and commerce with the newly 'discovered' worlds did not remain unchallenged. Not surprisingly, the search for a balance between the exercise of governmental authority over the sea and the idea of the freedom of the sea[106] soon evolved into one of the key issues on the political, strategic, economic and, not least, legal agenda of the international community.

The vigorous advocacy of Grotius for the open sea to be free for the use of all met with strong resistance by virtually the entire intellectual community of the time, including in particular his famous English counterpart John Selden,[107] and the controversy 'waxed and waned through the centuries'.[108] However, it was never in dispute that coastal waters may be subdued to some kind of dominium by the littoral power. 'The question at issue'—as Grotius himself admits—'does not concern a gulf or a strait in this ocean, nor even all the expanse of sea which is visible from the shore.'[109] And in 1625 he clarified that 'the empire of a portion of the sea ... [may reach] so far as those who sail in that part of the sea can be compelled from the shore as if they were on land'.[110] It was, however, another Dutch jurist, Cornelius van Bynkershoek, who, by virtue of his *De dominio maris dissertatio* (1703), eventually became the leading authority for the determination of the extent of the maritime belt which may legitimately come under the sway of the littoral State: *Imperium terrae finir ubi finitur armorum potestas.* Open for future (technological) developments, it took several more decades before the deliberately vague criterion of effective exercise of State authority was translated into the rather rigid three-mile limit, the alleged 'utmost range of a cannon ball'.[111] Although

---

[104] Eg Venice in the Adriatic, symbolized by an annual picturesque ceremony of 'espousing' (G Pace *De dominio maris adriatico* (1619)); Genoa on part of the Ligurian Sea (PB Borgo *De dominio serenessimae genuinsis reipublica in mari ligustico* (1641)). For details JHW Verzijl *International Law in Historical Perspective* (AW Sijthoff Leyden 1971) vol 4, at 11 ff.

[105] On the so-called King's Chambers and other claims to the Dominion of the British Seas see still unmatched TW Fulton *The Sovereignty of the Sea* (William Blackwood and Sons Edinburgh 1911), offering an amazing amount of 17th to 19th century State practice.

[106] DP O'Connell *The International Law of the Sea* (Clarendon Press Oxford 1982) vol 1, at 1.

[107] *De mare clausum* (1635 trans 1663).

[108] *The International Law of the Sea* (n 106) 14 ff with a succinct explanation of the distinction between imperium and dominium, crucial for the understanding of Grotius's writings.

[109] *The Freedom of the Seas* (n 102) 37.

[110] *De jure belli ac pacis* (n 56) book II, ch 3, para XIII.

[111] US Secretary of State Jefferson, letter of 8 November 1793 (JB Moore *A Digest of International Law* (Government Printing Office Washington 1906) vol 1, at 702).

never really matching the actual state of weapon technology, as a matter of reasonable-ness and convenience, the three-mile limit soon became the widely accepted principle for the determination of the outer limit of the territorial sea.[112]

9. GOING VERTICAL: APPROPRIATION AND DIVISION OF AIRSPACE

Traditional international law serves as a mediator for at least potentially conflicting interests of States. No wonder, therefore, that as long as the airspace was virtually inaccessible to man, (international) lawyers and State practice alike did not pay much interest in the eventuality of a vertical dimension of the State's spatial domain. The same is true—*mutatis mutandis*—for the earth's interior, the public law status of which has never attracted more than very marginal attention at all, up to the present day. Our perception is indeed still very much the same as the one exposed (in a private law context) by William Blackstone in the 1770s already: 'downwards, whatever is in a direct line between the surface of any land, and the center of the earth, belongs to the owner of the surface....'.[113]

It was only in the early 20th century that intellectual work slowly began to discover the airspace:

Whilst the technical expert from one century to another was engaged in investigating the problem of the navigation of the air, the jurist could afford to look on calm and unmoved as one experiment after another failed....So long as there were available only undirigible bal-loons, dangerous and expensive, absolutely unfit for regular traffic,[114] aerial navigation was therefore necessarily confined to some very unfrequent ascents, such as attractions at exhibi-tions, for pleasure trips or scientific excursions and most occasionally for military purposes;[115]

---

[112] Only in the late 20th century definitively replaced by today's 12 mile limit (UNCLOS (The United Nations Convention on the Law of the Sea) (1982) art 3).

[113] *Commentaries on the Laws of England* (Clarendon Press Oxford 1766) vol 2, ch 2, at 18; referred to by H Lauterpacht (ed) *Oppenheim's International Law* (8th edn Longmans, Green & Co New York 1955) at 462, as an 'universally recognized rule of the Law of Nations'. For details see *Die deutschen Staatsgren-zen* (n 74) 642 ff.

[114] The first free ascent of humans took place in Paris on 21 November 1783 in a hot-air balloon, con-structed by the brothers Josef and Etienne Montgolfier (Pilatre de Rozier and Marquis d'Arlandes).

[115] Isolated incidents of an early military use (battle of Fleurus 1794, siege of Venice 1849, battle of Solferino 1859) did not trigger any juridical reflections. The rather extensive use of balloons in the relief of the besieged city of Paris (Franco-German War 1870/71), however, led to some interesting juridical disputes, in particular in the field of international humanitarian law (threat of Bismarck to execute as spies all aeronauts). For extensive references see *Die deutschen Staatsgrenzen* (n 74) 622 ff.

it did not create situations and relationships demanding the immediate attention of the legislator.[116]

The main purpose of scattered 17th-century reflections on the subject[117] was indeed merely to strengthen one's own position in the heated debate on sovereignty over the sea. Exploiting the argument of the ocean's (allegedly) inexhaustible resources for his vigorous freedom plea, Grotius observed, 'The same thing would need to be said, too, about the air, if it were capable of any use for which the use of land is not required...'.[118] And Pufendorf on his part used exactly the same premise—the absolute inaccessibility of airspace—as a key argument for his opposite claim in favour of at least partial sovereignty over the sea 'so far as nature allows': 'Mention is made of the fowls of the heaven as well, yet since man has been denied the ability to be in the air to the extent that he rest in it alone, and be separated from the earth, he has been unable to exercise sovereignty over the air....'[119]

Although occasionally discussed, the Roman law maxim *cuius est solum eius est coelum* did not, as matter of fact, succeed to transgress the limits of the private law domain.[120] Instead, unanimity prevailed that, at least as far as the public law sphere was concerned,[121] the air was to be considered a *res omnium commune* and as such not susceptible of the exercise of any kind of sovereign rights by States.

It was only in the early years of the 20th century that a seminal paper by Paul Fauchille,[122] together with two comprehensive reports presented at the 1902 Brussels Session of the Institut de Droit International (*Régime juridique des aérostats*),[123] revived the discussion on the issue without, however, forging new intellectual paths. Clinging to the traditional argumentative pattern whereas *'l'air, par sa nature même, est insusceptible de propriété ou de souveraineté'*,[124] the overwhelming majority adhered

---

[116] JF Lycklama à Nijeholt *Air Sovereignty* (Nijhoff The Hague 1910) at 1.

[117] JS Dancko *De jure principis aereo. disputatio inauguralis* (Anhalt-Zerbst 1687) is probably the very first, although eccentric treatment of the subject (Synopsis of the original Latin text and German translation by Institute of Air and Space Law (Cologne University 2001)); a century later, J Pütter *Erörterungen und Beyspiele des teutschen Staats- und Fürstenrechts* (1793) vol 1, 10 f touches upon the issue in the context of the (hypothetical) distribution of competences between the (German) *Reich* and its constituent units (*Länder*).

[118] *De jure belli ac pacis* (n 56) book II, ch 2 and 3.

[119] 'De jure naturae et gentium. Libri octo' (1672) in JB Scott (ed and trans) *The Classics of International Law* (Clarendon Press Oxford 1934) vol 17, book IV, ch V, para 5.

[120] JC Cooper 'Roman Law and the Maxim "Cujus est solum" in International Air Law' in IA Vlasic (ed) *Explorations in Aerospace Law* (McGill University Press Montreal 1968) 54–102.

[121] For an opposite view (albeit for private law purposes) Commentaries on the Laws of England (n 113) 18.

[122] 'Le domaine aérien et le régime juridique des aérostats' (1901) 8 Revue Générale de Droit International Public 414–85.

[123] P Fauchille 'Régime juridique des aérostats' (1902) 19 Annuaire Institut de Droit International 19–86; E Nys (1902) 'Régime juridique des aérostats' 19 Annuaire Institut de Droit International 86–114.

[124] P Fauchille 'Régime des aérostats et de la télégraphie sans fil' (1906) 21 Annuaire Institut de Droit International 293–329 at 295.

to the succinct position that *'L'air est libre'*. Although security concerns soon gained some ground in the discussion of possible limitations of the freedom-of-the-air principle, the same remained not only widely accepted during the next few years,[125] but was even tagged by their protagonists as virtually 'uncontested'.[126] However, in a complete volte-face, the following decade witnessed a total abandonment of this solid legal doctrine: The successful launch by the Wright brothers of a power-driven and thus navigable aircraft (1903) and the potential consequences resulting from this technological revolution, sowed the first serious doubts over the correctness of the hitherto virtually unchallenged theory of unlimited aerial freedom.[127] And in the face of the devastating effects of First World War aerial warfare, it took hardly a year that States in the 1919 Paris Convention agreed on the following: 'The High Contracting Parties recognize that every Power has complete and exclusive sovereignty over the airspace above its territory.'[128]

Complemented by the duty of States to 'accord [in times of peace and under certain conditions] freedom of innocent passage above its territory to the aircraft of the other contracting States', an entirely new balance was sought between the (prevailing) national interest and—now, if at all, only coming second—the concept of *res omnium commune*. Although it is thus incorrect to assume that these provisions 'simply registered a principle... already sanctioned by customary international practice',[129] it is certainly true that the inclusion of airspace into State territory, reiterated and reconfirmed in the 1944 Convention on Civil Aviation,[130] soon entered the corpus of customary international law and has never seriously been challenged ever since. However, up to the present day no consensus could be reached on the exact location of the invisible frontier between airspace and outer space—unanimity prevailing that the latter should be kept free from sovereignty claims. Regardless of the never-ending dispute on this question,[131] the so-called Kármán Primary Jurisdiction

---

[125] K Hutchinson *Freedom of the Air* (Public Affairs Committee New York 1944) at 4. Still in 1910, Germany and France vigorously advocated for the time-honoured principle of a virtually unlimited freedom of the air.

[126] 'Régime des aérostats et de la télégraphie sans fil' (n 124).

[127] A proposal by Westlake, reverting explicitly to the 'cujus est solum ejus est usque ad coelom' principle to grant States a restricted 'droit de souveraineté sur l'espace aérien au-dessus de son sol' ('Régime des aérostats et de la télégraphie sans fil' (n 124) 299) was rejected by great majority at the IDI's Gent session (ibid 305). A similar position was held by H Hazeltine *The Law of the Air* (University of London Press London 1911).

[128] Convention Relating to the Regulation of Aerial Navigation (signed 13 October 1919, entered into force 29 March 1922) 11 LNTS 173, art 1.

[129] JHW Verzijl *International Law in Historical Perspective* (AW Sijthoff Leyden 1970) vol 3, at 75.

[130] Convention on International Civil Aviation (signed 7 December 1944, entered into force 5 March 1947) 15 UNTS 295 (so-called 'Chicago Convention').

[131] For details R Goedhart *The Never Ending Dispute: Delimitation of Air Space and Outer Space* (Editions Frontières Gif-sur Yvette 1996); G Oduntan *Sovereignty and Jurisdiction in Airspace and Outer Space: Legal Criteria for Spatial Delimitation* (Routledge New York 2012).

line of 1957,[132] locating the upper limit of State territory at a height of approximately 83 kilometres, still serves as some sort of authoritative guideline. Basically used for the transit of spaceships, rockets, and missiles only, the functional approach chosen by Kármán, must still be considered of sufficient precision to avoid conflicts between aeronautic and astronautic uses in this remote space at the intersection of the Mesosphere and the Thermosphere.

10. Spaces Beyond State Territory

Old maps occasionally designated uncharted territories (*terra incognita*) with the Latin phrase *hic sunt leones*. These times have long gone by and more than a century ago imperialistic expansion has brought the scramble for State dominion over the earth's landmasses to an end. The post-Second World War decolonization process (re-)distributed the territorial heritage of colonialism among newly independent States, without, however, leaving any blank spots of stateless domain on the world map, let alone creating new ones. Today, the only remaining exception in this respect is the 14 million km² Antarctic Continent. By virtue of the 1959 Antarctic Treaty,[133] pre-existing and partly overlapping territorial claims raised by a number of States were frozen (article IV), thus barring recognition of territorial sovereignty of any State over all land and ice shelves south of 60 degrees South (article VI). With respect to extra-terrestrial territories, a similar approach is followed. 'Outer space, including the Moon and other celestial bodies, is not subject to national appropriation by claim of sovereignty, by means of use or occupation, or by any other means.'[134] These treaty regimes, together with the one in existence for waters beyond national jurisdiction ('The High Sea'[135]), show a growing awareness of States that if history has taught us one lesson, then it might be that distributing competences and responsibilities by drawing lines on the ground between omnipotent and basically selfish political

[132] Developed by the Hungarian engineer and physicist Theodor von Kármán (1881–1963), this line relies on aerodynamic criteria: Where the thinning air does no longer allow the wings to generate enough lift to make an aircraft, travelling right below orbital velocity, to stay up, we have crossed the border between airspace and outer space.

[133] The Antarctic Treaty (signed 1 December 1959) 402 UNTS 71.

[134] Treaty on Principles Governing the Activities of States in the Exploration and Use of Outer Space, including the Moon and Other Celestial Bodies of 27 January 1967 (opened for signature 27 January 1967, entered into force 10 October 1967) 610 UNTS 205, art 2.

[135] United Nations Convention on the Law of the Sea 1833 UNTS 397, art 89: 'No State may validly purport to subject any part of the high seas to its sovereignty.'

entities is probably not the ultimate response to the urgent problems of an ever-more interdependent humankind.[136]

11. Conclusion

To be certain, Westphalian territoriality is not dead. On the contrary, territoriality is broadly respected today by all States, whereas in the past only a handful of (Western) powers enjoyed full territorial sovereignty.[137] For roughly the last 500 years, a bordered territory has been considered a suitable framework to organize governance over people. However, in recent years there are increasing signs that the traditional and rather categorical symbiosis between territory and power may no longer lay a legitimate claim for exclusivity. This is hardly deplorable since from an international law perspective, possession and transfer of territory have never been considered an end in itself. *L'obsession du territoire* of modern States[138] was always meant to serve people, not vice versa. One may recall in this context Robert Jenning's statement of timeless relevance: 'A territorial change means not just a transference of a portion of the earth's surface and its resources from one regime to another; it usually involves, perhaps more importantly, a decisive change in the nationality, allegiance, and way of life of a population.'[139]

Recommended Reading

Anderson, Malcolm *Frontiers: Territory and State Formation in the Modern World* (Cambridge Polity Press Cambridge 1996).
Blum, Yehuda *Historic Titles in International Law* (Martinus Nijhoff The Hague 1965).
Blumann, Claude 'Frontières et limites. Rapport général' in Société Française pour le Droit International (ed) *La frontière. Colloque de Poitiers 1979* (Pedone Paris 1980) 3–33.

---

[136] Recent developments indicate the emergence of new forms of even long-lasting 'territorial administration' by non-State actors. However, this complex issue is clearly transcending the history-oriented approach of this volume.

[137] K Raustiala 'The Evolution of Territoriality: International Relations and American Law' in M Kahler and BF Walter (eds) *Territoriality and Conflict in an Era of Globalization* (CUP Cambridge 2006).

[138] G Scelle 'Obsession du territoire' in JHW Verzijl (ed) *Symbolae Verzijl* (Martinus Nijhoff The Hague 1958) 347–61.

[139] *The Acquisition of Territory in International Law* (n 71) 3.

Buchanan, Allen and Margaret More *States, Nations, and Borders. The Ethics of Making Boundaries* (CUP Cambridge 2003).

Castellino, Joshua and Steve Allen *Title to Territory in International Law: A Temporal Analysis* (Ashgate Aldershot 2002).

De Visscher, Charles *Problèmes de confins en droit international* (Pedone Paris 1969).

Fulton, Thomas W *The Sovereignty of the Sea* (W Blackwood and Sons Edinburgh 1911).

Gottmann, Jean *The Significance of Territory* (The University Press of Virginia Charlottesville 1973).

Hill, Norman *Claims to Territory in International Law and Relations* (OUP London 1945).

Jennings, Robert Y *The Acquisition of Territory in International Law* (Manchester University Press Manchester 1963).

Johnston, Douglas M *The Theory and History of Ocean Boundary-Making* (McGill-Queen's University Press Kingston 1988).

Kolers, Avery *Land, Conflict and Justice: A Political Theory of Territory* (CUP Cambridge 2009).

La Pradelle, Paul Gouffre de *La frontière, étude de droit international* (Les éditions internationales Paris 1928).

Larkins, Jeremy *From Hierarchy to Anarchy. Territory and Politics before Westphalia* (Palgrave Macmillan New York 2010).

Milano, Enrico *Unlawful Territorial Situations in International Law. Reconciling Effectiveness, Legality and Legitimacy* (Martinus Nijhoff Leiden 2006).

Sassen, Saskia *Territory, Authority, Rights. From Medieval to Global Assemblages* (Princeton University Press Princeton 2006).

Schoenborn, Walther 'La nature juridique du territoire' (1929) 30 Recueil des cours 81–190.

Shaw, Malcolm (ed) *Title to Territory* (Ashgate Dartmouth 2005).

Shaw, Malcolm *The International Law of Territory* (OUP Oxford 2013 forthcoming).

CHAPTER 10

COSMOPOLIS AND UTOPIA

DOMINIQUE GAURIER

1. INTRODUCTION[1]

THIS chapter considers the various projects which have been planned over nearly six centuries, aimed towards a perpetual peace between the European nations. These projects essentially concerned European countries from the Middle Ages up to the eve of our times, that is, the contemporary period up to the mid-20th century, including the creation of the UN just after the First World War. Considerable anxiety was felt as no year passed without war between any of the European nations. Indeed, since the birth of nations, the rivalry between them was acute, each searching to establish domination over the other, although some countries were late to develop a true national feeling, like Italy, or Germany up to the 19th century. But others emerged earlier, like Spain, England, or most of the central Empire from the Habsburg dynasty, these rapidly became strong powers in opposition to each other, especially in coali-

[1] D Gaurier *Histoire du droit international. Auteurs, doctrines et développement de l'Antiquité à l'aube de la période moderne* (Presses Universitaires de Rennes Rennes 2005); J Brown Scott 'Introduction' in W Ladd *An Essay on a Congress of Nations for the Adjustment of International Disputes Without Resort to Arms* (OUP New York 1916) iii–xlv; Brown Scott gives a very interesting translation into English of the 12 articles proposed by the Abbé de Saint-Pierre, see ibid xxiv–xxvii.

tion against France, because the Habsburg King Charles V had obtained the imperial crown when King Francis I wanted it. Furthermore, there was a general policy among these nations to seek a true and equal balance between the nations up to the First World War.

Nevertheless, the different plans supported by some Utopians did not pursue the same objectives, their political views being mainly based on religious considerations or great fears; for example, the Turkish empire, with which France concluded several treaties[2]—so called 'capitulations'—since the beginning of the 16th century, or the Austrian Empire which openly was in opposition to France. Philosophers such as Jean-Jacques Rousseau and Immanuel Kant were interested in such an idea. Nevertheless, all these different plans were connected to one another, liaised and joined together to seek a permanent abolition of all kinds of wars. Therein lies Utopia.

Another concept also worth scrutinizing is the so-called 'Cosmopolis'. Immanuel Kant developed this idea of cosmopolitism with the view of building a peaceful community of nations supported by an alliance between free peoples and a federation of free States establishing a new comprehensive State, including one single people, in which wars were to be rejected.

The relationship between Utopia and Cosmopolis seems obvious, because both words include a Utopian meaning, but Utopia is a fiction, an ideal, unknown in the real world, as outlined by authors like Thomas More or Campanella.[3] On the other hand, Cosmopolis could be defined as a possible future, imaginary for sure, but an achievable world, reflected through a philosophical approach such as Immanuel Kant's. There is a difference between the two concepts. One is old and essentially oriented towards a reconstitution of a lost Christian commonwealth, or on the way to being lost forever, the *respublica Christiana* appealed by authors like Pierre Dubois, Sully, even Leibniz to some extent (see Section 6 in this chapter). The prospective view was supported by Idealists, who were hoping for a pacified world in a Europe divided into martial nations strongly opposed to one another (Castel de Saint-Pierre, with the realistic contradiction made by Leibniz, and the more philosophical approach of Immanuel Kant amongst others). Some other authors have different views: based on other convictions including religion, like William Penn, or the creation of a League of Nations, like President Woodrow Wilson.

It is difficult, if not absolutely impossible, to try to find a relation between these projects, because all must be considered independent from the others. But it is

---

[2] Such treaties begun with the first one concluded between Francis I and the Sultan Soliman on the 2 February 1536, followed by other same treaties which confirmed the agreements.

[3] T More *Utopie ou traité de la meilleure forme de gouvernement* (originally in Latin 1516; Droz Genève 1983); T Campanella *La Cité du Soleil* (originally in Italian 1602; Droz Genève 1972).

possible to classify them under some intellectual titles in order to give them a greater coherence rather than seeing them as a simple list of projects.

2. THE QUEST OF THE OLD CHRISTIAN COMMONWEALTH'S LOST WORLD

Christianity was first badly disrupted by the victory of the Islamic troops of Salah ad-Din (1138–93, the conquest of Jerusalem in October 1187), when they conquered the Holy Land and excluded the armies of the crusaded European nations from the Near-East countries. Whereas Christianity under the direction of the Pope of Rome saw itself in the beginning as a victorious faith when the crusaders were conquering the soil of Syria and Palestine, the Islamic reaction did not expect too much for fighting against this aggression and for expelling them from these countries. Nevertheless the idea of regaining a general power over the world never vanished among the Christian peoples, especially when the new Ottoman Muslim power emerged with the conquest of the rests of the Byzantine Empire in 1453 by Mehmet II 'The Victorious'.

The lost paradise was never forgotten, even if impossible to be regained, particularly when the Ottoman empire threatened the European kingdoms on several occasions, until the last one, besieging Austrian Vienna in 1683. If Christian countries expected to recover the lost ancient kingdoms of Jerusalem and Acra, hardly 150 years later, they were obliged to protect themselves from the heavy menace of the Ottomans.

This general context allowed the emergence of projects, like recovering of the lost countries, or sheltering the Christian European kingdoms from the Ottoman Empire. Three people set forth plans between the beginning of the 14th and the 17th centuries; Pierre Dubois, then George of Podébrady, and, 100 years later, the Duke of Sully, minister under Henry IV, King of France.

2.1. Pierre Dubois' *De Recuperatione Terre Sancte*[4]

Pierre Dubois was a lawyer. He practised as an advocate and procurator for the King of France in Coutances (Normandy). He wrote an opus which may be certified as the

---

[4] P Dubois *De recuperatione terre sancte, traité de politique générale* (CV Langlois ed) (Alphonse Picard Paris 1891).

first Utopia, in 1305, under the title *On the Recoverage of the Holy Land*, just at the time it became impossible to recover Palestine after the defeat of the Eighth Crusade conducted by King of France Louis IX (Saint-Louis). Only the first part of the work, the circular letter to Christian princes, is of interest for this chapter.

The arguments show three areas of interest. In the first, the author presents a war-and-peace theory and asserts peace as the ultimate goal, the supreme blessing, and the condition absolutely necessary for planning a possible re-conquest of the Holy Land. War against unbelieving people is a compulsory duty as a war against malefactors, because the origin of war lay in the sin created by Satan. However, Dubois does not define any criteria for defining what a 'legitimate' war could be; he only says that every war generates the following ones.

In the second argument, Dubois focuses on the means for asserting and warranting peace. Merely preaching peace is not in itself sufficient. Radical means should be used in order to make it possible to reach peace. In order to pursue such a goal, Christian people have to organize themselves, not through a universal monarchy, the realization of which is unreachable, but through a federation submitted to a general assembly, in which every nation would preserve an absolute independence regarding its own temporal affairs. At the head of this federation is the Pope of Rome, with his authority in the matter of establishing universal peace and punishing he wicked, whereas the German Emperor is set aside and the German Empire reduced to a single State like all others. According to its constitution, this Christian federation becomes dominant over the barbarian nation, and establishes peace in the world.

The third point concerns the organization of the international society. Within this federation of the Christian nations, all placed under sovereign princes' governance, it is necessary to install a superior authority, able to present sovereign princes or States with an international arbitration plan, such as developed in a general council summoned by the pope. Appeals might also be heard at the arbitral court of the pope. Here lies Dubois' weakness. He offers the pope the highest authority whilst Christian princes reject this at that time and would prefer to enforce their own authority in their countries. Moreover, the Canonical sanctions upheld by the arbitral court would notably be insufficient for the correction of the peace violators. Therefore Dubois does suggest their banishment to the Orient.

Pierre Dubois' plan did not appear to receive a decent hearing, mostly because of his disregard of the reality of European conflicts already born and to be solved before Europe could reach a political and national balance. Nevertheless, he perceived the growing strength of nations and the conflicts to be tackled to make a balance possible. He was certainly not a prophet but a man of his time, addressing Utopia as attainable, characterized by an unrealistic and impossible confederation of Christian nations. Dubois' plan could not enjoy a wide audience as it was palpably unrealistic.

2.2. George of Podébrady and his Plan for a Confederation of Christian Principalities[5]

George of Podébrady was a Czech noble born in 1421, who enlisted in the army, later became Regent and then King of Bohemia, when the infant king died in 1458. Supporting the Hussites and then perceived as a heretic for his attempt to become emperor of the German empire, he did not succeed and was excommunicated by Pope Paul II. His son-in-law, Matthias Corvin, King of Hungary, a fervent supporter of the Catholic church, expelled him from the throne in 1468. Podébrady died in 1471.

At the same time of his accession to the throne of Bohemia, Podébrady most likely also met a French manufacturer and inventor named Antoine Marini, the real creator of the plan attributed to Podébrady. Marini produced a scheme for a European federation and presented it to foreign princes on behalf of the King of Bohemia when Marini became his chancellor. Europe was at that time under threat from the Ottoman empire. Mehmet al-Fatih abolished the Byzantine empire and some three-quarters of a century later, in 1526, the Ottomans conquered Hungary in the battle of Mohács, maintaining the country under their domination for 150 years. For attempting to push this menace away, Marini together with Podébrady at first planned an alliance between the King of France, Louis XI, the King of Bohemia, and the Venice Republic, with a possibility that other princes might join. But prior to, and because of, the Ottoman threat, this potential alliance became a plan for a European confederation which had three goals: the establishment of a true peace in Europe, the creation of a European confederation, and the mandate of a crusade against the Ottomans.

The scheme of Podébrady, relying upon the provisions elaborated by Marini, had two parts. First of all, this idea linked up directly with a peace treaty and, in the first two articles of the settlement of confederation, it was phrased in terms of establishing a defensive alliance, called in Latin language *collegium, universitas, corpus,* or *congregatio*—every word meaning quite the same thing: that is, a collective compound in which kings and/or princes were assembled or united. Article 3 provided that offences against peace were not prejudicial to the alliance. The last two articles are most interesting, insofar as article 4 emphasizes that a State could be attacked by a non-confederated State. In such a case, the federal power would delegate emissaries in order to bring the question to settlement either by a judge of competence or by the federal judge. Article 5 went even further, providing that where a conflict emerged between two confederation non-member States, it had to be adjusted by a kind of a European covenant (*Entente*) amongst the nations, enlarging the genuine defensive alliance towards more general views.

---

[5] The most comprehensive presentation of the scheme of George of Podébrady was given in C Bernet 'Podiebard, Georg von' in T Bautz (ed) *Biographisch-Bilbiographisches Kirchenlexikon* (Verlag Traugott Bautz Nordhausen 2003) vol 21, col 1183–203.

The second part concerned the establishment of the confederation as planned, and sought to enforce a comprehensive peace based on justice, via the promotion and implementation of a jurisdictional power within the confederation. The scheme was therefore to create a so-called *consistoire* (*parlamentarium*, or *consistorium*), or a parliament, comparable to an international court of arbitration, placed under the control of the major part of the members of the confederation. This court was intended to be in office in 1464, whereas the leading council of the confederation was based in Basel for five years, then by roster in France, Italy, and so on. Peace between Christian nations was emphasized as the only way to guarantee a triumphant war against the Turks.

After all, the principle of peace as settled by Marini and Podébrady confirmed the old two-sided idea of peace: firstly peace between Christian nations and secondly in making war against the Turks, that latter being considered as the highest duty. The spirit of the crusades was definitely not yet rejected, in particular because of the pressing Ottoman threat on the countries located in Central Europe. Nevertheless, what was notable was a gradual fading from power of the figures of both the pope and the emperor.

Of course, this plan was never implemented, mainly because it did not address the general question about international peace; in fact, it only concerned minor, local, and incidental occasions, totally detached from the true Western European powers.

2.3. The 'Great Design' of the Duke of Sully[6]

Maximilien de Béthune, the Duke of Sully, was the Principal Minister of Henry IV, King of France, who in 1598 brought an end to religious wars which had torn the country into two opposed parties, Catholics and Protestants, from the beginning of the second part of the 16th century. Sully was himself a Protestant, allied with peaceful royal politics since a long time. He began to dictate his memoirs in 1612 and the complete opus of them was then published in 1640. Relying on official documents, assessments, and other documentation, he never hesitated to offer his personal ideas on all matters. Amongst the dreams he promoted, his 'Great Design' was the establishment of a 'most Christian Republic always peaceful in itself'. But prior to this, he sought after destroying the hegemony of the Austrian House through a great coalition of one half of the European countries against the other one.

Within the first half of his memoirs, he suggested a new arrangement of Europe, in which only six hereditary monarchies would remain: France, Spain, England, Sweden, Denmark, and Lombardy; plus six elective monarchies: Rome, Venice,

[6] M de Bethune Sully 'Mémoires des sages et royales oeconomies d'estat domestiques, politiques et militaires de Henry le Grand' in JF Michaud and JJ Poujoulat (eds) *Nouvelle collection des mémoires relatifs à l'histoire de France* (Didier Paris 1854) vol 2.

Poland, Bohemia, Hungary, and the German Empire; plus three federative Republics: the Netherlands (including Flanders), Helvetia, or an enlarged Switzerland, then Italy (including Genoa, Florence, Modena, Parma, and Piacenza). Two nations would be definitely excluded: the Muscovites because of their barbarity, and the Turks because of their so-called 'irreligion'. To the latter, a choice would be granted: either return home to the Far-East where from they are originated, or to adopt Christianity.

For keeping the peace perpetual within this 'most Christian Commonwealth', six special councils would be created in Danzig, Nuremberg, Vienna, Constance, Bologna, and in a town located along the Rhine river to be determined later. Near to those councils, a General Council of forty members 'well qualified and well circumspect', would sit by turns in one Central Europe town. This high assembly would treat of all litigious matters between the powers and, with the help of the six others assemblies, would recommend three possible solutions: (1) prevention from wars between neighbour States; (2) suppression of wars within each State, either civil or religious; and (3) ceasing of all squabbles by more powerful States against weaker ones.

Sully thus intended to support law rather than military strength, but he never considered a general disarmament, even suggesting leaving the armies of the confederation the task of resisting any power potentially threatening the peace.

French King Henry IV seemed to pay some attention to this plan, especially regarding the House of Austria. On his own part, Sully seemed to be fully conscious too that his scheme was totally utopian. It never came to pass.

3. Emeric De Crucé, His Quest for a General Peace Mixed with the Promotion of a Freedom of Commerce: *The New Cyneas*[7]

Emeric de Lacroix, or de Crucé (1590–1648), was a clergyman, practising as director of a Parisian school. Few things are known about his life; only the fact he became a clergyman in order to afford a good education, as he was poor. As a mathematics

[7] E de Crucé *Le nouveau cynée, ou discours d'etat représentant les occasions et moyens d'établir une paix générale et liberté du commerce par tout le monde* (A Fenet and A Guillaume eds) (Chez Jaques Villery Paris 1623; Presses Universitaires de Rennes Rennes 2004). A reproduction of the original edition of 1623 was published by the Editions d'Histoire Sociale (EDHIS) Paris 1976. See also P Louis-Lucas *Un plan de paix générale et de la liberté du commerce au XVIIe siècle* (PhD thesis Librairie du recueil Sirey Paris 1919).

teacher, he published his *Nouveau Cynée* in 1623. His main concern was about planning a complete programme for establishing an international organization, taking into account the principle of State sovereignty. He was the very first author to include non-Christian States like the Turkish Empire in such an organization. And he was the first to consider matters of economics and freedom of commerce as they related to peace.

The starting point of his work, however, remained morals; for example, he wrote that inhumanity is the source of all vices, that it is the most common vice to eradicate, and that life in and of itself ought to be valued above any doctrine. Therefore war is unjust and inhuman in and of itself: contrary not only to morals but to the interests of both States and individuals, because humanity should be understood as interdependent.

After scanning the four reasons of war—(1) martial honour, (2) benefits drawn from war, (3) compensations for all damage, (4) wars aiming to train the armies—and refusing to treat religion as a fifth, he presented war as the most dreadful thing, primarily caused by antipathies between people, relying on unavoidable and unjustified prejudice. Mutual tolerance should be established among States, since forcing anyone to convert under threat is an absolute nonsense.

He included the Ottoman empire as well as Christian nations in his vision. The general assembly heading his a commonwealth, being almost a European peace and supervision council, would dwell in Venice. Roles of precedence between States would be proposed as follows: the first place would be given to the pope because of his ecumenical call, the second to the Turkish sultan, the third to the German emperor, the fourth for the king of France because of his nation's military capacity, the fifth to the king of Spain, a place deemed totally unfit as the genuine site of that kingdom in Europe at that time. The council would act as a permanent authority and even a court of justice, taking a decision by a majority, rather than act as a simple court of arbitration. In short, he suggested that every nation unite with the injured party against the offender.

However attractive the idea of a united States in Europe might be, Cruce was too short of true juridical arguments to conceive such an assembly, thus remaining either too summary or vague on these points.

In the fourth and final part of his work, Cruce became a true advocate of freedom of commerce, from his point of view the sole way towards peace. He pleaded in favour of weight and measure units, as well as an international treaty towards a common currency value.

Leibniz is considered as having had a good knowledge of the *New Cyneas*, but he did not know its author. He was familiar with the book, which we should no longer consider as a whimsical piece of writing, but as something worth serious consideration in terms of a way to achieve and maintain peace among nations.

4. AROUND AND AGAINST THE UTOPIAN PLAN OF CASTEL DE SAINT PIERRE

4.1. The Project for Making Peace Perpetual in Europe of the Abbé Castel de Saint-Pierre[8]

As secretary of Prince of Polignac, the Abbé de Saint-Pierre went to Utrecht in 1712, where a treaty was concluded putting an end to the War of Spanish Succession. On the occasion, Saint-Pierre published his *Project for Making Peace Perpetual in Europe*; the first sketch of the work was drawn from 1707, two volumes followed, published in Utrecht in 1713, and a third volume came out in 1717. The complete work seems exceedingly verbose at about 1200 pages in total, and Saint-Pierre reworked it as a kind of a digest, published in Rotterdam in 1729. In a way, this abridgement forms a work separate from the complete version. Both were written at a time when the French King Louis XIV attempted to dominate the neighbouring countries with his armies.

There is a genuine affinity between the Saint-Pierre's and Sully's projects, but nevertheless only superficially. Saint-Pierre commended himself to this glorious patronage almost guaranteeing a better distribution of his plan. If Saint-Pierre certainly did not know the *Nouveau Cynée*, he supported many of the same ideas.

The larger work of Saint-Pierre involves two parts: part one comprises seven discourses in which the author makes two proposals, stating that the present constitution of Europe favoured all but ceaseless wars because of its inability to ensure a sufficient enforcement of the treaties, while the balance of power between the Austrian and the French houses did not provide sufficient security against foreign or civil wars, thus that States and commerce could be easily threatened. Seven ideas follow. The first discourse suggested arbitration which would help protect mutual commitments. From this stemmed the idea of a general union treaty between the eighteen major sovereignties of Europe in order to establish a perpetual congress like the United Provinces of the Netherlands or the Swiss Confederation, and certainly no more difficult to establish than the German body. In the second discourse, Saint-Pierre suggested resuming the *Great Design* supported by Henry IV, King of France, and proposed by his minister Sully, which, as it seemed to have already been accepted by a majority of the European sovereigns, would be worthwhile to resurrect. The third discourse discussed the advantages potentially to be drawn by the princes from such a treaty. The fourth discourse described how such European society would ensure a perpetual peace; and in the fifth discourse, Saint-Pierre points out that his project would make it easier to conclude such a treaty. In the sixth discourse, he

---

[8] Abbé Castel de Saint-Pierre *Projet pour rendre la paix perpétuelle en Europe* (Chez Antoine Schouten Utrecht 1713–17; Fayard Paris 1986).

dismissed and rejected all possible objections and attempts to break down the last difficulties which could rise as obstacles in the seventh and last discourse.

In part two, Saint-Pierre provided so-called fundamental articles shortened to five articles. Article 1 states that a perpetual peace would be henceforth secured between princes having undersigned the union treaty. In his comment on this provision, Saint-Pierre added that it was necessary for France and Spain to apply the treaty recently signed in Utrecht. Article 2 gives some details about the European organization, whereas article 3 discusses the mediation of the general assembly for settling the conflicts emerging between the allied nations in order to end war for ever. In the eventuality that this mediation does not succeed, the parties should rely upon the decision given by the plenipotentiaries of the other allies, who sit permanently and who decide by majority vote. Article 4 states that every nation, if preparing wars or negotiations contradictory to treaties, would be fought by the great alliance until they fulfil the judgments and ensure reparation for the prejudices caused by their hostilities. In his comment on this article, Saint-Pierre emphasizes that every prince who would know of his own interests would comply because of if he did not, all others could wage war against him.

The fifth and last article provides that all necessary or important decisions would be taken by the plenipotentiaries in order to achieve more security for the great assembly, as well as more strength and all other advantages. And nothing in the five articles might be modified without unanimous consent of all the partners.

In these five articles, very few details are given about the organization of the general assembly itself. These are to be found in one of the twenty-four fundamental articles; for example, article 5 provides that the seat of the general assembly is to be in Utrecht, and that twenty-two members would represent the European sovereigns with one vote each.

Saint-Pierre seems to have held a very optimistic view in his abridgement, deeming only five to six months to be sufficient to establish that alliance. If his Project was criticized by Leibniz and others, who supported the principle of a balance of power[9] and thus formed a large majority on the international scene of that time. Leibniz himself supported another plan advanced at his time, suggesting an emigration policy from Europe towards Asia and Africa, although this did not mention colonization. Leibniz sent to the King of France, Louis XIV, a project written in Latin under the title 'Consilium Ægyptiaticum' in which he suggests that the King could be more interested in conquering Egypt than invading the United Provinces of the Netherlands.[10]

---

[9] Such an idea of balance of power was firstly supported by F Guicciardini in his *History of Italy* (1537–40) book 1, ch 1; and J Bodin in his *Six Books on the Republic* (1576) book V, ch 6.

[10] Cf Ahmed Youssef, *La fascination de l'Egypte. Du rêve au projet*, L'Harmattan, Paris 1998; also in *Œuvres de Leibniz*, ed. by A. Foucher de Careil, Paris 1864, vol 5 (the complete volume).

Jean-Jacques Rousseau, the well-known author of *Emile*, *The Confessions*, and *The Social Contract*, wrote an *Extract from the Project of Saint-Pierre*,[11] in which he restated the five articles, disregarding the fundamental articles. But he seemed to be more pessimistic or more sceptical in a second work posthumously published, entitled *Judgement on the Project of Saint-Pierre*.[12] Being a dreamer like Saint-Pierre, he thought it impossible to compel the princes to commit themselves to peace without appealing to grounds such as ambition and self-interest. He seemed to justify the purpose of Saint-Pierre, recognizing at the same time that the arguments forwarded would probably not warrant a confederation as such, while they might at least justify an international organization for the peaceful settlement of conflicts on behalf of other agencies.

4.2. Was Leibniz ever a Utopian?[13]

It is easy to answer such a question: no, but we ought to explain this a little further. Gottfried-Wilhelm Leibniz (1646–1716) seemed quite soon to perceive that the term 'peace' did not mean a kind of quietism, but as a whole appealed to an ideal concentrated on establishing an international ability to combat a crime opposing the principles of any civilized society. During his youth, Leibniz developed some ideas on pacification because of his great concern about Germany falling into the hands of French King Louis XIV, who was perfectly aware of how to benefit from the dissension between the German princes after the breakup of the German Empire following the 1648 Westphalia Peace Treaties. He outlined a project in 1670, suggesting that European princes may do better by uniting to launch a crusade against the Ottoman empire, instead of fighting against one another. If this occurred, the Kingdom of France could campaign against Egypt and thus feed its hunger for conquest. Such a plan was presented to the king whilst he was in disagreement with the Turkish government. The king sent for the philosopher; but the dispute with the Turks was quickly settled and so the plan was never seriously examined, and thus joined all others which had something to do with a potential partition of the Ottoman empire.

From that time, Leibniz was conscious of the unattainability of such a perpetual peace when he eventually received the project elaborated by the Abbé de Saint-Pierre, to which he replied. Furthermore, when writing a foreword to his *Codex juris gentium diplomaticus*, the first of the two volumes published in 1693, he firmly insisted on the impossibility of such a perpetual peace which he pointed as being only the peace of cemeteries.

---

[11] cf J-J Rousseau *Collection complète des oeuvres* (Genève 1782) vol 23, at 3–52.

[12] cf ibid 53–71.

[13] GW Leibniz 'Codex juris gentium diplomaticus (Praefatio)' in GW Leibniz *Leibniz: Political Writings* (P Riley ed and trans) (Apud Joh. Christoph. Meisnerum Guelferbyti 1747; CUP Cambridge 1988) 165–76; see also GW Leibniz 'Caesarinus fuerstenerius' in GW Leibniz *Political Writings* (P Riley ed and trans) (1677; CUP Cambridge 1988) 111–20.

Nevertheless, in 1676, at the opening of the Nijmegen Peace Congress, in an anonymous publication—written in Latin—entitled *Caesarinus fuerstenerius, tractatus de jure suprematus ac legationis principum Germaniae* (Princely Caesar, Treaty on the Law of Supremacy and of Legation of the Princes of Germany), Leibniz firmly defended the old medieval idea of a 'Christian Commonwealth'.

He was thinking of some international federation, under the leadership of both the pope—as a spiritual leader—and the German emperor—as a temporal leader. Other princes would keep their sovereignty, since such a federation would only have the power of solving mutual conflicts through a permanent senate settled by a Christian council. But Leibniz never developed such a plan from his youth, although it seems he had kept some interest in the upholding of peace and general mutual understanding. He was himself known as a reader of the *Nouveau Cynée*, whose author he never met, and of the plan which the Abbé de Saint-Pierre sent him. He continued to maintain exchanges with Prince Ernst von Hesse-Rheinfels, who also suggested a pacification between Catholics and Protestants. Leibniz preferred the international Catholic court to sit in Lucerne while according to Hesse-Rheinfels it ought to sit in Rome under the presidency of the pope, as were the first bishops of Rome.

5. The Quakers and the Quest for a 'Godly Life'[14]

It is well known that the Quakers—the so-called Society of Friends—were dissenters in England and thus against by the Anglican Church. They in fact refused to take any oath, to serve in the army, or pay taxes. They were thus obliged to flee from their country to find shelter in the colonies in Northern America. William Penn was a member of the congregation and, as a friend of the Duke of York, the future King James II, he was awarded the concession of a large area along the Atlantic coast near the King's possessions which later became the province of Pennsylvania. When Penn travelled to Northern America, several Quakers from the Netherlands, Germany, and England, went with him.

It is not necessary to retell here the peaceful means of colonization, his religious tolerance, regular and equitable treaties with Indian tribes, etc. While Europe in 1693 was torn by wars on behalf of Louis XIV, King of France, against the German Emperor,

---

[14] W Penn 'Essay Towards the Present and Future Peace of Europe by the Establishment of an European Diet, Parliament, or Estates' in W Penn *Political Writings of William Penn* (Liberty Fund Indianapolis 2002) 401–19.

Penn published a short twenty-four article essay called *Essay Towards the Present and Future Peace of Europe by the Establishment of a European Diet, Parliament, or Estates*, in which he outlined a European federal organization.

Deeply impressed by the United Provinces of the Netherlands, he suggested the creation of a European diet composed of ninety members, twelve amongst them representing the German Empire, ten for Spain, six for Great Britain, four for Sweden, four for the Netherlands, etc. This diet would decide by a three-quarters majority, or at the very least a majority of seven. Its role would be to settle all possible conflicts occurring between the members. Many provisions regarded the procedure for voting.

Two provisions in articles 12 and 14 are especially interesting. First, Penn suggested that the room where the assembly was brought together would be a circle, so that all quarrels of precedence could be avoided; second, every orator would have to submit his interventions to the chairman beforehand, in order for the chairman to draw a digest of the arguments and submit the question to vote. The last article also provided Latin as the better common language between those following the Romance tradition, or French as an 'most easie [tongue] for Men of Quality'.[15] Such a scheme was never taken into consideration and remained unknown or forgotten, possibly because of its religious origin.

6. IMMANUEL KANT AND THE PHILOSOPHICAL APPROACH: THE PHILOSOPHICAL ESSAY ON PERPETUAL PEACE[16]

The essay by Immanuel Kant, the German philosopher, was published in 1795 in Kaliningrad in Russian Eastern Prussia. It was soon translated into French (1796), with a supplement added by the author. In fact, Kant returned to a plan drafted in 1793 in another work, *Theory and Practice*, in which he sketched as a conclusion 'a juridical state of *confederation*...according to a *law of nations* concerted in common'.[17] When it was published, the German empire was in great trouble as regards its constitution, and close to its end. Its final collapse occurred when Napoleon

---

[15] ibid 410.

[16] I Kant *Vers la paix perpétuelle* (bey Friedrich Nicolovius Königsberg 1795; Garnier-Flammarion Paris 1991); see also the translation which we have quoted in Introduction (n 1) xxxvi.

[17] I Kant 'On the Popular Judgment That May Be Right in Theory, but Does not Hold Good in the Praxis' in I Kant *Essays and Treatises on Moral, Political, and Various Philosophical Subjects* (London 1798) 159–239 at 219 (*Theory and Practice*) (original emphasis).

abolished it after the battle of Jena, 1806. Kant was horrified by the troubles affecting Europe in his lifetime and sought a common peace more on philosophical basis than on political one.

His essay has two sections: the first presenting six preliminary articles for the establishment of a perpetual peace, the second providing three definitive articles for implementation.

The six preliminary articles are as follows:

1. 'No treaty of peace shall be esteemed valid, on which is tacitly reserved matter for future war.'[18] Without such a precondition, it would only exist as a temporary ceasefire. Mental reservations of the parties which could emerge from the impossibility of stopping war due to lassitude of negotiating, only came from Jesuitical casuistry, therefore, let's say good faith shall be continuous and uncompromising.

2. 'Any state, of whatever extent, shall never pass under the dominion of another state, whether by inheritance, exchange, purchase, or donation.'[19] Because a State cannot be considered as a mere estate, it is first of all a human society and only its members are allowed to benefit from it.

3. 'Standing armies (*miles perpetuus*) shall in time be totally abolished.'[20] Armies are in fact very expensive and their maintenance tends to favour the exercise of war, since States which have them usually wish to use them.

4. 'National debts shall not be contracted with a view of maintaining the interests of the state abroad.'[21] When such a system of credit delays the immediate clearance of debts, a true treasury of war might be set up as a boost towards the launch of a war. Furthermore, the immediate clearance of debts avoids bankruptcy, not only for the State having fattened its coffers, but also for the other States which would commit just for nothing.

5. 'No state shall by force interfere with either the constitution or government of another state.'[22] Such interference would only be allowed in cases where a State causes sufficient annoyance to another State, otherwise the autonomy of others would be endangered.

6. 'A state shall not, during war, admit of hostilities of a nature that would render reciprocal confidence in a succeeding peace impossible: such as employing assassins (*percussores*), poisoners (*venefici*), violation of capitulation, secret instigation to rebellion (*perduellio*)….'[23] If the lesser confidence is impossible to be warranted, it is most probable one might go to war with which all would be destroyed. The perpetual peace would then be the peace of cemeteries. Consequently, all sorts of treachery are to be banned.

Three other articles follow in order to implement such a perpetual peace, which does not exist in the state of nature where war remains latent.

---

[18] I Kant *Project for a Perpetual Peace: A Philosophical Essay* (Vernor and Hood Cornhill 1796) at 2.
[19] ibid 3.   [20] ibid 4.   [21] ibid 6.   [22] ibid 7.   [23] ibid 8.

1. 'The civil constitution of every state ought to be republican.'[24] Here, Kant specifically states that 'republican' must not be equated with 'democratic', because that word refers only to the political principle of separation between executive and legislative powers. If democracy was in question, that is, where the people 'make' the law and the whole in such a way decide for the individual, it would become despotism. So a 'republican' constitution favours and enhances peace, because the individual is a citizen consulted on whether war is worth launching and then must think about the war's possible consequences.

2. 'The public right ought to be founded upon a federation of free states.'[25] It is then necessary to appeal to an alliance of peoples, rather than form single state of peoples because Kant thought it necessary to inquire the mutual right of these peoples. War is absolutely condemned when envisaged as a legal path. Peace is viewed as an immediate duty, which may be established through a mutual compact between peoples. Peace set up through such mutual compact is of course quite different from peace contracted after war: its aim is to avoid all future wars and to preserve the freedom of the States for their own interests and for the interests of other States. Therefore the idea of a federation might be progressively extended to all States, equivalent to the social and civic alliance, relying upon freedom.

3. 'The cosmopolitical right shall be limited to conditions of universal hospitality.'[26] In other words, Kant means that hospitality is equivalent to the right, for the foreigner, not to be treated as an enemy when arriving to another territory. It is not a right of residence, which would have necessitated a special treaty, but a simple right of visit, relying on the common possession of the lands allowing the mankind its borderless settlement with the consequent obligation to tolerate one another, because there is no different right of anybody to possess one place rather than another. Consequently, the interference with such a right in one single place affects the whole. Such a concept goes much further than the law of nations as developed by Grotius, Pufendorf, or Vattel. The right of universal hospitality, in fact, and the obligations to be taken on board, such as the changing of a single right of visit into a right of conquest—the foundation of international law—by itself goes further than the single will of the States and the restricted area of that international law to the single law of war. Kant seemed to be very close to the *Deutscher Bund* as it was organized in Germany after the peace of Vienna in 1815 in lieu of the German Empire.

In the second annex published in the second edition of his project, Kant added a so-called secret article, although it will be in opposition with the rules of the public law: 'The maxims of philosophers, on the conditions which render a perpetual peace possible, shall be consulted by those states armed for war.'[27] This provision should be kept

---

[24] ibid 13.   [25] ibid 21.   [26] ibid 28.   [27] ibid 43.

secret in order to preserve the dignity of the one who dictated it; nonetheless, philosophers would be kept free to speak when discussing the universal maxims concerning the conduct of war and the establishment of peace. Kant did not affirm philosophers must be kings, nor kings had to be philosophers, but he stated that freedom of speech for philosophers should warrant a reciprocal enlightenment of each other in their respective concerns, because they are not partisan.

7. Jeremy Bentham and his Plan for a Universal and Perpetual Peace (1786–89)[28]

Jeremy Bentham (1747–1832) wrote four fragments between 1786 and 1789 (supposed to be enclosed in a general work on international law). He relied on the preliminary articles of Kant, but took a liberal perspective. The first addresses the objectives of an international law, the second one the subjects concerned, that is, how far the dictates of the States would apply to individuals. The third addresses wars through their causes and consequences. The last one focuses on universal and perpetual peace. Bentham considered the rivalry between European countries, since the French Revolution 1789, which was thought by the monarchical regimes as a real threat.

A large part of his work had been devoted to codification of the law like European countries (France, Austria, Netherlands, etc.) begun to codify their civil and penal laws from the beginning of the 19th century on. He suggested that only the law should rule relationships between nations and thus imposed a code upon all nations. One of the objectives of that code was to plan possible agreements in order to minimize the scourge of wars.

To prevent wars, Bentham suggested to pass written international laws, since until then 'non-written' regulations (that is, customs) had governed the relations between nations. International treaties did not solve all difficulties, some of them remained totally unsolved: only a codification could improve the style of all laws both domestic and international.

This code of international law would be organized like the later German Civil Code promulgated in 1900, that is, divided into a general part and several specific parts. The general section, imposed by sovereigns to themselves, would then enclose their duties and rights duly established as regarding all other powers. Each specific part developed

---

[28] H Wheaton *History of the Law of Nations in Europe and America* (Gould, Banks and Co New York 1845) at 328–44; J Bentham 'Essay IV, A Plan for an Universal and Perpetual Peace' in J Bentham *Works of Jeremy Bentham* (J Browning ed) (William Tait Edinburgh 1843) vol 2, 546–60.

the rights and duties, which sovereigns considered to be preserved vis-à-vis other States, either exclusively against specified States, on grounds of legislative decisions or mutual advantage. Nonetheless, Bentham knew that such regulations would remain essentially 'moral', since they were not yet set under warrant of a court of justice which could have sanctioned them should they come into force.

Such means, however, would not be sufficient, since self-interest prevailed amongst nations, causing hostility between them. For that reason, Bentham suggested his plan for a universal and perpetual peace, based on two main elements: (1) cutting down and fixing the European nations armed forces, and (2) emancipation of all the colonies possessed by these nations.

Bentham thought it was difficult to achieve disarmament, especially as it remained a topic of discussion between two different States, each of them advocating the disarmament of the other, but not of itself. France, Spain, and the Netherlands could have kept their fleets and not have exceeded half of the English fleet if the agreements were mutual. But equity might prevail in order not to unfairly weaken the defence of a nation, and to secure that the accepted concessions seemed equitable. Anyway, every nation would be publicly requested to disarm, allowing public scrutiny of the real intentions of the States.

Regarding colonies, they should be unconditionally granted freedom due to their enormous cost in terms of maintenance of maritime forces particularly. Here Bentham paid special attention to the rivalry between France and Great Britain, trade being the source of wealth, while war is only a source of economic ruin. He proposed the establishment of an international court of justice competent to settle international conflicts, which would no doubt make it easier to agree to peace, although this court would not have coercive power. It is not very clear whether this court would be a simple diplomatic body, a kind of a diet, or a true court as such. In any case, all proceedings should be public. Such a jurisdiction could be able to suggest honourable issues for every party without being prejudicial to their own interests. Bentham provided some examples from the American Confederation, from the diet of the German Empire, even from the Swiss Confederation, in order to illustrate his purpose.

The first result of such a perpetual peace would be, according to Bentham, the lowering of the contributions paid by the populations themselves. Some troops provided by several States could finally be used to enforce compliance with a judicial decision of the court, but one should take into account that a free press can also encourage dissemination of the court's sentences.

Those considerations were published when the war broke out between European nations and was about to violate the positive law of nations flagrantly. In fact, Bentham did not foresee any tool for preserving peace, except a league of the European nations. He did not predict the possibility of more influential powers subduing this league to their own interests, hampering the independence of weaker States. Wheaton explains this programme, and adds that a perpetual right of supervision, constituting interference into the domestic politics of a nation, should not be registered in a possible international code, because of the cardinal value of the independence of the smaller States.[29] This is an essential rule, from his point of view, for the security of all, which above all depended on the balance of powers.

The cause of this project's failure certainly was to be found in the prerequisites: nations were not at all inclined to renounce their colonies, so that their disarmament was totally impossible when no other acceptable means had been taken for preventing war.

8. CONCLUSION: WAS UTOPIA A DEAD IDEA AFTER THE FIRST WORLD WAR?

What kind of uncompleted cosmopolis through the international organizations was actually realized?[30] One might think Utopian ideas would have passed away after the 19th century. Colonization left its cruel mark on indigenous people, living in Asia or Africa, and the century ended with the 1914–18 worldwide conflagration. There were still some alternative plans, but no longer as idealistic. They particularly focused on the creation of an international organization, which would deal only with the preservation of international peace. The international policy after the First World War actually made the project of perpetual peace more and more difficult, because nations did not stop fighting against other nations for self-preservation and because the world was then divided into many ideologically opposing factions. The proposed conferences or assembly of nations were to be considered as the last attempt towards avoiding war for as long as possible.

The written materials would obviously show that the sundry schemes of these authors could have been developed. Some of these projects were more or less advanced, including Ladd's,[31] giving a number of details on the organization of the international assembly and a shape for the future League of Nations.

It is interesting to examine the ideological foundations of the League of Nations, created just after First World War by President Wilson's proposal, which was inspired by the Quakers' faith and thus had some connection with the former Utopian ideals emphasized until then.

---

[29] *History of the Law of Nations* (n 28) 329–33.

[30] P Fiore *Le droit international codifié et sa sanction juridique* (A Chrétien trans) (Chevalier-Marescq et Cie Paris 1890) at 54–71; *An Essay on a Congress of Nations* (n 1); J Lorimer *Institutes of the Law of Nations: A Treatise of the Jural Relations of Separate Political Communities* (Blackwood and Sons Edinburgh 1883) vol 2, book 5, at 183–299.

[31] *An Essay on a Congress of Nations* (n 1).

In the United States of America and in Great Britain alike, a movement emerged to found a 'League to enforce Peace' under the chairmanship of ex-President William H Taft. His programme suggested that (1) all disputes between the members of the league should be settled by an international court of justice (other disputes being submitted to a council of conciliation); (2) economic and military forces should be used against any member resorting to hostilities without previous submission either to the international court of justice or to the council of conciliation; (3) conferences of the membership of the league should take place from time to time in order to for-mulate and codify rules of international law.[32] Many similar projects were also pub-lished by private individuals, thus encouraging governments to pay attention to the movement, for example, in Sweden, Denmark, and Norway. In the United States, President Wilson played a major role.

When the United States declared war on Germany, Wilson wanted to enshrine the victory of law over violence, to maintain international justice and to establish a definitive peace, earned by the rightful yearnings of the peoples and based on the necessary compensation of the major historical injustices and damages. He was also inspired by the attempt to establish a Pan-American compact, which would have made the Monroe Doctrine void. Yet he did not succeed. Speaking before the scien-tific Pan-American Congress in Washington on 6 January 1916, Wilson suggested the American republics unite with one another, in order to ensure their mutual political and territorial independence. If such proposals were to satisfy the smaller States (being placed at the same level as the greater nations), they were soon left aside, because of the direct US intervention in 1917 during First World War.

Rejecting the Monroe Doctrine, Wilson held that it caused European war based on the old idea of the balance of power. He endeavoured to support another idea, the nationality principle. He proposed that such a new idea might finally lay to rest the evils which tore apart European nations down so many centuries.

In a note dated 8 January 1918, Wilson sketched out in fourteen points[33] the general conditions likely to be concluded. The first six points formulated by the President Wilson himself were:

I. Open covenants of peace, openly arrived at, after which there shall be no private interna-tional understanding of any kind but diplomacy shall proceed always rankly and in the pub-lic view.

---

[32] Cf 'Appendix A: Proposals' in *Enforced Peace: Proceedings of the First Annual National Assemblage of the League to Enforce Peace* (Washington 26–27 May 1916) 189–90. The League to Enforce the Peace was an American organization established in 1915 at the outbreak of the First World War to promote an interna-tional body for world peace.

[33] W Wilson 'Wilson's Address to Congress, Stating the War Aims and Peace Terms of the United States (Delivered in Joint Session, 8 January 1918)' in A Shaw (ed) *State Papers and Adresses by Woodrow Wilson* (George H Doran Company New York 1918) 464–72.

II. Absolute freedom of navigation upon the seas, outside territorial waters, alike in peace and in war, except as the seas may be closed in whole or in part by international action for the enforcement of international covenants.

III. The removal, so far as possible, of all economic barriers and the establishment of an equality of trade among all the nations consenting to the peace and associating themselves of its maintenance.

IV. Adequate guarantees given and taken that national armaments will be reduced to the lowest point consistent with domestic safety.

V. A free, open-minded, and absolutely impartial adjustment of all colonial claims, based upon a strict observance of the principle that in determining all such questions of sovereignty the interests of the populations concerned must have equal weight with the equitable claims of the government whose title is to be determined.

VI. The evacuation of all Russian territory and such a settlement of all questions affecting Russia as will secure the best and freest cooperation of the other nations of the world in obtaining for her an unhampered and unembarrassed opportunity for the independent determination of her own political and national policy and assure her a sincere welcome, assistance also of every kind that she may need and may herself desire. The treatment accorded Russia by her sister nations in the months to come will be the acid test of their good will, of their comprehension of her needs as distinguished from their own interests, and of their intelligence and unselfish sympathy.

It must be noted here that the 'acid test' which was evoked by the President did not prevent some nations, like France and Great Britain, from supporting the armies of White Russia with their own finances. Thus, this test was promptly failed, showing that the President's dreams were obsolete as soon as expressed.

All of the remaining provisions firmly insist on the nationality principle: for Belgium (article VIII), for France (article IX as regards Alsace-Lorraine), for the different peoples of the Austro-Hungarian Empire (article X), for new Balkan States emerged from the Ottoman Empire (Serbia, Rumania and Montenegro, article XI), for Poland (article XIII), and for the non-Turkish peoples of the Ottoman Empire (article XII), the free passage through the Dardanelles being guaranteed for all nations. The last provision concerns the formation of an international association of nations and its role:

XIV. A general association of nations must be formed under specific covenants for the purpose of affording mutual guarantees of political independence and territorial integrity to great and small States alike.

A number of these provisions show that the nationality principle was firmly asserted and gave birth after First World War to numerous new nations through a dismemberment of the former Ottoman and Austro-Hungarian empires. Following the age-old desire of peoples for building their own nations, many 'nationalities' within these empires, like the Greeks, the Bulgarians, the Serbians, the Croatians, the Hungarians, the Czechs, laid claim to have their own nations and from now on to be recognized as free and independent countries. The nationality principle became the source of future difficulties between nations which remained until now unsolved, as it was seen through the dissolution of the former Federal Yugoslavian Republic. The 20th century ended badly.

It should also be added that the dismemberment of the central empires can be seen as the final revenge of last century against fear or the remnants of political rivalries in Europe, especially when Clemenceau provided for the dismemberment of the Austro-Hungarian and the Ottoman Empires when the peace was concluded in 1919. Whereas President Wilson foresaw that the principle of nationality could allow a harmonious development of the nation States, it finally ensured a lot of difficulties for European countries, even today, which are still enclosed in their 'selfish' interests. The beautiful idea of a community of nations debating together their common interests consequently seems to remain a *vœu pieux* today in the international organizations whatever they are.

However, there were two interesting ideas that were never really implemented. Russia was recognized as having its own path connected with its own political system; it could rejoin the '*Entente*' of nations if it wished to. All agreements should be made 'frankly and in the public view', that is, under the watchful eye of public opinion. However, this was never realized, because diplomatic bargains are still kept secret. The last provision which planned the establishment of a League of Nations, guaranteeing political and territorial independence of all members, 'small and great alike' offered a scheme not so far from Kant's cosmopolitan State above all based upon the law.

President Wilson confirmed such declarations twice in 1918, firstly in a message to the Congress dated 11 February, where he firmly rejected the balance of power principle, and secondly in a speech he hold in Mount-Vernon on the grave of Washington on 14 July. In this speech, he laid down four other interesting proposals:

I. The destruction of every arbitrary power that can…disturb the peace of the world.…

II. The settlement of every question…upon the basis of the free acceptance of that settlement by the people immediately concerned and not…of the material interest or disadvantage of any other nation.…

III. The consent of all nations to be governed in their conduct toward each other by the same principles of honor and of respect for the common law of civilized nations.…

IV. The establishment of an organization of peace…to which all must submit and by which every international readjustment that cannot be amicably agreed upon…shall be sanctioned.

Once more, when speaking about the future League of Nations, President Wilson considered the free States are not only governed by their government, but also by the opinion of the citizen of the world, which would be a factor of peace. During the first half part of the 20th century, French lawyers like Duguit and Scelle went still further, considering that citizens and not just States should be also subjects of the international law.

If ideals were never forgotten, the sense of reality unceasingly reminds us that a peaceful international society remains as a fiction covering the selfish interests governing every nation. No one ought to be prevented from dreaming of Utopia, but it ought to be recognized that it is a long way off.

Recommended Reading

Coudenhove-Kalergi, Richard N *Pan-Europe* (Presses Univérsitaires de France Paris 1988).

Gentz, Frédéric *De la paix perpétuelle* (MB Aoun ed and trans) (Librairie Duchemin Paris 1997).

Goyard-Fabre, Simone *La construction de la paix ou le travail de Sisyphe* (Vrin Paris 1994).

Von Holzendorff, Franz *Die Idee des ewigen Völkerfriedens* (Verlag von Carl Habel Berlin 1882).

Porada, Aleksandra 'The French Project of Pan-European Peace and their Practical Fiasco' in Lara Piccardo (ed) *L'idée d'Europe au XVIIIᵉ siècle* (Honoré Champion Paris 2009).

Raumer, Kurt von *Ewiger Friede: Friedensrufe und Friedenspläne seit der Renaissance* (Karl Alber München 1953).

Riot-Sarcey, Michèle (ed) *Dictionnaire critique des utopies* (Larousse-Bordas Paris 2002).

Senghaas, Dieter *On Perpetual Peace: A Timely Assessment* (Ewald Osers trans) (Berghahn Books New York 2007).

Slick, Tom *Permanent Peace: A Check and Balance Plan* (Prentice Hall Upper Saddle River NJ 1958).

Zinn, Howard *The Power of Nonviolence: Writings by Advocates of Peace* (Beacon Press Boston MA 2002).

CHAPTER 11

PEACE AND WAR

MARY ELLEN O'CONNELL

1. INTRODUCTION

LAW is valued for providing an alternative to the use of force in the ordering of human affairs.[1] In this sense, all of international law is law of peace,[2] peace being the antithesis of force, violence, and armed conflict. Still, at the heart of the international legal system is a specific set of rules, principles, and procedures prohibiting resort to force and mandating the use of peaceful means to settle disputes and to resolve societal problems. It is this more specific regime and its history that are the focus of this chapter. The creation of the peace regime in international law has required persistent and even courageous effort by those who believe humanity can forego the use of force with the aid of law. Working against them are those who believe that humanity is naturally disposed to engage in violence as well as those who believe in the utility of force to achieve important, even humane, goals.

The United Nations Charter, adopted in 1945, forms the basis of the contemporary peace regime. At the heart of the Charter's comprehensive approach is article 2(4), a rule generally prohibiting resort to force.[3] The Charter also establishes the United Nations Organization (UN), an institution for fostering interaction among States to

---

[1] E Zoller *Peacetime Unilateral Remedies: An Analysis of Countermeasures* (Transnational New York 1984) at 4.

[2] I Brownlie 'The Peaceful Settlement of International Disputes in Practice' (1995) 7 Pace International Law Review 257–79 at 257.

[3] The ICJ noted that both the United States and Nicaragua in their memorials to the court had referred to the United Nations Charter prohibition on the use of force in art 2(4) as a *ius cogens* norm. *Military and Paramilitary Activities in and against Nicaragua (Nicaragua v United States of America) (Merits)*

help resolve and prevent conflict. The UN's various organs are all mandated to support peace. The most powerful organ, the Security Council, has authority to respond to threats to the peace, breaches of the peace, and acts of aggression. To deter such crimes the Charter promotes the use of mechanisms for the peaceful settlement of disputes,[4] encourages economic development, and promotes respect for human rights. The purpose is to save 'succeeding generations from the scourge of war'.[5]

The story of how humanity reached the point of drafting the Charter could start at the beginning of recorded time and draw on all major cultures that embrace respect for human dignity and principles of non-violence.[6] The focus here will be narrower. Historians typically begin discussions of the Charter with the Just War Doctrine created by natural law theorists, drawing on early Christian (and therefore Jewish) thought, as well as classical Greek and Roman philosophy. The discussion will proceed to the rise of positivism in the 18th century, the associated decline of natural law theory, and the crisis that resulted respecting legal controls on resort to force in the absence of positive law. The international community has since developed positive law respecting peace, but as mere positive law, these restraints have been open to challenge over the ranking of value preferences. Of all the major subfields of international law, the law of peace and war may have the longest and most difficult history. Creating the peace regime has required and continues to require persons of integrity, courage, and commitment to stand by the law and the ideal of a more peaceful world.

2. Pacifism and the Rise of the Just War Doctrine

From the perspective of the current time, it may appear that all cultures must embrace resistance to non-violence, yet we have evidence that many ancient communities accepted war as a natural and normal part of life. Stephen Neff points to Confucianism as the first major tradition to develop the concept that peace is the normal condition

---

[1986] ICJ Rep 14, at 100–1 (para 190). Johnston refers to the Charter as the 'sacred text of the world community'. DM Johnston *The Historical Foundations of World Order: The Tower and the Arena* (Martinus Nijhoff Leiden 2008) at 164 and 708; see also D Bederman *International Law in Antiquity* (CUP Cambridge 2010).

  [4] See generally UN Charter ch VI.
  [5] This phrase is found in the first line of the UN Charter preamble.
  [6] See generally *The Historical Foundations* (n 3) and D Cortright *Peace: A History of Movements and Ideas* (CUP Cambridge 2008).

and war the abnormal.[7] Neff points to only one other ancient community as having developed this idea: early Christians.[8] The Christian insistence on 'the existence of a residual or background condition of peace in world affairs' was owing to 'a powerful strain of radical pacifism inherent in Christian doctrine...'.[9] According to Ian Brownlie, '[t]he early Christian Church refused to accept war as moral in any circumstances and until A.D. 170 Christians were forbidden to enlist. This period of extreme pacifism lasted for three centuries after Christ...'.[10]

Then, as Christianity became 'linked with the secular power of the [Roman] Empire', St Augustine introduced his just war theory.[11] Augustine, a 5th-century North African bishop, sought to move the Church away from the profound pacifism founded on an interpretation of the Gospel teaching to be peacemakers and to love even one's enemy.[12] To alter this, Augustine developed an argument drawing on his education in Roman and Greek philosophy and law. The Roman Cicero, who was influenced by the Stoics, taught that a just war could only be fought for a just cause to achieve peace.[13] The Stoics, in turn, had drawn on Aristotle who similarly taught that peace was the ultimate just cause of war.[14] Given that Christians are committed to peace, Augustine reasoned, fighting for peace could be a just cause of war. He concluded that using limited war when necessary as 'a means of preserving or restoring peace' is acceptable for Christians desiring to conform their conduct to their religious belief.[15] Augustine considered it just to fight in self-defence, to restore what was stolen, to respond to wrongdoing in an attempt to deter future wrongs, and to promote Christianity.[16]

This last cause, the promotion of Christianity, helped to transform pacific Christians to persons for whom fighting to preserve and promote the Church became a noble and virtuous thing.[17] Fighting in the crusades or fighting to conquer and colonize, all became justified under the argument that once all the world was converted to Christianity, peace would prevail and all fighting would end. A similar view developed in Islam: once the world was converted, peace would reign.[18]

---

[7] SC Neff *War and the Law of Nations: A General History* (CUP Cambridge 2005) at 31.

[8] ibid 39.   [9] ibid 39–40.

[10] I Brownlie *International Law and the Use of Force by States* (OUP Oxford 1963) at 5 (citation omitted).

[11] ibid; see also *War and the Law of Nations* (n 7) 3–5 and 10–11.

[12] WG Grewe *The Epochs of International Law* (M Byers trans) (de Gruyter Berlin 2000) at 108–11; A Nussbaum *A Concise History of the Law of Nations* (revised edn Macmillan London 1962) at 35.

[13] Neff recounts similar but earlier ideas in Confucianism: 'War was seen as a last resort, to counteract antisocial conduct and reinforce the norms which integrated the society into a harmonious whole'; *War and the Law of Nations* (n 7) 10.

[14] Aristotle *Nicomachean Ethics* book X, ch VII, 1177 b6; and *Politics* book VII, ch XIV.

[15] *The Epochs of International Law* (n 12) 107 (Latin rephrasing omitted); L Friedman (ed) *The Law of War: A Documentary History* (Greenwood Publishing Group Westport 1972) at 7.

[16] J von Elbe 'The Evolution of the Concept of the Just War in International Law' (1939) 33 American Journal of International Law 665.

[17] G Parker 'Early Modern Europe' in M Howard (ed) *The Laws of War: Constraints on Warfare in the Western World* (Yale University Press New Haven 1994) 40–58 at 43.

[18] *International Law and the Use of Force by States* (n 10) 5–6.

Christian warriors succeeded in establishing the Holy Roman Empire that lasted from the crowning of Charlemagne in 800[19] to the end of the Thirty Years War with the signing of the Peace of Westphalia in 1648. During this long period, scholars continued to develop the Just War Doctrine. The most influential just war scholar of the Middle Ages, St. Thomas Aquinas (1225–74), systematized Augustine's work, emphasizing core conditions for a just war: (1) right authority, (2) just cause, and (3) right intention.[20] After Aquinas, scholars conceived that princes could justifiably use war to respond to violations of sovereign territory, to treaty breaches, or to breaches of diplomatic immunity—many of the principles that would come to form the core of international law.

Even as justifications for war continued to multiply, some Christians sought to keep the ideal of pacifism alive. The 'Peace of God' movement, for example, began in 11th-century France, and sought to protect the weak in time of war and to limit the days for warfare.[21] The historian Geoffrey Parker has found evidence that, indeed, rulers did take seriously the limits on the right to engage in war due in part to the fact that Church teaching could be enforced through various sanctions. Bishops could compel obedience through the threat of excommunication or by withholding sacraments.[22] Gradually, however, the authority of the Church and its teaching began to wane. This development coincided with the rise of larger 'well-organized political units, monarchic and national in form, secular in government, and commercial, dynastic, and colonizing' that were replacing smaller principalities and less-well defined entities.[23] The political adviser, Niccolo Machiavelli (1492–1550), attacked the Just War Doctrine and its limits on war, arguing, '"that war is just which is necessary" and every sovereign entity may decide on the occasion for war'.[24]

The Spanish scholastics generally took a different view. They were aware of what the declining respect for the pope and emperor would mean for just war restraints. Francisco Vitoria (1480–1546), a Dominican monk, worked to develop a substitute for the central authority of church and empire. He came to see the law itself as the ultimate governor of human action as opposed to any individual.[25] He also, however, promoted the idea that all parties to a conflict could be fighting with the right intentions and, therefore, doing nothing morally wrong.[26] This argument might be entirely

---

[19] *A Concise History* (n 12) 20.

[20] *The Epochs of International Law* (n 12) 109; see also, Evolution of the Concept, (n 16) 669; and *International Law and the Use of Force by States* (n 10) 6.

[21] 'Early Modern Europe' (n 17); see also *A Concise History* (n 12) 17–18.

[22] J Dumas 'Sanctions of International Arbitration' (1911) 5 American Journal of International Law 934–57 at 937.

[23] *International Law and the Use of Force by States* (n 10) 11.

[24] ibid.

[25] 'Evolution of the Concept' (n 16) 674–5; *A Concise History* (n 12) 79–91. For a particular focus on Vitoria, his view of Native Americans, and the origins of international law, see A Anghie *Imperialism, Sovereignty, and the Making of International Law* (CUP Cambridge 2005).

[26] *A Concise History* (n 12) 80.

appropriate when considering the fate of a person's immortal soul but for constraining resort to war, it removed the Just War Doctrine's major objective constraint. If a leader deciding for war needed only to make up his own mind that his cause was just, rather than consulting with authorities on whether the cause was objectively just and the opponent's cause unjust, the constraint of just war was lost. Another Scholastic, Francisco Suárez (1548–1617), pointed out the absurdity of considering all parties to a conflict as having a permissible just cause based on a leader's subjective belief about his own cause. Suárez, however, had no solution for adjudicating the justice of competing claims among those who rejected papal authority.

Indeed, rather than seeming to be a problem, the idea of a subjectively just cause appealed to Protestant leaders. They believed one could rely on individual conscience when deciding for war, which was not unlike their approach to interpreting the Bible or their personal relationship with God. Alberico Gentili (1552–1608), an Italian Protestant who fled Italy for England and taught law in Oxford University, is particularly associated with the argument that individual leaders have the right to decide for themselves respecting the justice of a cause. Writing in 1593, he said

> [i]t is true, the prince is still considered as bound to examine the justice of his cause before he engages in war;…whatever the result of his decision may be, it never affects the legality of his action, since war is nothing more than a procedural device that may be resorted to even for the redress of a probable wrong without exposing either party to the blame of injustice.[27]

Hugo Grotius (1583–1645), a Protestant scholar and diplomat, understood the weakness of Gentili's argument. He saw the results of it in the brutal Thirty Years War that pitted Protestant rulers against Catholics for dominance in Europe. Everyone was fighting in a subjectively just cause. Grotius argued, in distinction to Gentili, that the cause must be objectively just, and not just only in the mind of a prince about his own cause. Grotius helped to preserve a Just War Doctrine with credible constraints and made the Doctrine the focus his of seminal work, *On the Law and War and Peace* (1625). Grotius believed in the Christian law of love and the optimistic view of people's capacity contained in Christianity.[28] He wanted to inspire greater humanity in the conduct of the war and encourage the establishment of a legal order for Western Europe after the war.[29] Building on the Scholastics, he proposed that people could understand what law required through reason rather than divine revelation or clerical interpretation. God remained the ultimate lawgiver, however, meaning law remained superior to the wishes of individuals or communities.

By 1648, European rulers were ready to end their long war and to agree to limits on resort to force. The peace treaties, known as the 'Peace of Westphalia', were negotiated

---

[27] 'Evolution of the Concept' (n 16) 678.
[28] H Lauterpacht 'The Grotian Tradition in International Law' (1946) 23 British Year Book of International Law 1–53 at 31, citing Grotius *De jure belli ac pacis* (1625) Proleg, at 23.
[29] *A Concise History* (n 12) 105.

over a period of three years in the 'first European Congress'.[30] The treaties committed the various kings, princes, and noblemen to refrain from resort to war in religious causes and to collectively enforce the treaties' provisions. The 300 members of the Holy Roman Empire were at last free to join alliances, giving rise essentially to their sovereign independence. All past disputes were deemed settled. Should any future disputes arise, the offended party was required to first try 'amicable settlement of legal discussion'.[31] After three years, if the disputants failed to reach a settlement, all other parties were to 'take up arms with all council and might in order to subdue the offender'. Arthur Nussbaum called this the 'first attempt at international organization for peace'.[32] The legal order that emerged through the Westphalian peace agreements owed much to Grotius:

On the one hand it has been argued, 'Grotius adapted the (old) Law of Nature to fill the vacuum created by the extinction of the supreme authority of Emperor and Pope'. On the other hand it has been affirmed that Grotius developed a system of international law which would equally appeal to, and be approved by, the believers and the atheists, and which would apply to all states irrespective of the character and dignity of their rulers.[33]

On the other hand, the new peace order contained the elements for a new challenge to legal restraints on war. The secularization of the legal regime and the establishment of equal, sovereign States undermined conceptions of community and community law. '[T]he Peace of Westphalia, while paying lip service to the idea of a Christian commonwealth, merely ushers in the era of sovereign absolutist states which recognized no superior authority'.[34]

3. Positivism and the Decline of the Just War Doctrine

Grotius seems to have considerably delayed but not wholly prevented the rise of subjectivism in decisions on resort to war. Indeed, Westphalia laid the basis for removing restraints from war by establishing the sovereign equality of each State. As equals,

---

[30] ibid 115.   [31] ibid 117.

[32] ibid; L Gross 'The Peace of Westphalia' in L Gross (ed) *Essays on International Law and Organization* (Transnational New York 1984) 3–21 at 3 and 7, citing DJ Hill *A History of Diplomacy in the International Development of Europe* (Longmans, Green and Co London 1925) vol II, at 602.

[33] 'The Peace of Westphalia' (n 32) 9, citing PH Winfield *The Foundations and the Future of International Law* (CUP Cambridge 1941) at 20; and W Van der Vlugt 'L'Oeuvre de Grotius et son influence sur le développement du droit international' (1925) 7 Recueil des cours 395–510 at 448.

[34] 'The Peace of Westphalia' (n 32) 18–19.

how could any State's leader sit in judgment of another, his co-equal? Even collective judgment necessary for collective enforcement action was being rejected. As a result, the enforcement mechanisms developed at Westphalia were never used. Ideas to create a peace order continued to be offered, most famously by the Abbé St Pierre and Immanuel Kant. Both men conceived of organizations of States to eliminate the interest in war. The actual trend in international relations, however, during this period was away from collectivities, federations, or organizations of States toward the ever-greater impermeability of the sovereignty of the individual State.[35]

Emmerich de Vattel (1714–67) proved highly influential in the development of the sovereignty doctrine. He was an international law scholar who earned his living as a contract diplomat for princes with an interest in enhancing the sovereign independence of their realms. Vattel wrote that resort to war was up to the individual leader and his conscience. International law, in his view, is not superior to States but rather a useful tool between States. Consistently with this orientation, Vattel advocated the use of various means of peaceful settlement, including arbitration, multi-state conferences, congresses, and inquiry. Disputes, he pointed out, arise from injuries received or from contests over rights. He counselled that a nation should insist on its rights, not submit to injury but always remember the rights of others.[36] Vattel cautioned against using peaceful methods when the 'safety' of the State was involved. He also revived the view that sovereigns could not sit in judgment of one another. True, he appealed to sovereigns' to consult their individual consciences before resort to war, but it was private conscience, not the community of States that mattered. In returning to a focus on the individual sovereign, Vattel was part of the new 'enlightenment' that looked to observation of the natural world for scientific laws. For international law that meant looking to the affirmative acts of States for evidence of the law—formal consent to treaties or acquiescence in customary rules.

The emphasis on positive acts began to exclude natural law. The theoretical shift meant a setback for the peace regime, given the fact that the Just War Doctrine is explained through natural law theory and that there were very few positive law restraints on war in the 18th century. By contrast, natural law theory recognized that some law bound States even without being created through positive acts. In natural law theory rules associated with moral principle, such as when resort to force could be justified, bound States even if their governments had not agreed to any such rule in a treaty or through acquiescence in a general practice.

Yet positivism never completely defeated natural law theory, especially in the area of peace and war. National leaders continued to declare the justice of their causes.[37]

---

[35] L Henkin *International Law: Politics and Values* (Martinus Nijhoff Dordrecht 1995) at 12.

[36] E Vattel *The Law of Nations or the Principles of Natural Law, Applied to the Conduct and to the Affairs of Nations and of Sovereigns* (CG Fenwick trans) (1758 edn The Carnegie Institution of Washington Washington DC 1916) at 222.

[37] 'Evolution of the Concept' (n 16) 684.

While often formalistic, the declarations nevertheless attested to the persistent belief that resort to war was not a completely unfettered sovereign prerogative. Moreover, some European Christian communities persisted in their adherence to pacifism. They, too, kept the moral question of war alive. Significant numbers of these Christian pacifists left Europe for the United States. They sought to escape war and military service, as well as to practise versions of Christianity that held pacifism and non-violence as central tenets. Quakers, Mennonites, and then a broad array of Protestant denominations provided popular support to politicians in the US willing to resolve disputes using peaceful methods. By the early 19th century, Christian pacifists in the United States were promoting arbitration as an alternative to war.[38] The United States and Britain included a commitment to arbitrate in the Jay Treaty of 1794 that settled outstanding issues left from the War of Independence.[39] President George Washington endorsed the Jay Treaty primarily because the commitment to arbitrate was likely to 'prevent war and to bring about the peaceful settlement of misunderstandings and quarrels'.[40] Starting with the St Croix River Arbitration of 1798, in which arbitrators adjudicated the boundary between present-day Canada and the United States, 536 arbitral awards were made pursuant to the Jay Treaty between 1794 and 1804.[41] The Jay Treaty is credited with starting the modern era of arbitration.

Despite the glorification of the War of Independence, American leaders also supported the peace movement both ideologically and institutionally. 'No other government permitted so many men of conscience to avoid military service. No other country erected so many constraints against a peacetime standing army. No other people defined their collective identity so firmly with the work of redeeming the world for peace'.[42] The peace movement in the US raised strong opposition to the War of 1812, fought by the US against Great Britain and Britain's Native American allies.[43] The US victory in 1815 dissipated much of the anti-war criticism, but the peace movement had by then been firmly established.[44] It was also in 1815 that William Low Dodge founded the world's first organization for the promotion of peace, the New York Peace Society. A number of other peace organizations were formed in the US in the years that followed. These were brought together in 1828 by William Ladd to form the

---

[38] MW Janis *The American Tradition of International Law: Great Expectations 1789–1914* (OUP Oxford 2004) at 98.

[39] The Jay Treaty arbitrations are considered the first law-based arbitrations (in contrast to diplomatic arbitration.); AM Stuyt *Survey of International Arbitrations 1794–1938* (Martinius Nijhoff The Hague 1939) at vii.

[40] M Curti *Peace or War: The American Struggle 1636–1936* (WW Norton and Co New York 1936) at 24.

[41] *The American Tradition* (n 38) 105, citing *A Concise History* (n 12) 128–9; *The Epochs of International Law* (n 12) 366. Claims commissions to settle property disputes between the US and Britain were also established, but without as much success.

[42] C DeBenedetti *The Peace Reform in American History* (Indiana University Press Indiana 1980) at 17.

[43] ibid 28.   [44] ibid 30.

American Peace Society (APS).[45] The APS combined Christianity and a belief in the peaceful resolution of international disputes by promoting negotiation, arbitration, and the formation of a congress of Christian nations.[46] Ladd's famous *Essay on a Congress of Nations* called for a two-tiered system of international justice: (1) a congress of ambassadors from certain States that would develop international law, and (2) an international court to arbitrate cases.[47]

Europeans who were committed to peace soon followed the American example. In 1816, British Quakers, working to end slavery and for other social reforms, founded the British Society for the Promotion of Permanent and Universal Peace.[48] French Christians formed the *Société de la morale chrétienne* in 1821, and Swiss peace advocates founded the *Société de la paix de Genève* in 1830.[49] American Elihu Burritt forged connections among the European peace societies and those in the US,[50] organizing several international peace congresses between 1848 and 1851.[51] The congresses focused primarily on means and methods to resolve international disputes that could substitute for war. The delegates were partial to both arbitration and international law.[52] Both alternatives were also promoted outside the peace organizations by American internationalists like the scholars Francis Lieber and David Dudley Field.

At the same time that peace advocates were taking these constructive steps, a critical debate was developing in the transatlantic movement. It was a debate that continues to resonate in international legal discourse on peace and war. In brief, in the mid-1800s, adherents of strict pacifism were being challenged by those who believed that some exceptions should be made to promote certain significant social issues or national self-defence.[53] Following violent incidents in the1830s, the American peace movement split between those supporting defensive war and those adhering to strict pacifism.[54] Anti-slavery proponents also divided between those who rejected war even to end slavery and those who believed war was the lesser of two evils. When the US Civil War began, some members of the peace movement joined the Northern effort to preserve the union and end slavery, but 1500 conscientious objectors including Quakers, Mennonites, and members of other small religious groups refused to fight despite their antipathy to slavery.[55]

Another issue that divided the international peace movement in similar ways concerned wars for colonial empires.[56] Americans were generally united in their

---

[45] ME Curti *The American Peace Crusade: 1815–60* (Duke University Press Durham 1929) 43; *The American Tradition* (n 38) 103–10.

[46] *The Peace Reform* (n 42) 38.

[47] *The American Peace Crusade* (n 45) 58.

[48] *Peace: A History* (n 6) 27.

[49] ibid 28.

[50] *The American Tradition* (n 38) 110, citing P Tolis *Elihu Burritt: Crusader for Brotherhood* (Archon North Haven 1968) at 1.

[51] *The American Peace Crusade* (n 45) 188.   [52] ibid 189.   [53] *Peace: A History* (n 6) 30.

[54] ibid 42.   [55] *The Peace Reform* (n 42) 58.   [56] *Peace: A History* (n 6) 47–8.

opposition to colonialism, but in Europe the dominant argument until the First World War held that Europeans were justified in fighting and conquering 'uncivilized' people.[57] Europeans saw a duty to bring the gift of civilization through imposing government institutions and supporting the work of Christian missionaries. Once 'civilized', colonized peoples could acquire sovereign statehood and participate fully in the international legal system. A critical part of this argument of justification for war and domination was the rise of positivism as the leading theory of international law in place of natural law theory. Natural law theory posits universal law and the equality of humanity. Positivism, by contrast, can premise law on the existence of certain institutions typically found within European States. Where the institutions did not exist, international law did not extend. According to Alexandrowicz: '[I]n the nineteenth century, the law of nations, which had been universal in the sixteenth, seventeenth and eighteenth centuries, abandoned the centuries-old universalist tradition based on natural law theory and "narrowed" [itself] to a regional (purely European) legal system'.[58] Anghie argues that the preference for positivism as the explanatory theory of international law in place of natural law can be traced to the support positivism gave to the justification of colonialism.[59]

Despite these rifts, peace advocates were united in other ways. They uniformly called for treaties committing States to arbitration, in step with the new trend in international law. Their efforts received a dramatic boost in 1872 as a result of the *Alabama Claims* arbitration. The US invited Britain to participate in arbitration on the question of whether Britain had failed to observe its neutral duties during the American Civil War. The British had failed to prevent the Confederate forces from purchasing three naval ships from a shipbuilder in Liverpool during the war. The ships did significant damage, and, the US argued, had extended the war. A few bellicose and likely ill-informed commentators demanded that the US follow up its initial demand to Britain for compensation with military action. Cooler heads prevailed and the two States agreed to resolve the dispute through arbitration. The US won the case, and Britain paid sizeable damages. The impact electrified the peace movement, which immediately held it up as a triumph of peaceful settlement on the basis of law. Lobbying for arbitration treaties expanded and by the 1880s saw efforts for a world court.[60] Not only did the *Alabama Claims* case energize the peace movement,

---

[57] A Orakhelashvili 'The Idea of European International Law' (2006) 17 European Journal of International Law 315–47 at 325–6; JT Gathii 'Neoliberalism, Colonialism, and International Governance: Decentering the International Law of Governmental Legitimacy' (2000) 98 Michigan Law Review 1996–2055 at 2019–20; A Anghie 'Finding the Peripheries: Sovereignty and Colonialism in Nineteenth Century International Law' (1999) 40 Harvard International Law Journal 1–80 at 54–5; and M Koskenniemi *The Gentle Civilizer of Nations: The Rise and Fall of International Law 1870–1960* (CUP Cambridge 2001) at 40.

[58] *The Epochs of International Law* (n 12) 466, citing H Alexandrowicz *An Introduction to the History of the Law of Nations of the East Indies (16th, 17th, and 18th Centuries)* (Clarendon Press Oxford 1967) at 2.

[59] 'Finding the Peripheries' (n 57) 54–5.

[60] *The Gentle Civilizer of Nations* (n 57) 40; D Caron 'War and International Adjudication: Reflections on the 1899 Peace Conference' (2000) 94 American Journal of International Law 4–30 at 4.

international law in general appeared to benefit. In 1873, for example, the International Law Association was founded in Brussels.

In addition to binding dispute resolution under international law, 19th-century peace advocates also promoted congresses and conferences of States to resolve disputes using international law. A congress drew up the Treaty of Paris of 1856[61] to settle the issues of the Crimean War and to establish the International Commission of the Danube, which included Turkey, thereby extending cooperation under international law beyond Europe. According to Nussbaum, the Treaty of Paris is 'second only to the treaties of Westphalia and Vienna in its importance for the history of international law'.[62] In the Berlin Congress of 1878, following the Russo-Turkish war, States attempted to resolve territorial disputes in the Balkans. The Berlin Congress of 1885 parcelled out the African continent among European States, ending their long-running belligerent competition.[63] Peace with African peoples was not on the agenda.

It was also in 1885 that the Austrian Baroness Bertha von Suttner (1843–1914) began her peace activism in Europe. She wrote several novels that served to galvanize interest in promoting peace and influenced Alfred Nobel's decision to create the Nobel Peace Prize.[64] Von Suttner brought popular attention to the Russian tsar's call for an international peace conference to be held in 1899 in The Hague.[65] The purpose of the conference was to 'make the great idea of universal peace triumph over the elements of trouble and discord'.[66] The tsar hoped to stem the arms race that was then underway, a race Russia could not hope to win. Von Suttner's best-known novel, *Die Waffen nieder* (*Lay Down Your Arms*) was an argument for peace through disarmament. The tsar must have been disappointed with the results of the 1899 conference, however, as no disarmament agreements were reached. Members of the international peace movements were certainly disappointed with the weak commitments to delay but not prohibit resort to war.[67] Ambitious peace campaigners had also hoped for a world court to be established for the resolution of disputes. States agreed only to the establishment of a secretariat to organize inter-state arbitration, though it was given the grand name, 'Permanent Court of Arbitration' (PCA). Still, peace campaigners like Von Suttner worked to bring positive attention to the PCA.

[61] General Treaty for the Re-Establishment of Peace between Austria, France, Great Britain, Prussia, Sardinia, and Turkey, and Russia (signed 30 March 1856) (1856) 114 CTS 409 ('Treaty of Paris').

[62] *A Concise History* (n 12) 190.

[63] ibid 193.

[64] See S Peter 'Bertha von Suttner (1843–1914)' in pt 6 of the present volume.

[65] Cf WI Hull *The Two Hague Conferences and their Contributions to International Law* (Ginn and Company Boston 1908) at 3.

[66] 'Rescript of Tsar Nicholas II, 24 August 1898, to Representatives of the Powers Accredited to Saint Petersburg' in S Cooper *Patriotic Pacifism: Waging War on War in Europe, 1815–1914* (OUP Oxford 1991) 221–2 at 222.

[67] *Peace: A History* (n 6) 41–2.

One of the leading international law scholars of the time, Lassa Oppenheim (1858–1919), had little patience with peace advocates like Von Suttner. Oppenheim, a German who moved to Great Britain for his health, taught in Cambridge University and became the Whewell Professor in 1908.[68] Oppenheim published a textbook on international law that has so far reached nine editions. Like Grotius's *De jure belli ac pacis*, Oppenheim's book divides international law into two parts: war and peace. Yet Oppenheim was a radical positivist, leaving him unable to find much law against war. He believed that part of the reason international law was not better respected by government officials and scholars, was owing to the lingering natural law theorists among the ranks of international lawyers. For him, all of international law could be explained by positive acts, in particular, consent. International law's claim to authority as law was due to state consent or self-limitation:

There is no doubt that these followers of Austin attribute to international law a lesser degree of binding force. But if [States] once consent to submit themselves to a rule of international law, [they] are bound by such rule to the same extent and degree as subjects are bound by rules of the municipal law of their state.[69]

Oppenheim distinguished international law rules from moral rules by the fact that international law rules are 'eventually enforced by external power', while moral rules are enforced only by conscience.[70]

Oppenheim could not, therefore, find an ultimate legal prohibition on war. State practice did not support it. The 1906 edition of his influential treatise contains the following passage:

[F]anatics of international peace, as well as those innumerable individuals who cannot grasp the idea of a law between Sovereign States, frequently consider war and law inconsistent. They quote the fact that wars are frequently waged by States as a proof against the very existence of an International Law. It is not difficult to show the absurdity of this opinion. As States are Sovereign, as consequently no central authority can exist above them able to enforce compliance with its demands, war cannot always be avoided. International Law recognizes this fact but at the same time provides regulations with which the belligerents have to comply.[71]

Many international lawyers came to share Oppenheim's view that the decision to go to war was the ultimate prerogative of the State and beyond legal regulation. Yet at the same time they viewed measures short of war and the conduct of war itself to be subject to extensive legal conditions.[72] The detailed legal rules attached to the use of force

[68] See M Schmoeckel 'Lassa Oppenheim (1858–1919)' in pt 6 of the present volume.

[69] L Oppenheim 'The Science of International Law' (1908) 2 American Journal of International Law 313–56 at 332.

[70] ibid 331.

[71] L Oppenheim *International Law: A Treatise* (Longmans, Greens, and Co. 1906) vol II, at 55–7 (note omitted).

[72] *The Epochs of International Law* (n 12) 525, citing A Bulmerincq 'Die Staatsstreitigkeiten und ihre Entscheidung ohne Krieg' (1889) 4 Holtzendorffs Handbuch des Völkerrechts 3–127 at 87.

short of war are exemplified in the 1842 correspondence between the United States and Britain over the scuttling of the ship *Caroline* in 1837 by British forces over Niagara Falls.[73] US Secretary of State Webster wrote to Lord Ashburton:

The President sees with pleasure that your Lordship fully admits those great principles of public law, applicable to cases of this kind, which this government has expressed; and that on your part, as on ours, respect for the inviolable character of the territory of independent states is the most essential foundation of civilization. And while it is admitted on both sides that there are exceptions to this rule, he is gratified to find that your Lordship admits that such exceptions must come within the limitations stated and the terms used in a former communication from this department to the British plenipotentiary here. Undoubtedly it is just, that while it is admitted that exceptions growing out of the great law of self-defence do exist, those exceptions should be confined to cases in which the 'necessity of that self-defence is instant, overwhelming and leaving no choice of means, and no moment for deliberation'.[74]

Beyond self-defence, States could use belligerent reprisals to respond to a legal injury but only following a prior demand for a remedy. In addition, the reprisal had to be proportional to the injury. The property of nationals, as well as the State, could be attached or retained. Indeed, it was preferred to treat State property as immune, but it, too, could be attached. States could take affirmative actions, such as the scuttling of the *Caroline*. Maritime reprisals were common,[75] as well as 'negative' or passive action such as denying rights and refusing to fulfil treaty obligations.

As Oppenheim indicates above, these detailed regulations on resort to measures short of war, also attached to war itself. In contrast to Oppenheim's view, however, the evidence indicates that statesmen still paid attention to the justice of war. In the making of a required declaration of war, leaders often cited the just cause of the war and the fact that it was being fought only as a last resort. Brownlie recounts that Japan cited the failure of attempts to negotiate with Russia at the start of the Russo-Japanese War in its declaration of war of 10 February 1904. The reference to the failed negotiations was an indication that war was a 'last resort'.[76] The war came to an end in 1905 thanks to the intervention of US President Theodore Roosevelt. His successful mediation was hailed by the peace movement and won him the Nobel Peace Prize in 1906. Also in 1906, the mechanism of inquiry was used by the United Kingdom and Russia to resolve the dangerous Dogger Bank dispute. Russian naval vessels had opened fire on six British fishing vessels. The incident nearly sparked a

[73] J Noyes 'The *Caroline*: International Law Limits on Resort to Force' in J Noyes et al (eds) *International Law Stories* (Foundation Press New York 2007) ch 9.

[74] 'Letter from Webster to Lord Ashburton (6 August 1842)' in H Miller (ed) *Treaties and Other International Acts of the United States of America* (Government Printing Office Washington 1934) vol 4, 454–5.

[75] *The Epochs of International Law* (n 12) 525.

[76] *International Law and the Use of Force by States* (n 10) 22.

war, but a commission of inquiry reported that the Russians mistook the vessels for submarines.[77]

This success in defusing the Dogger Bank incident led to further development of inquiry at the 1907 Hague Peace Conference,[78] when States again gathered in The Hague for another attempt at restricting war, promoting peaceful dispute resolution mechanisms, and advancing disarmament. This time the organizers invited Central and South American States, and Roosevelt sent his trusted Secretary of State, Elihu Root (1845–1937). Root had been a successful lawyer in private practice, was a committed pragmatist, and very much believed in the common sense of going to a court to resolve disputes.[79] In 1906, Root became the founding president of the American Society of International Law. He was not a pacifist. Yet, he believed war should be a last resort and that adjudication before arbitral tribunals or courts should be standard practice in international affairs as it was among the US states. Root arrived in The Hague with a blueprint for a court. The British had also become enthusiastic supporters of a world court. The Germans, however, had only just begun to establish an overseas empire and wanted no limits on their right to wage war.[80] As a result, no court was established in 1907. The delegates did manage one significant accomplishment for peace: they agreed to the first multilateral treaty outlawing a certain category of war, that is, armed conflict to collect contract debts.[81]

Root then took his enthusiasm for courts to the Americas and helped found the first international court, the Central American Court of Justice, in 1907. The Central American Court existed for ten years, resolving several important disputes. Root also continued his work promoting arbitration treaties and the advancement of international law. Between 1903 and 1914 over 100 arbitration treaties, some known as the 'Root treaties', were adopted. Root's successor in the State Department, William Jennings Bryan, took up the same cause of pursuing bilateral treaties for dispute settlement, adding the mechanisms of inquiry and conciliation to the 'Bryan treaties'.[82]

Despite the steadily growing body of positive law restricting war, when a secret Serbian nationalist group assassinated Archduke Franz Ferdinand, the Austro-Hungarian Empire's heir to the throne, a war engulfed Europe, drawing in colonies and the US. The Serbian Black Hand had formed over disappointment with the results of the Berlin Congress of 1878. Austria's conflict with Serbia seemed to be the very sort of dispute that should have been containable under the methods promoted

---

[77] Cf RN Lebow 'Accidents and Crises: The Dogger Bank Affair' (1978) 31 Naval War College Review 66–75.

[78] ibid.

[79] See generally PC Jessup *Elihu Root* (2 vols Dodd Mead New York 1938).

[80] The Gentle Civilizer of Nations (n 57).

[81] The Hague Convention II Respecting the Limitation of the Employment of Force for the Recovery of Contract Debts (signed 18 October 1907, entered into force 26 January 1910) (1907) 205 CTS 250.

[82] International Law and the Use of Force by States (n 10) 23.

for decades by peace advocates. Indeed, many in the United States and Europe worked passionately to prevent the war and then to end it through the use of peaceful means, especially mediation. Again, however, as over the issues of slavery and imperialism, the coalition that had supported a ban on war was split. Root, for example, advocated that the United States enter the First World War early on the side of the British.[83] The outbreak of war exposed the weaknesses and limitations of the practical peace reforms that dominated the pre-war period.

Despite the failure, Jane Addams (1860–1935), a social worker and committed Christian pacifist from Chicago, rose to great prominence as a leader of the peace movement by 1914. She took a very different view from Root about the war. She and Carrie Chapman Catt founded the Women's Peace Party, which advocated a mediated end to the conflict and no US participation. When older, established peace groups hesitated to support a strong line against the war, Addams formed several new peace organizations.[84] She believed women had a special role to play in war prevention:

As women we are the custodians of the life of the ages and we will no longer consent to its reckless destruction. We are particularly charged with the future of childhood, the care of the helpless and the unfortunate, and we will no longer endure without protest that added burden of maimed and invalid men and poverty-stricken women and orphans which war places on us.

... [W]e will no longer endure that hoary evil which in an hour destroys, or tolerate that denial of the sovereignty of reason and justice by which war and all that makes for war today render impotent the idealism of the race.[85]

While Addams was a progressive and friends with leading pragmatists, her commitment to peace was rooted in her Christianity, like America's traditional pacifists.[86] Addams worked for social reform, but believed that for social reform to succeed, peace was necessary. She wanted to move humanity to a new understanding of what should count as heroism. Statutes should not be erected to war heroes but to those fighting to create healthy societies. With her great gifts for organization and publicity, she promoted arbitration, mediation, and international institutions aimed at preventing war.[87] She helped to organize an international congress of women in The Hague in 1915 to promote an end to the war. Addams and a delegation of women visited capitals throughout Europe to persuade the warring parties to accept mediation by neutral countries. The United States, considered the leading neutral country of the time, was, however, already moving inexorably toward entering the war on the side of Great Britain. President Wilson did not offer to mediate.[88]

---

[83] ME O'Connell 'Elihu Root and Crisis Prevention' (2001) 95 American Society of International Law 115–18 at 115.

[84] J C Farrell *Beloved Lady: A History of Jane Addams' Ideas on Reform and Peace* (The John Hopkins Press Maryland 1967) at 140–1 and 150–3.

[85] ibid 140, quoting Jane Addams, 1915.

[86] ibid 141.   [87] ibid 148–50.   [88] ibid 159–69.

The American peace movement heavily criticized Wilson for backing away from neutrality and toward 'active preparedness' in the fall of 1915. The American Union Against Militarism was created in 1916 as a specific response to the President's policy. Yet, Wilson persuaded pacifists and progressives to support his re-election in 1916. Wilson's calls for a 'peace between equals' were immensely popular with pacifist progressives. They should have taken more careful note when Wilson sent General John Pershing into Mexico in 1916 as well as his failure to withdraw troops from Nicaragua. Soon after Wilson's second inauguration, he cut off relations with Germany, and Congress declared war on 2 April 1917.[89] Jane Addams continued to oppose the war in Europe even after the US entered it. She was heavily attacked in the press and fell swiftly from international prominence to obscurity.

As Europe emerged from the carnage, however, the proponents of congresses and courts appeared vindicated. The Treaty of Versailles, which ended the war, contained a multifaceted approach to ensuring the peace. It provided for a new international organization devoted to peace (the League of Nations); a world court; the break-up of the German, Ottoman, and Austro-Hungarian empires, and trials of the Kaiser for waging war in violation of treaties as well as of military officers in the defeated countries for war crimes.[90] The Covenant of the League of Nations, concluded as part of the treaty, required that all League members attempt peaceful settlement of disputes before resorting to war. In general, the Covenant created a presumption against resort to war.[91] A State failing to comply with an arbitral award could face sanctions or other enforcement action by the League. The Covenant also provided more generally for collective action against States using force unlawfully. The most radical provision of the Covenant was article 10, which prohibited all resort to force except in self-defence and pledged a collective response to violations. Article 15(7), however, appeared to permit resort to force to enforce legal rights in contradiction to article 10. The League never took action under article 10, but the issue was well known when the Charter of the United Nations was drafted twenty years later.

Perhaps more important for the general system of international law and the fulfilment of the efforts of many decades was the Permanent Court of International Justice (PCIJ). The PCIJ was the first international court open to all States for the resolution of disputes through the application of international law. The League and the PCIJ owed much to the American peace movement. Nevertheless, it was none other than Elihu Root who persuaded his former Republican Senate colleagues to vote against giving consent to the Versailles Treaty and US membership in the League. Root simply could not countenance the League Covenant's automatic

---

[89] *The Peace Reform* (n 42) 98.

[90] The Treaty of Versailles (signed 28 June 1919) (1919) 225 CTS 118; see also *International Law and the Use of Force by States* (n 10) ch IV.

[91] 'Covenant of the League of Nations' reprinted in ME O'Connell *International Law and the Use of Force* (Foundation Press New York 2008) at 139–41; see also RL Griffiths 'International Law, the Crime of Aggression and the *Ius Ad Bellum*' (2002) 2 International Criminal Law Review 301–73 at 303.

obligation in article 10 to join in collective action against unlawful uses of force.[92] Root was sent, however, to The Hague to join a committee of jurists advising the League of Nations on the formation of the PCIJ. By December 1920, the League adopted the Statute of the Permanent Court of International Justice. Root strove unsuccessfully for the rest of his life to persuade the Senate to give its consent to US membership in the PCIJ.

While the US failure to join the League has traditionally been linked to the organization's failure, the League did make progress toward a advancing the law of peace. Perhaps most importantly, it was open to States from all continents. It had fifty-eight members at its peak in the mid-1930s. The PCIJ decided fifty-six cases in eighteen years and moved the focus from arbitration to adjudication as the preferred method of interstate dispute resolution. In the midst of these developments, the US did wish to contribute to the advancement of peace in some respect. Secretary of State Frank Kellogg joined with his French counterpart to draft the 1928 Kellogg–Briand Pact or Pact of Paris, which outlawed war as an instrument of national policy.[93] The pact, like the Covenant, left some doubt about the right to resort to force to enforce legal rights; it undoubtedly permitted self-defence.

In addition to the League, and PCIJ, the architects of the post-war order believed that breaking up the German, Austrian, and Ottoman empires would eliminate some of the causes of war. It was, after all, angry Serb nationalists who had triggered the First World War. At the same time as these empires were being broken up, under the supervision of the victorious British, French and others, people living under colonial domination were demanding their own liberation. Mahatma Gandhi's non-violent movement for the independence of India was the development of years of reflection and experience in political organization. Gandhi (1869–1948) had grown up in the tolerant Jain religion. He had not always espoused non-violence; he had lobbied the British in South Africa to accept Indians as soldiers in the military effort to suppress the Zulu rebellion and other military service. Upon returning to India, however, Gandhi read the great Russian novelist, Leo Tolstoy, and was impressed by his 'anarchic pacifism' born of his deep commitment to Christianity.[94] Tolstoy's *Letter to a Hindu* helped to motivate Gandhi's campaigns of non-violent civil disobedience to rid the subcontinent of the British overlords.[95] Tolstoy, however, did not promote arbitration or international law as alternatives to war. 'He was dismissive of the established peace societies and scornful of the Hague Peace Conferences of 1899 and 1907. He considered arbitration and disarmament efforts futile, a diversion from the primary task of promoting worldwide refusal of military service'.[96] Gandhi himself, though a lawyer, seems not to have linked his own efforts

---

[92] *International Law and the Use of Force* (n 91) 126–7.
[93] *International Law and the Use of Force by States* (n 10) 57.
[94] *Peace: A History* (n 6) 198.
[95] ibid.   [96] ibid.

to international law. Interestingly, other peoples seeking an end to colonialism rarely adopted Gandhi's approach. The decades after 1945 became the years of national liberation struggle, often involving the use of military force, and justified as a lesser evil than imperialism.

4. TOTAL WAR AND A NEW JUST WAR DOCTRINE

National liberation was just one of the several just causes for resort to war advocated after the Second World War as exceptions to the robust peace regime established in 1945. The post-First World War peace regime had failed to prevent a catastrophe. The crimes of the Nazis and imperial Japanese discouraged all but the most committed pacifists to continue to call for alternatives to war in confronting fascism.[97] After the war, however, with some 60 million killed, communities reduced to rubble, and the natural environment devastated, the world was ready to commitment to peace.

New histories of the period are finally emerging questioning the common view of the Second World War as a 'good war'. The primary military action in Europe was between Germany and the Soviet Union, making 'World War II a clash of nearly equivalent evils'.[98] The firebombing of German cities and the use of an atomic bomb against Japan are finally being assessed under the law, rather than justified on the basis of cost/benefit analysis. It was this failure to apply international law in any sort of even handed way that led the prominent legal scholar, Hans Kelsen (1881–1973),[99] to criticize the Nuremberg Charter and Tribunal. Kelsen had advanced an elegant theory of international law as law superior to national law. He understood the Just War Doctrine to have persisted as an important part of international law. In this he contradicted his proclaimed commitment to positivism as the sole explanatory theory of international law.[100] The proponents of positivism had no argument to use against the dictators emerging in Europe with aggressive designs on other States.

---

[97] N Baker 'Why I'm a Pacifist, The Dangerous Myth of the Good War' *Harper's Magazine* (New York May 2011) 41 at 50.

[98] A Kirsch 'The Battle for History' *NY Times Book Review* (29 May 2011) 10, quoting N Davies *No Simple Victory: World War II in Europe, 1939–45* (Penguin New York 2007).

[99] See B Fassbender 'Hans Kelsen (1881–1973)' in pt 6 of the present volume.

[100] ME O'Connell *The Power and Purpose of International Law: Insights from the Theory and Practice of Enforcement* (OUP New York 2008) at 49 and 133–4.

Those designs were, after all, an exercise of state will. Nor could positivists argue why persons opposed to the absolute power of the State should not be treated as enemies of the State.[101] Kelsen, by contrast, credited Augustine, Aquinas, and Grotius as developing the idea of war being forbidden except in a good cause, regardless of state will.[102] Kelsen was alert to the quixotic position of scholars like Oppenheim who took the view that while war could not be restricted, measures short of war or reprisals could be heavily regulated.

To overcome the problem of self-judging in the application of the Just War Doctrine or any international law, Kelsen advocated an international judicial system. In this he was joined by Hersch Lauterpacht (1897–1960)[103] who wrote in his 1933 book, *The Function of Law in the International Community* that 'the decisive test is whether there exists a judge competent to decide upon disputed rights and to command peace'.[104] Kelsen was also an early advocate of individual accountability for violations of international law. This was in line with his view that States are ideational constructs only. The real human beings who lead States are the ones who bear responsibility.[105] That responsibility should be applied justly, however, to all serious law violators.[106]

Despite the importance and prominence of the Nuremberg and Tokyo Tribunals, as well as Kelsen's theories, US President Franklin Roosevelt did not ensure that courts would take centre stage after the war. Rather, he wanted a reformed League of Nations with a powerful security council as the centrepiece. Roosevelt had ordered work to begin on the new organization in 1938, long before the US was attacked by Japan. The new Charter prohibited the use of force for all States in article 2(4), except with Security Council authorization or in cases of self-defence to an armed attack until the Security Council could act. The Council received power to act in response to threats to the peace, breaches of the peace, and acts of aggression, and the drafters gave five permanent Security Council members the right to veto any resolution mandating action.[107] The veto was designed to assure that the US would not have to participate in operations of which it did not

---

[101] *A Concise History* (n 12) 276–8.

[102] H Kelsen *General Theory of Law and State* (A Wedberg trans) (The Lawbook Exchange Clark New Jersey 2008) 335–6.

[103] See I Scobbie 'Sir Hersch Lauterpacht (1897–1960)' in pt 6 of the present volume.

[104] H Lauterpacht *The Function of Law in the International Community* (OUP Oxford 1933) at 424.

[105] H Kelsen *Peace Through Law* (University of North Carolina Press Chapel Hill 1944) at 84–5.

[106] H Kelsen *Law of the United Nations* (F.A. Praeger New York 1950) at 713; H Kelsen 'The Legal Status of Germany According to the Declaration of Berlin' (1945) 39 American Journal of International Law 518–28; H Kelsen 'Collective and Individual Responsibility in International Law with Particular Regard to the Punishment of War Criminals' (1943) 31 California Law Review 530–71.

[107] Following the adoption of the Charter, the term 'war' dropped out of fashion. War ministries became defence ministries. Most governments and scholars concluded that armed reprisals were no longer lawful even for law enforcement.

approve—in contrast to article 10 of the League Covenant. The veto also ensured that the Soviet Union would join.

Roosevelt plainly had the Axis powers in mind, and the excuse those States had asserted for employing force in violation of the League Covenant and Kellogg–Briand Pact. They had claimed self-defence, *Lebensraum* in the case of Germany and access to natural resources in Japan's case. The new United Nations organization would permit unilateral self-defence only in cases where objective evidence of an emergency existed for the entire world to see: namely an actual armed attack. Other less tangible or immediate threats would receive Security Council scrutiny. The collective deliberation of the Council would be a better process for determining threats to the peace than the unilateral decision of the purported victim.

The new United Nations responded to other perceived weaknesses of the League. It put less emphasis on international law, removing, for example, the obligation on the League Council to enforce arbitral awards and decisions of the PCIJ. The UN Security Council has discretion with respect to ICJ judgments and plays no apparent role in enforcing arbitral awards or international law more generally. The new Security Council's job would be to enforce the peace, not the law.

5. Conclusion

In 2005, nearly every sovereign State joined in a World Summit Outcome document to renew their commitment to the United Nations Charter, promising to 'strictly' comply with the rules against the use of force.[108] The UN has existed almost three times as long as the League. No doubt some wars have been prevented. The use of war for conquest has virtually ended. Yet, the UN and its rules against war are widely disrespected. No attempt is even considered for stricter legal restrictions against war, such as outlawing civil war. The International Court of Justice continues to make important decisions, as did its predecessor the PCIJ, but its progressive provision, for compulsory jurisdiction on the basis of reciprocity has grown only very slowly. The United Kingdom is the sole permanent member of the Security Council that accepts compulsory jurisdiction. The US, the great champion of world courts, withdrew its acceptance in 1984, following the ICJ's decision that it could hear a case alleging that the US had violated article 2(4).

Ironically, it was Kelsen's protégé Hans Morgenthau who played perhaps the critical role in engendering disrespect and even antipathy toward the UN and

---

[108] UNGA Res 1 (15 September 2005) UN Doc A/Res/60/1.

international law in the US. Morgenthau had studied the work of Kelsen and Kelsen's rival in Germany, Carl Schmitt,[109] when Morgenthau was a student and young scholar of international law in Germany and Switzerland. He clearly preferred Schmitt.[110] Even after becoming a victim of Nazism like Kelsen, Morgenthau turned decisively away from international law and toward political science. He was confident that States, like men, lust for power and that international law cannot constrain them. In 1940, Morgenthau wrote an article highly critical of people's expectations for international law.[111] For him, international law, with its ineffective sanctions and inadequate theory, was too weak to command respect in the ultimate questions of power. The realist school of international relations theory owes many of its core ideas to Morgenthau, including its scepticism and even outright hostility toward international law.[112]

When a superpower pursues a foreign policy built largely on such 'realism', it is hardly surprising to see wide disregard for article 2(4). Add to this factor the current split among international law advocates between those supporting the Charter's limits on resort to force and those pressing for more exceptions to the Charter for humanitarian goals. These aspects of current international relations invite the question, what might renew the passion for peace embraced by so many for so long? History reveals that after cataclysms such as world wars, humanity does tend to recommit to peace, often looking to international law as the means. History also reveals, however, more hopefully, that a charismatic personality, a new Ghandi, could reignite the global imagination for world peace through law.

RECOMMENDED READING

Brownlie, Ian *International Law and the Use of Force by States* (OUP Oxford 1963).
Cortright, David *Peace: A History of Movements and Ideas* (CUP Cambridge 2008).
Grewe, Wilhelm G *The Epochs of International Law* (M Byers trans) (de Gruyter Berlin 2000).

[109]   See B Fassbender 'Carl Schmitt (1888–1985)' in pt 6 of the present volume.

[110]   See C Frei *Hans J Morgenthau: An Intellectual Biography* (Louisiana State University Press Louisiana 2001); see also *The Gentle Civilizer of Nations* (n 57) 436–7.

[111]   See HJ Morgenthau 'Positivism, Functionalism, and International Law' (1940) 34 American Journal of International Law 260–84.

[112]   'After half a century, the writings of Hans J Morgenthau continue to fill the minds, and often the hearts, of students of international politics. During the Cold War, his 'realist' approach ran as a leitmotif through political and academic discourse, his *Politics Among Nations* rising to become a "classic"'. D Philpott 'Moral Realism' (2002) 64 The Review of Politics 378–80 at 378 (reviewing Hans J Morgenthau (n 110)).

Johnston, Douglas M *The Historical Foundations of World Order: The Tower and the Arena* (Martinus Nijhoff Leiden 2008).

Neff, Stephen C *War and the Law of Nations: A General History* (CUP Cambridge 2005).

Nussbaum, Arthur *A Concise History of the Law of Nations* (revised edn Macmillan London 1962).

O'Connell, Mary E *The Power and Purpose of International Law: Insights from the Theory and Practice of Enforcement* (OUP New York 2008).

CHAPTER 12

RELIGION AND RELIGIOUS INTERVENTION

ANTJE VON UNGERN-STERNBERG

1. INTRODUCTION

THE role of religion in public international law is a complex one. First, religion may provide a source or a foundation of law and it may also influence concepts and norms of international law even if the latter was exclusively based on secular sources. Second, religion may characterize the relevant actors in international law such as rulers, peoples, States but also legal scholars. Third, religion may constitute the object of international law inasmuch as it settles issues raised by religion, for example the status of religious minorities. As a matter of course, these three aspects are interrelated. If influential, religious law and religious actors can shape the concepts and contents of international law. Conversely, the rules of international law determine the role religious concepts and religious actors may play.

All across these diverse aspects, two general developments—towards a secular legal order and towards an equal treatment of all religions in international law—can be discerned. The latter of these claims is easily explained: norms favouring the dominant religion are replaced by norms respecting the equality of all religions and denomination. International law, in this chapter, is meant to comprise the legal norms regulating the relations between relatively independent political units which are not subject of a superior authority possessing full legislative, executive, and judicative competences.[1] Thus, international law—dealing with war and peace, political and trade agreements, or diplomacy—is not confined to the relations between the modern States, but can be found throughout history, even if this chapter concentrates on early modern and modern times.

The term secularization, in this context, is not meant to characterize a sociological and political phenomenon, that is, the decline of religious beliefs or practices as a necessary corollary of modernization. This secularization theory modelled on a particular Western European experience of a particular time has rightly been called into question by today's sociology of religion.[2] By the same token, contemporary scholars stress the importance of religion as a factor influencing international relations and call for the integration of religion into the corresponding political theories.[3] In our legal context, secularization signifies that a legal order gets detached from religion.[4] Thereby, religion as a source and as a foundation of law is replaced by secular sources and foundations. Furthermore, religious elements of law making and law enforcement, for example legal functions for religious figures (priests as judges), religious rites (oaths, prayers, services), and the enforcement of secular goals by religious sanctions and vice versa, are abolished.[5] Indeed, this development may also be put into perspective. Empirically, one can refer to the influence of religious concepts on international law, not only from a Christian, but also from a Muslim or a Jewish point of view.[6] Normatively, the claim made by some that legal orders cannot accept religious arguments[7] may be rightly contested. As the following examples show, however, the process of secularization itself cannot be denied.

[1] Following W Grewe *The Epochs of International Law* (M Byers trans) (Walter de Gruyter Berlin 2000) at 7.

[2] J Casanova *Public Religions in a Modern World* (University of Chicago Press Chicago 1994) at 11–39; PL Berger *The Desecularization of the World. Resurgent Religion and World Politics* (Ethics and Public Policy Center Washington DC 1999) at 1–18.

[3] J Fox 'Integrating Religion into International Relations Theory' in J Haynes (ed) *Routledge Handbook of Religion and Politics* (Routledge New York 2009) 273–92.

[4] EW Böckenförde 'Die Entstehung des Staates als Vorgang der Säkularisation' in EW Böckenförde (ed) *Recht, Staat, Freiheit* (Suhrkamp Frankfurt 1992) 92–114 at 93.

[5] See the examples for possible ties between law and religion given by Y Dinstein 'International Law as a Primitive Legal System' (1986) 19 New York University Journal of International Law & Politics 1–32 at 17.

[6] N Bentwich *The Religious Foundations of Internationalism* (2nd edn George Allen & Unwin London 1959); JAR Nafziger 'The Functions of Religion in the International Legal System' in MW Janis and C Evans (eds) *Religion and International Law* (Martinus Nijhoff Leiden 2004) 155–76 at 162–6; S Rosenne 'The Influence on Judaism on the Development of International Law: An Assessment' in *Religion and International Law* (n 6) 63–94. MCW Pinto, however, rightly corrects Oppenheim's claim that international law has been the product of Christian civilization: MCW Pinto 'Reflections on the Role of Religion in International Law' in CA Armas Barea et al (eds) *Liber amicorum 'in memoriam' of Judge José Maria Ruda* (Kluwer Law The Hague 2000) 25–42 at 33.

[7] J Rawls 'The Idea of Public Reason Revisited' (1997) 64 The University of Chicago Law Review 765–807; J Habermas 'Religion in the Public Sphere' (2006) 14 European Journal of Philosophy 1–25.

It goes without saying that historiography itself may be considerably influenced by religion. There is no such thing as a neutral and omniscient observer, therefore the writings of international lawyers and historians are likely to reflect their respective cultural, ideological or religious background.[8] This might result in a particular interest in religion and in attempts to reappraise the role of Catholic scholars of international law[9] or to list the merits of Protestantism or Judaism.[10] The relationship between a scholar's background and his or her writings, however, is a very complex one and deserves a close look in every single case. Without such a detailed examination, it would be highly misleading to classify international lawyers or legal historians according to their religious affiliations, let alone to characterize international law as a Protestant or a Jewish discipline, simply because its leading scholars in the past had a Protestant or Jewish background (as, in fact, most of the intellectual elite of the time). In this chapter, the author's perspective is a secular Western European one—other perspectives can be found, for example in part three of this Handbook.

2. Secularization of International Law

One can distinguish three possible approaches for construing the relationships between a legal order and a religious one: the first considers both normatively interrelated, the second demands them to be strictly separate, and the third, while endorsing the separation in principle, empirically acknowledges their mutual influence and normatively accepts certain spheres of interrelationship.

With regard to international law, the first approach was prevalent throughout history until the 18th century. As opposed to our modern law, pre-modern legal orders are characterized in general by strong links between law and religion as well as other normative orders such as custom and morals,[11] which holds also true for international law. In Antiquity, legal sources and the sanctions incurred by infractions

---

[8] See M Koskenniemi *The Gentle Civilizer of Nations* (CUP Cambridge 2002).

[9] For example JB Scott *Catholic Conception of International Law* (Georgetown University Press Washington 1934) referring to Catholic de Vitoria—as opposed to Protestant Grotius—as the founder of the modern law of nations.

[10] For example PH Kooijmans 'Protestantism and the Development of International Law' (1976) 152 Recueil des Cours 79–117 linking the concept of human rights, the right of resistance, and the idea of international law itself to Protestant origins; P Weil 'Judaïsme et développement du droit international' (1976) 151 Recueil des Cours 253–335.

[11] 'International Law as a Primitive Legal System' (n 5) 16–18; D Kennedy 'Primitive Legal Scholarship' (1986) 17 Harvard International Law Journal 1–98 at 7–8.

were quite frequently seen as divine.[12] In medieval times, the scholastic concept of natural law was based on a hierarchical set of norms closely interrelated with religion: according to the terminology of Thomas Aquinas (1224/25–1274), eternal law (*lex aeterna*), the divine reason, constituted the highest source of law, followed by natural law (*lex naturalis*), that is, its earthly reflection recognizable to all men by human reason or divine revelation, in turn followed by human made law (*lex humana*), comprising *ius gentium*, 'conclusions' from natural law, and *ius civile*, positive law in the form of 'determinations' from natural law. Besides, divine law (*lex divina*) placed outside this hierarchy of norms could nevertheless define certain ultimate limits of human law. Thus, law in general and international law in particular (that is, treaties and customary law) was founded on and shaped by religion.[13] The development towards a secularized international law goes along two lines: in early modern times, scholars of international law start to argue for an increasing role of positive (man-made) law to the detriment of (religiously shaped) natural law, and they secularize natural law itself, that is, replace its links with religion by links to reason. With regard to the neo-scholastic Spanish school, this can be shown by the different role of natural and positive law in the teachings of Francisco de Vitoria (1483–1546) on the one hand, and Francisco Suárez (1548–1617) on the other.[14] According to the former, natural law is the first and highest source of international law. The rules derived from natural law are, however, complemented by rules based on consent, that is, treaties and custom. For the latter, whose teachings rest on the idea of voluntarism, this order is already reversed: international law is positive, human-made law, which is however founded upon and derives its stability from natural law.[15]

The Protestant humanists Alberico Gentili (1552–1608) and Hugo Grotius (1583–1645) severed international law from its Catholic scholastic foundations. Both remained devoted to the idea of natural law founded on divine law, but effectively reduced its religious content. According to Gentili, it is the 'agreement of all nations about a matter', a practice 'which native reason has established among all human beings' which constitutes natural law and the law of nations—a definition devoid of

---

[12] For a differentiated account of the role of religion, custom and reason in antique international law see DJ Bederman 'International Law in Antiquity' in *Religion and International Law* (n 6) 1–26.

[13] On Aquinas' concept of law, see F Wittreck *Geld als Instrument der Gerechtigkeit—Die Geldrechtslehre des Hl. Thomas von Aquin in ihrem interkulturellen Kontext* (Ferdinand Schöningh Paderborn 2002) at 68–75; *The Epochs of International Law* (n 1) 84–7.

[14] *The Epochs of International Law* (n 1) 189 ff; see also S Kadelbach 'Mission und Eroberung bei Vitoria: Über die Entstehung des Völkerrechts aus der Theologie' in M Lutz-Bachmann et al (eds) *Francisco de Vitoria und die Normativität des Rechts* (Frommann-Holzboog Stuttgart 2011).

[15] F de Victoria 'De indis et de iure belli relectiones' (1696) in JB Scott (ed) *The Classics of International Law* (Carnegie Washington 1917) vol 2, first relectio, s 3, para 1, at 151; F Suárez 'De legibus ac deo legislatore' in *Selections From Three Works of Francisco Suárez* in JB Scott *The Classics of International Law* (Clarendon Press Oxford 1944) book 2, ch 19, 341–50.

any religious reference.[16] As to Grotius, he did not only spell out the unthinkable, that is, that a theory of natural law does not presuppose the existence of God, which made him known to be the secularizer of international law.[17] He also essentially reduced the principles of 'true religion' to a belief in one God, thereby severing his system of international law from the teachings of a specific confession.[18] Due to the great success of his work *De jure belli ac pacis*, Grotius was thus the first to make a system of international law known to a wide public which was not based on a specific Christian creed and which could theoretically exist without religious foundations. Nevertheless, Grotius himself was still firmly rooted in Christianity and relied, in his treatment of international law, not only on citations from classical Greek and Roman authors, but also on numerous evidence found in the Bible.[19] If the doctrinal treatment of international law resembled, insofar, the scholastic tradition, its setting had also changed: international law was no longer an object of theologians like de Vitoria and Suárez, but of lawyers: both, Gentili and Grotius had studied law and worked in this profession, the former as a professor of law in Oxford, the latter as a public servant of the Netherlands and of France.

It was Emer de Vattel (1714–67),[20] the most widely read writer of international law in the 18th century, who, in his famous treatise *Le droits des gens*, effectively separated international law and religion. In his era, legal scholarship had already developed into a naturalist and a positivist strand, the former focusing on natural law, the latter on treaties and custom.[21] Thomas Hobbes (1588–1679), one of the most influential positivists, based his system of law entirely on human consent and left only a marginal role (the final origin of all legal obligations) for natural law. He was, however, a 'denier', not a secularizer of international law. A positivist approach towards

[16] A Gentili 'De iure belli libri tres' (1650) in JB Scott (ed) *The Classics of International Law* (Clarendon Press Oxford 1933) vol 2, book 1, ch 1, at 8; on Gentili in general, see A Nussbaum *A Concise History of the Law of Nations* (Macmillan New York 1954) at 94–101.

[17] H Grotius *De jure belli ac pacis* (1625) (R Tuck ed) (Liberty Fund Indianapolis 2005) book 1, Preliminary Discourse XI, at 89–90. Modern scholars have rightly pointed out that Grotius was not the first to formulate this thought, see *The Epochs of International Law* (n 1) 194; JB Schneewind *The Invention of Autonomy* (CUP Cambridge 1998) at 67–8.

[18] *De jure belli ac pacis* (n 17) book 2, ch 20, s XLV; *The Invention of Autonomy* (n 17) 66–70.

[19] MW Janis 'Religion and Literature of International Law: Some Standard Texts' in *Religion and International Law* (n 6) 121–44 at 123; KH Ziegler 'Biblische Grundlagen des europäischen Völkerrechts' (2000) 117 Zeitschrift der Savigny-Stiftung für Rechtsgeschichte, Kanonistische Abteilung 1–32 at 27–31.

[20] See E Jouannet *Emer de Vattel et l'émergence doctrinale du droit international classique* (Pedone Paris 1998). See the contribution by E Jouannet 'Emer de Vattel (1714–1767)' in this volume.

[21] *A Concise History* (n 16) 135–85; *The Epochs of International Law* (n 1) 349–60; KH Ziegler *Völkerrechtsgeschichte* (2nd edn CH Beck München 2007) at 163–5. These theories were not mutually exclusive, but rather show a difference in emphasis, see H McCoubrey 'Natural Law, Religion and the Development of International Law' in *Religion and International Law* (n 6) 177–89 at 185.

international law centring on State practice and treaties and thereby significantly diminishing religious influences can be found, for example, in the works of Richard Zouche (1590–1661) or Cornelius van Bynkershoek (1673–1743). Amongst the naturalists, Samuel Pufendorf (1632–94) established a system of secular natural law nominally still anchored in divine law, but effectively built on the precepts of reason. But Pufendorf, like Hobbes, attributed only a very limited role to international law. Instead, it was the naturalist de Vattel who construed international law on the basis of natural and positive law without relying on religious foundations, but—ultimately—only on the 'nature' of things.[22] If he nevertheless extensively treated 'piety and religion' in a chapter of its own, religion is dealt with as an object of law and for its positive or negative potentials.[23]

Thus, religion was dismissed not only as a source, but also as a foundation of international law. This secularization of international law has not seriously been challenged ever since neither by the increasingly dominant positivist nor by the remaining naturalist scholars.[24] However, the question of mutual influence and interrelationship of religious and secular sources or foundations of law was and still is of interest. It was, for example, quite common among Western scholars to identify international law as the product of civilized, that is, Christian nations.[25] Up until the 20th century, this could involve claims of Western superiority over, for example, the colonized nations.[26] In more recent times, scholars acknowledge the Christian influence on international law, while at the same time showing an interest in possible contributions of other religions[27]—a position which better reflects the principle of equality of religions and cultures.

[22]   E de Vattel 'Le droit des gens, ou principes de la loi naturelle, appliquée à la conduite aux affaires et des souverains' (1758) in JB Scott *The Classics of International Law* (Carnegie Institution Washington 1916) vol 3, at 1–9 (Introduction); 'Religion and Literature of International Law' (n 19) 126–8.

[23]   'Le droit des gens' (n 22) ch 12, 53–67.

[24]   On the latter, see A Orakhelashvili 'Natural Law and Justice' in R Wolfrum (ed) *Max Planck Encyclopedia of Public International Law* (OUP Oxford 2008) at <www.mpepil.com>.

[25]   See, for an example, H Wheaton *Elements of International Law with a Sketch of the History of Science* (Carey, Lea & Blanchard Philadelphia 1936) at 46; JK Bluntschli *Das moderne Völkerrecht der civilisierten Staaten* (Beck Nördlingen 1868) at 56.

[26]   See 'Natural Law and Justice' (n 24) paras 16–21.

[27]   See the contributions on the influence of Judaism (by S Rosenne) and Islam (by GM Badr) in *Religion and International Law* (n 6); CA Stumpf 'Christian and Islamic Traditions of Public International Law' (2005) 7 Journal of the History of International Law 69–80; I Bantekas 'Religion as a Source of International Law' in J Rehman and SC Breau (eds) *Religion, Human Rights and International Law* (Martinus Nijhoff Leiden 2007) 115–35; note also the ICJ's assessment that 'the traditions of Islam have made a substantial contribution' to the evolution of the regime of diplomatic law, *Case Concerning United States Diplomatic and Consular Staff in Tehran (United States of America v Iran)* [1980] ICJ Rep 1, para 86.

3. INTERNATIONAL RELATIONS BETWEEN ACTORS OF DIFFERENT FAITHS

If religiously motivated tendencies to distrust other religions influence international law, for example by outlawing treaties with 'infidels', this can impede international encounters between actors of different faiths. However, as the practice in the Christian and in the Muslim world shows, strict doctrine was modified by the need for pragmatic forms of cooperation. The Islamic conception of international law, as developed from the early 7th century onwards, proceeded from the assumption of a constant war (*jihād*) between the Muslim world (*dar al-islam*—'house of Islam') and the infidel world (*dar al-harb*—'house of war'), which runs counter the idea of treaties or diplomatic relations with nations of the latter.[28] Nevertheless, the necessity to cooperate with non-Muslims led to modifications of this idea. In this regard, Islamic law distinguished relations with the 'scriptuaries', that is, the peoples of the book like Christians and Jews, and the 'polytheists'. The permanent war against polytheists could technically be suspended by temporary peace treaties of up to a time limit of ten years (a period to be extended to twenty or twenty-five years in the 17th century), which effectively rendered short-term treaties of all sorts possible. War against the scriptuaries could be ended if they accepted Muslim protection and religious autonomy in exchange for paying a poll tax. The agreements between Muslim rulers and Jewish or Christian groups within and outside the Muslim world—provided they had an international character—constituted international treaties of principally unlimited duration. Treaties with scriptuaries as well as with polytheists had already been concluded by Mohammed himself, a practice to be continued afterwards. By the same token, diplomacy evolved from a mere auxiliary of warfare (delivery of the message of Islam before the fight, negotiations, exchange of prisoners of war) to a system of temporary missions rendering political relations between the Muslim and the non-Muslim world possible.[29] The conditions of those relations reflected the political strength of the parties involved. Notably the legal bonds between the Ottoman Empire and European States, which started with the treaty of 1535 between Suleiman the Magnificent and Francis I of France and were followed by other 'capitulations', are mostly characterized by unilateral concessions of the Sublime Porte facilitating

---

[28] On the following, see M Khadduri *War and Peace in the Law of Islam* (John Hopkins Press Baltimore 1955) at 175–222 and 239–50; M al-Shaybani *The Islamic Law of Nations* (M Khadduri trans) (John Hopkins Baltimore 1966) at 130–57; H Kruse *Islamische Völkerrechtslehre* (2nd edn Brockmeyer Bochum 1979) at 70–137; CH Alexandrowicz *An Introduction to the History of the Law of Nations in the East Indies* (Clarendon Press Oxford 1967) at 90–4. See the contribution of F Sahli and A El Ouazzani 'Africa North of the Sahara and Arab Countries' in this volume.

[29] MC Bassiouni 'Protection of Diplomats under Islamic Law' (1980) 74 American Journal of International Law 609–33.

Western trade, that is, granting freedom of commerce and navigation, tax privileges, as well as legal and religious autonomy.[30]

In the Christian world, treaty making with 'infidels', that is, with non-Christians, was also in dispute. One possible objection, the fact that the pagan partner would swear by his 'false' gods in order to confirm the treaty, had already been rebutted as irrelevant by Augustine of Hippo (354–430). But the medieval church principally condemned treaties with Muslims as *impia foedera* (ungodly alliances). This attitude, founded on suitable biblical references, was also motivated by the desire to unite the Christian world under papal authority.[31] However, political forces as well as scholarship emancipated themselves from this doctrine. Thus, in 1413, the King of (Christian) Poland concluded an alliance with (partly non-Christian) Lithuania aimed against the missionary crusades of the Teutonic order in Northern Europe. At the Council of Constance (1414–18), the Polish delegate Paulus Vladimiri justified this: in a case of extreme necessity, a Christian prince could make use of the assistance of infidels in order to defend his country. Even if the council did not subscribe to this view, the argument of necessity became influential for later legal reasoning.[32] The capitulation between Francis I and Suleiman the Magnificent in 1535, directed against Habsburg and the Holy Roman Empire, was considered treacherous by the rest of Europe, but effectively paved the way for other treaties with the Ottoman empire, for example by England and the Netherlands (fuelled by trade interests) or by the emperor himself (aimed at preventing further Ottoman attacks by the payments of tribute).[33] Furthermore, the letter of apology which Francis I sent to the pope in order to justify the capitulation, developed the modern idea that all humans belonged to human society regardless of their religion.[34] The arguments of necessity and equality also played an important role in the scholarly treatment of the matter. Writers like Gentili or Grotius,[35] by an independent reading of the biblical references, reached the conclusion that commercial treaties with infidels were lawful, whereas military alliances outside the Christian world could be considered legal (if at all) provided they were not directed against a Christian power. Gentili, who seems to have opposed all military alliances, warned that the involvement with 'infidels' could lead to the disrespect of the law of wars on their part.[36] Grotius, on the other hand, already proceeded from the assumption that 'the Right of making Alliances is common to all Men, and

---

[30] *A Concise History* (n 16) 63–5 and 121–3; KH Ziegler 'The Peace Treaties of the Ottoman Empire' in R Lesaffer (ed) *Peace Treaties and International Law in European History* (CUP Cambridge 2009) 338–64.

[31] 'Biblische Grundlagen' (n 19) 9, 11–12 and 16–17.

[32] *Introduction to the History of the Law of Nations* (n 28) 83–5.

[33] 'The Peace Treaties' (n 30) 342–64.

[34] Letter partly reproduced by E Nys *Les origines du droit international* (Alfred Castaignes Bruxelles 1894) at 162–3.

[35] On similar writings by Octavianus Cacheranus (in 1566) and John Henry Pott (in 1686), see *Introduction to the History of the Law of Nations* (n 28) 86–8.

[36] 'De iure belli libri tres' (n 16) book 3, ch 19, 397–403.

admits of no Exception on the Account of Religion.[37] At the same time, however, he stressed that alliances should serve Christianity and should not augment the power of the infidels.[38] It was de Vattel who abandoned this Christian bias and acknowledged full equality of all nations with regard to treaty making.[39]

Thus, the practice of interreligious international relations was also endorsed from a legal point of view. Other questions arising out of the encounter of different religions were equally solved in a pragmatic way. Treaty making, for example, used to involve the confirmation by oath up until the 17th century.[40] This, however, did not pose a problem since the parties of different faiths could swear separately by their respective gods—and the oath of an 'infidel' was still considered to be binding.[41] For parties from different Christian confessions, it was even possible to take a common oath, as, for example, the Peace of Münster (1648)[42] shows. Treaty invocations, regularly calling upon the Holy Trinity in agreements among Christian nations, were replaced by the formula 'in the name of God' in treaties between Christian and Muslim parties.[43] Furthermore, diplomatic law also accounted for religious differences. Most importantly, diplomats, whether on a permanent or on a temporary mission, had the right to freely exercise their religion in private.[44]

4. RELIGION AND WAR

Throughout history, religion has been a reason or a pretext to go to war. At the same time it provided strong arguments for limiting warfare. The doctrine of just war as developed by medieval theologians severely restricted the reasons to go to war and constitutes one of the most important influences of Christian thought on international *ius ad bellum*. Furthermore, today's *ius in bello* also evolved from religious precursors.[45]

[37]   *De jure belli ac pacis* (n 17) book 2, ch 15, s VIII.   [38]   ibid book 2, ch 15, s VIII–XII.
[39]   'Le droit des gens' (n 22) book 2, ch 12, para 162, 162 and ch 15, para 230, 191.
[40]   *A Concise History* (n 16) 18, 54 and 126.
[41]   Cf *Introduction to the History of the Law of Nations* (n 28) 166–7, for some examples, and *De jure belli ac pacis* (n 17) book 2, ch 13, s XII, on the legal assessment.
[42]   Confirmed by oath by the Dutch and the Spanish legates, see H Steiger 'Religion und die historische Entwicklung des Völkerrechts' in A Zimmermann (ed) *Religion und Internationales Recht* (Duncker & Humblot Berlin 2006) 11–50 at 43.
[43]   'The Peace Treaties' (n 30) 342–64.
[44]   'Le droit des gens' (n 22) book 4, ch 7, para 104, 384–5.
[45]   On these aspects of the just war doctrine and its influence on secular international law, see JT Johnson *Ideology, Reason, and the Limitation of War* (Princeton University Press Princeton 1975) at 40–6, 66–80 and 195–203; on Islamic rules restricting warfare see *War and Peace in the Law of Islam* (n 28) 83–137; *The Islamic Law of Nations* (n 28) 75–129.

If concentrating on religion as a justification for going to war, again a process towards a secularized reasoning and towards equality of religions can be depicted: in this context, secularization means that religious arguments have been eventually abolished from the legal discourse (in contrast to the political sphere where the term 'crusade', for example, has been revitalized in the war against terror[46]), whereas the principle of equality of religion outlaws that certain prerogatives—the right to fight heretics, to spread the faith, to intervene on behalf of religious minorities—are only acknowledged in favour of Christians. However, a methodological caveat applies. The general observation that the history of public international law has focused on theory while neglecting State practice,[47] also holds true for this subject. Little research has been done on the question of how wars were justified by the parties involved[48] and, in particular, how this fits into a legal doctrine.[49]

4.1. *Ius ad bellum* Doctrine

The development of *ius ad bellum* can be divided into three phases: first, the just war doctrine prevalent in the Middle Ages and in the early modern period, second, the era of a sovereign States' right to resort to war in order to pursue political aims culminating in the 19th century, and third,—beginning after the First World War—the prohibition of war unless justified by self-defence or collective peace enforcement.

According to the medieval doctrine,[50] (at least) three elements constituted the prerequisites of a just war: (1) *auctoritas principis*, meaning that only a sovereign entrusted with public authority could wage war; (2) *iusta causa,* that is, a valid legal claim of resorting to force; and (3) *recta intentio,* that is, the rightful intention as the subjective

---

[46] J Lears 'How War Became a Crusade' *New York Times* (New York 11 March 2003) 25.

[47] This observation is old, but still valid, see W Preiser *Die Völkerrechtsgeschichte, ihre Aufgaben und ihre Methode* (Franz Steiner Wiesbaden 1964) at 39; R Lesaffer 'International Law and its History: The Story of an Unrequited Love' in M Craven, M Fitzmaurice, and M Vogiatzi (eds) *Time, History and International Law* (Martinus Nijhoff Leiden 2006) 27–41 at 32–3 and 36–7.

[48] For a research agenda rather than results see K Repgen 'Kriegslegitimationen in Alteuropa. Entwurf einer historischen Typologie' (1985) 241 *Historische Zeitschrift* 27–49; A Tischer 'Offizielle Kriegsbegründungen in der frühen Neuzeit—Funktionen, Formen, Inhalte' (2004) 8 Militär und Gesellschaft in der frühen Neuzeit 48–54.

[49] Two of the rare exceptions are P Piirimäe 'Just War in Theory and Practice: The Legitimation of Swedish Intervention in the Thirty Years War' (2002) 45 The Historical Journal 499–523, R Lesaffer 'Defensive Warfare, Prevention and Hegemony. The Justifications for the Franco-Spanish War of 1635' (2006) 8 Journal of the History of International Law 91–123 and 141–79.

[50] On the just war doctrine(s) in general, see FH Russell *The Just War in the Middle Ages* (CUP Cambridge 1975); P Haggenmacher *Grotius et la doctrine de la guerre juste* (Presses Universitaires de France Paris 1983); R Tuck *The Rights of War and Peace. Political Thought and the International Order from Grotius to Kant* (OUP Oxford 1999); D Gaurier *Histoire du droit international. Auteurs, doctrines et développement de l'Antiquité à l'aube de la période contemporaine* (Presses Universitaires de Rennes Rennes 2005) at 240–72; SC Neff *War and the Law of Nations—A General History* (CUP Cambridge 2005) at 46–59.

element accompanying the objective just cause. In the early modern period, the doctrine was elaborated in two strands: the scholastic one, represented by writers like de Vitoria and Suárez, and the humanist one, embodied notably by Gentili and Grotius.[51] Both saw war as an instrument of justice, of law enforcement, of correcting a wrong.[52] But the scholastic tradition was still primarily concerned with questions of individual sin and the punishment of injuries whereas the humanist tradition already tried to define interests and rights of States which were to be enforced by war. This secularization of the just war doctrine continued by subsequent writers like de Vattel.[53] In Christian Europe, it was particularly under the (not yet secularized) just war doctrine that religious arguments—fight against heretics and infidels, mission, religious intervention—played a role, since they could establish the necessary just cause.

Interestingly, Muslim teaching also developed some restrictions on the *ius ad bellum* despite the assumption of permanent war against the infidels.[54] In contrast to the Christian just war doctrine, Islamic *jihād* did not require a religious or a secular wrong which was to be rectified by war. Instead, the religious purpose of spreading belief in Allah and creating a universal Islamic rule justified and demanded war in principle. However, a closer look reveals several limitations on the right to go to war: if 'polytheists' had to be fought until they converted, 'scripturaries' had the option of keeping their faith provided they submitted to Muslim rule and accepted to pay poll tax. Besides, factual circumstances led Islamic jurists to qualify the notion of permanent war and to accept its temporary suspension or even its dormant nature. Furthermore, *jihād* within the Muslim world, that is, against apostates (renouncing Islam) or dissenters (renouncing orthodox teaching), was restricted by considerations of proportionality.

4.2. Fight against Heretics and Infidels

The fight against heretics (Christians dissenting from the orthodox doctrine) and infidels (non-Christians) was a common phenomenon in medieval and early modern Europe.

To the medieval scholars, heretics were of much greater concern than infidels[55]—probably because they presented a bigger threat to the religious and

---

[51] On this difference, see *The Rights of War and Peace* (n 50) 16–108; 'Just War in Theory and Practice' (n 49) 508–11 and 515–16.

[52] *War and the Law of Nations* (n 50) 7 and 29.

[53] *Ideology, Reason, and the Limitation of War* (n 45) 208–58.

[54] On the following see *War and Peace in the Law of Islam* (n 28) 62–6 and 74–82. For a reading of an Islamic concept of war which is even equally restrictive as the Christian just war doctrine, see J Kelsay 'Religion, Morality, and The Governance of War: The Case of Classical Islam' (1990) 18 Journal of Religious Ethics 123–39.

[55] On the following see *The Just War in the Middle Ages* (n 50) 74–6, 199–201, 205, and 284–5.

political order based on Christian unity. According to Augustine, the persecution of heretics was justified. He based his argument on the phrase *compelle intrare* (Luke 14: 16–24), which in the biblical context referred to reluctant invitees of the Great Supper and which in Augustine's reading means that heretics shall be compelled to come into the orthodox church.[56] This reasoning, which Augustine himself did not put into the context of just war, was subsequently taken up by many writers in their attempts to justify wars against heretics or infidels. However, with regard to infidels, most notably Muslims, it eventually emerged in Christian doctrine, as spelled out by Pope Innocent IV (1195–1254), the canonist Hostensis (*c.* 1200–71) and Aquinas, that non-adherence to the Christian faith in itself was not a wrong justifying war. Hence, wars of conversion were prohibited and infidels could only be fought for the commission of a wrongful act. The fight against heretics, however, was considered justified. One argument supporting this difference was provided by Aquinas: the coercion of infidels was prohibited since belief must be voluntary, whereas heretics had given a promise to uphold the Christian faith and thus could be compelled to do so.

How did this theory square with the crusades, one of the outstanding examples of religiously motivated warfare in the Middle Ages and the early modern period? Crusades were military expeditions—into the Holy Land, against the Moors in Spain, against the Slavs in North-eastern Europe, or against heretics like the Albigensians in France—which were authorized by the pope and in which any Christian, after taking a vow, could participate with the view of enjoying indulgence.[57] As indicated above, the war against heretics was held to be legitimate per se, but the task of justifying the crusades against infidels according to the doctrine of just war remained.[58] And indeed, this was done with reference to the attacks of Muslims against the Byzantine Empire, to their occupation of the Holy Land, which was seen to belong to Christianity, and to their conquest of Spain. However, a similar reasoning was difficult with regard to the expansionist wars against the Slavs of North-western Europe who had not attacked, let alone conquered Christian territory. The apologetics of these forms of war were still couched in terms of the defence of Christianity, but it was also criticized by contemporaries that the idea of the crusade was extended far beyond the original fight in the Holy Land.[59] The prominent writings of Innocent IV, Hostensis, and Aquinas on just war doctrine only fragmentarily dealt with the crusades and, in doing so,

---

[56] ibid 23–5; H Maier 'Compelle intrare' in K Schreiber (ed) *Heilige Kriege* (Oldenbourg München 2008) 55–69 at 56 and 57–60.

[57] On the crusades in general see J Riley-Smith *What Were the Crusades?* (Macmillan London 1977); E-D Hehl 'Was ist eigentlich ein Kreuzzug?' (1994) 259 Historische Zeitschrift 297–336.

[58] On the justifications see *What Were the Crusades?* (n 57) 18–33; *The Just War in the Middle Ages* (n 50) 195–201 and 294–6.

[59] L Schmugge '"Deus lo vult?" Zu den Wandlungen der Kreuzzugsidee im Mittelalter' in *Heilige Kriege* (n 56) 93–108 at 97–106.

concentrated on the crusades in the Holy Land or the fight against heretics. By the same token, many of the papal crusading bulls failed to be included in the official decretal collections compiled by Dominicans and Franciscans. It seems that the leading scholastics were not prepared to justify all forms of war and it was also plausibly suggested that they were hesitant to involve the church directly in bloodshed.[60]

The scholars of the early modern period further developed the arguments concerning the fight against infidels. Confronted with the colonization of Southern and Central America, de Vitoria stressed that it was not justified to wage war against the Indians on the grounds that they refused to accept the Christian faith preached to them by the Spaniards.[61] This view was affirmed by Gentili and Grotius who wrote under the impression of the religious wars and the wars against the Ottoman Empire.[62] The scholars denied that not adhering to the Christian faith constituted a wrong in itself. Furthermore, they stressed that unbelief which was caused by ignorance and which had not been challenged by convincing proofs of the truth of the Christian faith did not amount to a sin (a point particularly dear to de Vitoria) and referred to the more general argument that—in contrast to the earlier reading of the passage of *compelle intrare*—Christian belief was a matter of free will and could not be enforced (a point made by Gentili). However, the humanist writers— in contrast to de Vitoria[63]—were also ready to accept a just cause which came close to the fight against infidels as such. Both acknowledged that war could be waged in order to punish sins against nature or god.[64] It is unclear, however, whether the examples given by them and by other scholars of the time—cannibalism, sexual misconduct, idolatry, blasphemy, atheism[65]—reflect contemporary imaginations about the life of the Indian aborigines or whether they represent a rather abstract compilation of possible sins perceived to be particularly dreadful. In any event, this line of argument, which frequently referred to those committing the aforementioned sins as 'beasts' or 'brutes', can be seen as a precursor of the modern distinction between 'civilized' and 'uncivilized' nations.[66] The argument that the fight

---

[60] *The Just War in the Middle Ages* (n 50) 294–6.

[61] 'De indis et de iure belli relectiones' (n 15) first relectio, s 2, paras 10–15, 142–6; on similar writings by other neo-scholastics, see J Fisch *Die europäische Expansion und das Völkerrecht: Die Auseinandersetzung um den Status der überseeischen Gebiete vom 15. Jahrhundert bis zur Gegenwart* (Steiner Stuttgart 1984) at 223–7.

[62] 'De iure belli libri tres' (n 16) book 1, chs 9 and 12, 38–41 and 53–7; *De jure belli ac pacis* (n 17) book 2, ch 20, s XLVIII.

[63] 'De indis et de iure belli relectiones' (n 61) s 2, para 16, 146–9.

[64] 'De iure belli libri tres' (n 16) book 1, ch 25, 123; *De jure belli ac pacis* (n 17) book 2, ch 20, ss XL–XLVI; on medieval precursors of this idea in the writings of Innocence IV, see *Die europäische Expansion* (n 61) 188.

[65] For example, by other writers—the scholastics Antonio de Córdoba, Juan Ginés de Sepúlveda, Bartolomé de las Casas, but also the positivist Richard Zouche—see *Die europäische Expansion* (n 61) 223–48.

[66] On this notion see also the contribution by L Obregón 'The Civilized and the Uncivilized' in this volume.

against heretics or infidels constituted a just cause for war, however, has no longer been put forward since the second half of the 16th century.

4.3. Mission

Another argument prevalent in the colonial context concerned the right to preach the Christian faith. The colonialist enterprises by Catholic Spain and Portugal effectively displayed considerable missionary zeal, as opposed to the Dutch colonial policy, for example, with its predominant focus on trade.[67] According to the early modern writers, however, mission in itself did not constitute a just cause for war since unbelief, as mentioned above, did not amount to an injury. Thus, the writers had to base their argument on the (illegal) hostile reactions by the infidels evoked by (legal) Christian missionary enterprises. De Vitoria, in particular, acknowledged a right to peaceful evangelization which could, if the missionaries met resistance by the Indians, be enforced by war. He effectively identified two related rights of the Spanish colonialists which could give rise to resort to war: first, a right to peacefully travel the Indian lands, to carry on trade with them and to be treated on an equal footing with other foreigners, which he found in the law of nations, and second, the aforementioned right to mission, which he based on the Bible.[68] However, these entitlements to free movement amounting to severe qualifications of State sovereignty were not accepted in State practice. Other neo-scholastics followed de Vitoria. Suárez, for example, argued at great length for the enforceable right of the pope and of the princes entrusted by him for preaching the Catholic faith to unbelievers—a privilege ultimately based on the Christian claim to truth and denied to unbelievers. But he also stressed that the mission should employ peaceful means and could only resort to force after being attacked or being repeatedly refused entrance into the realm of infidel princes. This was not only demanded by Christian teaching and practice, but also prevented to create the impression among the infidels that Christians claimed the right to violate international law.[69] However, the idea of a right to enforce a principally peaceful mission by military means was subsequently abandoned by humanist writers like Gentili and Grotius and not taken up afterwards.[70] Instead, mission on foreign territory was considered to require the permission of the territorial sovereign.[71]

---

[67] W Reinhard *Kleine Geschichte des Kolonialismus* (2nd edn Alfred Kröner Stuttgart 2008) at 44 and 68.

[68] 'De indis et de iure belli relectiones' (n 15) s 3, paras 1–4 and 6–12, at 151–53 and 154–58); on earlier claims of a right to mission, see *Die europäische Expansion* (n 61) 189 and 199.

[69] F Suárez 'De triplici virtute theologica, fide, spe, et charitate' in *Selections From Three Works of Francisco Suárez* (n 15) on faith, disputation 8, s 1, at 739–49; cf *Die europäische Expansion* (n 61) 224–41 (on Suárez and other scholastics).

[70] For an explicit refusal ('pretext of religion'), see 'De iure belli libri tres' (n 16) book 1, ch 25, 123.

[71] C Wolff *Jus gentium methodo scientifica pertractatum* in JB Scott *The Classics of International Law* (Clarendon Press Oxford 1934) vol 2, para 262, at 134–5; 'Le droit des gens' (n 22) book 2, ch 4, para 60, at 133.

4.4. Religious Intervention by Military Means

Religious intervention means the interference in the affairs of another State in favour of its subjects, motivated by religious concerns. Unlike the fight against heretics and infidels or the enforcement of a right to preach the Gospel, religious intervention may be construed without Christian bias, in a secularized and neutral manner, that is, justifying measures in favour of any religious minority. The idea was primarily discussed with respect to colonialism, the religious wars and the attempts to protect Christians within and against the Ottoman empire in the 19th century. It can refer to peaceful means as well as to the use of force.[72]

It was first of all de Vitoria who counted religious intervention (without using the term) among the arguments able to justify the use of force in America.[73] In doing so, he put forward two different grounds entitling the Spaniards to fight against oppressive rulers of the Indians: the first one, founded on Christian solidarity, allowing them to free their fellow (converted Indian) Christians from harassment and from pressure to abandon their faith, and the second one, founded on human solidarity as commanded by the Bible, calling them to rescue innocents from tyranny, for instance in the form of human sacrifice or cannibalism.[74] Both arguments were subsequently taken up by other scholars, who needed to justify religious intervention not only with regard to war, but also with regard to the emerging principles of State sovereignty and non-intervention.[75]

During the first period, the idea of an intervention in favour of subjects of a foreign State kept its Christian bias. According to writers like Suárez, Gentili, and Grotius, it was justified to wage war in order to protect Christians or would-be Christians if a ruler oppressed and persecuted them, in particular if he tried to prevent a conversion to Christianity or if he tried to compel them to abandon the Christian faith.[76] However, this was not accepted in the reverse case of a Christian ruler preventing his subjects to abandon their Christian faith. The reasons given for this difference essentially range from the argument of truth and entitlement by God (made by Suárez) or Christian allegiance (this point of de Vitoria is taken up by Gentili) to the already more secular aspect put forward by Grotius that the Christian religion it not destructive, but

[72] On religious intervention in general, see *The Epochs of International Law* (n 1) 177–81; S Chesterman *Just War or Just Peace? Humanitarian Intervention and International Law* (OUP Oxford 2002) at 7–33; GP van Nifterik 'Religious and Humanitarian Intervention in the Sixteenth- and Early Seventeenth-Century Legal Thought' in R Lesaffer and G Macours (eds) *Sovereignty and the Law of Nations (16th–18th centuries)* (Koninklijke Vlaams Academie van België voor Wetenschappen en Kunsten Brussels 2006) 35–60.

[73] Ancient and medieval precursors of this idea exist and are frequently referred to by most scholars writing on the topic; on respective ideas by Thomas Aquinas and other medieval writers, see *Die europäische Expansion* (n 61) 192–205.

[74] 'De indis et de iure belli relectiones' (n 15) s 3, paras 13–16, at 158–60.

[75] On this development, see *Just War or Just Peace?* (n 72) 16–23.

[76] 'De triplici virtute theologica' (n 69) disputation 13, s 5, paras 7–8, 826–27); 'De iure belli libri tres' (n 16) book 1, ch 15, 72; *De jure belli ac pacis* (n 17) book 2, ch 20, s XLIX and ch 25, s VIII.2.

beneficial to human society.[77] In addition to that, the scholars also recognized a more general title to war on grounds of humanity, that is, for the purpose of terminating the killing of innocents.[78] In a similar way, the Huguenot writer of the influential pamphlet *Vindiciae contra tyrannos* (1579) argued for the possibility and even the duty of a Christian prince to render assistance to subjects of neighbouring princes who are being persecuted on account of religion on the one hand or oppressed by manifest tyranny on the other hand.[79] In the European religious wars up until the Peace of Westphalia (1648), the argument of a military intervention motivated by religious solidarity among confessions seems to have played a certain role.[80] However, if confessional and military lines did not completely coincide, as in the Thirty Years' War, this reasoning had to be modified. Thus, the manifesto justifying the Swedish intervention in the Thirty Years' War (1630) referred to the aim of assisting the protestant estates of the Empire and of re-establishing their religious liberty, while at the same time not overemphasizing the confessional aspect (but concentrating on the more general argument of defence) so as to gain the approval of Sweden's Catholic ally France.[81] And the French intervention in 1635, directed against the Spanish Netherlands, very generally claimed to assist the oppressed population there.[82]

After 1648, the idea and the practice of religious intervention did not disappear.[83] It is true that the principles of State sovereignty and non-intervention became increasingly important[84] and that the peace treaties ending the religious wars to some extent accommodated the need to protect religious minorities.[85] Nevertheless, the secularized version of the right to religious intervention—disputed in post-Grotian scholarship—remained of theoretical and practical importance, especially with regard to the treatment of Christians within the Ottoman Empire. Writers like Christian Wolff (1679–1754) rejected the right to intervene on behalf of the subjects of another sovereign.[86] Others like de Vattel accepted a very limited right to intervention in order to help (but not to induce) a people to fight against tyranny and to defend its liberties in a civil war. The examples he listed show that he had cases of religious civil war in mind.

---

[77] *De jure belli ac pacis* (n 17) book 2, ch 20, s XLIX.

[78] 'De triplici virtute theologica' (n 69) disputation 13, s 5, para 5, at 825–6); 'De iure belli libri tres' (n 16) book 1 ch 25, 123; see also *De jure belli ac pacis* (n 17) book 2, ch 25, s VIII.

[79] SJ Brutus *Vindiciae, contra tyrannos: Or, Concerning the Legitimate Power of a Prince Over the People, and of the People Over a Prince* (G Garnett ed and trans) (CUP Cambridge 1994) at 173–83 and on the pamphlet and the identity of the writer, see 'Editor's Introduction' xix–lxxvi; A Esmain 'La théorie de l'intervention internationale chez quelques publicistes français du XVIe siècle' (1900) 24 Nouvelle revue historique de droit français et étranger 549–74 at 557–68; J Dennert *Beza, Brutus, Hotman: Calvinistische Monarchomachen* (Westdeutscher Verlag Köln 1968) at xvi–xxv.

[80] *Vindiciae, contra tyrannos* (n 79) 173–4 provides some examples.

[81] 'Just War in Theory and Practice' (n 49) 515–23.

[82] 'Defensive Warfare, Prevention and Hegemony' (n 49) 166–7.

[83] Contrary to the Grewe's assessment *The Epochs of International Law* (n 1) 181.

[84] R Grote 'Westphalian System' in *Max Planck Encyclopedia of Public International Law* (n 24).

[85] See Section 5.   [86] *Jus gentium methodo scientifica pertractatum* (n 71) para 258, at 132.

But in contrast to earlier conceptions the right to assistance was now devoid of any Christian bias.[87] The State practice of the 19th century, however, was clearly motivated by concerns for Christian minorities as several military interventions in the Ottoman Empire show: during the 1820s, Great Britain, France, and Russia jointly supported the (Christian) Greek insurgents' claim for autonomy and, after the Turkish refusal to concede, deployed military forces, which eventually led to Greek independence in 1830. In 1860, widespread massacres causing the death of thousands of Christians in Syria made all five European powers and the Ottoman Empire agree upon the deployment of European forces, which withdrew in 1861 after the violence had stopped. In 1876, when the Sultan refused to carry out the reforms in favour of the Christians in Bosnia, Herzegovina and Bulgaria called for by the European powers, Russia declared war on the Ottoman Empire, a war which resulted in local autonomy for Bulgaria and in the Austro-Hungarian occupation of Bosnia and Herzegovina.[88] The intervening powers regularly tried to justify their actions with regard to existing or newly created treaty provisions referring to the rights of religious minorities (which was, at times, rather difficult, given that the Treaty of Paris in 1856 expressly denied a right to intervene into the affairs of the Ottoman Empire). In the scholarly assessment of military religious interventions of the time, a rather cautious approach stressed the danger of abuse and accepted military action only in limited circumstances.[89] Others endorsed a broader notion of intervention[90] and emphasized the necessity for multilateral action.[91] In this context, at least the intervention in Syria (multilaterally agreed upon, not dominated by further strategic or political objectives) was considered legal according to contemporary international lawyers.[92] Today, the notion of religious intervention has been replaced by the more general, albeit controversial idea of humanitarian intervention which might comprise international action in favour of a particular group defined by ethnicity, nationality and religion.[93]

[87] 'Le droit des gens' (n 22) book 2, ch 4, para 56, at 131–2.

[88] *Just War or Just Peace?* (n 72) 24–33; SD Murphy *Humanitarian Intervention* (University of Pennsylvania Press Philadelphia 1996) at 49–55.

[89] R Phillimore *Commentaries upon International Law* (T & JW Johnson Philadelphia 1854) paras 474–75, at 340: 'only in the event a persecution of large bodies of men, on account of their religion'.

[90] Seminal: A Rougier 'La Théorie de l'intervention d'humanité' (1910) 17 Revue générale de droit international public 468–526; *Elements of International Law* (n 25) 91–4; EC Stowell *Intervention in International Law* (John Byrne Washington 1921) at 45–277.

[91] A Arntz 'Note sur la théorie du droit d'intervention' (1876) 8 Revue du droit international et de législation comparée 675–75 at 675.

[92] On Syria, S Kloepfer 'The Syrian Crisis, 1860–61: A Case Study in Classic Humanitarian Intervention' (1985) 23 Canadian Yearbook of International Law 246–60; for a more critical account I Pogany 'Humanitarian Intervention in International Law: The French Intervention in Syria Re-Examined' (1986) 35 International and Comparative Law Quarterly 182–90; *Just War or Just Peace?* (n 72) 26–32; H Köchler *The Concept of Humanitarian Intervention in the Context of Modern Power Politics* (International Progress Organization Wien 2001) at 7–13.

[93] FR Tesón *Humanitarian Intervention: An Inquiry Into Law and Morality* (Transnational Publishers Ardsley 2005) at 317–27 (examples of Rwanda and Bosnia).

5. INTERNATIONAL PROTECTION OF RELIGION

Religious diversity can be judged in both a positive and in a negative way. Apart from the modern perception of religious pluralism as a normative ideal, the enlightened rulers in the era of absolutism, for example, knew that attracting foreign settlers by granting tolerance to religious minorities (persecuted elsewhere) would promote trade and industry and would strengthen their own power since they could rely on the loyalty of the settlers.[94] Similarly, the treatment of the 'scriptuaries' by Muslim conquerors, that is, charging a poll tax instead of enforcing conversion, did not only entail financial, but also political advantages. However, the opposite view favouring religious homogeneity has dominated much of Western history—due to religious orthodoxy, the fear of instability and violence provoked by religious disputes, the perceived need of a common religious bond shared by all subjects, and the deep mistrust against other religions (as well as other nations or other ethnicities).[95] The treatment of religious minorities and of religion—an internal affair—becomes a matter of international law if it leads to military or non-military forms of intervention, and in particular if it forms a matter of international treaties[96] which nowadays provide for a universally recognized human right of religious freedom.[97]

The term 'religious intervention' as it was used, in particular, from the 18th to the beginning of the 20th century, did not only refer to military measures, but very broadly to all kinds of diplomatic and political efforts in favour of religious groups— mostly Christians or Jews—located in another State. Mistreatment and persecution of minorities in the Ottoman Empire gave rise to several protests by Western powers; for example, on behalf of the Christians in Crete (1866), or Macedonia (1903), and on behalf of the Armenians at the beginning of the 20th century.[98] Besides, the fate of the Jews in Central and Eastern Europe evoked sympathy and intercessions by the Western powers including the United States: Western governments objected, for example, to the expulsion of the Jews of Prague by Maria Theresa (1744/45) or against the discriminatory treatment of Jews and the failure to protect them against pogroms in Romania and Russia in the 19th and at the beginning of the 20th century.[99] This

---

[94] See eg J Whaley 'A Tolerant Society? Religious Toleration in the Holy Roman Empire, 1648–1806' in OP Grell and R Porter (eds) *Toleration in Enlightenment Europe* (CUP Cambridge 2000) 175–95.

[95] See eg M Goldie 'The Theory of Religious Intolerance in Restoration England' in OP Grell, JI Israel and N Tyake (eds) *From Persecution to Toleration—The Glorious Revolution and Religion in England* (Clarendon Press Oxford 1991) 331–86; M Linton 'Citizenship and Toleration in France' in *Toleration in Enlightenment Europe* (n 94) 157–74.

[96] On minorities in general, see the contribution by JE Nijman 'Minorities and Majorities' in this volume.

[97] PM Taylor *Freedom of Religion—UN and European Human Rights Law in Practice* (CUP Cambridge 2005).

[98] See *Just War or Just Peace?* (n 72) 25–6.

[99] N Feinberg 'The International Protection of Human Rights and the Jewish Question' (1968) 3 Israel Law Review 487–500 at 492–6; *Intervention in International Law* (n 90) 66–78.

protest, voiced either discreetly or publicly, was fuelled by general humanitarian concerns, but was also based on the international effects of these events, notably large-scale Jewish emigration to the United States, and on human rights. With regard to the latter, religious intervention very often involved either the attempt to create treaty rights or referred to existing treaty obligations which had been infringed.

The treaty-based human rights safeguarding religious groups or religion in general have several origins.[100] Some were obtained by a protecting power in favour of its nationals or fellow Christians living abroad, for instance merchants, pilgrims, or minorities in conquered territories. Notably the capitulations between European powers and the Ottoman empire accorded religious freedom to the Christians residing there. In this respect, France was recognized as the protector of all Latin Christians from 1535 onwards until other powers—England (1583), the Netherlands (1612), the Holy Roman Empire (1615), or Poland (1699)—followed suit. In 1774 (Treaty of Koutchouk-Kainardji),[101] Russia was granted respective rights for the Orthodox Christians. Other religious guarantees were brought about by the desire for peace after the religious wars of the 16th and 17th centuries. Some of them had a rather internal character like the Peace Treaty of Augsburg of 1555 (concluded by the Emperor and the Princes of the Schmalkaldic League, establishing the rule *cuius regio, eius religio* with regard to Catholicism and Lutheranism and creating a corresponding *ius emigrandi*), the Edict of Nantes of 1598 or the English Toleration Act of 1689 granting certain religious rights to the Huguenots and protestant dissenters respectively. The religious clauses of the Peace of Westphalia of 1648, however, were guaranteed internationally by the parties to the treaty and by the parties to other international treaties referring to it. Apart from recognizing a third, the Reformed, denomination in addition to Catholicism and Lutheranism, the treaty stipulated specific rights of religious minorities of those denominations: as a minimum, they were entitled to hold domestic worship, to attend service abroad and to raise their children in their faith. In some areas (defined according to the religious practice in the year of reference 1624), the minorities also had the right to hold 'private' services, that is, in a simple place of worship without spire, bells, and processions. Besides, the treaty contained a provision of non-discrimination which outlawed that a subject, on account of his denomination, was 'despised', expelled from a guild or craft or, more generally, refused certain civil

---

[100]   On the following, see J Fouques Duparc *La protection des minorités de race, de langue et de religion. Étude de droit des gens* (Dalloz Paris 1922) at 73–197; R Grote 'Die Religionsfreiheit im Spiegel völkervertraglicher Vereinbarungen zur politischen und territorialen Neuordnung' in R Grote and T Marauhn (eds) *Religionsfreiheit zwischen individueller Selbstbestimmung, Minderheitenschutz und Staatskirchenrecht—Völker- und verfassungsrechtliche Perspektiven* (Springer Berlin 2001) 3–52 at 4–32; SC Neff 'An Evolving International Legal Norm of Religious Freedom: Problems and Prospects' (1977) 7 California Western International Law Journal 543–90; P Thornberry *International Law and the Rights of Minorities* (Clarendon Press Oxford 1991) at 25–52. On the history of a national right of religious freedom, see A von Ungern-Sternberg *Religionsfreiheit in Europa* (Mohr Siebeck Tübingen 2008) at 7–31.

[101]   Peace Treaty of Koutchouk-Kainardji (signed 21 July 1774) (1774) 45 CTS 349.

or public rights.[102] Finally, treaties concerning cessions of territory frequently contained provisions in favour of religious minorities. A famous example is the Treaty of Oliva (1660),[103] which granted status quo to the Lutherans in Pomerania (ceded from Prussia to Sweden) and the right to domestic worship to Catholics in Latvia (ceded from Poland to Sweden). Similar stipulations were agreed upon, for instance, when France ceded territory to Holland in 1678, when Silesia was incorporated into Prussia from Austria in 1742, or when Great Britain took over the French possessions in Canada in 1713 and 1763.

The guarantees of these treaties were limited in several respects: they only entitled a particular religious minority (Catholics, specific protestant denominations, orthodox Christians), they were territorially confined, and they were restricted in scope. The rights of the religious minority in question regularly comprised freedom of conscience and of private worship, but did not include the free public exercise of religion and non-discrimination. Autonomy in civil and religious matters such as education, birth records, marriage and wills was, however, traditionally granted to the religious communities ('millet') in the Ottoman Empire.

Gradually, these limitations were abandoned in favour of a universally recognized human right of individual and collective freedom of religion. In the 18th century, Enlightenment and the American and French Revolutions advanced the idea that freedom of religion was no longer a matter of political expediency or of Christian allegiance, but a question of human rights. As a consequence, religious guarantees were increasingly couched in general and broad terms. Besides, the rise of nationalism led to a growing awareness for national and ethnic minorities also. The attempts by the Concert of Europe after 1815 and by the international community after 1918 to spread freedom of religion and religious non-discrimination were partly discredited, however, by their focus on the Ottoman empire and Eastern Europe, because this was considered a double-standard approach at the expense of the less powerful States and could serve as an excuse for not adhering to the guarantees to which they had subscribed. After the Congress of Vienna, the European powers, by method of 'conditional benefit',[104] achieved that several (South) Eastern European States committed themselves to freedom of religion and religious non-discrimination: the London Conference of 1830 recognized Greek independence after establishing, in its Protocol 3, that all inhabitants enjoy full religious freedom and equal access to public functions. Turkey was only admitted to the Concert of Europe by the Treaty of Paris in 1856[105] after the Sultan had guaranteed free religious exercise and religious

---

[102] Instrumentum Pacis Osnabrugensis (signed 24 October 1648) (1648) 1 CTS 119, art V, paras 31–32 and 34–35.

[103] Treaty of Oliva (signed 23 April 1660) (1660) 6 CTS 9.

[104] 'An Evolving International Legal Norm' (n 100) 557.

[105] General Treaty for the Re-Establishment of Peace between Austria, France, the United Kingdom, Prussia, Sardinia, Turkey and Russia (signed 30 March 1856) (1856) 114 CTS 409. The text of the respective provisions can also be found in *La protection des minorités* (n 100) 91.

equality by decree (*Hatt-i Hamayoun*)—which the treaty took formally note of. The creation of the four new States Serbia, Montenegro, Rumania and Bulgaria by the Treaty of Berlin in 1878[106] was equally made conditional upon extensive guarantees of freedom of religious exercise and non-discrimination. This new multilateral approach, however, did not prevent that the rights of Jews and Muslims were largely violated.

After the First World War, a further attempt for the multilateral protection of religious rights was developed within the League of Nations.[107] In the treaties concluded immediately after the War, the guarantees of free religious exercise and non-discrimination were imposed by the Allied Powers on the new States of Central and (South) Eastern Europe (for example Poland, Czechoslovakia, Serbia, Rumania, Greece) and on all of the besieged States except Germany (Austria, Hungary, Bulgaria, Turkey). They were supplemented by provisions in favour of national and ethnic minorities in general, and of particularly vulnerable minorities like the Jews in Poland, Greece, and Rumania, or the Muslims in Albania, Greece, and Yugoslavia. The protection of the religious minorities was now considered a matter of international concern: religious minorities issues could be addressed to the League Council, debated in the Assembly and brought to the Permanent International Court of Justice. One of the Court's advisory opinions effectively found that Albania had violated its commitment to the protection of minorities when it abolished its private school system run by religious communities.[108] However, apart from this single legal success, the League of Nations system of minorities' protection was not very effective. Like other elements of the international order established after the First World War, it lacked genuine acceptance and could not withstand the rise of nationalism and anti-Semitism culminating in the Second World War. After the Second World War, the human right of religious freedom and non-discrimination as enshrined, notably in the International Covenant on Civil and Political Rights or the European Convention on Human Rights, are no longer contested in principle.[109]

---

[106] Treaty for the Settlement of Affairs in the East (signed 13 July 1878) (1878) 153 CTS 171.

[107] H Rosting 'Protection of Minorities by the League of Nations' (1923) 17 American Journal of International Law 641–60.

[108] *Minority Schools in Albania* (Advisory Opinion) PCIJ Rep Series A/B No 64.

[109] On the remaining contested issues, for example the relationship of State and church or the condemnation of apostasy by many Muslim countries, see C Walter 'Religionsfreiheit in säkularen im Vergleich zu nicht-säkularen Staaten: Bausteine für ein integratives internationales Religionsrecht' in G Nolte et al (eds) *Pluralistische Gesellschaften und Internationales Recht* (CF Müller Heidelberg 2008) 253–92.

6. CONCLUSION

The history of religion and public international law is a history of secularization and of a development from an internal (in the Western world: Christian) towards a neutral perspective which treats all religions on an equal footing. In the process of secularization, religion is abandoned as a source and as a foundation of law, it becomes irrelevant as a factor characterizing international actors who engage in inter-religious relations, and it does no longer serve as a reason for justifying war in the guise of the fight against heretics, the defence of Christianity against Muslim attacks, or the enforceable right to mission. Moreover, the Christian bias of international law—outlawing all or certain treaties with infidels but not with Christians, assigning the right to fight heretics, to spread the faith and to intervene in favour of religious minorities only to Christians, and protecting solely the rights of Christian minorities—is replaced by the equal attribution (or non-attribution) of these entitlements. If this seems to support the classical interpretation of international law as a secularized legal order of sovereign and equal States established by the Peace of Westphalia,[110] this may be modified in two regards: international law cannot be separated from its historical, cultural, and religious origins. They should therefore be of particular interest to the scholarship of international law which could, at the same time, overcome its Western bias by also looking at non-Christian imprints on and interpretations of international law. Furthermore, the notion of sovereignty—a central aspect of the classical interpretation of the Westphalian system—has been restricted by religious matters which gave rise for religious interventions and for the formulation of religious rights.

RECOMMENDED READING

Alexandrowicz, Charles H *An Introduction to the History of the Law of Nations in the East Indies* (Clarendon Press Oxford 1967).

Esmain, Adhémar 'La théorie de l'intervention internationale chez quelques publicistes français du XVIᵉ siècle' (1900) 24 Nouvelle revue historique de droit français et étranger 549–74.

Fisch, Jörg *Die europäische Expansion und das Völkerrecht: Die Auseinandersetzung um den Status der überseeischen Gebiete vom 15. Jahrhundert bis zur Gegenwart* (Steiner Stuttgart 1984).

---

[110] L Gross 'The Peace of Westphalia, 1648–1948' (1948) 42 American Journal of International Law 20–41.

Fouques Duparc, Jacques *La protection des minorités de race, de langue et de religion. Étude de droit des gens* (Dalloz Paris 1922).

Grote, Rainer 'Die Religionsfreiheit im Spiegel völkervertraglicher Vereinbarungen zur politischen und territorialen Neuordnung' in Rainer Grote and Thilo Marauhn (eds) *Religionsfreiheit zwischen individueller Selbstbestimmung, Minderheitenschutz und Staatskirchenrecht—Völker- und verfassungsrechtliche Perspektiven* (Springer Berlin 2001) 3–52.

Haggenmacher, Peter *Grotius et la doctrine de la guerre juste* (Presses Universitaires de France Paris 1983).

Janis, Mark W and Carolyn Evans (eds) *Religion and International Law* (Martinus Nijhoff Leiden 2004).

Khadduri, Majid *War and Peace in the Law of Islam* (John Hopkins Press Baltimore 1955).

Kooijmans, Pieter H 'Protestantism and the Development of International Law' (1976) 152 Recueil des cours 79–117.

Nifterik, Gustaaf P van 'Religious and Humanitarian Intervention in the Sixteenth- and Early Seventeenth-Century Legal Thought' in Randall Lesaffer and Georges Macours (eds) *Sovereignty and the Law of Nations (16th–18th centuries)* (Koninklijke Vlaams Academie van België voor Wetenschappen en Kunsten Brussels 2006) 35–60.

Riley-Smith, Jonathan *What Were the Crusades?* (Macmillan London 1977).

Russell, Frederick H *The Just War in the Middle Ages* (CUP Cambridge 1975).

Scott, James B *The Catholic Conception of International Law* (Georgetown University Press Washington D.C. 1934).

Tuck, Richard *The Rights of War and Peace. Political Thought and the International Order from Grotius to Kant* (OUP Oxford 1999).

CHAPTER 13

THE PROTECTION
OF THE INDIVIDUAL
IN TIMES OF WAR
AND PEACE

ROBERT KOLB

1. INTRODUCTION

SINCE antiquity, public international law has dealt to some extent—at least secondarily—with rights and duties of individuals. Institutions such as postliminium or the suppression of piracy *iure gentium* bear testimony to this ancient lineage. In classical authors such as Grotius, we still find many passages, reminiscent of the medieval and scholastic world, where the status of individuals is at stake.[1] During the 17th–19th centuries, the question of torts committed against subjects of a foreign king and the ensuing remedy of the letters of reprisal were much discussed.[2] Since ancient

---

[1] See eg the chapter on the rights of parents, marriage, associations, and the rights over subjects and slaves: H Grotius *De iure belli ac pacis* (1625) book 2, ch 5.

[2] See eg *De iure belli* (n 1) book 3, ch 2; E de Vattel *Le droit des gens, ou principes de la loi naturelle appliqués à la conduite et aux affaires des nations et des souverains* (London 1758) vol 1, book 2, ch 18, paras 342 ff; see L Oppenheim *International Law* (RF Roxburgh ed) (3rd edn Longmans London 1921) vol 2 (*War and Neutrality*), at 47–8; G Clarke 'The English Practice with Regard to Reprisals by Private Persons'

times, the protection of merchants had been the object of keen attention. In the 19th century, the 'minimum standard of treatment' of foreigners was developed and international humanitarian law to take care of the victims of war emerged.

Thus, as a whole, the statement that the individual has long been deprived of standing in international law has been at least partially a doctrinal oversimplification. It gained popularity during the apogee of the state-centred phase of international law, at the end of the 19th century and at the beginning of the 20th. At that time, the national states developed and consolidated themselves on the European continent. As newly independent entities, often rooted in democratic institutions, they cherished their sovereignty. The State, dominated by its own constitution, became the dominant perspective of the times, the major political fact of the era. International society was thenceforth neatly separated from internal society. On the one hand was the State, with its vertical legal order and concentration of powers; on the other was the international space, with its horizontal legal order and its dispersion of power. This was at once order and anarchy. If the State was the dominant political feature of the times, a neat separation between its internal and external side was imposed also as to the 'subjects of the law' (legal persons). On the one hand, in municipal law, the relations between the State and its citizens, and among private persons; on the other hand, in international law, the relations between States or powerful entities (*ius inter potestates*). Rights and duties for individuals could therefore be only a matter for municipal law. These were essentially internal affairs. To be more precise, international law could 'indirectly' deal with individuals. Thus, a treaty could foresee that certain rights must be granted to certain persons; but in order to grant those rights as enforceable legal positions, the municipal law of the concerned State must enact the necessary legislation. The individual could thus not derive directly rights and duties from international law; international law could only oblige the States to take action in order to realize certain goals of protection.[3] This dual reality was framed in the known phrase of Oppenheim's *International Law* according to which the individual can only be the 'object' but not the 'subject' of international law.[4]

The dualistic model, described here with regard to the sources (vertical in municipal law: legislation; horizontal in international law: treaty and custom, the last being at those times framed as a tacit agreement) and the subjects (States and powers in international law; individuals in internal law), has been only a transient phase in the development of international law. Since the beginnings of the 20th century, many critical schools sought to re-assert a place for the individual in international law,

---

(1933) 27 American Journal of International Law 694–723 at 700 ff; WG Grewe *The Epochs of International Law* (M Byers trans) (Walter de Gruyter Berlin 2000) at 201–3; see also P Lafargue *Les représailles en temps de paix* (A Rousseau Paris 1899).

[3]   See eg G Jellinek *System der subjectiven öffentlichen Rechte* (Mohr Siebeck Freiburg 1892) at 310 ff; but see also A Peters 'Das subjektive internationale Recht' (2011) 59 *Jahrbuch des öffentlichen Rechts* 411–56.

[4]   *International Law* (n 2) vol 1, 460.

sometimes as the ultimate and true subject of all legal orders: one may here quote the Vienna School around Hans Kelsen[5] or the sociologic solidarism of Scelle.[6] Moreover, at the same time, many moderate authors rejected the 'dualistic' approach to international law, preferring 'monistic' constructions.[7] If international law and municipal law are part of one single great legal phenomenon, there is no reason to exclude that international law, as well as national law, could deal with individuals. These considerations were initially essentially theoretical. They gained practical momentum consequentially to the policies of oppression and the atrocities of the Axis Powers. Thus, since 1945, it was understood, politically as well as legally, that international law as well as municipal law could and should deal with the individual. Henceforward, the branches of international human rights law, international humanitarian law and international criminal law developed considerably. In a historical perspective, public international law thus first touched to the individual; than, during a short time-span the individual was eclipsed; and in the last phase the individual became an essential part of the international legal order.

The concrete approach of the law towards the individual, however, changed. It would be wrong to affirm summarily that classical international law did not seek the protection of individuals (even if this protection was generally achieved through some participation of the State, for example, the *lettres de marque*, whereas today it is autonomous, for example, through human rights complaints by the aggrieved individual himself). However, the amount and the modalities of the protection have undergone profound changes. The legal regime protecting the individual (or sanctioning him, which is but another aspect of a will to protect) has been considerably strengthened. Haphazard and punctual institutions of the past have been transformed in ever-growing and fully fledged regimes of protection. The modalities of protection have also changed. Modern international law is predicated upon the idea that the individual has 'fundamental rights': this stance can be seen in international human right law as well as in international humanitarian law (law of war). Fundamental rights are but a variant of 'subjective rights'. Now, the idea that a subject of the law is invested with a series of subjective rights which he may claim at its own will is a modern conception.[8] It did not exist in antiquity, or in the Middle Ages; it emerged

---

[5] On Kelsen and his doctrine, see A Truyol y Serra and R Kolb *Doctrines sur le fondement du droit des gens* (A Pedone Paris 2007) at 77 with further references; on his treatment of legal personality in particular, see JE Nijman *The Concept of International Legal Personality* (TMC Asser Press The Hague 2004) at 149 ff; R Portmann *Legal Personality in International Law* (CUP Cambridge 2010) at 173 ff.

[6] *Doctrines sur le fondement du droit des gens* (n 5) 94 ff; see also A Wüst *Das völkerrechtliche Werk von George Scelle im Frankreich der Zwischenkriegszeit* (Nomos Baden-Baden 2007); on the treatment of legal personality in particular *The Concept of International Legal Personality* (n 5) 192 ff.

[7] See eg the nuanced arguments presented by M Bourquin 'Règles générales du droit de la paix' (1931-I) 35 Recueil des cours 1–232 at 135 ff.

[8] For a powerful refutation C Donahue 'Ius in the Subjective Sense in Roman Law. Reflections on Villey and Tierney' in D Maffei et al (eds) *A Ennio Cortese* (Il Cigno Edizioni Rome 2001) 506–30;

in Enlightenment and is codified in the modern law, its hallmark being precisely the 'rights of man'. Modernity has shifted the paradigm. Antiquity and Middle Age think in categories of cosmic order. The law is a reflection of this order. It is therefore objective law. Modernity performs the anthropocentric revolution. The individual and his representation of the word become the centre of things. It was thus only a question of time for the 'subjective rights' of man to emerge. Doubtless, it is this relative absence of 'subjective rights' comparable to our own ones of today which renders more difficult for the modern man discovering the protections the old law granted to the individuals. These protections were more hidden in the wood of objective norms and were not formulated as powers of the individual under the guise of subjective entitlements. Therefore, only a studied eye will find the relevant links, whereas the time-constrained superficial observer will think that the era of protection of the individual in international law has started in 1945. With respect to a certain quality of protection, this is certainly true; but it is untrue if the question is considered from a global perspective avoiding retro-projection of modern legal tools and perspectives.

The protection of the individual is today performed mainly by two branches of international law: international human rights law and international humanitarian law. The first includes areas such as the protection of workers (International Labour Organisation (ILO)), refugees, internally displaced persons, indigenous peoples, etc. The second concerns protection of civilians, persons *hors de combat*, but also military persons still in combat: for example, when they are protected against the effect of certain weapons causing unnecessary suffering. This chapter will concentrate on the historical development of the law of war. It will focus on the phase prior to 1945 but include some short incursions into later times.

By approaching the subject-matter under the perspective of the protection of individuals, there is moreover the pitfall of not doing true and full justice to the history of certain branches of the law. Hence, international humanitarian law before 1945 was not the core of the branch of the law dealing with warfare. The older law was still centred on means and methods of warfare, that is, on military concerns. It was a law designed for military personnel and their fighting methods. The main point was to secure military honour (as derived from old chivalric traditions) and only as an annex to maintain some humanity in warfare. The civilian was largely absent from the law of war of that day. In other words, 'Hague Law' predominated largely over 'Geneva Law'. Moreover, this Hague Law remained under the sway of a largely applied exception of military necessity. It was understood at these days— even if not at all uncontroversial—that military necessity could derogate from any rule of the law of armed conflict. This body of law thus remained always under the control of a sort of subjectively appreciated *rebus sic stantibus*. This applied also to

M Villey 'L'idée du droit subjectif et les systèmes juridiques romains' (1946/47) 24/25 Revue historique de droit français et étranger 201–27.

the protection of individuals under the 'Geneva Law' limb. Hence, a much discussed question of the 19th century was that of a small military detachment happening to capture a great number of prisoners of war, which it could not keep under control or bring to a camp without putting into jeopardy its own security. Some authors propounded for the rule that the prisoners should then be released, eventually disarmed and even naked. Others argued that military necessity prevailed and that it was allowed to kill them. There is thus a danger of reconstructing the old law of war retroactively and anachronistically by putting too great an emphasis of the 'protection of war victims' or of 'individuals'. In this case, the law of war is excessively perceived and analysed through the lens of our individual-centred approach of today. In reality, the 'humanization' of international humanitarian law has been a slow progress. The same could be said for human rights law. Many forerunners of it can be found before 1945— and yet none is truly human rights law. In a somewhat retroactive perspective, all the punctual institutions that can be identified are nevertheless enrolled as nurses of infant human rights law. To some extent, this sort of anachronism seems inevitable.

2. The History of International Humanitarian Law (Law of War)

2.1. General Aspects

Rules as to the conduct of warfare (rather than the treatment of enemy persons) have existed since most ancient times in all civilizations. These rules are of four types: (i) rules of chivalry for combat tactics, oscillating between phases of peaks and then again phases of weakness; (ii) rules as to the prohibition of certain weapons, for example, poisoned ones; (iii) rules as to the protection of certain persons (for example, monks) or places (for example, temples) or objects (for example, fruit-trees); (iv) rules as to *commercia belli,* that is, conventions concluded between belligerents (armistices, truces, exchange of prisoners, etc.). In the *ius publicum europaeum* these rules were consolidated since antiquity and especially in the Middle Ages. But there existed such rules also in other civilizations: the Jewish (see the Old Testament), the powers of the Middle East (Persia, Mitanni, the Hittites, etc.), ancient India, ancient China, Black Africa, or Pre-Colombian America. Thus, for example, in the 'spring and autumn' period of ancient China (771 BC to 481 BC), characterized by the existence of a series of independent States, chivalry was at its heyday. Aristocrats fought the combat, each one followed by a number of commoners. War was highly ritualized and guided by ethical considerations. This ethic of war faded away in the next phase, those of 'States in War' (481 BC to 221 BC), where war became a struggle for conquest of territory and resources. The war became now licentious and brutal. Such oscillations between phases of constrained and then again unbridled war can be found in all civilizations. In some areas of the world quite special rules had emerged. Thus, in Pre-Colombian Mesoamerica, there has been an agreement among the Aztecs and some other powers to fight 'Flower Wars' where the object was essentially to capture prisoners alive for human sacrifice. Thus very specific rules of warfare developed for such wars. They were aimed at avoiding killing and privileging capturing.

The restrictions on belligerent violence of these ancient times do however not truly aim at the protection of 'individuals' in the modern sense of the word. In no ancient civilization a sacralisation of human life and integrity of limb, as it is in modern times, can be found. The limitations on belligerent licence flow from two considerations: (i) notions of military honour and chivalry, which can be found in all cultures; (ii) self-interest in limiting warfare, be it to secure a better peace by not inciting to hatred for excessive destruction committed on the vanquished community, to secure a better booty and conquered territories not entirely destroyed, or to extract financial advantages. Hence, for example, prisoners of war were initially killed, later enslaved and sold, still later released against ransom, and finally humanely treated in prisoners of war camps (Geneva Law). This evolution spans from antiquity to modern times. This is not to say that human treatment episodes could not occur: prisoners were graciously released or well treated (one may recall the legendary generosity of Saladin). This was not however a matter of culture, social norm or legal obligation. It was a matter of personal choice and policy.

The history of modern international humanitarian law has been exposed many times. Before passing to that history, it might be useful to insist on the importance of military necessity in the old law of war. This pivotal principle of the 19th century law did not only allow action derogating from the law, it also served to limit bellicose licence.

The law of war of the second part of the 19th century was replete with gaps and uncertainties.[9] The older 'usages' of war were considered not to be fully legal. They were a mixture of religious, moral and other practices, falling short of the modern legal concept, purportedly strictly scientific, which set its benchmark in the 19th-century positivistic ideal. On the other hand, legal codification was only at its earliest stages. Since one could not rely on a ready-made, lock, stock, and barrel set of

---

[9] This is also noted in various preambles of international instruments, eg the Brussels Declaration (Project of an International Declaration concerning the Laws and Customs of War (adopted 27 August 1874) published in D Schindler and J Toman (eds) *The Laws of Armed Conflicts* (Martinus Nijhoff Publisher Leiden 2004) at 21 ff) or the Oxford Manual (Laws of War on Land (adopted by the Institute of International Law at Oxford 9 September 1880) published ibid 29 ff).

precise rules, it became essential to encapsulate the whole subject matter within some guiding principles. Rapidly, 'military necessity' or 'war necessity' became the hallmark of the whole system. This 'necessity' obtains at once a positive, expansive, licence-to-violence role, and also a negative, restrictive, limiting-violence role. The equation reads as follows: (i) everything which is necessary to overpower the enemy must be granted to the military branch, and it would be pointless to attempt to prohibit it, even on account of humanity; (ii) but everything which is not so necessary remains alien to war and must be considered a superfluous, inhuman and prohibited, destruction. The first is thus always lawful; the second is always unlawful. In case of absence of concrete prohibitive rules, this principle offered criteria for deciding on lawful and unlawful means of warfare. The principle of necessity played an essential residual role in a legal environment where detailed rules were rare and gaps frequent. It kept clear from prohibitions all means and methods thought to be indispensable to achieve the war aim. The principle of humanity and all the restrictions on warfare blossomed in the second branch of necessity, the one of a restrictive nature. This restrictive 'necessity'-philosophy of the modern law of war is admirably summarized in the preamble of the St Petersburg Declaration (1868). Overall, 'necessity' was thus a complex principle inextricably linking together two opposite sides of the coin: it means first licence to act with regard to all violence indispensable for securing the war aim, but at the same time only that much violence and no more. The principle is dualistic, at once liberal and restrictive; it is thus at once flexible and firm. However, the principle could only produce increasingly significant clashes in a world where military conceptions and configurations of *raison d'état* widely differed: what could be common to a German militaristic conception of war (and thus of necessity), an Anglo-Saxon commercial conception of war (and thus of necessity), or a French, at that time more moderate, conception of defensive patriotic war (and thus of necessity)? Moreover, evolutions in warfare, new weapons systems, changes in the configuration of the relationships between civilians and combatants, all these and other factors constantly shift the demarcation lines between what appears 'necessary' or not at a certain time. Where exactly could the line be drawn at a certain moment? It was thus understood, at the turn of the century, that the 'necessity' criterion was too vague and open to abuses, and had to be complemented (and to some extent superseded) by a codification of particular rules in international conventions.

2.2. Specific Institutions

2.2.1. *Lieber Code*

The code of Francis (Franz) Lieber, a Prussian subject having left Prussia for the US and having settled as a professor of law at Columbia University, is the first comprehensive codification of the laws of war, drafted during the War of Secession. These instructions mainly codify the existing laws of war of the time. They served as an example for numerous pieces of legislation in the municipal law of various States, in the second half of the 19th century. Moreover, these instructions were used as a direct source of inspiration for the following efforts to draft international conventions on the laws of war. The Lieber Code served not only in the civil war, but was used by the US also in its international wars of the 19th century, in Mexico or in Cuba. The focus of the code is on military law, not on protection of individuals. It is a curious mixture of conservative (even harsh) and progressive elements. Its gist is not truly humanitarian in the modern sense. It rather reflected an acute sense of military honour and fairness. In that context a series of prohibitions were inserted into it, which it is possible, in the light of today, to interpret as expressing 'humanitarian' concerns. Hence, for example, article 11 recalls that the law of war 'disclaim all cruelty', going on to add quite significantly 'and bad faith' (which again shows the sense of honour). Article 15 underlines that direct destruction of life and limb is directed to armed enemies, and to other persons only when destruction is incidentally unavoidable in the armed contest. The civilian is largely absent from the code, it being understood that he is outside the war and not the object of attack.

2.2.2. *First Geneva Convention of 1864 on the Wounded and Sick*

The Geneva Convention of 1864 ('Convention for the Amelioration of the Condition of the Wounded in Armies in the Field')[10] is the offspring of the Solferino events and the initiative of Henry Dunant and Gustave Moynier. Dunant had been struck that so many soldiers died because of the absence of any organized sanitary service. With the large conscription armies of republican times, interest in care of individual soldiers had vanished. In the mass armies of the time, one solider could easily replace any other soldier. Moreover, the rudimentary sanitary services existing did not benefit from protection against attack. They did not have a uniform distinctive sign, which would make them recognizable. The 1864 convention in its ten articles addresses these questions. Its object is to secure care for wounded or sick military persons being thus *hors de combat*. Certain gaps left by the convention gave rise to additional articles adopted in 1868. The point was mainly to extend the benefit of the convention of 1864 to naval forces at sea. The 'Additional Articles relating to the Condition of the Wounded in War' were however not ratified and did not enter into force. There was in 1864 a first breakthrough in the humanitarian protection of individuals during war, even if restricted to military personnel in certain specific contexts.

---

[10] Convention for the Amelioration of the Condition of the Wounded in Armies in the Field (adopted 22 August 1864, entered into force 22 June 1865) published in *The Laws of Armed Conflicts* (n 9) at 365 ff.

2.2.3. *Declaration of St Petersburg of 1868*

The Declaration of St Petersburg ('Renouncing the Use, in Time of War, of Explosive Projectiles under 400 Grammes of Weight') is known today essentially for its preamble, in which the old Rousseau/Portalis maxim, namely that soldiers are enemies only by accident of the battlefield, found a glaring application. It reads as follows:

Considering: That the progress of civilization should have the effect of alleviating as much as possible the calamities of war; That the only legitimate object which States should endeavor to accomplish during war is to weaken the military forces of the enemy; That for this purpose it is sufficient to disable the greatest possible number of men; That this object would be exceeded by the employment of arms which aggravate the sufferings of disabled men, or render their death inevitable; That the employment of such arms would, therefore, be contrary to the laws of humanity.[11]

This text can be read as a first attempt at humanization of the law of war. It was directed against the Clausewitzian and other military doctrines having pleaded for a 'brutal', 'massive', or 'total' war in order to keep the armed contest as short as possible. To the maxim 'the most humane wars are the shortest ones', the declaration opposes or adds the maxim that the 'wars have to remain limited and humanitarian'. The fact that only military personnel is being directly considered by the declaration is in line with the conception of the time. The civilians are envisioned as being completely alien to the armed contest. The declaration thus limits itself to a military law perspective. The clause 'weaken the military forces of the enemy' at once shows this concentration on the military personnel and confirms implicitly that civilians are not to be made the object of attacks, being outside the sphere of belligerent violence. Overall, the declaration is one of the first hallmarks of a 'humanitarian' approach in the law of war. It consolidates within the Hague Law what had been achieved in the Geneva Law. It also admirably reflects the 'civilization' idea of the 19th century.

2.2.4. *Brussels Conference of 1874*

In 1874, the time had been considered ripe to try to codify the laws of warfare at the international level. Indeed, much national legislation had been adopted and was continuing to be adopted at a quick pace. Consequently, it was considered necessary to tame and to direct these different laws within the four corners of some internationally common law. However, there was finally no agreement at the Brussels Conference on some crucial points, in particular on the definition of combatants: could these only be military personnel of professional armies, or could civilians take up arms for fighting a patriotic war under certain conditions? Great powers leaned

---

[11] Declaration Renouncing the Use, in Time of War, of Explosive Projectiles Under 400 Grammes Weight (adopted and entered into force 11 December 1868) published in *The Laws of Armed Conflicts* (n 9) 91 ff.

towards the first, small powers towards the second. The Brussels Conference Draft[12] however inspired future attempts at codification. It directly served for the adoption of the Hague Conventions of 1899/1907. From the point of view of protection of individuals, the draft does not expand notably beyond the Lieber Code. It continues to be centred on military law, rather than on protected persons. It is however the first international draft to contain a section on the protection of prisoners of war (articles 23 ff).

2.2.5. *Oxford Manual of 1880*

Another effort of the same type is the manual of 'Laws of War on Land' prepared by Gustave Moynier for the Institut de droit international (1888).[13] The aim was to furnish to governments a practical manual, reflecting the customs of land warfare, in order to serve as a basis for national legislation in each State. Humanitarianism in this text is again directed essentially to the military personnel. The civilian remains largely absent, apart in occupied territories where some rudimentary protections are devised (especially in article 49). Article 7 recalls that 'it is prohibited to maltreat inoffensive populations'.

2.2.6. *Hague Conventions of 1899 and 1907*

The Hague Conventions (1899/1907) are the first comprehensive treaty codification of the laws of war on land and on the sea.[14] The most important piece is convention II of 1899; it led to convention IV of 1907, which is a revised version, both 'respecting the Laws and Customs of War on Land'. This convention took over the contents of the Lieber Code, the Brussels Draft and the Oxford Manual. It contains rules on the protection of prisoners of war (articles 4 ff), limits the permissible means and methods of warfare (articles 22 ff) and contains some (not sufficiently developed) rules on the protection of civilians in occupied territory (articles 42 ff). Its stress lies still on military law, that is, on what the military personnel may do when fighting, when occupying, and on the duties they have one with regard to the other among themselves. The modern 'protected person' is still absent. The most remarkable humanitarian feature in this convention is the famous 'Martens Clause':

Until a more complete code of the laws of war has been issued, the High Contracting Parties deem it expedient to declare that, in cases not included in the Regulations adopted by them, the inhabitants and the belligerents remain under the protection and the rule of the principles of the law of nations, as they result from the usages established among civilized peoples, from the laws of humanity, and the dictates of the public conscience.[15]

---

[12]   *The Laws of Armed Conflicts* (n 9) 21 ff.   [13]   ibid 29 ff.   [14]   ibid 41 ff.
[15]   Convention (IV) respecting the Laws and Customs of War on Land (adopted 18 October 1907, entered into force 26 January 1910) in *The Laws of Armed Conflicts* (n 9) 55 ff, Preamble.

The present clause flows from the principle of humanity. The laws of war contain a series of prohibitions for conduct during warfare. The clause secures that the gaps of the laws of war do not automatically lead to a licence for inhuman action according to the principle that 'all what is not prohibited is allowed'. The belligerent is required first to check if its prospected behaviour, even if not expressly prohibited in the positive body of the law, can be conciliated with dictates of humanity. If not, he should either abstain from it, or at least give due weight to potential humanitarian temperaments in the prospected action. The clause had no true practical weight before 1945. It became a part of positive law in 1949, but is still perhaps not as much taken seriously as it could and should.

2.2.7. *Geneva Conventions of 1906 and 1929*

A progress in humanitarian protection of military personnel was achieved in 1906 and later in 1929, through a development of the Geneva Law. The 1906 Convention for the 'Amelioration of the Condition of the Wounded and Sick in Armies in the Field'[16] develops the 1864 Convention in the light of the Additional Articles 1868 and of the Hague codification. The 1906 text is more detailed and more precise than the *torso* of 1864. There were new provisions, such as on burial of the dead, on transmission of information and on voluntary aid societies, which has in the meantime flourished. On the other hand, the provisions on aid to the wounded provided by the inhabitants were reduced to more realistic proportions. This convention was amended again in 1929 on the basis of the new experience of the First World War. New provisions were inserted on the protection of medical aircraft and the use (or abuse) of the distinctive emblem in times of peace. New protective emblems were also recognized; for example, the Red Crescent. Moreover, in 1929 a new Geneva Convention on the Treatment of Prisoners of War was adopted. The provisions of the Hague Convention had proved to be insufficient in the light of the First World War. Some important innovations in this convention had a distinctive humanitarian reach, namely the prohibition of reprisals (article 2) or collective penalties (article 46). Moreover, the convention expanded on the organization of prisoner's labour, the designation of prisoner's representatives and the control exercised by protecting powers.

2.2.8. *Improving Humanitarian Protection*

The protection of the individual during warfare was the main preoccupation of the ICRC (Geneva Committee) since its creation. The first great gap to fill after the 1864 Convention was that of prisoners of war who were not injured or sick. The ICRC took action during the Franco-Prussian War (1870–71) and in a series of later armed conflicts. Eventually, rules were adopted on that question in the Hague

---

[16] See Amelioration of the Condition of the Wounded in Armies in the Field (signed 22 August 1864, entered into force 22 June 1865) published in *The Laws of Armed Conflicts* (n 9) 365 ff.

Convention II of 1899/IV of 1907,[17] later in the Geneva Convention of 1929.[18] The next great gap was the protection of civilians, in and outside the context of combats. Some rules were devised for civilians in occupied territory, thus outside combat contexts (Hague Convention II/IV).[19] For the situation during combats, the ICRC concentrated much effort during the 1920s and 1930s. This was without immediate success: some important States did at that time strenuously resist to any international regulation on the matter. The breakthrough came only with Geneva Convention IV of 1949, after the appalling experiences during the World War. Finally, there was the gap in non-international armed conflicts. It was partly filled in 1949, in common article 3 of the Geneva Conventions, later in Additional Protocol II of 1977,[20] and still later by a conspicuous development of customary international law.[21] It is sufficiently known how precarious the application of these humanitarian norms is, especially in non-international armed conflicts. This is however no reason not to fight for their better dissemination and implementation.

2.2.9. *Geneva Conventions of 1949 and Evolutions since Then*

The adoption of the Geneva Conventions in 1949 (to which were later added the two major Additional Protocols of 1977) marked a radical departure from old conceptions and ushered in a new universe regarding the law of war. Essentially, the Geneva Conventions transform the law of armed conflict in a 'humanitarian law'. The protection of the individual war victims becomes the pivotal centre of the system; international humanitarian law ceases to be merely (or even essentially) the old 'military law'. The law is now clearly predicated on the idea of a thorough international codification of mandatory norms of behaviour engrafted on belligerents, norms moreover locked up against derogation and reprisals. These are the three main features of this third phase: (i) humanitarian protection; (ii) friendly and co-operative relationships with human rights; (iii) detailed international

---

[17] Convention (II) with Respect to the Laws and Customs of War on Land and Its Annex: Regulations Concerning the Laws and Customs of War on Land Land (adopted 29 July 1899, entered into force 4 February 1900) published in *The Laws of Armed Conflicts* (n 9) 55 ff; Convention (IV) Respecting the Laws and Customs of War on Land and Its Annex: Regulations Concerning the Laws and Customs of War on Land (adopted 18 October 1907, entered into force 26 January 1910) published in *The Laws of Armed Conflicts* (n 9) 55 ff.

[18] Convention Relative to the Treatment of Prisoners of War (adopted 27 July 1929, entered into force 19 June 1931) in *The Laws of Armed Conflicts* (n 9) 271 ff.

[19] arts 44, 45, 50 and 52 of Convention (II); art 50 of Convention (IV).

[20] Protocol Additional to the Geneva Conventions of 12 August 1949, and Relating to the Protection of Victims of Non-International Armed Conflicts (Protocol II) (adopted 8 June 1977, entered into force 7 December 1978) 1125 UNTS 609.

[21] J-M Henckaerts and L Doswald-Beck *Customary International Humanitarian Law* (3 vols CUP Cambridge 2005).

codification. The protective rules are now progressively extended to non-international armed conflict (article 3 common of the Geneva Conventions; Additional Protocol II of 1977; and other sources). Rules on means and methods of warfare, not revised since the Hague Codification and some punctual later treaties (for example, the Geneva Gas Protocol of 1925) are made the object of a new rules in Additional Protocol I of 1977, especially in articles 48 ff. As times goes on, the arm of international human rights law has grown longer. Thus, international humanitarian law and international human rights law start to interact together. The complex relationships of international humanitarian law and international human rights law are today on of the paramount fields of study in the context of the protection of the individual.

3. THE HISTORY OF INTERNATIONAL HUMAN RIGHTS LAW BEFORE 1945

3.1. General Aspects

Human rights law emerged in Europe in the wake of the subjectivist revolution of Enlightenment. Man, with his inalienable and pre-positive rights, was now put at the centre of the new 'natural law constructions'. However, for a long time, such rights were limited to 'civil society', that is, to municipal law, where they were guaranteed by Bills of Rights[22] and organs of judicial control. International society was since the Westphalian Peace (1648) progressively restricted to inter-state relations. Moreover, it was held to be a 'natural society', deprived of guaranteed individual rights.

Some degree of protection of individuals was nonetheless developed. It was often collective rather than individual (thus not a human rights device), and linked to nationality rather than granted to every human being (again unlike human rights). In the period of modern international law before the League of Nations (17th century to 1919), there were essentially three modalities of protection: (i) particular rights granted to individuals by treaty, such as a right of option for nationality; (ii) forcible or non-forcible humanitarian intervention; (iii) the

---

[22] Eg the Petition of Rights (England, 1628) or the Habeas Corpus Act (England, 1679); the Virginia Bill of Rights of 1776; or the Déclaration des droits de l'homme et du citoyen (France, 1789). Such a Bill of rights was proposed also for international law (and it became reality with the Declaration of 1948); H Lauterpacht *An International Bill of the Rights of Man* (OUP London 1945).

minimum standard of treatment for aliens. In the period of the League of Nations (1919–46), three new instruments were added to the old ones (but forcible human-itarian intervention was now progressively rejected): (i) the protection of workers through ILO; (ii) the protection of minorities through a series of particular trea-ties; (iii) the protection of formerly colonial peoples trough some supervision of the international 'mandates' (article 22 of the League of Nations Covenant). At the same time, a human rights movement proper was set in motion, as is shown by the work of the *Institut de droit international* of 1929. It would however be realized in positive law only through the Charter of the UN (1945), the Universal Declaration of Human Rights of 1948 (which was 'only' a resolution of the General Assembly and not, initially, binding law), the European Convention on Human Rights (1950), and later trough the UN Covenants of 1966. Apart from the mentioned regimes and institutions, there were some other new areas of action protective of the individual. Thus, for example, at the beginning of the 20th century, the law relating to refugees was in the phase of birth; and action had been taken to abolish slavery and slave trade.

3.2. Specific Institutions

3.2.1. *Rights of Nationality Option*

In ancient treaties, the right was granted to persons to retain their old nationality in case of cession or conquest of a territory.[23] The exercise of this right was sometimes linked to emigration.[24] The law relating to the option of nationality was fixed in an exemplary way in the Peace Treaty of Zurich (1859),[25] putting an end to the Italian War in which, accidentally, the battle of Solferino had taken place. The rights of option thereafter arrived at a peak in the peace settlement after the First World War.[26] The right of option was thus linked with the right to freedom of religion and to choice of nationality.

---

[23] See already F Stoerk *Option und Plebicit bei Eroberungen und Gebietscessionen* (Leipzig 1879); for more recent account, see Y Ronen 'Option of Nationality' in R Wolfrum (ed) *The Max Planck Encyclopedia of Public International Law* (OUP Oxford 2008) at <www.mpepil.com>.

[24] Conversely, emigration was sometimes the hallmark of religious freedom, in application of the principle *cuius regio, eius religio*. The person who wanted to retain his religious belief contrary to that of the new rules was granted the right to emigrate. This was the system of the Peace Treaties of Augsburg (1555) and of Westphalia (1648); for the Westphalian Treaties, see art 5 of the Treaty of Osnabrück (1648) and its confirmation in the Treaty of Münster (1648) para 47.

[25] Zurich, Austria–France (signed 10 November 1859) 121 CTS 145.

[26] See JL Kunz 'L'option de nationalité' (1930-I) 31 Recueil des cours 107–76.

3.2.2. *Humanitarian Intervention*

In the 19th century *ius publicum europaeum*, the practice emerged to allow humanitarian interventions in favour notably of persecuted Christians, notably in the Ottoman empire. In a series of old treaties, dating back to the 17th century, the Turks had accepted that France, Austria and Russia could protect orthodox or catholic Christians, even of Ottoman nationality, when domiciled on its territory. In the Treaty of Vienna of 1856 and the Treaty of Berlin of 1878, the Ottoman empire had formally promised to grant these Christians equality of treatment. It also guaranteed to offer them the necessary protection against assaults and inhuman treatment by Turkish nationals. It is on the basis of that particular law that the European powers intervened more than once in the empire, at a time when general international law did not prohibit the use of force. There was here, to some extent, a double permissive title for action: (i) the treaties granting supervisory rights to the powers; (ii) the freedom to use force in international relations, especially for cases of urgent necessity such as the protection of life and limb. However, humanitarian interventions, forcible or not, took place also in other areas, and even in Europe itself, for example, in the Two Sicilies. Overall, there is thus little doubt that a permissive custom of intervention existed at the time, condoned by the powers in Europe, and thus rooted in the *ius publicum europaeum* (to which Turkey had been admitted since 1856). Among the examples of such interventions are the intervention of France and Britain in Greece (1827) ('in order to stop the shedding of blood and mischiefs by the Turks') and that of France and Britain in 1856 in the Kingdom of the Two Sicilies following a series of politically motivated arrests and alleged cruel and arbitrary treatment of these political prisoners.

Even outside the larger European context, intervention was justified on the same lines. The intervention of the United States in Cuba in 1898 was, among other things, justified on humanitarian grounds. It is true that these interventions were never pursued *only* for purely unselfish reasons, but that should come as no surprise. It is also true that they were predicated on the protection of Christians, and were thus selective. However, some interventions also corresponded, at least in part, to genuine humanitarian concerns. They were rooted in an ideological stream of opinion, widely shared in the 19th century that was centred upon humanitarian values. This was part and parcel of the concept, widely held at that time, of 'civilized nations'. The idea of civilization, on which Europe prided itself, had given rise to the fight against slavery and diseases, to the effort to protect the wounded and sick in war (Henry Dunant's Red Cross Movement), and to a series of other agendas. It also found a kind of natural playground in the field of humanitarian intervention. At bottom, this humanitarian ideology finds its root in the idea of civic liberalism and of the rule of law, of paramount importance to the 19th century. By the end of the 19th century, doctrinal support for humanitarian intervention was split. Anglo-Saxon writers generally supported humanitarian intervention by invoking natural law precepts: one may

recall here ES Creasy,[27] WE Hall,[28] H Wheaton,[29] or TJ Lawrence.[30] Continental writers, on the other hand, had started to contest the principle as being incompatible with
positive international law and the equality of States: such was the position of P.
Pradier-Fodéré,[31] AW Heffter,[32] F von Liszt,[33] T Funck-Brentano and A Sorel.[34] Other
authors believed that humanitarian intervention could not 'be called legally right,
but [could] be morally justifiable and even commendable'; they were thought to be
an act of policy above and beyond the domain of law.[35] Still others, like E Arntz
thought that humanitarian intervention should be admissible, but that it should not
be exercised unilaterally. Rather, such a right should only be exercised in the name of
all humanity, presupposing a collective decision by all States except the tortfeasor, or
at least of the greatest number possible of civilized States.[36] Finally, the issue of
humanitarian intervention became intermingled with (and indeed pushed back by)
the newly developing *ius contra bellum* of the League of Nations Covenant, the Pact
of Paris (Briand–Kellogg) and the UN Charter. Under the charter, it was held that
humanitarian intervention could be lawful only if decided (or authorized) by the UN
Security Council (and eventually by the General Assembly under the Dean Acheson
Resolution). Action should thus be taken, but under a collective umbrella (see also
the notion of 'Responsibility to Protect'). Forcible action should be only the
ultimissima ratio. The Kosovo episode of 1999 showed that the concept of humanitarian intervention remains to some extent controversial. It was mentioned here as a
forerunner of international human rights only in the sense that it at least also served
to protect groups of individuals against persecution and death.

3.2.3. *The Minimum Standard of Treatment of Aliens*

The concept of a 'minimum standard of treatment of aliens'[37] was developed in the
diplomatic practice of States since the 18th century. It grew out of the old practice of

---

[27] ES Creasy *First Platform of International Law* (John van Voorst London 1876) at 297.

[28] WE Hall *A Treatise on International Law* (Clarendon Press Oxford 1880) at 247.

[29] H Wheaton *Elements of International Law* (2 vols B. Fellowes London 1836) at 69.

[30] TJ Lawrence *The Principles of International Law* (5th edn Heath Boston 1913) at 66.

[31] PLE Pradier-Fodéré *Traité de droit international public européen et américain* (A Durand & Pedone-
Lauriel Paris 1885–1905) vol 1, at 663.

[32] AW Heffter *Le droit international de l'Europe* (J Bergson trans) (HW Müller Berlin 1883) at 113.

[33] F von Liszt *Das Völkerrecht* (Haering Berlin 1898) at 122.

[34] T Funck-Brentano and A Sorel *Précis du droit des gens* (E Plon, Nourrit et Cie Paris 1877) at 223.

[35] CH Stockton *Outlines of International Law* (C Scribner's Sons New York 1914) at 100.

[36] See E Nys *Le droit international* (Marcel Rivière Paris 1912) vol 2, at 232, quoting Arntz; see also eg
WE Hall *A Treatise on International Law* (P Higgins ed) (8th edn Clarendon Press Oxford 1924) at 344.

[37] See A Roth *The Minimum Standard of International Law Applied to Aliens* (Sijthoff The Hague
1949); E Borchard *The Diplomatic Protection of Citizens Abroad* (The Banks Law Publisher New York
1915); the term 'minimum standard' comes from the idea that a State may treat foreigners as he treats its
own citizens, since discrimination may be resented as being unjustified (standard of national treatment).
However, this standard may not fall below a minimum of civilization. In other words, it would not be
allowable to mistreat foreigners simply because you also mistreat your own population. A 'minimum

reprisals for the torts committed on the subjects of a king abroad, initially often merchants. If *lettres de représailles* could he meted out in order to recover the losses illegally suffered by a citizen abroad, it was implicit that a ruler could first complain to the other that a tort had been committed and require that the matter be investigated and eventually the tort repaired. Hence, diplomatic protection developed under the umbrella of restrictive necessity: reprisals were not lawful if there had not been an attempt to obtain peaceful reparation from the wrongdoing collectivity.[38] The claim brought forward in such cases was, from the point of view of substantive law, that some rights of the foreigner under international law (that is, due to his State of origin) had been violated. This, in turn, progressively produced a catalogue of substantive rights, which has been progressively claimed in diplomatic protection. Roughly speaking, these rights concentrated around the following four spheres: (i) life, liberty and honour (for example, habeas corpus); (ii) property; (iii) freedom of religion and creed; (iv) denial of justice (fair trial: access to a local tribunal and also a substantively due process of law). The minimum standard of treatment was thus the international legal institution coming closest to modern human rights law. It differed structurally from human rights law only in the restricted entitlement to the granted rights: these were rights only of the foreigners. International law thus in that time uphold the rule that the treatment of its own nationals by a State was a domestic affair which it could not regulate. Conversely, the treatment of foreigners was not a simply domestic affair since the rights of other States (trough their nationals) were at stake. Hence, international law could deal with these aspects. After 1945, it has been claimed that the minimum standard was abandoned. It discriminatory edge (foreigners/nationals) was henceforth resented. Thus, the minimum standard has been held to have merged into the more general human right law movement and indeed it has been progressively retreating in State practice. However, diplomatic protection for violation of granted rights (be they minimum standard rights or human rights) has remained frequent.

3.2.4. *Workers Protection through ILO*

During the 19th century, the spread of industrial work had brought to a glaring light the necessity to improve the condition of the masses of industrial workers if social peace and justice were to be secured. The rise of communism had made that approach to some extent popular also in the spectrum of the moderate conservatives, since it

standard' must thus always be guaranteed; see H Kelsen 'Théorie générale du droit international public' (1932-IV) 42 Recueil des cours 248–9.

[38] See *Le droit des gens* (n 2) vol 1, book 2, ch 18, para 338: 'Son propre avantage [of the aggrieved party] et celui de la société humaine l'obligent à tenter, avant que d'en venir aux armes, tous les moyens pacifiques d'obtenir ou la réparation de l'injure, ou une juste satisfaction.…Souvent, même, il arrive que l'injure est faite par des subalternes, sans que leur Souverain y ait aucune part: et dans ces occasions, il est naturel de présumer qu'on ne nous refusera pas une juste satisfaction.'

was perceived as a bulwark against communist agitation. The Preamble of the Constitution of the ILO (1919), incorporated into the Versailles Treaty (Section XIII), expressed this endeavour in clear terms: universal peace could be established only if it was based on social justice; conditions of labour existed which involved such injustice, hardship and privation imperilled the peace and harmony of the world. Moreover, it was acknowledged that action could only be taken trough international cooperation: the failure of any nation to adopt humane conditions of labour was an obstacle for other nations which desired to improve conditions in their own countries (through 'social dumping'). The ILO was thus set up. Under its aegis, a series of conventions and control mechanisms were set up in order to improve the condition of workers. The conventions touched upon a series of typically 'human rights' questions in the area of labour: protection of women and children; non-discrimination; safety at work; freedom of association and belief; etc. There are today roughly 200 such protective treaties concluded under the arm of the ILO.

3.2.5. *Protection of Minorities*

The protection of minorities falls into two great phases. The *first phase*, from the times of the Treaties of Westphalia to the end of the First World War was based on a series of conventional provisions guaranteeing freedom of religion for certain religious minorities. These provisions were however relatively vague, haphazard, and fragmentary. They did not constitute a system for the protection of minorities. Moreover, there was no institutional control for their implementation. Such provisions can be found, amongst others, in the Treaties of Osnabrück and Münster (1648), protecting catholic or protestant minorities finding themselves in territories dominated by the 'adverse' faith ('*cuius regio, eius religio*'). Another example is the Treaty of Oliva (1660), by which Poland and the Great Elector (Prussia) ceded Pomerania and Livonia to Sweden, but at the same time guaranteeing the inhabitants of the ceded territories the enjoyment of their existing religious liberties. Such provisions can also be found in a series of treaties of the 17th and 18th centuries, such as Utrecht (1713) and Paris (1763) on the protection of religious minorities in the North American colonies, concluded between France and Great-Britain; the treaties between Russia and Poland (1773, 1775) on the protection of religious minorities; the treaty of Küçük Kaynardji (1774) between Russia and the Ottoman empire, on the protection of Christian minorities in Turkey; the Treaty of Vienna (1815), including clauses on the protection of Poles inhabiting States parties to the treaty; or in the Treaty of Berlin (1878), concerning the Turkish, Romanian, and Greek minorities in Bulgaria. The *second phase* is the system of protection created after the First World War within the framework of the League of Nations. Territorial changes in Europe, due to the collapse of the Austro-Hungarian and the Ottoman empires, brought to the fore acute problems of minorities in most parts of Eastern Europe. The peace treaties concluded with the various vanquished States of the region (Austria, Bulgaria, Hungary, Turkey) contained clauses for the protection of minorities. Further agreements of this type were concluded with the five States where the problems of minorities were acute: Poland, Czechoslovakia, Yugoslavia, Romania and Greece. For certain other States, the acceptance of obligations with regard to minorities was made the condition for their membership to the League (Albania, Estonia, Finland [Åland Islands], or Iraq). The obligations assumed spanned from fundamental freedoms to equality before the law, prohibition of discrimination, freedom to use one's own language, and freedom to run one's own minority schools. The undertakings assumed were the object of two guarantees. First, the States concerned had to recognize, in their respective legal orders, that provisions relating to minorities were fundamental laws not liable to be modified or abrogated by ordinary laws. Amendments had moreover to be approved by the Council of the League of Nations. Second, complains for breaches could be brought to the Council of the League of Nations and, if the dispute was between States and persisted, to the PCIJ. The minorities regime of the League worked approximately well at the beginning of the 1920, despite of many political tensions. It came into crisis at the end of the 1920s. One of the difficulties was that it was based on discrimination contrary to equality between States: some States, especially the vanquished ones, were subjected to international scrutiny of their minority obligations; other States were not subjected to such obligations.

3.2.6. *Protection of the People of Mandated Territories*

The territories detached from Germany and Turkey after the First World War were not annexed by the victorious powers but placed under the control of a trustee under the supervision of the League of Nations (article 22 of the League of Nations Covenant). The administration of these territories had to be performed with a view to insuring the well-being and development of such 'backward' peoples. The economic exploitation of the territory or its population was forbidden. The Council of the League of Nations was to control the way in which the mandated powers would perform their administration. In its task, the Council was assisted by a Permanent Mandates Commission (see article 22, § 9 of the covenant). The Commission and the Council received some petitions from the inhabitants of the mandated territories, through the channel of the mandatory government. The Mandates Commission or the council could then influence the policy of the mandatory power towards an improvement of the rights of the local inhabitants. Overall, this was only timidly done, but it must be noted that the Mandates Commission exerted a significant influence during the 1920s.

3.2.7. *The Resolution of the Institut de Droit International of 1929*

In the 1920s, the most progressive international lawyers fought for a generalization of the minorities protection regime. The regime of protection should first cast away the limitation to minorities in order to embrace all human beings. Second, the regime should not apply only to some States bound by a particular treaty, but to all States as a minimum standard of civilization. André Mandelstam, member of the *Institut de droit international*, has been particularly active in this effort.[39] After some drafts he presented to the *Institut de droit international*, this institution adopted in 1929 its resolution bearing the title 'Déclaration des droits internationaux de l'homme'.[40] The Preamble states that: 'Considérant que la conscience juridique du monde civilisé exige la reconnaissance à l'individu de droits soustraits à toute atteinte de la part de l'Etat...; qu'il importe d'étendre au monde entier la reconnaissance internationale des droits de l'homme'. Article 1 of the resolution then proceeds to require from States that they recognize to every person the right to life, to freedom, to property, and to grant the person the protection of the law without any discrimination. Article 2 concerns the freedom of religion or creed. Article 3 guarantees the free usage of one's own language and the related freedom to teach this language. Article 4 touches upon the right to access to different professions and schools, without discrimination. Article 5 concerns non-discrimination and material (not only formal) equality. Finally, article 6 prohibits any forfeiture of nationality for minorities on a State's territory, reserving only motives provided for in general laws, applicable to all persons. This resolution thus embodies a short Bill of Rights fusing together the minimum standard of treatment and the minority protection regimes. However, it constituted in 1929 only a recommendation to governments. It did not reflect, at that time, the positive law of nations. The treatment of its own nationals remained for every State a matter of domestic jurisdiction to the extent it had not undertaken international obligations by way of binding conventions. It was only with the Charter of the United Nations in 1945 that the legal position would change and that human rights became not only a matter of international concern, but also, progressively, a matter of positive international law.

4. Conclusion

Overall, it can thus be seen that a full-fledged protection of the individual at the international level arrives relatively late in legal history. It began in the 19th century and grew enormously in the 20th century. Keen attention for the fortunes of individuals

[39] AN Mandelstam 'La protection internationale des droits de l'homme' (1931-IV) 38 Recueil des cours 125–232 at 129 ff.

[40] Institut de Droit International 'Déclaration des droits internationaux de l'homme' (1929) 35 Annuaire 298–300 and 110–38.

supposes a high degree of civilization. At early stages, social ideology is caught up in the categories of group solidarity and *morale close*. Only through a long historical evolution morality develops into the more refined flower of compassion and care for the individual and its personal fate. The international society is no exception to that rule. Its all-embracing character and its great spatial extension explains its slower evolution. The grater a space is, and the slower time flows for it. It is therefore only in the last two centuries that the individual could fully catch the attention of its particular legal order, namely public international law.

RECOMMENDED READING

Best, Geoffrey *Humanity in Warfare: The Modern History of the International Law of Armed Conflicts* (Weidenfeld & Nicolson Ltd London 1980).

Bugnion, François *Le comité international de la Croix-Rouge et la protection des victimes de la guerre* (International Committee of the Red Cross Geneva 1994).

Burgers, Jan H 'The Road to San Francisco: The Revival of the Human Rights Idea in the Twentieth Century' (1992) 14 Human Rights Quarterly 447–77.

Hunt, Lynn *Inventing Human Rights: A History* (WW Norton & Company New York 2007).

Kolb, Robert *Ius in bello: le droit international des conflits armés: précis* (Helbing Lichtenhahn Basel 2009).

Lauren, Paul G *The Evolution of International Human Rights: Visions Seen* (University of Pennsylvania Press Philadelphia 2003).

Lauterpacht, Hersch *International Law and Human Rights* (Stevens London 1950).

Mandelstam, André N 'La protection internationale des droits de l'homme' (1931-IV) 38 Recueil des cours 125–232.

Meron, Theodor *The Humanization of International Law* (Martinus Nijhoff Publisher Leiden 2006).

Opitz, Peter-Joachim *Menschenrechte und Internationaler Menschenrechtsschutz im 20. Jahrhundert: Geschichte und Dokumente* (Fink München 2002).

Scott, James B 'La Déclaration internationale des droits de l'homme'(1930) 5 Revue de droit international (Paris) 79–99.

Sohn, Louis B 'How American International Lawyers Prepared for the San Fransisco Bill of Rights' (1995) 89 The American Journal of International Law 540–53.

Szabo, Imre 'Fondements historiques et développement des droits de l'homme' in Karel Vasak (ed) *Les dimensions internationales des droits de l'homme: Manuel destiné à l'enseignement des droits de l'homme dans les Universités* (UNESCO Paris 1978) 11–44.

Verdoodt, Albert *Naissance et signification de la déclaration universelle des droits de l'homme* (Warny Louvain 1964).

CHAPTER 14

TRADE, CHARTERED COMPANIES, AND MERCANTILE ASSOCIATIONS

KOEN STAPELBROEK

1. GROTIUS AND THE DUTCH EAST INDIA COMPANY

ON the morning of 25 February 1603, the Portuguese carrack 'Santa Catarina' was seized off the coast of Singapore by three ships of the United Amsterdam Company, falling under the command of Jacob van Heemskerk. In September 1604, the ship and its cargo were sentenced forfeited by the Amsterdam Admiralty Court and confiscated by the Dutch East India Company (*Vereenigde Oost-Indische Compagnie*, VOC).[1] The latter had been established by state charter in March 1602 on the foundations of the Amsterdam Company and other 'pre-companies'.[2]

---

[1] MJ van Ittersum *Profit and Principle: Hugo Grotius, Natural Rights Theories and the Rise of Dutch Power in the East Indies 1595–1615* (Brill Leiden 2006) 20–4. The verdict is in H Grotius *Commentary on the Law of Prize and Booty* (Liberty Fund Indianapolis 2006) 510–14.

[2] For a transcription and English translation of the charter, E Gepken-Jager, G van Solinge, and L Timmerman (eds) *VOC 1602–2002: 400 Years of Company Law* (Kluwer Deventer 2005) 17–38.

In the aftermath of the verdict, the twenty-one-year old Hugo Grotius—a distant family member of Heemskerk—was commissioned by the company directors to compose a public defence of the cause of the VOC. Grotius himself noted a few years later that the purpose of the text he wrote (which was discovered in 1864 and is now known as *De jure praedae*) was to explore issues of war and trade in the Indies that clearly were going to determine the future of the United Provinces.[3] In the context of negotiations with Spain over a truce during the Eighty Years' War, one chapter of the manuscript was prepared for separate publication as *De mare liberum*. This text, belatedly published in 1609, drew written critiques from British lawyers, first in 1610 contesting the rights of Dutch herring fishers in Scottish waters and between 1613 and 1615 in the context of a series of Anglo-Dutch negotiations over the legality of Dutch claims to exclusive trade rights.[4]

Grotius' perspective on the legal proceedings following the capture of the 'Santa Catarina' is not a theme to engage with here.[5] Neither is this the place to relate scholarly debate on the idea of the *ius gladii* in *De jure praedae* and modern rights traditions to the specific case of the VOC.[6] What is of interest is the influence of the legal principles put forward by Grotius within his Dutch context on the history of overseas company trade. It has long been accepted that both early modern state-building and the development of international law were historically related to company trade, yet no clear understanding exists of the nature of these links.

But the real challenge in this regard is not bringing together history and theory. From the late 19th century—coinciding with a hinging point in Dutch history and identity construction—Grotius may have been heralded as the person responsible for the establishment of international law.[7] However, understanding the role of legal notions in the actual historical creation and gradually evolving functioning of a new kind of commercial-political entity, requires a distinctly non-doctrinal focus.[8]

---

[3] He did so in his *Defensio capitis quinti maris liberi oppugnati a Gulielmo Welwodo*, see R Fruin 'Een Onuitgegeven Werk van Hugo De Groot' (An Unpublished Work by Grotius) (1868) 32 De Gids 1–37 and 215–54 at 3; and MJ van Ittersum 'The Long Goodbye: Hugo Grotius' Justification of Dutch Expansion Overseas, 1615–1645' (2010) 36 History of European Ideas 386–411.

[4] W Welwod *An Abridgement of All Sea-Lawes* (1613) and *De dominio maris* (1615). More famous is J Selden *Mare clausum* (1618); see GN Clark and WJM van Eysinga (eds) *The Colonial Conferences between England and the Netherlands in 1613 and 1615* (2 vols Brill Leiden 1940–51).

[5] See on this theme *Profit and Principle* (n 1) 24–30.

[6] R Tuck *The Rights of War and Peace: Political Thought and the International Order from Grotius to Kant* (OUP Oxford 1999) identified the theory of punishment in H Grotius *De jure praedae* (1604/05) as a progenitor to modern politics.

[7] Classically H Lauterpacht 'The Grotian Tradition in International Law' (1946) 23 British Yearbook of International Law 1–53; C van Vollenhoven *The Three Stages in the Evolution of the Law of Nations* (Nijhoff The Hague 1919), compare with R Fruin 'De drie tijdvakken der Nederlandsche geschiedenis' (The Three Stages in Dutch History) (1865) 29 De Gids 245–71. The stark contrast between the idea of the Grotian tradition and recent studies is discussed by G van Nifterik and J Nijman 'Introduction: Mare Liberum Revisited (1609–2009)' (2009) 30 Grotiana 3–19 at 8–9

[8] See CG Roelofsen 'Hugo de Groot en de VOC' in J Trapman (ed) *De Hollandse jaren van Hugo de Groot (1583–1621)* (*The Dutch Years of Hugo de Groot*) (Verloren Hilversum 1996) 57–66.

What deserves immediate attention in this chapter is the widespread common-sense notion that chartered companies were somehow designed as instruments of colonialism. From around 1900, overseas trade companies generally were deemed agencies of colonial conquest.[9] This is at odds with the combined legal, political, and economic views of the great majority of statesmen, company directors, and political writers who were involved in the early 17th-century creation of chartered companies. Notably, Grotius's early writings, which more than any other text of its time were concerned with delineating the legal and political principles of company trade, outlined the boundaries separating war, trade, and conquest.

If the history of company trade, then, is not as straightforward as might be expected, the aim of this chapter is to recapture the intellectual horizons under which companies like the VOC were conceived and in the next two centuries evaluated. In doing so, a key element is to make sense of how legal positions on company trade fit with 17th- and 18th-century political and economic thought on inter-state relations. Thus far, the legal aspects of overseas trade and the early stages of colonial rule have not been treated in this historical context.[10] The issue of Grotius and the VOC is a case in point. In contrast to the Dutch writer who holds a prominent place in the canon of international law, Grotius's early writings have been deconstructed as mere pieces of VOC propaganda.[11] While Grotius undoubtedly had his interested motives in writing what he wrote in his main legal treatises, this interpretation takes away from the intellectual challenge that Grotius himself saw in shaping the identity of the newly independent Dutch State.[12] It was within this process and with a long-

[9] The European literature, particularly from around 1900, contains many titles that aiming to reconstruct the origins of colonization assume an instrumental relationship between trade companies and territorial expansion.

[10] Their variety was categorized by J Fisch *Die europäische Expansion und das Völkerrecht: Die Auseinandersetzungen um den Status der überseeischen Gebiete vom 15. Jahrhundert bis zur Gegenwart* (Steiner Stuttgart 1984). J Fisch 'Law as a Means and as an End. Some Remarks on the Function of European and non-European Law in the Process of European Expansion' in WJ Mommsen and JA de Moor (eds) *European Expansion and Law. The Encounter of European and Indigenous Law in 19th- and 20th-Century Africa and Asia* (Berg Oxford 1991) 15–38 at 20–1 suggests that law turned from a mode of communication between societies, and a means towards realizing economic and political goals, into a an end in itself. Gradually, legal inequality and factual equality between European and indigenous parties transformed into legal equality and factual inequality. No general pattern, but the emergence through (eg common law) adaptations of an international plurality of legal regimes is discussed by LA Benton *Law and Colonial Cultures: Legal Regimes in World History 1400–1900* (CUP Cambridge 2002). WHJ Leue 'Legal Expansion in the Age of Companies: Aspects of the Administration of Justice in the English and Dutch Settlements of Maritime Asia, c. 1600–1750' in WJ Mommsen and JA de Moor (eds) *European Expansion and Law: The Encounter of European and Indigenous Law in 19th- and 20th-Century Africa and Asia* (Berg Oxford 1991) 129–58, argues there was an effective legislative void on restrictions of agency of the EIC and VOC in their Asian settlements. Cf CH Alexandrowicz *An Introduction to the History of the Law of Nations in the East Indies: 16th, 17th and 18th Centuries* (Clarendon Oxford 1967) and the thesis that the European rule of law tied together indigenous legal traditions into proper global international law.

[11] P Borschberg *Hugo Grotius, the Portuguese and Free Trade in the East Indies* (NUS Press Singapore 2011) and *Profit and Principle* (n 1).

[12] 'Een Onuitgegeven Werk van Hugo De Groot' (n 3) 8.

term outlook onto inter-state relations that this humanist historian turned political theorist worked towards an internally coherent system.[13]

Few economic historians now would disagree that the founding of the VOC would prove to be a watershed in the history of European overseas trade. Still, the reasons why this should be the case remain elusive.

2. PROFIT, POWER, AND SELF-PRESERVATION

Within the history of company trade, international lawyers traditionally have considered the empowerment of chartered companies to perform public or even sovereign acts. Companies soon after their creation became active treaty partners, in South-East Asia in particular. They also established titles over territory, primarily from the second half of the 18th century. The question to be asked before focusing on these issues is according to what broader logic companies acted when they became legal-political actors abroad.

Chartered companies have been researched extensively by economic historians.[14] One of the conclusions which emerged is that the motives that played a decisive role in the taking off of company trade cannot be phrased primarily in economic terms. Scholars agree that in the early 17th century, overseas trade was not a lucrative investment. In fact, the 'pre-companies', compared with the VOC, were often more profitable in terms of dividend payments.[15] The VOC has often been seen by economic historians as a failed enterprise because it did not make as large profits as shareholders at the time were promised and politicians suggested were being made.[16] The fact that the profit record was consistently under pressure, particularly in the case of the English East India Company, which was contractually obliged to annual payments to the government, gave rise to the idea that companies were forced to expand their activities. This required territorial occupation.[17]

---

[13] Hugo de Groot en de VOC (n 8) defends this approach as the basis for understanding Grotius' politics and diplomacy.

[14] The modern classic is N Steensgaard *The Asian Trade Revolution of the Seventeenth Century: The East India Companies and the Decline of the Caravan Trade* (University of Chicago Press Chicago 1974). Still providing a good overview L Blussé and F Gaastra (eds) *Companies and Trade. Essays on Overseas Trading Companies during the Ancien Régime* (Leiden University Press Leiden 1981); M Mollat (ed) *Sociétés et compagnies de commerce en Orient et dans l'Océan Indien* (SEVPEN Paris 1970).

[15] Eg 'Hugo de Groot en de VOC' (n 8) 60; cf 'Een Onuitgegeven Werk van Hugo De Groot' (n 3) 7, that the 'precompanies' often were *not* profitable.

[16] Noted by N Steensgaard 'The Companies as a Specific Institution in the History of European Expansion' in *Companies and Trade* (n 14) 245 and 249–51.

[17] Immediately after 1600 this became a VOC concern, see Section 5.

A different explanation of the companies taking on a political role from the one centring on profit ensues from the initial experience of the Dutch 'pre-companies'.[18] During their first voyages to Asia they witnessed that Portuguese power in Asia was not untouchable. While the Portuguese claimed exclusive jurisdiction and trade rights and attempted to aggressively defend them, they were unable to enforce their claims. In the context of the Dutch war against Spain, the States-General recognized overseas trade as providing a unique opportunity for the sea-borne population of the Dutch provinces to exert pressure onto its enemy.[19]

It is important to note that this explanation does not turn on the notion of the aggrandisement of power, commonly seen by economic historians as the counter pole to profit in accounting for the rise of company trade.[20] The VOC was not established as a war machine, for which there would have been no political support.[21] The combination of power and profit also does not capture the reasoning through which Dutch company trade was justified in the first decades after its founding. Rather, it was the case that the concepts of necessity and self-preservation coupled with the rhetoric of the Dutch Revolt against universal terror and Spanish monarchical abuse were transposed onto the domain of overseas trade.[22] Likewise, Grotius's justification of the VOC's depredations of enemy ships became a proxy for the identity of the new Dutch State, whose mission became to restore the *res communis* character of trade.[23] An important pointer in this regard lies in Pieter van Dam's *Beschryvinge van de Oostindische Compagnie*, of the late 17th century.[24] Van Dam accounted for the creation of the by then thriving VOC as a direct, but unintended effect of external Spanish threats, stimulating the Dutch to invent a new kind of livelihood that happened to neatly suit their natural condition and historical predicament. This contemporary outlook onto the causes leading to the establishment of the VOC favoured understanding the political, economic, and military benefits arising from trade, if not trade itself, as public goods.

In contrast to striking a dualistic balance of profit and power, this line of reasoning that was influential at the time derived the emergence of Dutch overseas profit-seeking from culturally ingrained resources for preserving the State and its population. The

[18] 'Een Onuitgegeven Werk van Hugo De Groot' (n 3) 7.

[19] 'Introduction: Mare Liberum Revisited' (n 7) 4.

[20] 'The Companies as a Specific Institution' (n 16) draws upon this dichotomous understanding.

[21] JA Somers *De VOC als volkenrechtelijke actor* (The VOC as an Actor under International Law) (Quint Gouda 2001) at 237–8; JA Somers and CG Roelofsen '"Mare liberum" and the Dutch East India Company: The Freedom of the Seas and Freedom of Trade as the Legal Bases of the Dutch Colonial State in the Indonesian Archipelago' (2004) 24/25 Grotiana 67–76 at 69.

[22] M van Gelderen *The Political Thought of the Dutch Revolt, 1555–1590* (CUP Cambridge 1992).

[23] E Wilson *The Savage Republic: De Indis of Hugo Grotius, Republicanism and Dutch Hegemony within the Early Modern World-System (c. 1600–1619)* (Nijhoff The Hague 2008); and E Wilson 'The VOC, Corporate Sovereignty and the Republican Sub-Text of De iure praedae' (2009) 26–8 Grotiana 310–40.

[24] P van Dam *Beschryvinge van de Oostindische Compagnie* (*Description of the East Indies Company*) (F W Stapel ed) (Rijks Geschiedkundige Publicatiën The Hague 1927) vol 1, at 7–9.

'intrinsic power' of the nation constituted a kind of right, it suggested.[25] Spanning the domains of political, legal, and economic argument, this logic provided a touchstone for Dutch state building (starting from resistance against Spain). How this type of argument related to company trade and its legal politics and whether within other European States similar justifications for expansionist overseas trade were generated is discussed below. What must be noted as well is that the political and economic rationale from which the legal positions of the big chartered companies were originally created diverges from the political thought that accompanied the intense rivalry among Europe's dominant States that gave rise to empire building in the 18th century.[26]

3. Chartered Companies in the History of Trade Organizations

The point about separating the age of company trade from European empire building (without denying that chartered companies paved the way for colonialism) has often been made.[27] The other side of the question has equally triggered much discussion: can the big chartered trade companies of the 17th century be understood as extrapolations of previous company systems?

In terms of organizational characteristics, the idea of a linear progress from the medieval company to the present-day multinational has steadfastly been rejected. Company history, in Steensgaard's words, was the unintended product of 'a unique encounter between political power and market oriented entrepreneurship' and is too 'rich in mutations and regressions' to be understood as the accumulated 'experience of generations'.[28] The same author argued that the chartered companies of the 17th

---

[25] I de Pinto *Second discours d'un bon Hollandais à ses compatriotes* (1779) at 11 and 27–32, written with an eye on inter-state stability in trade and war, formed a late version of this argument.

[26] See I Hont *Jealousy of Trade: International Competition and the Nation-State in Historical Perspective* (Harvard University Press Cambridge MA 2005).

[27] D Lombard 'Questions on the Contact between European Companies and Asian Societies' in *Companies and Trade* (n 14) 179.

[28] 'The Companies as a Specific Institution' (n 16) 246. For a legal perspective see S Tully *Corporations and International Lawmaking* (Nijhoff The Hague 2007) 33–9; K Nowrot *Normative Ordnungsstruktur und private Wirkungsmacht* (Berliner Wissenschafts-Verlag Berlin 2006) 100–10; and F Johns (ed) *International Legal Personality* (Ashgate Farnham 2010). WR Scott *The Constitution and Finance of English, Scottish, and Irish Joint-Stock Companies to 1720* (3 vols CUP Cambridge 1912); and CT Carr *Select Charters of Trading Companies, A.D. 1530–1707* (Selden Society London 1913) provide commentary on the charter history and organizational logic of regulative associations. W Hartung *Geschichte und Rechtsstellung der Compagnie in Europa: Eine Untersuchung am Beispiel der englischen East-India Company, der*

century effected a 'metamorphosis' of corporative structures, owing to institutional control by the State over company trade, generating new forms of finance and foreign trade policy.[29] How might this shift be explained?

As is well known, from late medieval times onwards, traders, and other economic professions organized themselves in the form of societies to spread risks. Precisely with regard to foreign enterprise, mercantile associations had the added advantage that participants could profit from shared knowledge and information and resources. Early forms of agency-networks and banking services arose through locally and transnationally organized structures, such as the Hanseatic League and the Italian trade communities that connected Northwest Europe to Byzantium during and in the aftermath of the religious crusades. Some of these organizations that functioned as economic partnerships also, again from medieval times, temporarily enjoyed governmentally delegated authority and property rights.[30]

In contrast to these economic partnerships, and forming a different kind of company organization, regulated companies functioned as unincorporated trade guilds— forming a chartered professional body of merchants with rights (for example, trade monopolies) and duties (notably fiscal ones). In late 17th-century England, regulated companies flourished and generated short-term economic partnerships, for instance within the Levant Company and the Muscovy Company.[31] From this context and the mixture of the two basic early-modern company models sprang the English East India Company (originally named The Company of Merchants of London Trading into the East Indies, EIC), which got its charter on 31 December 1600, more than a year before the Dutch 'pre-companies' merged into the VOC.

Yet the combination of economic partnership and regulative charter in the evolution of company structures cannot explain the above mentioned 'metamorphosis'. Most of these companies in England and elsewhere only lasted as a short-lived model. They functioned well while they facilitated the initial exploitation of new trade channels and the introduction of new products in domestic markets, but were not economically viable beyond this stage without protectionism.[32]

In response to his own questions about the structure of company history, Steensgaard identified three phases within the trade company 'movement' and suggested these to be decisively influenced by 'political events' (see Section 7). However, the model of two categories of external political events on the one hand and the fixed

niederländischen Vereenigten Oostindischen Compagnie und der preußischen Seehandlung (thesis Bonn 2000) argues that chartered companies *can* be seen as precursors to modern multinationals.

[29] *The Asian Trade Revolution of the Seventeenth Century* (n 14) 127.

[30] 'The Companies as a Specific Institution' (n 16) 247–8; PW Klein 'The Origins of Trading Companies' in *Companies and Trade* (n 14) 18–20 and 23–4.

[31] 'The Companies as a Specific Institution' (n 16) 248–9; R Robert *Chartered Companies and Their Role in the Development of Overseas Trade* (Bell London 1969); P Griffiths *A Licence to Trade: The History of English Chartered Companies* (Benn London 1974).

[32] 'The Origins of Trading Companies' (n 30).

rules of the market as a constant factor on the other providing the ingredients that make up company history seems overly generic and unspecified. If historically as well as organizationally the success of the main chartered companies seems demarcated from previous and later developments, it is hardly satisfactory to explain their rise within a wider world historical perspective of 'expansion and reaction'.[33] Instead of referring to an autonomous dynamic leading to the creation of independent States out of bankrupt colonial commerce, it is more instructive to grasp the specific interconnections between trade, finance, and sovereignty that arose in the history of company trade.

Steensgaard's conclusion that chartered companies 'represented a fusion of governmental and entrepreneurial interests' is the starting point for further investigation. In contrast to his idea that political events were external aspects impinging upon markets ending with the economic emancipation of post-colonial States, there was an earlier storyline. Deploying, for instance, Adam Anderson's late 18th-century conjectural history of commerce, late 19th-century writers highlighted the continuity in processes by which European States brought economic processes under their control. Within this general history and through the underlying subtext of politics absorbing commerce, company charters were described as a further instance of formally depersonalized power expropriating individual interest. Just as foreign trade followed from development of 'the trades' within a society, so staple rights and company charters successively intervened in this evolutionary development. Company trade followed from these interventions in the natural history of trade.[34]

Recently, essential parts of this 19th-century state-formation theory have been criticized for imposing an a-historical teleology onto historical reality. Against the notion of a 'division' within company history of a 'trading' and an 'imperial' period, but equally a rejection of the idea that companies were a manifestation of States controlling trade and expanding the horizons of control outside their domain of sovereignty, recent studies have reconsidered the governmental practices and legal personality of the VOC and the EIC in their time.[35] Rather than to separate States from commercial bodies invested with delegated rights, these studies suggest that European States them-

[33] Cf 'The Companies as a Specific Institution' (n 16) 245–6 and 264. Expansion and reaction as an overarching historical pattern rationalizes losses of power and profit as investments in the construction of the modern world market is central to HL Wesseling *Expansion and Reaction: Essays on European Expansion and Reactions in Asia and Africa* (Leiden University Press Leiden 1978). Alternatively, the evolution of mercantile organizations allows itself to be described as one process only in 'intermediate synthesis': JD Tracy *The Political Economy of Merchant Empires* (CUP Cambridge 1997) at vii.

[34] G Cawston and AH Keane *The Early Chartered Companies (A.D. 1296–1858)* (Arnold London 1896) at 2 with reference to A Anderson *An Historical and Chronological Deduction of the Origin of Commerce* (2 vols Millar London 1764); compare M Weber *Zur Geschichte der Handelsgesellschaften im Mittelalter: Nach südeuropäischen Quellen* (Enke Stuttgart 1889).

[35] PJ Stern *The Company-State: Corporate Sovereignty and the Early Modern Foundations of the British Empire in India* (OUP Oxford 2011); 'The VOC, Corporate Sovereignty' (n 23); D Zimmer 'Legal Personality' in *VOC 1602–2002* (n 2) 265–80.

selves were organized along the same lines as early-modern corporations. And if the argument is true that international legal personality as yet played a decisive role nei-ther in governing company behaviour nor in state development,[36] this condition, of States and companies forming comparably organized entities, made it fairly easy for companies with their roots in both hemispheres to autonomously modulate between the positions of being a 'mere merchant' and an 'independent sovereign', without needing to feign *imperium*.[37] The question remains how in this historical constellation a company like the VOC could transform itself into a new kind of entity.

4. Propriety—the Root Principle of Dutch Trade Expansion

Upon finding, just before 1600, that Portuguese claims to hegemony in the East could be defeated through naval prowess, the Dutch quickly developed overseas trade into a second front in their revolt against Iberian rule.[38] Under the protection of the States-General, the VOC deployed trade as a means to the acquisition of political liberty. Behind the naval-political appropriation of mercantile enterprise was the *landsadvo-caat* and chairman of the States of Holland Johan van Oldenbarnevelt. When ten-sions arose 'between mars and mercurius',[39] power and profit, and discussions about the VOC's identity and its interests broke out within the first decade of the VOC's existence, Grotius himself came to the rescue and made a concerted effort to recon-cile the military and commercial aims of the company.

In a set of memoranda written in 1608 and 1609, Grotius developed the VOC as an institutional embodiment of the right conception in *De jure praedae*.[40] Just like Heemskerk believed that the Dutch had no choice but to use their capacities as sea-men to make a living in whichever possible way, so Grotius had turned this common sense idea into a notion of propriety that was the cornerstone of his rival system to the Portuguese claims to trade and power.[41] The Dutch, as Grotius argued transpos-ing the theory of property in *De jure praedae* onto his campaign, had a right to engage

[36] JE Nijman *The Concept of International Legal Personality: An Inquiry into the History and Theory of International Law* (Asser Press The Hague 2004) at 29–84.

[37] *The Company-State* (n 35) 13.

[38] PJAN Rietbergen (ed) *De eerste landvoogd Pieter Both (1568–1615). Gouverneur-generaal van Neder-lands-Indië (1609–1614)* (The First Overlord) (2 vols Walburg Zutphen 1987) at 31–5. Taking into account the Portuguese and Asian perspectives: Hugo Grotius, the Portuguese and Free Trade (n 11).

[39] *De eerste landvoogd Pieter Both* (n 38) 33–7.

[40] ibid 35–7; *Profit and Principle* (n 1) 189–358.

[41] *Profit and Principle* (n 1) lv.

in maritime trade to provide their subsistence. This right, based on the principle of self-preservation, had been recognized by all philosophers in the history of human-kind. While the prolegomena of *De jure praedae* considered this right in abstract terms, Grotius' strategy for the VOC's development took it to its extreme the political consequences.[42]

The standard way to look at Grotius' right conception in hindsight now is to under-stand it as a cynical legitimization of aggressive warfare against the Portuguese out of a formal notion of individual natural rights to self-preservation.[43] While this is correct in one sense, in another sense, by recognizing the predicament of the Dutch sea faring nation around 1600, including its claimed sovereign status, one understands the char-acter of Grotius' argument and its hinging on the idea of propriety. This very notion of propriety defined legitimate interest as a relation between the intrinsic qualities and predispositions of a person (or a State), and the objects that the person or State could engage with (initially by use or occupation) in order to guarantee the conservation of the person or State.[44] Whereas the Portuguese legal argument and claims to monopoly trade rights derived directly from papal bulls and included a principle of moral supe-riority over non-Christian,[45] Grotius transformed propriety into the decisive category for *imperium*. In other words, the proper exercise of self-preservation entitled a person or State to the exercise of justice. A well-formed disposition of acting upon one's own intrinsic force created right. In developing this idea of right, Grotius not only put for-ward a theory of propriety that suited the Dutch Republic's struggle for independence, but also provided a framework for the development of international trade; one that had significant parallels with the fluidity of the federal structure of the Dutch Republic (which was copied into the structure of the VOC, which had different local chambers) and that might ultimately be seen as a commercial political 'reformation': the defeat of Iberian *reconquista*-driven *imperium* by an entirely different order.[46]

Writing to the directors of the VOC, Grotius described the combined political and economic importance of the VOC for the Dutch State, which, because of the scarcity of land could not rely for its subsistence on any other sources than trade, the primary sector of the Dutch economy.[47] The continuation of the charter of the VOC, even if

[42] J Salter 'Hugo Grotius: Property and Consent' (2001) 29 Political Theory 537–55.

[43] *The Rights of War and Peace* (n 6); *Profit and Principle* (n 1); *Hugo Grotius, the Portuguese and Free Trade* (n 11); *The Savage Republic* (n 23); 'Introduction: Mare Liberum Revisited' (n 7) 6–9 contrasts this reading with a more detached outlook on the provenance of the legal principles of *Mare Liberum*.

[44] *Commentary* (n 1) 22–4.

[45] ibid 306–62; see eg '"Mare liberum" and the Dutch East India Company' (n 21) 75; 'The VOC, Cor-porate Sovereignty' (n 23). Seraphim de Freitas defended the Portuguese claims still in 1625. Cf MF Lind-ley *The Acquisition and Government of Backward Territory in International Law* (Longmans London 1926) at 10–19 categorized rival outlooks on the legal status of indigenous ('backward') property titles.

[46] The proselytizing aspect of *reconquista* politics resulted also from the experience of unbridgeable cultural difference by discoverers of South America, see JH Elliott *The Old World and the New: 1492–1650* (CUP Cambridge 1970).

[47] CR Boxer *The Dutch Seaborne Empire* (Knopf New York 1965) at 5 traces this theme back to a peti-tion to Emperor Charles V in 1548.

that enterprise was not yet profitable, was required to secure the sovereign integrity of the United Provinces.[48] By giving a unified purpose to trade and the State and making the VOC the key agency in both, Grotius helped shape the VOC as an entirely new kind of institution. Rather than to choose between profit and power, a third way was chosen, one that would give a great boost to the development of the Dutch capital market and the international credit revolution. While the VOC had no dividends to pay, 'the profit motive was shoved a little into the future' and 'political liability became an economic asset, for it was only because of the support of the political authorities in the republic that the *bewindhebbers* became able to ignore the claim for return of the capital to the shareholders and so to make the investment permanent'.[49] While there is consensus among economic historians that the transformation of the VOC into the first ever joint-stock company did not take place by design, the legal-political vision of Grotius arguably enabled this development.[50]

5. FROM DOMINIUM TO TERRITORIAL IMPERIUM

Grotius' notion of propriety meant that the VOC could continuously choose to present itself either as a private or a public entity.[51] William Temple commented, in 1673, that the VOC 'managed its trade like a Commonwealth, rather than a Trade; and

---

[48] *De eerste landvoogd Pieter Both* (n 38) 35.

[49] 'The Companies as a Specific Institution' (n 16) 254; OC Gelderblom, JPB Jonker, and A de Jong 'An Admiralty for Asia: Isaac le Maire and Conflicting Conceptions about the Corporate Governance of the VOC' in JGS Koppell (ed) *The Origins Of Shareholder Advocacy* (Palgrave New York 2011) 29–60 emphasize that the VOC neglected shareholder interests and cannot be considered a precursor of the modern corporation.

[50] O Gelderblom 'The Organization of Long-Distance Trade in England and the Dutch Republic, 1550–1650' in O Gelderblom (ed) *The Political Economy of the Dutch Republic* (Ashgate Farnham 2009) 223–54; and JPB Jonker and OC Gelderblom 'Completing a Financial Revolution: The Finance of the Dutch East India Trade and the Rise of the Amsterdam Capital Market' (2004) 64 Journal of Economic History 641–72 explain how close interrelations between public and private finance safeguarded the development of the VOC and the Dutch Republic. See also LO Petram *The World's First Stock Exchange: How the Amsterdam Market for Dutch East India Company Shares Became a Modern Securities Market, 1602–1700* (thesis Amsterdam 2011). There has long been consensus that the transformation of the VOC into a joint-stock company did not occur by design, see F Gaastra 'The Shifting Balance of Trade of the Dutch East India Company' in *Companies and Trade* (n 14) 47–69. The contributions to part III of M Aymard (ed) *Dutch Capitalism and World Capitalism* (CUP Cambridge 1982) investigate the impact of the VOC on the Dutch economy.

[51] *Commentary* (n 1) 300–436. 'The VOC, Corporate Sovereignty' (n 23) 312 and 314 suggests that Grotius 'collapsed' the distinction between *dominium* and *imperium* to this end. See also *The Rights of War and Peace* (n 6) 9 and 82; and J van Goor 'A Hybrid State: The Dutch Economic and Political Network in

thereby raised a State in the Indies, governed indeed by the orders of the Company, but otherwise appearing to those Nations like a sovereign State'.[52] This fluidity was mirrored by the association in *De jure praedae* between *proprietas* (private property), based on *dominium* (the primitive and natural right to use the common), and the idea of *imperium* (jurisdiction and protection).[53] Importantly, legitimate self-preservation created a right to correct injustice by punishing the injurer, within the Grotian scheme. In practice, within 12 years after article XXXV of the original charter gave the VOC a mandate to conclude treaties with Asian rulers and thereby made it an actor under international law, the VOC had conquered Batavia and become a colonial State.[54] How did the change from trade expansion to political ownership in territorial affairs take effect?

As is oft-noted, Asia, unlike the West-Indies, was an equally old world as Europe, with highly sophisticated inter-state trade and political systems. The Portuguese conquests had shocked this trade system militarily, but no further than that.[55] While Portuguese trade in Asia was said to be predominantly 'redistributive' and based on military force, the forms of trade introduced by the Dutch and English companies have been labelled 'productive', a qualitative difference that was initially welcomed by various Asian rulers and populations that happily traded in Portuguese force for privileges to the newcomer companies.[56] When the Dutch and the English companies started to trade locally, participating in the intra-Asian textile and raw silk trade, this was part of a plan to increase profitability and complement the European spice trade. However, extending the intra-Asian trade was also part of a scheme, designed in 1608–9, by the prominent VOC Governor Cornelis Matelief (in correspondence with Oldenbarnevelt and Grotius) to create an Asian government of the VOC that would serve to enforce presumed monopoly rights in the spice trade that emanated, it could be argued, from contracts between the VOC and Asian rulers.[57]

Asia' in C Guillot, D Lombard and R Ptak (eds) *From the Mediterranean to the China Sea: Miscellaneous Notes* (Harrassowitz Wiesbaden, 1998) 193–214.

[52] W Temple *Observations upon the United Provinces of the Netherlands* (Gellibrand London 1673) at 204.

[53] 'Hugo Grotius: Property and Consent' (n 42).

[54] *De VOC als volkenrechtelijke actor* (n 21) 236–7.

[55] 'The Companies as a Specific Institution' (n 16) 253.

[56] *The Asian Trade Revolution of the Seventeenth Century* (n 14). '"Mare liberum" and the Dutch East India Company, (n 21) 69–72 sketches how the VOC bought its admission into existing trade structures by concluding contracts that could be considered treaties. JC van Leur *Indonesian Trade and Society* (Van Hoeve The Hague 1955) argued, from a Weberian perspective on state development, that the VOC became an ally to and subsequently absorbed the old Indonesian aristocracy into a new colonial reality. This position was characterized as mildly anachronistic in *The Asian Trade Revolution of the Seventeenth Century* (n 14), which presented a closer institutional analysis of comparative economic data.

[57] O Prakash 'The Portuguese and the Dutch in Asian Maritime Trade: A Comparative Analysis' in S Chaudhury and M Morineau (eds) *Merchants, Companies and Trade* (CUP Cambridge 1999) 182–5 sees Coen as a visionary; O Prakash *The Dutch East India Company and the Economy of Bengal, 1630–1720* (Princeton University Press Princeton 1985); MAP Meilink Roelofsz *Asian Trade and European Influence*

These contracts concluded with local rulers carried a lot of weight with the VOC. They protected against third party newcomers, from the Dutch point of view, the position achieved (and the territory gained) by defeating the Portuguese. It was in this way that Grotius' acknowledgement of the sovereignty of Asian forms of government—'those people have their own laws'[58]—ultimately became the platform from which Dutch commercial propriety transformed into licentious profit-seeking to the detriment of indigenous livelihoods and social structures. To start with, contracts provided a buffer against the entry of colonial commerce by third parties. *Mare liberum* clearly did not extend to the sphere of exchange relationships among public persons that had already entered in a *sui iuris* relationship of equals, or so the VOC argued.[59] In reality, Asian rulers were often forced to renew contracts against their will or otherwise pressured into contractual relationships with the VOC.[60] These same contracts would soon prove to be the stepping stone to the initial stages of colonial conquest, which are identified with the figure of Jan Pieterszoon Coen, the fourth Governor-General of the VOC from 1617 until 1629.[61] While Coen himself is remembered mainly for his austere and violent actions towards Asian rulers as well as towards European competitors, these actions relied on the strategy of concluding and enforcing exclusive contracts and transforming them into proper monopolies, which if violated immediately justified conquest.

In the process of concluding contracts with Asian rulers the VOC portrayed itself alternatively as a state representative, an independent governing body, or a legal person. Depending on the other contracting party, Governors adapted themselves to the customs and ceremonies of unequal relationships among Asian rulers at different levels.[62] Yet, in the aftermath of the creation of these contracts or treaties—which in non-European eyes were considered partnerships—these constructions allowed for almost imperceptibly hollowing out the sovereignty of the other party by claiming

---

in the Indonesian Archipelago between 1500 and about 1630 (Martinus Nijhoff The Hague 1962) historicized and corrected important parts in *Indonesian Trade and Society* (n 56), leading to a fuller appraisal of the Asian perspective and to a recognition of how Matelief's plan and Coen's execution impinged upon the existing trade system.

[58] See '"Mare liberum" and the Dutch East India Company' (n 21) 71.

[59] *The Colonial Conferences between England and the Netherlands* (n 4); *Profit and Principle* (n 1) 359–483.

[60] *De VOC als volkenrechtelijke actor* (n 21) 230 and 240–3; and '"Mare liberum" and the Dutch East India Company' (n 21) 74–6 argue that contracts held different culturally determined meanings for both parties. From most Asian perspectives, for instance, contracts did not bind future rulers. These gaps, plus strong ambiguities about whether Asian parties had entered into contract *sui iuris* (or as part of a *quid pro quo* arrangement against the Portuguese, not to mention through the use of threat or force) were grounds for future disagreement.

[61] *De eerste landvoogd Pieter Both* (n 38); '"Mare liberum" and the Dutch East India Company' (n 21); and *De VOC als volkenrechtelijke actor* (n 21) discuss the context. On Coen's operative legal-political mode L Kiers *Coen op Banda. De conquestie getoetst aan het recht van den tijd* (*Coen on Banda. The conquest examined through the laws of the age*) (Oosthoek Utrecht 1943).

[62] *De VOC als volkenrechtelijke actor* (n 21) 231–2 and 243–9. In practice, the need for adaptation overruled whatever article XXXV of the VOC charter might be stipulated.

monopoly trade rights and ultimately the right to punish violations of rights apparently contracted for, if necessary by conquest. Precisely the commercial requirement of profit (and the need to turn contracts into exclusive trade rights) added to the original simultaneously commercial and political mission of the VOC, in the hands of Coen, ultimately turned the VOC into a de facto State.[63] To what extent this outcome was planned or even desired remains speculation. One can agree with Gaastra that there may not have been a master plan, but definitely a system inherent to the development of the VOC's territorial *imperium* by Coen and his successors, a system built on contemporary legal principles that by themselves and through alignment with local indigenous law left a lot of space for opportunism and imperialism.[64]

6. Conditions and Legal Structure of English Company Trade

By the early 18th century, the EIC had gained supremacy among European nations in Asia after driving the Dutch out of the intra-Asian textile market. The main cause was that the decentralized British system gave larger discretionary powers to local officials, whereas the VOC relied on centralized bureaucratic price control—a remnant of the originally successful structures put in place through Matelief's plan. Between 1700 and 1740 this organizational factor played into the hands of the EIC, before colonial occupation on a large scale took place.[65]

From the beginning of the Seven Years' War, which Adam Smith would call 'altogether a colony quarrel',[66] territorial conquest became a direct focus of overseas trade expansion, particularly at the hands of the EIC, the strongest European actor. Recent research, however, has rejected the old commonplace that before 1756 the EIC (and trade companies in general) were predominantly concerned with trade, rather than politics. The same research has made a strong argument that the EIC organized itself from the start as a kind of government.[67] How did the EIC's charter and legal posi-

---

[63] *De VOC als volkenrechtelijke actor* (n 21) 247–50.

[64] FS Gaastra *The Dutch East India Company* (Walburg Zutphen 2003) 56–7. Leue adds that whether local courts followed 'any norms at all' cannot be proven ('Legal Expansion in the Age of Companies' (n 10) 143.)

[65] *The Dutch East India Company* (n 57); O Prakash *European Commercial Enterprise in Pre-Colonial India* (CUP Cambridge 1998); KN Chaudhuri *The Trading World of Asia and the English East India Company, 1660–1760* (CUP Cambridge 1978); and FS Gaastra 'War, Competition and Collaboration' in HV Bowen, M Lincoln, and N Rigby (eds) *The Worlds of the East India Company* (Boydell Woodbridge 2002) 49–68.

[66] A Smith *An Inquiry into the Nature and Causes of the Wealth of Nations* (OUP Oxford 1976) at 615.

[67] *The Company-State* (n 35).

tioning compare with the VOC's, which had developed into a territorial *imperium* driven by Grotius' and other political writers' views on Dutch State building? This question relates to the disputed issue to what extent English merchants before 1756 already changed, even deliberately disrupted, existing indigenous social and commercial structures.[68]

As argued above (Section 3), the EIC grew out of an organizational tradition of regulated companies that received their charters from the Crown. Within this tradition, profit and power combined well as separate logics, but did not mix. The English Crown required payments from the EIC (and private loans from merchants benefiting from the monopoly arrangement) in exchange for the charter privileges,[69] while in the Dutch case state protection created both a permanent capitalization of the company and effectively turned VOC shares into state bonds—lending the VOC a peculiar, state-authorized, autonomy.[70] Likewise, legally, the EIC was not the same kind of person as the VOC was perceived to be. While the VOC's mission was founded on the Grotian idea of propriety, which proved conducive to the expansion of overseas trade into territorial conquest, the EIC acted more straightforwardly as a commercial representative of *imperium* with a mandate to exercise power abroad on the one hand and the obligation to pay out profits and, later, shareholder dividends on the other. Precisely this derivative basis of rights and duties restricted the EIC's actions in Asia during most of the 17th century.[71] Moreover, at home the EIC's monopoly was always contested and associated with party political struggles about group interests and rival outlooks onto the development of commercial-political hegemony.[72]

The late 17th-century English debates about interlopers and the effects of imported textiles onto the development of the manufacturing sector in the domestic economy reflect these struggles. Similarly, charter renewals of the EIC were heavily negotiated affairs between government and circles of merchants, whereas in the Dutch Republic the continuity of the VOC as a commercial-political enterprise was secure. In sum, it

---

[68] As argued by S Sen *Empire of Free Trade: The East India Company and the Making of the Colonial Marketplace* (University of Pennsylvania Press Philadelphia 1998); and S Sen *A Distant Sovereignty: National Imperialism and the Origins of British India* (Routledge London 2002). *The Company-State* (n 35) argues emphatically that the EIC made an impact, not by peaceful apolitical business, but by interference with existing trade systems and political structures.

[69] On the early history and motives behind English overseas trade KR Andrews T*rade, Plunder and Settlement: Maritime Enterprise and the Genesis of the British Empire 1480–1630* (CUP Cambridge 1984); and KN Chaudhuri *The English East India Company: The Study of an Early Joint-Stock Company 1600–1640* (Cass London 1965).

[70] 'The Companies as a Specific Institution' (n 16) 256–8.

[71] 'Legal Expansion in the Age of Companies' (n 10) 136 downplays the long-term impact of these restrictions.

[72] SCA Pincus *1688: The First Modern Revolution* (Yale University Press New Haven 2009); *The Company-State* (n 35); TK Rabb, *Enterprise & Empire: Merchant and Gentry Investment in the Expansion of England 1575–1630* (Harvard University Press Cambridge MA 1967).

seems fair to conclude that while their different constitutions enabled both companies to assume governmental powers as well as to decline governmental responsibilities for the sake of profit, the EIC maybe called a 'company-state', whereas the VOC from its inception was considered a 'state-company'.

The relative advantages enjoyed by the VOC as a joint-stock company disappeared when between 1650 and 1720, the EIC was steadily reorganized. In 1657 Cromwell approved a charter that allowed the EIC to raise permanent capital. The year 1702 saw the creation of a more inclusive 'united' company out of the original EIC and its late 17th-century rival that had grown out of the 'Glorious Revolution'.[73] This fusion of companies not only dissolved a major dimension of party associated strife over the future of foreign trade, but also transformed the EIC into a joint-stock naval-imperial agency. Where the EIC previously had had to balance its rights and duties to emulate the VOC's actions, in the course of the 18th century it turned into an organ that raised the credit of the State in international financial markets and that extended the territorial reach of commercial empire through the export of English common law, which neatly accommodated a plurality of colonial legal systems out of sets of 'collective charters and grants [such as] bestowed on the Company by the Mughal Emperor'.[74]

7. European States and Company Objectives

Until the mid-18th century a great number and variety of companies was established. The charters and institutional characteristics of the main European national overseas trade companies have never been studied in comparison, but patterns can be distinguished.[75] Trade companies came, according to Steensgaard, came in three 'waves'.[76] Roughly, the periods in which companies were established can be associ-

---

[73] *The Company-State* (n 35); HV Bowen *Elites, Enterprise and the Making of the British Overseas Empire, 1688–1775* (Houndsmills Macmillan 1996).

[74] *A Distant Sovereignty* (n 68) xv; *Law and Colonial Cultures* (n 10).

[75] H Furber *Rival Empires of Trade in the Orient, 1600–1800* (University of Minnesota Press Minneapolis 1976). Anthologies providing overviews are *Companies and Trade* (n 14); *Merchants, Companies and Trade* (n 57); *Worlds of the East India Company* (n 65); J van Goor (ed) *Trading Companies in Asia 1600–1830* (HES Utrecht 1986); JR Bruijn and FS Gaastra (eds) *Ships, Sailors and Spices. East India Companies and Their Shipping in the 16th, 17th and 18th Centuries* (Nederlandsch Economisch-Historisch Archief Amsterdam 1993).

[76] 'The Companies as a Specific Institution' (n 16) 260–1 speaks of a 'conjoncture'; compare *European Commercial Enterprise* (n 65) 111–13.

ated with different political motives. Furthermore, in the 18th century, European trade companies were designed to fulfil certain geopolitical aims. Simultaneously, the economic question of what an overseas market does for the development of a national economy informs our understanding of why certain States developed their companies at a certain moment for certain specific reason.[77]

The trade companies established in the East Indies stood out organizationally and legally, for instance compared with the West Indies companies. While the latter were organized as normal trade companies, did not break into developed local trade systems, and did not overturn indigenous legal, political, and economic cultures, the former, in response to existing conditions, were organized as strongly protected monopoly traders that in reality competed with each other for global hegemony.[78]

The period between 1600 and 1628, in which the EIC, the VOC and also the French and Portuguese East Indies companies took shape, was the first stage in the development of company trade.[79] While the Dutch and English companies damaged Iberian political predominance in Europe a second stage ran from 1660 to 1673. Within this timeframe, post restoration England expanded its overseas trade towards Africa and North America, while France, under Colbert, attempted to emulate the EIC and the VOC by setting up an East and a West Indies company in 1664. The Dutch West Indies Company also stems from this era, as do the Danish East and West Indies Companies. Considering the French case it has been noted that the companies became a vehicle for individual profit-taking of merchants and failed to play a political role.[80] Importantly, these companies set up in the period until the Third Anglo-Dutch War were not based on the model of the permanently capitalized joint-stock venture, such as the VOC and the EIC had already developed into.

A third stage, dated from 1719 until 1734, is of special interest owing to its double-sided character. On the one hand Europe's dominant States, France, and Britain, discovered overseas trade as a possible means to dissolve state debt crises and boost the credit of the State. The famous French *Compagnie Perpetuelle des Indes* designed by John Law in 1719 breathed new life into a set of languishing existing companies and became a vehicle for a spectacular monetary reform experiment. In the same year, the English South Sea Company was transformed into a similar institution and shocked the private capital market in London. While the French and English megalomaniac

---

[77] 'The Origins of Trading Companies' (n 30).

[78] PC Emmer 'The West India Company' in *Companies and Trade* (n 14) 71–95.

[79] E Thomson 'The Dutch Miracle, Modified. Hugo Grotius's *Mare Liberum*, Commercial Governance and Imperial War in the Early-Seventeenth Century' (2009) 30 Grotiana 107–30, on the often abortive attempts to emulate Dutch trade policy including by Swedish and Danish competitors.

[80] PH Boulle 'French Mercantilism, Commercial Companies and Colonial Profitability' in *Companies and Trade* (n 14) 97–117.

banks broke, the link previously forged by the VOC between trade rivalry and financial speculation as a key to political power in global markets was irreversibly established.[81]

On the other hand, a number of other States set up trade companies, not to attain hegemony, but for different political purposes. The establishment of new overseas trade companies in Sweden and Prussia, but also the renewal of investments in the existing Danish company, took place with less government encouragement and statutorily highlighted the principles of transparency and shareholder representation.[82] If Europe's dominant States mixed power and trade in their competitive rivalry for empire, these companies followed the counter-model of 'pure trade'.

One explanatory factor for this divergence resides in the opinion of economic historians who have argued that companies in non-dominant States damage the development of the domestic market.[83] It also ought to be remembered that companies set up by weaker States were aggressively pushed out of the market, as the history of the short-lived Austrian Imperial Ostend Company (1717–31) shows.[84] Another suggestion worth taking into account is the idea that the establishment of trade companies by European States from the 1710s onwards represent rival ideas on the future of foreign trade and inter-state order in general. For instance, the development of 'pure trade' companies in Sweden and Denmark in the 1730s and 1740s ties in with a design for the reform of French foreign trade of the time, which, in response to British maritime supremacy, envisaged foreign 'neutral' States—like Denmark and Sweden that were in military terms increasingly useless allies to France—to act as the low-cost carriers of French production surpluses.[85] Traces of the effects of the interplay of alternative 18th-century designs for the rearrangement of international trade can be found not only in the history of company trade, but also in the history of the law of neutrality and of commercial treaties.[86]

[81] On these links, The Constitution and Finance of English, Scottish, and Irish Joint-Stock Companies to 1720 (n 28) and AB Dubois *The English Business Company after the Bubble Act, 1720–1800* (Commonwealth Fund New York 1938).

[82] 'The Companies as a Specific Institution' (n 16) 148; C Koninckx *The First and Second Charters of the Swedish East India Company (1731–1766)* (Ghemmert Kortrijk 1980).

[83] 'The Origins of Trading Companies' (n 30); and JL van Zanden *The Rise and Decline of Holland's Economy: Merchant Capitalism and the Labour Market* (Manchester University Press Manchester 1993).

[84] Still the main study is M Huisman *La Belgique commerciale sous l'Empereur Charles VI* (Lamertin Brussels 1902).

[85] A Alimento 'Competition, True Patriotism and Colonial Interests: Forbonnais' Vision of Neutrality and Trade' in K Stapelbroek (ed) *Trade and War: The Neutrality of Commerce in the Inter-State System* (Helsinki Collegium for Advanced Studies Helsinki 2011) 61–94.

[86] *Trade and War* (n 85); and A Alimento 'Commercial Treaties and the Harmonisation of National Interests' in A Alimento (ed) *War, Trade and Neutrality* (Franco Angeli Milan 2011) 107–28.

8. Conclusion: Company Trade and Global Markets

If in the first half of the 18th century, functionally different international trade orders were being prepared through the establishment of different kinds of national trade companies, the Seven Years' War signified the victory of the EIC, which, following its attempts to emulate the VOC's achievements, became the key colonial agency in Asia. Although it is therefore true that historically, company trade and colonial conquest are inherently related, the history of company trade itself from the outset is richer. The manner in which Grotius' legal innovations paved the way for Dutch trade expansion can be understood as a benchmark for the development of the EIC before 1756—and an enduring guide afterwards, when territorial expansion became a focus.

Grotius's approach to the parallel development of the VOC and the Dutch Republic and the usage of his thinking in the creation of *imperium*, when looked at through the lens of colonial history, by themselves amount to very little that can justify talk of a Grotian tradition in international law, such as was established in the early 20th century. Yet, once put in its own context one might recognize the Grotian notion of propriety—in however potentially expansionist way it might be and was interpreted—as an ordering principle of international trade and power.[87]

Within the Dutch context, the original Grotian idea which ensued from the ongoing war of independence was that differently constituted States (with different natural and cultural characteristics) took on different roles in the international sphere and were entitled to different courses of action. It befitted the Dutch nation to preserve itself at sea all over the world, so was the idea. Grotius' notion of propriety, the economic characteristics of the Dutch trade-based State and the role the Dutch were to play in an evolving inter-state system of trade and political relations also remained an implicit reference point until the end of the 18th century.

This one can glean, for instance, from the views of the Amsterdam financier and political writer Isaac de Pinto on trade as well as the VOC and the EIC.[88] Throughout his works, Pinto considered intercontinental trade as the prime mover of the economic progress and global integration of markets that European States had caused since the discovery of America. This idea he shared with most political writers of the time. However, writing in the 1770s, Pinto rejected any thoughts that the economic viability of overseas trade companies had decreased, that company monopolies affected domestic economic growth and that company trade subverted indigenous markets to the point that companies obstructed the natural development of trade on a global scale. Pinto's main focus was on the so-called problem of 'jealousy of trade',

[87] Cf PH Kooijmans 'How to Handle the Grotian Heritage: Grotius and Van Vollenhoven' (1983) 30 Netherlands International Law Review 81–92.

[88] I de Pinto *Letters on the American Troubles* (Boosey London 1776).

which he agreed with other political writers had unleashed the Seven Years' War.[89] From his perspective, solving the problem of inter-state competition required a solution in which States' 'intrinsic powers' combined into a long-term viable system of economic progress. Pinto treated the government of overseas trade as an index of the reform of inter-state trade relations and believed that if only the EIC were reformed and brought properly under the aegis of the State (as in the case of the VOC), the 'absurdity of *imperium in imperio*' and the struggles between government, shareholders, and company directors would be dissolved and the conjectural history of the modern commercial State could be completed. Pinto coupled this view with the idea of a European Union in which shared interests in global peace and trade inspired European States to give up trade rivalry. Trade ought to be left to the declined Dutch Republic, the cheapest carrier of other States' goods, representing no political threat to other States and act upon their own comparative advantages in producing goods for the international market.[90]

Prominent critics of company trade, Adam Smith, Guillaume Thomas François Raynal, and (later) David Ricardo engaged with the same political economic questions as Pinto, but held divergent views.[91] Smith in particular presented the VOC as a negative model for the future of the EIC. Driven by mercantile interests and organizationally controlled by shareholders, directors, and officials who were motivated by perverse incentives, the Dutch company had turned property into licentious behaviour, assumed governmental power to increase profits, and declined political responsibilities in setting up a system that was 'perfectly destructive' to local markets and societies. When the inefficiencies of company trade necessitated requests for further rights and privileges, as Smith represented Dutch history to suit his message to a British audience, States became deeply entrenched accomplices as well as unwitting victims of the inefficient, unequal and unjust pattern of global trade promulgated by company trade that was bound to cast a long spell onto world history.[92]

Beyond recognizing Pinto's defence and Smith's moral critique as directly opposed judgments of the effects of company trade on the history of commerce (as well as of the justice of colonial occupation), one may note that in grounding their judgment on the suitability of company trade for the nation's development they shared the same, originally Grotian, principle. In view of the fact that the late 19th- and early 20th-century liberal writers who inaugurated the idea of the Grotian tradition confronted much the same interrelations of war and trade as Pinto and Smith had, would it not make sense—as this chapter suggests—to understand the legal history

---

[89] *Jealousy of Trade* (n 26).

[90] *Letters on the American Troubles* (n 88) 52–3 and 73–89.

[91] S Muthu 'Adam Smith's Critique of International Trading Companies' (2008) 36 Political Theory 185–212.

[92] *Wealth of Nations* (n 66) 636.

of company trade itself as representative of, and also offering an ideal access point for grasping, the development of inter-state trade rivalry?

Recommended Reading

Alexandrowicz, Charles H *An Introduction to the History of the Law of Nations in the East Indies: 16th, 17th and 18th Centuries* (Clarendon Press Oxford 1967).

Benton, Lauren A *Law and Colonial Cultures: Legal Regimes in World History 1400–1900* (CUP Cambridge 2002).

Blussé, Leonard and Femme Gaastra (eds) *Companies and Trade: Essays on Overseas Trading Companies during the Ancien Régime* (Leiden University Press Leiden 1981).

Furber, Holden *Rival Empires of Trade in the Orient, 1600–1800* (University of Minnesota Press Minneapolis 1976).

Ittersum, Martine J van *Profit and Principle: Hugo Grotius, Natural Rights Theories and the Rise of Dutch Power in the East Indies 1595–1615* (Brill Leiden 2006).

Meilink Roelofsz, Marie AP *Asian Trade and European Influence in the Indonesian Archipelago between 1500 and about 1630* (Martinus Nijhoff The Hague 1962).

Somers, Jan A *De VOC als volkenrechtelijke actor* (The VOC as an Actor under International Law) (Quint Gouda 2001).

Steensgaard, Niels *The Asian Trade Revolution of the Seventeenth Century: The East India Companies and the Decline of the Caravan Trade* (University of Chicago Press Chicago 1974).

Stern, Philipp J *The Company-State: Corporate Sovereignty and the Early Modern Foundations of the British Empire in India* (OUP Oxford 2011).

CHAPTER 15

THE SEA

DAVID J BEDERMAN

1. INTRODUCTION

THE evolution of the law of the sea has had extensive intellectual and doctrinal effects on the development of international law as broadly conceived. For much of its history, the law of nations has been preoccupied with the creation and management of regimes to govern what is arguably the largest, most diverse, and most significant shared resource on the planet. The oceans not only account for three-fifths of the Earth's face, but also to be considered is the navigation and trade that flows on their surfaces, the bounty of their waters, and seabeds (both living and non-living resources), and the security imperatives of controlling this maritime domain. All of this contributes to the importance of understanding, in legal terms, how oceans have been used over time.

This chapter examines the history of the law of the sea from two separate, but linked, perspectives. First, I offer a chronological narrative, charting an intellectual history of international law's engagement with problems of ocean ownership and activities (Section 2). Drawing from global trends and perspectives, and reviewing some of the canonical writings on the subject, I tease out the main themes of discourse about legal regulation of the oceans, especially over the past half-millennia. The traditional historiographic approach to this subject has been through the optic of freedom of the seas as the key objective of law of the sea regimes. To some degree, I depart from that approach here, preferring to emphasize other tropes and themes of ocean management, especially over the past 500 years. There is a diversity of ways in which the law of the sea's history can be understood, and I explore many of them here.

The second perspective I offer here—albeit in a truncated form—is a more conventional doctrinal summary of the main currents for law of the sea regimes. Some of this narrative is, quite necessarily, woven into my intellectual history discussion of Section 2. But a more searching review of near-contemporary law of the sea doctrines—especially the current preoccupation with the juridical regimes of maritime zones—is undertaken in Section 3. My contribution largely focuses on historical developments with the law of the sea, prior to 1945. Some brief, concluding remarks follow in Section 4.

2. History of the Law of the Sea: Chronology, Ideas, and Trends

The history of the law of the sea is subject to the same rules of chronology and 'periodization'asanyotherhistoricalinquiry.Asafairlyconventionalmatterofhistoriography, the time periods of human history which are most relevant to major changes in the forms, functions, and doctrines of the law of the sea, include, first, classical antiquity; second, the Middle Ages and Renaissance; third, the first great European impulse of colonization and contact with the Americas, Africa, and Asia (*c.* 1480–1650); fourth, the period of early-Modern European nationalism and a second wave of colonialism culminating in the Seven Years War and the Napoleonic conflicts (1650–1815); and fifth, European hegemony and imperialism culminating in the First World War and embryonic efforts of codification of law of the sea principles in the inter-war Period (1815–1939). Of these five periods, the latter three (developments from 1500–1930) are arguably the most significant and will be given the greatest treatment here.

The very structure of this appraisal reveals a major objection: the existential Eurocentrism of the law of the sea. This has been observed by a number of scholars.[1] Under this criticism, the entire perspective for viewing developments in the regimes for ocean uses is an entirely European one, incorporating a wider international law apology and justification for European colonialism and imperialism. There is certainly some merit to this view. But a more nuanced approach would be to accept the logic that changes in the law of the sea are most likely to occur during periods of intensive globalization. These periods would include classical antiquity (and the first contacts between the Greek, Roman, Persian, and Chinese hegemonies), the first age of European exploration (1500–1770), and the age of European imperialism

[1] CH Alexandrowicz *An Introduction to the History of the Law of Nations in the East Indies* (Clarendon Press Oxford 1967) at 1–4; RP Anand *Origin and Development of the Law of the Sea* (Martinus Nijhoff The Hague 1983) at 1–6.

(1850–1914). In each of these periods, global contacts—the movement of people, goods, and ideas—accelerated dramatically.[2] It should come as no surprise that, during such periods, challenges would be made to regimes governing the main conduit of movement and transmission of global public goods (whether trade, resources, or security): the world's oceans.

Seen in this way, the history of the law of the sea is part and parcel of a wider vision for the law of nation's connection with globalization. At the same time, it has to be acknowledged that there is a 'dark side' to this history. Evolutions in existing trends and doctrines of the law of the sea have tended to feature conflict between a 'traditional' set of international law actors and concerns, poised against challengers to the existing order (the 'other').[3] So, aside from such banal concerns as the technicalities of periodization and the reliability of materials and texts, any authentic narrative for the law of the sea must also take into account wider trends of globalization and international law's engagement with outside polities and values.

2.1. Classical Antiquity

Another theme of the history of the law of the sea is answering the question of whether coherent doctrines for the management of ocean uses and resources can really occur during periods of empire or hegemony. Because of the Eurocentrism of this subject, this is the practical legacy of the Roman Empire—and of Roman law. But it would be a mistake to assume that the entire classical legacy of the law of the sea comprises dusty pronouncements from Justinian's *Institutes* or the obscure writings of Roman jurists. Roman law substantially incorporated the customs and practices of earlier seafaring peoples of the Mediterranean, most notably the Rhodians and their *Sea Code*. Additionally, there are well-documented contacts between Roman and Indian and Chinese merchants and the authorities that regulated such trade, and there was likely a highly developed set of norms governing sea trade in the Indian Ocean, long before any contact with Rome and its law.[4] In this context, it is important to realize that any divide between the 'public' law of the sea (those regimes for regulating ocean uses as between legitimate subjects of international law, such as States) and the 'private' maritime law (those doctrines regulating ocean commerce) are likely to be highly artificial. Nevertheless, the focus of this contribution will tend to be on the 'public' law of the oceans.

Indeed, the fundamental conceptual debate about the 'public' law character of the oceans derives from classical antiquity. Are the oceans capable of being 'owned' upon assertion of some form of dominion or jurisdiction? Or, do the seas—and all benefits

---

[2] DJ Bederman *Globalization and International Law* (Palgrave MacMillan New York 2008) at 1–10.
[3] A Orford (ed) *International Law and its Others* (CUP Cambridge 2006).
[4] *Origin and Development of the Law of the Sea* (n 1) 10–16.

associated with ocean use, including navigation and fishing rights—belong to all in common? In short, are the seas *res nullius* or *res communis*? The classical disquisitions on this topic would later exercise immense significance on the doctrinal debates of the 17th and 18th centuries, and, thereafter, plot the trajectory of doctrinal developments in this area.

Aside from a sparse record of classical Greek sources—some suggestive that Greek polities attempted to exercise dominion over sea areas in proximity to their coasts (such as Athens in parts of the Aegean)[5]—most of the classical writing is from Roman legal sources. The canonical statement in favour of a *res communis* position for the oceans is from Justinian's *Institutes*: 'By the law of nature then the following things are common to all men; air, running water, the sea, and, consequently the shores of the sea.'[6] From this statement it has been inferred from other Justianic sources (including the *Digest*) that Roman law adhered rigorously to the principle that title to ocean areas could not be acquired in any way, including prescriptive title by long possession.[7] Or, as the Emperor Antoninus is quoted in the *Digest*, 'I am indeed lord of the world, but the law is the lord of the sea'.[8] These statements have all been enlisted as the basis for an uncompromising *res communis* theory for freedom of the seas.

But it is entirely likely that such an interpretation would be inconsistent with the nature of Roman law and the realities of classical Roman state practice. For starters, the Justianic sources of Roman law are primarily concerned with private law, and so the distinction between the public law of the sea and the private maritime law cannot recede into the background. The statements from the *Digest* and *Institutes* may well reflect that, as between Roman citizens or private-law actors, there is no possibility of acquiring title to ocean areas (or their uses and products) and the freedom of the seas is enshrined. Put another way, in Roman law the seas were *res publica ex commercium*, inasmuch as they belonged to the Roman people or state under its public law and were entirely exempt from the operation of private law.[9] That is not the same thing as propounding, of course, that the Roman Republic (and later Empire) was required to open ocean areas under its control to competing polities, or, even worse, to subject itself to the outrages of pirates or brigands. In other words, as a matter of public international law, Rome was free to restrict ocean traffic and uses to its own citizens and state purposes.

---

[5] PB Potter *The Freedom of the Seas in History, Law, and Politics* (Longmans Green New York 1924) at 14–25.

[6] Justinian Inst II.1.1 and II.1.5. For the translation of this quote, see JT Abdy and B Walker (ed and trans) *The Institutes of Justinian* (CUP Cambridge 1876) at 78.

[7] Justinian Dig XLI.3.45.

[8] Justinian Dig XIV.2.9 (de lege Rhodia 9). For the translation of this quote, see B-M Emerigon *An Essay on Maritime Loans* (Philip H Nicklin & Co Baltimore 1811) at 286.

[9] G Butler and S Maccoby *The Development of International Law* (Longmans Green London 1928) at 40; JHW Verzijl *International Law in Historical Perspective* (AW Sijthoff Leyden 1971) vol 4, at 7.

It was thus no legal serendipity that the Romans called the Mediterranean *Mare Nostrum* ('Our Sea').[10] The classical sources are replete with references to assertions by Roman authorities of what may be characterized as 'sovereignty' over various ocean areas.[11] In perhaps the most famous instance, Pompey the Great was authorized by the Roman Republic in 67 BC to take all measures necessary to rid the Mediterranean of pirates and thus to 'restore the sovereignty (*imperium*) of the sea to the Roman people'.[12]

These concepts of ownership (*dominium*), power (*imperium*), and control or jurisdiction (*jurisdictio*) were all distinct in Roman law. And this has led to a fundamental theme in the intellectual history of the law of the sea. As framed in DP O'Connell's towering work, *The International Law of the Sea*,

[t]he question was whether the power to rule (*jurisdictio*) flowed from proprietorship of the marine terrain, or was independent of it. It was a critical question then [in both classical antiquity and the 17th century], and it remains a critical one today....[13]

Could jurisdiction and control over ocean uses (navigation and fishing) only come with ownership of the relevant maritime space? And, if ownership (proprietorship) of the seas was impossible, under natural law principles, did that mean there were no circumstances under which control could be exercised? Must the oceans be entirely and inalterably *mare liberum* or totally *mare clausum*? Or, was it possible to imagine splitting the atom of *imperium*, and allowing the separation of the concepts of ownership over the ocean space, as distinct from control over the ocean activity?

2.2. Middle Ages and Renaissance

It was during the Middle Ages that European polities, embracing inchoate notions of sovereignty, began to assert claims to ocean spaces in proximity to their land territories. But one must take care to distinguish, in this period, between rhetorical declarations of sovereign interests in maritime areas and the reality of State practice. As Pitman

---

[10] O Tellegen-Couperus *Short History of Roman Law* (Routledge London 1993) at 32.

[11] *The Freedom of the Seas in History, Law, and Politics* (n 5) 27–35; see also M Müller-Jochmus *Geschichte des Völkerrechts im Altertum* (Leipzig 1848) (repr Kessinger Berlin 2010) at 235–52; C Phillipson *International Law and Custom of Ancient Greece and Rome* (MacMillan London 1911) vol 2, at 372–80.

[12] Pliny the Elder *Natural History* vii.26; see also Plutarch *Pompey* xxv–xxvi (granting Pompey 'dominion' over the sea).

[13] DP O'Connell *The International Law of the Sea* (Clarendon Press Oxford 1982) vol 1, at 14–15; for a 17th-century view (discussed below), see H Grotius *The Free Sea [Mare Liberum]* (R Hakluyt trans) (Elzevier Amsterdam 1609) (repr Liberty Fund Indianapolis 2004) at 31 (some 'affirm a right over the sea [based on] protection and jurisdiction, which right they distinguish from propriety'); see also TW Fulton *The Sovereignty of the Sea* (Blackwood London 1911) (for English claims of dominion over the seas).

Potter observed, 'not what was said, but what was done provides us with our best information concerning the theories and principles of that era'.[14]

The emerging commercial city-States of Genoa and Venice were particularly aggressive with their rhetoric, variously referring to their control of maritime regions in the Ligurian and Adriatic Seas (respectively) as a 'seignory', 'royalty', 'full jurisdiction', or even 'empire'. Venetian claims were acknowledged by the leading secular and spiritual authorities of the time: the Holy Roman Empire and the Papacy. And, probably, to a degree not matched by other Mediterranean city-States, Venice was able to back up its rhetoric (including the annual, Ascension Day 'marriage' ceremony of the city to the sea, where *perpetuique dominii* was declaimed) with a sizable fleet, proximate colonies and trading posts, and robust maritime enforcement.[15] Genoese assertions of control in the Ligurian Sea—including the authority to interdict vessel traffic and collect tolls—were acknowledged by treaty with neighbouring States and were even regarded as so well established that the jurist, Baldus de Ubaldis (1327–1400), referred to them as '*inveteratissima consuetudo* (unassailable custom)'.[16]

In Northern Europe, similar claims were made by such larger territorial sovereigns as France, England, Denmark, and Sweden. Danish assertions of sovereignty to the Sound and Belts—the outlets of the Baltic into the North Sea—were a constant source of tension between that nation and other trading powers of the period (including the cities of the Hanseatic League). In England, claims of sovereignty to adjacent bodies of water (including the English Channel and North Sea) were commenced during Saxon times, and then maintained and extended after the Norman conquest. These declarations often involved the collection of fees or tolls, the procurement of licences for navigation through particular ocean areas, control of fisheries, and the conduct of maritime ceremonials (wherein foreign vessels were required to salute English ships at sea).[17] On occasion, these pretensions of authority were acquiesced in by other polities.

Until the beginning of the 17th century, little appeared in the scholarly literature of the law of nations on the subject of freedom of the seas. Such publicists as Nicholas Everard (writing about maritime taxes collected by the Count of Holland and Zeeland) and Alphonse de Castro (in a treatise on Venetian and Genoese claims), were dismissive of the civil law or Roman law basis for such assertions of sovereignty over maritime areas.[18] Other publicists—those more closely associated with national legal communities—tended to support sovereign assertions of authority to offshore areas. In this group was Henry de Bracton (*c.* 1210–68), whose treatise of 1260 was

---

[14] *The Freedom of the Seas in History, Law, and Politics* (n 5) 36.

[15] *International Law in Historical Perspective* (n 9) 11–15.

[16] G Gidel *Le droit international public de la mer* (Sirey Paris 1934) vol 3, at 137.

[17] CJ Colombos *The International Law of the Sea* (6th edn Longmans Green London 1967) at 48; *The Freedom of the Seas in History, Law, and Politics* (n 5) 38–41; *International Law in Historical Perspective* (n 9) 9–11.

[18] E Nys *Les Origines du Droit International* (Castaigne Brussels 1894) at 381–2.

influential in the course of developing subsequent English claims, especially later in the Tudor period. In a 1582 treatise, the French philosopher, Jean Bodin (1530–96), popularized a notion of State sovereignty that extended sixty miles from shore, an idea he ascribed to Baldus.[19]

Even in the face of what would later become the extraordinary claims of Spain and Portugal to maritime spaces in the East Indies and New World, strong objections were voiced among early international law publicists. Even within Catholic Spain itself, in *Controversiarum illustrium aliarumque usus frequentium libri tres* (1564), a prominent Spanish jurist named Fernando Vázquez y Menchaca (1512–69) attacked Venice and Genoa's claims to dominion over parts of the Mediterranean, defending the principle of freedom of the seas. His analysis extended to Spain's elaborately conceived set of claims to controlling navigation over extra-European trade, based on the 1493 Papal bull *Inter caetera* and the 1494 Treaty of Tordesillas,[20] which divided the world between Spain and Portugal. Vázquez, a humanist scholar who drew extensively on the Roman law tradition, rejected these bases for asserting sovereignty over what was essentially a *res communis*.

The last Renaissance publicist to be considered in this regard is Alberico Gentili (1552–1608).[21] Because of his Protestant beliefs he fled his native Italy and settled in England, where he became the Regius Professor of Civil Law at Oxford and a prominent practitioner in England's admiralty courts. In his *De iure belli libri tres* (1598), Gentili cleaved closely to the Justianic tradition of Roman law (as supplemented by other classical and humanist sources), even as he revived the distinction between dominion and jurisdiction.[22] While claims to sea-dominion were inadmissible, he held, it was possible to imagine that State necessity might impel certain forms of regulation being extended into ocean areas by coastal States.

By the end of the 16th century—the dawn of the early nation-state period in Europe and the close of the first, great epoch of trans-marine expansion and colonization—two trends are apparent in the history of the law of the sea. The first is the beginning of accretions of State practice, some of which is suggestive of assertive claims to sovereignty (including both jurisdiction and dominion) over ocean areas, with concomitant effects in limiting the freedom of the seas. The second is the continued influence of intellectual traditions from antiquity (including the primacy of Roman law) which resisted such claims. How these inclinations were resolved is part of the great debate on freedom of the seas in the 16th century.

---

[19] *The International Law of the Sea* (n 13) vol 1, 2–3.

[20] 'Hispanic-Portuguese Treaty (concluded 7 June 1494)' in WG Grewe (ed) *Fontes Historiae Iuris Gentium: Quellen zur Geschichte des Völkerrechts 1493–1815* (De Gruyter Berlin 1988) vol 2, 110–16 ('Treaty of Tordesillas').

[21] See the contribution by M Scattola 'Alberico Gentili (1552–1608)' in this volume.

[22] L Benton 'Legalities of the Sea in Gentili's *Hispanica Advocatio*' in B Kingsbury and B Straumann (eds) *The Roman Foundations of the Law of Nations: Alberico Gentili and the Justice of Empire* (OUP Oxford 2010) 269–82 at 275–6; *The Freedom of the Seas in History, Law, and Politics* (n 5) 52–5.

2.3. 'The Battle of the Books': Grotius, Selden, and their Contemporaries

The context for the 17th century's great debate on freedom of the seas was the competition between Portugal and the Dutch Republic for access to the trade riches of the East Indies. Portugal, relying on the Papal donation of 1493 and the division with Spain the following year, asserted near-monopoly authority over trade in spices and other products from all the East Indies and sought to exclude all competing merchants, especially those of the upstart Dutch. On their part, the Dutch established their own East India Company (*Vereenigde Oost-Indische Compagnie*) in 1602. Portugal and Holland thus competed for the trade attentions of a variety of well-organized polities and sovereigns on the Indian sub-continent, Indo-China, and the East Indies.[23]

This competition soon escalated into full-blown conflict between Portugal and the Dutch Republic. In February 1603, a Dutch squadron captured an exceedingly valuable Portuguese galleon, The Santa Catharina, in the straits of Molucca. The vessel was brought to Amsterdam and condemned as prize. At this juncture, a young Dutch jurist by the name of Hugo de Groot (Grotius) (1583–1645),[24] was approached to prepare an opinion on the legality of the capture. Some constituents within the Dutch East India Company were concerned that the taking of the Santa Catharina was tantamount to waging an unjust war. Grotius' resulting work-product (written in 1604–5) was a treatise later known as *De jure praedae commentarius* (Commentary on the law of prize and booty), which was only fully published in the 19th century. One chapter of *De jure praedae* did appear contemporaneously with the Santa Catharina controversy, and it was initially published anonymously in 1609 under the title, *Mare liberum*.[25]

Mare liberum is notionally divided into three sets of arguments. The first (chapters II–IV) deals with titles to sovereignty to East Indies territories. The second (chapters I, V–VII) concerns freedom of navigation in the Indian Ocean. The third (chapters VIII–XIII) relates to international trade. Grotius emphasized that he was explicating the 'primary' or 'first' law of nations,[26] based on Roman law foundations and humanist traditions, and borrowing substantially from the writings of Fernando Vázquez y Menchaca. Following Roman law precepts he held that the seas are incapable of occupation and that freedom of navigation is a natural right. Grotius does make a limited recognition of the difference between proprietary rights and the authority to protect and assert jurisdiction offshore, a legal distinction for which he cites Baldus but for which he may have been in Gentili's intellectual debt.[27] Even Grotius grudgingly concedes that the classical sources seem to have acknowledged

---

[23] *An Introduction to the History of the Law of Nations* (n 1) 42–9.

[24] See the contribution by P Haggenmacher 'Hugo Grotius (1583–1645)' in this volume.

[25] *Origin and Development of the Law of the Sea* (n 1) 77–81; CG Roelofsen 'Grotius and the International Politics of the Seventeenth Century' in H Bull, B Kingsbury, and A Roberts (eds) *Hugo Grotius and International Relations* (Clarendon Press Oxford 1990) 95–131, at 104–11.

[26] *The Free Sea* (n 13) 10, 20–1.   [27] ibid 31.

a limited form of occupation of the sea, provided that a 'public' easement was respected.[28]

It is apparent that Grotius' categorical position on freedom of the seas in *Mare liberum* was neither so intuitive (based on the sources available to him), nor so immutable. He appears to have ignored what may have been emerging State practice among European polities (Genoa, Venice, England, and Denmark, to name just a few jurisdictions), in favour of first principles—the 'primary' law of nations. Some scholars have thus suggested that Grotius adopted an Asian, not a European, view of freedom of the seas,[29] and aligned it with Roman law. And, unspoken in *Mare liberum* was another paradox: Grotius' client, the Dutch East India Company, was as aggressive in asserting monopoly power over trade with the East as the Spanish and Portuguese.[30] In short, the notion of 'closed seas' (*mare clausum*) was as popular, if not more so, than *mare liberum* at the beginning of the 17th century.

Indeed, Grotius would later recant, to some degree, the unqualified positions he took in *Mare liberum*. In the course of Anglo-Dutch negotiations in 1613 and 1615, concerning the Moluccan spice trade, the English had the temerity to cite *Mare liberum* to Grotius (as head of the Dutch delegation) as grounds for invalidating the exclusive monopoly that the Dutch were purporting to exercise in the East Indies. Grotius replied that such monopolies were merely future commercial arrangements, and did not violate of the law of nations if their terms were reasonable. This argument is repeated verbatim in Grotius' 1625 *De jure belli ac pacis* (On the laws of war and peace).[31] And, yet, despite these retractions, Grotius stood by the main thrust of his thesis in *Mare liberum*: that ocean areas were immune from claims of dominion and that freedom of navigation was a natural right of peoples and nations.[32]

This is apparent from Grotius' unpublished response to William Welwood's 1613 tract, *Of the Community and Propriety of the Seas*.[33] Welwood, whose works appeared between 1578 and 1622, was a professor at St Andrews University in Scotland, and the first to write a treatise in English on the law of the sea. Welwood emphasized that the law of nations is based on 'common consent',[34] and so he drew from what he collected as State practice from his time. He ultimately reached a compromise

---

[28] ibid 28 (citing the Roman jurists Celsus, Ulpian, and Labeo).

[29] *An Introduction to the History of the Law of Nations* (n 1) 44, 229.

[30] K Zemanek 'Was Hugo Grotius Really in Favor of Freedom of the Seas?' (1999) 1 Journal of the History of International Law 48–60 at 56.

[31] H Grotius *On the Laws of War and Peace (1625)* (FW Kelsey trans) (Classics of International Law series) (OUP Oxford 1925) vol 2, at 205 (passage II.2.24).

[32] WE Butler 'Grotius and the Law of the Sea' in *Hugo Grotius and International Relations* (n 25) 209–20 at 212–16; F Pauw *Grotius and the Law of the Sea* (Publications du Centre de droit international et de sociologie appliquée au droit international Brussels 1965).

[33] *The Free Sea* (n 26) 63, 75.   [34] ibid 69.

position in the face of Grotius' argument: that the principle of freedom of the seas may well apply to open ocean areas (what we would call the high seas today), but not to coastal areas and assertions of coastal State interests over fisheries.[35] In his reply manuscript, drafted around 1615, Grotius took issue with Welwood's characterization of the law of nations as being based on consent, and took a more nuanced approach to the use of customary norms.[36] Even more significantly, Grotius disputed Welwood's distinction in application between high seas and coastal areas, arguing that such was unsustainable and would lead inevitably to erosion of freedoms of navigation.[37]

A more sustained critique of Grotius' thesis was presented in a 1625 volume, *De iusto imperio Lusitanorum Asiatico* (On the Just Empire of the Portuguese in Asia), written by Serafim de Freitas (who was probably born in 1570 and who died in 1633), a Portuguese friar on the faculty of law at Valladolid.[38] Freitas's main contention was that the right to free trade and navigation, whatever its roots in the natural law espoused in Grotius' classical sources, had never become a part of the law of nations. A sovereign could thus exclude foreigners from his territories and thus could forbid his subjects to trade with them.[39] Even more significantly, Freitas hotly disputed Grotius' distinction (borrowed from Vázquez) between two branches of a law of nations: primary (immutable, natural) rules and secondary (customary or consensual) norms. Any notion of 'freedom of the seas', Freitas asserted, was permissive and could be altered by the whim of a sovereign.[40] Finally, Freitas resorted to a careful exegesis of the classical legal sources—especially the extract from Ulpian that Grotius so much relied upon—and concluded that while in Roman private law it was a nullity to assert dominion over the seas, in Roman public law such had been accomplished (at least to a limited degree) by the Roman empire.[41] In other words, it was possible for a territorial sovereign, by long usage, to establish a prescriptive right of 'quasi-occupation' over specific ocean areas for particular purposes.[42]

The similarities between Freitas' argument and that of the English publicist, John Selden (1584–1654), as enshrined in his 1635 tract, *Mare clausum* (Closed Seas), have been observed.[43] But such may have been purely coincidental. Selden actually had drafted his response to Grotius in the years immediately following the appearance of *Mare liberum* in 1609. But Selden's royal patron, King James I, forbade its publication for many years,

---

[35] ibid 74.   [36] ibid 106–7.   [37] ibid 126–7.
[38] CH Alexandrowicz 'Freitas *versus* Grotius' (1959) 35 British Yearbook of International Law 162–82; MB Vieira '*Mare Liberum* vs. *Mare Clausum*: Grotius, Freitas and Selden's Debate on Dominion over the Seas' (2003) 64 Journal of the History of Ideas 361–77.
[39] E Gordon 'Grotius and the Freedom of the Seas in the Seventeenth Century' (2008) 16 Willamette Journal of International Law and Dispute Resolution 252–69 at 261.
[40] 'Freitas *versus* Grotius' (n 38) 165; Mare Liberum vs. Mare Clausum (n 38) 365–6.
[41] '*Mare Liberum* vs. *Mare Clausum*' (n 38) 373–4.
[42] 'Freitas *versus* Grotius' (n 38) 174–5.
[43] '*Mare Liberum* vs. *Mare Clausum*' (n 38) 374, 377.

in fear of alienating the Dutch Republic and Kingdom of Denmark, both of which England was diplomatically cultivating during this period.[44] Even so, during the reign of King James I, royal proclamations were issued which purported to claim all fisheries along the British and Irish coasts and prohibiting foreign vessels from fishing in those proximate waters without a royal licence. Marshaling a wealth of humanist and biblical scholarship—in much the same manner as Grotius did in *De jure belli ac pacis*—Selden sought to make a full justification for the possibility of national occupation of, and dominion over, ocean areas. And, in a departure from Grotius' selection of international law sources, Selden employed evidence of European practice. Even while conceding that many such claims (especially those of Spain and Portugal in the New World and East Indies) were inchoate and spurious, Selden reserved the possibility that such assertions could be proven through evidence of continued occupation, possession or usage.[45]

The 'battle of the books' on freedom of the seas raged throughout most of the 17th century.[46] But, by the end of that century, the intellectual conflict was over. Grotius and the principle of freedom of the seas won a resounding victory. In large measure this had nothing to do with the academic merits of the positions taken, sources employed, or arguments arrayed on either side of the debate. Rather, as will be explained further below, it was the product of power politics: the ascendancy of maritime powers (especially Britain, the Netherlands, and France) at the expense of both coastal State or territorial imperial interests. But from the writings of this period it is apparent that there was an intellectual engagement (if not preoccupation) with, in Daniel Patrick O'Connell's words, 'the competition between the exercise of governmental authority over the sea and the idea of the freedom of the seas'.[47]

2.4. Mercantilism and Empire, Conflict and Codification (1700–1930)

With the dawn of the 18th century, the law of the sea emerged into a period of great stability and coherence that would persist for nearly 250 years. As just suggested, the intellectual discourse of the 16th and 17th centuries had reached a juncture where the principle of freedom of the seas was widely followed by most maritime powers, with the caveat that coastal States could exercise a narrow range of authority over navigation and fisheries very close to shore (what was often referred to as the 'maritime league' or 'cannon-shot' doctrine, more on which below).

---

[44] 'Grotius and the Freedom of the Seas' (n 39) 264–5.

[45] *The Freedom of the Seas in History, Law, and Politics* (n 5) 72.

[46] *Origin and Development of the Law of the Sea* (n 1) 107; *The International Law of the Sea* (n 13) vol 1, 12–13, 17–18 (discussing Conring, Gothofredus, Molloy, Pontanus, and Pufendorf).

[47] *The International Law of the Sea* (n 13) vol 1, 1.

This new synthesis in the contours of the law of the sea was best captured in the work of Cornelis van Bynkershoek (1673–1743), a Dutch jurist whose primary contribution to the literature was his *De dominio maris dissertatio*, published in 1702, and later revised in 1744.[48] In his volume, Bynkershoek concluded that '[today] no part of the ocean is possessed by anyone'.[49] Nevertheless, drawing from contemporary State practice (particularly the claims of Baltic nations), Bynkershoek recognized that possessory and usage claims to certain maritime belts could be strengthened within close proximity to shore (up to three or four nautical miles) by the assertion of force (from land-based fortifications) and by continuous navigation.[50] He essentially charted a middle course between Grotius and Selden, marking a compromise that would last centuries.

Bynkershoek's most remarkable contribution to the intellectual tradition of the law of the sea lay, however, in another dimension. He took strong issue with a bedrock assumption of the 'freedom of the seas' position: that ocean resources (whether viewed as navigation rights, access to fisheries, or use of other maritime assets) were essentially inexhaustible and limitless. Because of this, the theory posited, there was simply no justification for national assertions of dominion. Grotius embraced this view.[51] But Bynkershoek—even while he adhered to a robust vision of freedom of the seas—categorically rejected this. 'A *res communis*', he wrote, 'can be made almost useless by promiscuous use, as often happens in a sea which has been fished out'.[52] This comment neatly anticipates the phenomenon of what we would today call the 'tragedy of the commons'.[53] It was also a recognition of new economic realities for ocean uses, and the imperative that the principle of freedom of the seas be premised on sensible assumptions.

The intellectual synthesis that Bynkershoek crafted—if accommodation is really what it was—was thus attributable to a number of economic and geo-political factors. The leading one was the establishment of a paradigm for the law of the sea that carries on to this day.[54] That is the enduring competition between maritime State interests and those of coastal States, and the superimposition of that legal contestation in terms of ocean zones of control. Maritime States have a primary interest in assuring freedom of global trade and the ability to project power (through naval

[48] K Akashi *Cornelius van Bynkershoek: His Role in the History of International Law* (Kluwer Dordrecht 1998); *The Freedom of the Seas in History, Law, and Politics* (n 5) 85–6, 91; JB Scott 'Introduction' in C van Bynkershoek *De Dominio Maris Dissertatio* (1744) in JB Scott (ed) *The Classics of International Law* (OUP New York 1923) 13–22; see also the portrait by K Akashi 'Cornelius van Bynkershoek (1673–1743)' in this volume.

[49] 'Introduction' (n 48) 79.

[50] ibid 43–4.

[51] *The Free Sea* (n 26) 110–12.

[52] 'Introduction' (n 48) 91.

[53] G Hardin 'The Tragedy of the Commons' (1968) 162 Science 1243–48 (resources held in common inevitably degrade because no actor has an incentive to conserve them).

[54] *The Freedom of the Seas in History, Law, and Politics* (n 5) 171, 188.

assets) wherever and whenever they seek. Conversely, coastal States desire to ensure—for reasons of resource and national security—that ocean areas immediately contiguous to their land territory are under their exclusive control or sovereignty. Under this model, the farther one moves from shore, the less authority and power the coastal State should have, and the greater principle of freedom of the seas ought to prevail.

The 1700s witnessed two developments that would reinforce this paradigm. The first was the solidification of global trading networks and empires. Under the regime of mercantilism, countries such as Britain, France, Portugal and Spain sought to guarantee access to raw materials for domestic industries, and the protection of markets to the exclusion of any other economic rivals or competitors. So, despite the rhetoric of earlier centuries, the reality of 'freedom of the seas', at least in economic terms, was typically in the form of trade restrictions among competing national commercial empires. The commercial, and then industrial, revolutions in Europe (1700–1850) inevitably affected global peripheries by compelling their integration into a global trading system.[55]

The second development was the close integration of law of the sea principles with the dictates of maritime warfare. The 18th century saw, for nearly the first time, periods of truly global conflict emanating from European rivalries. These culminated in the Seven Years War (or Great War for Empire, 1756–63) and the Wars of the French Revolution and Napoleonic Wars (1792–1815). During this period, maritime powers also confronted—and largely defeated—that inevitable scourge of freedom of the seas: piracy. Organized brigandage at sea was an inevitable consequence of a globalized economy, competing national commercial empires, and the theoretical precepts of maritime freedom.[56] So, in the course of the 18th and early 19th centuries, the European powers (joined by the United States, and (later) by Latin American republics) were simultaneously challenged to develop rules of naval warfare consistent with the basic principles of freedom of the seas, while, at the same time, affording them freedom of action to suppress unlawful uses of open ocean spaces (piracy, and later, the slave trade).

The rules of naval conflict that mattered most to maritime powers were those pertaining to the capture of enemy and neutral shipping. There was certainly precedent for this preoccupation—after all, the opening salvo of the 'battle of the books' was the 1603 capture of the Santa Catharina by the Dutch. By 1815, there had developed a highly elaborate body of jurisprudence dealing with maritime captures, largely administered by domestic prize courts and applying an international customary law on this subject.

---

[55] An *Introduction to the History of the Law of Nations* (n 1) 124–9.

[56] ibid (n 1) 111–15; J Baer (ed) *British Piracy in the Golden Age: History and Interpretation, 1660–1730* (Pickering & Chatto London 2007); V Lunsford *Piracy and Privateering in the Golden Age Netherlands* (Palgrave Macmillan New York 2005); C Woodard *The Republic of Pirates Being the True and Surprising Story of the Caribbean Pirates and the Man Who Brought Them Down* (Harcourt New York 2007).

These prize tribunals—the most influential of which was the English High Court of Admiralty, presided over by Sir William Scott (Lord Stowell) during the Napoleonic Wars[57]—routinely dealt with such issues as where captures could be legitimately made and the potential enemy character of ostensibly neutral vessels and cargoes.[58] Both of these issues implicated profound freedoms of the seas, especially in wartime.

With the defeat of Napoleonic France, and the unquestioned supremacy of British naval power after the Battle of Trafalgar (1805), the law of the sea settled in to a century-long quiescence with few theoretical challenges being made to the principle of freedom of the seas. The 19th century's *Pax Britannica* marked the confirmation of doctrinal verities in the law of the sea: open trade, extremely limited coastal State authority (even in the face of such challenges as rampant smuggling), and predictable rules of maritime captures. During this period, Britain steadfastly refused to accede to any increases in coastal State authority and its position was vindicated in a number of diplomatic incidents and international arbitrations.[59]

Nor did the First World War materially change any of the essential premises of the law of the sea, even as the conflict utterly destroyed the old European order which had created this maritime system of empire, free trade, and colonialism. Prize courts adjudicated captures in much the same fashion as occurred a century before during the Napoleonic Wars. Naval blockades were applied as *sui generis, ius in bello* exceptions to the traditional freedom of the seas that would normally prevail during peacetime. Not even national security concerns about scarce resources (food and petrol, for example) would motivate coastal States in 1919 to assert new authority over offshore areas, as occurred in the aftermath of the Second World War with the Truman Proclamations in 1945.[60]

The first glimmerings of potential changes in the law of the sea came only with the League of Nations' efforts to generally codify international law. For the first time, attention was drawn to the need to clarify the law of the sea that had prevailed for centuries. One part[61] of this initiative was a project undertaken to codify the breadth and nature of the territorial sea regime—the law governing that band of waters just offshore a coastal State (what had been encompassed within the three-mile or cannon-shot rule). This culminated in the 1930 League Codification Conference, held at The Hague.

[57] H Bourguignon *Sir William Scott, Lord Stowell: Judge of the High Court of Admiralty, 1798–1828* (CUP Cambridge 1987) at 115–241.

[58] D Bederman 'The Feigned Demise of Prize' (1995) 9 Emory International Law Review 31; The Development of International Law (n 9) 56–7; JHW Verzijl, W Heere, and JPS Offerhaus *The Law of Maritime Prize: International Law in Historical Perspective* (Kluwer Dordrecht 1992) vol 11, at 1–31.

[59] The International Law of the Sea (n 17) 101–2; *Bering Sea Fur Seals Arbitration* (US v Great Britain) (1893).

[60] Proclamation 2667 of 28 September 1945, United States Policy Concerning Natural Resources of the Seabed and Fisheries on the High Seas, 10 Fed Reg 12305 (1945).

[61] The League also undertook studies of the international law of piracy and exploitation of products of the sea. See 'League of Nations Committee of Experts for the Progressive Codification of International Law, Questionnaire No. 7, adopted by the Committee at its Second Session held in January 1926, Exploitation of the products of the Sea' (1926) 20 American Journal of International Law Special Supplement 230–51.

Even after much preparatory work by a group of experts,[62] no agreement could be reached at the conference as to extending the breadth of a coastal State's territorial waters beyond three nautical miles. The great maritime powers—including the United Kingdom and United States—were opposed to such a measure. But in a draft resolution adopted by the conference in its Final Act, there was consensus that the legal regime prevailing in the territorial sea was tantamount to coastal State sovereignty, including authority and jurisdiction over the natural resources (fisheries, in particular) of that zone. Coastal State sovereignty was qualified by a rule of innocent passage (more on which below), allowing free navigation through territorial waters.[63] The 1930 Hague Codification Conference thus anticipated many of the doctrinal concerns and developments that would arise with the law of the sea after 1945.

3. DOCTRINAL DEVELOPMENTS

By the time of the 1930 Hague Codification Conference, the main doctrinal features of the law of the sea were formed in a way that would be fully recognizable today. These regimes were the natural product of the intellectual trends just discussed: the Eurocentrism of the law of the sea; the conceptual division between 'ownership' of ocean areas and 'jurisdiction' over maritime activities; the notional supremacy of freedom of the seas; the dynamic competition between coastal State and maritime Power interests; and the growing realization that ocean resources were not boundless.

The main feature of law of the sea regimes is, of course, the formalism that comes with the management of maritime zones emanating from shore. Beginning with the conception of territorial waters by Bynkershoek—a narrow band of sea immediately offshore a coastal State as defined by an objective measure—we today have a very complex set of interlocking zonal regimes. It very much matters 'where' in the ocean a particular event takes place, because such a location determines the relevant set of rules for legal conduct. The formalism of this system should, as O'Connell acknowledged, be balanced by pragmatism in the 'content' of the norms for each

---

[62] League of Nations Committee of Experts for the Progressive Codification of International Law, 'Questionnaire No. 2, adopted by the Committee at its Second Session held in January 1926, Territorial Waters' (1926) 20 American Journal of International Law Special Supplement 62–147.

[63] *The International Law of the Sea* (n 17) 103–6; *The International Law of the Sea* (n 13) vol 1, 21; League of Nations *Acts of Conferences for the Codification of International Law* 1930 (Geneva 1931) (LN doc C.351.M.145, 1930, V.); Report of the Second Commission, League of Nations Publication V. Legal, 1930.V. 9 (C.230, M. I 17, 1930. V).

zone, but that still belies the theoretical necessity of creating such a system in the first place. One can legitimately ask whether this deep structure for the law of the sea promotes stability or change for the entire intellectual enterprise.

For much of the time canvassed here, the primary maritime zone of contention was a coastal State's territorial waters. Once Bynkershoek's compromise position[64] was widely adopted, discussions as to the juridical character of territorial seas appeared to reflect a 'property' or 'territorial' view of the coastal State's rights in that zone. State practice from the 18th and 19th centuries—as manifested in treaties, diplomatic correspondence, and prize or revenue decisions[65]—seemed to concur that the waters immediately adjacent to a coastal State's land domain were 'considered as part of the territory of the sovereign'.

The consequence of this position was that any capture of a vessel in another country's territorial waters was a violation of that country's sovereignty, and was null and void. Additionally, having a definitive limit to territorial waters (one marine league or three nautical miles) led to formalistic resolutions of situations where 'limits in the sea' had to be observed and accommodated.[66] (The doctrine of hot pursuit, for example, proceeded on the assumption that an enforcement action at sea had to cease the moment that a suspect vessel entered another nation's territorial waters.[67])

Of course, the 'cannon-shot' rule was the principle that seemed to best enshrine the Bynkershoek compromise that brought synthesis to the Grotius—Selden debates of the early 1600s. As contemporary publicists have noted, though, the cannon-shot rule 'bore no necessary or logical relation to the question of the sovereignty of the seas. It was a convenient device for linking up diverse, albeit cognate questions...'.[68] In addition to promoting a formalism, the rule proceeded from a fiction—that the entirety of a coastal State's shoreline (and not just a harbour or port) was fortified with gun emplacements capable of projecting power offshore. Over time, the cannon-shot rule gave way to a measured distance of one marine league.[69] By the time of the Seven Years War, the wars of the American Revolution, and the Napoleonic Wars, this appeared to be the standard of international practice and was already reflected in domestic legislation and international agreements.[70] The three-mile rule

---

[64] See sub-s 2.4, at 12.

[65] *The Vrow Anna Catharina* (1802) 5 Ch Rob 15, 165 ER 809; *Church v Hubbart* 2 Cranch 187, 234; 6 US 187 US Supreme Court (1804).

[66] H Crocker *The Extent of the Marginal Sea: A Collection of Official Documents and Views of Representative Publicists* (US Department of State Washington 1919); P Jessup *The Law of Territorial Waters and Maritime Jurisdiction* (Jennings New York 1927).

[67] *The Freedom of the Seas in History, Law, and Politics* (n 5) 102–4.

[68] *The International Law of the Sea* (n 13) vol 1, 125.

[69] H Kent 'The Historical Origins of the Three-Mile Limit' (1954) 48 American Journal of International Law 537–53; DP O'Connell *The Influence of Law on Sea Power* (Manchester University Press Manchester 1975) at 24; W Walker 'Territorial Waters: The Cannon Shot Rule' (1945) 22 British Yearbook of International Law 210–31.

[70] *The International Law of the Sea* (n 13) vol 1, 129–39; Neutrality Act 1794 (US) 1 Stat 381–4.

was applied not only to adjudicate whether maritime captures were proper, but also the permissible extent of a coastal State's fisheries jurisdiction.

There were inevitable challenges to the notion that coastal States exercised sovereignty within territorial waters. As a doctrinal matter, one question was the right of foreign vessels (whether characterized as private shipping, State vessels, or warships) to traverse another country's territorial sea. This was the doctrine of innocent passage, and was largely confirmed in State practice by 1800.[71] Aside from a right of passage, there was also the corollary question of whether a coastal State could exercise any form of jurisdiction over a foreign vessel engaged in such a voyage. In 1876, the English Court of Crown Cases Reserved held that the captain of a foreign ship could not be tried for manslaughter committed in Britain's territorial sea (following a fatal collision).[72] In response, Britain legislated the Territorial Waters Jurisdiction Act,[73] purporting to assert criminal jurisdiction over incidents occurring in territorial waters. This was an immensely controversial move—especially by Great Britain, which had, historically, resisted any efforts to extend coastal State authority offshore.[74]

In any event, by the time of the Hague Codification Conference in 1930 it was beyond cavil that coastal States exercised sovereignty within their territorial seas, 'subject to the right of passage by the commercial vessels of other nations'.[75] Far more contentious, however, was the matter of whether foreign warships were free to traverse territorial waters under the innocent passage regime (as distinct from other conditions, such as transit passage—a set of rules developed only much later). In 1807, the United States took the position that the admission of foreign warships into its territorial waters, even in time of peace, could be refused on due cause.[76] The United States adhered to this position until its emergence as a superpower in the aftermath of the Second World War.[77]

In addition to problems arising under the doctrine of innocent passage, another scenario—common in the early 19th century—was that foreign smugglers would 'hover' their vessels just beyond the territorial sea limit, trans-ship their goods to smaller boats that would then proceed inshore, all the time hoping to evade revenue

---

[71] *The Twee Gebroederst* (1801) 3 Ch Rob 336, 352–4, ER 502.

[72] *R v Keyn* (Ferdinand) (The Franconia) [1876–77] LR 2 Ex D 63; [1876–77] LR 2 QBD 90 (English Crown Cases Reserved).

[73] The Territorial Waters Jurisdiction Act 1878 (UK) 41 and 42 Vict ch 73.

[74] *The International Law of the Sea* (n 13) vol 1, 61–4 (collecting contemporary criticism by publicists).

[75] *North Atlantic Coast Fisheries Arbitration (Great Britain v US)* (1910) Scott Hague Court Rep 141; *Proceedings of the North Atlantic Coast Fisheries Arbitration* (1912) vol 4, at 92; Barcelona Convention on the Regime of Navigable Waterways of International Concern (adopted 20 April 1921, entered into force 31 October 1922) 7 LNTS 27, 35, art 3.

[76] American State Papers, Foreign Relations vol 3, No 205 (Gales and Seaton Washington DC 1832) at 22 (HMS Leopard incident, 1807).

[77] *The Influence of Law on Sea Power* (n 69) vol 1, 138–9.

enforcement by the coastal State. This gave rise to the creation of a regime for a second maritime belt—now known as a 'contiguous zone'—in which the coastal State could exercise some forms of enforcement power and jurisdiction.

The initial State practice in favour of establishing a contiguous zone was Britain's 1736 Hovering Act,[78] later renewed in 1764, 1802, 1825, and 1853, which prescribed criminal penalties for vessels and individuals engaged in smuggling offshore, even beyond a maritime league.[79] These acts were justified by Lord Stowell (writing for the English High Court of Admiralty) as an exercise of 'the common courtesy of nations for their convenience to consider those parts of the ocean adjoining their shores as part of their dominions for various domestic purposes and particularly for fiscal or defensive regulations more immediately affecting their safety and welfare'.[80] Nevertheless, by the end of the 19th century, Britain repealed its Hovering Acts to conform with what it believed was the principle that no foreign vessel should be subject to any customs or revenue regulations beyond the three-mile limit.[81]

But by the late 1800s and early 1900s, the juridical regime of a contiguous zone had certainly entered into the customary international law of the sea. The United States had its own form of Hovering Act by 1799 (exercising customs jurisdiction out to four leagues, or 12 nautical miles),[82] and US courts recognized the authority of foreign nations to reasonably exercise such authority off their coasts.[83] The doctrine of the contiguous zone was given new life, at least in United States practice, during the prohibition-era of the 1920s with import bans on alcohol into the US. Other nations expressly agreed to US enforcement of prohibition laws by the boarding and search of their vessels, even beyond US territorial waters to a distance of one-hour's sailing from shore.[84]

By the time of the 1930 Hague Codification Conference, a crucial question for resolution was the breadth of the contiguous zone and its precise character. Proposals were made to have either a six- or nine-nautical-mile contiguous zone added to a three-mile territorial sea, where a coastal State 'may exercise the control necessary to prevent, within its territory or territorial waters, the infringement of its customs or sanitary regulations or interference with its security by foreign ships'.[85] This proposal

---

[78] Hovering Act (1736) 9 Geo II ch 35.   [79] *The International Law of the Sea* (n 17) 136–8.

[80] *The Le Louis* (1817) 2 Dods 210, 245, 165 ER 1464.

[81] Customs Consolidation Act 1876 (UK) 39 and 40 Vict ch 36, s 179

[82] Act of 2 March 1799 (US) 1 Stat 627, 668, ch 22, s 54.

[83] Church v Hubbart (n 65).

[84] Convention between the United States of America and Great Britain to Aid in the Prevention of the Smuggling of Intoxicating Liquors into the United States (23 January 1924) US Treaty Series No 685, arts 2 and 3; *The International Law of the Sea* (n 17) 140–3.

[85] *Acts of Conferences* (n 63); Territorial Waters (1930) 24 American Journal of International Law Supplement: Official Document 25–46 at 29.

was doomed by reference to a security zone, even though in the years running-up to the Second World War some nations proposed such a regime.[86] But, at The Hague, Britain objected in principle to any codification of the contiguous zone (much less delimiting its appropriate breadth), and this was only accomplished at the First UN Conference on the Law of the Sea in 1956 and the 1958 Geneva Convention on the Territorial Sea and Contiguous Zone.[87]

By 1945, the broad contours of the juridical status of territorial seas and contiguous zones were enshrined in the law of the sea. So, too, were the precedents for those maritime zones largely concerned with resource jurisdiction. Indeed, in the 'battle of the books' of the early 17th century, the primary contribution of the English publicists—including William Welwood and John Selden—was that dominion over the seas (at least for near-shore areas) was necessary for the protection of local fisheries. Emmerich de Vattel and JMG Rayneval, writing in the late 18th and early 19th centuries, argued that the resources of the seabed immediately offshore belonged to the coastal State.[88]

Unilateral decrees by northern European States of the 19th century established fisheries jurisdiction out as far as ten nautical miles. By the late 1800s, these same polities began to conclude bilateral fishing agreements which mutually established more modest fishery jurisdiction limits at three miles. This was as far as the United Kingdom would accede (consistent with its view about the breadth of the territorial sea), even though other countries were clamouring for extended fishery limits.[89] At the 1930 Hague Codification Conference, strong efforts were made—especially by Latin American countries—to create a new regime for a fisheries zone extending to twelve nautical miles, but to no avail.[90] Offshore oil and gas deposits were even the subject of bilateral treaties in the 1940s.[91] All of this anticipated the 1945 Truman Proclamations and the extraordinary developments in State practice which saw the creation of regimes for the continental shelf and exclusive economic zone, in the period from 1945 to 1982.

[86] 'Consultative Meeting of Foreign Ministers of the American Republics, Declaration of Panama (3 October 1939)' (1940) 34 American Journal of International Law Supplement: Official Documents 1–20 at 17–18, paras 1 and 4.

[87] Geneva Convention on the Territorial Sea and Contiguous Zone (adopted 29 April 1958, entered into force 10 September 1964) 516 UNTS 205; M McDougal and W Burke *World Public Order of the Oceans* (Yale University Press New Haven 1958) at 601; HA Smith 'The Contiguous Zone' (1939) 20 British Yearbook of International Law 122–5.

[88] *The International Law of the Sea* (n 13) vol 1, 468–9.

[89] *The Sovereignty of the Sea* (n 13) 693–740.

[90] *Le droit international public de la mer* (n 16) vol 3, 297–305; *The International Law of the Sea* (n 13) vol 1, 526–7.

[91] Treaty Relating to the Submarine Areas of the Gulf of Paria between Great Britain and Venezuela (adopted 26 February 1942, entered into force 22 September 1942) 205 LNTS 121.

4. Conclusion

The law of the sea's history can be viewed from a number of perspectives. It need not be regarded exclusively as a progress narrative of freedom, finely balanced with concerns as to resource security and naval necessity. Indeed, there is almost a dialectic phenomenon at work here over the past millennia. Theoretical and doctrinal syntheses (such as those by Justinian or Grotius or Bynkershoek) gave way—albeit over centuries—to new positions. Superimposed on these theoretical conditions for the development of the law of the sea—especially in light of the inherent Eurocentrism of the entire project—is a unique doctrinal structure. Law of the sea regimes emphasize a high degree of formalism, combined with a growing willingness to have State practice dictate the pragmatic consequences of ocean activities.

In the years since 1945, we have seen an increased tempo to changes in ocean regimes. The period from 1945 to 1982 was certainly the most tumultuous since the 'Grotian moment' for *mare liberum* in the early 1600s. Even after the comprehensive codification of the law of the sea in 1982 United Nations Convention,[92] we have witnessed startling efforts to refashion some sub-sets of rules for the system (most notably for high seas fisheries, environmental protection, underwater cultural heritage, and deep seabed resources). We may expect such selective efforts at progressive development of particular law of the sea regimes to intensify. It is also possible that we may be reaching a 'tipping-point', as in 1600 or 1945, where we encounter a 'revolutionary' climax for the system.

This contribution has sought to place ocean legal history's trajectory in a broader perspective. Far from being ancillary to the main currents of international legal history (especially bearing on questions of sovereignty, use of force, exercises of jurisdiction, and vindication of human rights), developments in the law of the sea have been central to the chief challenges confronting the discipline over the past 500 years. Any coherent account of international law must address the long, and distinguished, history of the law of the sea.

Recommended Reading

Alexandrowicz, Charles H 'Freitas versus Grotius' (1959) 35 British Yearbook of International Law 162–82.

Alexandrowicz, Charles H *An Introduction to the History of the Law of Nations in the East Indies (16th, 17th and 18th Centuries)* (Clarendon Press Oxford 1967).

---

[92] United Nations Convention on the Law of the Sea (adopted 10 December 1982, entered into force 16 November 1994) 1833 UNTS 396.

Anand, Ram P *Origin and Development of the Law of the Sea* (Martinus Nijhoff The Hague 1983).

Butler, Geoffrey and Simon Maccoby *The Development of International Law* (Longmans Green London 1928).

Bynkershoek, Cornelius *De Dominio Maris Dissertatio* (2nd edn 1744) in JB Scott *Classics of International Law* (OUP New York 1923).

Crocker, Henry *The Extent of the Marginal Sea: A Collection of Official Documents and Views of Representative Publicists* (US Department of State Washington 1919).

De Pauw, Frans *Grotius and the Law of the Sea* (Publications du Centre de droit international et de sociologie appliquée au droit international Brussels 1965).

Fulton, Thomas W *The Sovereignty of the Sea* (Blackwood London 1911).

Gidel, Gilbert *Le droit international public de la mer* (Sirey Paris 1934).

Grotius, Hugo *The Free Sea (1609)* (R Hakluyt trans) (Liberty Fund Indianapolis 2004).

Jessup, Philip *The Law of Territorial Waters and Maritime Jurisdiction* (Jennings New York 1927).

League of Nations *Acts of the Conference for the Codification of International Law* (League of Nations Geneva 1930).

League of Nations Committee of Experts for the Progressive Codification of International Law 'Questionnaire No. 2, adopted by the Committee at its Second Session held in January 1926, Territorial Waters' (1926) 20 American Journal of International Law Special Supplement 62–147.

McDougal, Myres S and William Burke *World Public Order of the Oceans* (Yale University Press, New Haven 1958).

O'Connell, Daniel P *The International Law of the Sea* (Clarendon Press Oxford 1982).

Potter, Pitman B *The Freedom of the Seas in History, Law, and Politics* (Longmans Green New York 1924).

Verzijl, Jan HW *International Law in Historical Perspective* (AW Sijthoff Leyden 1971) (vol 4—Stateless Domain).

Verzijl, Jan HW, Wybo Heere, and Polona S Offerhaus *The Law of Maritime Prize: International Law in Historical Perspective* (Kluwer Dordrecht 1992) (vol 11).

Vieira, Brito M 'Mare Liberum vs. Mare Clausum: Grotius, Freitas and Selden's Debate on Dominion over the Seas' (2003) 64 Journal of the History of Ideas 361–77.

Zemanek, Karl 'Was Hugo Grotius Really in Favor of Freedom of the Seas?' (1999) 1 Journal of the History of International Law 48–60.

PART III

REGIONS

I

AFRICA AND ARABIA

CHAPTER 16

AFRICA NORTH OF THE SAHARA AND ARAB COUNTRIES

FATIHA SAHLI AND ABDELMALEK EL OUAZZANI

1. INTRODUCTION

In his speech at the International Law Academy in the Hague in 1923, Baron Korff said: 'le droit international est aussi ancien que la civilisation en général, et il est réellement une conséquence nécessaire et inévitable de toute civilisation'.[1] This means that the history of international law did not start with the peace treaty of Westphalia in 1648, and that it was not only a European invention. Although in its current meaning, international law coincides with the concept of the nation-state, its origins go further back in history, and helped establish rules that regulate the relationships between independent political societies.[2]

Whatever the contribution of Greco-Roman antiquity and of Medieval Christianity to international law, we cannot ignore the contribution of other civilizations such as Islam, to this field. To say that international law is the proper purview of only one single civilization is unthinkable. In insisting on the Greco-Roman origins of

---

[1] M Korff 'Introduction à l'histoire du droit international' (1923) 1 Recueil des cours 5–23 at 21.

[2] MH Renault *Histoire du droit international public* (Editions Ellipses Paris 2007) at 3–4.

international law to claim it as essentially European, historians have omitted the contributions of other civilizations.

The alternation of war and peace has shaped relations between the Muslim and the Christian worlds, thus contributing in one way or another to the universal normative arsenal that is international law. A number of laws have been developed, especially in the Muslim world, during its domination over the Mediterranean basin and the extension of its influence which went deep into Asia, sub-Saharan Africa, and (Christian) Europe.[3] Romano-Germanic and Byzantine Europe certainly took advantage from those (Islamic) rules which constituted some of the basis of the theory of international law. If the fall of the Muslim kingdom of Granada in 1492 began the disintegration of the Christian and the Muslim worlds, it did not end in a total break. These States have continued negotiating in times of peace as well as in times of war, coming to agreements and signing common treaties in all areas, contributing therefore to the creation of international norms.

However, the conditions have been peculiar to both sides, since each lived and underwent problem and conflict imposed on it by its alliances from beyond its borders. The example of Moroccan alliance treaties[4] signed with some Western powers to resist the Ottoman forces which conquered Tlemcen (in Algeria) in 1556 and established its hegemony over all the Eastern Maghreb is a case in point. There is also the case of the alliances of some Iberian Muslim Kingdoms with the Christian nations around them to stop the expansionist desires of other neighbour Muslim Kingdoms; and the situation vice versa is also true.

Here we analyse North Africa's relationships with the other powers, mainly Christian; the main political directions these relations took; their characteristics; and the legal tools that were used to regulate relationships with other countries. But before doing so, it is important to offer an overview of the role which the area assumed in the history of international relations.

2. NORTH AFRICA IN INTERNATIONAL RELATIONS

North Africa has always been at the centre of international commerce. It was simultaneously the best export and import market for the goods that foreign countries needed.[5] North Africa was, therefore, not immune to international problems such as piracy on the

---

[3] An example for this development are the norms regarding war. Such norms were quite unknown to the other nations in the West.

[4] Some of these treaties are discussed below in Section 6.3 'Alliance treaties'.

[5] L Félix *Le statut international du Maroc d'après les traités* (A Pedone Paris 1928) at 6ff; H Ouazzani Chahdi *La pratique Marocaine du droit des traités* (LGDJ Paris 1982) at 13.

Mediterranean Sea, the wars in Europe, and the expansion of the Ottoman Empire. This could be explained by the numerous treaties,[6] mainly the bilateral ones, which were co-signed by the countries in this area. The history of international relations in this domain is therefore particularly rich.

Despite the fact that the relationships North Africa had with the rest of the world are as ancient as time, we have chosen[7] to deal with the period starting just after the fall of Granada because it was this event that really established a clear cleavage between North Africa and the rest of the world, and because it is close in time to the peace treaty signed in Westphalia, which is considered that 'the beginning of the contemporary international law'. Note though this phase did not really change anything in the strategic situation that North Africa occupied in the international relations.

2.1. The Strategic Location of North Africa in International Relations

This area is geopolitically of strategic importance, especially Morocco which is '… séparé de l'Espagne de seulement treize kilomètres (la largeur du détroit de Gibraltar) et dont le littoral atlantique le place sur les routes de l'Afrique Occidentale et de l'Amérique du Sud. Cette place au croisement des routes maritimes explique l'apparition, maintes fois répétée, d'"affaires marocaines" dans l'histoire des événements diplomatiques qui ont précédé la grande guerre.'[8]

As part of the Arab-Islamic world and as a strategic area, North Africa has become an important region in the history of international relations. To study its contribution to the creation of international norms requires taking two main factors into account: its belonging to two distinct worlds—the Arab-Islamic, and the European through its presence in Spain and Sicily[9]—and the envy with which it was viewed by

---

[6] See Section 6.3 'Alliance treaties'.

[7] We know that, according to Max Weber, any knowledge is selective and the glance of the researcher can embrace only one or some aspects of reality. But every choice needs to be justified, so we estimate it more relevant to be interested in the period after the fall of Muslim Spain which marks the beginning of the European conquests and the height of the conflicts between Mediterranean powers in which Ottoman Muslims became an important actor. For more details see M Weber *The Methodology of the Social Sciences* (EA Shils and HA Finch ed and trans) (Free Press of Glencoe Illinois 1949) at 72 ff.

[8] *Le statut international* (n 5) 12.

[9] E Moha says here: 'En effet, depuis l'antiquité, il n'y avait pas de délimitation bien précise entre les deux parties de cet espace (espace méditerranéen). Ni les religions, ni les prétendues différences ethniques, ni les systèmes politiques ne dressaient une frontière hermétique entre les peuples du Sud et ceux du Nord. L'Espagne et le Maroc avaient été durant longtemps les symboles de l'interpénétration et de liaison naturelle de part et d'autre du détroit de Gibraltar. Les Croisades et le caractère confessionnel qu'a donné l'inquisition à la Reconquista vont contribuer à diviser la Méditerranée en une zone européenne

Western powers as well as its Muslim neighbours, and all that this has engendered in the legal field.

However, when considering all this, a problem arises almost immediately: the problem relating to the value that international law confers on the treaties and common agreements that this area produced and undersigned. It is the legal status of these treaties that is put into question here.

2.2. The Legal Status of the Maghribi 'State Entities'

When the main players in this strategic region are not all under the same political authority, the study of their practices, mainly of the international treaties, would help in seeing that many international problems were dealt with in very similar ways by independent States like Morocco, and by regencies like Tunis or Algiers (Tunisia or Algeria). It is certain that the norms governing the treaties were different from one country to another, in that the regencies were obliged to submit them to the Ottoman authorities, while Morocco, an independent State, signed its own treaties itself. For Morocco, this was an independent and sovereign act, while for the other States, the treaties were subject to Ottoman will. It was this sovereignty that conferred on the Moroccan government the freedom to act in the international sphere.[10]

The North African States, except Morocco, were 'theoretically' dependent on the Ottoman Empire, but in fact they enjoyed a certain independence. Many jurists like the Italian Alberico Gentili (1552–1608) denied their quality as 'States' because of acts of piracy, while the Dutch Cornelius van Bynkershoek[11] refused to consider them as pirates. He wrote that

[t]he peoples of Algiers, Tripoli, Tunis, and Salee are not pirates, but rather organized states, which have fixed territory in which there is an established government, and with which, as with other nations, we are now at peace, now at war…they even have some respect for treaties.[12]

In fact, the Regencies of Algiers, and Tunis, contrary to Morocco, were from the beginning vassals to the Muslim conquerors. The dominance of many other powers, whether those of the Caliphates of Omar and Othman (two followers of the Prophet Mohamed and Khalifs), or those of the Oumayades (661–750), the Fatimides

---

chrétienne et une zone arabo-musulmane'. E Moha *Les relations Hispano-Marocaines* (Eddif Casablanca 1994) at 47.

[10] C de la Veronne 'Relation entre le Maroc et la Turquie dans la seconde moitié du XVIè siècle et le début du XVIIè siècle (1554–1616)' (1973) 15–16 Revue de l'Occident musulman et de la Mediterranée 391–401.

[11] See the contribution by K Akashi 'Cornelius van Bynkershoek (1673–1743)' in this volume.

[12] C van Bynkershoek *Quaestionum juris publici libri duo* (1773) in JB Scott (ed) *The Classics of International Law* (Clarendon Press Oxford 1930) vol 2, at 99.

(909–1171), or the Almoravides (1056–1147), or Al Mohades (1130–1269), or even those of simple local powers, made them vassals to these dynasties. But if these countries were legally tied to the sultan since the Ottoman conquest in the 16th century, their relationship gradually loosened; Algiers became an almost independent pirate centre, and Tunis became an almost independent kingdom. This is true despite the local currency and the prayers still being made in the name of the Ottoman sultan, and although he (the Ottoman sultan) continued to send to the new *Deys* the firmin of their nomination.[13] Yet Tunis became almost totally independent under the Husseiny Dynasty, a hereditary dynasty with which the French concluded a treaty on the protectorate of the country.[14] This dynasty remained undefeated until 1955 when the Tunisians voted for the change for a republic.[15] On the contrary, the status of Morocco has never been questioned, and the protectorate (from 1912–56) was but a parenthesis in its history.

Whatever their status was, when they signed an international treaty or an agreement, the North African States used to submit themselves to and respect the international laws. These agreements were made to find their ways into the basics of the Islamic doctrine as well as in the international practices.

3. The Theoretical and Doctrinal Foundations of the International Practices of the North African States

The contribution of Islamic civilization to international law through the practices of the North African States can neither be studied outside the way these States dealt with treaties, nor can it be separated from the Arab-Islamic way of thinking which, apart from all the divergences, had influenced some of the aspects of these practices.

Certainly, the initial problem which precedes any theoretical research is that of the historical causes. In law studies,

---

[13] B Tlili 'Kheiredinne' in CA Julien (ed) *Les Africains* (Editions Jeune Afrique Paris 1977) vol 8, at 133–67.

[14] The treaty Bardo installing the protectorate in Tunisia was signed on 12 May 1881 by the Bey Mohamed Es-Sadok. For more information see *Le journal officiel de la république française* 12 May 1881.

[15] The monarchy was abolished in Tunisia by the Constituent Assembly on 27 July 1956.

Le problème initial, qui précède toute recherche théorique, est celui des sources—de la cause historique. Dans le droit, les sources, en somme, ne peuvent être qu'instrumentaires et sociologiques. C'est par ces moyens d'expression que le droit devient accessible: sources proprement formelles, textuelles ou littérales. Cependant, la source réelle du droit n'est pas l'écrit qui le constate ou même l'intelligence individuelle qui le pense mais le milieu qui lui donne naissance.[16]

This chapter does not intend to analyse all the different sources. It limits itself to underlining the doctrinal productions which are of particular interest to the topic and which gave Islamic law, in general, and international Islamic law, in particular, its distinct character among the different Mediterranean legal systems.

From the commentaries on the Koran, there emerged a doctrine of international law which we can find in various works and in their interpretation. The Koran, the *Hadith* and *Sunnah* (the sayings and practices of the Prophet Mohammed and of the early founders of Islam) have become authoritative sources among Muslim theologians.

3.1. The Procedures

Two procedures can be identified: *Al Ijmaa* (consensus or unanimity) and *Qiyas* (reasoning through analogy). The first, *Al Ijmaa*,[17] was known in the early times of Islam. Its legitimacy stems from its origins in the different *Hadiths,* especially in one saying 'the Umma will never agree on error'. The unanimous agreement engenders the same obligatory effects as those of the Koran and the Hadith themselves. This procedure had functioned well in the early time of Islam, but it resulted in conflicts during the expansion of the Islamic Empire and the political dissent this brought forth. However, an idea that was sustained by a school of jurists which did not encounter any opposition could be considered to have received the blessing of *Al Ijmaa.*

It was the second procedure, the *Qiyas*[18] which came to be used most widely in the judgments of the *Cadis* (judges in Arabic); the *Fatwa* (ruling on a point of Islamic law given by a recognized authority); and the books of the doctrine. In fact, in order to respond to the enquiries of some Caliphs, the jurists pondered some specific studies relating to questions including those in relation to power or those concerning international law.

---

[16] E Rabbath 'Pour une théorie du droit international musulman' (1950) 6 Revue égyptienne de droit international 1–23 at 4.

[17] C Mansour *L'autorité dans la pensée musulmane: Le concept d'Ijma' (consensus) et la problématique de l'autorité* (Vrin Paris 1975) at 8 and 206.

[18] J Langhade and D Mallet 'Droit et philosophie au XIIè siècle dans l'Andalus: Averroès' (1985) 40 Revue de l'Occident musulman et de la Méditerranée 103–21.

3.2. The Contribution of the Muslim Philosophers

Many Muslim philosophers pondered the issue of international relations. The conducts relating to war from its outbreak to the signature of a peace treaty occupied a great deal of study and assumed a large place in their writings. We mention here Abu Nasr Al Farabi, (875–950), who was well known for his wide knowledge in the field of the universality of the human world. For Al Farabi,

La société modèle et parfaite, ou vertueuse, est, au-delà de la cité ou de la nation particulière, la réunion de tous les habitants de la terre, de même que la cité ou la nation heureuse est celle au sein de laquelle l'aide mutuelle des hommes et leurs divers groupements s'ordonne en fonction des choses qui conduisent véritablement au bonheur. La terre sera terre modèle quand les cités ou nations qui la composent s'aideront mutuellement dans le même but.[19]

Other Muslim philosophers should also be mentioned, such as Avicenna (930–1037) or Averroes (1126–98), who had developed particular notions relating to international law and which were conditioned by the relationship of the religious to the legal. However, one of the main issues in the field of international foreign relations between States remains the *SiyarSya* that are rules on 'the conduct in time of peace and war'. The most famous work is the well-known *Kitab Assiyar* (The Great Manners to Proceed) by Muhammed as-Saibani whom Hans Kruse called the 'Grotius of the Muslims'.[20]

4. Al-Siyar: Conduct in Time of War and Peace

This doctrine separated the world into 'believers and non-believers'. Inside the Muslim world there were believers; outside, the non-believers. For as long as Islam was not universal, war was the legal state between believers and non-believers. So any action in relation to foreigners was always conceived in terms of war: whether it was the 'right to go to war', or the 'right of war', or the end of war, 'the right to peace'. The act of war was seen in two ways: 'the right to go to war' or the 'law in war'.

---

[19] A Nasr Al Farabi (872–950) *Idée de la cité vertueuse* (RP Laussen, Y Karam and J Chlala trans) (Institut français d'archéologie orientale Cairo 1944) vol 1, ch 26. See A Truyol y Serra *L' histoire du droit international public* (Economica Paris 1995) at 35.

[20] H Kruse 'The Foundation of Islamic International Jurisprudence. Muhammed as-Saibani—Hugo Grotius of the Muslims' (1955) 3 Journal of the Pakistan Historical Society 231–67 at 231 and 265 cited in *L'histoire du droit international public* (n 19) 36.

4.1. The Notion of Jihad: 'The Right to go to War'

Generally, when we speak about the right to go to war, we evoke *Jihad* (the holy war) which is considered as an institution that is subject to the sovereignty of the law. If in the early period of Islam the *Jihad* basically existed to propagate Islam, since Islam was meant to be universal, the extension of the empire and its objectives were later put into question. The *Jihad* acquired another meaning. It was not then meant to defend Islam but to preserve the unity of the Muslim world.

The interpretation of the *Jihad* as a concept and an institution led to disagreements which arose among the legal consultants. Some Muslim classicists[21] maintained that in order to propagate and consolidate Islam, the *Jihad* is a collective and personal duty. The basis of this thought is found in the Koran itself.[22] This obligation, however, was relativized because the prophet Mohamed prohibited Muslims from going to war against other nations unless they had asked these people to convert to Islam: 'Soyez patients et tolérants avec les autres; ne leur faites la guerre qu'après les avoir invités à devenir musulmans. Que vous m'ameniez des musulmans, vaut mieux pour moi que de m'amener des épouses et des orphelins de ceux que vous aurez tués.'[23]

Therefore, the aim for Muslims in these instances is not to shed blood or wage wars, but only to combat those who attack. War was not even a coercive act of conversion, this relying on the Koranic principle that '[t]here shall be no compulsion in religion'.[24] The great jurisconsult (*Alim*) Ibn Taymiya wrote: 'Nous ne contraignons personne en religion; nous ne faisons la guerre qu'à ceux qui nous la font…; personne ne peut dire du Prophète qu'il aura contraint quelqu'un à épouser l'Islam; il n'y point d'intérêt dans un islam comme celui-ci.'[25] To other *Ulema* (legal consultants), the *Jihad* could not be considered a right except in self-defence, and only when Muslims were attacked or persecuted when they lived in a non-Muslim country. It is rather the right to protect one's community.[26]

The status of *Dar-al-Islam* or the 'ground of Muslim countries' implies the application of the *Sharia* throughout places under the Muslims rule. However, one of the questions asked during the occupation of Algeria was whether it was right to go to a Holy War (the *Jihad*) when an Islamic country, like Algeria, is conquered by a non-Muslim power, in order to liberate it. Therefore, in this instance, the *Ulema* were asked for a *Fatwa* to state whether a *Jihad* was to be waged against the Christian

[21] For more details see A Al Hassan Al-Quadûri 'Muskhtaçar de droit hanéfite' (1965) 5 Revue Tunisiènne de droit 123–49.

[22] *Holy Koran* At-Tawbah (the repentance) 9:73.

[23] See S Subhi As-Salih *Annudhum Al-Islamiya (Muslim Systems)* (Dar al-Ilm Li Al-Malayîn Beyrouth 1980) at 514.

[24] *Holy Koran* 2:256

[25] I Taymiya 'Risalat Al-Qital' (Letter of Al-Quital) in *Lettres d'ibn Taymiya (Rasâil)* in *Annudhum Al-Islamiya* (n 23) 518.

[26] The Prophet Mohamed said: 'Do not desire to meet the enemy; but ask God to keep you safe and sound.' See also M Ahmed 'Anthologie des Hadith' in *Annudhum Al-Islamiya* (n 23) 518.

invaders or to submit to them if they could guarantee for the Muslims the right to practise their religious rites.

The Algerian *Ulema* pronounced a *Fatwa* which was confirmed by the *Ulema* of Kerouan in Tunisia, those of Al Azhar in Egypt, and those of Taif in Hijaz (present-day Saudi Arabia).[27]

The obligation to wage a *Jihad* (war) was not totally rejected, but it was postponed because the Muslim world was then weak. This conciliating and wise judgment to submit to the occupying authority[28] even if it was not a Muslim one was reinforced by the *Ulema* of Tunisia and Morocco[29] when these two countries were invaded by the French. Rare were those *Ulema* who opted for the *Jihad* in these countries. Those who did were either from the countryside or the *Sufi*, a category of Muslims belonging to Muslim Brotherhood communities believing in and practising a radical/orthodox Islam.[30]

4.2. The Law in War

Concerning the law in war in the process of expansion and unification of the world, it was quite natural that certain principles and rules should be conceived in order to organize behaviour during war. These rules and principles are largely dominated by the concept of *Jihad*.[31] A moral and legal spirit should guide behaviour during war from the beginning to the signing of a peace treaty.

Before the start of hostilities, a message would be sent asking the enemy to convert and to adopt Islam. In cases where the enemies refused, they were either forced to pay *Al-Jizya*[32] or they were attacked. For Al-Quadûri:

---

[27] I. Roches *Dix ans à travers l'Islam: 1834–1844* (Librairie Académique Didier Paris 1904) at 236ff. L Roches, who cited this Fatwa, was himself a member of the committee who signed it. He was considered as a Muslim and was one of the companions of Emir Abdelkader.

[28] Obedience is a canonical duty for the Sunni *ulama* (scholar): obeying authority even if it is despotic, or an impious one, is better than chaos (*fitna*). Muslim jurists make obedience a synonym of the condition of being Muslim: each Muslim must carry in him the allegiance towards the Imam. See also I Taymiya (1263–1328) *Minhâj As-Sunna An-Nabawiya* (The Pathway of as-Sunnah an-Nabawiyyah) at 151–3.

[29] While asserting the same thing for the case of Morocco, Mohamed Tozy points out that the influence of *ulama* was limited, because their speech was confined to urban zones. M Tozy *Champ religieux et champ politique au Maroc* (Aix-Marseille III Aix en provence 1984) at 35.

[30] AH Green *The Tunisian Ulama 1875–1915: Social Structure and Response to Ideological Currents* (Brill Leiden 1978) at 130 and 132. 'It is perhaps significant that both men were of tribal origins, for example, since the rebel chiefs in other locales were tribal leaders. Moreover, each of them was a member of one or more Sufi brotherhoods, the affiliates of which appeared more inclined to oppose foreign invaders....'

[31] *L'histoire du droit international public* (n 19) 34.

[32] This is a tax that is due by 'the People of the Book' (ie the Christians and the Jews) living in Muslim countries.

Quand les musulmans pénètrent en territoire ennemi et assiègent une ville ou une forteresse, ils convieront les occupants à l'Islam. Si ceux-ci répondent favorablement à cet appel, ils cesseront de les combattre. Mais s'ils refusent, les musulmans les inviteront à payer l'impôt de la Jizya. Il n'est pas licite que l'Imam combatte ceux à qui n'est point parvenu le message de l'Islam. Il ne pourra le faire qu'après les y avoir appelés.[33]

Therefore, in the Islamic law of war, '[l]a déclaration était remplacée par l'exhortation à la soumission, institution dans laquelle on a pu voir le précèdent du *requerimiento* que les Espagnols dirigeront, en Amérique, aux indigènes, avant d'entreprendre les actions militaires.'[34]

During the war, the military forces were asked to respect a certain number of rules and conducts relating to the dignity and honour of the defeated people. Hence war was 'humanized' in a time when there was no morality and no law whatsoever. Concerning this question, Baron Michel de Taube wrote that

...à une époque où on ne trouve rien de pareil en Europe (sauf peut-être quelques déclarations théoriques de quelques théologiens), des principes d'un droit positif dans le domaine de la guerre, humains et raisonnables, sont formulés chez les musulmans.[35]

Similarly, one part of the doctrine states that:

L'Islam a, de toutes les civilisations (antiques), connu la réglementation la plus poussée et la plus générale en la matière. La minutie même de la réglementation a de quoi étonner. La conduite de la guerre, la distinction entre combattants et non-combattants et le traitement des prisonniers furent l'objet d'une législation fournie.[36]

During war, the distinction between the warriors and the non-warriors (soldiers and civilians) was therefore clearly established. The Muslim warriors were then subject to strict rules regulating their attitudes towards enemy warriors as well as towards civilians.[37]

The defeated (enemy) warriors were to be humanely treated. They were to be neither humiliated nor killed or tortured. During their captivity, these prisoners had to be cared for and allowed to worship and practise their religion freely.[38]

As for the non-warriors or civilians, different prescriptions guarantee them a large immunity. These people were generally those who could not fight: old men, the simple-minded, the disabled, women, children, monks, servants, and slaves.[39]

---

[33] 'Mukhtaçar de droit hanafi' (n 21) 125–6.

[34] *L'histoire du droit international public* (n 19) 34.

[35] M de Taube 'Etude sur le développement historique du droit international dans l'Europe orientale' (1926) 5 Receuil des cours 371–506 at 385.

[36] S Laghmani *L' histoire du droit des gens, du jus gentium impérial au jus publicum Europaeum* (A Pedone Paris 2004) at 20.

[37] A Rechid 'L'Islam et le droit des gens' (1937) 60 Receuil des cours 470–9.

[38] ibid.

[39] I Qayim al-Jawziya *Ahkam Ahl Ad-Dima* (Provisions of Ahl Ad-Dima) (Librairie Matba'At Jami'At Dimashq Damas 1961) at 5, 15 and 42–4. Other editions of the same book are available. See for example the edition of Dar Al-Hadith Cairo 2005.

The instructions of the Khalif Aboubaker summing up the incumbent obligations of the Muslim combatants are as follows:

Souvenez-vous que vous êtes toujours sous le regard de Dieu…que vous rendrez compte au jour dernier…. Lorsque vous combattez pour la gloire de Dieu, conduisez-vous comme des hommes, sans tourner le dos, mais que le sang des femmes ou celui des enfants et des vieillards ne souille pas votre victoire. Ne détruisez pas les palmiers, ne brûlez pas les habitations ni les champs de blé, ne coupez jamais les arbres fruitiers et ne tuez le bétail que lorsque vous êtes contraints de le manger. Quand vous accordez un traité ou une capitulation, ayez soin de remplir les clauses. Au fur et à mesure de votre avance, vous rencontrerez des hommes de religion qui vivent dans les monastères et qui servent Dieu dans la prière: laissez-les seuls, ne les tuez point et ne détruisez pas leurs monastères….[40]

In the same spirit, Al Quadûri says:

Il convient que les Musulmans ne commettent ni traîtrise ghadr, ni vol de butin de guerre ghulûl et qu'ils n'infligent pas aux ennemis des traitements atroces muthla. Ils ne doivent tuer ni femme, ni vieillard décrépit, ni impubère, ni aveugle, ni infirme, à moins que l'une de ces personnes ne donne des conseils pour la conduite de la guerre ou que la femme soit une reine. Il convient qu'ils ne tuent point les fous.[41]

However, what are the principles which regulate the conduct of the governors?

5. CONDUCT IN TIME OF PEACE

At the end of hostilities, the submission of the enemy after a victory or when victory became impossible for the enemy, certain rules of conduct were imposed to serve peace. In this instance, international Muslim law is closely dependent on public Islamic law since it was the status of the *Dhimmi* which would be taken as a basis for organizing peace relations with the foreign States.

It should be noted that the laws used at that time were well acknowledged in international law. They were the treaties ensuring the protection of foreigners. In this category of laws, we should point out the principles applied in *Dar-al-Islam* and the countries which would become Muslim after a conquest, which was seen as an opening-up of these countries to Islam. The conquests were called *Futuhat*. These *Futuhat* can be compared to the spirit of colonization of a civilization because the Muslims intended to bring to the conquered population the 'divine' message that was Islam.

---

[40] This is an instruction of Abu Bakr Esseddik (First Khalif) to the chiefs of his army sent to Syria right after the death of the Prophet Mohamed. Pour une théorie du droit international musulman (n 16) 16.

[41] 'Muskhtaçar de droit hanéfite' (n 21) 137, cited in *L' histoire du droit des gens* (n 36) at 30.

Among these principles, we mention the state of *Dhimmi*, the people who were 'put under the protection of Islam', or rather, under the protection of the Muslims. We also ought to cite the non-aggression pact called *Al-Ahd* (Act of faith to respect somebody, something, or an oath), or *Al Aman* (peace), an act insuring and offering protection for individuals as well as for groups or nations.

5.1. The Status of 'Dhimmi'[42]

Peace concerned first of all the legal condition of *Ahl Al Dimma*, meaning literally 'People of the Book',[43] or simply the Jews and the Christians who were permanently living in Muslim land. The basis of this status was an agreement by virtue of which the communities were subject to the Muslims authority except in religious and family matters. In return, these communities paid the *Jizya*, a tax on a person or a land tax if they were owner of a real estate.

The population of conquered lands would be exonerated from paying this tax if they converted to Islam; if not, they must all, except the old people, the disabled, the monks, and the children, pay *Al Jizya*, a tax which was already established and practised in the Eastern countries. The treaty concluded between the prophet Mohamed and the Christian community of *Najrân* was one of the first applications of this law. This is what historians cite as an example in this domain.[44]

In paying this tax, the non-Muslim population would in return enjoy protection offered by the Muslim authorities against any external/foreign aggression. The Muslim authority would also acknowledge, respect, and ensure the free practices of the judicial and legal autonomy of these people.

However, and with the expansion of the great conquests towards the East (from Mesopotamia to the frontiers of China and India), the law of protection was extended to the Zoroasters who were allowed to keep their cult and laws. Therefore, a community regime called the *Taifa* was created. In some social practices of this

---

[42] See *Ahkam Ahl Ad-Dima* (n 39) 5 and 15. The book we're referring to contains a reference to the issue of Ahl Ad-Dimma which deals with all aspects of the rules of conduct towards these people, both regarding war and peace, trade with them, the marriage between Muslims and their women, safeguarding their assets and property, etc.

[43] They were and still are considered as 'People of the Book' because for Islam the Thorah, and the Bible are God's holy words revealed by God to Moises and Jesus Christ in the same way the Koran was revealed to the Prophet Mohamed.

[44] The Christians of Najrân had received an ultimatum of the Prophet which asked them either to convert into Islam, to submit to him or to go to war. The Najrânites sent a committee to Medina to discuss the issues. The meetings ended by the conclusion of a treaty of submission with a promise that the Najrânites would pay the capitation. The interests of the clergy were therefore protected, and the religious tolerance insured. They also commited themselves to lend to the Muslim government weapons and animals in case a war or civil protests would burst out in Yemen. For more details, see M Hamidullah *Les documents sur la diplomatie musulmane à l'époque du Prophète et des Khalifes orthodoxes* (GP Maisonneuve Librairie Orientale et Américaine Paris 1935) at 78–81.

regime, people used to meet in two rows. The first comprises Muslims with no distinction as to their origins or language. The rows behind them comprise non-Muslims who were offered a legal status. There were also other legal classifications in the Muslim land like those mentioned by Hamidullah.[45]

This classification came about as a result of *Al Jizya* which was at the beginning imposed only on the Jews and the Christians (*Ahl Al Kitab* or people of the Book) but generalized to all non-Muslims afterwards. 'Le Prophète avait étendu son application aux Mages, ce qui laissa aux Califes les mains libres pour traiter les autres communautés non musulmanes comme des peuples soumis.'[46]

The protection in the name of *Dimma* and the status that emerged from it have common consensual origins which were the treaties signed right after the conquests. These treaties were easily comparable to those the Muslim States had signed with other nations, a '[s]ituation éminemment suggestive du droit international, qui n'a pas manqué d'imprégner tout le droit public de l'Islam'.[47]

5.2. The Respect of the 'Commitment' or Al-Ahd

Al-Ahd or 'the Commitment' is a concept that the Muslim authorities used in their relations with other nations. However, this concept, which constituted the basis of 'the theory of peace', could not be permanent because it was time-limited. But it is very important to underline the respect of the given word or oath taken because this was sacred for the Muslims. This action has its basis in the Koran itself.[48]

5.3. The 'Aman' Insurance

The insurance, or *Al Aman*, is a protection commitment that each Muslim can offer to any non-Muslim foreigner. It ensures the protection of the life, the freedom, and all the property of the non-Muslim foreigner living in a Muslim land. This foreigner can do everything that is not forbidden by the law. However, the period of this protection does (must not) exceed one year.

Therefore, this practice had, through the commercial exchanges between the Muslims and the non-Muslims, enabled certain Islamic concepts to permeate the thoughts of the Medieval institutions.

---

[45] For the classifications see ibid; *L' histoire du droit des gens* (n 36) 33.
[46] *Les documents sur la diplomatie musulmane* (n 44) 81.
[47] 'Pour une théorie du droit international musulman' (n 16) 20.
[48] A Hassan Ali Al-Mawardi *Al-Ahkam As-Sultaniya* (Matbaat Al-Watan Cairo 1297) at 133; see also *Holy Koran* 18:36, 8:60, 16:93, and 22:8.

These principles and mainly the *Al Siyar* were preserved in all the interaction between Muslim Arab or non-Arab countries. This is shown in the many treaties these people had together. [49]

6. The Writing Practices of the Treaties

It was during a period dominated by piracy, Europeans anxious to conquer some North African countries, a time of war and peace[50] between the Muslims and the Christians around the Mediterranean Sea, that the treaties which we are now going to discuss, were written and signed. We must remember that, at that time, the Portuguese had occupied a vast swathe of the 16th-century Moroccan Atlantic coast (from Safi to Larache), and the Spanish had occupied Ceuta and Melilla and the Algerian and Tunisian coasts until they were chased from these places by the Ottomans.

We have found many treaties and exchanges of letters which are in content and form similar to those which are signed in the current time by different nations. However, a number of factors—religious, economic, and political—have left a stamp on each of these agreements depending on the circumstances and the kind of dynamics governing the relationships between the different countries. We will see that realism dominated religious spirit, and political thinking yielded to economic pragmatism.

For the whole region, the legal heritage of the diplomatic history of these treaties reveals that three domains were covered by the treaties, epistolary exchanges or miscellanies. They were about commercial exchanges, peace, wars, and capitulations. If the treaties of surrender concerned the first two domains, they had certain unique traits.

It is important to underline the dominance of the bilateral nature of these agreements, because multilateral notions were introduced by the end of the 19th century with the North African States behaving more as subjects than as actors. The conference of Madrid in 1880 is revealing in this respect. Taking place from 19 May to 3 July 1880, with the participation of all European nations having representation in Morocco, the latter, relying on the help of Great Britain and the understanding of the US, asked for a limitation and a reform of the system of protection imposed on it. But the conference ended with a different result: it strengthened the power of protection by extending it to all the Western powers in place. The brutality of the French, supported

---

[49] Many of these treaties are dealt with the subsequent section 6, 'The writing practices of the treaties.'

[50] In order to stop the attacks of the privateers France sent esquadrons to bombard the ports of Algier (Algeria) in 1682, Tripoli (Libya) in 1765, and Salé (Morocco) in 1765.

by Germany, did not facilitate the task of the Moroccan delegation. By granting the Europeans the right to acquire properties in Morocco, this conference marked the end of its independence.[51]

If at the beginning peace treaties gave birth to concepts such as 'the truce of God' and 'the peace of God' (godly truce or godly peace), they subsequently paved the way to various domains to include clauses pertaining to the end of hostilities, promises of neutrality, commercial exchanges, legal status of people (institutions, freedom of religious cult, etc.), the liberation of captives, and so on. If the Western nations signed commerce and navigation treaties allowing them to regulate their relations with the North African nations, they did so mainly to obtain commercial concessions.

All the treaties signed from the early history until the end of the 18th century aimed essentially at the prevention of violence because that period was dominated by piracy. Their wordings or the way they were written were not very explicit. They included, in general, clauses relating to the buying and selling of goods, the choice of the indigenous brokers, or the organization of the consulates. Subsequent treaties were more explicit: they concerned freedom of navigation and traffic. They also contained clauses relating to the status of consuls and other diplomatic representatives and their people. We will distinguish here between the following kinds of treaties: commerce treaties, the concession treaties, capitulation treaties, and alliance treaties.

6.1. Commerce Treaties

Although Comte de Mas Latrie sustained that '[l]e commerce entre les nations chrétiennes et les nations musulmanes a toujours été, en dehors de la sphère religieuse, l'objet principal et le seul intérêt permanent des traités',[52] the objectives of these treaties were at the same time political and economic. Their clauses referred to the ending of hostilities, the liberation of the prisoners, the settlement of peoples, and religious and navigation freedom.[53] Concerning the ancient commerce treaties, Baron Boris Nolde wrote:

Les matières concernant directement le commerce international se trouvent enfouies dans les conventions dont le titre ne se réfère aucunement au commerce ou sont englobés dans des actes internationaux qui prétendent régir à côté des questions de commerce, d'autres questions.[54]

---

[51] CA Julien *Le Maroc face aux impérialismes* (Editions Jeune Afrique Paris 1978) at 69–90.

[52] JMJL de Mas Latrie *Traités de commerce et documents divers concernant les relations des chrétiens avec les Arabes de l'Afrique septentrionale* (Plon Paris 1868) at 2.

[53] E Rouard de Card *Les traités de la France avec les pays de l'Afrique du Nord, Algérie, Tunisie, Tripolitaine, Maroc* (A Pedone Paris 1906) at 6.

[54] B Nolde 'Droit et technique des traités de commerce' (1924) 3 Receuil des cours 295–461 at 296.

We must note here that the opening of the Arab and Muslim countries to the influence of the Europeans and the undertaking of the liberalization of commerce put them, mainly in the 19th century, in jeopardy. For Morocco

[l]e péril est accru par le traité de commerce de 1861[55] qui abaisse les taxes d'exportation en direction de l'Espagne, supprime certains monopoles, accorde le droit de pêche sur les côtes et permet aux commerçants espagnols de disposer de maisons, de magasins et de terrains, première dérogation au principe qui s'opposait formellement au droit de propriété par les étrangers.[56]

6.2. Concession Treaties

Concerning the concession treaties, it seems very important to emphasize that different Western European nations engaged in ferocious competition in order to reinforce and consolidate their respective positions. They insisted on having advantages at least equal to the other nations'. These treaties were made to give and ensure the right of Western companies to have certain commercial counters, exclusive commercial privileges with the local people, the choice to repair or build certain buildings, or the freedom and security for some commercial agents. We can cite many treaties signed between France and the different regencies of the Moroccan sultan which had as an objective concessions in favour of various African companies.[57]

These concessions, among others, have contributed to the foreign invasion of North Africa. To take Morocco as an example, the treaty of protectorate which the country signed in 1912 with France[58] did but confirm the situation in which France obtained supremacy in the economic field in this country.[59] It was the same with Tunisia whose concessions helped ensure a strong economic presence of the foreigners and a powerful impact of the consuls, especially that of the French and the British. This influence urged the *bey* (Turkish name for governor in Tunisia) to initiate a number of reforms, giving the 'Fundamental Pact' (*Ahd*

---

[55] Treaty of Commerce and Navigation between Spain and Morocco (signed 20 November 1861) 53 BFSP 1089.

[56] M Emerit 'Le Maroc et l'Europe: 1830–1894' (1965) 20 Annales, économies, sociétés, civilisations 635–40 at 637. Concerning this treaty, see also F Zaïm 'Le Maroc méditerranéen au XIXe siècle ou la frontière intérieure' (1988) 48 Revue de l'Occident musulman et de la Méditerranée 61–95 at 71.

[57] See for this point *Les traités de la France* (n 53).

[58] Bulletin Officiel, Empire Chérifien—Protectorat de la République Française au Maroc, 1 novembre 1912, at 1.

[59] A El Ouazzani *Pour une analyse comparative des élites politiques Maghrébines* (Aix-Marseille III Aix-en-Provence 1994) at 115. Example: The French bank Paribas obtained the right to control the Moroccan customs taxes to pay back the country's debt towards France. This gave France the power to have '*la main mise*' on the economy of the country. For more details see *Le Maroc* (n 51) 69–90.

Al Aman) of 10 September 1857[60] as an example in which he gave Léon Roches[61] the guarantee of the freedom of religious worship for non-Muslims, the establishment of courts for foreign criminals, the creation of a court of commerce with foreign participation, and mainly the right for non-Muslims to buy and own buildings in Tunisia.[62]

6.3. Alliance Treaties

For the Muslim world and according to the Islamic law and doctrine, a Muslim State must abstain from an alliance with a non-Muslim State against a Muslim one. Along the same lines of thought, the Christians prohibited any alliance of a Christian State with Muslim States which were considered impious. Moreover, some limitations to sell goods, especially when these were meant to increase the military power of the adversary, were imposed on the different States.

However, and as an example, Spain could not hope for the application of the testament of Isabella I who dreamt of a holy war in which North Africa would constitute the rationale for the conquest of other States to force Islam to retreat. Charles V did not commit himself in North Africa for fear that he would lose his hegemony over Europe.[63] On their part, François I and the Regent of Savoy in France aimed to sign an alliance treaty with the Ottoman Empire of Solomon the Magnificent against Charles V.

The menace of the Ottomans after their conquest of Algeria imposed a truce on the Moroccan and the Spanish. Morocco signed a treaty with the Spanish to preserve its independence from the Ottomans. 'Cette alliance durera jusqu'à la fin du 16 siècle quand les turcs renonceront définitivement à s'étendre en Méditerranée occidentale qui aura ainsi été préservée grâce à la coopération hispano-marocaine.'[64]

6.4. Surrender Clauses

'Les premières capitulations furent signées par l'Empire ottoman avec les Etats européens. Elles garantissaient beaucoup de libertés: liberté d'établissement, inviolabilité du domicile, liberté de circuler, liberté religieuse, exemptions fiscales, privilèges

---

[60] Le pacte fondamental (Ahd Al Amen) of 10 September 1857 <http://www.e-justice.tn/fileadmin/images/repertoire_musee/husseinite_avant_protec/Pacte_fondamental_1857_fr.pdf> (25 March 2012).

[61] See n 27.

[62] *Le Maroc* (n 51) 117.

[63] E Moha *Les relations Hispano-Marocaines* (Eddif Casablanca 1994) at 51.

[64] ibid 52.

judiciaires'.[65] However, if we generally consider immunities as guarantees offered to the foreign ambassadors in Muslim countries and therefore as a proof of respect of the diplomatic norms—they existed since antiquity—it is difficult not to interpret them as a sign of weakness of the State that issued them. We believe that the surrender clauses may indicate a sign of the weakness of a State which offers privileges to other States. Such treaties can be found among commerce treaties even if they included dispositions which constituted an infringement of the sovereignty of the State upon which they were used. Hence, the foreign consuls could offer their protection to Moroccan citizens, and when they did, the Moroccan people could completely escape from the authority of the sultan, who was thus weakened, and therefore forced to accept these kinds of treaties. We can refer here to the commerce treaty signed between Morocco and Spain on 20 November 1861 mentioned above. Article 15 of this treaty says that [66] 'les sujets *ou protégés espagnols*, tant mahométans, que chrétiens et israélites, jouiront également de tous les droits et privilèges accordés par ce traité et ceux qu'on accorderait à la nation la plus favorisée'.

Article 16 maintains that 'dans les causes criminelles ... qui seraient débattues entre sujets espagnols et les sujets ou citoyens d'autres nations étrangères...ces causes seront décidées au tribunal des consuls étrangers...sans aucune intervention du Gouvernement marocain'.[67]

7. Peace Treaties (Temporary Peace)

For the Muslims, peace, in theory, could not be permanent. It was limited in time and appears like a truce which could not exceed a period of ten years. The historiography of the Crusades is full of examples of truce treaties signed between Muslims and Christians. The object of these truces was always the necessity to cease war momentarily in order to recover the forces to start it again.[68]

More recently, Emir Abdelkader of Algeria signed two truce treaties with the French for the same reasons. The first treaty was signed with Desmichels on 26 February 1834,[69] and the second one, called the treaty of the Tafna, was signed with Bugeaud on 30 May 1837.[70]

---

[65] Morocco has also signed capitulations with the Europeans: with France in 1631, 1682 and 1767, with Spain in 1799 and with Great Britain and with the US in 1836 and 1856. See A Riziki Mohamed *La diplomatie en terre d'Islam* (l'Harmattan Paris 2005) at 206ff.

[66] Treaty of Commerce (n 55).   [67] *Les traités de la France* (n 53) 44–5.

[68] A Maalouf *Les croisades vues par les Arabes* (Jean-Claude Lattés Paris 1983).

[69] *Les traités de la France* (n 53) 89–90.   [70] ibid 92–4.

Historiography saw in the war waged by Emir Abdelkader nothing but a 'homogenous enterprise, or a simple conflict which opposes the one whom we should recognize as "the Great Indigenous Chief" or "the combatant of Faith" (meaning here Islam against the French commander)'.[71] In this way, the interpretation of the clauses confined itself to considerations and interrogations tending to find out the spirit of the treaties, and to overcome the ambiguities emanating from their Arabic and French versions[72] in order to reach the political objectives of each side and to make the other side responsible for the resumption of hostilities.

We might consider whether it would not be wise to investigate the arguments which were advanced by Emir Abdelkader to sustain his convictions to claim the *Jihad*, and who, in spite of the fact that he declared himself Caliph of the Sultan of Morocco, usurped the social title of Emir Al-Mouminin (the commander of the faithful people or Muslims) to justify the peace treaty he signed with the Christians.

For the French, the peace-making with Emir Abdelkader was based on a relatively clear idea insofar as the limited occupation of Algeria was maintained. The treaty was first meant to secure the French possessions by pacifying the other Algerian regions with the help of a local chief, seeking to eliminate the risk of permanent threat from the other local tribes who were autonomous and who did not accept the presence of the French in their country.

In justifying his decision to deal with Abdelkader, Desmichels said that

Le seul homme sur lequel je puisse jeter les yeux pour accomplir mon plan de pacification. Son esprit élevé, son énergie, la grande influence qu'il exerçait sur les arabes par sa naissance, par le respect dont il était entouré en sa qualité de marabout et par la vénération attachée au nom de son père, tout en lui répondait à mes desseins.[73]

In fact, the situation of the French in Oran, Arzew, and Mostaganem had become so difficult because of the harassment and the blockade by the Emir of their positions which forced them to ship everything in by sea. Therefore, the choice between ending[74] and continuing the conquest, and the idea of governing the regency with the help of a local chief, became more and more stark, especially as in France both Parliament and the government started questioning the French presence in Algeria.[75]

Emir Abdelkader was not in a strong military situation. He was confronted not only with the French but also with other local adversaries who became increasingly

---

[71] R Gallissot *La guerre d'Abd el Kader ou la ruine de la nationalité Algérienne (1839–1847)* (Rabat Faculté des Lettres et des Sciences Humaines 1964) at 119–42.

[72] See also CR Ageron *Politiques coloniales au Maghreb* (PUF Paris 1973).

[73] ibid 10.

[74] In France, this idea was mainly defended by the anti-colonials like Hypolite Passy, reporter of the Budget of the War, and Xavier de Sade, the liberal deputy of 'l'Aine' who declared on 3 April 1833 in the house of parliament that: 'tout accroissement de territoire ne comportait pas nécessairement un accroissement de puissance' and all the money alloted to the army in Algeria could be better used in France. CA Julien *Histoire de l'Algérie contemporaine: La conquête et le début de la colonisation 1827–1871* (Casbah Editions Alger 2005) at 106–7.

[75] ibid 106–15. The fact that the prescription of 22 July 1834, dedicating definitively 'the French possessions in North Africa', was taken five months after the treaty Desmichels could be very significant.

numerous. He was also supposed to provide his men with arms and gunpowder, but this he could not do without signing a treaty with Louis A Desmichels.[76] Consequently, Emir Abdelkader 'avait tout intérêt à se poser auprès des français comme le seul interlocuteur valable'.[77]

Did Emir Abdelkader accept French sovereignty over Algeria and give up his plan of liberating his country from the Christians? This idea seems to be less clear if we refer to what he told Léon Roches: 'En faisant la paix avec les chrétiens, ... je me suis inspiré de la parole de Dieu qui dit dans le Coran: "La paix avec les Infidèles doit être considérée par les musulmans comme une trêve pendant laquelle ils doivent se préparer à la guerre." '[78] The idea of peace dictated by necessity is therefore not to be excluded. It is even more probable to presume a real intention of both sides to divide Algeria between two authorities. It might have been so because, on the one hand, the treaty of Tafna which established such a division between the two authorities who, in order to coexist, must mutually help each other, could not be applied[79] in the long term. On the other hand, Emir Abdelkader, Chief of *Jihad*, and who declared himself 'Emir Al Mouminin', 'commander of the believers', could not remain in that difficult position indefinitely.

Anyway, war broke out shortly after, and when the situation of the Emir in 1842 became difficult, the idea of peace emerged again. Abdelkader wrote to the Sultan of Morocco in order to canvass his opinion about signing a peace treaty. In his answer to the Emir, the Sultan MY Abderrahman supported this idea by saying:

Nous savons que les Musulmans ont cruellement souffert de la guerre et ont subi de rudes échecs; qu'ils ont perpétué la razzia et le djihad, au grand préjudice de leurs enfants, laissant de côté pour ce but leurs propres affaires ... et que les Musulmans sont dans l'impuissance de tenir devant l'ennemi et l'Infidèle. Craignant la perte de Musulmans, j'ai cru devoir renouveler la paix. Donc, il est préférable d'en renouveler la demande. Il est plus sage de prendre en considération les Musulmans et ce qui est de nature à leur faire reprendre leurs forces.[80]

If such a vision has disappeared from the logic of the modern Muslim States, it has not completely disappeared from the mindset of the Islamist movements especially in the places which are, according to them, still occupied nowadays by *Dar al-Harb* (country at war) such as Afghanistan and Palestine.

---

[76] 'Treaty between Emir Abdelkader and General Desmichels (26 February 1936)'. A French translation is published in G Esquer (ed) *Correspondance du général Drouet d'Erlon, gouverneur général des possessions françaises dans le nord de l'Afrique (1834–1835)* (Champion Paris 1926) at 559–60; for a photograph of a certified copy of the 'secret' Desmichels Treaty, see CR Ageron, 'Premières négociations franco-algériennes' (September 1964) 163 Preuves 49.

[77] *Politiques Coloniales au Maghreb* (n 72) 72.

[78] *Dix ans* (n 27) 72.

[79] A Laroui *L'histoire du Maghreb* (Maspero Paris 1975) vol 2, at 73–4. See also Politiques coloniales au Maghreb (n 72).

[80] Lettre du Sultan du Maroc à Abdelkader 23 Chaoual 1257, début janvier 1842, Archives d'Outre-Mer, 18MI56, série E, liasse 212 (microfilm).

8. Conclusion

In fact, the impact of Islam on the contribution of North Africa in the production of the norms of international law has been relative. It must be associated with another reality, which is that of the relationships between powers and their competition for domination.

Throughout centuries of coexistence of Muslim empires and European nations, their reciprocal relations were guided by war strategies and by the power games which dominated the Mediterranean world. This area has always been a vast arena in which the Muslim and the non-Muslim powers have constantly confronted each other.

The armed struggle, whether it was direct or via the privateers and pirates, was a common strategy used by all nations. To try to find a proper rule in this logic of struggle for power would be pointless. In summarizing the logic of international law, Raymond Aron has shown how this field has always been dominated by war. He says that 'les relations internationales sont commandées par l'alternative de la paix et de la guerre…puisqu'il n'y a pas de civilisation qui n'ait connu, avec une fréquence variable, de guerres et de grandes guerres'.[81] Islamic civilization does not escape this logic.

If there is a contribution of Islam to international law, it is in the field of the protection of the laws of the persons, particularly in the laws of the *Dhimmi*, and more precisely in the laws of the religious minorities and the humane treatment of the war prisoners. Contrary to Christianity which used to justify the Inquisition in the name of the Church, Islam protected the Christians and the Jews living in Muslim lands in the name of the commandments written in the Koran and confirmed by the Prophet Mohamed.

But with the end of the Muslim empires and their division into small nation-states, Muslims have adopted the norms of the international law as they have found them defined by the Western orders stemming directly from the League of Nations.

Recommended Reading

Abdelmalek El Ouazzani, *Pour une analyse comparative des élites politiques maghrébines* (Aix-Marseille III Aix en Provence 1994).

Emerit, Marcel 'Le Maroc et l'Europe: 1830–1897' (1965) 20 Annales, économies, sociétés, civilisations 635–40.

Félix, Lucien *Le statut international du Maroc d'après les traités* (A Pedone Paris 1928).

Hamidullah, Muhammad *Les documents sur la diplomatie musulmane à l'époque du Prophète et des Khalifes orthodoxes* (GP Maisonneuve Librairie Orientale et Américaine Paris 1935).

Ibn al-Hasan al-Shaybani, Muhammad *Le grand livre de la conduit de l'état* (Kitab Essiyar Al-Kabir) (Muhammed Hamidullah trans) (Edition Turkiyé Diyanet Vakfi Ankara 1991).

---

[81] R Aron 'Sociologie des relations internationales' (1963) 4 Revue française de sociologie 307–20 at 308.

Julien, Charles-André *Le Maroc face aux impérialismes* (Editions Jeune Afrique Paris 1978).

Julien, Charles-André *Histoire de l'Algérie contemporaine, la conquête et le début de la colonisation (1827–1871)* (Casbah Edditions Alger 2005).

Laroui, Abdallah *Histoire du Maghreb* (Maspero Paris 1975) vol 2.

Latrie, Jacques MJL comte de Mas *Traités de commerce et documents divers concernant les relations des Chrétiens avec les Arabes de l'Afrique septentrionale* (Plon Paris 1868).

Maalouf, Amine *Les croisades vues par les Arabes* (Editions Jean-Claude Lattès Paris 1983).

Mallet, Dominique and Jaccques Langhade 'Droit et philosophie au XIIè siècle dans l'Andalus: Averroès' (1985) 40 Revue de l'Occident musulman et de la Méditerranée 103–21.

Mansour, Camille *L'autorité dans la pensée musulmane: Le concept d'Ijma'(Consensus) et la problématique de l'autorité* (Vrin Paris 1975).

Moha, Edouard *Les relations Hispano-Marocaines* (Editions Eddif Casablanca 1994).

Ouazzani Chahdi, Hassan *La pratique marocaine du droit des traités* (LGDJ Paris 1982).

Rabbath, Edmond 'Pour une théorie du droit international musulman' (1950) 6 Revue égyptienne de droit international 1–23.

Rechid, Ahmed 'L'Islam et droits des gens' (1937) 60 Recueil des cours 371–506.

Riziki, Abdelaziz Mohamed *La diplomatie en terre d'Islam* (L'Harmattan Paris 2005).

Roches, Léon *Dix ans à travers l'Islam 1834–1844* (Librairie académique Didier Paris 1904).

Rouard de Card, Edgard *Les traités de la France avec les pays de l'Afrique du Nord, Algérie, Tunisie, Tripolitaine, Maroc* (A Pedone Paris 1906).

Salih Subhi, As-Salih *Annudhum Al-Islamiya* (Muslim Systems) (Dar Al-Ilm Li Al-Malayîn Beyrouth 1980).

Taube, Baron Michel de 'Etude sur le développement historique du droit international dans l'Europe orientale' (1926) 11 Recueil des cours 341–556.

Veronne, Chantal de la 'Relations entre le Maroc et la Turquie dans la seconde moitié du XVIe siècle et le début du XVIIe siècle (1554–1616)' (1973) 15–16 Revue de l'Occident musulman et de la Méditerranée 391–401.

Zaïm, Fouad 'Le Maroc méditerranéen au XIXe siècle ou la frontière intérieure' (1988) 48–9 Revue de l'Occident musulman et de la Méditerranée.

CHAPTER 17

AFRICA

JAMES THUO GATHII

1. INTRODUCTION

In this chapter, I trace the two major trends in thinking about Africa's engagement with international law from a historical perspective—'contributionists' who empha-size Africa's contributions to international law on the one hand, and critical theorists who examine Africa's subordination in its international relations as a legacy that is traceable to international law, on the other.[1]

For contributionists such as Taslim Elias Olawale (hereinafter Elias), one time Judge of the International Court of Justice, 'inter-civilizational participation in the process of crafting genuinely universal norms' has historically involved Africa as a central player.[2] This emphasis on Africa's participation in the formation of international law amounts to contributionism. Contributionists, also referred to as an inter-civiliza-tional approach by some,[3] regard international law as the product of a number of civi-lizations rather than the sole product of European civilization. Contributionism emphasizes that Africa is 'an innovator and generator' of norms of international law.[4]

---

[1] M Mutua 'What is TWAIL?' (2000) 94 American Society of International Law Proceedings 31–40 at 32 (calling contributionists minimalist assimilationists, and critical theorists affirmative reconstructionists); see also O Okafor 'Newness, Imperialism and International Legal Reform in Our Time: A TWAIL Perspective' (2005) 43 Osgoode Hall Law Journal 171–91 at 176.

[2] See PS Surya *Legal Polycentricity and International Law* (Carolina Academic Press Durham NC 1996).

[3] Y Onuma 'When Was the Law of International Society Born?' (2000) 2 Journal of the History of International Law 1–66.

[4] J Levitt (ed) *Africa: Mapping New Boundaries in International Law* (Hart Oxford 2008).

Critical theorists, like Makau Wa Mutua, Siba Grovogui, Kamari Clark, Ibironke Odumosu, and Obiora Okafor, among others, by contrast focus on the manner in which modern international law continues the legacy of colonial disempowerment while providing spaces for resistance and reform. For critical theorists, a central question is how to 'defang international law of its imperialist and exploitative biases against the global South'[5] in general, and Africa in particular.

I proceed as follows: in Section 2, I exemplify how contributionists have sought to rewrite international law from an African perspective. I also discuss the distinguishing characteristics of contributionism. In Section 3, I examine the work of critical theorists in African international law historical scholarship. I end with a conclusion.

2. Contributionists Rewriting International Legal History: Assailing Eurocentricity to Accommodate Africa

In this section I will examine how contributionists have rewritten international legal history to assail Eurocentricity and accommodate African participation. Elias' work epitomizes and exemplifies this kind of contributionism. There are at least two aspectsw of Elias' critique of international law's Eurocentricity. First, Elias' work is unique in the manner in which it foregrounded an assertion of African identity against international law's claim to universality. Second, in so doing, his critique of international law's Eurocentricity undermined its central claim of universality as a constitutive foundation of the discipline. Elias heralded African scholars of international law in exposing the Eurocentricity of international law and in advancing corrective measures. As I will show below, Elias masterfully marshalled a variety of arguments to demonstrate that international law and its universality were not merely constituted by Europeans in Europe, but also by Africans. Elias' book *Africa and the Development of International Law* is an eloquent and extensive exposition of this tradition.

The importance of asserting an African identity in the post-Second World War period was to uphold the dignity, identity, and self-determination of the African race as an equal race to other races. The idea was to end the persistent prejudice that

---

[5] MW Mutua '(Book Review) *Africa: Mapping New Boundaries in International Law* by Jeremy I. Levitt' (2010) 104 American Journal of International Law 532–8 at 533.

Africans had no history, a view which in turn laid down a substantial basis for external slavery of Africans and colonial subjugation of Africa by European countries. Asserting the African identity was, however, not only an assault on stereotypes of African inferiority and backwardness,[6] but also on notions of Western and white supremacy as represented by colonial rule and other forms of Western subjugation and power over Africa.

Elias' work is therefore one of the most significant scholarly works of his period that makes the best case for rejecting and, therefore, redefining categories such as 'backward', 'uncivilized', and 'barbaric', assigned to African communities in international legal history.[7] Therefore, a major purpose of rewriting the history of international law for African scholars like Elias and Felix Okoye[8] was to correct the historical record: to rescue the African from his pre-assigned place in history by glorifying a bygone past where the African, much like the European, was a member of ancient kingdoms or political units equivalent to the 'modern' and 'civilized' Western States. It was in this sense that the scholars in the Elias tradition 'challenged the myths of black inferiority, servitude, backwardness'.[9]

By re-interpreting tropes of the African as uncivilized, barbaric, and backward, these African scholars realigned colonial categories thereby producing a post-colonial international law that made the racist and imperial connotations of the colonial discourse speak with race-blind meanings. Elias was advancing a project of colour and imperial blindness by advancing a claim of African 'dignity and self-respect of a kind that they had not known for generations'.[10]

2.1. Rewriting International Legal History from an African Perspective

Elias argued that prior to the colonial conquest, Africa was and has always been a participant in the international community. In so doing, he rejected the period of

---

[6] In addition, Elias must have been well aware of the insulting racism that confronted African diplomats in Western capitals like New York City in the 1960s and 70s.

[7] Hegel among other European scholars reinforced the exclusion of Africa from the universal future of conscious humanity embodied in Judeo-Christian historicity. See B Jewsiewicki and VY Mudimbe 'Africans' Memories and Contemporary History of Africa' (1992) 31 History and Theory 1–11. International scholars in the 19th century similarly adopted the view that Africa had no history. These scholars also emphasized that Africa was different from Judeo-Christian Europe because of general cultural inferiority and political disorganization which in turn barred Africa from membership in the family of nations.

[8] F Okoye *International Law and the New African States* (Sweet and Maxwell London 1972).

[9] B Davidson *Black Star: A View of the Life and Times of Kwame Nkrumah* (Allen Lane London 1973) at 12–13.

[10] ibid.

colonization as the move from a people without history to global incorporation, or as a transitory epoch from fragmented alienation to collective international solidarity. According to Elias, '[i]f we are to grasp something of the significance of Africa in current international affairs, we must begin with a brief account of the role which different parts of the so-called dark Continent played since recorded history in their internal as well as their external relations'.[11]

In the first part of chapter 1 of his book, *Africa and the Development of International Law*, titled 'Ancient and Pre-medieval Africa', Elias uses historical accounts to demonstrate how Carthaginian rulers (in present day Tunisia) acquired an extensive empire in Africa. According to Elias, the Carthaginian empire explicitly excluded Sicily, Sardinia, and Southern Spain by treaty.[12] Elias uses this treaty to make two claims. First, to underline the military power of Carthage as an African empire, and second, to demonstrate that Africa had contact with Europe prior to colonial conquest through an international convention as was typical in relations between States. As a result, he was laying a basis to dispel the image of Africa as a dark continent. In Elias' view,

it was mainly this exclusion [such as by the treaty precluding the expansion of the Cathargian empire into Europe and the closure of the North African coast west of Cyrenaica to foreigners] that must account for the lack of information in the writings of classical authors about the nature and extent of the Cathaginians' African trade.[13]

In this view, history mistakenly and inadvertently reflects Africa's otherwise true participation within the international community in the pre-colonial period. Elias concludes exuberantly that his 'outline should serve as an interesting background to the account now being given of how the Sahara may be said to have dominated the history of the north no less than it has done that of the south'.[14] Further on, Elias tells us that the '*universality* of trade in cloth and other luxuries (in beads for example) which together with the largely urban pattern of settlement distinguished the Guinea region from all other parts of Africa south of the "sudanic" belt'.[15] It is the interaction

---

[11] TO Elias *Africa and the Development of International Law* (Sijthoff Leiden 1974) at 3.

[12] ibid.

[13] ibid.

[14] ibid 5.

[15] ibid 6 (emphasis added). Historians have noted that the 'pattern of empirical information about Africa was itself [in the 18th century] a product of the peculiar relations built during the centuries of slave trade'. PD Curtin *The Image of Africa, British Ideas and Action, 1780–1850* (The University of Wisconsin Press Madison 1964) at 9. Information on trade was of importance because of the commercial links, especially in slaves, between the West African coast and European and other traders. Another important matter of commercial importance was 'an elementary knowledge of political structure…for traders, who had to deal with African authorities' (ibid 23). European travellers at the time therefore wrote with particular attention to matters of trade, commerce and the 'political' structure of African societies. Almost two centuries later, African jurists of international law found this information in part produced to serve the commercial interests of European traders. Unlike these traders and European audiences, these jurists used this information as evidence to back their assertions of African contact with the West prior to colonial conquest.

and contact of African trade at specific entry ports with Western traders that created universality in Elias' narrative. Hence, commerce between Africa and Europe is equated with universality. Whether or not the exchanges between Africans and Europeans were humane or equal is not the subject of his focus. For example, it is significant that Elias only talks about the slave trade in relation to its abolition. However, Elias has little to say about how international law was implicated in the history of slavery under international law in the 18th and 19th centuries. Elias also does not address or make any observations with regard to the ways in which images of backwardness and barbarism ascribed to Africans under international law justified colonial expropriation of African lands. After all, Elias' primary project was to dispel the falsity of these repugnant colonial categories rather than engage all the purposes they served.

The pre-colonial period in Elias' view offers ample evidence of the presence of 'internationality' or contact between Africa and Europe. The high degree of knowledge and practice of diplomatic law, as then known in Europe and Asia, within Africa is part of the historical evidence Elias uses.[16] It is apparent that his criteria of what constitutes 'international' only applies to interaction between medieval African kingdoms and States with those of Europe and Asia. If this is so, then perhaps Elias is as much to blame as Eurocentric international legal jurists for understating the influence of Euro-African contact in the pre-colonial and colonial periods that took place within an exploitative and extractive relationship.[17]

His book then moves on to a familiar historical narrative, from the scramble for Africa to treaty making to drawing up boundaries and the assumption of sovereignty over Africa by the colonizing powers. Significantly, rather than examine the imperial nature of the treaties entered between 'African' chiefs and European trading companies/powers supposedly ceding African land to these colonials, Elias uses the treaties as further evidence of the participation of African pre-colonial kingdoms in the international sphere. To Elias, it therefore seems that these treaties were a reflection of the freedom of African chiefs to enter into relationships with European countries. This unfortunately is the logic that British colonial courts used to find that African communities had sovereignty to cede their land to colonial authorities at a time when these communities were under the complete control and jurisdiction of colonial powers.[18] In fairness to Elias, one cannot argue that he was entirely unaware of the problematic origins of unequal treaties and the hesitation of some then newly independent States to be freed of obligations under such treaties. In other writings,

---

[16] *Africa and the Development of International Law* (n 11) 15.

[17] The point here is simply that the cultural Eurocentricism of international law was inseparable 'from the parallel project of colonial domination an elementary knowledge of political structure...for traders, who had to deal with African authorities'. See A Riles 'Aspiration and Control: International Legal Rhetoric and the Essentialization of Culture Note' (1993) 106 Harvard Law Review 723–40 at 737.

[18] For an extensive analysis, see J Gathii 'Imperialism, Colonialism and International Law' (2007) 54 Buffalo Law Review 1013–66.

Elias addressed concerns of newly independent countries arising from unequal treaties.[19]

Like Elias, there are other Third World scholars who have argued that though 'States' in the modern sense may be of European creation, there are political entities in Africa that predate European States.[20] Classical international lawyers like Henry Wheaton,[21] TJ Lawrence,[22] and James Lorimer[23] regarded international law as limited to the civilized and Christian people of Europe or to those people of European origin. African scholars of the immediate post independence did not reject the Christian or Western origins of international law. Instead, they argued that Africans participated in shaping it. For these African international lawyers, the imperial and mercantilist character of international law was never in the foreground.[24]

2.2. Sovereignty in Rewriting International Legal History

Elias' definition of sovereignty in international law is informed by his basic project of reclaiming, reconstructing, and rehabilitating the African past and making comparisons with its supposed European equivalent. Unsurprisingly, Elias first refers to sovereignty as the command of the sovereign. Sovereignty then forms the basis of the unbroken narrative from the past into the present.[25] Chapter 2 of *Africa and the Development of International Law* is a reconstruction of the African past.[26] Elias uses the anthropological research and work of Meyer Fortes and Evans Pritchard to show that African States and kingdoms had sovereigns just like European States.[27]

---

[19] See eg TO Elias 'The Berlin Treaty and the River Niger Commission' (1963) 57 American Journal of International Law 879–80.

[20] MTS Jewa *The Third World and International Law* (thesis University of Miami Coral Gables FL 1976) at 7.

[21] H Wheaton *Histoire des progrès du droit des gens en Europe et en Amérique* (Brockhaus Leipzig 1865); see also the contribution by LH Liu 'Henry Wheaton (1785–1872)' in this volume.

[22] On TJ Lawrence, see 'Aspiration and Control' (n 17).

[23] J Lorimer *The Institutes of the Law of Nations: A Treatise of the Jural Relations of Separate Political Communities* (Aalen Blackwood & Sons Edinburgh 1883–84).

[24] The second part of this chapter addresses how a different school of post-independence African international lawyers traced the imperial and mercantilist character of international law.

[25] NS Rembe *Africa and International Law of the Sea* (Sijthoff & Noordhoff Alphen aan den Rijn 1980) at 5 shares the view that sovereignty is a 'legal concept and one of the cardinal principles recognized in international law'. Rembe goes ahead to elaborate the internal and external attributes of state sovereignty. In part, he observes that 'the various attributes of sovereignty generate a feeling of unity and nationhood which is a condition of development' at 6.

[26] Elias also quotes another of his most often cited books, *The Nature of African Customary Law* (Manchester University Press Manchester 1956) in which he shows 'striking similarities' between African customary law and European or Western rule of law oriented regimes.

[27] According to SF Moore *Anthropology and Africa, Changing Perspectives on a Changing Scene* (University Press of Virginia Charlottesville 1994) at 30–1, Fortes and Pritchard were among a group of

Elias argues that the new political aggregations produced by colonialism 'closed the historic modes of international intercourse of indigenous States and kingdoms. They were supplanted by the new external relations governable by international law'.[28] To Elias, therefore, colonialism interrupted the manner in which African 'States' or kingdoms like Carthage interacted with European States in the pre-colonial period. Having already discussed these African-European trade and diplomatic links at length in chapter 1, Elias' next chapter portrays colonialism as an abrupt interruption to Euro-African contact. This interruption of African sovereignty according to Elias had consequences since

only sovereign states were at any time the subject of customary international law. The drama of international legal relations was being played out, so far as Africa is concerned, by European governments among themselves with regard to economic, technical and cultural matters. Customary law developing in many respects as a result of the continuous changes taking place in the continent, but the African dependencies were mere spectators in the game. African dependencies' contribution, if any, lay in the fact that they were suppliers of the raw material for evolving rules and practices of international relations during the heyday of colonial rule.[29]

This extract of Elias' book portrays Africa's sovereignty as being in abeyance during colonial rule. Independence restored the sovereignty of individual African States, while membership in the United Nations guaranteed their sovereign equality with all other States. It is for this reason that Elias is optimistic and confident about the 'equal participation' of African States within the United Nations. To Elias,

[i]ndependence has led to membership of the United Nations and its organs and the consequent widening of the international horizon of all member nations, resulting in the establishment of new institutions and processes and in the enlargement of participation in the making and development of contemporary international law. *No longer is the law of the world court to be confined within the sometimes narrow limits set for it by the older few; modern international law must be based on a wider consensus, in the sense that it must be a reflection of the principle legal systems and cultures of the world...* The contribution which the third world in general, and Africa in particular, is making to contemporary international law will in time increase both in quantity and quality especially within the framework of the United Nations.[30]

This quotation summarizes one of Elias' most enduring insights about modern international law. His emphasis helps us see that the equal participation and contribution of newly independent States within the international community were the most significant achievements of formerly colonized countries. As Elias argued in

'Africanists at Oxford, Cambridge, London and eventually Manchester [who] constituted a ready-made, informed audience for each other's work and ideas' continues Moore, '... [n]ot only were they all active in each other's seminars and in the international African Institute in London, but they were in close communication with colleagues in the research institutes in Africa...'.

[28] *Africa and the Development of International Law* (n 11) 19.
[29] ibid 21.   [30] ibid 33 (emphasis added).

his masterful work, *The United Nations Charter and the World Court*, 'universality rather than limited application…must now be the catchword in the expanding frontiers of international law under the United Nations Charter'.[31] Elias emphasized the 'equal dignity and worth' of all members of the United Nations and the need not only to abolish inequalities among them, but to ensure that both new and old States cooperate with goodwill to achieve the purposes of the United Nations.[32] Thus in Elias we see a commitment to a view of sovereignty and human dignity informed by the Charter of the United Nations. Elias calls this 'modern international law'.

Elias' contributionist project, unlike that of critical theorists, was therefore not that of exploring how the equality of nations within the United Nations era could play a role in disguising the unequal North-South relationships as other African international legal scholars of his time observed.[33] Elias' primary concern was the rehabilitation of Africa within the international community by correcting the image of Africa on the basis of its similarity with Western societies and its achievement of sovereignty. However, that approach did not unearth the various ways in which the colonial apparatuses of international law were carried forward into the United Nations era.[34]

Paradoxically, it may be surmised that the Elias school of contributionism saw decolonization as representing the emancipation of international law, as much as he celebrated it for emancipating Africa from colonial rule.[35] Such a view contrasts sharply with that of Antony Anghie's masterful study of the emergence of sovereignty in international law.[36] According to Anghie, sovereignty emerged not to maintain order among sovereigns as classical renditions would have it. Rather, sovereignty emerged from the encounter between the incommensurable cultural differences of Europeans and non-European.[37] In this view, sovereignty was forged as a doctrine to

[31] TO Elias *The United Nations Charter and the World Court* (Nigerian Institute of Advanced Legal Studies Lagos 1989) at 2.

[32] ibid 8.

[33] The author of *Africa and International Law of the Sea* (n 25) on his part opines 'that although state sovereignty presupposes legal equality, states may be greatly unequal in size, population, economic and military capabilities…[yet] despite the influence of other factors in inter-state relations, the concept of state sovereign equality of states remains an important aspect in the conduct of state relations' at 7. Rembe places hope in the fact that though African states lack real power 'their numerical strength has increased their voting power' at 7. Similarly, the economic inequality between newly independent and old States was not lost on mainstream scholars of international law who were in many respects much like Elias. For example, L Henkin et al (eds) *International Law Cases and Materials* (3rd edn West Publishing Minnesota 1993) at xxix argue that the 'growing gap between the economically developed and the economically less developed countries' was a major development of the post Second World War period that 'signaled a new departure in the evolution of international law'.

[34] For an excellent exploration, see A Anghie *Imperialism, Sovereignty and the Making of International Law* (CUP Cambridge 2005).

[35] I am grateful to an anonymous reviewer for pointing this out to me.

[36] Imperialism, Sovereignty and the Making of International Law (n 34).

[37] For Anghie, the 'sovereignty of the non-European entity is determined in 19th century international law by applying the standard of civilization to determine the status of territory; the sovereignty of

manage nations with different cultures and histories rather than to maintain order among sovereigns. Celebrating the use of the ability to enter freely into consensual treaties that comes with sovereignty thus reproduced the hierarchical relations between Europeans and non-Europeans that were predicated on the superiority of European ideas such as contract that were ostensibly replacing rather than replicating unequal colonial relations.[38] Anghie concludes that having emerged in a crucible of inequality, sovereignty carries within it both the agenda of decolonization as well as reinforcement of the historically unequal relations between European and non-European States.[39]

2.3. Some Concluding Remarks on the Contributionist Tradition

Contributionism as exemplified in the work of scholars like Elias, is primarily predicated on a rejection of Western frames of analysis that understate African involvement and participation in the making of international law. Elias emphasized how Africa is and has been a co-equal player-participant and shaper of international legal norms. Thus a major project of the Elias tradition is to displace the Eurocentric cultural or ethnocentric bias in international law. An important preoccupation of this scholarship is resisting the view that international law was a cultural achievement specific to Western European countries, rather than one shared by African kingdoms. In the process of establishing these claims of similarity, these scholars however failed to examine some of the particular ways in which international law justified expropriation by disguising it by making claims of European superiority based on racial, cultural, and indigenous difference. Scholars taking Elias' view may in effect have validated a kind of 'Africanity' that does not seriously engage the colonial origins of international law. But I would think this is precisely what Elias was trying to displace.

the non-European entity in the post colonial period is determined by the framework of contracts. There is a broad shift, then from status to contract' (ibid 241–2).

[38] Thus in presenting his argument about how the use of the doctrine of sanctity of contracts replaced conquest as the way in which Third World States continued to be dominated by Western corporations and States, Anghie notes that 'Contractual approaches to international law further serve to obscure the imperial past. The whole framework of contracts is crucial to the attempt to establish that international law is neutral, that the arbitrators are doing no more than enforcing the agreements that had been freely entered into by sovereign states on the one hand and MNCs on the other. The point, however, is that it is international law that legitimized, through doctrines of conquest and by upholding unequal treaties, the imbalances and inequalities in social and political power that are reflected in international contracts which are then characterized as expressing the free will of the parties' (ibid 241).

[39] According to Anghie, decolonization 'did not...resolve colonial problems. Instead, the enduring consequences of colonialism became a central issue for the discipline, rather than a peripheral concern, as the emergence of these "new states", as they were termed in the literature of the period, posed major questions of international law at both the theoretical and doctrinal levels'(ibid 197).

His revisionist legal historiography was to disallow any reading of international law as exclusively European or colonial. In this respect, he defended the unity and coherence of international law as a truly universal discipline. In this respect, Elias is a very different scholar than Mohammed Bedjaoui who saw modern international law as the overcoming of a colonial tradition. By contrast, Elias looks back in effect telling us if you want to understand 19th-century international law, do not just look to what European States were doing, or take the writings of Wheaton or Lorrimer to be definitive. Look to Africa too.

The argumentative strategy employed by scholars such as Elias was aimed at establishing accommodation for an African cultural heritage as a part of the international civilization that contributes to international law. Thus in this contributionist tradition, scholars sought to displace the view embodied in international law that Africans were neither Christian nor civilized and as such were not entitled to enjoy sovereignty over their land or their people. They sought to reverse the view in Eurocentric international law that Africa was backward and uncivilized and therefore never participated in the collective enterprise of building customary international law.

In the process of seeking to adapt international law to reflect African viewpoints and cultures, scholars like Elias invoked notions of liberal equality and assumed that these notions were grounded in neutral principles of general and indeed universal applicability. They therefore dismissed 'old' public international law scholarship as being in violation of liberal equality.

Coming from societies whose identity, culture, and entire way of life had been repressed for being supposedly backward, uncivilized and primitive, the commitment embodied in the decolonizing project of the Elias tradition was undoubtedly a major move forward from the racist images that had shaped international legal norms and practices. That at last the African was acknowledged as an equal to the white person cannot therefore be underestimated, as these scholars emphasized. This scholarship was in a large measure inspired by the work of liberal anthropologists especially in England in the 1940s and 1950s. This anthropological scholarship has sought to establish the specific ways in which the African had similar achievements to those of the white person. Human rights norms and the four Geneva Conventions of 1949[40] are good examples of shared legal concepts between African customary law

---

[40] Geneva Convention for the Amelioration of the Condition of the Wounded and Sick in Armed Forces in the Field (adopted 12 August 1949, entered into force 21 October 1950) 75 UNTS 31 ('Geneva Convention I'); Geneva Convention for the Amelioration of the Condition of Wounded, Sick and Ship-wrecked Members of Armed Forces at Sea (adopted 12 August 1949, entered into force 21 October 1950) 75 UNTS 85 ('Geneva Convention II'); Geneva Convention relative to the Treatment of Prisoners of War (adopted 12 August 1949, entered into force 21 October 1950) 75 UNTS 135 ('Geneva Convention III'); Geneva Convention relative to the Protection of Civilian Persons in Time of War (adopted 12 August 1949, entered into force 21 October 1950) 75 UNTS 287 ('Geneva Convention IV').

and public international law identified by scholars in this tradition as we shall see shortly.

For Elias, the 'intercourse between certain countries of Africa on the one hand, and those of Europe and Asia on the other...must have thrown up certain general principles of international behavior, certain universally accepted standards of international conduct between one state and another'.[41] Elias therefore comes to the conclusion, that

[t]he way is thus clear for the emergent states of Africa today to be willing and ready to enter into new international relationships with other states, without feeling too much like strangers in the international legal community...African customary law shares with customary international law the acceptance of the fundamental principle of *pacta servanda sunt (sic)* as the basis for the assurance of a valid world order. In sum, the ruler like the ruled, must be under the law.[42]

Another fascinating account of the similarity of African customary law and norms of international law is the analogy of the principles enshrined in the Geneva Conventions and the 'laws of armed conflict in pre-colonial Africa'. In an article that falls within the Elias tradition, Bello traces these similarities in minute detail.[43] Ali A Wafi in another remarkably similar article argues through direct comparisons between Sharia law and international human rights norms, that the latter are consistent with the former.[44] So in this respect, Elias' work opened up or became part of a tradition of revisionist historiography of international lawyers from newly independent States. Elias' project of revisionist historiography was also shared by the United Nations Institute for Training and Research (UNITAR). A seminar was organized in 1971 'to break new ground by bringing to light aspects of inter-state law which has existed in Africa prior to the scramble for colonial territories'.[45] The justification for the conference was stated as setting the record straight since,

for a long time an image has been conveyed of Black Africa before colonization as a collection of primitive tribes living under anarchy or under the arbitrary rule of a chief, perpetually at war with each other, yet, the existence of sophisticated forms of government in pre-colonial Africa is now beyond doubt.[46]

To arrive at an appropriate image of the African that could match if not surpass the Western 'standards' of civilization, it was strategic for these scholars to deploy a

---

[41] TO Elias *New Horizons in International Law* (Sijthoff & Noordhoff Alphen aan den Rijn 1981) 45.

[42] ibid (original emphasis).

[43] EG Bello 'Shared Legal Concepts between African Customary Norms and International Conventions and Humanitarian Law' (1984) 23 Revue de droit pénal militaire et de droit de la guerre 285–310.

[44] AA Wafi 'Human Rights in Islam' (1967) 11 Islamic Law Quarterly 64–75.

[45] S Prakash opined the purpose of the seminar was 'to arrest the possibility of African and Asian states retreating into an exclusive regional system of international law, like that called for in the early 19th century in Latin America' see *New Nations and the Law of Nations* (Leyden Sijthoff 1967) at 26.

[46] See M Brown *African International Legal History* (United Nations Institute for Training and Research New York New York 1975) at i.

variety of stylistic approaches. In deploying these approaches, they harnessed sympathetic scholarly work to their nationalist cause. However, in so doing, a few problems emerged: first, they overlooked the fact that the presumed African heritage or culture that they glorified had been Europeanized and changed to coincide with the goals of the colonial political economy; second, they ignored the fact that colonial rule was in a large measure justified on the basis of African primitivity in the universal hierarchy of civilization; third, they regarded colonial rule as being a brief interlude in Africa's historical development. In other words, Africa and Africans had survived colonial rule and any self-respecting African would fortify his/her African identity rather than continue to assume an imposed foreign one.

The upshot of these moves proceeded from the premise that international law could help in resolving the problems of newly independent African countries. In fact, this is a primary theme of the contributionist tradition. Today, contributionism is still a major approach to the study of international law among scholars studying Africa. This is best exemplified by the authors of a book, published in 2008, entitled *Africa: Mapping New Boundaries in International Law*,[47] who enumerate African contributions to international law. Critical theorists like Makau Wa Mutua have challenged contributionist accounts for failing to take into account the historical association of international law with colonial conquest and Western domination in Africa.[48] It is the views of these critical theorists that the next section examines.

3. THE CRITICAL TRADITION

Critical theorists, unlike contributionists, centre their analysis on the structural and economic underpinnings of the place of African States in the world. While contributionists identified the exclusion of Africa from contributing to international law, critical scholars of the immediate post-Second World War era in Africa focused on questions of power and wealth imbalances between African countries and the rest of the world as reasons to be sceptical of the possibilities for reform within or through the use of international law.

A primary project of this group of scholars was a critical examination of the imperial and colonial character of international law. They also had a critique of

---

[47] *Mapping New Boundaries in African International Law* (n 4).

[48] See MW Mutua 'Savages, Victims and Saviors: The Metaphor of Human Rights' (2001) 42 Harvard Journal of International Law 201–45; see also 'Book Review' (n 5) 532 (noting the contributionists tend to ignore the extent to which norms of international law developed by Africans find centrality in international law).

the post-colonial State as well as the international political economy. One of the scholars in this tradition captures the basic assumptions of this tradition as follows:

[I]nternational law is simply...transforming itself into [a] public and private law of neo-colonialism and imperialism, with some facade of progressiveness due to the narrow and nominal inclusion of human rights principles and de-recognition of the rightfulness of formal colonialism and overt forms of discrimination.[49]

For this tradition, self-determination through political independence was the onset of a new period of subjugation to the history of Europe through a statehood mod-elled along European lines. Hence, unlike contributionists, critical theorists saw self-determination not as a moment to return Africa to a past of glory with reciprocal exchanges with Europe, but rather as a moment of betrayal. In the critical tradition, the analysis of early African contact with Europe laid emphasis on issues such as the slave trade and colonial rule, while in the contributionist tradition, commerce and diplomatic relations with non-African States were emphasized. For the critical tradition, customary international law was therefore regarded not to have originated in the course of commercial and diplomatic links between Africa and Europe, but rather as having arisen as a consequence of industrial capitalism in the West and the territorial ambitions of Western powers. For the critical tradition, international law was regarded as a handmaiden of the expansion of the economic interests of colonizing countries.

In short, the critical tradition identified the shortcomings of public international law to be fourfold. First, its geographic origins in Europe which meant that international law embodied a value system exclusive to Europe and not shared by the outside world. Second, that international law had mercantilist economic foundations. As a result, scholars in the critical tradition argued in favour of an egalitarian international economic order not merely through the law-making process of the United Nations but also through a jettisoning of current rules that would among other things renounce, if necessary, foreign economic presence, subject foreign capital to domestic laws, abolish discriminatory trade practices in international economic relations, and ensure stable and fair price guarantees of primary commodities. Third, scholars in the critical tradition argued that the political goals of international law were imperialist. The scholars supported self-determination; non-interference in the internal affairs of newly independent countries in all spheres. For them non-intervention extended beyond armed intervention to all forms of outside intervention whether political, cultural, social or economic. Fourth, scholars in the critical tradition argued that international law had a Christian religious foundation.[50]

---

[49] SBO Gutto 'Violation of Human Rights in the Third World: Responsibility of States and TNCs' in F Snyder and S Sathirathai (eds) *Third World Attitudes toward International Law* (Nijhoff Dordrecht 1987) 275–92 at 287.

[50] UO Umozurike *International Law and Colonialism in Africa* (Nwamife Publishing Enugu 1979) at 9–10.

Unlike the contributionist tradition that regards independence as a means to restore Africa to its own history, the critical tradition regarded independence as a moment of betrayal for continuing the colonial relationship under the guise of political independence. More particularly, the World Bank and the International Monetary Fund were regarded as agencies for the preservation of dependence and colonialism. This school of thought expresses frustration at the failure of the nationalist struggle to transform colonial inequities between the North and the South and the failure of the now independent African States to correct post-colonial excesses and abuses by the North. The aspirations of this school of thought were strongly represented by the non-aligned movement, the struggles to advance the cause of the Third World in the then better funded United Nations Conference on Trade and Development (UNCTAD), and the Group of 77.

3.1. On the History of the Discipline

UO Umozurike's *International Law and Colonialism in Africa*[51] is one of the best texts to trace the history of the discipline in the critical tradition. Unlike within contributionism, here emphasis is laid on slave trade and colonialism as two of the foremost experiences the Africans had from contact with the Europeans. Umozurike contends that 'international law was used to facilitate or acquiesce in the imposition of both afflictions [slave trade and colonialism]'.[52] Umozurike then argues that while international law helped the establishment of slave trade and colonialism, it was now being used in their eradication.[53] The underlying thesis in Umozurike's account was that 'an evil system' (such as that embodied in international law) cannot 'alter its essential nature'. Umozurike, however, opined that, 'in the present age of international law, self-determination remains an important factor in securing rights internationally recognized'.[54] There is a frustration with the inequality of international relations in this tradition.

---

[51] ibid.

[52] ibid 1. According to another account of the history in this tradition, the world has gone through the following stages: (a) the crumbling of the feudal order and the emergence of mercantilist trade; (b) industrial revolution and the establishment of a world capitalist system that colonized the Third World (c) the crumbling of formal colonialism and the rise of a multilaterized world with a centre and a periphery. See OO Ombaka *Law and the Limits of International and National Reform: Institutions of the International Economy and Underdevelopment* (thesis Harvard Law School 1977).

[53] Umozurike wrote his thesis on self-determination at Oxford: see UO Umozurike *Self-Determination in International Law* (Archon Books Hamden CT 1972).

[54] ibid. On his part, Aguda states that 'until quite recently, the tragedy of the position was that the newly founded faculties in Africa were manned by Europeans and Americans most of whom lacked imagination and were too dogmatic to make any useful contribution to an African approach to international law. As we all know the joint major achievement of African countries was the formation of the Organization of African Unity which in the way of achievements has not turned out to be much worse

So whereas contributionists argued without caution in favour of full participation of African States in international organizations like the United Nations, in the critical tradition one can see some hesitation. Some scholars in the critical tradition went even further and called for a withdrawal from the exploitative international relations that characterized colonial relationships carried forward in the post-independence period. Rather than embrace the view that Africa had 'everything to gain through contact with the Europeans', the critical tradition condemned the international system as 'inhumane and immoral'.[55]

Umozurike traces the history of the transatlantic trade in African slaves and concludes quite exaggeratedly that it was 'carried out by Europeans exclusively'[56] and the profits that were accrued were so enormous as to form part of the foundation for the prosperity of the Western world. The certainty with which this assertion is made is of course subject to serious debate especially given that African and Arab traders were similarly involved in the transatlantic slave trade. In this tradition, the role of international law is not merely that of regulating relations between States, thereby reducing friction and promoting cooperation and development. Instead, international law in this tradition is regarded as the law that governed relations of the civilized and Christian Europe *inter se* and was therefore 'the law of which the so called "primitive people" kn[e]w nothing and therefore [it could] not protect them, [and] . . . was used to promote the trade in Africans for the economic benefit of Europeans'.[57] In another take on the history of international law, Umozurike[58] divides the history of international law into 'old' and 'new'.[59] He traces the history

than the United Nations Organization itself which has brought much skepticism as to its ability to attain its goals. But speaking for myself I think that OAU has achieved a lot, although like its elder brother—the United Nations—has failed to attain much that was hoped for'. T Aguda 'The Dynamics of International Law and the Need for an African Approach' in K Ginther and W Benedek (eds) *New Perspectives and Conceptions of International Law: An Afro-European Dialogue* (Springer Wien 1983) at 9.

[55]   *International Law and Colonialism in Africa* (n 50) x. Umozurike uses extensive historical reference to show how slave trade negated political, economic, cultural and social development, stultified the growth of civilization and destroyed what civilization there was, at 4.

[56]   ibid 14.

[57]   ibid.

[58]   UO Umozurike *Introduction to International Law* (Spectrum Law Publishing Ibadan 1993). A book he published for teaching international law (in Africa) 'that draws as many examples from the African situation while of course giving prominence to the popular cases and situations cited in western test-books' at vii. According to K Gunther, at a seminar on 'International law and African Problems' held in Lagos in 1967, it was recognized that, first 'that Africa as the newest continent had the duty to enrich international law with its own experiences, its values and ideas, in defense of legitimate interests, second, that traditional international law had to be re-evaluated in the African context [since] . . . Africans were living on borrowed knowledge and which hardly coincided with the interests of African states and finally . . . that one of the ways of encouraging the study of international law in Africa was the production of text books and the publication of materials and documents written and compiled from the African experience and point of view' ('Introductory Remarks, New Perspectives and Conceptions of International Law and the Teaching of International law' in New Perspectives and Conceptions of International Law (n 54) 4–5).

[59]   ibid 7.

of 'old' international law to antiquity—to ancient Egypt, China, India, Ghana, and other ancient African kingdoms—very much like Elias in the contributionist tradition. He acknowledges Grotius as one of the greatest European writers of international law. He uses Grotius' book, *Mare Liberum*, as an authority for the view that international law applied to all people and knew no religious or racial bounds.[60] Umozurike then traces the development of 'old' international law to the rise of European States in the 19th century. In his discussion of the Congress of Vienna (1815), Umozurike argues that a few of the European States 'arrogated themselves to the circle of the civilized world'[61] and it was at this point that 'the law of Christian states changed gradually to the law of civilized states through the use of military power'. European expansion to all points of the world and new inventions increased their hegemony over the rest of the world.

Umozurike then traces the proliferation of international law 'in its branches—law of the sea, outer space, international institutions, human rights among other subjects'.[62] Noting that a historical analysis of the development of international law reveals that it has been used to meet challenges and to promote and protect the interests of its active users, Umozurike calls on 'states ... [to] ... consciously evolve a more *relevant and just* law that will protect the interests of all states and peoples'.[63]

For Umozurike, the 'new' international law therefore emerged in the post-1960 period following decolonization and recognition of the 'principle of *peaceful co-existence* in a world of differing cultures' as 'emphasized in the principles of *sovereignty and consent*'.[64] Although the views of the history of international law in this critical tradition recognize the nature of international law as inimical in many respects to the interests of newly independent countries, the tradition nevertheless accepts international law in its new or post-1960 phase. In this respect, both the critical tradition and contributionists share the same view. All of them accept in varying degrees the possibility of using the post-United Nations international law to address the problems of the newly independent States. This is a too familiar trope across almost all areas of law in post-independent Africa—the aspiration for reform even while recognizing the daunting challenges of reforming the very structures and doctrines that subjugated Africa under colonial rule. Another point on which the critical tradition has similarities with the contributionist tradition is the strong emphasis on the rejection of racism within international law.[65] Both traditions condemn racism in its colonial and post-colonial forms and call for its eradication.

---

[60] ibid 8–9.   [61] ibid 9–10.   [62] ibid 11.
[63] ibid 11–12.   [64] ibid 13 (emphases added).
[65] Du Bois is one of the Africanists Umozurike frequently cites in *International Law and Colonialism in Africa* (n 50); at 37 for example, Umozurike states that '[i]nternational law was embedded in white racism and this promoted the interests of the whites while rigorously subordinating those of others. White racial discrimination was thus a fundamental element of international law during the period in question.'

3.2. On the Role of Sovereignty in the Critical Tradition

While in the contributionist tradition the denial of sovereignty on the part of Africans within colonial international law is considered somewhat inadvertent, in the critical tradition, the denial of sovereignty to Africans is regarded as a 'major legal technique for the imposition of colonialism'.[66] Umozurike, somewhat like Elias in the contributionist tradition then argues that African peoples were in fact sovereign because they like their Western counterparts 'observed certain norms of conduct in their external and internal relations … [but] did not possess sufficient military might to withstand the onslaught of the Europeans who were thus able to ignore or to deny their sovereignty'.[67]

In his analysis of the debates of European scholars who regarded Africa as *terra nullius* (which European States could freely occupy),[68] Umozurike cites the separate opinion of Judge Ammon in the International Court of Justice's decision in the first South West Africa Case who vigorously contested that idea.[69] Thus in the critical tradition, international law cannot decide the internal legitimacy or otherwise of the government of a State. The internal legitimacy of a State is a matter for municipal law applicable to that State. Legitimacy under municipal law is different and not subject to international law.[70] This assertion that internal legitimacy is a matter of internal self-rule in an interesting way served to legitimate African leaders who sought to ward off criticism of their abusive governance by claiming that certain matters were within their exclusive domestic jurisdiction. Thus the role served by the non-intervention norm for the critical tradition in post-independent Africa was analogous to the role cultural nationalism played for the contributionist tradition.

This streak of independence and self-determination was in part a strategy to exorcize and pre-empt the effects of what the critical tradition referred to as neo-colonialism in Africa. Umozurike quoted President Nkurumah's definition of neo-colonialism: 'The imperialists of today endeavor to achieve their ends not merely by military means, but by economic penetration, cultural assimilation, ideological domination, psychological infiltration, and subversive activities even to the point of inspiring and promoting assassination and strife.'[71] Umozurike, like other scholars in this tradition, used the analytical framework of John Hobson[72] and Lenin[73] in their espousal of imperialism. Lenin argued that capitalist expansion in peripheral areas

---

[66] ibid 19.   [67] ibid 21.   [68] ibid.

[69] *Legal Consequences for States of the Continued Presence of South Africa in Namibia (South West Africa) notwithstanding Security Council Resolution 276 (1970) (Advisory Opinion)* [1971] ICJ Rep 16 at 26.

[70] EK Quanshigah 'Legitimacy of Governments and the Resolution of Intra-national Conflicts in Africa' (1995) 7 African Journal of Comparative and International Law 248–304 at 248.

[71] *International Law and Colonialism in Africa* (n 50) 126.

[72] See eg ibid 31 citing JA Hobson 'Imperialism: A Study' (J Pott & Company 1908) at 24.

[73] See eg ibid 31 where he quotes VI Lenin *Imperialism, the Highest Stage of Capitalism* (Lawrence London 1934).

served the interests of private profit seekers, while Hobson argued that surplus capital from industrialized economies of the late 19th and early 20th centuries was economic imperialism.[74] The study of imperialism in Africa coincides with theories of dependency and neo-colonialism according to which colonial possessions were used by colonizing economies not only as sources of cheap inputs like cotton, but also as captive markets for the resulting products, with the consequence of stultifying the growth of native industries.[75] While dependency theory has received critical attention,[76] it is still widely believed among some 'progressive thinkers and activists in Africa and the development community in advanced capitalist countries, including academics and students of development'.[77] While Umozurike, like most other scholars in this tradition, analyses the aspirations of the New International Economic Order, there was a very clear streak of dependency thinking within this critical tradition of scholarship in international law in Africa.[78]

Some of the most vocal proponents of the critical tradition in Africa and elsewhere called for fundamental reform of the international political economy as a condition for Third World participation. Some scholars in this tradition in fact called for a complete rejection of the international legal order.[79] Mohammed Bedjaoui's *Towards a New International Economic Order*[80] is perhaps the most well-known text that best exemplifies both the case for rejection of the international legal order but also the optimism of reformism in this alternative tradition particularly the climate of the 1970s and 1980s. Declared Bedjaoui, '…the embryonic new order constitutes a challenge to international law. International law is thus "concerned" about the economic forces now at work on a world scale'.[81] He expressed disappointment that '…a very simple debate…has become extremely confused. This is regrettable because the stakes are now higher than ever and involve the establishment of the new interna-

---

[74] See generally 'Imperialism, Colonialism and International Law.' (n 18) 1013.

[75] See K Nkurumah *Neo-Colonialism: The Last Stage of Imperialism* (Nelson London 1965); W Rodney *How Europe Underdeveloped Africa* (Howard University Press Washington 1973).

[76] C Leys *The Rise and Fall of Development Theory* (East African Educational Publishers Nairobi 1996).

[77] ibid 150.

[78] Samir Amin was among the most vocal exponents of this radical dependency perspective. As recently as 1994, another leading proponent of the dependency analysis, C Leys, has since revised his thesis of underdevelopment in part since the East Asian miracle questions some of the fundamental assumptions of dependency thinking. In 1974, B Warren, a one-time editor of the radical African Political Economy Review resigned from the editorial board after he changed his radical political perspective by alleging that capitalist development was possible anywhere in the world. The economic reform programmes now advocated by the World Bank and other multinational financial institutions, referred to as the Washington Consensus, advocate market reform to replace the state in the management of the economy.

[79] RP Anand explores this theme in an article titled 'Confrontation or Cooperation: The General Assembly at Cross-Roads' in a book he published in 1984, *Confrontation or Cooperation? International Law and the Developing Countries* (Martinus Nijhoff Publishers Dordrecht 1987).

[80] M Bedjaoui *Towards a New International Economic Order* (Holmes & Meier New York 1979).

[81] ibid 97.

tional economic order, which is to say the lives of billions of human beings.'[82] Among the factors which, according to Bedjaoui, introduced confusion in the debate on the New International Economic Order (NIEO) is the misguided 'legal paganism'[83] that 'law is immutable'.[84] Bedjaoui claimed that the arguments of Western governments to the effect that NIEO constituted a departure from the traditional and immutable conception of sovereignty 'turn[ed] law into a new religion centered on itself'.[85] 'Legal paganism' in Bedjaoui's view perpetuates 'the supremacy of developed states'[86] since it focuses on the form of the legal concept while 'the social reality of developing countries [especially in meeting their "survival" needs][87] ... is lost sight of.'[88]

4. CONCLUSION

Contributionism remains an important and enduring feature of international legal scholarship in and on Africa today. In many ways, contributionism's efforts to use history to reclaim or claim a place in international legal history for Africa were as innovative for an international lawyer as they were important. They were innovative because contributionists sought to reject, and continue to reject, international law for its legacy and participation in the colonization of Africa, but seek to use its legal tools as best as they could to reform international law to serve African countries. Critical scholars such as those associated with Third World Approaches to International Law (TWAIL) focus on the dark sides of international law while expressing optimism in using international law to achieve egalitarian reforms. For example, in his important book *Imperialism, Sovereignty and the Making of International Law*, Antony Anghie traces how international law invented the sovereignty doctrine to legitimize colonial rule and how this legacy continues to date.[89] However, he does not in any way recommend a jettisoning of international law. He sees hope for reform. Many international lawyers in Africa today share this dual

---

[82] ibid.

[83] ibid 99, Bedjaoui refers to it as 'intoxication with sovereignty'. 'This intoxication in his view' is paving way to 'instability of legal situations' and anomy in the State's power of decision 'or in other words, a power of decision subject to no rules'.

[84] ibid 98. Notice that while in the first tradition, formalism was embodied in the view that law is the command of the sovereign, here Bedjaoui claims that it is embodied in law's immutability.

[85] ibid 100.

[86] ibid.

[87] ibid 103–4.

[88] ibid 99. Bedjaoui also explores an antinomy 'existing in law, which implies conservatism, and development, which calls for change' (at 97–8 and 109).

[89] *Imperialism, Sovereignty and the Making of International Law* (n 34).

sensibility—a sense that Africa and the Third World are treated differently in the international order, but at the same time a sense of hope that international law can lead to an alternative future.

One of the most significant ways in which the Elias tradition can be seen to have its influence is in the manner in which many contemporary international lawyers in Africa have stopped short of tracing Africa's social, economic, and political problems to international factors such as neo-colonialism. Rather than tracing Africa's social, economic, and political problems to external actors or factors, more and more scholarship has traced it to the poor economic policy choices on the part of African leadership, particularly their resistance to fully integrate their countries into the international political economy in the immediate post-independence period, and to the disastrous and authoritarian character of African leadership. The solutions for these problems chiefly centred on integrating African countries into world markets and adoption of political pluralism and respect for human rights. These solutions, especially insofar as they were centred on integrating Africa in the global economy, resonate extremely well with the contributionists method of historical recovery tracing Africa's forgotten participation in the evolution of international law. Thus as the contributionist tradition turned to history to trace Africa's integral location in international legal history, critical international lawyers have looked outward to international and regional integration for solutions to Africa's economic, social, and political problems.[90] The contributionist tradition also has much in common with contemporary international lawyers in Africa who continue to express optimism in the transformative possibilities that international law offers to Africa's various challenges.

However, not all international lawyers in Africa today share in this optimism of the potential egalitarian uses of international law. The critical tradition lives on the work of TWAIL scholars. These scholars have traced recurrent African problems like civil war, state collapse, and general economic, political, and social failure in sub-Saharan Africa to the legacy of unequal relations between the former colonial powers and their colonies as still embedded in international legal doctrines and practices as well as to contemporary abuses of power. Thus while international law provides a way of thinking about reform that could easily be deployed to disguise inequalities and projections of authority through claims of universality, interdependency, peace, and security, the critical tradition continues to live on in exploring the dark sides of both public and private international law and its contemporary legacies in national and international life. Such work has explored not simply the shortcomings of international law but the manner in which developed and developing country elites use doctrines and principles of international law such as sovereignty and self-determination to disguise the ways in which they

---

[90] J Gathii *African Regional Trade Agreements as Legal Regimes* (OUP Oxford 2011).

advance and protect their interests.[91] In short, to fully appreciate the Elias tradition, one has to locate it in relation to the critical tradition as I have tried to do in this chapter.

Recommended Reading

Anghie, Antony *Imperialism, Sovereignty and the Making of International Law* (CUP Cambridge 2005).

Brown, Mensa *African International Legal History* (United Nations Institute for Training and Research New York 1975).

Clarke, Maxine K *Fictions of Justice: The International Criminal Court and the Challenge of Legal Pluralism in Sub-Saharan Africa* (CUP Cambridge 2009).

Elias, Taslim O and Richard Akinjide *Africa and the Development of International Law* (Martinus Nijhoff Publishers Dordrecht 1988).

Gathii, James 'International Law and Eurocentricity' (1998) 9 European Journal of International Law 184–211.

Gathii, James 'Neoliberalism, Colonialism and International Governance: Decentering the International Law of Governmental Legitimacy' (2000) 98 Michigan Law Review 1996–2065.

Gathii, James 'A Critical Appraisal of the International Legal Tradition of Taslim Olawale Elias' (2008) 21 Leiden Journal of International Law 317–49.

Gathii, James *War, Commerce and International Law* (OUP New York 2009).

Ginther, Konrad and Wolfgang Benedek (eds) *New Perspectives and Conceptions of International Law: An Afro-European Dialogue* (Springer Wien 1983).

Grovogui, Siba *Sovereigns, Quasi-Sovereigns and Africans: Race and Self-Determination in International Law* (University of Minnesota Press Minneapolis MN 1996).

Gutto, Shadrack BO 'Violation of Human Rights in the Third World: Responsibility of States and TNCs' in Frederick Snyder and Surakiart Sathirathai (eds) *Third World Attitudes Toward International Law* (Nijhoff Dordrecht 1987) 275–92.

Levitt, Jeremy (ed) *Mapping New Boundaries in African International Law* (Hart Oxford 2008).

Maluwa, Tiyanjana *International Law in Post-Colonial Africa* (Kluwer The Hague 1999).

Mutua, Makau 'What is TWAIL?' (2000) 94 American Society of International Law Proceedings 31–40.

Mutua, Makau W 'Savages, Victims and Saviors: The Metaphor of Human Rights' (2001) 42 Harvard Journal of International Law 201–45.

Mutua, Makau W '(Book Review) Africa: Mapping New Boundaries in International Law by Jeremy I. Levitt' (2010) 104 American Journal of International Law 532–8.

Okoye, Felix *International Law and the New African States* (Sweet and Maxwell London 1972).

---

[91] J Gathii 'TWAIL: A Brief History of Its Origins, Its Decentralized Network and a Tentative Bibliography' (2011) 3 Trade Law and Development Journal 26–64.

Umozurike, Umozurike O *Self-Determination in International Law* (Archon Books Hamden Connecticut 1972).

Umozurike, Umozurike O *International Law and Colonialism in Africa* (Nwamife Publishing Enugu 1979).

Quashigah, Kofi E 'Legitimacy of Governments and the Resolution of Intra-national Conflicts in Africa' (1995) 7 African Journal of Comparative and International Law 248–304.

CHAPTER 18

OTTOMAN EMPIRE

UMUT ÖZSU

1. INTRODUCTION

INTERNATIONAL lawyers have long regarded the Ottoman Empire as having been central to the development of many of the most crucial rules, principles, and traditions of their discipline. Unsurprisingly, interest in Ottoman history and politics has only increased in recent years, driven by debates about Turkey's seemingly asymptotic accession to the European Union and its popular representation as a pivotal 'regional power' and 'emerging market'. The widely felt need to counter fears of an imminent 'clash of civilizations' by promoting a 'Turkish model' of multi-party democracy and free market capitalism adds fuel to this fire. Yet, much as Ottoman law has frequently been studied not on its own terms but in its relationship with 'Islamic law' or 'European law',[1] the international legal history of the Ottoman Empire remains a field in infancy—a field dominated by studies in historical sociology and economic and diplomatic history. Investigations have been undertaken into the reception of European law,[2] the international legal implications of darker episodes in late Ottoman history,[3]

---

[1] Cf R Miller 'The Legal History of the Ottoman Empire' (2008) 6 History Compass 286–96 at 287 ff.

[2] See eg E Örücü 'The Impact of European Law on the Ottoman Empire and Turkey' in WJ Mommsen and JA de Moor (eds) *European Expansion and Law: The Encounter of European and Indigenous Law in 19th- and 20th-Century Africa and Asia* (Berg Oxford 1992) 39–58; G Bozkurt *Batı Hukukunun Türkiye'de Benimsenmesi: Osmanlı Devleti'nden Türkiye Cumhuriyeti'ne Resepsiyon Süreci (1839–1939)* (Turkey's Absorption of Western Law: The Reception Process from the Ottoman State to the Republic of Turkey (1839–1939)) (Türk Tarih Kurumu Basımevi Ankara 1996).

[3] The Armenian genocide has attracted some (though not enough) attention. The most influential discussion is VN Dadrian 'Genocide as a Problem of National and International Law: The World War I

the somewhat thorny issue of legal relationship between the Ottoman Empire and the Republic of Turkey,[4] and even the question of whether it is possible to speak of a distinctly Turkish 'school' of international law.[5] Much has also been intimated over the years about the Ottoman Empire's fluctuating place in the 19th-century state system, particularly about its controversial admission to the Concert of Europe, or at least to its 'advantages', pursuant to the 1856 Treaty of Paris.[6] Nevertheless, there is as yet nothing that would warrant recognition as a comprehensive body of scholarship pertaining to the Ottomans' engagement with what we would now characterize as 'international law'.

What is perhaps most disconcerting about this dearth of scholarship is that relations between the Ottoman Empire and its non-Muslim allies and rivals were marked by remarkable ambiguities, being mediated by a class of instruments known generally to the early Ottomans as *ahdnameler* ('pledges', or, more literally, 'letters of promise') and to non-Muslim sovereigns as 'capitulations' (from *capitula*, for the 'chapters' into which they were typically divided). For centuries, the capitulations staged a kind of struggle between Ottoman and European (and eventually American) diplomats, functionaries, and jurists, their status being imprecise and contested. For the Ottoman sultans, as for at least some of the Arab, Mamluk, Turkic, and Byzantine rulers they succeeded,[7] the capitulations were at root imperial decrees—unilaterally granted and unilaterally revocable pledges to non-Muslim sovereigns with which political alliances or trading partnerships had been struck. The individual beneficiary of a

---

Armenian Case and Its Contemporary Legal Ramifications' (1989) 14 Yale Journal of International Law 221–334. A broader analysis of the 'Armenian question' is offered in M Toufayan 'Empathy, Humanity and the "Armenian Question" in the Internationalist Legal Imagination' (2011) 24 Revue québécoise de droit international (forthcoming, copy with author). Work on the international legal dimensions of other episodes has, however, only just begun; see eg U Özsu 'Fabricating Fidelity: Nation-Building, International Law, and the Greek-Turkish Population Exchange' (2011) 24 Leiden Journal of International Law 823–47.

[4] See eg E Öktem 'Turkey: Successor or Continuing State of the Ottoman Empire?' (2011) 24 Leiden Journal of International Law 561–83; E Zamuner 'Le rapport entre Empire ottoman et République turque face au droit international' (2004) 6 Journal of the History of International Law 209–31.

[5] B Aral 'An Inquiry into the Turkish "School" of International Law' (2005) 16 European Journal of International Law 769–85. Such efforts are not entirely without precedent: see eg PM Brown 'The Turkish Institute of International Law' (1943) 37 American Journal of International Law 640–2; C Bilsel 'International Law in Turkey' (1944) 38 American Journal of International Law 546–56.

[6] The most sustained legal engagement with the issue remains HM Wood 'The Treaty of Paris and Turkey's Status in International Law' (1943) 37 American Journal of International Law 262–74.

[7] I do not address these precedents in this chapter. However, for some of the Muslim cases, particularly interesting on account of their implications for Islamic legal doctrine, see PM Holt *Early Mamluk Diplomacy (1260–1290): Treaties of Baybars and Qalāwūn with Christian Rulers* (Brill Leiden 1995); BZ Kedar 'Religion in Catholic-Muslim Correspondence and Treaties' in AD Beihammer, MG Parani, and CD Schabel (eds) *Diplomatics in the Eastern Mediterranean 1000–1500: Aspects of Cross-Cultural Communication* (Brill Leiden 2008) 407–21; and also EA Zachariadou *Trade and Crusade: Venetian Crete and the Emirates of Menteshe and Aydin (1300–1415)* (Istituto Ellenico di Studi Bizantini e Postbizantini Venice 1983).

capitulatory grant—a *müstemin*, or non-Muslim foreigner, in Ottoman-Islamic parlance—was typically extended privileges of residence on or safe passage through Ottoman territory, made immune from the jurisdiction of Islamic courts, and provided with the benefit of tax exemptions and low customs duties.[8] The Ottoman chancery was given to choosing its words carefully. These privileges were not to be confused with permanent rights. And the Ottoman State was not to be seen as engaged with a non-Muslim entity on terms of strict formal equality. Among other things, this could have violated the letter of *Sharī'a*, skirting the prohibition against de iure recognition of non-Muslim States in classical Islamic law and thereby subordinating the Ottomans to an inter-state order for which even many dexterous Muslim jurists could find little normative justification.[9] A 16th-century Venetian merchant may have had little choice but to accept this formulation, working under the assumption that, when all was said and done, the capitulation that enabled him to ply his trade was a sultanic directive. But by the 19th century, many European and American jurists struggling to record the capitulations' historical evolution, or seeking to endow them with greater legal force, had grown accustomed to presenting them as treaties that imposed binding legal obligations upon both parties, the Ottoman sultan no less than the relevant non-Muslim power. Such jurists cast the capitulation not as a temporary and unilateral concession but as a lasting and bilateral treaty. As such, the capitulatory text was to be read not as a projection of Ottoman sovereignty so much as one in a set of instruments that bound Istanbul to an (unequal and stratified) international system spearheaded by a progressively integrated *droit public de l'Europe*.[10] Indeed, by the 19th century, Ottoman officials themselves sometimes

[8] For the terms of most capitulations, see N Sousa *The Capitulatory Régime of Turkey: Its History, Origin, and Nature* (Johns Hopkins Press Baltimore 1933) at 70–86; MH van den Boogert *The Capitulations and the Ottoman Legal System: Qadis, Consuls and Beratlıs in the 18th Century* (Brill Leiden 2005) ch 1.

[9] For this prohibition, see M Khadduri *War and Peace in the Law of Islam* (Johns Hopkins Press Baltimore 1955) at 51–4 and also 224–8; M Khadduri (ed) *The Islamic Law of Nations: Shaybānī's Siyar* (M Khadduri trans) (Johns Hopkins Press Baltimore 1966) at 10–14; see also M Hamīdullāh *Muslim Conduct of State* (revised edn Sh Muhammad Ashraf Lahore 1945) at 259–61.

[10] There were, of course, exceptions. Wheaton, for instance, admitted that, on 'careful examination', an early capitulation to France revealed itself to be not a 'reciprocal compact' but a 'gratuitous concession'. H Wheaton *Elements of International Law* (WB Lawrence ed) (6th edn Little, Brown & Co Boston 1855) at 508–9. Still, it was common to argue that, whatever their origins, the capitulations had by the 19th century come to acquire the binding force of treaties, in some cases by incorporation into treaties *sensu stricto*. See eg H Bonfils *Manuel de droit international public (droit des gens)* (P Fauchille ed) (5th edn A Rousseau Paris 1908) at 526. That Ottoman authorities of the period occasionally appear to have conceded this point complicates the matter further. SS Liu *Extraterritoriality: Its Rise and Its Decline* (Columbia University Press New York 1925) at 179–80. For recent consideration of the question, never resolved definitively, see eg H Theunissen 'Ottoman-Venetian Diplomatics: The 'Ahd-names. The Historical Background and the Development of a Category of Political-Commercial Instruments together with an Annotated Edition of a Corpus of Relevant Documents' (1998) 1 Electronic Journal of Oriental Studies 1–698 at 185–8 and 306–9; D Kołodziejczyk *Ottoman-Polish Diplomatic Relations (15th–18th Century): An Annotated Edition of 'Ahdnames and Other Documents* (Brill Leiden 2000) at 3–6; V Panaite *The Ottoman Law of War and Peace: The Ottoman Empire and Tribute Payers* (East European Monographs Boulder 2000) at 239–48; MH van den Boogert 'Consular Jurisdiction in the Ottoman Legal System in the Eighteenth Century' (2003) 22 Oriente Moderno 613–34 at 623–5.

referred to the capitulations as *imtiyazat* ('privileges'), or even as *imtiyazat-ı ecnebiye* ('foreign privileges'), although they still generally maintained that the capitulations were not to be confused with treaties.

This interpretational fluidity proved to be of tremendous material significance, given that European-Ottoman trade was channelled and regulated by way of capitulations. The claim that the capitulations constituted bilateral treaties—made with increasingly greater frequency after the mid-18th century, when the European law of treaties itself entered a period of refinement—underwrote ever more intense penetration of Ottoman markets and restricted the empire's capacity to exercise sovereign power over its territory. The extraterritorial consular jurisdiction the capitulations afforded came to be abused not only by the European merchants whose activities they facilitated but also by the increasingly large number of local 'protégés' with whom these merchants collaborated and to whom letters patent (*beratlar*) were granted. Predictably, by the final decades of the 19th century, Ottoman reform movements and incipient forms of Turkish nationalism had begun to target the capitulatory regime as a humiliating sign of Ottoman decline. No longer was the capitulatory grant a manifestation of state power on the part of a growing empire with legitimacy claims both to the Eastern Roman Empire and to the *dār al-Islām*. Instead, it was a reminder of how far, and how dramatically, the Ottomans had fallen—of their defeat at the hands of a technologically and administratively sophisticated West that had managed to leverage scientific ingenuity into imperial expansion.

The ambiguity surrounding the capitulations owed much to the contested status of the Ottoman Empire. On the one hand, the empire came under the influence of a variety of Western laws, both municipal and international, from the early 19th century onwards. Such processes both engendered and were engendered by relations of dependence and debt-accumulation similar in many respects to those in operation in colonial and quasi-colonial territories.[11] On the other hand, this protracted engagement with the West—coming to the fore explicitly with the French-inspired Tanzimat reforms of the mid-19th century and arguably reaching its zenith with the neo-Jacobin nation-building initiatives that followed the proclamation of a republic in 1923—betrayed the incremental marginalization of an otherwise powerful patrimonial State, not colonialism in any strict sense.[12] If it is true that, in the 19th century,

---

[11] From a variegated literature on the macro-level similarities, see especially CA Bayly *The Birth of the Modern World 1780–1914: Global Connections and Comparisons* (Blackwell Oxford 2004); H İslamoğlu and PC Perdue (eds) *Shared Histories of Modernity: China, India and the Ottoman Empire* (Routledge London 2009). For the international legal dimensions, see further RS Horowitz 'International Law and State Transformation in China, Siam, and the Ottoman Empire during the Nineteenth Century' (2004) 15 Journal of World History 445–86.

[12] For the argument that the Ottoman Empire boasted well-resourced bureaucratic apparatuses, with impressive recruitment standards and administrative techniques, at least as early as the 17th century, see R Murphey *Exploring Ottoman Sovereignty: Tradition, Image and Practice in the Ottoman Imperial Household, 1400–1800* (Continuum London 2008) ch 9; and also RA Abou-El-Haj *Formation of the Modern State: The Ottoman Empire, Sixteenth to Eighteenth Centuries* (2nd edn Syracuse University Press Syracuse 2005) esp at 61–72. These apparatuses were subject to considerable expansion and differentiation in

Ottoman Turkey was occasionally cast as the 'sick man of Europe', it is no less true that, even at this late stage, it still made a point of styling itself the Islamic world's 'eternal State' (*devlet-i ebed-müddet*). This precariousness was reflected in the fact that, while the Ottoman Empire was seldom recognized as a full member of the 'family of civilized nations', European jurists of the period often postulated an intermediate class for States of the kind it was deemed to exemplify. Just as James Lorimer broke humanity down into 'three concentric zones or spheres', with Turkey as an archetype of the kind of 'barbarous' State that found itself lodged between 'civilized' States and 'savage' peoples,[13] so too did Turkey figure prominently in Franz von Liszt's division of States into 'civilized' (*Kulturstaaten*), 'semi-civilized' (*halbcivilisierten Staaten*), and 'uncivilized' (*nichtcivilisierten Staaten*) groups in the opening pages of his 1898 textbook, *Das Völkerrecht*.[14] The capitulations, and the interpretational disputes to which they gave rise, confirmed and showcased this intermediate status.

While this chapter sketches some of the key treaties into which the Ottomans entered, as well as some of the most significant doctrinal developments that involved the empire, its principal focus lies with the capitulations. An ambitious State with multi-continental holdings, the legal authority of the Ottoman Empire was understood differently on different occasions. The capitulations illustrate the variability of the empire's status in the international legal system, demonstrating that this instability found expression in a distinct set of instruments for the regulation of political and economic relations with the West.

2. A Brief History of the Capitulations

The general parameters of the Ottoman capitulations' history are not difficult to trace. It is widely agreed that the Ottomans were in the habit of granting large numbers of capitulations to Genoese and Venetian (and also Florentine, Neapolitan, Ragusan, and other) merchants in the 14th and 15th centuries. A well-known case is the capitulation granted by Mehmed II to the Genoese after the Ottoman conquest of Constantinople

the 19th century, when new ministries (including, crucially, ministries of justice and foreign affairs) were established. For sustained treatment, see CV Findley *Bureaucratic Reform in the Ottoman Empire: The Sublime Porte, 1789–1922* (Princeton University Press Princeton 1980) at 167–90.

[13] J Lorimer *The Institutes of the Law of Nations: A Treatise of the Jural Relations of Separate Political Communities* (W Blackwood & Sons Edinburgh 1883) vol 1, at 101 ff.

[14] F von Liszt *Das Völkerrecht, systematisch dargestellt* (O Haering Berlin 1898) at 1–4. Of course, the Ottomans were proud of their own 'semi-sovereigns'; for a tellingly blunt discussion see YM Altuğ 'The Semi-Sovereign Dependencies of the Ottoman Empire' (1958) 8 Annales de la Faculté de droit d'Istanbul 8–28.

in 1453. Active in the city under Byzantine rule, the Genoese were invested with the privilege of conducting trade without a significant tax burden, and their ability to come and go, resolving their disputes in accordance with their own laws and customs, was recognized.[15] The adjudicative features of these early grants are intriguing, shedding light on the jurisdictional complexities fostered by even the earliest capitulations. While disputes between subjects of Latin powers were settled by local consuls, those between Latin merchants on the one hand and subjects of the sultan on the other seem at times to have been distributed between Latin consuls and Ottoman courts on the basis of the defendant's nationality. A Latin subject bringing an action against an Ottoman subject could take the matter to the Ottoman authorities, whereas an Ottoman subject with a claim against a Latin subject might go to the Latin consul, joint decisions by Latin and Ottoman authorities also apparently being an option.[16]

Far from being a piecemeal, irregularly applied affair, one with limited or merely local effect, these capitulations quickly developed into a far-flung regime of trade and diplomacy involving a large number of non-Muslim States. Merchants affiliated with a State to which a capitulation had been granted were authorized to operate full-scale *fondachi*, factories, and similar trading 'colonies' on Ottoman soil—a power on which chartered companies like the Levant Company, armed with the connections and commercial know-how needed to occupy the commanding heights of eastern Mediterranean trade, would eventually rely extensively for the purpose of facilitating rapid import and export of goods.[17] This provided a significant foothold in Ottoman economy and society, and also spurred the growth of new mechanisms of diplomatic intercourse.[18]

A capitulatory document involving France and conventionally dated to 1535 or 1536 was long regarded as the 'first' capitulation, and, as such, the *locus classicus* of the Ottoman capitulatory regime.[19] Such assessments are somewhat misleading. Quite

---

[15] K Fleet *European and Islamic Trade in the Early Ottoman State: The Merchants of Genoa and Turkey* (CUP Cambridge 1999) at 129.

[16] K Fleet 'Turkish-Latin Diplomatic Relations in the Fourteenth Century: The Case of the Consul' (2003) 22 Oriente Moderno 605–11 at 611. On the fluidity of such inter-imperial relations, see EN Rothman *Brokering Empire: Trans-Imperial Subjects between Venice and Istanbul* (Cornell University Press Ithaca 2012) chs 1–2; and also ER Dursteler *Venetians in Constantinople: Nation, Identity, and Coexistence in the Early Modern Mediterranean* (Johns Hopkins University Press Baltimore 2006).

[17] See generally M Epstein *The Early History of the Levant Company* (G Routledge & Sons London 1908); AC Wood *A History of the Levant Company* (OUP London 1935). For a revealing case study from a later period, see D Vlami 'Entrepreneurship and Relational Capital in a Levantine Context: Bartholomew Edward Abbott, the "Father of the Levant Company" in Thessaloniki (Eighteenth-Nineteenth Centuries)' (2009) 6 Historical Review 129–64 (examining the 'system of overlapping circles of relatives, social and business acquaintances, collaborators and "friends"' (at 156) through which such proto-corporations often operated).

[18] On the latter see D Goffman 'Negotiating with the Renaissance State: The Ottoman Empire and the New Diplomacy' in VH Aksan and D Goffman (eds) *The Early Modern Ottomans: Remapping the Empire* (CUP Cambridge 2007) 61–74 at 70.

[19] For the text see Traité de paix, d'amitié et de commerce, February 1535, reproduced in I de Testa *Recueil des traités de la Porte ottomane avec les puissances étrangères depuis le premier traité conclu, en 1536, entre Suléyman I et François I, jusqu'à nos jours* (Amyot Paris 1864) vol 1, 15–21. For assessments of its 'foundational' importance, see eg MA Desjardins *De l'origine des capitulations dans l'Empire ottoman*

apart from the fact that numerous capitulations had already been granted by the Ottomans to a variety of non-Muslim city-states, more recent scholarship has raised doubts as to whether the 1535–36 capitulation—the putative product of an anti-Habsburg alliance—was ever affirmed by the sultan. Jean de la Forêt, representative of France, and İbrahim Paşa, the Ottoman grand vezier, negotiated the document at some point in 1535 or the following year. But there is little evidence to suggest that Süleyman I confirmed the capitulation for subjects of François I formally (and İbrahim Paşa was executed shortly thereafter).[20]

Whatever may have been the precise status of the 1535–36 document, of doubtful legal status even for many European jurists,[21] capitulations granted to France over the course of the next two centuries bolstered the capitulatory regime significantly. A 1740 capitulation is key in this regard.[22] In addition to augmenting the immunities conceded to France in earlier grants, this was the first capitulation in which the sultan bound himself to concessions *in perpetuo*: unlike previous capitulations, generally couched as grants of limited duration that needed to be confirmed by each new sultan, the Porte here committed itself to a set of concessions whose effectiveness was not contingent upon formal acts of renewal.[23] The 1740 capitulation also granted most-favoured-nation status to France, with Louis XV being characterized as a 'sincère et ancien ami' of the sultan.[24] Finally, it was also notable for its exhaustiveness, comprising no less than eighty-five provisions on issues ranging from cooperation against North African pirates to free passage for pilgrims to Jerusalem.[25]

Scholars have emphasized different aspects of the 1740 capitulation. What is at least as revealing as the perpetuity of its privileges or the endowment of France with most-favoured-nation status,[26] though, is the fact that many later European and American

(A Picard Paris 1891) at 11–13; JB Angell 'The Turkish Capitulations' (1901) 6 American Historical Review 254–9 at 255–6; G Pélissié du Rausas *Le régime des capitulations dans l'Empire ottoman* (A Rousseau Paris 1902) vol 1, at 3 and 23; FE Hinckley *American Consular Jurisdiction in the Orient* (WH Lowdermilk & Co Washington 1906) at 8–9; PM Brown *Foreigners in Turkey: Their Juridical Status* (Princeton University Press Princeton 1914) at 33–7; Capitulatory Régime of Turkey (n 8) at 68–70. Such assessments have also been shared by Turkish scholars; see eg N Erim *Devletlerarası Hukuku ve Siyasi Tarih Metinleri* (International Law and Political History Texts) (Türk Tarih Kurumu Basımevi Ankara 1953) vol 1, at 5–7.

[20]   H İnalcık 'Imtiyāzāt' in B Lewis et al (eds) *The Encyclopaedia of Islam: New Edition* (Brill Leiden 1971) vol 3, 1179–89 at 1183 but see also J Matuz 'À propos de la validité des capitulations de 1536 entre l'Empire ottoman et la France' (1992) 24 Turcica 183–92.

[21]   For contextual analysis of Gentili's thoughts on the matter, for instance, see N Malcolm 'Alberico Gentili and the Ottomans' in B Kingsbury and B Straumann (eds) *The Roman Foundations of the Law of Nations: Alberico Gentili and the Justice of Empire* (OUP Oxford 2010) 127–45 at 138–45.

[22]   For the text see Lettres-patentes, 30 May 1740, reproduced in *Recueil des traités* (n 19) at 186–210.

[23]   ibid art 85, at 210.

[24]   ibid Preamble, at 187. For the general context in which this 'friendship' was revitalized, see especially FM Göçek *East Encounters West: France and the Ottoman Empire in the Eighteenth Century* (OUP Oxford 1987).

[25]   Lettres-patentes (n 22) arts 1, 11, 32, 54, and 81–2, at 189, 190–1, 195–6, 200, and 208–9.

[26]   E Eldem *French Trade in Istanbul in the Eighteenth Century* (Brill Leiden 1999) at 278–9; E Eldem 'Capitulations and Western Trade' in SN Faroqhi (ed) *The Cambridge History of Turkey* (CUP Cambridge

jurists, particularly of the late 19th century, argued that 1740 was the first step en route to the consolidation and crystallization of a mature capitulatory regime. Thus, writing with nearly a century and a half of hindsight, Travers Twiss observed that the 1740 document was 'the first which in terms bound [the sultan's] successors' and 'continue[d] to be operative in the present day',[27] a rather remarkable fact given that it was during the late 18th and 19th centuries that politico-economic relations between the Ottoman Empire and the West underwent their most thorough reconfiguration.[28] Edouard Engelhardt, the author of an influential study on the Tanzimat and eventually also a member of the Institut de droit international,[29] went further, suggesting that it was with the 1740 grant that Turkey submitted to the 'servitude des juridictions étrangères'—a period from which Engelhardt, writing in 1880, had yet to see it emerge.[30] In the hands of many such jurists, the 1740 capitulation, and others like it, was not a transitory and one-sided concession, but an enduring and bilateral treaty, or at least an instrument that could not be modified or supplanted by the sultan alone. Interestingly, it has since been suggested that the 1740 capitulation manifested a fundamentally altered appreciation of Mediterranean power dynamics,[31] a position that receives some support from the fact that the capitulation was made at a time of considerable turmoil within the empire.[32]

The Ottomans were far from oblivious to the dangers of these developments, and made a number of attempts to check them. Not the least significant were periodic

2006) vol 3, 283–335 at 320; AH de Groot 'The Historical Development of the Capitulatory Regime in the Ottoman Middle East from the Fifteenth to the Nineteenth Centuries' (2003) 22 Oriente Moderno 575–604 at 599; KH Ziegler 'The Peace Treaties of the Ottoman Empire with European Christian Powers' in R Lesaffer (ed) *Peace Treaties and International Law in European History: From the Late Middle Ages to World War One* (CUP Cambridge 2004) 338–64 at 349–50.

[27] T Twiss *The Law of Nations Considered as Independent Political Communities: On the Rights and Duties of Nations in Time of Peace* (2nd edn Clarendon Press Oxford 1884) at 389, 455, and similarly at 458.

[28] The 'Ottoman decline' thesis—in which the 18th century is frequently regarded as having played a pivotal role—has been subject to considerable criticism, not least on account of the sweeping, empirically questionable claims with which it has traditionally been accompanied. Still, the preponderance of evidence militates in favour of a general pattern of politico-economic incorporation and peripheralization. From a world-systems-theoretical perspective, see I Wallerstein, H Decdeli, and R Kasaba 'The Incorporation of the Ottoman Empire into the World-Economy' in H İslamoğlu-İnan (ed) *The Ottoman Empire and the World-Economy* (CUP Cambridge 1987) 88–97 at 92–4; R Kasaba *The Ottoman Empire and the World Economy: The Nineteenth Century* (State University of New York Press Albany 1988) at 18–35.

[29] E Engelhardt *La Turquie et le Tanzimat, ou histoire des réformes dans l'Empire ottoman depuis 1826 jusqu'à nos jours* (2 vols A Cotillon & Cie Paris 1882–84).

[30] E Engelhardt *Le droit d'intervention et la Turquie: Étude historique* (A Cotillon & Cie Paris 1880) at 15 (original emphasis).

[31] R Olson 'The Ottoman-French Treaty of 1740: A Year to be Remembered?' (1991) 15 Turkish Studies Association Bulletin 347–55 at 348.

[32] RW Olson 'Jews, Janissaries, Esnaf and the Revolt of 1740 in Istanbul: Social Upheaval and Political Realignment in the Ottoman Empire' (1977) 20 Journal of the Economic and Social History of the Orient 185–207 at 201 ff.

efforts to counter or clamp down on the proliferation of letters patent to those (often tangentially) associated with Western merchants, in some cases by issuing *berat*s to 'loyal' merchants, both Muslim and non-Muslim, with a view to reasserting control over the terms and conduct of international trade. Such efforts generally yielded no more than limited short-term results.[33] By the mid-19th century, many of the privileges offered in the capitulations had come to be enshrined, partly if not wholly, in bilateral and multilateral treaties. The 1838 Balta Liman Convention,[34] the most prominent early-19th-century free trade treaty with the Ottomans, provides a well-known example. The convention was concluded only a few years after the creation of an independent Greek kingdom and the Russo-Turkish War of 1828–29, not to mention France's seizure of Algiers and ongoing conflict in Syria and elsewhere with forces loyal to Egypt's Muhammad Ali. In addition to abolishing Ottoman monopolies and fixing import and export duties, the convention stipulated that '[a]ll rights, privileges, and immunities which have been conferred on the subjects or ships of Great Britain by the existing Capitulations and Treaties, are confirmed now and for ever, except in as far as they may be specifically altered by the present Convention.'[35] Not only did this provision associate the capitulations with treaties, but it reinforced the claim that the capitulations imposed binding legal obligations by conferring upon existing British privileges much the same perpetuity as that associated with the 1740 grant. A powerful demonstration for some of free trade doctrine's collusion with 'informal empire', the ultra-liberal regime made possible by the convention was appropriated by other powers and replicated before long in a number of other treaties.[36]

An even more lucid illustration of the felt need to entrench capitulatory privileges through treaty law is offered by the 1856 Treaty of Paris, the seventh article of which famously extended to the Porte the right 'à participer aux avantages du droit public

---

[33] Aİ Bağış *Osmanlı Ticaretinde Gayrî Müslimler: Kapitülasyonlar—Avrupa Tüccarları—Beratlı Tüccarlar—Hayriye Tüccarları, 1750–1839* (Non-Muslims in Ottoman Trade: Capitulations—*Avrupa Tüccarıs—Beratlı Tüccarıs—Hayriye Tüccarıs,* 1750–1839) (Turhan Kitabevi Ankara 1983) especially ch 2; B Masters 'The Sultan's Entrepreneurs: The *Avrupa Tüccarıs* and the *Hayriye Tüccarıs* in Syria' (1992) 24 International Journal of Middle East Studies 579–97; The Capitulations (n 8) at 105–12.

[34] Convention of Commerce and Navigation between Great Britain and Turkey (signed 16 August 1838) 88 CTS 77.

[35] ibid, art 1, at 79.

[36] See, famously, J Gallagher and R Robinson 'The Imperialism of Free Trade' (1953) 6 Economic History Review 1–15 at 11–12. But see also O Kurmuş 'The 1838 Treaty of Commerce Re-examined' in JL Bacqué-Grammont and P Dumont (eds) *Économie et sociétés dans l'Empire ottoman (fin du XVIIIe—début du XXe siècle). Actes du colloque de Strasbourg (1er–5 juillet 1980)* (Éditions du Centre national de la recherche scientifique Paris 1983) 411–17; Ş Pamuk *The Ottoman Empire and European Capitalism, 1820–1913: Trade, Investment and Production* (CUP Cambridge 1987) at 18–21 ff; R Kasaba 'Open-Door Treaties: China and the Ottoman Empire Compared' (1992) 7 New Perspectives on Turkey 71–89 at 73–5 and 78–82; D Quataert 'The Age of Reforms, 1812–1914' in H İnalcık and D Quataert (eds) *An Economic and Social History of the Ottoman Empire* (CUP Cambridge 1994), vol 2, 759–943 at 764.

et du concert Européens'.[37] The legal implications of this provision were notoriously nebulous, it being unclear whether the empire could be said to have thereby secured recognition as a full-fledged 'European' State, but the key power-political assumptions were never anything but obvious. It was widely believed that the treaty would neutralize the Black Sea, check Russian advances in the Balkans, and transfer Russia's long-standing claim to be the 'protector' of Turkey's Christians—a claim reinforced by treaty law[38]—to West European States.[39] This last objective dovetailed with article 9, which noted that the sultan had already issued a decree reaffirming his 'généreuses intentions envers les populations Chrétiennes de son Empire',[40] in particular through the institution of formal equality in regards to religious expression, legal adjudication, educational opportunity, and employment in the civil service.[41] Committed to countering intervention in their domestic affairs, Ottoman negotiators pressed for the formal abolition of the capitulatory regime, increasingly viewed as evidence of exclusion from the 'family of nations'.[42] Despite sustained pressure, though, the great powers refused to do away with the capitulations, deferring resolution of the matter while taking steps, in article 32, to bar unilateral renewals and replacements of 'Traités ou Conventions' in effect prior to the Crimean War.[43] Gone were the days when the

[37] General Treaty for the Re-Establishment of Peace (signed 30 March 1856) 114 CTS 409 ('Treaty of Paris') at 414.

[38] For the most significant treaty, see Treaty of Perpetual Peace and Amity (signed 10 July 1774) 45 CTS 349, arts 7 and 14, at 390 and 392–3. On Russian efforts to amplify the meaning of its terms, see RH Davison '"Russian Skill and Turkish Imbecility": The Treaty of Kuchuk Kainardji Reconsidered' (1976) 35 Slavic Review 463–83.

[39] See eg GDC Argyll *The Eastern Question: From the Treaty of Paris 1856 to the Treaty of Berlin 1878, and to the Second Afghan War* (Strahan & Co London 1879) vol 1, ch 1; H Temperley 'The Treaty of Paris of 1856 and Its Execution' (1932) 4 Journal of Modern History 523–43; AJP Taylor *The Struggle for Mastery in Europe 1848–1918* (Clarendon Press Oxford 1954) at 83–6.

[40] Treaty of Paris (n 37) at 414.

[41] For the decree see 'Hatti Humayoun relatif aux réformes de l'Empire Ottoman, 18 Février 1856' reproduced in G Noradounghian (ed) *Recueil d'actes internationaux de l'Empire Ottoman* (Librairie Cotillon F Pichon Paris 1902) vol 3, no 685, 83–8. Note that the wording of art 9 was contested, Ottoman negotiators resisting language that suggested quasi-contractual obligations growing out of the sultan's decree. RH Davison 'Ottoman Diplomacy at the Congress of Paris (1856) and the Question of Reforms' in *VII. Türk Tarih Kongresi (Ankara: 25–29 Eylül 1970)—Kongreye Sunulan Bildiriler* (Proceedings of the 7th Turkish Historical Congress (Ankara: 25–29 September 1970)) (Türk Tarih Kurumu Basımevi Ankara 1973) vol 2, 580–6 at 584–5.

[42] For standard 19th-century claims to the effect that extra-European States needed to 'apply' for 'membership' in the European 'family of nations', see eg WE Hall *International Law* (Clarendon Press Oxford 1880) at 34–5 (arguing that 'states outside European civilisation must formally enter into the circle of law-governed countries' by 'do[ing] something with the acquiescence of the latter, or of some of them, which amounts to an acceptance of the law in its entirety beyond all possibility of misconstruction'); TJ Lawrence *The Principles of International Law* (Macmillan & Co London 1895) at 58 (offering 'a certain degree of civilization' as an answer to the question of 'what further marks a community must possess, over and above the marks of sovereignty, before it can take its place among those states whose intercourse is regulated by the highly developed system of rules which we call International Law').

[43] Treaty of Paris (n 37) at 419.

empire could hazard the conceit of being a power confident in its eventual triumph and oblivious to the demands of permanent diplomacy.[44] It had secured the right to partake in the European state system's 'advantages', at least nominally, and had begun to comport itself accordingly: a foreign ministry had already been set up, and now it would be enlarged and augmented, with French being adopted as a key working language, its staff and procedures undergoing professionalization, and a spate of new embassies being established in Europe and elsewhere.[45] But the formalization and further entrenchment of the capitulations spoke to the fact that the Ottomans were now very clearly on the back foot, and that the empire's relationship with the European state system remained a strained and anomalous one.[46]

Historians of state-building and humanitarian intervention—the latter a phenomenon of largely, if not exclusively, 19th-century provenance—have recently turned their attention to late-19th-century Ottoman-Russian rivalries in the Balkans and Caucasus.[47] Although '[t]he assumption of a collective authority on the part of the powers to supervise the solution of the Eastern question—in other words, to regulate the disintegration of Turkey'—dates at least from 1856,[48] many such studies focus on the 1878 Congress of Berlin, the high-water mark of formal engagement with the 'Eastern question' and the diplomatic conclusion to the Russo-Turkish War of 1877–78. Thanks in no small part to successful lobbying by the Alliance israélite universelle, Berlin laid out an innovative set of minority protection guarantees.[49] It also conditioned recognition of Serbia, Montenegro, and Romania as de iure sovereigns—and Bulgaria as a de facto independent State—on conformity to these guarantees. The relevant provisions were substantively identical in each case, prohibiting, among other things, discrimination on the basis of faith 'en ce qui concerne la jouissance des droits civils et politiques, l'admission aux emplois publics, fonctions, et honneurs, ou l'exercice des différentes professions et industries'.[50] However, further requirements were introduced in the case

[44] Not until the final decade of the 18th century did the Ottomans begin to open permanent embassies in Europe. JC Hurewitz 'The Europeanization of Ottoman Diplomacy: The Conversion from Unilateralism to Reciprocity in the Nineteenth Century' (1961) 25 Belleten 455–66 at 460.

[45] ibid 462–4; see further CV Findley 'The Legacy of Tradition to Reform: Origins of the Ottoman Foreign Ministry' (1970) 1 International Journal of Middle East Studies 334–57; CV Findley 'The Foundation of the Ottoman Foreign Ministry' (1972) 3 International Journal of Middle East Studies 388–416.

[46] Cf JAR Marriott The Eastern Question: An Historical Study in European Diplomacy (Clarendon Press Oxford 1917) at 274 (suggesting that 'the Treaty of Paris marks indisputably the point at which Turkey finally passed into a state of tutelage to the European Concert').

[47] See especially D Rodogno Against Massacre: Humanitarian Interventions in the Ottoman Empire 1815–1914 (Princeton University Press Princeton 2012) chs 6–8; M Schulz 'The Guarantees of Humanity: The Concert of Europe and the Origins of the Russo-Ottoman War of 1877' in B Simms and DJB Trim (eds) Humanitarian Intervention: A History (CUP Cambridge 2011) 184–204.

[48] TE Holland The European Concert in the Eastern Question: A Collection of Treaties and Other Public Acts (Clarendon Press Oxford 1885) at 2.

[49] C Fink Defending the Rights of Others: The Great Powers, the Jews, and International Minority Protection, 1878–1938 (CUP Cambridge 2004) at 15–38.

[50] Treaty for the Settlement of Affairs in the East (signed 13 July 1878) 153 CTS 171 ('Treaty of Berlin') arts 5, 27, 35, and 44, at 176, 182, 184, and 187. Such provisions were not immune to criticism, or even

of Turkey. The Porte's heavy-handedness in suppressing rebellions in Bulgaria and else-where had raised the ire not only of Russia but also of the Western powers, 'bringing the fervor of humane impulse and of religious enthusiasm into one of the most confused problems of international law'.[51] As such, in addition to having to strengthen the right to offer evidence in Ottoman courts for all its nationals, to refrain from restricting the movement of clerics and pilgrims, and to adopt a variety of other measures to protect minorities and foreigners,[52] Turkey was compelled, by article 61, to undertake 'amélio-rations' and 'réformes' in Armenian-populated provinces.[53] Ottoman authorities largely ignored this stipulation in the years that followed. But the kind of politico-eco-nomic intervention made possible by the capitulations increasingly went hand in hand with diplomatic, and even military, intervention in the name of 'humanity'.[54] Interna-tional lawyers like André Mandelstam were, in fact, given to arguing that Berlin, for all its deficiencies, offered an illustration of '[l]'intervention collective d'humanité', an attempt to internationalize what might otherwise have been a solely domestic affair in the wake of 'une véritable guerre d'humanité'.[55]

The capitulations' survival was often justified with claims to the effect that the empire's legal codes were out of date, that its courts were rife with corruption, and that its legal traditions allowed for too much discretionary authority. So long as com-prehensive reforms were not undertaken for the purpose of introducing new codes and overhauling the administration of justice, the capitulations would remain indis-pensable for ensuring that nationals of non-Muslim States operating in the empire (and at least a faction of the local non-Muslims with whom they worked) were sub-ject only to 'civilized' European laws.[56] A belief in Turkey's financial instability

---

ridicule. Gladstone, for example, wrote that it was not 'a little amusing to observe with what edifying zeal all the great States of Europe united to force religious liberty upon those new-fledged bantlings of politics, on their first view of the light of day; and yet these great States have hardly in any case learned…to adopt it at home'. WE Gladstone *The Berlin Treaty and the Anglo-Turkish Convention* (Liberal Central Association London 1878) at 14.

[51] JP Thompson 'The Intercourse of Christian with Non-Christian Peoples' in JP Thompson *Ameri-can Comments on European Questions, International and Religious* (Houghton, Mifflin & Co Boston 1884) 104–31 at 105. The most influential illustration is WE Gladstone's widely circulated *Bulgarian Hor-rors and the Question of the East* (J Murray London 1876).

[52] Treaty of Berlin (n 50) art 62, at 189–90.

[53] ibid 189.

[54] The leading pre-1914 study made a point of underscoring the centrality of European engagement with the Ottoman Empire for the doctrinal emergence of humanitarian intervention: A Rougier 'La théorie de l'intervention d'humanité' (1910) 17 Revue générale de droit international public 468–526 at 472 ff.

[55] AN Mandelstam *La société des nations et les puissances devant le problème arménien* (Pedone Paris 1926) at 17–18 (de-emphasized from original).

[56] From an enormous contribution to the literature see F Martens *Das Consularwesen und die Con-sularjurisdiction im Orient* (H Skerst trans) (Weidmannsche Buchhandlung Berlin 1874) at 320 ff; T Twiss *On Consular Jurisdiction in the Levant, and the Status of Foreigners in the Ottoman Law Courts* (W Clowes & Sons London 1880) at 20–1 and 23–4; Institutes of the Law of Nations (n 13) at 313–14; J West-lake *Chapters on the Principles of International Law* (CUP Cambridge 1894) at 101–3; N Politis *La guerre*

occasionally accompanied such claims, at least after the empire's bankruptcy in 1875, following which a Public Debt Administration (*Düyun-u Umumiye*) was formed by European creditors to absorb government revenue.[57] The Young Ottomans, a group of liberal publicists and civil servants whose writings occasionally bled into proto-nationalism, tended not to launch systematic critiques of European legal and economic encroachment, given their overriding commitment to the empire's piecemeal Westernization.[58] But dissatisfaction, and a concomitant desire to formulate a cogent response, was clearly on the rise. Indeed, by the first years of the 20th century, penetrating scholars of imperialism could be found warning that the Ottoman Empire's dependence upon the West had reached critical levels. Just as Hobson cautioned in 1902 that most of the remaining Turkish dominions would succumb to 'a slow, precarious process of absorption'[59] (the 'absorption', when it finally came, proved neither slow nor precarious), so too did Lenin, strategizing laterally in 1917, group Turkey with China and Persia in a class of 'semi-colonial countries', free, perhaps, of formal colonialism but subject nonetheless to tremendous informal pressure.[60] Aware of the danger, Ottoman officials regularly sought to check encroachment, as when Gabriel Noradounghian, an Ottoman lawyer and diplomat of Armenian heritage who would eventually rise to the rank of foreign minister, voiced concern at the prospect of a Belgian push to enforce those clauses of an 1838 treaty that seemed to place criminal matters between Ottoman and Belgian nationals within the jurisdiction of Belgian consular courts.[61] The lease, the condominium, the protectorate—familiar

gréco-turque au point de vue du droit international: contribution à l'étude de la question d'Orient (Pedone Paris 1898) at 28 and 116–20. A telling illustration is offered by the remarks of a British official regarding the possibility that consular jurisdiction might be abolished in Tunis after France entered the territory and introduced its own system of courts. 'The institutions which have grown up under the Capitulations with Turkey have been found essential for the protection of foreigners under the peculiar circumstances of the Ottoman Empire', he observed, noting that 'the necessity for them disappears when Tribunals organized and controlled by an European Government take the place of the Mussulman Courts'. 'Mr. Plunkett to Earl Granville, October 19, 1882' in *Correspondence respecting the Establishment of French Tribunals and the Abrogation of Foreign Consular Jurisdiction in Tunis: 1882–83* (C 3843) (Harrison & Sons London 1884) 2–3 at 2.

[57] The classic study is DC Blaisdell *European Financial Control in the Ottoman Empire: A Study of the Establishment, Activities, and Significance of the Administration of the Ottoman Public Debt* (Columbia University Press New York 1929); see further H Feis *Europe the World's Banker 1870–1914: An Account of European Foreign Investment and the Connection of World Finance with Diplomacy Before the War* (AM Kelley New York 1964) at 332–41; R Owen *The Middle East in the World Economy 1800–1914* (Methuen London 1981) at 191–200; E Eldem 'Ottoman Financial Integration with Europe: Foreign Loans, the Ottoman Bank and the Ottoman Public Debt' (2005) 13 European Review 431–45 at 440–3.

[58] See generally Ş Mardin *The Genesis of Young Ottoman Thought: A Study in the Modernization of Turkish Political Ideas* (Princeton University Press Princeton 1962).

[59] JA Hobson *Imperialism: A Study* (J Nisbet & Co London 1902) at 236.

[60] VI Lenin 'Imperialism, the Highest Stage of Capitalism' in VI Lenin *Collected Works* (Y Sdobnikov trans) (Progress Publishers Moscow 1964) vol 22, 185–304 at 257–60.

[61] G Noradounghian 'Le traité turco-belge de 1838 et la compétence en matière pénale des autorités ottomanes envers les étrangers' (1906) 8 Revue de droit international et de législation comparée 119–35.

mechanisms such as these were 'devices of diplomacy', Hersch Lauterpacht later admitted, often employed as 'preparations for annexation' or offering 'means of acquiring sufficient power where downright annexation was thought to be politically inexpedient'.[62] The capitulations struck many, Ottoman and non-Ottoman alike, as having turned into yet one more mechanism of subjugation.

As the principal organ of the Young Turk movement that wrested control of the Ottoman government in 1908–9,[63] the Committee of Union and Progress (*İttihat ve Terakki Cemiyeti*) came of age during a period in which sharp critiques of the capitulatory regime gained wide currency. Officially committed though it was to a vision of shared Ottoman citizenship, the committee grew decreasingly reluctant after 1908–9 to advance policies designed to strengthen the Turkish-Muslim 'core' of Ottoman society (Muslims had long been characterized as the empire's *millet-i hâkime*, or 'ruling nation'). A point of particular sensitivity was the *en masse* displacement of Muslims to which a succession of Ottoman military and diplomatic defeats had given rise: large movements of Muslims from the Balkans, Caucasus, and Crimea had occurred more or less without pause since the 1860s.[64] The forced migration of Muslims during the Balkan Wars and the First World War only exacerbated these sensitivities, focusing ever larger portions of the Ottoman State's Turkish-Muslim citizenry around previously marginal modes of self-identification.[65] Turkish nationalism's popularization and normalization also owed much to the writings of European intellectuals sympathetic to economic nationalization. The work of Friedrich List, theorist of the aptly termed 'national system' of economics, a protectionist rival to 19th-century

---

[62] H Lauterpacht 'International Law and Colonial Questions, 1870–1914' in E Lauterpacht (ed) *International Law, Being the Collected Papers of Hersch Lauterpacht* (CUP Cambridge 1975) vol 2, 95–144 at 114.

[63] Over the course of 1908 and 1909, the committee deposed the reigning sultan, curtailed his successor's powers, and inaugurated a period of quasi-parliamentary rule by restoring the first Ottoman constitution of 1876. Attempts were then made to tighten Istanbul's grip over the provinces through a series of ham-fisted (and increasingly violent) state-centralization initiatives. For a detailed account of the *ancien régime*'s supplanting, see A Kansu *The Revolution of 1908 in Turkey* (Brill Leiden 1997) ch 4.

[64] The literature is large and growing. See eg KH Karpat *Ottoman Population, 1830–1914: Demographic and Social Characteristics* (University of Wisconsin Press Madison 1985) at 60–77; A Toumarkine *Les migrations des populations musulmanes balkaniques en Anatolie (1876–1913)* (Les éditions Isis İstanbul 1995) at 27–77; BG Williams 'Hijra and Forced Migration from Nineteenth-Century Russia to the Ottoman Empire: A Critical Analysis of the Great Crimean Tatar Emigration of 1860–1861' (2000) 41 Cahiers du monde russe 79–108; D Cuthell 'The Circassian Sürgün' (2003) 2 Ab Imperio 139–68.

[65] For a recent discussion see F Dündar *Modern Türkiye'nin Şifresi: İttihat ve Terakki'nin Etnisite Mühendisliği (1913–1918)* (The Key to Modern Turkey: The Ethnicity Engineering of the Committee of Union and Progress (1913–1918)) (İletişim Yayınları İstanbul 2008). That many Young Turks hailed from the Balkans was naturally of considerable importance; see especially EJ Zürcher 'The Young Turks: Children of the Borderlands?' (2003) 9 International Journal of Turkish Studies 275–85; and also EJ Zürcher *The Young Turk Legacy and Nation Building: From the Ottoman Empire to Atatürk's Turkey* (IB Tauris London 2010) chs 8–9.

British free trade doctrine, enjoyed residual influence.[66] But arguably the most illuminating figure is Alexander Helphand, the Second International theoretician and arms dealer credited with having proposed an embryonic form of the theory of uneven and combined development that would be picked up and developed by Trotsky. According to Helphand, a resident of Istanbul and advisor to the committee's inner circle in the 1910s, the Ottoman State had no choice but to abrogate the capitulations, do away with the Public Debt Administration, and ensure the construction of a thoroughly 'native' (that is, Turkish-Muslim) bourgeoisie, sovereign over capital accumulation and equipped to resist European imperialism.[67] So widely were such sentiments shared that Mahmut Esat, later to become the Republic of Turkey's minister of justice (and its agent before the Permanent Court of International Justice in the *Lotus* case), could structure his doctoral dissertation around the argument that the capitulations were incompatible with the specifically national character of the modern State.[68]

In 1914, only months before issuing the deportation orders that resulted in the Armenian genocide, the Committee of Union and Progress, by then little more than a *junta*, circulated a diplomatic note to States with which capitulatory agreements were in effect.[69] Coming at a time when Turkish-Ottoman newspapers regularly exhorted their readers to recognize that a 'people's integrity cannot be preserved by those old books of international law, but only by war',[70] the note argued that the capitulations, though originally consisting of unilateral and temporary concessions, had come over time to injure Ottoman sovereignty, hindering economic development and effective administration. The empire was therefore entitled to abrogate them, particularly in light of its demonstrated commitment to legal reform, and 'to adopt as the basis of relations with all States the general principles of international law'.[71] Only Berlin and

---

[66] Ş Pamuk 'The Ottoman Economy in World War I' in S Broadberry and M Harrison (eds) *The Economics of World War I* (CUP Cambridge 2005) 112–36 at 119; MŞ Hanioğlu *A Brief History of the Late Ottoman Empire* (Princeton University Press Princeton 2008) at 189. See, more generally, Z Toprak *Türkiye'de 'Millî İktisat' (1908–1918)* ('National Economy' in Turkey (1908–1918)) (Yurt Yayınları Ankara 1982) at 25–35.

[67] For Helphand's writings from this period, see Parvus Efendi *Türkiye'nin Malî Tutsaklığı* (Turkey's Financial Captivity) (M Sencer ed) (May Yayınları İstanbul 1977). For discussion see ZAB Zeman and WB Scharlau *The Merchant of Revolution: The Life of Alexander Israel Helphand (Parvus) 1867–1924* (OUP London 1965) ch 6; HL Kieser 'World War and World Revolution: Alexander Helphand-Parvus in Germany and Turkey' (2011) 12 Kritika: Explorations in Russian and Eurasian History 387–410.

[68] See M Essad *Du régime des capitulations ottomanes: Leur caractère juridique d'après l'histoire et les textes* (Fratelli Haim Stamboul 1928). The dissertation was defended in Fribourg in 1918.

[69] 'Ottoman Circular Announcing the Abrogation of the Capitulations, 9 September 1914' reproduced in JC Hurewitz (ed) *Diplomacy in the Near and Middle East: A Documentary Record: 1535–1956* (Octagon New York 1972) vol 2, 2–3.

[70] Quoted in M Aksakal *The Ottoman Road to War in 1914: The Ottoman Empire and the First World War* (CUP Cambridge 2008) at 21.

[71] Ottoman Circular (n 69) at 3. Interestingly, though, the English translation also effectively conflated 'treaties' with 'Capitulations'; see ibid 2.

Vienna recognized this move during the course of the war,[72] Germany in particular having previously promised to assist Turkey in doing away with the capitulations.[73] Mass celebrations broke out in Istanbul when the note was publicized, though many non-Muslim citizens, not to mention foreign investors, viewed it with scepticism and apprehension.[74]

An attempt was made by the Allies to reinstate the capitulations—whose abrogation they never recognized formally—in the Treaty of Sèvres, the peace treaty the defeated Ottomans signed in the aftermath of the First World War.[75] Sèvres, however, was never ratified, and was dismissed *tout court* by Mustafa Kemal's Anatolia-centred nationalist movement. And with Sèvres a dead letter from the outset, the fate of the capitulations still hung in the balance. At the 1922–23 Conference of Lausanne, where a definitive peace settlement with Turkey was negotiated,[76] İsmet Paşa, the chief Turkish delegate, advanced a number of arguments to secure the capitulations' abolition. To begin with, he declared, the documentary record supported the oft-repeated Turkish claim that the capitulations were 'essentially unilateral acts'; Turkey was therefore well within its rights to revoke them.[77] What is more, he went on to contend, even if the capitulations were to be characterized as treaties, the circumstances that had produced them had been marked by fundamental change, triggering the doctrine of *rebus sic stantibus* and releasing Turkey from its international legal obligations.[78] İsmet capped this point with a third, more wide-ranging argument to the effect that

---

[72] For details see N Bentwich 'The Abrogation of the Turkish Capitulations' (1923) 5 Journal of Comparative Legislation and International Law 182–8 at 183 ff; A Rechid 'La condition des étrangers dans la République de Turquie' (1933) 46 Recueil des cours 165–228 at 180–2; and, more generally, JA Mazard *Le régime des capitulations en Turquie pendant la guerre de 1914* (J Gaudet Alger 1923). Bolshevik Russia would follow suit in 1921.

[73] U Trumpener *Germany and the Ottoman Empire 1914–1918* (Princeton University Press Princeton 1968) at 28–9; see also R Bullard *Large and Loving Privileges: The Capitulations in the Middle East and North Africa* (Jackson, Son & Co Glasgow 1960) at 32.

[74] F Ahmad 'Ottoman Perceptions of the Capitulations 1800–1914' (2000) 11 Journal of Islamic Studies 1–20 at 18–20.

[75] 'Treaty of Peace between the Allied Powers and Turkey, signed at Sèvres, August 10, 1920' (1921) 15 American Journal of International Law Supplement 179–295, art 261, at 247.

[76] For the peace treaty, see Treaty of Peace (signed 24 July 1923) 28 LNTS 11. For the entire package of instruments comprising the settlement, see 'Treaty with Turkey and Other Instruments, signed at Lausanne, July 24, 1923' (1924) 18 American Journal of International Law Supplement 1–116.

[77] 'Annex: Memorandum Read by the Turkish Delegate at the Meeting of December 2, 1922, of the Commission on the Régime of Foreigners' in *Lausanne Conference on Near Eastern Affairs (1922–1923): Records of Proceedings and Draft Terms of Peace* (Cmd 1814) (His Majesty's Stationery Office London 1923) pt II, 471–80 at 478.

[78] ibid 478–9. This, incidentally, was a doctrine that had begun to come into its own in the late 19th century partly through great-power involvement in the 'Eastern question'. See G Haraszti 'Treaties and the Fundamental Change of Circumstances' (1975) 146 Recueil des cours 1–93 at 16–21; DJ Bederman 'The 1871 London Declaration, Rebus Sic Stantibus and a Primitivist View of the Law of Nations' (1988) 82 American Journal of International Law 1–40 at 4–22.

the capitulations had become 'an anomaly and an anachronism'.[79] Resembling argu-ments made by representatives of other States that had experienced or were still sub-ject to capitulatory regimes,[80] these positions ultimately carried the day. The Turkish delegation succeeded in securing the decisive abolition of the capitulations with arti-cle 28 of the peace treaty,[81] albeit only by reassuring the Allies of Ankara's commit-ment to legal reform[82] and agreeing to a five-year limitation of tariffs and related measures,[83] the temporary posting in Izmir and Istanbul of European 'counsellors',[84] and a number of other concessions. The centuries-long tradition of the Ottoman capitulations had come to an end, as a matter of form if not necessarily one of substance.

3. Conclusion

To assume that the capitulations were always and necessarily instruments of Euro-pean imperialism—instruments of imperialism *avant la lettre*, as it were—would be to fall prey to an unsustainable anachronism. It would, in fact, be tantamount to projecting into 15th-century Mediterranean commerce a critique of imperialism that surfaced in the late 19th century, established itself in the early 20th century, and was reformulated in neo-Marxian terms in the late 20th century. This is hardly a defensible approach, failing as it quite evidently does to capture the vagueness and mutability of capitulatory privileges—the intensity and frequency with which their

---

[79] Memorandum (n 77) at 479.

[80] A fascinating comparison of the Turkish argument at Lausanne with the Chinese argument at Ver-sailles only a few years earlier is provided in GW Keeton 'Extraterritoriality in International and Com-parative Law' (1948) 72 Recueil des cours 283–391 at 370–2 ff.

[81] Treaty of Peace (n 76) at 27.

[82] This was in keeping with calls for aggressive reform as a 'compensatory' measure; see eg LE Thayer 'The Capitulations of the Ottoman Empire and the Question of Their Abrogation as it Affects the United States' (1923) 17 American Journal of International Law 207–33 at 233 (arguing that '[i]t is highly import-ant, in view of past experience with the Turk, that any relinquishments be made progressive, the surren-der of each right being made expressly conditional upon the successful inauguration of a given reform').

[83] Commercial Convention (signed 24 July 1923) 28 LNTS 171.

[84] Declaration Relating to the Administration of Justice (signed 24 July 1923) 36 LNTS 161. Revealingly, though, the fact that these 'counsellors' were selected from states that had been neutral during the Great War irked some Allied jurists; see eg A Mestre *L'étranger en Turquie d'après le Traité de Lausanne* (Revue politique et parlementaire Paris 1923) at 22 (complaining that such officials would not represent 'directe-ment le point de vue français').

forms and functions changed, or were deemed to change, over time and space. Like most other international instruments, the legal status of a given capitulation was capable of being ascertained, if at all, only through close analysis of its terms, the factual context in which these terms were negotiated and drafted, and the procedure whereby the document as a whole was finalized and entered into force. Medium- to long-term patterns of trade and investment in favour of Western and pro-Western interests are well-documented, the substantive outcome of the mature capitulatory regime having clearly facilitated a significant degree of unequal exchange, and, by extension, of peripheralization and underdevelopment. Yet none of this means that the capitulations were 'imperialistic' through and through, at least not if this is taken to mean that the capitulations were from the outset an imposition from without. It is one thing to argue that, by the late 19th century, the capitulations had come to be understood as tools of Western imperialism, attracting both approbation and condemnation in the process. It is another thing entirely to deny that the capitulations were for the better part of their existence everyday mechanisms of governance—mechanisms which may have been overlaid with imperial and theological sanctification but which aimed above all to bolster trade, cement alliances, and delimit jurisdictional boundaries in a complex and competitive environment. Indeed, if anything, the capitulations began their career as instruments of *Ottoman*, not European, imperialism.

A sober, realistic account of the capitulations, one that captures the distinctive fluidity of Ottoman-European relations, may be developed on the back of the insight that each capitulatory document was first and foremost a site of contestation. Instead of working backwards from a year such as 1740, 1856, or 1923 so as to couch the entire history of the Ottoman capitulations as one of imperialism writ large (whether as 'Ottoman imperialism' or as 'Western imperialism', or as both), such an approach seeks to attend to the often considerable agency that both Ottoman and Western officials were able to exercise over the negotiation, implementation, and interpretation of the capitulations. There can be little doubt that both Ottomans and Westerners came over time to perceive the capitulations as sustaining far-reaching relations of domination and exploitation. There is, in particular, little way to make sense of the Ottoman desire to abrogate the capitulations—highly pronounced, even somewhat desperate, from the mid-19th century onwards—without taking seriously the fact that many Ottoman statesmen were given to holding the capitulations responsible for the empire's fragility and 'backwardness'. Even so, there is no point denying that the capitulations resist reduction to imperialism pure and simple, just as there is little point denying that some Ottoman authorities, including those of Turkish-Muslim heritage, threw their weight in favour of the capitulatory regime. As late as the first decades of the 19th century, the *Moniteur ottoman*, a quasi-official foreign-language gazette, was still able to laud the capitulations as the key to Turkey's economic development: 'In no part of the world does foreign merchandise pay so low an import duty as in Turkey', it proclaimed, going on to boast that 'for the space of three hundred years the Sultans have realized an object which civilized Europe is now earnestly labouring to accomplish'.[85]

The knotty, turbulent history of the capitulations encapsulates the full range of relations, both competitive and cooperative, that tethered the Ottoman Empire to the West, reflecting in miniature the vicissitudes of a State whose place in an increasingly Eurocentric international order was anything but stable. And the implications are far-reaching. For if capitulations and structurally analogous 'unequal treaties' were integral both to European expansion and to extra-European resistance in a number of different contexts, from China to Persia and from Japan to Siam, it was in no small part through the Ottoman experience that such mechanisms of extra-territoriality were popularized, entering into circulation as unique—and uniquely effective—legal commodities.

Recommended Reading

Aral, Berdal 'An Inquiry into the Turkish "School" of International Law' (2005) 16 European Journal of International Law 769–85.

Boogert, Maurits H van den and Kate Fleet (eds) 'The Ottoman Capitulations: Text and Context' (2003) 22 Oriente Moderno 575–727.

Boogert, Maurits H van den *The Capitulations and the Ottoman Legal System: Qadis, Consuls, and Beratlıs in the 18th Century* (Brill Leiden 2005).

Brown, Philip Marshall *Foreigners in Turkey: Their Juridical Status* (Princeton University Press Princeton 1914).

Eldem, Edhem 'Capitulations and Western Trade' in Suraiya N Faroqhi (ed) *The Cambridge History of Turkey* (CUP Cambridge 2006) vol 3, 283–335.

Engelhardt, Edouard *Le droit d'intervention et la Turquie: Étude historique* (A Cotillon & Cie Paris 1880).

İnalcık, Halil 'Imtiyāzāt' in Bernard Lewis et al (eds) *The Encyclopaedia of Islam: New Edition* (Brill Leiden 1971) vol 3, 1179–89.

Martens, Friedrich *Das Consularwesen und die Consularjurisdiction im Orient* (H Skerst trans) (Weidmannsche Buchhandlung Berlin 1874).

Panaite, Viorel *The Ottoman Law of War and Peace: The Ottoman Empire and Tribute Payers* (East European Monographs Boulder 2000).

Pélissié du Rausas, G *Le régime des capitulations dans l'Empire ottoman* (2 vols A Rousseau Paris 1902–5).

Rodogno, Davide *Against Massacre: Humanitarian Interventions in the Ottoman Empire 1815–1914* (Princeton University Press Princeton 2012).

---

[85] 'On Freedom of Commerce in the Ottoman Empire' repr in D Ross (ed) *Opinions of the European Press on the Eastern Question, Translated and Extracted from Turkish, German, French, and English Papers and Reviews* (J Ridgway & Sons London 1836) 1–9 at 4–6.

Rougier, Antoine 'La théorie de l'intervention d'humanité' (1910) 17 Revue générale de droit international public 468–526.

Sousa, Nasim *The Capitulatory Régime of Turkey: Its History, Origin, and Nature* (Johns Hopkins Press Baltimore 1933).

Twiss, Travers *On Consular Jurisdiction in the Levant, and the Status of Foreigners in the Ottoman Law Courts* (W Clowes & Sons London 1880).

Wood, Hugh McKinnon 'The Treaty of Paris and Turkey's Status in International Law' (1943) 37 American Journal of International Law 262–74.

II

ASIA

CHAPTER 19

CHINA

SHIN KAWASHIMA

1. INTRODUCTION

THIS chapter discusses how international law was received in China from the Chinese point of view. As is well known, China had treaty relations with Western countries, for example the Treaty of Nerchinsk of 7 September 1689.[1] However, it was only when William Martin translated Henry Wheaton's *Elements of International Law*[2] as *Wanguo Gongfa* (Immanuel CY Hsü translates it as public law of all nations), which was then published by the *Zongli Yamen* (government body in charge of foreign affairs during the late Qing Dynasty) in 1865[3] that China first received international

---

[1] This treaty was drafted in Latin officially, between Songgotu on behalf of the Kangxi Emperor and Fedor Golovin on behalf of the Russian tsars Peter I and Ivan V. It decided national borders and trade roads. On the Treaty of Nerchinsk between China and Russia ((signed 7 September 1689) (1689) 18 CTS 503), see K Yoshida *Roshia no Toho Shinshutsu to Neruchinsuku Joyaku (Russian Expansion for East and the Treaty of Nerchinsk)* (Toyo Bunko Tokyo 1984).

[2] See H Wheaton *Elements of International Law: With a Sketch of the History of Science* (6th edn Carey, Lea & Blanchard Philadelphia 1855); also the contribution by LH Liu 'Henry Wheaton (1785–1848)' in this volume.

[3] There are two theories regarding the publication year of the *Wanguo Gongfa* 1864 and 1865. In Japan, an example of the 1864 theory is S Satō *Kindai Chūgoku No Chishikijin To Bunmei (Intellectuals and Civilization in Modern China)* (The University of Tokyo Press Tokyo 1996) at 45; and LH Liu also adopted the 1864 theory in her book *The Clash of Empires: The Invention of China in Modern World Making* (Harvard University Press Cambridge MA 2004) at 108. An example of the 1865 theory is M Banno *Kindai Chūgoku Seiji Gaikō Shi (History of Modern Chinese Politics and Diplomacy)* (The University of Tokyo Press Tokyo 1973). However, as a conclusion, the 1865 theory is correct. This is especially because in the *Wanguo Gongfa*, the introduction of *Dongxun* is set in December of the third year of *Tongzhi*. See X Lin

law as text. In China, however, the translation *Wanguo Gongfa* is not used. Instead, the term *Guoji (Gong)fa* (international (public) law), which was brought back to China by intellectuals who studied in Japan in the early 20th century, has replaced it in the present day. This chapter discusses issues such as China's view of the international order before the reception of the *Wanguo Gongfa* as a text, circumstances before and after the reception of the text, circumstances surrounding the *Wanguo Gongfa* since then, the change of the term to *Guoji (Gong)fa* (international law), and its background.

2. RECOGNITION OF SPACE AND FOREIGN RELATIONS IN CHINESE DYNASTIES

2.1. *Dezhi* and *Jiaohua*

In a dynastic state, *dezhi* (rule by virtue) was assumed as a principle, and it was believed that the universal virtue of the emperor, who was given the Mandate of Heaven, spread all over the world. This is indicated by the words: 'Under universal heaven, all lands are the Emperor's lands; within the farthest limits of the land, all are the Emperor's subjects.'[4] It was believed that the virtue of the wise emperor spread out like grass flowing in the breeze, and that the people were influenced by his virtue.[5] This *hua* (voluntary change and reform under the influence of emperor's virtue) indicates those who benefit from the emperor's virtue and kindness, whereas *huawai* (area/people out of influence of emperor's virtue) are those who do not bask in such benefits. *Hua* is something that the people should perform voluntarily, and it should not be forced on them by the emperor. This was the case so long as the people of *huawai* did not disrupt the peace and stability of the society. If they did, the emperor would take action.[6]

Cong Wanguo Gongfa Dao Gongfa Waijiao: Wan Qing Guojifa De Chuanru, Quanshi Yu Yingyong (From Wanguo Gongfa to Diplomacy based on Public Law of All Nations: Propagation, Interpretaion and Applica-tion of International Law in the Late Qing Dynasty) (Shanghai Guji Chubanshe Shanghai 2009); also, regarding the English translation of the Chinese term *Wanguo Gongfa*, ICY Hsü translates it as 'public law of all nations'. See ICY Hsü *China's Entrance into the Family of Nations: The Diplomatic Phase, 1858–1880* (Harvard University Press Cambridge MA 1960).

  [4] 'Xiaoya: Beishan' in *Shijing (The Book of Songs)* ch 2, nos 205–15.
  [5] 'Qunzi zhi Defeng, Xiaoren zhi Decao. Caoshang zhi Feng, Bi Yan' in *Lunyu (The Analects of Confu-cius)* book 12 (*Yan Yuan*) verse 19.
  [6] The word '*huawai*' became an issue when Japan dispatched troops to Taiwan in 1871. However, this concept was originally based on the nationality principle. According to the logic of the dynasty, it was possible to have people of '*huawai*' living in its territory.

The emperor's virtue was regarded as 'universal' and guaranteed to have multiple interpretations. This framework was a useful logic to contain a diverse society, and the emperor held the interpretive authority. In other words, the relationship between the emperor and his subjects was not equal.

2.2. The Relationship between *Dezhi/Jiaohua* and the Frontier/Neighbouring Countries

From the viewpoint of space, the following could be said about the 'national borders' of Chinese dynasties. Although governance by Chinese dynasties held principles whose meaning included crossing borders, namely *dezhi* and *jiaohua*, their limits were recognized and enforcement of *jiaohua* was basically not implied. On the other hand, in reality, territories over which dynasties had effective control existed. Borders were established as needed for military operations, tax collection, and management of roads.

The concepts of *dezhi* and *jiaohua* were also applied to relations with the frontier and neighbouring countries. In other words, although it was believed that the emperor's virtue spread universally, in reality, many people did not benefit from it; and the number of such people increased as the distance between their residence and the emperor increased. Nonetheless, if they did not threaten peace, then a non-interference policy was adopted. If the head of the region paid homage to the emperor as a vassal, then he was seen as being morally transformed and became a king who was in a vassal relationship with the dynasty (*cefeng*). As for the neighbouring regions that have yet to form countries, the emperor gave the heads of those regions government posts (*tusi* and *tuguan*), and delegated authority to maintain order in their respective regions as the officers. Dynastic States tried to maintain relations with the surrounding regions of their territories through these ritualistic relationships.[7]

In places like Tibet, Mongolia, and Xinjiang, non-interference policy was approved due to 'rituals' that were conducted to show the vassal relationship between the emperor of the Qing Dynasty and the 'kings' (or authorities) of these respective regions. Therefore, order was maintained based on each region's 'customs'. Of course,

---

[7] Being in a vassal relationship with the Chinese dynasty meant that political powers sent envoys to the dynasty each time they were formed or when their leaders changed. By paying homage to the emperor as vassals, those living inside the dynasty's territories were given commensurate government posts, and those from outside the territories were given the title of king as well as the imperial seal and almanac. At times, these were awarded to the kings by envoys sent by the dynasty. However, whether both parties shared the understanding that these rituals were indeed 'vassal homage' is debatable. Even if the Chinese dynasty regarded such rituals as 'vassal homage', there is a possibility that the other envoys might have seen them as rituals similar to those conducted for their Kings. It should be kept in mind that many of the explanations derived from Chinese historical sources greatly reflect the views of the Chinese dynasty.

this was the Han group's point of view; from the viewpoint of the Tibetans and the Mongolians, they did not necessarily intend to build a relationship with Beijing by benefitting from the emperor's virtue.[8] For example, although the Dalai Lama recognized Qing's emperor as Buddha (Wenzhu), one of the patrons of Tibetan Buddhism, he did not think Tibet wholly belonged to the Qing Dynasty.

2.3. *Cefeng/Chaogong* and Borders

These concepts of *dezhi* and *jiaohua* were applied beyond the dynasty's territories, to relations with the surrounding countries. If the *qiu* (chiefs) of other countries benefitted from the emperor's virtue and came to pay homage to the emperor, they were given high-ranking government posts and high positions in the society (*guanjue*), thereby incorporating them into the Chinese bureaucratic system, and they were also appointed as kings. This was called the vassal relationship (*cefeng*), but this act was not intended to interfere in the domestic affairs of the surrounding countries, as in the case of the Chinese dynasty's relations with Korea at the end of the 19th century. The Chinese dynasty gave the title of kings, made the countries use the dynasty's calendar, and entrusted the kings to govern their own countries, and did not interfere in their domestic affairs as long as the surrounding countries did not make requirements of the dynasty; for example, requesting troops to support their battles with other countries. The ceremony of *cefeng* was basically conducted when new countries were created, or there was a successor to an old king requiring a transfer of title. Similarly, the *qiu* who had been called king presented the emperor with souvenirs to pay tribute to him, and the emperor gave him gifts in return (*huici*). These acts, known as the tribute system (*chaogong* or *jingong*) meant that the 'kings' from the surrounding countries yearned for the emperor's virtue, which then indicated that *jiaohua* was indeed being realized. Also, as long as the rules were being observed, the dynasty did not interfere in these countries' domestic affairs.[9] In reality, not many countries used the same era names as the Chinese dynasties, which changed whenever a new emperor was crowned. It should

---

[8] T Motegi 'Chūgoku Teki Sekaizō No Henyō To Saihen (Transformation of and Restructuring of the Chinese View of the World)' in W Iijima et al (eds) *Chūka Sekai To Kindai, Shirīzu 20 Seiki Chūgoku Shi (The Chinese World and the Modern Period, Series 20th Century Chinese History)* (The University of Tokyo Press Tokyo 2009); T Motegi 'Chūgoku Ōchō Kokka No Chitsujyo To Sono Kindai (Chinese Dynastic States' Order and Their Modern Period)' (2009) 682 Risō 83–93.

[9] Of course, the actual state of the dynasty's vassal relationship with the surrounding countries differed depending on the country and the period of time. Moreover, as the Qing Dynasty treated Russia as an 'ally', not all relations with foreign countries were positioned in the tribute system. Generally speaking, however, the Qing Dynasty adhered to its logic of *dezhi* and *jiaohua* in principle. See M Liao *Goshi Kara Mita Sinchō No Tsūshō Chitsujyo (Commercial Order of the Qing Dynasty from the Viewpoint of Mutual Trade)* (PhD thesis Hokkaido University Sapporo 2006); M Mancall *China at the Center: 300 Years of Foreign Policy* (Free Press New York 1984).

also be noted that in domestic affairs, the only countries that used the Chinese dynasty's concept, *Mingfen* (a kind of moral justification which provides hieratical relations) in their domestic affairs were Korea and perhaps the Ryukyus and Annam.

However, even if the emperor's virtue expanded to the surroundings, it was not necessarily the case that 'national borders' between the dynastic territories and the surrounding countries were assumed. Outside space where bureaucrats who passed the Imperial exam (*Keju*) made 'pilgrimage' (areas of local government agency in the Qing period) were the zones named *fanbu* (Tibet, Mongol, and Xinjiang), and areas ruled by *tusi*, which were provinces where Han officials made 'pilgrimage', except for Manchuria.

Naturally, dynastic territories changed. Sometimes they included areas of *yidi*, other times they became smaller. The territories as areas of effective control were allocated a certain amount of space, but the actual borders were not clear. Rather, they were established with contrasting density as necessary. For example, if there was military confrontation between the two sides, a military demarcation line was drawn. If tax had to be collected, a target area was set, and if there were roads, then there were boundaries to jurisdiction. The situation was the same in the coastal areas.

Beyond these circumstances, border lines in many sparsely populated regions were ambiguous. There were gray areas that could indeed be called *jiangyu*. And people who lived in these *jiangyu* played the role of a mediator between the dynasty and the neighbouring countries outside its territories, or among multiple countries.

2.4. *Cefeng/Chaogong* and Mutual Trade

Trade developed in these areas between 'national borders', and it was known as *hushi* (mutual trade). This was border trade basically without ceremonial rituals (*cefeng* and *chaogong*). Therefore *hushi* was based on foreign relationships that were different from those of *cefeng* and *chaogong*, which contained ceremonial rituals.

As Takeshi Hamashita argues, *chaogong* was certainly a political-diplomatic act accompanied by ceremonial rituals, but it was also an economic act.[10] Opportunities for *chaogong* were limited to once in a few years (sometimes permitted several times a year or once a year), and the places of entrance into port as well as envoys' routes to Beijing were designated. In Beijing, envoys were to pay homage to the emperor, present him with gifts, and receive gifts from him in return. In this sense, *chaogong* seemed like barter trade with little 'freedom'. In reality, however, many merchants

---

[10] T Hamashita *Kindai Chūgoku No Kokusaiteki Keiki: Chōkō Bōeki Shisutemu to Kindai Ajia (Modern China's International Opportunity: The Tribute and Trade System and Modern Asia)* (The University of Tokyo Press Tokyo 1990).

attended the envoys, and they traded in Beijing as well as in ports of entrance. Some of them could even go to places like Suzhou on buying trips while the envoys travelled from the port of entrance to Beijing and then back.

The Ming Dynasty basically unified foreign trade into trade accompanied by *chaogong*. Therefore, their stance was that countries could not trade if they did not conduct *chaogong*, and *hushi* was not permitted. The Qing Dynasty also adopted this principle of the Ming Dynasty. However, after the Qing Dynasty occupied Taiwan in 1683, this policy was changed and mutual trade without *chaogong* was permitted at four ports, including Ningbo and Guangzhou. There are still unclear aspects about the actual situation of *hushi* and its relations with *chaogong*, but at least we can think of a reason why trade with *chaogong* was still maintained thereafter.[11] One reason is that the surrounding States could have limited private trade with the Qing Dynasty. In countries that conducted *chaogong*, such as the Ryukus and Korea, it could be assumed that the kings monopolized trade with the Qing Dynasty and did not let the merchants of their own countries engage in *hushi*. Alternatively, there could have been goods that were only handled in *chaogong*, or tax exemption measures, but this subject requires further investigation.

2.5. The Canton System and Opium War

In 1757, the Qing Dynasty adopted a policy that limited trade with the Western countries to only take place in Guangzhou. Thereafter, the way of trade in Guangzhou was called the Canton System, and it became important as the limitation of trade in this system is regarded as a cause of the Opium War. In the first place, Western countries had mainly traded in Guangzhou before 1757, but it occurred within the framework of *hushi*, and was not officially related to *chaogong*.[12] To be sure, from the end of the 18th century to the early 19th century, when British envoys such as Macartney and Amherst visited China to negotiate the expansion of trade,

[11] Regarding *hushi*, see, for example, S Iwai 'Chōkō To Goshi (*Chaogong* and *Hushi*)' in H Wada et al (eds) *Higashi Ajia Kingendai Tsūshi 1 Higashi Ajia Sekai No Kindai 19 Seiki (Modern and Contemporary History of East Asia 1 The Modern Period of the East Asian World 19th Century)* (Iwanami Shoten 2010).

[12] Regarding the Canton Trade, the following studies have been referenced: W Cao 'Qingdai Guangdong Tizhi Zai Yanjiu (A Re-Study of the Guangdong System during the Qing Period)' (2006) 2 Qingshi Yanjiu 82–96; HB Morse *The Chronicles of the East India Company Trading to China, 1635–1834* (5 vols Clarendon Press Oxford 1926–29); EH Pritchard 'The Crucial Years of Early Anglo-Chinese Relations, 1750–1800' (1936) 4 Research Studies of the State College of Washington 96–442; WE Cheong *The Hong Merchants of Canton: Chinese Merchants in Sino-Western Trade* (Curzon Richmond 1997). In recent years, new horizons have gradually been developed by young Japanese scholars. For example, K Fujiwara '18 Seiki Chūyō No Kōshu Ni Okeru Kōgai Shōnin No Bōeki Sannyū Ni Kansuru Hukoku No Bunseki (Declarations Concerning outside Merchant Participation in Foreign Trade at Guangzhou during the mid-18th Century)' (2009) 91 Toyo Gakuho 411–38.

ceremonial rituals when meeting with the emperor (three kneelings and nine kow-tows) became a problem.

Hushi was trade under certain regulations such as paying taxes. There were no strict regulations on the volume of trade or on the goods, but still, trade with Western countries in Guangzhou was strongly regulated. Britain tried to break these restrictions by using opium, which ultimately led to the Opium War.

As a result of the Opium War and the Treaty of Nanjing[13] (*Jiangning*) of 29 August 1842, open ports were increased to five ports, and the Qing Dynasty lost its tariff autonomy. This, however, was nothing more than an expansion of *hushi* for the Qing Dynasty. Although the location for trade management with Western countries shifted from Guangzhou to Shanghai and changes were made to how taxes were collected, the 'newly' opened ports by the treaty were mostly previous *hushi* ports opened to Western countries before 1757, including Ningbo which was changed to Shanghai, and after the 1840s, the tribute relationships were still maintained.

3. TRANSLATION AND TEACHING OF INTERNATIONAL LAW

3.1. The Situation Before the Opium War

The first contact between Western international law and China is generally known to be the signing of the Treaty of Nerchinsk[14] on 7 September 1689.[15] Of course, there are arguments that contact between the two parties existed even before then.[16] The Treaty of Nerchinsk was equal, and it was mediated by a Jesuit missionary, Thomas Pereira. According to Pereira's diary, he lectured the Kangxi Emperor on matters of Western international law, such as sovereign equality and the meaning of signing treaties.[17] Needless to say, how these were interpreted by Kangxi is a different issue.

---

[13]   Treaty of Najing (concluded 29 August 1842) (1842) 93 CTS 465.

[14]   Treaty of Nerchinsk (n 1).

[15]   For this section, the author consulted the following source. *From Wanguo Gongfa* (n 3) 42–8.

[16]   AN Nussbaum *A Concise History of the Law of Nations* (Macmillan Company New York 1958) at 84–90. Also, Zhang Jianhua emphasizes the signing of the Peace Treaty of 1662 between the Dutch forces in Taiwan and Zheng Chenggong. See J Zhang *Wan Qing Zhongguoren De Guojifa Zhishi Yu Guojia Pingdeng Gainian (Chinese Knowledge of International Law and the Concept of Sovereign Equality in the Late Qing Dynasty)* (thesis Peking University 2003) at 11.

[17]   J Sebes *The Jesuits and the Sino-Russian Treaty of Nerchinsk 1689: The Diary of Thomas Pereira* (Institutum Histricum SI 1961 Rome) at 115–20.

By the 19th century, as negotiations over opium started to take place, China began referring to international law, which was regarded as the norm for international relations in the West. However, Chinese translation of international law was not systemic; rather, partial translation was done as needed. It is known that Lin Zexu, who took the post of the Imperial Inspector Minister in Guangzhou and Guangxi in 1839 and worked on the banning of opium, requested a partial translation of Emmerich de Vattel's *Le Droit des Gens*[18] of Peter Parker, an American optometrist staying in Guangzhou.[19] Moreover, regarding this book, it has been found that Lin also requested partial translation of his translator Yuan Dehui.[20] Furthermore, it is known that the text which Yuan relied on was not the original French, but instead he used the English translation by Joseph Chitty, *The Law of Nations*.[21]

Many preceding studies have actually criticized Lin Zexu's translation of the *Wanguo Gongfa*. This is because the translation was partial instead of systematic; it was explained orally instead of being written down, and sometimes the translation itself was incorrect.[22] It is difficult to judge how the translation during this period affected Lin Zexu's policy toward Britain, but from the perspective of the encounter between China and international law, it was important for at least the following three points. First, the translation by Yuan and others was based on the values and morals of Confucianism. Second, their translation created new words that impacted future generations; for example, 'right' was translated as *daoli*, and 'justice' was translated as *li*.[23] Third, both Parker's translation, '*Huada'er Geguo Luling*' (Law of Each Nation) and Yuan's translation, '*Fali Benxing Zhengli Suozai*' (Principles of the Law of Nature, applied to the Conduct and Affairs of Nations and Sovereigns) were selected and recorded as '*Geguo Luling*' in Wei Yuan's *Haiguo Tuzhi*, volume 52 (of 60 volumes), and also in volume 83 (of 100 volumes of the enlarged edition). Therefore, they were read not only in China, but also in surrounding areas that used Chinese characters.[24]

[18] The full title of this book by Emmerich de Vattel is *Le droit des gens; ou, principes de la loi naturelle appliqués à la conduite et aux affaires des nations et des souverains*. The first version was published in 1777, and republished in 1835–38 (Aillaud Paris). It was the leading work of the school of natural law at that time.

[19] P Parker 'The Tenth Report of the Ophthalmic Hospital, Canton, Being for the Year 1839' (1840) 8 Chinese Repository 634–5.

[20] H Chang 'The Earliest Phase of the Introduction of Western Political Science into China, 1820–52' (1950) 5 Yenching Journal of Social Studies 1–29 at 14.

[21] The full title is *The Law of Nations; or, Principles of the Law of Nature, applied to the Conduct and Affairs of Nations and Sovereigns*. One theory argues that it was published in 1833. See W Wang 'Lin Zexu Xu Fanyi Xifang Guojifa Zhuzuo Kaolue (A Study of Lin Zexu's Translation of Works on Western International Law)' (1985) 1 Zhongshan Daxue Xuebao (Shehui Kexue Ban) 58–67.

[22] *China's Entrance* (n 3) 123–5; 'The Earliest Phase' (n 20) 1820–52.

[23] R Svarverud 'Jus Gentium Sinense: The Earliest Chinese Translation of International Law with some Considerations Regarding the Compilation of Haiguo Tuzhi' (2000) 61 Acta Orientalia 203–37.

[24] Regarding these writings on international law recorded in *Haiguo Tuzhi*, Satō Shinichi argues that there are no records showing that these drew interest of the Chinese in this period, because the translation was fragmented and there were errors in the translation. See *Intellectuals and Civilization* (n 3) 202.

3.2. Conclusion of Unequal Treaties

Starting from the Treaty of Nanjing,[25] China signed a series of unequal treaties[26] with Western countries. Nevertheless, the conclusion of unequal treaties itself did not change the way China viewed the outside world. From Britain's point of view, treaties were based on the principle of sovereign equality, therefore other bilateral issues outside the treaties also had to be decided based on this principle. In contrast, from the Qing's point of view, treaty texts that showed sovereign equality were the exception, so there was no way that other matters outside the treaties should also be based on the principle of sovereign equality. The Qing avoided writing in treaties that the dynasty and Britain were equals, and it resulted in rejecting the stationing of British ministers in Beijing as well as avoiding to talk about the problem of audience of foreign ministers with the emperor. Qing did make compromises regarding regulations on sending documents between foreign consuls at open ports and local officials of the Qing Dynasty, but these were interpreted as a means to pacify the British and Western countries as *yidi* and end the war.

In future generations, the Treaty of Nanjing and other treaties were labelled as unequal treaties, and they became the symbol of Imperialist invasion of China. Generally, unequal treaties are explained from the following three points: unilateral extraterritoriality and consular jurisdiction, agreement tariff, and most-favoured-nation status. However, when the Qing Dynasty concluded the Treaty of Nanjing, it did not recognize the treaty to be unequal. For example, since the people of Qing were not permitted to travel abroad, Qing did not think about the Chinese people within British territories. Also, even if disputes between the British and Qing subjects occurred within Qing's territories, Qing thought it was more convenient for Qing that Britain themselves took care of their own people, as 'they stood on a lower level of civilization than Chinese in China'. Furthermore, according to *Tanglu*, law in the Tang period, dispute between foreigners in China was to be judged by foreign law. Therefore, consular jurisdiction did not contradict Chinese historical precedents.[27] Most-favoured-nation status was also regarded as universal benevolence equally provided to *yidi* by the emperor, which concept was called *Yishi Tongren*, and it was considered that it would cause more trouble if there were differences in the benefits provided to *yidi*. Also, as long as it was the emperor's virtue, it was something that only Qing could unilaterally provide, and not something that the other side could provide to Qing.

[25] Treaty of Nanjing (n 13).
[26] A Peters 'Unequal Treaties' in R Wolfrum (ed) *The Max Planck Encyclopedia of Public International Law* (Oxford University Press Oxford 2008) at <http://www.mpepil.com>.
[27] *China's Entrance* (n 3) 130.

3.3. Martin's *Wanguo Gongfa*

As stated above, it was when William Martin translated Henry Wheaton's *Elements of International Law* (1836) and published it as *Wanguo Gongfa* in early 1865 that China seriously and systemically translated Western international law.[28] This translation had a large impact, since there was no systemic translation of other works on international law for at least ten years thereafter. From the perspective of international law, the middle of the 19th century was a period of transition from international law based on natural law to one based on positive law, but Wheaton's work strongly holds elements of natural law. This view was that in the international community, there were universal systemic legal norms between States that could not be used for each State's own ends. These legal norms existed as something that was given, as in the order of nature. Therefore, there was a difference between individual treaties bilaterally signed between China and foreign countries, and this *Wanguo Gongfa*.

The process that led to *Wanguo Gongfa*'s translation could be explained by the following.[29] Martin was a Presbyterian missionary, and after he arrived in China in 1850, he was conducting missionary work in Ningbo. It is known that he became the interpreter of the American side during the negotiations for the Sino-American Treaty of Tianjin on 18 June 1858,[30] and contributed a text in the treaty about freedom to conduct missionary work. During the negotiation process, Martin witnessed Britain's violation of international law, and began to think that the Chinese government should acquire proficiency in diplomatic customs.[31] Martin went home once, then returned to China in 1862, and started to translate the *Wanguo Gongfa* in Shanghai.

Some preceding studies argue that Robert Hart had already translated parts of Wheaton's work as well as the American Consul's Manual when Martin began translating, but this is not correct. According to Hart's diary, Hart translated parts of Wheaton's work from July to August of 1863, after he became Maritime Customs Service Officer. The *Zongli Yamen* dispatched four envoys including Dong Xun and Xue Huan to make the translation request to Hart.[32] The translation work was finished on 7 August, and it was submitted to the *Zongli Yamen*. This date of submission

---

[28] There are many editions of this work. It is presumed that Martin relied on the 6th edition published in 1855. C Chang 'Bankoku Kōhō' Seiritsu Jijyō To Honyaku Mondai' (Circumstances over the Formation of Wanguo Gongfa and the Problem of Translation) in S Katō and M Maruyama (eds) *Nihon Kindai Shisō Taikei (Japan's Modern Philosophy System)* (Iwanami Shoten 1991) vol 15 (*Honyaku No Shisō (Philosophy of Translation)*), 381–400.

[29] *China's Entrance* (n 3); P Duus 'Science and Salvation in China: The Life and Work of W.A.P. Martin (1827–1916)' in KC Liu (ed) *American Missionaries in China* (East Asian Research Center, Harvard University Press Cambridge MA 1966); *The Clash of Empires* (n 3).

[30] On the Tianjin Treaty in 1858, see M Bannno *China and the West, 1858–1861: The Origins of the Tsungli Yamen* (Harvard University Press Cambridge MA 1964).

[31] WAP Martin 'Interesting from China' *New York Times* (New York 8 January 1864).

[32] KF Bruner, JK Fairbank, and R Smith (eds) *Entering China's Service: Robert Hart's Journals, 1854–1863* (Council on East Asian Studies Harvard University Cambridge MA 1986) 295–306.

indicates that Martin's translation of the *Wanguo Gongfa* was done earlier than the translation that was handed to the *Zongli Yamen*.

At this point, Martin was not requested to translate the *Wanguo Gongfa* by the *Zongli Yamen*. His translation work was finished in 1863. In the same year, when Wen Xiang, minister of the *Zongli Yamen*, was negotiating with France, he asked the American minister in Beijing Anson Burlingame to recommend literature on Western international law, and Burlingame mentioned Wheaton's work.[33] Since Burlingame knew about Martin's translation work, he recommended it to Wen Xiang. Martin immediately went to Beijing, and showed his translation manuscripts to Chong Hou, whom he had already met, and Chong delivered them to Wen Xiang. On 10 September 1863, Martin accompanied Minister Burlingame to visit the *Zongli Yamen*, and met with the heads of the *Zongli Yamen*, including Prince Gong I. After Wen Xiang checked the overlapping parts with Hart's translation, the *Zongli Yamen* certified this translation work to be beneficial, and ordered four secretaries (*zhangjing*) including Chen Qing and Li Changhua, to assist Martin in revising and editing the translation, which was completed in April 1864.[34] In early 1865, *Wanguo Gongfa* was published by the Beijing Chongshiguan, and Martin sent 300 copies of it to the *Zongli Yamen* with his compliments, which were then distributed to central and local offices.[35] This book evoked a strong response from East Asia, especially Japan.[36]

These episodes show that the *Zongli Yamen* was comparatively positive about translating the *Wanguo Gongfa*. The reason why the *Zongli Yamen* paid attention to the *Wanguo Gongfa* is certainly for the convenience of negotiations with France, but also it could have been related to the fact that it was trying to sign a series of treaties with Western countries besides Britain, France, the United States, and Russia in the 1860s. Banno Masataka argues that diplomacy during this period could be described as 'the beginning of diplomacy that followed the rules of modern diplomacy'.[37]

---

[33] *From Wanguo Gongfa* (n 3) 48–9.

[34] However, this *Wanguo Gongfa* is not a complete translation of Wheaton's work. Sections 17–19 in chapter 4 as well as the appendix are not translated. Also, rather than literally translating the original work, Martin's translation simplifies, or provides explanations beyond the original text, which Immanuel Hsü calls 'paraphrastic interpretation'. See *China's Entrance* (n 3) 238.

[35] Demand for *Wanguo Gongfa* increased afterwards, and various translations reprints were published. T Tian *Guojifa Shuru Yu Wan Qing Zhongguo (Import of International Law and China in the Late Qing Period)* (Jinan Chubanshe Jinan 2001) at 42; T Tian 'Ding Weiliang Yu "Wanguo Gongfa"' (William Martin and 'Wanguo Gongfa') (1999) 3 Shehui Kexue Yanjiu; *The Clash of Empires* (n 3) 117; Y Wang '"Wanguo Gongfa" De Jige Wenti' (Several Problems with Wanguo Gongfa) (2005) 3 Beijing Daxue Xuebao (Zhexue Shehui Kexue Ban) 78–86 at 78–9.

[36] In Japan, the book was reprinted in Edo during 1865, and since then works on *Wanguo Gongfa* written by other authors besides Wheaton were translated one after another. In 1873, when Mitsukuri Rinshō translated T Woolsey's work, he used the term 'kokusaihō' for the first time to translate the term 'international law', and in 1884, the University of Tokyo used the term 'kokusaihō' to name a department. Since then, the term 'kokusaihō' became commonly used. See Z Ohira 'Kokusai Hōgaku No Inyū To Seihō Ron' (Importing the Study of International Law and the Theory of Natural Law) (1938) 2 Hitotsubashi Ronsō 464–36.

[37] *History of Modern Chinese* (n 3) 278.

However, the purpose of the Chinese was to understand the *Wanguo Gongfa*, which was the norm of the West, and to confute their arguments.[38] It seems that the head of the Qing Dynasty recognized the usefulness of the *Wanguo Gongfa* due to an incident in February 1864. In February 1864, when Prussia and Austria declared war against Denmark over the Schleswig-Holstein Question, Prussian minister to China Guido von Rehfues used a German warship to capture a Danish commercial ship that was moored at Dagu. When the *Zongli Yamen* used the *Wanguo Gongfa* as a base to point out the illegality of such action and filed a protest to the Prussian minister, the latter admitted the mistake and released the Dane ship with compensation.[39] This was victory from 'negotiation' for the newly formed *Zongli Yamen*, and also an instance where it admitted the usefulness of the *Wanguo Gongfa*. Historical sources do not show direct causal relationship between this incident and the translation of the *Wanguo Gongfa*, but it is an important incident that became an opportunity for the *Zongli Yamen* to realize the utility of *Wanguo Gongfa* to conduct diplomacy with Western countries.

One thing to keep in mind, however, is that even at this point the Qing Dynasty did not think that it was obliged to obey the *Wanguo Gongfa*. The translation of the *Wanguo Gongfa* was based on the principle of gaining the upper hand over the West by using the tools of the West, and indeed, 'controlling foreign countries by using other foreign countries (*yiyi zhiyi*)'. This did not mean using Western tools as China's guiding principles, or 'changing China by using other foreign countries'. In that sense, the situation did not develop in the way that the American diplomats had expected; Qing's attitude did not change through the translation of the *Wanguo Gongfa*.

3.4. *Jingshi Tongwenguan* and Teaching of the *Wanguo Gongfa*

The Qing Dynasty established the *Zongli Yamen* in 1861 as a contact point for the four Western legations set up in Beijing as a result of the Treaties of Tianjin and Beijing during 1858–60. The *Zongli Yamen* was not an official body of the central government. Rather, it was a temporary institution, and most of its ministers overlapped with those of the *Junjichu* (Office of Military Secrets, known as the Grand Council). For this reason, it was strongly characterized as a temporary foreign office under the auspices of the *Junjichu*.[40] In 1862, the *Jingshi Tongwenguan* was established in Beijing as

---

[38] This is seen in the first Prince Gong's Address to the Throne. See *Tongzhi Chao Chouban Yiwu Shimo (Complete Record of the Management of Barbarian Affairs: Tongzhi Dynasty)* vol 27, at 25–6.

[39] ibid vol 26, at 29–36.

[40] China's first official Foreign Ministry was the *Waiwubu*, established in 1901. See S Kawashima 'Gaimu No Keisei: Gaimubu No Setsuritsu Katei' (The Formation of Foreign Affairs: The Process of

a subsidiary organization of the *Zongli Yamen*.[41] This was a school that taught foreign languages and a basic notion of international relations. Examples of its departments include the departments of English, French, and Russian. The students had to be younger than fifteen, and from *Baqi* (Peoples of Eight Flags). Teachers were recommended from the legations, but most of them were foreign missionaries. Martin became an English teacher in 1865, where others, such as John Bordon and John Fryer, taught English before him.

At the end of 1866, the *Zongli Yamen* decided to reform the *Tongwenguan*. The new policy was to teach the natural sciences like astronomy and mathematics, and to accept those who passed the Imperial examination as students so that they were educated by foreign teachers. This was strongly criticized by the bureaucrats. Nevertheless, *Zongli Yamen*'s reform proposal was ultimately accepted, and the *Tongwenguan* transformed from a language school to a comprehensive school. Afterwards, new subjects such as *Wanguo Gongfa*, *Fuguo Ce* (policy to increase national wealth), and world history were added. However, the tide of criticism toward the *Zongli Yamen* also strongly impacted the *Tongwenguan*.

Martin was also invited to teach *Wanguo Gongfa* and *Fuguo Ce* in October 1867, but he turned down the offer and returned home temporarily, and revisited Beijing on 26 November 1869. However, it was not until 1873 that he started teaching international law using Theodore D Woolsey's *Introduction to the Study of International Law*[42] as a textbook.[43] The work of translating the original book from English to Chinese was indeed appropriate for the *Tongwenguan*, which Martin often called the International Law and Language School.

However, the *Tongwenguan*'s curriculum shows that *Wanguo Gongfa* was not necessarily the core curriculum. Students belonged to one of the language departments (English, French, Russia, and German), and their curriculum was mainly to study their respective languages, Chinese, and mathematics. They could study other subjects after they decided to take either an eight-year or five-year course. *Wanguo Gongfa* was nothing more than an elective that was introduced only in the seventh year of the eight-year course, and in the final year of the five-year course.[44] There-

---

Establishment of the *Waiwubu*) in T Okamoto and S Kawashima (eds) *Chūgoku Kindai Gaikō No Taidō (Signs of Chinese Diplomacy in the Modern Period)* (The University of Tokyo Press Tokyo 2009).

[41] On the *Jingshi Tongwenguan*, see K Biggerstaff *The Earliest Modern Government School in China* (Cornell University Press Ithaca NY 1961); Z Sun *Qingli Tongwenguan Zhi Yanjiu (A Study of Qingli Tongwenguan)* (Jiaxin Shuini Gongsi Wenhua Jijinhui Taipei 1977); J Su *Qingli Tongwenguan* (self published 1978); J Su *Qingli Tongwenguan Ji Qishisheng (Qingli Tongwenguan and Its Teachers and Students)* (self published 1985).

[42] The full title of the book is TD Woolsey *Introduction to the Study of International Law: Designed as an Aid in Teaching, and in Historical Studies* (James Monroe and Company Boston 1860). It was probably used as a textbook for international law at Yale University.

[43] *From Wanguo Gongfa* (n 3) 126–7.

[44] See *Tongwenguan Timinglu (Curriculum of the Tongwenguan)* (Guangxu Wunian Tongwenguan Diyici 1879). This source also includes examination questions. For example, in the *Wanguo Gongfa* exam

fore, out of a 100 students at the *Tongwenguan*, only about ten students took the course on *Wanguo Gongfa*.[45] In this respect, it is difficult to say that the *Wanguo Gongfa* had a great importance in the *Tongwenguan*'s education curriculum. Nonetheless, it is also true that the school produced assistants for Martin's translation work of international law, such as Wang Fengzao, Lian Fang, and Qing Chang. They later became ministers in foreign embassies and leaders of the Foreign Ministry in the late Qing period.

3.5.   The Knowledge of *Wanguo Gongfa* and Diplomacy in the Modern Period

As mentioned above, the translation of the *Wanguo Gongfa* acted as a tool for negotiations with the West. As the Qing Dynasty started to dispatch ministers and contact with the West deepened, Qing was required to increase its understanding of the *Wanguo Gongfa*. Indeed, after the mid-1870s, demand for the *Wanguo Gongfa* did increase to a certain extent, and its knowledge was valued. However, as China felt more superior than the West because it valued *wulun* (the five Confucian filial-piety relationship) and faith, Qing's view of the world did not change that much.

In 1876, a year before Qing dispatched the first minister to Britain Guo Songtao, Martin and his students at the *Tongwenguan* (Lian Fang and Qing Chang) published *Xingyao Zhizhang*,[46] which was a handbook for sending diplomatic missions. Also in 1877, Martin and his students at the *Tongwenguan* (Wang Fengzao and Feng Yi) translated Theodore D Woolsey's *Introduction to the Study of International Law* and published it as *Gongfa Bianlan*.

Although *Xingyao Zhizhang* and *Gongfa Bianlan* contained various rules about sending diplomatic missions, in reality, Minister Guo did not take the letter of attorney with him, and a problem erupted regarding the status of Vice Minister Liu Xihong. Martin did show Guo *Xingyao Zhizhang* before he took the post, but perhaps the *Gongfa Bianlan* and *Xingyao Zhizhang* were not referred to the *Zongli Yamen*.

Nevertheless, Martin and his students at the *Tongwenguan* continued their translation work. These books were helpful for ministers dispatched abroad and for those involved in diplomatic negotiations. In 1880, JK Bluntschli's *Das moderne Völkerrecht*

---

in the fourth year of *Guangxu* (1878), a total of ten questions were asked. Examples include: (1) every independent country holds the right to send diplomatic missions. How do you demonstrate this? (2) When one country dispatches a diplomatic mission to another country, the receiving side may reject the mission. What is the cause of this?

[45] *From Wanguo Gongfa* (n 3) 130.

[46] *Xingyao Zhizhang* was the translation of C Martens *Le guide diplomatique: Précis des droits et des fonctions des agents diplomatiques et consularies* (FHGeffcken ed) (FA Brockhaus Leipzig 1866) vol 1.

der Civilisirten Staaten als Rechtsbuch dargestellt was translated as *Gongfa Huitong* (10 volumes). Also, during the Sino-French War in the early 1880s, the Convention respecting the Laws and Customs of War on Land was translated and used in Qing's negotiations with France. Furthermore, Martin's speech made in Berlin in 1881, *Trace of International Law in Ancient China*, was translated as *Zhongguo Gushi Gongfa Lunlue* by Wang Fengzao and it was published in 1884.[47]

Besides Martin and his students at the *Tongwenguan*, there was another person translating works on international law: John Fryer. Fryer mainly focused on British works, such as Edmund Robertson's section of international law in *The Encyclopaedia Britannica*, which was translated as *Gongfa Zonglun*.[48] Another example is the translation of Robert J Phillimore's *Commentaries upon International Law*[49] as *Guojifa Pinglun*. Parts of *Guojifa Pinglun* were also published as *Geguo Jiaoshe Gongfalun* and *Geguo Jiaoshe Bianfalun*.

3.6. Institut de Droit International and Martin's Presentation

While Martin and Fryer were working in China, the Institut de Droit International discussed the application of international law to 'Eastern countries', and the discussion was published in its *Annuaire de l'Institut de Droit International* and in *Revue de droit international et de législation comparée*.[50] In 1878, the fourth meeting of this organization

---

[47] This speech by Martin shows that he made strenuous efforts to explain the significance of the *Wanguo Gongfa* in accordance with Chinese history. Martin likened relations among the different countries of the Spring and Autumn period to international relations in the late Qing period, and compared norms such as *li* with the *Wanguo Gongfa*. However, the Spring and Autumn period was generally regarded as a time of chaos and confusion, so it was unacceptable to set the norm of this period as a model. Also, to begin with, it was difficult to liken a core concept of Confucianism such as *li* to Western concepts. Above all, it was difficult for Qing's intellectuals to see Qing and Western countries as equals, as in the relations among the different countries of the Spring and Autumn period. In *Shixi Jicheng* (dated 19 January 1877), which is a report written by Qing's first Minister to Britain Guo Songtao while in office, Guo compares the Spring and Autumn period with the international relations of the late 19th century. He stated: 'In recent years, major powers such as Britain, France, Russia, the United States, and Germany do compete with each other, but they have also created the *Wanguo Gongfa* to prioritize each other's faith, and value friendly relations. They value friendship, respect, and politeness for each other, so they have both deep characteristics and knowledge. This is far superior to relations among countries during the Spring and Autumn period.' However, the content of this report by Guo was later strongly criticized by the Qing bureaucrats. See *Intellectuals and Civilization* (n 3) 69–78.

[48] This book was co-translated with Wang Zhengsheng and published by Jiangnan Zhizaoju Fanyiguan.

[49] RJ Phillimore *Commentaries upon International Law* (WG Benning and Co London 1871–74).

[50] Regarding Martin's presentation, the author consulted M Harada 'Jyūkyū Seiki Ajia No Kokusaihō Jyuyō To Bankoku Kokusaihō Gakkai: Shin No Kokusaihō Jyuyō To Bankoku Kokusaihō Gakkai (The Reception of International Law and the Institut de Droit International in 19th Century Asia: Qing's Reception of International Law and the Institut de Droit International)' (thesis The University of Tokyo 2011).

was held in Paris, and a British scholar of international law and Vice President of the Association of Reform and Codification of the Law of Nations, Travers Twiss made a presentation.[51] On the application of international law to the East, he stated: 'People from the Ottoman Empire, Persia, China, and Japan are different from people of other uncivilized countries. Relations with Eastern countries differ depending on the level of civilization.'[52] Specifically on Japan and China, he stated:

Both countries are aware of their obligations toward foreign nationals and individuals, and this awareness is essentially the same as the European people's awareness of the basic principle of European international law—the principle that no authority can elude the obligations of a treaty without the other party's agreement.[53]

Therefore, according to Twiss, it was not impossible to incorporate Japan and China into the group of countries that receives international law.

On the other hand, at the seventh meeting of the Institut de Droit International, Hornung made a presentation titled 'Reform of the Judicial System in the East'. He pointed out the problems of the consular jurisdiction system at the time, and called for the establishment of mixed courts in all Eastern countries 'as the duty of civilized countries act as guardian for people whose progress has been slow'.[54] At this meeting, the establishment of mixed courts gradually became one of the focal points of the discussion. On China, Jan Helenus Ferguson, who also served as Dutch minister to China, made presentations titled 'Les réformes judiciaires en Chine et dans le Royaume de Siam' and 'Projet d'établissement de tribunaux internationaux pour la Chine', at the 12th meeting held in 1891 in Hamburg.[55] According to Ferguson, civil cases in China that were the most difficult and required most attention were: first, cases between Chinese and foreigners; second, cases between foreign residents in China from different home countries; and third, cases between foreign residents in

---

[51] (1879) 3 Annuaire de l'Institut de Droit International 300–5.   [52] ibid 301.   [53] ibid 302.

[54] As a matter of fact, J Hornung had published his comments on Martin's 1881 speech in Berlin, *Trace of International Law in China*, that was later translated as *Zhongguo Gushi Gongfa Lunlue* by Wang Feng-zao. Hornung stated: 'This big county is not following the West as fast as Japan. It is not catching up with our norms and institutions like Japan. However, China is doing a pretty good job while protecting the country's traditions. Its development that is slowly being realized will be stable. And it is not to say that China's progress has been terribly delayed.... We have seen Chinese people apply our science and technology, so there is no mistake that China has a big future ahead. According to Martin, China and the United States will soon become the world's strongest countries.... Martin predicts that China's deployment of weapons is purely for defense purposes and it will not pose danger to the West. However, China may one day become a major hegemony.... In any case, we should hope that this new state that has risen in Asia will place its power in its obligations of civilization and law. Also, in conclusion, we should pay respect to Martin for his honorable and difficult work of understanding Ancient China.' J Hornung 'Note additionnelle' (1882) 14 Revue de droit international et de législation comparée 242–3.

[55] JH Ferguson 'Les réformes judiciaires en Chine et dans le royaume de Siam' (1890) 22 Revue de droit international et de législation comparée 251–78; M Féraud-Giraud 'Les institutions judiciaires de l'Egypte' (1890) 22 Revue de droit international et de législation comparée 70–82; 'Analyse sommaire du rapport de M. Féraud-Giraud sur les institutions judiciaires de l'Egypte' (1889–92) 11 Annuaire de l'Institut de Droit International 337–47.

China from the same home country. He then argued that these problems could be resolved by setting up an international mixed court, and that the system used in Egypt should be revised and applied to China.

While working at the *Tongwenguan*, Martin often sent letters about his activities in China to European scholars of international law, and they were often published in *Revue de droit international et de législation comparée*. For example, in one article, he showed his motivation for the education of international law:

> I plan to start international law education with Woolsey's book. This book was written to be used by students, so it is better than Wheaton's collection of treaties. Students have the translation of Wheaton's book. I translated it into appropriate language, but ultimately I plan to have students read this book in original text. By starting from Woolsey, I am confident that students are able to gain a more complete knowledge of the subject as a whole.—In Beijing, June 20, 1872.[56]

In another article, Martin depicted China's reception of international law in the following way:

> The Chinese people to whom I handed the translation of Wheaton's book immediately realized the benefits that could be drawn of it. They understood that if they make a mistake, they could use such knowledge of laws and regulations to blame it on other countries' oppressive means. It was also easy for me to see what the Chinese did not understand. What they did not understand was that when they file a suit on Europe's compliance with international law, both parties must mutually assume suitable obligations. This is a high-level concept that is used in the practical stage, and not when they have just started learning international law.[57]

Here, Martin indicates that even though the Chinese were quick to understand international law as a tool for negotiations, they had difficulty understanding the concepts of the principle of reciprocity.

4. BUILDING OF A MODERN STATE AND THE *WANGUO GONGFA*

4.1. Qing's Double Standard in its Foreign Relations

From the 1870s to the 1880s, China's actual foreign relations started to undergo a big transformation. While maintaining existing tribute relationships, the Qing Dynasty

---

[56] WAP Martin 'Une université en Chine: Le présent et l'avenir de l'enseignement supérieur international à Péking' (1873) 5 Revue de droit international et de législation comparée 8–10.

[57] AMG Moynier 'Le Chine et le droit international' (1885) 17 Revue de droit international et de législation comparée 504–9.

also maintained treaty-based commercial relationships with Western countries. In other words, Qing held a double standard in its foreign relations. However, as the surrounding countries were colonized by the West or annexed by Japan, there was no choice but to gradually reduce its tribute relationships with the surrounding countries. In contrast, treaty relationships, which were originally limited to four countries (Britain, France, the United States, and Russia), expanded to include other Western countries that had commercial relations with China. Such treaties were all so-called unequal treaties.

By the mid-1880s, the only remaining country that was in a tribute relationship with Qing was Korea. Qing started to apply the double standard in its foreign relations to its relationship with Korea, and demanded Korea to open up to the West while maintaining the tribute relationship with Qing.[58] Qing entered into unequal relations with Korea in the field of commerce, opened a settlement (*zujie*) in Korea, and enjoyed the privilege of unilateral consular jurisdiction. In addition, in the 1880s, Qing stationed Yuan Shikai in Seoul not as minister or diplomat, but as a resident, and ordered him to be involved in Korea's domestic and foreign policies. Qing used the Western logic of a 'protectorate' and reorganized its tribute system into a modern one. Nevertheless, Qing took these unprecedented measures in order to maintain the tribute system and to guarantee its influence in Korea, which was geopolitically an important country.

Korea ended its tribute relationship with Qing in 1895 by signing the Treaty of Shimonoseki with Japan. Later, it entered into a treaty relationship with Qing with the conclusion of a treaty in 1899. As will be discussed below, by the second half of the 1890s, Qing's world view had started to change.

4.2. The 'Demarcation' of National Borders and 'China' as a Sovereign State

From the 1870s to the 1880s, the borders and territories were a challenging issue in China. The Taiwan Incident erupted between Qing and Japan in 1871. When the people of *Mudan* (Paiwan aborigines) from Southern Taiwan harmed the people of Japan's Yaeyama Islands who drifted ashore, Qing bureaucrats called the Paiwan aborigines 'people of *Huawai* (people outside civilization in Han's context)'. Japan judged this as a sign that Qing regarded Taiwan as *terra nullius* (no man's land) which it did not govern. Therefore, Japan dispatched troops to Taiwan. It was not that Qing had not understood the *Wanguo Gongfa* at this point, or that the

---

[58] T Okamoto *Zokkoku To Jishu No Aida: Kindai Shin Kan Kankei To Higashi Ajia No Meiun (Between Dependency and Sovereignty: Sino-Korean Relations in the Late Nineteenth Century and the Fate of the Far East)* (The University of Nagoya Press Nagoya 2004).

Minister of the *Zongli Yamen* who was in charge of negotiations mentioned the name 'people of *Huawai*'. Japan certainly tried to show its understanding of the *Wanguo Gongfa* by using its logic and advertising it both internally and externally.

In the 1870–80s, active discussions were held about how to defend Qing's territories, known as *Haifanglun* (assertion of naval defence) and *Saifanglun* (assertion of inland defence). This meant that disputes over national borders with Japan and Russia had erupted. After the Treaty of Nerchinsk of 1689, Qing's northern national borders were gradually demarcated. Also, as Russia advanced into Central Asia, disputes over national borders with Qing erupted, and the borders were demarcated by treaties such as the Treaty of Ili of 1881. Besides Japan and Russia, Qing also negotiated the border between Indochina with France, and the border between Burma with Britain, thereby demarcating its national borders. As a result of these negotiations, Qing did lose considerable parts of its territory, but it should also be noted that Xue Fucheng, who negotiated the border between Burma in the late 19th century and Tang Shaoyi, who negotiated the border between Tibet in the early 20th century, used the *Wanguo Gongfa* to conduct negotiations and worked to maintain China's sovereignty.[59]

In the process of demarcating new national borders, Qing adopted a policy to unify domestic governance that was pluralistic. In the 1880s, Qing set up Xingjiang and Taiwan as provinces, and in the 1890s, Manchuria as the Three Eastern Provinces (*Tongsansheng*), where immigration was initially prohibited because it was Qing's birthplace. Qing also sought to make Tibet into a province. These moves toward the unification of governance could be seen as Qing's intentionality for a modern sovereign State.

As 'China' as a sovereign State became established, people started to become aware of 'Chinese' as nation. Qing had not publicly approved overseas immigration until overseas travel was accepted by the Treaty of Beijing in 1860. However, Qing set up a consulate in South-East Asia and decided to protect the overseas Chinese living in the region.[60] This could also been seen as the approval of 'Chinese' who should be protected.

In this way Qing started to proclaim itself as a sovereign State, but it is not enough to discuss this phenomenon as simply Western impact. First, Qing's moves to set up provinces (*sheng*) and to protect overseas Chinese were not necessarily legitimized

---

[59] K Hakoda 'Chūei "Biruma-Chibetto Kyōtei" (1886 Nen) No Haikei: Shin Matsu Chūgoku Gaikō No Seikaku Wo Meguru Ichi Kousatsu (The Background of the Sino-British "Burma-Tibet Convention" (1886): A Study on the Characteristics of Chinese Diplomacy in the Late Qing Dynasty)' (2005) 88 Shirin 233–58.

[60] An exception was Siam, which rejected to enter into diplomatic relations with Qing. As a result, Qing could not set up a legation or a consulate, so overseas Chinese in Siam were treated at citizens of Siam. S Kawashima *Chūgoku Kindai Gaikō No Keisei (The Formation of China's Modern Diplomacy)* (The University of Nagoya Press Nagoya 2004).

under the logic that Qing should strive to become like a Western modern State.[61] The expansion of *sheng* and the protection of overseas Chinese were both understood according to the logic of expanding the Emperor's virtue and dynastic *dezhi* and *jiaohua*. Also, regarding the interpretation and uses of treaty privileges, the roles of people, called *Maiban*, who worked under Western merchants and Chinese local staff have started to draw attention.[62] In negotiations over the *Wanguo Gongfa* and treaties, we are required to not only examine the unilateral impact from the West, but also to grasp the issues from the interaction between the West and the Chinese side.

4.3. *Bianfa* and *Wanguo Gongfa*

Xue Fucheng thought it was problematic that Qing was seen as 'a country outside public law (*Gongfa*)' therefore it could not enjoy the rights that countries inside public law could enjoy.[63] However, as national salvation and protection became big issues after the First Sino-Japanese War, Qing's view of the world started to transform, and changes in its attitude toward the *Wanguo Gongfa* could also be seen. Specifically, it should be noted that *Kang Youwei* recaptured the world from *Yitong Chuishang* (governing the world hierarchically) to *Lieguo Bingli* (coexistence of nations of the world). This indicated change in Qing's thinking from one that believed Qing to be a key player of exceptional rank in the world to one that recognizes Qing as one of the many countries that stand side by side in the world. Therefore, according to the theory of social evolution, which was popular at that time, Qing was the inferior and the weak; in order for China to survive the competition of the international community, it had to work hard by itself.

The *Wanguo Gongfa* was used by revolutionaries, constitutionalist activists, and also by Qing as logic to emphasize its stance. However, the knowledge of international law that was used by a revolutionary polemic Hu Hanmin in discussions for the magazine *Minbao* no longer came from Martin, but from new scholars such as John Westlake, Franz Liszt, and Maptehe, or from Japanese scholars such as Takahashi Sakue and Terao Toru. Also, during this period the term *Wanguo Gongfa* quickly stopped being used, and it was replaced by the term *Guojifa* (international law).[64]

---

[61] T Okamoto and T Motegi 'Chūka Teikoku No Kindaiteki Saihen: Zaizai Kajin Hogoron No Taitō Wo Megutte (Modern Reorganization of the Chinese Empire: Regarding the Rise of the Theory to Protect Overseas Chinese)' in *Signs of Chinese Diplomacy* (n 40) 139–58.

[62] E Motono *Conflict and Cooperation in Sino-British Business, 1860–1911: The Impact of the Pro-British Commercial Network in Shanghai* (St Antony's Series Palgrave Macmillan Basingstoke 2000).

[63] F Xue *Lun Zhongguo Zazi Gongfawai Zhi Guo (Arguments on affect for China as a Country Outside Public Law)* (1892).

[64] *Intellectuals and Civilization* (n 3) 148–9.

This could be seen as the spread of Japanese translation of the term international law, as well as the spread of international law as positive law to China.

After the First Sino-Japanese War, a political reform movement known as the Hundred Days' Reform (*Wuxu Bianfa*) occurred for a short while in 1898. At *Jingshi Daxuetang* (later Peking University), which was set up at that time, various subjects of Western scholarship were incorporated into the curriculum, and Martin from the *Tongwenguan* was welcomed to teach there. However, the most important innovation was that international law was seen as Qing's legitimate knowledge. Qing declared the abolition of the Imperial exam in December 1901 (abolished in 1904), and in the following year one of the subjects tested in *Xiangshi* was world politics, which included public law. Also, in the 1904 charter of *Jingshi Daxuetang*, several schools were to be established in the *Jingshi Daxuetang*, and a course on 'negotiation law (international law)' was set up in the School of Politics and Law.[65] Since Qing decided to adopt the constitutional monarchy system, new schools of politics and law were established in various places, and at these schools international law was incorporated as an important part of the curriculum. The textbooks that were used in these schools were mainly from Japan, and they held characteristics of positive law.

On the other hand, Qing's students who studied abroad had contact with international law, and they brought back substantial knowledge to Qing. This trend had been seen from the 1870s. For example, students of Fuzhou Naval College who were sent to France made excellent grades studying international law. Ma Jianzhong, who studied international law at École Libre des Sciences Politiques as student supervisor submitted a proposal on training diplomats to Li Hungchang, and after returning to Qing, Ma became successful in conducting foreign negotiations under Li.[66] The *Tongwenguan* also sent students to Britain, France, and Germany twice in the second half of the 1890s. Furthermore, in the early 20th century when the United States used reparations from the Boxer Rebellion to open up opportunities to studying in the United States, highly capable intellectuals studied international law in major American universities. Gu Weijun and Wang Zhengting obtained degrees in international law from Columbia University and Yale University, respectively. They must have been influenced by American scholarship of international law, which values sovereignty.[67] It could be inferred that these became the foundation of diplomats who were successful during the period of the Republic of China.

[65] Guangxu 29, 26 November (13 January 1904), Zhang Baixi, 'Jingshi Daxuetang Zhangcheng (Futong Ruyuan Zhangcheng)'.

[66] M Banno *Chūgoku Kindaika To Ba Kenchū (China's Modernization and Ma Jianzhong)* (The University of Tokyo Press Tokyo 1985); T Okamoto *Ba Kenchū No Chūgoku Kindai (Ma Jianzhong's Modernization of China)* (The University of Kyoto Press Kyoto 2007).

[67] H Shinohara 'W.W. Wirobī To Senkanki Beichū Kankei: Shuken Kokka To Shite No Chūgoku' (W.W. Wiloughby and Sino-U.S. Relations during the Interwar Period: China as a Sovereign State) (1998) 118 Kokusai Seiji (Beichū Kankei) 9–26.

However, students who studied in Japan cannot be overlooked, considering their numbers and influence. Qing's abolition of the Imperial examination and provision of qualification equivalent to passing the Imperial exam to students who studied abroad encouraged students to study in Japan.

After the number of Chinese students studying in Japan reached almost 10,000 in the early 20th century, the knowledge of international law that the students gained did have a certain impact. Especially for Chinese intellectuals who started to foster awareness of 'China' as a State, and were increasingly conscious of the need to maintain the country's independence and to recover sovereign rights, international law was not only logic that justified the West's acts of aggression, but also logic that allowed Qing to defend itself and recover its lost sovereign rights. Huang Zunsan, who studied in Japan at the end of the Qing period left a detailed diary, in which he wrote that he got the concept of State and national territory and inviolability of territory, through learning international law.[68]

5. Conclusion

After the First Sino-Japanese War (1894–95), Qing was no longer a 'country outside the *Wanguo Gongfa*' and became aware of itself as one of many States that coexist in the international community. Qing clearly recognized this at international conferences, such as the Hague Conferences in 1899 and 1907. Being treated as a second- or third-rate power instead of a first-rate power due to the low level of Qing's development also gave a push to Qing to work toward building a modern State.

In the first half of the 20th century, 'national salvation' was the national goal, thus Qing's independence as a State and recovery of sovereign rights were demanded. International law was, on the one hand, a tool which the Western powers used to wrest sovereign rights from China, but during this period China actually relied on international law to maintain sovereign rights and took moves to recover sovereign rights that were lost. These tendencies could be seen in Chinese diplomacy at the Paris Peace Conference of 1919 and the Washington Naval Conference of 1921. From the 1910s to 1920s, China pursued a treaty revision diplomacy (*xiuyue waijiao*) that tried to recover lost rights and interests, but since entering World War I and becoming a victorious power, China took the rights and interests of defeated countries, such as Germany and Austria.

---

[68] Z Huang *Sanshi Nian Riji (Thirty-Year Diary)* (Changsha Hunan Yinshuguan 1933) vol 1 (*Liuxue Riji (Diary from Study Abroad)*), at 317.

On the other hand, at the League of Nations founded in 1919, China aimed to become a non-permanent member of the Council, and sometimes it acted as president of the Council. China also sent a judge to the International Court of Justice in The Hague, and showed a certain level of presence in the world of international law.

In considering the rapid spread of international law from the end of the 19th century, the transition from *Wanguo Gongfa* with characteristics of natural law to international law with characteristics of positive law, as well as the 'chain of knowledge' between East Asia and Japan is both important. How Japan's understanding of international law and international community that valued sovereign rights affected China is an issue for future research. Another important research topic is how the early 20th century Chinese diplomats' knowledge of international law was affected by the theories and schools of countries they studied in (mostly Europe and the United States).

Still, there is the question of whether we can simply consider that China, which understood the *Wanguo Gongfa* in a Chinese context in the second half of the 19th century, dovetailed with the international community's understanding of international law by the first half of the 20th century. As Western *Wanguo Gongfa*/the way of international law gradually became tolerant and flexible to include others including China, we can see the importance of mutual interaction between the Western society and the other worlds.[69] At the same time, it is also possible to set a hypothesis that China's own view of the international order and understanding of international law continued to exist in the first half of the 20th century, like overlapping layers of low-pitched sounds.[70] Or, these became more complex in the process of China's reception of Marxism. In that sense, as historians, we need to be careful about capturing the historical process from the second half of the 19th century to the first half of the 20th century as simple stages of 'evolution' or 'development'.

RECOMMENDED READING

Banno, Masataka *China and the West, 1858–1861: The Origins of the Tsungli Yamen* (Harvard University Press Cambridge MA 1964).

Bruner, Katherine F, John K Fairbank, and Richard Smith (eds) *Entering China's Service: Robert Hart's Journals, 1854–1863* (Council on East Asian Studies, Harvard University Cambridge MA 1986).

---

[69] G Xu *China and the Great War: China's Pursuit of a New National Identity and Internationalization* (CUP Cambridge 2005); Y Zhang *China in the International System, 1918–20: The Middle Kingdom at the Periphery* (Macmillan Press London 1991).

[70] See the following for how the tribute relationships until the second half of the 19th century were recognized by China during the first half of the 20th century. S Kawashima 'China's Re-Interpretation of the Chinese "World Oder," 1900–40s' in A Reid and Y Zheng (eds) *Negotiating Asymmetry: China's Place in Asia* (National University of Singapore Press Singapore 2009) 139–58.

Hamashita, Takeshi *Kindai Chūgoku No Kokusaiteki Keiki: Chōkō Bōeki Shisutemu to Kindai Ajia (Modern China's International Opportunity: The Tribute and Trade System and Modern Asia)* (The University of Tokyo Press Tokyo 1990).

Hsü, Immanuel CY *China's Entrance into the Family of Nations: The Diplomatic Phase, 1858–1880* (Harvard University Press Cambridge MA 1960).

Iwai, Shigeki 'Chōkō To Goshi (Chaogong and Hushi)' in Wada Haruki et al (eds) *Higashi Ajia Kingendai Tsūshi (Modern and Contemporary History of East Asia)* (Iwanami Shoten Tokyo 2010) vol 1 (*Higashi Ajia Sekai No Kindai 19 Seiki (The Modern Period of the East Asian World 19th Century)*).

Lin, Xuezhong *Cong Wanguo Gongfa Dao Gongfa Waijiao: Wan Qing Guojifa De Chuanru, Quanshi Yu Yingyong (From Wanguo Gongfa to Diplomacy based on Public Law of All Nations Diplomacy: Propagation Introduction of International Law in the Late Qing Dynasty, Interpretation, Explanation and Application of International Law in the Late Qing Dynasty)* (Shanghai Guji Chubanshe Shanghai 2009).

Liu, Lydia H *The Clash of Empires: The Invention of China in Modern World Making* (Harvard University Press Cambridge MA 2004).

Mancall, Mark *China at the Center: 300 Years of Foreign Policy* (Free Press New York 1984).

Sato, Shinichi *Kindai Chūgoku No Chishikijin To Bunmei (Intellectuals and Civilization in Modern China)* (The University of Tokyo Press Tokyo 1996).

Wheaton, Henry *Elements of International Law: With a Sketch of the History of Science* (Carey, Lea & Blanchard Philadelphia 1836).

CHAPTER 20

JAPAN

MASAHARU YANAGIHARA

1. INTRODUCTION

ACCORDING to the *History Book of Sui* (*China*) drawn up in 656 AD, a king of Japan sent an official letter in 607 AD to the second emperor of Sui saying that the letter was sent by *tianzi* (the Son of Heaven) of the country from which the sun rises to *tianzi* of the country into which the sun goes down.[1] The Chinese emperor was so angered with this letter especially because the title of *tianzi* could be used only by him, according to custom in China. This event is usually interpreted to mean that the king of Japan claimed equality with the Chinese emperor, but the latter rejected this.[2]

It has been a debatable and critical issue as to whether Japan was in reality incorporated in the Chinese world order in history, especially in the Muromachi period (in the 15th and 16th centuries) and the Tokugawa period (from the 17th century to the middle of the 19th century). The issue of whether Japan was just occupying a peripheral status in history in the world order in East Asia because China was, throughout

---

[1] Rekishigaku Kenkyukai (The Historical Science Society of Japan) (ed) *Materials of the Japanese History 1: Antiquity* (Iwanami Shoten Tokyo 2005) at 69 [in Japanese].

[2] We cannot find the similar passages in the *Chronicles of Japan* (*Nihon Shoki*) drawn up in 720. There are several interpretations concerning a big difference between the *History Book of Sui* and the *Chronicles of Japan*. For example, usually the country from which the sun rises and the country into which the sun goes down mean simply east and west according to Buddhist terminology, but some say that this expression had a meaning of extrication from a tribute system. Y Kawamoto 'Notes on Embassies to Sui China' (2004) 141 Shien or the Journal of History 53–77 [in Japanese].

most of history a tremendously powerful country in East Asia from a point of view of culture, economics, and politics, has also been much discussed.[3]

This chapter aims to clarify an 'international legal order' in pre-modern Japan from the 15th century to 1853 and the reception of modern European international law in Japan after 1853. The first point will be analysed particularly from the viewpoint of contrast with the Western and Chinese ideas of world order. The reception process from 1853 was also a complicated and constant conflict between the East Asian ideas and the Western ones.

2. International Legal Order in Pre-Modern Japan (15th Century to 1853)

2.1. Chinese World Order and Japan

2.1.1. *Idea of China as Central Empire*

The traditional world order in East Asia had been Sino-centric. A tribute, a seal of investiture, and an acceptance of the Chinese calendar were symbols of this idea in relation with neighbouring 'vassal' countries such as Korea, Ryukyu, Annam (Viet Nam), etc. A quite different idea of 'territory', *Hanto* ('*bantu*' in Chinese, the Chinese idea of territory), was dominant there. The virtue (*de*) of a Chinese emperor would in theory cover the entire world, with a rare exception in that some people could not understand the virtue and consequently did not enjoy the enlightenment from the emperor. Borders between China and the outer zone were established, but they were not at all a 'boundary', as understood in modern European international law, because of the inherent nature of *Hanto,* which was infinite in theory. It was not a 'territorial principle', but a 'personal principle' which dominated there as a general rule.[4]

In the Qing Dynasty, however, a dual structure was established: 'the south-east crescent', that is, the world of China, including Korea and Southeast Asia, and 'the north-west crescent', that is, the world of non-China, including Mongol, Tibet, and Sinkiang, as described by Mark Mancall. The 'north-west crescent' was also considered in theory under the control of the Chinese Dynasty.[5]

---

[3] Cf H Miyajima 'Paradigm Change of Knowledge of the Japanese History' (2010) 1029 Shiso 6–25 [in Japanese].

[4] T Motegi *International Order in Changing Modern East Asia* (Yamakawa Shuppansha Tokyo 1997) at 4–19 [in Japanese].

[5] M Mancall 'The Ch'ing Tribute System: An Interpretative Essay' in JK Fairbank (ed) *The Chinese World Order: Traditional China's Foreign Relations* (Harvard University Press Cambridge 1968) 63–89.

2.1.2. *Japan as Vassal Country*

It is still controversial whether Japan had been included in this Chinese world order or not. After an abolition of the Japanese missions to the Tang Dynasty in 894 there had existed no official relation between China and Japan until Yoshimitsu Ashikaga, Shogun at the Muromachi period, sent a letter to the Chinese emperor dated 13 May 1401 with a gift of local products, asking for the establishment of diplomatic relations with the Ming Dynasty. The second emperor of Ming replied to it in the letter dated 6 January 1402 admitting Japan into a tribute and investiture system, giving Yoshimitsu a title of 'the King of Japan', and distributing the calendar of the Ming Dynasty to him and his people.[6] Almost 900 years had passed after the Japanese five kings' tribute to China in the 5th century. The Japanese side regarded the relations with Ming as *Kango* (tally) trade, not as a tribute and investiture system, which took place sporadically until 1547.[7]

2.2. 'Seclusion' of Japan and 'Four Gates'

2.2.1. *'Seclusion' of Japan*

Japan maintained a policy of 'seclusion' or 'isolation' (*Sakoku*) for almost 250 years in the Tokugawa period, from 1639 to 1854. Japan was deemed to be almost completely separated from the external world. Trade with the Dutch at Dejima, an artificial islet, in Nagasaki, was the sole opportunity for Japan to have contact with foreigners.

We sometimes call the period from the latter half of the 16th century to the first half of the 17th century just before the period of seclusion, the 'Christian' century. The Portuguese brought *Tanegashima* (matchlock guns) to Japan in 1543 and then the Christian religion in 1549. The Spanish, English, and Dutch also came to Japan to preach Christianity and to trade. *Nanban* (Southern barbarian) culture flourished in Japan during this period. Many Japanese merchants, who were sometimes called *Wako* (Japanese pirates), established trade bases or Japanese communities in Korea and in Southeast Asian cities, especially Manila, Ayutthaya, Hoi An, etc. It was a period in Japanese history when Japan was wide open to the outside world, probably only seconded by the period from the 4th–7th centuries when many Chinese and Koreans settled in Japan and introduced advanced technology.[8] This openness was, however, gradually abandoned. Hideyoshi Toyotomi issued the deportation order of the Portuguese Jesuit priests in 1587. The Tokugawa government followed this basic

---

[6] T Tanaka (ed) *Zenrin kokuho ki, Shintei zoku zenrin kokuho ki* (Documents Concerning the Friendly Relations with Neighbouring Countries) (Shueisha Tokyo 1995) at 108–11 [in classical Chinese].

[7] Y Arano et al (eds) *Foreign Relations of Japan 4: Wako and the King of Japan* (Yoshikawa Kobunkan Tokyo 2010) at 1–27 [in Japanese].

[8] R Toby *History of Japan: Volume 9, Diplomacy of Sakoku (Seclusion)* (Shogakkan Tokyo 2008) at 10–11 [in Japanese].

policy, and finally in 1639 Japan became 'closed' to the external world. This isolation was suddenly endangered by the arrival of US commander Matthew Perry's four black ships in 1853.

The idea of seclusion is, however, now almost denied by most contemporary specialists in the history of Japan. The Tokugawa government had never issued a single edict of seclusion. The so-called seclusion[9] policy had, in fact, three factors. First, all Japanese people were prohibited from going abroad, and those living abroad were not allowed to return home. The second was the ban on Christianity and the deportation of foreign missionaries. The third was a prohibition of entry into Nagasaki Port of Western countries ships except Dutch ones.

It is, however, wrong to say that Japan was completely isolated from foreign countries during this period, especially when we take into consideration the relations with East Asia; with China, Korea, Ryukyu, and Ezo.[10] Japan was not closed at all to East Asia.[11] The theory of 'four gates', ideas of *Ikoku* and *Iiki*, and ideas of 'regions of correspondence' and 'regions of trade' are indispensable in understanding the real situation of Japan's relations with 'foreign' countries in the so-called seclusion period.

2.2.2. *Theory of 'Four Gates'*

The theory of four gates, initially formulated by Yasunori Arano in 1978, is now widely accepted among Japanese historians. Through the four gates which were open to the outside world, Japan mingled with foreign countries and foreign people. 'Matsumae Gate' open to the *Ainu* (indigenous people) in Ezo, 'Tsushima Gate' open to Korea, 'Nagasaki Gate' open to the Dutch and Chinese merchants, and 'Satsuma Gate' open to the Ryukyu Kingdom.[12]

Japan only had trade relations with the Dutch and the Chinese. No official diplomatic relations with the Netherlands and China existed. The Dutch merchants, deemed barbarians, were obliged to stay only at Dejima, but directors of the Dutch trading post, *Oranda kapitan* (Dutch captains), were asked to go to Yedo (Tokyo) every year to be received in audience by the Shogun and submitted *Oranda fusetsu gaki* (Dutch reports), in which the latest world news was written. No official diplomatic relations with China meant that Japan was attempting not to have a

---

[9] The term '*Sakoku*' was used for the first time when Tadao Shizuki published a Japanese translation of Engelbert Kaempfer's *The History of Japan* in 1801. The Tokugawa government never officially used this term even after 1801.

[10] Ezo, or Ezo-chi, was used in the Tokugawa period to mean the region where the *Ainu* lived. It included the most part of the present Hokkaido, Saghalien and the Kuril Islands. It was divided into East Ezo, West Ezo, and North Ezo in the beginning of the 19th century. Wajin-chi, Oshima Peninsula, was an antonym for it and was under the direct control of the Matsumae domain, as will be described later.

[11] RP Toby *State and Diplomacy in Early Modern Japan: Asia in the Development of the Tokugawa Bakufu* (Stanford University Press Stanford 1991) at 5.

[12] Y Arano 'The Shogunate State and Diplomacy' (1978) Rekishigakukenkyu Bessatsu Tokushu 95–105 [in Japanese].

tributary relationship with China, in sharp contrast with Korea. Information received from Chinese merchants, *Tosen fusetsu gaki* (Chinese ships reports), was also sent to Yedo.

Because Ezo, Korea, and the Ryukyu Kingdom were considered as *Ikoku* (foreign countries), three domains (*han*) in charge of these three gates, the Matsumae domain, the Tsushima domain and the Satsuma domain, had missions of checking; in other words, the means to contact each of the three foreign countries.

The relation between Japan and Korea was in fact not completely equal or reciprocal. The legal status of Tsushima domain(*han*)'s *Wakan* (guesthouse for Japanese) located in Busan, Korea, is still now wildly controversial. Was it really a guesthouse for the entertainment, trade, and residence of Japanese? Or was it a place for tribute of the Tsushima domain to the Korean king, because Korea recognized the Tsushima domain as her vassal country? Korea refused to allow Japan to send her *Tsushin-shi* (communication messengers or embassies) to Seoul, although Korea sent her *Tsushin-shi* to Yedo, in total twelve times from 1607 to 1811. The exact character of Korean *Tsushin-shi* is also highly controversial. It is perfectly true that these Korean embassies were recognized as official envoys, but the Tokugawa government proclaimed that Korean *Tsushin-shi* was a tributary mission to Japan, while Korea was insisting that *Tsushin-shi* was sent because of Japan's request.[13]

2.2.3. Ikoku and Iiki: *Ezo and Ryukyu*

It is also bitterly debated as to whether Ezo and the Ryukyu Kingdom in the Tokugawa period can be really considered as *Ikoku* (foreign countries).

Although Arano considered Korea, Ezo, and Ryukyu as *Ikoku*, the idea of distinguishing between *Ikoku* and *Iiki* (fringe land or rim land, not domestic area) was advocated by Katsumi Fukaya in 1989, and it is a now-popular view among historians. Claiming that it is sufficiently clear that Korea is typical *Ikoku*, Fukaya is of the opinion that the relation with the Dutch and the Chinese can be understood from a viewpoint of *Ikoku*. Ezo and Ryukyu had, however, been closely related with the Shogunate system and could not be completely separated as *Ikoku* from Japan, but on the other hand, they could not be wholly recognized as part of the Shogunate society, because they had unique and different culture patterns from Japan. He concludes that Ezo and Ryukyu should not be classified as *Ikoku*, but as *Iiki*.[14]

A distinction between *Ikoku* and *Iiki* appears to be completely clear and reasonable when we see a distinction between a country as independent entity and a region which is not an independent entity in the proper sense, but does not form a part of one country. We should, however, take into consideration that the

---

[13] *State and Diplomacy* (n 11) 25–44. The Tokugawa government was not allowed to send official envoys to Korea.

[14] K Fukaya 'General Remarks: The Shogunate State and Iiki/Ikoku' in E Kato et al (eds) *The Shogunate State and Iiki/Ikoku* (Azekura Shobo Tokyo 1989) 9–44 at 10–11 [in Japanese].

concepts of modern European 'sovereign and independent State' or 'sovereign States-system' did not exist in Japan or in the East Asian world at that time.[15] It is therefore important to recognize that a retrospective contrast between *Ikoku* and *Iiki* brought out from a perspective of the 'modern European State' is not sustainable.

More importantly, some specialists express serious doubts as to whether Ryukyu can be classified as *Iiki*, although it is almost indisputable that Ezo should be considered as *Iiki*. It follows easily from this that a simple contrast between *Ikoku* and *Iiki* is unlikely, but a distinction between the two concepts is useful in some respects, especially when this distinction subtly implies a remarkable and instructive contrast between Ezo and Ryukyu.

2.2.4. 'Regions of Correspondence' and 'Regions of Trade'

A new idea of *Tsushin no kuni* (regions of correspondence) and *Tsusho no kuni* (regions of trade) was developed by a senior councillor, Sadanobu Matsudaira, when the Russian envoy, Adam Laxman, came to Hakodate in Ezo in 1793 to request trade with Japan. Matsudaira refused to accept a diplomatic message despatched by the Russian empress, because Russia was not *Tsushin no kuni,* and therefore Japan could not have diplomatic relations with Russia. This idea was made clearer in 1804 in the written instructions delivered to the Russian envoy, Rezanov, saying that *Tsushin* and *Tsusho* were limited to China, Korea, Ryukyu, and the Netherlands. In the letter addressed to the Dutch minister in 1845 it was made explicit that the relations with Korea and Ryukyu were *Tsushin,* including the exchange of diplomatic documents or envoys, and the relations with China and Holland were *Tsusho,* as these included trade and the travelling to Japan of merchants from those states.[16]

The purpose of this idea is obvious: according to the traditional norm or ancestral law of Japan, the relations with the external world should be limited to these four 'countries', and Japan was not allowed to build up any type of relations with other countries.[17] Two points should be here taken into consideration. The first is Ezo. Ezo was not mentioned at all either in the 1804 instructions or in the 1845 letter. While an official diplomatic relation with *Iiki* was without any doubt impossible, judging from the very nature of the concept, *Tsusho* relations with Ezo might have been thinkable or acceptable, although the status of Ezo, especially before coming under direct control of the government in 1807, was both disputed and subtle, as will be explained later.

---

[15] Cf JK Fairbank 'A Preliminary Framework' in *The Chinese World Order* (n 5) 1–19 at 5.

[16] Gaimusho (ed) *Zoku tsushinzenran* (Complete Documents of Correspondence: The Second Series) (Yushodo Shuppan Tokyo 1985) vol 20, at 665 [in Japanese].

[17] *History of Japan: Volume 9* (n 8) 88–95 [in Japanese].

The second point is Ryukyu. *Tsushin* with Ryukyu means definitely that Ryukyu was regarded by the Tokugawa government as *Ikoku*, not as *Iiki* because *Tsushin* connotes official diplomatic relations. The status of Ryukyu according to this idea as well will be described in more detail in the next section.

2.3. 'Territory' of Japan

2.3.1. Hanto *and* Kegai no chi

Modern European international law is based mainly upon concepts of sovereignty, the modern State, the modern law distinguished from morals, the balance of power, and the system of States. Especially essential for it is a State with a defined territory, a 'territorial State'. International law could not exist without the existence of sovereign States defined by borders. 'Territory' defined by modern European international law is not the same either as was meant by 'territory' in Ancient and Medieval Europe, nor as was meant in Medieval or Early Modern East Asia.

Togai Ito, a Confucian scholar in the Tokugawa period, wrote in his 1729 book 'Heishoku Tan' that Ezo was not *Hanto* (territory), but *Kegai no chi*. The distinction between *Hanto* and *Kegai no chi* is reminiscent of a traditional Chinese concept of 'territory'. In contrast to *Hanto*, which means region under Chinese rule, *Kegai no chi* means region outside the enlightenment where the influence of benign rule is not exerted. Ito generally accepted this Chinese traditional idea of 'territory' and regarded Ezo not as *Hanto* but as *Kegai no chi*. Ito did not write further about *Hanto*, except to mention that Yakushima, a small island near Kagoshima, used to be *Kegai no chi*, but was now under a rule of the Satsuma domain, and was considered as *Hanto*.[18]

It is wholly clear that *Goki shichido* (five countries in the Kinki area and seven districts, *do*), administrative districts under a system of centralized government based on the *Ritsuryo* codes in Ancient Japan, including Tsushima, Oki, Yakushima, etc., were *Hanto* of Japan in the Tokugawa period. The status of Ezo and Ryukyu is especially controversial because these regions had not been included in these administrative districts.

2.3.2. Ezo and Ryukyu

Matsumae domain's control was twofold: *Wajin chi* (area of the Japanese) and *Ezo-chi* (area of Ainu). The Matsumae domain had direct control over *Wajin chi* which

---

[18] T Ito *Heishokutan* (Story of a Late Learning) (Yoshikawa Kobunkan Tokyo 1927) at 152 and 209 [in Japanese].

was a smaller area surrounding Hakodate in the Oshima Peninsular, but had only an exclusive right of trade with the Ainu in *Ezo-chi* which included the most part of Hokkaido.

It is an almost common view now to regard Ezo in the Tokugawa period neither as *Ikoku* nor as *Hanto*, but as *Iiki*. Ezo was not included in the territory proper of Japan, but was not under the administration of other countries such as Russia and China. Some kind of control over Ezo, even if it were not *dominium*, was considered to be exerted by the Matsumae domain, and by the Tokugawa government itself, which put *Ezo-chi* under its direct control in 1807.[19]

The status of Ryukyu in the Tokugawa period seems to have been profoundly puzzling.[20] The Ryukyu Kingdom delivered a tribute to China every two years, had a Ryukyu house at Fuzhou in China, and received Chinese envoys of investiture at the coronation of new kings at Naha. The kingdom was at the same time under the supervision and control of the Satsuma domain. Ryukyu's stipend of 120,000 *koku* of rice, assessed in terms of rice production, was added to the Satsuma domain's stipend in 1609. The Ryukyu Kingdom sent envoys to Yedo at the coronation of new Ryukyu kings and Japanese Shogun.

It is an unresolved dispute whether Ryukyu should be regarded as *Ikoku* or as *Iiki*. The fact that Ryukyu was classified in the beginning of the 19th century as *Tsushin no kuni* means that Japan had an official diplomatic relation with Ryukyu as was the case for Korea.[21] Here we ought to remind ourselves that concepts of modern European international law such as the sovereign State, territorial sovereignty, the sovereign States system, or the State boundary cannot be directly applied to East Asia in early modern times. That is definitely one reason why Ryukyu's status seems to be puzzling.

That is not, however, the only reason. We have several different interpretations about the status of Ryukyu in the Tokugawa period in relation with China and the Satsuma domain. Some scholars say that when we see written vows of the king of Ryukyu in 1611, the Ryukyu Kingdom was a vassal country to the Satsuma domain as *Ikoku* and gave a tribute to it. Some say that the Ryukyu Kingdom was annexed to Satsuma in 1609 and did not exist as *Ikoku* afterwards and that a tribute of Ryukyu paid to China was secretly controlled by Japan. Others are of the opinion that the Ryukyu Kingdom was under the military control of the Satsuma domain and at the same time under the Chinese tributary system. We can find here a dual subordination

---

[19] This direct control ended in 1821 and the second direct control began in 1855. K Fukaya 'Pre-modern Japan and East Asia' (2010) 1029 Shiso 170–87 at 182–3 [in Japanese].

[20] Cf RK Sakai 'The Ryukyu (Liu-ch'iu) Islands as a Fief of Satsuma' in *The Chinese World Order* (n 5) 112–34 at 112.

[21] A distinction between *Sanpu* (go up to Yedo) of Ryukyu embassies and *Raihei* (come to Yedo with gifts) of Korean embassies is subtle, but important. *Raihei* connotes an honoured guest. Cf 'Pre-modern Japan and East Asia' (n 19) 179.

or coexistence of two systems (*Ryozoku*) of the Japanese Shogunate system and the Chinese tributary system.

This issue is still now under much heated discussion. In the report of the Japan–China Joint History Research Committee (31 January 2010), the Japanese insisted that Ryukyu was under effective control of the Satsuma domain from the 17th century and that this fact was known to China, while the Chinese persevered that Ryukyu was an independent State until 1879, when Ryukyu was annexed by Japan.[22]

The status of Ryukyu is ambiguous when looked at from the perspective of modern European international law, although there appears to have been almost no serious issues concerning the status of Ryukyu at that time. Ryukyu's relations with Japan and China in the Tokugawa period were quite good.[23] There arose, however, a serious problem later in the last days of the Tokugawa government and in the beginning of the Meiji government.

2.3.3. *Four Complete Maps of Japan*

Maps might be one tool for recording a 'territory' or 'boundary', but they are no final authority. Four official maps of Japan (*Nihon sozu*) were drawn by the Tokugawa government: the Kan-ei Map (1638), the Shoho Map (1648), the Genroku Map (1702), and the Kyoho Map (1725). These maps were mainly based upon *Kuniezu* (provincial maps) of sixty-eight provinces under the Shogunate control.[24] What is at stake here is whether Ezo and Ryukyu were included in these maps.

While in the Kan-ei Map we do not find either Ezo or Ryukyu, Ezo is drawn in the Shoho Map. In this map, the Korean Peninsula is drawn as well, and the words 'Korea' and 'Sea of Busan' are inscribed. The third Genroku Map is the first to include both Ezo and Ryukyu. We also find *Wakan* (House of Japan), and *Soryoko* where *Wakan* was located. In the Kyoho Map, Ezo and *Wakan* were drawn, but Ryukyu was not included. Separate maps of isolated islands such as Ryukyu and Yakushima were drawn.

It is too hasty a conclusion to claim that based solely upon maps, Ryukyu was identified not as a part of Japan but put in the middle, between 'Self' and 'Others', and that the dual position of the Ryukyu was shown clearly in the representation of *Kuniezu* and *Nihon sozu*.[25] A reference to maps can thus only offer a limited role when defining a territory.

---

[22] Joint Research Committee of the Chinese and Japanese History (ed) *The First Report of the Joint Research of the Chinese and Japanese History* (Nihon Kokusaimondai Kenkyusho Tokyo 2010) [in Japanese and Chinese].

[23] 'In traditional East Asia, dual subordination was not so serious a problem as in modern times.' (T Ch'en 'Investiture of Liu-ch'iu Kings in the Ch'ing Period' in The Chinese World Order (n 5) 135–64 at 164).

[24] H Kawamura *Maps of Japan Drawn up by the Tokugawa Government* (Yoshikawa Kobunkan Tokyo 2009) at 48–58, 67, 85–94, 119–25, and 159–65 [in Japanese].

[25] A Kinda *A Landscape History of Japan* (Kyoto University Press Kyoto 2010) at 205.

2.3.4. Takeshima Ikken *(The Affair of Takeshima/Ulleungdo/Dagelet)*

Takeshima Ikken (the Affair of Takeshima/Ulleungdo/Dagelet) from 1693 to 1696 is an enormously important case to examine ideas of 'possession', 'border', and 'territory' in the Tokugawa period. This incident occurred at Ulleungdo, not in present-day Takeshima (Dokdo).

In 1693 the Oya family was engaged in a monopolistic fishery with the Murayama family around the Ulleungdo. It met with many Koreans engaged in fishing, and decided to bring two of these Koreans, Yong-Bok Ahn and Eo-Doon Park, back to Japan. This was at a time when the Korean government prohibited their people from travelling to Ulleungdo. The Tsushima domain repatriated two Koreans and initiated negotiations with Korea, asking them to prohibit their fishermen's passage to Ulleungdo. At the start, the negotiation between the Korean government and the Tsushima domain was a dispute about fishing rights, not an island possession dispute. By the second stage of negotiations, this became a dispute over whether there was one island belonging to Korea or Japan, or whether there were two islands, Ulleungdo and Takeshima, belonging to Korea and Japan respectively.

The final decision of the Japanese government in January 1696 was to prohibit passage of the Japanese to Ulleungdo, 'judging that it is in the best interest of Japan to maintain favourable relations with Korea'.[26]

This case is sometimes interpreted as issue of ownership over Ulleungdo or establishment of sovereignty. Although certainly there existed an idea of possession or border peculiar to Japan or to the East Asian World at that time, it would be misleading to apply modern European ideas of sovereignty or territory to the region at that time.

What kind of 'territory' idea or 'border' idea did exist in this region then? One suggestion is given by a statement issued by Masatake Abe, senior councillor, on 9 January 1696. He wrote that, 'the situation would have been different, if Japan had convincing evidence that Japan had taken that Island, or if some Japanese had lived there'.[27] Two factors are important to highlight that contribute to the claim that the territory belonged to Japan: inhabitance or some act of taking the island. Inhabitance is a perfectly clear concept. A letter of the Tottori domain addressed to the Tokugawa government dated 22 May 1693 also made mention of inhabitance.[28] But what would be an 'act of taking the Island'? Catching an abalone or a sea lion? Or does it mean an 'occupation', the same idea as in modern European international law? It is still not clear what Abe meant.

---

[26] Northeast Asia Division, Japanese Ministry of Foreign Affairs (ed) *Takeshima: 10 Issues of Takeshima* (Ministry of Foreign Affairs Tokyo 2008) at 6.

[27] T Koshi (ed) *Takeshima kiji* (News Articles of Takeshima) (1726) 9 January Genroku 9 (1696) [in Japanese].

[28] The Tottori Domain (ed) *Takeshima no kakitsuke* (Documents Concerning Takeshima) (1724) No 5 [in Japanese].

3. The Formation of Japan as a 'Modern State' According to Modern European International Law

3.1. The 'Opening' of Japan

3.1.1. *Latecomer*

From the end of the 18th century, Russian, French, and British ships came to Japan to request the 'opening' of Japan. The Tokugawa government responded to the official letter of the Dutch king, William II, in 1844 who sought a permit of foreign vessels' entry into Japanese ports, by saying that Japan would abide by ancestral law. It could not, however, maintain this position in the face of Perry's gunboat diplomacy in 1853, and it concluded the Kanagawa Treaty on 31 March 1854,[29] which was the first Western-style international treaty for Japan.[30]

Until this time, Japan had lived in her own world order, different both from the Chinese and from the European. While the Chinese world order was quite well known to Japan, Japan was a complete stranger to modern European international law at that time. During the so-called seclusion period, Japan received a lot of information about Western culture and civilization especially through the Nagasaki gate, but almost all of this was limited to the fields of science and technology. No information about international law had been officially brought to Dejima. Even in 1870, the third year of Meiji, the minister of foreign affairs was not aware of the rule on the breadth of territorial seas when Japan was advised by a Prussian minister to promulgate a neutrality declaration at the time of war between Prussia and France. As a 'latecomer' to modern European international law, Japan did her utmost to catch up with Western countries.[31]

3.1.2. *Reception of Modern European International Law*

In encounters with the Western countries which sought the opening of Japan and trade with Japan, and in the process of concluding treaties with the Western countries, the Tokugawa government realized slowly but very keenly Japan had to open up to Western culture and civilization, including modern European international law, and that a delimitation of 'territory' and 'border' of Japan, especially Ezo and Ryukyu, according to the theory of modern European international law, was urgent and pressing.

---

[29] Convention of Peace and Amity between the United States of America and the Empire of Japan (signed 31 March 1854, entered into force 21 February 1855) 111 CTS 377.

[30] See the contribution by K Akashi 'Japan–Europe' in this volume.

[31] M Yanagihara 'Japan's Engagement with and Use of International Law, 1853–1945' in H Steiger and T Marauhn (eds) *Universality and Continuity in International Law* (Eleven International Publishing The Hague 2011) 447–70.

Eventually, the Tokugawa government concluded the 1858 five treaties of commerce with the US,[32] the Netherlands,[33] Russia,[34] Great Britain,[35] and France,[36] although they were unbalanced, mainly due to a lack of knowledge regarding international law, and military inequality. The next goal of the government was clear: to obtain information about international law and to make Japan militarily stronger. Amane Nishi, who studied in Leyden from 1863 to 1865 under the guidance of Simon Vissering and who became professor at Kaiseijo, predecessor of the present University of Tokyo, offers a good case in point. Upon his return to Japan, he translated his Dutch lecture notes on international law into Japanese and submitted them to the government in August of 1866.

The new Meiji government continued efforts begun by the Tokugawa government to incorporate aspects of international law in Japan's dealings with outsiders after the Meiji Restoration in 1868. It was a basic policy of the Meiji government on treaty succession that the new government succeeded to all treaties concluded by the Tokugawa government, although the party name of Japan changed from *Taikun* (Shogun) to the *Ten-no* (emperor).

The Meiji government used every means at its disposal to incorporate international law. *Oyatoi Gaikokujin* (employed foreigners), teachers, and advisors in many fields, employed by the government, was one of them. Erasmus Peshine Smith, Karl Roesler, Henry Willard Denison, Charles William Le Gendre, Gustave Boissonade, and Alessandro Paternostro contributed in many ways to the development of the understanding of international law in Japan. Translations of international law textbooks in Japan were started by the reprint of Henry Wheaton's Chinese translation in 1865, which was done in 1864 by William Martin, the American missionary, with the help of Chinese assistants. A flood of Japanese translations followed.

The memorandum drawn up by the Japanese government during the negotiation with China concerning the abolition of the Ryukyu domain in 1879 offers a vivid contrast between the traditional Chinese customary rule and the 'contemporary public law'. The Chinese rule, the idea of China as central empire, was regarded here as null and void: an investiture given by the Chinese emperor was defined as ceremonial only and the true meaning of a tribute given to China was defined as solely that of a gift or trade. In contrast to this customary rule, a right of possessing the territory according to the contemporary public law—that is, modern European international law—comprised ruling over a region, taking the reins of government, and extracting taxes. Territorial sovereignty consisted in the fact of possession with an acquiescence to or

---

[32] Treaty of Amity and Commerce of Yedo (signed 29 July 1858, entered into force 4 July 1859) (1858) 119 CTS 253 ('Harris Treaty').
[33] Treaty of Friendship and Commerce (signed 18 August 1858) (1858) 119 CTS 313.
[34] Treaty of Friendship and Commerce (signed 19 August 1858) (1858) 119 CTS 337.
[35] Treaty of Peace, Friendship and Commerce (signed 26 August 1858) (1858) 119 CTS 401.
[36] Treaty of Peace, Amity and Commerce (signed 9 October 1858) (1858) 120 CTS 7.

dereliction of rival States.[37] A true motive of the memorandum is clear: Japan will henceforth be guided by contemporary international law, not by traditional Chinese rule. As a result, Ryukyu domain's 'territory' should be under the control of Japan.

Around ten years after the Meiji Restoration, the Japanese government was now profoundly confident that it had enough knowledge about modern European international law, and it insisted that the traditional Chinese rule should be entirely abolished in East Asia.

3.1.3. *Modern European International Law and 'Rule by Power'*

Although it might be said that modern Japan tried to accept contemporaneous European international law, tried to abide by it, and found no fault with it, there is some evidence that there were doubts as to international law's validity and utility for Japan.

A contemporary Chinese document shows that Arinori Mori, the Japanese Minister in China, in the negotiation with the Governor-General Hongzhang Li in Beijing concerning the status of Korea in 1876, said that serious matters of States were decided not by treaties but by power, because treaties dealt only with commerce. Therefore, international law was not useful. Hongzhang Li insisted that to break treaty agreements because of a threat of force was not permitted in international law.[38] This shows that the Japanese Minister had serious doubts as to the validity and usefulness of European international law, in striking contrast with Li. It is almost impossible to judge whether Mori's statement was accurate or not, because we cannot find any similar passage in the Japanese document recording the interview, but it does raise questions as to the total acceptance of international law by the Japanese at that time.[39]

It is, however, completely true that some Japanese regarded European international law as an imperative tool for use by the strong, otherwise it was useless. Takayoshi Kido, one of the three leaders of the Meiji Restoration, wrote in a diary entry dated 8 November 1868 that international law was a tool that ought not be permitted for the weak.[40] Another important person is Yukichi Fukuzawa, one of the most influential Enlightenment thinkers in the Meiji Period. He wrote in 1878 that a hundred volumes of international law textbooks were inferior to a couple of cannons, and a couple of peace treaties were inferior to a box of ammunition.[41]

---

[37] Gaimusho (ed) *Nihon gaiko monjo* (Documents on Japanese Foreign Policy) (Nihon Kokusairengo Kyokai Tokyo 1948) vol 12, at 191–200 [in Japanese].

[38] RL Wu (ed) *Complete Works of Hongzhang Li* (Wenhaichubanshe Taipei 1962) vol 5, at 106–7 [in Chinese].

[39] Gaimusho (ed) *Nihon gaiko monjo* (Documents on Japanese Foreign Policy) (Nihon Kokusairengo Kyokai Tokyo 1940) vol 9, at 170–80 [in Japanese].

[40] C Tsumaki (ed) *Diary of Takayoshi Kido* (Nihon Shiseki Kyokai Tokyo 1932) vol 1, at 138 [in Japanese].

[41] Keio Gijuku (ed) *Complete Works of Yukichi Fukuzawa* (Iwanami Shoten Tokyo 1959) vol 4, at 637 [in Japanese].

Officially, the Meiji government abided by international law as was shown in the declarations in the Sino-Japanese War in 1894 and the Russo-Japanese War in 1904. We should, however, remember that even in the latter half of the 19th century, international law did not enjoy universal acclaim among all Japanese politicians and scholars.

3.2. State Territory of Japan

3.2.1. *Border Delimitation*

When the British admiral James Stirling came to Nagasaki to request trade with Japan and asked the Magistrate of Nagasaki about the boundary of Japan in 1854, the Magistrate told him that Ryukyu was a vassal country of Japan, while Tsushima was located within the 'territory' of Japan.[42] This shows that Japan was asked to introduce the Western idea of 'territory' and to delimit her 'border' according to the concept of European international law in encounters with Western countries.

A truly remarkable document is found in the preparation materials of the 1871 Iwakura Mission to the US and European countries. Here we see Saghalien, Takeshima (Ulleungdo), and uninhabited islands as border delimitation issues, while Korea and Ryukyu were considered not as border delimitation but as diplomatic issues.[43] A distinction between border delimitation issues and diplomatic issues is highly political, especially when the matter regarding Ryukyu was classified not as a border issue but as a diplomatic one, which might lead to the conclusion that Ryukyu was considered not as Japanese territory but as a foreign country.

3.2.2. *Hokkaido and Okinawa*

The most important areas possibly to be defined as territory of modern Japan were Saghalien, Ezo, and Ryukyu. Article 2 of the 1855 Russo-Japanese Amity Treaty provides that a boundary between Russia and Japan be established between Etoropu Island and Urup Island.[44] This is the first boundary delimitation for Japan drawn by a treaty. The status of Saghalien is not clear at all in this treaty. It contains no direct article concerning Ezo, but it is a reasonable conclusion that Ezo was recognized as territory of Japan by international law because a frontier was set up between Etoropu Island and Urup Island. Two months later the Tokugawa government established the

---

[42] K Yanai (ed) *Tsukoichiran zokushu* (Synopsis of Foreign Relations: Supplementary Collections) (Seibundo Shuppan Osaka 1970) vol 3, at 99 [in Japanese]. The Magistrate also replied that a boundary issue with Korea was not among his duties.

[43] J Fujii (ed) *Documents Related to Iwakura Tomomi* (Nihon Shiseki Kyokai Tokyo 1934) vol 7, at 306–9 [in Japanese].

[44] Treaty of Commerce, Navigation and Delimitation between Japan and Russia (signed 7 February 1855) (1855) 112 CTS 467.

Magistrate of Hakodate, and the whole area of Ezo came under the direct control of the government.

The Meiji government took further necessary measures for Ezo. The Hakodate Court was established in 1868, but the most decisive step was to rename Ezo as Hokkai-do next year. This meant that Hokkai-do was now included in the Japanese traditional 'Goki-shichi-do'. In other words, Hokkai-do became territory of Japan in the accepted meaning, and Ezo as *Iiki* now disappeared. It should, however, not be forgotten that the Ainu people were considered to be a different race until the Assimilation Statute in 1899.

The status of Ryukyu in the Tokugawa Period was ambiguous. In the last days of the Period—that is, in the 1840s and the 1850s when Western countries such as France and United Kingdom came to Ryukyu to request friendship and trade— the Tokugawa government faced many difficulties in how to handle the issue. A basic policy of the government, which was a secession of the Ryukyu Kingdom from Japan, was decided with a pertinent and practical suggestion of the Satsuma domain. Hidetaka Godai, a Confucian scholar in Satsuma, wrote in a suggestion booklet *Secret Policy for Ryukyu* (1844) that even if Ryukyu were a fief of the Satsuma domain, it could not be considered to be a territory of Japan because it was a tributary country of China, and that Ryukyu had vassal country status within Japan. Following the idea of regarding Ryukyu as *Ikoku*, readily abandoned by Japan, the Tokugawa government demonstrated no commitment to the conclusion of amity treaties between the Ryukyu Kingdom and the US (1854),[45] France (1855),[46] and the Netherlands (1859).[47]

At the beginning of the Meiji period, the government assumed an ambivalent and equivocal attitude toward Ryukyu as to whether it should be considered as 'dual subordination' or as being a part of Japan. The 1871 Sino-Japanese Amity Treaty[48] is the first 'international' treaty between two countries. In appearance, the treaty was based upon equality between China and Japan and was concluded in a Western style treaty, especially when we look at article 1, which provides that *Hodo* (territories)[49] belong to

---

[45] Convention between the Lew Chew Islands and the US (signed 11 July 1854) (1854) 112 CTS 77.

[46] 'Convention entre la France et les Iles Liou-Tchou' in Ministère des Affaires Étrangères (ed) *Recueil des traités et conventions entre le Japon et les puissances étrangères 1854–1925* (Ministère des Affaires Étrangères Tokio 1934) vol 3, 654 ff.

[47] 'Traktaat tusschen Nederlanden en Lioe-Kioe' in ibid 658 ff.

[48] Treaty of Commerce and Navigation (signed 13 September 1871, entered into force 30 April 1873) 144 CTS 139.

[49] The meaning of *Hodo* did elicit afterwards considerable discussion between the two countries. It is doubtless that the Japanese representatives in charge of the treaty negotiation interpreted *Hodo* as territory in the meaning of European international law. Some researchers say that the Chinese representatives might have intentionally told the Japanese about a different meaning of *Hodo* in the negotiation process. Hongzhang Li made clear the meaning of *Hodo* in a Chinese interpretation to Arinori Mori in the 1876 negotiation; *Ho* means vassal countries such as Korea and *Do* means region under the direct control of China, or homeland. Cf Complete Works of Hongzhang Li (n 38) 107 [in Chinese].

the two countries respectively. We cannot, however, find any explicit article concerning Ryukyu in this treaty.

Kaoru Inoue, Vice-Minister of the Finance Ministry, wrote in his representation addressed to *Sei-in* (the Supreme Machinery of a State) in May 1872 that the same system used in Japan should be applied to Ryukyu, while it was written in the reply of *Sa-in* (Advisory Organ of Legislature) in June of that year that the Ryukyu Kingdom had been belonging both to Japan and China.

Just after that the Meiji government, however, unanimously espoused the policy of denying dual subordination. The imperial edict was promulgated on 16 October 1872 to appoint the king of Ryukyu as *Daimyo* of the Ryukyu domain, which meant an official abolition of the Ryukyu Kingdom. That also meant that the status as vassal country of the Satsuma domain was incontestably denied. The government gave an order to Ryukyu to sever relations with China in July 1876. Along the same lines with other domains where the domain (*han*) system was abolished and instead prefectures were established in August 1871, the Ryukyu domain was abolished and transformed into the Ryukyu Prefecture in March 1879, and the king of Ryukyu, or *Daimyo* of the Ryukyu domain, was obliged to move to Tokyo. This denotes the end of the Ryukyu Kingdom as a separate entity. A chain of measures taken by the government from 1872 to 1879 are called Ryukyu *Shobun* (Disposition).

A fiery academic discussion arose as to the *Shobun* especially in the 1950s and early in the 1960s. One interpretation is to regard it as 'invasive unification' or forcible annexation, while 'racial or national unification' is another.[50] The official view of the Meiji government was clear. Ryukyu had not been a country of subordination, or half-sovereign country, but had been a domain region of Japan; in other words, a territory of Japan from the Tokugawa period.[51] Ryukyu had certainly sent envoys to the Qing Dynasty to offer gifts, but had not paid any tax, while Ryukyu had been a fief of Satsuma. Here tax is considered as playing an overwhelmingly important role in deciding to which country Ryukyu had belonged. This is definitely not a traditional Chinese rule, but an idea from European international law.

The Meiji government also asserted that China admitted that Ryukyu did not belong to China during the consultation process about despatching Japanese troops to Taiwan in 1874. China insisted, however, on making an official protest against the annexation of Ryukyu conducted by Japan in March 1879. China refused to accept a proposal, in which Japan offered to cede two islands, Miyako Islands and Yaeyama Islands, to China, taking into consideration an arbitration of the former US President, Ulysses S Grant. This dispute continued unresolved until China did, in fact, abandon her claim during the Sino-Japanese War in 1895.

---

[50] K Tomiyama (ed) *World of the History of Ryukyu and Okinawa* (Yoshikawa Kobunkan Tokyo 2003) at 48–67 [in Japanese].

[51] M Matsuda 'Ryukyu Shobun (1879)' in F Shimomura (ed) *Documents Collection of the Meiji Culture 4: Diplomacy* (Kazama Shobo Tokyo 1962) 201–4 at 203 [in Japanese].

3.2.3. *Terra nullius and Inherent Territory*

This consultation between China and Japan from September to October 1874 also offers a remarkable discussion about *terra nullius*. Toshimichi Okubo, Extraordinary Minister of Japan, insisted that effective possession or control was essential for a territory and that there existed no effective control of any country in Taiwan. Thus, he considered Taiwan to be *terra nullius* and not as *Hanto* (territory) of China. [52]

The *Zongli Yamen* (ministry in charge of relations with foreign countries) of China asserted on the other hand that international law has been quite recently invented in Western countries, but that there was no mention there of China, and therefore it was useless to talk about international law in cases concerning Taiwan and China. According to this, international law, which had originated in Europe, was not applicable to China. China had her own rule and allowed the indigenous people in Taiwan to have their customs. China would conquer the people who resisted her, while she would accept the people who were obedient to her.[53] China thereby insisted that Taiwan belonged to her according to her traditional rule.

Here again, just as with the memorandum drawn up by the Japanese government in 1879, we can find a sharp contrast between the concept of modern European international law and the traditional Chinese world order. The point here is that Japan clearly asserted that Taiwan was *terra nullius,* and that an occupation of *terra nullius* could be carried out by Japan. No occupation was in fact attempted by the Japanese government, because its main target at that time was not Taiwan, but Ryukyu. According to the Japanese, Ryukyu was not *terra nullius*, but traditional Japanese territory, as has already been explained.

The theory of occupation of *terra nullius* was very widely applied by the Japanese government to neighbouring islands such as Ogasawara Islands (Bonin Islands) (1876), Iwo Island (1891), Senkaku Island (Diaoyutai) (1895), Minamitori Island (Marcus Island) (1898), Okidaito Island (1900), Nakanotori Island (1908),[54] and Okinotori Islands (Douglas Reef) (1931). While some problems existed in the case of Minamitori Island, there was no serious dispute with neighbouring countries at all concerning other islands.

Takeshima is not a case of occupation according to the official opinion of the current Japanese government. The Meiji government stipulated through a cabinet decision dated 28 January 1905 that Takeshima belonged to Japan and came under the jurisdiction of the Okinoshima branch of Shimane Prefectural government because the islands had been under continuous possession (*Senryo*) of Japan. This cabinet decision is considered to be a reaffirmation of Japan's intention to claim sovereignty over Takeshima. Japan insists that Takeshima is clearly an inherent territory of Japan

---

[52] Gaimusho (ed) *Nihon gaiko monjo* (Documents on Japanese Foreign Policy) (Nihon Kokusai Kyokai Tokyo 1939) vol 7, at 245 [in Japanese].

[53] ibid 221 and 230.

[54] The non–existence of Nakanotori Island was confirmed later.

(*wagakuni koyu no ryodo*), in the light of historical facts and based upon international law, similar to the Northern territories (Kuril Islands).[55]

In the confidential handbooks compiled from precedents in Japan and other countries, edited by the Treaty Division, Ministry of Foreign Affairs in October 1932 for the purpose of a handbook for the Foreign Ministry staff, only six precedents were taken up as precedents of island occupations, excluding Okinotori Islands and Takeshima.[56] Takeshima might have not been considered as precedent of *terra nullius* occupation by the Japanese Ministry of Foreign Affairs.

3.3. Treaty Revision

3.3.1. *Iwakura Mission*

It was a basic policy of the Meiji government on treaty succession that the new government succeeded to all treaties concluded by the Tokugawa government. In February 1869 (the second year of Meiji), however, the government notified its intention to revise treaties and sent an Iwakura mission to the United States and European countries to conduct negotiations for treaty revision. The result of this mission was not good. The Meiji government realized that treaty revision had costs as well as benefits, and that it was in the long-term interests of Japan to mould the nation along the lines of the West, that is, to modernize and civilize (*Bunmei Kaika*), and to increase her wealth and strengthen her military (*Fukoku Kyohei*).

3.3.2. *Treaties Concluded by the Ryukyu Kingdom*

What was the policy of the Meiji government on the amity treaties which the Ryukyu Kingdom had concluded with the US, France, and the Netherlands in the 1850s? Did the Meiji government succeed to all of them as with the unequal treaties concluded by the Tokugawa government? Or did the government deny them as null and void?

That was one of the critical topics under discussion between China and Japan in 1879. China asserted that the fact the Ryukyu Kingdom had concluded treaties with foreign countries in the 1850s showed that the Ryukyu Kingdom was an independent country.[57] The Japanese government replied that foreign countries which concluded treaties with Ryukyu did not know that Ryukyu did not have any power to conclude treaties. It continued to say that the then Tokugawa government governed in a purely feudal system and allowed local *Daimyos* to carry out services which could not have been allowed to them in a contemporary centralized system.

The Meiji government did not, however, adopt a policy of denying all treaties concluded by Ryukyu, but it promised foreign parties that it would implement all those

---

[55] *Takeshima* (n 26) 2.

[56] Gaimusho Joyakukyoku (ed) *Collections of International Law Precedents 2: Occupation of Islands* (Gaimusho Tokyo 1933) at 1–52 [in Japanese].

[57] *Nihon gaiko monjo* (n 37) 186–7.

treaties. It held the opinion that those treaties did not impose an enormous burden on Japan, but at the same time, they were as unequal as some treaties concluded by the Tokugawa government, to which the Meiji government agreed to succeed.[58] Taneomi Soejima, Foreign Minister, responded to the letter of Charles E de Long, US Minister at Tokyo, in a letter dated 5 November 1872, that the Ryukyu Islands had been dependencies of Japan for hundreds of years, and that to them the title of *Han* had been recently given and that the provisions of a compact between Ryukyu and the US would be observed by the government because Ryukyu was an integral portion of Japan.[59]

This idea of the Meiji government appears, however, to be not necessarily consistent with the basic policy of treaty revision. Because many of the treaties concluded by the Tokugawa government were unequal and intolerably burdensome for Japan, the Meiji government tried to revise them. One far more theoretically important issue is whether the Meiji government succeeded to treaties concluded by Ryukyu. It was impossible to succeed to them because according to the official idea of the Meiji government, Ryukyu had no official power to conclude treaties with foreign countries and therefore those treaties should be considered as null and void. These treaties cannot be theoretically put in the same category with those concluded by the Tokugawa government. How then can we satisfactorily explain that the Meiji government promised to implement those treaties?

One possible answer might be a ratification by the Meiji government. Because the Tokugawa government allowed local *Daimyos* to perform acts which could not have been allowed in a contemporary centralized system, the Meiji government decided to accept the content of the treaties and ratified them.[60]

4. Pseudo-Equality and New Order in East Asia

4.1. Pseudo-equality

4.1.1. *Japan as Great Power*

Japan seemed to have achieved a completely equal status as 'civilized nation' in the international community with Western countries early in the 20th century, as Lorimer's 'admirable' guess in 1883, when he said that 'should the Japanese ... continue their

---

[58] ibid 192–3.   [59] *Recueil des traités et conventions* (n 46) 662–3.

[60] According to a written statement of the Japanese Prime Minister (House of Representatives, Reply No. 193 dated 8 December 2006), the current Japanese government's position is that these are not treaties concluded officially by the Japanese government.

present rate of progress for another twenty years, the question whether they are not entitled to plenary political recognition may have to be determined.'[61]

An abolition of consular jurisdiction was finally achieved in 1899, and tariff autonomy was given to Japan in 1911. A conclusion of the Anglo-Japanese Alliance, the first equal alliance with the Great Power, was reached in 1902. Japan's predominant status was visible in some international conferences: Niichiro Matsunami served as vice president both in the 1899 London Conference and the 1900 Paris Conference of the Comité Maritime International, and the rights and interests of Japan in Korea were admitted by Western countries in the 1907 Hague Convention on the occasion of the secret messengers sent by the Korean emperor. Japan became an original permanent member of the League of Nations Council in 1920, and membership lasted until 1933, the year of her withdrawal from the League of Nations.

Mineichiro Adachi, judge of the Permanent Court of Justice (1930–34, president 1931–33) wrote in a 1912 article that when he was a high-school student in the late 1880s, Japan was considered as a country not included in the application of international law, but that now Japan occupied a respectable position in the world. He pointed out that whether or not Japan was a 'strong country' or 'great power', who would live by the rules of international law, was a major issue for the world, exactly the reverse situation from the 1880s.[62] Here we can find not only national pride or self-respect for Japan as a great power but also the greatest concern for Japan's important role in the international community.

4.1.2. 'Universality' and 'Fairness' of International Law: International Adjudication

Suspicions about the universality and fairness of international law arose among the Japanese people almost at the same time as Japan became aware that she was regarded as equal to the West.

One remarkable example is Japan's negative stance on international adjudication.[63] A noteworthy discussion was made in the draft process of the Permanent Court of International Justice (PCIJ). In the PCIJ Advisory Committee of Jurists

---

[61] J Lorimer *The Institutes of the Jural Relations of Separate Political Communities* (Blackwood Edinburgh 1883) vol 1, at 102–3. Lassa Oppenheim wrote in his famous 1905 textbook that only Japan in Asia was a full member of the Family of Nations. China, Korea, Thailand, and Tibet were considered to be partial members of the Family of Nations. L Oppenheim *International Law: A Treatise* (Longmans, Green & Co London 1905) vol 1, at 31.

[62] M Adachi 'Research on International Law' (1912) 11 Kokusaiho Gaiko Zasshi 209–15 [in Japanese].

[63] Cf K Taijudo 'Some Reflections on Japan's Practice of International Law during a Dozen Eventful Decades' (1975) 69 Proceedings of the 69th Annual Meeting of the American Society of International Law 64–9 at 68; H Owada 'Japan, International Law and the International Community' in N Ando (ed) *Japan and International Law: Past, Present and Future* (Kluwer Law International The Hague 1999) 347–78 at 356.

from June to July in 1920, two issues were critically discussed: first, the composition of the court, that is, issues regarding the nationality of the judges and second the jurisdiction of the court. Article 14(2) of the League of Nations Covenant ('The Court shall be competent to hear and determine any dispute of an international character which the parties thereto submit to it') was the main topic of discussion. In the final draft of the committee dated 24 July 1920, compulsory jurisdiction, that is, a competence of one party to institute proceedings without any consent of the other party, was included. Mineichiro Adachi was the only person who made a reservation to it under instructions from the Japanese government.

In the confidential report on PCIJ drawn up by the Ministry of Foreign Affairs on 1 September 1920 it was written that the 1905 Award of the Permanent Court of Arbitration (PCA) in the Yokohama House Tax Case was unfavourable to Japan. It emphasized that judges of PCA were mainly Western people and PCA did not admit Japan's claim because Japan had a different race and state of affairs from Western countries.[64]

Adachi wrote in a 1930 article that the PCIJ was necessary in the international society, even for Japan, but that in Japan there had been strong sense of disappointment in and deep suspicion of international adjudication at that time; in other words, there was a profound distrust of international law and Western lawyers. As late as 1930, it was his opinion that Japan should not accept the optional clause immediately. He insisted that Japan occupied a special position before the World Court.[65] It was in 1958 that Japan declared the acceptance of the optional clause of the International Court of Justice.

4.2. 'New Order' in East Asia

A basic policy of the Meiji government was to remake Japan as a civilized nation along the lines of the Western standard, or *Datsu-a Nyu-o* ('Quit Asia and Join Europe' or 'Out of Asia and Into Europe'). But Japan also tried to obtain a predominant status

---

[64] Gaimusho Jyoyakukyoku Daisanka 'Reports Relating to the Permanent Court of International Justice (Confidential) (1 September 1920)' Gaimusho Kiroku 2.4.2.3-1 [JACAR Ref. B06150567500] [in Japanese].

[65] It was Adachi's idea that a predominance of great powers including Japan was more important than the perfect equality of States. In other words, to equalize Japan with Western countries was the most serious issue for Japan, and no absolute insistence of independence of smaller countries could be allowed. M Adachi 'Diplomacy after the World War and Two Important Incidents' (1930) 89/532 Ginkotsushin-roku 16–23 at 21 [in Japanese]; cf M Adachi 'Address of Ambassador Adachi dated 16 May 1930' in *Private Papers of Mineichiro Adachi* (Modern Japanese Political History Materials Room, National Diet Library Tokyo 1998) vol 1084 at 19–20 [in Japanese].

amongst Asian, especially East Asian countries, in sharp contrast to the equal or pseudo-equal relations with Western countries. Japan concluded unequal treaties with Asian countries such as Korea in 1876,[66] and Thailand in 1898,[67] while the 1871 Sino-Japanese amity treaty was equal at least superficially. But gradually Japan tried to obtain various political and economic rights and interests from China, as was shown by the 21 Demands presented to China in 1915.[68]

Japan started, however, to insist on the possibility of a new order in East Asia from the late 1930s onwards. This may be referred to as 'quit European international law and join new international order in East Asia or Asia as a whole'. *Dai Toa Kyoei Ken* (a Greater East Asian Co-prosperity Sphere) declared on 26 July 1940, a new version of *Toa Shin Chitsujo* (New Order in East Asia) announced on 3 November 1938, was exactly this. However, two different ideas within the Japanese government should be distinguished at the initial stage: the idea of the Japanese military, and that of the Japanese Ministry of Foreign Affairs. The first idea is *Hakko-ichiu* (the whole world under one roof), which means in this case that the whole world is really one world under the reign of the Japanese emperor. Asia should be considered as a remote region separate from Europe and America, and in Asia, Japan should be a leading country in this new order. The second idea, of the Japanese Ministry of Foreign Affairs, was based upon respect for the sovereignty of and good relationships with all countries in the sphere.

It was a 'co-prosperity sphere', not a 'territory' in the traditional European international law sense that Japan asserted as *Dai Toa Kyoei Ken*. The idea had been greatly influenced by the *Lebensraum* theory in Germany. It was, however, claimed that it had its own purpose: decolonization of Asian nations, in other words, 'liberating Asia from the white domination', which can be deemed equally applicable to two different ideas of the military and the Japanese Ministry of Foreign Affairs.

These two different ideas competed severely within the Japanese government, but gradually the idea of the military gained the upper hand, especially after the outbreak of the war with the United States in 1941. It is still now disputable whether a real intent

[66] Treaty of Peace and Friendship of Kanghwa (Ganghwa) between Korea and Japan (signed 28 February 1876) in C de Martens and F de Cussy (eds) *Recueil manuel et pratique de traités et conventions sur lesquels sont établis les relations et les rapports existant aujourd'hui entre les divers états souverains du globe, depuis l'année 1760 jusqu'à l'époque actuelle* (Brockhaus Leipzig 1887) series II, vol II, 540–4.
[67] Convention concerning the Extension of the Territory of Hong Kong between China and Great Britain (signed 9 June 1898, entered into force 6 August 1898) in F Stoerk (ed) *Martens Nouveau recueil général de traités et autres actes relatifs aux rapports de droit international* (1895–1908) series II, vol 32, 89–90.
[68] Chinese National Welfare Society in America (ed) *The Shantung Question: A Statement of China's Claim Together with Important Documents Submitted to the Peace Conference in Paris* (Chinese National Welfare Society in America San Francisco 1919) at 33–6.

of the idea of co-prosperity was a new type of Asian colonization mapped out ingeniously by Japan.[69]

5. Conclusion

As quoted earlier, the Meiji government stated in the 1879 Memorandum that the then Tokugawa government governed in a purely feudal system and allowed local *Daimyos* to carry out services which could not have been allowed to them in a contemporary centralized system. This appears to show that the new government was tremendously self-confident, ruling over the country under modern European law and under modern European international law, and that there was not much continuity with the old order.

It is, however, too precipitate to conclude that the Tokugawa government, even in the closing days of the Shogunate system, was ignorant of European international law and paid no regard to it, preferring instead to remain secluded, and that the Meiji government established the initial diplomatic relations with the outer world and defined 'territory' and 'border' on the basis of European international law. The Tokugawa government, rather, had diplomatic or commercial relations both with the Netherlands and with East Asian 'countries' throughout its entire period, even though ideas of 'territory' and 'border' were not the same as European ones. Particularly after Russian, French, British, and American people started to come to Japan toward the end of the 18th century, the government was forced to come face-to-face not only with issues of diplomatic and commercial relations with outsiders, but also with Japan's 'territory' and 'border' issues in the meaning of modern European international law. Direct control of Ezo, frontier delimitation issues with Russia, and the status of the Ryukyu Kingdom are good and notable examples.

The efforts of the government were, however, not sufficient for Japan to be fully integrated into the Western States system. The Meiji government was phenomenally successful in accepting modern European international law, and Japan seemed to have achieved a totally equal status as a 'civilized nation' in the international community with Western countries early in the 20th century. Almost at the same time, however, suspicions about the universality and fairness of modern European international law emerged among the Japanese people.

---

[69] Gaimusho Hyakunenshi Hensaniinkai (ed) *Hundred Years of the Ministry of Foreign Affairs* (Hara Shobo Tokyo 1969) vol 2, at 630–1 and 637–8 [in Japanese].

Although modern Japan continued to play a role as a civilized nation, not as a barbarous people, for the whole period of 1853–1945 she could not keep up with the dramatic changes made in international law, especially concerning the outlawing of war or the prohibition of aggressive war beginning in the late 1920s. Japan invented, instead of a traditional European international law, an idea of the new order applicable to the Greater East Asian Sphere in the late 1930s, whose real meaning is still now in dispute.

Recommended Reading

Batten, Bruce *Nihon no 'kyokai': Zenkindai no kokka, minzoku, bunka* (Japan's 'Boundaries': State, Ethnicity, and Culture in Pre-modern Times) (Aoki Shoten Tokyo 2000).

Fairbank, John K (ed) *The Chinese World Order: Traditional China's Foreign Relations* (Harvard University Press Cambridge 1968).

Gaimusho Hyakunenshi Hensaniinkai (Editorial Committee of Hundred Years of MOFA) (ed) *Gaimusho no hyakunen* (Hundred Years of MOFA) (2 vols Hara Shobo Tokyo 1969).

Inobe, Shigeo *Ishin zenshi no kenkyu* (Research on the History before the Restoration) (2nd edn Chubunkan Shoten Tokyo 1942).

Ishii, Takashi *Nihon kaikoku shi* (History of the Opening of Japan) (Yoshikawa Kobunkan Tokyo 1972).

Ito, Fujio 'One Hundred Years of International Law Studies in Japan' (1969) 13 Japanese Annual of International Law 19–34.

Kokusaiho Jirei Kenkyukai (Research Committee of International Law Precedents) *Nihonno kokusaiho jirei kenkyu (3): Ryodo* (Research on International Law Precedents in Japan 3: Territory) (Keio Tsushin Tokyo 1990).

Lee, Keun-Gwan 'The "Reception" of European International Law in China, Japan and Korea: A Comparative and Critical Perspective' in Heinhard Steiger and Thilo Marauhn (eds) *Universality and Continuity in International Law* (Eleven International Publishing The Hague 2011) 419–46.

Liu, Lydia H *The Clash of Empires: The Invention of China in Modern World Making* (Harvard University Press Cambridge 2004).

Nishizato, Kiko *Shinmatsu chusonichi kankeishi no kenkyu* (A Study of Relations between China, Ryukyu and Japan in Late Qing Period) (Kyotodaigaku Gakujutsu Shuppankai Kyoto 2005).

Onuma, Yasuaki 'Japanese International Law in the Prewar Period' (1986) 29 Japanese Annual of International Law 23–47.

Owada, Hisashi 'Japan, International Law and the International Community' in Nisuke Ando (ed) *Japan and International Law: Past, Present and Future* (Kluwer Law International The Hague 1999) 347–78.

Svarverud, Rune *International Law as World Order in Late Imperial China: Translation, Reception and Discourse, 1847–1911* (Brill Leiden 2007).

Taijudo, Kanae 'Some Reflections on Japan's Practice of International Law during a Dozen Eventful Decades' (1975) 69 Proceedings of the 69th Annual Meeting of the American Society of International Law 64–9.

Toby, Ronald P *State and Diplomacy in Early Modern Japan: Asia in the Development of the Tokugawa Bakufu* (Stanford University Press Stanford 1991).

Toby, Ronald *Nihon no rekisi daikyukan sakoku toiu gaiko* (History of Japan: Volume 9, Diplomacy of Sakoku (Seclusion)) (Shogakkan Tokyo 2008).

Watanabe, Hiroshi *Nihon seijishisoshi: Junanaseiki kara jukyuseiki* (History of Japanese Political Thoughts: From the 17th to the 19th Centuries) (Tokyodaigaku Shuppankai Tokyo 2010).

Yamamuro, Shinichi *Shisokadai toshiteno Ajia* (Asia as an Ideological Topic) (Iwanami Shoten Tokyo 2001).

Yanagihara, Masaharu 'The Idea of Non-discriminating War and Japan' in Michael Stolleis and Masaharu Yanagihara (eds) *East Asian and European Perspectives on International Law* (Nomos Baden-Baden 2004) 179–201.

Yanagihara, Masaharu 'Japan's Engagement with and Use of International Law, 1853–1945' in Heinhard Steiger and Thilo Marauhn (eds) *Universality and Continuity in International Law* (Eleven International Publishing The Hague 2011) 447–70.

CHAPTER 21

INDIA

BIMAL N PATEL

1. INTRODUCTION

THIS chapter examines the history of international law in India between 1500 and 1945 and identifies those principles and practices which have disappeared after the independence of India or have become part of the regional system in one or another way. In other words, this historical analysis is confined to the colonization period when India[1] was under the rule of the European powers. One gets struck with the reality of today's prevailing law in India, as the English law enjoys a persuasive authority as an embodiment of written reason, and impresses its own character on a formally independent jurisprudence. The English law has also left lasting impressions on international law as practised by India after the independence. Between 1500 and 1945, international law in India grew up by degrees, completely marked by the absence of any attempt at codifying it, nourished,

[1] By 'India', I mean British India together with any territories of any native prince or chief under the suzerainty of Her Majesty, the Queen of Great Britain. Under the Interpretation Act of 1889, India ceased to be a cultural or a mere geographic expression and acquired a clearly defined political meaning. The exact number of princely States differs from record to record. For example, Sir Charles Tupper counted 629 feudatory States in 1886, *The Imperial Gazetteer* listed 693 in 1907, and Edward Haynes speaks of 'the 718 Princely States in India (c 1912)'. By 1920, the British authorities in Delhi could only count 587; and ten years later the Butler Commission had pared the number down to 562. In the first year of independence, however, the new national government of India recorded a final figure of 584 States, including those that had acceded to Pakistan. <http://princelystatesofindia.com/> (2 April 2012).

however, by the writings and thoughts of scholars, and the practice of the princely States.[2]

What salient features or developments bearing the most important influence on international law as evolved and practised in India can be identified? First, there was a systematic collapse of international law traditions which were observed as a matter of intercourse between princely States with the advent and penetration of British (and to a limited extent French, Dutch, and Portuguese) rule at all levels. In fact, one can observe that between 1600 and 1858, there were hardly any significant achievements noticed except for the preparation of some codes and digests. Since Hindu and Islamic laws have deeply penetrated into the political-socio-legal system of India, those codes and digests which were found to be not in consonance with the original Hindu or Islamic laws disappeared or were replaced during the colonization period. Secondly, much like in the ancient times, princely States[3] were convinced that interactions among them were necessary because in isolation they could not make progress or effectively counter the British influence. Various religious festivals and ceremonies, such as Aswamedha, the Rajasuya, the Vajapeya, the Punarabhisheka, and the Aindra Mahabhiseka sacrifices, which were practised in ancient times now were practised in different versions, and these ceremonies significantly enabled the interactions among the princely States and provided avenues for greater interactions between the executive authorities as well as normal people. These mechanisms enabled the princes and officials of princely States to discuss common problems and also were used to reach settlement on differences between them. With the independence of India, these practices have largely disappeared and it remains interesting to see what the means of communication between these princely States in the post-independence Indian history have become, and whether these traditions have had any contributory effect on the relations between the Union of India[4] and these

---

[2] The definition and meaning of the notion of 'princely State' and 'native State' have been subject to differences of opinion. For example, Sir William described a native State as 'a political community, occupying a territory in India of defined boundaries, and subject to a common and responsible ruler who has actually enjoyed and exercised, as belonging to him in his own right duly recognized by the supreme authority of the British Government, any of the functions and attributes of internal sovereignty. The indivisibility of sovereignty does not belong to the Indian system of sovereign states,…but the sovereignty of Native states is shared between the British Government and the Chiefs in varying degrees.' Sir William Lee-Warner *Native States of India* (MacMillan & Co London 1910).

[3] In 1928–29, 235 of 562 Indian principalities came under the category of States proper while 327 were grouped together under the heading of 'estates, Jaghirs and others'. Thus, it is impossible to identify the norms and rules of international law proclaimed and adopted by these States individually. M Ramaswamy 'The Indian States in the Indian Federation—A Juristic View' (1940) 3 The University of Toronto Law Journal 301–22 at 302.

[4] Before the Islamic conquest, India never became a really centralized political entity but was characterized by widespread decentralization. Inter-state relations in the pre-Islamic period resulted in clear-cut rules of warfare of a high humanitarian standard, of neutrality, and permanent or semi-permanent diplomatic relations. These rules were expressed in treaty law as well as in customary law embodied in religious charters.

princely States. Third, as far as self-determination, plebiscite, and the status of Indian princely States were concerned, these States prior to acceding to India (upon India receiving independence) did not seek the popular mandate of the people, as the princes often refused to recognize their people. As Chacko says, the implied principle in all these refusals apparently was that the sovereigns of the Indian State alone had the power to exercise the legal rights of accession to, or secession from, a political union.[5] Modern international law does not recognize such a right by the individual units of any nation to secede from, or accede to another, nation-state. Fourth, the grounds on which paramountcy of the British Empire rested being natural factors of geography, politics, economics, and history, social, religious, and cultural congruity, the method of automatic succession that has taken place may be called natural secession in international law. As the instrument of accession binds entities with a certain measure of sovereign powers, these should be construed as instruments of international law. Insofar as those instruments can function only on the sub-continent of India, they have only a regional value, and hence may be called 'regional international law'. Fifth, a close reading of the ancient Indian literature like the Srutis, the Dharmashastras and the Arthsastras show clear evidence of means and methods of international law as practised by the princely States. These relations were regulated by certain customs and practices. The history of foreign relations between princely States reveals the classical principles of international law which prevail in the modern world, namely, the rights of existence of self-preservation, of equality, of independence to territorial supremacy, of holding and requiring territory, of intercourse, and of good name and reputation. Some of the rights associated with the independence of a State were the power to exclusive control of its own domestic affairs, the power to admit or expel aliens, privileges, and immunities of diplomatic envoys in other States, and exclusive jurisdiction over crimes committed within its territory. The duties were the duty not to resort to war, to fulfil treaty obligations in good faith, the duty of non-intervention, the duty not to perform acts of sovereignty on the territory of another State, the duty not to allow in its territory preparations which are prejudicial to the security of another State, the duty not to intervene in the affairs of another State, and the duty not to foment civil strife in another States' territory. These rights and obligations exercised and fulfilled by the princely States originate from the religious scriptures of India, and thus one could see that despite the European influence and the need for princely States to collectively defend their independence (or obtain one), these legal principles and norms were practised and nourished by them.[6] The current international law which is being practised by India as an independent nation can be

---

[5] CJ Chacko 'India's Contribution to the Field of International Law Concepts' (1958) 93 Recueil des cours 117–222 at 196.

[6] J Briggs (*Transactions of the Royal Asiatic Society of Great Britain and Ireland*) underlines the importance of the correspondence as a historical document and praises the high qualities of the Marathas, particularly the religious tolerance of the Hindus.

considered to be a product of changes that took place in the society as well as principles and practices, which are slowly disappearing from the states institutions and life, and acquiring new meanings and shapes and influencing the new international law. In fact, the independent India has greatly benefited from the practices of princely States, which were themselves fully fledged States meeting the fundamental criteria of a State as provided in the Montevideo Convention.[7] By studying the practices of these princely States,[8] one is better equipped to understand the emergence of international law principles. It is remarkable that long before Hugo Grotius, the so-called father of modern international law, Ashoka the Great, tried to give by his actions a concrete shape to those ideals and principles, whose defence and vindication have become the first concern of international law in current international affairs.[9]

2. Principles of International Law Observed by the Princely States

The princely States strictly observed that each State has a will which is completely independent and free from external influences. But through the process of auto-limitation a State can restrict its powers and thereby limit its will. In short, the practice shows that they considered themselves not bound by international law because they were independent and sovereign but they can make themselves bound by rules of international law by restricting its powers. This auto-limitation theory is based upon a presumption

---

[7] Convention on the Rights and Duties of States (adopted 26 December 1933, entered into force 26 December 1934) 165 LNTS 19.

[8] Starting in the late 18th century, the British rule brought India into the framework of a new empire. The foreign relations of India were controlled and governed in London. The British Empire started depriving the princely States of their external sovereignty by various means and methods. Different from the pre-colonization period, their mutual relations were no longer based on international law proper. However, the princely States retained external sovereignty in their relations to States outside India, to be precise to European powers. In contrast, the commercial and cultural relations to non-European powers were based on principles and practices (customs) which were found to be mutually agreeable to the Indian and non-European States. Accordingly, it is wrong to say that the princely States cannot be considered as States in the sense of the current terminology of international law because of alleged lack of external sovereignty.

[9] This issue was discussed in the 1960 seminar at Delhi University about the contribution of Indian traditions to the development of international law. However, this seminar failed to discuss when exactly Indian traditions of inter-state conduct were still capable of exercising a direct influence on the global system of the law of nations. These traditions came to an end with the collapse of the independent state system in India at the end of the 18th and the beginning of the 19th century. CH Alexandrowicz 'Grotius and India' (1954) 3 Indian Yearbook of International Affairs 357–67.

that there exists a state will that, in fact is nothing but the will of the people who comprise it. The princely States' practices show that it was primarily the will of the ruler which was the will of the State. The period under examination also clearly shows that consent was (and still is) a basis of *inter se* relations between these States, that is, international law. Thus, the modern international law which recognizes the importance and utility of consensus as a basis of obligation in international law was the essential precondition of *inter se* relations during this period. In fact, the theory of consent as the basis of obligations widely prevailed in princely States' inter-state relations and was developed to promote their interests. Natural law had the greatest influence in their relations and practice of these States shows that they considered the natural law to be of universal application.[10] Princely States observed norms of inter-state relations because they considered themselves as independent States and were recognized as such by other princely States.[11] The inter-state relations were largely governed by a body of rules of law—international law—to govern their conduct as members of that community. Furthermore, while it remains fact that princely States met in general gatherings, outcomes of these meetings are not perfectly documented and preserved.

3. Disappearance of British Common Law from International Law Practice of Independent India

It has been observed that English common law was applied in many fields by the British Empire during their colonization of India. Upon independence, the Constitution of India did not alter that practice but provided for the continued operation of the law as it had been in force immediately before the entry-into-force of the Constitution. Therefore, in analogy with English common law, the municipal courts of India would apply the common law principles of international law, as well as the recognized principles of international customary law as a part of the law of the land. However, this continuity was short-lived because with the passage of time, several new laws came into being immediately after independence and they clarified or codified

---

[10] Today we believe that consent of States is a must—States are bound by rules of international law because they have consented to them. However, this practice did not prevail among the princely States. See HA Smith *Great Britain and the Law of Nations* (PS King London 1935) vol 2, pt 1, at 12–13.

[11] This is again a proof of what Brierly said: 'The ultimate explanation of the binding force of all law is that man, whether he is single, individual or whether he is associated with other men in a State, is constrained in so far as he is reasonable being, to believe that order and not chaos is the governing principle of the world in which he has to live.' JL Brierly *The Law of Nations* (6th edn Clarendon Press Oxford 1963) at 56.

some of the international customary law principles into national law. The judiciary of India also played an important role in holding or rejecting the applicability of English common law jurisprudence, *inter alia,* including then-prevailing and practised international law into Indian laws.[12]

4. THE DOCTRINE OF EQUITY, JUSTICE, AND GOOD CONSCIENCE

The application of the doctrine of equity, justice, and good conscience in India was marked by two characteristic features. Firstly, the application of personal laws to Hindus and Muslims was limited only to a few matters; namely inheritance, succession, marriage, and other religious usages and institutions, while all other cases were to be decided according to the customs followed by the community to which the suitors belonged. Secondly, the practice followed by the British Crown's courts and the East India Company's court greatly differed in this regard. The Crown's court applied personal law only to Hindus and Mohammedans and all other persons were adjudged by the English law which was *lex loci* in presidency towns. On the other hand, the East India Company's courts in *Mofusils* decided the cases of persons other than Hindus and Mohammedans according to customs and usages followed by the community to which they belonged. The cumulative effect of such a dual application of the doctrine of equity, justice, and good conscience was that it greatly helped the development of different branches of law in India through judicial legislation. This doctrine, which is obviously more applicable in private international law than public international law, is unique to the Indian sub-continent and still remains valid. The *Shrutis*, the *Smritis*, the *Dharmashastras*, the *Arthashastras,* and the *Puranas* establish that the States of ancient India had inter-state, or international, relations among themselves. These relations were carried out according to well-established customs, usages, and principles of life based on the *Advaita* system of philosophy.[13] These sources of international law continued to guide the relations of princely States.[14]

---

[12] SK Agrawala 'Law of Nations as Interpreted and Applied by Indian Courts and Legislatures' (1962) 2 Indian Journal of International Law 431–78 at 433.

[13] According to Bandopadhya, these customs, usages and principles of life were compendiously called the *Desh Dharma*. P Bandopadhyay *International Law and Customs in Ancient India* (Calcutta University Press Calcutta 1920) at 16.

[14] The authority of *Sruti* is primary, while that of the *Smriti* is secondary. *Sruti* literally means what is heard, and *Smriti* means what is remembered. This shows the distinction between hard laws and soft laws in ancient India.

5. Treaties as a Source of Regional International Law

The domain of operation of the treaties considered here was the sub-continent of India, and directly concerned only the British government, the British Indian government and the Indian States. The conclusion of these treaties was a procedure recognized by and observed under the generally accepted rules of international law governing international instruments. But the moment they came into effect, their scope became regional in character. It can be seen that India, like many developing countries, resisted accepting the validity of the customary international rule of law, so well recognized by the European powers, which permitted the latter the right of acquisition of non-Christian territory by discovery and occupation. It insisted that that part of international law which gave expression to the pattern of domination be no longer recognized. The theory of *terra nullius*, according to which the territories not in possession of a Christian prince were subject to acquisition by Papal grant or by discovery and occupation was not palatable to India.[15]

5.1. Sources of International Law in Pre-1945 India

There is sparse literature about how the princely States treated customary rules of international law in a domestic setting and what were their approaches in case customary rules of international law conflicted with domestic law. Treaties were the most important sources of inter-state law. We find an enormous amount of references to various treaties concluded between princely States and other States, and British India and other nations. However, the determination and interpretation of treaty provisions rested with the kings and not with judiciary. Treaties were negotiated and the States confirmed to be bound by the obligations flowing from those treaties. In independent India, treaties were negotiated by the executive and ratified by the cabinet, except a few cases which found ratification of the parliament and where the judiciary acquired an independent role in interpreting the obligations of the Indian State. Thus, the earlier customs which were widely followed among the princely States disappeared with the independence of India. In other words, the negotiation, execution, and interpretation of pre-1945 and post-1945 treaties were all

[15] S Prakash Sinha 'Perspective of the Newly Independent States on the Binding Quality of International Law' (1965) 14 The International and Comparative Law Quarterly 121–31 at 125; WS Armour 'Customs of Warfare in Ancient India' (1922) 8 Transactions of the Grotius Society 71–88.

markedly different. Did all elements of custom (such as long duration, uniformity, and consistency, generality of practice, *opinio iuris sive necessitatis*) exist in pre-1945 India? One can find that the motives of fairness, convenience or morality were more prevalent in pre-1945 inter-state relations. These motives have disappeared. Customary rules of international law in pre-1945 India developed as a result of diplomatic relations between princely States and British India and treaties between princely States, while the current customary international law also is developed as a result of practice of international organs and state laws, decisions of state courts and state military or administrative practices. There was no 'inter-state organization' comparable to the current world in the form of the UN. It is observed that courts in pre-1945 India made decisions based upon considerations of fair dealing and good faith, which may be independent of or even contrary to the law. Inter-state comity was another source of development of inter-state law. A number of matters of the governments of respective States were resolved on the advice of their legal advisors. In the pre-1945 period, these advisory opinions were one of the most important sources of inter-state law.

5.2. Sources of International Law in Ancient India and their Influence on Post-Independence India

Dharma in ancient India was not solely the deliberate creation of lawgivers and legislatures but largely social custom and practices observed under fear of divine sanctions. The sources of ancient Indian laws were revelations (*Sruti*, the Vedas), the tradition (*Smritis* or Dharmshastra), and the practice of those who knew the Vedas or customs (*Acahar*). Custom was an important source. It was considered to be a mixture of inter-caste practices. One of the critiques is that in the case of the ancient States of India there is little that is available on the nature of acts or statutes, or opinions and decisions of judicial forums. The writers and jurists of the princely States developed the law of nature in accordance with the values and conventions of their age. According to them, if there was a conflict between positive law and natural law, the latter would prevail. Even if we are critical of that finding, it must be admitted that natural law emphasized the importance of certain ideas and values lying 'behind' positive rules. India, having deep-rooted natural law traditions, embraced and developed human rights law and a system of punishment of war crimes, due to the influence of natural law. Thus, the idealist character of natural law has greatly influenced the pre-independence international law among the princely States. The Indian civilization and state practice demonstrates heavy emphasis on the rule of morality. In fact, the Indian legal literature has combined and explained the rule of law and the rule of morality as one. Thus, the Western philosophy which is captured in Oppenheim's definition of a legal rule[16] shows that a rule of morality is a rule which applies to conscience only and cannot be enforced by external powers, whereas the Indian traditions and practice read and practice both together. Regardless of periodization, the Indian policy-makers and rulers have given considerable weight to moral arguments. While the Western nations will appeal to the precedents, to treaties, and to opinion of specialists, Indian writers would appeal to the general feeling of moral rightness, as based on the long civilization history of India.

In Islam, it was believed that the law binds individuals rather than territorial groups. Thus Muslims wherever they went were under the jurisdiction of the Islamic State, as jurisdiction in Islam was based upon the *personal* rather than the *territorial* principle. This approach was bound to conflict with the development of inter-state law insofar as every State has a territory and exercises jurisdiction over its nationals and the concept of the latter, has primarily been territorial. However, as the ruler of an Islamic political unit, who was more often than not a monarch, was also bound by the Islamic law and movement beyond the territories of a State without the monarch in command was rare, this lacuna need not be exaggerated, particularly in an age when jurisdiction could be personal also. This legal principle which has been in existence since the Islamic civilization does conflict with present principles of international law; India, being the second largest Muslim country, and Indian Muslims follow this principle. Thus, as far as India and Indian Muslims are concerned, one can discern two approaches to international jurisdiction.

6. Concepts of International Law

6.1. Sovereignty

Although sovereignty in a unique form continued to exist in pre-1945 India, it shall be noted that the attitude of princely States towards international law, to employ the modern terminology, constituted a community-oriented consensus towards the fulfilment of international obligations rather than a sovereignty-oriented consent. As

---

[16] Oppenheim suggests that 'a rule is a rule of morality if by common consent of the community, it applies to conscience and to conscience only; whereas, on the other hand, a rule of law if by common consent of the community it will eventually be enforced by external power.' L Oppenheim *International Law* (H Lauterpacht ed) (8th edn Longmans, Green & Co London 1955) vol 1, at 8.

India was constituted from hundreds of princely States, the community approach of these princely States toward the British authorities continued to exist.[17] Sovereignty had a different meaning in 18th-and 19th-century India than it has now. The 18th-and 19th-century India had an active acceptance of double allegiance: In the native States of India, there existed a double allegiance of their subjects. The native rulers themselves were the subject of the Indian government. The natives of protected States owed not only allegiance to them, but also certain duties, ill defined, to the protecting State. This was typical of the Indian subcontinent, but this notion of sovereignty has disappeared in the modern State of India. It is observed that:

[T]he East India Company itself acted under two very dissimilar sorts of power, derived from two sources very remote from each other. The first source of its power is under Charters which the Crown of Great Britain was authorized by the act of Parliament to grant, the other was from several charters derived from the Emperor of the Moghuls.... As to those of the first description, it is from the British Charters that they derive a capacity by which they were considered as a public body, or at all capable of any public function....[18]

6.2. Recognition and Reciprocity

Reciprocity is the basis of current modern international law—no government can accept its legal claims to be honoured unless it demonstrates a corresponding willingness to honour the similar claims of its foreign counterparts. The pre-1945 Indian history shows that the reciprocity was expected by native/princely States vis-à-vis the British government and the East India Company, but the latter did not demonstrate the willingness to honour these expectations as the latter was in a much more powerful position than the former. Hence, with the advent of modern international law after the Second World War, the inequality in reciprocity faded away. In ancient and also during princely States existence, kings exercised full territorial sovereignty over their own lands, but in addition, there were instances in which they exercised limited sovereignty over others—protectorates, spheres of influence, leased territories. In ancient India, recognition came in various ways: when a State, having achieved independence, was invited to participate in great inter-state assemblage like *Asvamegha*, *Vajapeya*, *Rajasuya*.

[17] It is in this light that one should see India's leadership of the Movement of Non-aligned States (NAM) which challenged the sovereignty-oriented principle of consent, deeply rooted in the Western countries, by advocating a community-oriented consensus.

[18] Sir J MacDonell 'Sovereignty' in *The Encyclopaedia Britannica* (Encyclopaedia Britannica Company New York 1911) vol 25, 519–23.

7. International Law Making through Treaties

A treaty was an agreement concluded between by two kings who would exercise treaty-making powers on behalf of their States. It is evident that the kings and princes in ancient and pre-1945 India were regarded as the personification of sovereignty. So when in ancient India a king entered into some sort of transaction with another king, it was really a case of two States and not that of two individuals entering into an understanding or intercourse. In such a case there was no room for doubt that the king concerned was representing the people (in whom alone resided true sovereignty) and his State. This doctrine has lapsed with the emergence of independent India. In fact, the transactions which took place between the kings prior to independence and post-independence evidence this doctrine and must be accorded legal weight. Thus, the principles and norms which were followed by these principalities and constitute a body of conduct among these principalities ought to be considered as rules of international law (if dubbed into current context) or inter-state relations of ancient India.

8. Select Areas of International Law

8.1. Criminal Law

An examination of the criminal law system reveals that several principles and practices of the British era have ceased to exist. Prior to the Warren Hastings reforms, in the area of substantive criminal law, the British tended to exercise a much bigger scope of jurisdiction than the current international law recognizes. For example, not only the dacoits but family members of the dacoits were also made slaves and whole villages were fined, all under the disguise of stringent measures which were felt necessary to eradicate the evil of dacoity. The British Empire applied English laws in criminal matters in circumstances which were totally different from those of the English. Similarly, the harshness of English law was a reality in India but the redeeming features of English law and procedure were nowhere to be found.[19]

---

[19] That experience must be remembered when assessing the fact that India, together with China and other nations, does not recognize the jurisdiction of the International Criminal Court for regions and realities which are far away from the physical seat of that institution.

8.2. Religion and International Law

Prior to independence, the *Koran* and *Shastra* were consulted in deciding the disputes among the Muslims and Hindus. With independence, reforms were taking place and although *Koran*- and *Shastra*-based rules and norms determine cases such as inheritance, marriage, caste, and other religious usages, a uniform civil code was gradually entering in the legal system of India. The *Koran* and *Shastra* were consulted because the judges were Englishmen and they did not have knowledge of personal laws of Muslims and Hindus. Moreover, local traditions and customs of these two dominant communities were required to preserve them from English onslaught. *Dharma* is the core and centre of Hindu philosophical thought and political theory. It is no wonder therefore that Hindu law began with duties (*Dharma*) rather than with rights, as in the Western countries. In his study of *Kingship and Community in Early India*, Drekmeier shows that

[I]n Hindu political speculations, duty occupies the central position that in European thought belongs to conceptions of natural rights and freedoms—we are justified in saying that civil obligations rather than civil rights formed the basis of the relation of state and subject.[20]

These philosophical pronouncements underpinned the international law practice for the period prior to independence. However, much of today's international law, focused on rights first instead of obligations, is observed by post-independence India. International law in ancient India and pre-1945 may be defined as the body of customary rules or ethical principles based on the philosophy of the *Advaita* which regulated the relations of Indian States in their intercourse with one another. The above definition implies the following five prerequisites, viz: (1) The existence of sovereign independent States, based on the supremacy and universality of law which was the expression of the philosophy of *Advaita*; (2) the sanctity of treaties; (3) the existence of sanction; (4) the inevitability of intercourse among such States, and (5) the need for regulating such intercourse.[21]

8.3. Human Rights

Is the Indian intervention into neighbouring regions a unilateral use of force, or is it a part of India's rich civilization contributing to the protection and promotion of

---

[20] AK Pavithran 'International Law in Ancient India' (1973) 5 The Eastern Journal of International Law 220–42 at 230.

[21] It should be noted that inter-state rules and principles provided for religious sanctions rather than legal sanctions as understood in the West.

human rights?[22] With the Bangladesh War of 1971, the realization of the need to evolve norms and principles of international law to cover such situations began to dawn. Pre-independent India was full of social problems and evils, some of them were *sati* (self-immolation by a wife of a husband), the caste system, and untouchability, among others. To eradicate these problems, various social reform movements were launched which also attained measurable success. These social reform movements used to reinterpret the sacred texts of the Hindus and appealed to the conscience of people. Thus, the social problems and reforms have made great contributions to the modern international human rights law.[23] The struggle for independence provided equal opportunity to women. The Indian National Congress provided a common platform for men and women to play their role. This exposure empowered women to develop their own individuality and crusade for equal rights. The social reform movement lost its exclusive male basis and orientation, and women themselves founded an exclusively female association: the All India Women's Conference in 1926. They crusaded for various rights of women and advocated equality. Thus, the issues and problems unique to the Indian sub-continent's multiculturalism were addressed by equally unique means and mechanisms. Obviously, problems such as Caste were not found in monoculture societies of the West and the Islamic world. If these means and mechanisms would not have contributed to the typical problems, the universal aims of universal human rights instruments would have been difficult to achieve. In other words, the modern universal human rights instruments would have been devoid of universal or a truly multicultural input. If particularly Indian problems and solutions had not existed, then modern international law would neither have been able to claim universal approach nor would it have been able to appeal the entire human society. The joint family system, which is unique to India, has contributed to modern international business, trade, human rights, and humanitarian law, and many other branches of international law, as one could observe that practices and customs originated and were maintained by the joint family indirectly and directly contributed to the growth of and reflection in the modern international trade practices. It is, however, beyond the scope of this paper to analyse how the Indian joint family systems have contributed to the modern international law. Nevertheless, it must be accepted that the joint family system and principles are reflected in the overall Indian legal and

---

[22] As Frank and Rodley observe, 'international law, as a branch of behavioral science as well as normative philosophy may treat this event as the harbinger of new law that will henceforth increasingly govern inter-state relations. Perhaps India's example by its success has already entered into the nations' conscious expectations of future conduct.' TM Frank and N Rodley 'After Bangladesh: The Law of Humanitarian Intervention by Military Force' (1973) 67 American Journal of International Law 275–305 at 303.

[23] To promote and protect the rights of women, the UN has established various treaties and institutions. Similarly, in the pre-1945 period, several institutions were established in India to secure women a respected and proud place in society. Organizations like the Servants of India Society, Ramakrishna Mission, and Vishwabharati have done a great deal of work for the education of women to achieve the same ideals which much later were expressed in international instruments.

judicial system and jurisprudence which is in tandem and not necessarily in conflict with modern international law and jurisprudence centric to the nuclear family.

8.4. Cooperation among Princely States: A Prototype of Post-1945 International Organizations?

To address issues of common concern and to find solutions, after the Second World War, the nation states established several international and regional organizations. In ancient and pre-1945 India, as mentioned earlier, various religious ceremonies and sacrifices accelerated the process of such intercourse and strengthened people's conviction that greater and closer intercourse and not isolationism could alone offer dividends in the long run.[24] These mechanisms were ad hoc, unlike the concepts of administrative secretariats which are found in the international organizations. By performing these ceremonies on a particular day, the kings and States ensured some form of presence of other kings and state representatives and provided a platform to discuss issues of common concerns and interests on these occasions. Thus, ceremonies are nothing but 'annual conferences' of general bodies to meet and discuss the progress and chalk out a future course of action. When the kings met, they exchanged words of sympathy and fellow-feeling. Thus, these occasions served to strengthen inter-state amity and to ensure cooperation among States.

8.5. War and Peace

Princely States followed what Kautilya's advice commended a few hundred years before. For self-preservation, any mode of war is justified, including a peace treaty (*Sandhi*), *Mantra Yudha*, a war of intrigues (Cold War), and *Kutayudha* and use of barbarous tribes.[25] Modern international law imposes limitations and prohibitions as far as means and methods of warfare are concerned; however, the element of righteousness is uniquely found in the Indian history of warfare and worth re-examination today, especially when States resort to non-prohibited means of warfare but still have no regard for the righteousness of those means. Indian writers such as Kautilya, Kamandaka, and Manu all opposed war because of moral and

---

[24] International organizations were already conceptualized in the Kautilya period. Confederations of States appeared in the Indian sub-continent in the 18th century, to mention only the Maratha State, an association of rulers under the supreme government of the Peshwa at Poona. Moreover, the Moghul empire at the stage of its decentralization in the 18th century became a composite entity similar to the Holy Roman Empire. 'Grotius and India' (n 9) 309.

[25] ibid 32.

economic considerations, but as a last resort, going to war was not dismissed as an option. In ancient India, it was a practice to declare war if and when it became unavoidable. The declaration was crucial in India as it paved the way for the enemy to prepare for war.[26] The Indian custom of giving notice before engaging in battle[27] disappeared in the modern rules of warfare.[28] Prior to 1500 and even during 1500–1945, the rules of warfare observed by Indian kings and princely States were unique to Indian civilization and have made a significant contribution to modern international humanitarian law. These rules of warfare are genuine evidence of ancient chivalry and priestly influence and preaching. This is typical of the Indian civilization. There were strong religious sanctions for the observance of these rules, with penalties for breaches in this world and the next (to be experienced after reincarnation). As far as the rights to armed intervention either unilaterally or collectively in the modern day are concerned, one can find good reflections of similar reasons for intervention in the 1500–1945 India.[29] The modern concept of international law is essentially based on one uniform set of rules which governs all belligerents in a war. We have such a concept at present that is, the Geneva Conventions of 1949,[30] which have a universal application irrespective of considerations of different civilizations or opposing political ideologies of different States. This could not be said of medieval India, which became a battle ground of two civilizations, each having its own laws to govern inter-state conduct. Independent India has witnessed the disappearance of many principles and practices which were found in the Hindu scriptures and

[26] This practice has ceased to exist especially in modern international law. The wars in Iran and Iraq, Afghanistan, former Yugoslavia are all cases in reference.

[27] The beauty of Indian customs was that initially the envoys would be dispatched with the messages and if the opposite party denies, then a day, keeping in view the climatic conditions and auspicious day will be announced for battle.

[28] *Temperamenta belli*: rules for warriors were clearly laid out and practised by the warriors.

[29] Interventions were not outdated but practised even during the 1500–1945 for various reasons, some of which are also accepted in modern international law: (1) intervention on the basis of an implicit previous understanding; (2) intervention in self-defence, ie to ward off an imminent danger to the intervening power; (3) intervention on the ground of humanity; (4) intervention to prevent continued misrule in a state; (5) intervention in order to preserve the balance of power; (6) intervention by one or more powers at the request of one of the parties to a civil war. Indian rulers were fully aware of unjust battle or unrighteous warfare. And their distinction of a righteous war from an unrighteous war strikingly resembles the Grotian concept of just war. H Chatterjee *International Law and Inter-State Relations in Ancient India* (Mukhopadhyay Calcutta 1958) at 4.

[30] Geneva Convention for the Amelioration of the Condition of the Wounded and Sick in Armed Forces in the Field (adopted 12 August 1949, entered into force 21 October 1950) 75 UNTS 31 (Geneva Convention I); Geneva Convention for the Amelioration of the Condition of Wounded, Sick and Shipwrecked Members of Armed Forces at Sea (adopted 12 August 1949, entered into force 21 October 1950) 75 UNTS 85 (Geneva Convention II);Geneva Convention relative to the Treatment of Prisoners of War (adopted 12 August 1949, entered into force 21 October 1950) 75 UNTS 135 (Geneva Convention III); Geneva Convention relative to the Protection of Civilian Persons in Time of War (adopted 12 August 1949, entered into force 21 October 1950) 75 UNTS 287 (Geneva Convention IV).

princely States' functioning.[31] Under the Regulating Act of 1773,[32] the administration of India was centralized by making provisions for the appointment of a Governor-General and a council of four. Regarding the right to commence war or negotiate peace, the following provisions were made in the act: normally the subordinate presidencies could commence war or negotiate peace only with the consent of the Governor-General, but they could do so without the consent of the Governor-General when there was very urgent necessity provided they received orders directly from the Court of Directors of the British East India Company.

8.6. Trade, Commerce, and Economy

A rural economy and the self-sufficiency of the village communities, which were to a certain extent disintegrated during the British rule, are typical of the Indian subcontinent. The principle of international commercial, trade, and business run contrary to the objective of self-sufficiency, according to Adam Smith, David Ricardo, and John M Keynes, and the economic principles of world economic integration and interdependence they advocated. During the British rule, a slow but steady emergence of a tax regime consolidated to meet the needs of the British colonial administration. At the same time, the rural credit and the business of the moneylender, or micro-financer, emerged. This is a unique economic system applicable in India which finds resonance in current international financial and fiscal policies and principles. New versions with new means and mechanisms of financing have emerged but the principle and effective working system can be traced back to the Indian rural economy prior to independence. The British colonization led to the breakdown of the economic and social fabric of Indian self-sufficient village communities and the transformation of the whole pre-capitalist feudal economy of India into a capitalist economy. In other words, the rural economy of India was not powerful enough to withstand the forces of global capitalism. Even when all obstacles to cooperation were overcome under the pressure of the growing volume of trade, there remained the traditional reluctance of East Indian rulers to conclude treaties, a reluctance which has its roots in ancient traditions of Hindu polity. This shows a preference for

---

[31] For example, the dead body of a defeated king was returned to his home country. The classic example is the return of the body of Biswas Rao by Ahmad Shah Abdali after the battle of Panipat of 1761 AD, although according to the Durrani tradition the body should have been taken to the conqueror's country. In this context, it may be worth mentioning that in some cases when the law of the victorious State was more liberal than the law of the victim State, the victorious State renounced its liberal law in favour of the law of the victim State in order to retaliate. N Singh 'International Law in India (II): Mediaeval India' (1962) 2 Indian Journal of International Law 65–82 at 71.

[32] An Act for Establishing Certain Regulations for the better Management of the Affairs of the East India Company, as well in India as in Europe 1773 (UK) 13 Geo 3 c 63 ('Regulating Act').

informal and less legalistic relations which first disappeared but resurfaced again in the post-colonization period. It is easier to obtain a unilateral grant than to receive any concessions by treaty which is considered a limitation to the sovereignty of the conceding ruler. This shows an East versus West approach to international law.

9. EXECUTIVE AND JUDICIARY POWERS

In pre-colonial and ancient times, even during the early British colonization, there was no clear distinction between the executive and judiciary. The king exercised the executive and judicial function even in inter-state relations—the latter has disappeared with the advent of colonization. During the pre-independence phase, the high courts were not the interpreters and guardians of the fundamental rights which were prevailing in European nations; they were to have civil, criminal, and appellate jurisdiction. With independence, foreign relations were determined by the executive at federal level, hence the role of high courts significantly diminished in settling international disputes. The law declared by the Privy Council in the pre-constitution period is still binding on the High Courts except in those cases where the Supreme Court of India has declared law in its judgments. The contribution of the Privy Council to statute law, personal law, commercial laws, and criminal laws is of significant importance. Since these laws have been gradually expanded and codified, one could still see the impact of the Privy Council on international law practice as followed by India in these areas of law. It must be noted that until the Supreme Court of India takes a different view, the view taken by the Council is still binding—this particular *stare decisis* is applicable in India and a unique characteristic of regional law of India.[33] After the establishment of the Supreme Court on 26 January 1950, the decisions of the Privy Council have no compelling force on the court but are entitled to great respect.[34] Henceforth, the Supreme Court can decide independently.[35] The high courts are however bound unless they can point to a Supreme Court decision to the contrary.[36] As Indian high courts are frequently required to enforce and interpret

---

[33] As noted by Jois, the Privy Council's contribution and model is of eternal value, and a source of inspiration to all those concerned with the administration of India. R Jois *Legal and Constitutional History of India* (Fred B Rothman Bombay 1984) vol 2, at 198.

[34] *Chief Controlling Revenue Authority v Maharastra Sugar Mills Ltd* AIR (1950) SC 218; *State of Bihar v Abdul Majid* AIR (1954) SC 245.

[35] *Srinivas v Narayan* AIR (1954) SC 379.

[36] *Pandurang Kalu Patil v State of Maharastra* (2002) 2 SCC 490.

international law, it can be concluded that this ratio also applies to the international law cases and disputes in the jurisdiction of the High Courts of India. The jurisdiction of the Admiralty Court, established pursuant to the Charter of 1683, was not confined to mercantile and maritime cases as it was envisaged by the Charters of 1683 and 1686, but its jurisdiction was extended to civil and criminal cases. It became a general court of the land and the Supreme Court of the settlement. This practice ceased to exist with the independence of India. Admiralty Courts are no longer required to perform these tasks, but concentrate only on maritime and mercantile transactions and cases, as well as forfeiture of ships, piracy, trespass, injuries, and wrongs.

India's history until 1947 suggests that there was no clear separation between the executive and judiciary. The judiciary was under the control of the executive. Kings and princes were the law makers as well as law interpreters. Due to these historical reasons, the question of judicial independence did not arise in pre-independence India.[37] Thus, the foreign relations between Indian States and the settlement of disputes between the kingdoms or princely States were dealt with by the executive only. Various attempts were made by Great Britain during the colonization period to address difficulties and disputes arising between princely States and between princely States and individuals. However, none of these attempts provided a long-term solution which could be accepted by the rulers and population at large. During the judicial reforms (1787–93) by the British General Charles Cornwallis, attempts were made to ensure that all subjects received free and impartial justice. However, these reforms attracted floods of cases against other princely States and British institutions and individuals. This led to inordinate delays. Furthermore, Cornwallis entertained a notion that Indians were not worthy of trust. Probably his experience in the field of administration of criminal justice led him to this belief.[38] This is not surprising as the Privy Council administered justice to people thousands of miles away. It was separated from the people and their lives, by their customs and traditions. In such circumstances what is surprising is that the administration of justice at the highest level had so few blemishes. The Privy Council tried to inject the principle of equity and common law into the realms of Hindu and Mohammedan law. Quite often the decisions of the Privy Council were not in conformity with the accepted customs of the people. Another criticism is that it was too true to the ancient texts of personal laws and thus was responsible for the stagnation of personal laws of the people of India. The judiciary

---

[37] In the early days, the administration of justice in the settlements of the East India Company was not much developed. There was no separation between the executive and the judiciary. The judiciary was under the control of the executive, and the judges were not trained in law.

[38] It is unfortunate that General Cornwallis did not appreciate the fact that corruption was not confined to the Indians—the English servants were equally, if not more, corrupt. It has been observed that the American and the British subjects were excluded from the jurisdiction of the Indian judges. The reform introduced by Bentick was a great step forward in the 'Indianisation' of the administration of justice.

established in Bombay, Calcutta, and Madras contributed to the confusion and uncertainty regarding the fair and equitable implementation of the rule of law, which had profound implications for independent India. The Indian judges, it appears, did not enjoy equal status with the English judges during the British East India Company rule—a principle which has been abolished since the independence.[39] The Admiralty Court had jurisdiction to determine all cases, mercantile and maritime in nature, all cases of trespasses, injuries, and wrongs, committed on the high seas.[40] In Madras, the British East India Company established the corporation mainly for the purpose of municipal administration; however, it began to exercise jurisdiction as a court.[41] This shows that various mechanisms and various ad hoc institutions were established to resolve the disputes which invariably involved individuals and institutions of various princely States of India, which although under the suzerainty or colonization of the British East India Company, enjoyed independence to a significant extent and were considered states proper. Thus, the old norms and mechanisms for dispute settlement disappeared with the independence of India. The Supreme Court which was established in Calcutta in 1774 had various jurisdictions which involved national and international private and public law and norms. It had original jurisdiction, equity jurisdiction, admiralty jurisdiction, probate, and ecclesiastical jurisdiction and jurisdiction to supervise. With the establishment of the Supreme Court of Calcutta, for the first time the principle of separation of the judiciary from the executive was established in India. This was a major legal milestone in the Indian civilization as up until then, the executive and judiciary were one and no separation of powers existed between the two. The judges until this time were non-professional men, not conversant with the English laws, but who were administering justice according to English law. One could draw the conclusion, therefore, that with the advent of British colonization, the system of administration of justice as practised between princely States and which was exercised by the king collapsed and was largely taken over by non-professional men.

[39] They were not counted for the purpose of the quorum of the court fixed at three (there were five English and four Indian judges, who were called Black Judges). In the record of each day's proceedings, the name of each English judge was specifically mentioned but the Indian judges were collectively described as 'black justices'. The Indian judges played more or less a subsidiary role similar to that of assessors. Their main function was to acquaint the English judges with the local manners and customs and the caste systems of the local people. *Legal and Constitutional History* (n 33) 11. At times, the Governor and Council would also postpone cases involving serious crimes as they were aware of their lack of knowledge. Therefore, hesitation and delay continued.

[40] It had to decide cases according to the rules of equity and good conscience and the laws and customs of merchant law. Although all States are free to use the high seas, and although Queen Elizabeth of England emphasized in 1580 the freedom of the high seas and the principle that no State can claim sovereignty over them, the British East India Company challenged that concept because the Admiralty Court tried to exercise jurisdiction over the high seas too.

[41] It should be noted that the mayor's court exercised jurisdiction over European as well as Indian people, including in cases concerning religious matters. Incidents such as the conversion of a Hindu Woman (in 1730), the Oath in Bombay, Madras clearly attest to this practice of the mayor's court.

These men, not versed in law, could hardly be expected to know international law. This is one of the main reasons why there was a silent collapse of international law during the British era as it was practised before between the princely States. While Indian civilization was subjected to the administration of justice by these non-professional men, Western Europe was seeing the emergence of great international lawyers like Grotius, Bynkershoek, and Vattel among others. Since there was no counter-force practising and administering international law in the Indian sub-continent, the philosophy and rules promulgated by the Western international lawyers came to dominate the international scene. In contrast, before the British era there was a robust practice and administration of justice in the framework of ancient international law traditions of India. Therefore, there had been a counter-force in Asia, but this counter-force collapsed and with it, the great ancient international law traditions in India.

10. Private International Law

The questions which arose out of the merger of native States mostly relate to the execution of *ex parte* decrees of the British Indian courts in the courts of the merged States and vice versa. What Lord Selborne had laid down in the well-known case of *Sardar Gudayal Singh v Raja Faridkote* has become the accepted principle of international law. He observed, 'in personal action…a decree pronounced in absence by a foreign court, to the jurisdiction of which the defendant has not in any way submitted himself, is by international law an absolute nullity'.[42] And it must be regarded as such by the courts of any nation except in the country by which it was pronounced. The independence of India raised several issues with regards to partition, transfer of property, assets, liability, etc. With regards to the execution of a decree, it was observed that the execution of a decree of the court of one country could be directed not only against property in one dominion but also against the property in another. The principle applies not only for the purpose of passing the decree but also for its enactment. Although this interpretation is not in accord with the ordinary rules of international law, it had become somewhat necessary to meet the new situation. This practice, particularly restricted to India and Pakistan, does not find acceptance in international law but could be very useful, should such circumstances arise again in the future. When an Englishman died, leaving some property in India without leaving any legal representative, the practice followed was that the Governor and council of the town of residence of the deceased sold the property by public auction. The sale proceeds

[42] 'Law of Nations' (n 12) 451.

were deposited for the benefit of the legal representatives of the deceased in England. As the courts established in India had no royal authority, this practice of the British East India Company would lead to litigation in England. Often the Company had to pay damages as a result of the orders of the English courts. The Company very much desired to avoid such complications. It requested and was given by the Crown a grant of such powers conducive to the punishing of vice, administration of justice, and a better governing of effects of settlements abroad. This principle has disappeared as the current jurisprudence recognizes a limited right of recognition of foreign decrees in India.[43]

11. Conclusion

One may conclude that, unlike many other States of Asia which challenged some of the fundamental tenets of modern international law, India and the native States of India never challenged international law to the same degree. Rules and institutions established and practised in India, China, Egypt, and Assyria in ancient times, have an enormous and lasting impact on the international law. Anand wrote that these earlier legal systems of China, India, Egypt, Islam, or even Greece, were confined to their own civilizations, were not universal, and in any case 'have left no trace of continuity of history'.[44] This remark must be dismissed because it is not mindful of the impact of these civilizations on current international law. When India became independent, it considered itself bound by the existing treaties, at any rate those relating to extradition, boundary issues, and debts, as applicable instruments of international law.[45]

Recommended Reading

Agrawala, Sunil K 'Law of Nations as Interpreted and Applied by Indian Courts and Legislatures' (1962) 2 Indian Journal of International Law 431–78.
Alexandrowicz-Alexander, Charles H 'Grotius and India' (1954) 3 Indian Yearbook of International Affairs 357–67.

---

[43] *Legal and Constitutional History* (n 33) 16.

[44] RP Anand *Development of Modern International Law and India* (Indian Society of International Law New Delhi 2006) at 1.

[45] MK Nawaz 'International Law in the Contemporary Practice of India: Some Perspectives' (1963) 20 World Rule of Law Booklet Series 275–90 at 281.

Anand, Ram P *Asian States and the Development of International Law* (Vikas Publications New Delhi 1972).

Anand, Ram P *Development of Modern International Law and India* (Indian Society of International Law New Delhi 2006).

Armour, William S 'Customs of Warfare in Ancient India' (1922) 8 Transactions of the Grotius Society 71–88.

Bandopadhyay, Pramathanath *International Law and Customs in Ancient India* (Calcutta University Press Calcutta 1920).

Chatterjee, Hiralal 'International Law and Inter-State Relations in Ancient India' (Mukhopadhyay Calcutta 1958).

Dhawan, S S 'The Ramayana II International Law in the Age of Ramayana' *National Herald Magazine* (New Delhi India 21 January 1971).

Lanka, Sundaram 'The International Status of India' (1931) 17 Transactions of the Grotius Society 35–54.

Mani, Venkateshwara S *Handbook of International Humanitarian Law in South Asia* (OUP Oxford 2007).

Nawaz, Mahomed K 'International Law in the Contemporary Practice of India: Some Perspectives' (1963) 20 World Rule of Law Booklet Series 275–90.

Pannikkar, Kavalam M *Asia and Western Dominance* (Allen & Unwin London 1970).

Patel, Bimal N (ed) *India and International Law* (Brill Leiden 2005) vol 1.

Patel, Bimal N (ed) *India and International Law* (Martinus Nijhoff Publishers Leiden 2007) vol 2.

Pavithran, K 'International Law in Ancient India' (1973) 5 The Eastern Journal of International Law 220–42.

Ramaswamy, M 'The Indian States in the Indian Federation—A Juristic View' (1940) 3 The University of Toronto Law Journal 301–22.

Singh, Nagendra *India and International Law, Part A: Ancient and Mediaeval* (S Chand New Delhi 1973).

Singh, Nagendra *Juristic Concepts of Ancient Indian Polity* (Vision New Delhi 1980).

Singh, Nagendra 'Armed Conflicts and Humanitarian Laws of Ancient India' in Christophe Swinarski (ed) *Etudes et essais sur le droit international humanitaire et sur les principes de la Croix-Rouge en l'honneur de Jean Pictet* (Martinus Nijhoff Publishers Leiden 1984) 531–6.

Sinha, Sri Prakash 'Perspective of the Newly Independent States and Binding Quality of International Law' (1965) 14 International and Comparative Law Quarterly 121–31.

III

THE AMERICAS AND THE CARIBBEAN

CHAPTER 22

NORTH AMERICA: AMERICAN EXCEPTIONALISM IN INTERNATIONAL LAW

MARK W JANIS

1. INTRODUCTION

How has America been exceptional over history in its approach to international law? This chapter reviews a little of the story from the late 18th century, when the United States declared its independence from the United Kingdom, to the beginning of the 20th century, as the United States watched Europe descend into the First World War. The pages below, largely based upon material and observations drawn from a new book, *America and the Law of Nations 1776–1939*,[1] emphasize not the ways in which the American approach to international law has been similar to that in Europe, but how America has been different.

---

[1] MW Janis *America and the Law of Nations 1776–1939* (OUP Oxford 2010).

2. THE LAW OF NATIONS AND THE COMMON LAW

In the beginning, there was no international law, only the law of nations. The English philosopher, Jeremy Bentham, invented the term 'international'.[2] It is a word that has come to be applied to many things: international relations, international economics, international travel, international politics, etc. But in the first place it was meant only for international law. 1789 saw international law first appear in Bentham's book, *An Introduction to the Principles of Morals and Legislation*.[3] Bentham simply meant to replace one term, the law of nations, with another term, international law,[4] that he thought better characterized that branch of law, but he made two important false assumptions about his subject. First, he assumed that international law was exclusively about the rights and obligations of States *inter se* and not about the rights and obligations of individuals.[5] Second, he assumed that foreign transactions before municipal courts were always decided by internal, not international, rules.[6] Both of these assumptions flew in the face of Bentham's assertion that he was merely substituting the term international law for the term the law of nations.

Although Americans quickly adopted Bentham's new term,[7] they never adopted Bentham's philosophical conceptualization of the discipline. Instead, Americans followed in the intellectual footsteps of another Englishman, William Blackstone, the much more influential author of *Commentaries on the Laws of England* (1765–69). Blackstone, reflecting the English common law, explicitly referred to the law of nations as involving 'that intercourse which must frequently occur between two or more independent states, and the individuals belonging to each' and stated that the law of nations was 'adopted in its full extent by the common law'.[8] Blackstone's traditional notion of the law of nations encompassed, *inter alia*, the *lex mercatoria*, admiralty law, and the laws relating to piracy and ambassadors.[9] Not only did Blackstone's law of nations extend to ordinary matters, it applied equally to States and to individuals. It was Blackstone, not Bentham, who was the legal realist. In the 18th-century common law of America, individuals were ordinary subjects of the law of nations and their suits were within the usual jurisdiction of the courts.[10] Blackstone famously

---

[2] ibid 10–15.

[3] J Bentham *An Introduction to the Principles of Morals and Legislation* (J Burns and H Hart eds) (Methuen London 1970).

[4] ibid 296.

[5] ibid 296.

[6] ibid 296.

[7] *America and the Law of Nations* (n 1) 50, fn 66.

[8] W Blackstone *Commentaries on the Laws of England* (A Facsimile of the First Edition of 1765–69) (University of Chicago Press 1979) vol 4, at 66–7.

[9] ibid vol 4, 67–68.   [10] ibid vol 4, 67.

wrote, 'the law of nations is adopted in its full extent by the common law, and is held to be a part of the law of the land'.[11]

Thanks to Blackstone and the English common law, the law of nations was an intellectual inheritance of American lawyers at the time of the American Revolution (1775–83). The '[i]ncorporation of the law of nations…seemed so obvious…that there was no reason to question its propriety'.[12] In the writings of America's founding fathers, 'citations of Grotius, Pufendorf, and Vattel are scattered in about equal numbers'.[13] The law of nations was regularly included in American college curricula.[14] In 1773, Columbia established a chair in natural law. In 1774, John Adams (1735–1836) gave, as background reading on the law of nations, Grotius, Pufendorf, Barbeyrac, Locke, and Harington. A year later Alexander Hamilton (1757–1804) suggested Grotius, Pufendorf, Locke, Montesquieu, and Burlemaqui.[15]

From the outset, US courts found it useful to employ the law of nations in the fashion of Blackstone. In 1784, in *Respublica v De Longchamps*,[16] a Frenchman, De Longchamps, visited Francis Barbe Marbois, the French Consul General in Philadelphia, then the capital of the United States, to seek authentication of his background, especially his rank in the French army, to refute allegations in the press. When Marbois refused to support De Longchamps' claims, De Longchamps turned insulting, then threatening, and finally assaulted the French Consul General. Even worse behaviour followed two days later, when outside the coffee-house near Market Street, De Longchamps struck the walking stick of Marbois, precipitating a confrontation and inviting a duel. The Pennsylvania high court held that offences against foreign diplomats 'must be determined on the principles of the laws of nations, which form a part of the municipal law of Pennsylvania'.[17] Since De Longchamps' crime was 'an infraction of the law of nations [which] in its full extent, is part of the law of this State', Pennsylvania had the sovereign right to try and punish him. 'Whoever offers any violence to [a diplomat], not only affronts the sovereign he represents, but also hurts the common safety and well-being of nations; he is guilty of a crime against the whole world.'[18] De Longchamp's affirmation of Blackstone's principle that the law of nations is 'adopted in its full extent by the common law, and is held to be part of the common law',[19] became an accepted rule in the United States.

As Alexander Hamilton wrote in 1795, it was 'indubitable that the customary law of European nations is a part of the common law, and, by adoption, that of the United

---

[11] *Commentaries on the Laws* (n 8) vol 4, 67.

[12] HJ Bourguignon 'Incorporation of the Law of Nations during the American Revolution—The Case of the San Antonio' (1977) 71 American Journal of International Law 270–95 at 294.

[13] JS Reeves 'The Influence of the Law of Nations Upon International Law in the United States' (1909) 3 American Journal of International Law 547–61 at 549.

[14] DM Douglas 'The Jeffersonian Vision of Legal Education' (2001) 51 Journal of Legal Education 185–211 at 197 and 205.

[15] 'The Influence of the Law' (n 13) 551.   [16] *Respublica v De Longchamps* 1 US 111 (1784) at 114.

[17] ibid 114.   [18] ibid 114.   [19] *Commentaries on the Laws* (n 8) vol 4, 67.

States'.[20] Likewise US Attorney General Charles Lee (1758–1815) wrote to the US Secretary of State in 1797 respecting an arrest and prosecution of the Spanish Commandant of Amelia Island in then-Spanish Florida: 'The common law has adopted the law of nations in its fullest extent, and made it a part of the law of the land.'[21]

The most famous American enunciation of Blackstone's incorporation doctrine came in 1900 in the *Paquete Habana*.[22] Cuban nationals sued the US government under customary international law to recover the value of fishing boats seized and sold by the United States during the Spanish–American War. The Supreme Court held that:

[b]y an ancient usage among civilized nations, beginning centuries ago, and gradually ripening into a rule of international law, coast fishing vessels, pursuing their vocation of catching and bringing in fresh fish, have been recognized as exempt, with their cargoes and crews, from capture as prize of war.

Thus using ordinary international law to protect ordinary individuals in an ordinary American court, the Supreme Court ruled:

International law is part of our law, and must be ascertained and administered by the courts of justice of appropriate jurisdiction, as often as questions of right depending upon it are duly presented for their determination. For this purpose, where there is no treaty, and no controlling executive or legislative act or judicial decision, resort must be had to the customs and usages of civilized nations; and, as evidence of these, to the works of jurists and commentators, who by years of labor, research and experience, have made themselves peculiarly well acquainted with the subjects of which they treat. Such works are resorted to by judicial tribunals, not for the speculations of their authors concerning what the law ought to be, but for trustworthy evidence of what the law really is.

3. The Law of Nations and American Independence

Given the prominent position of the law of nations in 18th-century American law and given the even more prominent role of American lawyers in 18th-century American politics, it is no surprise that the law of nations served as the bedrock for assertions of American independence from British colonialism. The famous first two

---

[20]   Quoted in BM Ziegler *The International Law of John Marshall* (University of North Carolina Press Chapel Hill 1939) at 6.

[21]   C Lee Opinion of 26 January 1797, 1 *Opinions of the Attorney General 1791–1825* 68, 69.

[22]   *The Paquete Habana* 175 US 677; 20 SCt 290 (1900).

paragraphs of the US Declaration of Independence of 4 July 1776, drafted by Thomas Jefferson read:

When, in the course of human events, it becomes necessary for one people to dissolve the political bonds which have connected them with another, and to assume among the Powers of the earth, the separate and equal status to which the Laws of Nature and of Nature's God entitle them, a decent respect to the opinion of mankind requires that they should declare the causes which impel them to separation.

We hold these truths to be self-evident, that all men are created equal, and that they are endowed by their Creator with certain unalienable Rights, that among these are Life, Liberty, and the pursuit of Happiness. That, to secure these rights, Governments are instituted among Men, deriving their just powers from the consent of the governed, that whenever any form of Government becomes destructive of these ends, it is the Right of the People to alter or abolish it, and to institute new Government, laying its foundation on such Principles and organizing its Powers in such form, as to them shall seem most likely to effect their Safety and Happiness.

Thomas Jefferson (1745–1826) had studied the law of nations at the College of William and Mary. One of the most illustrious Americans of his generation, he served as Governor of Virginia, US Ambassador to France, Secretary of State to George Washington, Vice-President to John Adams, and third President of the United States (1801–9). In the Declaration of Independence Jefferson explained that he sought to 'appeal to the tribunal of the world…to place before mankind the common sense of the subject, in terms so plain and firm as to command their assent'. He looked not only to audiences in America and Britain, but also to those in France, the Netherlands, and Spain.[23]

In the Declaration, the law of nations also provided Jefferson with a bold and defiant definition of the sovereign position of the new United States:[24]

We, therefore, the Representatives of the United States of America, in General Congress, Assembled, appealing to the Supreme Judge of the World for the rectitude of our intentions, do, in the Name, and by Authority of the good People of these Colonies, solemnly publish and declare, That these United Colonies are, and of Right ought to be free and independent states; that they are Absolved from all Allegiance to the British Crown, and that all political connection between them and the State of Great Britain, is and ought to be totally dissolved; and that as Free and Independent States, they have full Power to levy War, conclude Peace, contract Alliances, establish Commerce, and to do all other Acts and Things, which Independent States may of right do.

A little more than a year after the Declaration, on 15 November 1777, Congress issued the Articles of Confederation, the first American constitution. Ratified in 1781, the Articles of Confederation served both as a domestic constitution and as a treaty allocating sovereign rights among the thirteen States. However, an ambivalent vesting of

[23] *America and the Law of Nations* (n 1) 25–6.
[24] D Armitage 'The Declaration of Independence and International Law' (2002) 59 William and Mary Quarterly 39–64 at 46.

sovereign powers between the States and the central government led to conflicts, including disputes about the right to apply and enforce the law of nations.[25] In 1779, Pennsylvania and Congress clashed over which had the power to condemn vessels in admiralty. Congress, by ten States to two (Pennsylvania and New Jersey in the minority), voted to take jurisdiction, resolving that it alone had 'the authority ultimately and finally to decide on all matters and questions touching the law of nations'.[26]

Along with international legal rights came international legal duties and it was the inability of the United States under the Articles of Confederation to live up to its obligations as a sovereign State under the law of nations which proved to be one of the principal causes of the downfall of that early form of US government. In the Peace of Paris, signed in 1783,[27] the United Kingdom acknowledged that the United States were 'Free, Sovereign and Independent States', thus confirming the New Republic's status at international law as a State equal to those in Europe.[28] In exchange, *inter alia,* the United States agreed with Britain 'that creditors on either side shall meet with no lawful impediment to the recovery of the full value in sterling money, of all bona fide debts heretofore contracted'.[29] However, in Virginia and Maryland, where many American debtors lived, statutes were enacted permitting them to pay off their creditors in depreciated state or US currency, in Maryland at about 60 per cent of real value, in Virginia at little more than 5 per cent.[30]

Even more troubling was the reluctance of many States to respect the promises of the Peace Treaty to return confiscated property of American Tories who had fought for the King.[31] New York, Pennsylvania, Virginia, and South Carolina, among other states, kept in place statutes discriminating against those Americans who had sided with the Crown in the Revolutionary War.[32] In retaliation, the United Kingdom refused to remove its troops from frontier forts or to negotiate a reciprocal trade treaty.

It was in the light not only of a considerable body of doctrinal and historical precedent about the law of nations, but also some very pressing international legal failures of the new United States under the Articles of Confederation, that the founding fathers in 1787 crafted a new organizing agreement, the US Constitution. Those meeting in Philadelphia to draft the document were not, as we have seen, bereft of formal training in the law of nations, but perhaps no one brought as much learning about the law of nations to Philadelphia's constitutional debate as James Madison (1751–1836), a young Princeton graduate and delegate from Virginia. Madison had

---

[25] RB Morris *The Forging of the Union: 1781–89* (Harper & Row New York 1987) at 62.

[26] ibid 68–9.

[27] Definitive Treaty of Peace and Friendship (signed 3 September 1783) (1783) 48 CTS 487, art I.

[28] P Onuf and N Onuf *Federal Union, Modern World: The Law of Nations in an Age of Revolution 1776–1814* (Madison House Madison 1993) at 113.

[29] Definitive Treaty of Peace and Friendship (n 27) art IV.

[30] *The Forging of the Union* (n 25) 196–201.

[31] Definitive Treaty of Peace and Friendship (n 27) art V.

[32] *The Forging of the Union* (n 25) 196–201.

devoted himself to a vigorous study 'of the most distinguished Confederacies, particularly those of antiquity' in order to improve his contribution to the writing of a new framework of government for the thirteen States.[33] Madison's *Notes* detailed six confederacies—the Lycian, Amphictyonic, Achaean, Helvetic (Swiss), Belgic (Dutch), and Germanic.[34] From his comparative study, Madison determined that the international legal failures of the US states demonstrated that,

[t]his evil has been so fully experienced both during the war and since the peace, results so naturally from the number and independent authority of the States, and has been so uniformly exemplified in every similar confederacy, that it may be considered as not less radically and permanently inherent in, that it is fatal to the object of the present system.[35]

The finished Constitution instituted a new concentration of sovereign authority in the central government to conduct international affairs. Article I (8) granted Congress the power, *inter alia*, to 'provide for the Common Defence and General Welfare of the United States', to 'regulate Commerce with foreign Nations, and among the several States, and with the Indian Tribes', to 'define and punish Piracies and Felonies committed on the high Seas, and Offences against the Law of Nations', to 'declare War, grant Letters of Marque and Reprisal, and make Rules concerning Captures on Law and Water', 'to raise and support Armies', and 'to provide and maintain a Navy'.[36] Article I (10) provided, *inter alia*, that 'No State shall enter into any Treaty, Alliance, or Confederation', nor 'grant Letters of Marque and Reprisal', nor

without the Consent of Congress, lay any Duty of Tonnage, keep troops, or Ships of War in time of Peace, enter into any Agreement or Compact with another State, or with a foreign Power, or engage in War, unless actually invaded, or in such imminent Danger as will not admit of delay.[37]

Article II (2) made the President 'Commander in Chief of the Army and Navy of the United States' and gave the President the 'Power, by and with the Advice and Consent of the Senate, to make Treaties, provided two thirds of the Senators present concur', as well as the power to 'nominate and by and with the Advice and Consent of the Senate, shall appoint Ambassadors'.[38]

   Article III (1) vested the judicial power of the United States in the Supreme Court and the inferior federal courts established by Congress.[39] The judicial power extended in article III (2) 'to all Cases, in Law and Equity, arising under this Constitution, the

---

[33] Quoted in JB Scott *James Madison's Notes of Debates in the Federal Convention of 1787 and their Relation to a More Perfect Society of Nations* (OUP Oxford 1918) at 5–6.

[34] J Madison 'Notes of Ancient and Modern Confederacies, Preparatory to the Federal Convention of 1784' in J Madison *Letters and Other Writings of James Madison* (JB Lippincott & Co Philadelphia 1867) vol 1, 293–315.

[35] ibid 320.

[36] 'The Constitution of the United States' in K Hall, W Wiecek, and P Finkelman (eds) *American Legal History: Cases and Materials* (OUP Oxford 1991) at 567–8.

[37] ibid 569.   [38] ibid 570–1.   [39] ibid 571.

Laws of the United States, and Treaties made, or which shall be made, under their Authority', as well as to, *inter alia*, 'Cases affecting Ambassadors, other public Ministers and Consuls' and to controversies between a State or its citizens and 'foreign states, Citizens or Subjects'.[40] Finally and crucially, there was the supremacy clause of article VI (2):

This Constitution, and the Laws of the United States which shall be made in Pursuance thereof; and all Treaties made, or which shall be made, under the authority of the United States shall be the supreme Law of the Land; and the Judges in every State shall be bound thereby, any Thing in the Constitution or Laws of any State to the Contrary notwithstanding.[41]

The international advantages of a stronger form of national sovereignty and a uniform approach to the law of nations were stressed by James Madison, John Jay, and Alexander Hamilton in their famous essays in favour of state ratification of the Constitution. *The Federalist Papers* have been repeatedly cited over more than two hundred years of constitutional interpretation.[42] In No 3, Jay wrote that

[u]nder the national government, treaties and articles of treaties, as well as the law of nations, will always be expounded in one sense and executed in the same manner—whereas adjudications on the same points and questions in thirteen states, or in three or four confederacies, will not always accord or be consistent'.[43]

Hence, 'either designed or accidental violations of treaties and of the law of nations' will be less likely 'under one general government than under several lesser ones'.[44] Madison, in No 42, similarly maintained that the 'power to define and punish piracies and felonies committed on the high seas and offenses against the law of nations belongs with equal propriety to the general government, and is a still greater improvement on the Articles of Confederation'.[45] In No 53, Madison felt that those elected to the new Congress should be 'acquainted with the treaties between the United States and other nations' and not 'be altogether ignorant of the law of nations'.[46]

The Federalists won the day. The Constitution, finally ratified by all thirteen States, came into force in 1789, the same year as George Washington's first administration. The US Constitution not only had roots in the law of nations and allocated sovereign powers over foreign affairs, it had international implications. For many Americans and Europeans the Constitution signaled a new model of the State, one which it was hoped would be more peaceful than before.[47] The US constitutional model contributed to America's 19th-century inclination towards utopian advocacy of international courts and organizations, culminating in Wilson's League of

---

[40] ibid 571.   [41] ibid 573.

[42] C Rossiter (ed) *The Federalist Papers* (New American Library New York 1961). Jay and Hamilton had studied law at Columbia.

[43] ibid 43.   [44] ibid 44.   [45] ibid 265.

[46] ibid 334.   [47] *Federal Union* (n 28) 65–89.

Nations, topics to which we turn below. At the time, however, the new US constitutional experiment had enough work to do avoiding entangling the New Republic in the many years of European turmoil engendered, also in 1789, by the French Revolution.

4. INTERNATIONAL LAW AND UTOPIA

Probably the most exceptional aspect of American international law is the belief long held by many Americans that the discipline embraces a utopian mission to substitute law and the courtroom for war and the battlefield. American utopian visions for international law and organization became widespread and influential in 19th-century America, largely as a result of the Christian peace movement.[48] Utopianism owed much to religious fervour as pacifism spread from a few groups like the Quakers to other American Protestant denominations.[49] Religious pacifism was reinforced by emerging secular concepts of internationalism.[50]

Some of the earliest texts of the 19th-century American Christian peace movement were penned by David Low Dodge (1774–1852), a Connecticut-born Presbyterian and New York merchant, whose self-study led him to pacifism in 1808. In 1809, Dodge wrote a much-heralded condemnation of war, *The Mediator's Kingdom not of this World but Spiritual, Heavenly, and Divine*. Dodge marshalled economic, political, and humanitarian rationales alongside religious objections to prove that war was wrong and unlawful.[51]

Dodge was a New Englander. This was no coincidence. The 19th-century peace movement was always stronger in New England than elsewhere in the United States.[52] The pacifism of many New Englanders, especially the conservative Federalists, was reinforced by the war of 1812. The interruption of New England's European commerce and British attacks on the coast of New England led many in the region to condemn all wars or at least all aggressive wars. At the abortive, possibly secessionist, Hartford Convention (December 1814–January 1815), delegates from the New

---

[48] FH Hinsley 'The Modern Pattern of War and Peace' in CH Alexandrowicz (ed) *Grotian Society Papers—Studies in the History of the Law of Nations* (Martinus Nijhoff The Hague 1972) 76–89 at 89.

[49] P Brock *Pacifism in the United States from the Colonial Era to the First World War* (Princeton University Press Princeton 1968) at 449.

[50] ACF Beales *The History of Peace: A Short Account of the Organized Movements for International Peace* (Dial Press New York 1931) at 8.

[51] *Pacifism in the United States* (n 49) 450–66.

[52] ibid 469.

England states of Massachusetts, Connecticut, Rhode Island, New Hampshire, and Vermont boldly resolved that '[r]arely can the state of this country call for or justify offensive war'.[53] Dodge's most influential book was published in the heat of war. *War Inconsistent with the Religion of Jesus Christ* appeared in 1814 and showed seven reasons why war was inhuman, eight why it was unwise, and eleven why it was criminal, and concluded with this call to action:

All who earnestly desire and look for the millennial glory of the church should consider that it can never arrive until the spirit and practice of war are abolished. All who love our Lord Jesus Christ in sincerity cannot but ardently desire that wars may cease to the ends of the earth and that mankind should embrace each other as brethren. If so, is it not their duty to do all in their power to promote so benevolent an object?[54]

Not long after Dodge's evangelistic pacifist works came the efforts of Noah Worcester (1758–1837), a New Hampshire-born Unitarian minister in Massachusetts. Worcester, a veteran of the American Revolutionary War, came gradually to his anti-war position. The War of 1812, Worcester wrote, was 'the occasion of perfecting the revolution in my mind in regard to the lawfulness of war'.[55] In 1814, the same year of Dodge's key essay, Worcester published *A Solemn Review of the Custom of War,* which was to become a classic, probably 'the most widely distributed of all Peace literature'.[56] Worcester later explained that he 'became thoroughly convinced that war is the effect of delusion, totally repugnant to the Christian religion, and wholly unnecessary except as it becomes necessary from delusion'.[57]

Worcester applauded the peaceful tradition of the Quakers and Shakers,[58] attacked the depravity occasioned by war upon armies and general populations,[59] and showed how war was contrary to the spirit and teachings of Christianity.[60] He envisioned peace societies spreading to every Christian nation and serving as the vehicles for educating public opinion about the horrors of war.[61] '[L]et lawyers, politicians and divines, and men of every class, who can write or speak, consecrate their talents to the diffusion of light, love and peace.'[62]

When the War of 1812 came to a close, the New England Federalists, now seen as unpatriotic, watched their party slide into political oblivion, but the anti-war sentiment of Dodge and Worcester persisted. So did the idea of peace societies. No sooner was the war against England over in 1815, than Dodge in New York, Worcester in Massachusetts, and two Quakers in Ohio independently founded the world's first

---

[53] T Dwight *History of the Hartford Convention* (N & J White New York 1833) at 351–2, 373 and 378.

[54] DL Dodge *War Inconsistent With the Religion of Jesus Christ* (Ginn & Co Boston 1905) at 120.

[55] H Ware *Memoirs of the Rev. Noah Worcester, D.D.* (J Munroe Boston 1844) at 64.

[56] *The History of Peace* (n 50) 45.

[57] *Memoirs of the Rev. Noah Worcester* (n 55) 66–7.

[58] N Worcester *A Solemn Review of the Custom of War, Showing that War is the Effect of Popular Delusion and Proposing a Remedy* (11th edn SG Simpkins Boston 1833) at 7–8.

[59] ibid 9–10.   [60] ibid 10–17.

[61] ibid 17–24.   [62] ibid 21.

popular peace societies.[63] More state peace societies followed in New England in Maine, New Hampshire, Vermont, Rhode Island, and Connecticut, and, further afield, in Pennsylvania, North Carolina, and Georgia.[64]

Next in the line of Americans dedicated to the elaboration of a utopian model for international law was William Ladd (1778–1841). Born in Exeter, New Hampshire, and graduated in 1797 from Harvard College, Ladd first followed the sea and then settled down in Maine on his family's prosperous farm. His conversion to the peace movement came in 1819, in part due to a reading of Worcester.[65] Ladd made two important contributions to the American utopian movement. First, in 1828, he consolidated the various state peace societies into a national federation, the American Peace Society, of which he served first as executive officer and then its president. He was instrumental in the publication of the society's monthly journal, first called the *Harbinger of Peace* in 1828, and later the *Calumet* in 1831, the *American Advocate of Peace* in 1835, and the *Advocate of Peace,* when in 1837, the American Peace Society moved from Hartford to Boston.[66]

Second, in 1840, Ladd published his *Essay on a Congress of Nations,* which, like Worcester's *Solemn Review,* was to be long remembered. In 1872, Elihu Burritt characterized Ladd as 'the Apostle of Peace' and termed his *Essay's* High Court of Nations 'the noblest and loftiest bar that could be established on earth'.[67] In 1916, James Brown Scott called Ladd's *Essay* an 'abiding title to fame'.[68] In 1935, in a dispassionate and 'scientific' study, Georg Schwarzenberger concluded that there was a 'direct line' in the history of ideas about international organization 'from Ladd to the achievements of Geneva [the *Alabama* arbitration below], and even further, on the foundations of his Equity Tribunal, to a real League of Nations'.[69]

In his *Essay*, Ladd claimed originality only on 'the thought of separating the subject into two distinct parts':

1st. A congress of ambassadors from all those Christian and civilized nations who should choose to send them, for the purpose of settling the principles of international law by compact and agreement, of the nature of a mutual treaty, and also by devising and promoting plans for the preservation of peace, and meliorating the condition of man. 2d. A court of nations, composed of the most able civilians in the world, to arbitrate or judge such cases as should be brought before it, by the mutual consent of two or more contending nations: thus dividing entirely the diplomatic from the judicial functions, which require such different, not to say opposite, characters in the exercise of their functions. I

---

[63] *Pacifism in the United States* (n 49) 458–9 and 472; *The History of Peace* (n 50) 45–6. A year later a British peace society was founded by Quakers in London. ibid 46.

[64] JB Scott 'Introduction' in W Ladd *An Essay on a Congress of Nations* (OUP Oxford 1916) iii–xlv at vii.

[65] ibid iii and v.

[66] ibid vii–viii.

[67] ibid iii.

[68] ibid viii.

[69] G Schwarzenberger *William Ladd: An Examination of an American Proposal for an International Equity Tribunal* (Constable London 1935) at 7 and 37.

consider the Congress as the legislature, and the Court as the judiciary, in the government of nations, leaving the functions of the executive with public opinion, 'the queen of the world'.[70]

Ladd's proposal that the new international organization be divided into legislative, judicial, and executive branches, was a logical step to be taken by an American familiar with comparable provisions for separation of powers in the US Constitution. It also reflected the re-emergence of international arbitration, an encouraging development stimulated by the Jay Treaty. Concluded by the governments of the United States and the United Kingdom, the Jay Treaty was a means for resolving the many disputes still remaining after Britain's formal acknowledgment of American independence in 1783, that generated a surprising number of arbitral awards, some 536 between 1799 and 1804.[71]

Despite the international arbitral progress of the times, Ladd still deserves to be reckoned a visionary. His proposed international court was to go much further than international arbitration had gone before. Moreover, Ladd was writing not only as an intellectual, but also as a leader of a popular American peace movement with considerable influence, particularly between 1835 and 1853.[72] Peace societies were numbered along with anti-slavery, temperance, and missionary societies as 'important 19th century reforms...urged on Christian grounds and advocated with Christian slogans'.[73]

By the 1840s, the American utopian movement for the peaceful reign of international law and organization had already moved from the individual speculations of Dodge and Worcester and the state peace societies, and to William Ladd and the nation-wide American Peace Society. The logical next step was agitation and organization for an international crusade for peace. The person, more than any other, who took that step was 'the learned blacksmith', Elihu Burritt (1810–79). Before he became an advocate for world peace, Burritt was already celebrated in America and England as a gifted linguist who spoke fifty languages.[74] In 1840, the same year as Ladd's *Essay,* Burritt was discovered by Massachusetts Governor Edward Everett, who publicized Burritt's achievements and introduced him to the poet, Longfellow. Longfellow suggested that Burritt work at Harvard, but Burritt chose instead to take to the profitable lecture circuit, where he extolled the potential and realities of self-culture and the

---

[70] *An Essay on a Congress of Nations* (n 64) xlix–1.

[71] AN Nussbaum *A Concise History of the Law of Nations* (Macmillan New York 1954) at 128–9; HJ Schlochauer 'Jay Treaty' in R Berhardt *Encyclopedia of Public International Law* (North Holland Amsterdam 1981) vol 1, 108–11 at 110.

[72] C Phelps *The Anglo-American Peace Movement in the Mid-Nineteenth Century* (Columbia University Press New York 1930) at 12.

[73] ibid 13.

[74] *The Inquirer* (London UK 15 April 1843) 227–8. The figure may have been inflated. Tolis, one of Burritt's biographers, opines that 'the number of languages he could read (he spoke more of them) was closer to thirty than fifty', though admitting that even this was 'no mean accomplishment'. P Tolis *Elihu Burritt: Crusader for Brotherhood* (Archon Books Hamden 1968) at 16–17.

self-made man, topics already made popular in America by the Unitarian minister, William Ellery Channing.[75]

Burritt, like Dodge and Worcester before him, came to the idea of world peace by his own contemplations. Up until 1843, Burritt was apparently unaware of the active peace movements in nearby Hartford and Boston. Preparing a lecture on the earth's anatomy, he became persuaded that the interdependency of the different parts of the globe made an argument against war. He lectured on this topic at the Tremont Theatre in Boston and, speaking to an audience that included some peace advocates, was recruited to the cause of peace. Burritt inaugurated a weekly newspaper, the *Christian Citizen* and, later in Worcester and then in England alongside the Quaker, Edmund Fry, established the paper, *The Bond of Universal Brotherhood*.[76]

Burritt threw his enthusiasm and considerable organizational talent into a peace movement that was already taking on an international, or at least an Anglo-American, character. In 1841, the Boston Convention of the Friends of Peace resolved to call an international peace conference. That meeting, the first Universal Peace Convention, was held in June 1843. The venue was London where it was hoped delegates would attend from all over. There were 292 from the United Kingdom, 26 from America, but only six from the continent.[77] This was all too typical. Despite missionary work on the continent, the American and London Peace Societies were unable to foster any European peace societies before the 1860s except ones in France and Switzerland.[78]

The Anglo-American nature of the peace movement may explain why the Dutch scholar, PH Kooijmans, perhaps looking too narrowly at continental Protestantism, insisted that Protestantism after the time of Grotius had made little impact on the development of international law.[79] A similar predilection was expressed by another continental scholar, who dismissed the 'peace societies and federalist and pacifist movements with their strongest base within the Anglo-American world' as 'incompatible with an attempt to conceptualize the post-Napoleonic system in terms of legal rules'.[80] One suspects that some continental civil lawyers, then as now, have trouble with common law moralizing and are personally more comfortable drawing a black line between the 'science' of law and the 'emotions' of morality and religion, a

---

[75] M Curti *The Learned Blacksmith: The Letters and Journals of Elihu Burritt* (Wilson-Erickson New York 1937) at 1–7; *Elihu Burritt* (n 74) 3–27; D Camp 'World's First Champion of Peace' (1906) 10 Connecticut Magazine 499–602.

[76] *The Learned Blacksmith* (n 75) 28, and 20–1 (Journal entries of 23 May 1843 and 28 June 1843); 'World's First Champion of Peace' (n 75) 602–3.

[77] *The History of Peace* (n 50) 66–7.

[78] ibid 50 and 54–55.

[79] PH Kooijmans 'Protestantism and the Development of International Law' (1976) 152 Recueil des cours 79–118 at 109.

[80] M Koskenniemi *The Gentle Civilizer of Nations: The Rise and Fall of International Law 1870–1960* (CUP Cambridge 2002) at 35.

line often and cheerfully crossed by many Anglo-Americans or, as called by some, 'Anglo-Saxons'.[81]

Surveying the scene in 1845 and 1846, and especially concerned about the possibility of war between Great Britain and the United States over the fate of the Oregon Territory, Burritt was convinced that it was necessary to supplement the existing state and national peace societies with an international peace organization. In May 1846, Burritt left America for England. Expecting to stay in Britain for four months, he remained for four years. Early on, in July 1846, Burritt founded The League of Universal Brotherhood. Key to the League was a pledge by each member to a 'bond' promising to elevate 'man, as a being, as a brother, irrespective of his country, colour, character, or condition' and never to enlist in the armed forces or support any war. By the end of Burritt's stay in England in 1850, the League had come to number about 25,000 Americans and a similar number of Britons, but, despite much effort, only a few others.[82]

Burritt's most remarkable contributions were made as a propagandist, able to reach a broad public with his ideas about peace.[83] His immediate objective in the late 1840s was to dampen the sparks of international conflict that could inflame countries into war. In speeches, pamphlets, and newspapers, Burritt argued not only against war over Oregon, but also against the Mexican–American War, and the possibility of war between England and France.[84]

Burritt went to Paris in August 1848 to organize a new peace conference, but the July Revolution made the city an unhappy venue.[85] Unable to hold the peace conference in Paris, Burritt turned instead to Brussels where his Popular International Peace Congress opened on 20 September 1848. Burritt addressed the meeting on the need for a congress and a court of nations, a project that he acknowledged he had inherited from William Ladd.[86] Paris made up for its revolution of 1848 by hosting in 1849 what may have been 'the most stupendous of the whole series' of international peace conferences.[87] Victor Hugo delivered the inaugural address.[88]

The 1849 Paris Conference welcomed more than 600 delegates, this time many from outside England and America. It marked the moment when the peace movement moved from its Anglo-American religious foundations to take on an international character.[89] Third and fourth peace conferences followed in Frankfurt in 1850 and in London in 1851. Burritt organized mass meetings in England and the continent

---

[81] See MW Janis 'Book Review of WG Grewe The Epochs of International Law' (2010) 57 Netherlands International Law Review 495–507 at 502, 504 and 506.

[82] The Learned Blacksmith (n 75) 29–32; 'World's First Champion of Peace' (n 75) 603; The History of Peace (n 50) 73.

[83] Elihu Burritt (n 74) 132.

[84] The Learned Blacksmith (n 75) 28–32.

[85] The History of Peace (n 50) 76; The Learned Blacksmith (n 75) 38.

[86] 'World's First Champion of Peace' (n 75) 603; The Learned Blacksmith (n 75) 37–9.

[87] The History of Peace (n 50) 78.

[88] ibid 78.   [89] ibid.

and did what he could to moderate the difficulties involving Austria and Denmark over Schleswig-Holstein and the great powers in the Crimea.[90]

Burritt lobbied tirelessly and at remarkably high levels for his peace proposals. In 1849, he urged on Alexis de Tocqueville, then the French Foreign Minister, the cause of peace. The author of *Democracy in America* responded favourably, but 'although personally his sympathies were with all efforts to accomplish such a desirable end he feared that its attainment was far distant'.[91] Much less satisfying were Burritt's meetings with the Germans.[92] In 1854, Burritt had an audience at the White House with Franklin Pierce. The President and Burritt, it seemed, were of quite the same persuasion.[93]

However, even as Pierce and Burritt spoke, this phase of the American utopian movement for international law and organization was coming to an end. Undermining the cause of Burritt and the other peace advocates was the problem of slavery and the political battles about it that would soon lead to the American Civil War.[94] It was the tragic flaw of the early American peace movement that the crusader for world peace was often also the same person as the crusader for the abolition of slavery. Ultimately, the struggle to abolish slavery in America meant war between the States.[95]

If slavery were an injustice and wrong, what should the Christian peace advocate do about it? Were there times when violence, even war, might be justified to right a great wrong? As the Civil War approached, Burritt and the other Christian peace reformers lost support throughout the North as the use of force to eradicate slavery began to be seen by many as a necessary evil. In 1856, William Lloyd Garrison argued: 'Peace or war is a secondary consideration.... Slavery must be conquered—peaceably if we can, forcibly if we must.'[96]

When in April 1861, the Civil War engulfed the nation, Burritt and the other American utopian peace advocates found themselves isolated from the very public opinion in which they so believed.[97] In January 1862, Burritt wrote to his English friend, Edmund Fry, and complained that 'war-fever' in America had cut off his revenues from peace lecturing. Burritt was despondent and even a bit fearful.[98] In a few months, Burritt abandoned war-torn America for England. He would return and live long enough to see peace restored in the United States and to begin again his utopian advocacy of international law and organization.[99] Thanks to Burritt and his prede-

---

[90]   *The Learned Blacksmith* (n 75) 39–41.

[91]   ibid 59–61 (Burritt's Journal 15 July 1849).

[92]   ibid 62 (Burritt's Journal 19 July 1850).

[93]   ibid 82–3 (Burritt's Journal 24 March 1854).

[94]   Another affliction, the Crimean War, beset the English peace movement. *The History of Peace* (n 50) 96–104.

[95]   See the contribution by S Drescher and P Finkelman 'Slavery' in this volume.

[96]   Quoted in *The History of Peace* (n 50) 105–6.

[97]   ibid 104–10; *Pacifism in the United States* (n 49) 689–712.

[98]   Letter of Elihu Burritt to Edmund Fry, 22 January 1862, manuscript in author's collection.

[99]   On Burritt's activities after 1865, see *Pacifism in the United States* (n 49) 921; *Elihu Burritt* (n 74) 269–92; *The Learned Blacksmith* (n 75) 150–241.

cessors Dodge, Worcester, and Ladd, the plans for an international court had been drawn durably enough that they would survive the conflagration of the Civil War.

The importance of the American religious utopians who flourished between 1815 and 1860 is easily missed nowadays when the international law enterprise is dominated by legal professionals. However, the impact of religious optimism and organization was crucial in contributing to a social climate in the 19th century where there was a remarkable general agreement among Americans that the law of nations was fundamentally a good thing. The utopian ambitions of Dodge, Worcester, Ladd, and Burritt fashioned an international-law-friendly popular sentiment that deeply influenced American leaders in the late 19th and early 20th centuries.

After the Civil War, some Americans returned to the thought that war's days might well be numbered. The great law codifier, David Dudley Field remarked at the 1876 Centennial Celebration in Philadelphia:

The history of international law since July 4, 1776, shows that, notwithstanding the prevalence of almost universal war during the last quarter of the past century and the first fifteen years of the present, there has been a general tendency of the nations to approach each other more closely, to avoid war as much as possible, and to diminish its severity, when it occurs.[100]

In 1910, John W Foster, President Harrison's Secretary of State and grandfather of President Eisenhower's Secretary of State, John Foster Dulles, opined that all three of America's 19th-century foreign conflicts—the War of 1812, the 1846 Mexican War, and the 1898 Spanish–American War—could have been avoided if the disputes precipitating them had 'been submitted to arbitration and decided without recourse to war'.[101]

Most important of all for the optimism of the time was the judgment of the Alabama arbitral tribunal, probably the most influential event of 19th-century American international law. Delivered in 1872, the Alabama judgment was the work of an ad hoc tribunal composed of five judges: Charles Francis Adams, Sir Alexander Cockburn, Count Frederic Sclopis, Jacques Staempfli, and Baron d'Itajubá, named by each of the United States, Great Britain, Italy, Switzerland, and Brazil. The panel was empowered by Great Britain and the United States in 1871 to decide whether the United Kingdom had violated international law when it permitted British companies to build Confederate warships, notably the cruisers Alabama, Florida, and Shenandoah, which preyed on Union shipping during the American Civil War. After the North's victory over the secessionist South in 1865, the United States demanded that the United Kingdom pay compensation for the losses caused by the British-built warships.

---

[100] DD Field 'American Contributions to International Law' (1876) 14 Albany Law Journal 257–61 at 258.

[101] JW Foster 'Were the Questions Involved in the Foreign Wars of the United States of Such a Nature that They Could Have Been Submitted to Arbitration of Settled Without Recourse to War?' in *Proceedings of International Conference Under the Auspices of American Society for Judicial Settlement of International Disputes: December 15–17, 1910* (Waverly Press Baltimore 1912) 44–68.

After hearing argument, the *Alabama* tribunal ruled that Britain had owed the United States a duty of 'active due diligence' to prevent private parties from supplying the southern rebels, but had failed to observe her international obligations as a neutral State.[102] The United States claimed about $21 million in direct and $4 million in indirect damages caused by the attacks of the *Alabama* and her sister Confederate raiders; the United Kingdom acknowledged only about $8 million in direct damages.[103] The arbitrators split the difference, ordering Great Britain to pay the United States some $15,500,000.[104] The full sum was proffered in British Treasury Bonds on 9 September 1873. The American receipt was framed and hung in 10 Downing Street.[105]

The *Alabama* arbitration was an exceptionally encouraging development for American international law enthusiasts. Some years earlier, in 1865, Lord Russell, the British Foreign Secretary, had refused to arbitrate the *Alabama* claims on the grounds that the British government were 'sole guardians of their own honor'.[106] War between the two countries was not an outlandish possibility. The United States and Great Britain had already fought twice in the Revolutionary War (1775–83) and the War of 1812 (1812–15). It seemed credible that a third Anglo-American conflict might break out, a struggle not only about compensation for the Confederate maritime attacks, but also to settle possession of Canada, a part of the British Empire much coveted by some Americans.[107]

The eventual success of the *Alabama* arbitration became an important popular demonstration that it was possible for powerful States to arbitrate important disputes and thereby avoid war. General Ulysses S Grant (1822–85), President of the United States during the *Alabama* arbitration, was so encouraged by the tribunal's deeds that the old warrior predicted 'an epoch when a court recognized by all nations will settle international differences instead of keeping large standing armies'.[108] David Dudley Field turned to the *Alabama* proceedings to demonstrate the probability of the eventual success of international arbitration.[109] The *Alabama* judgment, now largely forgotten, was at the time profoundly influential. In the words of Samuel Eliot

---

[102] H Blomeyer-Bartenstein 'Due Diligence' in R Bernhardt (ed) *Encyclopedia of Public International Law* (North Holland Amsterdam 1987) vol 10, 138–43.

[103] US Department of State *Papers Relating to the Treaty of Washington* (Government Printing Office Washington DC 1872) vol 4 (Geneva Arbitration) at 41–2.

[104] WW Bishop *International Law* (3rd edn Little Brown Boston 1971) at 1023–7.

[105] GJ Wetter *The International Arbitral Process: Public and Private* (Oceana Dobbs Ferry New York 1979) vol 1, at 170–1.

[106] CC Hyde *International Law Chiefly as Interpreted and Applied by the United States* (Little Brown Boston 1922) vol 2, at 120.

[107] SE Morison *The Oxford History of the American People* (OUP Oxford 1965) at 726–9.

[108] CD Davis *The United States and the First Hague Peace Conference* (Cornell University Press Ithaca NY 1962) at 13–14.

[109] DD Field 'International Law' (1873) 8 Albany Law Journal 277–81 at 279.

Morison, 'never before had disputes involving such touchy subjects of national honor been submitted to the majority vote of an international tribunal'.[110]

Emboldened by the *Alabama* decision, peace activists began to push anew for an international peace congress that would formulate a universal code of international law and create an international organization devoted to the promotion of peace. The activists included Elihu Burritt, who returned to the United States in 1870, after seven years in England.[111] It may be that the idea for a new peace congress sprang from a meeting between Burritt and the Secretary of the American Peace Society, Reverend James B Miles, in 1870, when both were stranded by a storm in New Bedford, Massachusetts. Burritt's health did not permit him to cross the Atlantic again, but Miles went to Europe to promote the scheme. The overseas response being favourable, Miles and others gathered at David Dudley Field's house in New York on 15 May 1873. There they resolved to organize a congress in Brussels in October and to constitute an International Code Committee in the United States to muster American support.[112]

Field's International Code Committee led to the establishment, also in 1873, of the Association for the Reform and Codification of the Law of Nations, an organization now known as the International Law Association. Unlike the *Institut de droit international*, founded the same year but more academically oriented, the Association welcomed

to its membership, not only lawyers, but shipowners, underwriters, merchants, and philanthropists, and received delegates from affiliated bodies, such as Chambers of Commerce and Shipping, and Arbitration or Peace Sections, thus admitting all who are interested in the improvement of international relations.[113]

Though broad-based in its membership both by occupation and by nationality, the Association was in large measure the product of the American peace advocates.[114]

High aspirations for international courts were shared by many Americans in the late 19th century. To inspire them there were the excellent example of the *Alabama* arbitration, many other successful international arbitrations, the new International Law Association, the on-going American Peace Society, and the Universal Peace Union. The last was the publisher of the influential magazine, *The Peacemaker*, which began to advocate general arbitration treaties, a permanent international arbitral court, and gradual disarmament.[115] It was argued that the cause of peace would be

---

[110]   *The Oxford History of the American People* (n 107) 729.

[111]   *The Learned Blacksmith* (n 75) 150–1.

[112]   KH Nadelmann 'International Law at America's Centennial: The International Code Committee's Centennial Celebration and the Centenary of Field's International Code' (1976) 70 American Journal of International Law 519–29 at 522–3.

[113]   International Law Association *Report of the First Conference, held at Brussels, 1873, and of the Second Conference, held at Geneva, 1874* (West, Newman & Co. London 1903) at v.

[114]   ibid iv–v.   [115]   *The United States* (n 108) 8–15.

much advanced if a permanent arbitral court were available to which countries could submit their disputes.[116]

The Russian Tsar, hard pressed by the cost of the global arms race, called for an international peace conference. It met at The Hague in 1899. The United States, as well as the United Kingdom, pressed for a permanent and universal court of arbitration. Although Germany at first resisted such notions, in time she weakened her opposition, and the delegates adopted the Convention for the Pacific Settlement of International Dispute.[117] This Hague Arbitration Convention, somewhat modified by a second Hague Conference in 1907, required its parties 'to use their best efforts to insure the pacific settlement of international differences'.[118] States were first to rely on the good offices or mediation of friendly third States to settle their disagreements, that is, on informal diplomatic procedures, but if good offices and mediation proved unsuccessful, then the convention provided for the establishment of international commissions of inquiry, which were to 'elucidat[e] the facts by means of an impartial and conscientious investigation' and then issue nonbinding reports.[119] The convention also established the first permanent panel of international arbitrators, the Permanent Court of Arbitration (PCA), from which States could designate specific arbitrators to sit on ad hoc tribunals that could hear cases submitted voluntarily by States and render legally binding awards.[120]

The establishment of the PCA owed much to the 19th-century American peace movement. The specific proposal leading to the PCA came from the British delegate to the 1899 Hague Peace Conference, Lord Pauncefote, who had read a pamphlet describing the peace movement and its plans for an international court. Pauncefote, believing that aspirations for disarmament were unrealistic, felt that it was 'possible that there should be a movement in the direction of a court of arbitration'.[121] The influential pamphlet, *International Justice*, was the work of David Jayne Hill (1850–1932), then US Assistant Secretary of State, and later Ambassador to Berlin.[122] Hill was a staunch advocate of international arbitration.[123] His pamphlet, read by Pauncefote, had first been published as an article in the *Yale Law Journal* in 1896,[124] where Hill explicated a resume of the peace and codification movements.

---

[116] S Amos *Remedies for War* (Harper & Brothers New York 1880) at 123.

[117] The United States (n 108) at 146–72; D Bederman 'The Hague Peace Conferences of 1899 and 1907' in M Janis (ed) *International Courts for the Twenty-First Century* (Martinus Nijhoff Dordrecht 1992) at 9.

[118] The Hague Convention for the Pacific Settlement of International Disputes (signed 29 July 1899) (1899) 187 CTS 410, art 15.

[119] ibid arts 2–14.

[120] ibid arts 15–57.

[121] JB Scott *The Hague Court Reports* (OUP Oxford 1916) at xiii–xiv.

[122] ibid.

[123] A Parkman *David Jayne Hill and the Problem of World Peace* (Bucknell University Press 1975).

[124] DJ Hill 'International Justice' (1896) 6 Yale Law Journal 1–19.

So, finally was the international court project moved from theory to practice. The PCA was hailed by one of its creators as the 'greatest achievement' of the first Hague Conference.[125] John W Foster confidently predicted that the

nations will, with greater frequency, carry their differences to the Hague; and the Temple, for the construction of which the generous American citizen, Mr. Carnegie, has provided the means, bids fair to be thronged with suitors appealing to reason and international justice for the protection of their national rights.[126]

Mr Carnegie's 'Temple' is the Peace Palace, presently the home of the International Court of Justice, as well as that of the still extant PCA. Joseph Choate, the First Delegate of the United States to the Second Hague Peace Conference, wrote in 1913 that there were preparations for a third Hague Conference in 1915, along with plans to 'celebrate the completion of a century of unbroken peace between ourselves and all other great nations of the earth'. No third Conference was held. The century of unbroken peace was missed by a year.[127] The Great War began.

The effect of the First World War on American attitudes to international law was profound. Watching 'civilized' Europe slip into such a dreadful loss of life and treasure for so little good reason shook the intellectual foundations of those Americans who believed in the inevitability of progress and cared deeply about the law of nations. Beginning in 1914, American idealists knew they would need to think again about any great expectations for international law. As Europe's armies began to kill millions, it was plain that the 19th-century promise of the law of nations had not been kept.

Key to the transformation of American expectations for international law was Woodrow Wilson (1856–1924), President of the United States (1913–21). As an academic political scientist and President of Princeton University and Governor of New Jersey, Wilson showed little interest in international law.[128] Only when Wilson became President of the United States in 1913, did he begin to take a rather different view. He had famously remarked to a Princeton friend a few days before moving to Washington: 'It would be the irony of fate if my administration had to deal chiefly with foreign affairs.'[129] Probably to Wilson's surprise, international law emerged as a necessary part of his new job. As President of a neutral United States during the first years of World War I, Wilson had to be deeply concerned about international law, especially violations of it. In his 'Fourth of July Address' in 1914, after the assassinations in Sarajevo in June, but before the beginning of hostilities in August, Wilson was already speaking of the importance of upholding treaty obligations.[130]

---

[125]   JH Choate *The Two Hague Conferences* (Princeton University Press 1913) at 31–2.
[126]   JW Foster *Arbitration and the Hague Court* (Houghton Mifflin Boston 1904) at 76.
[127]   *The Two Hague Conferences* (n 125) 92.
[128]   *America and the Law of Nations* (n 1) 159–165.
[129]   AS Link *Wilson the Diplomatist* (Johns Hopkins Press 1957) at 5.
[130]   W Wilson 'A Fourth of July Address (1914)' *The Papers of Woodrow Wilson* (AS Link ed) (Princeton University Press Princeton 1979) vol 30, 248–56 at 253.

When the European war broke out, Wilson appealed to all Americans to remain 'neutral in fact as well as in name during these days that are to try men's souls'.[131] Soon after, on 22 August 1914, Wilson's principal advisor, Colonel House, whom Wilson called 'my second personality...my independent self', advised:

Germany's success will ultimately mean trouble for us. We will have to abandon the path which you are blazing as a standard for future generations, with permanent peace as its goal and a new international ethics code as its guiding star, and build up a military machine of vast proportions.[132]

A few months later, Wilson echoed Colonel House in a speech to the American Bar Association: 'Our first thought, I suppose, as lawyers, is of international law, of those bonds of right and principle which draw the nations together and hold the community of the world to some standards of action'.[133]

Faced with attacks on trans-Atlantic shipping by German U-boats, Wilson invoked 'the whole fine fabric of international law' as justification for permitting Americans, still neutral in the combat, to travel on Allied shipping for to do otherwise, international law 'might crumble under our hands piece by piece'.[134] This policy, however, began to edge Wilson and the United States nearer to war. On 7 May 1915, off Ireland a German submarine sank the British passenger liner *Lusitania*, costing more than a thousand lives, including 128 Americans.[135]

The descent to war quickened in early 1917, when the German government, in hopes of winning the conflict, adopted the fateful decision to begin unrestricted submarine warfare. Colonel House, for Wilson, urged the Germans to relent, but on 31 January 1917, the German ambassador notified US Secretary of State Lansing that no such reversal was possible. On 3 February, Wilson told Congress he was breaking diplomatic relations with Germany. On 25 February, a submarine sank the British passenger liner *Laconia* with two American deaths. On 1 March 1917, it became known that the German Foreign Minister had proposed in the so-called Zimmerman Telegram that Mexico fight alongside Germany and win back Texas, Arizona, and New Mexico from the United States. Soon thereafter, three US merchant ships were sunk by German submarines. On 20 March, Wilson's Cabinet voted unanimously for war with Germany.[136]

When, on 2 April 1917, Wilson went to Congress for a declaration of war against imperial Germany, he entered into a brief but decisive phase of involvement with

[131] W Wilson 'An Appeal to the American People (19 August 1914)' ibid 393–4 at 394.
[132] Quoted in R Hofstadter 'Woodrow Wilson: The Conservative as Liberal' in R Hofstadter *The American Political Tradition and the Men Who Made It* (Vintage New York 1974) 307–66 at 308 and 340.
[133] W Wilson 'Remarks to the American Bar Association (20 October 1914)' in *Papers of Woodrow Wilson* (AS Link ed) (Princeton University Press 1979) vol 31, 184–7 at 184.
[134] 'An Appeal to the American People' (n 132) 345.
[135] *Wilson the Diplomatist* (n 129) 56.
[136] T Knock *To End all Wars: Woodrow Wilson and the Quest for a New World Order* (Princeton University Press Princeton 1995) at 105–7.

international law. Far from a subject of little interest, no longer just a matter of presidential concern, international law became, for war-president Woodrow Wilson, a passionate engagement. Indeed, the progressive development of international law and organization became his chief justification for bringing the United States into a bloody and much regretted conflict.

To understand Wilson's final passion for international law, it will help to comprehend his personal anguish in launching the United States into the horrors of Europe's Great War. And to understand that anguish, it is useful to remember Wilson's boyhood acquaintance with an equally awful conflagration, the American Civil War. Thomas Knock captures the young Wilson:

Thomas Woodrow Wilson's earliest memory was of hearing, at the age of four, that Abraham Lincoln had been elected President and that there would soon be a war. His father, the Reverend Dr. Joseph Ruggles Wilson, was one of Georgia's most prominent Presbyterian ministers and, despite his Yankee heritage, an ardent Southern sympathizer. Both of Wilson's parents were Northerners; in the 1850's, they had moved from Ohio to Staunton, Virginia (where Wilson was born in 1856), and eventually to Augusta, Georgia, where the Civil War overshadowed Wilson's childhood. As his eighth birthday approached, he witnessed the solemn march of thousands of Confederate troops on their way to defend the city against Sherman's invasion. He watched wounded soldiers die inside his father's church and pondered the fate of the ragged Union prisoners confined in the churchyard outside. Soon he would see Jefferson Davis paraded under Union guard through the streets and would recall standing 'for a moment at General Lee's side and looking up into his face'. Wilson once commented, 'A boy never gets over his boyhood, and never can change those subtle influences which have become a part of him'. It is an important fact that he experienced, at an impressionable age, the effects of a great war and its aftermath.[137]

The son of a Presbyterian minister and a Presbyterian minister's daughter, Wilson, in the words of Richard Hofstadter, was reared 'to look upon life as the progressive fulfilment of God's will and to see man as 'a distinct moral agent' in a universe of moral imperatives'.[138] Wilson 'never aspired to be a clergyman, but he made politics his means of spreading spiritual enlightenment, of expressing the powerful Protestant urge for "service"'.[139] During the Great War, international law became Wilson's mission.

The echoes of the Civil War and his powerful Protestant sense of moral mission were plain two years after America's declaration of war when Wilson went to the US Senate looking for its advice and consent to the League of Nations Covenant[140] which he had personally negotiated in Paris. Wilson spoke of Congress's assent to sending troops to fight in France:

---

[137] ibid 3.   [138] 'Woodrow Wilson' (n 132) 308.   [139] ibid.
[140] League of Nations Covenant (concluded 28 June 1919, entered into force 10 January 1920) (1919) 225 CTS 195.

Let us never forget the purpose—the high purpose, the disinterested purpose—with which America lent its strength, not for its own glory but for the defense of mankind. I think there is nothing that appeals to the imagination more in the history of man than those convoyed fleets crossing the ocean with the millions of American soldiers aboard—those crusaders, those men who loved liberty enough to leave their homes and fight for them upon the distant fields of battle, those men who swung into the open as if in fulfillment of the long prophecy of American history. What a halo and glory surrounds those old men whom we now greet with such reverence, the men who were the soldiers in our Civil War! They saved a Nation! When these youngsters grow old who have come back from the fields of France, what a halo will be around their brows! They saved the world! They are of the same stuff as those old veterans of the Civil War.[141]

What would justify this great sacrifice? Three years before, Wilson had already invoked international adjudication with religious enthusiasm.[142] Once the war began, Wilson went further, moving from merely advocating an international tribunal, to the idealistic promotion of a fully fledged international government, the League of Nations:

If it be in deed and in truth the common object of the Governments associated against Germany and of the nations whom they govern, as I believe it to be, to achieve by the coming settlements a secure and lasting peace, it will be necessary that all who sit down at the peace table shall come ready and willing to pay the price, the only price, that will procure it; and ready and willing, also, to create in some virile fashion the only instrumentality by which it can be made certain that the agreements of the peace will be honored and fulfilled. That price is impartial justice in every item of the settlement, no matter whose interest is crossed, and not only impartial justice, but also the satisfaction of the several peoples whose fortunes are dealt with. That indispensable instrumentality is a League of Nations formed under covenants that will be efficacious.[143]

Wilson's conversion to the promise of international law and organization was remarkable. After years of doubt about the potential of the law of nations, he had become fully committed to an extreme utopian form of the discipline, a belief in world government. Arguing that 'International Law [was] Completely Changed',[144] Wilson wrote that

[i]nternational law up to this time has been the most singular code of manners. You could not mention to any other government anything that concerned it unless you could prove that your own interests were involved....In other words, at present, we have to mind our own business.[145]

---

[141] *Woodrow Wilson's Case for the League of Nations* (H Foley ed) (Princeton University Press Princeton 1923) 20–1.

[142] Woodrow Wilsons' speech in Des Moines, Iowa, 1 February 1916 is quoted in JB Scott *An International Court of Justice* (OUP Oxford 1916) at ii.

[143] W Wilson '27 September 1918 [Address in New York]' in D Day (ed) *Woodrow Wilson's Own Story* (Little Brown Boston 1952) 284–9 at 285.

[144] *Woodrow Wilson's Case* (n 141) 103.

[145] ibid 103–4.

But, once the United States joined the League of Nations, Americans would be able to 'mind other people's business and everything that affects the peace of the world, whether we are parties to it or not. We can force a nation on the other side of the globe to bring to that bar of mankind any wrong that is afoot in that part of the world which is likely to affect the good understanding between nations, and we can oblige them to show cause why it should not be remedied'.[146] This was supra-nationalism, a thoroughgoing imposition on state sovereignty. Even now Wilson's goal of having Americans 'mind other people's business' rings out of tune with majority American sentiment.

The apotheosis of Wilson's vision of a new international law came in his famous Fourteen Points speech of 8 January 1918. This eloquent statement of American war aims not only hastened peace with Germany and the other central powers, but charted Wilson's proposed ethical course for international relations:

We entered this war because violations of right had occurred which touched us to the quick and made the life of our own people impossible unless they were corrected and the world secured once for all against their recurrence. What we demand in this war, therefore, is nothing peculiar to ourselves. It is that the world be made fit and safe to live in; and particularly that it be made safe for every peace-loving nation which, like our own, wishes to live its own life, determine its own institutions, be assured of justice and fair dealing by the other peoples of the world as against force and selfish aggression. All the peoples of the world are in effect partners in this interest, and for our own part we see very clearly that unless justice be done to others it will not be done to us. The program of the world's peace, therefore, is our program; and that program, the only possible program, as we see it, is this.

The most important was article 14:

A general association of nations must be formed under specific covenants for the purpose of affording mutual guarantees of political independence and territorial integrity to great and small states alike.[147]

The Fourteen Points proved critical in the final days of the war. Germany gambled in the spring of 1917 that launching unrestricted submarine warfare, although it would probably bring America into the war, would finish off England and France before American troops could arrive in Europe in considerable number. Things looked brightest for Germany in early 1918, when, with Russia beset by revolution and out of the war, Germany moved her eastern armies to the Western front in an attempt to finally crush the Allies. However, English and French forces held the line outside Paris in July, and by the fall of 1918, the United States arrived in full force. When the Allies broke through the German lines and approached the German border, Germany

---

[146] ibid 104.

[147] W Wilson 'Address to Congress, Stating the War Aims and Peace Terms of the United States (Delivered in Joint Session, 8 January 1918)' in A Shaw (ed) *State Papers and Adresses by Woodrow Wilson* (George H Doran Company New York 1918) 464–72 at 470.

agreed to surrender on the terms of Wilson's Fourteen Points. On 11 November 1918, a Pre-Armistice Agreement brought hostilities to a halt.[148]

Wilson's discovery of international law and organization came at a crucial time for the discipline. Many of its adherents had grown disheartened by the outrages of the Great War. Indeed, the leaders of the American Society of International Law decided not to hold an annual meeting in 1918, 1919, and 1920, years in which, one would have thought, discussion and promotion of international law would have been especially useful. Incredibly, in 1918, the Executive Council of the American Society of International Law, including Elihu Root and James Brown Scott, resolved:

> The Executive Council of the American Society of International Law consider that the very existence of international law is now at issue. The Committee on the Annual Meeting has therefore refrained from calling the members of the Society from the active work on which most of them are engaged to meet for the discussion of questions of law. The only greater question of international law today is whether that law should continue to exist.[149]

By 1918, it was Wilson, who had once held so little hope for international law, who had become international law's most fervent advocate. International law's long-standing proponents, Brown and Root, severely disillusioned by the Great War, were doubting their discipline. Wilson's sense of personal responsibility had transformed him into a passionate believer in the absolute necessity of transforming international law and organization and making them the principal justification for the loss of life of the Great War. Arthur Link has remarked that 'Wilson's uncommon concern with the fundamental principle of national and international life sometimes led him to over-simplify the vast complexities of international politics'.[150] Coming to expect too much of international law and organization, Wilson, by 1918, had finally and decisively become a 'Wilsonian'. It was the 'Wilsonian' Wilson who would travel to Paris to try to put his Fourteen Points into practice. He did so with a faith in himself and in his presidential role that had already been elaborated in 1900, deep in his academic years at Princeton: 'When foreign affairs play a prominent part in the politics and policy of a nation, its Executive must of necessity be its guide: must utter every initial judgment, take every first step of action, supply the information upon which it is to act, suggest and in large measure control its conduct'.[151] Sadly, Wilson's absolutism joined to his passionate conversion to the cause of international law and organization, would divide the nation along political lines and undermine the American consensus that the law of nations was, generally, good for the country. Wilson selected five American plenipotentiaries for the Paris Peace Conference himself, Colonel House, US Secretary

---

[148] *Wilson the Diplomatist* (n 129) 106–8.

[149] 'Minutes of the Meeting of the Executive Council: 27 April 1918' (1918/1919) 12/13 Proceedings of the American Society of International Law at the Meeting of Its Executive Council 5–21 at 14.

[150] *Wilson the Diplomatist* (n 129) 18.

[151] W Wilson *Congressional Government: A Study in American Politics* (15th edn Houghton Mifflin Boston 1900) at 22.

of State Lansing, General Tasker Bliss, and the diplomat Henry White. Wilson's decision to go himself to Paris was regretted by many, including Secretary of State Lansing, who noted in his diary that Wilson 'is making one of the greatest mistakes of his career, and will imperil his reputation'.[152] Harold Nicolson concluded that Wilson ought to have remained in Washington to keep in touch with and reconcile American political opinion, and that his presence in Paris 'was a serious misfortune'.[153] When Wilson set sail from New York on 4 December 1918, he left behind both William Howard Taft and Henry Cabot Lodge, key Republicans who had supported the war. Wilson seemed little concerned to garner Republican support for either the League of Nations or for international law.[154]

Wilson would have found Republican support useful in Europe, as well as in America. Many were not so keen on the League of Nations as Wilson. The French, especially, were suspicious, seeing the peace conference as a way to end the war with Germany and to re-establish a balance of power in Europe. Clemenceau, the French Prime Minister, rebutted Wilson's belief in a League of Nations by referring 'to Wilson's noble *candeur*, a word that can mean either candour or pathetic naiveté'.[155] The French prepared an agenda for the peace talks, paying hardly attention to the League, Wilson rejected it.[156] Lloyd George, the British Prime Minister, was more sympathetic, and with British support, Wilson succeeded in putting the League first and foremost. Wilson himself served as chair of the commission on the League that met first on 25 January 1919. To the surprise of many, Wilson suggested that the commission prepare a draft of the League Covenant in only two weeks, but on 14 February 1919, the same day he set sail for the United States, Wilson was able to offer a draft League Covenant to the Versailles Conference.[157]

Wilson's principal achievement was article 10 providing for collective security.[158] Articles XII to XV set up a scheme of international arbitration and adjudication, calling for the creation of a Permanent Court of International Justice. When Wilson left Paris by train for Brest to sail home, Colonel House noted: 'He looked happy as well indeed he should.'[159] Wilson had succeeded in setting up a form of international organization and adjudication, the dream of the 19th-century American utopians. However, Wilson, a late-comer to the movement, was unfamiliar with its history. Thomas Knock has insightfully remarked:

---

[152]   Quoted in H Nicolson *Peacemaking 1919* (Universal Library New York 1965) at 73.
[153]   ibid 69–74.
[154]   M Macmillan *Paris 1919* (Random House New York 2003) at 5–6 and 87–8; *To End All Wars* (n 136) 199–204.
[155]   ibid 23.
[156]   ibid 55.
[157]   ibid 83–91.
[158]   *Wilson the Diplomatist* (n 129) 120.
[159]   *To End all Wars* (n 136) 226.

As President of the United States he would incorporate into his own program their proposals for arbitration of international disputes and disarmament, and others pertaining to
world federation. At length, however, Wilson's impact on the peace movement would prove
greater than its impact on him.[160]

To the dismay of both the peace movement and himself, Wilson failed to persuade
most Americans that these new creations of international law were good things.
Home for a month, Wilson began his battle against the now-dominant Republicans
about the very wisdom of international law and organization. He did not do so effectively. In the words of one commentator, the Draft Covenant 'expressed Wilson's lone
handed radically executive approach to foreign policy'.[161] The British were already
suspicious of Wilson, feeling, correctly as it turned out, that Wilson was speaking
neither for the Senate nor for the majority of the American people in his readiness to
commit the United States to a powerful international institution.[162] Back in Paris on
14 March, Wilson returned to international rather than domestic politics. On 28 April
1919, he secured adoption of the Covenant of the League of Nations from the peace
conference.

Then, between May and October 1919, Wilson fought and lost his personal campaign for the League in the United States. Failing to win the support he sought in the
Senate, Wilson set off on a national speaking tour on 3 September 1919, aiming to rally
American popular opinion behind the Versailles Treaty and the League of Nations.
According to Secretary of State Lansing, Wilson was 'very angry' at the Senate, and
'that he was going to go to the people at once and that if [the Senate] wanted war, he
would "give them a belly full"'.[163] Wilson delivered forty speeches in twenty-one days,
more than he had ever given before.[164] He was exhausted.

On 25 September 1919, in Pueblo, Colorado, Wilson's health finally broke. After
making what would be not only the last speech on his trip, but his last prolonged
public speech ever, Wilson cancelled the last stops on his tour and returned to
Washington. On 2 October 1919, the President suffered a debilitating stroke. His
public life was effectively over.[165] Wilson, sick and intransigent, refused to compromise with Lodge and the Republicans. The Senate voted down the Treaty of
Versailles on 19 November 1919, and rejected it again on 19 March 1920.[166] Wilson's
passionate cause, the League of Nations, was left a shambles. Its intellectual
context, America's 'Wilsonian' vision of international law, was in no better
condition.

---

[160] ibid 12.

[161] J Cooper Jr *Breaking the Heart of the World: Woodrow Wilson and the Fight for the League of Nations*
(CUP Cambridge 2001) at 54.

[162] *Peacemaking 1919* (n 152) 205–7.

[163] *Breaking the Heart of the World* (n 161) 152.

[164] ibid 158–9.   [165] ibid 189–98.   [166] ibid 234–375.

RECOMMENDED READING

Armitage, David 'The Declaration of Independence and International Law' (2002) 59 William and Mary Quarterly 39–64.

Beales, Arthur CF *The History of Peace: A Short Account of the Organized Movement for International Peace* (Dial Press New York 1931).

Bourguignon, Henry J 'Incorporation of the Law of Nations during the American Revolution—The Case of the San Antonio' (1977) 71 American Journal of International Law 270–95.

Brock, Peter *Pacifism in the United States from the Colonial Era to the First World War* (Princeton University Press Princeton 1968).

Choate, Joseph H *The Two Hague Conferences* (Princeton University Press Princeton 1913).

Cooper, John M Jr *Breaking the Heart of the World: Woodrow Wilson and the Fight for the League of Nations* (CUP Cambridge 2001).

Curti, Merle E *The Learned Blacksmith: The Letters and Journals of Elihu Burritt* (Wilson-Erickson New York 1937).

Davis, Calvin D *The United States and the First Hague Peace Conference* (Cornell University Press Ithaca 1962).

Dodge, David L *War Inconsistent With the Religion of Jesus Christ* (Ginn & Co Boston 1844).

Foley, Hamilton (ed) *Woodrow Wison's Case for the League of Nations* (Princeton University Press Princeton 1923).

Janis, Mark W *America and the Law of Nations 1776–1939* (OUP Oxford 2010).

Knock, Thomas J *To End All Wars: Woodrow Wilson and the Quest for a New World Order* (Princeton University Press Princeton 1995).

Ladd, William *An Essay on a Congress of Nations for the Adjustment of International Disputes without Resort to Arms* (OUP Oxford 1916).

Link, Arthur S *Wilson the Diplomat* (Johns Hopkins Press Baltimore 1957).

Nadelmann, Kurt H 'International Law at America's Centennial: The International Code Committee's Centennial Celebration and the Centenary of Field's International Code' (1976) 70 American Journal of International Law 519–29.

Phelps, Christina *The Anglo-American Peace Movement in the Mid-Nineteenth Century* (Columbia University Press New York 1930).

Reeves, Jesse S 'The Influence of the Law of Nations Upon International Law in the United States' (1909) 3 American Journal of International Law 547–61.

Rossiter, Clinton (ed) *The Federalist Papers* (New American Library New York 1961).

Schwarzenberger, Georg *William Ladd: An Examination of an American Proposal for an International Equity Tribunal* (Constable London 1935).

Worcester, Noah *A Solemn Review of the Custom of War, Showing that War is the Effect of Popular Delusion and Proposing a Remedy* (SG Simpkins Boston 1833).

CHAPTER 23

LATIN AMERICA

JORGE L ESQUIROL

1. INTRODUCTION

THIS chapter focuses on the international law most relevant to Latin Americans, from the wars of independence beginning in 1810 to the middle of the 20th century. The most renowned development was, no doubt, the assertion of a uniquely Latin American international law, equal in rank to general international law. It was premised on the different practices and treaties of American States. However, this was not the only important creation of international law in the region. A range of local events spurred distinct doctrinal developments. For instance, the international recognition of internal belligerents, conferring legal personality on revolutionaries, was reputedly forged in the Spanish American wars of independence. The modern definition of *uti possidetis*, affirming colonial administrative demarcations as the borders of newly independent States, was fitted to resolve territorial disputes among Latin American States. No less, the series of regional conferences starting with the Congress of Panama in 1826 foreshadowed later regional and international organizations. Indeed, a number of familiar constructs of modern international law are linked to Latin America.

2. RECOGNITION OF BELLIGERENCY

The earliest international recognition of internal rebels is often traced to the Spanish American wars of independence, from 1810 to 1826.[1] This period marks the first appreciable application of the international legal concept of belligerency, before the doctrine expressly existed. The Spanish American 'republics in arms' operated internationally prior to any formal acknowledgement of their existence as sovereign States or duly constituted governments.[2] This form of 'recognition' was novel in the early 19th century.[3] The revolutionary wars of the period, it can be said, set in motion belligerency's later theorization. In brief, it came to be seen that, once certain factual preconditions were met, third-party States could and arguably should recognize the international standing of rebels, granting them the same belligerent rights as sovereigns.[4] This legal doctrine presented a rather incomplete picture of historical events, however. It omitted many weighty considerations of foreign policy that were inseparable from recognition decisions. No doubt related to these failings, the doctrine is now seen as a conceptual relic of a bygone era.

As it was developed, however, belligerency status applied to an advanced stage of armed rebellion or civil war.[5] Recognition could be express or implied: it could come from third-party States or the incumbent government. Its application purportedly rested on a purely factual determination. Its elements were typically armed conflict of a general character; control over a substantial portion of territory; conduct of hostilities in accordance with the rules of war; elements of a regular government, and, a necessity for a third-party State to pronounce itself on the question at hand.[6] Debate abounded over the right versus the duty to recognize internal belligerents.[7] It also

[1] H Lauterpacht *Recognition in International Law* (CUP Cambridge 1947) at 179–80; H Wheaton *Elements of International Law* (1866 edn, RH Dana ed) (GG Wilson ed) (William S Hein & Co Buffalo NY 1995) para 23 RH Dana fn 15; A Bello *Principios de derecho internacional* (3rd edn Imprenta del Mercurio Valparaíso 1864) republished as A Bello *Derecho internacional* (Ministerio de Educación Caracas 1954) at 374–8.

[2] *Principios de derecho internacional* (n 1) 374–8; L Moir *The Law of Internal Armed Conflict* (CUP Cambridge 2002) at 6–7.

[3] FL Paxson *The Independence of the South American Republics: A Study in Recognition and Foreign Policy* (Ferris and Leach Philadelphia 1903) at 17–44; WE Kane 'American Involvement in Latin American Civil Strife' (1967) 61 American Society of International Law Proceedings 58–69 at 60; El Marqués de Olivart *Del reconocimiento de beligerancia: y sus efectos inmediatos* (Tipolitografía de L Péant e hijos Madrid 1895) at 19–21; G Weeks 'Almost Jeffersonian: U.S. Recognition Policy toward Latin America' (2001) 31 Presidential Studies Quarterly 490–504.

[4] *Recognition in International Law* (n 1) 176–85.

[5] *Elements of International Law* (n 1); *Recognition in International Law* (n 1) 175–85; J Lorimer *The Institutes of the Law of Nations* (W Blackwood & Sons Edinburgh 1883) at 141–50.

[6] J Brown Scott (ed) *Resolutions of the Institute of International Law* (OUP New York 1916) at 158–9; *Elements of International Law* (n 1); *Recognition in International Law* (n 1).

[7] *Del reconocimiento de beligerancia* (n 3).

extended to questions over the indicia of acts constituting an implied recognition.[8] In summary, the doctrine purported merely to give legal effect to an existing situation of fact. Belligerency status, nevertheless, vested insurgents with international personality and relieved the incumbent government of responsibility for insurgents' acts. It could thus constitute an important prior step to third-party State recognition of rebel claims to independence or a new government.[9]

In essence, what later became belligerency doctrine closely reflected the relationship of Spanish American rebel forces with the US and Great Britain,[10] in the period prior to formal recognitions of independence.[11] At the time, the military struggle was ongoing, and rebel success was far from certain.[12] Nonetheless, the rebellious colonies were conducting their own governments, sending emissaries to foreign States, and controlling significant portions of territory. Spain consistently proclaimed its colonies were in illegal revolt and desperately sought European assistance.[13] Any formal recognition would have clearly been seen as a violation of Spanish sovereignty.[14]

The official policy of the US and Britain at the time was one of strict neutrality. In the US, there was considerable public support for Spanish American independence.[15] The US government, however, delayed any official recognition, in a conciliatory bid to obtain the territory of Florida from Spain.[16] By 1820, the latter traded this concession, and acknowledgement of the US' Western claims, for a pledge from the US not to recognize the rebellious provinces prematurely.[17] Notwithstanding, the US consistently maintained consuls or agents in Buenos Aires and Caracas for six years following the 1810 revolts.[18] After that, while maintaining representatives, their status was more informal. Emissaries from the Spanish American forces were also regularly received in Washington DC.

In addition, several official pronouncements in the US supported the Spanish American rebels' international status. The US President James Madison issued a proclamation of neutrality in 1815.[19] It was expanded in 1817 by his successor, James Monroe, recognizing the two sides' rights as legitimate parties to a civil war.[20] Past a

---

[8] *The Independence of South American Republics* (n 3).

[9] *Del reconocimiento de beligerancia* (n 3) 2.

[10] *Recognition in International Law* (n 1) 175–6.

[11] *The Independence of South American Republics* (n 3).

[12] ibid 244–6.

[13] ibid 114.

[14] ibid 101.

[15] SF Bemis *Latin American Policy of the United States: An Historical Interpretation* (Harcourt Brace New York 1943) at 34–5.

[16] ibid 36–47.   [17] ibid 43.

[18] *The Independence of South American Republics* (n 3) 111, 113, and 121–2.

[19] American State Papers, Foreign Relations vol 4, No 277 (Gales and Seaton Washington DC 1834) at 1.

[20] Message of President Monroe to Fifteenth US Congress, 2 December 1817, American State Papers, Foreign Relations vol 4, No 289 (Gales and Seaton Washington DC 1834) at 130.

certain point in the hostilities, it was maintained, third-party States could formally recognize the advancing revolutionaries.[21] Indeed, the then US Secretary of State, Richard Rush stated that his government 'considered the contest in the light of a civil war, in which parties were equal'.[22] In addition, the US Congress in 1817 and 1818 extended earlier laws on neutrality relative to 'any prince, state, colony, district or people with whom the United States are at peace'.[23] Finally, the US Supreme Court in a series of admiralty cases at the time effectively recognized the Spanish American rebels' belligerency rights.[24]

Great Britain, by comparison, sent few emissaries to the rebellious colonies but was engaged in robust trade and investment in the region.[25] In addition, it allowed for open ports to rebel flags, commerce with rebellious provinces, and communications with rebel governments.[26] These interactions were apparently justified on the factual conditions on the ground: that is, the rebels' extensive military control.[27] In this way, it can be said, both the US and Great Britain recognized, de facto, the state of belligerency in Spanish America. Since this recognition was implicit at best, there is no precise date. Significantly, though, the US first declared neutrality in 1815, and Great Britain prohibited munitions sales to Spain, and to the rebels, in 1819.[28] Both actions put Spain and its rebellious colonies on an equal footing.

The origins of belligerency doctrine have also been attributed to the American Revolution, during which France and Holland recognized the de facto rights of the North American revolutionaries.[29] The concept was first made explicit, however, during the US Civil War when Great Britain recognized the belligerency of the Confederate South in 1861.[30] The Union government protested that Britain had done so

---

[21] JQ Adams, Secretary of State 'Notes to President Monroe' in *MSS, Monroe Papers, Department of State* (24 August 1816); JQ Adams, Secretary of State 'Notes to Mr Anderson' in *MSS Inst Ministers* (27 May 1823); H Clay *Debate in House of Representatives* (March 1818); 'Speech of Hon HC Lodge of Massachusetts in the Senate of the United States', *Secession of Panama, Congressional Record* (5 January 1904) 529–31.

[22] *The Independence of South American Republics* (n 3) 122.

[23] US Congress, 3 Stat 370–1 (1811–23), 3 March 1817, ch 58; US Congress, 3 Stat 447–50 (1811–23), 20 April 1818, ch 88; 30 Annals of US Congress (1816–17) at 39–40, 734; 31 Annals of US Congress (1817–1818) at 519–22.

[24] *The Divina Pastora* 17 US 52 (1819); *The Nuestra Señora de la Caridad* 17 US 497 (1819); *The Santisima Trinidad and the St Ander* 20 US 283 (1822).

[25] FG Dawson *The First Latin American Debt Crisis* (Yale University Press New Haven 1990).

[26] *Recognition in International Law* (n 1); *Del reconocimiento de beligerancia* (n 3) 10–12; JN Pomeroy *Lectures on International Law in Time of Peace* (TS Woolsey ed) (Houghton, Mifflin and Company Boston 1886).

[27] *Reflections on the State of the Late Spanish American Colonies and on the Expediency of the Recognition of their Independence by Great Britain* (J Hatchard & Son London 1823).

[28] *Recognition in International Law* (n 1) 179 and 182; *The Law of Internal Armed Conflict* (n 2) 6–7.

[29] *The Independence of South American Republics* (n 3); F Wharton (ed) *The Revolutionary Diplomatic Correspondence of the United States* (Government Printing Office Washington 1889) vol 1, ch 8, at 453–5.

[30] *Recognition in International Law* (n 1) 184–5.

prematurely.[31] Although the South ostensibly satisfied the preconditions for recognition of belligerency, the North denied the legitimacy of the doctrine's narrow requirements for international standing.[32]

The doctrine remained quite relevant in Latin America. It pointedly re-emerged during the Cuban wars of independence.[33] These were fought over successive periods: unsuccessfully at first in the Ten Years War of 1868–78 with independence finally won in 1898 with US help to Cuban rebels.[34] This last conflict is also known as the Spanish-American War. After the mysterious explosion of the USS Maine in Havana harbour, the US intervened. Within one month Spain had surrendered. More to the point, the US had refused to recognize the belligerency status of Cuban insurgents throughout this period, not acknowledging any status until actual independence through its own intercession in 1898.[35] Only the government of Peru, then at war with Spain, recognized the Cuban state of belligerency in 1869.[36]

By the mid-20th century, the belligerency doctrine was soundly discredited. At best, it became quite irrelevant in the calculations of States' foreign policy.[37] Its demise in modern international law practice is often attributed to its non-application during the Spanish Civil War, from 1936–39.[38] There, despite the fact that all apparent prerequisites had been met, the major world powers withheld recognition from the Nationalist forces.[39] This circumstance has come to be understood as falling beyond the mere irrelevance or even manipulation of the doctrine's factual preconditions. Rather, it has been perceived as resulting from the doctrine's potentially perverse effects. Instead of preserving neutrality and containing war, it could actually precipitate greater conflict.[40] Once the Spanish Nationalists were recognized, apparently the thinking went, other European fascist governments could more easily come to their aid and possibly conflagrate hostilities into a full-scale continental war.[41]

---

[31] G Bemis *The Hasty Recognition of Rebel Belligerency and Our Right to Complain of It* (A Williams & Co Boston 1865).

[32] *The Institutes of the Law of Nations* (n 5); CF Adams 'Mr Adams to Lord Russell (London, 18 September 1865)' in United States Department of State (ed) *Papers Relating to Foreign Affairs, Accompanying the Annual Message of the President to the First Session Thirty-Ninth Congress* (US Government Printing Office Washington 1866) pt 1, 554–60.

[33] *Del reconocimiento de beligerancia* (n 3) 2.

[34] TS Woolsey 'The Consequences of Cuban Belligerency' (1895–96) 5 Yale Law Journal 182–6.

[35] Declaration of James Buchanan, President of the United States of America, Lawrence, Commentaires II, 325; *Del reconocimiento de beligerancia* (n 3) 99.

[36] *Del reconocimiento de beligerancia* (n 3) 27 and 33.

[37] Cf JL Esquirol 'Can International Law Help? An Analysis of the Colombian Peace Process' (2000) 16 Connecticut Journal of International Law 23–93.

[38] Q Wright et al *The International Law of Civil War* (P Falk ed) (Johns Hopkins University Press Baltimore 1971) para 11.

[39] J de Yanguas Messia *Beligerancia, no intervención, y reconocimiento* (Artes Gráficas Grijelmo SA Bilbao 1938) 21–2, 61–4, and 75–85; NJ Padelford 'International Law and the Spanish Civil War' (1937) 31 American Journal of International Law 226–43.

[40] N Berman 'Between "Alliance" and "Localization": Nationalism and the New Oscillationism' (1994) 26 New York University Journal of International Law and Politics 449–91.

[41] ibid.

3. THE RIGHT OF DIPLOMATIC ASYLUM

Possibly the best known international law doctrine related to Latin America is the right of diplomatic asylum. It was made famous in the *Colombia v Peru* (Haya de la Torre) case at the International Court of Justice in 1950. The action involved Colombia's grant of asylum at its Lima embassy to Raúl Haya de la Torre, the leader of Alianza Popular Revolucionaria Americana, the Peruvian socialist party. The Peruvians demanded his surrender on charges of terrorism and other crimes. Colombia insisted, instead, on the political nature of the charges and Peru's obligation to provide safe passage out of the country for the asylee. The ICJ invalidated the grant of asylum and the request for safe passage on the basis of binding treaty law. More importantly, the Chilean Judge Alejandro Alvarez wrote his now-famous dissent in favour of treaty interpretation in this case 'in accordance with the nature of asylum in Latin America'.[42]

This latter mode of asylum refers to the protection of individuals at foreign embassies and legations. It effectively extends asylum-granting jurisdiction to a State's diplomatic premises abroad. While its origins can be traced to antiquity, diplomatic asylum was more formally recognized in practice and in treaties in Latin America.[43] Its broad acceptance is often explained by the prevalence of political volatility, especially in the mid-19th century.[44] Indeed, the practice has been defended pragmatically as well as on humanitarian grounds.

The right of diplomatic asylum was the subject of four separate regional conventions. The first was the Convention on Asylum at Havana in 1928.[45] It upheld the right to asylum 'to the extent in which allowed, as a right or through humanitarian toleration, by the usages, the conventions or the laws of the country in which granted'.[46] Questions remained regarding the definition of a political offender versus a common criminal. States objecting to another State's grant of diplomatic asylum could insist on the common criminal nature of the asylum seeker's offences.[47] The second was the Convention on Political Asylum adopted at the Seventh International Conference of American States in 1933.[48] It attempted to settle the definitional ambiguity by committing resolution of the question to the State granting asylum. An ancillary question remained as to the definitiveness of the designation of political offence by the granting State. It was argued that the granting State could only provisionally qualify the

---

[42] *Asylum Case (Colombia v Peru)* (Haya de la Torre Case) *(Jurisdiction)* [1950] ICJ Rep 266 at 298.

[43] C Urrutia-Aparicio *Opúsculo sobre el derecho de asilo diplomático con anotaciones históricas, doctrinarias y judiciales* (Talleres Gutenberg Guatemala 1952) at 1–16.

[44] CN Ronning *Law and Politics in Inter-American Diplomacy* (Wiley New York 1963) at 90.

[45] Convention Fixing the Rules to Be Observed for the Granting of Asylum, Adopted by the VIth International Conference of American States (signed 20 February 1928) 132 LNTS 323.

[46] ibid art 2.

[47] *Law and Politics in Inter-American Diplomacy* (n 44) 97.

[48] Convention on Political Asylum (entered into force 28 March 1935) OAS Treaty Series No 34 (1933).

offence, for purposes of considering the asylum petition.[49] A third Treaty on Asylum and Political Refuge was signed in 1939, at the Second Montevideo Congress. It clarified that asylum-granting States were not required to admit refugees into their territory, unless the asylee was not admitted to any other State. In the aftermath of the Haya de la Torre case, a fourth convention was signed at the Tenth Inter-American Conference in 1954.[50] It required territorial States to give safe passage out of the country for political offenders granted diplomatic asylum. It indirectly settled the question of the definitiveness of the characterization of political offence by the asylum-granting State.[51]

Not all Latin American publicists have endorsed the doctrine or its nature as a legal right.[52] Diplomatic asylum was deplored by some as an open invitation to foreign intervention.[53] Foreign powers, through their embassies, could side with one faction or another in internal political conflict. The quintessential example is the French and British blockade of Venezuelan ports in 1858.[54] Military action was used to force the Venezuelan government to give safe passage out of the country to former president General José Tadeo Monagas, granted diplomatic protection by these European nations. The event is reputed to be the first classic case of diplomatic asylum.[55] Notably, it was not a Latin American initiative at all. Rather, it was the interpretation of French and British diplomatic officials of international law.[56]

Indeed, the right to diplomatic asylum may conflict with another Latin American shibboleth of international legality, non-intervention. This may explain why some Latin States did not ratify the diplomatic asylum conventions.[57] It has also been noted that while the US rejected the international law-based right to diplomatic asylum, and did not ratify any of the conventions, it still engaged in the practice.[58] In the cases asylum was granted, it was defended by the US on the basis of 'local toleration' or, later, on humanitarian grounds.[59] Possibly sensitive to increasing charges of imperialism, the practice by the US was significantly curtailed after the 1930s.[60]

---

[49] *Law and Politics in Inter-American Diplomacy* (n 44) 97–8.

[50] Convention on Diplomatic Asylum (entered into force 29 December 1954) OAS Treaty Series No 18 (1954).

[51] ibid 98–9.

[52] S Planas-Suárez *El asilo diplomático* (Imprenta López Buenos Aires 1953) at 15–18.

[53] ibid 15–18.

[54] ibid 382–91.

[55] ibid 15–18; Ministerio de Relaciones Exteriores de Perú *Congresos Americanos de Lima* (Imprenta Torres Aguirre Lima 1938) vol 2, at 5–104.

[56] *El asilo diplomático* (n 52) 380.

[57] Convention Fixing the Rules to Be Observed for the Granting of Asylum (n 45); Convention on Political Asylum (n 48); Convention on Diplomatic Asylum (n 50).

[58] American Law Institute (ed) *Restatement of the Law, Third: The Foreign Relations Law of the United States* (3rd edn American Law Institute Washington DC 1987) vol 1, para 466, Reporters' Notes 3.

[59] ibid.

[60] *Law and Politics in Inter-American Diplomacy* (n 44) 93.

4. American and Pan American Conferences

Notable in the Americas is the series of international conferences throughout the 19th and especially the 20th centuries.[61] These constituted regularly programmed events not for the purpose of settling accounts after a war or, solely, for setting the terms of military alliances.[62] Rather they dealt with a whole host of practical issues. At least two different cycles are discernible. The first originated with attempts by Simón Bolívar, the liberator of northern South America, to create greater political union among the newly independent States at the Congress of Panama in 1826.[63] The second cycle arises from the more vigorous participation of the United States, beginning in 1889 in Washington DC.[64] These regular encounters are recognized as early precedents for the Hague Peace Conferences of 1899 and 1907, as well as the League of Nations of 1918.[65] More directly, these conferences produced the first hemispheric international organizations: the Commercial Bureau of the American Republics in 1889 (renamed the International Bureau in 1901), the Pan American Union of 1910 now defunct,[66] and, later, the still-extant Organization of American States chartered in 1948.[67]

The initial Congress of Panama of 1826 launched the so-called American conferences.[68] Of the eight independent Latin American States at the time, four attended: Colombia (then including Ecuador, Panama, and Venezuela), Guatemala (then including Costa Rica, El Salvador, Honduras, and Nicaragua), Mexico, and Peru. Great Britain and Holland attended as observers.[69] The US was also invited, and President John Quincy Adams, abandoning the traditional US isolationist stance, supported sending representatives.[70] The US Congress, however, was concerned that the Congress of Panama could lead to military alliances with the Spanish American republics, a breach of neutrality with Spain, the recognition of Haitian independence,

---

[61] *Inter-American Conferences 1826–1948*, Congress and Conference Series No 56, Organization of American States (Washington DC 1949).

[62] JM Yepes *La contribution de l'Amérique Latine au développement du droit international public et privé* (Recueil Sirey Paris 1931) at 12.

[63] E Gil *Evolución del panamericanismo* (J Menéndez Buenos Aires 1933).

[64] J Brown Scott (ed) *International Conferences of American States 1889–1928* (OUP New York 1931).

[65] ibid xii.

[66] AS de Bustamante 'The Progress of Codification under the Auspices of the Pan American Union' (1926) 20 American Society of International Law Proceedings 108–201 at 110.

[67] *International Conferences of American States 1889–1928* (n 64) xii–xiii.

[68] N Carbonell *Las conferencias internacionales Americanas* (Montalvo y Cardenas La Habana 1928) paras 7–54.

[69] RF Seijas *El derecho internacional Hispano-Americano (público y privado)* (El Monitor Caracas 1884) at 19.

[70] *International Conferences of American States 1889–1928* (n 64).

and the liberation of Cuba and Puerto Rico, including the abolition of slavery on these islands—a perceived threat to Southern slave-holding States.[71] In the end, one of the US delegates died en route, and the other, delayed by the approval of the US Congress, did not arrive in time.[72] In any case, only Colombia ratified the resulting conventions.[73] Of the four treaties produced at the Congress of Panama, the main one was the Treaty of Perpetual Union, League, and Confederation, which along with the others never came into effect due to an insufficient number of ratifications. It contained provisions on mutual defence, a regional army, and the principle of arbitration. In addition, a code of public law of the Americas was discussed, of which the congress's treaties would become part.[74]

Subsequent attempts for a second conference in Mexico in the 1830s were not successful. The so-called First American Congress, after the Congress of Panama, had to wait until 1847 in Lima. There was also the Continental Congress in Santiago, Chile in 1856, attended by Ecuador, Chile, and Peru.[75] Its objective was to establish a permanent council for mutual defence and to obtain additional ratifications.[76] The effort was precipitated by the filibustering activities of William Walker, a private US citizen who had successfully invaded Nicaragua for a period in 1855.

In addition, the US territorial conquests in the Mexican–American War of 1846–48 further led to a more defensive 'Latin' American consciousness distinct from the prior general American focus.[77] Indeed, it is during this period that the term 'Latin America' reputedly gained currency to designate the former Spanish and Portuguese American colonies.[78] With this new inflection, the first cycle of conferences continued with a Second American Congress back in Lima in 1864.[79] A further American Congress of Jurisconsults also in Lima was held from 1877–80 on the topic of private international law.[80] A Bolivarian Congress of 1883 in Caracas honoured the centenary of Simón Bolívar, reaffirming territorial integrity and the principle of *uti possidetis*.[81] Closing out this series was the Montevideo Congress of 1888–89 on intellectual property and

---

[71] Senator Hayne of South Carolina 'Address to U.S. Senate, On the Panama Mission' in *Congressional Debate* (March 1826) vol 2, pt I, at 153 and 165–70; El derecho internacional Hispano-Americano (n 69) 25–7; *Las conferencias internacionales Americanas* (n 68) 20.

[72] *International Conferences of American States 1889–1928* (n 64); *El derecho internacional Hispano-Americano* (n 69) 19 and 25.

[73] ibid 510.

[74] *International Conferences of American States 1889–1928* (n 64) xxii–xxiv.

[75] GA Nuermberger 'The Continental Treaties of 1856: An American Union "Exclusive of the United States"' (1940) 20 The Hispanic American Historical Review 32–55.

[76] ibid.

[77] C Calvo *Colección completa de todos los tratados, convenciones, capitulaciones, armisticios y otros actos diplomáticos: de todos los Estados de América Latina* (A Durand Paris 1862).

[78] A Ardao *Génesis de la idea y el nombre de América Latina* (Centro de Estudios Latinoamericanos Rómulo Gallegos Caracas 1980).

[79] *Congresos Americanos de Lima* (n 55).

[80] *Las conferencias internacionales Americanas* (n 68) 32–40.

[81] ibid 45–7.

private international law.[82] These 19th-century conferences produced various treaties. Yet, with the exception of the 1888–89 Montevideo conventions, none entered into effect.

A second cycle of international conferences began in 1889 with the support and participation of the US, the so-called Pan American conferences.[83] At the first one in Washington, DC, nineteen of the then twenty-one American States were present. No binding agreements ensued, only recommendations concerning a host of economic matters. A plan for binding arbitration was adopted; territorial conquest by one American republic against another was denounced; and a Commercial Bureau of the American Republics was created. The Pan American Conferences addressed a wide array of practical matters and other issues. The conferences continued on a regular basis, approximately every five years, interrupted by the two World Wars.

The optimism surrounding Pan Americanism began to fade, however, in the early 20th century. Many Latin Americans began to see it as a cover for US interests.[84] As such, it fell into disrepute in some quarters. It did not help that during the early 20th century, the US was conducting its most imperialist foreign policy. In the face of continual military interventions, it was unlikely that US participation at diplomatic conferences could be seen as anything other than mere rhetoric. As a result, some Latin American leaders began to speak of Hispano-Americanismo or other forms of Latin Americanism.[85] The period of the 1920s and 1930s is generally recalled as the height of Latin American idealism and the turn to Latin-American-ness as the source of a regional identity, propelling significant works of literature, philosophy and law.

5. American International Law

Probably the most dramatic project of international law in the region was the claim to a separate, American international law.[86] In its strongest expression, this particular law would rank equal to, and in cases of conflict, trump general or European

[82] ibid 20.

[83] ibid; *International Conferences of American States 1889–1928* (n 64) vii–xv; JB Lockey *Pan Americanism: Its Beginnings* (Macmillan London 1920).

[84] L Quintanilla *A Latin American Speaks* (Macmillan New York 1943) at 131–47.

[85] See eg CP Iñíguez 'José Ingenieros: El tránsito del positivismo al Latinoamericanismo' in CP Iñíguez (ed) Pensadores Latinoamericanos del siglo XX: Ideas, utopía y destino (Siglo XXI Buenos Aires 2006) 113–26 at 124.

[86] H Caminos 'The Latin American Contribution to International Law' (1986) 80 American Society of International Law Proceedings 157–60; *La contribution de l'Amérique Latine* (n 62) 87–102.

international law.[87] It was to apply to relations among American States as well as between European and American States.[88] From a contemporary perspective, the claim to American specificity is primarily understood as an historical oddity. It has been received as simply incorrect, or at best, an indefensible overstatement of regional uniqueness.

One of the concept's earliest proponents was the Argentine jurist Amancio Alcorta, who in 1883 defended the norms and practices observed by Latin American nations.[89] In 1884, the Venezuelan jurist Rafael F Seijas published a treatise on Hispanic-American international law, upholding its distinctiveness especially in light of European non-observance of general international law with respect to Latin America.[90] The overall notion became part of the Third Latin American Scientific Congress in Rio de Janeiro in 1905 and was advocated by the Chilean publicist and later judge on the International Court of Justice, Alejandro Alvarez.[91] The thesis was again considered at the First Pan American Scientific Congress in Santiago, Chile in 1908.[92] Its most definitive statement, however, was the Declaration of American Principles at the Eighth Pan American Conference of 1938 in Lima.[93] In addition, as noted above, Alvarez famously memorialized its existence in his 1950 dissent in the International Court of Justice's *Haya de la Torre* case.

As its most famous proponent, Alvarez believed—at least in his early writings— that Alcorta had not sufficiently stated American law's separate existence, fundamental characteristics, or constitutive sources.[94] He also thought this regional international law was not limited to the treaties, practices, and pronouncements of Latin American States, but also included the United States.[95] As such, it was for him closely allied with Pan Americanism. The force of Alvarez's claim, moreover, was that American international law was as equally international law as the dominant European version.[96] As he explained it, it consisted of norms applied to situations arising in the Americas and not in Europe, as well as from situations arising in both Europe and the Americas but for which different norms were applied in the latter.[97] Among its doctrines, the most

---

[87] A Álvarez 'Latin America and International Law' (1909) 3 American Journal of International Law 269–353.

[88] A Alcorta *Cours de droit international public* (L Larose et Forcel Paris 1887) vol 1, at 51.

[89] A Alcorta 'La ciencia del derecho internacional' (1883) 7 Nueva Revista de Buenos Aires 406–37 at 413–18; *Cours de droit international public* (n 88) vol 1, 374–8.

[90] *El derecho internacional Hispano-Americano* (n 69) 25–7 and 508.

[91] HB Jacobini 'International Law in Latin America' (1975) 7 Lawyer of the Americas 605–13.

[92] V dos Santos, Relatório Geral—Trabalhos das secções do Congresso, vol 5: Sciencias jurídicas e sociais, 9a. sessão, 314; M de Sá Vianna *De la non-existence d'un droit international américain* (L Figueredo Rio de Janeiro 1912) at 3–6.

[93] CA Sánchez i Sánchez *Curso de derecho internacional público Americano: Sistematica i exegesis* (Editora Montalvo Ciudad Trujillo RD 1943) at 691–6.

[94] 'Latin America and International Law' (n 87) 352.

[95] ibid.

[96] *Curso de derecho internacional público Americano* (n 93) 148–55.

[97] 'Latin America and International Law' (n 87) 349–52.

commonly cited are: non-intervention by third-party States; compulsory international arbitration for State to State disputes; territorial limits based on *uti possidetis iuris* of 1810; third-party right to recognition of internal belligerents; right of diplomatic asylum; the principle of *ius soli* in nationality laws; freedom of national rivers navigation; coastal security jurisdiction; freedom of neutral trade in times of war, and a few others.[98]

In addition, during the early 20th century, there was a flurry of doctrinal pronouncements by Latin American publicists.[99] Various principles of international law were proclaimed: for example, the Drago Doctrine, the Calvo Doctrine, the Estrada Doctrine. Most of these statements of foreign policy were expressions against outside intervention and foreign imperialism in domestic affairs. They addressed abuses committed by Europe and the US in pursuing complaints by their nationals for unpaid debts, investment disputes, 'denials of justice' in local courts, and the like. The supporters of a separate regional law were quick to claim these non-intervention doctrines as part of the corpus of American international law.

Still, not all Latin American publicists were of a single mind.[100] Much debate ensued regarding whether there was, alternatively, a separate American international law, American problems of international law, or simply principles of international law originating in Latin America.[101] For its critics, the elements of American international law heralded by its proponents were merely local contributions to the general evolution of universal international law. There were also disagreements over whether or not the US properly belonged to the group. Alvarez had firmly included the US and re-interpreted the outwardly imperialist Monroe Doctrine as a main principle of a joint Americas international law.[102] The topic provoked a goodly amount of debate.[103]

Some of the main objections to American international law were recorded by the Brazilian jurist and delegate at numerous international conferences, Manuel de Sá Vianna.[104] Sá Vianna argued, among other things, that Latin American States in their first century of independence were incapable of producing such a corpus of international law.[105] The reasons ranged from internal political instability, border disputes,

---

[98] *Curso de derecho internacional público Americano* (n 93) 130–53; H Arias 'Nationality and Naturalisation in Latin America from the Point of View of International Law' (1910) 11 Journal of the Society of Comparative Legislation 126–42; 'Latin American Contribution to International Law' (n 86) 158; E Hasani 'Uti Possidetis Juris: From Rome to Kosovo' (2003) 27 Fletcher Forum of World Affairs 85–98.

[99] *Curso de derecho internacional público Americano* (n 93) 120–9.

[100] D Antokoletz *Doctrine de Monroë et l'Amérique Latine* (Émile Larose 1905) at 16–17.

[101] *Curso de derecho internacional público Americano* (n 93) 124–9.

[102] A Álvarez 'The Monroe Doctrine from a Latin American Perspective' (1917) 2 St Louis Law Review 135–46; *Doctrine de Monroë et l'Amérique Latine* (n 100) 157–62; I Fabela *Las Doctrinas Monroe y Drago* (Universidad Nacional Autónoma de México 1957).

[103] *Curso de derecho internacional público Americano* (n 93) 12–29.

[104] *De la non-existence* (n 92).

[105] ibid 61–5.

lack of significant commercial exchange, lack of communication, and linguistic and cultural differences.[106] He noted that Latin American States were barely recognized, in their own right, as proper subjects of international law, even if their independence had been formally accepted. The proof was the repeated military and other forms of intervention in Latin American States by the major European powers and the United States.[107] No less, he opposed American international law on strategic grounds.[108] After the long struggle for admission into the society of nations—culminating in extensive Latin American participation in the then recent Second Hague Peace Conference of 1907—it seemed like a step backwards to argue for a separate American international law.[109]

The historical context of these debates represents precarious times for Latin American sovereignty. This is a period of transition from European to US imperialism.[110] The US became increasingly capable and willing to exercise military might. The Roosevelt Corollary of 1904, pronounced by US President Theodore Roosevelt, revived the Monroe Doctrine and expressed the intention to enforce it unilaterally.[111] Both supporters and detractors of an American international law must have had this situation uppermost in their minds. Thus, irrespective of the conceptual difficulties surrounding a particularistic international law, this project reveals a geo-politically meaningful deployment of international legality.[112] It offered a means for addressing both US and European imperialism.[113] It also showcased Latin American statesmen and publicists as equal creators, and enforcers, of international law.[114]

In passing, I should note that collecting historical constructs of international law from Latin America, as I have tried to do here, is not meant to support either the existence or non-existence of a separate American international law. Rather, it simply describes the main international law forms employed by Latin Americans. An American international law is one of these forms. Insistence on a singular universal international law is another.[115] In this second case, international concepts may be no less

---

[106] ibid 35.   [107] ibid 33.   [108] ibid 82–3.

[109] ibid 61–2; C De Armond Davis *The United States and the Second Hague Peace Conference: American Diplomacy and International Organization, 1899–1945* (Duke University Press Durham 1975) at 272.

[110] CG Fenwick 'Intervention: Individual and Collective' (1945) 39 American Journal of International Law 645–63 at 651–2.

[111] SF Bemis *Latin American Policy of the United States: An Historical Interpretation* (Harcourt, Brace & Company New York 1943) at 142–67.

[112] L Obregón 'The Colluding Worlds of the Lawyer, the Scholar and the Policymaker: A View of International Law from Latin America' (2005) 23 Wisconsin International Law Journal 145–72; A Becker Lorca 'International Law in Latin America or Latin American International Law? Rise, Fall and Retrieval of a Tradition of Legal Thinking and Political Imagination' (2006) 47 Harvard International Law Journal 283–306.

[113] JL Esquirol 'Alejandro Álvarez's Latin American Law: A Question of Identity' (2006) 19 Leiden Journal of International Law 931–56.

[114] 'La contribution de l'Amérique Latine' (n 62) 9.

[115] A Becker Lorca 'Universal International Law: Nineteenth-Century Histories of Imposition and Appropriation' (2010) 51 Harvard International Law Journal 475–552.

idiosyncratically adapted to local circumstances, yet in unacknowledged ways.[116] Indeed, a part of this latter mode is the characterization of Latin American particularities as merely contributions to or influences on universal international law. Regardless, both approaches mobilize the identity of international law in support of different constructions of legal authority.

6. Non-Intervention

Non-intervention in international law is often associated with Latin America, paradoxically because of the frequency of European and US military and diplomatic intervention in the region. From national independence until 1945, the US alone intervened militarily no less than sixty-eight times, counting all instances of territorial incursions.[117] In addition, the European powers blockaded ports and forcibly intervened on numerous occasions, including a four-year French occupation of Mexico in 1862.[118] In response, the principle of non-intervention was developed by Latin American publicists and by governmental declarations against interference with national sovereignty.[119] The topic was also the subject of numerous regional conferences, the most famous of which was the Montevideo Convention of 1933 on the Rights and Duties of States.

The circumstances for foreign intervention were of two main types. Initially, there were attempts to recolonize Latin American republics by European monarchies. In this connection, the Monroe Doctrine of 1823 was an early US foreign policy pronouncement against new European territorial acquisitions in the Americas. The first Congress of Panama in 1826, moreover, sought to operationalize this doctrine by establishing a common defence against any form of foreign subjugation.[120] The first American Congress in Lima in 1847–48 included a treaty provision to this same effect.[121] Neither of these conventions came into effect, however. Moreover, none of these pronouncements prevented the European powers from forcibly intervening to collect debts or defend their interests.

Indeed, the main rationale for intervention in Latin America in the 19th and early 20th centuries was to collect on foreign pecuniary claims. Independence from Spain

---

[116] ibid.

[117] RF Grimmett *Instances of Use of United States Armed Forces, 1798 to 2001* (Congressional Research Service Washington 2002).

[118] *Las doctrinas Monroe y Drago* (n 102) 87–193.

[119] A van Wynen Thomas and AJ Thomas Jr *Non-Intervention: The Law and Its Import in the Americas* (Southern Methodist University Press Dallas 1956) at 55–64.

[120] ibid 55–6.   [121] ibid.

had introduced a range of liberal economic and immigration policies, welcoming significant foreign investment and European immigrants.[122] These increased contacts invariably led to international friction, especially with nationals of the major powers. In the event of loss or harm to them, foreign nationals not infrequently turned to their home country foreign offices for redress. The latter placed pressure on Latin American governments on behalf of their citizens, whether in connection with private disputes, the repayment of public debt, or in matters of local politics. This practice was also referred to as 'diplomatic interposition'.[123] The actual measures ranged from formal protests and withdrawal of diplomatic representation to forcible intervention, such as naval blockades and military invasion.[124]

On the one side were capital-exporting countries armed with doctrines of State responsibility and on the other were capital-importing States defending rights to non-intervention and the equality of States.[125] Still, there were important differences even within capital-importing States. Ruy Barbosa, chief of the Brazilian delegation at the 1907 Hague Peace Conference, argued that outlawing forcible intervention might negatively affect credit to Latin America.[126] Alvarez also thought that intervention was justified when peaceful means had been exhausted.[127]

Regardless, Latin American publicists generally became the principal expositors of the doctrines of non-intervention.[128] Chief among them was Luis M Drago, Argentine Minister of Foreign Affairs. Drago denounced forcible intervention in the case of collecting on public debts.[129] Reacting to the British, German, and Italian invasion of Venezuela in 1902, he argued that military intervention to collect debts could ultimately lead to a recolonization of the Americas by European powers.[130] His position was that the collection of unpaid sovereign bonds in no case justified intervention by a foreign power. It was not a far-fetched observation, considering that in 1862 France occupied Mexico, on the rationale of collecting on unpaid public debt.

Drago's fellow countryman, the Argentine diplomat and jurist, Carlos Calvo, expanded on this position.[131] Calvo was already an eminent publicist at the

---

[122] *The First Latin American Debt Crisis* (n 25).

[123] FG Dawson 'The Contribution of Lesser Developed States to International Law: The Latin American Experience' (1981) 13 Case Western Reserve Journal of International Law 37–82.

[124] ibid 48.

[125] J Castaneda 'The Underdeveloped Nations and the Development of International Law' (1961) 15 International Organization 38–48.

[126] *The United States and the Second Hague Peace Conference* (n 109) 182 and 257.

[127] 'Latin America and International Law' (n 87) 335.

[128] WE Kane 'American Involvement in Latin American Civil Strife' (1967) 61 American Society of International Law Proceedings 58–68 at 64–5.

[129] AS Hershey 'The Calvo and Drago Doctrines' (1907) 1 American Journal of International Law 26–45 at 31.

[130] LM Drago, *Cobro coercitivo de deudas públicas* (Coni Hermanos, Buenos Aires 1906) at 9–26; LM Drago 'Les emprunts d'état et leurs rapports avec la politique internationale' (1907) 14 Revue Générale de Droit International Public 251–87.

[131] 'The Calvo and Drago Doctrines' (n 129) 3.

time.[132] In his later years, and in reaction to the Drago doctrine, his letters evidence an expansion on the declaration against foreign intervention for any reason. Calvo advanced the thesis that foreigners have no greater rights than nationals in cases of loss of life or property.[133] In practice, this would mean no military intervention or diplomatic interposition by foreign governments on behalf of their nationals for pecuniary claims of any kind. Calvo's doctrine would require treatment equal to nationals, limiting aliens to the local courts and institutions. More importantly, he advanced this position as a principle of international law. It should be noted that Calvo himself was not a proponent of a separate American law of nations.[134] Still, his non-intervention principle was widely incorporated into Latin American treaties, constitutions, legislation, and agreements between Latin American States or individuals and foreign parties.[135]

Other comparable doctrines were articulated by Latin American publicists and diplomats. For example, the Venezuelan Rafael F Seijas, mentioned earlier, wrote against the abuse of diplomatic intervention by foreign powers on behalf of their nationals.[136] He advocated a strong exhaustion of the local remedies rule, excepting only cases of flagrant denial of justice in the local courts as a justification for diplomatic intervention.[137] Even then, Seijas endorsed State responsibility only during wartime and when compensation was also available to nationals.

Later in the 20th century, the Estrada Doctrine, named after the Mexican Secretary of Foreign Affairs, also became part of the Latin American pantheon of non-intervention.[138] It declared Mexico's position in 1930 against both formal recognitions and non-recognitions of foreign governments.[139] Taking a position on recognition—especially of a government claiming power through the use of force—could be considered an act of intervention by either extending or withholding approval. Henceforth, Mexico would limit itself to maintaining or not maintaining relations with foreign governments—but not making official declarations as to whether or not it formally recognized such government.

Not all of these new doctrines cut the same way. Notably, the earlier Tobar Doctrine of 1907, named after the Ecuadorian Minister of Foreign Affairs Carlos R

---

[132] C Calvo *Le Droit International Théorique et Pratique* (5th edn A Rousseau Paris 1896) vol 1, at 264–355.

[133] ibid 267.

[134] 'The Contribution of Lesser Developed States to International Law' (n 123) 57.

[135] See MR Garcia-Mora 'The Calvo Clause in Latin American Constitutions and International Law' (1949–50) 33 Marquette Law Review 205–19; DR Shea *The Calvo Clause: A Problem of the Inter-American and International Law and Diplomacy* (University of Minnesota Press Minneapolis 1955) at 21–32.

[136] *El derecho internacional Hispano-Americano* (n 69) 48.

[137] ibid 518.

[138] *La opinión universal sobre la doctrina Estrada expuesta por el Gobierno de México, bajo la presidencia de Don Pascual Ortiz Rubio* (Instituto Americano de Derecho y Legislación Comparada México 1931).

[139] J Irizarry y Puente 'The Doctrines of Recognition and Intervention in Latin America' (1953–54) 28 Tulane Law Review 313–42 at 322.

Tobar, endorsed a practice of denying recognition to de facto governments.[140] It would limit recognition to transitions in keeping with the national constitutional order. Allowing this review power to third-party States, however, resembled the kind of interventionism historically afflicting Latin America. It was the opposite of what the Estrada Doctrine came to represent. Notably, a version of the Tobar Doctrine was incorporated into the Central American Peace and Amity Treaties of 1907 and 1923.[141]

The topic of non-intervention, furthermore, was formally addressed at the Third Pan American Conference of Rio de Janeiro of 1906 where a resolution was passed to advocate for its recognition at the Second Hague Peace Conference, scheduled for the following year. The reasoning was that such a principle must be endorsed by the creditor nations, and not just the debtors, if it were to have any practical effect. At the Conference, the US did not support the general Latin American position in favour of the principle as expressed in the revised Drago Doctrine, requiring unconditional renunciation of force in the collection of debts.[142] Instead, the US advanced the milder Porter Doctrine, proposed by the US delegate, which was successfully included in the Second Hague Convention Respecting the Limitation of the Employment of Force for the Recovery of Contract Debts of 1907.[143] Forcible intervention remained legal if the defaulting State did not agree to arbitration, frustrated the process, or refused to submit to a final arbitral award.

The principle of non-intervention was also prominently raised at the Fifth Pan American Conference in Havana in 1928.[144] The Commission of Jurists, meeting a year earlier at Rio de Janeiro in 1927, had included a preparatory draft that 'No nation has a right to interfere in the internal or foreign affairs of an American Republic against the will of that Republic'. The United States opposed the project, and it was withdrawn. The principle was ultimately adopted however in the 1933 Montevideo Convention on the Rights and Duties of States. Calls for compulsory international arbitration, in lieu of force, can also be traced to these debates.[145] Ultimately, the United States agreed to the Montevideo Convention, withdrawing its reservation in 1936.[146] This shift coincided with the US initiative at the Conference

---

[140] ibid 317.

[141] CL Stansifer 'Application of the Tobar Doctrine to Central America' (1967) 23 The Americas 251–72.

[142] 'Alejandro Alvarez's Latin American Law' (n 113) at 948; *The United States and the Second Hague Peace Conference* (n 109) 255.

[143] J Brown Scott 'The Work of the Second Hague Peace Conference' (1908) 2 American Journal of International Law 1–28 at 15; *The United States and the Second Hague Peace Conference* (n 109) 284–5.

[144] 'Intervention: Individual and Collective' (n 110) 654.

[145] *La contribution de l'Amérique Latine* (n 62) 68–9.

[146] 'The Contribution of Lesser Developed States to International Law' (n 123) 63.

for the Maintenance of Peace in Buenos Aires the same year, reaffirming the principle of non-intervention and introducing Franklin Delano Roosevelt's good neighbour policy toward Latin America.[147]

7. CODIFICATION OF INTERNATIONAL LAW

The codification of international law is another widely recognized Latin American undertaking. Its chief result was the Havana Convention on Private International Law of 1928, incorporating the Bustamante Code.[148] The codification of public international law, by contrast, progressed along topic-specific treaties. The Bustamante Code was an attempt to harmonize the conflicts of private law rules across the Americas.

The original impetus for international law codification in the region is commonly traced to the first Congress of Panama in 1826.[149] However, it was the Conference of Lima of 1877 which produced the first systematic efforts, compiling a large portion of private international law. The Lima conference adopted the controversial European or nationality rule for conflicts of personal status laws.[150] It was ratified only by Peru and never went into effect.[151] The subsequent Convention of Montevideo on Civil and Commercial Law of 1888–89 marked a shift from the law of nationality to the law of domicile.[152] It covered rules on conflicts in the areas of civil, commercial, criminal, procedural, and intellectual property law.[153] The various treaties produced were ratified in their entirety by Argentina, Bolivia, Paraguay, Peru, and Uruguay. A number of other countries, including European ones, later acceded to one or more of these treaties.[154]

Codification began in earnest, however, at the Second Pan American Conference of 1901–2 in Mexico City. Delegates endorsed a proposal for the codification of both public international law and private international law.[155] The means for codification

---

[147] 'Intervention: Individual and Collective' (n 110) 656; C Saavedra Lamas *La Conferencia Interamericana de Consolidación de la Paz* (Ministerio de Relaciones Exteriores y Culto Buenos Aires 1938).

[148] Convention on Private International Law (signed 20 February 1928) 86 LNTS 111 at 120.

[149] 'Latin America and International Law' (n 87); 'The Progress of Codification' (n 66) 110.

[150] 'The Doctrines of Recognition and Intervention in Latin America' (n 139) 96.

[151] *La contribution de l'Amérique Latine* (n 62) 26.

[152] ibid 27; 'The Doctrines of Recognition and Intervention in Latin America' (n 139) 98–9.

[153] *La contribution de l'Amérique Latine* (n 62) 27.

[154] 'The Doctrines of Recognition and Intervention in Latin America' (n 139) 97.

[155] 'The Progress of Codification' (n 66) 110.

was a three-, and later, seven-person commission consisting of five prominent jurists from the Americas and two from Europe.[156] The Third Pan American Conference of 1906 in Rio de Janeiro created the International Commission of American Jurists, changing the method for producing drafts of codification.[157] This new body consisted of representatives trained in the law, one from each of the twenty-one American republics.[158] This body of legal experts compiled various preliminary studies and proposals for public and private international law codification.[159]

The International Commission first met in 1912 in Rio de Janeiro.[160] Unfortunately, World War I intervened, and all of these efforts were placed on hold. The Fifth Pan American Conference of 1923 in Santiago de Chile called for the continuation of this work.[161] The International Commission met again in Rio de Janeiro in 1927,[162] producing working drafts for the next Pan American conference the following year.[163] At the Sixth Pan American Conference in Havana in 1928 the Bustamante Code was adopted.[164] It was named after its main drafter, the Cuban jurist Antonio Sánchez de Bustamante y Sirven.[165] Bustamante was engaged by the American Institute of International Law to produce a draft proposal.[166] The Institute, then headed by James Brown Scott and Alejandro Alvarez, was commissioned by the Pan American Union for this work.[167]

The Bustamante Code was later enacted as part of the national legislation of many Latin American countries. It has been criticized, on several grounds, as overly restrictive on the validity of commercial contacts; limiting party autonomy to contract for the governing law; and failing to introduce a uniform rule on personal status.[168] Indeed, a main issue concerning the latter was the choice between national law and

---

[156] *La contribution de l'Amérique Latine* (n 62) 31.

[157] JM Yepes *La codificación del derecho internacional Americano* (Imprenta Nacional Bogotá 1927) at 13.

[158] ibid 4.

[159] J Brown Scott 'The Codification of International Law in America' (1925) 19 American Journal of International Law 333–7 at 333–4; 'International Commission of Jurists (Sessions Held at Rio de Janeiro, Brazil, 18 April to 20 May 1927)' (1928) 22 Special Number American Journal of International Law Special Supplement 234–329.

[160] *La contribution de l'Amérique Latine* (n 62) 32–3.

[161] *La codificación* (n 157) 10–13.

[162] ibid 13.

[163] 'International Commission of Jurists' (n 159).

[164] Convention on Private International Law (n 148); EG Lorenzen 'Uniformity Between Latin America and the United States in the Rules of Private International Law Relating to Commercial Contracts' (1940–41) 15 Tulane Law Review 165–76 at 166.

[165] 'The Progress of Codification' (n 66) 117.

[166] *La codificación* (n 157) 27.

[167] International Commission of Jurists (n 159) 234–5.

[168] 'Uniformity Between Latin America and the United States' (n 164) 166.

the law of domicile.[169] For Latin Americans this debate involved nothing less than their national sovereignty.[170] National law potentially opened the door to foreign interference and even military intervention. [171] In addition, it was seen as an impediment to the social assimilation of foreign immigrants.[172] Under a form of personal law, these new Americans would continue to look to their sovereigns of origin for their laws, protection, and allegiance. By contrast, the law of domicile was seen by its proponents as protective of host country sovereignty and national identity. Indeed, the law of domicile was argued by some as the 'American' rule, in contraposition to the larger weight of scholarly authority.[173] The latter represented the opinions of European jurists and the interests of European sovereigns. Through this jurisprudential means, Europe maintained links with its emigrant citizens and their affairs in the Americas. Nonetheless, in light of the failure at uniformity, a subsequent convention was held in Montevideo in 1940.[174] Its promoters included some of the more prominent dissenters from the Bustamente Code.[175] The final text expanded upon the earlier Montevideo Convention of 1888–89, reaffirming the rule of domicile in conflicts cases.

Not all Latin Americans favoured the law of domicile however.[176] A main issue, for some, was concern over the continuing application of national family law over their own citizens abroad.[177] Latin Americans establishing domicile in jurisdictions with legalized divorce could obtain a foreign divorce decree and then seek legal recognition in their home countries. This concern was partially allayed, during codification debates, by a purported exception for divorce to the law of domicile. This debate also drew on legal theory. Defenders of national law argued that national legislation was the crystallization of local customs.[178] Therefore, the law appropriate to individuals was the one arising from their own nation's customs. The proponents of the law of domicile did not necessarily discount the organic nature of law but rather emphasized the new interrelationships and communities which immigrants had voluntarily chosen. In short, private international law codification was not only a technical feat, but it involved controversies regarding, *inter alia*, immigration, sovereignty, family law, and other areas.

---

[169] AS de Bustamante y Sirven *La nacionalidad y el domicilio* (Imprenta El Siglo XX La Habana 1927).

[170] C Saavedra Lamas *La Crise de la Codification et la Doctrine Argentine du Droit International* (Les Éditions Internationales Paris 1931) at 747–53.

[171] ibid 158–76.

[172] *La contribution de l'Amérique Latine* (n 62) 27–8.

[173] *La Crise de la Codification* (n 170) 158–66.

[174] E Rabel 'The Revision of the Treaties of Montevideo on the Law of Conflicts' (1940–41) 39 Michigan Law Review 517–25.

[175] *La Crise de la Codification* (n 170) J Irizarry y Puente 'Treaties on Private International Law' (1943) 37 American Journal of International Law Supplement 95–9.

[176] *La codificación* (n 157) 45–8.

[177] ibid 56–62.   [178] ibid 30–1.

8. CENTRAL AMERICAN COURT OF JUSTICE

The Central American Court of Justice operated from 25 May 1908 until 12 March 1918. It was initially located in Cartago, Costa Rica. It was later transferred to San José, the Costa Rican capital, in 1911.[179] This new institution was an early model of a permanent court of international law with compulsory jurisdiction.[180] The Central American Court departed from piecemeal international arbitration, such as provided by the Permanent Court of International Arbitration.[181] It has been noted that '[t]his was the first international court in modern history to be endowed with continuing functions'.[182] Previous international efforts had fallen short, as recently as the Second Hague Peace Conference of 1907.[183] Publicists have generally upheld the Central American Court's place among significant developments in international law.[184] However, it is primarily recalled as a premature step in the natural progression of international institutions.[185]

The court itself was established as part of the Central American Convention of Peace and Amity of 1907, in Washington DC, convened by the US and Mexico subsequent to hostilities between Nicaragua and Honduras.[186] It was attended by all five Central American republics: Costa Rica, El Salvador, Guatemala, Honduras, and Nicaragua. The treaty establishing the court was signed on 20 December 1907 and was ratified in 1908 by all five signatory States. A declaration by Guatemala at the convention reserved 'the right of resort to the good offices and friendly mediation of their Excellencies, the Presidents of the United States of America and Mexico, in the event of any difficulty in the execution of the findings of the court.[187] The court consisted of five justices, one from each constituting State. It was mandated to decide cases according to the principles of international law.[188] Over its ten-year history, a total of ten cases came before the court. Five were brought by individuals, all of which were deemed inadmissible.[189] According to Manley O Hudson,

---

[179] J Eyma *La Cour de Justice Centre-Américaine* (E. Sagot Paris 1928) at 39–40.

[180] 'The First Case Before the Central American Court of Justice' (1908) 2 American Journal of International Law 835–41; *La Cour de Justice Centre-Américaine* (n 179) 28–34.

[181] The Hague Convention for the Pacific Settlement of International Disputes of 1899 (entered into force 4 September 1900) (1899) 187 CTS 410.

[182] MO Hudson 'The Central American Court of Justice' (1932) 26 American Journal of International Law 759–86 at 785–6.

[183] *La Cour de Justice Centre-Américaine* (n 179) 44.

[184] N Politis *La justice internationale* (Hachette Paris 1924) at 141.

[185] *La Cour de Justice Centre-Américaine* (n 179) 44–5 and 171–6.

[186] 'The Central American Court of Justice' (n 182) 761; *La Cour de Justice Centre-Américaine* (n 179) 18.

[187] 'The Central American Court of Justice' (n 182) 767.

[188] 'Convention for the Establishment of a Central American Court of Justice' (1908) 2 American Journal of International Law Supplement: Official Documents 231–24 at 228–9 (art XXI).

[189] 'The Central American Court of Justice' (n 182) 768.

[i]n the decisions of the court, there is little to indicate an attempt to formulate any special doctrines of Central American public law, though the views of the court, particularly in El Salvador v. Nicaragua, were influenced by the tradition of confederation in Central America.[190]

The Central American Court, nonetheless, clearly constituted a bold move especially in terms of its extensive jurisdiction.[191] It, quite exceptionally, covered any and all controversies arising among the contracting States: under the treaty, they agreed to 'bind themselves to submit all controversies or questions which may arise among them, of whatsoever nature and no matter what their origin may be'.[192] The court could also initiate proceedings on its own responsibility. In addition, it had jurisdiction over disputes, of an international character or a treaty violation, between contracting States and citizens of a different State. The individual's claim need not have been supported by his home government. The claimant was required, however, to show that local remedies had been exhausted or that there had been a denial of justice. The treaty establishing the court also contained an annex, providing an optional article on jurisdiction. The 'optional clause' provided for jurisdiction over conflicts between the legislative, executive, and judicial branches of a national government 'when as a matter of fact the judicial decisions and resolutions of the National Congress are not respected'.[193] All States, except Costa Rica, ratified the optional clause, although there was some debate as to whether this clause ever entered into effect.

The most prominent cases handled by the court were two related complaints by Costa Rica and El Salvador for violation by Nicaragua of rights under international treaties.[194] In 1914, Nicaragua negotiated the Bryan-Chamorro treaty with the United States, ceding to the US the right in perpetuity to build a trans-oceanic canal across Nicaragua, the right to build a naval base off Fonseca bay, and leasing several Caribbean islands for a renewable ninety-nine-year period.[195] The US objective was, rather than actually constructing a canal, to prevent a new transoceanic canal from being built through Nicaragua, which could compete with its recently completed Panama Canal.[196] Nicaragua agreed to the sum of US$ 3 million in consideration for its concessions. In March 1916, Costa Rica filed suit claiming that Nicaragua had breached

[190]   ibid 767–8.

[191]   J Brown Scott 'The Central American Peace Conference of 1907' (1908) 2 American Journal of International Law 121–43 at 141 and 143.

[192]   'Convention for the Establishment of a Central American Court of Justice' (n 188) 231 (art I).

[193]   'The Central American Court of Justice' (n 182) 766.

[194]   La Cour de Justice Centre-Américaine (n 179) 109–56.

[195]   'Convention Between Nicaragua and the United States Regarding the Nicaraguan Canal Route and a Naval Base on the Gulf of Fonseca' (1916) 10 American Journal of International Law Supplement: Official Documents 258–60; La Cour de Justice Centre-Américaine (n 179) 103–9.

[196]   GA Finch 'The Treaty with Nicaragua granting Canal and other Rights to the United States' (1916) 10 American Journal of International Law 344–51 at 346.

its right to prior consultation, provided for under the Cañas-Jerez Treaty of 1858 between the two nations, by unilaterally entering into the Bryan-Chamorro Treaty with the US.[197] The violation, it argued, rendered the later treaty void. El Salvador also filed a complaint alleging violations of the 1907 Central American Peace and Amity Treaty.[198] Ultimately, on 30 September 1916 and 9 March 1917, the court agreed with the claimants.[199] It did not go as far as to invalidate Nicaragua's treaty with the US.[200] However, it ordered Nicaragua to restore the status quo *ex ante*. Nicaragua refused to comply.[201] The United States entered into a separate protocol with Costa Rica in 1923 agreeing to consult in the event of the construction of a trans-oceanic canal.[202] That protocol was apparently never ratified in the US Senate.

The court's ten-year charter, established by treaty, expired in 1918 without renewal. Indeed, a year prior to its final term, the court's continuation was denounced by the government of Nicaragua, apparently for good measure. A subsequent round of Central American peace and amity treaties took place in 1922–23. They once again revived a Central American court. This time it was in the form of an International Central American Court of Justice, which was to convene only when needed. The latter consisted simply of a regular process for ad hoc arbitration among States. This second institution was clearly a step backwards from the previously more ambitious court. Its predecessor was more in line with later developments such as the Permanent Court of International Justice, established in 1922 under the League of Nations, and its successor the International Court of Justice, established in 1946.

The storied Central American Court drew from the regional history of political confederation and common cultural identity. It emerged, however, during a period of formal independence of the several Central American States, as the product of peace negotiations ending regional hostilities. As a result, rather than part of a unified political regime, it was created to resolve the international disputes of separate sovereigns. In addition, a different impetus for the court can be found in the international institutional interests of the United States. The Central American tribunal embodied the model of international dispute resolution backed by the US at the Second Hague Peace Conference of 1907.[203] The US position did not ultimately prevail at The Hague, but it did resurface in the Central American treaty that same year. Furthermore, the court's ultimate dissolution

---

[197] *La Cour de Justice Centre-Américaine* (n 179) 109–25.

[198] ibid 125–56.

[199] 'Judicial Decisions Involving Questions of International Law, El Salvador v. Nicaragua, Central American Court of Justice' (1917) 11 American Journal of International Law 674–730.

[200] 'The Central American Court of Justice' (n 182) 780.

[201] PM Brown 'Costa Rica v. Nicaragua' (1917) 11 American Journal of International Law 156–60; *La Cour de Justice Centre-Américaine* (n 179) 157–70.

[202] 'The Central American Court of Justice' (n 182) 780.

[203] *La Cour de Justice Centre-Américaine* (n 179) 43–4 and 53–8.

was also intertwined with US interests.[204] The court foundered on Nicaragua's non-compliance with the decision against its treaty with the US. Notably, the latter did not encourage a particularly conciliatory stance by Nicaragua toward the court's decision. By that time, the court's usefulness, at least from a US foreign policy perspective, was seemingly diminished. Indeed, the history of the Central American Court cannot be understood without reference to the prevailing US interests in Central America at the time.

9. CONCLUSION

The most renowned developments of international law in the region clearly respond to the political and intellectual concerns of their day. It is these interconnections that this survey has especially attempted to stress. Moreover, there is a notable thread running through many of the examples here. It is the issue of foreign interference in the affairs of relatively weak States. In this connection, much of international law in Latin America has come to define the very elements of modern sovereignty and statehood.

RECOMMENDED READING

Alcorta, Amancio *Cours de droit international public* (L Larose et Forcel Paris 1887).

Alvarez, Alejandro 'Latin America and International Law' (1909) 3 American Journal of International Law 269–353.

Bello, Andrés *Principios de derecho internacional* (3rd edn Imprenta de la Patria Valparaíso 1864).

Bustamante y Sirven, Antonio S de *La nacionalidad y el domicilio* (Imprenta El Siglo XX La Habana 1927).

Calvo, Carlos *Le droit international théorique et pratique* (5th edn A Rousseau Paris 1896).

Drago, Luis María 'Les emprunts d'état et leurs rapports avec la politique internationale' (1907) 14 Revue Générale de Droit International Public 251–87.

Eyma, Jean *La Cour de Justice Centre-Américaine* (E Sagot Paris 1928).

Lamas Saavedra, Carlos *La crise de la codification et la doctrine Argentine du droit international* (Les Éditions Internationales Paris 1931).

---

[204] J Brown Scott 'The Closing of the Central American Court of Justice' (1919) 12 American Journal of International Law 380–2 at 382.

Planas-Suárez, Simón *El asilo diplomático* (Imprenta López Buenos Aires 1953).

Sá Vianna, Manuel *La non-existence d'un droit international Américain* (L Figueredo Rio de Janeiro 1912).

Seijas, Rafael F *El derecho internacional Hispano-Americano (público y privado)* (El Monitor Caracas 1884).

Yepes, Jesús María *La codificación del derecho internacional Americano y la conferencia de Rio de Janeiro* (Imprenta Nacional Bogotá 1927).

Yepes, Jesús María *La contribution de l'Amérique Latine au développement du droit international public et privé* (Recueil Sirey Paris 1931).

CHAPTER 24

....

THE CARIBBEAN

....

DAVID S BERRY

1. INTRODUCTION

....

THE history of the Caribbean is complex.[1] The peoples and islands of the Caribbean have been subject to territorial and commercial ambitions on the part of a number of powers, including the Spanish, Portuguese, French, English, Dutch, Danish, and Americans. Each power had its own impact upon the Caribbean, and the relations of the various powers shaped both the region and the metropolitan centres. The following pages seek to describe a series of important, formative events from a regional perspective, concentrating on the Caribbean itself and reflecting upon both the impact of external powers, and the contribution of regional and local actors to the development of international law. Although many of the islands described in this chapter did not obtain independence until after the mid-1960s, their influence upon global affairs was felt from the earliest periods.

Following a rough chronological order, the chapter seeks to highlight some of the key issues and themes of Caribbean legal and historical development from the time of first contact between Europeans and the indigenous peoples of the region to the early 20th century. It represents the first exploration of this field of the history of international law, and therefore primarily relies upon the traditional historical

---

[1] The word 'Caribbean' has several meanings and could be deemed to refer to all lands in and around the Caribbean Sea/Basin. However, given the scope of other chapters in the current volume, the focus of the present chapter remains limited primarily to the islands of the Caribbean Sea and excludes the surrounding continental territories.

narrative.[2] It introduces the Spanish arrival in the Caribbean and Americas and sketches the consequences of that 'discovery' and the subsequent European conflicts over title and spheres of control for the treatment of the 'New World' and its peoples.[3] Section 2, following the present introduction, traces the attempts that were made to divide the Old World from the New, by means of papal bulls and 'lines of amity' between rival powers, and explores the new forms of mercantilism (chartered trading companies) and militarism (privateers) that resulted. Section 3 examines two key engines for Caribbean wealth—slavery and sugar production—and traces the gradual and piecemeal abolition of the slave trade and slavery. The horrors of slavery have been felt globally, but the Caribbean has been and remains uniquely shaped by it. Section 4 highlights the effect of maritime actors in the Caribbean—including contraband traders, pirates, and privateers—and their role in maintaining a distinction between the European and Caribbean spheres. Such privatization of force was a central part of Caribbean history and was joined by a kind of privatization of sovereign powers, as shown in Section 5 which looks at the role of chartered trading companies. Section 6 briefly examines the impact of two pivotal revolutions—the American and Haitian revolutions—and is followed by some brief conclusions.

2. Spanish Exploration, Claims to Title, and World View

Christopher Columbus' act of setting foot on the small island of Guanahani in The Bahamas on 12 October 1492 engendered far-reaching changes in religious, political, and legal thought.[4] His arrival in the Caribbean set in motion a notional division of the globe, brought European conflict outside of the continent, and ushered in an era where private actors were used to fulfil State ambitions.

The already diminished unity of Christendom arguably disintegrated during the course of the bitter struggles of the great European nations to discover, conquer, and

---

[2] Although in places questioning the traditional narrative this chapter generally presents a broad overview of the region's historical events and themes. It is meant to be introductory, and for this reason relies upon and cites secondary sources.

[3] 'Discovery' and 'New World' are contested terms in light of the pre-existing indigenous civilizations in the region. 'Discovery' refers to a method of acquisition of title to territory but also, along with 'New World', serves to critically emphasize European views about the novelty of the Caribbean.

[4] For descriptions of Columbus' voyages, see Sir A Burns *History of the British West Indies* (2nd edn George Allen & Unwin London 1965) chs 2–4.

convert the territories and inhabitants of the Americas and Caribbean.[5] The Holy See prioritized the claims of two great Catholic powers, Spain and Portugal, over all other Christian nations.[6] In a series of papal grants dating from 1452, Portugal had been granted rights to explore and conquer heathen lands, to enslave their inhabitants, to appropriate their lands and goods, and to engage in missionary activities.[7] But following the return of Columbus from the Caribbean in March 1493, Pope Alexander VI was moved to issue five edicts in favour of Spain, in May and September of 1493. The first three edicts were superseded by the fourth, issued on 4 May 1493. This fourth papal bull, entitled *Inter caetera*, granted the Spanish rights to all lands discovered, or to be discovered, beyond a line drawn from north to south 100 leagues west of the Azores and Cape Verde Islands, with the sea and lands west of the line given to Spanish exploration in exchange for a feudal obligation to convert the inhabitants to the Christian faith. The fifth, *Dudum siquidem*, extended the previous grants to include 'all islands and mainlands whatever, found or to be found...in sailing towards the west and south', and cancelled all other grants previously made, even if followed by actual possession.[8] Since these papal bulls left the definitive determination of the navigational frontier to Spain and Portugal, these two powers mutually agreed to a demarcation line 370 miles westwards of the Cape Verde Islands by means of the Treaty of Tordesillas of 1494.[9] The difference between the original demarcation line and that agreed in the Treaty of Tordesillas brought a considerable part of the South American continent, including Brasilia, into the Portuguese sphere, but purportedly left the rest of the Americas and Caribbean in Spanish hands.[10]

2.1. Papal Bulls

The meaning and legal effect of these papal bulls was, and remains, subject to considerable controversy. Suggestions that they were meant to grant full title—literally to divide the world in two and grant all westward lands to Spain—were countered by arguments that they only mandated Christian conversion of heathens in the west by Spanish kings. Support for the latter view was drawn from the limitation expressed in *Inter caetera* that the grant excluded 'islands and mainlands...discovered and to be

[5] Grewe WG *The Epochs of International Law* (M Byers trans) (de Gruyter New York 2000) 141–2.

[6] For a discussion of rivalries between the Iberian powers and the papacy in this context, see AP Rubin 'International Law in the Age of Columbus' (1992) 39 Netherlands International Law Review 5–35.

[7] *The Epochs of International Law* (n 5) 230–1.

[8] JH Parry, PM Sherlock, and AP Maingot *A Short History of the West Indies* (4th edn MacMillan Education London 1987) at 7.

[9] 'Hispanic-Portuguese Treaty/Tordesillas' (7 June 1494) in WG Grewe (ed) *Fontes Historiae Iuris Gentium: Sources Relating to the History of the Law of Nations* (de Gruyter New York 1988–1995) vol 2, 110–16; see also 'Hispanic-Portuguese Treaty/Sargossa' (22 April 1529) in ibid 117–34.

[10] *The Epochs of International Law* (n 5) 233–5.

discovered…in the actual possession of any Christian king or prince'.[11] Later scholars, perhaps imposing more modern conceptions upon past events, suggest that the Pope's decrees merely granted 'inchoate' title to the lands, which would be perfected following occupation.[12]

The consequences of the papal bulls were easier to measure. European views of the New World were greatly influenced by the source of their authority over it.[13] Spain and Portugal relied upon the papal bulls as extending, on an exclusive basis, their European territories across the globe. The French, English, and Dutch, in contrast, at least initially viewed the New World as 'foreign' to *all* Europeans, and not claimable simply by way of a papal decree, or by means of an Iberian bilateral treaty.[14] The English Crown, for example, granted letters patent to John Cabot in 1496 over areas of North America potentially covered by the papal bulls, and in 1532 Francis I did not reject the claims of the French protestant Huguenots regarding their rights of freedom of trade and navigation in the purportedly Spanish sphere.[15] In 1580 Queen Elizabeth directly contradicted Iberian claims to the New World in her famous letter to the Spanish envoy in London, Mendoza. In speaking of the effect of the papal bulls, the Queen stated:

[T]his donation of what does not belong to the donor and this imaginary right of property ought not to prevent other princes from carrying on commerce in those regions or establishing colonies there in places not inhabited by the Spaniards. Such action would in no way violate the law of nations, since prescription without possession is not valid. Moreover all are at liberty to navigate that vast ocean, since the use of the sea and the air are common to all. No nation or private person can have a right to the ocean, for neither the course of nature nor public usage permits any occupation of it.[16]

This English position with respect to freedom of navigation was later echoed in Hugo Grotius' 1609 treatise, *Mare liberum*, written in support of the claims of Dutch East India Company.[17] It also should be noted that the texts of *Inter caetera* and the Treaty

---

[11] 'Bull Inter Caetera of Pope Alexander VI' (4 May 1493) in *Fontes Historiae Iuris Gentium* (n 9) vol 2, 103–9.

[12] *The Epochs of International Law* (n 5) 236–7. On inchoate title cf *Island of Palmas Case* (Netherlands v US) (1928) 2 RIAA No XX 829.

[13] See eg A Pagden *Lords of All the World: Ideologies of Empire in Spain, Britain and France c. 1500–c. 1800* (Yale University Press New Haven 1995) ch 2.

[14] E Mancke 'Empire and State' in D Armitage and MJ Braddick (eds) *The British Atlantic World 1500–1800* (2nd edn Palgrave Macmillan New York 2009) 193–213 at 196–7.

[15] 'The First Letters Patent Granted to John Cabot and His Sons' (1496) reproduced in JA Williamson *The Voyages of the Cabots and the Discovery of North America* (Argonaut Press London 1929) 25–7; *The Epochs of International Law* (n 5) 244–5 (Huguenot petition).

[16] 'Queen Elizabeth of England to the Spanish envoy in London Mendoza' (1580) in *Fontes Historiae Iuris Gentium* (n 9) vol 2, at 151. For a full quotation of the statement and for discussion of its ramifications see EP Cheney 'International Law under Queen Elizabeth' (1905) 20 The English Historical Review 659–72.

[17] R Feenstra (ed) *Hugo Grotius Mare Liberum: 1609–2009* (Brill Leiden 2009); see also R Jennings and A Watts (eds) *Oppenheim's International Law* (9th edn Longman London 1996) vol 1, at 721–2.

of Tordesillas did not expressly grant rights of control over or possession of the oceans, although such grants had existed in earlier papal bulls.[18]

2.2. Lines of Amity

The Spanish and Portuguese claims, although fiercely resisted by the French, Dutch, and English, also posed a potential threat to the balance of power in Europe. As a result European States between 1494 and 1648 sought both politically and legally to distinguish actions and events taking place in the overseas colonial sphere from those taking place in Europe. 'Lines of amity' were drawn, beyond which different rules were to apply, so that the European sphere of peace would not be disrupted by military conflicts in the Americas or the Caribbean.[19]

A geographical delimitation of 'lines of amity' was first established by oral agreement during the Cateau-Cambrésis peace negotiations of 1559: 'apparently to the effect that west of the prime meridian and south of the Tropic of Cancer might should make right, and violence done by either party to the other should not be regarded as in contravention of treaties'.[20] The idea of 'no peace beyond the line' (as succinctly expressed by Sir Francis Drake), was generally accepted in both State practice and subsequent treaties until the mid-18th century, although the exact position of the lines was subject to some disagreement.[21] The distinction between the European sphere and the sphere 'beyond the line' was manifested in the means of conflict. As noted by Grewe, the struggle 'beyond the line' was undertaken by private actors, 'with or without a formal letter of mandate from their sovereign'.[22]

The strength of these lines of amity should not be overemphasized, since contests between colonial powers in Europe directly affected relations beyond the line, and important events in the Americas and Caribbean shaped and modified metropolitan

---

[18] *The Epochs of International Law* (n 5) 257; eg 'Sanction of the Portuguese Monopoly of Navigation by Nicholas V in the Bull "*Romanus pontifex*"' (1455) in *Fontes Historiae Iuris Gentium* (n 9) vol 1, at 642–6 [vesting ownership over oceans]. For a seminal 20th-century assertion of ownership over an aspect of the Caribbean Sea, namely, the continental shelf, by Great Britain (on behalf of Trinidad) and Venezuela see the Treaty relating to the Submarine Areas of the Gulf of Paria (adopted 26 February 1942, entered into force 22 September 1942) 205 LNTS 121.

[19] *The Epochs of International Law* (n 5) 152–4.

[20] FG Davenport *European Treaties Bearing on the History of the United States and its Dependencies* (Carnegie Institution Washington DC 1917) vol 1, at 220 (as cited in *The Epochs of International Law* (n 5) 155).

[21] *The Epochs of International Law* (n 5) 155–9 and 250.

[22] ibid 273–4. On Grewe, his historical writings, and his relation to Carl Schmitt and the Nazi ideology see B Fassbender 'Stories of War and Peace: On Writing the History of International Law in the "Third Reich" and After' (2002) 13 European Journal of International Law 479–512.

policies.[23] But as a theoretical construct the papal bulls and the lines of amity allowed a notional division of Europe from the Americas and Caribbean—creating an 'other' where legal rules and human relations were different.[24]

2.3. Indigenous Peoples

The difficulties faced by Europeans in characterizing the territories and the legal regimes of the Americas and Caribbean also extended to the inhabitants. There was significant doctrinal debate about the status of indigenous persons at the time of early contact with the Europeans. This debate was shaped by colonial ambitions, and in turn itself shaped the development of international law.[25] However the debate did not discourage the uniform practice of Europeans of neither formally recognizing the equality of indigenous peoples nor respecting their property. Instead indigenous peoples and their lands were treated as *res nullius*.[26]

Spanish writers such as Francisco de Vitoria, Bartolomé de las Casas, and Francisco Suárez (together sometimes called the 'Spanish School'), advocated a potentially more benign, humanist approach towards indigenous peoples, by relying in their writings upon the basic Christian principle of equality of human beings.[27] According to Vitoria, for example, indigenous peoples were part of the universal community of mankind and could exercise all of the essential natural rights. However Vitoria's writings did not support the complete equality, let alone independent authority, of indigenous peoples, since he also recognized a natural right of free interaction on the part of Spain with indigenous peoples. This natural right

---

[23] *The Epochs of International Law* (n 5) 303.

[24] For an argument distinguishing the spatial division of the world between Spain and Portugal on the basis of *rayas* on the one hand, and the English and the French on the basis of 'lines of amity' on the other, see C Schmitt *The Nomos of the Earth in the International Law of the Jus Publicum Europaeum* (Telos Press Publishing New York 2003) at 90–1 and 94. For a brief account of Schmitt's life and work, see B Fassbender 'Carl Schmitt (1888–1985)' in pt 6 of the present volume.

[25] Eg A Anghie 'Francisco de Vitoria and the Colonial Origins of International Law' (1996) 5 Social and Legal Studies 321–36 at 322.

[26] Schmitt links the non-recognition of indigenous personality to the 'freedom' resulting from the 'lines of amity', which 'set aside an area where force could be used freely and ruthlessly'. He notes: 'It was understood, however, that only Christian-European princes and peoples could share in the land-appropriations of the New World and be parties to such treaties.... Everything that occurred "beyond the line" remained outside the legal, moral, and political values recognized on this [European] side of the line.' *The Nomos of the Earth* (n 24) 94.

[27] Eg CG Marks 'Indigenous Peoples in International Law: The Significance of Francisco de Vitoria and Bartolome de las Casas' (1992) 13 Australian Yearbook of International Law 1–51; D Kennedy 'Primitive Legal Scholarship' (1986) 27 Harvard International Law Journal 1–98; 'International Law in the Age of Columbus' (n 6); *Lords of All the World* (n 13) ch 2. Note that de las Casas has been criticized as favouring the African slave trade: *History of the British West Indies* (n 4) 118–19.

included the right to trade with, preach to and, in certain circumstances, settle next to, indigenous persons and, if frustrated in doing so, to wage war against them.[28] As a result, Vitoria's writings could be used to justify the conquest and subjugation of indigenous peoples by the Spanish if they refused to allow European trade or resisted Christian conversion.[29] No doubt influenced by such views, Spanish con-quistadors as early as 1514 read a formal proclamation (*requerimiento*) to the indig-enous peoples they met which graphically set out the consequences of their failure to convert to the Catholic faith—including war, confiscation of property, and enslavement.[30]

But the Spanish were not alone in not recognizing the full juridical personality of indigenous persons. The English Crown, in granting letters patent to English explor-ers, had no difficulty in awarding title to 'lands not possessed by Christians'.[31] As a result, generally speaking, to the extent that indigenous inhabitants existed on Carib-bean territories, European settlers did not regard them as an obstacle to acquisition of sovereignty. Whether as a result of theories of ineffective possession, as espoused by Vattel, or superior use, as espoused by John Locke, or simply as a result of not being recognized as possessing international legal personality, their lands were treated as *terra nullius* (land juridically vacant), subject to discovery and occupation.[32] Where indigenous resistance was encountered, however, Europeans entered into treaties and informal alliances with indigenous groups; later, when Europeans gained mili-tary superiority, they purported to derive title through conquest.[33]

The reliance upon mutually exclusive forms of title by the Europeans reveals fun-damental inconsistencies with respect to the legal status of indigenous peoples.[34] Dis-covery and occupation are original forms of title, exercised over lands juridically vacant. Conquest and cession are derivative forms, which must be acquired from an

[28] *The Epochs of International Law* (n 5) 146–7, 205, 242.

[29] Eg F de Vitoria 'De indis et de jure belli relectiones' (1696 edn) in JB Scott (ed) *The Classics of Inter-national Law* (Carnegie Institution Washington DC 1917) 151–62 (lawful bases for Spanish acquisition of title to indigenous land), 165–87 (justifications for warfare against indigenous peoples). For descriptions of the Spanish depredations against the indigenous peoples see eg *History of the British West Indies* (n 4) 120–2.

[30] See eg 'Requerimiente (Proclamation Read to the American-Indian Natives by the Conquistadores After their Landing)' (1513) reproduced in *Fontes Historiae Iuris Gentium* (n 9) vol 2, at 68–70.

[31] See eg the letters patent of John Cabot cited in 'The First Letters Patent' (n 15) above.

[32] See eg *The Epochs of International Law* (n 5) 400 (Vattel); J Tully 'Aboriginal Property and Western Theory: Recovering a Middle Ground' in EF Paul, FD Miller Jr and J Paul (eds) *Property Rights* (CUP Cambridge 1994) (Locke); *Lords of All the World* (n 13) ch 3.

[33] On the complex nature of European-indigenous alliances and their implications for notions of ethnicity see NL Whitehead 'Carib Ethnic Soldiering in Venezuela, the Guianas, and the Antilles, 1492–1820' (1990) 37 Ethnohistory 357–85.

[34] See D Berry 'Legal Anomalies, Indigenous Peoples and the New World' in B Saunders and D Haljan (eds) *Whither Multiculturalism? A Politics of Dissensus* (Leuven University Press Leuven 2003) 235–71; *Lords of All the World* (n 13) ch 3.

internationally recognized authority. The first assumes no, and the second full, juridical status.[35] The reliance upon *both* by the same European powers demonstrates a
disregard for, or at least expedient view of, the rules of international law.

This issue of the status of indigenous persons in the Caribbean remains important
today, and has been raised in the fields of indigenous title and international human
rights law. The issue merits further research, particularly in the English speaking Caribbean, where rules of British colonial constitutional law regarding the effect of conquest, for example, allow for the preservation of existing laws (potentially including
indigenous rights) so long as those laws were not repugnant to the fundamental principles of English law nor superseded by the legislation of the conquering country.[36]

2.4. Later Spanish Claims to Title and Repartimientos

On his first two voyages Columbus claimed by discovery on behalf of the Spanish
Crown the islands of San Salvador (The Bahamas), Cuba, Haiti, Hispaniola, Jamaica,
and Puerto Rico. But on his third voyage, in 1498, after returning from Trinidad,
Columbus found the Spanish colony in Hispaniola in open revolt against his brother,
Bartolomé. This revolt raised questions about the status of indigenous persons, which
were resolved by classifying the indigenous inhabitants as servants and estate
labourers for the settlers under the *repartimiento* system. *Repartimientos*, given legal
form by royal decree in 1503, subjugated the indigenous peoples under a system of
forced tribute and labour in return for conversion and protection.

Against those that resisted, the Spanish waged war. But even those indigenous persons who submitted were decimated, either by despair and suicide, or by European
diseases and other practices.[37] The resulting diminished indigenous labour force
both frustrated the early development of Hispaniola and encouraged Spanish settlement of other islands, such as Jamaica in 1509. The settlement of Cuba by the Spanish
in 1511 was followed by an attempt to settle Puerto Rico in 1512, against the fierce
resistance of the indigenous inhabitants, the Caribs. But in 1513 Spanish attention was
shifted from the islands of the Caribbean by the discovery of Balboa that it was possible to cross the Isthmus of Darien in Central America (then called 'Castilla del Oro')
to reach what later became known as the Pacific Ocean. The exploration of the Western Caribbean and Gulf of Mexico thenceforth became part of the broader race
between the Portuguese and the Spanish to reach the East.[38]

---

[35] See *Lords of All the World* (n 13) ch 3 for an argument that originally flawed titles were cured by
prescription.

[36] Eg Sir K Roberts-Wray *Commonwealth and Colonial Law* (Stevens & Sons London 1966) at 541.

[37] *A Short History of the West Indies* (n 8) 6–10.

[38] ibid 12–13.

3. Sugar Production and Slavery

3.1. The Spanish and Portuguese

Sugar is said to have been brought to the Caribbean by Columbus on his second voyage in 1493.[39] It was not until several years later, however, that the Spanish commenced sugar production. The first sugar mill was built in Hispaniola in 1508 and the first samples were sent to Spain around 1515. By 1523 there were approximately twenty-four working mills on the island, which represented a considerable capital investment.[40] Nevertheless, labour shortages proved to be a serious difficulty even when supplemented by the capture of the indigenous inhabitants of The Bahamas and Pánuco.

The Spanish turned to West African slaves as their principal source of labour, and in 1510 the Spanish government ordered 250 slaves to be sent to Hispaniola to work in the gold mines.[41] Shortly thereafter, however, the enslavement of 'indigenous' peoples was forbidden, following the campaign against their reckless exploitation by Fray Antonio de Montesinos, both in Santa Domingo and before the Spanish Court. The resulting Laws of Burgos of 1512, the first colonial code, although allowing the continuation of a weaker form of the *repartimiento* system, made clear that at law indigenous peoples were free, not slaves.[42] The Laws of Burgos recognized the indigenous inhabitants of the West Indies as subjects of the King of Castile, who therefore could not be enslaved. However, they did not alter the Spanish views about the suitability of West Africans for enslavement, on the formal basis that they could be viewed as subjects of other kings. As summarized by Parry and others, the voices raised in the West Indies on behalf of the Indian, although loud, were largely ineffective; but for the West African slaves 'no one spoke at all'.[43]

These developments ushered in the African slave trade. The nature of this trade must be distinguished from earlier versions of slavery in its immense scale, its triangular trade model, and in its essentially racist nature.[44] Unlike earlier enslavement practices—which most often resulted from the defeat of a people in war and subjected all of the vanquished to enslavement, regardless of colour, sex, social origin, or religion—the Atlantic slave trade was based on profit and racism.[45] Only black Africans were enslaved for the transatlantic trade.

---

[39] Eg *History of the British West Indies* (n 4) 132.

[40] *A Short History of the West Indies* (n 8) 17.

[41] ibid 18.

[42] ibid 23. Although in practice indigenous enslavement continued beyond this period: eg 'Carib Ethnic Soldiering in Venezuela' (n 33).

[43] *A Short History of the West Indies* (n 8) 25.

[44] A Cassese *International Law in a Divided World* (Clarendon Press Oxford 1986) at 52; AM Trebilcock 'Slavery' in R Bernhardt (ed) *Encyclopedia of Public International Law* (Elsevier Amsterdam 1992–2000) vol 4, 422–6 at 422.

[45] *International Law in a Divided World* (n 44) 52–3.

The Spanish slave trade to the Caribbean was regulated through a royal 'house of trade'—the *Casa de Contratación*—which developed in 1503 and which served as a government bureau for inspecting and licensing ships, cargoes, merchants, passengers, and crews passing to and from the West Indies. From 1518, in order to deter Portuguese smuggling, the Spanish Crown began to grant private licences to traders to import slaves into the West Indies. However because the supply of slaves was insufficient and haphazard, and given the difficulties of shipping sugar to a distant market, sugar production did not become the dominant industry in the West Indies until much later.[46]

3.2. The English, the French, and the Dutch

French and English colonies in the Caribbean became interested in the commercial cultivation of sugar when it became clear that they would not be able to compete with Virginia in the cultivation of tobacco. Sugar was an advantageous crop since it could only be grown in the tropics. But since neither the French nor English colonists had the skill, knowledge, or equipment that was necessary for commercial production of sugar, they turned for assistance to the Dutch, who had experience from Brazil. The Dutchmen therefore became the founders of the sugar industry in the English and French West Indies from the late 1630s, providing technical knowledge and equipment to Barbados, and settling in the French West Indies.[47]

Four of the colonial powers in the Caribbean—the Portuguese, Dutch, English, and French—acquired slave bases in West Africa and sought to establish a monopoly over trade in slaves with their colonies, with any surpluses to be sold to the Spanish.[48] The Dutch in particular played a crucial role in satisfying the Caribbean-wide need for slave labour after they captured most of the Portuguese slave barracoons in West Africa in the 1630s.[49] In exchange for slaves, Caribbean colonies traded locally produced commodities, which were transported to Europe for sale—thus completing the slave trading triangle, which started in Europe with manufactured goods and weapons, which were traded in Africa for slaves, who were then traded in the Caribbean and Americas for commodities.[50]

From 1595 the Spanish sought to regulate the slave trade through a regime of *Asientos*, licences to trade in slaves.[51] This system continued until 1640, when Portugal revolted against Spanish rule. The Dutch thereafter took over the slave trade, along

---

[46] *A Short History of the West Indies* (n 8) 18.
[47] ibid 61–3.
[48] Cf ibid 83–4.
[49] ibid 66–7.
[50] 'Slavery' (n 44) 422.
[51] *A Short History of the West Indies* (n 8) 84.

with other contraband. In England, Charles II granted a charter to an English company in 1663, the Company of Royal Adventurers of England Trading into Africa,
which took on the purpose of slave trading. The larger and more powerful Royal Africa
Company continued this purpose in 1672 and subsequently, following the Treaty of
Utrecht of 1713, the South Sea Company obtained the Spanish American *Asiento*.[52]

The sugar trade was highly regulated in the English colonies, through a trilogy of
statutes: the Navigation Act of 1660,[53] the Staple Act of 1663,[54] and the Plantation
Duties Act of 1673.[55] Their combined effect was, on the one hand, to dramatically
restrict non-English trade for the colonies, but on the other, to provide a guaranteed
market for colonial goods. The acts were enforced by the Courts of Vice-Admiralty,
which were set up in the colonies by the consolidating Navigation Act of 1696.[56]

The French West Indies followed a similar pattern, with the *Compagnie des Indies
Occidentales* holding a monopoly on all trade, including the slave trade, from 1664 to
1674, when the company ended. From 1679 the *Compagnie d'Afrique*, and a succession of other companies, held monopolies on the slave trade. Foreign ships were
forbidden to visit the French islands and the law set down severe penalties for foreign traders and French colonists who engaged in contraband trade.[57]

The overall effect of these policies of restrictive trade was dramatic for the Dutch
West Indies Company, which suffered major setbacks. The company went into bankruptcy in 1674 as a result of the combination of the Treaty of Westminster of 1654[58]
(which restored Dutch slaving stations to Portugal, thereby enabling English trade
there), the recapture of the Gorée and Cape Coast Castle barracoons by the English
in 1664, and the wars with England and France.[59]

3.3. Wealth and Influence

The influence of the slave-produced wealth of Caribbean colonies over their metropolitan authorities should not be underestimated.[60] The profitability of Caribbean
sugar production in the English West Indies, for example, led to the creation of agents
and powerful planters' lobbying groups in London long before these existed for

---

[52] ibid 85–6; 'Empire and State' (n 14) 203–4.
[53] 'Navigation Act (1660)' in A Browning (ed) *English Historical Documents* (Routledge London 1966)
vol 6 (1660–1714), 533–7.
[54] Staple Act (1663) 15 Car II c 7.
[55] Plantation Duties Act (1673) 25 Car II c 7.
[56] JH Parry and PM Sherlock (eds) *A Short History of the West Indies* (3rd edn MacMillan Press Ltd
London 1971) at 77.
[57] ibid 77–9.
[58] Treaty of Westminster (5 April 1654) Dum VI ii 74.
[59] *A Short History of the West Indies* (n 56) 79.
[60] For a view of the economic impact of slavery upon British industrialization, see eg W Darity Jr 'British Industry and the West Indies Plantations' (1990) 14 Social Science History 117–49.

American colonies.[61] As early as 1680 the sugar planters from Barbados were the 'wealthiest group of men in British America', with their shipments being 'worth more than the total value of exports to England from all of the American mainland colonies'.[62] Caribbean absentee sugar planters held several dozen seats in the House of Commons by the middle of the 18th century and represented the most powerful colonial lobby in London.[63] Further, the profits generated by slave plantations directly influenced British foreign policy, allowing it to expand its colonial possessions and to finance wars. Such profits could even help determine the outcome of wars, a fact that led Britain to sack French and Spanish plantations so as to deprive those nations of colonial trade.[64] Slaves also played a direct role in wars, serving in the British army in the Americas during the Seven Years War, the American Revolution, and the French Revolution. In the words of Christopher Brown, 'Slavery, therefore, not only produced political power, it also defined political interests, for individuals as well as for the state.'[65]

3.4. The Beginnings of Abolition of the Slave Trade

By the mid-18th century, economic challenges inspired the English Caribbean colonies to consolidate power and protect their interests in London through powerful pressure groups, including the Society of West Indian Merchants and the Society of West Indian Planters and Merchants. The English also attempted to rival the French and Dutch by creating their own free ports, in Jamaica and Dominica, following the British Free Ports Act of 1766.[66]

However, the English slave trade started to decline as a result of two forms of challenge, economic and humanitarian. English economists strongly attacked the slave trade by calling attention to the financial disincentives associated with it. Some, for example, questioned the high prices caused by the monopolies in the West Indian sugar system. Others noted that the slave trade was being used by Britain's competitors—including the French, Spanish, and Portuguese colonies in the Caribbean, and the Americans—to generate significant wealth at the expense of British interests.[67] Moreover the profits from sugar production were falling generally, and the conquest of

---

[61] 'Empire and State' (n 14) 208–9.

[62] DW Galenson 'The Atlantic Slave Trade and the Barbados Market, 1673–1723' (1982) 42 Journal of Economic History 491–511 at 492; see also H McD Beckles 'The "Hub of Empire": The Caribbean and Britain in the Seventeenth Century' in N Canny (ed) *The Origins of Empire: British Overseas Enterprise to the Close of the Seventeenth Century* (OUP Oxford 1998) 218–40.

[63] CL Brown 'The Politics of Slavery' in D Armitage and MJ Braddick (eds) *The British Atlantic World 1500–1800* (2nd edn Palgrave Macmillan New York 2009) 232–50 at 235.

[64] ibid 235 and 242.

[65] ibid 235.

[66] *A Short History of the West Indies* (n 8) 112–14.

[67] *International Law in a Divided World* (n 44) 52–3.

India brought a cheap source of manpower not dependent upon slavery. Although there are differing views on the viability of the sugar industry on the eve of abolition, Ryden has argued that the English planters faced two challenges following their decision to expand the trade after the Haitian revolution: overproduction and intense international competition from other producers, including those in the Spanish territories of Cuba and Puerto Rico, and in the French territories of Guadeloupe and Martinique.[68] The result was that abolition took place 'at a time when foreign competition and the mercantilist policy worked against the slave economy'.[69]

Economic motivations were not the only factor encouraging suppression of the slave trade. Abolition itself was expensive and other policy objectives, including security and strategic interests, supported it.[70] The revolution in Haiti, for example, prompted concerns about increasing the number of new slaves from Africa.[71] In addition an abolitionist agenda provided justifications for the British to visit and inspect of foreign vessels, thereby ensuring their domination of the world's oceans.[72]

Further, humanitarian critics attacked the institution of slavery itself, both politically and in the law courts. Such challenges relied upon the Christian doctrine of equality, the same doctrine that played an important role in helping to ameliorate the Spanish treatment of indigenous peoples in the 16th century. This doctrine, which had not discouraged three centuries of African slavery, became instrumental when the Quakers, Moravian Brethren, and the Puritans took on the abolitionist agenda. The French Revolution and the principles in the Declaration of the Rights of Man also played a role in raising public consciousness against slavery (albeit not immediately in the French colonies).[73] The cruelties of plantation slavery also became more widely known.[74]

Early legal challenges, several involving Caribbean territories, had limited effect. For example, little justice was provided in the case of the slave Katherine Aucker, who had been tortured by her Barbadian master and mistress and turned out of the household, but who had not been discharged and therefore could not serve elsewhere in England. A Middlesex County Court judge merely granted her the 'liberty to serve any person until such time as [her master] shall return from Barbadoes'.[75] However in the famous case of *Somerset v Stewart,* Lord Mansfield upheld the right of a slave,

---

[68] DB Ryden 'Does Decline Make Sense? The West Indian Economy and the Abolition of the British Slave Trade' (2001) 31 Journal of Interdisciplinary History 347–74 at 368.

[69] ibid 374.

[70] JS Martinez 'Antislavery Courts and the Dawn of International Human Rights Law' (2008) 117 Yale Law Journal 550–641 at 557–8.

[71] B Brereton 'Haiti and the Haitian Revolution in the Political Discourse of Nineteenth-Century Trinidad' in M Munro and E Walcott-Hackshaw (eds) *Reinterpreting the Haitian Revolution and Its Cultural Aftershocks* (University of the West Indies Press Kingston 2006) 123–49 at 125.

[72] *The Epochs of International Law* (n 5) 564–6.

[73] *International Law in a Divided World* (n 44) 52–3.

[74] Eg 'Hub of Empire' (n 62) 232–3.

[75] Middlesex Country Records, Sessions Books no 472 (February 1690).

James Somerset, not to be forcibly removed to Jamaica and sold into slavery after his escape and recapture.[76] The Chief Justice held that the positive law of England did not support a claim for the return of a slave in such circumstances, and thus discharged him, concluding that '[t]he state of slavery is of such a nature, that it is incapable of being introduced on any reasons, moral or political; . . . it's so odious, that nothing can be suffered to support it, but positive law.'[77] The *decidendi* of the Chief Justice's judgment was limited in scope, and was modified by subsequent decisions.[78] But this did not prevent the case from having a profound impact upon British society, where at that time approximately 10,000 black slaves resided, the property of West Indians.[79]

Nevertheless it was not until the Abolition of the Slave Trade Act that the illegality of the slave trade in Britain and her colonies became clear.[80] At a time when more than one-half of the slave trade was in British hands, this statute had tremendous consequences. Over the next few years the laws in Britain became increasingly severe for slave traders, with slave trading becoming a felony in 1811, and being declared to be a form of piracy in 1827, which made it punishable by death.[81] Further, during the war with France, British warships searched foreign vessels in order to ensure that they were not violating the rules of neutrality and used these exercises as a mechanism to suppress the slave trade. As demonstrated in the case of *The Amedie*, if slavers were caught and could not demonstrate the legality of their actions, their slaves were freed and their vessels awarded as prize.[82] A later case, *Forbes v Cochrane*, extended this principle to grant freedom to a slave who set foot on a British ship in international waters and thereby came under her laws.[83]

Other States with interests in the Caribbean abolished the slave trade around the same period, Denmark doing so in 1804, Holland in 1814, France in 1818, and Spain in 1820. The United States banned importation of slaves into its territory in 1808, but a substantial illegal trade continued in the South. Slave trading continued in Cuba until 1865 and in Brazil until much later.[84] Bilateral treaties aimed at suppressing the slave trade were concluded as early as 1814, including the Additional Articles to the Paris Peace Treaty concluded between Britain and France, and the second Paris Peace Treaty of 1815.[85] A multilateral instrument, the 'Declaration Against the Slave Trade',

---

[76] *Somerset v Stewart* (1772) Lofft 1, 98 ER 499.

[77] ibid 510.

[78] Eg *The Slave, Grace* (1827) 2 Hag Adm 94, 166 ER 179 (while a slave is free in England, if he returns to a slave jurisdiction without manumission he reverts to slavery).

[79] *A Short History of the West Indies* (n 8) 153.

[80] 47 Geo III c 36 sess I (1807).

[81] *A Short History of the West Indies* (n 8) 156.

[82] *Amedie, Johnson, Master* (1810) 1 Act 240, 12 ER 92 (B); see also *United States v Libellants of Schooner Amistad* 40 US 518, 15 Pet 518 (1841).

[83] [1824–34] All ER Rep 48 (KB).

[84] *A Short History of the West Indies* (n 8) 156; 'Slavery' (n 44) 423.

[85] Additional Articles to the Paris Peace Treaty of 30 May (signed 30 May 1814) (1814) 63 CTS 193; Additional Article to the Treaty of Vienna (signed 20 November 1815) (1815) 65 CTS 257; *The Epochs of International Law* (n 5) 558.

was included in the General Act of the Congress of Vienna of 1815; it committed the signatories to employ all means to abolish the slave trade in their own territories, and to do everything possible to induce other governments to take similar steps.[86] Further bilateral treaties in 1817 between Britain, on the one hand, and the Netherlands, Portugal, and Spain, on the other, allowed a mutual right to search vessels and established mixed courts to try and condemn captured slave ships.[87] Additional States joined these mixed courts of justice or mixed commissions, which heard more than 600 cases and freed almost 80,000 slaves during their brief tenure.[88] These arrangements were followed by the Treaty for the Suppression of the African Slave Trade, which in 1841 obliged the four powers to forbid all trade in African slaves engaged in by their subjects, with their capital, or under their flag.[89] Further, the treaty attempted, albeit unsuccessfully, to characterize the slave trade as a form of piracy internationally. In 1890 the General Act of the Brussels Conference relative to the African Slave Trade brought about a more widespread, formal and more effective abolition of the slave trade.[90]

3.5. Abolition of Slavery

Agitation for the abolition of slavery per se developed in Britain but was resisted in the Caribbean. However slave revolts occurred in Barbados, Guiana, and Jamaica in the 1820s, and in 1831 there was a large uprising in Jamaica.[91] In 1833 the Emancipation Act entered into force for England and her colonies.[92] The act substituted for slavery a four to six year period of 'apprenticeship', depending upon work category, which required the former slave to work three-quarters of the week (40.5 hours) without pay, and one-quarter of the week with pay.[93] This pay could be used by the slave to buy freedom before the end of the apprenticeship.

France followed suit in abolishing slavery fifteen years later, starting with the enactment of a law in 1836 that freed all slaves who were brought into France, and ending

---

[86] *The Epochs of International Law* (n 5) 512, 554.

[87] 'Antislavery Courts' (n 70) 576.

[88] ibid 595–6.

[89] *The Epochs of International Law* (n 5) 561–2; Treaty of London for the Suppression of the African Slave Trade (signed 20 December 1841) (1841) 92 CTS 437.

[90] General Act of the Brussels Conference Relating to the African Slave Trade (signed 2 July 1890) (1890) 173 CTS 293; 'Slavery' (n 44) 423; *The Epochs of International Law* (n 5) 567–8.

[91] *A Short History of the West Indies* (n 8) 157–61.

[92] ibid 161; Slavery Abolition Act 1833 (UK) 3 and 4 Will 4 c 73.

[93] *A Short History of the West Indies* (n 8) 168. This apprenticeship period was subsequently reduced, ending in 1838.

with complete emancipation in 1848 throughout the French colonies.[94] Portugal, the Netherlands, and the US banned slavery in 1858, 1863, and 1865, respectively. Spain banned slavery for its Cuban colony in 1870, and it was banned in Brazil in 1871. However it took another fifty years for a multilateral convention to extend the abolition of slavery to a global level, with the creation of the 1926 Convention to Suppress the Slave Trade and Slavery.[95]

4. Smugglers, Pirates, and Privateers

From the earliest periods in the Caribbean, State interests 'beyond the line' were to a large extent expressed through private actors, from individual traders, to chartered trading companies, to privateers (state-sanctioned mercenaries). As a result, the most active contestation of Spanish and Portuguese claims to sovereignty over the New World came at the hands of English, French, and Dutch merchant adventurers, explorers, privateers, and pirates.[96] Often operating outside the law, these actors absorbed risks that governments either could not, or would not, afford.[97]

4.1. Early Contraband Traders

In order to satisfy the enormous demand for slaves, smugglers, and contraband traders started to bring slaves from West Africa to the Spanish Caribbean without licences in the early 16th century.[98] The English joined them by the middle of the century, with John Hawkins, for example, organizing four trading voyages to the Caribbean between 1562 and 1568, to carry cloth, general merchandise and slaves from West Africa in defiance of Spanish and Portuguese regulations.[99]

---

[94] ibid 162.

[95] 'Slavery' (n 44) 423–4; Slavery Convention (adopted 25 September 1926, entered into force 9 March 1927) 60 LNTS 253.

[96] 'Empire and State' (n 14) 199.

[97] Eg KE Lane *Blood & Silver: A History of Piracy in the Caribbean and Central America* (Ian Randle Kingston Jamaica 1999) at 202.

[98] *A Short History of the West Indies* (n 8) 29; *History of the British West Indies* (n 4) 129–31, argues that piracy in the region was a direct result of the monopolistic trade restrictions of the Spanish and the severe punishment for their breach.

[99] *A Short History of the West Indies* (n 8) 34–5.

4.2. French Pirates and Privateers

French sailors were probably the earliest pirates in the region. After the Spanish conquest of Mexico in 1519–21, French pirates turned their energies to the lucrative Spanish treasure ships. The Spanish reaction, by 1525, was to require Spanish ships to travel in convoys, and by 1552 merchant ships had to travel armed, at their own expense. By 1561 a bi-annual *flota*, or fleet system, was instituted. The expenses for such protective measures were not borne by the Spanish Crown, which was reluctant to finance a navy 'beyond the line'.[100]

Franco-Spanish hostilities, and the defensive alliance between Portugal and France established by the Treaty of Lyon in 1536, ushered in a new era in the West Indies, that of the privateer, the state-sanctioned mercenary.[101] Privateers were legally (if not so easily factually) distinguishable from pirates because they acted under the higher authority of the State, and not entirely for private gain.

Private, although ultimately state-sanctioned, force against foreigners had been permissible from the time of the Middle Ages under the law of reprisals. The law of 'special reprisals', for example, allowed an injured national who had unsuccessfully sought vindication of his rights or compensation from the government and courts of a lawbreaker's country, to forcibly extract compensation from the wrongdoer's countrymen after obtaining authorization in the form of a letter of reprisal (*lettres de représailles*). The victim of a lawful reprisal could then claim damages from his own sovereign.[102] 'Special reprisals' provided one of the historical roots for the institution of privateering.[103] 'Privateers' were private ships and ship captains who were authorized under *lettres de marque* by a belligerent to participate on its side of a maritime war.[104]

Privateers were vital to European powers which did not possess sufficient naval forces until well into the 18th century and thus relied upon private mercenaries to supplement their naval strength. Privateering also satisfied the interests of those engaged in it. Merchant ships were required to be armed for self-defence in any event, and a successful defence against and capture of a pirate ship allowed a privateer (but not a regular merchant) to gain legal title over the prize.[105] Pirates and privateers were both considered enemy ships, and thus could be taken as prize; any State could seize a pirate ship.[106]

Attacks by French privateers on Spanish shipping in the 16th century, especially on the fleets returning to Spain with silver, imposed a heavy toll upon Seville. Not only did trade with the Caribbean require extensive and expensive naval protection with cruiser squadrons, but attacks by privateers and pirates also mandated heavy

---

[100] *Blood & Silver* (n 97) 16–18.
[101] *A Short History of the West Indies* (n 8) 30.
[102] *The Epochs of International Law* (n 5) 201.
[103] On the use of general reprisals, from the mid-17th to the 19th century, see ibid 368–70.
[104] ibid 203.   [105] ibid 312–13.   [106] ibid 306.

fortification and other protective measures throughout Spanish Caribbean colonies. After 1552 French privateers, with royal warships among them, moved to The Bahamas and cruised against Spanish shipping.[107] Former pirates became officially sanctioned as privateers, including the famous François Le Clerc, alias 'Jambe de Bois' (Leg of Wood), the first known peg-legged pirate.[108] In 1553 Le Clerc and his men crossed the Atlantic with a fleet of ten French warships and systematically burnt and pillaged the port towns of the Caribbean. In 1554 they destroyed Santiago de Cuba, and in 1555 Sores did the same to Havana, razing it to the ground and causing great consternation in Spain.[109] By 1555–56 Spanish cruiser squadrons under the command of Pedro Menéndez de Avilés were assigned to protect home-bound fleets. By 1564–66, Spanish regulations required fleets to sail in convoys, cruiser squadrons (*armadillas*) to be permanently based in the Caribbean, and the principal colonial harbours to be heavily fortified, including with garrisons.[110]

4.3. Strong-armed Contraband Trading

French corsairs also turned to strong-armed contraband trading with Spanish settlements, a form of trading pursued by the English in 1558–68.[111] The exploits of John Hawkins, an Englishman, provide an example of strong-armed contraband trading. In 1564, on his second voyage to the West Indies, Hawkins raided the West African coast and took 400 slaves from Portuguese custody. He sailed to the Caribbean to trade in slaves but was refused the licence to do so in Margarita. He then sailed to the next port, the settlement of Burburata (on the coast of Venezuela), but was not warmly received by the citizens, who sent for approval from the Governor for trade. Hawkins waited impatiently for ten days for the arrival of the Governor, who granted a trade licence, but under unappealing conditions. Hawkins balked at the terms and put ashore one hundred armed men to force the elimination of this tax. The resulting sale was more profitable.[112]

Francis Drake continued this approach when accompanying Hawkins on his third slaving voyage. Drake was fired upon by the Spanish on his arrival at Riohacha, returned fire, destroyed the Governor's house, landed his men, took hostages, and drove the townspeople into the hills. Such violence set the terms of trade and most of Drake's slaves were successfully bartered for pearls and local produce. However Drake and Hawkins suffered substantial setbacks at the end of their voyage and suffered heavy losses at the hands of the Spanish fleet. The unprofitable

[107] *A Short History of the West Indies* (n 8) 30–1; *Blood & Silver* (n 97) 23.
[108] *Blood & Silver* (n 97) 23.
[109] *A Short History of the West Indies* (n 8) 32; *Blood & Silver* (n 97) 23–4.
[110] *A Short History of the West Indies* (n 8) 36.
[111] *Blood & Silver* (n 97) 27–8 and 31–2.   [112] ibid 33–4.

nature of the voyage resulted in a pause in the English contraband slave trade until the next century.[113]

4.4. English Piracy

Instead the English turned to straightforward piracy. English raiders such as Drake allied themselves with French corsairs against their common Catholic foe and also struck up alliances with runaway African slaves (camaroons or *cimarrones*), since they had no ports in the region. In 1573 Drake and Guillaume Le Testu, a French corsair, allied themselves with camaroons in order to attack and plunder a Spanish treasure-laden mule train, making the survivors very wealthy. Between 1570 and 1574, ten pirating expeditions harried Spanish Caribbean ports and ships. In 1575 an enterprising Englishman, John Oxenham, extended the range of pirates by crossing the Panamanian Isthmus and harassing the Spanish in the Pacific.[114]

4.5. English, French, and Dutch Privateering

After war broke out with Spain, the English pursued privateering in the Caribbean. Some 76 English expeditions to the West Indies took place between 1585 and 1603, during the hostilities.[115] Drake returned in 1585 with a major fleet of twenty vessels. He captured Santo Domingo and Cartagena and, although failing to disrupt the Spanish treasure convoy, materially damaged both the possessions and prestige of Spain.[116] The Spanish reacted with more regular naval patrols, increased armaments on merchant ships, and the building of coastal fortifications.[117] As a result, when Drake and Hawkins returned in 1595 they encountered stiff resistance from the Spanish and were unsuccessful in taking San Juan del Puerto Rico.[118]

In 1596 however, France, England, and the Netherlands formed an alliance against Spain at the Treaty of The Hague and 'a joint English and Dutch fleet promptly destroyed a whole American convoy lying in the Cadiz harbour, thus stopping communication between Spain and the Indies for nearly two years'.[119] The French made peace in the Treaty of Vervins in 1598, and the English followed suit in 1604 in the Treaty of London. In the mid-17th century, Spain and Portugal abandoned their

---

[113]   ibid 36–8.   [114]   ibid 38–41.   [115]   ibid 47–8.

[116]   *A Short History of the West Indies* (n 8) 39–41.

[117]   *Blood & Silver* (n 97) 48.

[118]   *A Short History of the West Indies* (n 8) 41–2.

[119]   ibid 42. For more on Dutch privateering and piracy, including the seizure of the Spanish treasure fleet by Piet Heyn in 1628, see *Blood & Silver* (n 97) at 62–8.

hegemonic claims to the extra-European world through a series of treaties.[120] Such reconciliation in the Caribbean was influenced by the actions of privateers.

4.6. The Decline of Privateering and Piracy

The boundary between privateers and pirates became easily blurred, as the same persons played both roles at different times and did not operate fully under the control of the metropolitan powers. The English Governor of Jamaica, Thomas Modyford, for example, refused to stop issuing letters of marque to privateers on the grounds that they were needed for the security of the island.[121] In 1668 Modyford commissioned the famous pirate leader, Henry Morgan, to carry out a reconnaissance in Cuba and then to attack Puerto Bello. Morgan and his men took Puerto Bello by surprise, locked the garrison in the fort, blew it up, pillaged, tortured prisoners, and brought back 250,000 pieces of eight to Port Royal, in Jamaica, which he then used as his base of operations.[122]

Perhaps as a result the Anglo-Spanish Treaty of Madrid of 1670[123] not only recognized the English presence in the Caribbean but 'bound both parties to abstain from pillage and to revoke all letters of marque and reprisal'.[124] Efforts to prevent piracy nevertheless remained unsuccessful until 1685, when a small frigate squadron was sent to Jamaica for the purpose of hunting down the pirates. Port Royal itself sank beneath the seas following an earthquake in 1692.[125]

Other islands, such as Tortuga, also served as bases for buccaneers.[126] The appointment of d'Ogéron as governor of Tortuga for the *Compagnie des Indies* in 1665 led to the conscious organization of the pirates into a colony. Saint-Domingue, on the Western side of Hispaniola, became a base for settlers under d'Ogéron, and Tortuga was tolerated as a base for buccaneers. From this base *la confrérie de la côte* (the brotherhood of the coast) conducted raids on Spanish possessions throughout the Caribbean.[127]

However following the Peace of Ryswyck of 1697,[128] and towards the end of the 18th century, the age of the buccaneers came to a close.[129] As noted by Parry and others, 'at

---

[120] 'Empire and State' (n 14) 202–3.

[121] ibid 203.

[122] *A Short History of the West Indies* (n 8) 75. On Port Royal, Henry Morgan, and other Jamaica-based pirates see *Blood & Silver* (n 97) at 102–26.

[123] Treaty of Madrid (signed 8 July 1670) (1670) 11 CTS 383.

[124] *A Short History of the West Indies* (n 8) 76.

[125] ibid 77–8; see also *Blood & Silver* (n 97) at 172–3 [survivor's account].

[126] *Blood & Silver* (n 97) at 97 identifies the origin of the term 'buccaneers' as '*boucaniers*', the name given to the makers of beef jerky (*viande boucanée*) who lived on the North coast of Hispaniola.

[127] *A Short History of the West Indies* (n 8) 78–9; *The Epochs of International Law* (n 5) 309.

[128] Treaty of Ryswyck (signed 20 September 1697) (1697) 21 CTS 409.

[129] *The Epochs of International Law* (n 5) 314–15. But see *Blood & Silver* (n 97) at 167–95 [describing the last buccaneers, from the 1680s to 1730]

no other time in Western history can a few thousand desperadoes have created a reign of terror over so vast an area, or have exercised so great and so continuous an influence upon the policy of civilized states'.[130] The actions of buccaneers had exacted a considerable toll upon the Caribbean. Henry Morgan and his men alone, for example, during the period from 1655–61 had sacked eighteen cities, four towns, and nearly forty villages across the Caribbean.[131]

5. THE ROLE OF CHARTERED TRADING COMPANIES

Chartered trading companies existed from the 15th century but took on an increasingly prominent role in the 17th century. Being neither purely private commercial enterprises, nor for the most part State organs, they filled a much needed intermediate position in State relations 'beyond the line'. Acting under royal charters, trading companies exercised delegated powers, including exclusive and monopolistic rights of trade with designated territories or regions. In some cases they exercised full administrative authority on behalf of the sovereign, including the ability to exert such sovereign powers as those of sending and receiving envoys, dispatching warships, men, and war materials, building and maintaining fortifications, waging wars (on non-Christian peoples and other trading companies), and minting coins.[132]

Grewe has argued that the ambiguous legal status of these companies allowed them to exist in a kind of intermediate position between full State sovereignty and private ownership. As a consequence, the authorities of the various empires could come into contact (and conflict) in far flung areas of the world without such actions entailing the more serious consequences that would occur at the State-to-State level in the European sphere. These companies could go to war with one another without automatically provoking a war between their respective sovereigns (although the latter in fact sometimes happened), and trading companies could maintain peaceful relations between themselves during times of conflict between their home States.[133]

The Dutch West India Company provides an example. Formed after the end of the Twelve Years' Truce in 1621, it was given a monopoly over trade with the Americas and West Africa (where Dutch slavers already possessed a 'factory'), and was used by the Dutch to plunder and conquer Spanish and Portuguese interests.[134] The attacks of the Dutch in the Caribbean taxed Spain almost to the breaking point. In 1628, for

---

[130] *A Short History of the West Indies* (n 8) 82.   [131] ibid 82.
[132] *The Epochs of International Law* (n 5) 299–303.
[133] ibid 303–4.
[134] *A Short History of the West Indies* (n 8) 48.

example, Piet Heyn, in command of thirty-one ships, surprised the homeward bound *flota* off Mantanzas, and captured all of the ships, yielding a profit of 15 million guilders. This capture enabled the Dutch to refinance their Brazilian offensive and 'ruined Spanish credit in Europe'.[135] The Dutch West India Company showed little interest in settlement during this period, but captured the key islands of Curaçao (valuable for its salt pans), Saba, St Martin, and St Eustatius, between 1630 and 1640.

The French established the *Compagnie des Isles d'Amérique* in 1626, which was active in St Christophe and other West Indian islands, and settled Martinique and Guadeloupe in 1635.[136] Since these latter islands were inhabited by war-like Caribs, however, those colonies developed slowly. Although Swedish, Danish, Portuguese, and Prussian trading companies also came into existence, their influence upon international relations was less prominent.[137]

6. Pivotal Revolutions in the Caribbean

6.1. The American Revolution

Perhaps surprisingly, the American Revolution provoked a *negative* reaction from the English Caribbean colonies, which generally saw the war in 1776 as a threat to their interests. Although the Caribbean colonists shared similar views and grievances with the American rebels, they were far less hostile to the taxes raised for their much-needed imperial defence. The Caribbean islands were rich and vulnerable, had small, loyal free populations, and were influenced by many overseas landowners. As a result, with the exception of a few Bermudans, the British West Indians generally refused to join the American revolutionaries.[138]

However, the English colonies were unable to remain outside of the conflict. France and Spain, in 1778 and 1779 respectively, joined the fighting with the intention not only of assisting the revolution in North America but also of seizing or plundering the British possessions in the Caribbean. The French and Dutch also provided substantial support for rebels in the American Revolution via islands such as Martinique and St Eustatius, including gunpowder, ammunition, clothing, and materials.[139]

---

[135] ibid 50.

[136] ibid 51; *The Epochs of International Law* (n 5) 301. It was replaced by the Compagnie des Indes Occidentales in 1644.

[137] *The Epochs of International Law* (n 5) 301.

[138] *A Short History of the West Indies* (n 8) 116.

[139] RJ Singh *French Diplomacy in the Caribbean and the American Revolution* (Exposition Press Hicksville NY 1977) at 7–8.

British naval vessels, in contrast, were engaged in the Americas, and so the English Caribbean colonies faced food shortages and tremendous trade difficulties. Several English territories were captured during the war, and others, such as Jamaica and Barbados, faced commercial strangulation in the face of the superiority of French and Spanish forces in the Caribbean.

After the end of the war, under the Treaty of Versailles, Great Britain recovered a number of its colonial possessions. But overall the conclusion of hostilities did not advantage either the English Caribbean colonies, which faced new competition from the United States as a foreign power outside of the English colonial system of trade preferences, or the United States, which lost its privileged trading position in the Caribbean.[140] As an independent State, however, the US gained its own territorial possessions in the Caribbean.[141] It also went on to exercise a profound influence upon Latin American and Caribbean States, both by propping up weak governments or installing new ones so as to best secure US commercial interests.[142]

6.2. The Haitian Revolution

Following the American Revolution, the fearful planters of Saint-Domingue (Haiti) sent delegates to the French Estates General in 1789 seeking greater 'liberty' to proceed against free persons of colour and slaves.[143] The white planters represented a tiny minority of the population, numbering approximately 30,000 persons, when compared to the 30,000 free persons of colour and 450,000 slaves.[144] However the post-Revolution French National Assembly refused their request, siding instead with the *Amis des Noirs*, a society similar to Clarkson's abolitionist society in England. The Assembly by decree of 15 May 1791 provided that persons of colour born of free parents, if otherwise qualified, should be entitled to vote for the provincial and colonial assemblies. The colonists were outraged and refused to obey the decree; the governor refused to enforce it, and there was even talk of secession from France.[145]

In August 1791 the discontent of the slave population manifested itself in open revolt, first in the northern plain, and then in most of the rest of the provinces. Chaos reigned, and the French sent a revolutionary Jacobin army in 1792. The Jacobin leader,

---

[140] *A Short History of the West Indies* (n 8) 120; CW Toth 'Anglo-American Diplomacy and the British West Indies (1783–1789)' (1976) 32 The Americas 418–36.

[141] See eg Treaty of Peace Between Spain and the United States (signed 10 December 1898) (1898) 187 CTS 100 (*inter alia*, Puerto Rico); Convention Between the United States and Denmark Providing for the Cession of the West Indies (signed 4 August 1916) (1916) USTS No 629 (US Virgin Islands).

[142] Eg *A Short History of the West Indies* (n 8) ch 17.

[143] ibid 138–9.

[144] R Forster 'France in America' (2000) 23 French Historical Studies 239–58 at 247.

[145] *A Short History of the West Indies* (n 8) 140.

Sonthonax, faced with royalist resistance, decided to ally his forces with the revolted slaves, who in June 1793, at his instigation, entered and sacked the town of Cap Français. In August a decree of conditional emancipation was proclaimed for the slaves and was confirmed by the French National Convention in 1794.[146]

These events raised grave concerns for the Spanish government in Santo Domingo and for the British in Jamaica. Both sent forces to invade Saint-Domingue in 1793 after their countries went to war with France. British forces occupied part of Saint-Domingue but were unable to achieve complete victory because of a lack of reinforcements, following the start of the second maroon war in Jamaica.[147]

Instead Toussaint L'Ouverture seized leadership in Saint-Domingue. He directed his energies against the English and by 1798 had forced them out. He then turned against the mulatto faction of the west and south and defeated its leader Rigaud. For his victories, Toussaint was appointed Governor-General by the French directorate in 1799 and by 1800 was supreme within the colony. But Toussaint lost favour with Napoleon after he defied orders and invaded Spanish Santo Domingo in 1801. Napoleon sent General le Clerc to retake Saint-Domingue and to capture Toussaint, who was sent to Europe and imprisoned.[148]

Napoleon's forces were unable to completely recapture the island. Instead, the challenges of mountain fighting, yellow fever, food shortages, and the lack of troop replacements took their toll. Moreover resistance stiffened when Napoleon's forces, after regaining control over Guadeloupe, reintroduced slavery and the slave trade. By the end of 1803 the French forces surrendered to the British in Jamaica. In Saint-Domingue, Dessalines, one of Toussaint's former generals, embarked on a campaign to exterminate the remaining whites and in 1804 proclaimed himself an independent ruler—the Emperor of Haiti. Following Dessalines' death in 1806 the new State was divided between his rival successors.[149] It took several decades, however, for Haiti to receive widespread international recognition. France, for example, recognized it in 1825 (and required Haiti to pay 150 million French francs); the US only recognized it in 1862.

The Haitian Revolution had a tremendous impact upon the broader Caribbean, inspiring slave insurrections and revolts across the region: uprisings in Jamaica by the maroons and St Vincent by the Caribs in 1795–96, slave and maroon revolts in Surinam in 1798, rebellion in Grenada in 1795–97, the 'Brigand's War' in St Lucia in 1796–97, and mutinies and unrest in Dominica in 1802 and 1809, Jamaica in 1808, and Barbados in 1816.[150] By providing the example of a new State arising from slave revolt, Haiti shook the international community and strongly influenced both sides of the

---

[146] ibid 141. The convention of 1794 abolished slavery and the slave trade in all French territories but this was reversed by Napoleon in 1802: 'Slavery' (n 44) 423. On the political views related to slavery in the colonies in France at this time, see *Lords of All the World* (n 13) ch 6.

[147] *A Short History of the West Indies* (n 8) 142.

[148] ibid 142–4.   [149] ibid 144–5.   [150] ibid 138.

anti-slavery movement.[151] The Haitian Revolution, in the words of Jeremy Popkin, 'directly challenged the system of racial hierarchy that had prevailed throughout the Atlantic world since the beginning of the colonial era'.[152]

7. CONCLUSION

The history of the Caribbean illustrates several important developments in the broader history of international law and international relations. Although tradition-ally seen as the object of imperial ambitions, in a very real sense the territories and peoples of the Caribbean helped to change European views about the world and the nature and scope of international law. The voyages of Columbus set in motion a con-test between European powers during which attempts were made to divide the Old World from the New. Papal bulls such as *Inter caetera* set the deeply contested theo-retical backdrop, which was later supplemented by various concrete actions, from treaties such as the Treaty of Tordesillas, to the 'lines of amity' between rival powers, to new forms of mercantilism (chartered trading companies), and militarism (privateers). These developments both reflected, and shaped, imperial policies and actions in Europe and the Americas. The economies of the Caribbean also initiated, and then later helped to terminate, what is now accepted as one of the most funda-mental violations of the rules of international law—the crimes of slavery and slave trading. The horrors of the institution of slavery, under which approximately 15 mil-lion Africans were captured, enslaved and shipped to the New World, left a deep imprint upon the peoples and countries of the region, and today the practice is pro-hibited and punished under both domestic and international legal systems.[153] The Caribbean is also the site of two successful revolutions, both of which had profound consequences for the region and Europe. The American Revolution of independence disrupted the privileged trading position of the English Caribbean colonies, and the second revolution, the slave revolt which produced the State of Haiti, shook the globe by both challenging the institution of slavery and establishing a precedent for inde-pendent Afro-Caribbean nations. In light of such historical developments, it is fair to say that the Caribbean has shaped not only our view of the world, but also of ourselves.

---

[151] See eg 'Haiti and the Haitian Revolution' (n 71).

[152] JD Popkin *Facing Racial Revolution: Eyewitness Accounts of the Haitian Revolution* (University of Chicago Press Chicago 2007) at 1.

[153] 'Slavery' (n 44) 423–5.

Recommended Reading

Burns, Andrew Sir *History of the British West Indies* (2nd edn George Allen & Unwin London 1965).

Grewe, Wilhelm G *The Epochs of International Law* (Michael Byers trans) (de Gruyter New York 2000).

Lane, Kris E *Blood & Silver: A History of Piracy in the Caribbean and Central America* (Ian Randle Kingston Jamaica 1999).

Parry, John H, Philip M Sherlock, and Anthony P Maingot *A Short History of the West Indies* (4th edn MacMillan Education London 1987).

Rose, John H, Arthur P Newton, and Ernest A Benians (eds) *The Cambridge History of the British Empire* (CUP Cambridge 1929).

Southey, Thomas Captain *Chronological History of the West Indies* (3 vols 1st edn 1827, repr Frank Cass & Co London 1968).

Trebilcock, Abigail M 'Slavery' in Rudolf Bernhardt (ed) *Encyclopedia of Public International Law* (Elsevier Amsterdam 1992–2000) vol 4, 422–6.

PART IV

EUROPE

CHAPTER 25

FROM THE LATE MIDDLE AGES TO THE PEACE OF WESTPHALIA

MARTIN KINTZINGER

1. INTRODUCTION

THERE are two different ways in Western Europe of analysing and categorizing medieval history as part of the development of international law: from the point of view of the history of law on the one hand and from the one of the general history of the Middle Ages on the other. The difference seems to be simple: strictly taken, the premodern era in general and the Middle Ages in particular have not necessarily been part of the history of international law, which came into existence only in the 17th century with the Peace of Westphalia. But is the analysis of international law therefore unimaginable for any historical period before that point in time?

A written international law, systematically arranged within a collection of juridical definitions and normative orders, did not in fact exist before 1648. However, premodern and medieval times were in fact always aware of the meaning and importance of international law, here defined more widely, since distinctive forms of political and social order came into existence.

The difference between the two disciplinary views on the history of international law is even more complicated. Whether the Middle Ages are judged to be part of the history of international law or not will depend on who is asking the question: history is not a fact to be discovered, but a narrative which tells us about the past.

From the point of view of a general and cultural history of the Middle Ages, international law is surely to be regarded as part of historical reality, although it existed neither as an academic discipline at universities nor as collections of texts in printed volumes. But it was undoubtedly present in the reflections of learned men in the Middle Ages and, not least, in political and diplomatic contemporary practice. Finally, international law in medieval Western Europe is to be described as a historical reality before its formal existence, that is, in the classical sense of a phenomenon *avant la lettre*.

Yet within the development of international law, a medieval period has still figured in handbooks on the history of international law. In a book published in 1984 but essentially written in the years of the Second World War, Wilhelm Grewe described the main features of the history of international law from the Middle Ages until 1494, termed *Ius gentium: Grundzüge der mittelalterlichen Völkerrechtsordnung* (Ius gentium: main features of medieval international law). Following this, he identified a special period of further development which directly led to 1648: *Ius inter gentes: Die Völkerrechtsordnung des spanischen Zeitalters* (Ius inter gentes: international law in the Spanish era).[1] Another handbook, frequently quoted even now, was published by Karl-Heinz Ziegler in 1994. He starts with Greek and Roman antiquity, then differentiates between a period of change between antiquity and the Middle Ages (400 to 800 AD), the early and high Middle Ages (800–1300) and the late Middle Ages (1300–1500), followed by the Spanish era (1500–1648).[2]

The most recent handbook on this subject, published by Dominique Gaurier in 2005, first presents the contributions of Greek and Roman antiquity ('*les apports grecs et romains*'), then the time of the Middle Ages ('*les temps médiévaux*'), before introducing well-known authors on the theory of international law from the late 14th to the 16th and 17th centuries as 'great founders' ('*les grandes figures fondatrices*').[3] Other current publications could be quoted here as well. It is evident that the methodological approach to the subject has changed from a focus on temporal periods and a supposed chronological development to a focus on individual authors and the development of ideas and conceptions. Gaurier continues with chapters on great subjects ('*les grands thèmes*'), famous events ('*quelques grands moments*'), and continuities of

---

[1] WG Grewe *Epochen der Völkerrechtsgeschichte* (Baden-Baden 1984). For the history of the book, see B Fassbender 'Stories of War and Peace: On Writing the History of International Law in the "Third Reich" and After' (2002) 13 European Journal of International Law 479–512. Cf H Steiger 'Völkerrecht' in O Brunner, W Conze, and R Koselleck (eds) *Geschichtliche Grundbegriffe* (Klett-Cotta Stuttgart 2004) vol 7, 97–140.

[2] KH Ziegler *Völkerrechtsgeschichte* (CH Beck München 1994).

[3] D Gaurier *Histoire du droit international. Auteurs, doctrines et développements de l'Antiquité à l'aube de la période contemporaine* (Presses Universitaires de Rennes 2005).

ideal imaginations ('*la permance d'un rêve ancien*'). Nowadays, the history of international law is an independent interdisciplinary field of research. It no longer simply deals with the past of a current present but with the genesis of current ideas of international normativity through the pre-modern and the modern eras until now.

2. Chronologies

The focus of historical interest and research is doubtless very often determined by experiences and challenges affecting and influencing historians during their own time. In the last decades of the 20th century, the history of ideas of peace and of practices of peacemaking was predominant in historical research. Widely unexpected conflicts in international politics which led to real wars even within parts of Eastern Europe, changed the situation. The history of war now became a favourite subject of historical research, no longer as a traditional military history of causes but as a cultural history of conflict, violence, and war based on current methodological standards. Finally, the emergence of new dimensions of international terrorism from 9/11 onwards shifted the focus on the history of international conflicts, including battles and wars, and strategies of peacemaking and peacekeeping.

These major strands of historical research influenced different disciplines of history, and particularly medieval history. In contrast to former prejudices, partly still quoted by the mass media, research on medieval history has abandoned the idea of the Middle Ages as a dark period of violence without control or order. On the contrary, it has intended to prove the specific conditions and developments of medieval cultures of war and peace. The question of whether a normative legal order might have existed and the idea of an international judicial framework thus became relevant. The more the International Court of Justice at The Hague became established and international diplomacy and policies became important parts of the public interest, the more interdisciplinary research might have had an interest in the study of the history of international law in pre-modern times. Yet, studies on the history of political decision-making ignored international law as part of medieval history and studies on the history of international law did as much ignore medieval history as part of the history of law.

The title of the present chapter 'From the Late Middle Ages to the Peace of Westphalia' seems to be specific in its chronology, but it really needs further explanation. Particularly the chronology itself and attempts at periodization should be taken with caution. To begin with, what might be a period 'before 1648'? We cannot really be satisfied with concluding historical processes by positing a fixed date or an alleged break. History went on after 1648 and so did the development of international law until now. Is 1648 really that important a date and is it in fact helpful to strictly differentiate between 'before' and 'after' in the history of international law? Learned texts on international law even from the 18th century, for instance, are impressive examples of citations and receptions both of the terminology as well as of historical examples from the Middle Ages onwards. But to see the end of a period in 1648 appears to be a widely accepted opinion in interdisciplinary discussions.

Another question seems to be even more bewildering: when did the history of international law in the Middle Ages start? Even understanding this as *'avant la lettre'* does not help: which elements of historical reality and which instruments of political and diplomatic practice or scholarly theory might be taken as testimony and when did they start to become functional and to be of greater influence?

Other chapters in this volume offer arguments about when the history of international law began in world history. In the context of global cultural history, the European Middle Ages are certainly not its origin. For European medievalists, the articles on non-European history in the present volume are extremely interesting and helpful. Up to now, there is plenty to discuss among those two disciplinary traditions dealing with the same subject.

Nowadays, global history is obviously a well established subject in the history of international law. But in cultural history and even in political history it is, in fact, not. To put it more precisely, while global history has come to be a standard methodological approach in historical research in the United States and particularly in Asia, it is hardly one in Europe and not yet widely used in Germany.

Moreover, global history mostly concerns contemporary and not pre-modern history. In 2009, an instructive volume on world history in the 15th century was published in France.[4] It offers many insightful contributions, especially ones on the history of diplomacy, peacemaking and international relations, but none of them deals with international law. A volume on world history in the Middle Ages, published in Germany in 2010, established a new standard within that genre of historiography because of its intercultural conception, as it includes Christian Europe as well as the Muslim Orient, their cultures and the intercultural influences between them.[5] One contribution is interested in 'theology, law and philosophy in Islam', whereas the articles on the European Middle Ages are restricted to political theory, theological doctrines, conceptions of salvation, disciplines of scholarly knowledge and the emancipation of reason—but they hardly consider international law, neither as practice nor as theory.

---

[4] P Boucheron in collaboration with J Loiseau, P Monnet, and Y Potin (eds) *Histoire du Monde au XVe siècle* (Fayard Paris 2009).

[5] J Fried and ED Hehl (eds) *Weltdeutungen und Weltreligionen 600 bis 1500* (Wissenschaftliche Buchgesellschaft Darmstadt 2010).

To conclude, it is a relatively new approach to ask for the development of international law within a history of the European Middle Ages. But as already mentioned, this largely has to do with what kind of questions we ask and what we want to know about historical reality, which does never explain itself voluntarily. As evidence of this conclusion, an opus magnum of no less than 800 pages was published by Heinhard Steiger in 2010 under the title *Die Ordnung der Welt* (The Order of the World), with the subtitle *A History of International Law in the Carolingian Period*.[6]

As Steiger explains in his work, he is very carefully looking for an adequate description of his subject and for a terminological setting that is based on contemporary sources and yet is faithful to the technical language of current historical and juridical research in order to not be misinterpreted. It is, therefore, for instance, problematic to use 'international law' without further explanations because the term did in fact not exist in the Middle Ages and is nowadays normally and exclusively used for the modern era from 1648 onwards. To put it briefly: Steiger is neither asking for a fixed order nor for a written form of international law. He describes diplomatic contacts between those who held political power in their hands and is thus necessarily less concerned with systematic and programmatic structures than with the large evidence from historical research on the Middle Ages.

Steiger creates a pragmatic definition of what international law might have been in the early and high Middle Ages: 'normativity of inter-power relations'. Those inter-power relations include legal norms as well as other elements of cultural norms which were adhered to in contacts between emperors, kings, nobles and their power-brokers. He therefore first differentiates between 'powers' (*Mächten*) in order to analyse forms of contacts and communications, then distinguishes between power, law, diplomacy, negotiations and treaties to describe the instruments of contemporary actions, and finally focuses on war, order, peace, and friendship to find out what the leading idea of practical power-politics was. He does not primarily focus on learned traditions and serial citations from antiquity to the Middle Ages, or on the history of leading ideas, but on the practical function of international contacts, politics and law.

International law during the Carolingian period and at the beginning of the European Middle Ages is now no longer unknown or underestimated as a simple and more or less dark link between Roman antiquity and later pre-modern history. In other words, Heinhard Steiger is presenting evidence of international law in practice and of its meaning and interpretation in theory during the early Middle Ages. This is the most recent narrative of the history of international law we have as a solid foundation for further research.

---

[6] H Steiger *Die Ordnung der Welt. Eine Völkerrechtsgeschichte des karolingischen Zeitalters (741 bis 840)* (Böhlau Köln 2010).

Insight into the history of international law in high and late medieval times, and comparative studies with a European as well as a global perspective, are still needed. They will hopefully lead to more than just an intensified cooperation of legal history and medieval or pre-modern history. More than other subject, the history of international law is of necessity a field of interdisciplinary research. Consequently, current historical discussions and recent studies on the history of diplomacy as well as on foreign policy and international relations, for instance, are of great relevance for the history of international law. They all belong together as important elements of historical reality.[7] In general history, a methodological problem of interdisciplinary discussions appears even earlier than in the history of international law: in the history of the Middle Ages, it is very often not quite obvious what is meant by the terms 'foreign policies' or 'international relations', that is, terms referring to a political order which did not yet know a developed state system nor any specific formal competence in foreign affairs.

A seminal proposal by the German historian Dieter Berg in 1997 is often quoted on this topic: any legal act of a ruler that transcends the borders of his reign should be defined as foreign policy.[8] This definition is undoubtedly useful for studies on historical subjects, but is not sufficient for legal history. Even up to now, historians of the Middle Ages often participate in the idea that international law was still unknown in the Middle Ages, because in medieval sources they are observing a process of finding norms to organize international contacts and conflicts. Those contemporary norms could have been, for example, specific arrangements on how to behave at the court of another prince, how to arrange a meeting of two kings from different kingdoms, how to make sure that those meetings have a real political effect, or how to express one's own message by symbolic gestures in contact with others from abroad. Such cultural practices were in fact essential in order to make international political communication successful. But cultural practices were, in fact, not able to substitute the norms of international law.

In fact, the medieval attempt to develop a concept of international communication consequently does not mean that the people at that time were ignorant of the tradition and theoretical conception of international law as it had been established in antiquity. Diplomatic practices such as the declaration of neutrality or safe conduct were well-known procedures in the Middle Ages. They were approved by tradition

---

[7] cf C Märtl and C Zey (eds) *Aus der Frühzeit europäischer Diplomatie. Zum geistlichen und weltlichen Gesandtschaftswesen vom 12. bis zum 15. Jahrhundert* (Chronos Zürich 2008); D de Villepin (ed) *Histoire de la diplomatie française* (Perrin Paris 2005); S Dünnebeil and C Ottner (eds) *Aussenpolitisches Handeln im ausgehenden Mittelalter: Akteure und Ziele.* (Böhlau Wien 2007).

[8] D Berg *Deutschland und seine Nachbarn 1200–1500* (Oldenbourg München 1997) vol 40, at 1; concerning international law cf at 4 and 55. It is surprising, that even today this book is the only one on this topic. Others have been announced, for instance by the French historian Robert Delort, but not yet published.

and they were flexible enough to be adjusted to specific, current challenges. Finally, both belong to those elements of medieval political practice that lead more or less unchanged to early modern times.[9]

Such norms could not be prescribed by men, neither by way of a governmental decision nor by one of consensus. Kings and princes might have used such ideas of universal norms in their practice of representation, diplomats might have used them in their everyday acting, learned lawyers might have explained them and commented on them—but none of them did so. To put it succinctly, to the contemporary mind, international norms, and therefore international law, must have been established by divine creation. Men could therefore not do more than to discover it, to describe it and to thus turn it into general knowledge and practice. Seen in this context, it is not surprising that people in the Middle Ages were systematically searching for the idea of an international law as a priori norma.

Thus, there is strong continuity with modern times. The search for a generally accepted practice of international law is still on the agenda of international institutions even at the beginning of the 21st century. Clear evidence of the continuation of these procedures in modern times is, for instance, international meetings of governors, kings, or presidents. As an expression of the personal political relationship between the leading figures of two countries (or at least its staging in public), images of these meetings—now in photos, in the Middle Ages through elaborated illustrations in manuscripts that were mainly added to the texts of chronicles—have always been taken as symbolic expressions of friendship, peace, and consensus. Such meetings are documented from the 9th century onwards, and in recent historical research those of the late Middle Ages are at the centre of attention. They are mostly interpreted as the final act of a special realisation of foreign affairs, and scholarship has more recently concentrated on their staging as ceremonies, rituals and symbolic acts.[10]

In recent studies, meetings between kings and princes are understood as a personal contact between rulers from different countries. Meetings between a king and princes of the same realm, however, are not taken into account within the same context. Asking for international relations between kingdoms may at first sight not lead to the analysis of their internal structures. But those structures should not be

[9] cf JF Chanet and C Windler (eds) *Les resources des faibles. Neutralités, sauvegardes, accomodements en temps de guerre (XVIe–XVIIIe siècle)* (Presses Universitaires de Rennes 2009); M Kintzinger 'Cum salvo conductu: Geleit im westeuropäischen Spätmittelalter' in RC Schwinges and K Wriedt (eds) *Gesandtschafts- und Botenwesen im spätmittelalterlichen Europa* (Thorbecke Ostfildern 2003) 313–63; M Kintzinger 'Der neutrale Ort: Konstruktion einer diplomatischen Realität. Ein methodisches Experiment' in N Bock, G Jostkleigrewe, and B Walter (eds) *Faktum und Konstrukt. Politische Grenzen im europäischen Mittelalter: Verdichtung—Symbolisierung—Reflexion* (Rhema-Verlag Münster 2011) 111–39.

[10] cf G Schwedler *Herrschertreffen des Spätmittelalters: Formen—Rituale—Wirkungen* (Thorbecke Ostfildern 2008).

underestimated in their importance for external political and diplomatic activities, as are hierarchies of obedience and social networks or mutual connections within a feudal system. It necessarily was always the king who could claim the exclusive competence to establish foreign relations in his own authority. Whenever princes or bishops came to an arrangement with foreign kings or princes who made them take part in their alliances, they had to declare not to support nor join any of their allies' activities against their own king. Such a retention of loyalty followed from the internal order of obedience within the realm but also was of direct consequence for the management of external relations and became an element of international law in political practice.

Also relevant in this context is the principle of consensus mentioned above. In order to make it clear that medieval kingship was under no circumstances absolute, that is, independent from legal control—because the king inevitably had to come up with an agreement with the princes of their realm in order to act legally and to be able to rely on their loyalty—modern historians have used the term 'consensual government'.[11] Consequently, the principle of consensus between the participants of an internal political order, the king and the princes of a realm, was transferred to international relations. Foreign policy in its procedures and practical instruments has very often been derived from internal policy and it took a long time for specific institutions of diplomacy (permanent embassies, for instance) and foreign policy to become established.

Even strategies of legitimation were taken from the tradition of internal relations. Treaties between kings emphasized their consensus and friendship (*amicitia*). Symbolic representations of such ideas became more and more important for and evident in the public presentation of treaties and alliances. Current historical research on international policy in the Middle Ages therefore does not only deal with concepts and practices of diplomacy and political decision making but also with the traditions and functions of symbolic cultures. They were a fundamental link between the courts of kings and princes, secular as well as ecclesiastical, all over Europe. Whenever there was no common language between the noble representatives of both sides, and with the decline of the knowledge and practice of Latin at the courts, the communication by symbolic gestures, ceremonies, and stagings became more and more important as a leading instrument of international communication. Of course, receptions of ambassadors, meetings of princes, or the final public act of announcing a treaty were prepared in detail behind the stages by the

---

[11] B Schneidmüller 'Konsensuale Herrschaft. Ein Essay über Formen und Konzepte politischer Ordnung im Mittelalter' in PJ Heinig et al (eds) *Regionen und Europa in Mittelalter und Neuzeit: Festschrift Peter Moraw* (Duncker & Humblot Berlin 2000) 53–87; JM Moeglin 'Le Saint Empire: contrat politique et souveraineté partagée' in F Foronda (ed) *Avant le contrat social: Le contrat politique dans l'Occident medieval, XIIIe-XVe siècle* (Publications de la Sorbonne Paris 2011) 173–91.

envoys of both sides. But to be accepted as a true and guaranteed commitment, treaties between princes always needed the final representative act of publication, proving the value of the written document. But those acts of publication focused on a sophisticated description of the performance of the princes' meetings. Symbolic culture was therefore inevitable for diplomatic and political acts in international communication.

At the same time, other instruments of international diplomacy were developed in a more formal and juridical sense, like the principle of not obstructing an ambassador, which was instituted within the norms of canon law by declaring ambassadors inviolable (*legati inviolabiles*). Even in their practical value, norms like this can only be understood by their symbolic meaning: physically violating an ambassador, as someone's official representative, meant to symbolically violate the authority he represented. Acting against a king's ambassador meant to directly hurt the king himself, not only because the ambassador represented his king in a physical way, but because the king increasingly became defined by the difference between his own personal, physical, nature and his official position. As was explained by scholarly theory, the king had two bodies, so to speak, and so did the emperor and even the pope. This particular situation led to several incidents related by contemporary chronicles, as for instance one of a meeting at the court of Emperor Frederick I at Besançon in 1157. A representative of the papal court presented a letter from Pope Hadrian IV conveying that the archbishop of Lund had been attacked by unknown forces while travelling as the pope's ambassador. He therefore accused the emperor of not having protected the archbishop, although the pope had given him exclusive privileges (*beneficia*) in order to make him responsible for the church's protection all over the world. Even though it was probably not the intention of those acting in such situations, the interdiction of obstructing an ambassador led to a worldwide diplomatic practice of protection, and was thus evidently an element of international law.

Finally, with respect to recent debates on intercultural communication in history, the contacts and meetings between European kings and rulers from outside of Europe are becoming objects of comparative studies, as for instance those between Christian and Muslim rulers. This is a new approach to pre-modern history calling for new methods of historical analysis and interpretation which will probably lead to a new reading of global history.[12] What makes it 'new', is the methodological difference to the older approaches to a history of the world which studied

---

[12] cf W Drews 'Transkulturelle Perspektiven in der mittelalterlichen Historiographie: Zur Diskussion welt- und globalgeschichtlicher Entwürfe in der aktuellen Geschichtswissenschaft' (2011) 292 Historische Zeitschrift 31–59; C Gratloup *Faut-il penser autrement l'histoire du monde?* (Armand Collin Paris 2011) on the Middle Ages at 88 and 91–5.

individual countries or kingdoms, whereas global history intends to describe comprehensively the universal horizon of interactions, transcultural communications, processes of mobility and migration, and the creation of a worldwide field of activity.

The difference between 'world history' and 'global history' is comparable to the one between 'law of nations' (*droit des gens, Völkerrecht*—as direct translations from the Latin *ius gentium*) and 'international law' (as a recent terminology in interdisciplinary legal research). Consequently, current disciplinary research on the history of law normally prefers to define its subject as 'international law', and no longer as 'law of nations'.

The importance of an international law within a concept of a new global history is certainly evident and indeed poses an ambitious methodological challenge for historical research as well as for legal studies: global history as a subject of research and as a part of historical and current reality necessarily calls for norms that are of international validity, that is, those that are to be respected all over the world. An encoded symbolic culture based on the consensus within the international social and political noble elite functioned in fact as such a norm in pre-modern Europe. It acquired practical value no later than the high Middle Ages (during the 10th and 11th centuries), and it remained important until the 17th and 18th centuries.

Within the pre-modern period of European history, things changed fundamentally as historic developments and transformations took place and new experiences, discoveries, and challenges brought renewed knowledge and an awareness of traditional subjects. If such processes are to be qualified as forms of a progress to modernity, they might still be viewed with suspicion: no pre-modern international law in a modern sense existed during the Middle Ages and the early modern period, but there were norms and practical measures by which people managed international communications and conflicts and which were theoretically and functionally equivalent to international law.

Once more, periodization poses a problem: were the origins international law to be found in the Middle Ages from the 17th century onwards even before its formal existence, and which period of the Middle Ages might be marked here as the beginning of an elaborated, international symbolic culture at the European courts in the 10th and 11th centuries? Or did it already start with the first establishment of a political order in central Europe under Carolingian rule in the 8th and the 9th centuries? Did actual practice and a first theory of international law in the Middle Ages rely on each other, when considering the circumstances of successive development? Was there a specific medieval practice of international law or did it change from the later Middle Ages to the early modern period? Did it profit from the development of an increasingly centralized monarchy in the Western kingdoms from the early 13th century onwards or from the establishment of novel princely territories in the Holy Roman Empire during the 15th and 16th centuries?

3. CATEGORIES

According to the most recent publications on the topic, the beginnings of international law in the Middle Ages can be dated to the Carolingian period. The above quoted seminal publication by Heinhard Steiger from 2010 has led to a new state of knowledge in this regard. Nevertheless, many issues remain to be dealt with, that is, the analysis of the development of international law in Western European civilization from the middle of the 9th to the beginning of the 16th century and further until 1648. To start with, all we can do is try to find out which methodological arguments and which categories of description may be useful to conceptualize the current history of international law in the Middle Ages and the early modern period. The categories established by Heinhard Steiger (*Zwischen-Mächte-Beziehungen, Zwischen-Mächte-Recht, Zwischen-Mächte-Verbindungen*)[13] are of great practical value for further studies on the whole pre-modern period, and in particular the Middle Ages. Three methodological remarks should be made here. First: a collection of key words of contemporary descriptions of the subject such as *'ius gentium'*, 'international law', *'droit des gens'*, or *'Völkerrecht'* is needed. One then must differentiate the key words taken from contemporary sources from those belonging to modern research. It will be quite important to make clear whether or not it is possible to use words such as 'nation', 'national' and 'international', 'State' and 'government'. They are part of contemporary life and it is common knowledge that neither nations nor States in a modern sense existed during the Middle Ages. On the other hand, we do have to make it as clear as possible what we mean by our descriptions and by the words we use. Therefore there might not be an alternative to the use of the word 'international' and one might use it without necessarily implying that political nations existed in the Middle Ages. The term 'international law' can and should be used in the sense of a transformation from the Latin and medieval *'ius gentium'*, although the older 'law of nations' or *'droit des gens'* is nearer to the Latin origin. Up to now, no other terminology is available. This might be briefly compared to the use of terminology in other contexts: 'natural law' or 'positive law' as translations for *ius naturale* or *ius positivum* are generally accepted as well. The term 'inter-power relations' might not yet be established but will undoubtedly be so after further study of Heinhard Steiger's new book; it really is as distinct a description as 'diplomacy', 'contact', and even 'foreign policy', and 'international relations' to define what is meant by practical measures, instruments, and consequences of acting according to international law in the Middle Ages.

Second, in addition to collecting key words it is necessary to focus on the practical functions of diplomacy and international relations described by the terms, and to remain open to the surprises offered by historical sources. Their testimony might be unexpected by us, but our description of them through adequate language should

---

[13] Inter-powers relations, inter-powers law, inter-powers associations.

always follow their intention and not vice versa. Who would have seriously expected the Carolingians to practise inter-power relations? But they did, in fact.

Third, being historians, we should always and in each case of analysis keep in mind the historical contexts of our subjects. Evidently, there was a wide range of traditions, challenges, orders, norms and expectations which made people act as they did in specific historical situations. Political and diplomatic actions in the Middle Ages certainly followed concrete aims, as they do nowadays, but, under all circumstances, they had to respect ritual ceremonies, symbolic meanings and the rules of court life and courtly diplomatic practice. Consequently, the history of international law in the Middle Ages should no longer be understood as a more or less dark pre-history of modern progress but as an important period of development which substantially helped to instigate modern international law.[14]

4. CITATIONS AND CODES

To start with a recapitulation, as part of the history of international law, the beginning of the late Middle Ages is to be regarded as marked by the establishment of an organized political system of governments and their foreign relations in the high Middle Ages during the 12th and 13th centuries. The classic and the contemporary definition of international law, however, was much older and has been received from Roman antiquity through learned ecclesiastical tradition: the term and meaning of *ius gentium*, originally invented by Cicero (106–43 BC). To put it briefly, the Roman interpretation of international law was quite different from the one of the Middle Ages and especially the one of modern times. Even Cicero provided two different definitions, the *ius belli ac pacis* and the *ius gentium*, which is of particular interest here. For the Romans, *ius gentium* was the law they gave to people who had been conquered by them before. Fundamentally, it was their own law, the law of the Romans, which they considered to be the best possible law for all people. Thus international (private) law substantially was a right of predominance.[15]

This is the reason why medieval scholars who knew about the old, traditional meaning of the Roman *ius gentium* did not decide to use this terminology when they were looking for a practical definition of a just and legal order to describe and organize international political communication, contact, and conflict. They intended to find a specific kind of order which had not been given by man, did not depend on

---

[14] Cf MS Anderson *The Origins of the Modern European State System, 1491–1618* (Longman London 1998).

[15] Cf M Kaser *Ius gentium* (Böhlau Köln 1993) at 4 and 10.

force, and was strong enough to remain free of any political influence. It was supposed to be valid as a general order which everyone had to obey. And because this order was also supposed to be useful for international and global and intercultural contacts, the theological definition, normally favoured by them, was not what they sought.

They discovered a suitable and simple explanation in Cicero which they were able to use for their own purposes: international law is based on natural law which is given by nature to every human being and all people and nations. International law as natural law thus offers the greatest justice possible. From Isidor of Sevilla in the early 7th century to late medieval political theory, this definition remained valid. In the theory of noble exclusive communities of the 14th and 15th centuries, a social understanding of natural law helped to explain that noblemen were all equal to each other within their *aequitas*. Within the same framework of meaning, scholastic authors from the 11th and 12th centuries onwards used the theological model of a just war (*bellum iustum*). This had been established by Augustine (354–430) in the early 5th century due to the frightening experience of the fall of Rome in 410. Once again based on Ciceronian texts, the idea of the just war in medieval interpretation established a strong connection between justice and social as well as political norms.

Two remarks are necessary here. First, it is undoubtedly evident that all authors cited above were not simply quoting others but responding to former argumentations from learned tradition and then developing their own concepts from them. And second, they were not able to take any theoretical norms from elsewhere to substantiate their political practice, simply because there were none. On the contrary, they developed their theoretical concepts in order to describe a reality which was already there. In the development of international law, theory followed practice. At all times, theoretical concepts of international law reacted directly to given challenges such as contacts and conflicts, and on that background continued to construct learned concepts as manuals for political and diplomatic practice.

In the 13th century, Thomas Aquinas (*c.* 1225–74) was thus the successor of Augustine in shaping a sophisticated theory on just war as well as on the different categories of law, including international law. Later scholastic authors in the 14th and 15th centuries followed him, as did eventually the famous authors of so-called Spanish late scholasticism from the early 16th century. They implemented a new strategy by interpreting international law as part of positive law (as was first done by Thomas Aquinas) and no longer exclusively as an element of natural law. And they arrived at a new consequence by defining international law as equal to all human beings and thus related to human rights. But the connection of international and natural law and the fundamental legitimization of their own ideas that rested on the long tradition from Augustine and Thomas Aquinas remained very important for them.

Spanish late scholasticism was the last elaborated scholarly theory of international law before the period of the Thirty Years' War and the Peace of Westphalia. It was developed from scholastic ideas of the 13th century and this is why this school of thought is still characterized by that name, although it unfortunately is slightly unclear how independent and conceptualized its ideas were. Still, there was no direct link between the ideas of Thomas Aquinas and the scholarly representatives of his thought in the early 16th century. Confronted with special challenges in their own time, the authors of Spanish late scholasticism went back to arguments which others before them had proposed in similar situations. About 100 years earlier, at the beginning of the 15th century, nearly the same situation had occurred, leading to comparable results. At the Council of Constance (1414–18), the conflict between the kingdom of Poland and the Teutonic Order became a subject of dispute. In 1410, Poland and Lithuania (both connected through rule by a personal union) had surprisingly won the Battle of Tannenberg (Grunwald/Žalgiris), and now the jurists of the King of Poland intended finally to prove that the role of the order in Eastern Europe had been one of an intruder and occupier.

One of the most important points of conflict was the question of whether the government of a non-Christian country—as the order considered Lithuania to be—could be legitimate and whether treaties between Christian kings and non-Christian allies were to be respected. The leading jurist of the Polish crown and rector of the university of Cracow, Paulus Vladimiri (1370–1435), painstakingly argued as follows: (1) there is no superior authority, either of the emperor or of the pope or of anyone else, over non-Christian countries and their governments; (2) all fighting and war has necessarily to be justified as a just war (*bellum iustum*) and is otherwise illegitimate; (3) these fundamental arguments were taken exclusively from international law (*ius gentium*) as well as natural and human law (*ius natural et humanum*). Vladimiri doubtlessly reacted to reality in explaining the interest of the king of Poland and Lithuania through a theoretical construct. Thus he acted as much in a strategic way as an advocate in a forensic dispute does against the specious arguments of the opposite site. Furthermore, however, he obviously intended to derive a manual from his theory for practically managing actual conflicts of international politics and diplomacy. Thus he was the first in the late Middle Ages to argue explicitly in an international political conflict with reference to the terminology and the meaning of international law. In earlier times, comparable disputes had always been carried out by presenting oppositional arguments of claimed or dismissed authorities, or of symbolic rank or superiority.

By arguing as he did, Vladimiri not only put an end to that kind of old-fashioned definition of superiority but opened up the practice of learned disputes on the subject of international law to a new understanding of superiority and sovereignty, as well as to a new awareness of the principal equality of all governments in the world (unconcerned whether central or peripheral, European or not, belonging to the Christian religion or not) within the context of international political and diplomatic communication. If one were to look for the first idea of the new approach to global history and post-colonial reflections, in which much current research in cultural history is interested, it might possibly be found here in the disputes of the early

15th century.[16] Later development proceeded from that point and so did the authors of Spanish late scholasticism.

The contemporaries of the 16th century faced completely different challenges, but the methods used by intellectual work on the theoretical definition of international law as a useful preparation for actual practice continued. That was the reason why in particular the Dominican and learned theologian Francisco de Vitoria (c. 1483–1546) got into trouble at the court of the Emperor Charles V (1500–58). His application of the theory of international law to the political practice of the Emperor's politics in the New World led to different consequences than did the intentions of those who simply disregarded law and justice in order to maximize economic effects. Unfortunately, they were the ones who managed to win the quarrel in practice and to marginalize the ideas of international law as a learned, normative theory.[17] The emperor felt real and personal sympathy for Vitoria. However, he was obviously unable to enforce his arguments as a matter of governmental policy in the New World. In a particular way, Charles represents the fundamental change during his time: after the conquest of the New World he initially proclaimed self-confidently to be the sole ruler of an empire on which the sun never sets, and in 1520 he declared himself superior to the entire world. But eventually, in 1556, he was not able to accept the transformations, eventually becoming the first emperor to abdicate his throne.

Nevertheless, Vitoria caused a renewed interest in the history of the idea of international law. In recent studies, he has therefore been called the founder of a global philosophy. According to his theory, natural law leads to international law by positing the idea of a law which belongs to all human beings equally and which is, in other words, the right of man. The most pressing contemporary challenge for Vitoria was the necessity of integrating the New World within the already existing social and political order. In fact, the Spanish conquest had discovered an elaborate yet closed social and governmental order that was, of course, completely different to the one of the European kingdoms and did not know the Christian God. It could not possibly be just to deny the right of existence to the people living there, who increasingly came to be dominated by the power and arbitrariness of the European conquerors. Vitoria definitely rejected the legal arguments the conquistadors pretended to respect in order to completely subdue their new colony. Astonishingly, he did so not only through theological arguments as the basic condition for defending a global natural law and human right. He argued in a juridical way, quoting legal texts from the tradition of scholarly Roman law, and he found a new definition of international law, which fundamentally made it clear that international law belongs to all peoples: 'That, which is created by natural reason among all peoples, is called international

---

[16] Cf C Gauvard 'Contrat, consentement et souveraineté en France' in *Avant le contrat social* (n 11) 232–30.

[17] Cf A Brendecke *Imperium und Empirie. Funktionen des Wissens in der spanischen Kolonialherrschaft* (Böhlau Köln 2009).

law' (*Quod naturalis ratio inter omnes gentes constituit, vocatur ius gentium*).[18] Therefore international law must inevitably be either natural law or affiliated with natural
law. Such an affiliation (*derivatur*) was new in this context and it finally allowed Vitoria to combine his newly defined international law with the traditional Roman right
to hospitality—and to conclude that it is therefore illegitimate to oppress the American Indians in the New World as the Spanish did in their colony. In addition, he
changed the word for the peoples he found in the Roman law (*gentes*) to the one for
political nations (*nationes*), which had not been in general use in Europe before the
end of the 15th century.

According to Vitoria, international law is valid not only because of respective treaties and a consensus among human beings, but because of the fact that the whole
world resembles a unique political community in which the general laws and the
norms of the peoples are valid in peace as well as in time of war (*quod ius gentium non
solum habet vim ex pacto et condicto inter homines, sed etiam habet vim legis. Habet
enim totus orbis, qui aliquo modo est una res publica, potestatem ferendi leges acquas et
convenientes omnibus, quales sunt in iure gentium. Ex quo patet, quod mortaliter pec-
cant violantes iura gentium—sive in pace, sive in bello*).[19]

Also Christian theology gave rise to ideas of human rights. However, it did not
recognize their exclusive or paramount validity. References to non-Christian ideas of
a priori values and norms were thus increasing. They led Vitoria to a genuinely global
understanding of natural law and thus to a new, sustainable definition of international law.

Vitoria is the best known and most influential representative of Spanish late scholasticism, together with the Jesuit Francisco Suárez (1548–1617), a learned theologian
as well, who, one generation later, reflected on and continued the ideas of Vitoria, in
particular those concerning the theory of international law.[20] While Vitoria was a witness to the Spanish conquest of the New World, which caused an extremely deep fis-
sure in the traditional knowledge of the world, Suárez was a famous commentator
(*doctor eximius*) on the consequences of the conquest for Europe. In his theoretical
writings, he focused on the history and interpretation of natural law and his studies
were of great influence to later authors of the 17th and 18th centuries.

As had been apparent for a long time, Suárez claimed that any international norms
were necessarily not regarded as having been given by mankind by any authority nor
by a consensus. In contrast, it should be defined as 'a priori', in the sense of having
been given by God or by nature. Consequently, in the writings of Suárez, the universal
law that is superior to all human laws and obligatory to obey for everyone is either

---

[18] F de Victoria *De Indis recenter inventis et de jure belli Hispanorum in Barbaros relectiones* (1539) at
s 3 pt 2.

[19] F de Victoria *Relectio de potestate civile* (1528) at no 21.

[20] For the following context cf M Kintzinger 'Bellum iustum—gerechter Krieg oder Recht zum Krieg?'
in U Lappenküper and R Marcowitz (eds) *Macht und Recht. Völkerrecht in den internationalen Beziehungen* (Ferdinand Schöningh Paderborn 2010) 3–30.

divine law (*lex aeterna*) or natural law (*lex naturalis*). While natural or divine law is intangible to human beings, international law, in contrast, belongs to positive law (*ius positivum*). Thus for those responsible for governmental policies it demands a serious commitment to apply international law responsibly to the challenges of their reality.

Even scholastic authors who had written on the topic much earlier had already come to nearly the same conclusion. It is obvious that an answer to the question of whether international law existed was needed in late medieval society. This question found its own ways to articulate itself and it culminated in a specific scholarly theory which achieved a conceptual independence. The context here was the same as the later one for the authors of late Spanish scholasticism: it was the fundamental question of whether in a global political world a supreme power existed which did not relate to the well-known quarrels between emperors, kings, and popes, but to the substantial discussion of how to imagine sovereignty.

The idea of 'aequitas', the justice of equality, played an important role here. In the early 14th century, Engelbert of Admont (*c.* 1250–1331) explained that, because the world is the creation of God, there should not be any hierarchy or subordination in international communication, that is, among political powers, emperors, and kings. Within any political and social order, one would always be superior, but in external relations it must not be the same. *Superioritas* consequently was not supposed to exist in global politics, emperors, and kings were thus forced to find a new way of how to cooperate and to reach a consensus in international politics.

Although theological reasons and natural law remained important, the argument here is different: *superioritas* (not mentioned but implied as a leading idea as well as practical element of international law) is not just given, but has to be established by a *consensus omnium*. What is occurring here is similar to the modern idea of decision making.

The scholastic discussion on superiority was initiated by contemporary experiences and developments: in those circumstances, theory already followed practice. The main question of those who dealt with the idea of Engelbert was not how to establish a sophisticated model, but to give an answer to a question of everyday political experience: what is to be done when emperors and kings get into conflict? How can fighting be avoided and how can conflicts be ended? Where can an authority be found that is able to make others stop their disputes and that can restore peace? It was the well known Italian lawyer Baldus de Ubaldis (*c.* 1327–1400) in the middle of the 14th century who gave the answer. He said that no power and no men are able to do so, but that there is a general and legal principle to be accepted as a leading norm. 'That which all people are commonly using, which is always good and useful and equal to all people'—that is what we are looking for, and it is called *ius gentium*. A new definition of international law had been found, in reaction to actual conflicts in Italy and all over Europe, in the tradition of scholastic thinking, but in a unique shape. It used an old word as its subject, but it created quite a new, functional meaning for it.

Ius gentium thus did no longer mean a right of predominance but became a set of legal instruments to achieve consensus.

It has to be conceded that Baldus' brilliant idea did not quite manage to be directly applied to political practice. But it is certain that his idea became quite familiar at royal courts, as did other thoughts by the same author, for instance the model of the king as emperor in his own reign. Although originally from a Burgundian jurist of the mid-13th century, Jean de Blanot (who died in 1281), whose proposition '*Rex Franciae in regno suo princeps est*' had often been quoted during the following centuries as '*Rex Franciae Imperator in regno suo*', Baldus established the following general statement: '*Rex in regno suo est imperator regni sui*'.[21] Understood in that way, the idea of the king as sovereign in his own kingdom could be and has been widely adopted. Sovereignty strictly meant not to accept or tolerate any other political power above one's own and to refuse any influence from another king or ruler within one's own kingdom, not even by the pope and particularly not by the emperor of the Holy Roman Empire. To be the emperor in his reign therefore made the King of France equal to the emperor.

Attributed to the States by the Peace of Westphalia in 1648, sovereignty in the Middle Ages remained an exclusive personal quality of those kings who were successfully able to claim to be sovereigns as emperors in their kingdoms. The discussion about sovereignty took place nearly everywhere in the late Middle Ages and the early modern period. It helped to consolidate a king's reign within his own country as well as to make him equal to other kings from abroad, to fundamentally reorganize the conditions of international political and diplomatic communication.

Testimonies to this development are usually not theoretical explanations but chronicles showing texts and images of what took place when two or more princes and kings met each other or had a meeting with the emperor. Distinct representations of how to express one's own sovereignty were created, for instance, by using a white horse instead of a dark one or by respecting and claiming specific rituals of court ceremonies. Under these circumstances, international law came to be expressed in quite surprising ways in the late Middle Ages. In the perception of contemporaries, international law as a learned theory could not be separated from political and diplomatic practice in all of its forms.

This remained true even for the early modern period, when the beginning of the modern State came to be based on more elaborated theories of the sovereignty of a prince. The importance of rituals and ceremonies at the court as expression of the practice of international law nevertheless remained high and even increased.

---

[21] cf M Kintzinger 'Der weisse Reiter. Formen internationaler Politik im Spätmittelalter' (2003–2004) 37 Frühmittelalterliche Studien 315–53 at 337–8, 344–5, and 352; M Kintzinger 'Superioritas: Rechtlichkeit als Problem bei internationalen Konflikten' in S Esders (ed) *Rechtsverständnis und Konfliktbewältigung: Gerichtliche und außergerichtliche Strategien im Mittelalter* (Böhlau Köln 2007) 363–78 at 373–4; M Kintzinger 'Rex superior: Die Internationalität der Hofkultur und die Regionalität ihrer Konfliktlösung im westeuropäischen Spätmittelalter' in S Dauchy and M Vec (eds) *Les conflits entre peuples: De la résolution libre à la résolution imposée* (Nomos Baden-Baden 2011) 23–50.

The complex relations between Emperor Charles V and Francis I (1494–1547), king of France, can only be understood by a close examination of the concurrence of their representative performances.[22] The conflict of prestige between the German king as Roman Emperor and the King of France originated in the 10th century but had always been reinvented under current conditions.[23] That was the case in the 16th century as well. Conditions were different and the fighting between two Christian parties in Europe, Catholics and Protestants, was new. But the fundamental problems were the same as before and so were the instruments of self-expression.[24] The public performance of representations and representatives in conflict simply gave an up-to-date answer to the ancient question: how could international law be represented by diplomacy?

From a modern point of view, this result may seem to be modest. Therefore we should ultimately not forget those who tried to achieve more and who failed doing so. King Georg Podiebrad of Bohemia (1420–71), for instance, who in 1462 published the project of an international court to mediate peace in cases of conflicts between European kings. Compared with current institutions, this idea is surprisingly modern. He proposed to establish a board of princes who were to judge (like a court of justice) the actions of their 'colleagues'. Equality (*aequitas*) was paramount for that peace-project, as was justice, peace-keeping, international cooperation, and consensus. Again, the fundamental commitment to international law was ultimately based on natural law.

Why did that project not have a chance of being realized in practical political life? The answer is simple and is to be given with reference to the contemporary understanding of the practical value of international law. A sovereign king like the King of France, Louis XI (1423–83), nominated as the president of the international court, was by no means willing to accept equality if it meant that he himself was to be a part of a group of others. The conclusion is evident: in late medieval international law, theory continues to follow practice and theoretical concepts did not yet necessarily shape practical politics.

Before the Peace of Westphalia, there were hardly any changes in the relationship between theory and practice of international law. To conclude what has been pointed out in the history of international law in the Middle Ages and in the early modern period, it is not yet certain whether there were any fundamental changes before 1648. Studies of the history of foreign relations marginalize the date of the French invasion

---

[22] M Kintzinger 'Inszenierungen der Kaiserherrschaft bei Karl V: Überlegungen zum Verhältnis von imperialer Tradition und universalen Herausforderungen' (2011) 38 Francia 207–27.

[23] JM Moeglin *Kaisertum und allerchristlichster König, 1214–1500* (Wissenschaftliche Buchgesellschaft Darmstadt 2010); R Große *Vom Frankenreich zu den Ursprüngen der Nationalstaaten, 800–1214* (Wissenschaftliche Buchgesellschaft Darmstadt 2005).

[24] R Babel *Deutschland und Frankreich im Zeichen der habsburgischen Universalmonarchie, 1500–1648* (Wissenschaftliche Buchgesellschaft Darmstadt 2005). L Schorn-Schütte *Konfessionskriege und europäische Expansion: Europa 1500–1648* (CH Beck München 2010); J Hélie *Les relations internationales dans l'Europe Moderne: Conflits et équilibres européens, 1453–1789* (Armand Colin Paris 2008).

into Northern Italy in 1494 which for a long time had been taken as the beginning of a new era. The establishment of formal embassies in northern Italy in the last decades of the 15th century is no longer seen as a substantial change within the history of diplomacy.

The beginning of the Reformation in the 16th century and its long-lasting political consequences—as well as the era of confessional conflicts between religious parties in the so-called time of confessionalism, unknown to the Middle Ages—should not be underestimated here. Those conflicts established a new quality of difference and exclusion and they did so both within the kingdoms as well as in international contacts and communication and therefore led to the beginning of one of the great struggles of the 17th century.

As stated above, the unexpected resignation of Emperor Charles V in 1556 might also be discussed here, in the context of the history of colonization, expansion, the discovery of the New World, and of diverse international conflicts over how to make a profit from those discoveries. The theory of defining and explaining international law had finally been established by Spanish late scholasticism in the first half of the 16th century. Since then, things seem to have progressed until the European world was affected by the outbreak of the Thirty Years' War in 1618. From then on, the search for theoretically constructing as well as practically dealing with the diplomatic and political instruments of an elaborated international law was intensified and finally led to the founding of the classic modern period of international law with the ideas of Hugo Grotius and others and with the fundamental and substantially new norms of the Treaty of Muenster/Osnabruck in 1648.

Yet it must be concluded that the medieval theory and practice of international law is of fundamental interest for the research and the understanding of later and even of modern and current international law, not as just the origin of later developments or as a kind of 'forerunner', but as a long period of the unique construction and progression of a well-proven and functional international law under contemporary conditions.

5. Conclusion

International law as such did not exist in medieval European history as a codified legal norm as it did from 1648 onwards. But of course, cooperation and conflicts between different kings and princes were frequent and they regularly caused challenges for those acting together. How to behave during the contact, how to organize the communication, how to come to agreements, how to finish fighting and to make peace and, not the least, how to make sure that agreements would last for some time? The search for norms in international political and diplomatic communication was a major political objective throughout the whole Middle Ages, from the Carolingian period up to the 15th century. At all times, practical challenges came first and theories of international norms always followed practice. The instruments of a symbolic culture at the courts were useful to organize international diplomacy, as for instance during meetings between princes or at ceremonies of reception. The ancient tradition of a Roman ius gentium was not continued. Medieval theory had to discover international law again. It did so by describing a natural law given by God or nature to every human being. Scholastic texts from the 13th century onwards testify to the development of an international law based on natural law. At the same time debates ensued about the superiority of kings over each other and therefore about the definition of sovereignty. To be a sovereign prince then meant not to accept any superiors. Finally, sovereign princes could not accept the emperor's nor the pope's nor anyone else's superiority, but only an idea of an a priori and superior universal norm. This idea had first been described by Italian legal authors in the late 14th century, and in the following on the occasion of an international conflict in Eastern Europe at the beginning of the 15th century. It was finally developed into a first doctrine of international law by authors of Spanish late scholasticism in order to react to the discovery of the New World.

RECOMMENDEND READING

Gaurier, Domenique *Histoire du droit international: Auteurs, doctrines et développement de l'Antiquité à l'aube de la période contemporaine* (Presses Universitaires de Rennes Rennes 2005).

Heneccius, Johann G *Grundlagen des Natur- und Völkerrechts* (Peter Mortzfeld trans, Christoph Bergfeld ed) (Insel Frankfurt am Main 1994).

Jucker, Michael, Martin Kintzinger, Rainer Schwinges, et al (eds) *Rechtsformen internationaler Politik: Theorie, Norm und Praxis vom 12. bis 18. Jahrhundert* (Duncker & Humblot Berlin 2011).

Kaser, Max *Ius gentium* (Böhlau Köln 1993).

Laghmani, Slim *Histoire du droit des gens du* jus gentium *impérial au* jus publicum europaeum (Pedone Paris 2003).

Lappenküper, Ulrich and Reiner Marcowitz (eds) *Macht und Recht: Völkerrecht in den internationalen Beziehungen* (Ferdinand Schöningh Paderborn 2010).

Steiger, Heinhard *Die Ordnung der Welt. Eine Völkerrechtsgeschichte des karolingischen Zeitalters (741 bis 840)* (Böhlau Köln 2010).

CHAPTER 26

FROM THE PEACE OF WESTPHALIA TO THE CONGRESS OF VIENNA

HEINZ DUCHHARDT[*]

1. INTRODUCTION

THERE are many ways one can reconstruct the history of international law over an extended period of time: one can, for example, follow the 'leading' scholars in the field and set out their outlines in a chronological manner and/or compare and contrast them in a more differentiated way. A drawback of this line of investigation is that certain 'lesser' scholars may be overlooked and that not enough weight would be given to the interdependency between theory and practice. An alternative approach could be to focus on what—allegedly—has been described as turning points in the history of international law, in this case the great peace congresses held between the Peace of Münster (1648)—as complemented by the Treaties of Münster and

* Translation by Uta Protz.

Osnabrück—and the Congress of Vienna (1814–15).[1] The disadvantage here is that the theory of international law would not be given adequate attention. An alternative approach was taken by Wilhelm Grewe in *Epochen der Völkerrechtsgeschichte*, one of the standard works on the history of international law, which departs from the respective States and then, in a broadly chronological manner, discusses the issues that led them into conflict and required regulation.[2] I have decided to follow a similar approach here and to address the issues central to inter-state relations and their legal foundation by way of a thematic approach; it is, at least to my mind, the method that best links politics with theory.

2. INTER-STATE RELATIONS AS THE BASIS OF INTERNATIONAL LAW

Let me introduce my discussion—as Grewe did—with some brief reflections on the impact inter-state relations had on international law.[3] The Peace of Westphalia (1648), as little as it could achieve a European security system as once called for by Richelieu (1585–1642) or a settlement of all inter-state disputes apparent at the time, at least succeeded in rebalancing the Central European system of power: it transferred the never particularly robust Holy Roman Empire into a new order, a constellation which accorded France and Sweden, the two guarantors of the Peace of Westphalia, a considerable degree of influence and curtailed the position of the Holy Roman Emperor in important respects. The declaration of war and the conclusion of peace, for example, were henceforth subject to the approval of the *Reichstag*. Further, the German princes were each granted the right to form alliances (*ius forderis*); it was a privilege they had long claimed for themselves and had to an extent already come to

---

[1] The Peace of Münster: Treaty of Peace between Spain and the Netherlands (signed 30 January 1648) (1648) 1 CTS 1. The Treaties of Münster: Treaty of Peace between the Holy Roman Empire and France (signed 24 October 1648) (1648) 1 CTS 271; and Osnabrück: Treaty of Peace between the Holy Roman Empire and Sweden (signed 24 October 1648) (1648) 1 CTS 198. Together, these treaties form the Peace of Westphalia.

[2] WG Grewe *Epochen der Völkerrechtsgeschichte* (Nomos Baden-Baden 1984).

[3] A still reliable source is D McKay and HM Scott *The Rise of the Great Powers 1648–1815* (Longman London 1983); also worth consulting is HM Scott *The Birth of a Great Power System 1740–1815* (Pearson Longman Harlow 2006); for a major contribution to the study of the history of international relations see H Duchhardt and F Knipping (eds) *Handbuch der Geschichte der Internationalen Beziehungen* (Schöningh Paderborn 2007) vol 2 covers the period up until the Peace of Westphalia; vol 4 (1997) the 18th century from the Great Northern War; and vol 5 (2004) the period 1785–1830; vol 3—covering the period from the Peace of Westphalia to the Great Northern War—is forthcoming.

experience. In short, the Peace of Westphalia remained until the end of the *ancien régime* the most important legal text governing inter-state relations in Central Europe, the undisputed point of reference, minor variations aside, for all peace treaties concluded until the 1790s. Whether one can describe the Peace of Westphalia, as many British and American social scientists like to do, as the point of departure of a 'Westphalian system', however, remains—also in light of what will follow—open to debate. What is certain is that the historian struggles to hold back his reservations, even when he is aware that several publication projects—such as the Consolidated Treaty Series and the multi-volume *Recueil des instructions données aux ambassadeurs de France*— took the Peace of Westphalia as their starting point.[4]

The Peace of Westphalia certainly did not herald a new golden age of peace, especially as it could neither end the Franco-Spanish War (1635–59)—which was only accomplished by way of the Treaty of the Pyrenees in 1659[5]—nor achieve a general peace assured by a European security system.[6] This was above all due to the fact that no other than the two guarantors of the Peace of Westphalia soon embarked on a campaign of outright aggression: Sweden, determined to maintain an inflated military apparatus yet unable to raise sufficient tax revenue at home, to generate additional income abroad, and France, driven by a new ruler, Louis XIV (1638–1715), to assert territorial claims and to take the lead in Europe. Indeed, it is not without reason that some texts—such as the one by Grewe—refer to the period after the Peace of Westphalia as the 'French Age', characterized by French military aggression against all of France's immediate neighbours (apart from England, which was protected by the Channel), the introduction of a Europe-wide network of diplomatic representations, and the implementation of a propagandistic court ritual at Versailles which other States soon sought to emulate.[7] But there was another side to the coin: while Versailles served as a 'prototype', it also consolidated resistance among Europe's Catholic and Protestant powers. Their collective opposition, though, could not stop Louis XIV from installing the Bourbon dynasty in Habsburg Spain at the end of the War of the Spanish Succession (1701–14). Moreover, the second guarantor of the Peace of

---

[4] H Duchhardt '"Westphalian System". Zur Problematik einer Denkfigur' (1999) 269 Historische Zeitschrift 305–15. See also B Fassbender 'Westphalia, Peace of (1648)' in R Wolfrum (ed) *The Max Planck Encyclopedia of Public International Law* (Oxford University Press Oxford 2012) at <http://www.mpepil.com>.

[5] Treaty between France and Spain (signed 7 November 1659) (1659) 5 CTS 325 ('Treaty of the Pyrenees').

[6] On the Treaty of the Pyrenees see the following two conference proceedings: H Duchhardt (ed) *Der Pyrenäenfriede 1659. Vorgeschichte, Widerhall, Rezeptionsgeschichte* (Vandenhoeck & Ruprecht Göttingen 2010) and M Gantelet et al (eds) *La paix des Pyrénées et son impact en Lorraine et au Luxembourg/Der Pyrenäenfriede und seine Auswirkungen auf Lothringen und Luxemburg* (Presse Universitaire du Luxembourg Luxembourg 2010).

[7] There exists an abundant literature on Louis XIV and his court at Versailles. For a recent addition see C Quaeitzsch '*Une société de plaisirs*'. *Festkultur und Bühnenbilder am Hofe Ludwigs XIV. und ihr Publikum* (Deutscher Kunstverlag Munich 2010).

Westphalia, Sweden, though less consistent in its actions than France, exposed itself as a force which was determined to change the balance of power in Europe. If the First Northern War (1655–60) was testimony to this, then the Great Northern War (1700–21), which was to engage all States bordering the Baltic Sea and which was to result in the decline of Sweden and the rise of Russia, was to later affirm this.

The ambitions of the Ottoman Empire placed additional pressure on the European balance of power, as did the Anglo-Dutch Wars, which were fought throughout the 17th and 18th centuries. Having first flexed their muscles in the 1660s, the Ottoman forces stepped up their offensive in the 1680s, only to meet substantial European resistance, such as before Vienna in 1683. The Holy League (1684) and the Treaty of Karlowitz (1699)[8] must be mentioned as turning points here; they showed the Sublime Porte that expansion in the shadow of Central European conflicts had become increasingly difficult and that the Ottoman Empire better adhered to the rules that were to form the basis of international law. Furthermore, while Europe faced conflict in the East, it also saw the rise of conflicts in the West, naval disputes which were driven by the quest to have command of the sea and to dominate the profitable maritime trade. The Anglo-Dutch Wars, however, were also about the balance of power in Europe and were to constitute a particular challenge for scholars of international law.

The Treaties of Utrecht/Rastatt/Baden (1713–14)[9] and Nystadt (1721)[10] finally brought peace to Europe.[11] While the United Kingdom arguably benefited most from these treaties, the European continent, drained by years of conflict, demanded just one thing at this time: peace to recuperate. It is against this backdrop that the 1720s can be described as a *pax britannica*, a period when London controlled and led the other powers, but also as a phase in which the European powers attempted for the first time—by way of congresses in Cambrai (1722) and Soissons (1728–29)—to prevent future conflicts. The efforts of the French cardinal-minister Fleury (1653–1743) yielded only limited success, though, as Bourbon-ruled Spain sought to revise the outcomes of the War of the Spanish Succession. Like the Ottoman Empire, Spain thus was to be a constant challenge to the post-war order. France, in turn, having recovered from the disaster of Louis XIV's last war, took the election of a Polish king as an opportunity to again assert territorial ambitions. That all happened against the background of the great political theories of the day, the idea to establish a balance of

---

[8] Treaty of Peace between the Ottoman Empire and the Holy League (signed 26 January 1699) (1699) 22 CTS 219 ('Treaty of Karlowitz').

[9] Treaty of Peace and Friendship Between France and Great Britain (signed 11 April 1713, entered into force 18 April 1713) (1713) 27 CTS 477 ('Treaty of Utrecht'); Treaty of Peace Between the Emperor and Spain, and France (signed 7 March 1714) (1714) 29 CTS 1 ('Treaty of Rastatt'); Treaty of Peace between the Emperor and Spain and France (signed 7 September 1714) (1714) 29 CTS 141 ('Treaty of Baden').

[10] Treaty of Peace between Russia and Sweden (signed 30 August 1721) (1721) 31 CTS 339 ('Treaty of Nystadt').

[11] As to the Treaty of Utrecht, see L Bély's definitive study *Espions et ambassadeurs au temps de Louis XIV* (Fayard Paris 1990). There, unfortunately, exist no comparable studies for the treaties of Rastatt and Baden.

power, which since the Treaty of Utrecht (1713) had almost become a principle of international law. It subsequently took until the extinction of the male Austrian line of the Habsburg dynasty (1740) for the European powers to enter into conflict again, disputes that were driven by German ambition, above all Prussia's quest to secure part of this heritage and by Bourbon and British competition over overseas interests. The latter led, for the first time, to a major European conflict being fought outside Europe. Before long the new was to become the norm: conflicts involving European powers in Europe were to have a regular impact on territories outside Europe and define colonial politics; vice versa, conflicts involving European powers outside Europe were to be regularly exploited by third powers to advance interests in Europe—the prime example here is the American War of Independence where the two Bourbon States intervened, directly and indirectly, to weaken Britain's position in Europe.

While the Treaty of Aix-la-Chapelle (1748)[12] was more of a milestone than a turning point, the Seven Years' War (1756–63) shaped the European balance of power up until the French Revolution (1789–99). It firmly established Prussia and Russia as major European powers, confirmed Britain's command of the sea and predominance as a colonial power, and validated the demise of France, which some historians have interpreted as the origin of the French Revolution. The Seven Years' War thus laid the foundation for a new European order: an order which turned the age-old antagonism between Vienna and Versailles into a matter of the past (*renversement des alliances*) and the alliance of Austria and France into a matter of the present. At the same time, it also exposed first rifts in the alliance between Berlin and St Petersburg, which effectively were to leave Prussia without an alliance partner upon the death of Frederick the Great (1712–86). Prussia subsequently attempted to compensate for this by aligning itself with Germany's minor princely states, but the *Fürstenbund*, which it had established in 1785, was to already cease existence again in 1790. Despite their commitment to different alliances, however, the European powers did not fail—usually under the pretext of maintaining an equitable balance of power—to also act together; the most extreme example of this is the first partition of Poland in 1772, when Russia, Prussia, and Austria all secured important long-term interests for themselves. Curiously it is an act, later much condemned by scholars of international law, that the press reacted to with little criticism at the time.[13]

The outbreak of the revolution in France fundamentally changed the European balance of power. It not only saw other States exploit this situation elsewhere, as reflected in the subsequent partitions of Poland in 1793 and 1795, but also saw them misjudge the strength of the revolutionary movement, which swiftly was to find an echo outside France. In addition, they underestimated the emergence of a new type of warfare and soon had to acknowledge that their disciplined armies all but lacked the strength to successfully withstand the vigour of peoples' armies. Still, this revolutionary 'spook'

---

[12] Treaty of Aix-la-Chapelle (signed 18 October 1748) (1748) 38 CTS 297 ('Treaty of Aix-la-Chapelle').
[13] See T Cegielski *Das Alte Reich und die Erste Teilung Polens 1768–74* (Steiner Stuttgart 1988).

would probably have passed had there not been this charismatic army general from Corsica, Napoleon Bonaparte (1769–1821), who catapulted himself to the head of the French State, who over the next fifteen years conquered—Britain and Russia excluded—almost every State in Europe, and who ultimately made Paris the centre of contemporary politics. Once Napoleon had crowned himself emperor in 1804, he organized and staged what previous generations had called a 'universal monarchy': a superpower, which controlled an entire continent in terms of politics and culture. It was inevitable that the other powers would eventually join forces to set an end to this dream, which in all its principles opposed the notion that unity rested in diversity. The War of the Sixth Coalition (1813–14) marked the end of Napoleon's rule and while the Congress of Vienna did not restore the pre-revolutionary order, it drew important consequences out of the largely unjust politics pursued by the major powers during the *ancien régime*: it introduced—and this constituted a clear paradigm shift[14]—a framework for concord, which had its problems, but brought peace to Europe for a couple of decades.

3. Impetus and Theme in International Law: War

3.1. The Right to Conduct War

The development of modern international law, understood as a law that governs the relationship between sovereign States, has long been in the making and would not have been possible without the conflicts of the 16th and 17th centuries. The overseas wars and the French Wars of Religion (1562–98), in which the Spanish crown—if one allows for the use of this term for the Iberian composite monarchy at this time already—was involved, created an additional need for regulation, which extended beyond the code of ethics stipulated by the Holy Scripture and the laws codified in Late Antiquity. The focus of early international law reflected this, which during the age of the Baroque and Enlightenment, following the 'Spanish' exponents of second scholasticism and Hugo Grotius[15] (1583–1645), was primarily concerned with the *ius ad bellum*

---

[14] This is the main argument of PW Schroeder in *The Transformation of European Politics, 1763–1848* (Clarendon Press Oxford 1994); the book sparked intensive international debate: see eg P Krüger and PW Schroeder (eds) *'The Transformation of European Politics, 1763–1848': Episode or Model in Modern History?* (Lit Verlag Münster 2002).

[15] H Grotius *De iure belli ac pacis libri tres* (Paris 1625), as readily accessible in JB Scott (ed) *Classics of International Law* (Clarendon Press Oxford 1925) vol 3; see also the contribution by P Haggenmacher 'Hugo Grotius (1583–1645)' in this volume.

and *ius in bello*. The latter took on a particular urgency in the aftermath of the Thirty Years' War (1618–48), which had destroyed large parts of Europe. As to the *ius ad bellum*, which governed which legal entities were entitled to conduct war, this had in discussions conducted parallel to the Dutch War of Independence (1568–1648) been limited to holders of 'sovereignty', as coined by the French jurist and political philosopher Jean Bodin (1529–96); non-sovereign rulers and political units with only limited sovereignty had thus been denied the right to conduct war. The definition changed the status of the territorial estates, such as the Pomeranian *Landstände*, which had still participated in the conferences, leading to the Peace of Westphalia.[16] The same applied to the many princes and free cities, which received their fiefdoms from the Holy Roman Emperor and were no longer considered sovereign rulers. What had seemingly been a clear-cut division was complicated again by the Peace of Westphalia: it gave the German princes the so-called '*Bündnisrecht*', in other words the right to conduct their own foreign affairs, which some jurists immediately interpreted as 'sovereignty'. The issue being a most complex one, it was to take until the large congresses after the Peace of Westphalia to settle whether the German princes should be regarded sovereign rulers or not. Linked to this query was the question as to whether they should be entitled to receive and send ambassadors (*ius legationis*); the matter was so contentious that it sparked a fierce pamphlet war at the Congress of Nijmegen (1678–79).[17] It resulted in the German princes being permanently denied the right to participate in multilateral peace congresses as independent parties. The same applied to the associations representing the imperial circles (*Reichskreise*), established since the 1650s, which were also refused to participate as fully accredited political units. Similarly, the Hanseatic League, which represented the interests of an international array of trading cities and which had long acted as a 'legal person' on the international stage, was now—because no sovereign State and due to its partial dissolution—by and large excluded from inter-state affairs, a fact, however, which did not prevent it from being included in international agreements well into the 18th century.[18] As to the members of the Imperial Diet, their status was eventually reviewed: were they able to demonstrate that they were independent political units, which they generally did by wearing a royal crown not linked to the imperial realm; they were, after all, allowed to participate in multilateral peace congresses.

---

[16] H Langer 'Die pommerschen Landstände und der westfälische Friedenskongreß' in H Duchhardt (ed) *Der Westfälische Friede. Diplomatie—politische Zäsur—kulturelles Umfeld—Rezeptionsgeschichte* (Oldenbourg Munich 1998) 485–99.

[17] H Bots (ed) *The Peace of Nijmegen 1676–1678/79/La paix de Nimègue 1676–1678/79* (Holland Universiteits Pers Amsterdam 1980) (proceedings of the conference marking the tricentennial anniversary of the Treaties of Nijmegen, Nijmegen, 14–16 September 1978).

[18] H Duchhardt 'Die Hanse und das europäische Mächtesystem des frühen 17. Jahrhunderts' in A Grassmann (ed) *Niedergang oder Übergang? Zur Spätzeit der Hanse im 17. Jahrhundert* (Böhlau Cologne 1998) 11–24.

3.2. War in Europe—War Overseas?

The only exceptions to its inter-state character international law allowed for after the Peace of Westphalia were agreements between States and trading companies, which in some regions of the world enjoyed a kind of veiled sovereignty and to which the English crown even extended the *ius belli ac pacis* (the right to conduct war and conclude peace) and *ius legationis* (the right to receive and send ambassadors). It consequently was not uncommon for the heads of some of the trading posts to put on an extraordinary display of splendour which made them look little less than the monarchs they represented. This indicated just how powerful the British East India Company and the Dutch East/West India Companies were in international politics, whose main function it was, according to Grewe, to prevent the transfer of the European notion of the State to territories outside Europe.[19] Indeed, there were cases where some of the European trading companies were at war with each other, but where their conflict did not impinge on peace in Europe. This observation reflects that from the end of the 18th century there was a degree of regularity for European conflicts to continue outside Europe. It was by no means a given, though, as the hemisphere beyond the Pillars of Hercules had long been regarded as an area subject to its own laws, a sphere 'beyond the line' to which the 'strict norms of international law as determined by the political circumstances of Europe' did not apply.[20] If one considers, however, that the main opponents in Europe—excluding the Habsburg emperor, who only developed an interest in colonies and world trade after the transition of the Spanish Netherlands to his realm in 1713—were also colonial powers, it follows that decisions in Europe had to take interests beyond Europe—such as the fight over lucrative resources in Africa, the Americas, and Asia—into account. There were even conflicts in Europe, such as the wars of 1739 and 1755, which took their departure from conflicts in the colonies or at sea. It resulted in the trading companies demanding to have their voices heard at congresses, moreover the need for separate agreements to be drawn up that reflected the complex circumstances faced overseas, a world only understood by those who had experienced it.

3.3. Types of War

The right to conduct war was one side of the coin. The other was—and still is—the enduring question concerning the *iusta causa* of war, the question as to when and under

---

[19] *Epochen* (n 2) 351; further toWG Grewe and C Schmitt *Der Nomos der Erde im Völkerrecht des Jus Publicum Europaeum* (Greven Cologne 1950), see also J Fisch *Die europäische Expansion und das Völkerrecht. Die Auseinandersetzungen um den Status der überseeischen Gebiete vom 15. Jahrhundert bis zur Gegenwart* (Steiner Stuttgart 1984).

[20] *Epochen* (n 2) 346.

which circumstances a war is legal under international law. It was Grotius, referring back to scholars from the late scholastic period, who set the standard here: according to him, just causes to conduct war included the defence of a territory, its people, and its material objects against an aggressor, the recovery of a captured territory, its people and its material objects, and retribution. By contrast, he defined military action to achieve territorial enlargement, political independence, or rule over others as unjust causes to conduct war.

While Grotius' interpretation found no explicit reflection in the politics of his time, it soon was to become the standard against which wars were to be judged: the outrage over the wars of Louis XIV (War of Devolution, 1667–68; Dutch War, 1672–78) and Frederick the Great (First Silesian War, 1740–42), which merely served to make territorial gains, can be traced back to the influence of Grotius, as can, on the other hand, the arguments put forward by the two rulers (succession to the duchy of Brabant, claims by the House of Hohenzollern to principalities in Silesia) to make their actions look legal.

Grotius made no allowance for preventive war, which in 1756—to mention the most striking example—Frederick the Great claimed to make use of when he attacked Saxony and started the Seven Years' War. This type of war, which by definition was a construct, enabled rulers to go to war even when there existed—according to Grotius—no just reason for doing so. Well into the 20th century it was a much used excuse to legitimize military action.

Preventive war was a kind of intervention, the interference, for whatever reason, of one State in the affairs of another. Whereas such early scholars of international law as Christian Wolff (1679–1754)[21] and Emer de Vattel (1714–67)[22] considered religious motives as an unjust reason for intervention, Vattel—despite his respect for freedom and the right to self-rule—considered liberation from a despotic ruler as a possible just reason for intervention. It was a view that found an echo among revolutionaries, just as the question of intervention—now involving the great powers—was to remain on the agenda until well after the French Revolution.

The Franco-Spanish War having still been declared in the traditional manner in 1635 (with heralds reading out the declaration of war in ceremonies held along the enemy's border), it was by now more common for wars to be declared by legal notice. Reduced to an administrative act, it also entailed that diplomatic representatives were recalled. At the same time, it was not unknown for wars to be conducted without war having been declared; in the 18th century this increasingly took the form of reprisals, followed by a declaration of war at a much later date. In

---

[21]   CH Wolff *Ius gentium methodo scientifica pertractatum* (Magdeburg 1749), as readily accessible in JB Scott (ed) *Classics of International Law* (Clarendon Press Oxford 1934) vol 13; and M Thomann et al (eds) *Christian Wolff: Gesammelte Werke* (Olms Hildesheim 1972) vol 25; see also the contribution by K Haakonssen 'Christian Wolff (1679–1754)' in this volume.

[22]   E de Vattel *Le droit des gens, ou principes de la loi naturelle* (1758), as readily accessible in JB Scott (ed) *Classics of International Law* (Carnegie Institution Washington 1916) vol 5; see also the contribution by E Jouannet 'Emer de Vattel (1714–1767)' in this volume.

certain circumstances, though, reprisals themselves were regarded as declarations of war.[23]

If the ritual surrounding war receded at this time, it still remained an important aspect of inter-state relations. This was especially so when States looked for confrontation. The most telling example here is Britain's insistence on the flag salute, whereby non-British ships had to salute British ships on the *oceanus britannicus*. The refusal of the Dutch navy to do so led to no less than three wars; indeed, in the declaration of war 1659, the British stated the refusal of the Dutch to salute as the main reason to go to war. What titles and orders of precedence are in diplomacy, the flag salute is at sea.

3.4. Neutrality

An area of great interest to scholars of international law has traditionally been that group of States *qui in bello medii sunt*, which do not conduct war. Why Grotius avoided using the Latin version of the term 'neutrality', although well-known during his lifetime, remains unknown; one reason might be that he strove to write in classical Latin prose, to which the term *neutralitas* was unknown, of course. As in all of his work, he distinguished between just and unjust wars, whereby he left it to each 'neutral' State to determine whether it considered a war to be based on a just or an unjust cause. If a State was seen to conduct war based on an *iniusta causa*, it was to be denied all support; if, by contrast, it was regarded as conducting based on a *iusta causa*, it was to be given the unhindered right to do so. As to less clear-cut cases, Grotius advised 'neutral' States to limit their exposure and risk, to conclude agreements with each of the belligerents, setting out the details of their particular relationship.

Already contemplated by Machiavelli (1469–1527), the subject of the role of neutral States during wartime was nothing new. Bodin had reflected on it with a positive undertone and Johannn Wilhelm Neumayr von Ramssla[24] (1570–1644) had written a dissertation on it five years before Grotius' *De jure belli ac pacis libri tres* was published in 1625. Judging from the rich body of surviving texts, neutrality governed by legal agreement shaped inter-state relations until the French Revolution, whereby it remains open whether, and if so to what extent, this was due to the influence of Grotius. In the post-Westphalian era, however, the question of whether a war was based on a just or an unjust cause became redundant to neutral States and was no longer referred to in the agreements they concluded with belligerents; rather, neutral States

---

[23] *Epochen* (n 2) 432.

[24] JW Newmayr von Ramsla *Von der Neutralitet und Assistentz oder Unpartheyligkeit und Partheyligkeit in Kriegszeiten* (Erfurt 1620).

came to take no position and to engage with belligerents in an equal and impartial manner. If one considers that it was the interest of States, as opposed to moral and religious interests, that determined the post-Westphalian order, this development—as already discussed by Cornelis van Bynkershoek (1673–1743),[25] Emer de Vattel, and Martin Hübner (1723–95),[26] who respectively examined the right of belligerents to cross the territory of neutral States—was both logical and comprehensible. It also was the precondition for institutional neutrality to become conceivable, and for 'armed neutrality' to emerge, as was the case in 1780 when a group of States formed a 'neutral alliance to defend the rights of neutral States by armed force'.[27] Only at the time of the French Revolution, when *confessions*—in this case avowal to a certain type of State—became important again, did the term 'neutrality' find application in yet another context.

3.5. The Laws of War

Whether Grotius can also be regarded as the authority who defined the *ius in bello*, the laws of war, for the modern period shall at least for the present remain an open question here. Judging from the preliminary discourse to *De jure belli ac pacis libri tres*, in which Grotius elaborated on the disastrous decline in the conduct of war, the appalling disrespect of morals and laws during the French Wars of Religion, as already discussed by Balthasar Ayala (1548–84)[28] in 1582, one would expect him to argue for a humanization of war. Indeed, Grotius writes of a 'degenerate conduct of war' that would even cause barbarians to be ashamed. What derives from this is a twofold approach to the resolution of conflict: on the one hand, the preference to deter rulers from conducting war, especially when based on a futile reason, and to settle differences by way of negotiation, a compromise, a third-party verdict, a draw, or even a duel between the rulers in question; on the other hand, in the case where all preventive measures fail, the promotion of a shared understanding that there exists a set of laws that applies during war. Its most important objective was to moderate and humanize the conduct of war and to limit its expansion in time and space. It did not explicitly assure the safety of civilians, though, nor did it explicitly prohibit the destruction of enemy property and religious sites. The proposed legal system

---

[25] C van Bijnkershoek *Quaestionum iuris publici libri duo* (1737), as readily accessible in JB Scott (ed) *Classics of International Law* (Clarendon Press Oxford 1930) vol 1; see also the contribution by K Akashi 'Cornelius van Bynkershoek (1673–1743)' in this volume.

[26] M Hübner *De la saisie des bâtiments neutres ou droit qu'ont les belligérantes d'arrêter les navires des peuples amis* (The Hague 1759).

[27] *Epochen* (n 2) 450.

[28] B Ayala *De iure et officiis bellicis et disciplina militari libri tres* (1582), as readily accessible in JB Scott (ed) *Classics of International Law* (Carnegie Institution of Washington Washington 1912) vol 2.

therefore corresponded only partially with what Grotius had considered elsewhere as acceptable with regard to war.

Set out on no more than one page, a closer look at Grotius' *opus magnum* reveals that he revoked his arguments for such a legal system just a few pages later, citing existing laws, Christian charity, and the need for belligerents to act with moderation. One can criticize Grotius for his lack of coherence, or praise him for his willingness to address the tension between the *ius gentium naturale* and the *ius gentium voluntarium*. Whatever view one takes, post-Grotian thinking on the laws of war and the protection of civilians, in particular, has since moved a long way. Frederick the Great was to later boast that his wars were not even noticed by the civilian population. The development of new types of war, such as the 'cabinet war', which aimed to outmanoeuvre rather than to defeat the enemy, reflected this new thinking on the protection of civilians during wartime. It did not mean, however, as exemplified by the Seven Years' War, that large-scale battles disappeared altogether. Post-Grotian writing on the laws of war also expressed itself, *unisono*, against the killing of prisoners of war. Again, theory translated into practice and it did not take long for 'cartels' to be established to govern the exchange of prisoners of war; each rank being accorded an agreed price, the cartels attempted to achieve as even an exchange as possible.[29] Less common, by contrast, was the long-term detention of prisoners of war, especially of specialists like seamen, which the enemy was more likely to integrate into his own ranks than to leave idle. But it was also in another respect that the laws of war reached well beyond Grotius: they condemned the use of chemical and cluster weapons long before the Hague Conventions (first negotiated in 1899) translated this principle into law.

4. The Peace of Westphalia as a Turning Point in the History of International Law

Most historians and historians of international law assume that the Peace of Westphalia was of fundamental importance to the development of laws of peace.[30] There is little one can say against this, except that there have been important changes as to

---

[29] For examples see H Duchhardt *Krieg und Frieden im Zeitalter Ludwigs XIV* (Schwann Düsseldorf 1987) at 46–52.

[30] A wealth of important literature was published on the occasion of the 350th anniversary of the Peace of Westphalia in 1998; for a review see J Arndt 'Ein europäisches Jubiläum: 350 Jahre Westfälischer Friede' (2000) 1 Jahrbuch für Europäische Geschichte 133–58; 10 years later, in 2008, a conference was

how peace has been concluded and framed within international law.[31] If war has its rituals, the same applies—perhaps even more so—to peace.

The Peace of Westphalia—consisting of the Peace of Münster and the Treaties of Münster and Osnabrück—regulated who was entitled to attend a peace congress. Indeed, it had not been a given that princes of the Holy Roman Empire—as well as such lower ranks as the free imperial cities and imperial knights—were admitted to the 'congress'. At the same time there existed the expectation, which the admission of the princes and lower ranks turned into a rule, that each political unit involved in a military conflict—whether large or small, Protestant or Catholic, a monarchy or a republic, with a large army or a small one—should be entitled to represent its concerns. This rule was modified again at the Congress of Nijmegen, when the admission of the princes was revoked; they also were not consulted at smaller peace congresses (for example, Breda 1667) or when a settlement had already been reached ahead of a congress (for example, Utrecht 1713, Paris 1763, and Paris 1783). Still, the Peace of Westphalia established peace congresses as the principle forum for conflict resolution; they were to remain of central importance at least until the Congress of Vienna.

Further, the Congresses of Münster and Osnabrück also instituted the form of negotiation that was to characterize the practice of international law until the Congress of Vienna. If at the time of Charles V (1500–58) rulers had still met in person to negotiate peace, they no longer attended and represented themselves at peace congresses after 1648. Along with this development plenary sessions were replaced by more private meetings and ceremonial pomp by professional politics. Only the Congress of Vienna was to be an assembly of emperors, kings, and other statesmen again. Rather, rulers were represented by plenipotentiaries, in general three for each of the great powers, belonging to different strata of society, and holding different qualifications. These, in turn, adopted the titles, ceremonial, and other rights of the sovereigns they represented. It was an act that repeatedly resulted in dispute, over the form and language of written authorities, the use of titles, and the order of precedence. It no doubt was due to details like these that the congresses preceding the Congress of Vienna took as long as they did. At the same time, it was no mere vanity that was at stake here but, it should be emphasized, the very foundations of a State's power and rights.

The plenipotentiaries—to return to the main argument—never met in plenary sessions, but sought to advance their arguments and interests in meetings under four, sometimes more, eyes. Key to this process was the written documentation of everything that was said; it is for this reason that the peace congresses of the early modern

held in Osnabrück to take stock of this research; for the conference proceedings see I Schmidt-Voges et al (eds) *Pax perpetua. Neuere Forschungen zum Frieden in der Frühen Neuzeit* (Oldenbourg Munich 2010).

[31] See, also with reference to the next paragraph, H Duchhardt 'Peace Treaties from Westphalia to the Revolutionary Era' in R Lesaffer (ed) *Peace Treaties and International Law in European History: From the Late Middle Ages to World War One* (CUP Cambridge 2004) 45–58.

period produced such large quantities of paper. It remains one of the outstanding tasks for the historians to systematically compile and interpret—like the *Acta Pacis Westphalicae*, one of the largest editing projects of the last fifty years—the papers produced at the other peace congresses. However ambitious, such a project would set an end to no more than haphazard collections of papers—generally published privately shortly after the event they record—being available to the historian. Negotiations focused on the conversations each party had held and on the positions written assurances had been obtained on, all of which were exchanged; the form of negotiation only became easier at the Congress of Vienna, when specialized committees were established to address specific topics, each involving only those plenipotentiaries who had a proven interest in the topic under debate. Likewise, responses, replies and rejoinders were exchanged, whereby a so-called 'protest' was able to render a claim or counter-claim futile. It was a practice that emulated the procedure followed by High Courts in earlier centuries.

4.1. The Mediator

Mediators played a key role in the negotiations between belligerents as well as in the production and distribution of position papers and treaty texts. Their legal status changed substantially after the Peace of Westphalia. If the apostolic nuncio Fabio Chigi (1599–1667) and the Venetian diplomat Alvise Contarini (1597–1651) had still been widely accepted as mediators in Münster, who not only acted as couriers, but also contributed substantially to the peace negotiations (with the suggestions expressed by the representative of the Holy See being received with considerable scrutiny), the legal status of the mediator was to become a matter of intensive inter-state debate during the so-called 'Dutch phase' of the history of international law (with the exception of the Treaty of Karlowitz,[32] all of the decisive treaties negotiated between the 1660s and the War of the Spanish Succession were concluded in Dutch cities).[33] It resulted, as duly recorded in several documents at the time,[34] in a considerable curtailment of the authority of the mediator. Distrust in the ability of the mediator was also expressed in the academic writing of the time: only few scholars—next to the established Samuel von Pufendorf[35] (1632–94), the younger Johann Friedrich

---

[32] Treaty of Karlowitz (n 8).

[33] The term 'Dutch phase' is taken from CG Roelofsen 'Von Nimwegen (1676–79) bis Utrecht (1712–13): Die "niederländische Epoche" in der Geschichte des europäischen Kongreßwesens' in H Duchhardt (ed) *Städte und Friedenskongresse* (Böhlau Cologne 1999) 109–16.

[34] H Duchhardt *Studien zur Friedensvermittlung in der Frühen Neuzeit* (Steiner Cologne 1979) at ch 10, 89–117 ('Friedensvermittlung im Völkerrecht des 17. und 18. Jahrhunderts: Von Grotius zu Vattel').

[35] S von Pufendorf *De jure naturae et gentium libri VIII* (Lund 1672); see also the contribution by K Haakonssen 'Samuel Pufendorf (1632–1694)' in this volume.

Wilhelm Neumann,[36] Ernst Friedrich Meurer,[37] and Friedrich von Stephani[38]—were prepared to accord mediators competencies that extended beyond the role of notary and courier to that of arbitrator and decision-maker. In the second half of the 17th century, the role of the mediator thus became ever more precarious, last but not least because the great powers were simply too proud to place their destiny into the hands of a 'smaller power'; moreover, a mediator who did not even have the moral authority the representatives of the Holy See had once brought to the conference table.[39] The consequence of this development, as apparent in the political field and the literature on international law, was that one dispensed with mediators. Already the case when the War of the Spanish Succession was settled, it became the norm in the 18th century. A rare exception was the Treaty of Teschen (1779),[40] where France and Russia—respectively allied to the adversaries—acted as 'mediators'.

Whether the Peace of Westphalia fundamentally changed the way language was used in the negotiation of peace treaties is less certain. While there existed the general expectation that peace treaties would be formulated in Latin, as happened—with the exception of the separate peace between Spain and the Netherlands, which was set out in Spanish and Dutch—with the *instrumenta pacis* of 1648, there existed no 'binding' language of negotiation in Münster/Osnabrück as yet. The general assumption, however, that French replaced Latin after 1648 cannot be upheld; from the Treaties of Nijmegen (1678/79) to the Treaty of Ryswick (1697)[41] and the Treaties of Rastatt and Baden (1714)[42], there have time and again been peace treaties which have been written in Latin. Still, it is probably correct to observe that French became the prominent language in inter-state diplomacy after 1648.[43]

4.2. The Peace Treaty

The peace treaty, the result of verbal and written negotiations often lasting years, had to meet—whether formulated in Latin, French, Spanish, or even German—certain formal criteria. Ideally set out like a medieval charter, it generally contained an *invocatio*—an appeal to a supernatural agency as well as the names and titles of the

---

[36] JP Felwinger and JFW Neumann *De Mediatoris officio, eiusque requisitis* (Altdorf 1676).

[37] EF Meurer *Mediator* (Jena 1678).

[38] F von Stephani *De officio et jure mediatorum pacis* (Frankfurt (Oder) 1702).

[39] See eg *Studien zur Friedensvermittlung* (n 34) at ch 10, 23–88 ('Arbitration, Mediation oder bons offices? Die englische Friedensvermittlung in Nijmwegen 1676–1679').

[40] Treaty of Teschen (signed 13 May 1779) (1779) 47 CTS 153.

[41] Treaty of Peace Between France and The Netherlands (signed 20 September 1697) (1697) 21 CTS 347.

[42] Treaty of Rastatt (n 9); Treaty of Baden (n 9).

[43] G Braun 'Verhandlungs- und Vertragssprachen in der "niederländischen Epoche" des europäischen Kongresswesens (1678/79–1713/14)' (2011) 12 Jahrbuch für Europäische Geschichte 103–30.

signatory parties (and those of their plenipotentiaries), which right into the 18th century acted as legal persons rather than political units—and a kind of *arenga*—which graphically bemoaned the horrors of war, the loss of Christian blood, and sometimes also described in metaphorical language how the respective rulers simultaneously arrived at the decision to conclude peace (as in the Treaty of Utrecht between England and France).[44] The set phrase *respublica Christiana*, which had been used in both a supra- and inter-denominational manner, was in the decades after the Peace of Westphalia gradually replaced by other phrases, interestingly referring not so much to the balance of power, as emphasized in political pamphlets,[45] but to peace and security in Europe, which was to be restored.[46] Following the preamble, the conditions for peace were set out, which after the experiences of 1648 were to be formulated in as precise a manner as possible. They were succeeded by details about the ratification of the treaty, the sanctions to be applied in case of contravention of the treaty, the signatures of the diplomats, and the date and place where the treaty was signed.

Unlike in the medieval period and the first half of the early modern period, when the validity of peace treaties was limited to the lifetime of their signatories or a set period of time (usually five, nine, twelve, or one-hundred years), the peace treaties of the second half of the early modern period not only included no indications of liability nor details of compensation, but were also considered infinite.[47] Indeed, it was only in the case of the Ottoman Empire that peace treaties were still limited, but then they served short-term ceasefires rather than long-term peace. As to the guarantee of peace, the provision of hostages was, with the exception of the Treaty of Aix-la-Chapelle,[48] discarded after the Peace of Westphalia. Third States occasionally offered guarantees, but this was by no means the rule; rather, the signatory parties had come to believe that their own power, or that of their allies, was sufficient to guarantee peace. In reality it was only when there was a considerable imbalance in power that the weaker of the signatory parties contemplated asking a stronger ally for a guarantee. This occurred, for example, after the War of the Spanish Succession (1701–14) when guarantors supported Portugal in its efforts to conclude peace with the Bourbon states.

Peace treaties could also provide for commissions, generally composed of representatives from two powers (the Treaty of Aix-la-Chapelle provided for a French-British

---

[44] Treaty of Utrecht (n 9).

[45] H Duchhardt 'The Missing Balance' (2000) 2 Journal of the History of International Law 67–72.

[46] H Duchhardt 'Europa als Begründungs- und Legitimationsformel' in WEJ Weber and R Dauser (eds) *Faszinierende Frühneuzeit. Reich, Frieden, Kultur und Kommunikation, 1500–1800. Festschrift für Johannes Burkhardt zum 65. Geburtstag* (Akademie Verlag Berlin 2008) 51–60.

[47] Oblivion (*oblivio*) was considered the supreme law (*suprema lex*); see also J Fisch *Krieg und Frieden im Friedensvertrag: Eine universalgeschichtliche Studie über Grundlagen und Formelemente des Friedensschlusses* (Klett-Cotta Stuttgart 1979).

[48] Treaty of Aix-la-Chapelle (n 12).

commission), to implement what had been set out in the peace treaty (for example, new boundaries) or to negotiate whatever had been impossible to negotiate during the peace congress (for example, the establishment of a cartel to govern the exchange of prisoners of war).[49] As late as in the last decades of the 17th century, voices could be heard who wanted the Pope to act as an arbiter (or even super-arbiter).[50] While arbitration did not completely disappear from inter-state relations (England reverted to it on several occasions in the second half of the 17th century), it played a much less significant role than made out by the political press.

Following ratification, peace treaties had to formally and publicly be proclaimed by the signatory parties, the respective rulers or, as was the case in the Netherlands, the States-General. This could be elaborate affairs, such as in Münster in February 1649. The treaty text would then be lodged with *parlement* for approbation or—as was the case in England, Spain, and Portugal—be brought to the attention of the houses of representatives. Although not always explicitly mentioned in the treaty text, disarmament, reflected in the reduction of soldiers and the military budget, usually followed the conclusion of peace. In the case of England, for example, it was not only empty coffers, but also pressure from parliament which ensured that peace treaties were followed by disarmament.

4.3. The Ottoman Empire

A word should be added with regard to the relations between the Ottoman Empire[51] and the States of Western, Central, Southern, and Eastern Europe under international law. While relations between States belonging to the *christianitas* were based on the principle of *aequalitas*, and while their existence was even at times of disagreement, such as over ceremonial matters, not called into question, this was different in the case of Ottoman-European relations. The principle of *aequalitas* did not apply here and there existed no provisions under international law that allowed the Ottoman Empire and the European States to meet at eye level; rather, there simply existed the Ottoman Empire's claim that it was superior to its Christian partners, a notion that reflected in its unwillingness to conclude permanent peace treaties and to define its borders. Only after the conclusion of the Treaty of Karlowitz,[52] which set an end to the disastrous defeats suffered by the Ottoman forces, did the Sublime Porte—in what came to be known as the 'tulip period' in Ottoman

---

[49] A Reese 'Den Krieg verschieben—verkürzen—ersetzen? Die französisch-englischen gemeinsamen Kommissionen vor dem Siebenjährigen Krieg' in H Duchhardt (ed) *Zwischenstaatliche Friedenswahrung in Mittelalter und früher Neuzeit* (Böhlau Cologne 1991) 245–60.

[50] *Epochen* (n 2) 424.

[51] See the contribution by U Özsu 'Ottoman Empire' in this volume.

[52] Treaty of Karlowitz (n 8).

history—move closer to European notions of international law and open up to 'Western' influences.

4.4. Congresses to Guard Peace

Other than the congresses held during warfare to broker peace, a few congresses were also held, with war in sight, to guard peace. The two most notable examples are the Congresses of Cambrai and Soissons held in the 1720s, which respectively sought to establish a European security system based on the abdication of territorial claims. The negotiations were unsuccessful, though, and the congresses dissolved without lasting results. Still, they provided a model that diplomats in the age of Metternich (1773–1859) were to develop one-hundred years later.

5. DIPLOMACY

'Normal' inter-state relations in Europe as well as with the Ottoman Empire were established and maintained by 'permanent' diplomats, who carried a letter of credence from the sovereign they represented and resided at and reported from the court they had been sent to.[53] This reads a lot simpler than was the reality actually: this was due, on the one hand, to the fact that the term 'diplomat' stood for a great variety of officials holding different ranks and, on the other hand, to the fact that the terms 'diplomat' and 'spy' were often still aligned, making diplomats look more like adversaries than advocates of peace. As far as diplomats were of noble stock, as the vast majority of them were, they generally served abroad with the expectation to then pursue a gleaming career at their own court; it explains why so few of them had any interest in extending their stays abroad.[54] Many nobles even hesitated to accept posts abroad, or only did so *contre coeur*, as the pay did not suffice to maintain social obligations at home. To be a diplomat was for many a financial disaster which weighed heavily on their private assets.

As to the diplomatic ranks used at the time, the diplomatic manuals compiled by Abraham de Wiquefort (*c.* 1598–1682) and François de Callières (1645–1717) provide

---

[53] MS Anderson *The Rise of Modern Diplomacy 1450–1919* (Longman London 1993).
[54] See A Pečar *Die Ökonomie der Ehre. Höfischer Adel am Kaiserhof Karls VI.* (Wissenschaftliche Buchgesellschaft Darmstadt 2003) on this tension.

valuable information.[55] They belonged, like Jean Rousset de Missy's (1686–1762) *Mémoires sur le rang et la préséance entre les souverains de l'Europe* (Amsterdam 1746), to the 'set reading' of a diplomat. At the top of the diplomatic hierarchy stood the *ambassadeur*, a high-ranking official which only a major power could dispatch. Medium-sized and smaller States could only send an *envoyé* or even *resident*, who no longer had to be of noble stock. Indeed, in the case of the English diplomatic service, nobles were the exception rather than the rule. Underlying diplomatic relations was the understanding that corresponding posts would for the most part be filled at the same level, that the French ambassador in Vienna enjoyed the same powers and privileges as the imperial ambassador in Versailles. If a State decided to dispatch a lower-ranking diplomat—such as a *resident* rather than an *envoyé*—it usually was an indication that relations had deteriorated.

Further, the practice continued to dispatch 'temporary' diplomats, so-called special envoys, abroad. These were important to attend special functions, but also to intervene when an ally looked to change sides. At the time of church elections, the court of the Holy Roman Emperor also made use of special envoys to ensure that no Francophile candidate would be elected and that the *neo-electus* would receive Imperial assurances right after his election.[56] The *Repertorium der diplomatischen Vertreter aller Länder seit dem Westfälischen Frieden*, a publication project started in the 1930s, provides an insight into the manifold reasons special envoys have been dispatched for in the past.[57]

Diplomats had to report back regularly—in either open or enciphered format—about developments and people in the State to which they had been dispatched. Some diplomats also maintained, further to the formal correspondence they had to maintain, correspondence with other officials, occasionally even with the sovereign they represented; Eugene of Savoy (1663–1736), for example, maintained a whole network of secret correspondence.[58]

As already mentioned, every diplomat had the same ceremonial rights as the sovereign he represented. This repeatedly led to conflicts, such as in London in the 1660s when the Spanish and French ambassadors had such a fierce row over the order of precedence that it ended in bloodshed. The best strategy to avoid conflict was to avoid each other. This applied especially to peace congresses, where diplomats met day after day and where the many official events resembled powder kegs.

---

[55] JC Waquet *François de Callières, L'Art de négocier en France sous Louis XIV* (Editions Rue d'Ulm Paris 2005).

[56] H Wolf 'Der kaiserliche Wahlkommissar und die Entwicklung von Verfahren und Zeremoniell bei der frühneuzeitlichen Bischofswahlen' in C Dartmann et al (ed) *Technik und Symbolik vormoderner Wahlverfahren* (Oldenbourg Munich 2010) 183–200.

[57] L Bittner (ed) *Repertorium der diplomatischen Vertreter aller Länder seit dem Westfälischen Frieden (1648–1715)* (Stalling Oldenburg 1936) vol 1.

[58] M Braubach *Die Geheimdiplomatie des Prinzen Eugen von Savoyen* (Westdeutscher Verlag Cologne 1962).

Going back to the time of Louis XIV, France built up a network of diplomats much larger than that of any other State. The many volumes of the *Recueil des instructions données aux ambassadeurs de France* are a testimony to this history. Unlike many other States, France also dispatched diplomats to smaller courts, courts that it considered important for political or strategic reasons. It was a policy most other States could not afford, especially when it came to the dispatch of diplomats to the many German courts. Other States, such as Russia, had yet another problem: they first had to establish a diplomatic service, a challenge which not infrequently led them to draw on the talent of their neighbours. The Sublime Porte, by contrast, ceased to dispatch resident diplomats to Europe at this time. It was a development that was to have serious consequences for all foreign diplomats on the Bosporus: if they had already led a perilous existence there, they now witnessed long-established norms being abandoned and the immunity of the diplomat being placed in question.[59] Wiquefort went so far as to speak of a total disrespect of international law in the Ottoman Empire.

At times diplomats succeeded in developing norms of international law away from the peace congresses. One such case was the agreement over how far a coastal State's sovereignty extended into its adjoining waters, a topic of intensive debate since the beginning of the 18th century. If the dominant sea powers had repeatedly—and unsuccessfully—tried to claim entire oceans in the past, they came, at the end of the 1780s, to agree on what constituted a State's territorial water. There was discussion over a two- or three-mile-zone, the views of Hermann Conring (1606–81) and Johann Gryphiander (1614–52), both experts on international law, that the matter should be decided according to local custom, and the idea to either use sight distance or cannon range as a criterion.[60] In the end agreements were reached that soon became accepted international law: involving the British, French, and Russian States, they defined territorial water according to cannon range. It was to take another couple of decades, until the 19th century, for the three-mile limit to be introduced.[61] The case illustrates that diplomats could also be effective during peacetime, that they could advance issues important to international law that could not be advanced during wartime. The most impressive proof to this effect is the Jay Treaty (1794),[62] which American and British diplomats negotiated in London and which settled several key conflicts between the two countries.[63] Critically, it named the Saint Croix River as the boundary line between American and British interests in the north-east of North America.

[59] LS Frey and ML Frey *The History of Diplomatic Immunity* (Ohio State University Press Columbus OH 1999).

[60] The first to set out cannon range in any comprehensive detail was C van Bynkershoek *De dominio maris* (The Hague 1703).

[61] *Epochen* (n 2) 387.

[62] Treaty of Amity, Commerce and Navigation between Great Britain and the United States (signed 19 November 1794) (1793–95) 52 CTS 243 ('Jay Treaty').

[63] The Jay Treaty is named after the American chief negotiator John Jay (1745–1829).

6. International Law as an Academic Discipline

Academic writing on international law was concentrated in certain geographical areas in the early modern period. It was no accident that the first steps were taken by practitioners and scholars in the Netherlands, a political unit which time and again, either due to religious or to societal reasons, had been ravaged by war and which had to assert itself on the international stage. Equally, it was no coincidence that it was in the Netherlands that the law of the sea took its beginning. Some of Grotius' main texts on international law focused on the sea,[64] as did Bynkershoek's,[65] who took a special interest in piracy.[66] It probably is characteristic of the second half of the early modern period that academic writing on international law evolved in the smaller political units, States whose survival depended on legal detail rather than military force.[67] Over many generations Leiden University thus produced a large number of leading scholars of international law. German-speaking universities tried to follow suit, such as Halle (as associated with Christian Wolff), Kiel (where a chair of international law was established shortly after the foundation of the university in 1665), and, above all, Göttingen (as associated with Georg Friedrich von Martens, 1756–1821). In Switzerland, Jean-Jacques Burlamaqui (1694–1748) made a significant contribution to international law, as did Johannes Loccenius (1598–1677) in Sweden, and Martin Hübner in Denmark. Whereas Loccenius[68] focused on questions of piracy, Hübner[69] wrote an insightful text on the protection of neutral ships during warfare.

But writing on international law was never limited to the universities as Gottfried Wilhelm Leibniz's (1646–1716) *Codex juris gentium diplomaticus* of 1693 and Emer de Vattel's *Le droit des gens, ou principes de la loi naturelle* of 1758 exemplify. Born in the Swiss principality of Neuenburg and later in the service of the Elector of Saxony, Vattel wrote with *Le droit des gens* an early modern bestseller, a landmark text which first made use of the term '*société des nations*' (rather than some similar term with Christian connotations), moreover set out the premise that subjects of different religious belief constituted no threat, neither to morals nor the State.[70]

---

[64]   eg H Grotius *De mari libero* (Leiden 1633).   [65]   *De dominio maris* (n 60).

[66]   *Epochen* (n 2) 356.

[67]   It is worth citing Grewe at greater length in this context (*Epochen* (n 2) 411): 'It is no doubt curious that the French phase of the history of international law has nothing representative to offer.' Also, the Oxford jurist Richard Zouch (c. 1590–1661) has to be excluded from the above general statement.

[68]   J Loccenius *De iure naturae et navali libri tres* (Ex Officina Joannis Janssonii Stockholm 1652).

[69]   *Epochen* (n 2) 439 fn 37.

[70]   ibid 332 f.

Progress in international law also would not have been possible without the many scholars who dedicated themselves to the editing of early theoretical texts and the records of the major peace congresses. Worth mentioning is the Huguenot publicist Jean Dumont (1667–1727), active at the imperial court in Vienna, whose multivolume *Corps universel diplomatique du droit des gens* was published between 1726 and 1739. In some respects it remains an indispensable source of reference even today. Carl Wilhelm Gärtner (1700–60) and Johann Gottfried von Meiern (1692–1745), the latter director of the archive in Hanover, saw to the early compilation of the records of the Peace of Westphalia.[71] Last but not least, there is Martens' important *Recueil des principaux traités* from the end of the 18th century that ought to be mentioned.

7. International Law in a New Age

7.1. The French Revolution and its Impact on International Law

To refer to the French Revolution and the age of Napoleon as a mere episode in the history of international law would be an exaggeration. Still, the revolutionaries tried, at times with direct reference to Vattel, whom they much revered, to move international law forward.[72] An issue they actively sought to progress was the long debated idea of 'natural borders', which in several cases had already entered inter-state agreements. Further, they took an active interest in the right to intervention, arguably to ensure freedom and human rights, in reality to extend French hegemony. As already mentioned, the idea of the right to intervention was to enjoy— albeit against a different background—a revival after the Congress of Vienna. War thus assumed the character of a crusade and made the unwritten laws governing the 'controlled' conduct of war a thing of the past. Likewise, France undermined the established notion of neutrality in that it concluded a series of neutrality agreements in the late 1790s which explicitly allowed for its troops to cross neutral territory.[73]

---

[71] A Oschmann 'Johann Gottfried von Meiern und die *Acta pacis Westphalicae publica*' in H Duch-hardt (ed) *Der Westfälische Friede: Diplomatie, politische Zäsur, kulturelles Umfeld, Rezeptionsgeschichte* (Oldenbourg Munich 1998) 778–803.

[72] For a much cited statement by Vattel see *Epochen* (n 2) 381.

[73] ibid 446.

7.2. The Congress of Vienna as a Turning Point in the History of International Law

The course for the future of international law was thus only set at the Congress of Vienna. It therefore is no exaggeration to speak of the twenty-five years between the outbreak of the French Revolution and the fall of Napoleon as a 'peculiar transitional state', characterized by such illegal acts as the execution of the Duke of Enghien (1772–1804) during the French Consulate and the bombardment of Copenhagen by the British fleet in 1807.[74]

The most important innovation was arguably that the term *nations civilisées*[75] found entry into international law. It first emerged in opposition to the slave trade and replaced Christian notions of community as 'the uniting spirit of international law'.[76] Instead, inter-state relations were to be governed by the idea of a much more comprehensive community of 'civilized nations', which certain States, however, found difficult to accept.

As indicated, the term *nations civilisées* goes back to the initiative to make the slave trade illegal.[77] It did not ostracize slavery as yet, though, but moved in that direction. A noble idea, the abolition of slavery was to prove a major challenge for some of the colonial powers, Spain and Portugal, in particular. Britain, by contrast, where an anti-slavery movement had formed in the 1780s, already made the slave trade illegal in 1807. It also showed that private organizations had come to take an interest in international law; henceforth they were to also have an impact on politics. Academic writing on international law has since praised the condemnation of the slave trade as one of the major achievements of the Congress of Vienna.[78] Indeed, it was the first time that human rights were guaranteed by international law. However, whether Britain pursued international agreement on the abolition of the slave trade because of humanitarian concerns or because of economic reasons remains to be answered.[79] The term 'nations civilisées' having found entry into international law, it is worth pointing out that the term 'neutrality' was also given a new quality at the Congress of Vienna. It was on this occasion that Switzerland, which for so long had refrained from entering any conflict, was accorded the status of a neutral State. It was to remain the only State with such status for some time, but served as a model for similar creations in the future (for example, the Vatican).

---

[74] ibid 485.

[75] See the contribution by L Obrégon 'The Civilized and the Uncivilized' in this volume.

[76] *Epochen* (n 2) 335.

[77] See the contribution by S Drescher and P Finkelman 'Slavery' in this volume.

[78] For an overview on academic writing on international law see K Strupp and HJ Schlochauer (eds) *Wörterbuch des Völkerrechts* (De Gruyter Berlin 1960–62) vol 3, at 276.

[79] For literature on this point see H Duchhardt *Gleichgewicht der Kräfte, Convenance, Europäisches Konzert* (Wissenschaftliche Buchgesellschaft Darmstadt 1976) at 146.

Another major innovation was laid down in the Vienna Protocol of 24 June 1814, a document signed shortly before the start of the Congress of Vienna. It decreed the unification of the Dutch Republic, the Austrian Netherlands (Belgium), and the Prince-Bishopric of Liège (Belgium) into the United Kingdom of the Netherlands and stipulated that all public offices were to be open to all citizens, disregarding religious affiliation. This was, in principle, a constitutional matter, but was to have an immediate effect on international law: for a State to be a *nation civilisée*, it henceforth had to be, at least in theory, a State neutral to confessional matters.

A third major innovation was the reorganization of diplomatic ranks, a source of permanent conflict in the past. The French Revolution no doubt had provided valuable groundwork here: if nations were equal, then respective diplomatic ranks had to be equal. A commission was thus appointed at the Congress of Vienna, which reported back three years later at the Congress of Aix-la-Chapelle (1818). If orders of precedence had previously been influenced by the power of the States that had dispatched diplomats, they now were simply set out according to date of arrival and alphabetical order. Only the papal nuncio, as a kind of doyen, was granted precedence to all.

Of major importance, at least in the decades immediately after the Congress of Vienna, was also the Concert of Europe. Initially supported by the Quadruple Alliance of Austria, Britain, Prussia, and Russia, as signed in Paris on 20 November 1815 (Treaty of Paris), it later—following the Congress of Aix-la-Chapelle—also engaged France. First discussed at the Congress of Châtillon (1814), the Concert of Europe was to meet at regular intervals to settle international conflicts by negotiation rather than force. This being so, it still reserved the right to intervention. Unlike in earlier centuries, however, when similar collaborative initiatives had all been futile, the Concert of Europe produced immediate results: based on the principle of legitimacy, the Congresses of Aix-la-Chapelle (1818), Laibach (1821), and Verona (1822) instituted a new international order and gave intervention the semblance of a 'just' measure. That the latter was subject to considerable criticism from liberal jurists like Johann Caspar Bluntschli (1808–81) is another matter.

The Congress of Vienna—together with its successor congresses—laid the foundation for the future. It therefore does not surprise that contemporary scholars of international law like Johann Ludwig Klüber (1762–1837) immediately set out to publish the conference documents.[80] Subsequent generations took a different view: while they duly acknowledged the impact the congresses had on humanitarian (abolition of the slave trade) and economic (introduction of the freedom of movement, especially on rivers) issues, they also questioned the great powers' claim to (and practice of) the right to intervention. The latter was particularly controversial when it was

---

[80] JL Klüber *Acten des Wiener Kongresses* (9 vols Erlangen 1816–35).

directed against liberal and democratic opposition movements which either appeared to or de facto did undermine a regime.[81]

8. Conclusion

The period in the history of international law discussed here is arguably one of the most exciting in the whole of the history of international law. It illustrates that from the 16th century onwards the early modern State and State system required a set of rules that transcended such 'old' instruments of inter-state relations as, for example, arbitration. From the beginning of the 16th century, drawing on 'Spanish' exponents of second scholasticism, there thus emerged, headed by Grotius—the 'father of modern international law'—an intensive debate about the *ius ad bellum* and the *ius in bello* as of concern to political actors at the time. Mirroring the negotiations leading to the Peace of Westphalia, the need for action became ever more urgent: on the one hand there was the need for 'peace-making', on the other hand the need for such formalities as 'peace treaties'. European expansion and the emergence of colonial empires called for further rules; taking a long-term perspective, one is no doubt right to observe that the Seven Years' War—which was a global military conflict involving most of the great powers—and the experience of revolution shifted the focus of international law from a preoccupation with war to a preoccupation with peace (Kant published his influential discourse on perpetual peace in 1795) and from a principal interest in inter-state competition to a principal interest in inter-state cooperation (whereby the family of States soon came to transcend the *orbis europaeus* and to include States in North and South America). Added to this should be the observation that from the time of the French Revolution international law, as challenged by private interest groups, advanced humanitarian and socio-political issues that would not have been of interest to 17th-century jurists primarily concerned with the laws of war. One can thus conclude that international law in the 150 years discussed here progressed in its traditional—regarding such questions as military intervention and diplomatic ranks—as well as into new fields: it is a development that continues to have ramifications even today.

---

[81] M Vec 'Intervention/Nichtintervention. Verrechtlichung der Politik und Politisierung des Völkerrechts im 19. Jahrhundert' in U Lappenküper and R Marcowitz (eds) *Macht und Recht. Völkerrecht in den internationalen Beziehungen* (Schöningh Paderborn 2010) 135–60.

RECOMMENDED READING

Anderson, Matthew S *The Rise of Modern Diplomacy 1450–1919* (Longman London 1993).

Duchhardt, Heinz and Franz Knipping (eds) *Handbuch der Geschichte der Internationalen Beziehungen* (9 vols Schöningh Paderborn 1997–), in particular vol 2 by Heinz Schilling (2007), vol 3 by Klaus Malettke (forthcoming), vol 4 by Heinz Duchhardt (1997) and vol 5 by Michael Erbe (2004).

Fisch, Jörg *Krieg und Frieden im Friedensvertrag: Eine universalgeschichtliche Studie über Grundlagen und Formelemente des Friedensschlusses* (Klett-Cotta Stuttgart 1979).

Grewe, Wilhelm G *Epochen der Völkerrechtsgeschichte* (Nomos Baden-Baden 1984).

Lesaffer, Randall (ed) *Peace Treaties and International Law in European History: From the Late Middle Ages to World War One* (CUP Cambridge 2004).

Schmitt, Carl *Der Nomos der Erde im Völkerrecht des Jus Publicum Europaeum* (Greven Cologne 1950).

Steiger, Heinhard *Von der Staatengesellschaft zur Weltrepublik? Aufsätze zur Geschichte des Völkerrechts aus vierzig Jahren* (Nomos Baden-Baden 2009).

CHAPTER 27

FROM THE CONGRESS OF VIENNA TO THE PARIS PEACE TREATIES OF 1919

MILOŠ VEC

1. INTRODUCTION

THE beginning and the end of the era this chapter deals with are marked by two famous congresses and their subsequent treaties, the localities of which have become their synonyms: Vienna in 1815 and Paris in 1919. In between, numerous smaller gatherings happened in Europe, which dealt with now-forgotten treaties, few wars, and major interventions; Europe externalized its conflicts. International law doctrine developed remarkably. It was the period which has often been regarded as the one in which European jurisprudence had reached its zenith and German lawyers played a great part in this process, particularly with regard to international law.[1] International law as practice and doctrine, formulated by European jurists, spread all over the

---

[1] M Koskenniemi 'Between Coordination and Constitution: International Law as a German Discipline' (2011) 14 Redescriptions 45–70; A Carty 'The Evolution of International Legal Scholarship in Germany during the Kaiserreich and the Weimarer Republik (1871–1933)' (2007) 50 German Yearbook of International Law 29–90.

world and extended both in regulatory matters and in scope. It was a legitimization narrative for various actions of European and global politics in a century that left its traces on legal thinking and political practice.[2] 'Legitimization narrative' in that sense means that the normative order of international law presupposed justifications while generating them at the same time; the 'legitimization narrative' of international law thus contained possibilities of critique, rejection, and resistance which were beyond the facticity of its juridical positivism.[3]

Not surprisingly, the history of international law has to deal with the problem of Eurocentrism[4] and hegemonic perspectives.[5] Furthermore, the development of 19th-century international law is often attached to some master narratives of modern society. Some of the most famous concepts are universalization, professionalization, the rise of science, juridification/legalization, and positivism. By telling the following story about 19th-century international law, I undertake a critical discussion to see if these assumptions are all true and if so, in what way and at what cost.

2. Conceptual and Doctrinal Foundations and Changes; Expansion of International Law

The 19th century is said to have seen the birth of the modern world; it is the age of 'Die Verwandlung der Welt' as global historian Jürgen Osterhammel[6] put it. International law took part in this big global transformation. Its spread and growing importance was supported by the fact that the 19th century was not only the century of nationalism and the national State, as often told, but also of many internationalisms.[7]

---

[2] See eg MCR Craven 'What Happened to Unequal Treaties? The Continuities of Informal Empire' in MCR Craven and M Fitzmaurice (eds) *Interrogating the Treaty* (Wolf Legal Publishers Nijmegen 2005) 43–80.

[3] R Forst and K Günther 'Die Herausbildung normativer Ordnungen' (2010) 1 Normative Orders Working Papers 2–3.

[4] M Koskenniemi 'Histories of International Law: Dealing with Eurocentrism' (2011) 19 Rechtsgeschichte 152–76.

[5] A Kemmerer 'The Turning Aside: On International Law and Its History' in RA Miller and RM Bratspies (eds) *Progress in International Law* (Martinus Nijhoff Leiden 2008) 71–93 at 77.

[6] J Osterhammel *Die Verwandlung der Welt. Eine Geschichte des 19. Jahrhunderts* (CH Beck München 2009).

[7] J Paulmann 'Reformer, Experten und Diplomaten: Grundlagen des Internationalismus im 19. Jahrhundert' in H von Thiessen and C Windler (eds) *Akteure der Außenbeziehungen* (Böhlau Köln 2010) 173–97; J Paulmann 'Searching for a "Royal International"' in MH Geyer and J Paulmann (eds) *The Mechanics of Internationalism: Culture, Society, and Politics from the 1840s to the First World War* (OUP Oxford 2001) 145–76.

2.1. Terms and Subjects

First and most evidently, the language of international law changed.[8] Latin ceased to be the language of academic discussions in international law. Only a vanishing minority of authors published some Latin treatises on international law in the 19th century. Moreover, jurists were aware of the problems which the term *ius gentium* would have implied for the labelling of their field of work, and therefore they dropped it. It was Jeremy Bentham who shifted the English denominations from 'law of nations' to 'international law' at the end of the 18th-century.[9] The French, Italian, and Spanish lawyers followed and developed terms which are still valid in the 21st century: *droit international, diritto internazionale,* and *derecho internacional* were sometimes used as substitutes, but in most cases were options for labelling the juridical order between States.

Although Bentham was valued as a legal philosopher by many Germans jurists, the German term *Völkerrecht* persisted. Kant had famously suggested the term *Staatenrecht* (law of States) instead of *Völkerrecht* arguing that not the people but the States were legal subjects in this field of law.[10] Obviously, Kant's doctrine was widely appreciated and discussed in general.[11] Both the idea of freedom as the sole principle of law and law as the foundation of society were enthusiastically welcomed by his contemporaries. International law doctrine was influenced by him, too, yet probably less than other areas of legal thinking. Nobody objected to the idea that this field of law should be named after its subjects, yet under late 18th- and 19th-century international legal doctrine, only States were regarded as subjects of international law. In German, the terms *Volk* and *Staat* were often treated as synonyms; however, with regard to pure doctrine, the term *Staatenrecht* would have been correct. Other authors even suggested terms like *ius cosmopoliticum, ius publicum civitatum, Internationalrecht, Staatsvölkerrecht, äusseres Staatsrecht,* and *internationales Staatsrecht.* Discussion went on for some decades, but language is hard to change, and one of the main 19th-century authorities, Robert von Mohl, was probably right when he concluded that *Staatsrecht* and *Staatenrecht* could be confused acoustically too easily.[12] Thus Germany is one of the countries that still derives the term of the legal doctrine ('Völkerrecht') from the subject this doctrine is dealing with (in the understanding of the 18th and 19th centuries when 'Volk' and 'Staat' were considered identical); this is also the case in the Netherlands

---

[8] H Steiger 'Völkerrecht' in O Brunner, W Conze, and R Koselleck (eds) *Geschichtliche Grundbegriffe* (Klett Cotta Stuttgart 1992) vol VII, 97–140.

[9] MW Janis 'Jeremy Bentham and the Fashioning of "International Law"' (1984) 78 American Journal of International Law 405–18.

[10] I Kant *Die Metaphysik der Sitten. Erster Theil, metaphysische Anfangsgründe der Rechtslehre* (2nd edn Friedrich Nicolovius Königsberg 1798) at 246.

[11] J Rückert 'Kant-Rezeption in juristischer und politischer Theorie' in MP Thompsen (ed) *John Locke und/and Immanuel Kant* (Duncker & Humblot Berlin 1991) 144–215.

[12] R von Mohl *Encyklopädie der Staatswissenschaften* (2nd edn Laupp Tübingen 1872) at 405.

(*Volkenregt*)[13] and some Scandinavian countries (*Folkeret*).[14] Yet in the French- and English-speaking world, the early modern terms of *droit des gens, droit des nations,* and 'law of nations' can still be used alternatively even though they are less common.

However, other denominations like *droit des peuples, droit des nations,*[15] or *droit public d'Europe,*[16] and *droit public externe/ius publicum externum* vanished at the latest in the early 20th century. Jurists still held the assumption that international order addresses the order of the external relations of the State as opposed to its internal legal system. One of the irritating consequences of the often very radical and clear differentiation was that the interdependencies between both were made invisible. Domestic and foreign policy, national and international law seemed separated and disconnected in this dualism (this doctrine was most prominently and elaborated formulated by Heinrich Triepel in 1899).[17] The connections that exist in reality disappeared and still disappear in these conceptualizations.[18] Whereas most 19th-century authors followed the doctrinal dualism of the 'foreign'/'international' and the 'domestic' quite enthusiastically, at least some of them were aware of the loss such distinctions carried with them.[19] This change in terminology went along with the formation of international law as a juridical discipline not only distinct from other academic subjects but also from other juridical disciplines; according to the majority of the 19th-century maritime law jurists, 'international law' excluded international private law and international criminal law *in extenso*.[20]

These disappearances and transformations marked a slow-going, but deep change in lawyers' perspective. How did that transition work? What instruments were used to achieve it. And how universal were they in terms of the norm?

2.2. A Community of (European) States: Criteria, Inclusions, and Exclusions

Europe was not only in the geographical centre of this legal order but it also defined the criteria of belonging to international society. Classical international law was

---

[13] G de Wal *Inleiding tot de Wetenschap van het Europesche Volkenregt* (J Oomkens Groningen 1835); H Cock *Natuur- Staats- en Volkenregt* (Lau Leyden 1837).

[14] JLA Kolderup-Rosenvinge *Grundrids af den positive Folkeret* (Gyldendal Kjøbenhavn 1835); H Matzen *Forelaesninger over den positive Folkeret* (JH Schultz Kjøbenhavn 1900).

[15] S Algernon *Discours sur le Gouvernement* (Louis et Henri van Dole La Haye 1702) vol I, at 26.

[16] H Steiger 'Ius publicum Europaeum' in F Jaeger (ed) *Enzyklopädie der Neuzeit* (Metzler Stuttgart 2007) vol 5, 1148–54.

[17] H Triepel *Völkerrecht und Landesrecht* (Hirschfeld Leipzig 1899).

[18] JE Nijman and A Nollkaemper 'Beyond the Divide' in JE Nijman and A Nollkaemper (eds) *New Perspectives on the Divide between National and International Law* (OUP Oxford 2007) 341–60 at 341.

[19] C Frantz *Der Föderalismus* (F Kirchheim Mainz 1879) at 372.

[20] F von Liszt *Das Völkerrecht* (M Fleischmann ed) (12th edn Springer Berlin 1925) at 1.

developed by 17th- and 18th-century European jurists, and understood only States as legitimate subjects of international law. Thus the question of who could be considered as sovereign was crucial to international law. Juridical criteria went together with cultural presuppositions, inclusions, and exclusions. Juridical constructions like federations and confederations as well as dependant political subjects in 19th-century political order were particular challenges.

The European States were seen as independent actors, yet at the same time they formed a legal community which aimed at a very limited integration of outside actors. This idea implied clear rejections of utopian dreams of a universal State—the 18th-century ideas of Wolff, Vattel, and Kant were criticized and sometimes even condemned. The basis and scope of this international community was geographically clear only insofar as the (western and central) European States and the United States of America[21] belonged to this international society; however, its underlying criteria were nevertheless discussed and disputed. Lawyers frequently mentioned the common history and Christian religion of the continent,[22] the existing foundation of treaties and the shared ideas of legal consciousness and mutual recognition as common basis of these countries to form 'the' international society.[23]

Out of this definition two problems arose. Firstly, who belonged technically to this international legal community? The legal status of Russia and the Ottoman Empire posed particular challenges to this issue of European boundaries in the 19th century, yet the latter is said to have been admitted to the international society by the Treaty of Paris in 1856[24] which shifted the criteria of inclusion from 'European' to 'civilized'.[25] Africa and Asia entered the scope of international law, but only few Asian States such as China, Japan, Siam, and Persia were seen as legitimate members of the growing international society. Latin American States seemed to have fewer difficulties in entering. Other actors like Indian tribes or nomad peoples were unanimously seen as being outside this community.

Secondly, the exclusion from the community did not determine how to handle these actors. Doctrine made various proposals and conceptualized different degrees of exclusion and discrimination of what they saw as 'the other', or at least those in a peripheral, position.[26] The practice sometimes went together with these multiple discriminatory concepts as the so-called 'uncivilized' or 'barbarians' were not treated on

---

[21] MW Janis *America and the Law of Nations, 1776–1939* (OUP Oxford 2010).

[22] CM Kennedy *The Influence of Christianity upon International Law* (Macmillan Cambridge 1856); MF Lucas 'De l'influence et du rôle du christianisme dans la formation du droit international' (1893) Revue des Facultés catholiques de l'Ouest 556–84.

[23] J Fisch *Die europäische Expansion und das Völkerrecht* (Steiner Stuttgart 1984) at 285.

[24] General Treaty for the Re-Establishment of Peace between Austria, France, Great Britain, Prussia, Sardinia, and Turkey, and Russia (signed 30 March 1856) (1856) 114 CTS 409 ('Treaty of Paris').

[25] E Augusti 'The Ottoman Empire at the Congress of Paris' in LB Varela, PG Vega and A Spinosa (eds) *Crossing Legal Cultures* (Meidenbauer München 2009) 503–17.

[26] L Nuzzo 'Un mondo senza nemici. La costruzione del diritto internazionale e il controllo delle differenze' (2009) 38 Quaderni Fiorentini 1311–81.

the basis of reciprocity or full equality (see the practice of the 'unequal treaties') by the 'family of civilized nations'. In other cases, treaty relations were maintained by the Europeans although it was without any doubt that the subjects did not belong to international society.

2.3. Diplomacy and Congresses as Multipartite Political Instruments

The Congress of Vienna established a European order which lasted for some decades and was finally terminated by the Crimean War. Its language referred to 'fraternity' and 'legitimacy' as authoritative narratives which highlighted the personal bonds between the ruling monarchs. Technically, the system based upon diplomacy, international law and the threat of intervention. In the words of Eric Weitz, 'Vienna centered on dynastic legitimacy and state sovereignty with clearly defined borders'.[27] As Mathias Schulz pointed out, the Vienna Concert could be regarded as some kind of 19th-century Security Council.[28] This concept went along with the official approval of political unequality of the state actors because some States established their political hegemony (also) juridically against this background. International lawyers hesitated to approve this political order thoroughly. Instead, they discussed some principles of the Vienna order like the 'balance of power' most critically in terms of their possible juridical content—thus, one may even say that this principle was 'de-juridified'.[29] Only the fight of international law against slavery (see the Declaration of 8 February 1815; Treaty of 20 December 1841),[30] the establishment of the principle of free navigation on rivers (articles 108 and 113), and the dissolution of the problem of the diplomatic ranks of ambassadors and plenipotentiaries[31] were later seen as real advancements of those years.[32]

---

[27]   ED Weitz 'From the Vienna to the Paris System: International Politics and the Entangled Histories of Human Rights, Forced Deportations, and Civilizing Missions' (2008) 113 American Historical Review 1313–43 at 1314.

[28]   M Schulz *Normen und Praxis. Das Europäische Konzert der Grossmächte als Sicherheitsrat 1815–60* (Oldenbourg München 2009).

[29]   M Vec 'De-Juridifying "Balance of Power"' (2011) European Society of International Law Conference Paper Series <http://papers.ssrn.com/sol3/papers.cfm?abstract_id=1968667> (15 February 2012).

[30]   Treaty of Vienna Act XV, Declaration Relative to the Universal Abolition of the Slave Trade (concluded 18 February 1815) 63 CTS 473 ('Vienna Treaty'); Treaty of London between Austria, Great Britain, Prussia and Russia for the Suppression of the African Slave Trade (concluded 20 December 1841) 92 CTS 437.

[31]   M Vec '"Technische" gegen "symbolische" Verfahrensformen? Die Normierung und Ausdifferenzierung der Gesandtenränge nach der juristischen und politischen Literatur des 18. und 19. Jahrhunderts' in B Stollberg-Rilinger (ed) *Vormoderne politische Verfahren* (Duncker & Humblot Berlin 2001) 559–90.

[32]   JC Bluntschli *Das moderne Völkerrecht* (CH Beck Nördlingen 1868) para 312 at 182.

After Vienna, frequent congresses came up to maintain and adjust the international order according to the political needs (concern for equilibrium).[33] A canonization of political events which organized multilateral state interests was fixed as follows: Aachen 1818, Troppau 1820, Laibach 1821, Verona 1822, London 1830–33, London 1850–52, Paris 1856, Berlin 1856, Berlin 1878, Berlin 1884–85, The Hague 1899 and 1907. Thus 19th-century European politics had found some organizational pattern for the negotiation of its interests and for conflict 'resolution' in a world in which courts for this kind of conflicts did not exist. International law proved to have developed genuine patterns of conflict management that should not be simply understood as inferior to other areas of law.[34] It enabled Europe, a continent of multiple political and economic tensions, to maintain a period of relative peace in the sense of the absence of war.[35] At the same time, the exercise of force was seen as a legitimate and even beneficial instrument for the resolution of inter-state disputes. However, this perspective changed slightly at the beginning of the 20th century as the Drago-Porter Convention established a relative interdiction of force in 1907.

Both the model of multilateral gatherings and the doctrine of balance of power had been carried over from earlier times (the epoch which is classically attached to the idea of balance of power is the 18th century[36] and particularly the Treaty of Utrecht). Henceforth the above-mentioned conferences were instruments that combined international law with raison d'état and sought to prevent further revolutionary turnovers. Against this background intervention was seen as a legitimized political instrument to protect the needs of the European continent. It was practised for various needs and attached to legitimization narratives, ranging from political stability and humanity[37] to intervention for the sake of financial interests (intervention in the internal affairs of debtor States).

International law did not fully approve these political inter-state practices. Some of them were not even legalized, which would mean that political actors tried not to present their actions as a part of the newly emerging international law. For example, in fields such as international debt regulation they avoided any pretence of showing a type of behaviour that might be interpreted as a general legal pattern.[38] Therefore,

[33] WP Schroeder 'The Nineteenth Century System: Balance of Power or Political Equilibrium?' (1989) 15 Review of International Studies 135–53.

[34] M Vec 'Verrechtlichung internationaler Streitbeilegung im 19. und 20. Jahrhundert?' in S Dauchy and M Vec (eds) *Les conflits entre peuples* (Nomos Baden-Baden 2011) 1–21.

[35] J Dülffer, M Kröger, and RH Wippich *Vermiedene Kriege* (Oldenbourg München 1997).

[36] F Dhondt 'Law on the Diplomatic Stage: The 1725 Ripperda Treaty' in V Draganova and S Kroll (eds) *Inszenierung des Rechts* (Meidenbauer München 2011) 303–23.

[37] DJB Trim and B Simms (eds) *Humanitarian Intervention: A History* (CUP Cambridge 2011); I Kreutzmann *Missbrauch der humanitären Intervention im 19. Jahrhundert* (Baltica Glücksburg 1999); M Swatek-Evenstein *Geschichte der 'Humanitären Intervention'* (Nomos Baden-Baden 2008).

[38] L Heimbeck 'Law, Finances and Politics: The Significance of Economic Contexts for the Formation of Norms' in Inszenierung des Rechts (n 36) 253–73.

legal rules drawn from present cases were not meant to be applied to future ones, and States were thus able to maintain their freedom of political action.

However, in other fields of politics, actors wished to legalize their actions using international law as the instrument to achieve this purpose. Thus they claimed, as in the cases of the interventions of the Vienna Concert, the lawfulness of their steps. Yet this claim was attacked from various sides: other politicians and international lawyers branded the interventions as illegal. The doctrine of international law thus tried at the same time both to formulate legal principles and rules for the international order. Those rules' starting point was state sovereignty which generally did not allow any interference into internal affairs by third powers; thus the juridical doctrine carried the liberal 18th-century political assumption of 'essential separateness of individuals from each other'.[39] This principle was acknowledged and international lawyers did not question it; even the 'tension between State freedom and international order'[40] was hardly discussed in early classical international law. However, at the same time, international lawyers agreed that no principle existed without exception and even sovereignty would underlie such restrictions in distinct cases. Thus, regarding the issues of 19th-century state sovereignty and interests for intervention, the question was not whether exceptions existed but which exceptions did, or rather whether there was a distinct problem that corresponded to these exceptions. With regard to the last issue, little agreement was to be found among international lawyers.[41] They tried to develop criteria and enumerated catalogues which were supposed to be helpful in recognizing such a general rule. In many cases, historical examples served to illustrate and prove the legitimacy or unlawfulness of interventions and interventionist rules. Yet they could not achieve any agreement on this question of lawful exceptions from the general principle of non-intervention. Guiseppe Carnazza Amari noted in 1873: '[j]amais peut-être thème du droit des gens ne fut plus diversement étudié, plus énergiequement discuté, plus différemment développé et décidé que le principe de non-intervention.'[42]

Other landmark congresses followed in the decades after the Vienna order had eroded: Paris in 1856, the Berlin congress of 1878, the Berlin West African Conference of 1884–85, and finally the Hague Peace Conferences in 1899[43] and 1907.[44] Europe negotiated its political order and global affairs using law and multilateral diplomacy and it was at least quite successful in externalizing war. Conflict prevention worked in

---

[39] M Koskenniemi *From Apology to Utopia* (CUP Cambridge 2009) at 74.

[40] ibid 119.

[41] M Vec 'Intervention/Nichtintervention. Verrechtlichung der Politik und Politisierung des Völkerrechts im 19. Jahrhundert' in U Lappenküper and R Marcowicz (eds) *Macht und Recht. Völkerrecht in den internationalen Beziehungen* (Schöningh Paderborn 2010) 135–60.

[42] G Carnazza-Amari 'Nouvel exposé du principe de non-intervention' (1873) 5 Revue de droit international et de legislation comparée 352–89 and 531–65 at 352.

[43] A Eyffinger *The 1899 Hague Peace Conference: 'The Parliament of Man, the Federation of the World'* (Kluwer Law International The Hague 2000).

[44] A Eyffinger *The 1907 Hague Peace Conference: 'The Conscience of the Civilized World'* (Judicap The Hague 2007).

many cases. Jost Dülffer thus pointed out that the European political actors used various diplomatic and legal instruments to prevent wars.[45] Yet this order finally failed in 1914 when the interest in expanding Empires and the mood for starting a war overruled the wish for peace.

2.4. Conferences

The well-known statement that European diplomacy had already used the instrument of multipartite conferences in the 17th and 18th centuries might hide the important observation that this instrument underwent a fundamental change ever since. Congresses and particularly so-called conferences amounted to much more than mere political instruments.[46] With the agglomeration of international relations, these gatherings were used to discuss and handle new topics and themes. They became more frequent, and they attracted not only notorious politicians, jurists, and diplomats, but also professionals from other areas. A symptomatic break can be seen in the first sanitary conference to standardize international quarantine regulations which took place in Paris in 1851.[47] The expression 'more frequent' shall mean here that while conferences were held only once a year in the 1830s, one can count hundreds after 1900—per annum.[48] The impact of the industrial revolution, of technical and scientific improvement in traffic and communication driving this change cannot be underestimated.[49]

2.5. New and Expanding Fields of Regulation

These conferences treated various topics regarding trade, economy, and sciences. Thereby, these fields—including the standardization of weights, measures, and time—also became subjects of international law. The role of consulates, consular law, and consular jurisdiction increased. Older subjects like commerce and the treaties regulating it came into the focus of international law and politics; cooperation became a powerful idea in this field.[50] International society declared war on piracy and abol-

---

[45] *Vermiedene Kriege* (n 35).

[46] RG Gruber *Internationale Staatenkongresse und Konferenzen* (Puttkammer & Mühlbrecht Berlin 1919).

[47] C Tapia and J Taieb 'Conférences et Congrès Internationaux de 1815 à 1913' (1976) 5 Relations Internationales 11–35 at 31.

[48] ibid 12.

[49] M Vec *Recht und Normierung in der Industriellen Revolution* (Klostermann Frankfurt 2006) 21 ff.

[50] R Pahre *Politics and Trade Cooperation in the Nineteenth Century: The 'Agreeable Customs' of 1815–1914* (CUP Cambridge 2008). See also G Thiemeyer *Internationalimus und Diplomatie. Währungspolitische Kooperationen im europäischen Staatensystem 1865–1900* (Oldenbourg München 2009).

ished privateering formally by the Paris declaration of 1856.[51] More treaties of friendship, trade, and navigation than ever before were concluded. Lawyers, economists, and politicians had high expectations regarding their potential achievement for human societies in general.[52] The discussion on 'free trade' and its consequences displayed antagonistic positions in national economy and international law. Yet it seemed that the various protagonists agreed on the assumption that international law generally worked as an important instrument which they could mobilize for economic goals. This was also true for other fields of growing global entanglements where the progress of human societies led to new internationalisms like cooperations, organizations, institutionalizations, all of them connecting the multiple actors of states and civil societies.

International law had undoubtedly expanded significantly. It gained new challenges for regulations and conferences were the instruments to master them. Many of the issues were efforts to standardize norms that already existed on a national level and also on the international one, helping to facilitate commerce by the reduction of transactions costs; for example in the field of taxes and railroads,[53] or the traffic of sugar.[54] Here, in the field of communications and economy, international cooperation and competition through national and international law-making took place simultaneously.[55]

Yet international law was not only challenged by technical and economic development but philanthropic and moral objectives extended its scope too. Condemnation of slavery (Treaty of Vienna 1815; Treaty between Austria, Great Britain, Prussia, and Russia for the Suppression of the African Slave Trade, 1841) and humanization of warfare (foundation of the Red Cross after the battle of Solferino, 1859; Geneva Convention for the Amelioration of the Condition of the Wounded in Armies in the Field,[56] 1864; Declaration of Brussels,[57] 1874) were included into the agenda of 19th-century international law.[58] Moreover, the first transnational efforts for the exten-

---

[51] M Kempe *Fluch der Weltmeere—Piraterie, Völkerrecht und internationale Beziehungen 1500–1900* (Campus Frankfurt 2010).

[52] R Klump and M Vec 'Große Erwartungen. Völkerrecht und Weltwirtschaft im 19. Jahrhundert' in R Klump and M Vec (eds) *Völkerrecht und Weltwirtschaft im 19. Jahrhundert* (Nomos Baden-Baden 2012) 1–16.

[53] W Kaufmann *Die mitteleuropäischen Eisenbahnen und das internationale öffentliche Recht* (Duncker & Humblot Leipzig 1893).

[54] W Kaufmann *Welt-Zuckerindustrie* (F Siemenroth Berlin 1904).

[55] G Ambrosius *Regulativer Wettbewerb und koordinative Standardisierung zwischen Staaten* (Franz Steiner Stuttgart 2005); I Hont *Jealousy of Trade. International Competition and the Nation-State in Historical Perspective* (Harvard University Press Cambridge MA 2001).

[56] Convention for the Amelioration of the Condition of the Wounded in Armies in the Field (adopted 22 August 1864, entered into force 22 June 1865) 129 CTS 361.

[57] 'Project of an International Declaration Concerning the Laws and Customs of War, adopted by the Conference of Brussels (27 August 1874)' in (1907) 1 American Journal of International Law Supplement 96–103.

[58] F Lentner *Das Recht im Kriege* (LW Seidel & Sohn Wien 1880).

sion of social policy and the welfare State were included into this new field of law.[59] International law fought white-slave traffic (*traité des blanches*)[60] and pornography around 1900, thereby including European civil society's moral perspective aims and transformed its goals into positive regulations and general principles of international law.

These agendas were often not at all or only loosely connected to one another. As a result, those new fields of regulation displayed a fragmentation of the upcoming regulatory agenda of modern international law which followed various needs in a very contingent way.

However, at the same time, both the reach of international law and of the juridification of conflicts of interest were also clearly limited. Efforts to build legal regimes often conflicted with strong political interests to avoid derogating sovereignty in essential fields. This was particularly true for military interests which contradicted wishes for the limitation of the amount of arms (England refusing to limit its fleet)[61] or supported the use of technological innovations notwithstanding their cruelty or particular harmfulness (dumdum or expanding bullets, submarines). Often, the efforts in norm enforcement indicated the (missing) political interest in a consequential juridification of areas like warfare.

2.6. International Organizations

These new fields of regulation developed together with the foundation of a set of international organizations. Yet these organizations were highly limited in their scope as their names clearly indicate; consider for example the Central Commission for the Navigation of the Rhine[62] established in 1815 and often regarded as the first international organization.[63] However, later foundations like the International Committee of the Red Cross (1863) or the Universal Postal Union (1874) sound less particular to us and they brought about a change in the making and the implementation of decisions.[64] Particularly administrative unions were armed with permanent institutions (*bureaux*),[65] limited possibilities of autonomy including

---

[59] E Francke 'Der internationale Arbeiterschutz' (1904) 10 Jahrbuch der Gehe-Stiftung 35–70.

[60] LA Zapatero 'Vom Kampf gegen die Sklaverei und den Mädchenhandel hin zum Verbot des Menschenhandels' in F von Herzog and U Neumann (eds) *Festschrift für Wilfried Hassemer* (CF Müller Heidelberg 2010) 929–44.

[61] V Ritter-Döring *Zwischen Normierung und Rüstungswettlauf. Die Entwicklung des Seekriegsrechts, 1856–1914* (Nomos Baden-Baden 2012).

[62] M Vec 'Das Prinzip der Verkehrsfreiheit im Völkerrecht' (2008) 30 Zeitschrift für Neuere Rechtsgeschichte 221–41.

[63] B Reinalda *Routledge History of International Organizations* (Routledge London 2009) 3 ff.

[64] CA Riches *Majority Rule in International Organization* (Johns Hopkins Press Baltimore 1940).

[65] G Moynier *Les bureaux internationaux des Unions universelles* (Cherbuliez Genève 1892).

jurisdiction,[66] and even the exercise of coercion. They were the forerunners of modern international organizations, the first of which was the International Telecommunication Union, established in 1865.[67] The Central Commission for the Navigation of the Rhine was established earlier. Also, the Pan-American Conferences founded the International Union of American Republics and agreed in the course of their attempts for regional integration in 1890 on the establishment of an office representing the Union.[68]

Thus, the second conclusion to be drawn is that 19th-century international law led to some institutionalization. There obviously was a kind of international organization before the 'age of international organization' (seen through the eyes of political scientists), yet the foundational change was according to Wolfgang Friedmann,[69] the shift from international law of coexistence to international law of cooperation.

This extended cooperation in state practice went hand in hand with a paradigm shift in international legal theory. Many mid-19th-century authors criticized their forerunners and colleagues for following ideas which no longer suited the current state of international relations. They argued that international legal theory should leave the paradigms of coexistence and sovereignty as major principles. Instead, they should acknowledge the transformation of international relations which had underwent a change to higher cooperation. Thus, the international community should be the new and decisive principle of the discipline. This idea was promoted by Carl von Kaltenborn, Robert von Mohl, Lorenz von Stein, and Fedor Martens,[70] whereas others dismissed it and its related constructions as not sufficiently juridical.[71] Around 1900, the idea of the international community had already been regarded as an epoch in the history of international law. Nevertheless it had revivals in the 20th-century legal and sociological doctrine,[72] and it succeeded in being established as a weighty counterpart to sovereignty with which it has to be balanced in every single case.

---

[66] S Kneisel *Schiedsgerichtsbarkeit in Internationalen Verwaltungsunionen (1874–1914)* (Nomos Baden-Baden 2009).

[67] M Herren *Internationale Organisationen seit 1865* (Wissenschaftliche Buchgesellschaft Darmstadt 2009).

[68] C Graf Fugger Kirchberg-Weißenhorn *Der Panamerikanismus und das amerikanische Völkerrecht* (GJ Manz München 1931) at 4; R Büchi *Die Geschichte der panamerikanischen Bewegung* (JU Kern Breslau 1914) at 44.

[69] W Friedmann *The Changing Structure of International Law* (Stevens & Sons London 1964) at 60–3.

[70] C Baron von Kaltenborn von Stachau *Kritik des Völkerrechts* (Gustav Mayer Leipzig 1847); R von Mohl 'Die Pflege der internationalen Gemeinschaft als Aufgabe des Völkerrechts' in R von Mohl (ed) *Staatsrecht, Völkerrecht und Politik* (Laupp Tübingen 1860) vol 1, 579–635; W Załęski *Zur Geschichte und Lehre der internationalen Gemeinschaft* (Laakmann Dorpat 1866); L von Stein 'Einige Bemerkungen über das internationale Verwaltungsrecht' (1882) 6 Schmollers Jahrbuch 395–442; F von Martens *Völkerrecht* (C Bergbohm ed) (Weidmann Berlin 1883 and 1886).

[71] P Heilborn *Das System des Völkerrechts* (J Springer Berlin 1896) at 397.

[72] AL Paulus *Die internationale Gemeinschaft im Völkerrecht* (CH Beck München 2001).

3. POSITIVISTIC UNIVERSALIZATION OF INTERNATIONAL LAW?

However, the often-told story of international law claims more than such a mere expansion of fields of regulation. First, the story supposes a positivistic turn and secondly, a globalization of international law.

3.1. Sources: Treaties, Codification, and International Legislation

Nineteenth-century international law acknowledged a variety of sources of international law, but a formal or official definition comparable to article 38 of the ICJ statute did not exist. Contemporary jurist's classical doctrines listed the following sources: treaties, protocols, and declarations of the great powers, national laws and statutes, jurisdiction of international courts, writings of law teachers and international customary law.[73] Thus, a 'plurality of equivalent sources' with no clear hierarchy was involved in the law-making process which produced a horizontally and vertically pluralistic international order.[74]

In these sources, taken from a leading encyclopaedia of 1870, natural law had already been excluded or had at least been made 'invisible' (as natural law may be regarded to have survived as part of the quoted 'writings of the law teachers'). This separation was a long and complicated process that did not proceed in all discourses at the same speed. Nevertheless, with regard to its sources and methods, the discipline of positivistic jurisprudence was founded after 1800.[75]

At least in Italy and France, the academic culture of jurisprudence promoted the study of international law in the context of natural law until the mid-19th century.[76] Some authors even identified international law with international morality.[77] The

---

[73] AF Berner 'Völkerrecht' in JC Bluntschli and K Brater (eds) *Deutsches Staats-Wörterbuch* (Expedition des Staats-Wörterbuchs Stuttgart 1870) vol XI, 76–96 at 94–6.

[74] S Besson 'Theorizing the Sources of International Law' in S Besson and J Tasioulas (eds) *The Philosophy of International Law* (OUP Oxford 2010) 163–85 at 164.

[75] J Schröder *Recht als Wissenschaft* (CH Beck München 2001) at 189ff.

[76] The titles for France include G de Rayneval *Institutions du droit de la nature et des gens* (Leblanc Paris 1803); CLS Michel *Considérations nouvelles sur le droit en général* (Delaunay Paris 1813); LB Cotelle *Droit de la Nature et des Gens* (Gobelet Paris 1820); for Italy eg P Baroli *Diritto Naturale Privato E Publico. Volumes V–VI: Diritto Naturale Pubblico Esterno* (Feraboli Cremona 1837).

[77] G Atkinson *International Morality; or, the Touchstone of the Law of Nations* (G Woodfall and Son London 1851); PD Pontsevrez *Cours élémentaire de morale* (Hachette Paris 1886) at 120: 'La morale internationale ou droit des gens'.

frequent reprints or new editions of Vattel and Burlamaqui until the 1860s[78] also demonstrate a vivid interest in natural law doctrine.

However, international legal doctrine developed differently in England. In the early 19th century, the state of legal education was rather poor there and international law was 'essentially directed by practical men'.[79]

Only after 1870 did an 'autonomous' study of international law begin in these nations. Other late 19th-century international legal authors placed explicit natural law ideas in their writing by referring to 'the social' idea or certain values; jurisprudence was thus made ethical in some way. Therefore, it is hard to make a clear distinction between legal positivism and natural law thinking in 19th-century international law;[80] it seems 'that there is no clear distinction to be discerned'.[81] Other exclusions from international law (doctrine) had also left their traces. Since the late Enlightenment, international lawyers had emphasized[82] that international law should clearly be distinguished from international morality[83] or international diplomacy,[84] thus they formalized the discipline. Yet at the same time they refuted the arguments of the so-called deniers of international law. This took largely place in the theory of sources of international law and in their exclusion of legitimate arguments. The 'deniers' claimed that the true and only source of inter-state regulation could be found in the internal legal order of States and therefore they did not accept the idea that an autonomous sphere of international law existed. This position was proclaimed by jurists like Gustav Hugo,[85] Georg Friedrich Puchta,[86] Georg

---

[78] For two late editions, see JJ Burlamaqui *The Principles of Natural and Politic Law* (J Nourse London 1763, 7th edn JH Riley & Co Columbus Ohio 1859); E de Vattel *Le droit des gens ou principes de la loi naturelle* (Aillaud Paris 1863).

[79] C Sylvest 'The Foundations of Victorian International Law' in D Bell (ed) *Victorian Visions of Global Order* (CUP Cambridge 2007) 47–66 at 50; M Lobban 'English Approaches to International Law in the Nineteenth Century' in MCR Craven, M Fitzmaurice and M Vogiantzi (eds) *Time, History and International Law* (Martinus Nijhoff Leiden 2007) 65–90.

[80] See the paradigmatic case study on Bulmerincq by L Mälksoo 'The Context of International Legal Arguments' (2005) 7 Journal of the History of International Law 181–209 at 208.

[81] C Sylvest 'International Law in Nineteenth-Century Britain' (2004) 75 British Year Book of International Law 9–70 at 12.

[82] DHL von Ompteda *Literatur des gesamten sowohl natürlichen als positiven Völkerrechts. Erster Theil* (Montag Regensburg 1785) at 6.

[83] GF Martens *Einleitung in das positive Europäische Völkerrecht* (Dieterich Göttingen 1796) at ix and 2; C Welcker 'Encyklopädische Uebersicht der Staatswissenschaften' in C von Rotteck and C Welcker (eds) *Staats-Lexikon* (Hammerich Altona 1834) vol 1, 1–42 at 39; AW Heffter *Das Europäische Völkerrecht der Gegenwart* (2nd edn Schroeder Berlin 1848) at iv; LA Warnkönig *Juristische Encyclopädie* (Enke Erlangen 1853) at 557.

[84] Cf F von Liszt *Das Völkerrecht* (5th edn Haering Berlin 1907, 12th edn M Fleischmann ed Springer Berlin 1925) at 117 ('internationale Courtoisie' versus 'international law').

[85] G Hugo *Lehrbuch eines civilistischen Cursus* (8th edn August Mylius Berlin 1835) vol 1, at 73.

[86] GF Puchta *Das Gewohnheitsrecht, Erster Theil* (Palm Erlangen 1828) at 142 'man sollte von einer Völker- oder Staatenmoral, aber nicht von einem Völkerrecht sprechen'.

Wilhelm Friedrich Hegel,[87] John Austin,[88] George Cornewall Lewis,[89] Adolf Lasson,[90] and Philipp Zorn.[91] Consequently, some of them such as Hegel and Zorn preferred to use terms like *Außenstaatsrecht* (external public law; *droit public externe; diritto pubblico esterno*) instead of 'international law'.

However, the renunciation and separation of international law from natural law doctrine had immediate consequences for the legal sources. Nineteenth-century doctrine avoided evocations of 'natural law' as a legitimate source but it held still valid that 'reason', 'law of reason', 'justice', or 'the nature of things' could work as legal sources or at least as legitimate arguments when discussing the existence of a rule or principle in international law. Thus, the expulsion and extermination of natural law mainly took place in terminology whereas functional equivalents enabled natural law to subsist on a somehow subterranean level.

Nevertheless, with regard to sources both theory and practice started to focus more on empirically observable references in inter-state behaviour like treaties and customary law. The self-understanding of international law reflected this shift in so far as the geographical space and European history gained more weight than in natural law doctrine which constructed its arguments in a universalistic manner. International law was understood as a universal set of norms which was of European origin; the first contributions to the history of international law[92] in the 19th century strongly supported this point. Thus the denomination of the scope of international law changed systematically according to some formula that displayed these historical and geographical references: *droit des gens européen* indicated a culturally founded self-understanding with reference to the continent of its origin[93] to which others explicitly added civilization and Christendom, claiming that their subject could also be named 'Christian law of nations' (*christliches Völkerrecht*).[94] Europe with its customs and political and cultural relations were at the theoretical centre of the emergence of international law.

---

[87] GFW Hegel *Grundlinien der Philosophie des Rechts* (Nicolaische Buchhandlung Berlin 1821) para 330 and addition 191.

[88] J Austin *The Province of Jurisprudence Determined* (Murray London 1832) at 147 ('*law of nations* or *international law*' is 'a law improperly so called').

[89] GC Lewis *A Treatise on the Methods of Observation and Reasoning in Politics* (Parker London 1852) vol 1, at 44 ('international law is not law in the strict sense').

[90] A Lasson *Princip und Zukunft des Völkerrechts* (Hertz Berlin 1871) at 22.

[91] Cf J Schmidt *Konservative Staatsrechtslehre und Friedenspolitik. Leben und Werk Philipp Zorns* (Aktiv Druck und Verlag Ebelsbach 2001).

[92] R Lesaffer 'International Law and its History: The Story of an Unrequited Love' in *Time, History and International Law* (n 79) 27–41.

[93] KH Lingens 'Europa in der Lehre des "praktischen Völkerrechts"' in I Dingel and M Schnettger (eds) *Auf dem Weg nach Europa* (Vandenhoeck & Ruprecht Göttingen 2010) 173–86.

[94] L Freiherr von Neumann *Grundriss des heutigen europäischen Völkerrechtes* (1st edn Kaiserlich-königliche Hof- und Staatsdruckerei Vienna 1856, 2nd edn W Braumüller Vienna 1877, 3rd edn W Braumüller Vienna 1885).

It is quite clear that international law's expansion and development—or as Isambert, Wheaton, Bluntschli, Pierantoni, Calvo, and others put it prominently in their titles—'progress'[95] had to be founded on treaties; customary law was not an adequate instrument for the emergence of new principles and rules that were needed under this historical-teleological premise. Treaties had to master the regulatory challenge, and many more than ever before were concluded.[96] The number of international agreements grew dramatically. State practice of the earlier centuries which had been only occupied with war and peace seemed poor in comparison. New and extended treaty collections appeared.[97] Fedor Fedorovitch Martens enthusiastically proclaimed a new epoch, the era of 'social-commercial treaties', had begun.[98] Thus good reasons support the claim of the existence of a 'Treaty-Making Revolution of the Nineteenth Century'.[99]

Not only did the frequency, density, and topics of international agreements increase, but the doctrine of treaties also changed. Multipartite (multilateral) open regulatory treaties had been invented as new regulatory model. As legislation in the proper sense was impossible in the 19th century and codification in international law seemed unlikely, these *traités-lois* could serve as a substitute. Famous long-lasting treaties like the one on the Universal Postal Union were concluded. Contemporary jurists praised this model as the beginning of an 'international legislation'[100] or as the beginning of a 'world law'.[101]

In contrast, 'real legislation' was much harder to achieve and it failed in most attempts. Major attempts were made by private individuals, including Francis Lieber (*Instructions for the Government of Armies of the United States in the Field*, 1883), Alphonse de Domin-Petrushevecz (*Précis d'un code du droit international*, 1861), Johann Caspar Bluntschli (*Das moderne Völkerrecht der civilisirten Staaten als Rechtsbuch dargestellt*,

---

[95] FA Isambert *Tableau des progrès du droit public et du droit des gens* (Paulin Paris 1823); H Wheaton *Histoire des progrès du droit des gens en Europe et en Amérique* (3rd edn Brockhaus Leipzig 1853); JC Bluntschli *Die Bedeutung und die Fortschritte des modernen Völkerrechts* (CG Lüderitz Berlin 1866); A Pierantoni *Il progresso del diritto pubblico e delle genti* (Nicola Zanichelli Modena 1866); C Calvo *Le droit international théorique et pratique précédé d'un exposé historique des progrès de la science du droit des gens* (4 vols 3rd edn Guillaumin Paris 1880–81); S Brie *Die Fortschritte des Völkerrechts seit dem Wiener Congress* (Schletter Breslau 1890); Sir HE Richards *The Progress of International Law and Arbitration* (Clarendon Press Oxford 1911).

[96] M Lachs 'Le développement et les fonctions des traités multilatéraux' (1957) 92 Recueil des cours 226–333 at 233; A Nussbaum *A Concise History of the Law of Nations* (revised edn Macmillan New York 1961) 196–200.

[97] P Macalister-Smith and J Schwietzke 'Literature and Documentary Sources relating to the History of Public International Law' (1999) 1 Journal of the History of International Law 136–212.

[98] *Völkerrecht* (n 70).

[99] E Keene 'The Treaty-Making Revolution of the Nineteenth Century' (2012) 34 International History Review (forthcoming, copy with author).

[100] AS Hershey *The Essentials of International Public Law* (Macmillan New York 1914) at 21; JB Moore 'International Law: Its Present and Future' (1907) 1 American Journal of International Law 11–12 at 12; WG Miller *Lectures on the Philosophy of Law* (C Griffin & co London 1884) at 88.

[101] RL Bridgman *The First Book of World Law* (Ginn Boston 1911).

1868). They were the forerunners of further attempts at codification which were carried out by international institutions, governments, and finally the international community itself, particularly at the Hague Peace Conferences. At these conferences, delegates supported massive attempts to formulate binding agreements on disarmament, peaceful adjustment of international differences, and on the laws and customs of war on land and the regulations annexed thereto. Although the parties failed to find an agreement on reducing and limiting armaments, the procedure and outcome was remarkable—the development of humanitarian principles and peaceful settlement of disputes were prominently set on the agenda of a global community of States.

3.2. Which Positivism? Which Universalism?

In that sense, international laws basis became broader; many new and extended treaties gave a positivistic turn to the factual regulation of international relations. Some of the multipartite treaties were nearly global.

Did this process constitute the development of positivism and universalization? Furthermore, is this development sufficient to label the epoch by using these terms?

The optimistic mood and the progressive narratives among 19th-century international lawyers should not withdraw our attention from the fact that most of the quoted regulations were quite specific in their subject and their objective. Particularly, regarding the issue of positivism, there was little universalism in subject or scope. The Convention on the grape phylloxera of 1882 (vine fretter) is an illustration of that fact.

3.3. Natural Law Lessons

As to the general rules of international relations, where did they come from? Of course, already in the 19th century, international lawyers knew general principles and concepts which could help to conceptualize conflicts and interests.[102] In the 18th century these rules and meta-rules stemmed from moral philosophy and particularly from natural law. This constellation did not really change during the 19th century. Although natural law was abolished terminologically and substituted by legal philosophy and subsequently by legal theory, I find it hard to claim a consequent positivistic turn in the academic field. The new discipline of the theory of international law did indeed refrain from the term 'natural law'. Yet non-positivistic concepts were still held to be the foundation of international law; sometimes they were derived as sub-

---

[102] M Vec 'Rechtsprinzipien in der Völkerrechtswissenschaft des 19. Jahrhunderts' in R Lieberwirth and H Lück (eds) *Akten des 36. Deutschen Rechtshistorikertages* (Nomos Baden-Baden 2008) 445–63.

sidiaries from Roman law, sometimes from private law. However, most authors like Heffter[103] or Wheaton still referred freely to the axioms of learned German *ius publicum universale*; they refreshed the easier accessible European enlightenment writings of Burlamaqui, Vattel, and Wolff, who were Grotius' successors. A field where this fact is borne out was the so-called fundamental rights and duties of States.[104] Thus one needs to consider to what extent universalization and positivism mutually excluded each other in 19th-century international law.

4. JURIDIFICATION

It is considered more correct to speak of a juridification of international relations which occurred in 19th century without any precedence. International law's expansion into new subjects and the emergence of new regulatory regimes have already been mentioned.

4.1. Disciplinary Shifts

This process went hand in hand with disciplinary shifts. Jurists excluded other disciplines in the construction of international law and international order. They gained, for example, a monopoly on the definition of peace. International law obtained importance with the new tasks; its voice became stronger; and it strove for autonomy with respect to other legal and non-legal disciplines.

4.2. Proximity and Distance to Politics

At the same time, international law sought both proximity to and distance from politics. Proximity meant that counselling should be useful for the defence of States' rights, for power politics, and various other objectives. Simultaneously, distance was emphasized to underline the autonomy of the legal and academic viewpoint.

---

[103] IJ Hueck 'Pragmatism, Positivism and Hegelianism in the Nineteenth Century' in M Stolleis and M Yanagihara (eds) *East Asian and European Perspectives on International Law* (Nomos Baden-Baden 2004) 41–55.

[104] M Vec 'Grundrechte der Staaten. Die Tradierung des Natur- und Völkerrechts der Aufklärung' (2011) 18 Rechtsgeschichte 66–94.

International law should be something different from the affirmation of inter-state practice. It claimed to be a distinct justification narrative (*Rechtfertigungsnarrativ*)[105] that implied the possibility of critique through selective, fragmented construction of justification. International lawyers thus tried to draw a sharp distinction between international law and political science.[106]

4.3. Flexible Legal Doctrines

Constructions like 'sovereignty' were part of larger juridical systems; they had to be consistent according to the methodological standards of the discipline. Thus, these discourses on key concepts and general principles of international law served to guarantee the coherence of the discipline.

Yet at first glance the constructions and the key concepts often sounded clearer than they really were. Theory was often very flexible and it voluntarily left space for interpretations and exceptions.[107] Classical international legal doctrine created procedural law 'instead of proposing material rules'.[108] Furthermore, the implementation of norms served both as a challenge to and the possibility of adopting standards like 'equality' to the needs of so-called real international life with its hegemonic structures. In 'real international life' the claim of pre-eminence obviously had a long juridical and political tradition which let this effort seem legitimate. Thus key concepts and general principles of international law contributed not only to the coherence but also 'to complementing international law and *filling its gaps*'.[109]

4.4. International Judiciary and Arbitration

This juridification went along with an 'enthusiasm for the international judiciary and for arbitration'.[110] Contemporaries understood the successful dispute settlement between Britain and the United States in the Alabama case in 1872 as a highlight

---

[105] 'Die Herausbildung normativer Ordnungen' (n 3) 10.

[106] *Literatur des gesamten sowohl natürlichen als positiven Völkerrechts* (n 82) para 2, at 6.

[107] L Benton 'From International Law to Imperial Constitutions: The Problem of Quasi-Sovereignty, 1870–1900' (2008) 26 Law and History Review 595–619.

[108] *From Apology to Utopia* (n 39) 155.

[109] S Besson 'General Principles in International Law—Whose Principles?' in S Besson and P Pichonnaz (eds) *Les principes en droit européen—Principles in European Law* (Schulthess Zürich 2011) 21–68 at 49 (original emphasis).

[110] D Kennedy 'International Law and the Nineteenth Century: History of an Illusion' (1996) 65 Nordic Journal International Law 385–420 at 415.

of international arbitration. The essential use of international arbitration is said to have been reborn with the Jay Treaty in 1794. This is, however, a historically rather questionable perception.[111] Yet the Alabama case initiated high expectations for the instrument of international dispute settlement which were shared both by lawyers and public opinion and which intensified around 1900 when the Hague Peace Conferences appeared as the culminating point in a cultural development where political realism and pacifist hopes met. International law became increasingly ethically focused in these years. Instead of the very formal and technical perspective of its classical early 19th-century masterminds like Martens or Klüber, the interest in incorporating moral rules and values grew remarkably around the turn to the 20th century.

4.5. Leeway for Non-juridification

Yet there were also areas where international law was hardly admitted as a regulatory instrument like the regulation of state debts[112] or the consequent interdiction of force. The question of avoidance of law would be an interesting topic to research.

Hence, juridification of international relations had many limits. It is thus necessary to distinguish carefully between different regulatory regimes; any generalizations on the interrelation of law and politics in the 19th century can only be overly fussy. Consular jurisdiction[113] or mixed tribunals and colonial international law[114] showed clearly how juridical systems could be used for political ends and how they altered political orders. In the colonial context, acquisition and possession of land were justified by conferences, treaties (Berlin 1884–85), and legal doctrines ('terra nullius'; *occupatio*) that combined the belief in correct juridical procedures with political interests for territorial rights abroad. Political power was not only disciplined by international law but the latter was also used widely for politics' interests which thus shaped laws' language and axioms.[115]

---

[111] K-H Lingens 'Der Jay-Vertrag (1794) als Geburtsstunde der modernen internationalen Schiedsgerichtsbarkeit?' in *Les conflits entre peuples* (n 34) 65–82.

[112] L Heimbeck 'Das Gleichgewicht wahren' *Frankfurter Allgemeine Zeitung* (Frankfurt Germany 29 December 2011) 8.

[113] J Berchtold *Recht und Gerechtigkeit in der Konsulargerichtsbarkeit. Britische Exterritorialität im osmanischen Reich 1825–1914* (Oldenbourg München 2009); J Ulbert and L Pijac (eds) *Consuls et services consulaires au XIXe siècle* (DOBU Hamburg 2010).

[114] L Nuzzo 'Kolonialrecht' (2011) European History Online (EGO) <http://www.ieg-ego.eu/nuzzol-2011-de> (15 February 2012); L Nuzzo *Origini di una Scienza. Diritto internazionale e colonialismo nel XIX secolo* (Klostermann Frankfurt 2012); L Nuzzo 'A Dark Side of the Western Legal Modernity: The Colonial Law and Its Subject' (2011) 33 Zeitschrift für neuere Rechtsgeschichte 205–22.

[115] A Anghie *Imperialism, Sovereignty and the Making of International Law* (CUP Cambridge 2005).

5. THE RISE OF SCIENCE AND PROFESSIONALIZATION

The doctrine of international law expanded enormously in the 19th century. I have not described this expansion in any detail as it would take too much space to do it justice. One should consider the development regarding textbooks,[116] treaty collections, journals (Revue de droit international et de législation comparée, 1869; Revue générale de droit international public, 1894),[117] the increase of teaching of international law, the foundation of chairs and institutes at universities and international academic institutions (Institut de Droit international and Association for the Reform and Codification of International Law, later International Law Association, both founded in 1873).[118] A growing European-American community of international lawyers was happy about this development and their institutionalized ambition was 'de devenir l'organe de la conscience juridique du monde civilisé'.[119] This reference to a plurality of political entities did not preclude loyalty to particular European States and their interests.

On the one hand, leading lawyers from overseas like Andres Bello, Henry Wheaton, and Carlos Calvo promoted European legal doctrine. Thus, they took an active part in the globalization and globalization of international law.[120] On the other hand, they converted these standards in favour of their particular political interests, like the promotion of Latin American independency or rather the construction of regional international law in the case of Alejandro Alvarez. The history of international law as a research subject was born; the myth of its birth in 1648 was further manifested in various disciplines.[121]

Yet at the same time jurists still excluded some areas from public international law. Around the turn of the century they claimed that international private law and

---

[116] 'Literature and Documentary Sources' (n 97); P Macalister-Smith and J Schwietzke 'Bibliography of the Textbooks and Comprehensive Treatises on Positive International Law of the 19th Century' (2001) 3 Journal of the History of International Law 75–142.

[117] IJ Hueck 'Die Gründung völkerrechtlicher Zeitschriften in Deutschland im internationalen Vergleich' in M Stolleis (ed) *Juristische Zeitschriften* (Klostermann Frankfurt 1999) 379–420.

[118] G Rolin-Jaequemyns 'De la nécessité d'organiser une institution scientifique permanente pour favoriser l'étude et le progrès du droit international' (1873) 5 Revue de droit international et de législation comparée 463–91; AH Fried 'Organisiert die Welt!' (1906) 8 Die Friedens-Warte 1–3.

[119] art 1 of the *Institute de Droit International's* 1873 Statute.

[120] A Becker Lorca 'Universal International Law: Nineteenth-Century Histories of Imposition and Appropriation' (2010) 51 Harvard International Law Journal 475–552; S Kroll Normgenese *durch Re-Interpretation—China und das europäische Völkerrecht im 19. und 20. Jahrhundert* (Nomos Baden-Baden 2012); UM Zachmann *Krieg und Ordnungsdenken im völkerrechtlichen Diskurs Japans 1919–60* (Nomos Baden-Baden 2012).

[121] A Osiander 'Sovereignty, International Relations, and the Westphalian Myth' (2011) 55 International Organization 251–87 at 265.

international criminal law were no longer a part of the discipline. Their perspective was historical, practical, and positivistic. This self-perception was thus true insofar as lawyers referred to European history and rejected utopian ideas. Eternal peace and *civitas maxima* were no popular visions for a regular international lawyer. Nevertheless, values and political ideas still played a role in their writings. 'International morality', *moralité internationale* was sometimes even used as synonym for international law.[122] Today, many of these ideas do not come across very sympathetic from a political point of view. Whereas some protagonists might be labelled as liberal internationalists,[123] this hardly works with others. Furthermore, whereas some authors followed a very technical concept of international law, others devote their legal systems emphatically to ideas like 'international community'—these trends also changed over time. Yet these concepts often meant nothing but Christendom, culture, and civilization, with negative connotations for each.[124] The use of force was seen as legitimate instrument to distribute these aims universally; the terra nullius doctrine constituted an option for expansion.

As the First World War began, many international lawyers were nationalist supporters of their respective countries. Violations of norms were justified, enemies were slandered. International law discourse was intensified through the needs and wishes of the situation. Hence, international cooperation was terminated with some countries while simultaneously intensified with others.

The Paris treaties constructed a very different order than the one which had been designed in Vienna; the old order was dismissed and new principles like self-determination[125] offered a chance of bringing 'just peace' to all peoples and of distributing the burden of war to the culprits.

The set of rules and norms called international law gained more density, coherence, and relevance in the 19th century. However, a single treaty that could serve or be interpreted as a European constitution did not exist. Treaties and academic writing took up many tasks and tried to resolve them in the framework of the political,

---

[122] G Atkinson *International Morality; or, the Touchstone of the Law of Nations* (G Woodfall and Son London 1851); PD Pontsevrez *Cours élémentaire de morale* (Hachette Paris 1886) at 120 ('La morale internationale ou droit des gens').

[123] M Koskenniemi *The Gentle Civilizer of Nations* (CUP Cambridge 2001) at 4.

[124] E Keene *Beyond the Anarchical Society: Grotius, Colonialism and Order in World Politics* (CUP Cambridge 2002) at 109–19; G Gozzi *Diritti e civiltà. Storia e filosofia del diritto internazionale* (Il Mulino Bologna 2010) at 133–66; GW Gong *The Standard of 'Civilization' in International Society* (Clarendon Press Oxford 1984); B Bowden *The Empire of Civilization: The Evolution of an Imperial Idea* (University of Chicago Press Chicago 2009); J Osterhammel '"The Great Work of Uplifting Mankind": Zivilisierungsmission und Moderne' in J Osterhammel and Boris Barth (eds) *Zivilisierungsmissionen* (UVK Konstanz 2005) 363–425.

[125] J Fisch *Das Selbstbestimmungsrecht der Völker* (CH Beck München 2010); J Fisch (ed) *Die Verteilung der Welt. Selbstbestimmung und das Selbstbestimmungsrecht der Völker. The World Divided: Self-Determination and the Right of Peoples to Self-Determination* (Oldenbourg München 2011); L Palleit *Völkerrecht und Selbstbestimmung. Zum Begriff des Selbstbestimmungsrechts der Völker in der deutschen und österreichischen Völkerrechtswissenschaft 1918–33* (Nomos Baden-Baden 2008).

social, and economic surroundings. Many inter-state regulations looked very specific; the growth of positive treaty law did not take place in all fields with identical speed. Nevertheless, some general rules and principles were identified by international lawyers and the political actors. These general rules can be understood as foundations, elements, and forerunners of a global legal constitution, a constitutionalization of international law *avant la lettre*. Yet, the leading idea which was promoted was not necessarily the rule of law. Around 1900 lawyers primarily aimed at 'organization'.[126] International law and international order was to bring to a higher degree of integration through 'organization' which was understood as the genesis of new rules and institutions in various fields.[127] In particularly, international administration was an area where wishes for more intensive state cooperation ('internationalism') met with contemporary political realities.[128] Thus the new field of international administrative law, promoted by von Stein,[129] Martens and others, received a high degree of acceptance or even enthusiasm by other international lawyers. Its assumption also embraced the hope that this form of pragmatic internationalism would help to promote peaceful cooperation and prevent war. This was one of 19th-century international lawyer's illusions[130] as the outbreak of the First World War showed. At least, many of the cooperative endeavours endured wartime and were transformed into the legal and political system of the League of Nations in the inter-war period.

6. Conclusion

Europe was a political and legal community with much ambivalence, many tensions, and a lot of common interests during the 19th century. This statement sounds trivial but it illustrates how hard it is to combine internationalism, imperialism, and law in the period of the so-called first globalization. International law and its makers contributed a lion's share to this process. On the one hand law expanded and favoured a juridification of international relations; yet simultaneously some doctrines discriminated particular actors structurally.

---

[126] P Kazansky 'Les premiers éléments de l'organisation universelle' (1897) 29 Revue de droit international et de législation comparée 238–47; E Duplessix *L'Organisation Internationale* (Larose & Forcel Paris 1909); W Schücking *Die Organisation der Welt* (Kröner Leipzig 1909).

[127] PS Reinsch *Public International Unions* (Ginn and Co Boston and London 1911).

[128] J Claveirole *L'Internationalisme et l'Organisation Internationale Administrative* (Waton Saint-Étienne 1910).

[129] 'Einige Bemerkungen' (n 70).

[130] 'International Law and the Nineteenth Century' (n 110) 385–420.

Telling this story, one has to be aware of the specifics of this normative order. Compared to other fields of law, institutions in international law seemed weak, conflict resolution through courts poor, and legislation a joke. However, legal history has to refrain from traditional 19th-century state-centred categories and it should be pointed out the irritating legal and normative pluralism which can be found in international relations in all epochs, and which I would call 'multinormativity' (*Multinormativität*[131]).

In our days, the nation-state and its statutory law are no longer at the centre of legal theory; modern legal theory encourages instead a fragmented system of national, international, and private norms.[132] Legal history can contribute to the awareness that the self-perception of 19th-century international lawyers is not always accurate. The assumption of a general process of positivism cannot be maintained. Progress and peace were ideologies and normative expansion and juridification of international relations were complex movements which crept towards our modernity.

RECOMMENDED READING

Anghie, Anthony *Imperialism, Sovereignty and the Making of International Law* (CUP Cambridge 2005).

Dülffer, Jost *Regeln gegen den Krieg? Die Haager Friedenskonferenzen von 1899 und 1907 in der internationalen Politik* (Ullstein Frankfurt am Main 1978).

Dülffer, Jost, Martin Kröger, and Rolf-Harald Wippich *Vermiedene Kriege: Deeskalation von Konflikten der Großmächte zwischen Krimkrieg und Erstem Weltkrieg* (Oldenbourg München 1997).

Fisch, Jörg *Die europäische Expansion und das Völkerrecht: Die Auseinandersetzungen um den Status der überseeischen Gebiete vom 15. Jahrhundert bis zur Gegenwart* (Steiner Stuttgart 1984).

Kennedy, David 'International Law and the Nineteenth Century: History of an Illusion' (1996) 65 Nordic Journal International Law 385–420.

Koskenniemi, Martti *The Gentle Civilizer of Nations: The Rise and Fall of International Law 1870–1960* (CUP Cambridge 2001).

Koskenniemi, Martti *From Apology to Utopia: The Structure of International Legal Argument. Reissue with New Epilogue* (CUP Cambridge 2009).

Schroeder, Paul W *The Transformation of European Politics 1763–1848* (Clarendon Press Oxford 1994).

Schulz, Matthias *Normen und Praxis. Das Europäische Konzert der Großmächte als Sicherheitsrat, 1815–60* (Oldenbourg München 2009).

---

[131] M Vec 'Multinormativität in der Rechtsgeschichte' (2008) 16 Jahrbuch der Berlin-Brandenburgischen Akademie der Wissenschaften 155–66.

[132] U Sieber 'Rechtliche Ordnung in einer globalen Welt. Die Entwicklung zu einem fragmentierten System von nationalen, internationalen und privaten Normen' (2010) 41 Rechtstheorie 151–98.

Steiger, Heinhard *Von der Staatengesellschaft zur Weltrepublik? Aufsätze zur Geschichte des Völkerrechts aus vierzig Jahren* (Nomos Baden-Baden 2009).

Vec, Miloš *Recht und Normierung in der Industriellen Revolution. Neue Strukturen der Normsetzung in Völkerrecht, staatlicher Gesetzgebung und gesellschaftlicher Selbstnormierung* (Klostermann Frankfurt am Main 2006).

Weitz, Eric D 'From the Vienna to the Paris System: International Politics and the Entangled Histories of Human Rights, Forced Deportations, and Civilizing Missions' (2008) 113 American Historical Review 1313–43.

CHAPTER 28

FROM THE PARIS PEACE TREATIES TO THE END OF THE SECOND WORLD WAR

PETER KRÜGER

1. INTRODUCTION

THE end of the First First World War in 1918–19 was an epochal event with far-reaching consequences. It revealed like few other occasions in modern history the terrible extent of new difficulties and exposed past failures to establish an international order capable of securing peace. Moreover, it sped up the process of modernization all over the world. One of the momentous results was a rapidly growing international interdependence fostered by technical progress and by a considerable scarcity of raw materials and food. This development caused an extraordinary extension of governmental tasks, machinery, and power, and created a huge task for international law, difficult to assess in its dimensions and not to be solved without the sustained support by all the governments involved. What was needed was a framework for effective international cooperation within which measures could be designed to secure peace and to facilitate transnational or international initiatives to improve political, economic, social, and cultural cooperation. The interaction between foreign and domestic policy became much closer, and the willingness to effect internal structural change, in particular by the defeated States, became ever more urgent when dealing with problems of war and peace. Resistance to such modernizing change became one of the most serious problems because protests against it were directed increasingly against international interdependence which was seen as a threat to national and cultural autonomy, and in some cases even to racial identity. These protests, however, were intermixed with justified resistance to modern impulses towards an isolation of human beings and a standardization of their biographies. Thus, international law and politics were confronted with a new task; namely, to make the aspirations of the people a guideline for legal activities by acknowledging as fundamental values not only human dignity, freedom, and self-determination but also cultural diversity. The feeling of insecurity, in particular among the people of the States defeated in 1918, was largely caused by the sudden end of the war and the abrupt change from expected victory to defeat. The military debacle aggravated a deep and far-reaching general crisis of the State and its constitution, a crisis which in Germany was intensified by the revolution of November 1918. What happened in and to Germany, also with regard to international law, had repercussions worldwide.

2. Concluding Peace

On 3 October 1918 the German Government asked President Wilson to establish peace on the basis of his 'Fourteen Points' of 8 January 1918 and later pronouncements.[1] With this clever move, the Germans gave Wilson an important advantage to realize his ambitious peace programme, which implied a substantial progress of international law, above all by establishing the first universal organization of States, the League of Nations. Wilson increased the pressure on the German Government by emphasizing that democratization of Germany and the establishment of a democratically elected German parliament were essential conditions for peace and constituent parts of a modern international order. This nexus gained increasing importance for the development of international law in the years to come, and intensified the connection between foreign and domestic policy. In order to prevent economic disaster and to reorganize fiscal and economic relations, closer contacts between banking and commerce, desired by both, were indispensable and proved

---

[1] W Wilson 'Wilson's Address to Congress, Stating the War Aims and Peace Terms of the United States (Delivered in Joint Session, 8 January 1918)' in A Shaw (ed) *State Papers and Adresses by Woodrow Wilson* (George H Doran Company New York 1918) 464–72.

effective in the development of the credit system as well as for reaching an under-standing concerning relatively liberal economic principles. The 'most favoured nation' clause was on the march.

After the armistice (11 November 1918), the Paris Peace Conference started on 18 January 1919 as a kind of pre-conference. The British delegation represented the Commonwealth as a whole, but was accompanied by representatives of Canada, Australia, South Africa, New Zealand, and India as members of the Commonwealth. These countries became signatories of the peace treaties and members of the League of Nations. The Commonwealth was a unique institution but did not become a model in international law as a new form of an association of States. Russia was not invited at all due to the fact that the victors were unable to find a common position on how to deal with this hotbed of revolution. The delegation of Germany, the first and most important adversary, was summoned on 7 May 1919 in order to receive the draft treaty. Oral negotiations were refused. The Treaty of Versailles was signed on 28 June 1919 after an ultimatum by the victors.[2] Their attitude can be explained by their under-standable embitterment because of the long duration of the war, the new forms of warfare and weapons, the heavy casualties, the German breaches of international law, and the massive devastation of infrastructure caused by German warfare.

The peace treaties with Germany's allies were concluded with each of them separately, one after the other. Like the Treaty of Versailles, they were prepared by the victors in secret negotiations, not least in order to avoid publicity and public influence in open procedure—as originally provided for in President Wilson's programme—that might have prevented dictated treaty clauses. The Treaty of Saint-Germain-en-Laye (signed on 10 September 1919)[3] was imposed on Austria, which after the dissolution of the Austro-Hungarian Empire was a small State. Austria's wish to be united with Germany was denied, particularly by France, despite the fact that the right of every people to self-determination had become one of the most spectacular new doctrines of international law, many controversies about its exact meaning and scope notwithstanding. Wilson had elevated that right to one of the basic principles of peacemaking after the war. Since the Hungarian case was more complicated, the next peace treaty was concluded with Bulgaria at Neuilly (27 November 1919).[4] In comparison, the conditions imposed on Bulgaria were not so harsh. In the Treaty of Trianon (4 June 1920),[5] Hungary had to accept bitter territorial losses, contrary to the armistice

---

[2] Treaty of Versailles (signed 28 June 1919) (1919) 225 CTS 188. A Sharp *The Versailles Settlement: Peace-making in Paris 1919* (Macmillan London 1991) ch 5. The historical framework is set out by WG Grewe *The Epochs of International Law* (M Byers trans) (de Gruyter Berlin 2000) at 573–98.

[3] Treaty of Saint-Germain-en-Laye (Treaty of Peace between the Allied and Associated Powers and Austria) (signed 10 September 1919) (1919) 226 CTS 8.

[4] Treaty of Neuilly-sur-Seine (Treaty of Peace Between the Allied and Associated Powers and Bulgaria) (signed 27 November 1919) (1919) 226 CTS 332.

[5] Treaty of Trianon (Treaty of Peace Between The Allied and Associated Powers and Hungary) (signed 4 June 1920, entered into force 26 July 1921) 6 LNTS 187.

conditions. The new borders caused a severe problem of national minorities. About one-third of the Magyar population now had to live in the victorious neighbouring countries. The last and most short-lived of the Paris peace treaties was concluded at Sèvres on 10 August 1920 with Turkey.[6] The treaty would have made Turkey a territorially downsized State under foreign tutelage. General Mustapha Kemal was able to organize protest against the conditions of this treaty, completed in draft already in April 1920, by establishing a new parliament at Ankara in the spring of 1920, the 'Grand National Assembly' which made him president in January 1921. These events amounted to a veritable coup d'état. After Greece, one of the main beneficiaries of the treaty, had attacked Turkey but had been defeated, and after complicated and depressing diplomatic manoeuvres, peace negotiations were resumed and concluded by the Treaty of Lausanne (24 July 1923).[7] Compared to the Treaty of Sèvres, that treaty definitely provided better conditions for Turkey.[8]

As a result of the peace treaties, a broad zone of new or substantially enlarged States had emerged in Europe between the Baltic Sea and the Aegean, and each case provided its fair share of demands and controversies. Given that it had been one of the main objectives of international law after 1918 to provide legal guidelines and solutions of a general character, the peace treaties caused a surge in legal activity in order to make the varying settlements compatible with each other. The only practicable way to cope with this situation would have been to make the League of Nations a kind of parent organization for all existing States while upholding their independence. To join a world order consolidated in this way became for several States both in Europe and in Asia a kind of *Realpolitik* that stimulated the development of modern structures at home and secured for them a certain international order and protection after the First World War. To a certain degree it became attractive, or even seemed necessary, to belong to the signatories of the peace treaties—of course on the right side and only as long as domestic culture was not impaired. This kind of politics was practised for instance by Siam (from April 1939 on, Thailand), one of those regional powers trying hard to increase its strength and to regain certain territories. Siam managed to start modernizing the State as well as society and to improve its position by joining the Allies, declaring war on Germany and Austria-Hungary (22 July 1917), and sending a small contingent of troops to Europe. Consequently Siam became a signatory to the peace treaties and a founding member of the League of Nations.[9]

---

[6] Treaty of Sèvres (The Treaty of Peace Between the Allied and Associated Powers and the Ottoman Empire) (signed 10 August 1920) 113 BFSP 652. However, this treaty was never ratified by the Turkish Government and was eventually superseded by the Treaty of Lausanne.

[7] Treaty of Lausanne (Treaty of Peace with Turkey) (adopted 24 July 1923, entered into force 30 August 1924) 28 LNTS 11.

[8] *The Versailles Settlement* (n 2) 39, 142–52, and 168–75; *Documents on British Foreign Policy* first series, vol XVIII, 972–3.

[9] K Strupp and J Hatschek (eds) *Wörterbuch des Völkerrechts und der Diplomatie* (de Gruyter Berlin 1929) vol 3, at 444.

China attempted a similar move in August 1917 to gain support against Japan—in vain,[10] because Japan was too strong and too important to the Allies. Great Britain needed assistance from the Japanese navy and promised as a quid pro quo to support the Japanese policy of conquest as well as Japanese political and economic dominance in China. There were more such deals. They indicated a grave disregard for international law even on the side of the Allied Powers. In the long run such an attitude contributed to the emergence of radical and revolutionary mass movements. In 1921, Mao Tse-tung and Tchou En-lai became prominent among the founders of the Communist Party in China, as did Ho Chi Minh in Vietnam in 1930, and so two future focal points for revolution and international confrontation were created. Japan had obtained an important international position during the First World War and afterwards as a permanent member of the League of Nations Council.[11] This was a comfortable starting point for a breathtaking and brutal expansion of power without a counterweight in East Asia before the last stage of the Second World War and the rise of revolutionary China. The situation was different in the Pacific region under the influence of the United States.

A problem of its own was the Middle East, compounded by international haggling about spheres of influence and a new order in the region triggered by the establishment of a Jewish State in Palestine following the Balfour Declaration (2 November 1917),[12] and by the fact that Hijas (Saudi Arabia) remained the only independent State in the area. From the perspective of international law and policy, the Middle East was a highly unstable region with an uneven structure. It constituted a dangerous bequest of this post-war period to the next following the Second World War.[13]

In Latin America, the conditions for international cooperation were better, though rather limited.[14] Pan-American conferences received a new impetus from the United States from 1889. In view of the diverging interests, the US approach at the Pan American Conference at Santiago (25 March–3 May 1923) was appropriate—to concentrate on peaceful mediation ensured by means of international law and on better cooperation in matters of customs and trade (Gondra Treaty, 3 May 1923).[15] However, this approach was not pursued intensively enough.

Finally, in the transitional period of 1918–1921 there was a group of small countries in the contested Baltic district of Europe eager to become independent States, namely Estonia, Latvia, and Lithuania. They were given a chance to achieve that goal after the

---

[10] ibid 751–62. For context, see M Stolleis and M Yanagihara (eds) *East Asian and European Perspectives on International Law* (Nomos Baden-Baden 2004); C Aydin *The Politics of Anti-Westernism in Asia* (Columbia University Press New York 2007); see also the contribution by S Kawashima 'China' in this volume.

[11] See the contribution by M Yanagihara 'Japan' in this volume.

[12] 'The Balfour Declaration' in JN Moore (ed) *The Arab-Israeli Conflict* (Princeton University Press Princeton 1974) vol III, at 32.

[13] *Versailles Settlement* (n 2) 175–83.

[14] See the contribution by JL Esquirol 'Latin America' in this volume.

[15] Treaty to Avoid or Prevent Conflicts Between the American States (Gondra Treaty) (signed 3 May 1923, entered into force 8 October 1924) (1923) 33 LNTS 25; US Department of State (ed) *Foreign Relations of the United States 1923* (US Government Printing Office 1935) vol I, 297–320.

Baltic provinces had been separated from Russia in the peace treaty concluded with Germany and Austria-Hungary at Brest-Litovsk (3 March 1918).[16] Shaken by turmoil and outside interventions after the end of the war (armistice of 11 November 1918),[17] they established themselves with some difficulties as States internationally recognized by their membership in the League of Nations in September 1921.[18]

3. THE LEAGUE OF NATIONS

The Covenant of the League of Nations,[19] which constituted part I of the peace treaties concluded with Germany and her allies, offered important innovations in international law after the end of the First World War. First of all, it meant the breakthrough to a universal, and not merely a European, community of States. The main task was to create a system of securing peace and solving international problems as well as providing for common action of the member States in the future. This was to include disarmament and armament control, collective security, protection of minorities, and the peaceful settlement of international conflicts (articles 8–17). However, the prohibition of war in article 15 remained incomplete. Furthermore, there was a first and very cautious approach to establish and to promote international organization and solutions of problems in social, economic and cultural affairs, and traffic. In addition, there were cautious attempts to promote de-colonization and development by a system of mandates administered under the control of the League for the former colonies of Germany and the Ottoman empire. The aim of the mandates was to extend the reach of the 'civilized world' by a just treatment of the native populations of the territories in question, by measures against the 'traffic in women and children, and the traffic in opium and other dangerous drugs' as well as 'the trade in arms and ammunition', and by the obligation of the administering powers 'to secure and maintain fair and human conditions of labour for men, women, and children' (articles 22, 23, and 25 of the League of Nations Covenant).

Self-determination and human rights were not dealt with explicitly in the Covenant but belonged to the core of the views which guided the instrument. The organs of the League were the Assembly, constituted by representatives of all member States,

---

[16] Treaty of Brest-Litovsk (signed 3 March 1918) (1918) 223 CTS 81.

[17] 'Conditions of an Armistice with Germany, 1918' (1919) 13 American Journal of International Law Supplement 97–108.

[18] J Hiden *The Baltic States and Weimar Ostpolitik* (CUP Cambridge 1987) pt I.

[19] cf n 2; see also the contribution by A Peters and S Peter 'International Organizations: Between Technocracy and Democracy' in this volume.

and the powerful Council made up of the representatives of the 'Principal Allied and Associated Powers' together with the representatives of initially four additional member States chosen by the Assembly. Another organ was the Secretariat, the importance and practical work of which has often been underrated. This organizational model was adopted by the successor of the League, the United Nations, in 1945. Further, a Permanent Court of International Justice was to be established at The Hague to judge all international cases presented to the court in accordance with its statute.[20] The court was founded in 1920. An optional clause in the statute (article 36) invited all governments to recognize, by way of a unilateral declaration, as compulsory and without special agreement the jurisdiction of the court in all legal disputes concerning questions of international law.[21] According to article 18 of the covenant, every treaty or international engagement entered into by any member of the League had to be registered with the Secretariat and be published by it in order to be binding on the parties. The League officially came into existence on 10 January 1920 when the Treaty of Versailles entered into force. The League existed until 1946 but its finest days were over by 1930 when it started to lose its influence.

The intensification of international interdependence as a result of industrialization and modernization that occurred before 1914 led to a major problem of international law after the First World War.[22] It was considerably increased by the devastation, burdens, and hostilities of the war. The principal question was how to arrange the future co-existence of the victors and the defeated States, above all in Europe. The realization of the idea of an international organization seemed to offer the basic answer in the long run, but it was unable to solve the acute problem of reaching a pragmatic arrangement between the two groups of States. Germany and her allies were treated like outlaws. As if to reinforce this state of affairs, another fundamental modification of international law was introduced. The long-established clause of oblivion was replaced in the Treaty of Versailles by quite the opposite;[23] namely, by clauses providing for 'penalties', including sanctions for acts in violation of the laws and customs of war to be imposed by military tribunals (articles 227–230 of the Versailles Treaty). Wilhelm II, the former German Emperor, was arraigned for 'a supreme offence against international morality and the sanctity of treaties' (article 227). However, none of the tribunals provided for in these clauses became effective. An alarming innovation was the appropriation of private assets, as was the obligation to make

---

[20] See the contribution by CG Roelofsen 'International Arbitration and Courts' in this volume; also O Spiermann *International Legal Argument in the Permanent Court of International Justice: The Rise of the International Judiciary* (CUP Cambridge 2005).

[21] Germany was one of the few major powers which made a declaration in accordance with the optional clause (23 September 1927), *Reichsgesetzblatt 1928* pt II, 19–20.

[22] M Vec *Recht und Normierung in der Industriellen Revolution: Neue Strukturen der Normsetzung in Völkerrecht, staatlicher Gesetzgebung und gesellschaftlicher Selbstnormierung* (Klostermann Frankfurt 2006) at 388–98 (English summary).

[23] Treaty of Versailles (n 2).

reparations for 'all damage done to the civilian population of the Allied and Associated Powers and to their property during the period of the belligerency of each as an Allied or Associated Power against Germany by such aggression by land, by sea and from the air' (article 232).[24] That burden was much heavier than traditional war indemnities. Altogether, it was a discriminating peace. As things stood, collapse was inevitable, considering the terrible dimensions of this modern, and finally worldwide, war.

4. INTERNATIONAL LAW AND THE ERA OF UNDERSTANDING

In a statement of what had been accomplished and what was missing in the realization of international law, politics, and order during peacemaking in 1918/20, the fact that Europe lacked a truly new order should figure prominently, notwithstanding the innovations brought about by the peace treaties. The dangerous gap soon became obvious. Efforts to fill it started in 1923/24, particularly in the development of new possibilities of international law to strengthen common projects and cooperation in Europe. This was necessary because among the victors, the difference between announcing high standards of international law and their practice of neglecting them, sometimes even in dealing with each other, indicated the danger of a decay of international law. The First World War and its aftermath ushered in an unusually condensed period of change, not only in Europe. The gradually increasing power and the attraction of radical change as proposed by the new communist movements in Asia hinted at the explosive force of delayed change.

The high standards of the new international order established in the peace treaties and the League Covenant required a durable foundation. This was particularly important to France as Germany's neighbour. The French security treaties with the United States and the United Kingdom of 28 June 1919 were supposed to become the cornerstone of the French security system. Both treaties failed when the US Senate decided not to approve the Treaty of Versailles, and together with it, US membership in the League of Nations.[25] The security of France suffered a setback, but even more so the whole post-war international order.

---

[24] For the pre-armistice agreement of 5 November 1918, see *Versailles Settlement* (n 2) 12–18. See also HJ Schröder (ed) *Confrontation and Cooperation: Germany and the United States in the Era of World War I, 1900–1924* (Berg Providence 1993).

[25] *Versailles Settlement* (n 2) 110–13; S Jeannesson *Poincaré, la France et la Ruhr 1922–1924* (Presses universitaires de Strasbourg 1998) at 27–9; C Fischer *The Ruhr Crisis 1923–1924* (OUP Oxford 2003) at 11–12.

The League of Nations as well as international policy were kept busy by intensive efforts of the French government to obtain an adequate substitute for the failed treaties which France thought it needed as a defence against Germany. Using demands for reparations as a justification until the climax of the Ruhr crisis in fall 1923, the French applied increasingly violent measures against Germany. The possible disruption of international relations in Europe and in particular the possible economic and political consequences prompted Great Britain and the United States to arrange a new basis for the payment of reparations. A clear signal was the British note addressed to the French Government of 11 August 1923 challenging the legality of the French occupation of the Ruhr area.[26] Step by step, transition arrangements were discussed to move from the threat of intra-European antagonism to the possibility of mutual understanding, with resolute American support in the background.

Another factor which gained increasing importance for international law was the growing influence of domestic affairs on foreign policy. Germany could barely come to terms with its sudden defeat, the breakdown of the empire, and the abrupt change of its constitution from monarchy to Republic. Deep political cleavages emerged about the responsibility for the catastrophe and for the far-reaching constitutional changes which had taken place within a few months, but which probably would need many years or perhaps even generations to be accepted and assimilated into the country's cultural traditions. For these reasons, foreign policy became a part of domestic policy. Rational cooperation in international politics was even more important and urgent in order to find a balance of interests with the former enemies, otherwise the whole system established in 1919–20 was put at risk—the peace treaties, the League, the new standards of international law. Among the victors themselves there were tendencies to neglect the requirements of that new international order, and Germany was strong enough to challenge that system.

Under these difficult circumstances it was indispensable that both sides, Germany as well as France, ought to be prepared to learn from their menacing experiences with the Ruhr crisis and to come to an agreement regarding the most pressing problem—reparations. In October 1923, the British Foreign Office had proposed to the Americans a common policy aiming at an international settlement of the reparations problem. A group of experts was established to examine all essential aspects of that problem and to elaborate a plan for German reparations payments, the so-called Dawes Plan. The drafting of the plan took place in the time between 14 January and 9 April 1924. The plan marked a new approach in international law to economic and financial problems and to the settlement of long-term payments. It meant a breakthrough to a rapprochement of the former enemies. The Dawes Plan was adopted at

---

[26] PO Cohrs *The Unfinished Peace after World War I: America, Britain and the Stabilisation of Europe* (CUP Cambridge 2006) ch 7; cf also n 25.

a conference in London (16 July–16 August 1924).[27] New to international law were the numerous arbitration clauses and controls of the German economy, including the liability of the German National Railways and National Bank. Furthermore, the States participating in the conference decided to appoint an American citizen, Seymour Parker Gilbert, as 'Agent General for German Reparations Payments', a remarkable solution to one of the thorniest problems of peacemaking at Versailles and an example of a pragmatic development of international law. The Reparation Commission was no longer a tool of the victorious European States, and the arbitration clauses confirmed Germany's policy, pursued since 1921 (arbitration treaty with Switzerland)[28] to strengthen systematically arbitral dispute settlement in international law. This thorough change in the relationship between the victorious and the defeated, a transition to cooperation, offered a great opportunity. It was the beginning of a remarkable period of international understanding in Europe with an emphasis on securing peace, political cooperation, and economic recovery. As the experts stressed in their report of 9 April 1924, '[w]e have not concealed from ourselves the fact that the reconstruction of Germany is not an end in itself. It is only part of the larger problem of the reconstruction of Europe'.[29]

That period of understanding lasted from 1923/24 until the spring of 1930. It made possible remarkable progress in international law. New treaties with legal improvements had been agreed to and were brought into connection with the League Covenant. A few days after the Dawes Plan had become effective (30 August 1924), the British Prime Minister James Ramsay MacDonald requested in the Assembly of the League that Germany join the League. The German application for membership (29 September 1924) caused extended debates. The security problem of France became acute again. The leading officials of the German Foreign Office were not unprepared. Since April 1923, a blueprint of the later treaties of Locarno was ready as an offer to France but was not accepted by the then German Foreign Minister Frederic von Rosenberg. After a new minister, Gustav Stresemann, had taken office, the German security initiative for central Europe was launched in January and February 1925 in London and Paris, and slightly later, in Rome and Brussels.[30] The initiative was supported by the British Embassy in Berlin. The crucial point of the resulting negotiations was the German proposal for a permanent demilitarization of the German

---

[27] *Die Sachverständigen-Gutachten. Die Berichte des von der Reparationskommission eingesetzten Sachverständigenkomitees vom 9. April 1924* (Deutsche Verlagsgesellschaft für Politik und Geschichte Berlin 1914) (texts in French, English and German); *Unfinished Peace* (n 26) ch 10.

[28] *Akten zur deutschen auswärtigen Politik 1918–1945* series A, vol V, 478–9.

[29] *Sachverständigen-Gutachten* (n 27) 49.

[30] *Documents on British Foreign Policy* first series, vol XXVII; *Akten zur deutschen auswärtigen Politik* series A, vol XIV, at xxxix–xlvi; M Breuer and N Weiß (eds) *Das Vertragswerk von Locarno und seine Bedeutung für die internationale Gemeinschaft nach 80 Jahren* (Lang Frankfurt 2007) at 77–110. For context, see M Habicht *Post-War Treaties for the Pacific Settlement of International Disputes* (Harvard University Press Cambridge MA 1931); and JL Brierly *The Law of Nations: An Introduction to the International Law of Peace* (Clarendon Press Oxford 1950) ch III.

Rhineland. This needed to be discussed with France and Belgium, since the status of the Rhineland concerned the former enemy States in the region, as well as with Great Britain and Italy as European Great Powers. Besides, arbitration treaties against the threat of war were to be negotiated between Germany and her Eastern and Western neighbours.

Two aspects illustrate the pre-eminent importance of the issue of the demilitarization of the Rhineland in the framework of the Locarno system of treaties. First, demilitarization was repeatedly demanded by France. The Rhineland was the area in which France could first react in case of any German attempt to prepare for military operations against Poland and Czechoslovakia. Demilitarization also seemed to be the only effective protection for France. The so-called Rhine Pact, therefore, was the core of the Locarno Treaties.[31] The demilitarization of the Rhineland acted as a stimulus for international law, with the creation of a new device, the formation of a demilitarized zone as a means to secure peace. Second, this course of events emphasized the character of the League of Nations as a predominantly European organization. The League was the best that international law had to offer to the Europeans. After the catastrophe of the First World War, it seemed capable of providing them with the institutions and instruments necessary for securing peace, the conciliation of conflicts, the balancing of interests, and the deepening of cooperation in Europe. The League created a common sphere of law useful to the several States. It introduced into international law a hierarchy of norms, with the Covenant at the highest level.[32]

A new aspect of international law was the goal to overcome the preponderance of military alliances and counter-alliances. Consequently, agreements concerning the peaceful balancing of interests became increasingly important. The provisions of the Locarno Treaties,[33] particularly regarding demilitarization, the territorial status quo, and the inviolability of the borders, were effectively interwoven with the articles of the League Covenant. This was an innovation in international law which strengthened its effectiveness in international politics—as long as the powers adhered to compromise, cooperation, and the peaceful settlement of disputes. Exceeding the

---

[31] Arbitration Convention between Germany and Belgium, done at Locarno, 16 October 1925 (signed 16 October 1925, entered into force 14 September 1926) 54 LNTS 305; Arbitration Convention between Germany and France, done at Locarno, 16 October 1925 (signed 16 October 1925, entered into force 14 September 1926) 54 LNTS 317; Arbitration Treaty between Germany and Poland, done at Locarno, 16 October 1925 (signed 16 October 1925, entered into force 14 September 1926) 54 LNTS 329; Arbitration Treaty between Germany and Czechoslovakia, done at Locarno, 16 October 1925 (signed 16 October 1925, entered into force 14 September 1926) 54 LNTS 343; Final Protocol of the Locarno Conference (signed 1 December 1925) 54 LNTS 297.

[32] Art 20 of the Covenant reads: 'The Members of the League severally agree that this Covenant is accepted as abrogating all obligations or understandings inter se which are inconsistent with the terms thereof, and solemnly undertake that they will not hereafter enter into any engagements inconsistent with the terms thereof. In case any Member of the League shall, before becoming a Member of the League, have undertaken any obligations inconsistent with the terms of this Covenant, it shall be the duty of such Member to take immediate steps to procure its release from such obligations.'

[33] Cf n 30. For text, see *Reichsgesetzblatt 1925* pt II, 975–1009.

rules of the League Covenant, the Rhine Pact included a commitment of France, Belgium, and Germany under no circumstances to attack, invade or wage war against each other (article 2). Compared to the Covenant, the notion of a 'war of aggression' was more clearly defined. The role of the League Council was strengthened by the Locarno Treaties. Germany accepted explicitly that rights and duties laid down in the Treaty of Versailles and its supplementary arrangements (in particular, the Dawes Plan) were not affected by the Treaties of Locarno. The importance of the Rhine Pact for European politics was emphasized by the fact that the four major European powers belonged to the signatories, powers which constituted—after Germany had joined the League (8 September 1926)—four of the five permanent members of the League Council. By this conjunction of Great Power politics and international organization, the Locarno era became the most successful period of the League. It demonstrated how the structural tension between the international politics of sovereign States, and a universal legal and peace system could be reconciled. However, the precondition was the general willingness to promote such an arrangement. This willingness decreased rapidly after 1930, not least under the pressure of domestic change in Germany.

The Locarno treaties were important in stimulating the preparation of a general disarmament conference. Their economic importance has often been ignored although they provided an impulse towards a certain liberalization of international commerce and finance in Europe and to endeavours to improve the international economic system with the support of international law. The first World Economic Conference at Geneva (4–23 May 1927) was a great success. It was an expert conference that aimed at the promotion of obligatory principles to guide the international economy and at exploring options of a development of production and trade.[34] The exigencies of growing international interdependence paradoxically also led to an insistence on national competences. But that first world conference intensified the economic activities of the League of Nations and provided new tasks for international law. New committees were created and diplomatic conferences convened, for instance against bans on imports and exports. This development was one of the main roots of the later General Agreement on Tariffs and Trade (GATT) (30 October 1947).[35] The statement at the very end of the Final Protocol of the Locarno Conference proved to be no empty formula: the agreements of Locarno indeed contributed strongly to facilitate solutions to political and economic problems of the time.

[34] M Schulz *Deutschland, der Völkerbund und die Frage der europäischen Wirtschaftsordnung 1925–1933* (Krämer Hamburg 1997) at 89–107. For context, see DH Aldcroft *Europe's Third World: The European Periphery in the Interwar Years* (Ashgate Aldershot 2006) chs 1 and 3; DH Aldcroft *The European Economy 1914–2000* (4th edn Routledge London 2001) chs 1–3; H Berding (ed) *Wirtschaftliche und politische Integration in Europa im 19. und 20. Jahrhundert* (Vandenhoeck & Ruprecht Göttingen 1984) at 149–68.

[35] General Agreement on Tariffs and Trade (signed 30 October 1947, provisionally applied 1 January 1948) 55 UNTS 194.

The last success of Locarno politics—and a remarkable example of the use made of international law for the solution of difficult and highly technical problems—was the final regulation of reparation payments on the basis of the Young Plan (Hague Conferences of August 1929 and January 1930).[36] The agreement provided for the foundation of the Bank for International Settlements (BIS) in Basel as an administrator of reparation payments and the commercialization of reparation bonds.[37] The bank was to advance the urgently needed cooperation of the central banks, 'and within limitations of the sound use of credit, to contribute to the stability of international finance and the growth of world trade'.[38] Initially the German Central Bank director Hjalmar Schacht wanted to make the BIS a kind of world bank as it was founded in 1944 in Bretton Woods. This did not happen, but nevertheless the BIS was an important step towards the international banking system realized after the Second World War.[39]

The first universal Conference on Concerted Economic Action (Tariff Truce) of the League (Geneva, 17 February–24 March 1930) was meant to be the next important step in the process initiated with the 1927 World Economic Conference. However, under the pressure of the world economic crisis and rapidly rising protectionism, the conference did not achieve very much. This was a first sign of the decay of inter-war international law. The last World Economic Conference of the League at London (12 June–27 July 1932) was a debacle and was adjourned *sine die*.[40]

5. A Period of Decay: International Law and Politics in the 1930s

Three outstanding tasks of international politics arose in Europe after the First World War. Two of them have already been dealt with—the necessity of a promotion of a policy of international cooperation, rapprochement, peace, and security, and the

[36] 'Report of the Committee of Experts Settlement of the Reparation Problem (7 June 1929)' (1930) 24 American Journal of International Law Supplement 81–143 ('Young Plan').

[37] Hague Agreement Regarding the Complete and Final Settlement of the Question of Reparations, with Annexes and Protocol Concerning the Approval in Principle of the Report of the Experts (signed 20 January 1930) 104 LNTS 243; Convention Respecting the Bank for International Settlements (signed 20 January 1930) 104 LNTS 441.

[38] P Krüger *Die Aussenpolitik der Republik von Weimar* (Wissenschaftliche Buchgesellschaft Darmstadt 1985) at 483–506 (quotation at 484).

[39] D Lefort 'Bank for International Settlements (BIS), Basel, Switzerland' in R Blanpain and M Colucci (eds) *International Encyclopaedia of Laws: Intergovernmental Organizations—Suppl 36* (Kluwer Alphen aan den Rijn 2009) at MN 44.

[40] *Europäische Wirtschaftsordnung* (n 34) 210–27 and 325–32.

strengthening of rules advancing a market-oriented international economy. A third task proved most important for international relations because of its explosive force—the solution of the complicated problem of disarmament. Disarmament ranked high as an obligation of the member States of the League (article 8 of the Covenant). Similarly as in the two other fields, the discussion was connected with the Locarno process. In December 1925, the League Council invited several States, including the non-members Germany, the USSR, and the United States, to the inauguration of a preparatory commission for a disarmament conference.[41] The invitation to the Soviet Union revealed a remarkable change in her international position since 1919, a change that became more marked in the following years; for instance, on the occasion of the conclusion of the 1928 Kellogg–Briand Pact.[42] France wanted to make security a precondition of disarmament and to use the Geneva Protocol on the Peaceful Settlement of International Conflicts (2 October 1924) as a basis.[43] Due to British resistance, this Geneva Protocol was never ratified, but it remained a reference standard up until Aristide Briand's plan for Europe of 1929–30, Europe's last chance before the Second World War.[44] The Protocol developed a comprehensive system of obligatory peaceful settlement of disputes, and of sanctions in the case of breaches of its rules. According to the Protocol, 'aggressors' were those States which did not observe the Protocol.

The first disarmament conference only convened (on 2 February 1932) when the era of understanding was already over. It ran into severe difficulties in the summer of 1932, caused above all by disarmed Germany's demand for equality in terms of its military capacities, and ended in a showdown for the future of international law. The crucial question was whether progress was still possible in disarmament, and more generally in international cooperation, or whether this failure to reach an agreement on (dis)armament would usher in a period of decay of international relations, possibly ending in ever graver violations of international law by the National Socialist Germany.

More successful than the Europeans and the League was the United States. At the Washington Naval Conference (12 November 1921–6 February 1922), the US achieved, outside the League framework, an arms limitation for the leading navies against a threatening arms race.[45] This was combined with confidence-building measures for the Pacific area, a guarantee of the Pacific possessions of the United States, Great Britain, Japan, and France, and a securing of the 'Open Door Policy' (allowing all

[41]   *Aussenpolitik* (n 38) 336.

[42]   Kellogg–Briand Pact (concluded 27 August 1928, entered into force 24 July 1929) 94 LNTS 57; *Aussenpolitik* (n 38) 409–10. For context, see J Jacobsen *When the Soviet Union Entered World Politics* (University of California Press Berkeley 1994); C Baechler *L'aigle et l'ours. La politique russe de l'Allemagne de Bismarck à Hitler 1871–1945* (Lang Bern 2001) ch V.

[43]   'Geneva Protocol on the Peaceful Settlement of International Conflicts' (1924) Société des Nations Journal Officiel Spec Supp 23, 502–6.

[44]   J Bariéty (ed) *Aristide Briand, la Société des Nations et l'Europe 1919–1932* (Presses universitaires de Strasbourg 2007) at 339–96.

[45]   US Department of State (ed) *Foreign Relations of the United States 1921* (US Government Printing Office Washington 1938) vol I, 18–87; *1922*, vol I, 1–384.

European nations and the United States economic access to China). Japan had to give back the control of Shantung (Shandong) and Kiauchau (Jiaozhou), which it had gained by the Treaty of Versailles, to China. The London Naval Conference (21 January–22 April 1930) extended the arms limitation to the smaller types of warships.[46]

In general, a weakening of the Peace Treaties of 1919–20 and the League of Nations came about in the beginning of 1930. Consequently, the post-war order in Europe, established by means of international law, was endangered. Symptomatic was the growing disinterest in and even animosity towards the League and its mission of peaceful conciliation. Japan reacted to the protest against her invasion in Manchuria (1931) and the proclamation of the Manchu State (Manchukuo) (1932) by leaving the League (27 March 1933). Italy also ended its membership in the League in 1937 after having been condemned for annexing Ethiopia (Abyssinia). Even more important for the fate of the League was Germany's decision in October 1933 to leave both the Disarmament Conference and the League.[47] That move fitted into a wave of actions directed against the existing European order and international law, including the conclusion of bilateral 'non-aggression pacts' and similar treaties. Hitler's spectacular move, which wrecked the Disarmament Conference, was presented as an answer to the disagreement about Germany's military equality. By leaving the League, Germany also renounced the Rhine Pact because German membership in the League was a precondition of the entry into force of that Pact. No harsh reaction of the League Council followed. In 1935, the United Kingdom concluded a naval treaty with Germany. Even after Hitler, contrary to all treaty obligations, had sent troops into the demilitarized Rhineland (7 March 1936), no policy of containment was formulated as an answer, although the security of France, Poland, and Czechoslovakia depended upon that demilitarization. Subsequently, Germany became even more important to Mussolini's Italy, while a German–Japanese alliance was initiated with the 'Anti-Comintern Pact' (25 November 1936).[48] Having left the League, Italy joined the alliance (6 November 1937) and also concluded a 'Pact of Friendship and Alliance' ('*Stahlpakt*') with Germany (22 May 1939)[49] after the Reich had become its most powerful direct neighbour through the incorporation of Austria (March 1938) and the Sudeten Land (Munich Agreement of 29 September 1938),[50] and the destruction of Czechoslovakia (March 1939).[51]

---

[46] *Documents on British Foreign Policy* second series, vol 1, chs 1 and 3 and app I.

[47] *Akten zur deutschen auswärtigen Politik* series C, vol I/2, 905–12.

[48] Agreement Against the Communist International (Komintern) (signed 25 November 1936) 140 BFSP 529.

[49] Germano-Italian Pact of Amity and Alliance (signed 22 May 1939) ('Steel Pact') reprinted in WG Grewe (ed) *Fontes Historiae Iuris Gentium: Sources Relating to the History of the Law of Nations* (De Gruyter Berlin 1988) vol 2, 1118–21.

[50] Agreement for the Cession by Czechoslovakia to Germany of Sudeten German Territory (signed 29 September 1938) 142 BFSP 438 ('Munich Agreement').

[51] AP Adamthwaite *The Making of the Second World War* (Allen & Unwin London 1985); C Joerges and NS Ghaleigh (eds) *Darker Legacies of Law in Europe: The Shadow of National Socialism and Fascism Over Europe and Its Legal Tradition* (Hart Oxford 2003).

6. The Second World War

While Japan and Italy had been forerunners in the disregard and destruction of international law, Germany's destructive activity was even worse. Germany started what would become the Second World War with its invasion of Poland on 1 September 1939. The attack had been made possible by an agreement with the USSR, the 'Hitler–Stalin Pact' (or 'Molotov-Ribbentrop Pact') of 23 August 1939.[52] Poland, Estonia, Latvia, and Lithuania disappeared as independent States.[53] The whole area was divided between the USSR and Germany. Finland resisted successfully until she was forced to sign a peace treaty in Moscow (12 March 1940). Stalin did not occupy the country because he wanted to avoid British and French intervention. The USSR was excluded from the League in 1939. Both in Germany and the USSR, the wars were accompanied by violence and cruelty directed against minorities and anybody opposing those in power. In Germany, the anti-semitism of the National Socialists culminated in the Holocaust—the systematic discrimination, persecution, deportation, and murder of the Jewish People. Referring to the American Monroe Doctrine, Hitler proclaimed a German *Grossraum* (grand space) which should be respected, by way of non-intervention, by other powers, in particular the United States.[54] This German *Grossraum* policy was another aspect of the decay of international law.

President Franklin D Roosevelt emphasized the connection and interplay between the constitutional order of a State and its foreign policy principles.[55] In his message to the US Congress of 6 January 1941, he proclaimed the 'Four Freedoms' that democracies should fight for: freedom of speech, freedom of worship, freedom from want, and freedom from fear.[56] He argued for a new concept of collective security in international law, which should defend these human freedoms, to be set against the policy of violence of the dictators. Contrary to the years of 1919–20, the United States now became the driving force behind a new world order. However, it had to accept the Soviet Union as an ally, and to support it militarily in its fight against Germany.

[52] 'Treaty of Non-Aggression between Germany and the Union of Soviet Socialist Republics' (signed 23 August 1939, entered into force 23 August 1939) in JAS Grenville *The Major International Treaties 1914–1945: A History and Guide with Texts* (Methuen New York 1987) at 195.

[53] Cf *Europe's Third World* (n 34); E Mühle (ed) *Germany and the European East in the Twentieth Century* (Berg Oxford 2003); L Mälksoo *Illegal Annexation and State Continuity: The Case of the Incorporation of the Baltic States by the USSR* (Nijhoff Leiden 2003).

[54] M Schmoeckel *Die Grossraumtheorie: Ein Beitrag zur Geschichte der Völkerrechtsgeschichte im Dritten Reich, insbesondere der Kriegszeit* (Duncker & Humblot Berlin 1994); PMR Stirk *Carl Schmitt, Crown Jurist of the Third Reich* (Edwin Mellen Press Lewiston NY 2005); B Fassbender 'Stories of War and Peace: On Writing the History of International Law in the "Third Reich" and After' (2002) 13 *European Journal of International Law* 479–512.

[55] R Dallek *Franklin D. Roosevelt and American Foreign Policy, 1932–1945* (OUP New York 1995); R Dallek *The American Style of Foreign Policy: Cultural Politics and Foreign Affairs* (Knopf New York 1983).

[56] US Department of State (ed) *Foreign Relations of the United States 1941* (US Government Printing Office Washington 1958) vol I, doc 1.

In the Atlantic Charter of 14 August 1941,[57] President Roosevelt and the British Prime Minister Winston Churchill proclaimed a liberal policy and order for a world of free and self-determined peoples. The United States and the United Kingdom, the Charter said in its fourth principle, will endeavour to further the enjoyment by all States of access, on equal terms, to the trade and to the raw materials of the world. With their pledge for the 'establishment of a wider and permanent system of general security' (in the eighth principle of the Charter) they paved the way for a new world organization to replace the League of Nations and a new international law. The Allied Governments, including the USSR, consented to the Atlantic Charter at the London Conference of 24 September 1941.[58] The Soviets, however, insisted on all their far-reaching war objectives which clearly were not compatible with the 'Four Freedoms'. This had consequences for the post-war condition of international law and for the effectiveness of the United Nations Organization.

Under the title of 'The United Nations', the 26 Allies issued a common declaration[59] in Washington on 1 January 1942 in which they stated their principles and aims in fighting Germany, Japan, and Italy until a complete victory was achieved. Under the aspect of international law, the notion of 'complete victory' was meant to permit deep interference with the domestic structure of the enemy State. In order to justify these aims, the Allies professed to be engaged in a common fight for the fate of humanity. The 1942 'Declaration by United Nations' was later supplemented with more specific war aims, in particular the unconditional surrender of the enemy, war crimes trials, and the establishment a new universal organization to protect peace and security. At the Dumbarton Oaks Conference in Washington, DC (21 August–7 October 1944), the United States, the USSR, the United Kingdom, and China agreed on a draft of the later United Nations Charter. However, a number of controversial points, especially concerning the voting procedure of the Security Council—the successor of the League Council—remained open.[60] This demonstrated the growing influence of the USSR as a result of its ongoing march into Central Europe.[61] Faster progress than in political questions was made by the four powers with regard to a new world economic order. Following the conference of Bretton Woods in New Hampshire (1–22 July 1944), attended by forty-four delegates of the United Nations, it was decided to stabilize world currencies by fixing the exchange rate of the dollar as a reserve currency and by

---

[57] Declaration of Principles (signed and entered into force 14 August 1941) 204 LNTS 381 ('Atlantic Charter').

[58] ibid 341–78.

[59] Declaration by United Nations (done 1 January 1942, entered into force 1 January 1942) 204 LNTS 381.

[60] Cf B Fassbender 'Dumbarton Oaks Conference (1944)' in R Wolfrum (ed) *The Max Planck Encyclopedia of Public International Law* (Oxford University Press Oxford 2008) at <www.mpepil.com>.

[61] US Department of State (ed) *Foreign Relations of the United States 1942* (US Government Printing Office Washington 1958) vol I, 1–38 and *1944* vol I, 614–923.

establishing an International Monetary Fund (IMF)[62] and an International Bank for Reconstruction and Development (IBRD, or World Bank).[63] The agreements on the IMF and the World Bank came into effect on 27 December 1945; they offered a fresh impulse for a world economic system guided by the idea of open markets.

When Roosevelt, Stalin, and Churchill met at Yalta in the Crimea (4–11 February 1945),[64] the 'Big Three' engaged largely in defining their respective spheres of influence—the scale of this endeavour was a novum in international law—and in drawing up borders, not least those of the zones of occupation in Germany. The principles of the Atlantic Charter were specified in a 'Declaration on Liberated Europe'[65] according to which all liberated peoples should be enabled 'to destroy the last vestiges of nazism and fascism and to create democratic institutions of their own choice'. 'This', the Declaration further said, 'is a principle of the Atlantic Charter—the right of all peoples to choose the form of government under which they will live'.[66] The three politicians also reached a compromise on the issue of voting in the Security Council of the new world organization. The USSR won her demand for a right of veto of extensive range for each of the permanent members of the Security Council accepted and gained two additional seats in the General Assembly for the Ukrainian and the Byelorussian Soviet Socialist Republic. The invitations by the four principal powers to the United Nations Conference on International Organization (UNCIO) at San Francisco (25 April–26 June 1945) could now be dispatched. On the last day of the Conference, fifty States signed the Charter of the United Nations.[67] Following the required procedure of ratification, the Charter entered into force on 24 October 1945. The League of Nations was formally dissolved on 19 April 1946. Germany capitulated on 7 May 1945 in Reims, France. [68] The signing ceremony was repeated on 9 May 1945 in Berlin. Japan followed on 2 September 1945[69] while Italy had already agreed to an

---

[62] Articles of Agreement of the International Monetary Fund (adopted 22 July 1944, entered into force 27 December 1945) 2 UNTS 39.

[63] Articles of Agreement of the International Bank for Reconstruction and Development (adopted 22 July 1944, entered into force 27 December 1945) 2 UNTS 134; US Department of State (ed) *Proceedings and Documents of the United Nations Monetary and Financial Conference, Bretton Woods, New Hampshire, July 1–22, 1944* (US Government Printing Office Washington 1948).

[64] US Department of State (ed) *Foreign Relations of the United States: Diplomatic Papers. The Conference of Berlin* (US Government Printing Office Washington 1960) vol II, 1567–81 (Protocol of Proceedings and Communiqué of Yalta Conference).

[65] Declaration on Liberated Europe made by President Roosevelt, Prime Minister Churchill, and Premier Stalin at the end of the Yalta Conference and released to the press on 12 February 1945; US Department of State (ed) *Foreign Relations of the United States: The Conferences at Malta and Yalta, 1945* (US Government Printing Office Washington 1945) at 971.

[66] Declaration of Principles (n 57).

[67] Charter of the United Nations (concluded 26 June 1945, entered into force 24 October 1945) 59 Stat 1031; TS 993; 3 Bevans 1153.

[68] Act of Military Surrender (8 May 1945) (1945) Gazette of the Control Council for Germany Supp 1, 6.

[69] Instrument of Surrender (signed and entered into force 2 September 1945) 139 UNTS 387.

armistice with the Allied Armed Forces on 3 September 1943 after Mussolini's fall in July 1943.[70]

7. CONCLUSION

The structure of the United Nations Organization followed that of the League. Its principal organs are the General Assembly, the Security Council, the Economic and Social Council, the Secretariat, and the International Court of Justice. However, compared to the League Covenant, the UN Charter is a more comprehensive and consistent document, particularly concerning the concept of war which was more in line with modern forms of inter-state violence. The UN Charter is more oriented to the status quo than the League Covenant which in article 19 had subscribed to the idea of 'peaceful change'.[71] In 1945, international law had to be re-established, and cautiously adjusted to new conditions, after a period of force, terror, and atrocities. Dangerous problems surrounding the possibility of peaceful co-existence emerged, in view of the deep controversies among States, cultures, and ideologies after the Second World War which affected the power structure in whole regions, or even continents. Since Eastern and Central Europe was now dominated by the Soviet Union with its dictatorial communist constitution, the conflict with the community of free States in the West, characterized by open societies and democratic constitutions, was predictable. The 'Cold War' did not come as a surprise. The fault line of the divided Europe ran through the divided Germany and its divided capital, Berlin.

RECOMMENDED READING

Aldcroft, Derek H *The European Economy 1914–2000* (Routledge London 2001).

Aydin, Cemil *The Politics of Anti-Westernism in Asia* (Columbia University Press New York 2007).

Breuer, Marten and Norman Weiß (eds) *Das Vertragswerk von Locarno und seine Bedeutung für die internationale Gemeinschaft* (Lang Frankfurt am Main 2007).

---

[70] 'Italian Military Armistice, 3 September 1943' (1946) 40 American Journal of International Law Supplement 1.

[71] Art 19 of the Covenant read as follows: 'The Assembly may from time to time advise the reconsideration by Members of the League of treaties which have become inapplicable and the consideration of international conditions whose continuance might endanger the peace of the world'; cf art 14 of the UN Charter.

Cohrs, Patrick O *The Unfinished Peace after World War I: America, Britain and the Stabilisation of Europe, 1919–1932* (CUP Cambridge 2006).

Jacobson, Jon *When the Soviet Union Entered World Politics* (University of California Press Berkeley 1994).

Joerges, Christian and Navraj Singh Ghaleigh (eds) *Darker Legacies of Law in Europe: The Shadow of National Socialism and Fascism over Europe and Its Legal Traditions* (Hart Oxford 2003).

Lappenküper, Ulrich and Reiner Marcowitz (eds) *Macht und Recht: Völkerrecht in den internationalen Beziehungen* (Schöningh Paderborn 2010).

Sharp, Alan *The Versailles Settlement: Peacemaking after the First World War, 1919–1923* (2nd edn Palgrave Macmillan London 2008).

Steiger, Heinhard *Von der Staatenwelt zur Weltrepublik? Aufsätze zur Geschichte des Völkerrechts aus vierzig Jahren* (Nomos Baden-Baden 2009).

Stolleis, Michael and Masaharu Yanagihara (eds) *East Asian and European Perspectives of International Law* (Nomos Baden-Baden 2004).

V

ENCOUNTERS

CHAPTER 29

CHINA–EUROPE

CHI-HUA TANG

1. INTRODUCTION

SINCE ancient times, China has been the cultural, economic, and military leader in East Asia. Because of China's privileged position in this region, the surrounding peoples and cultures have been deeply influenced by China, and over the course of the last two thousand years, East Asia has developed its own unique world order.

Following significant advancements in geographic knowledge and travel, the modern West became increasingly more involved in East Asia. During the early 16th century, the Western and Eastern world orders came into contact, leading to an exchange of ideas and practices, some exchanges resulting in conflict, others in an integration of cultures.

The Sino-British Opium War (1839–42) was a watershed in China–Europe relations. Prior to this, the Chinese world order exercised the leading role in exchanges between the East and West. Following the Sino-British Treaty of Nanking (29 August 1842),[1] the Western concept of international law became the more dominant of the two aforementioned 'world orders'. As a result of the Sino-Japanese War (1894–95), and especially of the Boxer Uprising, which brought about the signing of the Boxer Protocol (7 September 1901),[2] China abandoned its traditional concept of the world order, while fully accepting Western concepts of international law and order.

---

[1] Treaty of Nanking (signed 29 August 1842) (1842) 93 CTS 465.
[2] 'Final Protocol between the Powers and China, signed 7 September 1901' (1907) 1 American Journal of International Law Supplement 388–96 ('Boxer Protocol').

In order to maintain its sovereignty and enhance its international status, China participated in international organizations while also employing Western principles of international law. Nonetheless, China suffered more oppression by 'unequal treaties' than nearly any other large nation. From the waning years of the Qing Dynasty (1644–1911) to the Beijing Government (1912–28), the Nationalist Regime (1928–49), all the way down to the advent of the People's Republic of China, China toiled for decades to free itself of the unequal treaties, win back its complete sovereignty, and claim equality of international status. During this process, the Chinese involvement in international affairs and among the international law community made significant developments. China's increasing involvement in the international community also affected the global development of international law.

This chapter emphasizes the relationship between China and Europe concerning international law. First, this chapter explores the process of China's encounter with international law. Second, it considers China's use of international law to secure treaty revisions and the consequent impact that this process had on international law. Finally, it looks at China's involvement in international conventions and organizations, as well as at the process of China's improving status among the international community.

2. China's Encounter with International Law

The traditional Chinese world order was based on ideas and constructs significantly different to that of Europe. Since China was surrounded by smaller, weaker countries with less developed culture, the main principle of the Chinese empire was that 'all-under-Heaven' was presided over by the 'Son of Heaven', the Chinese Emperor. Under such a system, there can be no competitor nor equal in the world to the Chinese Emperor; therefore, there was no international law in the East Asian world. The relationship between China and other countries was regulated by Chinese ritual.[3]

John King Fairbank describes Chinese relations with surrounding areas, and with non-Chinese peoples, as generally coloured by the concept of Sinocentrism and an assumption of Chinese superiority. The Chinese tended to think of their foreign relations as giving expression externally to the same principles of social and political order that were manifested internally within the Chinese State and society. China's

---

[3] T Wang 'Zhongguo yu Guojifa: Lishi yu Dangdai' (International Law in China: Historical and Contemporary Perspectives) in T Wang (ed) *Wang Tieya Wenxuan* (Selected Papers of Wang Tieya) (Zhongguo Zhenfa Dahsue Press Beijing 2003) at 229.

foreign relations were accordingly hierarchic and non-egalitarian, like Chinese society itself.

The grades and concentric hierarchy of China's foreign relations included other peoples and countries that may be grouped into three main zones: the Sinic Zone, the Inner Asian Zone, and the Outer Zone. All the surrounding non-Chinese States and peoples were expected, in theory, to be properly tributary to the Son of Heaven in the Central Country.[4]

Under the so-called tributary system, non-Chinese rulers participated in the Chinese world order by observing the appropriate forms and ceremonies (*li*) in their contact with the Son of Heaven. Taken together, these practices constituted the tribute system. Under its regulations during the Qing period:

> non-Chinese rulers were given a patent of appointment and an official seal for use in correspondence; they were given a noble rank in the Qing hierarchy; they dated their communications by the Qing calendar, that is, by the Qing dynastic reign-title; they presented tribute memorials of various sorts on appropriate statutory occasions; they also presented a symbolic tribute (*gong*) of local products; they or their envoys were escorted to court by the imperial post; they performed the appropriate ceremonies of the Qing Court, notably the kowtow; they received imperial gifts in return; and they were granted certain privileges of trade at the frontier and at the capital.[5]

Fairbank's tributary system theory combines tribute and trade, and states that China required each country that wished to trade with China become China's tributary State. Then, and only then, could that country become a part of China's world order. In other words, China convinced other countries to give tribute by offering trade benefits, providing China with a degree of loose control, and furthered the political ideology that all countries were subordinate to China in the tributary system.

However, Fairbank's theory has been recently challenged and modified by numerous scholars. Some contest the beginning date of the tributary system, while others argue that Fairbank's model of the tributary system is too simple and is little more than a caricature of the actual system. Essentially, many scholars argue that Fairbank's model shows a stagnant and arrogant China, which should bear the brunt of the blame in the China-European conflict. Fairbank's argument shows the discourse hegemony of western world, legalizing the Western impact and Chinese response paradigm.

Japanese scholars also challenged Fairbank's theory on the Western impact. Takeshi Hamashita argues European countries traded with China and then joined the traditional China-centered East Asia trading system themselves. They purport that

---

[4] J King Fairbank (ed) *The China World Order: Traditional China's Foreign Relations* (Harvard University Press Cambridge MA 1968) at 2.

[5] *The China World Order* (n 4) 10–11.

this system was never broken, even under European pressure and did recover quite well.[6]

Liao Ming-shu challenges the concept of tributary trade. She argues that the Qing dynasty's trading system was *hushi* (a system of mutual trade), not the tributary system. Even after the Treaty of Nanking, the *hushi* System was still maintained, contrary to Fairbank's theory that the tributary system was transformed into the treaty system following the Treaty of Nanking.[7] Fairbank's theory of China's traditional world order has been, and is still being, constantly modified in recent years.

China's encounter with the European system of international law began in the 17th century. The most evident case was when Zhen Chengong (Kokxin) signed a treaty with the Dutch East Indian Company commander of Zeelandia, Taiwan, Frederick Coijett, on 1 February 1662, following a nine-month siege in which the Dutch were made to surrender. The treaty was drafted entirely in the form common in Europe at the time.[8]

The Sino-Russian Treaty of Nerchinsk of 7 September 1689 is a more famous case.[9] This treaty's original copy was in Latin, and carbon copies were in Manchu, Mongolian, and Russian. Its form, signature, sealing, and exchange were all strictly according to the customary European practice. Its context reflected the principle of sovereign equality of modern international law. Thomas Pereira, a Portuguese Jesuit missionary and one of the interpreters of the Qing delegation, wrote in his diary that he introduced some concepts of international law to Emperor Kang-xi. However, this assertion lacks direct evidence. Chinese scholars believe the international law principles did affect the negotiations of the Treaty of Nerchinsk, but that it hardly proves that Emperor Kang-xi accepted international law instead of the traditional Chinese world order. Kang-xi had no intention of making the Treaty of Nerchinsk a precedent of future treaties with foreign countries. In fact, prior to 1839, there is no record verifying Chinese adoption of international law in any official Qing documents.[10]

Before the Opium War, Commissioner Lin Cexu arrived in Canton during the spring of 1839 to enforce the law prohibiting opium addiction. In an effort to better understand European rules of war, Lin asked Dr Peter Parker, a medical missionary at Canton, to translate part of Emerich de Vattel's *Le droit des gens; ou,*

---

[6] See T Hamashita, *China, East Asia and the Global Economy: Regional and Historical Perspectives* (Routledge London 2008) ch 2.

[7] M Liao 'Qingdai Duiwai Tongshan Zidu' (Foreign Trade System of Ching Dynasty) in *Jindai Zhongguo, Dongya yu Shijie* (Modern China, East Asia and the World) (Shehui Keshue Wenshian Press Beijing 2008) vol 2, 443–66.

[8] 'Treaty between Koxinga and the Dutch Government' in W Campell *Formosa Under the Dutch: Described from Contemporary Records* (Kegan Paul, Trench, Trubner London 1903) 455–6.

[9] Treaty of Nerchinsk (signed 7 September 1689) (1689) 18 CTS 503.

[10] 'Zhongguo yu Guojifa' (n 3) 238.

principes de la loi naturelle appliqués à la conduite et aux affaires des nations et des souverains, which dealt with war, blockades, and detainment. Lin used some of the principles gathered from this work later in negotiations with the British, but the effect of Lin's translation of international law was quite limited. These translated sentences became a part of Wei Yuan's well-known book *Hai-guo tu-zhi* (Illustrated treatise on the Maritime Kingdoms).[11] After the Opium War, China's interest in international law seemed to vanish.

After the Second Opium War (1856–60), the Qing Dynasty decided on a policy of 'bridling and reining in' (*Jimi*) the powerful European powers while concentrating on pacifying internal rebellions, and the Qing established the Zongli Yamen (Foreign Office) to handle relations with the West. A new school, the Beijing Tongwenguan, was established under the Zongli Yamen's auspices in 1862, and its original purpose was to train the translators needed in Sino-Western diplomacy. William AP Martin, head teacher of the Tongwenguan, translated Henry Wheaton's *Elements of International Law* into Chinese in 1864. This book was the first complete translation of a European masterpiece on international law.[12]

In the spring of 1864, the Prussian Minister rode aboard a battleship on his journey to Peking. While approaching China they came across three Danish merchant ships and captured them as spoils of war. The Zongli Yamen protested against this action and pointed that the capture venue was in China's territorial waters, and therefore, should be subject to China's jurisdiction. The Prussian Minister conceded and released two ships and compensated the third one. This case was solved peacefully according to the principles of international law. The Zongli Yamen was impressed deeply by the usefulness of international law and then printed and distributed William Martin's translated book.[13]

William Martin and his Tongwenguan colleagues and students further translated several other international works. Martin taught international law in the Tongwenguan and attracted the attention of some high-ranking officers. However, there was only very limited practical use of international law following this episode.

After the Sino-Japanese War of 1894–95 and Boxer Rebellion of 1900, the Qing government was determined to reform its political and legal system, and sent numerous students abroad to study. Hundreds of students who studied in Japan brought modern international law doctrines back to China. In the early 20th century, international law became a popular tool in China's sovereign recovery campaign.

[11] 'Zhongguo yu Guojifa' (n 3) 239.

[12] LH Liu *Clash of Empires: The Invention of China in Modern World Making* (Harvard University Press Cambridge MA 2004); see further the contribution by LH Liu 'Henry Wheaton (1785–1848)' in this volume.

[13] 'Zhongguo yu Guojifa' (n 3) 243–4.

3. China's Treaty Revision Campaign and International Law

From 1842 to 1943, China's sovereignty was impeded upon by the so-called unequal treaties.[14] After its acceptance of international law, the Chinese adopted the principle of sovereign equality in an effort to rid itself of the burden of those treaties. Basically, there were two approaches to reaching this end, abrogation and revision of the unequal treaties. Dr Sun Yat-sen made famous the slogan 'abrogation of the unequal treaties' in the 1920s, which became a powerful political propaganda tool helping revolutionary parties (Kuomintang of China and Chinese Communist Party) summon popular support to win political power, but this approach had very limited practical importance. From the viewpoint of international law, China's treaty revision campaign was much more significant.

In the late Qing period, eighteen countries entered into treaty relations with China and enjoyed various privileges, which were detrimental to Chinese sovereignty. Soon after the republic was established in 1912, the cabinet of the Chinese government passed a resolution that any new treaty signed should offer equal rights and privileges to each signing party. However, the Japanese forced China to accept the Twenty-one Demands and to sign the Sino-Japanese Treaty of 25 May 1915,[15] which encroached heavily upon China's sovereignty. This treaty became a well-known national humiliation and provoked modern Chinese nationalism directed against Japan.

After the First World War, the Chinese government requested entrance to the Paris Peace Conference of 1919 and the Washington Conference of 1921 so as to revise those treaty clauses restricting China's sovereignty, but this was met with scant sympathy, and no concrete resolution was concluded. In the meantime, the Soviet Union announced two generous offers of unconditional relinquishment of former Tsarist Russia's treaty privileges in China. Dr Sun Yat-sen and many Chinese accepted the Soviet offers, and entered into an alliance with the Soviet Union under the premise of anti-imperialism and abrogation of unequal treaties.

The Beijing government, then China's central government, employed the principal of vital change of circumstances (*clausula rebus sic stantibus*) as the means of its treaty revision campaign. At the Paris Conference, Wellington Koo, one of the Chinese delegates, cited this principle in regards to the dispute with Japan over Germany's treaty rights in Shandong. Koo argued, on 28 January 1919, at the Council of Ten, that the Sino-Japanese Treaty of 1915 was invalid, and 'even if the treaties and notes

---

[14] A Peters 'Unequal Treaties' R Wolfrum (ed) *The Max Planck Encyclopedia of Public International Law* (Oxford University Press Oxford 2008) at <http://www.mpepil.com>.

[15] 'Sino-Japanese Treaties and Exchanges of Notes of 25 May 1915' (1916) 10 American Journal of International Law Supplement: Official Documents 1–66.

had been entirely valid, the fact of China's declaration of war on Germany (during the First World War) had altered the situation in such a way that on the principle of *rebus sic stantibus,* they could not be enforced today'.[16] Two weeks later, the Chinese delegation presented a memorandum on the Shandong problem again emphasizing this principle. However, the council decided that Germany's treaty privileges over Shandong should be inherited by Japan.

The second case of China's reference to this principle dealt with Chinese rights in Mongolia. After the Chinese Revolution of 1911, Outer Mongolia declared independence from China. As the result of negotiations among China, Russia and Mongolia, a treaty of tripartite was signed in June 1915. Accordingly Outer Mongolia became an autonomous area of China, and many trading privileges were extended to Russia. Two years later, when revolution broke out in Russia, the Chinese government gradually recovered its influence in Outer Mongolia. In the end of 1919, by calling on the principal of vital change of circumstances, Beijing declared the treaty of tripartite invalid and, therefore, so was the autonomy of Outer Mongolia.

During the Washington Conference of 1921–22, this principle was referred to several times in issues concerning China. One of China's main purposes at that conference was to abolish the Sino-Japanese Treaty of 1915. Public opinion supported the Beijing government's reference to the principle of vital change of circumstances to this end. Chinese delegates requested that the conference declare the treaty invalid since it violated the Nine-Power Treaty. Japanese delegates declared on 2 February 1922 that the Japanese government could not accept China's assertion of the invalidity of the Sino-Japanese Treaty of 1915. However, in considering the vital change of circumstances since the conclusion of that treaty, Japan would voluntarily abandon three articles of that treaty.

In early 1923, the Chinese parliament resolved to abolish the Sino-Japanese Treaty of 1915. Furthermore, a prominent law professor at Beijing University argued that unilateral renouncement of a bilateral treaty was legally untenable, and he suggested that China employ the principle of vital change of circumstances to denounce the treaty.

After the May 30th Incident in 1925,[17] public opinion in China rose against the treaty system. The Beijing government sent a memorandum to the treaty powers proclaiming that since all the Sino-foreign treaties had been concluded several decades ago, the circumstances had undergone 'vital changes' both in China and in the outside world; therefore, these treaties ought to be revised. The treaty powers replied that they would consider China's request provided the Chinese government could prove its will and ability to execute treaty responsibilities.

---

[16] J Guangyao and M Jianbiao (eds) *Guweijun Yanjiangji* (Wellington Koo's Diplomatic Speeches) (Shanghai Cishu Press Shanghai 2006) at 20.

[17] At the so-called May 30th Incident in 1925 ended a series of nationwide anti-foreign demonstrations in China in the killing of thirteen demonstrators by the British Police in Shanghai.

As a result of the ineffectiveness of the treaty revision requests and growing eagerness of the Chinese to abolish the unequal treaties, the Beijing government resorted to another course of action. Wang Zhenting, then the Minister of Foreign Affairs, summoned the Committee of Diplomatic Affairs in early 1926, and they devised a formula which combined the principal of vital change of circumstances with the revision clause embedded in each treaty (usually set for every ten years) to ask each power to revise the treaties one by one. This formula became the main tool of the Chinese treaty revision campaign thereafter.

In 1926, three treaties were due to be revised. The Beijing government notified France, Japan, and Belgium accordingly, and expressed its desire to revise its treaties with those countries. China's goal was not only to revise the commercial clauses according to international customs, and so it insisted that old treaties be terminated by the revised date. France and Japan accepted the proposal but delayed negotiations using a myriad of excuses. Belgium rejected China's proposal on the basis of article 46 of the Sino-Belgian Treaty of 1865, which stated that only Belgium had the right to raise the revision clause; therefore, China had no right to renounce a bilateral treaty.

Prior to 27 October, the due date of revision, no compromise had been reached. The Beijing government announced on 6 November that the Sino-Belgian Treaty was terminated. The vital change of circumstances was one of the prime reasons for China's decisive action. Belgium strongly protested and brought a lawsuit to the Permanent Court of International Law at The Hague concerning article 46 of the Sino-Belgian Treaty of 1865.

The Beijing government was in an awkward position. It considered bringing China's case to the Assembly of the League of Nations, referring to article 19 of the League's convention about the right to revise unsuitable treaties. Beijing decided to consult with four top international law experts, Walther Schücking, Giuseppe Motta, Nicolas Politis, and Robert Lansing, about how to defend China's case at The Hague. Schücking believed China could refer to the principle of vital changes of circumstances, and win considerable sympathy in The Hague.

Politis wrote a very detailed memorandum. He believed Belgium had a very strong position on article 46, and that China should refer to the principle of vital changes of circumstances to claim that the Treaty of 1865 was legally discredited. China should further prove that in the negotiations, it had tried every possible way to replace the outdated old treaty with a more suitable new treaty, and only after confirming that Belgium had no intention of revising the old treaty, China renounced the old treaty as a last resort. Belgium soon altered its position and proclaimed its willingness to negotiate a new treaty with Beijing, and to rescind the lawsuit at The Hague.[18]

---

[18]   C Tang *Bai Feichu Bupinden Tiaoyue Zebi de Beiyang Xiuyue Shi (1912–1928)* (Treaty Revision Campaign of the Beijing Government, 1912–1928: Out of the Shadow of the 'Abrogation of Unequal Treaties') (Shehui Keshue Wenshian Press Beijing 2010) at 367–406.

This case greatly strengthened China's position and set a valuable precedent for China's ability to attack outdated treaties. From 1926 to 1928, the Beijing government pursued its new treaty revision formula and achieved numerous positive results. It renounced two treaties, and forced several countries to negotiate new treaties with China.

The Nationalist government, which originally insisted on abrogation of all unequal treaties, after replacing the Beijing government as China's central governing body, adhered to the Beijing government treaty revision formula. After unifying China in mid-1928, the Nationalist government issued its declaration on concluding new treaties on 7 July, which under the pretence of the abrogation of unequal treaties, was actually employing the principle of vital change of circumstances and the revision clauses of each treaty. Within six months, it concluded a dozen new treaties with the powers.

The Manchurian Incident of 18 September 1931[19] was a watershed for China's treaty revision campaign because it altered the priority of China's diplomatic efforts to resisting the Japanese invasion. China accused Japan of illegally invading Chinese Manchuria and breaking the Convention of the League of Nations. The League sent the Lytton Commission to investigate and suggest a solution. When the Assembly of the League confirmed the Lytton Commission's report, which suggested that Manchukuo was a puppet regime of Japanese Kwantung Army, and should not be recognized, Japan announced that it was withdrawing its membership from the League. Most members of the League refused to recognize Manchukuo, which allowed China to cultivate friendships with those countries so as to check Japan's intrusion into China proper, but the treaty revision had to be postponed.

As the conflicts between China and Japan escalated, the Marco Polo Bridge Incident[20] broke out in the summer of 1937. China appealed to the Nine Powers Treaty (6 February 1922)[21] and the Brussels Conference was summoned. Chinese delegates referred to the principle of the sanctity of treaty obligations, accusing Japan of breaking the Nine Powers Treaty and invading China's territory and encroaching upon its sovereignty. China sought the help of the Great Powers to place sanctions on Japan. On the treaty issue, China moved from calling on the principle of vital change of circumstances to employing the principle of the sanctity of treaty obligations.

Japan did the exact opposite. When China devoted herself to treaty revision, Japan insisted on the principle of the sanctity of treaty obligations. When China referred to the principle of the sanctity of treaty obligations, Japan called on the principle of vital

[19] The so-called Manchurian Incident refers to a bomb attack by Japanese military in Manchuria which is often seen as the beginning of Japan's invasion of China.

[20] The Marco Polo Bridge Incident refers to an armed encounter between Japanese and Chinese troops triggering the Second Sino-Japanese War (1937–45).

[21] 'Treaty between all Nine Allied Powers Relating to Principles to be Followed in Matters Concerning China 6 February 1922' (1922) 16 American Journal of International Law Supplement: Official Documents 64–8.

changes. In October 1938, when the Japanese army occupied Hankow and Canton, two major Chinese cities, the American government accused Japan of breaking the Open Door Doctrine. The Japanese prime minister asserted that Japan was building a 'new order' of East Asia, and that other countries should recognize that new order. The Japanese foreign minister renounced American protests by saying that there was a vital change of East Asia's circumstances; therefore, the Nine Powers Treaty was outdated.

China's foreign minister indicated the vital change of East Asia that the Japanese claimed was caused by illegal actions of the Japanese military; hence, it was unfitting to refer to the principle of vital change of circumstances to abolish the Nine Powers Treaty. American and British governments both protested the Japanese announcement along the same line later on.

A retrospective glance at China's treaty revision campaign during the 1920s and 1930s reveals that the main trend was the development of its treaty-revision formula, which combined the principles of vital change of circumstances and employment of the revision clause of each treaty. This formula ingeniously combined the strength of the principle of vital change of circumstances with the revision clause embedded into each treaty. The latter unequivocally indicated the date of each treaty to be revised. Since most treaties were to be revised every ten years, China endeavoured to revise all her unequal treaties within the coming decade. However, calling on the revision clause did have limitations, as some treaties contained no such clause, and this clause affected only commercial and tax business according to the common customs of international practice. The former principle offered China a solid legal case to indicate the outdated and unethical status of the unequal treaties, which became the main source of Sino-foreign conflict at the time and, therefore, made it imperative to revise the treaties completely.

In the mid-1920s, the Beijing government developed this powerful formula, which was further backed by the popular support of its people and the appeal of 'abrogation of the unequal treaties' of the Nationalist government, and pushed steadily forward in its pursuit of achieving equal treaty rights on the international stage. At first, the Beijing government only wished to revise treaties one by one in their due time, but gradually this formula developed into a unilateral termination of the treaty if the power refused to revise the treaty. The Belgium case set a successful precedent. The Nationalist government followed this formula, even if it did not acknowledge doing so.

China's resorting to the principle of vital change of circumstances had a close connection with Sino-Japanese relations. Following the Twenty-one Demands negotiations, the Chinese government and the public resisted and boycotted the Sino-Japanese Treaty of 1915. At the Paris Conference, Wellington Koo first referred to this principle in an attempt to contend with Japan for the Shandong rights. At the Washington Conference, Chinese delegates requested the abolition of the Sino-Japanese Treaty of 1915. In the 1920s, many scholars suggested that China referred to this principle so as to abolish the Sino-Japanese treaty. The Japanese, conversely, referred to the principle of the sanctity of treaty obligations to offset China's case. A reversal of positions took place following the Manchurian Incident of 1931. China chose to emphasize the sanctity of treaties and Japan insisted upon the vital change of circumstances. The enactment of international law not only occurred between China and Europe but also China and Japan. This point becomes even more thought provoking when one takes into account that China imported its knowledge of international law mostly from Japan as late as the early 20th century.

The vital change of circumstances was quite a controversial principle in the international law circle. After the First World War, Germany, Turkey, and Persia all referred to this principle in an attempt to relieve their treaty burdens, and their cases have been well researched; however, China's use of this principle in revising treaties has been mostly neglected until recently. The main reason is that Kuomintang of China and Chinese Communist Party have been ruling China since 1927, and they emphasized the importance of Dr Sun Yat-sen's slogan of 'abrogation of the unequal treaties' while understating the importance of the Beijing government's treaty revision formula. This ideological bias hindered academic research in the history and law of Chinese international relations.

4. China's Involvement in International Organizations and International Law

4.1. The Hague Peace Conference

Another topic involving China's encounter with international law is China's involvement in international organizations. China's international position had descended to a low ebb due to the signing of the Boxer Protocol of 1901. It barely escaped the fate of being partitioned, but instead became a so-called 'semi-colony', exploited by the Great Powers. Hence, on the one hand the Qing government, endeavoured to reform its legal system wishing to be accepted as a civilized nation. On the other hand, China positively participated in the international society as a sovereign State, hoping to be accepted by the powers as an equal member of the State system.

At the turn of the 20th century, imperialism had become the mainstream of international politics. In the meantime, the international peace movement also began gathering momentum. Two Hague Peace Conferences were prominent examples. China eagerly participated in both conferences, hoping to ease the imperialist pressures upon her.

The first Hague Peace Conference was convened by Tsar Nicholas II of Russia, and held in 1899. Twenty-six countries sent delegations to discuss issues concerning disarmament and international arbitration. The Qing government appointed Yang Ru, its minister to St Petersburg, to take part. Yang brought some attachés, including an interpreter, Lu Zhengxiang, with him. While this conference did not reach any concrete results on the armament issues, it did conclude some agreements on the peaceful settlement of international conflict and attempt to civilize warfare. By the end of the conference, China had signed several conventions, including the Red Cross Conventions of 1864. It was the very beginning of China's active participation in international conventions and organizations.

One of the main results of the first conference was the establishment of the Permanent Court of Arbitration (PCA). Its expenditures were shared by member States according to the Universal Postal Union's share. China assumed the lion's share voluntarily.

The second Hague Peace Conference held in 1907, and forty-four States, almost all the sovereign States at that time, took part. China appointed Lu Zhengxiang, then the minister to The Hague, to attend. Lu's attitude to that conference was generally cautious. Early in 1907, Lu suggested the Qing Court sent a special envoy to the conference and proclaimed that

this Conference concerns the international array of powers…an international conference is a non violent battlefield for every country…on this occasion the most important thing is to be superior to other countries. A country's ranking during this occasion implies its ranking in the world.[22]

He concluded that China also should send an ambassador in order to confront other countries. The Qing Court then appointed Lu the Ambassador for the Hague Peace Conference and promoted Qian Xun, China's attaché to the embassy in Holland to collaborate with Lu. The court also invited John W Foster (1836–1917), a former Secretary of State and advisor to China's embassy in America, to represent China in the conference due to Foster's distinguished reputation.

The second Hague Peace Conference took place from June to October 1907. The Chinese delegation agreed on most of the issues, but Lu opposed all issues concerning Chinese sovereignty, especially the issue of the new international court proposed by the US. It was said that the permanent court was neither permanent nor a court due to its inefficiency. The US proposed to set up a new court staffed by seventeen standing judges. A standing judge's term was twelve years. Of the forty-five member countries, the US, Germany, France, the UK, Austria, Italy, Russia, and Japan could send one standing judge. The remaining thirty-seven countries could send their judges to fill in the remaining nine seats. According to the degree of development in each country's legal system, the term of that country's judge varied from one, two, four, to ten years. The Turkish judge's term was ten years but China's

---

[22] Lu to Foreign Ministry, 13 March 1907, Waijiaobu (Ministry of Foreign Affairs) Archives, 02-21-002-02-043 (Academia Sinica Taipei Taiwan).

only four years because of the disparity between the countries' legal systems. China was treated as a third-class country. Lu thought that the court reflected all countries' perspectives on China. It would be a significant problem if there were to be no Chinese judge in the court when discussing an issue relating to China. Lu argued in the conference that China had always been a first class country with respect to the size of its population and territory. In the old court, China, Russia, and Germany were all allocated 25 shares. The new ranking should also accord an equal number of shares, otherwise China would not accept its new ranking. In addition to China, Brazil, and Mexico also opposed this proposal, so the proposal was not passed.

Lu reported to the Foreign Ministry saying that Japan endeavoured to make China a 'third-class country'. Lu said:

I have read the first draft of the Conference. China was ranked as first class. The Japanese congressman argued that China's judicial system is radically different from other civilized countries. This is why every country has the power of consular jurisdiction in China and Chinese civil servants do not have the right to interfere with foreign affairs....It would be ridiculous if a country could not bring a foreigner on its soil to trial despite having equal judicial power to other countries in judging international affairs.[23]

After the conference, Lu submitted a memorandum saying that some conventions had been signed in the conference, but each country harboured mutual suspicions and scepticism.

I think we cannot hope for peace; war is forthcoming...I can foresee that the three continents, namely Europe, America and Asia, will be well-matched in strength...Japan seems to be the police officer to look after the foreign powers' interests in China.

He argued that the way for China to survive was to play the powers against one another, and suggested forming an alliance with the US and Germany.[24]

This was the first time China took an active role in the international community. Chinese diplomats were extremely sensitive to China's international status and were shocked by its status as a 'third-class country'. In autumn 1907, Chinese ministers posted in Europe urged the Foreign Ministry to forward their joint memorandum in order to urge the Qing Court to amend the judicial system and become a constitutional country. They argued that:

Because every country in North and South America sees China's as the most uncivilised judicial system, European countries also agree on this viewpoint. Now China must amend the system to secure its sovereignty and to stop other countries' criticisms. We have to investigate other countries' legal systems and amend ours at the same time. Meanwhile, we should recruit legal experts to help us. If we want to be a great power, our constitution has to reach the quality of most countries' constitutions. If we do not amend the judicial system, the

---

[23] Lu to Foreign Ministry, 22 July 1907, Waijiaobu Archives, 02-21-010-01-002.
[24] Lu to Foreign Ministry, 16 January 1908, Waijiaobu Archives, 02-21-004-01-003.

constitution will not be effective. We do not know which class China will be in during the third Hague Peace Conference.[25]

Lu was reappointed Minister to Holland in 1908 and signed the Sino-Dutch Consular Agreement with the Dutch minister in Beijing in 1911. Then he was instructed to go to Russia to revise the Sino-Russian Treaty of Commerce of 1881 and was appointed Minister to Russia. During the 1911 Revolution, Lu was the first Minister who supported the Republican government and sent a telegram to ask the Qing Court to abdicate the throne. Lu was appointed the Foreign Minister of the Republic of China and reformed the foreign ministry, thus laying the foundation of the Republic of China's foreign affairs.

The third Hague Peace Conference was scheduled to convene in 1914. Every country was to send all proposals to The Hague for research in 1912. After the second Hague Conference, Qian Xun continued to submit memorandums to petition the Qing Court to prepare for the third conference as soon as possible. Qian suggested sparing no effort in amending the judicial system and cultivating experts during the years before the third conference. Qian also petitioned researching and publishing all conventions signed in the second conference; however, the Qing government did not respond.

After the 1911 Revolution, Foreign Minister Lu was keen to prepare for the third conference. On 24 September 1912, Lu stepped down from the post of Prime Minister and organized a society on international law. On 30 September, Lu said every country's judicial experts commented on international matters in the former Hague Peace Conferences and every matter was decided efficiently. He wanted to devote himself to the study of international law in order to help China gain an equal footing with the other nations and then initiated this international law society in preparation of the third Hague Peace Conference. The Foreign Ministry also requested President Yuan Shikai to instruct high-ranking officials to prepare for The Hague Peace Conference. On 2 October, Yuan instructed Lu to take care of the preparations.

Lu then organized the Preparatory Committee for the third Hague Peace Conference. He argued that

the establishment of the Hague Peace Conference was to stop wars, but this is very unlikely, so the purpose changed to advance the civilization of war regulations. Thus, the army and navy are involved. The legal field is also involved because some countries criticized China's legal system as not well-developed.

He then sent a dispatch to invite the Army, Naval and Judicial Ministries to send official who understood foreign languages to the committee meeting. The Preparatory Committee convened on 12 December 1912. The purpose of the Preparatory Committee, Lu reported, was that since the Chinese delegation was not

---

[25] Lu and other Ministers in Europe to Foreign Ministry, 15 August 1907, Waijiaobu Archives, 02-21-002-03-051.

adequately prepared for the first and second Hague Peace Conferences, and was unable to effectively participate in discussions; therefore, he believed it mandatory that China be adequately prepared for the upcoming third conference. Lu then set regulations, and collected documents and relevant works.

The committee meeting began by researching the conventions of the second Hague Peace Conference which were not signed by all member countries, starting with the First Geneva Convention for the Amelioration of the Condition of the Wounded and Sick in Armed Forces in the Field, 1864.[26] By March 1913, preparations for all relevant issues were completed and the president ordered the relevant ministries to make necessary amendments. The Preparatory Committee continued to discuss and passed the Convention Respecting the Laws and Customs of War on Land on 5 June 1913.[27]

The Committee then discussed the Status of Enemy Merchant Ships at the Outbreak of Hostilities and passed it on 23 October. Lu also stated that

the Qing worried that the state could not afford new responsibilities, and the people could not follow international agreements, thus it decided not to participate in any international community. The Republic should be nice to its neighbors and allow foreigners to advance their understandings of the Republic. If a new convention is passed during the Conference, China should sign it immediately.[28]

On 6 November, the Committee discussed the Conversion of Merchant Ships into War-Ships and the Laying of Automatic Submarine Mines.[29] By 18 December, the latter was passed. On 19 February 1914, the Convention Relative to Certain Restrictions with Regard to the Exercise of the Capture in Naval War was discussed and was signed on 27 March.[30] On 3 April, the Committee discussed the Creation of an International Prize Court,[31] but on 8 June decided not to ratify it. By then every Hague convention of 1907 had been discussed and presented to the president in early 1915. Finally, all the passed conventions were ratified in early 1916, and sent to The Hague in May of 1917.

On 14 August 1917, the Chinese president declared war on Germany and Austria and proclaimed that the Republic of China's government would follow the war regulations made during The Hague Peace Conference. At the time, China had already

[26] Convention (I) for the Amelioration of the Condition of the Wounded and Sick in Armed Forces in the Field (adopted 22 August 1864, entered into force 22 June 1865) 129 CTS 361.

[27] Convention (IV) Respecting the Laws and Customs of War on Land and its Annex: Regulations Concerning the Laws and Customs of War on Land (adopted 18 October 1907, entered into force 26 January 1910) 187 CTS 227.

[28] Record of 25th meeting, 23 October 1913, Waijiaobu Archives, 03-35-003-01-025.

[29] Convention (VII) Relating to the Conversion of Merchant Ships into War-Ships (adopted 18 October 1907, entered into force 26 January 1910) 205 CTS 319; Convention (VIII) relative to the Laying of Automatic Submarine Contact Mines (adopted 18 October 1907, entered into force 26 January 1910) 205 CTS 331.

[30] Convention (XI) Relative to certain Restrictions with regard to the Exercise of the Right of Capture in Naval War (adopted 18 October 1907, entered into force 26 January 1910) 205 CTS 367.

[31] Convention (XII) Relative to the Creation of an International Prize Court (adopted 18 October 1907) 205 CTS 381.

sent the signed conventions to the Dutch Foreign Ministry, and these conventions all became effective after a period of 60 days. The Beijing government printed out collection of conventions of The Hague Peace Conference and sent a copy to every ministry in order to enable it to carry them out.

From 1899 to 1917, China participated in and prepared for the Hague Peace Conferences, and signed a number of international conventions. The Hague Peace Conferences were the first time that China participated in international conferences and organizations. The conventions of The Hague and Red Cross were the first international treaties to which China was a signatory, and as such this was a watershed for modern Chinese diplomatic history. In the course of preparations for the third Peace Conference, enough experience was accumulated that China could enter the First World War and attend the Paris Peace Conference of 1919. During this period, China's attempts at internationalization to enter into the Western-led international community indicate that China was a civilized and a sovereign State capable of using Western-style international conventions and international law, take part in international activities, as well as uphold international responsibilities. These efforts, together with domestic attempts at constitutionalism, judicial reforms and revolution, forced foreign powers to treat China with equality and revise the Unequal Treaties.

4.2. The League of Nations

Three years after the founding of the Republic, the First World War broke out in 1914. China proclaimed its neutral status and requested that all warring countries not engage in conflicts in their settlements within China. Using the pretext of the Anglo-Japanese Alliance, Japan declared war on Germany, but it ignored China's neutrality and attacked Jiaozhou Bay. Japan even attacked beyond the war zone designated by the Chinese government and occupied the Qingdao-Jinan railway. Finally, it imposed the Twenty-one Demands on China in May 1915. China was forced to negotiate with Japan with Foreign Minister Lu as China's main negotiator. After the Sino-Japanese Treaty of 1915 was signed in May 1915,[32] Lu suggested to Yuan that entering The First World War was the only chance to save China. However, Yuan's successor Duan Qirui accepted Japan's terms resulting in an increase in Japan's influence in China following President Yuan's passing.

During the 1917 discussions on whether the Beijing government should enter the First World War, Liang Qichao strongly argued that China should imitate Italy, which joined the Crimean War with the intent to raise its international status. Liang argued that we have to be very active to follow the international trend and plan our country's future development and endeavour to stand on the side of the international commu-

---

[32] Sino-Japanese Treaties (n 15).

nity. The Entente Powers offered favourable terms to persuade China to enter the war. On 14 August 1917, after China declared war on Germany and Austria, the acting British minister replied that due to this decision, Sino-British relations would be significantly improved and that the UK could help China to become a great power. China could not contribute much to the Entente Powers because China was suffering from civil war. This irritated the Entente powers because China did not fulfil the responsibilities of being one of the Entente powers and this undermined China's status following the war.

After China's entry into the First World War, the Beijing foreign ministry started to prepare for the peace conference after the war. On 8 January 1918, US President Woodrow Wilson proclaimed the Fourteen Points for Peace in Congress.[33] Wellington Koo, minister to London, and Shi Zhaoji, minister to Washington, both suggested that China cooperate with the US, and both of them were highly interested in the fourth article: 'a general association of nations must be formed under specific covenants for the purpose of affording mutual guarantees of political independence and territorial integrity to great and small states alike'.

During the 1919 Paris Peace Conference, the Chinese delegation took an active role in the commission of the League of Nations in order to gain higher status in the new international order. The commission was put in charge of drafting the League's Covenant. The Big Five sent two representatives and the other nine countries sent one (the Chinese representative was Wellington Koo). US President Wilson chaired the commission.

While drafting the Covenant of the League of Nations and discussing the organization of the Council, Koo argued that the Council should be represented by the Great Powers as well as the minor countries. Koo also supported Japan's suggestion of 'racial equality'. After the covenant was passed Wilson brought it back to the US, accepted Congress' amendments and continued to discuss the covenant in Paris.

In addition to focusing on the covenant, China also strived for a seat on the Council. The primary organs of the League were the Assembly, the Council and the Secretariat with the Council acting as the chief decision-making organ. The permanent members of the Council were the United States, Great Britain, France, Italy, and Japan, and these five selected the four seats of the first term non-permanent members. Koo, in the commission, suggested that the standard to select the non-permanent seats should be in accordance with the ranking of every State's population, size of territory, and the advancement of commerce in its continent, a proposal which was vetoed by several countries led by Japan. Belgium, Brazil, Greece, and Spain were selected. The Chinese were very dissatisfied with this, and Chinese pundits suggested that China should not join the League if it could not get a seat in the Council.

---

[33] W Wilson 'Wilson's Address to Congress, Stating the War Aims and Peace Terms of the United States (Delivered in Joint Session, 8 January 1918)' in A Shaw (ed) *State Papers and Addresses by Woodrow Wilson* (George H. Doran Company New York 1918) 464–72.

The first Assembly of the League convened in November 1920. The Beijing government transferred Koo's post from Washington to London so that he could also act as the Chinese representative to the League. Koo fought for a Council seat with the hope to amend China's unequal status and to decrease Japan's influence in the Council on the Shandong issue.[34] In the subcommittee, while discussing how to elect the non-permanent country membership, Koo stated that every continent should have a set number of representatives. This proposal was referred to as Fenzhouzhuyi. Due to Koo's efforts, his suggestion became a tentative consensus in the Assembly, and China was selected as one of the four non-permanent members along with Spain, Brazil and Belgium. One scholar has argued that the fact that China was elected as a non-permanent member in the Council was a sign that western countries saw China as a member of the international family.[35] It was seen as a glorious achievement.

In addition to appointing Koo as the Chinese representative of the Council, Beijing set up an office in Geneva. The 14th meeting of the Council convened in August 1921 with Koo as the chairman. As a result of which, Koo was also the acting chairman of the second Assembly in September 1921, and toasted every member country in the opening ceremony. In the Assembly, China was re-elected as a non-permanent member of the Council.

Koo returned to Beijing after the Washington Conference (1921–22) and took the post of Minister for Foreign Affairs. The Chinese minister to Rome, Tang Zaifu, succeeded Koo's position in the League. During the third Assembly, a number of countries strived for seats on the Council which endangered China's seat; however, Koo gained enough support and the number of the non-permanent member seats was increased to six, China was still elected as a non-permanent Council member.

In 1923 China's international reputation deteriorated due to domestic unrest. During the fourth Assembly of September 1923 the Chinese representative publicized the Fenzhouzhuyi, but China was not able to keep its seat on the Council as it was given to Persia. During the fifth Assembly in 1924, the Chinese representative again publicized the Fenzhouzhuyi and even announced that China would secede from the League if it did not get a seat on the Council, but China still failed to regain its seat. In 1926, Germany sought membership of the League and a permanent seat on the Council. In March 1926 a special Assembly convened to discuss this matter, but Spain, Brazil, and Poland also wanted to have their permanent seats in the Council. Beijing also instructed the Chinese representative to take this opportunity to vie for a seat.

---

[34] The Shandong issue concerns a dispute about art 156 of the Versailles Treaty ((signed 28 June 1919, entered into force 10 January 1920) (1919) 225 CTS 188) regarding the transfer of the former territorial rights, titles and privileges of Germany in the Shandong Peninsula to Japan. This dispute resulted in the non-signing of the Versailles Treaty by China. See on this F Schorkopf 'Versailles Peace Treaty (1919)' in *The Max Planck Encyclopedia of Public International Law* (n 14).

[35] Z Yongjin, *China in the International System, 1918–1920: The Middle Kingdom at the Periphery* (Macmillan London 1991) at 193–4.

However, Brazil opposed this proposal so that Germany could not join the League of Nations. Then a reorganizational committee was set up to discuss the German case and the committee decided that Germany should join the Council and have a permanent seat. Finally, the number of non-permanent seats was increased to nine under the premise that three seats were to be up for election each year, and that Fenzhouzhuyi be considered as a guideline for choosing these seats. China was elected into the Council that year as a two-year member.

In 1928, after it had nominally reunited China, the Nanjing-based Nationalist government was highly concerned about its international status. Unfortunately, the first time that Nanjing represented China during the ninth Assembly of the League of Nations, China was not elected as a member of the Council, which was a great embarrassment to them. This was seen a serious insult to Nanjing. In the 10th Assembly of 1929, China's representative Wu Chaoshu was elected as one of the six deputy chairmen, which was perceived by Nanjing as evidence of its rise in international status. In the 1930 11th Assembly, China endeavoured to fight for a seat on the Council; however, the result was a disappointment.

As of September 1931, Nanjing had already consolidated its sovereignty on Chinese soil, which brought a commensurate increase in its international reputation. China was elected onto the Council as a three-year, non-permanent member that year. In 1934, China's term was due but China did not get re-elected due to Japan's firm opposition (although Japan claimed to have seceded from the League in 1933, according to the Covenant, it required two years to take effect). The League was helpless to stop the Sino-Japanese War, which began in 1937, and was equally unable to avert war again in 1939 as the Second World War broke out. The League's commitment to international security was a failure.

China also participated in the Permanent Court of International Justice at The Hague. In February 1920, the League's Council discussed a proposal to establish a permanent international court. In December, the first Assembly of the League passed the Statute of the Permanent Court of International Justice.[36] In September 1921, at the second Assembly of the League, eleven judges and four deputy judges were elected. Wang Chonghui, then the Dean of the Dali Yuan (High Court of Justice), was elected deputy judge. He went to Europe at the beginning of 1921 to attend the Covenant Amending Committee as the Chinese representative.

The Assembly of the League of Nations of 22 September 1924, envisaging the creation of a standing organ called the Committee of Experts for the Progressive Codification of International Law, which consisted of seventeen experts, was to prepare a list of subjects 'the regulation of which by international agreement' was most 'desirable and realizable', and thereafter to examine the comments of governments on this list and report on the questions which 'were sufficiently ripe', as well as on the procedure to be

---

[36] Statute of the Permanent Court of International Justice (entered into force 20 August 1921) 6 LNTS 379.

followed in preparing for conferences in view of finding solutions. This was the first attempt on a worldwide basis to codify and develop whole fields of international law rather than simply regulating individual and specific legal problems.

In April 1925, the League Committee for the Progressive Codification of International Law was summoned in Geneva. Wang Chonghui attended as an expert and raised issue on 'the responsibility of states for damage done in their territory to the person and property of foreigners'. This issue had been accepted and further discussed in 1927, did not pass the Codification Conference, which met at The Hague from 13 March to 12 April 1930.

4.3. The United Nations

After the outbreak of the Pacific War in December 1941, China's contribution to the fight against Japan was viewed as invaluable. Franklin D. Roosevelt and Winston Churchill met in Newfoundland in August 1941 and issued the Atlantic Charter. The charter proposed to establish a standing security organization. In January 1942, representatives from 26 countries signed the declaration of the United Nations to jointly fight against fascism and to close cooperation after the war. In January 1943, the Sino-American and Sino-British unequal treaties were abolished. Due to Roosevelt's insistence, China was listed as a world power while the member States were planning to form a post war international security organization. On 30 October 1943, the American, Russian, British, and Chinese representatives signed the Moscow Declaration, which recognized China as one of the Big Four. The November Cairo Conference, furthermore, confirmed China's status as one of the Big Four.

The Big Four planned the Washington Conversations on International Peace and Security Organization in Dumbarton Oaks from 21 August to 7 October 1943. In fact, Britain, the Soviet Union and the United States decided everything in the first phase of the meeting from 21 August to 28 September. China was only permitted to attend the second phase of meeting from 29 September to 7 October with America and Britain, which only confirmed the decisions already made during the first phase. However, China raised seven amendments concerning the UN in the second phase of meeting. They were: (1) that the maintenance of peace and security must accord to justice and the principles of international law, so as to prevent the newly established international organization from being reduced to a tool of power politics; (2) to guarantee political independence and the territorial integrity of each country, and to increase the confidence of each country, particularly that of small nations; (3) to define 'invasion' as specifically as possible; (4) to organize an international air force as the symbol and means of the Security Council; (5) to allow the Assembly to initiate policy and amendments of international law for the good of promoting security in accordance with the principles of international law; (6) that the international court should arbitrate forcefully; and (7) to promote education and cultural corporation. After discussions, the US and Great

Britain accepted the first, fifth, and seventh points, and these three points were written into the United Nations Charter. The three powers agreed on the sixth point, but postponed a decision on the third point, and rejected the second and fourth points.[37]

Besides concerning itself with international law, China's participation in this conference signalled its status as one of the Big Four. Furthermore, this significantly helped China to become a permanent member on the UN Security Council. The Nationalist government appointed the ambassador to Britain, Wellington Koo; the ambassador to the United States, Wei Daoming; Deputy Foreign Minister, Hu Shize; and the Head of the Military Representative Group in the US, Shang Zhen, as China's delegation to the United Nations.

China's greatest concern was its status in the international community. Was it qualified to be one of the Big Four? What was China's status in this international organization? Wellington Koo and Wang Chonghui both argued that China should participate in the Big Four so as to reap the privileges afforded by it, but Wang Shijie was opposed. Wang argued that the Big Four should not enjoy privileges which would nurture other countries grievances against China. China must not strive for membership in the Big Four because China cannot enjoy the same amount of privileges as America, Britain, and Soviet Union do. While the delegation was having its own meeting, Wei Daoming argued that China was better off being viewed as an ordinary member. Finally, Koo struck a chord when he argued that now China's role in the Big Four has to be confirmed and he endeavoured to raise China's international status.

The San Francisco Conference was convened in April 1945 to draft the Charter for the forthcoming United Nations. On the eve of the conference, Wang and Koo were still debating. Wang argued that China ought not be a member of the Big Four, and its status would be more secure as a spokesman of the second-class powers. But Koo's belief was that China's best interests had to be with the Big Four. At the San Francisco Conference, China opposed imperialism and colonialism, and wished to facilitate colonies' independence and to help the colonies to gain independence from their metropolitan States. In the Trustee Committee, China emphasized that every colony's eventual goal was independence instead of autonomy. This suggestion was declined by the US, Britain, France, the Netherlands, and Australia but was supported by minor States. The proposal was finally passed and recorded in the Charter of the United Nations.

Following China's participation in The Hague Peace Conference, the League of Nations and the United Nations, China endeavoured to protect its sovereignty and to protect neutral States' security by employing international law. China had high expectations that international law could stop aggression and protect minor States by the power of international community.

---

[37] J Guangyao, 'Gu Weichun yu Zhongguo canja Dunbadun Xiangshuyuan Huiyi' (Wellington Koo and China's Participation on the Dumbarton Oaks Conference) in J Guangyao (ed) *Gu Weijun yu Zhongguo Waijiao* (Wellington Koo and Diplomacy of China) (Shanghai Guji Press Shanghai 2001) 294–8.

5. Conclusion

This chapter discussed the interrelations of international law between China and Europe beginning in the 15th century and ending in 1945 in three sections. The first section outlined China's traditional perspectives on world order and the introduction of international law to China. Section 2 focused on how China extricated itself from the unequal treaties. Finally, Section 4 discussed China's participation in international organizations including a brief discussion of international law.

China's approach to the modern world evolved from the traditional view of the Celestial Empire to a full recognition of equality with the Western countries. Although it signed Western-style treaties, China still maintained the tributary system with other Eastern countries. After the period of 1895–1901, China was forced to abandon the traditional idea of the Celestial Empire and accepted without reservation the viewpoints of Western international law. This enabled China to use international law to protect China's sovereignty and independence and to raise its international status.

The Chinese government and populace's efforts to extricate itself from the restrictions of the treaties was encouraged by the idealism of US diplomacy. At the 1919 Paris Conference, China's delegation submitted the Questions for Readjustment memorandum but was totally neglected. China submitted this issue again at the Washington Conference but gained only lip service.

Due to its disillusion with the United States, China then turned to the Soviet Union. Between 1923 and 1927, the Nationalist and Communist Parties pursued the line of 'Down with Imperialism' and 'Abrogation of the Unequal Treaties'. Meanwhile, the Beijing government kept revising treaties and left many thought-provoking cases referring to principles of international law.

China's entrance into the world of international law was dogged by the diplomacy of imperialism. However, the most serious threat to China came not from the West, but from Japan's challenge to become the leading country in East Asia. Japan applied western international law in Okinawa, Taiwan, and Korea in order to challenge the status of China's metropolitan State. During the late Qing period, China acquired knowledge of international law from Japan and amended its judicial system in order to raise its international status. Thereafter, China was capable of using Western international law against Japan and competed with Japan in the arena of international law. After he First World War, China became one of the standing members of the United Nations Security Council.

Some scholars have argued that Japan's Greater East Asia Co-Prosperity Sphere idea was the legacy of a traditional East Asian world. Presently, China and Japan are still competing for the leading role in East Asia. If China regains its supreme position in East Asia, will it restore to prominence the traditional Chinese world order?

It is the opinion of this author that research concerning China's approach to international law following the First World War should go beyond the Sino-European encounter. It is necessary to also delve into research on the Sino-Russian and Sino-Japanese encounters.

RECOMMENDED READING

Hamashita, Takeshi *China, East Asia and the Global Economy: Regional and Historical Perspectives* (Routledge London and New York, 2008).

King Fairbank, John (ed) *The China World Order: Traditional China's Foreign Relations* (Harvard University Press Cambridge MA 1968).

Liao, Minshu 'Qingdai Duiwai Tongshang Zhidu' (Foreign Trade System of Qing Dynasty) in *Jindai Zhongguo, Dongya yu Shijie* (Modern China, East Asia and the World) (Shehui Keshue Wenshian Press Beijing 2008) vol 2, 443–66.

Lin, Shuezhong *Cong Wangguo Gongfa dao Gongfa Waijiao: Wanqing Guojifa de Changru, Quanshi yu Yuniong* (From International Law to International Law Diplomacy: The Importation, Interpretation and Practice of International Law in the Late Qing Dynasty) (Shanghai Kuji Press Shanghai 2009).

Svarverud, Rune *International Law as World Order in Late Imperial China: Translation, Reception and Discourse, 1847–1911* (Brill Leiden 2007).

Tang, Chi-hua, Beijing Zhengfu yu Guoji Lianmeng, 1919–1928 (The Beijing Government and League of Nations, 1919–1928) (Dongda Press Taipei 1998).

Tang, Chi-hua *Bai 'Feichu Bupinden Tiaoyue' Zebi de Beiyang Xiuyueshi (1912–1928)* (Treaty Revision Campaign of the Beijing Government, 1912–1928: Out of the Shadow of the 'Abrogation of Unequal Treaties') (Shehui Keshue Wenshian Press Beijing 2010).

Wang, Dong *China's Unequal Treaties: Narrating National History* (Lexington Books Lanham 2005).

Wang, Tieya 'International Law in China: Historical and Contemporary Perspectives' (1990-II) 221 Hague Academy of International Law, Recueil des cours 195–369.

Zhang, Yongjin *China in the International System, 1918–1920: The Middle Kingdom at the Periphery* (Macmillan London 1991).

CHAPTER 30

JAPAN–EUROPE

KINJI AKASHI

1. INTRODUCTION

THE present chapter discusses the Japanese contribution to the development of international law after Japan's 'encounter' with it. It might be argued that 'international law' of European origin extended its application to non-European regions since the age of European voyages of 'discovery'. While, as several chapters in this handbook exhibit, the periods of its expansion and the modes of its application differ from one region to another,[1] in East Asia the Europeans up to the 18th century made efforts in adapting themselves to the regional 'international' system without seeking a way to impose their own ideas of international relations and law on the indigenous rulers and peoples.[2] ('East Asia' in the present chapter signifies China and other bodies politic under the direct influence of the Chinese civilization such as Chinese writing and Confucianism. The region thus comprises the present States of China, Japan, (North and South) Korea, Taiwan, Vietnam, and so on.) The same applies to the encounters between the Japanese and the Europeans and, even in

---

[1] While, for example, the application of international law to the South American continent began immediately after the 'discovery' of the new continent, the same phenomenon commenced with regard to the East Asian nations only in the middle of the 19th century notwithstanding the fact that the Europeans had intercourses with them much earlier. This is due to the attitudes of the Europeans that at first they did not claim any superiority of their legal system, nor of their civilization, over those of the region.

[2] J Fisch *Die europäische Expansion und das Völkerrecht* (Steiner Stuttgart 1984) at 37–8.

mid-19th century, the Dutch representatives met Shogun with the traditional courtesy required by the Japanese.

The attitudes of the Europeans changed through the process of the imperial expansion in the 19th century. The European powers and the United States explained the existence of international law to the indigenous rulers and claimed that the law should be applied to the relations among them. For the Asian rulers and officials, the European claim was felt as coercion or compulsion. It is therefore understandable that the Japanese officials who negotiated with the Western envoys about opening the secluded country showed passive attitudes towards the application of international law.

In evaluating such passive attitudes in light of the history of international law, we tend to conclude that Japan did not play any positive role in its development. It might be true. Yet we should bear in mind that it is one thing that a nation was forced to take part in the world where international law functioned, it is quite another how such a nation made use of it. The Japanese history, indeed, exhibits these different two aspects.

The purpose of the present chapter is to explore whether and how the Japanese contributed to the development of international law after they encountered it by describing the two aspects. In order to fulfil this purpose, we first confirm the traditional Japanese view on 'international relations' and 'law'. The discussion then proceeds to how Japanese officials and scholars accepted, and made use of, international law.

Before approaching the main subject of discussion, we should clarify the period of 'encounter' in the present chapter. The present writer proposes that it spans from 1853 when the American fleet under the command of Commodore Matthew Calbraith Perry arrived at Uraga Channel at the mouth of the Bay of Yedo (Tokyo) to the first decade of the Japanese Imperial government (until the end of the 1870s) via the collapse of the Tokugawa Shogunate government in 1868.

2. Before the 'Encounter': Japanese Traditional Ideas on 'International Relations' and 'Law'

2.1. Japanese Idea of 'International Relations' before the 'Encounter'

The first record regarding the arrival of Europeans in Japan dates back to 1543 when two Portuguese carrying firearms were found in a Chinese ship that drifted ashore at Tanegashima Island. In 1549, a Jesuit missionary came to Kagoshima, and a Portuguese vessel anchored at the port of Hirado near Nagasaki in the following year. (All these places are located in the south-west part of the country.) Japan in this way began its intercourses with the Europeans in the middle of the 16th century.

Yet the Japanese 'international' relations did not start by such encounters. There are numerous historical records showing much older and closer relations among the bodies politic in the East Asian region. The first written record in which we find Japan (called in those days Wa) is *Han Shu*, the official record of the Former Han Dynasty edited in the 1st century AD, which is regarded as one of the most important records of Chinese ancient history. This record tells us that the people of Wa in the 1st century BC lived separately in more than one hundred small countries and regularly paid tribute to the rulers of the Former Han. The books of the official history of the Later Han Dynasty edited around 432 recorded that a king of Wa sent an envoy to the capital city of the dynasty in 57 AD, and the Chinese emperor handed him down a seal of king. It is also recorded that Himiko, a ruling queen of Wa, in 239 dispatched a mission to Daifangjun, a Chinese stronghold located in the mid-west area of the Korean Peninsula from the beginning of the 3rd century until 313, and the lord of Daifangjun sent his delegation to Wa next year. Moreover, a king of Wa sent his envoy to the dynasty of Wei in 243.[3]

As these examples suggest, there existed 'international' relations among bodies politic in the East Asian region in the early period of recorded history. However, they were not the expressions of something similar to the modern international relations based on the sovereignty of States, but of the Sinocentric tributary system, the premise of which was that China kept a predominant status in the region economically, militarily and even culturally. This premise was, indeed, the foundation of the 'Sinocentrism'. (As current historians have been developing discussions on the meaning, structure, and nature of the Sinocentrism, any definitive explanation thereof shall be avoided here).[4]

The relation between China and Japan was suspended between 502 (when a king of Wa was conferred the title of 'General for the Eastern Conquest') and 600 (when the first Japanese envoy to the Sui Dynasty was dispatched). It did not, however, mean that Wa completely broke off any foreign relations in this period; rather, it actively embarked on the armed intervention in the conflicts inside the Korean Peninsula.

---

[3] The records concerning Japan found in the descriptions of Chinese official history are available in English in the following work: R Tsunoda and LC Goodrich *Japan in the Chinese Dynastic Histories: Later Han through Ming Dynasties* (PD & I Perkins South Pasadena CA 1851); see also the English translation of *Nihongi* (or *Nihonshoki*), one of the most important historical sources in Japan edited in the early 8th century: WG Aston (ed) *Nihongi: Chronicles of Japan from the Earliest Times to A.D. 697* (WG Aston trans) (Allen & Unwin London 1896; repr Routledge Abingdon 2011).

[4] As regards Sinocentrism, see the contributions by C-H Tang 'China' and M Yanagihara 'Japan' in this volume. The established theory on Sinocentrism has been strongly influenced by JK Fairbank. See eg JF Fairbank (ed) *The Chinese World Order: Traditional China's Foreign Relations* (Harvard University Press Cambridge 1968); D Twitchett and JK Fairbank *The Cambridge History of China* (CUP Cambridge 1980) vol 2; but the Fairbankean view, especially on the understanding of *yi* (barbarian), is fiercely rebutted by Liu; see LH Liu: *The Clash of Empires: The Invention of China in Modern World Making* (Harvard University Press Cambridge 2004).

This is the period when the Japanese-styled 'small Sinocentrism' was developed.[5] It was expressed in the following manner.

The official history of the Song (Sung) Dynasty edited in 488 contains a record concerning a king of Wa who invaded and conquered the peoples living in the northern and southern part of Japan in the 5th century. Those who were conquered were subjected to, and discriminated by, the people of Wa. In so doing, the king of Wa let himself be at the conceptual center of the Japanese styled Sinocentric order.

Apart from these ancient examples, an expression of the Japanese 'small Sinocentrism' in the early modern age can be clearly seen in the foreign policy of Hideyoshi Toyotomi who subjugated most of Japanese local rulers by the end of the 16th century. (Japan in those days had been suffering from an 'era of wars' since the middle of the 15th century.) He asked the kingdoms ruling the Ryūkyū Islands (the mainland of which is Okinawa) and the Korean Peninsula to recognize his suzerainty.

The Ryūkyū Islands were unified in 1429 and became a kingdom. It kept tributary relation with the Ming Dynasty and thus formed a part of the Sinocentric order. The kingdom therefore rejected the request by Toyotomi to send troops when he was about to invade Korea and China. (The Japanese troops under the command of Toyotomi actually invaded the Korean Peninsula with the intention to conquer China under the Ming Dynasty from 1592 to 1598 with the truce period from 1593 to 1597.) After the death of Toyotomi (1598), the lord of Satsuma (present-day Kagoshima, the southernmost fief of the main part of Japan) attacked and conquered the kingdom in 1609. The vanquished were obliged to pay tribute to the conqueror and to send their envoy to Yedo, the capital city of Japan under the Tokugawa Shogunate government. Meanwhile, the kingdom maintained its tributary relations with the Ming Dynasty, and its succeeding dynasty, Qing, as well. The Ryūkyū Kingdom in this way was under the double (or even triple) suzerainty and was integrated into both Sinocentrism and the 'small Sinocentrism', while keeping the appearance of an independent kingdom.

Korea's 'international' status was much more complicated than that of Ryūkyū, since the Korean Dynasty itself asserted the superiority of its own in the region, that is, the Korean 'small Sinocentrism', while accepting tributary relations with China. This, as a matter of course, created problems in its relations with Japan.

During the years under the sway of Toyotomi and thereafter, the negotiations between Japan and Korea were carried out through the family of Sō, the lord of Tsushima Island located between Japan and the Korean Peninsula. Sō recognized the suzerainty of both Japan and Korea and both were in the position claiming the superiority in the region. It was thus Sō's fundamental policy that it should avoid the collision of the two superior powers. In the case of Toyotomi's demand to send a Korean envoy to Japan to show obedience to him, the first envoy was finally dispatched in 1590 but the understandings of the

---

[5] M Sakayori 'Kai-shisō no Shosō' (Some Aspects of the Idea of 'Flowery'-'Barbarous') in Y Arano, M Ishii and S Murai (eds) *Ajia no naka no Nihonshi V* (The Japanese History in Asia V) (Tokyo University Press Tokyo 1993) 27–58 at 44–6.

two sides were different; Toyotomi considered it as the expression of accepting his demand, while the Koreans, according to their self-estimation, visited Japan to 'celebrate' the unification of Japan by Toyotomi. A similar situation occurred when the Japanese ruler repeatedly demanded Korea 'to be his guide for conquering China'. The Koreans understood it as a request to grant the Japanese the right of passage to China through their territory. These mutual misunderstandings were caused by the manipulation by Sō who gave each of the parties different explanations in order to avoid the clash of its two suzerains. (It is worthwhile mentioning here that China, as the center of the Sinocentric system of the East Asian region, did not intervene in the disputes between Japan and Korea until the Western powers expanded their imperialism into this region, because China had little concern with the relations between a Chinese tributary entity and a non-tributary entity.)

This way of communication between Japan and Korea through the commonly sub-ordinated entity was maintained in the era of the Japanese seclusion policy (*Sakoku*).[6] In 1635, the Tokugawa Shogunate government issued an order for the interdiction of overseas journeys by the Japanese, and in 1639 an order prohibiting Portuguese vessels from entering Japan, which de facto effectuated the policy. From that year on and until the reopening of its door in the middle of the 19th century, Japan severed its ties with the rest of the world except China, the Netherlands, Korea, and Ryūkyū.

As Japan in the secluded era is discussed somewhere else in this volume,[7] the present writer limits himself to pointing out that the relations between Japan and the Netherlands, the sole European counterpart of the Far Eastern country in this era, were regulated by the logic of the Japanese traditional ideas.[8] The Tokugawa government kept Japan's door open to the Netherlands because it considered that the Dutch people did not have any intention to propagate Christianity in Japan. Their activities were completely controlled by the Japanese government and their relations with the Japanese rulers were regulated by the idea of 'small Sinocentrism'.[9]

---

[6] The first occasion when the term '*Sakoku*' was used in the official documents seems to have occurred in 1858 when a high rank Japanese official charged with naval defence made a report on Harris, the first American consular general to Japan, who was about to revisit Yedo. It may safely be submitted that the term '*Kaikin*' (the prohibition of voyage), instead of *Sakoku*, had usually been used until the final stage of the Tokugawa government. See Y Arano, '*Kaikin to Sakoku*' (The Prohibition of Voyage and the Seclu-sion) in Y Arano, M Ishii, and S Murai (eds) *Ajia no nakano Nihonsi II* (The Japanese History in Asia II) (Tokyo University Press Tokyo 1992) 191–222 at 207–13.

[7] About the 'seclusion' or 'isolation' (*Sakoku*) of Japan, see the contribution by M Yanagihara 'Japan' in this volume.

[8] During the seclusion period, especially in the 18th century, the Japanese scholars developed and systematized their traditional view of cosmology relying on the written materials describing the ancient history culminating in the establishment of the Japanese Imperial family and the nation (eg *Kojiki* of 712 and *Nihon-shoki* of 720).

[9] Rutherford Alcock, the first English minister to Japan (July 1859–December 1864 at Yedo) who played an important role during the final years of the Tycoon government, described that even after the aboli-tion of the seclusion policy, 'American, Dutch, and Russian agents had, on one or two occasions, travelled along the high road, either from Nagasaki or Hakodadi [Hakodate: KA], on their way to and from the

The above discussion confirms that from the ancient times until the 'encounter' with the Western powers in the middle of the 19th century, Japan did not have any idea similar to the modern concept of sovereignty and to the 'international' relations based on sovereign equality.

2.2. Japanese Idea of 'Law' before the 'Encounter'

In the Middle Ages, especially in the Kamakura Period (1192–1333), the concept of 'law' in Japan was equated with that of 'reason'. (*Dōri*, literally, 'way' and 'reason'. It thus means 'the way it should be'.) It was commonly conceived that 'law' might not arbitrarily be legislated by rulers. Hence, 'reason' restrained the authority of rulers. 'Reason' in those days meant the rules of morality, the essential part of which denoted the common sense in the ordinary life of warriors (*Bushi* or *Samurai*) that had evolved since the Heian Period (794–1185).

In the early modern period, however, we find another picture of the concept of 'law', which was quite different from the medieval image of law in Japan. The new concept can be summarized in a Japanese maxim '*Hi-Ri-Hō-Ken-Ten*', which may be translated as 'irrationality, reason, laws, authority, the Heaven'. 'Irrationality' means something opposite to 'reason', that is, something rational which may be affirmed by everyone's common sense. 'Laws' were not the laws of Buddhism, nor of Nature, but statutes legislated by the Shogunate government. The concept of 'authority' referred to the power and authority of the emperor and Shogun. The 'Heaven', originating from ancient Chinese philosophy, was the supreme and almighty God.[10] '*Hi-Ri-Hō-Ken-Ten*' indicates that 'irrationality' shall be overcome by 'reason', 'reason' by 'laws', 'laws' by 'authority', and 'authority' by the 'Heaven'.[11]

In this hierarchical order, we observe two features. First, as 'laws' were superior to 'reason', the order between the two in medieval Japan was modified; second, both 'laws' and 'reason' were inferior to the 'authority' of the ruler. These were the characteristics of the concept of 'law' in Japan in the early modern period; and the second point was obviously incompatible with the principles of the European modern law, including the 'rule of law' with the purport that even the rulers shall be restrained by law.

capital for purposes of negotiation, as the Dutch formerly carry tribute'. R Alcock *The Capital of the Tycoon: A Narrative of a Three Years' Residence in Japan* (Longman London 1863; repr Scholarly Press St. Clair Shores MI 1969) vol 1, at 400.

[10] S Takigawa *Hi-Ri-Hō-Ken-Ten* (Irrationalness, Rationalness, Law, Authority, the Heaven) (Seiabō Tokyo 1964) at 19–25.

[11] H Asako et al (eds) *Nihon Hōseishi* (The History of Japanese Law) (Seirin Shoin Tokyo 2010) at 108.

3. The 'Encounter' and the Japanese 'Acceptance' of the European Law of Nations

3.1. The 'Encounter'

We have confirmed in the preceding section the conceptual preconditions in Japan when the European powers tried to reopen the door of the nation which maintained its seclusion policy since the beginning of the 17th century.

Japan was forced to enter into diplomatic relations with Western powers after the American fleet appeared at the mouth of the Bay of Yedo in 1853 and 1854. As already mentioned, the Netherlands formally maintained commercial relations with Japan. Other nations also sent delegates to Japan, including the Russian envoys Adam K Laksman in 1792 and Nikolaj P Rezanov in 1804 and the French fleets under the command of Captain Bénigne E Fornier-Duplan in 1844 and of Admiral Jean-Baptiste TM Cécille in 1846. But the Americans were the first who were ready to resort to armed force to change the long-sustained Japanese policy of seclusion.[12] Moreover, the United States was the first nation that forced Japan to regulate the diplomatic relations between the two nations by international law and to conclude a treaty in the Western style.

In view of the above-mentioned traditional Japanese idea of 'international relations' and 'law', international law should have been perceived by the Japanese officials who negotiated with the Americans as perplexing. But the long-secluded people quickly understood that their traditional policy could no longer be maintained, for they were not totally ignorant of the state of affairs in the world. In effect, even in the years of seclusion, the Tokugawa government could acquire information of the outside world through various sources.[13] They were therefore capable of taking into account the reality of the contemporary world, especially the Western invasion of China, when Shogun and his councillors deliberated opening the door of Japan.

The deliberation itself was intense but after the decision to open the country and conclude a treaty with the United States, the Japanese internal turmoil intensified.

---

[12] In 1846, seven years prior to Matthew C Perry's expedition, American commodore James Biddle came with two US warships to Uraga Channel and attempted to create trade relations between the US and Japan. His effort was finally unsuccessful and Perry seems to have learned from this bitter experience of Biddle how to deal with the Japanese officials. On the expedition of Perry's squadron, see, the first volume of MC Perry *Narrative of the Expedition of an American Squadron to the China Sea and Japan Performed in the Years 1852, 1853, and 1854* (FL Hawks ed) (AOP Nicholson Washington 1856) vol 1.

[13] A good example of the source of information during the Japanese seclusion era was 'Oranda Fūsetsu Gaki' (the Dutch news reports) provided by the Captains (representatives) of the Dutch factory in Nagasaki.

'Respect the Emperor, expel the foreigners', was the slogan of the factions that tried to subvert the Tokugawa government, which symbolized the hatred and fear of the Japanese people towards the Westerners. The anti-Shogunate factions, however, soon realized the military superiority of the Western powers after the armed conflicts between the Westerners and the Japanese feudal lords (*Daimyō*) who belonged to such factions.

Having recognized the reality, all Japanese political factions understood that the abolition of the seclusion policy was unavoidable. Then, the enthusiasm for obtaining the 'scientific' knowledge of the Western 'civilization' flared up in both the pro-Tokugawa and anti-Tokugawa factions. It should be pointed out that this was not the first occasion that the Japanese people attempted to obtain such knowledge. Not only the reports supplied to the Shogunate government by the Dutch but also the Chinese translations of Western books were the channels to the European civilization for Japan. Except books containing descriptions about Christianity, the Tokugawa government imported from China books about Western science and technology.[14] Yet an important feature is observable in the contents of the imported science and technology during the 'encounter' period: while the imported Chinese translations during the seclusion era had been works in natural science and technology,[15] those which the Japanese people tried to obtain during the 'encounter' period were not limited to such 'pure' science or its application. It was felt that the Western knowledge in such fields as law, government, and economy was a matter of necessity to maintain intercourse with the Westerners. International law was, as a matter of course, considered to be one of the new important issues that the rapidly changing nation should learn.

3.2. 'Acceptance'

It was logically difficult for the secluded Japanese people to accept the system of international law based on the equality of sovereign States, since the pre-'encounter' cosmology—which was set up based on the regional 'international' system of concentric circles, the center of which was Japan—was quite different from that commonly understood by Europeans. The psychological consequence of the 'encounter' for the people who had been secluded from the outside world for more than two centuries

---

[14] About the Chinese books imported to Japan during the Tokugawa period, see O Ōba *Edojidai niokeru Tōsen Mochiwatasisho no Kenkyū* (Studies on Chinese Books Imported to Japan by Chinese Vessels in the Yedo Period) (The Institute of Oriental and Occidental Studies (Kansai University) Suita 1967); M Kawakatsu *Nihon Kinsei to Higashi Ajia Sekai* (The Early Modern Japan and the East Asian World) (Yoshikawa Kōbun-kan Tokyo 2002) at 259–330.

[15] The works on the system of law, government, and economy invented and developed in China were allowed to be imported.

should be the feeling that they were forced to open their country and to accept the European concept of law for the newly established international relations. The feeling of 'being forced', however, did not necessarily mean reluctant attitudes towards international law. The Japanese people, especially the officials who had direct intercourse with Westerners, were indeed quite active in acquiring knowledge, and a radical change in cosmology seems to have been smoothly accomplished.

The Japanese enthusiasm for obtaining knowledge of the Western civilization, especially that of international law, materialized through four channels: foreign books, Japanese students and officials sent to Western countries, 'Oyatoi Gaikokujin' (employed foreigners), and Western envoys sent to Japan.

First, as regards books of international law, two kinds of works were imported: Chinese translations and textbooks written in European languages. The most important work of the former type imported to Japan during the 'encounter' period is Henry Wheaton's *Elements of International Law*. It was first translated into Chinese by William Martin, an American Protestant missionary, and published in mid-1860s in China.[16] The Chinese translation was imported to Japan in either 1865 or 1866, and both the original English and Chinese versions were later translated into Japanese. In a similar way, TD Woolsey's *Introduction to the Study of International Law*[17] and JC Bluntschli's *Das Moderne Völkerrecht als Rechtsbuch* were made accessible in Japan in 1878 and in 1881 respectively. The first Japanese translation directly from the English version of Charles de Martens' *Guide diplomatique* was made and published by Gen-ichirō Fukuchi in 1869. A Japanese translation of James Kent's work appeared in 1876 and of Henry Halleck's in 1878, both of which were made without the help of Chinese translations. Other Japanese translations of textbooks, such as AW Heffter's (in 1877), S Amos' (in 1879), and WE Hall's (in 1888), were also made available.

Second, among Japanese students and officials sent abroad, the most important to the history of international law is Amane Nishi. He was dispatched to Europe with his colleague Mamichi Tsuda[18] and studied at Leyden where he did research in various fields, including international law, under the guidance of Professor Simon Vissering. After his return from Europe, Nishi made a translation of his notes from lectures at Leyden and published them under the title 'Bankoku Kohō' (literally, 'the public law of ten thousand States') in 1868.

Third, the foreigners employed by the Tokugawa government and feudal lords played an important role in the process of Japan's Westernization. As already mentioned, the Japanese seclusion policy did not mean complete isolation from the out-

---

[16] In this regard, see also the contribution by LH Liu 'Henry Wheaton (1785–1848)' and S Kawashima 'China' in this volume.

[17] Woolsey's textbook, however, was first translated into Japanese by Rinshō Mizukuri directly from the original text in 1873.

[18] Tsuda later published 'Taisai Kokuhō-ron' (On the Western Public Law). This was the translation of his notes of the lectures given by Vissering at Leyden and was the first work that introduced Western jurisprudence to Japan.

side world and there existed some official channels for acquiring information about contemporary foreign affairs. Such information was supplied by the Koreans, the Chinese, the Dutch, and even by Westerners of other nationalities who came to Japan as members of the Dutch factory, such as the Germans Engelbert Kaemper (1651–1716) and Philipp Franz von Siebold (1796–1866). During the 'encounter' period, however, a wave of foreigners other than diplomats came to Japan, and about 200 foreigners were employed as teachers of languages and/or technologies in the final years of the Tokugawa period (1854–1868) either by the Shogunate government or by feudal lords.[19] After the collapse of the two-and-a-half-centuries-long authoritarian regime, Westerners continued to serve in the newly established Imperial government, among others as counsellors advising on foreign policy from the viewpoint of international law. The list of foreigners who were employed by the Japanese ministry of foreign affairs included Peshine Smith, an American who served from 1871 to 1876 as the first *Oyatoi Gikokujin* in the ministry; Hermann Roesler, a German (Rostock) professor who was invited as a counsellor on public international law in 1878 (until 1893) but made great efforts to draft Japanese 'modernized' laws, *inter alia* constitutional law, civil law and commercial code; and Henry W Denison, an American who served from 1880 to 1914 as a counsellor on public international law.[20]

Among the three channels mentioned above, by far the most important, albeit only at the primary stage of the 'encounter', for the acquisition of the practical

---

[19] Among the *Oyatoi Gaikokujin* employed by the Tokugawa government, the majority was formed by the French and, when the regime was collapsed, there were 84 French employees in the government. (This was due to the fact that Léon Roches, a French minister in Yedo (April 1664–June 1868), succeeded in establishing good relations with the collapsing government.) AW Burks 'The West's Inreach: The Oyatoi Gaikokujin' in AW Burks (ed) *The Modernizers: Overseas Students, Foreign Employees, and Meiji Japan* (West View Press Boulder CO 1985) 187–206 at 190.

[20] The primary concern of foreign policy for the new Japanese Imperial government were the 'unequal' treaties concluded with the Western powers by the former government. See A Peters 'Unequal Treaties' in R Wolfrum (ed) *The Max Planck Encyclopedia of Public International Law* (OUP Oxford 2008) at <www.mpepil.com>. The focal points of inequality contained in them were the consular jurisdiction (The importance of the issue of consular jurisdiction seems to have been expressed in the fact that the dissertation of Tsurutarō Senga presented to the Berlin University dealt with it; see T Senga *Gestaltung und Kritik der heutigen Konsulargerichtsbarkeit in Japan* (Phd thesis Frederick William University Berlin 1897). This issue was introduced to the Westerners by Alessandro Paternostro, an *Oyatoi Gaikokuji* of Italian origin; see A Paternostro 'La revision des traités avec le Japon au point de vue du droit international' (1891) 23 Revue droit international et législation comparée 5–29 and 176–200.) and the lack of tariff autonomy of Japan. For revising them, Japan should prove that it can stand on an equal footing with them. The Japanese national policy thus was aimed at building up a 'civilized' (namely, 'Westernized') nation and the application of international law was one of the major issues to show its capacity to be 'civilized'. As its logical consequence, after the treaties were 'equalized' at the beginning of the 20th century (the abolition of consular jurisdiction in 1899, the recovery of tariff autonomy in 1911), there would be no need of *Oyatoi Gaikokujin* in the field of foreign affairs, including international law. The fact, however, is that, as the case of Thomas Baty, an English man who served for the ministry of foreign affairs and died in Tokyo in 1954, the Japanese government continued to employ Westerners with the purpose of using them in its foreign relations until the Second World War.

knowledge of international law was the fourth channel: namely, Western diplomats in Japan.

The first Western envoy dispatched to Japan based on a treaty was Townsend Harris, a US Consul General who engaged in establishing a substantially revised treaty relation between the two countries.[21] In his journal[22] which chronicled his experience, ranging from weather and day-to-day life to diplomatic negotiations, during his mission in Japan (August 1856–June 1859 at Shimoda, July 1859–May 1862 at Yedo), we witness his importance to Japanese officials as a provider of information and expertise of international law, especially the law of legation. The following examples from his journal may serve as the evidence for such an evaluation.[23]

The Japanese officials adopted new formalities such as exchanging salutes and the ceremony for handing over full power in response to Harris' requests to conform to international comity on various occasions.[24] The formalities to hand over a letter from the US President to the Tycoon, which had been disputed since the commencement of the diplomatic relations between the two countries, were finally accepted in accordance with the US envoy's request.[25] Harris explained his 'undoubted rights under the laws of nations'[26] and the rights of ministers and consuls[27] to his Japanese counterparts. Finally, he acquainted the Japanese officials with the role of arbitrator and with the laws of neutrality.[28]

While, based on Harris' journal, it may be pointed out that the concept of international law for the Japanese officials was at most 'the practice of Western nations or the laws adopted commonly among nations', and that in their minds the conceptual distinction between municipal and international law was dubious,[29] the fact remains that the Japanese officials were very keen on collecting any concrete knowledge concerning inter-

[21]   Harris' efforts resulted in the treaty between the two countries signed at Shimoda on 17 June 1857 and the treaty of amity and commerce singed at Yedo (Tokyo) on 29 July 1858.
[22]   T Harris *The Complete Journal of Townsend Harris* (ME Cosenza ed) (Doubleday, Doran and Company New York 1930). The edition made use of in the present chapter is its revised edition (Rutland Vermont 1959) at xix and 616.
[23]   See also the journal of Henry Heusken, a Dutch native who served for Harris as a Dutch-English interpreter (the only communicable European language for the Japanese in those days was Dutch), but in fact advised and assisted other Western envoys as well as many Japanese acquaintances beyond his official task. H Heusken *Japan Journal: 1855–61* (JC van der Corput and RA Wilson eds and trans) (Rutgers University Press New Brunswick NJ 1964). This journal also witnesses the credibility of the descriptions by Harris.
[24]   See *The Complete Journal of Townsend Harris* (n 22) especially 344–5.
[25]   See ibid 447–58.
[26]   ibid 456–7.
[27]   ibid 507.
[28]   ibid 515. Harris proposed also, and the Japanese officials agreed to, a stipulation on the role of the US President as 'the mediator of the Japanese when asked to do so' and an article stating that 'American men-of-war and consuls should assist Japanese vessels and their crews so far as the laws of neutrality permit'.
[29]   S Kōzai 'Bakumatsu Kaikoku-ki niokeru Kokusaihō no Dōnyū' (Japan's Initial Encounter with International Law in the Late Tokugawa Period (Kōzai's translation)) (1975) 97 Hōgaku Ronsō (Kyōto Law Review) 1–38 at 31.

national law. In short, the Japanese officials had little interest in abstract or conceptual issues of international law, and what they really wanted was practical knowledge that was indispensable to maintaining 'peaceful' relations with the Western powers.

Japan, after the abolition of its seclusion policy, swiftly obtained the knowledge of international law through the various channels. The nation then commenced to utilize the newly acquired knowledge in its diplomatic practice.

3.3. Utilization

Ernest Mason Satow, an English diplomat who stayed in Japan for more than two decades (1862–83), affords the proof of the swiftness of the Japanese in making use of the knowledge of international law. His journal,[30] kept during his mission to Japan, reports, for example, an incident at Namamugi in the vicinity of Yokohama on 14 September 1862, only several months after Harris' departure from Japan. In this incident, some liegemen of the powerful feudal lord of Satsuma put an English merchant to death by sword (two of his company were injured). After the incident, the Tokugawa government, instead of the lord of Satsuma, undertook the negotiation with the English diplomat.[31] Satow also reports the Simonoseki incident in which the same attitude of the 'central' government is observable; the incident was caused by a cannon fired on some Western vessels from a bastion of Simonoseki, a part of the fief of Chō-shū in Western Japan;[32] the Tokugawa government assumed responsibility in place of the local lord.[33] These reported practices may exemplify the correct and swift understanding on the Japanese side as to what a 'central' government should do according to international law. Moreover, the fact that the reports and diaries of other Western diplomats dispatched to Japan later than Harris recorded much fewer occasions to teach international comity and law[34] may also suggest the swiftness of the Japanese in acquiring the newly introduced knowledge, as well as Harris' importance in the primary stage of the 'encounter'.

The above-mentioned cases are those in which the Tokugawa government relied on international law. Satow also touched upon the *Stonewall-Jackson* case in which the

---

[30] EM Satow *A Diplomat in Japan* (Seeley London 1921).

[31] The Namamugi Incident and its consequences resulting in the payment of the indemnity by the Shogunate government are reported by Satow (*A Diplomat in Japan* (n 30) 50–83). Kagoshima, the capital city of Satsuma, was, however, later bombarded by an English fleet and the English exacted the reparation (ibid 84–94). This shows that, while the Shogunate government was trying to exhibit the legitimacy of its own as the sole representative of Japan, the European legations observed the de facto independence enjoyed by some mighty feudal lords.

[32] Satuma and Chō-shū later formed the core part of the anti-Tokugawa faction and the liegemen, mostly of low rank, seized the central power of the new Imperial government.

[33] *A Diplomat in Japan* (n 30) 135.

[34] See eg *The Capital of the Tycoon* (n 9).

new Imperial government invoked international law against both the former government and the Western powers. This case took place during the continual warfare
between the Tokugawa faction and the Imperial government which was founded
with the Imperial Declaration of Restoration on 3 January 1868.[35] Before its collapse,
the Tokugawa government had made contracts for purchasing an ironclad warship,
the *Stonewall-Jackson*, from the United States and another two from France. When the
US-made vessel was about to be delivered to the original purchaser, the Imperial
government requested the supplier to refrain from handing it over based on the
laws of neutrality. The request for the observance of the laws of neutrality was com-
municated to other Western governments, too.[36] The United States granted it and the
delivery was suspended. There are other examples in which the Japanese government
actively relied on the rules of international law.[37]

Moreover, the case of *Takeaki Enomoto* is of interest. (Enomoto later held an
important position in the Imperial government and successfully negotiated with
Russia in concluding the 1875 Treaty for Exchanging the Kuril Islands and Sakhalin.)
Even after the decisive defeat of the Tokugawa faction (1868), the stiff resistance
organized by the liegemen of the Tokugawa Shogunate and pro-Tokugawa feudal
lords continued. Enomoto, who had studied in the Netherlands from 1862 to 1867 as
a loyal liegeman to the Shogunate and had been well disciplined also as a naval officer,
took command of a fleet of the collapsed Tokugawa navy and made a strong final
stand at the city of Hakodate, situated in the southern part of Hokkaidō. He had
reportedly planned to create an independent republic in Hokkaidō and in fact asked
the Western envoys to maintain their neutrality and to recognize his party as a belligerent according to international law. Although his plan finally proved to be unrealizable, his request was admitted by some of the envoys.[38]

3.4. Enthusiasm about International Law

It is submitted that the issues discussed above show, notwithstanding the fact that
both the abolition of the Japanese seclusion policy and the application of international law to the relations between Japan and the Western powers were, from the
Japanese point of view, forced, that, immediately following the 'encounter', the Japanese officials and scholars were enthusiastic about obtaining the practical rules, not
conceptual or abstract issues, of international law, and swiftly applied them to actual

---

[35] The *Stonewall-Jackson* case is reported in *A Diplomat in Japan* (n 30) 404.
[36] The idea of requesting Western nations for the observance of obligations in accordance with the
laws of neutrality is said to have stemmed from the advice by the English legation. *A Diplomat in Japan*
(n 30) 330.
[37] Such an example is to be found in, e.g. the negotiations between the Japanese officials and the Western envoys on the recognition of the Imperial government. See *A Diplomat in Japan* (n 30) 307–25.
[38] On Enomoto's resistance, see eg *A Diplomat in Japan* (n 30) 395–408.

cases.[39] While there may be various reasons why Japan could change its traditional policy and was enthusiastic about adapting itself to the new reality brought by the Westerners, the analysis in the present section shows the essential importance of the information obtained through several channels. At the initial stage of the 'encounter', the cognizance of the complete alteration of the power relations between the West and the East, which was brought to it especially through its uninterrupted relations with the Netherlands, was crucial to Japan.[40] At the same time, Western diplomats played an essential role for Japan by introducing Japanese officials to practical and concrete rules of international law.

As the discussion in the next section will show, Japan maintained the same attitude towards Western powers and international law after the 'encounter' period, and its motivation was basically the same as before, viz to prove its civility as a nation in the Western style. The target, however, became more manifest, namely the revision of the unequal treaties.

4. After the 'Encounter'

4.1. Until the First World War: Law Abidance

4.1.1. *Participation in International Institutions*

In the years following the 'encounter' period, the Japanese government, with the purpose of proving its equal footing with the Western powers, began to participate in the activities of Western-made international institutions.

In 1877, due to the humanitarian atrocities in the internal warfare (*Seinan Sensō*, the final and largest uprising by the former liegemen, led by Takamori Saigou, dissatisfied with the Imperial government), *Hakuai-sha* ('the society of philanthropy') was established, which would change its name to the 'Japanese Society of Red Cross' in 1887. Immediately after the recognition of accession to the International Commit-

---

[39] It should also be mentioned that neither in Harris' journal nor in other accessible chronicles by the Western envoys any passage referring explicitly to abstract ideas of international law appears.

[40] Alcock recorded as follows: 'Japan, there seemed reason to believe, was better advised, and better able, perhaps, to understand and appreciate the changes which had completely altered the relative positions of Europe and the East. Partly, it would seem, from their greater quickness and aptitude for seizing the true meaning and significance of such facts as come before them; but greatly also owing to the continued relations they had maintained with the Dutch. A door was thus kept open by which they could get reliable information of what was really passing in the world beyond. There seems little doubt that so far back as 1845, after the close of the first war with China, the Dutch set themselves seriously to work to prepare the Japanese mind for inevitable changes.' *The Capital of the Tycoon* (n 9) 205–6.

tee of Red Cross, the Japanese Red Cross was invited, as the first Asian participant, to the fourth International Conference of the Red Cross held at Karlsruhe in September 1887. Meanwhile, Japan acceded to the Geneva Conventions in 1886.[41]

In the same year when *Hakuai-sha* was established, Japan acceded to the General Postal Union, which was established in 1874 and the name of which was changed to Universal Postal Union in 1878, as the first Asian State party. As regards the International Telecommunication Union which was originally created as the International Telegraph Union in 1865, Japan first attended its conference as an observer in 1871 and formally acceded to it in 1879.

4.1.2. *Japan and Wars*

In order to publicize its civility to the Westerners, Japan utilized wars, and the task was carried out by Japanese publicists too. During the Sino-Japanese War (1893–94), Japanese legal counsellors (Nagao Ariga and Sakuyé Takahashi) specializing in the laws of war accompanied the Japanese Imperial Army and Navy and they later published books describing the records of the war in European languages.[42]

These publications accomplished their purpose. They were highly praised as the proof of Japanese law-abiding attitudes by the Westerners,[43] including Thomas E Holland, an Oxford professor who was a leading figure in defending Japan. In his work published in 1898, he states that Japan 'has conformed to the laws of war, both in her treatment of the enemy and in her relations to neutrals, in a manner worthy of the most civilized nations of Western Europe'.[44]

The Japanese decision, however, to behave respectfully towards the laws of war was not only based on an appeal of innocence to the Western nations. During the war, Japan assured the uninterrupted neutral trade carried out by the Westerners using Chinese ports (especially Shanghai) and showed its respect for their keen trade interests.[45] Japan in this way pursued its diplomacy focused on keeping favourable relations with the Western nations and its law-abiding attitude was in tune with its diplomacy. This was the Japanese realist approach to the international politics then dominated by the Western powers.

---

[41] About the early history of the Japanese Red Cross, see N Ariga *La Croix-Rouge en Extrême-Orient: exposé de l'organisation et du fonctionnement de la Société de la Croix-Rouge du Japon* (Présenté à l'exposition universelle de 1900 par la Société de la Croix-Rouge du Japon) (A Pedone Paris 1900).

[42] See especially N Ariga *La guerre sino-japonaise au point de vue du droit international* (Pedone Paris 1896) and S Takahashi S *Cases on International Law during the Chino-Japanese War* (CUP Cambridge 1899).

[43] Takahashi published a compilation of the book reviews on his work. S Takahashi *Äusserrungen über völkerrechtlich bedeutsame Vorkommnisse aus dem Chinesisch-Japanischen Seekrieg und das darauf bezügliche Werk: 'Cases on International Law during the Chino-Japanese War'* (Reinhardt München 1900).

[44] TE Holland *Studies in International Law* (Clarendon Oxford 1898) at 128; in contrast with Japan, Holland considered that China 'has given no indication of her acceptance of the usages of civilized warfare' although the Chinese 'have shown themselves to be well versed in the ceremonial of embassy and the conduct of diplomacy'; at 129: Finally, Holland concluded that 'a respect for the laws of war they have not yet attained'.

[45] WM Langer *The Diplomacy of Imperialism 1890–1902* (2nd edn Knopf New York 1951) at 173–4.

The same strategy for obtaining the Western appraisal was taken by the Japanese government during the Russo-Japanese War (1904–05) on a larger scale[46] and this was also fairly successful.[47]

4.2. The Inter-war Period: Frustration

Japan's law-abiding attitude was maintained until the First World War and Japan participated in the Versailles Conference as a new major power. But its self-confidence as such turned into frustration.

The first and evident instance of Japan's dissatisfaction arose during the drafting process of the Covenant of the League of Nations. The delegation of Japan, as a non-white rising power, negotiated at Versailles for the insertion of a clause on the equality of all human races into the Covenant.[48] The new power from the East advocated this idea for the period of post-white, or post-Euro-American, domination. The Japanese efforts, firstly to create a specific article on the issue and secondly to insert a new paragraph to preamble, were, though US President Wilson sometimes showed support for Japan, finally rejected completely by the Western powers and only produced frustration on the Japanese side.[49] Japan had to admit the persistent reality of the white domination of international politics.[50]

---

[46] See eg H Nagaoka 'La guerre russo-japonaise et le droit international' (1904) 36 Revue droit international et législation comparée 461–515; H Nagaoka 'Étude sur la guerre russo-japonaise au point de vue du droit international' (1905) 12 Revue générale de droit international public 603–36; N Ariga *La guerre russo-japonaise au point de vue continental et le droit international d'après les documents officiels du grand état-major japonais* (P Fauchille pref) (Pedone Paris 1908); S Takahashi *International Law Applied to the Russo-Japanese War with the Decisions of the Japanese Prize Court* (Stevens and Sons London 1908).

[47] See especially S Takahashi *Reviews of Dr. Takahashi's Recent Work, 'International Law Applied to the Russo-Japanese War'* (Tokyo Print Tokyo 1909); see further AS Hershey *The International Law and Diplomacy of the Russo-Japanese War* (Macmillan New York 1906); JA White *The Diplomacy of the Russo-Japanese War* (Princeton University Press Princeton NJ 1964).

[48] The background of the Japanese proposal was as follows. From the late 19th century, a boycott of Japanese immigrants had been in effect in the United States, especially in the western states, such as California. (The heat of the boycott of Chinese immigrants had already been burning since the 1870s.) In 1907, the US law on immigration was revised and, in response to the revision, a gentlemen's agreement was concluded between Japan and the United States, according to which the Japanese government committed itself to abstain from issuing passports for entry into the US mainland to Japanese emigrant workers except in the case of re-entry or for special categories of workers. There was also a problem of a similar nature between Japan and Australia, caused by the 'White Australia Policy'.

[49] On the text of the Japanese proposal, see S Tachi *Kokusai-Renmei Kiyaku Ron* (Comments on the Covenant of the League of Nations) (Kokusai Ren-mei Kyōkai Tokyo 1932) at 11–14.

[50] Whether the Japanese government really believed the universal value of the equality of all races and stood against racial discrimination was rather dubious. In the case of the American boycott of immigrant workers from Asia, the Chinese government concluded a treaty with the United States on the formal restriction of Chinese emigrants to the United States. The Japanese government persistently rejected

Notwithstanding this bitter experience, Japan was among the original forty-five member States of the League of Nations, became a permanent member of its council, and was thus recognized as one of the major powers in the world. With such a prestigious status of their country, the Japanese were active on the international stage during the first decade of the League's existence. For example, Michikazu Matsuda was among the legal experts dealing with the codification of international law at the League and Yōtarō Sugimura was a member of the legal committee for drafting the rules of aerial warfare at The Hague. Moreover, in the newly established Permanent Court of International Justice, Japanese judges always appeared on its bench until 1942.[51]

However, Japan's newly recognized status did not eradicate its frustration with international politics. The League of Nations was not only a forum of international cooperation but also an arena of imperialism. Japan participated in the worldwide competition among the imperial powers. In the course of the growth of Japanese imperialism in East Asia, Japan colonized Taiwan, the Korean Peninsula, and caused the Manchurian Incident in September 1931. The independence of the Manchurian State was declared on 1 March 1932 and Japan recognized the new State on 15 September of the same year. Faced with Japanese military expansion in China, the League sent an investigation team which subsequently submitted to the League a report (the Lytton Report) which was publicized in early October 1932. The report rejected the independence of Manchuria and opposed the Japanese view, while it acknowledged

such a treaty, since the conclusion of a treaty of the same kind would mean the acceptance of the same status as China, and other non-white nations as well. As a new imperial power from Asia, Japan could not accept such a shameful treatment. Evidently, Japan discriminated against other Asian nations. See Y Ōnuma 'Harukanaru Jin-ken Byōdō no Shisō' (The Far Distant Idea of the Equality of Human Rights) in Y Ōnuma (ed) *Kokusai-hō, Kokusai-Rengō to Nippon* (International Law, the United Nations and Japan) (Kōbundō Tokyo 1987) 427–80 at 436–9 and 475.

[51] The first Japanese judge of PCIJ was Yorozu Oda, who served it from its establishment (1921–30). The second was Mineichirō Adachi, whose missions before coming to PCIJ enumerates not only working in Japanese embassies but also works as an expert of international law, including especially his membership of the Advisory Committee of Jurists for drafting the Statute of PCIJ in 1920. He was elected as a judge of PCIJ in September 1930 and its President in January of the following year. (His service on the court was interrupted by his death at Amsterdam on 28 December 1934, for which the Dutch government expressed its condolences by according a state funeral.) The third and the last Japanese PCIJ judge was Harukazu Nagaoka, who, after the death of Adachi, was elected as successor to his compatriot on 14 September 1935, though Japan had officially withdrawn from the League already on 27 March 1935. (This was possible because Japan retained its status as a State party to the Statute of PCIJ and participated in the meetings of the Assembly and the Council of the League electing the judges of PCIJ. See MO Hudson *The Permanent Court of International Justice 1920–1942: A Treatise* (Macmillan New York 1943) 254 ff.) Nagaoka's term should have expired in 1939 when Adachi's original term was over, but the fact is that, due apparently to the postponement of the third general election of judges, he held his seat until 15 January 1942 when his letter of resignation was transmitted from the President of PCIJ to the Secretary-General of the League. (On the Japanese judges of PCIJ, see K Akashi 'Japanese Predecessors of Judge Oda in the World Courts: Works and Method' in N Andō, E McWhinney and R Wolfrum (eds) *Liber Amicorum Judge Shigeru Oda* (Kluwer Law International The Hague 2002) vol 1, 9–22.)

the 'special interests' of Japan in the region.[52] In the following year, like Germany and Italy, Japan seceded from the League and adopted the policy for continuing its imperialist expansion.

Meanwhile, the Japanese imperialism was not developed in a theoretical vacuum. Its theoretical and legal expression in the field of international law was the theory of *Dai-Tōa Kokusai-hō* (Great East Asian International Law), which is touched upon elsewhere in this handbook.[53]

5. Conclusion

The Japanese since the ancient times had embraced a unique view on 'international relations' and 'law' which was in principle incompatible with international law based on the sovereign equality of States. After the forced and unavoidable abolition of the sustained seclusion policy, Japan swiftly adapted itself to the reality imposed by the Western powers and, at least in its appearance, reached the rank of a 'civilized nation' within half a century since its drastic policy change without being colonized. Japan recognized the importance of international law for surviving in the world of Western domination, even though the nation sometimes expected too much of it.

Throughout the years from the 'encounter' period up to the Second World War, the Japanese officials and scholars continuously received the contents of international law made by the Westerners. Even the theory of 'Great East Asian International Law' seems to be a modified version of the German 'Grossraum' or 'Lebensraum' theory. In this sense, the Japanese kept passive attitudes towards the development of international law, even though they tried to, and could in effect, utilize it, and took part in the international institutions and activities with the Western powers. Accordingly, if it is asked whether the original Japanese ideas on 'international relations' and 'international legal order' had 'any influence and impact on the body of international law as it emerged from the encounter', the answer should be negative.

---

[52] On the deliberations over the Lytton Report inside the League, see H Kobayashi *Kokusai Chitsujo no Keisei to Kindai Nippon* (The Formation of International Order and the Modern Japanese State) (Yoshikawa Koubun-kan Tokyo 2002) 185–206.

[53] See the contribution by M Yanagihara 'Japan' in this volume. See also K Akashi 'Dai-Tōa Kokusai-hō Riron-Nihon niokeru Kokusaihō Riron Juyō no Kiketsu' (The Theory of the Great East Asian International Law: A Result of the Acceptance of International Law in Japan) (2009) 82 Hōgaku Ken-kyū (Journal of Law, Politics and Sociology) 261–92. For a succinct overview of the theory in English, see K Akashi 'Methodological Aspects of Japan's Encounter with the Modern Law of Nations: A Brief Outline for Reconsidering the Function of the "Persistent Spectre"' (2010) 11 Keio Law Review 1–13 at 9–13.

We may, however, not underestimate the importance of the Japanese historical experience in accepting international law. Having been taught an almost completely different cosmology, and having a different idea of 'law' from those of the Western society, the Japanese officials and scholars swiftly understood the contents of international law and made use of them. Besides the reasons particular to the Japanese,[54] there were some inherent features of international law which can explain the Japanese swiftness in accepting it. The present writer would like to suggest that they were, *inter alia*, its logically understandable structure and the concreteness of its rules. These features helped the Japanese comprehend the contents of international law. In other words, these features ensured its universal applicability.

There have been some criticisms on the intrinsic and ideological character of international law, viz its Eurocentrism. They have been developed in the perspective of critique of Western-domination or of a relativization of the Western values in line with the so-called 'inter-civilizational approach' or 'transcivilizational perspective'.[55] It cannot, and may not, be denied that the expansion of international law was accomplished with the help of armed forces in the name of 'civilization'. Yet the smooth acceptance of international law in Japan exemplifies the universal applicability of the concept and logic of international law. To put it differently, it is worthwhile asking ourselves whether it would have been possible that the traditional concept of 'international relations' and 'law' in East Asia become universally applicable.

Finally, the conclusion of the present chapter is that while the Japanese encounter with international law did not have any specific significance for the creation or development of specific rules and principles of international law, the process of encounter with, and acceptance of, international law in Japan demonstrates the universal applicability of its logic, however easy it is to criticize its inherent Eurocentric character.

---

[54] Alcock points out the particular intellectual character of the Japanese shown in the process of receiving international law. 'Long isolation has given to this branch of the earth's great family a development which they may claim with some reason as peculiarly their own. Their outer life, their laws, customs, and institutions have all something peculiar—a *cachet* of their own which may always be distinguished. It is neither Chinese nor European, nor can the type be said to be purely Asiatic. The Japanese seem rather to be like the Greeks of the ancient world, forming a link between Europe and Asia; and put forth claims to be ranked inferior to neither race in *some* of their best qualities; yet very strangely blending many of the worst characteristics of both.' [emphasis by Alcock] *The Capital of the Tycoon* (n 9) 222–3.

[55] As regards the 'inter-civilizational approach', see Y Onuma 'When was the Law of International Society Born? An Inquiry of the History of International Law from an Intercivilizational Perspective' (2000) 2 Journal of the History of International Law 1–66; Y Onuma 'A Transcivilizational Perspective on International Law' (2009) 342 Recueil des cours de l'Académie du droit international 81–418.

Recommended Reading

Akashi, Kinji 'Japanese Predecessors of Judge Oda in the World Courts: Works and Method' in Nisuke Andō, Edward McWhinney, and Rüdiger Wolfrum (eds) *Liber Amicorum Judge Shigeru Oda* (Kluwer Law International The Hague 2002) vol 1, 9–22.

Akashi, Kinji 'Japanese "Acceptance" of the European Law of Nations: A Brief History of International Law in Japan c. 1853–1900' in Michael Stolleis and Masaharu Yanagihara (eds) *East Asian and European Perspectives on International Law* (Nomos Baden-Baden 2004) 1–21.

Burks, Ardath W (ed) *The Modernizers: Overseas Students, Foreign Employees, and Meiji Japan* (West View Press Boulder CO 1985).

Fairbank, John King (ed) *The Chinese World Order: Traditional China's Foreign Relations* (Harvard University Press Cambridge 1968).

Fisch, Jörg *Die europäische Expansion und das Völkerrecht* (Steiner Stuttgart 1984).

Liu, Lydia H *The Clash of Empires: The Invention of China in Modern World Making* (Harvard University Press Cambridge 2004).

Onuma, Yasuaki 'When was the Law of International Society Born?—An Inquiry of the History of International Law from an Intercivilizational Perspective' (2000) 2 Journal of the History of International Law 1–66.

Onuma, Yasuaki 'A Transcivilizational Perspective on International Law' (2009) 342 Recueil des cours de l'Académie du droit international 81–418.

Schirokauer, Conrad *A Brief History of Chinese and Japanese Civilizations* (Harcourt Brace Jovanovich New York 1978).

Schmitt, Carl *Der Nomos der Erde im Völkerrecht des Jus Publicum Europaeum* (Duncker und Humblot Berlin 1950).

Sims, Richard *French Diplomacy towards the Bakufu and Meiji Japan 1854–95* (Curzan Press Richmond 1998).

Svarverud, Rune *International Law as World Order in Late Imperial China: Translation, Reception and Discourse, 1847–1911* (Brill Leiden 2007).

CHAPTER 31

INDIA–EUROPE

UPENDRA BAXI

1. INTRODUCTION

MUCH has been said and written about 'India' and 'Europe' in many a disciplinary tradition, especially philosophy, religion, culture, and history. Even so, this 'much' is simply not enough from at least some Indological perspectives.[1] In contrast, writings on the Europe–India interface in the making of international law are relatively sparse. And such writing as does exist fails to quite explicitly address what 'India' and other colonized nations and peoples may have contributed to the evolution of law and international law in 'Europe'. In this register remains singular the work of Charles Henry Alexandrowicz who pioneered understanding of the distinctively Indian contributions to the making of modern international law.[2] This chapter is dedicated to his memory.

Many expressions have been used for 'international law'—such as 'public international law', the 'law of nations',[3] 'transnational law', 'the common law of mankind',[4] and even the 'law of peoples'.[5] The term 'international law' was for a long while reserved to principles, standards, and norms that governed the conduct of 'civilized' States in

---

[1] See W Halbfass *India and Europe: An Essay in Understanding* (State University of New York Press Albany 1998).

[2] CH Alexandrowicz *An Introduction to the History of the Law of Nations in the East Indies: (16th, 17th and 18th Centuries)*(Clarendon Press Oxford 1967); see further CH Alexandrowicz *The Afro-Asian World the Law of Nations: Historical Aspects* (1968) 123 Recueil des cours 117–214 at 123–4.

[3] See E de Vattel *The Law of Nations or Principles of Natural Law* in JB Scott (ed) *Classics of International Law* (Carnegie Institution Washington DC 1916); JL Brierly *The Law of Nations: An Introduction to the International Law of Peace* (Clarendon Press Oxford 1928).

[4] See CW Jenks *The Common Law of Mankind* (Prager New York 1958).

[5] J Rawls *The Law of Peoples* (Harvard University Press 1999).

relation to each other. Today it applies to all States. The second description is designed to distinguish the 'public' character of international law as distinct from private international law or conflict of laws; although the categories 'private' and 'public' have been much contested,[6] public international law has become a term of art.

The second conception invites engagement with 'nations' rather than 'States'. For some scholars (such as James Leslie Brierly) the distinction was important because while colonizing or imperial state formation counted as a single legal person under international law, it ruled over many nations and the law of nations had to have some regard for the ruled nations claims for recognition, personality, or status within such formations. In contrast, Emer de Vattel, writing in 1773, scrutinized the idea of the law of nations from the perspective of the justification for the application of principles of the law of nature going beyond custom and consent of States.[7] In any event, the term 'law of nations' emerges as richer than 'international law' at least in the sense that 'nation' (ties of birth, belonging, language, religion, shared cultural as well as civilizational traditions everywhere) antedates the advent of the idea of a 'State'. The fact that some European States signed 'treaties' with Indigenous nations (despite predatory intent) suggests an acknowledgment of their equal juridical existence and status.

Further, from the perspective of human history the colonial epoch, however significant, cannot be regarded as being more than a brief interlude in the historical life of the colonized nations. Thus viewed, it also becomes clear that much of the current rhetoric about 'new nations', and their acceptance of international law, do not make much sense in terms of 'old' and 'new'. Nations which have now joined international political and economic organizations since the mid-20th century onwards are 'new' only from the limited perspective of the history of international law, not the law of nations. Deprivation of their political freedom by colonial powers cannot be said to have extinguished their 'nationhood' in any significant use of that term; nor, indeed, is there any compelling need to regard 'Western' and colonial powers as being significantly 'old' nations. History is a great equalizer, and at any rate, to the realities and perplexities of the post-Westphalian international law and contemporary human rights norms and standards, all nations come as relative strangers.

The expression—the common law of mankind (C Wilfred Jenks)—marks the importance of a truly multicultural conception of international law. He asks: How may we 'deduce a sufficient consensus of general principles from legal systems as varied as the common law with its own variants of the Islamic Law, Hindu Law, Jewish Law, Chinese Law, African law in its varied forms, and Soviet Law, to give us the basic foundation of a universal system of international law?'[8]

The quest here is framed in terms of a *juridical* (hu)mankind. Important as this endeavour remains even today, perhaps even more important is the idea, attributed

---

[6] For a critique of this distinction, see U Baxi 'Mass Torts, Multinational Enterprise Liability and Private International Law' (1999) 276 Recueil des cours 297–426.

[7] See the contribution by E Jouannet 'Emer De Vattel (1714–1767)' in this volume.

[8] *The Common Law of Mankind* (n 4) 3.

to the American philosopher Hartley Burr Alexander, that the common law articulates the will of mankind, issuing from the life of the people.[9]

In contrast, John Rawls seeks an ethical grounding of international law (via a second original position) in which peoples will enunciate the basic principles of the law of nations. Peoples in this thought experiment have no means of knowing which state of society they might be born in or live under; this 'veil of ignorance' then will yield an agreement by all over the basic principles of justice and a fair scheme of social cooperation which all States should observe. 'Peoples', in Rawls's conception, are collective moral agents; they do not appear here as inert elements alongside 'territory' as *constituted* elements of the state law but rather as *constitutive* elements. As such agents, they have a capacity to distinguish between what may be thought of as *'rational'* in contrast to what may be named as *'reasonable'*. If the making of the old European empires (or for that matter some new empires) may thus be thought *rational* by its authors and their normative cohorts, the law of peoples however provides ways, means, and grounds that entail critique of the empires as unreasonable. Rawls is not concerned with the historical or juridical reason but with moral reason. This contribution allows no scope for a fuller mention even of multifaceted critiques of the Rawlsian positions; suffice it to say for the moment that the notion of the 'law of the peoples' marks a paradigm shift if only because it provides a 'tribunal of reason' (to borrow a phrase from Kant) adjudging claims to legality in international state conduct.

Thus underlying concerns about nomenclature remain deeper questions about *what* and *whose* narratives histories international law may offer, and *why* (that is for what good reasons).

2. THE PLURIVERSES OF 'PUBLIC INTERNATIONAL LAW'

Questioning the idea about authorship of 'international law' as a sole creation of 'Europe' must remain the first step towards a study of 'Europe–India' interfaces. Doing this would not deny the obvious fact that the term 'international law' had no linguistic counterpart among the non-European others but would rather contest a particular way

---

[9] The quotation is from an inscription on the Eastern *façade* of the main Department of Justice building in Washington, DC, overlooking 9th Street NW. The building was completed in 1935. The full quote is: 'The common law derives from the will of mankind, issuing from the life of the people, framed by mutual confidence, and sanctioned by the light of reason.' According to the Library of Congress, the inscription is attributable to Hartley Burr Alexander (1873–1939), a poet, philosopher, scholar, and architectural iconographer.

of practising sociolinguistics. The proposition that India lacked the idea of international law because that term came into being in the 'West' is as helpful as saying that 'Europe' had no idea of or about religion because it lacked the word 'Dharma'! To state the obvious, neither the idea of religion nor that of law is exhausted by naming practices, in languages as well as vernaculars. Much the same holds for 'human rights'. Non-European others had their own ways of articulating equal concern about the nature and scope of sovereign power and relations between nations and peoples. Studying these ways remains only possible when we put an end to monological ways of doing 'histories' of international law as the stories of its European origins and development.

The idea that only in Europe occurred certain critical events leading to the making of a Westphalian 'international law' is justified from the perspective of a regional history but it is misleading when presented as the only history there is. Of course, several ways of thinking and events shape the beginnings of the idea of Europe. The differentiation between temporal and spiritual governance as giving birth to the modern idea of a State is a critical event. The Westphalian international law moves away (to adapt Michel Foucault) from the practices of the governance of soul to those of governance of bodies. Nor may one deny the fact and world-historical pertinence of three 'great' revolutions—the American, the French, and the Marxist-Leninist, though the pride of place remains always accorded by historians of 'international law' and human rights to the first two. Further, the heritage of Judeo-Christian discursive tradition as reworked by the Enlightenment provides new narratives of progress about liberties, freedoms, rights, and justice, testifying fully to the power of a universalizing public reason.

It is understandable that European historians and jurists regard this regional history as providing some privileged narratives concerning the origins of 'international law'. However, an equal regard for other regional histories calls into question claims of exclusive authorship of the values, standards, and norms of 'international law'. Such a threshold acknowledgement will, surely, entail different notions about civilization: the Indigenous or First Nations peoples millennia ago provided, and still provide, some profound grounds for questioning the 'Western' image of civilization as a form of 'mastery' over human and natural nature. Further, the non-European others have their own distinctive—and not inferior—histories of what it may mean to speak of being 'enlightened' as, for example, Gautam Buddha and Lord Mahavir fully exemplify. The invention of non-proselytizing religious traditions—for instance, Buddhism and Hinduism—does not create any 'empire' by the power of the sword. This kind of cultural diffusion on a global scale indeed may not simply be brushed aside in doing histories of 'international law'. Nor may be disregarded within Europe different understandings of the idea of the Enlightenment or internal critique of the making of the Westphalian international law of 'civilized' nations manifest memorably in the writings of Francisco de Vitoria.[10]

---

[10] For Vitoria, see the contribution by A Brett 'Francisco de Vitoria (1483–1546) and Francisco Suárez (1548–1617)' in this volume.

The endless enterprise to subject sovereign power to a modicum of normative and ethical corpus of restraints names a universal phenomenon informing, and progressively transforming the many worlds of international law.[11] We may begin to grasp this historic fact only when we begin to recognize that, far from being any Occidental accident or thought-experiment of the Christian ius naturale and the 'Enlightenment', 'Europe' actually corresponds rather well with the civilizational and cultural traditions of the 'non-West' peoples and their effective histories—an aspect highlighted briefly later in this text.

For the moment, we may do well to recall with Charles Alexandrowicz that the doctrine of *mare liberum* (freedom of the high seas) remained deeply ingrained in the doctrine and practice of the 'East Indies', which was fully acknowledged by Hugo Grotius.[12] Nor does it at all trivialize this discourse to say further that the pivotal histories of the immunity of diplomatic agents were fully affirmed millennia before by the 'Indian', and other equally significant traditions of non-European others. Further, economic historians of pre-colonial India suggest, for example, that *lex mercatoria* is scarcely a distinct European project or product. The typical inventions of commercial instruments, banking, insurance, and forms of arbitral dispute resolution were not unknown to 'India', as economic historians reveal.[13]

It is on this register that one may speak about the pluriverses of the making of international law which afford some new approaches to doing histories of the making of 'international law' and call for epistemic humility rather than arrogant Eurocentric, and heavily belaboured, claims of exclusive authorship.

3. DIFFERENT 'HISTORIES'

Writing about 'Europe' and 'India' international law interface leads us further to pursue further histories at least in terms of histories of ideas as mediated or intermediated by institutional arrangements and practices. Summarily, I present some concerns (approaches and orientations) at least in the following six ways.

---

[11] See eg A Nussbaum *A Concise History of the Law of Nations* (Macmillan New York 1947).

[12] See eg CH Alexandrowicz *An Introduction to the History of the Law of Nations in the East Indies* (OUP Oxford 1967); see also CH Alexandrowicz 'Grotius and India' 3 (1954) The Indian Year Book of International Affairs 357–67; see furthermore the contribution by P Haggenmacher 'Hugo Grotius (1583–1645)' in this volume.

[13] See T Raychaudhry, I Habib, and D Kumar *The Cambridge Economic History of India c. 1200–c. 1750* (CUP Cambridge 1982) vol 1; CA Bayly *Rulers, Townsmen and Bazaars: North Indian Society in the Age of British Expansion, 1770–1870* (OUP Oxford 1988).

First, doctrinal or *juristic* histories study the evolution of the norms and standards of authoritative obligations arising from custom, treaty, or related state practices. Second, *institutional* histories offer, in the main, the forms of internal differentiation fostering technical as well as political collaboration and cooperation among States functioning under specific treaty and customary regimes; these also include adjudicatory institutions as well as a network of arbitral and related dispute-handling organizations. This approach is often known as the history of international organizations. Third, *axiological* histories elaborate, from the perspective of justice and related values, ways of adjudging state conduct and the standards and norms otherwise established by custom, treaty, and other similar auspices. To some extent, they also provide and promote critical auspices for the renovation of extant normative postures of 'international law'. Fourth, histories oriented to the ongoing exploration of *international relations* take us beyond 'law' to inter-/trans-governmental spheres of action. Often but not always these are also the histories of political and economic relations between nations at times making, and at times unmaking other histories of 'international law'. Fifth, histories of *ideas* or mentalities (ideologies) provide a different genre, so do some recent histories of the idea of human rights. Sixth, finally, and without being exhaustive, some distinctive 'subaltern' histories privilege the voices of human suffering and communities in resistance.

Obviously these categories need to be further nuanced in their own distinctive terrains—a task that I will not here pursue. Even so, I maintain that it would be simply unhistorical to even whisper a suggestion that the second, third, fourth, and fifth approach are the singular products of European 'modernity'. Careful historians of ancient civilizations predating the European such as Indian and Chinese, but above of all of the Indigenous peoples of the Earth, surely fully suggest otherwise. To put it differently, the 'law of nations' was not unknown to the non-European others.

At the same time approaches summated under rubrics first, second, and fourth above are cultural products as well as artefacts of power and domination specific to the emergence of the Westphalian public international law conceived as demarcating theory and practice of 'international law' amongst sovereign and equal States (their customs, conduct, practices, processes, and institutions). In this view, then, those political communities denied or deprived of their right to self-governance and determination would necessarily remain prefigured as *objects* of international law. Raising this question even in its most rudimentary form exposes some imperialist and colonizing attributes of this approach. The DNA of normative or doctrinal and juridical histories of international law necessarily remains held within Eurocentric canon, constraint, and compulsion. Summarily put, these have little or no purchase on the comparative normative histories elsewhere, especially of the ancient Indigenous peoples and the colonized ones.

Today, and at long last, the threat of climate change has prompted an awareness of the global nature of our communal existence. This has led to a begrudging recognition of the wisdom of the Earth's ancient peoples and their civilizational values which encouraged the virtues of a primordial respect for Nature, rather than mastery over it. The so-called Huntington-like 'clash of civilizations' completely ignores a different genre of 'clash' now resurgent in a declaration of human rights which encompasses the rights of Mother Earth, as exemplified by the Ogoni, Zapatista, and above all the Cochabamba 2010 Declarations. Alternate eco-histories of international law are beginning to emerge only in the catastrophic contexts of climate change and global warming.

The 'metahistories' of the origins and sources of 'international law, crystallizing the monopoly of the narrative voice of self-proclaimed Westphalian 'civilized nations' of Europe now stands displaced and dissipated, if not entirely destroyed. Increasingly, a new *opinio iuris* or global *sensus communis* now redresses the erstwhile deafness to the voices of human and social suffering.

Approaches to the study of international law histories may no longer ignore the socio-ethical conviction, or the steady growth in collective moral human sentiment represented by the languages, logics, and paralogics of contemporary human rights. It is now recognized that the making of the Westphalian international law is a profoundly genocidal narrative as poignantly observed by Eduardo Galeano.[14] And the Subaltern Studies movement for South Asia alerts us fully to the default of Europe-centred settings or habits of thought. This faultline—or, to deploy a contemporary techno-scientific metaphor, a genetic marker—disempowers the voices of non-Europeans, the voices of suffering peoples colonized, and the practices of resistance articulated also by anti-colonial and imperialist thinkers.

Within the wider conext of human history, the stories of the making and unmaking of international law values, norms, and standards remain of little interest except as providing some sub-plots to humankind's endeavours. Surely, even as this reminds us of the marginality of 'international law' unless the historians of 'international law' explore in greater depth history *in* international law, rather than just pursue the history *of* international law.[15] Important remains in this context a fuller attention to the nascent spheres of anthropological analyses of human rights as well as the economic anthropology of the Empire.[16]

[14] See D Fischlin and M Nandorfy (eds) *Eduardo Galeano: Through the Looking Glass* (Black Rose Books Montreal 2002).

[15] See M Craven 'Introduction: International Law and Its Histories' in M Craven, M Fitzmaurice, and V Maria (eds) *Time, History and International Law* (Martinus Nijhoff Leiden 2007) 1–27.

[16] See as to latter, eg R Birla *Stages of Capital: Law, Culture, and Market Governance in Late Colonial India* (Duke University Press Durham 2009).

4. SOME METHODOLOGICAL CONCERNS

These remarks bring us to the doorstep of some concerns about method. Both 'India' and 'Europe' remain 'imagined communities'; neither exists as an invariant 'essence'. There are as many 'Europes' as 'Indias', and the awkwardly named large historical entities, 'India' and 'Europe', remain historically opaque, if not incoherent. Rather than in any sense 'pre-given', this politics of naming remains inherently troubled. Put differently, if 'India' of today bears little resemblance to ancient and medieval Hindu and Islamic political communities and formations, 'Europe' also exists in its own fragments. If 'provincializing Europe' remains a necessary imperative of historiographic imagination (as Dipesh Chakrabarty maintains),[17] 'cosmopolitizing' pre-colonial India also remains an equally pressing task. A new history of 'international law' cannot but afford equal dignity of discourse both to time and space within 'Europe' and 'India'. Narratives of colonizing space paradigmatically depict the geographies of injustice, lack of rights, and injustice constituted by the versatile colonizing corpus, genre, and grammar of conquest and occupation of territories, resources, and peoples. And yet, to undertake a large historical observation, pre-colonial empires and even some geographies of power in the post-colonial age offer examples of a different kind of colonization of space, the latter rendered often acutely visible by human rights-based critiques of post-colonial domination or governance. What sense then will a historian of international law make of the geographies of injustice and contestations over the denial of the right to have rights (to here invoke a contested phrase of Hannah Arendt)?[18]

Colonial/colonizing international law celebrates the logics of predatory conquest-the ongoing appropriation of the space of life of the non-European others. This confiscation of space assumes various forms—from genocidal occupation, institutionalized apartheid, and other forms of domination of the 'outer space' of the colonized peoples on the one hand, to conquests over the inner space (symbolized via 'Christianity' and 'Civilization'), on the other. How may writing histories of the Westphalian international law take more fully into account these multiple forms of 'spatiality' still remains an open question.

The time dimension of the making of the 'Westphalian' international law values, norms, and standards also requires further elucidation. Anthropologists of time speak to us about time categories such as 'enduring', 'cyclical', 'erratic', 'retarded', 'accelerated', and 'deceptive' as well as 'explosive'.[19] How may one write the 'history' of international law in terms of such temporalities? How may the addition of 'messianic' time of the

---

[17] See D Chakrabarty *Provincializing Europe: Postcolonial Thought and Historical Difference* (Princeton University Press Princeton 2000).

[18] See P Birmingham *Hannah Arendt and Human Rights* (Indiana University Press Bloomington 2006).

[19] See A Gell *The Anthropology of Time: Cultural Constructions of Temporal Maps and Images.* (Berg Oxford 2001).

European 'civilizing mission' help us in re-exploring the Europe–India interface? In this context, a further complexity stands ushered in by the notion of civilizational time: the imagery of a 'deep time'—a notion crossing continents and millennia as an intermix of different civilizational times.[20]

5. RE-SITUATING THE 'TWAIL' PROJECT?

The community of Third World and International Law (TWAIL) scholars has offered a full critique of the hollowness of the 'Eurocentric' notion that colonizing European nations were 'civilized' nations even by their own proclaimed Enlightenment values, norms, and standards which they created for themselves. TWAIL scholars vigorously contest the modes of global-knowledge production via which the colonizing 'Europe' fostered ways of designating the non-European as ethical infants in contrast to European ethical Enlightenment giants, who paradigmatically constructed the colonized self as 'savages' and as 'uncivilized', peoples and persons unfit or incapable for self-governance and self-determination, as beings (as Georg WF Hegel[21] infamously said) lacking 'history'. Even Immanuel Kant sought to justify a 'moral tutelage' which may in the long run bring them to a 'common standard of civilization'. There is no question that forms of ingrained racism were ever present at the European-Indian interface, at least in the metaphor of a 'Divine Right to Empire' claimed by the colonizing European nations, peoples, and States.

The TWAIL scholarship would, indeed, remain marginal to the dominant Eurocentric traditions of historiography of international law and relations were it to rest content with an ideological statement. However, it assumes an importance as alternative ways of writing history and the history of international law begin to be seen as legitimate. For example, Anthony Anghie insists that we attend closely to the task of telling stories—of 'histories of resistance to colonial power . . . from the vantage point of peoples who were subjugated, and the unique histories of non-European peoples'.[22] Gerry Simpson speaks to us about the regimes of legalized hegemony manifest in the reciprocal and dialectical relations between 'great powers' and the 'outlaw States'. Both scholars critique colonial historiography. Anghie insists, with formidable

---

[20] WC Dimock *Through Other Continents: American Literature across Deep Time* (Princeton University Press Princeton 2006); R Higgins 'Time and the Law: International Perspectives on an Old Problem' (1997) 46 International and Comparative Law Quarterly 501–20; M Koskenniemi 'Why History of International Law Today?' (2004) 4 Rechtsgeschichte 61–6.

[21] See the contribution by A von Bogdandy and S Dellavalle 'Georg Wilhelm Friedrich Hegel (1770–1831)' in this volume.

[22] A Anghie *A Imperialism, Sovereignty, and the Making of International Law* (CUP Cambridge 2005).

evidence, that the 'colonial history of international law is concealed even when it is reproduced'; and Simpson likewise challenges the 'linearity' of the older traditions, and argues for the development of a theoretical and intellectual history of international law and relations that would address the struggle between two conceptions of international society—the 'pluralist and the anti-pluralist' approaches.[23]

I single out these two TWAIL contributions (without here dwelling on the work of TWAIL as well Marxian scholarship) not only because they offer an ideological critique or exposé of the false consciousness of Europe's civilizing mission in the making of 'modern' international law, but also because they offer a model or a map of how alternative histories may be imagined and practised by way of contesting the first five types of practising history of international law while exemplifying the sixth.[24] These TWAIL analyses inaugurate many acts of reading the dominant histories of 'international law', regardless of some internal and friendly critique.[25] How far these may affect or refashion mainstream practice remains an open question; this is one reason for my view that we draw our conceptions of alternative histories not just from within inside the frameworks of the dominant but from a larger reservoir of cultural and civilizational resources of the subordinated peoples who, through literature and arts, provide new aesthetic forms of critiquing domination. While attending to the realms of the specifically political, an alternate history also needs to attune to the growth and development of new communities of sentiment among and across the violated non-European others; in that respect, Edward Said, EP Thompson, Eduardo Galeano, and Jacques Rancière, remain foremost exemplars. Put differently, a further task confronting the TWAIL discursive traditions summons us towards anthropological and ethnographical understanding of the making of the post-Westphalian international law.

6. Different Itineraries

Some commonalities in the international law of global primitive accumulation include genocidal violence (systematic massacre) directed against Indigenous peoples especially in the conquest of the 'New World';[26] the inscription of inherent inferiority

---

[23] G Simpson *Great Powers and Outlaw States: Unequal Sovereigns in the International Legal Order* (CUP Cambridge 2004).

[24] See Section 3 above.

[25] U Baxi 'New Approaches to the History of International Law' (2006) 19 Leiden Journal of International Law 555–66.

[26] E Galeano *Open Veins of Latin America: Five Centuries of a Pillage of a Continent* (C Belfrage trans) (Monthly Review Press New York 1973).

to the colonized peoples, incapable of access to the faculties of reason and will; the accompanying faith in a global civilizing mission (the 'White Man's Burden'); the expansive archive of the unsustainable exploitation of the resources (land, labour, and capital) for the Industrial Revolution in the 'West'; and an unapologetic celebration accompanied with some troubled justifications of the public virtues of predatory forms of colonizing 'governance'.

That said, we must not disregard the fact that colonization has many different histories. Not all countries and peoples of 'Europe' participated equally in the scramble for a new empire. And those that did differed in the constructions of the colonized self, as can be seen via the different 'Anglophonic' and 'Francophone' colonizing modes. Global imperial rivalries furnish different itineraries of occupation and domination. Further, and also of necessity in terms of 'Europe–India' interfaces, I will only speak here about the four 'Cs' of predatory European formations—Conquest, Commerce, Christianity, and 'Civilization'. These neat terms provide many a register of complexity and contradiction.

The second 'C' (commerce) may not be conceived outside the forms of conquest colonization. Construction of a new slavery (in fields, farms, factories, and imperial wars) stands accompanied by forms of the great Indian disapora—forms of indentured labour transmigrated, servicing the needs of the British Empire. This newly minted transnational imperial regime constitutes many an anxious reflexive moment for historians of international labour law.

The European (including the Portuguese, French, and British) conquests of 'India' occurred via commercial corporations variously subject to domestic legislative and executive oversight. The British East India Company maintained its own armed forces which gradually conquered 'India' via several battles and wars from 1757 to 1818, and in the process entered into several treaties with various Indian rulers. The remarkable invention of a corporate form as a vessel and vehicle of the British imperialism in India (and also elsewhere in Asia) requires critical attention at least from those who seek to frame categories of alternative ways of doing international law histories. How does it come to pass that juridical histories of international law could have ever maintained, with positivist innocence, that only 'States' are the subjects of international law? What explains their reluctance to acknowledge the roles played by state-like yet state-transcendent European mercantile corporations fully invested with the power to wage wars and to sign treaties? How can many eminent 'historians' of international contemplate any consideration of otherwise much-celebrated doctrines of 'just war' in the corporate sovereign acts of hostility against the duly established sovereign rulers of 'India'? And how may we call the doctrinal or juridical histories of international law of this period in any sense as the law of 'civilized' nations when all evidence suggests that what occurred was a consolidation of 'Euro-mercantile' predation?

Questionable, also, is the claim that unlike other sites of colonization where non-European others were regarded as moral infants or even as 'savages', 'India' was never regarded as a *terra nullius*. What may then help us to differentiate the Mogul conquest and governance of India (13th–16th centuries CE) from the Company Raj? Both display equal measures of imperial cruelty, thus surely the question of how they differ is of some historical pertinence. For these and related reasons I suggest 'acts of reading' (to adapt a seminal phrase of Jacques Derrida), rendering the making of the Westphalian regime in the imagery of an *international 'law' of global primitive accumulation*.

The other two 'Cs' also mingle and cohabit the production of this 'law'. Civilization equals Christianity. The international law of *primitive accumulation* remains animated by an evangelical motif of a deepening universalization of Christianity as a world historic project.[27] European 'mercenaries' and 'evangelists' took different approaches to subjugation of the colonized subjects. If the latter were primarily concerned with the expansion of Christianity as a universal religion, the former were specialists in loot and plunder of the resources of the occupied nations who antedated by several millennia the formation of a 'civilized Europe'. Yet of course, even as the missionaries often developed an internal critique of early and middle phases of Euro-colonization in 'India' and elsewhere, they were not entirely averse to the emerging international law of primitive accumulation which provided them both a shield and sword necessary for the pursuit of their 'redemptive' tasks.

Obviously a more detailed understanding or narrative of the itineraries of collaboration and complicity is signified by the four 'C's, outside which the form and grammar of international law of global primitive accumulation remains difficult of grasp. Put differently, even historians of international law in the several senses indicated above, need to move cautiously, rather than polemically, in understanding the contexts of convergence between European 'Christianity' and 'Civilization'.

7. International Law of 'Cosmopolitan' Imperial Governance

Perhaps a second phase of the Euro-international law occurs in an Age of Empire, where the metropolitan governments begin to administer the colonies directly. 'Europe–India' international law interface illustrates this formation at least in some ways. I have in mind here the ending of the 150-year Company Raj in India inaugurated by the trial of Warren Hastings, and in turn impelled by an urgency of response

---

[27] See S Moyn *The Last Utopia: Human Rights in History* (Belknap Press Cambridge MA 2010).

in the wake of what some Anglo-British historians still continue to call the 'Great Indian Mutiny'—in stark contrast to some nationalist Indian historians who regard it as a first struggle for Indian independence.

The Proclamation of Queen Victoria of 1 November 1858,[28] which enforced the ending of the Company Raj, emerges as an important marker of imperial cosmopolitan international law. In the first place, it anticipates the elements of the international law of succession by announcing 'to the native princes of India, that all treaties and engagements made with them by or under the authority of the East India Company are by us accepted and will be scrupulously maintained, and we look for the like observance on their part'. Second, follows an assurance 'that we shall respect the rights, dignity and honour of native princes as our own'. Third, is the assurance of religious toleration: 'We declare it to be our royal will and pleasure that none be in any wise favoured, none molested or disquieted, by reason of their religious faith or observances, but that all shall alike enjoy the equal and impartial protection of the law....' Fourth, there follows a statement of amnesty for 1857 insurgents, all those who have been 'misled, but who desire to return to the path of duty' prefaced by a note of indirect apology: 'We deeply lament the evils and misery which have been brought upon India by the acts of ambitious men.' Fifth occurs an assurance to administer the government for the benefit of all subjects 'resident therein' because in 'their prosperity will be our strength, in their contentment our security, and in their gratitude our best reward'. The history and hermeneutic complexity of this proclamation—and subsequent legal, constitutional, and governance transformations—lie outside the scope of this chapter.[29] However, a few remarks are necessary for my claiming this as a marker of cosmopolitan imperial international law.

The first imperial recital at least normatively constructs native Indian rulers as being subjects of international law capable of signing international treaties, and the second recital likewise expands the horizons of the law of state succession in Euro-international law. The relations of 'paramountcy' established by further agreements (excluding foreign affairs, defence, and currency), however, render these more than 500 entities as 'quasi' subjects of an imperial international law. Forms of autonomous governance thus assured to native princes generate a distinctive formative history of Indian private international law, matters even today of peripheral concern to historians of this sphere.

---

[28] Proclamation by the Queen in Council to the Princes, Chiefs, and People of India (1 November 1858) reprinted in A Berriedale Keith (ed) *Speeches and Documents on Indian Policy, 1750–1921* (Oxford University Press London 1922) vol I, 382–6.

[29] See, eg TR Metcalf *The Aftermath of Revolt: India 1857–70* (Princeton University Press Princeton 1964); B Chandra, A Tripathi, and B De *Freedom Struggle* (National Book Trust New Delhi 1972); B Chandra et al *India's Struggle for Independence* (Penguin Books New Delhi 1989); AR Desai *Social Background of Indian Nationalism* (Popular Book Depot Bombay 1959); S Sarkar *Modern India: 1885–1947* (Macmillan Delhi 1983).

Leaving this aside, the British Indian Independence Act of 1947,[30] among other things, crucially marks a reversion of sovereign status to these entities entailing the negotiation of further instruments (known as 'instruments of accession') by these new sovereigns, accepting integration with a post-colonial formation constitutionally named as the sovereign democratic republic of India. As is generally well-known, the accession by the Maharaja of Jammu and Kashmir (in the context of invasion by the then newly formed State of Pakistan, which eventually leads to the formation of a separate entity named as 'Azad Kashmir') remains a tragic legacy of the cosmopolitan imperial law formation, disrupting many a juridical history of recognition of States under international law, and the associated approaches to the law of peace and war.

Moving on, the third imperial recital assurance of the Proclamation now disorients the Missionaries, who at one end of the spectrum regard the 1857 happenings or events as failures of their obligations of faith, and at the other end, remain discontented with the 'secularization' of governance.[31]

The fifth recital marks an itinerary of importation of a new discursive normativity of the standards of metropolitan legality in the governance of a new British Raj. While this bears no reference even to some contemporaneous standards of public 'international law', it remains directed to the forms of social reproduction of loyal subjects, millions of whom were later to forfeit their lives amidst the unspeakable horrors of the First World War. How may we grasp this paradigm shift—from the mercantilist era to a cosmopolitan colonial governance—in terms of an emergent history of new 'international law', even when serving the ends of cosmopolitan imperial governance?

8. Sourcing International Law

The Europe–India interface offers fertile ground in terms of sourcing normative obligations for state conduct in times of peace and war. Ancient 'Indian' ways of thought reveal the profundity of approaches towards fashioning what the holders and wielders of sovereign power could do and ought to do or refrain from doing.

---

[30] An Act to make provision for the setting up in India of two independent Dominions, to substitute other provisions for certain provisions of the Government of India Act, 1935, which apply outside those Dominions, and to provide for other matters consequential on or connected with the setting up of those Dominions 1947 (UK) 10 & 11 Geo 6 c 30 ('Indian Independence Act').

[31] As fully described by an Algerian scholar; see B Belkacem 'A Wind of Change: The New British Policy in Post-Revolt British India' (2008) 30 Atlantis—Journal of the Spanish Association of Anglo-American Studies 111–24.

'Europe' offers equally rich histories via various avatars of theistic and secular natural law doctrines. Very broadly speaking, if the theistic natural law tradition outsources these obligations to God (His Will or Reason), many secular versions of natural law tradition derive of binding norms from human reason or from the laws of Nature. The positivist doctrine that derives exclusively obligatory norms, maxims, and principles from the consent (will) of the States is of a rather recent European origin.[32]

Central to 'India' remains the idea of *Dharma*, an idea laced with a huge hermeneutic investment of philosophical cultural capital, and political contestation. Without entering this formidable territory of thought and practice, I may here only suggest the following elements of understanding for the present context.

First, *Dharma* is *sanatan,* that is, eternal, law (roughly the same sense that St Thomas Aquinas gave to it) governing the cosmos and as such is impervious to human reason and will. Second, it is also natural law in the sense that obligations owed under the name of *Dharma* flow from, the 'nature of things', independent of human will and reason. Third, however, inunctions and imperatives of *Dharma* as extending to human conduct emerge as dictates of practical reason varying with *Desh and Kala* (region and time respectively); indeed, the imageries of cyclical millennial cosmic time variously articulated in the diction of the four *yugas* reinforce the perspective in which eternal law continually redefines *dharmic* obligations. Fourth, *Dharma*'s origins do not lie in any revealed Word of a singular Supreme Being contained in a single Holy Book; rather its sources derive from a variety scriptural and literary sources (epics such as the *Ramayana* and the *Mahabharata*, for example). '

Fifth, *dharmic* discourse provides narrative scope for justificatory practices of projects of ethical violence (including the just war—*dharnma-yuddah*—discourse), but also for its other—an ethical project directed towards *Ahimsa*—articulating a non-violent grammar of practices of domination as well of resistance. This development stands more specifically extended and enriched by the Buddhist and Jainist discursive traditions, and especially in our times in the figuration of Mahatma Gandhi. India–Europe interfaces remain scarcely understandable outside Gandhi's unique invention of non-violent mass civil disobedience reflected variously beyond as with the two other are legendary 'Ms' (Nelson) Mandela, and Martin (Luther King), as well as heroic struggles for self-determination and of human rights by the Buddhist Monks, in Viet Nam, Cambodia, Tibet, and Burma.

How may the notion of *Dharma* be extended for use as a source of obligations among sovereigns and peoples in 'India?' A specific explanation of the normative origin of restraints on sovereign power and obligations of those ruled occurs via complex schema of *varna* and castes. If the four *varnas* being *Brahmin, Kshtriya, Vaishya,* and *Sudras* signify a timeless schema of *homo hierarchicus* (to refer to a much-contested naming by Louis Dumont), castes remain infinitely various and

---

[32] J Bernstorff *The Public International Law Theory of Hans Kelsen: Believing in Universal Law* (CUP Cambridge 2010).

somehow assigned to each of the four *varnas*. Thus stand fully opposed the imageries of *Kshtriya dharma* and *Rajdhrama* in the charismatic *Bhagwat Gita*: Lord Krishna in a conversation with Prince Arjuna in the midst of a mighty battle-field urges him to follow *Kshatriya dharma*, avenging the perfidious conduct of his own family/kinsfolk. But this specific order of caste-based obligations stands further subsumed in a wider notion of *Rajdharma* extending a complex of normative restraints extending to the holders and wielders of sovereign power. In the *Gita*, *rajdhrama* emerges as a heavy mix of epistemological (ways of knowing truth), ontological (the nature of self or Being), and metaphysical (cosmological) considerations.

This notion, in turn, constitutes its other—*praja-dharma* (the pious obligation of the subjects of sovereign) was the principal source of normative obligations of the rulers and the ruled. Furthermore, the question remains whether the discursive traditions of *praja-dharma* offer any narrative scope for 'natural' rights, if only because its constitutive elements were not manifestly based on any 'theory' of social contract nor a 'right to rebel'. The problem of the justification of 'tyrannicide' which so overwhelmed Catholic 'concilar' theory in late Middle Ages does not feature as an aspect of *praja-dharma*.

One way to read the *Gita*—a classic text of all times—is via the metaphor of *dharma-yuddha*. The *Gita* offers some comprehensive articulation of just war as an instrument of last recourse to *a-dharmic* regime, which pursues force and fraud against its 'Other' and isimpervious to any kind of just 'mediation'. The *Gita*, of course celebrates the doctrine of 'just war' as *dharma in extremis* as it were, a state of affairs which permits departures from the rules of warfare . There is also room for thinking that many a standard and norm of what passes under the rubric 'humanitarian international law' was fully anticipated in ancient India.[33] To recall the regime of obligations of avoidance of unnecessary suffering in the conduct of war, we need to read the canons of *rajdharma* which millennially antedate the notion of *tempermenta belli*—developed especially by Hugo Grotius and since then . Neither any forms of nostalgic recall of a hoary past of 'Hindustan', nor any simple-minded critique of the arrogance of 'European' jurists and publicists, can be justified.

If Emperor Ashoka remains an icon of *ahimsa* (justice as prohibiting violent conduct by rulers in dealing with other rulers and with all peoples), Emperor Akbar lays the foundation of tolerance and respect for minority rights by a deeply syncretic form of secularism. Neither reduced royal relations to an order of mere statecraft, as some hurried readings of Kautilya's *Arthasastra* may lead us to believe. The problem constituted by 'just war' remains shared in a equal measure at the 'Europe–India'

---

[33] See *An Introduction to the History* (n 2); JW Spellman *Political Theory of Ancient India: A Study of Kingship from the Earliest Times to circa A.D. 300* (Clarendon Press Oxford 1964); UN Ghosal *A History of Indian Political Ideas: The Ancient Period and the Period of Transition to the Middle Ages* (OUP London 1959).

interface and beyond. Much the same can be said about the advance of Mogul Rule in India in the Middle Ages, which brought some distinctive *Shari'a*-based notions of just rule. How can historians of 'international law' of peace and war, and even the communities of the old and new TWAIL scholarship, proceed in order to grasp paradigmatic variations of the history of ideas about Europe–India interfaces? Furthermore, any suggested variance between concerning the pre-eminence of theistic natural law tradition needs to take seriously at least two forms of the making of Indian civilizational tradition.

'India', not unlike Europe, then, resourced 'international law' by an appeal to the higher law. Unlike 'Europe', however, the nature and forms of higher law does not, in my view, signify a difference not of degree but rather of *kind*. It is important to acknowledge that notions of *rajdhrama* proved capacious enough to accommodate some forms of 'positivist' approaches. For example, Kautilya speaks about various types of *sandhis* (treaties and agreements) corresponding to forms of righteous, predatory (greedy), and demonic conquests, and *Arthasastra* fully develops the notion of concentric circles of power (the theory of Mandala) offering a corpus of normative constraint on Hindu emperors.[34] This contribution ought not be considered a matter of antiquarian interests especially in contemporary contexts of the outlawing of war save in self-defence under the UN Charter, or the myriad acts of collective 'humanitarian intervention' with or without the UN mandate. Furthermore, the old and new international relations theory about balance of power in a multipolar world ordering may find unexpected insights in this classic text of 4th century BC.

Space constraints prevent any further pursuit of the positivist tradition within the approaches to *rajdhrama*. Nor is it possible here to trace how these helped or hindered the three centuries-long interaction with the Mogul Empire save by saying that a distinct body of state practice and conduct also emerged in the new Empire. The early Europe–India interfaces did not as fully emerge in 'India'; this despite its long-lasting encounter with the British, and enclave encounters with France in the south (Pondicherry) and with the Portuguese in Goa, and Dadra Nagar Haveli in the western region (which endured even into the first two decades of an independent India.) Historians of cosmopolitan imperial law must surely ask: How did the pre-colonial and British Raj state practice adapt and respond to a long exposure to British traditions of positivist 'international law'. A fascinating archive of the 'Indian' understanding of the positivist tradition in international law stands offered in its participation in the International Court of Justice which had to opine or rule upon the various contentions raised in particular by Portugal.

Even before decolonization, the role of India as an original member of the ILO, and on other sites, requires more careful examination than now already at hand. Were we to turn our scope to the inter-war (the First World War, and the Second, as

---

[34] CH Alexandrowicz 'Kautilyan Principles and the Law of Nations' (1965–1966) 41 British Year Book of International Law 301–20 at s 3 and 4.

well as the Cold War) the India–Europe interface offers a very different 'history'. Indeed, India offers several complex and contradictory registers in the making of contemporary international law. Thus, for example, modern India offers the first exercise of the right to self-determination against the British Empire; invents 'Nehru Doctrine'[35] against an erstwhile 'Monroe Doctrine'; remains the first nation-state as early as 1951 to refer a territorial (Kashmir) dispute between it and Pakistan; co-invents a doctrine of Panchashila with Egypt and Indonesia; advances the cause of decolonization, including the cause of self-determination; advances the UN General Assembly Uniting for Peace Resolution in the context of the Koran War; actively participates in the enunciation of human rights instruments and ethos in the UN, remaining in the forefront with other ex-colonial nations and peoples in advancement of internationally codified human rights; leads and participates in the UN-based movements against apartheid and race-based practices in South Africa and related countries; actively participates in UN Peace-Keeping Forces worldwide. All this is addressed by Bimal Patel in this volume and elsewhere. There is no simple way to cover the UN-based and contemporary India–Europe interface in one chapter.

9. A Non-concluding Remark

The phrase 'Europe–India' interface offers many different perspectives on the history of 'international law.' Doctrinal or juridical history writing, important as these remain, remain imbued with the belief that 'international law' is a 'gift'—of the 'West' to the 'rest'! In this conception, the millennial or 'deep' time of the non-European others stand ignored. Even other approaches suggesting a greater concern for acknowledging civilizational plurality in making and unmaking some dominant and hegemonic conceptions thus offered but these fail to imagine the early authorship of core international law norms by the non-European others.

I have not attempted to trace the 'genealogies' of the creation of both the Westphalian and post-Westphalian' spheres as well as of the old or new 'Empires'. Nor have I thus far invoked Marxist interpretations, decoding the materiality of international law into social relations of production and their reproduction. Such studies exist, directing attention both within and across nations to cite imperialism as a leitmotiv of the Westphalian public international law. Even today almost all traditions of

---

[35] The principal characteristic of this doctrine were: 'opposition to colonialism ad racism, non-interference with Asian affairs ny non-Asian powers, no further colonization or aggression in Asia, no entanglement in power blocs…': see Richard Falk, Samuel S Kim, and Saul Mendolvitz (ed) *International Law* (Transaction Press Somerset NJ 1966).

history writing avoid alternative histories of, and about, 'international law' with regard to former and extant socialist societies, as if these did not exist at all. Marxian-Leninist approaches to 'international law' may be viewed as merely 'ideological', but of course the liberal perspectives are not devoid of even ideology either. Susan Marks, BS Chimni, and Bill Bowring (among significant TWAIL others) alert us to the impoverishment of international history-writing thus induced and fully caused. By way of a minor footnote to their rich corpus, I suggest a new way of doing 'international law' histories, distinct from histories of international law formations of primitive global capital accumulation, of cosmopolitan imperial law and now of 'neoliberal' international law, even amidst the complex and contradictory aftermath of global financial meltdowns and Eurozone crises. These histories may not allow for inclusion some of the more seismic shifts, from the Czech to the Arab Spring movements, offering some 'post-Rawlsian' narratives of the law of the peoples.

As one untutored in the arts and crafts of history writing, I remain aware that 'historians' of 'international law' properly so named may respond to this contribution by ignoring it. Even so, a cache of large questions still remain unanswered: How may the sources of subaltern 'international law' contribute to the new approaches of doing this history? How may one 'feminize' sovereignty and State via acts of reading the hidden transcripts of the past and present? What sense, if any, may we make in reading of histories of labour movements and struggles, within, across, and even beyond the Europe–India interface? How may TWAIL-genre alternate histories? How may one ascribe ancient civilizational traditions (at least in terms of histories of ideas and movements) to any remaking of some new future of international law? Do any of these perspectives offer fruitful points of departure?

In summary, three types of problems remain inherent in any practice of a new historiography of 'international law': the Herculean, Promethean, or even Sisyphus-like endeavours. Acts of cleansing the Augean stables of 'classical' international law remain, I suggest, comparatively less arduous. I remain less sanguine concerning any suggestion that TWAIL and post-TWAIL approaches entail any Sisyphus-like endeavours. The Promethean imagery perhaps marks some future and even funerary itineraries of the corpus and genre of international human rights as we know these today. In sum, the India–Europe interfaces map and mark, *faute de mieux*, some new emergent histories of 'unmaking' and 'remaking' international law—surely a task worthy of historians of the future.

Recommended Reading

Alexandrowicz, Charles H 'Doctrinal Aspects of the Universality of the Law of Nations' (1961) 37 British Year Book of International Law 506–15.

Alexandrowicz, Charles H 'Kautilyan Principles and the Law of Nations' (1965–1966) 41 British Year Book of International Law 301–20.

Anand, Ram P *New States and International Law* (Vikas Publishing House Delhi 1972).

Belmekki, Belkacem 'A Wind of Change: The New British Colonial Policy in Post-revolt India' (2008) 30(2) Atlantis—Journal of the Spanish Association of Anglo-American Studies 111–24.

Chimni, Bhupinder S *International Law and World Order: A Critique of Contemporary Approaches* (Sage Publications New Delhi 1993).

Crawford, James *The Creation of States in International Law* (Clarendon Press Oxford 1979).

Curtis, Michel *Orientalism and Islam: European Thinkers on Oriental Despotism in the Middle East and India* (CUP Cambridge 2009).

Gong, Gerrit W *The Standard of Civilization in International Society* (OUP Oxford 1984).

Ishay, Michelin *The History of Human Rights: From Ancient Times to the Globalization Era* (2nd edn University of California Press Berkeley California 2008).

Kennedy, David 'International Law and the Nineteenth Century: History of an Illusion' (1997) 17 Quinnipiac Law Review 99–136.

Koskenniemi, Martti *From Apology to Utopia: The Structure of International Legal Argument* (Finnish Lawyers Pub Co Helsinki 1989).

Martinez, Jenny S *The Slave Trade and the Origins of International Human Rights Law* (OUP Oxford 2012).

Otto, Dianne 'Subalternity and International Law: The Problem of Global Community and the Incommensurability of Difference' (1996) 5 Social & Legal Studies 337–64.

Pagden, Anthony 'Human Rights, Natural Rights, and Europe's Imperial Legacy' (2003) 31(2) Political Theory 171–99.

Thomas, Jeremy 'History and International Law in Asia: A Time for Review?' in Ronald Saint John Macdonald (ed) *Essays in Honour of Wang Tieya* (Nijhoff Dordrecht 1994) 813–58.

Westlake, John *Chapters on the Principles of International Law* (CUP Cambridge 1894).

Young, Robert JC *Postcolonialism: An Historical Introduction* (Blackwell Publishers Oxford 2001).

CHAPTER 32

RUSSIA–EUROPE

LAURI MÄLKSOO[*]

1. INTRODUCTION

THERE are two alternative ways to look at Russia's encounter with Europe in the history of international law. One way is to look at Russia as one of the European countries—a unique European country, for sure, but then a number of European countries have had their historical *Sonderweg*. If so, then to look at Russia's encounter with Europe in international law may not be so fundamentally different from looking at Poland's, Spain's, Scandinavia's, or even Britain's role in the development of international law. This approach puts Russia's claimed or real Europeanness at the foreground of research; the emphasis is on unity and similarities rather than differences with the rest of the European State community. When Russia made contributions to international law, it did so as a European—even if idiosyncratically so—power. Another perspective is to put Russia's uniqueness—and thus, differences from Europe—at the foreground of the historical research. International law is about regulating conflicts between States and conflicts are caused by differences—perceived or real—rather than similarities. In a number of ways, Russia has been a *sui generis* case in the history of international relations. Being the country with the largest territory in the world, stretching geographically from the Baltic Sea to Siberia and Far East, it

* Research for this chapter has been supported by a grant of the European Research Council and grant no 8087 of the Estonian Science Foundation. The author would like to thank participants in the January 2011 Interlaken workshop and the semiotician Mikhail Lotman for useful comments on an earlier draft.

has until today preserved its independent role and status in the international community. Of the former European Great Powers, Britain, France, and Germany are all members of the supranational European Union while today's Russia is not. The opinion that Russia is not just part of Europe but is unique has been influential in Russia and Europe alike, to the extent that a number of prominent thinkers in Russia continue to argue that Russia constitutes a unique 'Eurasian' civilization.[1] In this reading, Russia's encounter with Europe has been an encounter of two 'worlds', autonomous cultural-political spaces.

We do not need to make an immediate choice between these two contradicting approaches. It is enough that we are aware of their continued relevance. Hopefully the material that we will discuss in the following will eventually give a historically nuanced answer to the question of Russia's Europeanness. Yet it is also fair to admit that in some ways the approach chosen in this chapter represents the Baltic perspective on the Russian history. The contestable nature of some of the arguments and interpretations contained here is understood. If the present chapter motivates other researchers to lay out different accents and approaches, that would only be beneficial to the study of the history of international law in Russia.

Russia's encounter with Europe has been a central theme in the Russian public discourse for the last three centuries.[2] It is fair to say that during that time, Russia has been existentially more preoccupied with Western Europe than Western Europe has been preoccupied with Russia. With this background in mind, Russia's encounter with Europe in terms of international law can best be analysed with the help of the concepts of 'centre' and 'periphery'. Of course, these concepts—'centre' and 'periphery'—have not been directly used in international legal documents and doctrines of the past. Nor are they used in the official language of international law today. For the purposes of this chapter, the concepts of 'centre' and 'periphery' and their use in Russia's historical context are borrowed from the semiotic works of Yuri Mikhailovich Lotman (1922–93),[3] the founder of the Tartu-Moscow school of semiotics, and the relevant historical research done on Russia.[4]

From the point of view of the history of international law, 'centre' and 'periphery' are not just metaphors, though. When international law was dominated by the European

[1] See eg SS Sulakshin 'Civilization Genesis in Global Historical Time' (Draft of speech given at the 'Forum of Civilizations' conference October 2010).

[2] M Malia *Russia under Western Eyes. From the Bronze Horseman to the Lenin Mausoleum* (Harvard University Press Harvard 1999); IB Neumann *Russia and the Idea of Europe* (Routledge London 1996).

[3] YM Lotman *Istoria i tipologia russkoi kul'tury* (History and Typology of the Russian Culture) (Iskusstvo St Petersburg 2002) at 254 f.

[4] See A Toynbee *A Study of History. A New Edition Revised and Abridged by the Author and Jane Caplan* (OUP Oxford 1972); D Lieven *Empire. The Russian Empire and its Rivals* (Nota Bene Yale 2002) at 226–7; GS Starodubtsev *Istoria mezhdunarodnogo prava i ego nauki* (History of International Law and Its Scholarship) (Izdatel'stvo Rossiiskogo universiteta druzhby narodov Moscow 2006) at 45.

powers, it included a specific 'standard' for distinguishing between 'centre' and 'periphery'. This standard was made up by the language of 'civilization'. The standard settled what constituted developed 'normality' and what underdeveloped barbarity; who received status and who was marginalized as not worthy of full status.[5]

2. Russia and International Law until the Late 17th Century

2.1. Contacts with and Influences from Byzantium

For at least the past three centuries, Russia has been carrying a dialogue of civilizations with Europe, but perhaps conducted greater self-reflection about Europe and modernization. One of the particularities of Russia was that although the Scandinavian Varangians were crucial in consolidating statehood in the lands of Rus, the country's first major dialogue was with Byzantium, the Eastern Roman empire. The encounters of the Princes of Kievan Rus with Byzantium were a mixture of co-operation and conflict. Over the 10th century, the Kievan princes conducted a number of military campaigns against Byzantium. One result of these campaigns were four treaties concluded between Byzantium and Kievan Rus—in 907, 911, 944 (945), and 971 (972). The first treaty is known only through the chronicle; texts of the other treaties have survived.

The nature of these treaties suggests that, subjectively, Byzantium must have regarded the Kievan Rus princes as unequal, even though the 'barbarians' of the North reached a number of military victories against 'civilized' Byzantium.[6] The treaty of 907 regulated the way Kievans were to visit and live in Constantinople. Among other restrictions, the Kievans were mandated to be accompanied by an imperial official.[7] The treaty of 911 regulated criminal and civilian matters related to the lives of Kievans who had settled in Byzantium. Thus, this treaty followed the pattern of Roman *ius gentium*, 'private international law'. It seems evident that the initiative for such stipulations must have come from Byzantium and followed the Roman legal tradition.[8] While the treaty of 945 made some amendments to the previous two

---

[5] GW Gong *The Standard of 'Civilization' in International Society* (Clarendon Press Oxford 1984).

[6] M de Taube 'Études sur le développement historique du droit international dans l'Europe orientale' (1926-I) 11 Recueil des cours 341–535 at 406.

[7] VM Shumilov *Kratkii kurs istorii mezhdunarodnogo prava* (Short Course in the History of International Law) (State University Voronezh 2006) at 17.

[8] The Byzantines had concluded a very similar treaty with the Bulgarians in 716.

treaties, the fourth treaty of 972 contained the pledge of Prince Svyatoslav to live in eternal peace with the Byzantenes.

The most lasting influence of the Eastern Roman empire was that in 988, Kievan Rus accepted Christianity from Byzantium. Initially, baptism affected primarily the rulers and remained only formal, as far as the general population was concerned. In 1054, the Christian Church split into Western and Eastern (Orthodox) parts led by Rome and Constantinople respectively. In 1453, the Turks conquered Constantinople and the headquarters of Orthodox Christianity fell in Muslim hands. At that time, Muscovy remained the sole Orthodox Christian power on earth.

One significant event that had influence on the future normative relations between Muscovy and Western Europe was that Muscovy rejected the Act of Union of 1439. The Greek Metropolitan of Moscow, Isidore, had signed this act recognizing the pope's supremacy in the whole Christian Church. The act had also been signed by the East Roman Emperor John VIII Palaeologus.[9] However, the people of Muscovy rejected the union. Moreover, Muscovy interpreted Constantinople's fall in 1453 as the God's punishment for Eastern Rome's falling back in terms of true faith in 1439. With the decision to stay apart from the Latins and not to recognize the pope's supremacy in the Christian world, Muscovy also put itself outside the so-called *respublica Christiana*, since at that time, community between European princes was based on religious unity. Of course, in Latin Europe, Reformation soon followed, and the Christian unity was split between the Catholics and the Protestants. Yet Muscovy's exclusion from the *respublica Christiana* seemed to have additional historical, cultural, and geographical dimensions. Tsar Ivan Grozny's attempt in the Livonian War (1558–83) to conquer the Baltic provinces for Muscovy did not help in establishing friendly relations with the Western Christians either. In 1570, as a hostile power, Muscovy was not invited to the conference in Stettin that otherwise regulated legal matters at the Baltic Sea.[10] Maximilian de Sully's (1560–1641) 'Grand Design', a utopian plan for a 'Very Christian' united Europe (1638) explicitly left out of the united Europe the 'Scythian prince' of Muscovy.[11]

In the late Middle Ages, the main normative disputes were religious ones. Theological arguments between political entities at that time were in a way a precursor to future international legal arguments. Having remained the sole Orthodox power, Muscovy for a while entertained the idea of Orthodox messianism (Moscow as the 'third Rome'). The pope's envoy Possevino, who visited Muscovy under Ivan Grozny's rule, recounted that 'these people believe that the whole world is under his sovereignty and all people are his slaves'.[12] This idea remained predominant in Muscovy. Yet at the same time, the Muscovite Tsar made some efforts to assure its Western neighbours that he did not entertain universalistic territorial ambition of the

---

[9] *A Study of History* (n 4) 271.
[10] 'Études sur le développement' (n 6) 485.
[11] ibid 487.   [12] ibid 479.

Byzantine Emperors. In 1576, Tsar Ivan IV instructed his ambassadors to the court of the Habsburg Western 'Roman Emperor' to explain that his claim to the title 'Tsar' was based on the fact that he had conquered the 'tsardoms' of Kazan and Astrakhan. In 1582, Ivan IV calmed the papal envoy: 'We do not want the realm of the whole Universe.'[13] Carl Schmitt (1888–1985)[14] famously argued that all political concepts of the modern theory of the State were secularized theological concepts.[15] One may ask whether some roots of Russia's later preoccupation with State sovereignty can be found in the rejection of the Latin (religious) supremacy in the 15th century. In any case, the rejection of the unification of the Christian churches—on Latin terms—may have introduced the foundation of mistrust towards certain normative initiatives of the West even later. Even today, Russia's reluctance to accept certain Western concepts of international law (for example, human rights law) without reservations may be influenced by its historically developed mistrust towards the intentions of Western Christianity.

2.2. Latin Europe: Contacts and Influences

One of the results of not being counted as part of *respublica Christiana* was that Muscovy did not participate in the Westphalian settlement of 1648. The Peace of Westpahlia was a matter between European Catholic and Protestant powers. The Orthodox Muscovy in the Eastern periphery of Europe was neither participant of the Thirty Years' War nor invited to settle it. Nevertheless, in the Treaty of Osnabrück, the Grand Prince of Muscovy was mentioned 'on the part of Sweden'.[16] The exact historical background of this reference is not clear. The late Middle Ages had constituted a serious break in Russian princedoms' relationship with Latin Europe. The main cause for this was the Mongol conquest of Rus between the 1240s and 1480. The only significant Russian principality that remained relatively independent from Mongols was Novgorod. (However, it was annexed by Muscovy in 1478.) Already in 1189, Novgorod had negotiated a treaty with Gotland. Treaties with German Hanseatic towns and Gotland in 1270, with the Swedes in 1323, with the Norwegians in 1326, and with Lithuania in 1440 followed.[17] Besides Novgorod, Smolensk concluded a treaty with Riga and Gotland in 1229. Michael Taube in particular makes the point that the Mongol invasion suppressed in the lands of Rus

---

[13] *A Study of History* (n 4) 273.

[14] See the contribution by B Fassbender 'Carl Schmitt (1888–1985)' in this volume.

[15] C Schmitt *Politische Theologie. Vier Kapitel von der Lehre zur Souveränität* (9th edn Duncker & Humblot Berlin 2009).

[16] Treaty of Peace between Sweden and the Empire (24 October 1648) (1648) 1 CTS 198, art 17, para 11 'ex parte serenissimae reginae regnique Sueciae omnes eius foederati ... rex Poloniae, rex et regnum Lusitaniae, magnus dux Muscoviae'.

[17] *Istoria mezhdunarodnogo prava* (n 4) 47–54.

political and legal developments that otherwise would have led to further integration with Latin Europe.[18] In Taube's view, one should not overemphasize the theologico-normative differences between the Orthodox Rus and the Latin West prior to the invasion of the Mongols. The fact that free Novgorod continued to trade with the Hanseatic League and concluded sophisticated treaties of commerce with the Germans and Swedes while the rest of the lands of Rus were subjugated and cut off from these developments, seems to prove Taube's point. The comparison between Novgorod and its nemesis, Muscovy, is also intriguing from the point of view of the development of Russia's domestic governmental structures. Mediaeval Novgorod had developed a populist type of *veche* democracy while Muscovy successfully built on two autocratic traditions. On the one hand, there was the Byzantine idea that the Tsar (*basileus*) was by definition above any independent Church authority, which was not a great starting point for the idea of the separation of powers. On the other hand, there was the Mongol tradition of ruthless suppression of one's own people by the rulers and constant readiness to wage war with neighbours. Muscovy appeared to be more successful than other Russian principalities under the Mongols—for example, its arch-rival Vladimir—partly because it borrowed most efficiently from the Mongol tradition. Russian lands were not reunited through negotiations or peaceful mergers; they were reunited by brutal force. A particularly heavy type of autocracy was developed that was to leave its mark on the future of Russia for centuries to come. In the framework of speculative history, Yuri Lotman also compared Novgorod and Muscovy and argued that, had the former prevailed over the latter, a more 'contractual' legal culture, thanks to Hanseatic influences in Novgorod, could have emerged in Russia.[19] One aspect of the Muscovy tradition was that the Tsar did not feel at all bound by law, not even vis-à-vis the Court members and nobility. In Western Europe, the contractual type of feudal law developed, and the power of the king became legally restricted, at least vis-à-vis the nobility. In Muscovy, the autocrat remained beyond any earthly law; his authority was absolute. Tsar Ivan Grozny was convinced that the fact that his rule was absolute and divine made him inherently superior to Western European powers. For example, Ivan wrote a letter to Queen Elizabeth I in which he expressed his disappointment about the fact that he had thought that she was a true sovereign but then he learned that not only did she have to rely on the advice of others—even worse, she had to accept the advice of merchants and was therefore apparently just a 'common girl' (*poshlaya devitsa*).[20] To the Swedish king Erik XIV, Ivan Grozny wrote that he was as elevated from Erik as heaven was from the earth.[21] Yet at the same time, as Fyodor Fyodorovich Martens correctly pointed out, England managed in the 16th century

---

[18] 'Études sur le développement' (n 6) 481.

[19] Y Lotman *Semiosfera* (Semiosphere) (Iskusstvo St Petersburg 2000) at 385. However, for a view that emphasizes more Muscovy's perspective, see Y Alekseev *'K Moskve khotim': Zakat boyarskoi respubliki v Novgorode* (Lenizdat Leningrad 1991).

[20] F de Martens *Recueil des traités et conventions* (St Petersburg 1892) vol 9, at 23.

[21] 'Études sur le développement' (n 6) 480.

to establish privileged and asymmetrical commercial relations with Muscovy[22] that can be retrospectively characterized as centre–periphery relations. This was the time when the language of international law first starts to come up in Western–Russian dealings. In 1583, English envoy Jeremy Bowes, discussing the Treaty of Alliance desired by Muscovy, raised in his rhetoric the 'spirit of Christianity, international law and good faith'.[23] Yet relations remained volatile. For example, Tsar Feodor's behaviour in 1588 towards the English envoy Fletcher in 1588 was so humiliating that Queen Elizabeth wrote back to the Tsar that 'no sovereign in Europe allows himself such a behaviour with Our Majesty'.[24] One difference that remained was that in Muscovy all land belonged, directly or through the Orthodox Church, to the Tsar, which meant that political power and property were in the same hands.[25] No one's property on land was autonomous from the Tsar. The tradition of not knowing how to keep political power and ownership of economic resources apart has arguably negatively influenced the development of Russia's democracy even beyond the 20th century.[26] Now, how are these domestic peculiarities relevant to the analysis of international law? Hersch Lauterpacht developed the point that when international law was established in Europe, princes and scholars borrowed heavily from Roman concepts of private law.[27] This was not necessarily a conscious decision or a random act of will. Via glossators and post-glossators, Roman law had simply become part of the history and culture in Latin Europe. Nations in international law were comparable to autonomous persons in the domestic legal order and were therefore entitled to sovereignty. Treaties were like contracts and, according to private law analogy, the maxim of *pacta sunt servanda* applied. Considering the absence of permanent courts in the international community, the next step would have been dispute settlement, negotiation, and arbitration between the sovereigns. The bottom line is that European international law in its post-1648 version rested on the idea of legal equality between the subjects of law, States. Other nations which did not have that kind of tradition of Roman law at home and joined or re-joined the 'European family of nations', had to some extent accept the ideas and solutions produced in another culture. One of the big historical questions in international law affecting not just Russia but other non-Western regions as well is: what has been the impact of domestic legal ideas and solutions on the understanding of international law? How

---

[22] *Recueil des traités et conventions* (n 20) vol 9, 69.

[23] ibid 37.

[24] ibid 61.

[25] R Pipes *Russia under the Old Regime* (2nd edn Penguin Books London 1995).

[26] E Lukasheva *Chelovek, pravo, tsivilizatsii: normativno-tsennostnoe izmerenie* (Human Being, Law, Civilizations: Normatibe and Value-related Dimension) (Norma Moscow 2009) at 326.

[27] H Lauterpacht *Private Law Sources and Analogies of International Law* (Longmans Green & Co London 1927).

can you project law vis-à-vis other nations if, domestically, the idea of the 'rule of law over all men' has not been highly valued and developed? How do such nations see international law? How can a State power that domestically does not conclude equal contracts with private actors, respect international treaties concluded with other sovereigns? Of the international relations theories, realism treats sovereign nations as 'black boxes', whereas liberalism would argue that domestic understanding of normativity has inevitably affected the nation's understanding of international law.[28] Yuri Lotman has explained that deep in the cultural 'code' of the country, Russia has historically tried to replace jurisprudence with moral or religious principles. In Russian literature, heroes oppose Grace (*milost'*) to Law (*zakon*), and seek the former rather than the latter. According to Lotman, in this antithesis of grace and law, the Russian idea stands in opposition to the Latin spirit that is permeated by the spirit of laws (*fiat justitia, pereat mundus; dura lex sed lex*). Lotman argues that in Russian literature there is a strong tendency to see in law a dry and inhuman principle opposed to such informal and positive notions as grace, sacrifice, and love. The antithesis of state law and personal morality, politics and holiness was emphasized.[29] Even in 1989, leading liberal Russian legal thinkers lamented that Russia had not stopped with its historical tradition of 'legal nihilism'.[30] In the movie '12' made by Nikita Mikhalkov—a contemporary Russian film director known for his conservative patriotism—a member of the jury, a simple Russian man, declares that Russians will never start to live 'by law' because doing so would mean that life would become 'boring'. In any case, 'joining' the international community as it became historically developed in (Western) Europe by the mid-17th century, did not just mean accepting 'international law', ideas, and practices following from the idea of sovereign equality in intra-European affairs. Joining 'international community' also meant questioning one's own domestic law and order and comparing it to European models. The nations reading Pufendorf and Vattel usually also went through the process of reception of European law domestically.[31] In terms of the reception of European legal and constitutional ideas, a comparable dynamics happened historically in Russia, Japan, and Turkey (with Peter the Great, Meiji Restoration, and Atatürk). In that way, relationships between the centre (Europe) and the periphery (newcomers to the international system) were established.

---

[28] See further D Armstrong, T Farrell, and H Lambert (eds) *International Law and International Relations* (CUP Cambridge 2007) and the programmatic statement contained in the title of the article by AM Slaughter and W Burke-White 'The Future of International Law is Domestic' (or, the European Way of Law) (2006) 47 Harvard Journal of International Law 327–52.

[29] *Semiosfera* (n 19) 143.

[30] VA Tumanov 'O pravovom nigilizme' (On Legal Nihilism) (1989) Sovetskoe gosudarstvo i pravo 20–7.

[31] See the contributions by K Haakonssen 'Samuel Pufendorf (1632–1694)' and by E Jouannet 'Emer de Vattel (1714–1767)' in this volume.

3. Russia and International Law From the Late 17th Century Until 1917

3.1. Peter the Great: Giving up Muscovy's Isolation, Successfully Becoming 'Part of Europe'

In the case of Russia, Muscovy joined the European state system and discourse on international law under the Tsar and later Emperor Peter the Great (1672–1725). Peter's opening a window to Europe was a process, not a single event. (Not even the Great Nordic War or the Nystad Peace Treaty of 1721[32] that finished the war were it). Taube emphasizes one important change that, from the viewpoint of international law happened during the rule of Peter I—the launch of permanent embassies, both of European powers in Moscow and of Muscovy in European capitals.[33] Moreover, under Peter the Great, Muscovy considerably intensified concluding treaties with foreign powers. Muscovy became part of the system of European alliances. For example, in 1686, Muscovy and Poland concluded a treaty of 'perpetual peace', making Muscovy join the anti-Turkish alliance.[34] Formerly isolationist and even anti-European, Muscovy became known as Russia. The Russian–Austrian Treaty of Alliance, also directed against Turks and Tatars, was concluded in 1697. Treaty relations were not restricted to European powers, however. Already in 1689, Muscovy had concluded the Border Treaty with China in Nerchinsk.[35]

After his *incognito* study trip to the Netherlands, Tsar Peter was eager to modernize Muscovy. One of the things Peter thought Muscovy needed was European law. It seems that by this he meant simultaneously legal philosophy and constitutional and international law. At that time, these fields were seen as part of the same natural law—consider, for example, the ideas of Samuel von Pufendorf (1632–94). Peter was so impressed by Pufendorf's intellectual influence in Europe that he even called himself 'Russia's Pufendorf'.[36] If anything, this moniker demonstrates how important the project of legal modernization of Muscovy was to Peter the Great. Nevertheless, Peter also wanted to remain the autocrat of Russia. In this sense, the encounter with European ideas of public law must have been for him like an encounter with

---

[32] Treaty of Peace between Russia and Sweden (signed 30 August 1721) (1721) 31 CTS 339.

[33] 'Études sur le développement' (n 6) 489.

[34] ibid 490.

[35] Treaty between China and Russia (signed 7 September 1689) (1689) 18 CTS 503; see further H Scheu *Das Völkerrecht in den Beziehungen Chinas zu den europäischen Seemächten und zu Russland. Ein Beitrag zur Geschichte des Völkerrechts* (difo-druck schmacht Frankfurt aM 1971).

[36] DW Treadgold *The West in Russia and China. Religious and Secular Thought in Modern Times Volume I: Russia 1472–1717* (CUP Cambridge 1973) at 89.

another 'language'. When Peter was visiting London and was surprised to see self-conscious men wearing wigs and gowns and moving around in the House of Lords, he asked who these people were. The answer was 'lawyers'. Peter was recorded to have responded (jokingly): 'I have but two in my whole dominions and I believe I shall hang one of them the moment I get home.'[37]

Peter the Great's Muscovy joining the European State system and making its first arguments 'in the language of European international law' happened of course at the same time. During the Great Nordic War (1700–21) that Muscovy waged against Sweden, the Tsar commissioned one of his diplomats, Petr Shafirov (1670–1739), to write a pamphlet defending Russia's actions in historical, legal, and moral terms. The pamphlet entitled 'A Discourse Concerning the Just Causes of the War between Russia and Sweden'[38] was published in 1717. The essence of this treatise was a peripheral nation looking for recognition and justification from the centre. The treatise was an appeal to 'all Christian and civilized Nations'. Shafirov lamented about Russia's peripheral treatment by Europe; it was as if Russia did not belong to civilized nations and was one of the Oriental lands, like 'India and Persia'.[39]

Shafirov's message to Western Europeans was straightforward: we are also a civilized nation, we want recognition from the centre, we want to be part of 'it'. Yet Shafirov, speaking in the name of a peripheral nation, spoke the language of *ius publicum europaeum* with an idiosyncratic accent. To start with, the discourse directed towards the 'civilized world' differed somewhat from the domestic discourse. For example, in the Russian version of the booklet, Petr Shafirov (or PS) called himself a 'slave' to the Tsar; however, that 'title' was thoughtfully omitted in the English version of the pamphlet.[40] Shafirov's historical argument—namely, that ancient Russian chronicles mentioned that Livonian lands had once, centuries ago, belonged to Rus—carried strong apologetic overtones and was difficult to verify. Nevertheless, it is noteworthy that although Russia had already succeeded with a *fait accompli* and conquered the formerly Swedish/German Baltic lands, it nevertheless felt like having to make this kind of appeal, however apologetically constructed its arguments were. That was the two-faced nature of the European discourse on civilization—ultimately, the test of one's civilization was superior force plus willingness to speak about it in a 'civilized' legitimizing way. Back in the Middle Ages, Mongols had the force but they did not care about the European normative discourse (just as

[37] J Quigley *Soviet Legal Innovation and the Law of the Western World* (CUP Cambridge 2007) at 60.

[38] See PP Shafirov *Rassuzhdenie, kakie zakonnye prichiny Petr I, tsar i povelitel' vserossiiskii, k nachatiu voiny protiv Karla XII, korolya shvedskogo, v 1700 godu imel* (A Discourse Concerning the Just Causes of the War between Sweden and Russia: 1700–21) (Zertsalo Moscow 2008).

[39] PP Shafirov *A Discourse concerning the Just Causes of the War between Sweden and Russia: 1700–21* (Oceana Publications Dobbs Ferry NY 1973) at 2 (of the Russian text).

[40] *Rassuzhdenie* (n 38) 8, 10. For the ethymology of the word 'slave' in Muscovy and Russia, see MT Poe *'A People Born to Slavery'. Russia in Early Modern European Ethnography, 1476–1748* (Cornell University Press 2000).

Muscovy's Ivan Grozny did not in the 16th century). Muscovy's Tsars of the mid-17th century did not have the muscle to break the window to Europe and would they have had that, we do not know whether they would have bothered to justify it in European normative terms. Peter the Great's genius was to realize that in order to be successful and recognized as European/civilized, Muscovy needed both: a combination of superior military force and the willingness to 'sell' the conquest in European normative-legitimizing terms. In any case, it is clear that Peter's Russia needed to adapt and start speaking the language of international law that had been exercised in Western Europe already for four hundred years.[41]

3.2. Russia's Role in International Law from the Early 18th Century until 1917: International Legal Practice

With the Peace of Nystad[42] which Russia concluded with the defeated Sweden in 1721, Russia became a European power and a considerable weight in the calculations concerning the balance of power in Europe. In terms of the history of international law, we should distinguish between the normatively relevant diplomatic history—the history of international law proper—and the history of the international law scholarship/doctrine. We will first turn our attention to the first.

Having settled to the newly built capital on the Baltic Sea, Saint Petersburg, the Romanov Emperors adopted a nearly total course towards Europeanization of Russia. The successful Empress Catherine II was ethnically German, and the emperors during the first half of the 19th century, especially Nicholas I, desired to model Russia on disciplined and Protestant Prussia. Many leading diplomats and influential officials in the government in St Petersburg were Baltic Germans, by cultural and historical background the most 'European' of the Emperors' subjects. However, it was often observed that the self-proclaimed Europeanness of Russia concerned primarily the elites and that the majority of the Russian people remained faithful to their own ancient ways and traditions.

During the 18th and 19th centuries, Russia contributed significantly to the development of international law in Europe. As a leading military power, imperial Russia often made European history, altering the course and direction of wars and peace settlements. The examples of Russia's contributions to the development of international law include the following.

In 1779, Russia de facto guaranteed the balance of power in Central Europe, especially between Prussia and Austria who could not agree on the predominance in the

---

[41] VE Grabar *Materialy k istorii literatury mezhdunarodnogo prava v Rossii (1647–1917)* (Materials on the History of International Legal Writings in Russia 1647–1917) (Zertsalo Moscow 2005) at 1.

[42] Treaty of Peace (n 32).

German lands. Empress Catherine II was invited to become the guarantor of the Treaty of Teschen[43] that was concluded between the German States. Since the Treaty of Teschen reconfirmed the validity of the Treaty of Westphalia, one can even say that in 1779 Russia became the guarantor of the Peace Treaty of Westphalia.

In 1780, Empress Catherine II successfully proclaimed the principles of armed neutrality—that during military conflicts (such as the American War of Independence that was going on at that time), the ships of neutral nations had to remain untouched by warring parties. This principle found rapid support among other affected European nations, although the leading maritime power, England, felt somewhat restricted by it.[44] The principle of the rights of neutrals was made part of treaty law at the end of the Crimean War (1853–56), via the Paris Peace Treaty.[45]

Another, more dubious face of international law was the partition of Poland which was carried out by Prussia, Russia, and Austria at the end of the 18th century. What is striking from a contemporary perspective is that the three partitions of Poland were prepared and executed via meticulous treaties that read like extensive entries in a cadastral register.[46]

Another of Russia's contributions was its role at the Congress of Vienna in 1815, after the defeat of Napoleon.[47] This was an unprecedented attempt to create a non-permanent international organization that would take care of the European balance of power for decades to come. Together with Prussia and Austria, Russia formed an anti-revolutionary and arch-conservative Holy Alliance in Vienna. Michel de Taube attempts to make the point that while Catherine the Great's 1780 initiative on armed neutrality was Russia's 'progressive' contribution, the conservative role Tsar Alexander I's Russia played in Vienna and afterwards was something primarily negative.[48] At the same time, Russia's conservative role as the 'gendarme of Europe', suppressor of the revolution in Hungary and uprisings in annexed Poland do not come as a surprise. Tsarist Russia's normative ideals abroad simply followed from Russia's domestic self-understanding as an uncompromising autocracy. Isaiah Berlin, himself a Jewish émigré from the Russian Empire, characterized that period in the following emphatic way: 'Russia was to the democrats of this period very much what the fascist powers were in our own time: the arch-enemy of freedom and enlightenment,

[43] Treaty of Teschen (signed 13 May 1779) (1779) 47 CTS 153.

[44] See C Bergbohm *Die bewaffnete Neutralität. Eine Entwicklungsphase des Völkerrechts im Seekriege* (Laakmann Dorpat 1883).

[45] General Treaty for the Re-establishment of Peace (signed 30 March 1856, entered into force 27 April 1856) (1856) 114 CTS 409 ('Paris Peace Treaty').

[46] F de Martens *Recueil des traités et conventions* (St Petersburg 1875) vol 2, 305–358.eg

[47] D Lieven *Russia against Napoleon. The True Story of the Campaigns of 'War and Peace'* (Viking London 2010).

[48] 'Études sur le développement' (n 6) 494–5. For the same point, see *Istoria mezhdunarodnogo prava* (n 4) 67.

the reservoir of darkness, cruelty and oppression, the land most frequently, most violently denounced by its own exiled sons.'[49]

During the 18th and especially 19th centuries, Russia also fought for the principle of humanitarian intervention, especially in favour of Orthodox peoples who lived in the Ottoman empire. It is interesting to note that this doctrine emerged at the time when otherwise in the European understanding of international law, non-intervention was the leading principle, at least vis-à-vis other European powers. However, Taube points out that Russia had borrowed the doctrine of the right to intervene in favour of the Orthodox believers from Byzantium.[50] In 1783, at the request of the local King the Russian protectorate over Georgia was established—in order to defend this ancient Christian State from attacks by Persia and the Ottoman Empire. However, in 1801 Georgia was annexed by Russia. Moreover, already in 1711, Peter the Great had concluded a secret pact with Kantemir, the hospodar of Moldova and vassal of the Ottoman empire, in which Kantemir recognized that Moldova was to become Russia's protectorate. With the Kücük Kainarca (Koutchouk-Kainardji) Peace Treaty of 1774,[51] the Ottoman empire recognized Russia's special rights and prerogatives vis-à-vis the Orthodox Christian population of the Ottoman empire.[52] The Treaty of Paris that was concluded at the end of the Crimean war (1853–56) transformed this 'right to intervention' into a general right of the members of the Concert of Europe, not just Russia individually.

During the second half of the 19th century, Tsarist Russia played a remarkable role in the development of international law of war. The St Petersburg Declaration of 1868[53] prohibited the use of explosive projectiles under 400 grams weight. Russia was one of the initiators of the 1874 Brussels conference on the codification of the laws of war. The Brussels conference was ultimately not successful but laid foundations for the codification of the laws of war in the future. Finally, the famous 1899 Hague Peace Conference was convened at the initiative of the Russian Tsar Nicholas II. Russia's leading international lawyer, Fyodor Fyodorovich Martens (1845–1909) played a crucial role at the conference and by formulating the famous Martens clause made the deal between European Great Powers and smaller States possible. During the second Hague Peace conference in 1907, the Russian delegation continued to play a decisive role. Russia's stance in 1907 was also more nuanced; the country no longer automatically represented idealistic 'pacifist' positions.

---

[49] I Berlin *Russian Thinkers* (Penguin Books London 1994) at 11.

[50] 'Études sur le développement' (n 6) 493.

[51] Treaty of Perpetual Peace and Amity between Russia and Turkey (signed 10 (21) July 1774) (1774) 45 CTS 349 ('Kücük Kainarca').

[52] ibid 493.

[53] Declaration Renouncing the Use in Time of War of Explosive Projectiles under 400 Grammes Weight (signed 11 December 1868) (1869) 138 CTS 297 ('St Petersburg Declaration').

3.3   Russia's Role in International Law from the Early 18th Century until 1917: The Doctrine (Interpreted through the Lens of Yuri Lotman's Theory)

Fyodor Fyodorovich Martens put Russia on the world map of international law, also in terms of international law scholarship.[54] No other person represents the role and the impact of Tsarist Russia on international law since the 1870s to the early 20th century as completely as Martens, a scholar and a diplomat. It took quite a long time for Russia to make the leap from Shafirov to Martens. One fascinating aspect about Martens was that there was not too much in terms of international law scholarship in Russia between Shafirov's 1717 attempt and Martens who started to publish extensively in the 1870s. The Baltic German professors at the University of Doprat,[55] especially August Bulmerincq, hardly made any effort to speak internationally in the name of Russia and instead pursued the German cultural agenda in the Baltic provinces. In this sense at least, the Baltic German professors of the University of Dorpat did not really count as 'Russian' scholars.

What were the reasons why international law scholarship was not highly developed in Russia after Shafirov and before Martens? One could, however, reverse the question: why should it have been? How could it have been? If international law was a language born in Western Europe, in the periphery the idea was to acquire it, not to teach or preach it. After all, Russia's first university, the University of Moscow, was opened only in 1755. Important ideas needed time for gestation. By Martens' time, Russians felt that the country had passively learned and been stimulated enough, and it was time to reverse the flow of information. In any case, the reception of the work of Martens in the rest of the world—both 'civilized' and 'uncivilized' alike—was unparalleled to Russia's public intellectuals of the time and was only surpassed by the works of the great Russian novelists.

If the law of nations was a language and Shafirov had made an attempt, with an accent, to speak that language, then Martens mastered it superbly. When Shafirov was trying to make the point that Russia 'too' was civilized, Martens already spoke in the name of 'the' (European, Christian) civilization. A central idea of his theory of international law was that this law bound only civilized (European, Christian) nations while the 'non-civilized' (Asian and African) nations remained outside its regulation. While most other European theorists of international law in Martens' time pursued the same logic of civilized versus uncivilized, there was a particular intensity and ferocity in Martens' approach. In terms of pursuing the project of European

---

[54] See also the contribution by L Mälksoo 'Friedrich Fromhold von Martens (Fyodor Fyodorovich Martens) (1845–1909)' in this volume.

[55] See L Mälksoo 'The Science of International Law and the Concept of Politics: the Arguments and Lives of the International Law Professors at the University of Dorpat/Iur'ev/Tartu 1855–1985' (2005) 76 British Year Book of International Law 383–501.

civilization and imperialism, Russia speaking with the voice of Martens had become 'more Catholic than the Pope(s)'. The arch-imperialists of the time, the British, seemed already to bother less to make that point, at least in the context of treatises of international law. It was as if the one who was the more recently converted was also the most eager proselytizer.

Yet the paradox was that Martens' life became what it did exactly in pursuit of European analogy and civilization. The Dean of St Petersburg University's Faculty of Law, Ivanovskii, had made him study international law instead of criminal law which young Martens had initially preferred—'so that we would have our own Martens'.[56] Not just figuratively speaking, *nomen* was *omen*. Martens' project of publishing fifteen volumes of Russia's treaties with other European powers—Austria, Germany, England, and France—alluded to the early 19th-century Martens' collection of treaties in Germany. (Unfortunately Martens died in 1909 and could not finalize the enormous work.)

However, Martens' vehement point that Russia was European/civilized whereas Turkey, China, and Japan, for instance, were doomed to be uncivilized, may have also reflected insecurity about Russia's own true identity and suppressed normative ideals. Was that the historical role and fate of Russia, to excel at the reception of the ideas of others? Slavophiles and Russian nationalists had started to doubt that aping Western Europe was Russia's normative destiny. In this context, Dostoevsky even famously declared: 'In Europe we were hangers-on and slaves whereas in Asia we will go as masters.'[57] When projected onto Russia's own domestic context, the doctrine of Martens was ambivalent at best. Being a liberal, Martens defined the standard of civilization through the respect of individual rights by the respective State—an explosive and subversive thesis in the context of Tsarist Russia where even patriotic conservatives agreed that the state of individual rights in the empire left, to put it mildly, much to be desired. Yet—to pursue a classical Russian question—whose fault was that? At the moments of pessimism, critical liberals admitted that many Russians did not even seem to care about their rights. Thus, Chernyshevsky lamented in 1859: 'There is no European country in which the vast majority of the people is absolutely indifferent to the rights which are the object of desire and concern only to the liberals.'[58]

In his Russian textbook of international law, Martens has a passage where he suggests that Russia still has things to learn from other, 'more educated peoples'.[59] Although Martens had a mixed reputation in the West of having been expressed his country's *politique juridique extérieure*, his diaries reveal that he was in opposition

---

[56] Referring to the leading German positivist of the late 18th century, Georg Friedrich von Martens (1756–1821).

[57] *Empire* (n 4) 220.

[58] *Russian Thinkers* (n 49) 3.

[59] FF Martens *Sovremennoe mezhdunarodnoe pravo tsivilizovannykh narodov* (Contemporary International Law of Civilized Nations) (Yuridicheski kolledzh MGU Moscow 1996) vol 1, at 158.

to the Tsarist State (while continuing to serve it). The diaries also touch on the subject of Martens being a man from the (over-represented) imperial periphery. (Being born to ethnic Estonian parents and having spent his childhood in the Baltic province of Livonia, Martens could only be a 'political' Russian). In one particular passage in the diary, Martens complained that Tsarist Russia was no longer eager to promote non-ethnic Russians.[60] Indeed, after 1917, when most of the international lawyers of the Tsarist era were forced to emigrate, it turned out that many of them, especially the St Petersburg school, were representatives of Russianized German/Baltic families—Boris Nolde, Michael Taube, André Mandelstam, etc.[61]

The pragmatic side of Russia speaking the language of civilized versus uncivilized nations during the 18th and 19th centuries was that this was the period of the Russian Empire's extensive expansion towards the East and South. When Britain and France colonized overseas, Russia continued to expand as land empire in the Far East, Central Asia, and the Caucasus.[62] A theory of international law only belonging to civilized peoples was practical and handy; it paid off. Paradoxically, with all its talk about progress, civilization, and codification of the laws of war, the late 19th-century international law accepted conquest (as long as other imperial powers were willing to recognize it from the viewpoint of the logic of balance of power).

At this point, we should take a step back in our discussion of Russia's relationship with Europe in international law, particularly in terms of centre–periphery relations. One helpful reminder would be that international law has never been an isolated phenomenon. I would like to draw here parallels with ideas expressed in the work of Yuri Mikhailovich Lotman who focused mostly on the exchange of literary texts between the West and Russia.

Lotman argued that dialogues were usually asymmetrical.[63] In the dialogic exchange, one may distinguish the following scheme: the first participant (transferer) commands a considerable amount of accumulated experience (memory), and the second (receiver) is interested in acquiring this experience.[64] At the beginning, new alien texts stimulate and bring the receiver out from the sphere of inertia. Then the stage of passive saturation will follow. The language will be acquired, the texts adapted. Texts are transferred from the 'foreign' language (in the broader semiotic

---

[60] Archive of the Foreign Policy of the Russian Empire Moscow Fond no 340, opis no 787 entry of 13 March 1907 at 113.

[61] See GS Starodubtsev *Mezhdunarodno-pravovaya nauka Rossiiskoi emigratsii* (International Legal Scholarship of the Russian Emigration) (Kniga i biznes Moscow 2000); MA Taube '*Zarnitsy*'. *Vospominania o tragicheskoi sud'be predrevolyutsionnoi Rossii (1900–17)* (Lightnings. Memoirs on the Tragic Fate of Russia before Revolution 1900–17) (Rosspen Moscow 2007).

[62] In the 19th century, Count Constantine von der Pahlen justified Russia's conquest of Central Asia exactly in terms of the superiority of European civilization. See *Empire* (n 4) 219.

[63] YM Lotman *Universe of the Mind: A Semiotic Theory of Culture* (Introduction by U Eco) (IB Tauris & Co Ltd London 1990) at 268.

[64] YM Lotman *Istoria i tipologia russkoi kul'tury* (History and Typology of the Russian Culture) (Iskusstvo St Petersburg 2002) at 47.

meaning of the word 'language') into 'one's own'. At the same time, they will make transformations based on the laws of the receiving culture. The memory of the receiver also saves texts in 'alien', not understandable language.

The next stage is already the command of the foreign language and easy use of it; production of new texts based on its rules. However, after that phase comes the really crucial moment—the foreign tradition will be transformed on the basis of 'indigenous' semiotic substance of the receiver. The alien becomes 'own', transforming and often changing the ways of the indigenous. At that moment, roles may be reversed: the receiver becomes the giver, and the first participant may, in reverse, become the receiver.[65] The response may also be directed to another receiving subject, not the initial stimulator.

Lotman also maintained that the dialogue of cultures was characterized by sharp struggle for mental independence. Once again, dialogic partnership is usually asymmetrical. At the beginning, the dominant party, claiming central position, attributes to the receiver the position of periphery. The receivers themselves understand their position in a similar way (at the same time referring to their youth, the role of beginners, etc.).[66] However, getting closer to the culminating moment, the 'new' culture starts to affirm its 'old age' and claim the central position in the cultural world.

Lotman writes about the 'rebellion of the periphery against the centre' of the semiosphere.[67] The moment when the receiver of texts suddenly changes direction and becomes an active translator, goes together with the rise of national self-consciousness and the rise of hostility towards the formerly dominant power.[68] Explosion may be interpreted as the moment of the collision (clash) of two languages alien to each other: assimilating and assimilated.[69] When ideas spread from the centre to the periphery, there was sometimes only an appearance of unification. If in the centre meta-structure steps up as 'one's own' language then in the periphery it appears to be an 'alien' language, not capable of adequately reflecting the real semiotic practice of the place. It is as a grammar of a foreign language. At the periphery, the relationships between semiotic practice and norms are conflictuous.[70]

To follow Lotman's model, one can argue that Peter the Great (with his spokesperson Shafirov) introduced European international law to Russia as initially alien language, and Russia of the time of Fyodor Fyodorovich Martens had learned to speak it flawlessly, perhaps even more flawlessly than anyone spoke it at that time in the historic centre. Later on, in the context of the Stalinist campaign against Western influences, the Soviet international law scholar Vsevolod Nikolaevich Durdenevskyi wrote in 1949 about the late 19th-century Russian contributions to international law: 'Roles, in that way, changed: when earlier we translated Klüber and Heffter, then now Bergbohm translates Martens, young Bustamante studies Martens, experienced Liszt

---

[65] ibid 48.   [66] ibid 49.   [67] ibid 51.
[68] ibid 52.   [69] ibid 118.   [70] *Universe of the Mind* (n 63) 259.

learns from Hrabar. Russian scholarship becomes very visible. It reached the level of and became superior to the Western scholarship.[71]

Yet in Martens' time, the language of international law that Russia spoke remained the same language that had been established elsewhere. This does not diminish Tsarist Russia's contributions to the development of the laws of war in the late 19th century. Nevertheless, Russia's original 'answer' and 'explosion'—former periphery's response to the former centre in the language of international law—came only after Martens, with Russia's communist revolution of 1917. Now new Soviet Russia no longer 'contributed to' but fundamentally changed international law.

3.4. The Impact of Russia's October 1917 Revolution on International Law

Russia's Bolshevik Revolution of October 1917 had a considerable impact on the development of international law. Following Lotman's scheme, we can call it the rebellion of a former periphery against the centre. The message that revolutionary Russia sent out was at least as much directed to the rest of the world (the former 'uncivilized') as to the European centre (the '*über*-civilized').

One aspect of Russia's Bolshevik revolution was that the revolutionaries denied the universality of international law. Anyway, they argued, European-dominated international law had not been universal to start with—since the nations had been divided into categories of 'civilized' and 'uncivilized'. Now, however, was the first time that someone detached itself from the centre and turned its back on the West. Soviet Russia suggested creating its own type of 'Soviet international law' with Soviet Russia as its new centre. One of the first original Soviet theoreticians of international law, Evgeny Alexandrovich Korovin, in the 1920s explicitly rejected the idea of the universality of international law.[72] This was not yet the ultimate end of *ius publicum europaeum* but in 1917, Russia cut herself out of it, possibly for the next one hundred years.

Contemporary Western scholarship has rediscovered its interest in the Soviet theory and practice of international law.[73] Occasionally neo-Marxist in its normative

---

[71] VN Durdenevskii 'Vklad russkoi nauki v mezhdunarodnoe pravo, Vestnik Moskovskogo Gosudarstvennogo Universiteta. (Contribution of the Russian Scholarship to International Law; quoted in Starodubtsev's History of International Law and Its Scholarship) 1949 at 79 in *Istoria mezhdunarodnogo prava* (n 4) 117.

[72] EA Korovin *Das Völkerrecht der Übergangszeit. Grundlagen der völkerrechtlichen Beziehungen der Union der Sowjetrepubliken* (Stilke Berlin 1929) at vii, 7–8, and 13. The Russian original was published in 1923.

[73] See eg B Bowring *The Degradation of the International Legal Order? The Rehabilitation of Law and the Possibility of Politics* (Routledge New York 2008); J Quigley *Soviet Legal Innovation and the Law of the Western World* (CUP Cambridge 2007); C Miéville *Between Equal Rights. A Marxist Theory of International Law* (Brill Leiden 2005); M Head *Evgeny Pashukanis. A Critical Reappraisal* (Routledge London 2007).

foundations, this literature emphasizes the positive and revolutionary challenges and amendments that Soviet Russia made to international law. This new scholarship is in stark contrast to the Soviet-era legal sub-discipline of *Ostrecht* which was, quite suitably to the atmosphere of the Cold War, hostile towards Soviet approaches to international law.

In a way, Russia after 1917 was the first wave of decolonization: Russia strongly detached herself from Western European liberal bourgeois concepts of law and good society. The inhuman in the old normative system was rejected as alien. It was quite symptomatic that the person and ideas of Fyodor Fyodorovich Martens were largely forgotten, even taboo, during the Soviet period in Russia.[74] He had become alien for new Russia. Of course, the ideas that Lenin and his co-revolutionaries had borrowed from Marx and Engels were initially also 'European'. Yet as the Russian philosopher Nicholas Berdyaev pointed out, the religious zeal and energy with which the Bolsheviks carried out the Marxist programme was also an expression of historic Russian Messianism; even the way the Bolsheviks fought the Christianity had something heretically religious about it.[75]

It was as if Russia had for two centuries enjoyed the membership in the club of the 'civilized', suffered stoically occasional patronizations and humiliations as still not enough 'civilized'/European, and finally came to the conclusion that 'your civilization/international law was *wrong*'. Perhaps it took someone who was half in, half out (a periphery rather than centre) and who had used the argument of the superiority of the 'European' civilization mainly as a tactical compromise, to challenge the power structure of the old normative order.

After 1917, the Bolsheviks rejected bourgeois law, including bourgeois international law. Concrete examples of the 'Soviet legal innovations' as John Quigley calls them, include the following.

First was the emphasis of the right of peoples to self-determination and the rejection of forcible annexations. With the Decree on Peace of 25 October 1917, the Bolshevik government declared its ideal of democratic world without annexations. The Soviet government called for a 'just and democratic peace', a peace 'without annexations', by which it meant 'without the seizure of the lands of others, without the forcible incorporation of other nationalities'. The Soviet government opposed 'any incorporation to a large and powerful State of a small or weak nationality without a precise, clear, and voluntary expression of consent' by that nationality, 'regardless of whether the nationality lives in Europe or in distant overseas countries'.[76] Moreover,

---

[74] VV Pustogarov *Our Martens. F.F. Martens, International Lawyer and Achitect of Peace* (Introduction by WE Butler) (Kluwer The Hague 2000) at 3–4.

[75] NA Berdyaev *Istoki i smysl russkogo kommunizma* (Sources and Meaning of the Russian Communism) (YMCA-Press Paris 1955).

[76] Quoted in J Quigley *Soviet Legal Innovation and the Law of the Western World* (CUP Cambridge 2007) at 137.

the suggestion in Decree on Peace that peace could be concluded by individual military units on the front and not necessarily by the governments, demonstrated the revolutionary anarchical thinking of the Bolsheviks.

In the Declaration of the Rights of the Peoples of Russia (15 November 1917), the Soviet government decreed that all the nationalities had the right to decide their own political orientation.[77]

Another revolutionary aspect was the renouncement of the previous regime of capitulations. Namely, the colonial powers had enjoyed a number of important extra-territorial rights in non-Western countries. (In his time, Martens had written a major work about this system, strongly justifying it.)[78] Tsarist Russia had enjoyed territorial rights in Persia, China, Turkey, and Afghanistan. However, in 1919, the Soviet government issued a unilateral declaration, renouncing these rights and denounced the capitulatory system.[79] The Soviet government continued to denounce capitulations as a violation of the rights of those countries where the major powers maintained such regimes. In treaties concluded in 1921 with Turkey[80] and Persia,[81] Soviet Russia denounced capitulations regimes. Other nations followed suit. With regard to China, Russia ended the capitulations regime in 1924, other European nations in 1928, Britain and the US in 1943.[82]

The Soviet government denounced both unequal treaties and secret pacts between imperialist Powers. The treaty collection published by Martens since 1874 was filled with examples of secret stipulations ('*stipulation secrète*' and even '*très-secrète*') that Russia had concluded with other European powers. The phenomenon of secret pacts continued to be a European practice during the First World War. For example, France and Britain had, in the secret 1916 Sykes–Picot Treaty,[83] agreed on spheres of influence in the former Ottoman empire. After they had come to power in Russia, the Bolsheviks published more than one hundred such treaties they had found in Tsarist archives.[84] Public opinion was deeply shocked by the revelation of secret dealings at odds with the positions the same States adopted in public.[85] Thus, article 18 of the Covenant of the League of Nations was the direct result of the Soviet publication of

---

[77] ibid 47–8.

[78] FF Martens *O konsulakh i konsul'skoi jurisdktsii na Vostoke* (On Consuls and Consular Jurisdiction in the East) (St Petersburg 1873); FF Martens *Das Consularwesen und die Consularjurisdiction im Orient* (H. Skerst Berlin 1874).

[79] *Soviet Legal Innovation* (n 76) 52.

[80] Treaty of Friendship between Turkey, the Socialist Soviet Republic of Armenia, the Azerbaijan Socialist Soviet Republic, and the Socialist Soviet Republic of Georgia, with participation of Russia (concluded 13 October 1921, entered into force 11 September 1922) 120 BFSP 906 ('Treaty of Kars').

[81] Treaty of Friendship between Persia and the Russian Socialist Federal Soviet Republic (signed 26 February 1921) (1922) 9 LNTS 383.

[82] *Soviet Legal Innovation* (n 76) 136.

[83] Sykes-Picot Agreement (concluded 16 May 1916) 221 CTS 323.

[84] *Soviet Legal Innovation* (n 76) 49.

[85] ibid 133.

the secret First World War treaties, and Soviet jurists justifiably claimed credit for the Soviet role in that.[86] In August 1918, the Soviet government terminated 'unjust trea-ties' regarding the partition of Poland, and recognized Poland's right to statehood.[87]

Thus, Soviet Russia was perhaps the main power that made possible the demise of the international law of the era of European colonialism. It showed successfully and convincingly what was wrong with the 'old' international law. Moreover, the Soviet pressure changed the West and made its policies more social—for instance, the crea-tion of International Labour Organization after the First World War can be traced back to the fear of Soviet influence. Later on, the USSR had a decisive impact on the way the UN's human rights pacts were worked out in 1966, especially the fact that social and economic rights were included in the whole package.

Yet the recent Western literature that enthusiastically praised the Soviet influence on and progressive contributions to international law tends to downplay the more negative aspects. One of them was that the Bolshevik revolutionaries were actually not 'people of law'—they were, at least in their own minds, 'people of justice'. In other words, they saw law as a tactical tool not a strategic goal. They intended to remake the world based on their ideas of justice, not some sort of a 'new rule of law'. One aspect of this thinking was that while the Soviets criticized colonialism in the West, they failed to see it in Russia's own backyard. This led to hypocrisies in Soviet foreign policy. Especially in the territory of the former Tsarist Russian Empire, the Soviet government undertook forcible annex-ations (Georgia 1921), supported military *coups d'état* (Estonia 1924), concluded secret pacts leading to annexations (the secret protocols of the Hitler Stalin Pact of 1939),[88] and violated treaties like the 1933 Convention for the Definition of Aggression that it had herself solemnly initiated.

The other aspect that the neo-Marxist literature praising Soviet achievements in international law fails to sufficiently take into account are the mass crimes that the Soviets committed against the Russian people and the other peoples of the former Tsarist empire. One can perhaps admire certain aspects of the Leninist theory in an abstract way but one should not do so by diminishing the unprecedented human cost of the communist experiment in Russia and the neighbouring countries.

Thus, the conclusion regarding the impact of the Soviet revolution in interna-tional law is mixed. The Bolsheviks had a number of valuable substantive points that changed international law but they advanced them from an anti-legal and anti-indi-vidualist revolutionary platform. On paper at least, the Soviet project made the inter-national law of the 20th century more human (in the sense of 'social'). John Quigley is essentially correct when he emphasizes that it was Soviet Russia that for the first

---

[86] ibid 134.

[87] *Kratkii kurs istorii mezhdunarodnogo prava* (n 7) 35.

[88] Treaty of Non-Aggression Between Germany and the Union of Soviet Socialist Republics (signed and entered into force 23 August 1939) in JAS Grenville *The Major International Treaties 1914–1973* (Methuen London 1974) 195–96 ('Molotov–Ribbentrop Pact').

time in the modern history forced the individualist West to an ideological compromise, thus changing, among other things, the orientation of international law of the 20th century. Yet even Russia herself finally turned away from that project in 1991. Thus, the conservative Baltic German law professor and expatriate from the Tsarist empire, Axel Baron Freytagh-Loringhoven may have been prophetically right when he wrote in 1919: 'The civilized world will have to be thankful to Russia that it has demonstrated at the cost of unimaginably high number of victims that socialist ideas cannot be realized in practice.'[89]

4. Conclusion

Russia's historical relationship with Europe (and the West) in the framework of international law can be characterized as the relationship of the periphery and the centre. Initially, from the early 18th century onwards, Russia was a European periphery that had successfully attached itself to the Western European centre. Russia benefited enormously from belonging to the 'civilized' European peoples. This enabled Russia to continue its territorial expansion in Central Asia, Far East, and Caucasus; to the extent that the Russian Empire became the world's largest State. During the late 18th and 19th centuries, Russia contributed significantly to international law. The Hague Peace conference of 1899 was convened at Tsarist Russia's initiative and Russia's international law spokespersons, especially Martens, became leading voices in expanding international law. Yet Russia's attitude towards international law as it had been developed in Europe could only be ambivalent—the Tsarist rulers were willing to accept the external aspects of international law but they were not prepared or successful in going along with the reverse side of the coin—giving rights to its own population. They loved State sovereignty but neglected the rights of their 'subjects'. Certain idiosyncratic cultural and historical elements were suppressed in the name of the country's (especially elite's) 'Europeanness'.

Thus, what happened in 1917 was a rebellion of the periphery against the centre. The Russian Bolsheviks criticized the colonial international law as corrupt and unjust. In a way, it was the Bolsheviks who delivered the lethal blow to the old international law of 'civilized nations'. In doing so, they inspired with their revolutionary energy the upcoming elites outside Europe, in the world colonized by the Europeans. The circle of the main subjects of international law—States—expanded when the principle of self-determination started to do its historical work. Since the USSR took

---

[89] AF von Freytagh Loringhoven *Russland* (Max Niemeyer Halle 1919) at 34.

up the legacy of the Tsarist empire too easily and never properly admitted that Russia too had been a colonial power, the Bolshevik leaders hoped that their anti-colonialist project would territorially affect primarily Western European empires. Nevertheless, Russia had to eventually apply the same anti-colonialist principles in its own territory which finally led to the collapse of the USSR in 1991. In that way, the centre and the periphery had mutually changed positions and influenced each other like major pieces in a historical kaleidoscope.

RECOMMENDED READING

Bergbohm, Carl *Die bewaffnete Neutralität 1780–83. Eine Entwicklungsphase des Völkerrechts im Seekriege* (C Mattiesen Dorpat 1883).

Butler, William E *Russia and the Law of Nations in Historical Perspective. Collected Essays* (Wildy, Simmonds & Hill Publishing London 2009).

Grabar, Vladimir *The History of International Law in Russia, 1647–1917: a bio-bibliographical study* (William E Butler ed and trans) (OUP Oxford 1990).

Grzybowsky, Kazimierz *Soviet Public International Law: Doctrines and Diplomatic Practice* (Sjithoff Leiden 1970).

Lieven, Dominic (ed) *The Cambridge History of Russia. Volume II: Imperial Russia 1689–1917* (CUP Cambridge 2006).

Mälksoo, Lauri 'The Science of International Law and the Concept of Politics. The Arguments and Lives of the International Law Professors at the University of Dorpat/Iur'ev/Tartu 1855–1985' (2005) 76 British Year Book of International Law 383–501.

Mälksoo, Lauri 'The History of International Legal Theory in Russia: a Civilizational Dialogue with Europe' (2008) 19 European Journal of International Law 211–32.

Martens, Fyodor (ed) *Recueil des Traités et Conventions conclus par la Russie avec les puissances étrangères* (Imprimerie du Ministère des Voies de Communication St Pétersbourg 1874–1909) vols 1–15.

Quigley, John *Soviet Legal Innovation and the Law of the Western World* (CUP Cambridge 2007).

Taracouzio, Timothy A *The Soviet Union and International Law. A Study based on the Legislation, Treaties and Foreign Relations of the Union of Socialist Soviet Republics* (Macmillan New York 1935).

Taube, Michel de 'Études sur le développement historique du droit international dans l'Europe orientale' (1926) 11(1) Recueil des cours 341–535.

Taube, Michel de 'L'apport du Byzance au développement du droit international occidental' (1939) 67 Recueil des cours 233–339.

Triska, Jan F and Robert M Slusser *The Theory, Law, and Policy of Soviet Treaties* (Stanford University Press Stanford 1962).

CHAPTER 33

NORTH AMERICAN INDIGENOUS PEOPLES' ENCOUNTERS

KEN COATES

1. INTRODUCTION

THE law is fundamental to the meeting of Indigenous and European peoples through-out North America. This has been the case from the earliest encounters along the East Coast of the continent, to the present time. The colonial processes in North America involved European powers claiming Indigenous territories as their own. But what was long perceived as a one-sided arrangement dominated by Europeans has come to be understood as a much more complicated interaction involving Indigenous concepts of law and land ownership, military and commercial alliances, formal and informal treaties, European attempts to define Indigenous legal rights, and Aboriginal protests relating to personal and collective legal status. The contours of the European–Indigenous encounter in North America, from the outset, have been shaped by legal assumptions, agreements, contests, and negotiations.[1]

---

[1] The best survey of this subject is J Analya *Indigenous Peoples in International Law* (OUP New York 1996); see also R Williams *The American Indian in Western Legal Thought: The Discourse of Conquest* (OUP New York 1990) and A Anghie *Imperialism, Sovereignty, and the Making of International Law*

There are few fields of international law that are as dynamic, in terms of historical inquiry and the application of historical analysis in the court room, as the study of Indigenous–European legal encounter. Scholars have, from the time of the first European forays into the uncharted waters across the Atlantic, puzzled over the nature of the legal obligations of the colonial powers, the legal status of Indigenous peoples, and the appropriate legal framework for managing relations between Indigenous peoples, the colonizers, and the European fragment colonies in the New World.[2] Throughout this long and complex history, the study of the legal aspects of Indigenous peoples of North America in encounter with Europe has been influenced by international and global considerations of core concepts, values, and legal relationships.[3]

Beginning in the mid-19th century, when European powers and their colonial offshoots sought to understand the political and social demise of Indigenous peoples in most parts of North America, the analysis of international Indigenous law followed a fairly simple pattern. Scholars lauded European law as being inherently superior to any informal constructs that might have shaped Aboriginal societies. In this initial formulation, the incorporation of the Indigenous peoples of North America into the European legal and political system was viewed as an inevitable and positive outcome of colonization, and a crucial step in the civilization of the backward and pagan inhabitants of the New World.

Analysts began in the 20th century to offer a contrary view of the role of the law in the history of Indigenous–newcomer encounter. Historians and legal historians adopted the view held strongly by many Christian missionaries that the colonial powers had abused their powers, not dealt fairly with Indigenous rights and aspirations, used the law as an instrument of State domination. Historians examining aspects of Indigenous-newcomer encounter documented how European and colonial powers ignored their national laws and values and used legal processes to strip Indigenous peoples of their rightful authority. In this formulation, colonial and international law was an instrument of domination.[4]

(CUP Cambridge 2005); for a broader historical context of the evolution of Indigenous experiences, see K Coates *A Global History of Indigenous Peoples: Struggle and Survival* (Palgrave Macmillan London 2004); G Bennett *Aboriginal Rights in International Law* (Royal Anthropological Institute London 1978).

[2] For a contrarian view of the initial encounter, see C Sale *The Conquest of Paradise: Christopher Columbus and the Columbian Legacy* (Plume London 1991).

[3] C Tennant 'Indigenous Peoples, International Institutions, and the International Legal Literature from 1945–1993' (1994) 16 Human Rights Quarterly 1–55.

[4] There is a very large literature on Indigenous–newcomer relations in North America. For a general overview of contact situations, examine FP Prucha *The Great Father: The United States Government and the American Indians* (2 vols University of Nebraska Press Lincoln 1984 and 1986); and J Miller *Skyscrapers Hide the Heavens: A History of Indian-White Relations in Canada* (University of Toronto Press Toronto 2000); see also R Nichols *Indians in the United States & Canada, A Comparative History* (University of Nebraska Press Lincoln 1998); on the broad global literature on Indigenous peoples, see S Totten and R Hitchcock *Genocide of Indigenous People: A Critical Biographical Review* (Transaction Publishers New Brunswick NJ 2011).

The evolution of historical and legal historical scholarship in the 1960s saw marked changes in the understanding of the role of international law in Indigenous affairs in North America. Researchers demonstrated that Indigenous leaders demanded a great deal, negotiated well, understood the political and conceptual role of alliances and treaties, and sought to develop lasting legal relationships with the colonial powers and the new North American nation-states. The new scholarship highlighted the influence that Indigenous peoples exerted over settler societies and documented how, in many instances, they were partners with European powers and interests in trade, war, and political settlements. The new literature emphasized Aboriginal agency and engagement with the intricacies of cross-cultural and international relations in North America.[5]

As North American Indigenous peoples fight for rights and land claims, historians and legal historians are engaged directly in contemporary struggles and debates. This, in turn, has politicized the scholarly writing on the topic, particularly as a new group of academics drawing more directly on Aboriginal oral and cultural traditions entered the field.[6] The rich and diverse academic work on the history of international law relating to Indigenous rights and encounter in Europe has had a marked effect on the understanding of the global significance of legal history and the intersections between history, law, and politics in the contemporary world.[7]

2. INDIGENOUS PEOPLES IN CONTACT WITH EUROPE

The complexity of the Indigenous–European counter is rarely appreciated in full. From the time of initial contact—dated to 1000 AD and the arrival of the Vikings in the Northeast—various European powers came in contact with the Aboriginal

[5] The key scholarship was tied to the study of the fur trade and other early encounters, see R White *The Middle Ground: Indians, Empires, and Republics in the Great Lakes Region, 1650–1815* (CUP Cambridge, 1991); B Trigger *Natives and Newcomers: Canada's 'Heroic Age' Reconsidered* (McGill-Queen's Montreal 1986); AJ Ray *Indians in the Fur Trade: Their Role as Trappers, Hunters, and Middlemen in the Lands Southwest of Hudson Bay, 1660–1870* (University of Toronto Press Toronto 1998); and R Fisher *Contact and Conflict: Indian-European Relations in British Columbia* (University of British Columbia Press Vancouver 1992).

[6] K Coates 'Writing First Nations into Canadian History: A Review of Recent Scholarly Works' (2000) 81 Canadian Historical Review 99–115.

[7] For a very good introduction to the historical and historiographical issues in the history of Native-newcomer relations in North America, see B Trigger and W Washburn (eds) *The Cambridge History of the Native Peoples of the Americas* (2 vols CUP Cambridge 1997).

peoples on the continent. The relationships with the Spanish, French, and English are generally well appreciated. Much less is generally known about the encounters involving other colonizing powers, including the Dutch in the north-east and the Russians along the Pacific Coast. The diversity of the European–Indigenous encounter was more than matched on the other side of the frontier. There were (and are) dozens of linguistic groups across the continent and hundreds of specific and localized cultures. These societies ranged from the semi-sedentary in the north-east and around the Great Lakes to the highly mobile peoples of the Arctic and sub-Arctic. The plains peoples built their seasonal round around the movements of the buffalo; West Coast societies relied on annual salmon cycles. Some of the cultures lived most of the year in extended family groups, while, in others, communities of many hundreds of people were common. European observers, and the international legal fraternity, tended to lump all Indigenous peoples into a single culture group, even though they appreciated that there were major differences. The nature of the contact experience varied dramatically as well. In some instances, early contacts were destructive for the Aboriginal people, marked by bitter and often violent conflicts, land dispossessions, the spread of imported diseases, and eventually European domination. As European conflicts spread to North America, strong and long-term alliances between individual European powers and First Nations groups produced strong political and military collaborations. Other newcomer–Aboriginal relationships, particularly in British North America, proceeded more collaboratively, typically around mutually beneficial trading relationships. In remote regions—the High Arctic, across the vast sub-Arctic, and in the desert and near-desert regions of the West—isolation and a lack of competition for land limited engagement. No single pattern of engagement characterized the European–Indigenous encounter and no single model of intergovernmental, legal, or alliance arrangements emerged across the continent.

3. Indigenous Views of the Aboriginal-European Encounter

Aboriginal groups in North America, having inhabited the continent for more than 7000 years in most areas, had well-developed social, cultural, and economic systems. Far from being the savages and primitive peoples often described, Indigenous cultures had sophisticated worldviews, stable political and governance systems, and complex alliances with neighbouring groups. Europeans did not immediately see the richness of the internal structures and found little that compared directly to the emerging European State systems.

First Nations and newcomers came to rely on each other extensively, forcing both sides to find political means of organizing their relationships. The language and formality of the alliances, made with much ceremony, gift giving, and assurances of lasting support, established the practice of nation-to-nation relationships. Chiefs and councils were accorded respect and high status by the colonial officials, who relied heavily on the Aboriginal soldiers and the logistical support they provided. The Aboriginal leadership had limited knowledge of the national system that lay behind the colonial apparatus. What they did know was that their allies needed their support and relied heavily upon their contributions.[8]

Positive relations at this early stage reinforced Aboriginal assumptions about their partnerships with Europeans and about the strength and status of their formal arrangements. These were codified into treaties of alliance or surrender and in long-functioning trading partnerships that carried considerable authority on both sides of the frontier. The formality of treaty negotiations, annual payments, and rituals of alliance celebrated the relationships and reinforced the power of Aboriginal leaders. More than anything, the military and trading alliances that dominated in the eastern and north-eastern part of the continent established the reality of nation to nation negotiations and gave Aboriginal people the clear expectation that they had a permanent role in the emerging societies of North America. The law and rhetoric of Aboriginal sovereignty survived in the United States, where notions of tribal control of reserve lands stayed strong and received legal sanction in the 19th century, but found less of a toe-hold in then British North America.[9]

The centrality of nation-to-nation arrangements and the apparent (to First Nations) formal equality of Aboriginal peoples and newcomers did not survive the 19th century. With the resolution of European conflicts in North America with the end of the War of 1812 in the north-east and the settlement of Russian and Spanish territorial aspirations in the Far West and South subsequently stripped the Aboriginal–newcomer relationships of their urgency. The government of Britain and the colonial authorities worried less about US-American invasion. The United States turned its attention from American–European relations to the internal dynamics of the rapidly moving settlement frontier. The assertive US-American State expanded its control westward, largely through military intervention and one-sided treaty arrangements with displaced Aboriginal groups. Chiefs participated in treaty negotiations and were represented at regular treaty-related events, but the threat of

[8] C Calloway *New Worlds for All: Indians, Europeans, and the Remaking of Early America* (WW Norton New York 1998); F Jennings *The Founders of America: How Indians Discovered the Land, Pioneered in it, and Created Great Classical Civilizations, How They were Plunged into a Dark Age by Invasion and Conquest, and How They Are Reviving* (Norton New York 1994).

[9] F Jennings *The Invasion of America: Indians, Colonialism, and the Cant of Conquest* (WW Norton New York 1981); J Axtell *The Invasion Within: The Contest of Cultures in Colonial North America* (OUP New York 1986); and J Axtell *Natives and Newcomers: The Cultural Origins of North America* (OUP New York 2000).

military power made it clear that an imbalance of authority had replaced the partnerships of old.[10]

First Nations passed from military and political allies to wards of the State in less
than two generations. Government and colonial officials who had counted on Aboriginal warriors to fight their Eurocentric battles now struggled to find an enduring
place for First Nations within the new North America. Many assumed that the Aboriginal peoples were doomed, a perception reinforced by the rapid decline in
population related to imported diseases. Survivors found themselves on government-
controlled reserves and reservations, save for those remote regions where the har-
vesting lifestyles remained viable. Government paternalism replaced affirmation of
alliance and equality; cultures of poverty and colonial administration took hold.
Aboriginal peoples and leaders surrendered neither their dignity nor their belief in
their political, if not military, equality.[11] From the perspective of the dominant Euro-
pean-fragment societies, however, the legal, moral, and political right rested with the
colonial and national governments.

4. KEY ELEMENTS IN INTERNATIONAL LAW PERTAINING TO INDIGENOUS PEOPLES

European States and neo-European societies in North America did not awaken to the
reality of Aboriginal legal rights in the mid to late 19th century. The conquest and
occupation of North America was part of a global expansion of Europe. The expansion, too, was wrapped in a veil of legality and legal debate, for the challenge of taking
over, by means peaceful or violent, lands occupied by non-European peoples carried
with it a variety of legal and moral challenges. The questions were fundamental: were
the strange societies encountered in distant lands 'people' or 'civilized' by European
standards? Did the standard laws of State authority and private property hold for
Indigenous peoples who lived without agriculture or husbandry and whose authorities lacked formal written codes, structured legal systems, and formal land records?

Early writers, particularly Bartolomé de las Casas and Francisco de Vitoria,[12]
argued passionately that Indigenous peoples merited equitable treatment before the

---

[10] H Berman 'The Concept of Aboriginal Rights in the Early Legal History of the United States'
(1977–78) 27 Buffalo Law Review 637–67.

[11] FP Prucha *American Indian Treaties: The History of a Political Anomaly* (University of California
Press Los Angeles 1997); *The Great Father* (n 4).

[12] On the life and work of Francisco de Vitoria, see the contribution by A Brett 'Francisco de Vitoria
(1480–1546) and Francisco Suárez (1548–1617)' in this volume.

law. De las Casas excoriated European governments for their brutal treatment of Aboriginal populations and for the imposition of colonial authority over functioning societies.[13] Vitoria, like de las Casa, asserted the humanity of Indigenous peoples and argued that they warranted equitable treatment with Europeans.[14] The work of these legal scholars, coming at the formative stages of the development of international law as a field of professional inquiry, provided an important foundation for further scholarship on the meaning of international encounter.[15] Hugo Grotius, one of the key figures in the development of international law, drew significantly on the writings of de las Casas and Vitoria.[16]

Generations later, legal scholars would resurrect the writings of Vitoria and others to demonstrate that intellectual support for Indigenous rights lay deep in Europe's past. At the time, however, governments had other priorities. The key European colonies in the Western hemisphere, particularly Mexico, Peru, and Brazil, produced dazzling quantities of precious metals and gems. The wealth elevated Spain and Portugal to world-leading stature and convinced other States that the newly discovered lands might likewise produce the vast wealth needed to enrich the monarchical powers of Europe. God and Christianity featured prominently in the early conversations about Indigenous peoples' legal and moral rights, with supporters, like de las Casas and Vitoria, claiming that the natural order ordained by God took precedence over more worldly and political considerations. Injunctions against European domination over Indigenous peoples, however, found little favour among imperial States who viewed their expansion into the New Worlds to be ordained by their Christian heritage.[17]

The Christian church's characterization of the Indigenous peoples as primitive pagans justified ignoring any claims to equality of treatment. The 'unproductive' use of territory, by which Europeans meant the failure to develop agriculture and animal husbandry, made it obvious to the colonial powers that the land was available for the taking. The twin doctrines of 'right of discovery' and '*terra nullius*' paved the way for the rapid occupation of Indigenous lands. The 'right of discovery' concept held that the first European power to identify and make claim to newly

---

[13] B de las Casas *History of the Indies* (AM Collard ed and trans) (Harper Row New York 1971); PS Vickery *Bartolomé de las Casas: Great Prophet of the Americas* (Paulist Press New York 2006).

[14] AT Serra (ed) *The Principles of Political and International Law in the Work of Francisco de Vitoria* (Ediciones Cultura Hispánica Madrid 1946). F de Vitoria *De indis et de jure belli relectiones* (1696) in JB Scott (ed) *The Classics of International Law* (The Carnegie Institution of Washington Washington 1917).

[15] For a very insightful commentary on Vitoria, see also *Imperialism, Sovereignty, and the Making of International Law* (n 1) ch 1.

[16] See, specifically, JB Scott *The Spanish Origin of International Law* (Clarendon Press Oxford 1934); G Marks 'Indigenous Peoples in International Law: The Significance of Francisco de Vitoria and Bartolomé de las Casas' (1992) 13 Australian Year Book of International Law 1–51.

[17] These ideas are explored in detail in R Williams *The American Indian in Western Legal Thought: The Discourse of Conquest* (OUP New York 1990) and LC Green and O Dickason *The Law of Nations and the New World* (University of Alberta Press Edmonton 1989).

found lands earned the right to own and develop the area. This, understandably, urged European nations to redouble efforts at exploration and discovery. *Terra nullius* described the widely held belief—reinforced by courts and governments–that Aboriginal land was not occupied and was, therefore, open to claim by right of discovery.[18]

Legal commentators, including individuals such as Grotius[19] and Domingo de Soto,[20] argued in the 16th and 17th centuries, that Christianity, military might and self-interest did not justify the occupation of Aboriginal lands. Procedures appropriate to the humanity of Indigenous peoples, including treaties or conquest through a war, had to be followed. The mere assertion of sovereignty and domination over Aboriginal populations was, to these writers, inappropriate. At this crucial early stage in the European settlement of North America, therefore, European powers wrestled, often minimally, with moral, ethical, and legal questions about their authority. Justifications for conquest—including an open-ended category of 'just war'—were readily at hand if conflict with an Indigenous group arose or if an Aboriginal population resisted the arrival of newcomers.

The emergence of the modern State in the post-Treaty of Westphalia era (1648), created a new intellectual environment for reviewing and evaluating Indigenous rights. The emerging 'law of nations' doctrines advanced by Emmerich de Vattel[21] and others focused on the legal divide between individuals and the nation. Indigenous peoples, as a sub-national communitarian group, did not fit easily into a model of governance and legal principles that soon defined the western legal tradition. Aboriginal peoples, in this construction, might have rights as individuals, depending on their capacity for equality before the law, but not as corporate entities and not, as Indigenous leaders would have it, as nations in their own right. That North American Indigenous peoples lacked the agricultural, urban, and industrial capabilities of even the Central American Aboriginal populations made it impossible for most thinkers to categorize them as 'States' in the legal sense of the world.[22]

---

[18] Several of the best studies on this concept, based on Australian examples, are by Henry Reynolds, and include *Frontier: Aborigines, Settlers and Land* (Allen and Unwin Sydney 1987); *Dispossession: Black Australia and White Invaders* (Allen and Unwin Sydney 1996); and *The Law of the Land* (Penguin Sydney 2003).

[19] H Grotius *De jure belli ac pacis libri tres* in JB Scott (ed) *The Classics of International Law* (2 vols Clarendon Press Oxford 1913–25).

[20] D de Soto *De iustitia et iure* (Salamanca 1556).

[21] E de Vattel *Le droit des gens ou Principes de la loi naturelle: appliqués à la conduite et aux affaires des nations et des souverains* (Carnegie Institution of Washington Washington 1916 reprint of the 1758 edn).

[22] L Gross 'The Peace of Westphalia, 1648–1948' (1948) 42 The American Journal of International Law 20–41.

5. Sovereign Partners

Political and military necessities created different relationships with Indigenous peoples and European governments. Beginning in the late 18th century, primarily through a series of treaties and a vital British proclamation, the colonial authorities created a series of legal standards that would later become the cornerstone of Indigenous rights. Treaties began along the early Eastern settlement frontier, primarily to settle violent conflicts and to respond to Indigenous participation in European conflicts in North America. The treaties provided many assurances of land, peaceful co-existence, and government support. Many of the treaties provided brief and unclear guarantees of support and protection. For most of the First Nations involved, these treaties created a direct and powerful connection with the British monarch or with the government and people of the US.[23] Most of the early treaties were quickly abrogated or simply ignored, primarily by the European people and authorities but also by the Indigenous peoples. Nonetheless, the treaty processes treated First Nations as political authorities, recognized the Aboriginal peoples as corporate entities, recognized that they had laid claim to traditional territories, and provided some measure of commitment support.[24]

Aboriginal claims to formal recognition gain greater solidity with the Royal Proclamation of 1763.[25] This famous statement, one of the Intolerable Acts that sparked the American Revolution, sought to quell violence on the western frontier. With the Seven Years War with France resolved, British authorities resolved to limit western expansion, ensure peace with Aboriginal peoples, and save money. The Royal Proclamation effectively closed off western lands to spontaneous settlement, insisting that

[23] British Colonial authorities signed treaties with several Indigenous groups in Eastern North America, including The Great Treaty of 1722 Between the Five Nations, the Mahicans, and the Colonies of New York, Virginia, and Pennsylvania; Deed in Trust from Three of the Five Nations of Indians to the King, 1726; A Treaty Held at the Town of Lancaster, By the Honourable the Lieutenant Governor of the Province, and the Honourable the Commissioners for the Province of Virginia and Maryland, with the Indians of the Six Nations in June, 1744; Treaty of Logstown, 1752; The Albany Congress, and Treaty of 1754; Treaty with the Western Nations of Indians, at the Camp before Pittsburgh, 12th Day of August 1760; the Treaty of Fort Stanwix, or The Grant from the Six Nations to the King and Agreement of Boundary Line—Six Nations, Shawnee, Delaware, Mingoes of Ohio, 1768. The texts of these treaties can be found at <http://earlytreaties .unl.edu> (5 April 2012). British authorities also signed a series of peace and friendship treaties with the Mi'kmaq between 1725 and 1779. Starting in 1778, with the Delawares, the Government of the United States signed treaties with such groups as the Chickawa, Six Nations, Wyandot, Cherokee, Chocktaw, Shawnee, Creeks, and Oneida. On the hotly contested Mi'kmaq treaties, see K Coates *The Marshall Decision and Aboriginal Rights in the Maritimes* (McGill-Queen's Montreal 1999); W Wicken *Mi'kmaq Treaties on Trial: History, Land and Donald Marshall Junior* (University of Toronto Press Toronto 2002).

[24] For a broad overview of legal relations, see H Berman 'Perspectives on American Indian Sovereignty and International Law, 1600–1776' in O Lyons and J Mohawk (eds) *Exiled in the Land of the Free: Democracy, Indian Nations, and the US Constitution* (Clear Light Santa Fe 1992) 125–88; see also F Jennings *The Ambiguous Iroquois Empire: The Covenant Chain Confederation of Indian Tribes with English Colonies from its Beginnings to the Lancaster Treaty of 1744* (WW Norton New York 1900).

[25] Royal Proclamation (7 October 1763) reprinted at RSC 1985 App II No 1.

treaties be signed with Aboriginal peoples before newcomers could move into an area. The proclamation was a critical affirmation of Aboriginal control, if not sovereignty as internationally recognized, over traditional territories. Indigenous leaders took the proclamation as a major commitment to Indigenous control and as a sign that partnership, not military domination, would govern future relationships. Frontier settlers and developers took it as an affront to their liberty and independence.[26]

The Royal Proclamation had an uneven history after 1763. It did not survive the American Revolution in the US. The government of the United States signed treaties with many Indian groups across the south and west, typically after armed conflict. Frontier settlement continued to have a life of its own, and the newcomers' needs and interests took precedence. In British North America (progressively incorporated into the new Dominion of Canada), the Royal Proclamation remained in force, but more due to the limited settlement of the areas west of the Great Lakes than a deep commitment to the spirit of the proclamation. The Robinson Treaties were signed in Upper Canada in the 1850s, providing a measure of protection for Aboriginal peoples.[27] British Columbia, which faced substantial settlement pressure beginning in the 1850s, was deemed not to be covered by the proclamation since the area had not been discovered by Europeans as of 1763. When western settlement in Canada began in earnest in the 1870s, the government of Canada opted for a series of treaties on the western plains, partially to honour the Royal Proclamation and, even more, to avoid the costly and ruinous Indian wars that had plagued the American west.[28]

Even as the treaty frontier expanded across the United States and, later, into Canada, political and legal processes were redefining Aboriginal legal rights. Aboriginal communities rarely had the resources or the opportunity to bring their issues before the courts. US Supreme Court Chief Justice John Marshall laid the foundation for long-term recognition of Indigenous legal rights in the United States in a series of decisions (*Johnson v M'Intoch,*[29] 1823; *Cherokee Nation v Georgia,*[30] 1831; *Worcester v Georgia,*[31] 1832) that recognized the subordinate legitimacy of Indian nations and the authority of tribal governments on their reserve lands. These crucial rulings drew heavily on the writing of Emmerich de Vattel[32] and wrestled with questions about the

---

[26] B Gremont *The Iroquois in the American Revolution* (Syracuse University Press Syracuse 1972); R Allen *His Majesty's Indian Allies: British Indian Policy in the Defence of Canada 1774–1815* (Dundrun Toronto 1996) examines this issue from the Canadian side of the border.

[27] Robinson Treaty Made in the Year 1850 with the Ojibewa Indians Of Lake Superior Conveying Certain Lands to the Crown, 7 September 1850, and Robinson Treaty Made in the Year 1850 with the Ojibewa Indians Of Lake Huron Conveying Certain Lands to the Crown (signed 9 September 1850). The text of the treaties can be found at <http://www.aadnc-aandc.gc.ca/eng/1100100028978> accessed 5 April 2012.

[28] JR Miller *Compact, Contract, Covenant: Aboriginal Treaty-Making in Canada* (University of Toronto Press Toronto 2009).

[29] *Johnson v M'Intoch* 21 US (8 Wheat) 543 (1823).

[30] *Cherokee Nation v Georgia* 30 US 1, 5 Pet 1, 8 L Ed 25 (1831).

[31] *Worcester v Georgia* 31 US 515 (1832).   [32] Cf *Le droit des gens* (n 21).

status of Indigenous populations at the point of contact, the loss of sovereignty over their land through conquest, voluntary surrender of land, and the resulting primacy of the nation-state. Importantly, Marshall and other legal commentators of the time drew a sharp distinction between those populations, like the Cherokee, that exhibited control over settled lands, and those many others who moved across vast territories and had not established substantial control over their lands. Indigenous groups, therefore, were not 'nations' (even subordinate ones) unless they had established Europe-like lifestyles, economic systems and political structures.[33] In British North America/Canada, the law ran in a different direction, limiting the authority of band governments, affirming the dominance of the State in what was effective a ward or guardian relationship, and rejecting the idea that Aboriginal peoples or communities had legal power independent of the government.[34]

6. LAWS OF DOMINATION

By the late 19th century, consideration of Indigenous rights had dropped out of most of the discussions about international law. International law addressed questions of nation to nation relationships. Since Indigenous peoples did not have nation-state status, their aspirations and legal issues were properly the responsibility of national and imperial legal systems. The rapidly changing field of international law struggled to keep up with the emergence of new States, the independence of former colonies, and the growing complexity of the global political and legal order. In this intellectual and legal environment, the rights and claims of Indigenous peoples attracted little attention. International law was within the purview of nation-states, and was not applicable to subordinate political entities that existed under national or imperial law.[35]

The treaty arrangements, alliances, and peaceful coexistence that governed most Indigenous newcomer relations until the early 19th century did not survive. The dual

---

[33] *Cherokee Nation v Georgia* 30 US 1, 5 Pet 1, 8 L Ed 25 (1831); RK Newmyer *John Marshall and the Heroic Age of the Supreme Court* (Louisiana State University Press Baton Rouge 2001); R Faulkner *The Jurisprudence of John Marshall* (Princeton University Press Princeton 1968).

[34] There were comparable developments in New Zealand, see J Belich *Making Peoples: A History of the New Zealanders: From Polynesian Settlement to the End of the Nineteenth Century* (University of Hawaii Press Honolulu 2002); see also C Orange *The Treaty of Waitangi* (Allen & Unwin Auckland 1987).

[35] For background on this important era, see D Kennedy 'International Law in the Nineteenth Century: History of an Illusion' (1997) 99 Quinnipiac Law Review; and A Carter *The Decay of International Law?: A Reappraisal of the Limits of Legal Imagination in International Affairs* (Manchester University Press Manchester 1986).

forces of mass immigration and industrialization transformed much of North America. Indigenous peoples were overrun by millions of settlers, farmers, ranchers, miners, and others. Aboriginal people emerged as either the unfortunate victims of progress or impediments to prosperity. In the latter instance, Indigenous communities saw treaties and agreements abrogated or implemented unevenly. Even worse, they experienced displacement and military intervention. The idea of Aboriginal peoples as victims took root in this time period. Missionaries sought to educate the Indigenous children for engagement in the new economy.

Governments and charities provided the basic necessities, often decrying the lack of adaptability in the Aboriginal communities. If they were victims of progress, it appeared to be a cultural flaw, a reflection of how poorly Indigenous culture intersected with technology, work and opportunity. What Francis Jennings, writing about the colonial era in Massachusetts described as the 'cant of conquest' took hold, rationalizing the continent's rapacious appetite for Indigenous lands.[36] That Aboriginal peoples had trouble on the reserves and reservations reinforced the idea that the disappearance of the Indigenous population was preordained. For some, reserves and reservations provided Aboriginal people with the opportunity to regroup and rebuild, protected from the depredations of the general population. For many more, these remaining Indigenous lands were where the Aboriginal people would go to die.

With such sombre forecasts of current and present possibilities, Aboriginal people found even less interest in their legal standing, although many Indigenous groups tried to use the courts to secure a resolution of their grievances. The courts stood strongly behind governments and legislatures, rejecting claims to recognize broad Aboriginal rights and accepting the authority of the government to manage Aboriginal affairs. There was no Canadian and American consensus on how best to proceed. In 1887, the United States government introduced the Dawes Act,[37] which attempted to turn commonly held property into fee simple title, and which sought to eliminate the special legal status of Native Americans.[38] Canada, in 1876, passed the Indian Act,[39] which codified the ward-like status of First Nations in the country, establishing administrative oversight of band governments and giving the federal government the authority to manage Indigenous affairs.[40]

Aboriginal people, particularly in Canada, did not have full legal rights (the right to vote came in 1960).[41] Indeed, governments used their guardian-type powers to

---

[36] *The Invasion of America* (n 9).

[37] Dawes General Allotment Act (1887) US Statutes at Large, vol XXIV, 388–91.

[38] W Washburn *The Assault on Indian Tribalism: The General Allotment Law (Dawes Act) of 1887* (Lippincott New York 1975).

[39] Indian Act SC 1876 c 18.

[40] For an excellent source on American jurisprudence relating to Indigenous peoples, see FS Cohen *Handbook of Federal Indian Law* (R Strickland ed) (University of New Mexico Press Albuquerque 1971).

[41] Act to Amend the Canada Elections Act SC 1960, c 7.

outlaw major cultural practices, including the potlatch and the Sun Dance, to regulate Aboriginal governments off reserves, and to control economic activities. In a major 1927 legislative move, the government of Canada denied First Nations the right to hire lawyers or even to meet for the purposes of challenging the government.[42] The United States, drawing on Marshall's pivotal decisions, accepted the concept of 'domestic dependent nations' and acknowledged Aboriginal autonomy.[43] This was not backed up with financial support, however. Few Native American groups had the resources to make much progress. In both countries, aggressive measures designed to weaken Indigenous cultures provided the strongest possible signals of government objectives. By the early 20th century, Indigenous peoples in North American increasingly understood the law to an instrument of colonization and cultural domination, ensuring that they posed no threat to the political and legal status quo.

7. INDIGENOUS APPEALS TO INTERNATIONAL LAW

Long before Aboriginal peoples appreciated the coercive power of European legal systems, they understood the potential power of international conventions. Assuming that they had nation-to-nation partnerships with their European allies, a small number of Indigenous groups made direct representations to their monarch, believing that the Kings and Queens would recognize and honour the language included in alliance and treaty documents. Such petitions, however, did not and could not alter colonial priorities and policies. That Aboriginal groups saw themselves as political and legal partners, however, spoke clearly to their view of their formal relationships with the European powers.[44]

As a new international regime evolved, particularly after the First World War, Indigenous leaders saw yet another opportunity. The League of Nations, a loose union of countries seeking means of controlling military conflicts and resolving disputes, offered a new forum for Aboriginal protests. Efforts by Deskaheh and the Council of the Iroquis Confederacy to secure the attention of the League of Nations were quickly rebuffed.[45] The campaign, however, alerted governments, supporters and other Aboriginal groups to the possibilities of international law. The still nascent

---

[42] Act to Amend the Indian Act RSC 1927 c 98; *Skyscrapers Hide the Heavens* (n 4) covers the evolution of Indian policy in Canada.

[43] *Cherokee Nation v Georgia*, 30 US 1 (1831).

[44] The best survey of this long and complicated process is *Indigenous Peoples in International Law* (n 1).

[45] L Hauptman *The Iroquois Struggle for Survival* (Syracuse University Press Syracuse 1986).

nation-state configuration of the world, transformed by the independence of European colonies and shaken by the early rumblings of decolonization movements, clearly required international mechanisms to bring order to the growing post-imperial complexity of the world. By the 1930s, select Indigenous groups in North America had attempted to use national and international systems. Lobbying and legal efforts produced few results, but demonstrated a significant awareness among Aboriginal peoples of the possibilities of the law as a tool in their political struggle.

Clearly, however, national governments and the broader legal fraternity in Canada and the United States devoted little attention to the conceptual and theoretical aspects of their legal relationships with Aboriginal groups. Governments honoured, at least in part, their obligations under 19th-century treaties, but largely ignored the promises and assurances in the pre-1900 accords. Efforts focused on practical considerations related to health care, education, and economic opportunities for Indigenous peoples. Few Europeans devoted much time to the legal aspects of Aboriginal affairs globally or in North America. Slight and slow improvements in Indigenous living conditions at least ended the discussion of the inevitable demise of Indigenous peoples and cultures. By far the greatest effort focused on encouraging Aboriginal assimilation.

8. International Indigenous Law as a Political Force

Indigenous legal conditions and realities changed dramatically after the Second World War. The racial and ethnic horrors of Nazi Germany and the Pacific War drew global attention to the destructive forces of racism. After the failed efforts to use international governance to create fairness and justice on a global scale, national governments sought to create a more powerful international governance system. The creation of the United Nations in 1945 represented a watershed development in the codification and promotion of individual and collective rights. The Universal Declaration of Human Rights[46] attacked the very foundations of racially based legislation, while the Convention on Genocide[47] drew attention to calculated government efforts designed to undermine the rights, living conditions and even existence of distinct cultural groups. The new international regime broadened the understanding of the role of law from one that mediated between individuals and their State and between

---

[46] UNGA Res 217 A (III) (10 December 1948) UN Doc A/810, 71–7.

[47] Convention on the Prevention and Punishment of the Crime of Genocide (opened for signature 9 December 1948, entered into force 12 January 1951) 78 UNTS 277.

States to one that recognized the separate legal rights, needs and aspirations of sub-national groups.[48]

It soon became event that Aboriginal groups understood the significance of the new international political regime. Whereas governments, including Canada and the United States, had repeatedly resorted to national and regional laws to restrict Aboriginal freedoms and to limit their citizenship rights, attention now shifted to improving living conditions and eliminating the more egregious efforts to control Aboriginal populations.[49] A major Canadian rewriting of the Indian Act in 1951,[50] for example, captured the spirit of the new age, removing restrictions on political and legal rights and eliminating the government's right to restrict cultural and social activities. Aboriginal people had volunteered in large numbers for military service in both Canada and the United States, returning home to fewer rights than they had enjoyed while in uniform. This, in turn, drew attention to fundamental contradictions between national norms, international rights agreements and the realities of Aboriginal life on the continent.

Movement on the international stage proved slow, in large measure because of the intense political attention to other human rights debates with nation-states. Globally, post-war attention focused on the decolonization movements. The sequential liberation of dozens of former colonies and the emergence of once dependent States into political independence across Africa and throughout Asia attracted political and legal attention. At few moments in world history have there been so many loosely connected political transformations, all tied to the new international rights regimes and the growing expectations of self-determination. The destruction of most of the world's colonial system provided a model for minority and Indigenous groups still struggling for recognition and a resolution to their challenges.[51]

Small improvements emerged. The long-standing organizations working in support of Indigenous rights expanded in membership, became more secular, and lobbied more effectively. Organizations such as the International Work Group on Indigenous Affairs and Survival International drew attention to specific legal and cultural conflicts. These organizations provided a developing world forum for the articulation of a global political and legal agenda that would lift Indigenous issues

---

[48] See eg A Bozeman *The Future of Law in a Multicultural world* (Princeton University Press Princeton 1971); RP Anand *New States and the Development of International Law* (Vikas Publishing House New Dehli 1972); and P Thornberry *International Law and the Rights of Minorities* (Clarendon Press Oxford 1993).

[49] As this relates to the US, see C Wilkinson *American Indians, Time, and the Law: Native Societies in a Modern Constitutional Democracy* (Yale University Press New Haven 1988); for Canada, see JR Miller *Lethal Legacy* (McClelland and Stewart Toronto 2004).

[50] Indian Act ('An Act Respecting Indians') SC 51 c 29.

[51] G Alfredsson 'International Law, International Organizations and Indigenous Peoples' (1982) 36 Journal of International Affairs 113–24; for an interesting perspective on the rights of sub-national ethnic groups, see T Franck 'Postmodern Tribalism and the Right to Secession' in C Brölmann, R Lefeber, and M Zieck (eds) *Peoples and Minorities in International Law* (Martinus Nijhoff Leiden 1993)

out of the realm of national politics and into the more influential realm of basic human rights.

The International Labour Organization (ILO) issued a declaration on Indigenous rights in 1957. ILO Convention No 107[52] reflected the still-prevalent paternalism of the 1950s, and reflected the belief that national governments and the dominant societies in individual countries knew what was best for Indigenous peoples. The declaration emphasized the rights of Indigenous peoples as workers and their social and economic conditions, and called on national governments to invest more heavily in education, health care, and basic living conditions. The ILO document reflected developments underway in Canada and the United States with the governments focusing on quality of life issues. These programmes, and the ILO declaration, had strong statist, social democratic, and assimilationist elements. They appealed, in the main, to prosperous governments and countries that, for reasons of guilt and basic social justice, had neglected their Aboriginal populations. ILO Convention No 107 did not alter the way in which Indigenous rights were viewed within the international legal framework.

In the wealthier nations, governments made major investments in Aboriginal affairs, and bureaucracies, without yielding any ground on the legal front. There was little appetite for wholesale recognition of Indigenous rights or a major improvement of their legal situation. Existing authority remained, particularly the dependent nations notion of sovereignty in the United States. The global effort paralleled the national social justice ethos, seeking to use international conventions to force governments to do better by Indigenous populations and to use international watchdog organizations to draw attention to breaches in the growing global consensus around the rights and needs of Indigenous peoples.

Conditions changed rapidly in the 1960s, driven by the dramatic rise of Aboriginal activism. Groups like the American Indian Movement in the United States challenged the legitimacy of national governments.[53] In Canada, the patient First Nations peoples, responded in 1969 to the unexpected suggestion that Aboriginal legal status and the authority of the Indian Act be eliminated in favour of full equality with other Canadians.[54] First Nations fought back, producing an outcome 180 degrees at variance with the government of Canada's intensions. These Aboriginal protest movements found inspiration in the writings of Franz Fanon, the revolutionary efforts of Che Guevara, and the expanding decolonization movements.[55]

---

[52] Convention Concerning the Protection and Integration of Indigenous and Other Tribal and Semi-Tribal Populations in Independent Countries) (adopted 26 June 1957, entered into force 2 June 1959) 328 UNTS 247.

[53] D Banks and R Erdoes *Ojibwa Warrior: Dennis Banks and the Rise of the American Indian Movement* (University of Oklahoma Press Norman OK 2004).

[54] H Cardinal *The Unjust Society* (Hurtig Edmonton 1969).

[55] R Torres 'The Rights of Indigenous Populations: The Emerging International Norm' (1991) 16 Yale Journal of International Law 127–75.

The political challenge had a strong legal element across North America. Indigenous groups that did not have signed treaties lobbied strongly for agreements. Aboriginal leaders threatened to interrupt resource developments on lands not yet ceded to national governments. The signing of the Alaska Native Claims Settlement Act in 1969 designed to expedite the development of Prudhoe Bay oil reserves in Alaska, ushered in a new era of legal and constitutional discussions between Aboriginal peoples and national governments.[56] Similarly, First Nations in Canada chafed under the many restrictions on their personal freedoms. As late as the 1960s, they did not have the right to vote, consume alcohol, hunt and fish for traditional purposes, or own land on their reserves. In a series of incremental legal battles, Indigenous people used the courts to secure their rights as Canadians and Americans, while simultaneously asserting their collective rights as Indigenous peoples.

By the 1970s, Indigenous rights had emerged as a significant branch of national and international law, both because of the practical issues at play across North America and the profound conceptual and theoretical issues associated with Indigenous rights and aspirations. Academics and practitioners devoted much more effort to framing and explaining the issues. Indigenous organizations flooded the courts with literally thousands of cases. The effort focused on using the courts and parallel political processes to define and entrench Indigenous rights within national legal and constitutional frameworks. The North American effort attracted a great deal of global attention, as Indigenous groups participated in and shaped international Aboriginal political groups and as courts looked to Canadian and American legislation, and legal judgments for workable precedents.[57]

That the world paid attention to North American developments reflected the continued activism of Indigenous peoples. The broad engagement of the American Indian Movement and the creation of the World Council of Indigenous Peoples and the International Indian Treaty Council drew attention to mistreatment of Indigenous groups in other countries. As Aboriginal leaders pointed out, the presence of laws, treaties and government promises had provided little security for Indigenous peoples. Critics argued that government 'lawlessness' routinely characterized the exercise and protection of Aboriginal rights, rendering the detailed treaties, legislation and legal judgments of little real effect. Indigenous politicians recognized the multilayered hypocrisy of the Canadian and US governments on Aboriginal matters. These same governments were active critics of apartheid in South Africa, supported expanded rights for ethnic minorities in other countries,

[56] For a review of the situation in Alaska, see T Berger *Village Journey: The Report of the Alaska Native Review Commission* (Greystone Books Vancouver 2010).

[57] The best assessment of the global aspects of the Indigenous rights movement is J Berger *Report from the Frontier: The State of the World's Indigenous Peoples* (Zed Books London 1987); see also, *A Global History of Indigenous Peoples* (n 1).

improved legal arrangements for women and homosexuals in their countries, and positioned themselves as champions of human rights generally.[58]

Aboriginal peoples recognized the political value of the growing international interest. Presenting their cases in the court of international public opinion proved effective in gaining the attention of politicians and the public at large. Indeed, the emerging global support for Aboriginal peoples and their legal rights had much greater impact at the political than the legal level. As leading proponents of human rights, both Canada and the United States could be embarrassed by revelations about their failure to attend to the legal aspirations of their Aboriginal citizens. One of the most telling examples involved a Mik'maq woman, Sandra Lovelace, who attacked discriminatory elements in the Canadian Indian Act by appealing to the United Nations in 1977.[59] Under the Indian Act, an Aboriginal woman who married a non-Aboriginal man automatically lost her Indian status. An Aboriginal man who married a non-Aboriginal woman both kept his own Indian status and conferred that same status on his wife. The public condemnation of the Canadian law sparked a political response. Bill C-31[60] restored status to the women and their children.

This collective and uncoordinated effort brought sweeping changes in the legal and constitutional status of Aboriginal peoples. Historic treaties were reaffirmed and, in some instances, government malfeasance in the treaty process was acknowledged. In the United States, sacred sites legislation provided Indian groups with control over key cultural locations. The Alaska claims settlement was followed by an equally agreement covering the James Bay Cree in northern Quebec, clearing the way for a massive hydroelectric project.[61] This, in turn, was followed by negotiations covering the entire Canadian North and a more complicated process in British Columbia. Key court decisions, like the Boldt judgment in Washington State, recognized Aboriginal resource rights and sparked a continent-wide re-evaluation of Indigenous access to hunting, fishing and other resources.[62] Legal struggles redefined the authority and autonomy of Aboriginal governments. Through these processes, some communities gained recognition of their rights to run their own police forces and Aboriginal courts.

By the last decade of the 20th century, a veritable revolution in Aboriginal rights and legal recognition had occurred. The revision of ILO Convention No 107, as ILO

---

[58] George Manual, the author of *The Fourth World: An Indian Reality* (Collier-Macmillan Toronto 1974), was one of the founders of the global movement.

[59] *Sandra Lovelace v Canada*, UN Doc CCPR/C/13/D/24/1977 (views adopted 30 July 1981).

[60] Bill C-31: An Act to Amend the Indian Act SC 1985 *c* 27.

[61] B Richardson *Strangers Devout the Land: The Cree Hunters of the James Bay Area versus Premier Bourassa and the James Bay Development Corporation* (Chelsea Green Publishing Toronto 2008).

[62] A Harmon *The Power of Promises: Rethinking Indian Treaties in the Pacific Northwest* (University of Washington Seattle 2008).

Convention No. 169 (1989),[63] included an explicit recognition that the earlier statement was paternalistic and assimilationist. Convention No 169 provided much stronger support for Indigenous land and resource rights, political autonomy and full participation in national decision making.[64] The declaration of 1993 as the International Decade of the World's Indigenous People signalled a new level of recognition for the aspirations of Aboriginal populations.[65] The 1982 constitutional process in Canada produced dramatic change, including constitutional recognition of Aboriginal rights in section 35 of the Constitution Act of Canada, which protected 'existing Aboriginal and treaty rights'.[66] This provision in the Constitution ensured national attention to the existence and authority of Indigenous rights.

Aboriginal legal contestation brought significant changes to North American legal environments and processes. As oral cultures, Aboriginal peoples did not have an archive of legal codes, land agreements, and treaties. Instead, their oral traditions provided the core of Indigenous legal, social, and political life. The struggle to bring oral history and cultural norms into the courtroom proved difficult but ultimately successful. While judges initially resisted the introduction of such evidence, it soon became commonplace to have elders, leaders, and academic experts provide testimony and for courts to take the information as vital to the final decisions. In a series of decisions relating to the management of resources, the modern application of treaties, sentencing of Aboriginal offenders, internal Indigenous government systems, membership arrangements, cultural practices, and sacred sites, the courts relied heavily on their assessments of Indigenous cultures and social processes.

The encounter between been Indigenous and European peoples and governments produced new law, at both the domestic and international levels. In the 1970s, analysts argued that the impact of Aboriginal legal and political systems had been more pronounced than previously understood. The Iroquois Confederacy, one of the most powerful alliances in pre-European North America, was claimed to have provided some inspiration for the constitution of the United States of America. Subsequent analysis undercut this assertion.[67] The hundreds of court cases brought by Aboriginal claimants changed Canadian and American law in a process of chaotic incrementalism.

---

[63] ILO Convention C169: Indigenous and Tribal Peoples Convention (Convention Concerning Indigenous and Tribal Peoples in Independent Countries) (adopted 27 June 1989, entered into force 5 September 1991).

[64] L Swepston, 'A New Step in the International Law on Indigenous and Tribal Peoples: ILO Convention No. 169 of 1989' (1990) 15 Oklahoma City University Law Review 677–714.

[65] UNGA A/Res/48/163 (adopted 21 December 1993). This was extended into a Second Decade of the World's Indigenous Peoples.

[66] R Dussault and G Erasmus *Partners in Confederation: Aboriginal Peoples, Self-Government, and the Constitution* (Royal Commission on Aboriginal Peoples Ottawa 1993).

[67] E Tooker 'The United States Constitution and the Iroquois League' in JA Clifton *The Invented Indian: Cultural Fictions and Government Policies* (Transaction Publishers New Brunswick NJ 1990).

Legal and political struggles compelled a re-evaluation of the place of Indigenous peoples within the history, legal and political, of North America. It became increasingly clear that Aboriginal peoples had played a larger role than assumed in shaping the evolution of North America. Indigenous peoples forced national governments and legal systems to respond to their circumstances and aspirations. Over decades, they forced the governments to reconsider the laws and regulations and, in many instances, to adapt them to accommodate Aboriginal aspirations. This, in turn, created the recognition of a broader set of Indigenous rights, which rested on Aboriginality and their special status as the original peoples in North America. Canadian political scientist Alan Cairns defined Aboriginal peoples as being 'Citizens Plus', having the rights and responsibilities of all Canadians and a separate set of legal rights emerging out of treaties, Indigenous-specific laws and government commitments to Aboriginal rights.[68] The American situation differed, in large measure because of the long-standing acceptance of Indian sovereignty, which specifically recognized the separate status of Indian peoples and communities. The increasing application of that special status through Indian government initiatives and cultural reassertion brought a gradual public recognition of the special status of American Indians although, ironically, the primary manifestation was the rapid expansion of Indian-owned casinos.[69]

The long-standing interest of North American Aboriginal peoples in global Indigenous rights ensured active engagement in efforts to secure recognition for Aboriginal aspirations. The United Nations, through the UN Sub-Commission on Prevention of Discrimination and Protection of Minorities, began investigating the possibilities of a separate declaration on the rights of Indigenous peoples. The initial work commenced in the early 1970s, but the preparation of major report by José Martinez Cobo, completed in 1981–83, raised the profile of Indigenous rights within international law.[70] In 1982, the United Nations established the Working Group on Indigenous Populations. This process, opposed by the Canadian and American governments but strongly supported and pushed by North American Indigenous groups, involved more than two decades of negotiations and international collaborations. The emergence of the UN Draft Declaration on the Rights of Indigenous Peoples[71] in 1993 was a watershed moment. The draft declaration spoke most eloquently to the situation of Indigenous peoples in the developing world, where many lived in precarious conditions and lacked even the most fundamental legal protections.

The UN draft declaration moved slowly through the international political processes and appeared for a time to be destined for failure. Four of the opposing

---

[68] A Cairns *Citizens Plus: Aboriginal Peoples and the Canadian State* (UBC Press Vancouver 2000).

[69] Y Belanger (ed) *First Nation Gaming* (University of Manitoba Winnipeg 2011).

[70] J Martinez Cobo *Study of the Problem of Discrimination Against Indigenous Populations* (United Nations New York 1981–84).

[71] Draft Declaration on the Rights of Indigenous Peoples (1994) UN Doc E/CN.4/Sub.2/1994/56.

national governments—Canada, the US, New Zealand, and Australia—were among the most liberal in their approach to Aboriginal rights, arguing that the draft declaration put at risk the delicate treaty, legal, and political arrangements with Indigenous peoples that had been constructed over decades. Aboriginal leaders countered that the Draft Declaration was 'aspirational' and did not represent a legal code that they expected to be implemented within individual countries. When the draft declaration reached the floor of the United Nations in 2007, it secured overwhelming support.[72] Canada, the United States, Australia, and New Zealand maintained their opposition and refused to sign. Continued pressure and the realization, in effect, that the UN Declaration lacked the force of law and need not have an impact on national legal and political practice convinced the governments of Canada (2009) and the United States (2010) to sign up to the declaration.[73]

The UN Declaration represented a transitional point in the history of Indigenous law. That the governments of the United Nations, including the recalcitrant Canadian and American authorities, accepted the bold assertions of Indigenous aspirations marked a major shift from the historic approach to Aboriginal affairs. There was no rapid move in Canada or the United States to bring the Declaration into the legal struggles in North America. After all, existing legal structures and processes had produced a latticework of Aboriginal law that respected both general Indigenous and treaty rights and that recognized, in limited ways, Aboriginal sovereignty and rights of self-government.[74]

9. CONCLUSION

Despite the transitions and legal changes, the legal standing of Indigenous peoples remains uncertain. Canadian governments routinely challenged the assertion that Aboriginal peoples lived in organized societies before the arrival of European peoples,

---

[72] United Nations Declaration on the Rights of Indigenous Peoples (adopted 13 September 2007) UNGA A/Res/61/295.

[73] J Gilbert 'Indigenous Rights in the Making: The United Nations Declaration on the Rights of Indigenous Peoples' (2007) 14 International Journal on Minority and Group Rights 207–30.

[74] For thoughtful discussions of the role of history in the legal process, see AJ Ray 'Native History on Trial: Confessions of an Expert Witness' (2003) 84 Canadian Historical Review 253–73; AJ Ray 'Aboriginal Title and Treaty Rights Research: A Comparative Look at Australia, Canada, New Zealand, and the United States' (2003) 37 New Zealand Journal of History 5–21; AJ Ray 'Regina v. Marshall: Native History, the Judiciary, and the Public' (2000) 29 Acadiensis 138–46.

a legal position that Indigenous claimants found fundamentally offensive.[75] That the courts and governments finally recognized the stability and structures of pre-contact Indigenous cultures was a major turning point in Indigenous legal affairs and produced a new level of equality before the law. The full meaning of this change, and the long-term legal implications for Indigenous peoples, remain to be determined.

Important questions remain about the role and interactions of legal history, international law, and Indigenous rights in North America.[76] For generations, the history of the Aboriginal–European encounter focused on a subset of historical process, including military conflict, political alliances, economic relations, and the role of missionaries in Indigenous life. The broader and more conceptual questions of international law and the interplay of legal issues and domestic realities have attracted less attention. The rules-building process, through the creation of regulations, treaties, legislation, and promises to Indigenous peoples, created a matrix of understanding and misunderstanding that needs to be documented and defined with much greater precision. It is important, further, to understand how Indigenous legal concepts and structures interacted with European and North American national legal systems.[77]

International law played a critical role in the evolution of the global order and, specifically, in the relationships between Indigenous and non-Indigenous peoples. The fundamental purpose of the law is to define the structure of critical relationships and to outline the terms and conditions under which land and private property is maintained and social relationships are defined. International law both regulates and outlines relations between distinct political entities. The historical inequality between European and Indigenous peoples ensured that the legal relationship lacked balance and meant that the Aboriginal communities bore the brunt of the weaknesses of the evolving system. The role of the law and Indigenous–European legal encounters provide useful means of exploring the complex social situations that existed through the encounter situation.

Military metaphors have long been influential in describing legal frontiers, which are portrayed in terms of battles, conflicts, victories, and losses. In the case of Indigenous peoples and international law, the military rhetoric does an injustice to the nature of the legal encounter. The comprehensive processes are more subtle, involving assumptions about Indigenous rights and cultures, the integration of European legal values into administrative processes, and the cultural misunderstandings that

---

[75]   R Fisher 'Judging History: Reflections on the Reasons for Judgment in Delgamuukw vs. B.C.' (1992) 95 BC Studies 43–54; and A McEachern *Reasons for Judgement: Delgamuukw v. B.C.* (Supreme Court of British Columbia Smithers 1991).

[76]   S Razack *Looking White People in the Eye: Gender, Race, and Culture in Courtrooms and Classrooms* (University of Toronto Press Toronto 1998).

[77]   For a very useful paper on the relationship between international law and Indigenous affairs in the US, see—'International Law as an Interpretative Force in Federal Indian Law' (2003) 116 Harvard Law Review 1751–73; J Corntassel and TH Primeau 'Indigenous "Sovereignty" and International Law: Revised Strategies for Pursuing "Self-Determination"' (1995) 17 Human Rights Quarterly 343–65.

are always possible in fluid cross-cultural situations.[78] There are occasionally formal legal cases, typically brought by Indigenous groups seeking to protect their rights. These actions, however, represent only the tip of the legal iceberg and undervalue the complex social, political, and cultural interactions that play out away from the courtroom.

Legal historians and the study of legal history have a great deal to contribute to the understanding of Indigenous–European encounter in North America and, equally, to the resolution of outstanding legal claims and issues. The legal complexities and subtleties of the encounter experience speak to the continuing influence of European values, the responsiveness of Indigenous peoples, and the multiplicity of local solutions to the imposition of a broad European system on the continent. That these historical influences remain so important in contemporary legal processes only reinforces the value of understanding historical patterns and imbedded cultural values and assumptions. Legal historians have long understood that legal structures and processes serve as instruments of power systems and as windows on social, economic, and cultural changes within and between societies.

By the 1980s, with the establishment of the processes that led to the UN Declaration on the Rights of Indigenous Peoples,[79] Aboriginal aspirations had emerged as a formidable global force and as a key issue in the articulation of an international law regime for the modern era. The UN Declaration represented a symbolic end to the Indigenous struggle for recognition. Across North America, however, Aboriginal groups continue to assert their rights as Indigenous nations, debate self-determination and autonomy, and seek to articulate and negotiate special status within the existing nation-state regime. In this instance, the theory and conceptualization of international law is significantly in advance of the practice of both national and international legal systems. The coming years will determine if the high profile political accomplishments of Indigenous leaders can be transformed into practical and active rights and processes that provide an appropriate place for Aboriginal issues within the international legal arrangements.[80]

RECOMMENDED READING

Anaya, James *Indigenous Peoples in International Law* (OUP New York 1996).
Bennett, Gordon *Aboriginal Rights in International Law* (Royal Anthropological Institute London 1978).

[78] J Borrows *Recovering Canada: The Resurgence of Indigenous Law* (University of Toronto Press Toronto 2002).

[79] Declaration on the Rights of Indigenous Peoples (n 72).

[80] J Anaya 'Divergent Discourses About International Law, Indigenous Peoples, and Rights Over Lands and Natural Resources: Toward a Realist Trend' (2005) 16 Colorado Journal of International Environmental Law and Policy 237–50.

Coates, Ken *A Global History of Indigenous Peoples: Struggle and Survival* (Palgrave Macmillan London 2004).

Cobo Martinez, José *Study of the Problem of Discrimination Against Indigenous Populations* (United Nations New York 1981–84).

de las Casas, Bartolomé *History of the Indies* (Andrée M Collard ed and trans) (Harper Row New York 1971).

Green, Leslie C and Olive Dickason *The Law of Nations and the New World* (University of Alberta Press Edmonton 1989).

Tennant, Chris 'Indigenous Peoples, International Institutions, and the International Legal Literature from 1945–1993' (1994) 16 Human Rights Quarterly 1–57.

Truyol Serra, Antonio (ed) *The Principles of Political and International Law in the Work of Francisco de Vitoria* (Ediciones Cultura Hispánica Madrid 1946).

Vattel, Emer de *Le droit des gens ou Principes de la loi naturelle: appliqués à la conduite et aux affaires des nations et des souverains* (Carnegie Institution of Washington Washington 1916 repr of the 1758 edn).

Williams, Robert *The American Indian in Western Legal Thought: The Discourse of Conquest* (OUP New York 1990).

PART IV

INTERACTION OR IMPOSITION

CHAPTER 34

DIPLOMACY

ARTHUR EYFFINGER

1. INTRODUCTION

1.1. Perimeters

Diplomacy, as a keen diplomat observed long ago,[1] is an instrument of power. For centuries on end the wielding of power in Europe was based on territory and the wealth this generated. The ownership of land and its buying power was felt to justify the execution of exclusive rights. Notably, it legitimized the ruler's sovereignty and his prerogative to diplomacy and to wage war, that is the continuation of diplomacy by other, forceful, means. For centuries on end, the State was virtually the exclusive holder of these prerogatives. Theoreticians identified the State with the most perfect form of society. The role of diplomacy was the juggling and balancing of the competing interests of these state-champions of autonomy.

Over the past half-century all this has changed dramatically. History has overhauled the premise. As paramount generator of wealth, territory has been replaced by trade and capital markets, and in recent decades by information technology and the tertiary service sector. New competing actors assert their rights in new forums and in forms and processes of 'diplomatic' negotiating tailor-made to their specific interests. In a parallel process of social renewal, time-honoured State sovereignty is ideologically being challenged by the concept of universal human rights and, in terms of

---

[1] F de Callières *De la Manière de Négocier avec les Souverains* (Pour la Compagnie Amsterdam 1716).

organization, by a host of international and regional bodies, by global governance and civil society.

As ever, life in its countless complexities has shown little patience with limping tradition. In its restless stride, it has overrun the boundaries of the public and private spheres. International contacts have expanded well beyond inter-state contacts, and these in turn long broken through the perimeters of classical, conventional diplomacy. As we speak, intergovernmental organizations, the spokesmen of civil society (non-governmental organizations, NGOs), and financial and economic institutions have all become global players in the integrated network of overlapping interests that makes up world diplomacy today. They enter into partnerships in debating climate change, biodiversity, preventive diplomacy, or post-conflict peace building. Political challenges by non-state actors have generated new types of conflict. The world's fabric is under reconstruction and humanity in search of new directions and normative guidance.

The above process is as irreversible as its outcome is unpredictable. Is our generation witnessing the end of the Westphalian states system? Are we recapturing the multilayered medieval society, when bankers, guilds, Hanse, and knighthood conversed with kings and emperors? Are we heading for a global 'civil society'? Or is our age a new transition phase *within* the system, as when dynastic rule gave way to constitutional rights, and these in turn to parliamentary control? Will the States system absorb all change to valiantly challenge global issues?[2]

The answers to these penetrating questions lie in the lap of the gods and will not be offered, nor expected, in these pages. Quite the contrary: the above appraisal serves precisely to justify the demarcation of this chapter. Institutionalized diplomacy, that is, the entertaining of international relations in a continuous process and by qualified officials, was the wilful creation of the State, both to express and to protect its sovereignty. This chapter sets out to discuss the full span of that discipline's unchallenged and unimpaired functioning, from its origins at the dawn of the states system until the emergence of the current twilight zone (1450–1950).

1.2. Diplomacy: A Political Device

The overarching purpose of diplomacy is to protect and further one's interest vis-à-vis foreign actors. It is the assessment of what analysts such as Hobbes or Grotius identified as man's two paramount drives, his urge for self-preservation and his social appetite. All civil society and commerce grew from these drives. Diplomacy, therefore, long preceded documented history.[3] The two drives, accordingly, mirror

---

[2] J Black *A History of Diplomacy* (Reaktion London 2010) at 248–63.
[3] ibid 17–22.

mainstreams of diplomacy, often verified as the warrior type and the merchant type. Throughout history, both types have found expression in endless variety. Early commentators often linked these types to national characters, deeming these in turn determined by climate, region, or size.[4] Be this as it may, the pertinence of self-interest puts diplomacy in the political sphere, that is, outside that of moral philosophy.[5] Diplomatic practice is conditioned by political power and follows suit wherever it is taken.[6]

Three complementary elements of old have made up the discipline: representation, negotiation, and the gathering of information, the 'intelligence' aspect.[7] The proportional weight of these elements is ultimately a matter of contingencies determined by the overall political climate, the strength of relations, and the prevailing type of diplomacy.

1.3. The Law of Diplomacy

Even if diplomacy, as an executive tool of foreign policy, is at heart a political device, the law has been its steady companion. The law of diplomacy is indeed one of the oldest and most impressive, if admittedly also most complex domains of international law. From time immemorial, it was well understood that the proper functioning of the diplomatic agent had to be wrapped in guarantees and protected by safety valves. In the communications between States definite conventions developed. From it grew a fascinating amalgam of non-binding customs and arrangements, such as courtesy and protocol, along with a distinct set of binding rules of law. At its core are the concepts of immunity and inviolability, aimed at defining the legal rights and duties of the sending and receiving State, with a view to facilitating the envoy's functioning.[8] In 1961 this rich tradition, which encapsulates some of humanity's most precious customary law, was comprehensively codified in the much acclaimed and widely applied Vienna Convention on Diplomatic Relations.[9]

---

[4] For an amusing appreciation of the national traditions of diplomacy, see H Nicolson *Diplomacy* (Thornton Butterworth London 1939) at 127–53.

[5] ibid 50.

[6] ibid 60 ff.

[7] Art 3 of the 1964 Vienna Convention ((signed 18 April 1961, entered into force 24 April 1964) 500 UNTS 95) adds to this the protecting of interests of nationals and, echoing the UN Charter, the explicit promoting of friendly relations.

[8] MS Anderson *The Rise of Modern Diplomacy 1450–1919* (Longman London 1993) at 24–6; *A History of Diplomacy* (n 2) 62–3.

[9] Vienna Convention on Diplomatic Relations (n 7).

1.4. Diplomacy: Its Legislative and Executive Branches

In monitoring international relations, conventional inter-state diplomacy diverges into two distinct branches: the legislative aspect of formulating a policy, and the executive part of policy implementation.[10] The legislative aspect is at the discretion of a State's central organ, its administration. The executive part is usually entrusted to a specialized taskforce—in our day and age the foreign ministry and its diplomatic staff—from the well-understood perception that each branch requires specific skills, which do not by definition overlap. As critics have stipulated, precisely the blurring of these two spheres has time and again compromised international relations.

1.5. The Balancing of Interests

Professional diplomacy boasts distinct techniques and a toolkit that reflects the world's accumulated experience with human nature and the human condition. In effecting its objectives, diplomacy is committed to peaceful *means*, short of the use of force, if not necessarily towards peaceful *ends*. Even so, and inasmuch as commerce and trade are held to profit from peace, it is in neutralizing dispute and in balancing and levelling conflicting interests that, historically, diplomacy has consummated its role and effectively served international society. Not by coincidence, Western diplomacy's paramount concept constitutes the theory of the balance of power.[11] The concept was familiar to domestic politics from the days of Polybius (*c.* 150 BC), in analogy to the medical 'balance of humours'. It was first applied in modern times within the *Quattrocento* world of Italian city-States.

Following successive bids for world hegemony by Habsburg Spain and Bourbon France, the balance was adopted as the overriding instrument of European policy at Utrecht (1713). It had a special appeal to a world imbued with the thought of Newton and Boyle. Reason and 'political arithmetic' suggested a benign political order. In practice, state-actors found the mechanism fairly elusive—and doctrine proved of little help. A balance is by nature easily tipped and a precarious instrument to base durable equilibrium on. Its appliance with a view to freezing change and protecting vested interests hampered the natural flow of society; neither did it serve social justice.[12] The peaceful balancing of interests is never easy under the best of circumstances. It never was within a single civilization, and the global interacting of widely diverging traditions from 1850 onwards only exacerbated the challenge.

---

[10] *Diplomacy* (n 4) 12–13.

[11] *The Rise of Modern Diplomacy* (n 8) 149–203.

[12] An account of early balance systems in *A History of Diplomacy* (n 2) 20.

1.6. A Tradition of Secrecy and Elitism

Old prejudices die hard. Diplomacy is often identified with 'secrecy' and 'elitism'. Both objections cut some ice, yet both elements have their justification, the first in substance, and the second in historical circumstance. To politicians the media may be a valuable asset. Bismarck, for one, understood this perfectly well. By adroitly stirring up mass hysteria in the volatile French media, he forced the hand of Napoleon III to have France rashly declare war on Prussia (1870). Diplomats, by contrast, do not seek the limelight of their own accord. Much like courts of law, negotiators can do well without the fickle *vox populi*. Privacy facilitates freedom of speech and fosters compromise.[13] Our world's insistence on all-out openness all too readily discredits the assets of negotiating *à huis clos*.

A tragic victim of misconception of the role of secrecy and of the different spheres of policy and diplomacy was Woodrow Wilson. On the surge of his Fourteen Points Rule (1918), Wilson sailed to France to make short shrift of 'European diplomacy of secrecy'. At Versailles he soon found efficient diplomacy hard to chime with democratic control—and ended up in a private study, excluding the vanquished powers, most of his allies, and the press alike. Wilson was not the first to discredit 'secrecy' all too rashly. In their zeal to bring down the establishment, all revolutionary movements, from the American and French Revolutions to socialism and communism, bellowed their disdain for conventional diplomacy, only soon to recant. The art of manoeuvring at the conference table is a discipline better left to experts.

2. THE RISE OF MODERN DIPLOMACY

2.1. International Relations: Three Concepts[14]

Three political concepts have steered European history of international relations: the empire or universal monarchy; the states system; the supranational order. The first and third concepts embodied steadfast, time-honoured ideals; the States system never did. It was the consequence of social crisis and imposed by political necessity, for lack of alternative, and in breach of tradition.

---

[13] *Diplomacy* (n 4) 14.
[14] H Spruyt *The Sovereign State and Its Competitors. An Analysis of Systems Change* (Princeton University Press Princeton 1994).

The concept of the universal, hegemonic empire—the dream of the Roman legacy—was the utopian *Leitbegriff* in Europe up to early modernity. A long forlorn cause ever after the division of Charlemagne's empire (843), the notion was kept alive in the illusory *Translatio Imperii*; still glorified in Dante's *De Monarchia* (c. 1300), the ideal faded with time, if reluctantly; the ambition was never quite abandoned.

The concepts of supranational order and international organization can likewise be traced back to (idealist) literature of the early modern period.[15] Only towards the end of the 19th century the concept became *salonfähig* and a factor of acute political interest—then to be implemented, with qualified success, in the 20th century.

The concept of the states system grew from the political and moral bankruptcy of the bipolar medieval power constellation of empire and church in the face of socio-economic renewal at the dawn of the modern nation-state. The concept drew its *raison d'être* and rationale from forestalling universal hegemony. It was this concept that prompted modern sedentary diplomacy and down the centuries remained its steady companion. This concept, therefore, constitutes the backdrop of our narrative.

2.2. Resident Envoys and Sedentary Missions

The rise of modern diplomacy is intricately linked to the fascinating world of the Italian *Quattrocento*.[16] Here, way ahead of Europe across the Alps, a fabric of sovereign city-States had emerged that thrived on trade and commerce with the Levant and controlled silk routes and international banking. This world's keen political insights and aspirations were underpinned in the works of shrewd early 16th-century observers like the Florentine Niccolò Machiavelli and Francesco Guicciardini.

It was a cynical world perhaps, ruled by princes, usurpers, and oligarchs, and a chronically unstable crucible of intrigue and scheming. Still, the common sense of merchant and banker readily perceived the profits to be reaped from levelling powers in equilibrium of peace. Political expansionism and keen commercial rivalry prompted the first modern application of the classical concept of the balance of power.

From that same bedrock sprung the notion of sedentary embassies, and for similar pragmatic reasons. Throughout Antiquity and the Middle Ages diplomacy had been episodic, an ad hoc phenomenon spurred by representation at coronation or wedding ceremonies, by acute conflict or the conclusion of treaties and negotiating of alliances. No need for permanency had ever arisen, let alone for a specific functionary

---

[15] CL Lange *Histoire de l'internationalisme* (3 vols Aschehoug Kristiana 1919); J Ter Meulen *Der Gedanke der internationalen Organization in seiner Entwicklung* (3 vols Nijhoff The Hague 1929–40); *The Rise of Modern Diplomacy* (n 8) 204–90.

[16] *Diplomacy* (n 4) 26–30; *The Rise of Modern Diplomacy* (n 8) 1–40; *A History of Diplomacy* (n 2) 43–6.

with definite qualifications, tasks or status. However, the old formula sufficed no longer for Italian city councils, on which the urgency of reliable intelligence services imposed itself on a daily basis.

Competing expansionism of Florence, Milan, and Venice is credited with having generated the concept of the resident envoy and permanent mission in the 1430s.[17] Earlier experience with consuls in the Levant, a tradition launched by Venice as early as 1197, may have suggested the formula. The concept spread quickly—in Italy, that is. By 1460 Savoy had an *orator et ambaxiator continuus et procurator* in Rome. By 1500 Venice had two merchants as permanent envoys in London.

At first, no need to reciprocate was felt on the northern side of the Alps.[18] Not only did the intensity of contacts not yet warrant the step, state machinery had not yet reached that sophistication. Actually, the institution was looked at askance and felt to express hostility rather than friendship: it was tolerated rather than encouraged. Until Francis I, France declined the concept as token of distrust and weakness and positively despised these envoys as sleuths and spies. The juncture, therefore, was not necessarily seen as a paradigm shift by contemporary observers.[19] Only with time did the institution became widely accepted. At first, social background and status of the permanent envoys were well below that of the traditional ambassadors, aristocrats in the *Herrschernähe.*[20] Rulers kept entrusting ad hoc embassies to their tried and trusted intimates. The new institution's somewhat questionable antecedents and objectives will have accounted for this.

Titles of sedentary envoys varied widely. Names ran from *orator* to *procurator* to *legatus* to *ambaxiator.*[21] By 1600 Gentili distinguished three classes.[22] The 'corps' of permanent envoys was motley of different standing. Petrarch, Boccaccio, Macchiavelli, Giucciardini, Jordaens, Rubens—they all served as diplomats. Rome, long the diplomatic epicentre,[23] produced the first monograph on the new functionary, Bernard du Rosier's *Ambaxiator Brevilogus* (1436). In 1490 Ermolao Barbaro published his *De Officio Legati* in Venice. Only much later Jean Hotman (*La charge et la dignité de l'ambassadeur,* 1604) and Francis Thynne (*The Perfect Ambassador,* 1652) followed suit in France and Britain respectively.[24]

A new era of diplomacy was heralded with the Italian Wars (1494–1559). Habsburg aspirations to absorb the cisalpine commonwealth made France interfere in the Italian power play. Charles VIII's campaigns were vicious affairs. War at the scale here presented was, if not by right, on account of its sheer cost reserved for States only, and

---

[17] *A History of Diplomacy* (n 2) 30 assumes a leading role for Milan.
[18] *The Rise of Modern Diplomacy* (n 8) 10.
[19] *A History of Diplomacy* (n 2) 47.
[20] ibid 26 and 47–8.
[21] *The Rise of Modern Diplomacy* (n 8) 6.
[22] A Gentili *De jure belli libri tres* (1598). See *The Rise of Modern Diplomacy* (n 8) 5.
[23] *A History of Diplomacy* (n 2) 28–9.
[24] *The Rise of Modern Diplomacy* (n 8) 26–7.

well beyond the purse of cities, guilds, or knighthood.[25] To curb the Habsburg Empire Charles leaned heavily on his Genovese bankers. It was a historic turn: the 'pact of necessity' of State and capital would prove indissoluble.

Peace was only secured by the bankruptcy of the antagonists. France's bare survival determined the course of history against the hegemonic empire, and accelerated the growth towards a system of sovereign States. Diplomacy was scaled up too, in an array of otherwise short-lived leagues that may perhaps count as the opening of a European Balance System.[26] The modern State, capitalism, and political interdependence had all assumed new dimensions.

2.3. The Institutional Framework

From 1550, the exchange of permanent missions and the rise of a professional class of diplomats changed the discipline. Firstly, it generated a diplomatic bureaucracy.[27] Chanceries were launched and archives kept of reports, such as of the legendary *Relazione* of Venetian ambassadors. The Papal Chancery that issued decretals was reputed for its legal expertise. Secondly, diplomacy as 'intelligence' gathering generated a network of espionage. The quest for sensitive information made the diplomat's correspondence a keen target for interception. Early records are colourful: dispatches were sent in duplicate, by different routes, or sewn into clothing. Couriers were disguised as merchant or wandering scholar.

Codes and ciphers were ubiquitous.[28] Already by 1550 Rome employed a secretary in charge of cipher systems to serve its *nuncios*.[29] The obvious rejoinder was codebreaking by specialized *cabinets noirs* (Paris) or Black Chambers (London).[30] The 16th century produced expert monographs on the issue, like Von Trittenheim's *Polygraphia* (1516), Della Porta's *De furtivis litterarum notis* (1563), or De Vigenère's *Traité des chiffres* (1586). A later benchmark was Antoine Rossignol's *Le grand chiffre* (c. 1650). It brought about the coming of age of the law of diplomacy.

2.4. Privileges and Immunities

Until the 15th century, the alpha and omega of the law of diplomacy had been the diplomatic agent's personal inviolability or sacrosanctity. The rise of permanent

---

[25] cf GP Geoffrey *The Military Revolution. Military Innovation and the Rise of the West, 1500–1800* (CUP Cambridge 1988) ch 1; C Tilly *Coercion, Capital and European States, AD 990–1990* (Basil Blackwell Cambridge Massachusetts 1990); R Bonney *The European Dynastic States 1494–1660* (OUP Oxford 1990).

[26] M Sheehan *The Balance of Power. History and Theory* (Routledge London 1996).

[27] *The Rise of Modern Diplomacy* (n 8) 20–3.

[28] ibid 22–3 and 43.   [29] ibid 34–5.   [30] *A History of Diplomacy* (n 2) 108–9.

missions imposed the need for extension of protection to include the envoy's family, household, residence, and correspondence. It would prove a tantalizing conundrum.

The first legal device developed to comprehensively deal with the above issues was the concept of extraterritoriality, first proposed in 1575 by the French lawyer Pierre Ayrault.[31] It was abandoned as abusive interpretation led to the claim of so-called *franchise de quartier* for whole embassy quarters, where contraband and petty crime abounded to the bewilderment of authorities. Another right, precious in the days of religious strife, was impaired by similar deceit: the *droit de chapelle*. As abuse turned whole embassies into places of asylum, the concept was dropped.

The envoy's personal sacrosanctity lay enshrined in tracts by Bartolus (1354) and Da Legnano (1360). Still, practice was entirely different. Henry VIII had a papal *nuncio* arrested for spying. Granvelle spent time in prison for displeasing Francis I. The integrity of the discipline, the secrecy surrounding this 'mystery of State', and the *virtú* of these 'licensed spies' were widely contested. Suspicion was well founded. Madrid sent envoys to conspire against Elizabeth I and, in 1584, had William of Orange, the charismatic leader of the Dutch Revolt, assassinated.[32] British ambassadors intrigued with Huguenots in Paris. The concept of personal immunity remained a vexing issue, until in Grotius' days (*c.*1625) its nature and extent were legally defined. Still, abuse abounded. As late as in 1717 the Swedish ministers in London and The Hague were arrested for sedition. Accepted rules of universal application had to wait till the 20th century.

The two pragmatic grounds for the aristocratic, eliitary tradition of diplomacy had been reliability and means. Permanent envoys were often seriously handicapped by irregular and arbitrary payment. Complaints are ubiquitous, and include Grotius himself. Scholars or merchants, when acting as envoys, often found themselves financially left out in the cold, liable to debts and subsequent actions by creditors. From this circumstance grew the concepts of immunities from civil or criminal proceedings.[33] Insolvency also made envoys liable to bribes by the host country. Gifts (free lodgings, horses, gold chains) were effective means to corrupt. But then, diplomats had their share of guilt. Through the ages, they mistook exemption from custom duties as licence for smuggling.

The same interplay of theory and practice, claim and abuse applied to diplomatic premises. In the days of the St Bartholemew's Day massacres (1572) French Huguenots took shelter in the Dutch embassy.[34] Embassies figured as safe havens for dissidents and were dens of uproar. As a consequence, acceptance of the immunity of

---

[31] *The Rise of Modern Diplomacy* (n 8) 24; *A History of Diplomacy* (n 2) 18; ER Adair *The Exterritoriality of Ambassadors in the Sixteenth and Seventeenth Centuries* (Longmans London 1929).

[32] *A History of Diplomacy* (n 2) 59–60.

[33] *The Rise of Modern Diplomacy* (n 8) 53–5.

[34] ibid 53–5.

premises also was a slow process. To conclude, for centuries on end immunities were arranged on a bilateral and ad hoc basis.

3. The Westphalian Experience

3.1. The States System

The Westphalian Peace Conference (1644–48) that put an end to the ideological clash of the Thirty Years War constituted a critical benchmark in the history of European diplomacy. As a diplomatic accomplishment it was an unprecedented *tour de force*.[35] It tremendously enhanced the prestige of the discipline, enlarged its expertise, and refined its techniques and procedures.

The acquiescence of belligerents in the military deadlock and their grudging resignation to come to terms—prompted by exhaustion rather than lofty ideals of peace—was historic in itself. It put an end to one of Europe's most complex eras of crisis. For well over a century, and in a merciless clash of dynastic, national and religious interests, Protestantism had challenged Catholicism; Bourbon and Vasa dynasties had defied Habsburg supremacy, and German nobility had contested imperial centralism.

Westphalia was a watershed: it undid the universal claims of papacy and empire, the dream of a single Christianity, and the last vestiges of overlapping sovereignty on varying titles that were the relics of the medieval world. It embraced the exclusive principle of territorial sovereignty and reserved the prerogative of diplomatic relations for States. Westphalia formally replaced universalism with a society of commonwealths that interacted along shared norms and values embedded in legal precepts of universal application, such as the principle of non-intervention. It accepted—or paid lip-service to—the formal equality of States, thus introducing a horizontal and ideologically clear cut international order: the states system.

Of essence to our discussion, 1648 was a *negotiated* result that relied on the diplomatic device of the balance, now shouldered by ample reflection and theory. The label of 'anarchical society'[36] along Hobbesian lines does not quite fit this system. Keen political and economic competition was kept in check by sophisticated alliance strategy.

---

[35] *A History of Diplomacy* (n 2) 66.
[36] H Bull *The Anarchical Society. A Study of Order in World Politics* (2nd edn Macmillan Basingstoke 1988).

Tolerance did not come easily, or wholeheartedly. It was imposed by necessity, for lack of alternative, upon actors who, within their domestic domain of 'internal' sovereignty insisted on absolutism and non-negotiable coercion. Given the endemic strife for hegemony, the states system would require non-stop dialogue and recurrent shifting and rebalancing—from Utrecht 1713 to, most recently, Paris 1990. In this process, historians generally discern three phases: a first period of dynastic policies in the *ancien régime* (1648–1815), a second phase of congress policies of the Concert that broke down in 1914, finally, the phase of international organization guided by the principle of national self-determination. For three centuries the system checked hegemonic aspirations and curbed anarchy—if amidst serious hiccups. By resolute action and in a purposeful manner diplomats at Westphalia raised the scaffolding of this imposing architecture.

3.2. The Negotiation Process

With hindsight, and from the point of negotiating policy and techniques, the Peace Congress left a great deal to be desired. Negotiating had not been the parties' first option anyway. It had taken them years to reach that point. Propositions made by the Vatican in the 1630s and by the emperor around 1640 had been firmly rejected. Informal talks started in 1641 through Danish mediation. Even so, throughout the protracted negotiations (1644–48), delegates delayed proceedings from sheer opportunism, eagerly awaiting decisive action on the battlefield. Deliberations were suppressed each spring awaiting that season's military campaigns.

Political power-play and blackmail were considered perfectly legitimate ways of applying pressure. Rather than welcoming interdependence delegations stressed differences, preferring competition to cooperation. Vehement differences included bloody encounters of staff. Prestige took precedence over substance. The formal opening was delayed six months on account of *préséance*-issues. Antagonists stood head to head, brandishing sovereignty and honour, not wanting to lose face by the slightest concession. The sheer impossibility of having France, Sweden, and the Vatican share the same conference table imposed two venues: Munster for the Catholic and international issues, Osnabruck for the Protestant parties and the cornered empire.[37] Nor was Westphalia a multilateral conference truly. All talks were bilateral, and most were indirect. At Munster the papal nuncio mediated; in Osnabruck, where parties did not accept papal meddling, Venice procured mediation.

The instruments of mediation and good services were not yet legally defined.[38] Cherishing hidden agendas, the mediators did not exactly exercise scrupulous neu-

---

[37] Cf K Hamilton and R Langhorne (eds) *The Practice of Diplomacy* (Routledge London 1995) 80.
[38] T Princen *Intermediaries in International Conflict* (Princeton University Press Princeton 1992).

trality. Even so, they were not to be envied. France risked complete failure by deliberately insulting Venice and persistently undermining the position of the nuncio on account of Rome's political aspirations.

Proceedings were delayed by the lack of mandate of delegations that had to stick to the letter of their instructions. It left no latitude for compromise and made them entirely dependent on slow, often intercepted communications with their home base. On top came the quarrels within delegations. The noblemen or patricians at their head rarely bothered to enter into the debate, a phenomenon described by Juan de Vera's *El Ambajador* (1620),[39] and willingly left technicalities to their assistants. These were mostly lawyers, who, if luminaries in their profession, lacked political genius and were treated with perfect disdain by their superiors. The composition of the French, Swedish, and Dutch delegations reflected friction and clashing interests at home. The overall atmosphere at the conference breathed mistrust and intrigue. With gifts or female charms considered perfectly acceptable instruments to gain influence, bribe and espionage were in the order of the day.

Negotiations at Westphalia may have been fairly rudimentary, delegates proved themselves veritable masters in the subtle art. Negotiation, to be sure, may aim at dispute resolution, but it may also serve as an effective excuse to postpone unwelcome solutions. The process may mislead by hiding problems or introducing doubts. In the international arena of clashing cultures and traditions, negotiating is by definition an unpredictable process that requires versatility and dexterity. Maximizing profit does not always pay; to accept an immediate small loss may well turn out more profitable in the long run.[40]

An intelligent Dutch observer in French service readily drew his conclusions. In his manual *L'ambassadeur et ses fonctions* (1681), Abraham de Wicquefort called for the separation of politics and diplomacy, and the recruiting of competent professional diplomats with full mandate to make binding decisions.[41]

4. Power Politics

4.1. *Raison d'état*

The lust for power is innate to politics and has many faces. Sixteenth-century Habsburg supremacy was based on intermarriage and succession strategies. Seafaring Portuguese,

---

[39] A History of Diplomacy (n 2) 72.

[40] WFG Mastenbroek *Negotiate* (Basil Blackwell Oxford 1989); FC Iklé *How Nations Negotiate* (Harper New York NY 1964).

[41] A History of Diplomacy (n 2) 83 and 112.

Dutch, and British aspired at colonies to serve their commercial interests. France, the paramount State in Europe after Westphalia, was a continental power. Its calculations were directed at territorial gains.[42] By 1630, in its uphill fight to dismantle the Habsburg conglomerate from justified fear of being surrounded, Catholic Louis XIII, in a critical move, broke the deadlock of a century by crossing the borderlines between confessions and join forces with Lutheran Swedes and Calvinist Dutch. In defiance of papal dogma, the Cardinals Richelieu and Mazarin even found a willing ally in the Ottoman empire. Henceforward, *raison d'état*, and nothing else, dictated French policy. It heralded a new era, which revealed Bourbon aspirations at hegemony. Until 1713 the Bourbons aspired to the continent, henceforth they dreamt of the world.

4.2. 'Heroic' Diplomacy

Styles of diplomacy are determined by political objectives. The French Age emphatically presented the 'heroic' type. As formulated by Rohan in his *De l'interest des princes* (1638) this amounted to 'war by other means'. Hypersensitive to status and honour, it took the slightest concession or penchant to conciliation as token of weakness.

French warrior diplomacy had some distinct success. Never before or after was Europe to such an extent dominated by a single tongue and culture of diplomacy. French replaced Latin as diplomatic language, to hold sway until 1945.[43] Still, from the first, French diplomacy of intimidation evoked resentment. The Dutch Stadholder, William III of Orange, who became King in England, spearheaded resistance from The Hague, 'The Whispering Gallery of Europe'.[44] At Utrecht (1713), the European Alliance rallying against French dominance implemented the Balance of Power mechanism.

Amply discussed in literature—from Philippe Duplessis-Mornay's *Discours* (1584), Paolo Paruta's *Discorsi politici* (1599), and Giovanni Botero's *Relazione* (1605), to Alberico Gentili's *De jure belli* (1612) and Paul de Lisola's *Bouclier d'Etat* (1667)—the concept had been adroitly applied before.[45] Thus 16th-century Venice claimed to balance Valois–Habsburg rivalry. From 1659 Britain reserved for itself the mediating role of 'tongue' of the balance. In 1713 the mechanism was first tested as the Charter of Europe in the cauldron of high politics, and as the 'natural' antidote to power conflict 'in the light of reason'. Hegemonic aspirations were abjured as 'un-European' and 'uncivilized'. Optimism at Utrecht was based on its steadfast belief in man's capacity to steer the international 'machinery' and monitor collective security.[46] The device proved as hazardous in practice as controversial in theory. Critics protested its lack of morality and dynamism. In political reality the equilibrium proved hard to maintain.

---

[42] *Diplomacy* (n 4) 51–4.   [43] ibid 226–33.

[44] *A History of Diplomacy* (n 2) 71.

[45] *The Rise of Modern Diplomacy* (n 8) 149–58.

[46] *A History of Diplomacy* (n 2) 85–9.

4.3. *Préséance* and Prestige[47]

By 1650 inter-state diplomacy had come of age: a veritable *corps diplomatique* had sprung up.[48] Diplomacy had become the adjunct of an aristocratic elite that enjoyed well-defined privileges and agreed on conventions and etiquette. Embassies were prestigious centres that rivalled in hospitality and patronage of the arts. Hierarchy was strict: after Pope, emperor, and heir-apparent, hereditary monarchs preceded elective ones. These in turn were followed by the republics, proudly headed by Venice and the Dutch. On the oceans, British and Dutch navies keenly contested the first salute and lowering of colours. Among envoys similar hierarchy ruled, the title of ambassador being a precious privilege. Career diplomats, mostly lawyers, were found in junior ranks. Consular posts were bestowed on merchants.[49]

'French' diplomacy was all about representation, infinite ceremonial and elaborate protocol. Status was the essence of being. Diplomats emphatically represented monarchs. To *l'état, c'est moi* the most modest envoy embodied *le roi soleil*. An ambassador's entry occasioned public spectacles. Versailles was built to impress. *Préséance*, 'the most delicate article of political faith', was this world's great preoccupation. The signing of treaties, processions, seating orders at banquets, all meetings gave 'just cause' for ceremonial war. A medal was struck to immortalize Louis XIV's victory over Spain in a violent clash of coaches in London, one out of many, but one that counted fifty casualties.[50] To counter preoccupation with *préséance*, at the Peace of Ryswyck (1697) the 'Round Table Conference' was devised. Publications like Selden's *Titles of Honour* (1614), Finet's *Philoxenis* (1656), Howell's *Treatise of Ambassadors* (1664), or De Wicquefort's *L'Ambassadeur et ses fonctions* (1681) attest to this culture.[51] An interesting publication in this context is the report by Johan Nieuhof of the contacts of the *Vereenigde Oostindische Compagnie* (VOC, Dutch East India Company) with China (*Legatio Batavica*, 1656).[52]

4.4. Professionalism on the Rise

After Utrecht (1713) common sense returned. Ceremonial and *préséance* became less obsessive, excuse for rivalry was substituted by the quest for consensus. The art of negotiating was refined, witness François de Callières *De la manière de négocier avec les souverains* (1716) or Antoine Pecquet's *Discours sur l'art de négocier* (1737).[53] Callières (1645–1717), a first-rank diplomat whose signature features on the Peace of

---

[47] *Diplomacy* (n 4) 178–201; *The Rise of Modern Diplomacy* (n 8) 15–20 and 56–68.
[48] *A History of Diplomacy* (n 2) 67–8.
[49] ibid 74 and 115.   [50] ibid 77.   [51] ibid 76.   [52] ibid 67.   [53] ibid 112.

Ryswyck, deemed the European States members of the same republic: before turning to arms, nations should exhaust reason and persuasion. He pressed for career diplomats, insisted on integrity,[54] and advised against a diplomat's interference in internal affairs.

Hesitantly, Callières' call for professionalism was complied with. Novelties reflected the changing perspective and growing technicality: the first boundary treaty illustrated by a map (1718);[55] the compilation of treaty series such as Léonard's French collection (1435–1690), Leibniz' *Codex juris gentium diplomaticus* (1693), or Dumont's impressive European survey (1721).[56] In 1701 in Rome a training centre for diplomats was opened, in 1712 a Paris *Académie politique*. Colbert recruited interpreters, Berlin had its *Kabinettsministerium* (1733). Still, the secrecy of court diplomacy, such as Louis XV's *Secret du Roi* (1745), was not conducive to the idea. Sycophancy counted more than technical expertise.[57]

In a steady process immunities were widened and defined. Bynkershoek's *De foro legatorum* (1721) and Vattel's *Le droit des gens* (1758) attest to this progress. As from 1750 precedence was arranged by seniority. At sea the firing of guns for salute replaced the lowering of colours.[58] Even so, the Vienna *Règlement* (1815) that solved endless riddles came as a great relief.

4.5. The American and French Revolutions

The world of conventional diplomacy was severely upset by the American and French Revolutions. The bid for independence by the British colony (1775–83) was an unprecedented step.[59] Its success transplanted the European State model to the Western hemisphere. Still, American revolt was a rejection of the *ancien régime*, including its diplomacy, in favour of the republican ethos. Jefferson, himself an envoy to France (1801–09), from fear of corruption abjured a diplomatic service.[60]

The French Revolution (1789–1814) was of a different nature altogether.[61] It marked a fundamental change of ideology by a leading European nation in the toppling of a prestigious dynasty. It was a far more radical proposition. The Girondins categorically ruled out relations with other governments, cancelled treaties and abjured all diplomacy as 'secret'. Thermidor Terror (1794), missionary expansionism

---

[54] An evaluation of the aspects of cunning and integrity in theory from O Maggi *De Legato* (1596) to J Cambons *Le Diplomate* (Hachette Paris 1926) in *Diplomacy* (n 4) 106–12.

[55] *The Rise of Modern Diplomacy* (n 8) 97–8.

[56] *A History of Diplomacy* (n 2) 80; *The Rise of Modern Diplomacy* (n 8) 94–6.

[57] *The Rise of Modern Diplomacy* (n 8) 73–80 and 90–1; *A History of Diplomacy* (n 2) 100, 107, and 113.

[58] *The Rise of Modern Diplomacy* (n 8) 68.

[59] *A History of Diplomacy* (n 2) 127–31.

[60] ibid 119.   [61] ibid 131–44.

and strategic opportunism legged up the military. Napoleon, for all his military genius, proved the archetype of the provocative diplomat.[62] His diplomacy was as imperialistic in its bullying as it was dynastic in its nepotism. The turmoil did produce one lasting asset: the nation-state. The concept was widely embraced as a hallmark of identity and cement of cohesion.

5. The Concert of Europe

5.1. The Vienna Congress

After Waterloo, repulsion of war and revolutionary ideology was ubiquitous. At the Vienna Congress (1814–15)—the first truly multinational and perhaps most successful major conference in the history of the Westphalian System—the leading powers 'in the Name of Europe' devised a Concert System of collective security in Tsar Alexander's Holy Alliance (1815).[63] For all its grandiloquence, it was a sensible proposition in view of recent experience. It was conservative in its insistence on order.[64] It was pretentious in guaranteeing stability. It even spoke of arrogance in investing on its *petit comité* the moral authority to monitor the small and deploy forcible intervention. It was also modern in its level-headed acceptance of national differences and in advancing consensus, trust and respect as means to bridge gaps. Yet, critically, Tsar Alexander I, Castlereagh, and Metternich failed to appreciate the durable impact of the revolutionary concept of nationality—and never consulted diplomats.

5.2. The Vienna *Règlement*

A historic moment was the adoption, in an Annex to the Congress Act, of the so-called Vienna *Règlement* (1815).[65] A controversial document, the outcome of months of bargaining, and soon amended by the Aix-la-Chapelle *Protocol* (1818), it marked a first codification of widely diverging national diplomatic custom. It adopted alternation

---

[62] ibid 140–4.

[63] Classical studies are H Nicolson *The Congress of Vienna. A Study in Allied Unity, 1812–1822* (Constable London 1946); P Schroeder *The Transformation of European Politics 1763–1848* (Clarendon Press Oxford 1994).

[64] *A History of Diplomacy* (n 2) 144–50.

[65] Congress of Vienna, Final Act (1815) 64 CTS 453 annex 17; *Diplomacy* (n 4) 31–3; *A History of Diplomacy* (n 2) 153–4.

as procedure in signing treaties. Above all, it comprehensively codified the complex ranking of diplomats, to end centuries of conflict.

The *Règlement* distinguished three classes of agents in order of precedence: ambassadors, envoys and *chargés d'affaires*. The 1818 *Protocol* inserted yet another category, that of minister resident, as third in line. The rank of ambassador ('extraordinary and plenipotentiary') was strictly reserved for agents between the Great Powers. Envoys, the second rank, also with plenipotentiary powers, headed missions in smaller countries. This was the rank allotted to the majority of diplomats until the Second World War. With the adoption of the principle of equality of States in the UN Charter (1945), most legations were upgraded to embassies. As a consequence, as of 1945, both the second and third ranks virtually eclipsed. The *Règlement* assigned the highest precedence and the title of dean (*doyen*) to the most senior diplomat within the *corps diplomatique*, as determined by date of entrance or presentation of credentials. In Roman Catholic States this role was reserved for the papal nuncio.

5.3. Merchant Diplomacy

The 'long' 19th century (1815–1919) is often presented as the classical period of diplomacy.[66] Its great protagonist in the international arena was Britain. British policy changed diplomacy dramatically. It identified its interest with calm and its profit with optimizing conditions for commerce. It steered a businesslike *laissez faire* policy of adroit bargaining and fair dealing, open to compromise and conciliation. If mistaken for weakness by inveterate 'heroic' diplomats at Berlin's Wilhelmstrasse, it proved infinitely more effective than French imperialism. Not accidentally, the century saw long spans of peace, only briefly stirred by the Crimean War (1853–56) and the Franco-Prussian War (1870–71).

The Great Powers' insistence on the strictest maintenance of the balance within Europe made powers try their luck at power display outside Europe. Diplomacy followed the tracks of colonialism, still accelerated by industrialization. A striking feature of 19th-century diplomacy, therefore, was its global expansion and cultural diversification. Time and distance have always been crucial to diplomacy.[67] The challenges offered by the Digital Age recall those posed by printing press in the 15th century, journals in the 18th, telegraph, steamer, and railway in the 19th, or aircraft in the mid-20th century. In the 19th century, Western diplomatic customs spread worldwide. At first, this was a fairly unilateral process.[68] With time, growing sensitivity to

---

[66] Seen from the Western perspective, that is. *A History of Diplomacy* (n 2) 152.

[67] ibid 95–8 on early European conditions.

[68] ibid 158. On the varying response in China, Japan and Korea see A Eyffinger 'Caught between Tradition and Modernity; East Asia at The Hague Peace Conferences' (2008) 1 Journal of East Asian and International Law 1–48.

non-Western cultures rendered contacts reciprocal. Through standardized training, expert diplomats for specific regions emerged.

5.4. The Balance Questioned

Modernity did not only bring blessings to diplomacy. Quite the contrary: it seriously affected the social fabric and prompted calls for reform. 'Vienna' intended to simplify the complex balance by creating a two-tiered system. By 1815, however, the credibility of the balance as such was seriously undermined. Critics dismissed it as at odds with political reality and as pretext for forceful intervention. Ideologically the concept was challenged from many quarters.[69] Each in its way contributed to the uprooting of *ancien régime* society.

A first challenge voiced the soul of British tradition: the Free Trade ideology of Cobden and Bentham. British Liberals dismissed the balance as a delusion of war-loving monarchs, and discredited diplomacy's secrecy and aristocratic privilege. As Montesquieu before, they relied on the exchange of goods and intellect as incentives to harmony between nations. To have no foreign policy was the best of policies.

On the Continent, more utopian and radical theories verified history with class struggle. They insisted on change in the overthrow of balance, national boundaries and diplomacy alike. In concurring mainstreams of socialism, communism, and anarchism, and whether inspired by Bebel, Marx, or Bakunin, this 'internationalism' preached the revolution of the masses, the building blocks of society.

This second, 'internationalist' ideology clashed with a third one, every inch as radical, which intriguingly had far greater appeal to the masses: nationalism. Its ideologist, Hegel, identified the Family of Fatherlands with the fulfilment of Europe's destiny to implement world peace. Spread by missionaries like Mazzini and Von Treitschke, this ideology radicalized public opinion.[70] Mass media demanded democracy and the breakup of an elitist world of secrecy.[71]

5.5. The Supranational Order

And there was more. In Waterloo also lay the roots of the supranational order. In massive reaction to the unprecedented onslaught a peace movement emerged worldwide. Religious and moral concerns in the Mennonite and Quaker traditions merged with utilitarian concepts of liberal sociology and Kantian speculation. Pacifism contested heavy taxation, demanded disarmament and advocated arbitration. It

[69] *The Rise of Modern Diplomacy* (n 8) 189–96.
[70] ibid 136–41.   [71] ibid 142–8.

submitted propositions for leagues, codes, and tribunals, actuating a theoretical quest of centuries. Overkill well beyond the 'necessities of war' at Balaklava and Gettysburg prompted Lieber Code (1863), and the Red Cross (1864), and Petersburg (1868) Conventions. Within two decades, the 'Hague' and 'Geneva' branches of humanitarian law were developed: the temperance of war and the care for its victims. In 1874, at Brussels, a first, abortive attempt was made at codification of war on land.

In this process, the pioneering research of two think tanks of legal reform, the *Institut de droit international* and the International Law Association, (both founded in 1873) was pivotal. For all raving nationalism, these bodies claimed, the true spirit of the age was *l'esprit d'internationalité*. Humanity went from independence to interdependence, from patriotism to international solidarity. If nationalism served kings and dynasties, internationalism served peoples and democracy; if the first caused polarization, the second inspired cooperation; if the one meant war and barracks, the other peace and wealth. The days of cabinet wars and backroom diplomacy were over. The shared values of all peoples were to be embedded in normative codes of universal appliance expressing humanity's collective conscience. It took a new cataclysm for this ideal to be institutionalized in the League of Nations.

5.6. The Erosion of a Culture

An immediate, dramatic effect of socio-political change was the erosion of conventional diplomatic culture. Foreign affairs had of old been the prerogative of monarchs. Its officials and diplomats were recruited from the royal entourage, as was felt perfectly justified. Patronage warranted family pedigrees of diplomats all over Europe, such as the Hertslets, Nelidovs or Cambons.[72] The diplomatic establishment constituted an international class with definite group consciousness. Raised at Eton, the Vienna *Theresianum*, or the Petersburg Imperial *Lycée*, and trained in reputed university corps like the Heidelberg *Saxoborussians*, these diplomats were steeped in the world of protocol and etiquette, dress codes, proper comportment—and art collecting.[73] German-speaking diplomacy thrived on finesses of lineage within *Uradel* and *Briefadel*. It was a world in which the creation of international crisis after mid-July, the Spa season, was considered 'not done'.

For all its conventionalisms, this *corps diplomatique* breathed distinct cosmopolitanism in its sophisticated linguistic and social fluency. Recently historians have highlighted the cultural connotations of this particular phase of diplomacy.[74] The

---

[72] ibid 120.

[73] A tradition of long standing. *A History of Diplomacy* (n 2) 70.

[74] TG Otte '"Outdoor Relief for the Aristocracy"? European Nobility and Diplomacy, 1850–1914' in M Mösslang and T Riotte (eds) *The Diplomats' World. A Cultural History of Diplomacy, 1815–1914* (OUP Oxford 2008) 23–57.

shocking entrance of French Republican 'bourgeois' diplomats after 1870 tore this fabric apart. Their commercial links and interests raised suspicion of corruption in this world of—otherwise economically surprisingly well-informed—noblemen.

Inside attempts at streamlining services did not bring much.[75] In the end, external pressure for reform and parliamentary control (as complied with in the publication of Blue Books)[76] eroded this natural habitat and prerogative of the aristocracy. By 1890, with industrialization and capitalism undermining land-based wealth, this outdated but moderate world gave in to middle-class pressure. In expanding Foreign Offices a new class of expert military, naval, economic and cultural *attachés* made its entrance.[77] The expert bureaucrat replaced the gentleman amateur. It also opened the floodgates to mass politics and frenzied nationalism that would steer Europe towards the abyss.

5.7. The Hague Peace Conferences[78]

The Hague Peace Conferences of 1899 and 1907 epitomized the 19th-century diplomatic legacy. They encapsulated all earlier efforts towards law codification, humanitarianism, and the implementation of courts and tribunals. It is trite to downgrade these encounters on account of their few palpable results. For this, there were many reasons, notably the overall climate of distrust that paralyzed European politics after 1870. Yet, the conferences stand out as the first world summits of 'civilized' nations (25 in 1899, 44 in 1907 when the Latin-American republics attended) on the vexing political issues of the day. They tell of a global clash of cultures and ideologies, of representatives of absolutist regimes who felt out of their depth in democratic debate, of politicians, diplomats, military men, and legal luminaries uncomfortably crossing swords.

The gaps proved far too wide to be bridged overnight: reactionary Austrian diplomats dismissed lawyers as mere technicians. American and British naval delegates perfectly ridiculed humanitarian concepts. German lawyers summarily dismissed compulsory jurisdiction. Yet after three months of splendid isolation in The Hague woods, these 'Hundred Chosen' agreed on the profit reaped from personal encounters and prolonged talks—and easily decided on a sequel. They found out that these meetings, in order to bear fruit, required careful preparation—and acted upon it. In

---

[75] *The Rise of Modern Diplomacy* (n 8) 110–28.   [76] ibid 114.

[77] ibid 129–36; *A History of Diplomacy* (n 2) 171–2.

[78] J Dülffer *Regeln gegen den Krieg? Die Haager Friedens-Konferenzen 1899 und 1907 in der internationalen Politik* (Ullstein Berlin 1981); A Eyffinger *The 1899 Hague Peace Conference:'The Parliament of Man, the Federation of the World'* (Kluwer Dordrecht 1999); A Eyffinger *The 1907 Hague Peace Conference: 'The Conscience of the Civilized World'* (Judicap The Hague 2007).

their futile efforts to reach agreement, they noted that the unanimity principle posed a serious obstacle: a single minor power could undo weeks of painstaking labour. In trying to launch a world court they were baffled by the recalcitrant dilemma of representation and election. Legal luminaries stood head to head over whether arbitration was the instrument of peace or of justice. After bitter fights between Great Powers and small, old Powers and new, progress surrendered to the idol of State sovereignty. Yet one agreed on a bottom-line consensus in endorsing the 'rule of the principles of the law of nations, as they result from the usages established among civilized peoples, from the laws of humanity, and the dictates of the public conscience'.[79] The accumulated experience of success and setback paid off in the institutionalization of the conference system and international organization after the cataclysm. Intellectually speaking, at The Hague the international era was born.

6. New Diplomacy and the League

6.1. The Incompatibility of the Old and New Order

Versailles hailed a new epoch of diplomacy, heralded by the world's new leading nation. Dismissing 'old diplomacy', US President Wilson, in his Fourteen Points speech (1918), championed all the assets of Anglo-Saxon liberal internationalism.[80] In his moral, legalistic approach Wilson advocated a League of Nations, 'open covenants openly arrived at', disarmament, and nationality as criterion for State sovereignty. The League's showpieces were the innovative paradigm of collective security, the world court, and the device of (economic) sanctions to outlaw aggressors. The idol of state sovereignty remained unimpaired, yet the binding force of treaties was conditioned by their registration and publication by the League Secretariat (which incidentally incited secret protocols and side letters). Wilson's brainchild emphatically aspired at moral guidance of its member-States.[81]

---

[79] Cf the preamble of the Convention (IV) Respecting the Laws and Customs of War on Land and its Annex: Regulation concerning the Laws and Customs of War on Land (signed 18 October 1907, entered into force 26 January 1910) (1910) 187 CTS 227 ('1907 Hague Convention IV').

[80] G Kennan *American Diplomacy* (University Chicago Press Chicago 1984); KA Clements *The Presidency of Woodrow Wilson* (University Press Kansas State Lawrence Kansas 1992); MW Janis *America and the Law of Nations 1776–1939* (OUP Oxford 2010) 167–75. On the pitfalls of 'public diplomacy' see *Diplomacy* (n 4) 84–103; *A History of Diplomacy* (n 2) 188–9.

[81] Wartime propositions for a league in *The Rise of Modern Diplomacy* (n 8) 280–7.

It is trite to put down the failure of the League to Axis Powers and Communism, to leftovers of Versailles, reparation claims, economic depression, and failing financial markets.[82] Clearly, Wilson's idealism was lost on the totalitarian regimes of communism, Fascism, and Nazism. In amoral ideology they willfully headed for conflict, as their cynical reply to the idealists' appeasement policy in the late 1930s pointed out.[83]

Still, half-heartedness of self-focused democracies likewise affected the credibility and stability of the supranational order. Voting down Wilson's proposition, the US Senate left the historic experiment fatally crippled. It entrusted its interests to Kellogg–Briand Pact (1928) and Saavedra Lamas Treaty (1933), relying on Britain's stewardship of the League. The UK, in two minds and while paying lip-service to Wilson's ideal, never lost sight of the balance, as Locarno (1925) amply demonstrated. Rather than relying on collective security, it entrusted its naval interests to a bilateral treaty with France, thereby obliging French military dominance on the Continent (1928). France, in turn, built its own *cordon sanitaire* against Germany.

The outcome was a double circuit of parallel and overlapping tracks and institutions.[84] The League Council watered down to a political showcase for prime ministers of the Great Powers. Ideological issues were left to the Assembly of small fry that met once a year. Exploiting the Council's antagonism, representatives of smaller nations in the Assembly played the gallery to optimize media exposure. The League was held hostage by the keen rivalry of States within its respective organs. The Secretary-General had his share of in-fighting with nationally recruited officials. A major handicap from the first, therefore, was the *incompatibilité d'humeurs* of the old and the new order.

6.2. The Inevitable Failure

Still, with the coming of the League, diplomacy would never be the same. In the inflammable political climate nations soon acknowledged the organization's mediating role. With the rise of technical commissions and the proliferation of legal, social and administrative organs a new class of professional experts in Geneva replaced the old diplomat-in-disrepute. Within twenty years, the experience with international bureaucracy and multilateral conference techniques grew impressively. The codification of international law progressed by leaps and bounces. The merits of the League

---

[82] *A History of Diplomacy* (n 2) 201–4.
[83] ibid 192–4.
[84] J Kaufmann *Conference Diplomacy* (Macmillan London 1996).

in the field of humanitarian law, concerning mandates, refugees, and minorities, were impressive by all standards.

The experiment of the League was as imperative as it failure was inevitable. It collapsed from lack of political will and identification with an overarching common interest. Even so, there never was a way back. Substantial ideological progress was made in 1945 when the UN substituted non-committal co-existence with the positive duty for cooperation, and made universal human rights prevail over State sovereignty. This formula turned its Charter into a constitution of mankind—to overrule Westphalia.

6.3. Summit Diplomacy

For all its pros and cons, new diplomacy was there to stay. Wilson's talks with Clémenceau, Lloyd George, and Orlando opened the era of what Winston Churchill in 1950 called summit diplomacy. The openness and mandate political leaders brought to the conference table accelerated negotiating processes and broke bureaucratic stalemates.

Over the past century, summit diplomacy has become the plaything of politicians. The concept, otherwise, has a long tradition, prior to, and unaffected by sedentary representation. Even so, it has always been controversial. Early commentators like De Commines (1559)[85] and Callières (1716) succinctly pointed out the risks of replacing circumspect diplomats by passionate politicians.

Legendary summits like that of Francis I and Henry VIII on the Field of the Cloth of Gold (1520) were presumably of a foremost ceremonial nature.[86] Far less innocent, however, was the secret treaty concluded by Wilhelm II and Nicholas II on the Tsar's yacht off Björkoe in 1905. Dictators acting as their own ambassadors often produced devastating results: Napoleon, Stalin, and Hitler are pertinent cases in point. Hitler's meetings with Mussolini and Franco were mere propaganda shams. Still, democratic leaders such as Lloyd George and Churchill likewise favoured personal dialogue, perhaps somewhat overrating the 'personal chemistry' and the psychological impact of ceremonial and prestige as incentives to commitment.

Summits profited much from technological progress, air travel and mass media. Yet external influence put aside, its popularity reflects the pretensions of politicians vis-à-vis diplomats—and is eroding a time-honoured profession. Summits involve risks: history tells painful stories of misunderstanding and failure due to linguistic

---

[85] J Bastin (ed) *Les mémoires de Philippe de Commynes* (Bruxelles 1944).
[86] *The Rise of Modern Diplomacy* (n 8) 10; *A History of Diplomacy* (n 2) 24 and 53.

shortcomings or debonair neglect of dossiers.[87] Apprehension to lose face leads to vague, non-committal *communiqués*. The volatility of public opinion has wrecked many careers. Yet politicians become easily addicted to media hype, for electoral gain or to swing political barometers.

The four wartime meetings of Allied Leaders to ward off crisis did much to boost public confidence. Still, Stalin made sure the venues were well within the Soviet sphere of influence.[88] Politicians as a rule chose their places of venue with care. Border-rivers have a long history in diplomatic encounter. The Peace of the Pyrenees (1659) between France and Spain was concluded in a pavilion on a border-island in a river featuring separate bridges. Napoleon and Alexander I famously met on a raft in Niemen River near Tilsen (1807).[89] Capitals of small, neutral nations, like Switzerland, Belgium, or Norway lend their repute for hosting summits from this consideration. The current reputation of The Hague as 'judicial capital' harks back to the peace conferences. Its choice, however, was a last-minute move, actuated by the deadlock between the Great Powers that ruled out major capitals, and the unavailability, for varying reasons, of Geneva, Brussels, and Oslo.

7. The Codification of Custom

In its Cambridge Regulation (1895) the *Institut* attained a first, tentative codification of diplomatic tradition. Subsequent benchmarks were the regional Havana Convention (1928) of the Pan-American Union and a Draft Convention drawn up in 1932 by the Harvard Research Project. In 1954 the International Law Commission resumed these efforts. From its endeavours generated the pivotal Vienna Conventions on Diplomatic Relations (1961) and on Consular Relations (1963).[90] Both were eminently timely undertakings given the multiplication of young sovereign States that did not boast diplomatic expertise. Encompassing the world's rich, multifaceted tradition the 1961 Convention on Diplomatic Relations stands out as a gem of legal genius and as one of the most successful accomplishments of codification in the UN Era.[91] It

---

[87] R Cohen *Negotiating Across Cultures: Communication Obstacles in International Diplomacy* (US Institute of Peace Washington DC 1997).

[88] *A History of Diplomacy* (n 2) 209.

[89] *The Rise of Modern Diplomacy* (n 8) 10 for more instances.

[90] Vienna Convention on Consular Relations (signed 24 April 1963, entered into force 19 March 1967) 596 UNTS 261.

[91] E Denza *Diplomatic Law: Commentary on the Vienna Convention on Diplomatic Relations* (3rd edn OUP Oxford 2008); M Hardy *Modern Diplomatic Law* (Manchester University Press Manchester 1968);

eminently combines existing practice with a progressive development of the law on the basis of generally accepted legal principles. As the convention states (article 2), there is no 'right' of legation. Diplomatic relations take place by mutual consent: reciprocity is a cardinal feature of tradition.[92] Formal prerequisite is mutual recognition—from which otherwise diplomatic relations do not follow automatically. Consent implies the licence by the receiving State to have the sending State execute State functions on its territory, by granting it certain privileges and immunities. These functions include representation, the protection of the mission State's interests, negotiating, information gathering, and the promotion of friendly relations (article 3). The receiving State's paramount duty is the adequate protection of the mission's staff (article 1).

Prerequisite to the sending of the head of mission is this official's acceptance by the receiving State, its *agrément* and accreditation. Acceptance is at the discretion of the receiving State, which is under no obligation to motivate refusal of a *persona non grata* (article 4). The same holds for termination procedures: the sending State may notify the receiving State of an official's leave. The host State may without further substantiation notify the sending State its staff member is no longer welcome.

The receiving State pledges not just to grant the mission facilities required for its functioning (within the restrictions of its national security, article 25), but to the best of its abilities protect its premises (article 30) from external interference, intrusion, damage, or impairment of its dignity. This includes immunity from the search of premises or means of transport (article 22) and extends to the mission's archives and correspondence—the diplomatic bag shall not be opened or detained (article 27)—and to the agent's private files (article 31).

The convention warrants the personal inviolability of the diplomatic agent (article 29), who shall be treated with due respect, not be liable to arrest or detention and be duly protected from attack. Besides, diplomatic agents enjoy immunity from jurisdiction of local courts, a stipulation that is qualified by their duty to respect the receiving State's laws and regulations (article 41). They shall enjoy immunity from criminal jurisdiction (article 31): found guilty of criminal offence they may be declared unwelcome. The same applies to civil and administrative jurisdiction: here immunity is qualified, but never with respect to official acts. Furthermore, agents are exempt from dues, taxes (articles 23, 34), and custom duties (article 37), or from giving evidence in court (article 31).

Immunities are enjoyed from the moment the agent enters the receiving State or his appointment is notified to its foreign office, to expire upon leave (article 39).

I Brownlie *Principles of Public International Law* (7th edn OUP Oxford 2008) ch 17; GV McClanahan *Diplomatic Immunity, Principles, Practices, Problems* (Hurst London 1989).

92 *A History of Diplomacy* (n 2) 68–9.

Termination of a mission may follow recall, the outbreak of war between the States, or a State's extinction (article 39).

8. Conclusion

The 1961 Vienna Convention epitomizes the intellectual harvest of millennia of troubled human intercourse. More apposite, it embodies the diplomatic legacy of the Westphalian Era and of half a millennium of State practice. In Vienna, therefore, our narrative finds its natural ending. At the dawn of a new era of infinite challenge and stunning complexity, the convention's acclaim world-wide suggests it may serve as anchor for wandering humanity. In its restraint and tentative guidance it is a beacon of wisdom. Yet none of this can close our eyes to its limitations in dealing with contemporary problems. Many other forms of diplomacy await codification. As incidents over the past fifty years suggest, diplomacy itself is losing some of its aura of immunity. The symbolism of embassies is evaporating, the taboo being broken. There is, in short, ample ground for concern about the future of the discipline. Still, precisely its history presents comfort, more than any convention can. For one thing, history definitely belies diplomacy's reputation of stubborn conservatism. Down the centuries, in coping with perplexing reality, the discipline has shown remarkable resilience and flexibility. And to top it all, the diplomat himself stands out as the true chameleon.

Recommended Reading

Anderson, Mathew S *The Rise of Modern Diplomacy, 1450–1919* (Longman London 1993).

Black, Jeremy *A History of Diplomacy* (Reaktion London 2010).

Bull, Hedley *The Anarchical Society. A Study of Order in World Politics* (2nd edn Basingstoke Macmillan London 1977).

Denza, Eileen *Diplomatic Law: Commentary on the Vienna Convention on Diplomatic Relations* (3rd edn OUP Oxford 2008).

Grewe, Wilhelm G *The Epochs of International Law* (De Gruyter Berlin 2000).

Hamilton, Keith and Richard Langthorne *The Practice of Diplomacy: Its Evolution, Theory and Administration* (Routledge London 1995).

Holsti, Kalevi J *Peace and War; Armed Conflicts and International Order 1648–1948* (CUP Cambridge 1991).

Koskenniemi, Martti *The Gentle Civilizer of Nations. The Rise and Fall of International Law 1870–1960* (CUP Cambridge 2002).

Lauren, Paul G (ed) *Diplomacy: New Approaches in History, Theory, and Policy* (Collier Macmillan London 1980).

Mattingly, Garrett *Renaissance Diplomacy* (Cape London 1970).

Morgenthau, Hans *Politics Among Nations: The Struggle for Power and Peace* (Brief edn McGraw-Hill New York 1967).

Mowat, Robert B *A History of European Diplomacy, 1815–1914* (Arnold London 1927).

Nicolson, Harold *Diplomacy* (OUP Oxford 1939 reprinted 1963).

Roberts, Ivor (ed) *Satow's Guide to Diplomatic Practice* (6th edn OUP Oxford 2009).

Sheehan, Michael *The Balance of Power: History and Theory* (Routledge London 2000).

Visscher, Charles de *Théories et réalités en droit international public* (Pedone Paris 1953).

Watson, Adam *The Evolution of International Society* (Routledge London 1992).

CHAPTER 35

DISCOVERY, CONQUEST, AND OCCUPATION OF TERRITORY

ANDREW FITZMAURICE

1. INTRODUCTION

EUROPEANS employed a spectrum of legal arguments to justify empire and colonization over the 500 years from the first voyage of Columbus to the collapse of empire in the 20th century. There was a remarkable stability in these doctrines over those 500 years, even while they were subjected to ceaseless reinterpretation. The dominant doctrines were discovery, conquest, cession, and occupation. Publicists and princes frequently appealed to a right of discovery but that argument was rarely taken seriously by jurists. Occupation and cession were the most potent of these legal arguments. Colonial titles were usually gained through conquest, but conquest was not popular as a legal argument in part because it too readily recalled the Spanish Black Legend of the conquest of the Aztecs and Incas but also because occupation and treaty were particularly suited to agricultural colonization. The reality of conquest was clothed in the more acceptable language of peaceful occupation. There was a significant gap, therefore, between the language of the law of nations and the practice of States. On matters of empire, international law appeared to be more a system of rhetoric than a system of justice. The exception to this rhetorical role, however, was when the law of nations and international law were employed to oppose European conquests. Following the rise of post-colonial studies in the past thirty years, historians have sought to show how international law was complicit in the extension of European empires.[1] They have, as a consequence, tended to present critiques of empire as rhetorical sanitization and thus as further justification of empire. The argument of occupation was frequently employed, however, to state that the land of non-European peoples was already occupied and could not justifiably be seized either by conquest or occupation. The conventions of international law and the law of nations were thus tools which could be turned to a number of different and sometimes conflicting ends.

2. DISCOVERY

The 'doctrine of discovery' may be a useful shorthand when applied to the justifications of empire employed by States, but it is misleading if applied to the history of the law of nations which has largely been opposed to the principle of discovery.[2] Princes, of course, claimed rights to territory on the basis of prior discovery from the voyages of Columbus right through to the 19th century. But jurists were generally sceptical of these claims. The Spanish based their claim to the whole West coast of the Americas on the right of discovery recognized in the Papal Bull of 1494. Even publicists of rival powers would sometimes recognize these claims. The great English compiler of voyage accounts, Samuel Purchas, rejected the papal donation but accepted the legitimacy of the Spanish discovery:

[I] question not the right of the Spanish Crowne in those parts... The Castilian Industry I honour (as appears in the former relations) their Right may, for that which is actually in their Possession, without this Bull, plead Discoverie even before this [that is, the Donation of Alexander] was written.[3]

---

[1] See eg A Anghie *Imperialism, Sovereignty and the Making of International Law* (CUP Cambridge 2005); M Koskenniemi *The Gentle Civilizer of Nations. The Rise and Fall of International Law 1870–1960* (CUP Cambridge 2001); RA Williams *The American Indian in Western Legal Thought* (OUP Oxford 1990).

[2] For legal historians' use of the concept of the 'doctrine of discovery', see eg *The American Indian* (n 1) 325; L Behrendt, RJ Miller, and T Lindberg (eds) *Discovering Indigenous Lands: The Doctrine of Discovery in the English Colonies* (OUP Oxford 2010).

[3] S Purchas *Hakluytus posthumus or Purchas his Pilgrimes* (London 1625) vol 1, book 2, ch 1, at 20.

Writers on the law of nations, however, cast doubts on both the legitimacy of the donation and title based upon discovery, beginning with the great Spanish theologian Francesco de Vitoria.[4] Vitoria wrote 'On the American Indians' to assess the claims that the conquistadors had put forward to justify their conquests. In response to the claim that the pope was 'empowered to constitute the kings of Spain as kings and lords of those lands', Vitoria argued that he had 'no temporal power over these barbarians, or any other unbelievers'.[5] He then immediately turned to the question of discovery. For Vitoria the 'Third unjust title' was 'that possession of these countries was by right of discovery'. 'The title by right of discovery', he argued, 'was the only title alleged in the beginning, and it was with this pretext alone that Columbus of Genoa first set sail'.[6] He proceeded to argue that this title seemed just because '[a]ll things which are unoccupied or deserted become the property of the of the occupier by natural law and the law of nations' and the Spaniards 'were the first to discover and occupy these countries'. In his usual dialectical fashion, he concluded: 'But on the other hand, against this third title, we need not argue long' because 'the barbarians possessed true public and private dominion' so that 'the goods in question here had an owner'.[7] Subsequent jurists, opposed occupation to discovery. Vitoria, by contrast, virtually equated the two. The title by discovery (*inventio*) appeared right, he argued, because occupation (*occupatio*) gives title. Vitoria was not so much opposing the argument of discovery in the justification of title as opposing the idea that the Americas remained undiscovered when there were people living there clearly in possession of their goods and affairs. In Vitoria's understanding of the *ius gentium*, therefore, discovery was a legitimate basis to title but one could not claim a right of discovery in a land that was already occupied by another people.

When we turn to Grotius' understanding of the law of nations, on the other hand, we find a deep scepticism concerning the idea that rights could be based upon discovery and this scepticism was to endure through the law of nations and international law into the 20th and 21st centuries.[8] Grotius distinguished between the arguments of discovery and occupation and opposed discovery with the right of occupation. In his writings on the East Indies, Grotius demolished each of the Portuguese and Spanish claims to *dominium* and *imperium* in the Indies, devoting a chapter to each claim: first, the claim to dominion based upon discovery, then by the 'pope's gift', then 'by title of war' or conquest, and finally by religion. In response to the claim to 'title by invention', or discovery, Grotius followed Vitoria's reasoning that the 'Indians' 'have, and always had, their kings, their commonwealth, their laws, and their liberties': that

---

[4] See the contribution by A Brett 'Francisco de Vitoria (1483–1546) and Francisco Suárez (1548–1617)' in this volume.

[5] F de Vitoria 'On the American Indians' in F de Vitoria *Political Writings* (A Pagden and J Lawrance eds) (CUP Cambridge 1991) 231–92 at 262.

[6] ibid 264.

[7] ibid 265.

[8] See the contribution by P Haggenmacher 'Hugo Grotius (1583–1645)' in this volume.

is, lawful society was already constituted in a manner demonstrating that the 'Indians' understood the operation of natural law.[9] But he then extended Vitoria's analysis, and departed from it, arguing that discovery never provides title 'for to find [that is, possess] is not to see a thing with the eyes but to lay hold of it with the hands'.[10] By introducing the distinction between seeing something and taking hold of it with the hands, Grotius opened up the distinction between discovery as seeing, and occupation, taking hold of it. He concluded: 'Vitoria therefore rightly saith that the Spaniards got no more authority over the Indians for this cause than the Indians had over the Spaniards if any of them had come formerly into Spain.'[11]

Grotius established this distinction between discovery and occupation precisely for the purpose of combating the huge claims of the Spanish empire. He understood that recognition of the right of discovery in the law of nations would impede rather than facilitate European colonization. To permit European powers to claim sovereignty, by right of discovery, over large areas of territory which they did not exploit would dramatically reduce the territory that could be exploited by other powers. The right of discovery was an impediment to empire and its critics recognized this problem over a number of centuries (although it does not follow that every critic of the right of discovery was an apologist for colonization). Grotius' distinction between discovery and occupation was seminal to these critiques. Pufendorf, for example, echoed Grotius, arguing 'the bare seeing a thing, or the knowing where it is, is not judged a sufficient Title of Possession', although Pufendorf, as we shall see, widened the gap by applying an even more stringent test for title by occupation than a mere taking of things with the hands.[12]

The distinction between discovery and occupation entered the practice of colonizers at the same time it was being made by jurists. Samuel Wharton argued that occupation and cession were the only legitimate titles to land. Wharton was a leader of the Suffering Traders, a group of Pennsylvania land speculators between the Seven Years War and the American Revolution. He claimed that only Native Americans had legitimate titles to land, through occupation, and these titles had been purchased by the land speculators. It was, accordingly, important for Wharton that the claims of European sovereigns to American land had to be diminished. Discovery of the lands by European princes, he claimed, conferred no title, 'as all civilians, &c. agree'.[13] Wharton understood that to base the Crown's rights upon discovery would impede further colonization (and indeed that was precisely the Crown's intention in the Declaration

---

[9] H Grotius *The Free Sea: With W Welwod's Critique and Grotius's Reply* (D Armitage ed and R Hakluyt trans) (Liberty Fund Indianapolis 2004) 13–15.

[10] ibid 13.

[11] ibid 15.

[12] S Pufendorf *De jure naturae et gentium libri octo* (CH Oldfather and WA Oldfather trans) (OUP Oxford 1934) vol 2, at 391.; see furthermore the contribution by K Haakonssen 'Samuel Pufendorf (1632–1694)' in this volume.

[13] S Wharton *Plain Facts* (Printed and sold by R Aitken Philadelphia 1781) at 10.

of 1763). His fears were well founded. When in 1823 Chief Justice Marshall based the sovereignty of the United States of America upon the right of discovery and conquest he did so in order to rule that private citizens could not purchase land off Native Americans.

The distinction between discovery and occupation was perpetuated by Emerich de Vattel.[14] Vattel, however, conceded a minor role for discovery as a first step in the creation of title, and in this sense he retreated from the absolute scepticism expressed by Grotius and Pufendorf. Vattel agreed that it was not possible for a nation to claim right by discovery if it does not occupy. He accepted, however, that discovery could give a preliminary claim to exclude other claimants from a territory if it is followed by occupation. The title of discovery, he wrote, 'has been commonly respected, provided it was soon after followed by a real possession'. For Vattel a real possession meant cultivation. He warned, however, that a country must not attempt to use this right of discovery to appropriate to itself that 'which it does not really occupy, and in this manner reserve to itself much more than it is able to people or cultivate'.[15]

Vattel was followed by a number of 18th- and 19th-century philosophers and jurists in the minor role he allowed to discovery in the creation of title. While discussing colonization, Adam Ferguson conceded that, if nations agreed to the principles amongst themselves, various kinds of symbols and so-called rights of discovery could be treated as a form of occupation in the short term when claiming new territories. He added, however, that no such agreement is sufficient to 'exclude' the rights of 'any stranger who is not a party' to the convention, 'much less a plea sufficient to deprive the native, however rude or barbarous, of the inheritance of possession to which he is born'. He argued that such symbolic acts and discoveries cannot, therefore, be justified 'either from the principle of occupancy, or the principle of labour'.[16]

Nineteenth-century jurists in international law were largely divided between Grotius and Vattel in their discussions of discovery: that is, between those who were sceptical that discovery conferred any rights at all on the discoverer, and those who acknowledged a minor role for discovery as the first step in occupation. Both natural law, with its recognition of occupation, and positivism with its acknowledgement of facts, mitigated against the idea that acts of discovery, and their associated symbolism, could hold an important status in law. German civil lawyers in the first half of the 19th century were sceptical of discovery. These jurists included Georg Friedrich von Martens (1756–1821), Johann Ludwig Klüber (1762–1837) and Auguste Wilhelm Heffter (1796–1880). Martens, one of the great codifiers of the law of nations, wrote that '[t]he simple fact of having been the first to discover or visit an island, etc., subsequently abandoned, would seem insufficient [to establish title], as all nations acknowledge.' 'Crosses, plinths and inscriptions', he added, do not suffice for the

---

[14] See the contribution by E Jouannet 'Emer De Vattel (1714–1767)' in this volume.
[15] E de Vattel *The Law of Nations* (S & E Butler Northampton MA 1805) at 159.
[16] A Ferguson *Principles of Moral and Political Science* (Edinburgh 1792) vol 2, at 212.

acquisition or preservation of property in a country where 'we do not cultivate'.[17] Within the *Vormärz* historical school of public law, Klüber agreed, arguing that 'discovery ... will not suffice'.[18] He associated the idea with the long-discredited Papal donation. Heffter, professor of law at Bonn, Halle, and Berlin, observed that 'simple declarations and uncertain signs of a projected appropriation' could not be 'regarded as a valid title, albeit that the practice of nations sometimes acknowledges similar measures'.[19]

Such acknowledgement could also come from jurists. Writing in 1846, the British civil lawyer and international jurist, Sir Travers Twiss, acknowledged that discovery '[i]s not recognized in the Roman law, nor has it a place in the systems of Grotius or Puffendorff.' But, according to Twiss, '[a]mong the acts which are accessorial to occupation, the chief is Discovery. The title, however, which results from discovery, is only an imperfect title.'[20] The context within which Twiss made this concession was the dispute over the Oregon territory in the American north-west, where Russia, Britain, and the United States competed for sovereignty over the territory from the latitude 51° north to 65° north. In the same year that Twiss wrote, Daniel Dickinson, Senator for New York, acknowledged a similar place for discovery in a speech on the Oregon dispute to the United States Senate. Dickinson paraphrased the Monroe Doctrine when he declared that: 'But, sir, this is not a mere struggle for the Oregon ... it is a contest between two great systems—between monarchy and freedom—between the darkness of the Old World and the sunlight of the New—between the mines and manufactories of Europe and the fertile fields of the distant West.'[21] Ironically, the United States based part of its argument upon the Spanish claims to the right of discovery of the west coast of America north of 42° which passed to the US by virtue of the Adams-Onís treaty of 22 February 1819. They also claimed rights based upon the exploits of American explorers and merchants in the Oregon in the late 18th and early 19th centuries. Thus Dickinson was able to argue: 'The first discovery ... carries with it all the advantages of a perfect discovery. Though occupation should follow, it need not immediately succeed discovery. But there must be an intent to follow up the discovery by occupation.'[22]

Jurists in the second half of the 19th century were similarly sceptical regarding discovery as earlier generations had been and, as they turned to the earnest codification and professionalization of international law, they formalized a minimal role for

---

[17] GF von Martens *Précis du droit des gens moderne de l'Europe* (JP Aillaud Paris 1831) vol 1, at 118–19.

[18] JL Klüber *Droit des gens* (JP Aillaud Paris 1831) at 211.

[19] AG Heffter *Le droit international public de l'Europe* (Cotillon et Fils Paris 1866) at 143; on Heffter, see E Nys *Droit international. Les principes, les théories, les faits* (2nd edn Alfred Castaigne Bruxelles 1904) vol 1, at 289–90.

[20] T Twiss *The Oregon Territory* (D Appleton & Co New York 1846) at 115; see also T Twiss *The Law of Nations* (OUP Oxford 1861) at 162: 'Discovery is only an inchoate title.'

[21] DS Dickinson 'On the Oregon Question' speech delivered in the senate, 24 February 1846 (Washington 1846) 1–15 at 15.

[22] ibid 4.

discovery in the conventions. Sir Robert Phillimore, probably the most the eminent British international lawyer of his generation, agreed with Vattel, and his colleague Twiss, that: '*Discovery*... furnishes an *inchoate* title to *possession* in the discoverer.' He added that 'the fact of authorized discovery may be said to found the *right to occupy*' but if that right was not exercised it would lapse.[23] With an historical view, Henry Sumner Maine observed that '[a]ll discovery is now disregarded, unless it be followed by acts showing an intention to hold the country.'[24] The legal status of discovery was further diminished at Otto von Bismarck's Berlin Conference of colonial powers (1884–85), called to debate the rules by which Africa would be carved up. Article 35 of the General Act of the Berlin Conference stipulated that for a power to take possession a territory it must occupy and exercise 'adequate authority to enforce respect for acquired rights'.[25] Article 35 gave recognition in international diplomacy to the long-standing conventions in the law of nations which opposed the right of discovery.

The *Institut de droit international* devoted a number of meetings and many papers in the aftermath of the conference to the matter of what principles had been established in international law. Edouard Engelhardt, the French plenipotentiary minister at the Berlin Conference, was prominent in those discussions. He argued that the act of the conference would bring the legal abuses of the past to an end, writing disdainfully that the 'fact of discovery' had given rise to 'singular disputes' because 'certain explorers claimed territories which they said they were the first to see'.[26] The eminent jurist and political theorist, Johann Caspar Bluntschli (1808–81), wrote, in the year after the conference, that 'temporary or artificial occupation can only create an artificial right'. He understood precisely that the right of discovery would impede rather than extend empire:

If a power, such as, for example, England in America or Australia, such as Spain and Portugal in South America, such as the Low Countries in the islands of Oceania, extends its pretended sovereignty over immense spaces, inhabited and occupied by savages, and cannot, in reality, neither cultivate nor govern those territories, that state does not walk toward the aims of humanity; it retards, on the contrary, the realization of those aims in preventing other nations from establishing themselves in those countries.[27]

Bluntschli then referred his readers to the General Act of the Berlin Conference as the foundation for his principles.

The French jurist Charles Salomon wrote *L'occupation des territoires sans maître* in direct response to the conventions established at the Berlin Conference. He devoted

---

[23] R Phillimore *Commentaries upon International Law* (2nd edn Butterworths London 1871) vol 1, at 269.

[24] HS Maine *International Law* (Henry Holt New York 1888) at 67.

[25] —'The General Act of the Berlin Conference' in HM Stanley *The Congo and the Founding of its Free State* (Sampson Low London 1885) vol 2, 378–458 at 457.

[26] E Englehardt 'Etude sur la déclaration de la Conférence de Berlin relative aux occupations' (1886) 18 Revue de droit international et de législation comparée 573–86 at 575.

[27] JC Bluntschli *Le droit international codifié* (Guillaumin Paris 1886) at 178.

a large portion of his treatise to the history of the justification of European expansion which he divided into three periods: the first dominated by the Papal bulls, the second dominated by the right of discovery (for example, the hoisting of flags, the use of ceremonies) but which also saw the development of the doctrine of occupation; and the third period, Salomon's own, on which the theory of occupation was perfected as the theory of effective occupation.[28] Salomon admitted that his notion of a second period in which empire was justified by discovery, rather than bulls, was within limits that were not 'well determined'. Indeed, he observed that the claim to the right of discovery and the use of signs marking discovery (flags, crosses, plinths) continued to be employed by governments into the 19th century even though no jurist regarded them as a holding any status in the law of nations.[29]

Vattel's qualified acceptance of Grotius' views on discovery became 20th-century orthodoxy. In Lassa Oppenheim's view discovery 'made an *inchoate* title'.[30] The inchoate titles 'perishes' unless the State 'effectively occupies' the territory within a reasonable period of time. For Theodor J Lawrence this title was even weaker. He observed that '[o]ccupation is not effected by discovery.' 'The utmost that can be said for discovery to-day' is that other nations would be bound by 'comity' to wait a respectful time to see if discovery was followed by occupation.[31]

3. CONQUEST

All writers on the law of nations conceded that there are just causes for war, and therefore for conquest, but remarkably few argued that European empires presented any of those causes. For natural law writers it was inevitable that just war and conquest must be possible because, by definition, anything that was contrary to the law of nature would justify some use of force. For Thomistic writers on the *ius gentium*, such as the 16th-century School of Salamanca, the primary natural law was human sociability and anything that breached that law could be a justification for force. Thus Vitoria argued that if the American Indians refused the presence of the Spanish by refusing their trade or friendship, there would be a just cause for war.[32] In making this claim Vitoria has frequently been seen as having justified the Spanish conquests but this understanding rests on a very selective reading of Vitoria (which, as we shall see,

---

[28] C Salomon *L'occupation des territoires sans maître* (A Giard Paris 1887) 31–101.
[29] ibid 78.
[30] L Oppenheim *International Law* (Longmans London 1920) vol 1, at 386.
[31] TJ Lawrence *The Principles of International Law* (DC Heath and Co Boston 1915) at 152.
[32] 'On the American Indians' (n 5) 278–80.

may have its origin with Pufendorf). Vitoria was very careful to avoid stating that the Indians had refused the rights of communication and friendship and elsewhere he suggested that it had been the Spaniards, on the contrary, who had violated the laws of sociability.[33]

Alberico Gentili,[34] the Regius Professor of civil law at Oxford, argued that it is just to wage war against those 'who wearing the human form, live the life of the most brutal of beasts', and citing Cicero's *De officiis* he observed that 'some men differ very little from the brutes. They have the human form, but in reality they are beasts.'[35] However Gentili also condemned the Spanish for pretending that the right of trade and friendship had been violated:

[t]he warfare of the Spaniards in that part of the world seems to be justified, because the inhabitants prohibited other men from commerce with them; and it would be an adequate defence, *if the statement were true*. . . . But the Spaniards were aiming there, not at commerce, but at dominion. And they regarded it as beyond dispute that it was lawful to take possession of those lands which were not previously known to us; just as if to be known to none of us was the same thing as to be possessed by no one.[36]

Hugo Grotius echoed Gentili on this point and he also agreed with Vitoria that the conquest of the Americas had been unjust. Grotius understood natural law as a law of self-preservation as much as a law of sociability. Accordingly, he argued that the law of nature favoured the right to fight war: 'The end and aim of war being the preservation of life and limb, and the keeping or acquiring of things useful to life, war is in perfect accord with those first principles of nature.'[37] Grotius was a humanist by training and he wrote in the context of what is often referred to as the 'new humanism' of Machiavelli and the 16th-century Tacitists, such as Lispsius and Montaigne. From this position, Grotius argued that when we speak of 'just war' we must take a broad view of what constitutes 'moral goodness' and justice. Such questions are not 'black and white', most laws, and most human action, concerned some intermediate space between the two. Indeed, he pointed out, 'war may be just from the point of view of either side'.[38] Even armed with such moral relativism, Grotius was unable to find that the Spanish acted within the bounds of just war when they conquered the Americas. On this question he paraphrased Gentili:

[t]here were no cause truly that they should pretend war. For they who pursue the barbarians with war, as the Spaniards do the people of America, are wont to pretend two things: that they are hindered from trading with them, or because they will not acknowledge the

---

[33]   F de Vitoria 'Letter to Miguel de Arcos' in *Political Writings* (n 5) 331–3.

[34]   See the contribution by M Scattola 'Alberico Gentili (1552–1608)' in this volume.

[35]   A Gentili *De jure belli libri tres* in JB Scott (ed) *The Classics of International Law* (OUP Oxford 1933) vol 1, at 41.

[36]   ibid 89; my emphasis.

[37]   H Grotius *De jure belli ac pacis* in JB Scott (ed) *The Classics of International Law* (OUP Oxford 1925) at 52.

[38]   ibid 566.

doctrine of true religion. As for trading, the Portugalls obtained it of the Indians, so that in this behalf they have no reason to complain.[39]

On 'the other pretence', namely that of conquest in the name of religion, he cited Cajetan on the doctrine that Vitoria adopted: namely, that for infidel countries, 'the lords thereof, although infidels, are lawful lords, whether they be governed by regal or political government, neither are they deprived of dominion of the lands or goods for their infidelity'.[40] In *On the Law of War and Peace*, Grotius expanded on these thoughts in a chapter 'On Unjust Causes of Wars' which drew heavily on Vitoria.[41]

While writers on the *ius gentium* and law of nations condemned the arguments of the Spanish conquistadors, the arguments of those same writers could be employed as justifications of conquest. The Virginia Company publicist Robert Gray echoed Gentili in his declaration that 'a Christian King may lawfullie make warre upon barbarous and savage people'. The Virginian colonist William Strachey similarly appealed to the Roman law right to repel violence with violence: 'to draw our swordes, et vim vi repellere'. And the poet John Donne argued, in the manner of Grotius, that American colonists could turn to the principle of self-preservation to justify force: 'the Law of Nations may justifie some force, in seeking' the means of sustenance.[42]

Despite, or perhaps because, of the appeals to conquest in the writings of colonial publicists, the critique of European colonial practices became even more pronounced in the law of nations. This increasingly sceptical tone is evident when we turn from Grotius to Pufendorf. One of the striking differences between the two writers is in how they read Vitoria. Whereas Grotius understood Vitoria to have been attacking the Spanish conquests, Pufendorf interpreted Vitoria as an apologist for empire and developed his own profound critique of colonial rationalizations. According to Pufendorf, 'Franciscus a Victoria, *Relectiones de Indis*, Pt.V, § 3, does not win many to his position when he discusses the adequate grounds on which the Spaniards felt themselves entitled to subdue the Indians.'[43] He continued: 'It is crude indeed to try to give others so indefinite a right to journey and live among us, with no thought of the number in which they come, their purpose in coming, as well as the question of whether ... they propose to stay but a short time or settle among us permanently.'[44] Pufendorf was able to put Vitoria's discussion of the rights of 'natural communication' in doubt because, in common with the modern natural law writers, his understanding of natural law rested less upon the supposition of a universal human fellowship and more upon the notion of the universal rule of self-interest.

---

[39] *Free Sea* (n 9) 18.

[40] ibid 18–19; see also 'On the American Indians' (n 5) 263–4.

[41] *De jure belli ac pacis* (n 37) 546–56.

[42] R Gray *A Good Speed to Virginia* (London 1610) [C4]r; W Strachey *The Historie of Travell into Virginia Britannia* (LB Wright and V Freund eds) (Hakluyt Society London 1953) at 25–6; J Donne *A Sermon Preached to the Honourable Company of the Virginian Plantation* (London 1622) at 25–7.

[43] *De jure naturae et gentium* (n 12) 364.

[44] ibid 364–5.

Immanuel Kant entered into this debate firmly taking the position that 'universal hospitality' was a 'cosmopolitan right' and he accordingly rejected Pufendorf's position on the issue.[45] For Kant the possibility to seek commerce with others provided the opportunity for peoples to 'enter peaceably into relations with one another' and so bring 'the human race ever closer to a cosmopolitan constitution'. Importantly, however, and in agreement with Pufendorf, Kant was able to reflect on the fact that the right to communicate with other peoples had been grossly abused by European colonizers 'the injustice they show in *visiting* foreign lands and peoples (which with them is tantamount to *conquering* them) goes to horrifying lengths'. And it was this abuse of the right of commerce that led to the perception of other lands as *res nullius*: that is, as lands belonging to no one. Kant immediately continued: 'When America, the negro countries, the Spice Islands, the Cape, and so forth were discovered, they were, to them, countries belonging to no one, since they counted the inhabitants as nothing.'[46]

For 19th-century jurists, conquest was a vexed question. Writers on the law of nations had argued themselves to a position in which it was almost impossible to imagine that empire could be established justly through conquest. The Berlin Conference provided further acknowledgement for this position, elevating 'effective occupation' as the ideal of colonial practice. 'It is doubtful', argued Paul Pradier-Fodéré (1827–1904) writing on conquest just prior to the Berlin Conference, 'that force can give birth to a right'.[47] Writing in the aftermath of the conference, Henry Bonfils (1835–97) outlined the just means of acquiring territory and confidently declared under the subhead *'Conquête'*: 'Conquest. It is not a mode of acquisition. A violent taking of possession is a pure fact, simple and brutal.'[48] While the theory of just acquisition of imperial territory had become increasingly sceptical of conquest, the fact of conquest remained, as Bonfils had noted. International law, if it sometimes stood on principles, was founded also on dealing with facts, and there were two ways in which the fact of conquest was discussed. The first was in the debate over how to deal with the goods of an enemy. For many international jurists, conquest was simply a problem of what to do when the goods of an enemy in war came under the power of the conqueror and they generally concluded that property rights should be respected whether or not the conquered people were 'civilized'.

The second problem of conquest was to determine the legal status of a conquest of long standing, regardless of how unjust it may have been. Most jurists agreed that if something was held by someone for long enough, no matter how they came by it, that thing became the property of the holder. This was the principle known as 'usucaption' or 'prescription' and it performed the useful function of bringing right into line

---

[45]   See the contribution by E Jouannet 'Immanuel Kant (1724–1767)' in this volume.

[46]   I Kant 'Toward Perpetual Peace' in I Kant *Practical Philosophy* (MJ Gregor trans) (CUP Cambridge 1996) 328–30.

[47]   P Pradier-Fodéré *Principes généraux de droit, de politique et de legislation* (Guillaumin Paris 1969) at 561.

[48]   H Bonfils *Manuel de droit international public* (3rd edn Rousseau Paris 1901) at 300.

with fact. Prescription was recognized in Roman law and Grotius adopted it in his law of nations.[49] Vattel declared that prescription was 'a celebrated question' in relations between nations and it remained such through to the 19th century.[50]

Chief Justice Marshall employed the principle of prescription in *Johnson v M'Intosh*, the landmark 1823 United States Supreme Court judgment which ruled that the absolute title to Indian lands was held by the US government. Marshall acknowledged that North America had been conquered rather than merely occupied and that however 'opposed to natural right' had been the treatment of Native Americans, the passing of time had established a 'system' which could not be overturned:

> However extravagant the pretension of converting the discovery of an inhabited country into conquest may appear; if the principle has been asserted in the first instance, and afterwards sustained; if a country has been acquired and held under it; if the property of the great mass of the community originates in it, it becomes the law of the land and cannot be questioned.[51]

Shortly after this judgment, Henry Wheaton,[52] the eminent American jurist of international law, was able to cite *Johnson v M'Intosh* immediately following his discussion of prescription. According to Wheaton, European colonizers simply assumed that 'the right of the native Indians was subordinate' so that 'the primitive title of the Indians has been entirely overlooked', but that title had subsequently 'been almost entirely extinguished by force of arms, or by voluntary compact'. Thus at the same time conquest was rejected from the present practice of the law of nations, prescription was employed to justify 'ancient' conquests.[53] Ironically, while contemporaries continued to conquer through another name, namely occupation, those 19th-century conquests (for example, in Australia, New Zealand, and Africa) would later be recognized *as* conquests (as they were too by some contemporary critics), retrospectively frowned upon, and justified through the law of prescription.

4. OCCUPATION

The idea that subjects, or individuals, possess rights was central to European political consciousness from late medieval times. Rights theories were based on natural law and therefore made claims to universal application. It was this universal notion of

---

[49] *De jure belli ac pacis* (n 37) 227–9.
[50] *The Law of Nations* (n 15) 251–6; *Manuel de droit international public* (n 48) 299.
[51] *Johnson's Lessee v M'Intosh* 21 US 543, 8 Wheat. 543 (1823) at 591–2.
[52] See the contribution by LH Liu 'Henry Wheaton (1785–1848)' in this volume.
[53] H Wheaton *Elements of International Law* (6th edn Little Brown and Co Boston 1855) at 218–20.

rights which impeded the arguments of discovery and conquest. Europeans therefore sought a justification of their encroachments on other peoples' lands that would be proofed against the rights-based critiques. In such circumstances, the best justification would itself have to come from the rights tradition and this is precisely why apologists for European expansion seized upon the argument of occupation. Occupation became the single most important justification for European empire over the five centuries following the discoveries by Columbus. Occupation was initially introduced into thinking about European empire, however, as a means of critiquing the claims of the Spanish empire in the Americas rather than as a justification of empire.

Occupatio in Roman law was the principle whereby anything that belonged to nobody became, 'by natural reason', the property of the first person to take it: '*Quod enim nullius est, id ratione naturali occupanti conceditur.*'[54] Medieval jurists introduced *occupatio* into discussions of civil law, in part as an explanation of the origin of property. They also employed the term '*res nullius*' to refer to that law. Discussions of *occupatio* in Roman law did not use the term '*res nullius*' simply, it would seem, because '*nullius*' in classical Latin did not require the '*res*' that it already implied (although *res publica* was employed). In medieval Latin, '*nullius*' became clearer with its subject '*res*' which the grammar of most European languages would require.[55] This grammatical innovation was the first step in a process of the reification of *occupatio* in the modern *ius gentium* and law of nations.

Francesco de Vitoria was the first writer to address the justice of European expansion employing the Roman law of occupation. According to Vitoria, one of the possible reasons it could be just to conquer the Americas was 'by right of discovery (in iure inventionis)'. The right of discovery, he argued, was sustained by the Roman law of occupation: 'All things which are unoccupied or deserted become the property of the occupier by natural law and the law of nations [*ius gentium*], according to the law *Ferae bestiae* (*Institutions* II, 1.12).' As we have seen, he then pointed out that 'the barbarians possessed true public and private dominion.'[56] For Vitoria, as an Aristotelian, the question of what constituted a just society was whether that society demonstrated an understanding of the laws of nature and whether it exploited those laws to build communities. The question of occupation was an expression of that Aristotelian understanding of sociability.

Vitoria's defence of non-European societies was easily inverted as an attack. If the measure of a just society was whether it had understood and exploited the laws of nature, it was possible merely to reverse the description of non-European peoples

---

[54] T Mommsen (ed) *The Digest of Justinian* (University of Pennsylvania Press Philadelphia PA 1985) vol 4, at 487a.

[55] This tendency is apparent in the 12th century glossator Azo of Bologna and in his imitator Henry Bracton. See H Bracton *De legibus et consuetudinibus angliæ* (London 1569) f.8r–v*; and Azo *Summa perutilis* (Constantin Fradin Lyon 1530) book 2, folio 273.

[56] 'On the American Indians' (n 5) 264–5.

from being civil, from having occupied their territory, to being savage. Savage or bar-barian people did not understand natural law—they sinned against it—and they did not, therefore, occupy the land upon which they lived. Arguments of this nature were employed from the early 17th century by writers who were acutely conscious of Vitoria's writings and the limitations he imposed. John Donne observed in his ser-mon before the Virginia Company: 'In the law of Nature and Nations, a land never inhabited, by any, or utterly derelicted and immemorially abandoned by the former Inhabitants, becomes theirs that will possesse it.'[57] North America, according to the English publicists, was just such a land: 'Who will think', demanded the colonist William Strachey:

[i]t is an unlawful act, to fortefye, and strengthen our selves (as Nature requires)...in the wast and vast, unhabited groundes of theirs amongst a world of which not one foot of a thousand, do they either use or know how to turne to any benefit, and therefore lyes so great a Circuit vayne and idle before them?[58]

The argument that occupation of the land was the basis of a just society, and so justi-fied European expansion, found its highest expression in John Locke's essay 'On Property' in his *Two Treatises*. Locke's theory of property has sometimes been con-trasted with 'occupation theory', although it was rather an extension of the idea of occupation.[59] Locke transformed the meaning of occupying something from signify-ing a mere presence to the improvement of the thing which becomes property. In this understanding property could no longer remain as a simple relation to something. The thing itself was transformed and the meaning of property had to change accord-ingly. For Locke use creates not only property but value. Value was the basis for his progressive theory of history which is absent in Vitoria. According to Locke, the more intensively we labour on nature the more value we add to our property. Through this process one person and one society surpasses another in the degree to which the potential held in nature is released. He was thus famously able to conclude:

[A]n Acre of Land that bears here Twenty Bushels of Wheat, and another in *America*, which, with the same Husbandry, would do the like, are, without doubt, of the same natural, instrin-sick Value. But yet the Benefit Mankind receives from the one, in a Year, is 5.*l*. and from the other possibly not worth a Penny...Tis *Labour* then which *puts the greatest part of Value upon Land*.[60]

This so-called 'agriculturalist argument' became the foundation for much of the European discourse legitimizing empire from Locke's day through to the 20th cen-tury: it justified not only agricultural societies but also commercial and industrial

---

[57] *A Sermon* (n 42) 25–7.
[58] *Historie* (n 42) 25.
[59] On the contrast between occupation theory and Locke's theory of property, see J Waldron *The Right to Private Property* (OUP Oxford 1988) at 173. Waldron recognizes that Locke's account of the origin of property is a gloss on what he describes as 'First Occupation Theory'.
[60] J Locke *Two Treatises of Government* (P Laslett ed) (CUP Cambridge 1960) at 298.

empire. On this philosophical foundation, jurists writing on the law of nations and international law sought to extrapolate and codify the law of occupation.

This path was not smooth, however, and one of the greatest challenges to the theory of occupation was a dramatic revision of the understanding of natural law amongst 17th-century jurists and philosophers. For medieval and 16th-century writers on natural law property had its origin in occupation, from people first taking things from what was common in nature. They were able to hold this property by virtue of the relation between individuals and nature, without the existence of any formally established civil society, albeit that society was itself natural.

Shaped by the wars of religion, 17th-century natural law writers, including Grotius, Hobbes and Pufendorf, argued that self-preservation, rather than sociability, was the primary natural law. According to this theory of 'unsociable sociability', nature was violent and society was created not from mutual love but from mutual fear, from a need to escape the dangers of a war of all against all. For these 'modern' natural law theorists, property could only be a creation of agreement or law, it could only come into existence as a consequence of civil society.[61] In a state of nature a person could not call something hers or his when it could be taken from her or him at any moment. If law was the origin of property the particular form that property might take would simply depend on the nature of the law. Occupation was no longer a necessary part of the understanding of property. This, indeed, was Thomas Hobbes' understanding of property and he makes no mention of occupation. The greatly diminished role for occupation amongst the modern natural lawyers makes it all the more surprising that it subsequently came to be central to the justification of European empires. The endurance of occupation in the understanding of property can be attributed to the codification of civil law and to the restoration of occupation in modern natural law in the writings of Grotius and Pufendorf. Both authors, having insisted on law as the origin of property, then almost perversely argued that the first law every society made regarding property was that occupation was the origin of all property. As Pufendorf put it: 'Hence we apprehend the first Agreement, that Men made about this Point, to have been, that what any Person had seiz'd out of the common Store of Things ... none else should rob him of.'[62] It is unclear why Grotius and Pufendorf restored occupation to a central place in understanding property when their assumptions did not require it. It may be that they had to produce an account of property that was consistent with the conventions of civil law in which occupation continued to hold a central place. Hobbes, of course, did not have to deal directly with civil law because English legal practice was predominantly based upon the Common Law (with civil law only employed in the ecclesiastical and Admiralty Courts).

While Pufendorf acknowledged that occupation was the first law made regarding property, he nevertheless insisted that any society had a right to dispose of its

---

[61] *De jure belli ac pacis* (n 37) 189; *De jure naturae et gentium* (n 12) 366.
[62] *De jure belli ac pacis* (n 37) 189–90; *De jure naturae et gentium* (n 12) 367.

property and the territory it occupied in the manner it saw fit. Thus, he pointed out, a community may legitimately decide to employ proprietorship whereby individuals possess things for their own use or they may rather hold some or all of the goods and land in 'positive community': that is, in a communal ownership. In *both* cases, Pufendorf insists, all claims by outsiders to those goods are excluded.[63] He implicitly rejected here the argument used by colonizers that native peoples who had not established individual proprietorship had failed to establish dominion. The implications of this argument were more explicitly developed by Christian Wolff[64] who conceded that 'things are occupied for the sake of their use' but responded that

[i]f, indeed, separate families should be accustomed to wander about after the manner of the Scythians [the classic early modern example of barbarity] through uncultivated wilds...the intention of wandering, which is governed by that intended use gives sufficient evidence of the occupation of the lands subject to their use, although they have not established a permanent abode on them.[65]

Eighteenth-century jurists and philosophers began to use the term '*res nullius*', which had been employed in the medieval explanation of '*occupatio*', as a short-hand for the doctrine of '*occupatio*' itself. Thus textbooks of Roman law and discussions of the law of nations contained the sub-heading '*Res nullius*'. In his textbook *Summary of the Roman Law*, published in 1772, John Taylor, Rector of Lawford in Essex, included the large subheading '*RES NULLIUS*' which he defined as 'Things that lie in common; parts of the world not yet discovered, animals not claimed'.[66] *Res nullius* were things which had been taken by no one and could therefore become the property of the first taker, and this understanding, as Taylor indicated, could apply to the vast empires being carved out by European States. But *res nullius* could also be things understood as Grotius had understood the sea: that is, things that could be taken by no one because they were common. Consistent with Vitoria's use of *occupatio*, the doctrine of *res nullius* was also employed to argue, as we have seen in the examples from Wolff, Kant and Ferguson above, that things which had been occupied by a people, whether they were European or not, could not be occupied by others: that is, that the territory of even savage peoples could not be treated as *res nullius*. Georg Friedrich von Martens declared that '[t]he right of property is the same for all men, natural law does not authorise Christian people to claim territory already effectively occupied by savages against their will, even if practice offers too many examples of seeming usurpations.'[67] On these usurpations, he cited Abbé Raynal, whose collaborative work (with Diderot

---

[63] *De jure naturae et gentium* (n 12) 536.
[64] See the contribution by K Haakonssen 'Christian Wolff (1679–1754)' in this volume.
[65] C Wolff *Jus gentium methodo scientifica pertractatum* (1764) in JB Scott (ed) *The Classics of International Law* (OUP Oxford 1934) vol 2, at 158.
[66] J Taylor *Summary of the Roman Law* (Printed for T Payne London 1772) at 244.
[67] *Précis du droit des gens* (n 17) 117.

amongst others), the *Histoire philosophique des établissements des Européens aux Indes*, was one of the Enlightenment's most strident critiques of European empire.[68]

The doctrine of occupation reached its peak in the context of the creation of international law in the 19th century. Nineteenth-century jurists employed a synthesis of natural law and positivism as well as historical approaches to the law, but even the more rigorous positivists acknowledged the law of occupation merely by virtue of the fact that it was a recognized convention in the law of nations. At the same time, the language of occupation occupied the centre of a debate about whether empire was just. In this context, occupation was employed not only to justify empire but also to argue to that if territory was already occupied by a people it could not be annexed by European powers. The German jurist Klüber argued: 'A state can acquire things which belong to nobody (*res nullius*) by occupation.'[69] But he warned that 'no nation is authorized by its qualities, whatever they may be, notably not by a higher form of culture of whatever kind, to ravish another nation of its property, not even that of savages or nomads'. Similarly, Heffter declared:

[o]ccupation could only be applied to goods which, though susceptible to ownership, have no master. [Occupation] can't be extended to people who could only be subjected [in a way that is] . . . either voluntary or forced. Occupation is notably applied to areas or islands which are not inhabited or not entirely occupied, but no power on earth has the right to impose its laws upon wandering or even savage peoples.[70]

This debate over the justice of empire increasingly focused on precisely what constituted occupation. For Vitoria, occupation and discovery were barely distinguished. Grotius separated the two by distinguishing seeing with the eyes and taking with the hands. Locke added labour and value to what it meant to take with the hands. By the time the first professional body of international jurists was established in 1873, the *Institut de droit international*, the effort to codify international law led to a taxonomy of occupation which included not only *res nullius*, but also *territorium nullius* and *terra nullius*. Each of these terms was employed in order to distinguish the particular conditions in which occupation may be possible and also to distinguish different possible degrees of occupation.

The term *territorium nullius* was first employed in international law (although it had previously been used in canon law), in the context of the carve up of Africa in the 1880s. From the 1870s, European powers showed growing interest in claiming various parts of Africa as new colonies, or protectorates, and as they did so they increasingly came into conflict over competing claims. The German Chancellor, Otto von Bismarck, called a meeting of all the powers in Berlin which would establish rules for the claiming of new territory. The Berlin Conference resoundingly endorsed the

---

[68] On Raynal's scepticism of empire, see S Muthu *Enlightenment against Empire* (Princeton University Press Princeton NJ 2003) at 72.

[69] *Droit des gens* (n 18) 209; see also *Précis du droit des gens* (n 17) 117.

[70] *Le droit international* (n 19) 142.

principle of 'effective occupation' as the basis for all claims to territory. The jurists of the *Institut de droit international* devoted their meetings after the conference to establishing what new principles had been established in Berlin. Some jurists argued that the measure of whether occupation of a territory could be possible would be whether the people in that territory possessed territorial sovereignty. A people who were not subject to territorial sovereignty were *territorium nullius*, and therefore open to the first taker. The concept *territorium nullius* would perform the same function that *res nullius* had performed in civil law.

The *Institut de droit international* met in Brussels in September 1885 and commissioned Ferdinand Martitz, a relatively young German professor of ecclesiastical and international law, to chair a committee to study more deeply the question of effective occupation. According to Martitz's report, '[a]ll regions are considered to be *territorium nullius* which do not find themselves effectively under sovereignty…no matter whether the region is inhabited or not.' 'It is an exaggeration', he declared, 'to speak of the sovereignty of savage or semi-barbarian peoples'. Moreover, 'international law does not recognize rights of independent tribes'. For this reason, he concluded, '*territorium nullius* is not the same thing as *res nullius*'.[71] Whereas *res nullius* could be anything, *territorum nullius* was confined solely to the question of sovereignty and it was around this question of sovereignty that discussions of occupation revolved. In international law, a land could not be *res nullius*, that is the people who lived there could possess property (unless one took the view, as many did, that property came from sovereignty), and yet if it lacked territorial sovereignty it would be *territorium nullius*.

Territorium nullius was the focus of scepticism about empire as much as it was a justification of empire. Edouard Engelhardt objected that it was dangerous to apply this rule to inhabited regions.[72] Under what conditions, he asked, would a State be regarded as part of the community of nations? What is the situation of a State, such as Morocco, that recognizes some of the rules of the law of nations and not others? Other societies, he insisted, are outside the law of nations and yet still deserve respect. This, he added, was the situation of the American States conquered by the Spanish in the 16th century. He argued that even in the case of 'savage peoples', who are completely outside the law of nations, it would nevertheless be 'exorbitant to consider their territory as *territorium nullius*'.[73]

Both sceptics and apologists for African expansion agreed that the occupation of African territory must be accompanied by treaties. Thus treaties and cession were not perceived to be an alternative to the legal argument of occupation but an extension of it. For the apologists, treaties were implied by the idea of *territorium nullius*. While a

---

[71] M de Martitz 'Occupation des territoires—Rapport et projet de résolutions présentés à l'Institut de droit international' (1887) 19 Revue de droit international et de législation comparée 371–6 at 373–4; Martitz's report was also published in (1888) 9 Annuaire de l'Institut de droit international 243–51.

[72] 'Sixième commission—Examen de la théorie de la conférence de Berlin sur l'occupation des territoires' (1889) 10 Annuaire de l'Institut de droit international at 177.

[73] ibid 178; see also 'Etude sur la déclaration de la Conférence de Berlin' (n 26).

territory being occupied might be void of territorial sovereignty, it was not necessarily void of sovereignty or property and it was expected that treaties should be made with the sovereign powers and property holders in order to protect existing rights. *Territorium nullius* was the legal rationalization of protectorates, a means of recognizing sovereignty and property in the territory being occupied and simultaneously subsuming it under a supposedly higher form of sovereignty. For the sceptics of African colonization, treaties which were freely consented to and fully understood by both parties, were the only means in which it might possibly be just to occupy such territory.[74] The consensus among jurists on the necessity for treaties in the occupation of heavily populated territory was mirrored in the extraordinary number of treaties that were made in Africa in this period, particularly in the race between colonial agents, such as between Brazza and Stanley in the Congo, to be the first to make those treaties with the subject peoples. The taxonomy of occupation was extended further with the growth of interest in the Polar Regions in the late 19th and early 20th centuries. Claims over the Polar Regions presented dramatically different legal and political challenges to those recently faced in Africa. Whereas in Africa legal arguments had been sought that would justify the occupation of densely populated territories, in the polar regions, for example on the island of Spitzbergen where much of the debate focused, the claims concerned land that had little or no population. Jurists employed the term *terra nullius* to describe unpopulated regions that had been taken by no one and could become the property of the first taker.[75] The term *terra nullius* had been employed a very few times in international law in the second half of the 19th century and, like *territorium nullius*, it was used in 18th-century canon law, but its currency exploded in the debate over the Polar Regions.[76] It was impossible, of course, effectively to occupy large areas of the Polar Regions, such as the Antarctic, so *terra nullius* was also used to describe areas that belonged to no one and should remain so because they could not be occupied.[77] Interest focused, however, on the areas, such as

[74] G Jèze *Étude théorique et pratique sur l'occupation* (V. Giard Paris 1896) at 103; *L'occupation des territoires sans maître* (n 28).

[75] C Piccioni 'L'organisation du Spitzberg' (1909) 16 Revue générale de droit international public 117–34 at 118; JB Scott 'Arctic Exploration and International Law' (1909) 3 The American Journal of International Law 928–41 at 941; F Despagnet *Cours de droit international public* (4th edn L Larose Paris 1910) at 590–1; FB Sayre *Experiments in International Administration* (Harper New York 1919) at 92; R Redslob *Histoire des grands principes du droit des gens* (Rousseau Paris 1923) at 528; G Smedal *Acquisition of Sovereignty over Polar Areas* (Ch Meyer trans) (I Kommisjon Hos Jacob Dybwad Oslo 1931) Skrifter om Svalbard og Ishavet no 36, 6.

[76] An early reference can be found in 1885 in relation to the conflict between Spain and the United States over the Contoy Islands in 1850: HE von Holst *The Constitutional and Political History of the United States* (J Lalor trans) (Callaghan and Co London 1885) vol 4, at 51. Holst claims that 'Barringer, the American ambassador at Madrid, was unquestionably right when he said that Contoy was not, in an international sense, a desert, that is an abandoned island and hence *terra nullius*'.

[77] See eg DH Miller 'Political Rights in the Polar Regions' in WLC Joerg (ed) *Problems of Polar Research: A Series of Papers by Thirty-one Authors* (American Geographical Society New York 1928) 240*.

Spitzbergen and East Greenland, where some foothold was being established and European powers were brought once again into competition.[78] Whereas *territorium nullius* had been employed to describe territory devoid of sovereignty, but not people, *terra nullius* was employed to describe land where there was literally no one, or where a country, as Kant had said, could be said to belong to no one, since the people who lived there, such as the Inuit, counted as nothing. Through to the 1930s the concept of *terra nullius* remained largely confined to discussions of the Polar Regions. In the 1930s, however, the Joint Seminar in International Law at Columbia University began to investigate whether the application of the concept of *terra nullius* could be expanded. This group included Philip C Jessup (1897–1986), Charles Cheney Hyde (1873–1952), and their students James Simsarian and Oliver J Lissitzyn. The group, through Jessup, wrote to jurists and historians in former colonial societies to inquire whether the concept of *terra nullius* had been employed to justify the occupation of those territories. The Australian historian Sir Ernest Scott received a letter in 1938 from Jessup posing this question and in response Scott wrote an article explaining the doctrine of *terra nullius* as it had been employed in the colonization of Australia.[79] In responding to Jessup's question Scott introduced the term to the consideration of the occupation of Australia for the first time. As the law of occupation had been used historically to discuss the justice of colonization in Australia, it was easy to anachronistically fit the relatively new term in international law, *terra nullius*, to that historical fact. Having gathered evidence for a wide application of *terra nullius*, the Columbia professors began to publish a series of works in which *terra nullius* expanded from a discussion of the Polar Regions to become emblematic of the doctrine of occupation more generally.[80] Students of the Columbia seminar produced a volume in which they took their object as the 'endeavours of the leading European maritime states, in the period 1400–1800, to acquire dominion over *terra nullius*'.[81] As it expanded in scope, *terra nullius* lost the initial focus of its meaning and rapidly assumed the signification that had also been attributed to *territorium nullius* so that rival concept progressively disappeared from the vocabulary of international law. *Terra nullius* proved to be a potent conceptual tool. Twenty years after he wrote to Scott, Jessup published (with Howard J Taubenfeld) *Controls for Outer Space and the Antarctic Analogy*. As the title suggests, Jessup and Taubenfeld examined similarities in the legal conflicts over the Antarctic and Space and they employed the tools of '*terra nullius*' and '*res*

---

[78] LV Staël-Holstein *Norway in Arcticum: From Spitzbergen to Greenland?* (Levin and Munksgaard Copenhagen 1932).

[79] See Sir E Scott 'Taking Possession of Australia—The Doctrine of *terra nullius* (No-Man's Land)' (1940) 26 Journal and Proceedings. Royal Australian Historical Society pt 1, 1–19.

[80] See eg J Simsarian 'The Acquisition of Legal Title to terra nullius' (1938) 53 Political Science Quarterly 111–28.

[81] AS Keller, OJ Lissitzyn, and FJ Mann (eds) *Creation of Rights of Sovereignty through Symbolic Acts* (Columbia University Press New York 1938) at v.

nullius' to assist the comparison.[82] At precisely the historical moment that decolonization was gaining momentum a new frontier of expansion opened in Space. The legal and political arsenal that had been developed in tandem with European expansion now moved to this new frontier, and the law of occupation maintained its central position in that new legal context.

5. Conclusion

The history of the conventions employed to justify European expansion from the 16th to the 20th centuries is a triumph of the idea of occupation over its rivals discovery and conquest. Occupation prevailed over the rival legal understandings of empire because the theory of occupation developed in tandem with the progressive, or stadial, theory of history. When articulated in terms of the imperative to exploit nature, occupation justified the European understanding of historical time. The progressive understanding of history that came to accompany the theory of occupation could be employed to establish a taxonomy, a series of fine distinctions, between the different kinds of political rights that could be established according to the status of the territory being occupied. At the same time, claims based on discovery and conquest could leave, to the European mind, large swathes of the globe unexploited.

Finally, occupation triumphed as a convention in international law because it could be employed not only to justify European expansion but also to condemn it. The status of occupation was raised by the fact that opponents and supporters of empire agreed over the terms upon which territory could be justly appropriated. Where they differed was more in the description of the peoples who were potentially to be occupied rather than in the question of what constituted a just appropriation.

It is necessary, therefore, to revise the image of international law as a mere agent of European expansion. It was an agent of empire, without question, but it was also a discourse in which profound debates were conducted over the justice of empire and in which tools were created that could be employed to defend the rights of non-European peoples as much as to attack them. The status of empire in international law, therefore, reflects the ambivalence about empire more broadly in the history of Western political thought. The liberal tradition presents us with the tools to critique empire as much as it presents the tools of expansionism.

---

[82] PC Jessup and HJ Taubenfeld *Controls for Outer Space and the Antarctic Analogy* (Columbia University Press New York 1959) see eg at 18, 34–9, 181, and 257–8; see also PC Jessup *The Use of International Law* (University of Michigan Press Ann Arbor 1959) at 148–9.

Recommended Reading

Anghie, Antony *Imperialism, Sovereignty and the Making of International Law* (CUP Cambridge 2005).

Bell, Duncan (ed) *Victorian Visions of Global Order: Empire and International Relations in Nineteenth Century Political Thought* (CUP Cambridge 2007).

Benton, Lauren *A Search for Sovereignty: Law and Geography in European Empires, 1400–1900* (CUP Cambridge 2010).

Haakonssen, Knud *Natural Law and Moral Philosophy: From Grotius to the Scottish Englightenment* (CUP Cambridge 1996).

Kingsbury, Benedict and Benjamin Straumann (eds) *The Roman Foundations of the Law of Nations: Alberico Gentili and the Justice of Empire* (OUP Oxford 2010).

Koskenniemi, Martti *The Gentle Civilizer of Nations. The Rise and Fall of International Law 1870–1960* (CUP Cambridge 2001).

Pagden, Anthony *The Fall of Natural Man* (CUP Cambridge 1982).

Pagden, Anthony *Lords of all the World: Ideologies of Empire in Spain, Britain and France c1500–c1800* (Yale University Press New Haven 1995).

Tuck, Richard *The Rights of War and Peace: Political Thought and the International Order from Grotius to Kant* (OUP Oxford 1999).

Williams, Robert A *The American Indian in Western Legal Thought* (OUP Oxford 1990).

CHAPTER 36

COLONIALISM AND DOMINATION

MATTHEW CRAVEN

1. INTRODUCTION

To speak today of the 'colonial origins of international law' is arguably no longer a standpoint of dissent, or of a radical revisionism, but one which is situated in the centre-ground of accounts of international legal history.[1] What is made of that observation is a matter upon which there remains a not insignificant divergence of opinion, but a consciousness that the emergence of the European states system in the post-Westphalian era was not merely incidentally related to the expansion of mercantile empires and the taking of colonial possessions, but was rather intimately connected with it, is one that is widely shared. It is no longer possible to read Grotius without attending to the fact that much of his work seemed to be written as an 'apology for the whole Dutch commercial expansion into the Indies',[2] or engage with the

---

[1] See generally A Anghie *Imperialism, Sovereignty and the Making of International Law* (CUP Cambridge 2004); C Mieville *Between Equal Rights: A Marxist Theory of International Law* (Brill Leiden 2005); J Fisch *Die europäische Expansion und das Völkerrecht* (Steiner Stuttgart 1984); WG Grewe *The Epochs of International Law* (M Byers trans) (De Gruyter Berlin 2000); M Koskenniemi *The Gentle Civilizer of Nations: The Rise and Fall of International Law 1870–1960* (CUP Cambridge 2002).

[2] R Tuck *The Rights of War and Peace: Political Thought and the International Order from Grotius to Kant* (OUP Oxford 1999) at 79.

historic formation of notions of war, sovereignty and territory and not notice the role they assumed in the violent expansion of European empires.

At certain points of time, of course, the relationship between the development of nascent legal doctrine and the practice of colonial rule has been entirely transparent. Just as Vitoria's famous lectures from 1532—*De Indis Noviter Inventis* and *De Jure Bellis Hispanorum in Barbaros*[3]—addressed themselves to the titles the Spanish put forward in order to justify their domination in the New World, so also, some 360 years later, Westlake, Martitz, Hornung, and other members of the newly formed Institut de Droit International were to debate the terms under which territory in Africa might be brought under colonial rule.[4] On other occasions, and far more frequently, colonialism has remained a significant background theme, providing the setting for doctrinal debates over freedom of the high seas, the use of force, title to territory, recognition, and statehood. Dealing with its legacy, of course, was also a central preoccupation in the 20th century both informing institutional initiatives (mandates and trusteeships) and emergent doctrine such as that relating to self-determination, sovereignty over natural resources, human rights, the law of armed conflict, state succession, and the boundary delimitation (*uti possidetis iuris*). There is, it might be suggested, scarcely a single area of international law that has not, in some manner or other, been informed by this history.

Yet even if there is broad concurrence in the view that the history of international law is intimately related to the history of colonial rule, there is, as I have already suggested, considerably less agreement over 'how' one may plausibly articulate, or account for, that relationship. For some, the relationship is almost an incidental one—the expansion of European empires and the development of international law being the product of an intra-European rivalry whose centre of gravity remained firmly European.[5] For others, the relationship is taken to be far more central, but here again the contrasts are marked. For Tony Anghie, for example, European international law not only provided a means of legitimizing imperialism, but was also profoundly shaped by that encounter, encoding within its disciplinary structures (especially sovereignty) the discriminatory features of cultural difference.[6] For China Mieville, by contrast, colonization was to be understood not so much in terms of its content, but in terms of the imperialism of its form:

Colonialism is in the very form, the structure of international law itself, predicated on global trade between inherently unequal polities, with unequal coercive violence implied in the very commodity form. This unequal coercion is what forces particular content into the legal form.[7]

---

[3] F De Victoria *De Indis et De Iure Belli relectiones* (E Nys ed) (Carnegie Institution Washington 1917).

[4] See *The Gentle Civilizer of Nations* (n 1) 149–52.

[5] Eg *The Epochs of International Law* (n 1); C Schmitt *The Nomos of the Earth* (Telos Press Publishing New York 2006).

[6] *Imperialism* (n 1) 6–7.

[7] *Between Equal Rights* (n 1) 178.

The instantiation of an international legal order governed by principles of sovereign equality and reciprocity thus formed a central facet of the emergent mercantilist, then capitalist/imperial, system in which the colony represented merely the most visible form of the accumulatory impulse that lay at its heart.

For all their differences, two particular assumptions have remained common in such accounts: one of which is reliance upon a conceptual separation between the material and ideological facets of international relations—between state practice and the (potentially oppositional) discourse of international law.[8] The other being a tendency to reify notions of State and sovereignty as the key architectural features of international relations, whose existence from the Peace of Westphalia onwards is taken to be both 'given' and historically 'constant'.[9] These are obviously related—the distinction between the ideological superstructure of international legal thought and the material impulses upon which it worked finding its rationality in the pre-existence of a particular structure of power in the form of the nation-state. The difficulty, of course, is that such an account not only leaves un-theorized the forms of knowledge and technologies of rule that underpinned the emergence of the 'state' as an object of inquiry: how was it that international law came to be regarded as the servile adjunct to imperial rule? Was this not, historically, something which was generated in the same story?

The concern of this chapter thus would be to provide an outline sketch of this putative 'relationship' between international law and colonial practice across the 16th–19th centuries in a way that both avoids the indulgence of believing that the law of nations was somehow abstracted from the material processes of colonial rule (that it was, in that sense, purely ideological), and treats with scepticism the claim that the institutions of 'State' or 'sovereignty' can be taken as historically continuous phenomena.[10] This means, on one side, attempting to situate the discourses on the law of nations 'inside' an account of the evolving technology of government and rule rather than seeing them as a form of external critique or mode of validation. On the other hand, it also means trying to conceptualize the process of colonization not simply in terms of a straightforward 'extension' of a pre-formed European sovereignty to the non-European world, but one whose dynamics were shaped by, and shaped in turn, changing conceptions as to the nature and character of governmental authority.

---

[8] Eg J Fisch 'The Role of International Law in the Territorial Expansion of Europe 16th–20th Centuries' (2000) 3 International Center for Comparative Law and Politics Review 4–13; D Armitage *The Ideological Origins of the British Empire* (CUP Cambridge 2000); A Pagden *Lords of All the World: Ideologies of Empire in Spain, Britain and France, c. 1500–c. 1800* (Yale University Press New Haven 1995).

[9] Eg H Wheaton *History of International Law in Europe and America* (Gould New York 1842); *Between Equal Rights* (n 1) 169.

[10] Cf M Foucault *Security, Territory, Population: Lectures at the Collège de France, 1977–78* (M Senellart ed, G Burchell trans) (Picador New York 2007) at 277.

In concrete terms, thus, I want to draw attention to two aspects of this history: one being the slow accretive process by which ideas of sovereignty were to form and mutate during the period between 1500 and 1900—from a notion of sovereign authority centred upon the coercive authority of the monarch, to the modern imagination of the 'nation-state'. The other being the parallel transition from a post-feudal mercantile economy to one centered (in Europe at least) upon industrial production and finance capital. In its most raw terms, the argument is that this history may be understood, albeit somewhat schematically, in terms of a shift in the conceptualization of the juridical politics of space from one marked by the notion of *dominium* to that of *imperium*. *Dominium* and *imperium* of course being seen operate here not merely as the juridical brackets that frame the 'colony', but also as having direct relationship to their etymological counterparts—domination on one side, and empire on the other.

2. Discovery and Conquest

For nearly a century prior to Columbus' voyage to the Americas, the Crowns of Castile, and Portugal had been sponsoring expeditions down the West Coast of Africa to the Canary Islands, Cape Verde, and the Azores, the overt purpose of which was to locate a direct source for the gold, spices, and silk whose supply had hitherto been dominated by the Arab traders and the merchants of Venice and Genoa. In the process, they had routinely sought, in accordance with the spirit of the *reconquista*, the blessing of the pope[11] and had respectively been rewarded with the authorization, in accordance with the stipulations of Hostiensis, to 'search out and conquer all pagans, enslave them and appropriate their lands and goods'.[12]

Columbus' voyage in search of an alternative route to the East Indies was not, in that sense, novel. Nor indeed was the subsequent involvement of the pope who was called upon to 'arbitrate' between the respective Castilian and Portuguese claims to the territory subsequently 'discovered'. Yet Pope Alexander VI's famous *inter caetera divinae* of 4 May 1493 (the fourth of five) was significant nevertheless. According to the Bull, the Pope purported to 'give grant and assign' to the kings of Castile and Leon in perpetuity exclusive jurisdiction over 'all... remote and unknown mainlands and islands... that have been discovered or hereafter may be discovered by you or your envoys' lying west of a line running from Pole to Pole 100 leagues west of the meridian

---

[11] FG Davenport *European Treaties Bearing on the History of the United States and its Dependencies* (Carnegie Institution Washington Washington DC 1917) vol 1, at 11; E Nys *Les Origines du Droit International* (Thorin Paris 1894) at 284–6.

[12] 'The Bull Romanus Pontifex (Nicholas V), 8 January 1455' in *European Treaties* (n 11) 9–26 at 12.

of the Azores and Cape Verde.[13] If the demarcation seemed clear enough, it was clouded by the fact that it excluded those territories already under the jurisdiction of other Christian powers, and was also silent on the question of Portuguese jurisdiction to the east. The two powers were thus forced to seek agreement as to their respective dominions—the subsequent Spanish–Portuguese Treaty of Tordesillas (7 June 1494)[14] diving the world again along the same lines, but a little further to the West. A further treaty was also required—the Treaty of Saragossa (1529)—to identify the respective line in the Pacific in which, incidentally, the much treasured Spice Islands (the Moluccas) were effectively 'sold' by Spain to Portugal for 350,000 ducats.[15]

These events themselves were revealing enough: in the first instance, whilst the involvement of the Pope seemed to signal the residual authority of the papacy as the moral and political centre of the late-medieval *respublica Christiana*, the subsequent agreements, by contrast, not only heralded its decline as the ultimate author of claims to power and jurisdiction, but marked the increasingly disputatious character of claims to overseas dominions brought about by the expansion of long-distance mercantile trade. The formalities of the Papal grant, even if important in signifying the persistence of a latent theological structure in legal and political thought was only the beginning of the story (as the subsequent claim to the establishment of New France by Francis I amply demonstrated). Apart from anything else, any such grant was made explicitly dependent upon the symbolic appropriation of land by subsequent acts of 'discovery' and occupation.

In the second place, the divisional lines that were put in place (*rayas*) were not, as Schmitt points out, lines separating the realm of Papal authority from that which was beyond his sway, but were rather global lines operating as 'internal divisions between two land-appropriating Christian princes within the framework of one and the same spatial order'.[16] In this sense the *Inter caetera divinae* departed from the earlier lines that had been drawn in 1443 and 1456 that extended only *usque ad indos*, and affirmed an outlook which was to bring the entirety of the globe within the contemplation of (European) political authority. Thirdly, it was to signal a good deal about the prevailing conception of political authority that was to undergird such acquisitions. That the Pope purported to 'gift, grant, or assign' the territories in question to the Kings of Leon and Castile was to look back in an obvious sense to a mediaeval theological universe of Papal authority, to feudal notions of investiture[17] and to the crusading mandate that had underpinned the *reconquista*. It also, however, looked forwards towards the emergence of a patrimonial conception of territorial sovereignty in which Roman civil law notions of property (*dominium*) came to structure notions of

---

[13] *European Treaties* (n 11) 64 and 68.
[14] ibid 84.
[15] ibid 146 and 169.
[16] *The Nomos of the Earth* (n 5) 92.
[17] See *The Epochs of International Law* (n 1) 231–2.

royal power for purposes of conceptualizing its expansion. Sovereignty and *dominium*, for such purposes, could be regarded as equivalent.

Each of these ideas were reflections of the broader social movements of the time. At the forefront, here, was the uneven, but nevertheless, steady decline of feudalism within Europe prompted, amongst other things, by the emergence of towns with their markets, merchants, exchanges, and guilds, the introduction of money into the agrarian economy, and a new technology of commerce (bills of exchange, joint stock companies, notaries, etc.).[18] Whilst the commodification of the rural economy and the associated decline in seigniorial rents was to signal the dissolution of the feudal political economy, it also stimulated the search for new sources of revenue—on one side through the centralization of governmental authority, the establishment of monopolies and systems of taxation and, on the other, through the sponsorship of long-distance maritime enterprise in the hope of cutting into the existing circuits of trade for the supply of high-value, high-return, goods.[19]

With the era of a mercantile absolutism just around the corner, Vitoria's famous reflections on the Spanish conquest of the West Indies might best be understood to be of a transitional character.[20] In one direction, and following in the footsteps of Bartolomé des las Casas, he was to deny the Spanish claim to possession on the basis of Papal mandate or discovery, asserting in the process not merely the limits of Papal authority (*imperator non est totius orbis dominus*[21]) but the essential humanity, and thus equality, of the inhabitants of the West Indies vis-à-vis the conquistadors from Spain. His innovation, here—to imagine a world governed by uniform principles of natural law ascertained by reason—was tempered only, however, by his subsequent endorsement of the justness of the Spanish conquest as having been based upon what he saw to be a legitimate *casus belli*. His understanding of the conditions under which a just war might be pursued, however, was particularly significant. War could not be waged, in Vitoria's mind, merely for purposes of imperial expansion, for the pursuit of the personal glory of the Crown, or indeed to enable the forcible conversion of pagans to the faith.[22] The only effective ground was 'a wrong received', for which principles of commutative, rather than distributive, justice were applicable. What constituted a 'wrong', however, was of importance insofar as it reflected back upon those 'natural' precepts of the *ius gentium* that governed the interaction between different peoples around the globe. Here Vitoria was to lay down, as primary, principles of sociability, and commercial interaction. The Spanish had a right, he claimed, 'to travel into the lands in question and to sojourn there'.[23] Further to this:

---

[18] See generally F Braudel *The Wheels of Commerce* (S Reynolds trans) (Collins London 1982).

[19] P Anderson *Lineages of the Absolutist State* (NLB London 1974) at 15–42.

[20] *Between Equal Rights* (n 1) 174–5.

[21] 'First Relectio' in *De Indis* (n 3) 115–62, s II-1 ('The Emperor is not lord of the whole world', translation at 337).

[22] 'Second Relectio' in *De Indis* (n 3) 163–87 at 170.   [23] 'First Relectio' (n 21) 151.

The Spaniards may lawfully trade among the native Indians, so long as they do no harm to their country, as for instance, by importing thither wares which the natives lack, and by exporting thence either gold or silver or other wares of which the natives have in abundance. Neither may the native princes hinder their subjects from carrying on trade with the Spanish; nor, on the other hand, may the princes of Spain prevent commerce with the natives.[24]

If, then, the natives were to prevent the Spanish from enjoying such rights of travel or commerce, the Spanish would be entitled to 'defend themselves' by force, to build fortresses and, ultimately, wage war, seize cities and provinces by way of retribution.[25] The same would be the case, he suggests if the Indians were to prevent the Spanish from preaching the Gospel.[26]

As has been suggested elsewhere, whilst Vitoria articulated these as universal principles he does not appear to have had in mind the possibility that the Indians, for their part, might avail themselves of similar rights.[27] Certainly as far as the preaching of the gospel goes, it was almost inconceivable that the Moors or Saracens would have the same right to wage war in defence of their faith.[28] Yet in some ways what is more revealing is the emphasis he places upon the institutions of commerce and property rather than those of Christianity. If faith, and the dominion of the Pope, could not serve as the governing conditions for relations with the non-Christian world, then some other framework of analysis needed to be set in its place. And Vitoria's choice here—to imagine a world of individual and communal property rights through which one could address almost all relevant questions (from the implications of discovery to the legitimacy of conquest)—was significant in two different ways.

In the first place, Vitoria's imagined world was not a purely hypothetical one, but in many senses reflected a pre-existent reality. The global circuits of trade which had for several centuries brought to Europe the gold, silk, and spices in search of which Columbus had crossed the Atlantic,[29] was only comprehensible if one started from an understanding of a global *diviso rerum* enabling the sequence of transactions and exchanges to take place.[30] Commerce, more than anything else, pushed attention towards the conditions under which both individuals and princes might claim to 'own' that which they found in their possession. And this, of course, not only challenged received precepts of Christian thought (the prohibition on usury, the belief that 'God made everything to be owned by all'), but was a concern that was to subsequently occupy jurists and political theorists such as Grotius and Locke for another few centuries.

---

[24] ibid 152.   [25] ibid 154–6.   [26] ibid 157.

[27] See *Imperialism* (n 1) 26–7; *The Role of International Law* (n 8) 8.

[28] 'Second Relectio' (n 22) 173.

[29] See *The Wheels of Commerce* (n 18) 114–34; JL Abu-Lughod *Before European Hegemony* (OUP New York 1989).

[30] See generally M Koskenniemi 'Empire and International Law: The Real Spanish Contribution' (2011) 61 University of Toronto Law Journal 1–36 at 16–29.

In the second place, just as Vitoria seemed to open out an entirely new imperial vision in which the emphasis was placed upon the 'informal' control of resources through private-law relationships of property and exchange rather than formal annexation,[31] it was also a vision resonant of a distinctively feudal imaginary. Whilst Vitoria understood that the conditions of political-legal coercion were centralized in the hands of the prince (in the sense that only sovereigns in his view could authorize the waging of war), and whilst the ruler was not entitled to intervene in his subjects enjoyment of private property (except for purposes of the common good), it was nevertheless not the case that political and economic power were yet entirely separated. Authority and possession remained intertwined through a conception of *dominium* that was understood to be both public and private,[32] encompassing matters of both jurisdiction and ownership. As he was to suggest in his Second Relectio:

[E]ven if we assume that the Indian aborigines may be true owners, yet they might have superior lords, just as inferior princes have a king and some kings have the Emperor over them. *There can in this way be many persons having dominium over the same thing;* and this accounts for the well-worn distinction drawn by the jurists between dominion high and low, dominion direct and available, dominion pure and mixed.[33]

It was thus possible to conceptualize the jurisdiction of the prince being exercised over his domain in a manner entirely analogous to that exercised by the lord over his manorial possessions, just as it had formerly been possible to envisage the dominions of the prince to be subordinate to the temporal 'dominion' of the Pope. All were, in a way, a seamless part of the same order, within which the (putatively) private institution of property remained entwined. And in the same respect, Vitoria seemed to be reflecting upon the semi-feudal character of Spanish colonial enterprise itself. The *capitulaciones* which structured the relationship between the *conquistadors* and the Spanish crown—in which the colonists were granted land, booty, and titles in return for of tax revenues and fees—envisaged, in effect, the creation of an 'empire of tribute'[34] in which authority would be vested in a local landed elite who would organize the administration of their petty fiefdoms through a feudal land tenure system in which natives were assigned to estates (the *economienda*) and threatened with slavery if they failed to fulfil the conditions of the requirement.[35] That the Spanish Crown subsequently developed an extensive colonial bureaucracy, monopolizing transatlantic trade through the *Casa de Contratación* and regulating the *economienda* system and the trade in slaves was only, arguably, a function of the degree to which spatial disaggregation threatened to sever the ties of loyalty upon which the entire system depended.

---

[31] ibid 32.
[32] 'First Relectio' (n 21) in *De Indis* (n 3) 128.
[33] ibid 130 (emphasis added).
[34] R Blackburn *The Making of New World Slavery* (Verso London 2010) at 129–34.
[35] E Wood *Empire of Capital* (Verso London 2003) at 42.

3. MERCANTILE COLONIALISM

If the declining authority of the Papacy had been signalled by Vitoria's reflections on the Spanish conquest, this was only to reflect upon the appearance of a new governmental rationality in the following century, which was aligned on one side with the centralization of sovereign power (*raison d'état*) and underpinned, on the other, by a competitive mercantilism that took as its end the enrichment of the State.[36] The practice of mercantilism, broadly outlined in the work of those such as Montchrestien, Mun, and Serra found its expression in a variety of institutions and policies: the surveillance and control of imports and exports, the creation of free 'internal' markets (through the dismantlement of urban protectionism), the imposition of duties on foreign goods (for example, the Colbert reforms of 1664, 1667), controls over shipping (for example, the Navigation Act of 1651[37]), the regulation of currency exchange and controls over the export of bullion, the granting of monopolies, and the control of public finance through the establishment of central banks. At its centre, however, were two key ideas: first, that the accrual of wealth, particularly in the form of bullion, was dependent upon a positive balance of trade the achievement of which would become an end of government itself; and secondly, that the conditions of competition necessitated a balance of power amongst European nations which would be secured, in the final measure, by means of a military-diplomatic armature.

The significance of this new rationality for purposes of colonial expansion was several. In the first instance, it took as its centre ground the problem of trade: although, as in France, one side of the equation could be addressed through the enhancement of local production and the encouragement of exports, as a whole it was to direct attention to the role of overseas commerce in the accumulation of pecuniary surpluses. And it was clear that it was long-distance trade that provided the unrivalled means 'for the rapid reproduction and increase of capital'.[38] Whilst, furthermore, this did not rule out the conquest or settlement of overseas territories, this was by no means a necessary measure[39] and, indeed, could often be seen to be an obstacle to commerce rather than its facilitator.[40] The French, British, and Dutch thus all joined Vitoria in disputing the competence of the Pope to divide the globe between Portugal and Spain and sought, where possible, to limit Spanish and Portuguese claims in order to break their monopoly over commerce in the West and

---

[36] *Security, Territory, Population* (n 10) 285–306.

[37] Navigation Act (9 October 1651) reprinted in H Scobell (ed) *A Collection of Several Acts of Parliament, Published in the Years 1648, 1649, 1650, and 1651* (John Field London 1653) pt 2, at 165–9.

[38] *The Wheels of Commerce* (n 18) 408.

[39] G Arrighi *The Long Twentieth Century: Money, Power, and the Origins of our Times* (Verso London 1994) at 141.

[40] For its significance in relation to maritime relations see GN Clark 'Grotius's East India Mission in England' (1935) 20 Transactions of the Grotius Society 45–84; CH Alexandrowicz 'Freitas *Versus* Grotius' (1959) 35 British Yearbook of International Law 162–82 at 165–6.

East Indies.[41] The French commissioners were to emphasize this point whilst negotiating the Treaty of Cateau-Cambresis of 1559,[42] as did the British[43] and Dutch in the terms of the letters patent or Charters granted to their own explorers. The letters patent granted to Cabot by Henry VII,[44] and Gylberte by Elizabeth I,[45] as with the General Charter issued by the states-General of the United Netherlands in 1614,[46] merely limited the respective grants by reference to land already occupied by another Christian power. Increasingly, thus, even if Spanish dominion within parts of the West Indies had to be taken as a fait accompli, the grounds upon which claims to dominion might be based were increasingly narrowed. Discovery could no longer suffice in itself—particularly if it merely involved the symbolic planting of stones or the erection of flags.[47] Actual occupation was needed in order to justify the limitations that were otherwise being placed upon the 'right of commerce',[48] and this theme was to become central to the subsequent discourse that premised title upon the effective use of land.

In the second place, since mercantilism took as its starting point the notion of national wealth understood in aggregate terms, not only was it blind to the internal distribution of wealth, but also encouraged an association between the interests and material wealth of the merchant class and the nation as a whole. This was, indeed, to find institutional recognition in the development of the chartered trading companies (the first of which being the Muscovy Company of 1555) whose role in colonial expansion over the following two centuries would be critical. Whilst trading partnerships had long been a staple feature of overseas trade, the chartered companies were innovative politico-economic amalgams: constituted on one side as joint-stock companies[49] but also endowed, on the other, with public prerogatives—generally rights of monopoly, but not infrequently rights to conquer and colonize. It was arguably by means of these public prerogatives that companies such as the East India Company (1600), the London and Plymouth Companies (1606), and Dutch East India Company (1604), to name but a few, were to increase the size of the respective Dutch and British overseas possessions enormously. The apparent 'harmony of interests'[50] upon which such arrangements rested, however, had certain consequences. In the first instance it was obviously to obscure the distinctions made by those such as Gentili

---

[41] A Pearce-Higgins 'International Law and the Outer World 1480–1648' in J Holland Rose et al (eds) *Cambridge History of the British Empire* (CUP Cambridge 1929) vol I, 183–4.

[42] *European Treaties* (n 11) 219–21.

[43] *The Ideological Origins* (n 8) 107–8.

[44] Letters Patent, 3 February 1498.

[45] Letters Patent, 11 June 1578.

[46] M Brumbaugh and J Walton (eds) *Inducements Offered by the States General of Holland to Settlers on the Hudson* (Christopher Sower Philadelphia 1898) at 4–5.

[47] *The Nomos of the Earth* (n 5) 131.

[48] *The Epochs of International Law* (n 1) 249–50 and 396.

[49] *The Wheels of Commerce* (n 18) 439–55.

[50] cf EH Carr *The Twenty Years' Crisis 1919–39* (Macmillan London 1940) at 42–61.

between public and private war, between piracy and privateering, and between public and private property.[51] Just as Vitoria had imagined the conquistadors to be, at one moment, private merchants exercising rights of travel and trade, and at another, the enforcers of public right, so also Grotius was later to advocate, in his *de jure praedae*, a right on the part of individuals (and private companies of course) to resort to violence in punishment of 'wrongs'. That this meant that private trading companies were entitled to aggressively pursue their commercial interests in the East Indies, and engage in hostilities and secure prize if they were unjustifiably prevented from doing so,[52] was only such as to reflect upon the fact that the distinctions in question (between public war and private enterprise) had yet to be made meaningful. That the same putative 'harmony of interest' was later to have the consequence of potentially bringing the entire imperial project into disrepute—most critically exemplified perhaps by the celebrated impeachment of Warren Hastings, India's Governor-General, at the hands of Burke[53]—was only an indication of the subsequent movement here in which the idea of 'public corruption' came to signify the (advocated) separation between, on the one hand, the exercise of duties of public office and, on the other, the accrual of private wealth.

In the third place, the focus on overseas trade also directed attention towards its necessary conditions, and in particular, to the status of the high seas and the navigation routes that provided access to the new markets. Whilst there had long been disputes over the control of European maritime zones (the Adriatic, the Baltic, the Ligurian sea, or the *Oceanus Brittanicus*), the Papal Bulls upon which Spain and Portugal based their claims only occasionally made mention of occupation or jurisdiction over the seas. In contrast to Nicholas V's *Romano Pontifex* of 1455 which granted to the crown of Portugal exclusive rights in relation to the Guinea trade including the right to exercise exclusive jurisdiction in relation to both the land and sea, the *Inter Caetera* edict, had merely prohibited the undertaking of voyages to the Indies without permission of the Crown of Castile.[54]

The debate that was to ensue following the publication of Grotius' *Mare Liberum* in 1609 was conducted at two different levels. On one level, and that which specifically informed the work of Selden,[55] his English interlocutor, the question seemed to be that of the possibility of enclosure in which rights over proximate maritime resources (principally fish) and local security were at the forefront. In Grotius' own terms, however (and that of de Freitas[56] his Portuguese critic), the question was more directly

---

[51] A Gentili *De Iure Belli Libri Tres* (1612 edn JR Rolfe trans) (Clarendon Press Oxford and Milford London 1933) vol II, at iii and 15.

[52] *The Rights of War and Peace* (n 2) 79–90.

[53] See generally, NB Dirks *The Scandal of Empire: India and the Creation of Imperial Britain* (Belknap Press Cambridge MA 2006).

[54] *European Treaties* (n 11) 72–4.

[55] J Selden *Mare Clausum* (excudebat Will. Stanesbeius, pro Richard Meighen London 1635).

[56] S de Freitas *De justo imperio Lusitanorum Asiatico* (1627).

concerned with long-distance navigation and trade, and the implications for the latter of claims to *dominium* over colonial possessions and the sea routes leading to them. The two sets of arguments were obviously related, however, insofar as each appeared to turn upon the question of ownership. For Grotius (who, of course, was writing at the behest of the Dutch East India Company), the sea was incapable of being subject to ownership insofar as it was not open to being consumed or transformed through possession.[57] Like the air, the 'sea is common to all, because it is so limitless that it cannot become a possession of any one, and because it is adapted for the use of all, whether we consider it from the point of view of navigation or fisheries'.[58]

Just as an individual was incapable of establishing ownership over something which was by definition limitless, so also was the *respublica* incapable of doing the same.[59] For Selden, by contrast, the sea was capable of enclosure through the medium of public navies and policing, much in the same way as local *dominium* was exercised over rivers and internal waters—what was in question was not 'control of the element of water, but control over the unchanging geographic sphere'.[60]

Perhaps most significant here is the politico-juridical organization of this argument. The difference between Selden and Grotius seemed to be one that turned upon a differentiation between jurisdiction and ownership—between what the Romans might have referred to as *imperium* (the public powers of the magistrate) and *dominium* (private rights of ownership). That it was a distinction neither appeared to recognize fully (and indeed which Grotius momentarily explicitly denied) was only such as to confirm the continuity of an essentially feudal equation of political and economic power ('sovereignty', despite Bodin's strictures, continued to be equated to ownership). At the same time, however, it was apparent that something new had appeared: as Schmitt points out, the real point was not whether the seas were *res nullius* or *res omnium*, but rather whether they represented a domain of law, or a domain of (lawless) freedom; and so far as the seas were thus to acquire particular legal status as 'free', was only such as to create two separate global orders each with its own related concepts of 'enemy, war, booty and freedom'.[61] In one sense, Schmitt's perception of an antithesis between the normative orders of land and sea might be associated with two distinct logics of imperialism—one expressed through a political logic of territorial expansion and colonial rule, the other through an economic logic of mercantile trade and navigational freedom.[62] Of course, however, they were far

[57] H Grotius *Mare Liberum* (1608) (JB Scott ed) (OUP New York 1916) at 22–9.

[58] ibid 28.

[59] Contra, H Grotius *De jure belli ac pacis* (JB Scott ed) (Clarendon Press Oxford 1925) vol II, ch iii, s iv, at 206–7 and s xiii, at 212–13.

[60] *The Epochs of International Law* (n 1) 268.

[61] *The Nomos of the Earth* (n 5) 172–84.

[62] For discussion of the antithesis of territorial and capitalist logics of imperialism see D Harvey *The New Imperialism* (OUP Oxford 2003) at 26–30 and 183; A Callinicos *Imperialism and Global Political Economy* (Polity Cambridge and Malden MA 2009) at 71–3.

from distinct: just as the mercantile communities saw as their enemy the monopolies and barriers to trade that ensued from (foreign) colonial rule or patrimonial claims over the seas, so also was it evident that advocacy of free navigation tended to coalesce in those places in which maritime strength would ensure eventual monopolistic control. The change in stance of the English crown in relation to the enclosure of the high seas, on that score, perfectly accords with the growing strength and size of its merchant fleet.[63] What was, perhaps, of more significance was the emergence of the 'sea' as a law-governed domain, in which absent outright ownership, the maritime powers increasingly sought to exercise powers of police—evidenced, in one direction by the subsequent enclosure of the territorial sea and, in another, by the increasing exercise of superintendent powers over the high seas whether under the Portuguese *cartaz* (a 17th-century version of the navicert)[64] or more generally in relation to piracy and slavery.[65]

4. Settler Colonialism

If, as has been suggested, one side of mercantilist thought was largely concerned with external trade, the other side focused upon the problem of enhancing the local conditions of production—of putting the population to work (through the regulation of migration and vagrancy and the introduction of 'poor laws'), controlling what would be produced (through subsidies and land regulation) and maximizing the productive output of land (through new agricultural techniques). This not only brought, as Foucault suggests, the population as a productive resource within the boundaries of governmental activity,[66] but also had its implications for the use of land. If the productive output of land itself had to be maximized it was a proposition which found its immediate expression in the long history of enclosures in England, and elsewhere in Europe, in which common land was given over to private ownership in order to be made more productive.[67] That the 'improvement' of land had impelled the dispossession of an agrarian population in England was to have particular significance for the development of settler colonialism in the 17th century—and not merely insofar as it provided the motive and means for such settlement (specifically the

---

[63] One may note, here, the critical change in position adopted by the British at the end of the 17th century. See *The Nomos of the Earth* (n 5) 177–8; *The Ideological Origins* (n 8) 100–24.

[64] 'Freitas *Versus* Grotius' (n 40) 176–80.

[65] See generally L Benton *A Search for Sovereignty* (CUP Cambridge 2010) at 104–61.

[66] *Security, Territory, Population* (n 10) 67–9.

[67] See K Polanyi *The Great Transformation* (Beacon Press Boston 1957) at 34–8.

existence of a dispossessed 'surplus' agrarian population who would settle in the colonies as indentured servants), but also its intrinsic rationality.

Settler colonialism as it was to develop in the hands of the British and Dutch in the early part of the 17th century differed from the earlier mercantile colonialism of the Portuguese insofar as it was concerned not merely with the establishment of local trading stations, but with the expansion of the dominion of the State and the volume of its productive land.[68] Sped by the appearance of new class of colonial merchants seeking to secure control over the production of sugar or tobacco,[69] the new settlements and plantations in the West Indies, Virginia, New England, and New Netherlands were thus, in the first instance, stations for production and consumption: they were to be supplied with (slave) labour, equipment, and an apparatus of security,[70] and would contribute to the general economic prosperity both by the consumption of produce from the imperial centre, and through the supply of new materials. Their integration within the metropolitan political economy, however, was always dependent upon the latter's control over trade—in the case of the British, for example, through the sequence of Navigation Acts from 1651 onwards—and this increasingly became the principle source of tension as the conditions of self-government intensified. Yet if the central idea was to settle and expand the dominions of the State, the operative means for doing so was not immediately understood in terms of straightforward conquest or annexation.[71] Rather, it was through the technology and practice of individual land appropriation (or what Marx called 'primitive accumulation').

The early charters granted to settlers in the Americas were, on the face of it, profoundly paradoxical. In one sense they were little more than feudal land grants faintly premised upon the idea that Christianity and civilization would be bought to the natives.[72] The first Charter of Virginia granted by James I, for example, authorized the settlers 'to make habitation, plantation and deduce a colony' on lands or islands that are 'either appertaining to us, or which are not now actually possessed by any Christian prince or peoples'. The terms of the 'grant' declared that 'they shall have all the Lands, Woods, Soil, Grounds, Havens, Ports, Rivers, Mines, Minerals, Marshes, Waters, Fishings, Commodities, and Hereditaments'[73] that subsist within fifty miles of each settlement, and that land was to be held under common socage with one fifth of all gold or silver ore to be paid to the Crown.[74] The curiosity here is not simply that

[68] *Empire of Capital* (n 35) 103.

[69] See R Brenner *Merchants and Revolution* (Princeton University Press Princeton 1993).

[70] See eg 'Charter of Privileges to Patroons, 7/17 June 1629' in W MacDonald (ed) *Select Charters and other Documents Illustrative of American History, 1606–1775* (Macmillan New York) 43–9.

[71] *The Rights of War and Peace* (n 2) 120–6.

[72] ibid 110.

[73] 'First Charter of Virginia, 10/20 April 1606' in *Select Charters* (n 70) 1–11 at 3.

[74] *Select Charters* (n 70) 1, 2, and 3. See also 'Patent of the Council for New England, 3/13 November 1620' in *Select Charters* (n 70) 23–33 at 28 and 'First Charter of Carolina, 24 March/3 April 1622/3' in *Select Charters* (n 70) 120–5.

no mention was made of the native inhabitants (except by implication),[75] nor that there was little precision as to where the colony itself would be 'deduced', but that the conditions under which the grant itself was made were entirely invisible. This may have been to suggest that the grants were premised upon the idea that the territory in question was effectively *res nullius*.[76] Yet, insofar as *res nullius* merely signified the possibility of things being bought into personal possession through occupation,[77] this was clearly not an effective condition for the original grant. The grants were suggestive, in other words, of a curious inversion in which the public authority to grant land seemed to precede the conditions precedent for the establishment of that authority in the first place—a form of appropriation before the fact.

Yet this inversion was to highlight a specific facet of the process of settlement—namely that the process by which sovereignty and jurisdiction came to be claimed was largely indistinguishable from the specificity of private acts of occupation and/or purchase of land.[78] There were two overt reasons for this: first of all because even if the settlements were originally conceived as a project of the royal State, the agents who would carry it forward were the industrious private settlers rather than the military forces of public authority.[79] In the second place it was evident that even if in some cases the 'grants' of charter or of patent preceded the fact of settlement,[80] in many others they clearly followed it as a process of ex post facto validation.[81] Either way, however, the governing rationality was one conditioned by the possibility of assuming individual rights of possession of land that had yet to be brought under the jurisdiction of the colonizing power. And it was here that the theme of land-improvement was to assume particular prominence.

Whilst Vitoria had insisted upon the existence of native title to land—and thus thrust the emphasis of justification upon the possibility of conquest—Grotius was not only to develop the latter theme much more generously (allowing, amongst other things, the right to punish those 'who act with impiety towards their parents'[82]), but was signal the opening out a new ground of appropriation that turned upon the conditions of its use:

[I]f within the territory of a people there is any deserted and unproductive soil, this also ought to be granted to foreigners if they ask for it. Or it is right for foreigners even to take

---

[75] In 'Patent of the Council for New England' (n 74) 25, however, it was noted that a 'wonderful Plague' had brought 'Destruction, Devastacion and Depopulacion' to the natural inhabitants of New England, leaving it open to be possessed and enjoyed unhindered.

[76] Eg J Elliott *Empires of the Atlantic World: Britain and Spain in America 1492–1830* (Yale University Press New Haven 2006) at 32; *Lords of All the World* (n 8) 76–7.

[77] On which see L Benton 'Acquiring Empire through Law' (2010) 28 Law and History Review 1–38.

[78] Cf 'Grant of Province of Maine, 3/13 April 1639' in *Select Charters* (n 70) 65–7 (in which the grant was accompanied by the following: 'Wee Doe by theise Presents ... take the same into our ... possession').

[79] EM Wood *The Origin of Capitalism: A Longer View* (Monthly Review Press New York 2002) at 164.

[80] Eg 'Charter of Maryland, 20/30 June 1632' in *Select Charters* (n 70) 53–9.

[81] Eg 'First Charter of Carolina' (n 74) 120.

[82] *De jure belli ac pacis* (n 59) vol II, ch xx, s xl, at 505.

possession of such ground, for the reason that uncultivated land ought not to be considered as occupied except in respect to sovereignty [*imperium*], which remains unimpaired in favour of the original people.[83]

In one respect Grotius was merely drawing upon a tradition of thought that had been well established since the time of More who, in his *Utopia*, had already advocated the settlement of foreign shores where land was unused.[84] But in a deeper sense he was also giving expression to the overt rationality underpinning the contemporaneous Dutch settlement of Guiana and Manhattan.[85] In its Charter of Privileges to Patroons of 1629, for example, the Dutch West India Company had declared that private individuals were 'at liberty to take up and take possession of as much land as they shall be able properly to improve'.[86] Even if the same Charter went on to specify that they 'shall be obliged to satisfy the Indians for the land they shall settle upon',[87] this only went so far as to emphasize that what was being authorized, was the settlement of land beyond the immediate confines of Dutch jurisdiction.

Two aspects of this are noteworthy. In the first place it was to reflect back upon practice of 'symbolic' possession associated with the right of discovery. If unsettled land was open to be occupied, then that would go just as easily for territory which had simply been marked by earlier discoverers as it would for territory newly found.[88] Title by discovery alone was effectively ruled out. Secondly, the underlying rationality of a right to appropriate 'deserted' or 'unproductive' land was one that not merely accorded with the precepts of mercantilism (to whit the maximization of domestic production), but also had buried within it a further implication: the right to appropriate land that was not being used productively enough. This was to find explicit recognition in the subsequent work of Locke who was to remark, with America in mind, that even if land had come to be enclosed, it might nevertheless still be taken into possession by another if it were 'left to waste'.[89] That this rationality led, on occasion, to squatting (Plymouth) or the unauthorized purchase of land (Rhode Island and Providence)[90] is perhaps unsurprising. In the second place, however, in working through the distinction between the public and private aspects of occupation (what he referred to as *occupatio duplex*), and in suggesting that the taking of possession (*dominium*) might leave unimpaired the jurisdiction (*imperium*) of the original people, Grotius seemed to leave in the air the question as to how Dutch or British

[83] *De jure belli ac pacis* (n 59) vol II, ch ii, s xvii, at 202.

[84] T More *Utopia* (1516) (P Turner trans) (Penguin London 1972) at 81.

[85] *The Rights of War and Peace* (n 2) 104–8.

[86] 'Charter of Privileges' (n 70) s xxi, at 49.

[87] ibid s xxvi, at 49–50.

[88] See *The Epochs of International Law* (n 1) 395–401.

[89] J Locke *Second Treatise of Government* (1690) (CB Macpherson ed) (Hackett Indianapolis 1980) at 24; see further *Empire of Capital* (n 35) 109–15 and 157–61.

[90] See E Keene *Beyond the Anarchical Society: Grotius Colonialism and Order in World Politics* (CUP Cambridge 2002) at 66.

sovereignty might come to be established over their respective settlements in the Americas? The answer, it seems, was to be found in Grotius' differentiation between forms of jurisdiction (*imperium*). Jurisdiction was primarily that exercisable in relation to persons, and only secondarily did it take the form of jurisdiction over territory.[91] This ordering of jurisdiction seemed, in some ways, to be descriptive of how he saw the settlement of the Americas: the personal jurisdiction over the Dutch and British settlers transmuting itself subtly into territorial jurisdiction as the settlements came to be established—whether by individual acts of 'occupation' or by the collective purchase of land from the original owners. Either way, however, sovereignty appeared to proceed from the fact of private appropriation rather than the other way round.

Emer de Vattel, who was later to return to the same theme almost a century later, was to fill out the sketch provided by Grotius albeit in slight amended guise:

We have already observed (§ 81) in establishing the obligation to cultivate the Earth, that these Nations cannot exclusively appropriate to themselves more land than they have occasion for, or more than they are able to settle and cultivate. Their removing their habitations through these immense regions cannot be taken for a true and legal possession; and the people of Europe, too closely pent up, finding land of which these nations are in no particular want, and of which they made no actual and constant use may lawfully possess it, and establish colonies there. We have already said, that he Earth belongs to the human race in general, and was designed to furnish them with subsistence: if each nation had resolved from the beginning to appropriate to itself a vast country, that the people might live only by hunting, fishing, and wild fruits, our Globe would not be sufficient to maintain a tenth part of its present inhabitants. People have not then deviated from the views of Nature in confining the Indians within narrow limits.[92]

Whilst Vattel retains the same core theme, several notable shifts in the terms of debate are apparent here. In the first place, and most obviously, the discussion is now framed in terms of the rights and obligations of nations: it is no longer a matter of private appropriation, but appropriation of a public nature equivalent to, but different from, conquest. When laying claim to vacant territory, the nation acquires 'empire' or 'sovereignty' at the same time as 'dominion'—'it can have no intention' he explains elsewhere, 'in settling in a country, to leave to others the rights of command'.[93] But at the same time as pushing the emphasis towards the rights of sovereignty, he opens up at the same time, a gap between public and private modes of territorial acquisition, in which the question of agency was therefore to become significant: under what authority were the colonists settling the land in question? Did they possess national character or were they merely emigrants? Was the

[91] *De jure belli ac pacis* (n 59) vol II, ch iii, s ix, at 206–7. For this interpretation see *The Rights of War and Peace* (n 2) 107–8.

[92] E de Vattel *The Law of Nations or Principles of Nature Applied to the Conduct and Affairs of Sovereigns* (Samuel Campbell New York 1796) book I, ch xviii, s 209, at 160–1.

[93] ibid book I, ch xviii, s 205.

intention to establish a colony under the sovereignty of the imperial power, or to establish a new nation on vacant land?

In the second place, by drawing attention to such questions, Vattel was not merely to reflect upon the growing demands for self-government in the colonies, but also to a subtle transformation in the prevailing governmental rationality that was to articulate itself increasingly forcefully in a distinction being drawn between the proper realm of governmental action and that of private intercourse. Whilst, as yet, the coming separation of the economic system from general social relations was not fully apparent, Vattel's contribution may be seen as one marked by a concern not so much as to enhance the end of the State through the organization and expansion of productive circuits, but rather to limit its authority by reference to the same precepts. The issue, as he puts it, was not so much the appropriation of territory for purpose of settlement and production, but rather the prior 'usurpation' of land by those who were not in a position to use it properly. If this was to emphasize the importance of 'effective control' for purposes of claiming title, it was also to hint at an entirely new rationality for colonial government—to enable the exploitation and use of land by bringing it within the ambit of an independent, self-regulating, market economy.

5. Imperialism, Political Economy, and the Scramble for Africa

If the early theorists of imperialism (Hobson, Lenin, Kautsky, Luxemburg, Bukharin, and Arendt) disagreed as to what it was they were seeking to describe, they were nevertheless uniform in their perception that it was a phenomenon to be associated with the final three decades of the 19th century.[94] During that period the visible enthusiasm for colonial acquisitions had led to an estimated 4.5 million square miles and 66 million inhabitants being incorporated within the British Empire; France gained 3.5 million square miles and 26 million people; Germany 1 million square miles and 26 million people; and Belgium, through Leopold's Congo Free State, 900,000 square miles and a population of 8.5 million.[95] The precise causes of the scramble were, of course, obscure: whether it was driven by the collapse in commodity prices and under-consumption within Europe,[96] the unravelling of the free trade

---

[94] See A Brewer *Marxist Theories of Imperialism: A Critical Survey* (Routledge London 1980); *Imperialism and Global Political Economy* (n 62).

[95] C Hayes *A Generation of Materialism, 1871–1900* (Harper New York 1941) at 237.

[96] R Luxemburg *The Accumulation of Capital* (Routledge London 2003).

arrangements put in place in the aftermath of the Cobden–Chevallier agreement of 1860, or by the emergence of the trusts, cartels, and monopolies associated with the rise of 'high finance'[97] were points of difference. Nevertheless, there was no doubt that the apparent over-accumulation of capital in Europe had encouraged the speculative interest in overseas investment (in trade, mining, manufacturing, railways, telegraph systems etc) which had, in turn, fed through into a self-reinforcing logic of acquisition: colonies and protectorates had to be acquired in order to 'protect' overseas trade and investment from the dangers posed by the monopolistic or protectionist policies of rival colonial powers.

At the centre of this account of the late 19th-century 'turn' towards colonial acquisition was the Berlin Conference of 1884–85 which, in many respects, appeared to stand as a symbol of this new Imperial era.[98] Articles 34 and 35 of the Final Act were particularly resonant here insofar as they sought to lay down the terms under which colonial powers might 'take possession' of land in Africa:

Article XXXIV   Any Powers which henceforth takes possession of a trace of land on the coasts of the African continent outside of its present possessions, as well as the Power which assumes a Protectorate there, shall accompany the respective act with a notification thereof, addressed to the other Signatory Powers of the present Act, in order to enable them, if need be, to make good any claims of their own.

Article XXXV   The Signatory Powers of the present Act recognize the obligation to ensure the establishment of authority in the regions occupied by them on the coasts of the African Continent sufficient to protect existing rights, and, as the case may be, freedom of trade and transit under the conditions agreed upon.[99]

The limitations of those articles were made all too apparent when the members of the *Institut de Droit International* were later to discuss their implications: not only were they territorially limited (specifically to the coasts of Africa), but they did not resolve either the question as to the necessity of native consent (as the US representative at the Conference, Kasson, had insisted they should) or whether the obligation to ensure the 'establishment of authority' subsisted in equal measure for protectorates as it did for possessions over which sovereignty was definitively asserted. In the eyes of some, the provisions appeared to endorse the idea that African territory was effectively to be regarded as *territorium nullius* for purposes of colonization; in the view of others such a conclusion was implicitly denied.[100] In fact, when read as a whole, the final Act

---

[97]   JA Hobson *Imperialism: A Study* (J Pott New York 1902); R Hilferding *Finance Capital: A Study in the Latest Phase of Capitalist Development* (M Watnick and S Gordon trans) (Routledge London 1981).

[98]   See generally *Between Equal Rights* (n 1) 250–6; *The Gentle Civilizer of Nations* (n 1) 121–7.

[99]   General Act of the Berlin Conference Respecting the Congo (signed 26 February 1885) (1885) 165 CTS 485.

[100]   J Fisch 'Africa as terra nullius: The Berlin Conference and International Law' in S Förster, W Mommsen, and R Robinson (eds) *Bismarck, Europe and Africa: The Berlin Africa Conference 1884–85 and the Onset of Partition* (OUP Oxford 1988) 347–74 at 355; A Fitzmaurice 'The Genealogy of *Terra Nullius*' (2007) 129 Australian Historical Studies 1–15.

assumes a thoroughly ambivalent character: whilst in part it was concerned with allowing colonization to proceed without conflict, there was also a distinctively anti-colonial thread within it.[101] This was true, in particular, of the plans for the 'conventional regime of the Congo' (which spread across the entirety of the African Continent from East to West) which sought the establishment of a 'neutral' central African zone of free commerce over which Leopold's Congo Free State would exercise a superintendent responsibility. That such a zone never materialized and, in fact, dissolved into one of the most brutal of colonial regimes is, perhaps, only emblematic of the general contradictions that underpinned the agreement in the first place.[102]

Two aspects of the story of the Berlin Conference might be usefully highlighted here. The first is the apparent confusion that the Conference sought to resolve concerning the precise modes by which colonies and protectorates might be acquired, and which, at the same time, brought into contemplation the nature and significance of 'native sovereignty'. The second is the curious connection that seemed to exist between the two modes of colonial engagement in question—formal colonization on the one hand, and the pursuit of free trade on the other.

Before turning to these two dimensions of the international legal framework of 19th-century colonialism, two particular aspects of its environment are worth highlighting. In the first place was the decline of mercantilism as an animating philosophy, and the rise in its place, of a new rationality of government organized around the idea of the self-regulating market and the institution of free trade. In the hands of Smith, Ricardo, and Say, the spirit of *laissez-faire* government was to find a new regulating force in the natural laws of economic life which would become its 'indispensable hypodermis'.[103] This presaged the gradual decline of formalized colonial monopolies, the winding up of the old charter companies (the East India Company being replaced by direct rule in 1858) and the rise of an increasingly fervent mercantile free-trade lobby.[104] Paradoxically enough, however, colonization proceeded apace, gaining velocity in the 'neo-mercantilist' decades at the end of the century.

Secondly, the industrial revolution as it was to take shape in Europe had both led to the 'political emancipation of the bourgeoisie' as Hannah Arendt put it,[105] and to the emergence of nationalism as a political ideology and practical project. Whether prompted as a palliative to the collective anomie of an increasingly urban industrialized workforce, or as a project associated with the creation of a skilled and mobile

---

[101] R Robinson 'The Conference in Berlin and the Future in Africa 1884–1885' in *Bismarck, Europe and Africa* (n 100) 1–34.

[102] SE Crowe *The Berlin West African Conference 1884–85* (Longmans, Green and Co London 1942) at 4–5.

[103] M Foucault *The Birth of Biopolitics: Lectures at the Collège de France 1978–79* (M Senellart ed, G Burchell trans) (Palgrave Macmillan New York 2008) at 16.

[104] See B Porter *Critics of Empire: British Radicals and the Imperial Challenge* (Macmillan London 1968).

[105] H Arendt *The Origins of Totalitarianism* (Harcourt New York 1968) at 123.

labour force, 'nationalism' not only spoke about the intrinsic value of ethnic or linguistic homogenity, but also about the desirability of government by consent ('le plébiscite de tous les jours' as Ernest Renan was to put it).[106] This placed two potential constraints on colonial expansion: in one direction it seemed to demand the consent of those who were to be subjugated by alien rule, in another it pointed to the impossibility of the full integration of colonial territories within the juridico-political conception of the nation-state.

5.1. Formalities of Colonial Acquisition

If, by the time of Vattel, the formal rationality of colonial acquisition had largely reduced itself to questions of conquest or occupation, the conceptual frame of territory, understood in terms of an analogy with property (organized around the primary and derivative modes of acquisition) was increasingly problematic. Political economy seemed to demand a separation between sovereign authority and private ownership to which end a differentiation between *imperium* (sovereignty or jurisdiction) and *dominium* (property) was important. The ethos of nationalism, furthermore, emphasized the relationship between the conditions of sovereignty (popular consent) and the spatial terrain over which sovereignty was exercised (who were the people?). As Arendt was to suggest, this was to pose a formidable obstacle to the expansion of empire: since a conquering power would 'have to assimilate rather than to integrate, to enforce consent rather than justice',[107] no nation-state, she was to suggest, 'could with clear conscience ever try to conquer foreign peoples', since the imposition of law upon others was fundamentally inconsistent with its own conception of law as 'an outgrowth of a unique national substance'.[108]

This was not to say, of course, that conquest was out of the question—indeed the forcible annexation of territories such as Burma (1826), Malacca (1824), Singapore (1819), Algeria (1830), Natal (1843), Basutoland (1868), New Zealand (1840), and the Transvaal (1901) was to belie any pretension otherwise. But Arendt's point remains: confronted by the theoretical and logistical difficulties of merging the juridico-political identity of the metropole with that of its colonial possessions (as pursued, largely unsuccessfully by France in relation to Algeria), colonial powers were encouraged to turn either to ideas of federalism, or to alternative, more flexible, modes of rule that defied any pretension of annexation. Within the sprawling British Empire at the end of the century, thus, one was to find not merely a plurality of institutional forms (protectorates, protected States, crown colonies, dominions, leased territories, con-

---

[106] E Renan *Qu'est-ce qu'une nation? Conférence faite en Sorbonne, le 11 mars 1882* (Lévy Paris 1882) at 27.
[107] *The Origins of Totalitarianism* (n 105) at 125.
[108] ibid 126–7.

dominia, suzerains, etc.) all of which had attenuated relations with the metropole, but also the emergence of the idea of an imperial 'commonwealth' that was at once internally divided, yet externally unitary. In reflecting upon the legal form of British India, for example, Westlake was to explain that:

[t]he colonial and other dependencies of a state are not in a personal union with it ... [n]either are they in a real union with the parent or supreme state, because they do not stand side by side with it as equals. ... They form with it one dominion or set of dominions, represented abroad by the parent or supreme state.[109]

This was, in one sense, to make relative the language of sovereignty: it assumed a different meaning depending upon whether one was focusing upon the inside, or the outside of imperial rule, looking towards the multiple forms of internal 'dominion' or outwards to the unity of the 'supreme State'. One thing was clear though, just as the determination to differentiate categorically between public and private action seemed to encourage the articulation of increasingly rigid conceptions of State and sovereignty,[110] Empire for its part seemed to represent a resistant strain, formulating itself in terms of a loose amalgam of governmental or jurisdictional powers secured only by the privilege of exclusivity.[111]

That imperial expansion seemed to be managed through an increasingly diverse set of institutions was, in part, a function of the extent to which the natives themselves were brought into account. However problematic, by the time of the Berlin Conference colonial powers had increasingly sought to justify their claims to African territory on the basis of treaties of cession or protection signed by local sovereigns.[112] The rationality for this, of course, was not that indigenous sovereigns in Africa could be treated as possessing full legal agency as, apart from anything else, they appeared not to be 'fit subjects for the application of legal technicalities'. It would, be absurd, as Thomas J Lawrence was to suggest 'to expect the king of Dahomey to establish a Prize Court, or to require the dwarfs of the central African forest to receive a permanent diplomatic mission'.[113] Rather, they were to be assimilated to primitive societies due, or destined to be, civilized,[114] capable nevertheless of authorizing their own subordination. The theme of inclusion and exclusion was pervasive. Even those committed to denying native sovereigns any form of legal agency nevertheless catalogued and categorized those non-legal forms for purposes of bringing them within the field of thought and action. Some differentiated, thus, between legal relations as might exist between European States and non-legal, moral or ethical, propositions that governed relations with the non-civilized world,[115] others between the relations governing States

---

[109] J Westlake *International Law* (CUP Cambridge 1904) vol I (Peace) at 41.

[110] Cf *The Epochs of International Law* (n 1) 467.

[111] Eg J Westlake *Chapters on the Principles of International Law* (CUP Cambridge 1894) at 128–33.

[112] M Lindley *The Acquisition and Government of Backward Territory in International Law* (Longmans London 1926).

[113] TJ Lawrence *The Principles of International Law* (DC Heath and Co Boston, 1895) at 58.

[114] See G Gong *The Standard of Civilization in International Society* (Clarendon Press Oxford 1984).

[115] *Chapters on the Principles of International Law* (n 111) 137–40.

enjoying full membership and those enjoying merely partial membership in the family of nations.[116]

The teleological ordering of societal forms which underpinned the liminal subjectivity of the natives was to have significance for colonial practice in two different respects. In the first place, it was to orient itself to the practice of colonial rule: if civilized States, as Westlake was to note, were those marked by the kinds of institutions of government, private law, and public administration found in Western Europe, colonial rule itself was to identify those conditions as being its objective.[117] If the marks of sovereignty were not pre-existent, they were to be produced. In the second place it was also to provide a new conceptual ground for colonial acquisition: this was not conquest, nor was it possession of vacant land (*res nullius*), but control premised upon the capacity to transform (civilize) the natives. What was being brought into European control was not merely land and resources (as had been the case in settler colonialism), but also, and perhaps more importantly, people and markets. From that perspective it was not the case, thus, that the native inhabitants could be regarded as inexistent, or the entirely dispensable subjects of colonial occupation, since they also seemed to occupy the role of potential producers and consumers. As John Kasson, the American delegate at Berlin was to insist:

> [i]t is not sufficient for all our merchants to enjoy equally the right of buying the oil, gums and ivory of the natives....Productive labour must be seriously encouraged in the African territories, and the means of the inhabitants of acquiring the products of civilized nations be thus increased.[118]

When seen in this light, the otherwise apparently disconnected features of the Berlin Conference appear perfectly congruent: the concern for the problem of 'slavery' or for the well-being of the native populations being driven, neither by a purely humanitarian idealism, nor by a cynical desire to justify colonial intervention, but by the underlying logic of producing free labour as the generative condition for the market economy.

If the natives primarily came into contemplation as potential producers and consumers, it was also tolerably clear that their 'voluntary consent' was far from necessary in order to substantiate colonial rule, despite Kasson's claims to the contrary.[119] The reason for this was not just the obviously questionable character of

---

[116] H Wheaton *Elements of International Law* (Clarendon Press Oxford 1866); L Oppenheim *International Law: A Treatise* (Longmans London 1905).

[117] See S Humphreys *Theatre of the Rule of Law: Transnational Legal Intervention in Theory and Practice* (CUP Cambridge 2010) at 109–21.

[118] Berlin General Act, Annex 14, Protocol 5 in R Gavin and J Betley (eds) *The Scramble for Africa: Documents on the Berlin West African Conference and Related Subjects 1884/1885* (Ibadan University Press Ibadan 1973) at 220.

[119] Protocol of 31st January 1885 in *The Scramble for Africa* (n 118) 240.

that consent, but an appreciation that the category of sovereignty qua 'possession' was, if anything, to be avoided. A notable illustration is to be found in the debate at Berlin over the extent to which the obligation in article 35 of 'ensuring the establishment of authority' was applicable to 'protectorates'. Unlike Germany, and to a lesser extent France, Britain had not pursued a policy of seeking to colonize and administer every territory over which it enjoyed rights of protection, and in many cases, it had merely sought to monopolize trade under title of agreement, but yet only exercise, in the process, a form of consular jurisdiction over British Nationals (which, in accordance with the terms of the Foreign Jurisdiction Act of 1843,[120] was all that could be exercised in relation to those not subject to recognized forms of government).[121] Even if British practice was peculiar on this score (and of 'doubtful legality' as Wilhelm Grewe was to claim),[122] its implications were nevertheless revealing. In the first instance it was to recognize that colonial rule could, at least potentially, assume a form that neither resolved itself in a claim of 'ownership', nor in the active administration of territory. As Westlake was to explain, the new breed of colonial protectorates that had appeared (for example, Gambia, Sierra Leone, Uganda, North and South Nigeria, and Somaliland) were those in which the colonial power did not yet claim to be 'internationally its territory', but yet were designed 'to exclude all other states from any action within it'.[123] If such a claim to jurisdictional exclusivity short of ownership was hard to recognize in terms of the received categories of territorial acquisition, it was perhaps only to indicate the limits of those categories as a way of conceptualizing the character of imperial rule.

A second matter signified by this practice was that it revealed an essential continuity between different forms of imperial rule. If one was to set aside the frame of *dominium* as a structuring category, and focus instead upon the question of jurisdiction, then it was immediately apparent that imperial rule could be understood as exercised through a gradated system running from, at one end, the establishment of regimes of consular jurisdiction to, at the other end, direct administration and rule over nationals, natives and foreigners alike. The essential fluidity of the idea and practice of jurisdiction, and its capacity to express itself in both territorial and non-territorial forms, was a perfect complement to an imperialism of commercial expansion that related itself, only very ambivalently, to the intensively administered structures of the colony.

[120] Foreign Jurisdiction Act of 1843, 6 and 7 Vict c 94.
[121] WE Hall *A Treatise on the Foreign Powers and Jurisdiction of the British Crown* (Clarendon Press Oxford 1894).
[122] *The Epochs of International Law* (n 1) 473.
[123] *International Law* (n 109) 123–4.

5.2. Imperial Free Trade

The central tension that ran through discussions at the Berlin Conference, and which arguably underpinned the inchoate form of the colonial protectorate was, of course the apparent conflict between, on the one hand a commitment to the expansion of trade and commerce (which, for many, could only expand if made free), and on the other, the expansion and intensification of colonial rule. This found its institutional expression in the distinction that appeared in practice between colonial rule, on the one hand, and the regimes of extra-territorial or consular jurisdiction that were to be put in place in China, Japan, Siam, Zanzibar, Muscat, and the Ottoman empire on the other. The distinction between these two institutional forms seemed profound. In the first instance, whereas colonies were understood to be marked by the assertion of territorial authority on the part of the colonial power, regimes of consular jurisdiction were, by contrast, premised upon its absence—there was no claim to sovereignty and foreigners were merely immunized from the application of local law.[124] Secondly, whereas colonial rule would have seen the establishment of national preferences, prohibitive tariff barriers and de facto, if not formal, monopolies on trade, the regimes of consular jurisdiction by contrast seemed to be designed to do precisely the opposite. Thus, in case of China, in the aftermath of the first Opium War in 1842, a network of bilateral treaties were put in place all of which sought to secure the necessary conditions for the exercise of freedom of commerce. European merchants were provided security in their commercial transactions through the comforting blanket of consular jurisdiction in which all disputes, whether civil or criminal, familial or commercial, would be governed by the laws of the State of nationality and heard by a resident consul (sometimes sitting alone, sometimes in a mixed court). Tariffs on all trade were regulated by the same means, fixed by treaty and gathered by European customs agents. The replication of similar provisions in treaties with the majority of European powers (with liberal use of most-favoured-nation clauses), and their extensive application to both nationals and *protégés* (who might hail from other parts of the colonial empires), meant that a large proportion of foreign trade was conducted under the terms of such regimes.[125]

For all of the theoretical differences that marked this activity from the parallel processes of formal colonization, there were several obvious points of connection.[126] It was clear from the outset that the regimes of consular jurisdiction were not entirely incompatible with the establishment of colonies by way of lease (Port

---

[124] See F Piggott *Extraterritoriality: The Law Relating to Consular Jurisdiction and to Residence in Oriental Countries* (Kelly & Walsh Hong Kong 1907); FE Hinckley *American Consular Jurisdiction in the Orient* (WH Lowdermilk and Co Washington 1906); G Keeton *The Development of Extraterritoriality in China* (Longmans London 1928).

[125] See PK Cassel, Grounds of Judgment: Extraterritoriality and Imperial Power in Nineteenth-Century China and Japan (OUP Oxford 2012).

[126] See *The Epochs of International Law* (n 1) 474–7.

Arthur, Weiheiwei), regimes of protection (Morocco), or mere occupation (Egypt). As time progressed, furthermore, territorial divisions became more resilient resulting in the establishment, sometimes formally sometimes informally, of 'spheres of influence' in which European powers mutually recognized their respective rights of commercial preponderance within designated zones. Siam, for example, was effectively divided between the British and the French on this basis, neither of which purported to exercise anything other than consular jurisdiction, but both enjoying otherwise the privileges of colonial predominance. As Westlake was to point out, the sphere of influence was not itself 'a recognized form of aggrandisement' and had no particular effect in relation to third parties.[127] It was, at best, a 'shadowy form of earmarking'.[128] But he was also to note how spheres of influence were occasionally subtly reshaped into claims of sovereignty—his example being the 'remarkable' agreement of the 12 May 1894 in which Britain purported to grant the Congo State a lease over territory, its only claim to which being that it fell within its sphere of influence as recognized in a treaty with Germany and Italy. His conclusion that Britain, in fact, had no basis upon which to act as lessor of the territory in question, did little more than confirm a particular direction of travel: namely that spheres of influence were liable to 'harden' over time and formalize themselves in regimes of protection,[129] just as the latter themselves were liable to harden into a fully fledged colonies.

6. Conclusion

In the course of this chapter, I have alluded to a series of shifts in the operative rationality of governmental thought and practice: in economic terms from feudalism through mercantilism to modern political economy; in political terms from the emergence of absolutism to the territorial nation-state and the plural bracket of Empire; in legal terms from the scholasticism of Vitoria, through the natural law of the humanists to the anthropologically informed positivism of the 19th century. Each of these shifts I take to be important in their own right, but more is disclosed, as I have sought to show, through their relationship to one another: in the way in which they shed light on the different technologies of colonial rule, shaping both its form and content at various different moments in time.

[127] *Chapters on the Principles of International Law* (n 111) 188.
[128] *International Law* (n 109) 128.
[129] *A Treatise on the Foreign Powers* (n 121) 230.

The key theme that I have sought to sketch out, is the shift from a conception of colonial rule framed in terms of *dominium*, to one structured around the idea of *imperium*. To some extent talking about a move from *dominium* to *imperium* means reading into the vocabulary of Roman law much more than is apparent in its bare terms. It was clearly not the case that late 19th century colonialism experienced a retrocession to the forms of Roman imperialism, or indeed that the vocabulary of Roman law was an indispensable adjunct to colonial rule. I find it, nevertheless, a useful expression to the extent that it reveals a shift in the discourse and practice of colonial rule from a moment at which the technology of expansion could be articulated in terms of the straightforward acquisition of property (whether original or derivative), to one in which relations of property became the active object of colonial rule rather than its precondition. Colonialism was not just about acquiring things as property, but about turning things into property. If, originally, *dominium* and *imperium* lacked a decisive point of differentiation, not only were they later to be set apart, but the rationality of *imperium* was increasingly organized around the idea of establishing the conditions for the enjoyment of private property and exchange. Understood as pure jurisdiction empire knew no boundaries, and followed 'meekly in the train of exported money'[130] but yet at the same time had to reach back to neo-feudal ideas of 'ownership' in order to sustain the exclusivity of governmental authority that exported money demanded.

Recommended Reading

Alexandrowicz, Charles H *An Introduction to the History of the Law of Nations in the East Indies* (Clarendon Press Oxford 1967).

Anghie, Antony *Imperialism, Sovereignty and the Making of International Law* (CUP Cambridge 2004).

Arendt, Hannah *The Origins of Totalitarianism* (Harcourt, Brace & World New York 1968) 123–157.

Armitage, David *The Ideological Origins of the British Empire* (CUP Cambridge 2000).

Benton, Lauren A *Law and Colonial Cultures: Legal Regimes in World History, 1400–1900* (CUP Cambridge 2002).

Benton, Lauren A 'Acquiring Empire through Law' (2010) 28 Law and History Review 1–38.

Cassel, Pär K *Grounds of Judgment Extraterritoriality and Imperial Power in Nineteenth-Century China and Japan* (OUP Oxford 2012).

Fisch, Jörg *Die europäische Expansion und das Völkerrecht* (Steiner Stuttgart 1984).

Grewe, Wilhelm G *The Epochs of International Law* (M Byers trans) (De Gruyter Berlin 2000).

Koskenniemi, Martti *The Gentle Civilizer of Nations: The Rise and Fall of International Law 1870–1960* (CUP Cambridge 2002).

---

[130]   *The Origins of Totalitarianism* (n 105) 135.

Koskenniemi, Martti 'Empire and International Law: The Real Spanish Contribution' (2011) 61 University of Toronto Law Journal 1–36.

Mieville, China *Between Equal Rights: A Marxist Theory of International Law* (Brill Leiden 2005).

Pagden, Anthony *Lords of all the World: Ideologies of Empire in Spain, Britain and France, c. 1500–c. 1800* (Yale University Press New Haven 1995).

Schmitt, Carl *The Nomos of the Earth* (Telos Press Publishing New York 2006).

Tuck, Richard *The Rights of War and Peace: Political Thought and the International Order from Grotius to Kant* (OUP Oxford 1999).

CHAPTER 37

SLAVERY

SEYMOUR DRESCHER AND
PAUL FINKELMAN

1. Introduction

SLAVERY is one of the oldest known human institutions. Evidence of it is found in archaeological sites and in ancient legal records. With a few minor exceptions, slavery has existed throughout the world, in all cultures and societies. Virtually all ancient legal codes, including the Mesopotamian, Babylonian, Roman, and biblical, defined and justified slavery. Only in the 18th and 19th centuries—after more than four millennia of known human history—did slavery come under sustained juridical and political attack.

Although the substance of slavery has varied from place to place, and over time, systems of slavery include most, or all, of the following conditions: (1) slaves are property, and can be sold, traded, given away, bequeathed, inherited, or exchanged for other things of value; (2) the status of slave is inheritable, usually through the mother; (3) formal legal structures or informal agreements regulate the capture and return of fugitives slaves; (4) slaves have limited (or no) legal rights or protections; (5) slaves may be punished by slave owners (or their agents) with minimal or no legal limitations; (6) masters may treat, or mistreat, slaves as they wish, although some societies required that masters treat slaves 'humanely' and some societies banned murder and extreme or barbaric forms of punishment and torture; (7) masters have unlimited rights to sexual activity with their slaves; (8) slaves have very limited or no appeal to formal legal institutions; (9) slaves are not allowed to give testimony against their masters or (usually) other free people, and in general their testimony is not given the same weight as a free person's; (10) the mobility of slaves is limited by owners and often by the State; (11) owners are able to makes slaves into free persons through a formal legal process (manumission), but often these freed persons are not given full legal rights; (12) slave ownership is supported by laws, regulations, courts, and legislatures, including provisions for special courts and punishments for slaves, provisions for the capture and return of fugitive slaves, and provisions and rules for regulating the sale of slaves. All of these aspects of slavery have been part of the development of the international law regulating slavery.

In almost all legal systems, slaves are considered moveable property—in English legal terms chattels or 'things'—to be bought and sold by individual masters, corporations, or institutions (often the churches). In some places, the State might also own the slaves as well, but in that context the State is acting like an individual owner, just as the State might own real estate or vehicles. By 1890, chattel slavery had disappeared in Europe and the New World, and was no longer acceptable under existing rules of international law. However, in European colonies in Africa, and later in the Soviet Union and Nazi Germany, new systems of 'State slavery', 'corporate slavery', and 'slave-like conditions' emerged in the late 19th century through to the mid-20th century. These included brutal systems of massive forced labour in Belgian, French, German, and British colonies involving Africans working in mines and plantations, Soviet Gulags, and massive forced labour and actual slave labour in Nazi Germany. Convict labour in the American South, while not affecting nearly as many people, was also a new form of State-forced labour.

Even where slavery itself was prohibited many States have accepted and enforced the status of slaves under concepts of both private and public law. Thus, in the English *Somerset's Case*,[1] Lord Chief Justice Mansfield ruled that a slave could not be held in Britain against his will, but at the same time stated that '[c]ontract for sale of a slave is good here; the sale is a matter to which the law properly and readily attaches, and will maintain the price according to the agreement.'[2] Similarly, Sir William Scott (later elevated as Lord Stowell) of the British High Court of Admiralty recognized in *Le Louis* that, while the African slave trade violated English law, it did not violate international law. He held it would be 'deemed a most extravagant assumption in any Court of the Law of Nations, to pronounce that this practice, the tolerated, the approved, the encouraged object of law, ever since man became subject to law, was prohibited by that law, and was legally criminal'.[3] In the US, Chief Justice John Marshall used this logic in *The Antelope*,[4] acknowledging that the African slave trade violated American law and was 'contrary to the law of nature', but concluding that it was 'consistent with the law of nations' and 'cannot in itself be piracy'.[5] Pennsylvania

---

[1] *Somerset v Stewart* (1772) Lofft 1, 98 ER 499.   [2] ibid 509.
[3] *Le Louis* (1817) 12 Dods 210, 165 ER 1464 at 1477.
[4] *The Antelope* 23 US 66, 10 Wheat 66 (1825).   [5] ibid 101 and 122.

(1780) and New York (1799) absolutely banned the importation of new slaves, but used concepts of comity and international law to allow visitors a limited sojourn with their slaves.

In our own time, persons illegally held in slave-like conditions of forced labour and constricted mobility are not slaves in the true sense. People kidnapped, trafficked, or held against their will are treated like slaves by those holding them, but their servitude is not supported by formal institutions, and if they escape their illegal bondage, the law will protect them from their captors. The distinction here is between slavery as a legal and economic system and individual acts of enslavement, based on illegal private coercion and force.

2. The International Law Elements of Slavery

The international law elements of slavery fall into eight general categories: (1) acceptance of enslavement as a legitimate status based on internationally accepted criteria; (2) the willingness to accept the slave status of persons from other jurisdictions under some theory of conflicts of law or comity; (3) international recognition of the trade or commerce in slaves; (4) a general view, in the ancient world, that anyone could be enslaved, without regard to race, ethnicity, religion, or economic status, under internationally recognized rules of warfare, custom, and economics; (5) a changing notion in the Western world of who might be enslaved, moving from a universality to limiting enslavement to non-Christians, then non-Europeans, then just to Africans, and finally to the international prohibition of all enslavement; (6) international regulation leading to the end of commerce in slaves; (7) general condemnation of enslavement which denies comity to foreign owners because slavery is contrary to natural law and most municipal law, and only tenable under local positive law; and (8) the modern view that under international law enslavement is unacceptable exploitation that constitutes a crime against humanity.

The historical evolution of the international law of slavery can be seen as a series of mirror images of these concepts. Thus, under the first category, in the ancient world, almost no one questioned the legitimacy of enslavement. The biblical story of Joseph (whether true or entirely fictitious) illustrates this concept. When Joseph's brothers sell him to a caravan, the purchasers accept at face value that those selling Joseph may legitimately do so. Slavery was so ubiquitous that there was no reason to question the status of anyone presented as a slave. Most ancient slaves were not of course sold into bondage by their jealous brothers. Rather, enslavement was most commonly the result of warfare or debt. Under internationally accepted rules of the ancient world, soldiers and civilians captured in warfare might be legitimately killed, but their captors might impose the more humane consequence of enslavement. But, under the sixth category, neither prisoners of war nor captured civilians may be summarily killed, and thus their enslavement is not a humane alternative to death, but an impermissible violation of fundamental human rights constituting a crime against humanity. Thus after the Second World War German and Japanese leaders were prosecuted for crimes against humanity for enslaving civilians and prisoners of war.

Similarly, under category 2, when slavery was generally acceptable under international law and the comity of nations, masters could travel with their slaves, knowing that they would be entitled to their property interest in their slaves along with other forms of property. Starting in the 18th century, slavery was no longer universally acceptable (category 7) and thus it became more problematic to apply the concepts of comity to the slave property of visiting masters. Courts in 18th-century France and Great Britain freed slaves of visitors on the theory that no metropolitan laws existed to uphold the status of a slave. Starting in the 1830s, northern-state courts in the United States often liberated slaves of visiting southern masters. In the modern world, where slavery is universally condemned, slave status created in one nation would not be recognized in other countries.

The transition from universal acceptability (category 4) to limiting enslavement to certain religions, races, or ethnicities (category 5) reflects the transition from the ancient to the modern world in the international conceptualization of slavery. In the ancient world *anyone* could be enslaved. A Roman soldier—even a general—could be captured and enslaved; similarly, a slave could become free and rise in society. As Moses I Finley observes, although most classical slaves were 'barbarians' from other cultures, there were also 'Greek slaves in Greece [and] Italian slaves in Rome…'.[6] Europeans enslaved each other throughout the ancient world and well into the modern period. With the fall of Rome enslavement was gradually limited to European pagans. As Europe became Christian, only non-Europeans could be slaves. Expansion to Africa and the Americas allowed for enslavement based solely on race—first Africans and Indians, and by the 18th century, only Africans. By the end of the 19th century, generally accepted concepts of international law prohibited slavery everywhere in the Western world. The German, Japanese, and Soviet reintroduction of slavery in the 1930s and 1940s violated accepted rules of international law, while also resurrecting older categories of vulnerability to enslavement based on ethnicity, race, and status as civilian and military prisoners of war. Ironically, in the modern world human trafficking, which is illegal everywhere, and unacceptable under international law, has led to slave-like conditions for people of all races, cultures, and ethnicities.

The first element of slavery targeted for suppression was the trans-oceanic slave trade (the transition between categories 3 and 4). After becoming the focus of a sustained civil and political mobilization its abolition became a crusade in Europe and

---

[6]   MI Finley *Ancient Slavery and Modern Ideology* (Penguin Books New York 1983) at 118.

America. In 1815, slave trading was the first economic activity to be formally condemned in an international treaty as repugnant to the principles of humanity and universal morality.[7] Its practitioners were also the first category of law breakers to have their cases adjudicated before international courts.

At the Nuremberg tribunals after the Second World War, enslavement was among the first activities to be prosecuted as a 'crime against humanity'. Reflecting the long history of its suppression, slavery is the first specific violation of human rights listed in *The Universal Declaration of Human Rights* (1948). Slavery's salience as a consensually condemned condition ensured that many other human rights campaigners would endeavour to designate their targets for criminalization as slave-like conditions.

3. Before Anti-slavery and Abolitionism

3.1. Gradual Restriction of Enslavement

Slavery's importance to world history and international law derives from its antiquity and ubiquity. In various forms it was identifiable in almost every culture, reaching back to the very origins of humanity. As Sir William Scott recognized in *Le Louis*, 'personal slavery arising out of forcible captivity is coeval with the earliest period of the history of mankind', was found in the 'earliest and most authentic records of the human race', and was embedded in the traditions of the 'most polished' peoples of classical civilization.[8] Above all, it was an integral component of the most prestigious and durable juridical legacy of antiquity—Roman civil law, where slavery was given universal status. 'Roman juristic references to slavery being *contra naturam*' were followed by the observation that it was an 'institution of the *ius gentium* (law common to all peoples) and what natural reason prescribed for all men'.[9] Warfare and trade were the most common methods for acquiring and distributing slaves. The rationale that conquest entailed the right to kill or spare and dispose of the conquered remained at the core of the universal rationale for enslavement. Bondage also grew out of local criminal laws and even civil arrangements, as debtors (or their family members) could be enslaved to creditors. Once the enslavement took place, the slave was commodified and subject to sale.

---

[7] Declaration Relative to the Universal Abolition of the Slave Trade (signed 8 Februrary 1815) (1815) 63 CTS 473.

[8] *Le Louis* (n 3) 1477.

[9] Cicero *De officiis* 3.5.23 quoted in *Ancient Slavery and Modern Ideology* (n 6) 99–100.

During the medieval period, the boundaries of enslavement were gradually restricted by religious affiliation, but the enslavement of infidels in a just war offered ample scope for the continuation of the institution. For captives from abroad, the legitimacy of the initial enslavement was usually unimportant. Few medieval purchasers worried how Britons, Celts, or Slavs came to be enslaved, when Vikings brought them to the Mediterranean. From the standpoint of Roman law, an imported captive's status was defined by the *ius civile* of the place where the initial enslavement took place. This perspective defined European attitudes towards Africans later transported to Europe and the Americas.[10] In the Southern Mediterranean basin, sub-Saharan Africa, central Asia, and throughout the Muslim world enslavement and the slave trade continued unabated into the modern world.

The shift away from the universality and ubiquity of slavery began in Europe in areas located at the greatest distance from the Mediterranean zone of intermittent warfare and violent contact between Christian, Muslim and the non-monotheistic regions of Africa and Eurasia. By the beginning of the 16th century, slavery had yielded to regimes of contractual systems of labour in north-western Europe. Encouraged by the expansion of medieval European urban notions of 'free air', juridical commentaries began to take note of the absence of slaves within their polities. Whether attributed to communal, royal, or religious inspiration, English, Dutch, and French jurists and communal governments claimed that as soon as slaves reached the soil or breathed the air of their nations they became free.[11]

3.2. Prisoners of War as Slaves

Strengthening this notion was the observation that, in contrast to antiquity, Christian nations had abandoned the principle that all civilian populations or prisoners of war were at the disposal of warring neighbours. Nevertheless, the development of principles of liberating soil entailing the prohibition of slavery was still regarded as a peculiar local innovation. Those engaged in developing international law supported the legitimacy of enslaving non-Christians 'beyond the line' of Christian Europe. After 1450, Iberian jurists easily applied this legal ideology to the Portuguese and Spanish empires, easily applying institutionalized slavery in the metropolis to overseas colonies. Located at the frontier of interreligious warfare and mutual enslavement, human bondage continued, as did both de facto and de iure slavery.

---

[10] Y Rotman *Byzantine Slavery and the Mediterranean World* (Harvard University Press Cambridge MA 2009) at 26.

[11] S Drescher *Abolition: A History of Slavery and Antislavery* (CUP New York 2009) at 23; see also S Peabody *'There are No Slaves in France': The Political Culture of Race and Slavery in the Ancien Régime* (OUP New York 1996); and S Peabody 'An Alternative Genealogy of the Origins of French Free Soil: Medieval Toulouse' (2011) 32 Slavery and Abolition 341–62; for the American context, see P Finkelman *An Imperfect Union: Slavery, Federalism and Comity* (University of North Carolina Press Chapel Hill 1981).

The Portuguese pioneers of the African slave trade to Europe and the Americas understood Portuguese-African relations in terms of religious warfare. Roman civil law, inflected by canon law, justified the enslavement of captives in a just war. From the standpoint of civil law the status of captives purchased from abroad had already been determined. As the Portuguese explored the African coast, its inhabitants were seamlessly conflated with Saracens. As early as 1452 the papacy granted the Portuguese monarch the 'full and free permission to invade, search out, capture and subjugate the Saracens and pagans and any other unbelievers and enemies of Christ wherever they may be…and to reduce their persons to perpetual slavery' for purposes of conversion.[12] The fact that the Portuguese were in no position to invade Africa on a large scale strengthened the rationalization for slave trading as the best available means for the conversion and salvation of Africans. For the Portuguese the purchase of African slaves constituted an integral part of the *ius gentium*, especially in the kingdom of the Congo, where Portugal quickly established formal diplomatic relations.[13]

3.3. African and American Slave Trade

The transatlantic slave trade and African slavery's judicial legitimacy in the Americas was integrally related to Africa's initial independence vis-à-vis Europe. The contrast with the Spanish policy towards the enslavement of Native American populations is striking. Although the enslavement of Amerindians began with the second voyage of Columbus, by the mid-16th century there was an imperial consensus against their further enslavement. The conquistadors' rapid domination of the most densely populated areas of the Americas, combined with the enormous mortality wrought by disease and exploitation, led Bartolomé de las Casas and other Spanish clergy to denounce the enslavement of the Indians and induce the monarchy to prohibit the further enslavement of Amerindians who voluntarily surrendered to Spanish domination. Under the usual terms of just war principles enslavement was still legitimate when a native population refused to accept submission and conversion. Thereafter Indian enslavement continued only at the unconquered peripheries of the New World empires. As the transatlantic slave trade increased by more than tenfold between the mid-16th and the early 19th centuries there were no major challenges to the legitimacy of slavery in the Iberian empires. There was never a public debate over the legitimacy of the African slave trade or over slavery itself which legally existed everywhere in the Spanish and Portuguese empires.[14]

---

[12] JF Maxwell *Slavery and the Catholic Church* (Barry Rose Chichester 1975) at 53.

[13] JK Thornton *The Kingdom of Kongo: Civil War and Transition, 1641–1718* (University of Wisconsin Press Madison WI 1983); and D Birmingham *Portugal and Africa* (St Martin's Press New York 1999).

[14] *Abolition* (n 11) 64–6.

North of Iberia slavery had vanished long before the launching of overseas colonial ventures in the 17th century. Nevertheless, northern European political, legal, and religious authorities offered no sustained opposition to overseas slaving or slave holding 'beyond the line' of metropolitan Europe. To rationalize this system with their metropolitan 'freedom principle' these polities developed dual legal systems regarding slavery. Following the Portuguese example, the French monarchy formally sanctioned a French slave trade for purposes of conversion. Lacking an indigenous metropolitan slave code like the Portuguese, the French monarchy created colonial Black Codes. In Paris, a 'Court of Conscience' at the Sorbonne ruled that nothing in the Bible, the canon law, or the civil law's *ius gentium* prohibited the legitimate ownership of slaves.[15] Holland and Great Britain explicitly authorized trade and colonizing companies to formulate legal codes appropriate to their overseas situations. The premise of new needs for new settlements 'beyond the line' prevailed in all the new European colonies. In 1584 England allowed colonies, 'in remote, heathen and barbarous lands', to make particular laws and statutes 'agreeable to the laws of England'. All British governments during two subsequent centuries found slavery and the slave trade within in all of their dominions to be 'agreeable'.[16]

3.4. Slavery and the Law of Nations

Early modern European commentators on the law of nations regarded the development of overseas slave systems as relatively insignificant. Echoing the traditional categories of medieval civil law, slavery retained its traditional place as an integral and consensual element of the law of nations, in conformity with natural reason, logically derived from the quasi-universal phenomena of war, captivity, and poverty. Ayala Balthazar, Cornelius van Bynkershock, Hugo Grotius, Samuel von Pufendorf, and other legal theorists all agreed that the law of nations sanctioned slavery. Sir Thomas More considered slavery integral to society and his *Utopia* (1516) assumed that every household would have slaves, either imported from another country or local residents convicted of crimes.[17] Similarly, the English libertarian philosopher, John Locke provided for slavery in his draft of the Fundamental Constitution of Carolina (1669)[18] and his *Two Treatises on Government* (1690)[19] sanctioned slavery. The very nature of war still gave victors the power of life or death potentially attenuated by enslavement.

---

[15] DB Davis *The Problem of Slavery in Western Culture* (Cornell University Press Ithaca NY 1966) at 197.

[16] *Abolition* (n 11) 75.

[17] T More *Utopia* (Printed for Richard Chiswell London 1684) at 68 and 138.

[18] J Locke *The Fundamental Constitution of Carolina* (London 1670) para 109.

[19] J Locke *Two Treatises on Government* (Printed for Whitmore and Fenn and C Brown London 1821) at 1 and 205–7 *et passim*.

European restraints on exercising the power of enslavement were noted as a fortunate exception to the general rule that slavery remained integral to the law of nations. If the institution could be limited or modified by municipal law it still remained part of the world's rational legal order.[20] Significantly, where major early modern commentators on the law of nations congratulated Europeans on having attenuated the unlimited rights of enslavement by conquest their focus was entirely metropolitan.

Despite the Atlantic World expansion of slavery and the slave trade, international law theorists paid little attention to this new development in world history. Here the contrast between the lawyers' treatment of slavery and piracy is striking. In no other aspect of early modern international law can the domination of Antiquity be seen as in the comparative treatment of slavery and piracy. The civil law tradition unequivocally declared that pirates were *hostis humani generis*—common enemies of the human race. Piracy was designated, without hesitation, as an affront to the consensual law of nations and pirates could be summarily hung.[21]

Those who had to deal with the maritime aspects of international law could not so easily elude the increasing involvement of Europe in the slave trade. Charles Malloy's *De Jure Maritimo et Navali* (1682) still confidently assumed that slavery was a general if not quite universal institution. Under certain conditions, he reiterated, enslavement was consistent with 'natural justice by covenant' (voluntary) or by 'transgression' (involuntary).[22] European princes had universally agreed (the consensual requisite) 'to esteem the words, *Slave, Bondman* or *Villain* as barbarous'.[23] In England, trover could not be maintained even for a 'More [Moor] or other Indian'.[24] Yet Englishmen traded in slaves in Africa and the New World. 'Beyond the line' rationalized the difference. Natural and mathematical laws had more certitude than civil law, and human activities were subjected to different 'certitudes' in different latitudes.[25] It was not only the legal tradition but the ubiquity of slavery that weighed upon lawyers and philosophers. From a global perspective Europe's rulers appeared as committed to perpetuating bondage on the eve of the American Revolution as they had been when the Portuguese purchased their first slaves on the coast of Africa three centuries earlier. In 1772 Arthur Young, a political arithmetician, estimated that of the earth's 775 million inhabitants all but 33 million could be classified as unfree. That year Francis Hargrave successfully represented James Somerset, warning Lord Mansfield and the people of England that if Stewart's right to hold Somerset as a slave was recognized in England, slavery 'with its horrid train of evils' would invade their island 'at the

---

[20]   *The Problem of Slavery* (n 15) 114–20.

[21]   Compare Emerich de Vattel's discomfort at having to even discuss slavery as part of the *ius gentium* with his zest in sanctioning of the casual dispatch of pirates to their fate. E de Vattel *The Law of Nations, or the Principles of Natural Law Applied to the Conduct and to the Affairs of Nations and Sovereigns* (1758) art 152 and 233.

[22]   C Molloy *De Jure Maritimo et Navali; or a Treatise of Affairs Maritime, or of Commerce* (3rd edn printed for John Bellinger and George Dawes London 1682) at 353.

[23]   ibid 355.   [24]   ibid.   [25]   ibid 426–27.

discretion of every individual foreign and native'. He predicted it would come 'not only from our colonies and those of other European nations, but from Poland, Russia, Spain, and Turkey, from the coast of Barbary, from the Western and Eastern coasts of Africa, from every part of the world, where it still continues to torment and dishonor the human species'.[26] Similarly, Adam Smith told his law students at Glasgow, they should not be deceived by the absence of slavery in their one small corner of the globe. Slavery was found on every continent, and was likely to endure for ages, if not forever.[27]

4. Abolition and International Law

4.1. Conflicts of Laws over Slavery

In the half-century after Smith's lectures, developments in conflicts of laws theory and world trade dramatically affected the international law of slavery. The larger debate—and the greater impact on international law—focused on the African slave trade. But, before that issue developed, issues over conflicts of laws marched through the courts and legislatures of Europe and the United States.

Under traditional notions of international law and comity, the status of a person did not change when that person was brought to a new jurisdiction. For example, people married in one country would be considered married in another, even if the other country might not have allowed them to marry in the first place. To offer a modern illustration, a State which requires that women be at least sixteen before they can marry, is unlikely to prosecute a twenty-one year old husband if he enters the jurisdiction with his fifteen-year-old wife, if that marriage was legal where they were married. But this simple concept of comity and status breaks down when the status violates the public policy or positive law of the forum State. Thus, a State might not recognize a polygamous marriage, even if it was legal where it was performed.[28]

In the 18th century this problem arose when Europeans, colonists, or foreigners brought slaves to the metropolis. Courts in both France and Britain ruled that slaves brought within their jurisdiction could not be held against their will, because slavery

[26] Francis Hargrave *An Argument in the Case of James Sommerset a Negro, Lately Determined by the Court of King's Bench: Wherein it is Attempted to Demonstrate the Present Unlawfulness of Domestic Slavery in England. To Which is Prefixed a State of the Case* (Printed for the Author London 1772) at 11, reprinted in P Finkelman (ed) *Slavery, Race and the American Legal System, 1700–1872* (Garland New York 1988) series 1, vol 1, at 11.

[27] A Smith *Lectures on Jurisprudence* (RL Meek, DD Raphael, and PG Stein eds) (Clarendon Press Oxford 1978) at 186–7.

[28] See *Reynolds v United States* 98 US 145 (1878) upholding polygamy prosecutions.

had never been established in those places. In the absence of positive law, such a status could not be recognized. In *Somerset v Stewart* Lord Chief Justice Mansfield famously set out the standard for why a slave brought to England was free:

So high an act of dominion [as holding someone in slavery] must be recognized by the law of the country where it is used. The power of a master over his slave has been extremely different, in different countries. The state of slavery is of such a nature, that it is incapable of being introduced on any reasons, moral or political; but only positive law, which preserves its force long after the reasons, occasion, and time itself from whence it was created, is erased from memory: it's so odious, that nothing can be suffered to support it, but positive law.[29]

By 1840 most of the free states of the United States adopted the *Somerset* principle, although some also provided limited exemptions for travelling masters. Before 1840 a number of southern States also recognized the principle, holding that slaves voluntarily taken to free States had become free. However, by the eve of the American Civil War, most southern States no longer applied the *Somerset* principle to slaves who had lived in free jurisdictions. In *Dred Scott v Sandford*[30] the US Supreme Court ruled that the *Somerset* principle would not apply to federal territories or federal courts.[31]

While the *Somerset* principle was primarily applied within the British Empire and the between American states, it also led to international conflicts. After the American Revolution, about 20,000 blacks fled with the British armies. In the Treaty of Paris (1783) and Jay's Treaty (1794) Britain agreed to return 'property' owned by Americans. But, the British refused to return thousands, on the grounds that they had offered freedom when they left America. Similar issues arose in 1841, when a group of slaves on the Creole, a US coasting vessel, seized the ship and sailed it to the British Bahamas. The British returned the ship but refused to return the slaves to the United States, asserting they were free under the *Somerset* precedent. Britain refused to extend comity to America and the incident simmered for years, as American administrations unsuccessfully demanded a return of the slaves.

The clearest example of the international law conflicts over slavery between the two nations involved the slave John Anderson, who killed a white man while escaping from Missouri. He made his way to Canada, where the United States tried to extradite him for murder. British and Canadian abolitionists argued that since slavery violated natural law, Anderson had a right to defend his freedom. The case became a *cause célèbre* in England and Canada, but Anderson ultimately reached England, where he remained free.[32] In the United States were there were similar cases that might be

---

[29] *Somerset v Stewart* (n 1) 510.

[30] *Dred Scott v Sandford* 60 US 393; 19 How 393 (1857).

[31] See P Finkelman *An Imperfect Union: Slavery, Federalism and Comity* (University of North Carolina Press Chapel Hill 1981); for a history of this issue in the United States; on the conflicts of laws issue in Dred Scott v Sandford, see P Finkelman *Dred Scott v Sandford: A Brief History* (Bedford Books Boston 1995).

[32] See P Finkelman 'International Extradition and Fugitive Slaves: The John Anderson Case' (1992) 18 Brooklyn Journal of International Law 765–810.

classified as 'domestic international law', as governors in free states refused to return fugitive slaves charged with crimes or free people charged with helping fugitive slaves escape. On the eve of the Civil War, in *Kentucky v Dennison*,[33] the US Supreme Court castigated Ohio for refusing to return a free black charged with stealing in Kentucky because he helped a slave escape from that state. But the court would not force Ohio to cooperate in the extradition.

All of these cases were premised on the notion that slavery was illegitimate, and could only exist under positive, statutory, law. No state or nation was required, on theories of international law or comity, to give force to slave status created in another jurisdiction. This was a vast change from the earlier period, when all jurisdictions recognized slavery and upheld its status under international concepts of comity.

4.2. The Anti-slavery Movements

The other major slavery-related international law issue in this period involved the movement to abolish the African slave trade. For the first time opposition to the trade became the policy of a sovereign nation, Great Britain, which also was the world's strongest economic, naval, and international diplomatic power. This movement dovetailed with the rise of a British movement to end slavery itself, first in the empire and then in the world. While attacks on the trade were launched almost simultaneously on both sides of the Atlantic (in the United States, Great Britain, and France), Britain became the largest, the longest, and the most indispensable agent of change. In America opposition to the trade and to slavery itself was muted by the overriding fact that slaveholders dominated the nation's political structure, slaves constituted the nation's most valuable form of private property after real estate, and the American constitution protected slavery in numerous ways. In 1794 France's revolutionary government declared an emancipation throughout the empire. However, in 1802 Napoleon restored slavery everywhere but Haiti, the site of the only successful slave revolution in history. By the second quarter of the 19th century the United States and France became the two nations that most fiercely resisted the internationalization of abolitionism.[34]

The internationalization of anti-slavery grew directly out of the British abolitionist movement. Launched in 1787, the first campaign against the British slave trade evolved to amass more popular support than any other British reform movement for the next half a century. A similar movement developed in the US. During the American Revolution all of the newly independent states prohibited the African slave trade, on economic grounds and for political and philosophical reasons. By 1787, five states

---

[33] *Kentucky v Dennison* 65 US 66; 24 How 66 (1860).
[34] *Abolition* (n 11) 115–80.

had either abolished slavery or passed gradual abolition acts. At the Constitutional Convention there were significant and angry debates over the African slave trade. Some delegates attacked the trade as immoral, while others defended it on grounds of history, economics, and international law. South Carolina's Charles Pinckney, citing ancient Rome and Greece, declared that slavery was 'justified by the example of all the world'.[35] Ultimately the constitution prohibited Congress from abolishing the trade before 1808, but did not require that the trade be banned then. From 1794 to 1803, Congress passed three acts prohibiting American citizens and ships from participating in the trade. But imports from foreign (usually British) traders remained legal. In 1808, Congress completely banned the trade. By 1822 the United States had made slave trading piracy, punishable by death.[36] However, as noted above, in *The Antelope*, Chief Justice John Marshall refused to apply the ban to foreign traders who inadvertently brought slaves into the US.[37]

In 1807 Britain prohibited its nationals from participating in the transatlantic slave trade, ending importations into Britain's New World colonies, but not in Africa and Asia. In 1814 another popular mobilization induced the British government to internationalize the campaign against the slave trade.[38] Its first achievement, at the Congress of Vienna, was a treaty provision condemning the traffic as 'repugnant to the principles of humanity and universal morality'.[39] It expressly recognized the article's radical departure from existing practices and beliefs, and 'the interests, the habits and even the prejudices' of those who benefited from the trade. Therefore the declaration did not 'prejudge the period that each particular Power may consider most advisable for the definitive Abolition of the Slave-Trade'. Thus the trade remained legal as a matter of international law.[40]

The British also pursued a series of bilateral treaties that allowed mutual rights of search to the signatories. Effectively this meant that the British Navy, the largest and most powerful pursuer of slavers, would be searching vessels sailing under foreign flags. During the Napoleonic wars the British navy had exercised belligerent rights of search and seizure against enemy ships carrying slaves. Under significant abolitionist pressure bounties were offered to naval ships for captured slaves adjudicated at a Vice-Admiralty Court established in Sierra Leone.[41]

---

[35] Pinckney quoted in P Finkelman *Slavery and the Founders: Race and Liberty in the Age of Jefferson* (2nd edn ME Sharpe Armonk NY 2001) at 28.

[36] P Finkelman 'The American Suppression of the African Slave Trade: Lessons on Legal Change, Social Policy, and Legislation' (2008–9) 42 Akron Law Review 433–67; and P Finkelman 'Regulating the African Slave Trade' (2008) 54 Civil War History 379–405.

[37] *The Antelope* (n 4).

[38] *Abolition* (n 11) 205–44.

[39] *Declaration* (n 7).

[40] JS Martinez 'Antislavery Courts and the Dawn of International Human Rights Law' (2008) 117 Yale Law Journal 550–641 at 575.

[41] D Eltis *Economic Growth and the Ending of the Transatlantic Slave Trade* (OUP New York 1987) at 102–11.

The power of the international law tradition became evident after the return of peace. The decision in *Le Louis* (1817), confirmed the power of the 'law of nations' to protect foreign slave ships against seizures not covered by mutual treaties in peacetime. A British ship seized *Le Louis* on the pretext that France had prohibited the trade after Waterloo. Reflecting popular opposition in Britain to this brutal and horrific traffic, Sir William Scott specifically separated his own 'moral apprehensions' from his decision that an English court could not support the seizure of the French ship because all sovereign nations had an equal right to the 'unappropriated parts' of the ocean in peacetime. Despite enormous public opposition to the African trade, Parliament had not declared it to be piracy. History weighed heavily. Slavery, 'arising out of forcible captivity is coeval with the earliest periods of the history of mankind'. Slavery was found, without condemnation, in humanity's most 'authentic records' from the most cultivated peoples of antiquity through early Christianity to Scott's own time when treaties, monopolies, and public laws facilitated the trade. The slave trade was universally recognized by all nations, which were entitled to continue or end it on their own terms. The consensual and reciprocal premises of the law of nations set sharp limits on action against the slave trade.[42]

Nineteenth-century legal treatises and texts echoed Justice Scott's opinion in *Le Louis*. Since the 'law of nations' was treated as a measure of consensus on slavery, international law could only view the progress of abolition as a passive register of change among the sovereign States. Eight years after *Le Louis*, Chief Justice John Marshall of the US Supreme Court adopted Scott's logic in *The Antelope*. Noting that 'the detestation' of this 'abhorrent', 'unnatural traffic' was 'growing daily', Marshall nevertheless held that its violence to natural law or public sentiment could not alter the mandate of a judge. The law of nations was 'the law of all' and by that test the question went in favour of 'the legality of the trade'. And thus the trade 'could not be pronounced repugnant to the law of nations'. Only the common consent of all nations could modify international law.[43]

As the main engine of abolitionist initiatives after 1815 the British government followed a number of strategies to circumvent the limitations imposed by the existing international law. Britain first attempted to obtain multinational agreements on the model of the Congress of Vienna. The Congresses of Aix-la-Chapelle (1818) and Verona (1822), and a multinational negotiation in London (1840) all foundered on the breach of sovereignty required by the right of search. Meanwhile, from 1815 until the end of the century Britain negotiated more than one hundred bi-national treaties to suppress the trade by allowing mutual searches, or securing agreements to declare the trade to be a form of piracy. The refusal of the United States to acquiesce in a mutual right of search and the limited cooperation of France precluded final closure of the transatlantic trade until late in the century.

---

[42] *Le Louis* (n 3) 1476 and 1477.
[43] *The Antelope* (n 4) 115, 116, and 120–1.

4.3. Mixed Commissions

One innovation of the treaty system that affected international law was the creation of multilateral courts (or 'mixed commissions') to adjudicate the disposal of slave ships and recaptured slaves. The magistrates were drawn from the signatories of each country. In case the two judges could not agree on a given case a third judge would be selected by lottery. Anti-slavery now added a dimension to international law hitherto absent from the prosecution of piracy. A formal institution, consisting of international representation and rules of adjudication, was added to the repertoire of international law. The treaties eventually included the United States, but never France. The courts heard more than 600 cases involving 80,000 Africans.[44]

The system has been hailed as a precursor of the international courts of the 20th century. However, two of the most important commissions were located in Havana and Rio de Janeiro, the principal New World destinations of slavers after the Anglo-American abolitions. However, these two commissions sent many of the liberated Africans (*emancipados*) to work for long terms of apprenticeship from which they never emerged. Most significantly, these mixed commissions appear to have had very little impact on the development of later international law theory. In this sense they may have acted more as harbingers rather than originators in the development of the international justice system.

Mixed commissions were primarily the projection of a British naval and global power in the half-century following the victory over Napoleon.[45] As noted above, such processes caused major changes in both the theory and practice of international law. The mixed commissions were both an extension of *Pax Britannica* and a widely recognized shift in the operation of the law of nations. Most international law commentators stressed the limitations on anti-slavery expounded by Scott and Marshall rather than slavery's questionable expansion in the tropical towns of Havana and Rio de Janeiro. *Pax Britannica* and British anti-slavery also affected the development of international law in a far more significant way. In response to British pressure, weaker rulers often signed treaties and then evaded enforcement, sometimes for decades. Meanwhile, British governments escalated diplomacy to virtual warfare, with naval blockades and even bombardments to ensure compliance with their demands to end the slave trade—in Portugal in 1842, in Brazil in 1850, and in various parts of West Africa.

4.4. *The Amistad Case*

Notions of international law in the United States, the other major player in the drama over the illegal African slave trade, further complicated suppression. The United States, dominated by Southerners, refused to fund a naval force sufficient to effectively patrol

---

[44] 'Antislavery Courts' (n 40) 579 ff.
[45] L Benton 'Abolition and Imperial Law, 1790–1820' (2011) 39 Journal of Imperial and Commonwealth History 355–74.

the African coast but at the same time, invoking international law, refused to allow British ships to stop and inspect American-flagged vessels. This allowed smugglers to evade British naval patrols by falsely flying an American flag and also protected actual American ships involved in the illegal trade from being stopped by the British.

International law, and the presence of British authorities in Havana, did lead to the outcome in *United States v The Amistad*,[46] the most dramatic slave-trade case in the United States, and perhaps in the whole Atlantic world. *The Amistad* was transporting slaves from one part of Cuba to another in 1839, when the slaves, who had been recently, and illegally, imported from Africa, revolted, killed the crew, took charge of the ship, and ordered their owners, who survived the revolt, to steer the ship east, towards Africa. During the day the owners did this, but at night they reversed course, heading north and west, hoping to reach the United States' South. Instead, the ship was discovered by a US Coast Guard vessel in Long Island Sound, and towed to Connecticut. This began a two-year saga ultimately leading to the US Supreme Court. Spain, acting under the Treaty of San Lorenzo (1795), which is better known as the Pinckney Treaty,[47] demanded that the Africans—who became known as the 'Amistads'—be returned to Cuba so they could be tried for murder and mutiny or be re-enslaved, the Cuban owners claimed the Amistads as their property, while the crew of the US Coast Guard vessel claimed salvage rights in the ship and its contents, including the Africans. Based in part on evidence provided by British officials stationed in Havana, the US Court in Connecticut ruled that the Amistads had been illegally imported to Cuba and thus they were never legally slaves and therefore the Pinckney Treaty did not apply them. The US Supreme Court upheld this ruling, and the Amistads went free, and were ultimately repatriated to Africa. This case illustrates the complexity and force of international law at this time. Because Cuba no longer allowed the slave trade, the recently imported Africans went free. However, a Cuban-born slave cabin boy on the ship was returned to Cuba, under the Pinckney Treaty, because he was legally a slave under Cuban law and under international law.

5. A New Line: Civilization

Euro-American emancipation ended the transatlantic trade and led to a new conceptual and diplomatic line between the 'civilized' world of Europeans and the 'semi-civilized' or 'uncivilized' regions of Afro-Asia.[48] As late as 1840, abolitionist leaders in Britain proposed the extension of the bilateral treaty network against the slave trade

---

[46] *United States v The Amistad* 40 US 518; 15 Pet 518 (1841).
[47] Treaty of San Lorenzo (signed 27 October 1795) 53 CTS 9 ('Pinckney Treaty').
[48] On the concept of civilization, see the contribution by L Obregón 'The Civilized and the Uncivilized' in this volume.

to the states along the African coast. The plan included pursuing and arresting suspected slavers in national waters close to the coast and even into navigable rivers.
Some African rulers, when first confronted by British agents, attempted to negotiate
limitations on the Royal Navy on the basis of international maritime law. The British
Navy then intimidated the rulers into signing treaties and peremptorily burned the
slave barracoons. After some initial metropolitan hesitations about transgressing
international law the pattern became set: naval officers would attempt to negotiate a
treaty. If that proved impossible, they might employ force and then negotiate abolition treaties post facto. This was not unlike the earlier Spanish model of empire
building in the Americas.

Even long established African States like Dahomey were intimidated. Unlike the
British actions against the Luso-Brazilian States, no permission to engage in hostilities was requested or granted by Parliament. It was better to finesse legal qualms
than to risk encountering the hurdles of the law of nations. Various British governments frequently considered declaring slavery equivalent to piracy, but rejected the
idea on familiar grounds. 'Though a greater moral crime than piracy', slaving was
not, 'like piracy, a crime which by the general and established law of nations any
and every nation may punish, whatever may be the country to which the offenders
belong'.[49]

The most significant outcome of the pre-emptory pattern of British policy was
that by the late 1840s metropolitan public opinion regarded African polities as not
entitled to inclusion as sovereign nations under international law. Admission into the
circle of civilization rested on presumptions of consent and reciprocity among the
civilized. A new line of exclusion grew out of public debates on the implications of
unequal treaties with Asian societies. Since African states were regarded as even less
civilized than their Asian counterparts, the logic of exclusion applied with greater
force to African States.

By the 1860s and 1870s, the professionalization of international law reinforced the
reformulation of the limits of the law of nations along the lines of civilization.[50] International lawyers developed a cluster of characteristics that placed a nation within the
magic circle of the civilized: a common millennial history and intellectual tradition
(classical/Christian), a secularized religious culture, a common set of manners, a
common legal culture, sometimes a common biological or genealogical heritage,
and, of course, membership in a common scientific international law association. In
this regard slavery and anti-slavery became decisive markers of civilization during
the late 19th century.

---

[49] R Law 'Abolition and Imperialism: International Law and the British Suppression of the African
Slave Trade' in DR Peterson (ed) *Abolitionism and Imperialism in Britain, Africa, and the Atlantic* (Ohio
University Press Athens OH 2010) 150–74.

[50] M Koskenniemi *The Gentle Civilizer of Nations: The Rise and Fall of International Law 1870–1960*
(CUP Cambridge 2001) ch 1.

By 1850 all European and New World societies had prohibited the slave trade. Spanish Cuba alone held out de facto, ignoring large-scale slave smuggling for another decade. By 1875 all the slaveholding countries of the Americas had either emancipated their slaves or were committed to gradual abolition. There was now a sharper distinction between a 'free soil' Western world and the complex and persistent variants of slavery in Afro-Asia, from Morocco to the Pacific. This differentiation between the worlds of civilized anti-slavery and uncivilized servitude was ratified in the half century after 1840. The signs were already evident in Anglo-African diplomatic relations in the early 1840s, when Foreign Minister Palmerston designated Afro-British treaties as 'agreements' or 'arrangements', to 'mark the distinction between agreements with barbarous Chiefs and the international Compacts of Civilized States'.[51] Naval officers on the African patrol wavered only between treating African slavers as criminals or children, but in any event, found it to be 'absurd to invest these petty barbarians the rights of civilized states and to observe the forms of diplomacy in dealing with them'. Since Africans had never acknowledged 'the law of nations' they were neither bound by it nor entitled to its protections. For the rest of the 19th century Europeans would simultaneously sign and devalue treaties/agreements with Africans. Since the combined textual and nationalist arguments against identifying slavers with pirates were too formidable to overcome, Britain comfortably classified slaving as the practices of savages or barbarians.

6. International Law and Anti-slavery

6.1. The Slow Death of Slavery

Before the last quarter of the 19th century, anti-slavery was incorporated into the law of nations only as an intra-Euro-American development and as the exception to the rule laid down in the original *ius gentium*. The oceans and shorelines of the world were the theatre of action and arguments over the scope of international law in shutting down the slave trade. The institution of slavery itself remained firmly within the orbit of municipal and imperial sovereignty as extensions of metropolitan jurisdiction. Ironically, the prospect of emancipation more frequently acted as a deterrent than a stimulus to Western imperial expansion into areas where slavery remained a major institution.

---

[51] James Stephen's minute on the Kataba Treaty of 6 September 1841 quoted in *Abolition and Imperialism* (n 49) 166.

Before 1870, British and French empire-builders had little interest in tropical Africa and Asia. In 1880 Britain could already claim an empire unequalled in human history. But its extension in Western regions of North America, South-East Asia, and the Pacific entailed neither an expansion into the zones of slavery nor an invocation of abolitionist principles as a justification for such expansion. The legal logic of anti-slavery discouraged British and French expansion into tropical Africa after the ending of the slave trade. The laws leading to their respective colonial emancipations in the 1830s and 1840s required both empires to eliminate slavery in all future territories they acquired. Thereafter, any expansion entailed juggling between measures designed to pacify slave-holding elites who agreed to accept European rule, and renegotiating relationships between masters and slaves. This complex process most often resulted in a minimalist approach to emancipation, with a bureaucratic preference for allowing liberation by quiet filtration rather than by sweeping proclamations.[52]

This policy of a gradualist 'slow death of slavery' coincided with the formation of a new ethos within the emergent international law profession on the eve of the scramble for Africa. The profession wished to align international law with the metamorphosis of Western European imperialism from empires of slavery to empires of personal liberation. With the combined emancipations of slaves and serfs in the United States and Russia in the 1860s and the adoption of gradual emancipation in the Spanish empire and Brazil in the 1860s and 1870s, it seemed that all of Western civilization could be identified as an international empire of anti-slavery. For the international lawyers of the 1870s and 1880s, individual freedom and human rights became fundamental and consensual objects of protection by international law. This meant linking individual civil liberty to personal rights of migration, trade, and religious freedom. This cluster of rights was now conceived to be 'under the collective juridical guarantee of all civilized States'.[53]

In this frame of reference the West alone had so far reached a collective anti-slavery consciousness via a long civilizing process. Embracing a theory of evolutionary stages, international lawyers easily identified less civilized zones in Asia, and above all in Africa, because they lacked the political organization, the cultural traditions (including anti-slavery), and the consciousness that allowed for full membership in the legal community of nations.

6.2. The Scramble for Africa and the Brussels Act

This perspective, already evident in British dealings with African rulers during the ending of the transatlantic slave trade, accelerated when the European powers began

---

[52] *Abolition* (n 11) 387–96.
[53] *The Gentle Civilizer of Nations* (n 50) 54–6.

the 'scramble for Africa' in the 1880s. The scramble for Africa evolved from diplomacy in Europe's capitals and the actions of small European interest groups in Africa and Western Europe. The first international conference on Africa (Berlin 1884), was not the outcome of humanitarian concerns, unlike the earlier slave trade congresses, but was convened to minimize conflicts over claims to sovereignty and to create free trade in the Congo. In a sense, it was intended to reverse the historical pattern of intra-European conflict over colonization. Instead of the rule of 'no peace beyond the line' it was intended to prevent intra-European wars 'beyond the line'. As Ronald Robinson concluded, 'the leading powers... were clearly intent on avoiding surges of colonial liabilities'. Among other advantages, imperial powers did not have to immediately enact anti-slavery laws in a protectorate. Slavery and the slave trade were barely and belatedly added to the agenda of the conference. Britain was simultaneously able to ensure that the status of its protectorates as non-sovereign spheres was reaffirmed, and, stimulated by its Anti-Slavery Society, burnish its anti-slavery credentials by proposing to make the slave trade 'a crime against humanity'. The final Berlin Act declared the slave trade 'was forbidden by international law', but provided no machinery for implementing the declaration.[54]

The Berlin Conference and its aftermath enabled the new generation of international lawyers to reaffirm the pedigree of international law as a unique product of European history and culture. The *Institut de Droit International*, while always assiduously avoiding intra-European issues, unhesitatingly offered opinions on matters of pan-European interest such as freedom of navigation in the Congo or conditions for the effective occupation in Africa. Whether or not lawyers no longer accepted the axiom that the slave trade was in conformity with the law of nations, they still did not collectively intervene to strengthen the slave trade resolution by supporting the British proposal to have slaving declared 'a crime against humanity'.

However, international lawyers now rallied around the line of civilizational exclusion. 'Uncivilized' natives could be safely left to the consciences of the States under whose sovereignty they might fall. Thus late 19th-century textbooks emphasized the exclusion of uncivilized populations from international law, while making room for the gradual universal extension of individual human rights. Imperialism was reconceived reducing individual dependency within the framework of an indefinite period of collective dependency during the civilizing process.[55]

The most tragic outcome of the lawyers' advocacy of European domination in Africa came precisely where internationalization appeared to have won its most innovative victory in Berlin—the creation of an independent state of the Congo under the authority of the *Association International du Congo* (AIC). Under the rule

---

[54] R Robinson 'The Conference in Berlin and the Future in Africa, 1884–1885' in S Förster, WJ Mommsen, and R Robinson (eds) *Bismarck Europe, and Africa: The Berlin Africa Conference 1884–1885 and the Onset of Partition* (OUP Oxford 1988) 1–34 at 22–3.

[55] *The Gentle Civilizer of Nations* (n 50) 127 citing J Westlake *Chapters on the Principles of International Law* (CUP Cambridge 1894).

of King Leopold II of Belgium, the civilizing mission became a reign of terror, as the Belgians dragooned tens of thousands of Congolese into forced labour that resembled slavery without individual ownership. During the peak years of the campaign to expose the enormous atrocities of Leopold's regime, the international law community remained almost silent over this introduction of state created forced labour that was as bad as slavery or worse. Similarly most international lawyers ignored atrocities in the French and German colonies in Africa, including the German annihilation order in Southwest Africa, in 1906. Labour practices in British colonies by companies and entrepreneurs verged on slavery and both the British government and international lawyers turned a blind eye to this new form of bondage. A sustained attack on these situations would have undermined the assumption/goal of the inseparability of European public law and civilization. It was left to other groups to expose or protest the atrocities.[56]

The power of anti-slavery as a stimulus to popular mobilization re-emerged four years after the Berlin Conference. In 1888, a century after the first popular petition against the British slave trade, a Catholic cardinal, Charles Lavigerie, launched a new anti-slavery campaign, couching his plea as a crusade against Muslim slave traders. His European speaking tour inspired the formation of national organizations throughout Catholic Western and Central Europe. The campaign culminated in the Brussels Conference in 1889, which included diplomats from thirteen European nations, the United States, Leopold's Congo Free State, the Ottoman empire, Zanzibar, and Persia. The Brussels Act of 1890[57] was the first comprehensive multilateral treaty directed specifically against the African slave trade. It explicitly identified European imperialism as an agent of international anti-slavery and it established procedures for detaining and trying slavers. Continued French resistance to the British mixed commission model left enforcement in the hands of national courts. Arguing that it would infringe national sovereignty, a number of European nations and the Ottoman empire weakened another British proposal, to create an oversight bureau to gather information and monitor enforcement.[58]

Despite its anti-slavery provisions, the Brussels Act was a testimonial to the primacy of national sovereignty. Fulfilment of its major provisions was always qualified by 'as far as possible'. Its preamble, pledging to bring civilization to Africa, did not forbid the violent conquest of additional territories in pursuit of ending the slave trade. Nor did it discourage massive mobilizations of coerced native labour for the purpose of accelerating the economic development of occupied regions.[59] Ironically,

---

[56] See A Hochschild *King Leopold's Ghost* (First Mariner Books New York 1999); *The Gentle Civilizer of Nations* (n 50) 165–6; and K Grant *A Civilised Savagery* (Routledge New York 2005); LJ Satre *Chocolate on Trial: Slavery, Politics, and the Ethics of Business* (Ohio University Press Ohio 2005).

[57] General Act of the Brussels Conference (signed 2 July 1890) 173 CTS 293.

[58] S Miers *Britain and the Ending of the Slave Trade* (Africana Publishing New York 1975) ch 6.

[59] S Miers *Slavery in the Twentieth Century* (Altamira Press New York 2003) at 20–5.

the attempt to end slavery in Africa led to new forms of forced labour and exploitation that resembled slavery.

6.3. After the First World War

The next major international step against slavery came in the wake of the First World War. With chattel slavery reduced to a vestige of its former magnitude Western nations superseded the Berlin and Brussels Acts with a new international convention against slavery under the aegis of the League of Nations. The Slavery Convention of 1926 was designed to pursue the slave trade into its still-inaccessible corners of the uncivilized world. It also committed the signatories to attack slavery 'in all its forms': child trafficking, concubinage, debt-bondage, and forced labour.[60] Opposition to the inclusion of forced labour, on grounds of infringement of national sovereignty, led the drafters to transfer that problem to the International Labour Organization. The Slavery Convention of 1926 replaced all prior agreements on slavery and the slave trade. France, adhering to its century old tradition of rejecting the Right of Search, again refused to allow a blanket equation of the seaborne slave trade with piracy.[61]

Slavery was now defined as 'the status or condition of a person over whom any or all of the powers attaching to the right of ownership are exercised'. This basic definition has since remained unaltered. When the Slavery Convention of 1926 was amended by the Supplementary Convention of 1956,[62] it did not alter the definition of slavery. It only obliged States to abolish related servile conditions of debt, or bondage, or serfdom, or institutions which transfer a woman to another person or group for payment, or by inheritance, or of any practice in which children are delivered to others for exploitation.[63]

Most members of the League of Nations, as well as the United States, signed the 1926 convention during the interwar period. It was the first international treaty directed against slavery as well as the slave trade. The inclusion of the ambiguous phrase, 'all its forms', left 'slavery' open to embrace an ever-widening range of practices, now designated as conditions 'analogous to slavery'. In the context of its signing it was still viewed as a European-sponsored instrument for ensuring the elimination

[60] Convention to Suppress the Slave Trade and Slavery (concluded 25 September 1926, entered into force 9 March 1927) 60 LNTS 253.

[61] ibid 124–6; RC Redman 'The League of Nations and the Right to Be Free From Enslavement: The First Human Right To Be Recognized as Customary International Law' (1994) 70 Chicago-Kent Law Review 759–802.

[62] Supplementary Convention on the Abolition of Slavery, the Slave Trade and Institutions and Practices Similar to Slavery (signed 7 September 1956, entered into force 30 April 1957) 266 UNTS 3.

[63] D Weissbrodt and Anti-Slavery International 'Abolishing Slavery and its Contemporary Forms' (2002) UN Doc HR/PUB/02/4; see also J Allain 'A Legal Consideration "Slavery" in the Light of the *Travaux Préparatoires* of the 1926 Convention' (paper delivered at WISE Hull 23 November 2006) at 4.

of the last vestiges of the slave trade and slavery in areas of the world that lay beyond the sovereignty of the nations pledged to eliminate the institution. The reports submitted to the League by the colonial powers in 1926 celebrated their own national histories of enlightened rule in promoting freedom. Many lauded their imperial achievement in overcoming the hurdles of native ignorance, laziness, and cultural backwardness. The formal prohibition of slavery now seemed to be a consensual part of international law and an anticipation of its rapid extinction from the world.[64]

When the 1926 Slavery Convention was signed, the next development in the history of slavery was probably inconceivable to any student of international law. Within two decades slavery 'in all its forms' reached greater proportions in the heart of Europe than had existed in the whole New World a century earlier. By 1931, the British House of Lords was debating the reappearance of slave labour in the Soviet Union—what came to be called the Gulag Archipelago. Millions of forced labourers toiled in camps that stretched for thousands of miles across the Eurasian landmass. Even more massive was the explosive expansion of slave labour in Nazi Europe which extended the zone of enslavement westward to the coast of the Atlantic Ocean and eastward into the heart of the Soviet Union. Immediately after it invaded Poland in 1939, Germany decreed a general obligation to labour under terms entirely dictated by the conquerors. During the next four years, approximately 12 million foreigners were forcibly transported to work in Germany. This does not include coerced labourers set to work for German military, governmental, and civilian agencies outside the official boundaries of the *Reich*, or hundreds of thousands of Jews, Romani, and Eastern Europeans who were used as slave labour in death camps and concentration camps.[65]

The closest analogue to the dynamics of the Nazi German system may lie in the history of ancient Roman slavery. Rome made heavy and continuous demands on its citizens in ever-expanding wars of conquest. Enslaved captives became the substitute labourers of choice for the uprooted citizen-soldiers of the Republic. The same combination of militarization, vulnerability to enslavement, and profitability re-emerged full blown in the heart of 20th-century Europe. With 14 million Germans called to arms an enormous labour gap had to be filled quickly. At least as many European workers were forcibly imported into Germany in five years as all the Africans brought to the Americas in the 400 years of the Atlantic slave trade.[66]

The Germans openly analogized their coerced labourers to slaves. Nazi ideology regarded upwards of 200 million Europeans as racially destined for servility or outright extermination. German leaders did not hesitate to identify their round-ups as slaving expeditions or their captives as slaves. In 1942 Heinrich Himmler told senior SS officers of the need to 'fill our camps with slaves—in this room I mean to say things

---

[64]   DB Davis *Slavery and Human Progress* (OUP New York 1984) at 311.
[65]   ibid 309–15; and *Abolition* (n 11) 426–49.
[66]   *Slavery and Human Progress* (n 64) 430–1.

very firmly and very clearly—with worker slaves, who will build our cities, our villages, our farms without regard to any losses'. Nor were the managers of the labour system unaware that they were contravening the recent trajectory of the law of nations. Indeed, for those groups designated by the Nazis for proximate destruction, either through conditions of labour or immediate extermination, historians had to invent a new term—genocide—and a new category of 'less than slaves'.[67]

Belligerents on both sides—the Germans, the Japanese, and the Soviets—reintroduced the ancient concept that prisoners of war could be enslaved. Unlike ancient Rome, prisoners of war on the Eastern front of Europe (or in Asia) were not sold off to individuals or seized as a legitimate booty of warfare by soldiers. Instead, military prisoners and civilians were sent to work camps or factories, where many were literally worked to death in slave-like conditions. After 1945 the Soviet Union refused to repatriate tens of thousands (or more) of German prisoners of war and others seized during the war, and as late as the 1950s many were still slaving away in the Soviet Gulag. This was clearly in violation of international law and the laws of war, but no international body investigated this or had any power to influence Soviet policy.

7. POST-WAR

During the Second World War, the Allies made it clear that enemy perpetrators would be tried for war crimes. In August 1945, the United States, Great Britain, the Soviet Union, and France created an International Military Tribunal to bring to justice those most responsible for enslavement and many other crimes. At the most famous trial, in October 1945, the German leaders tried for 'crimes against humanity' were charged with violation of the 1926 Convention to Suppress the Slave Trade and Slavery,[68] to which Germany was a party. Because of the lack of prior provisions for enforcement, the new United Nations provided for the organization of the trials.

The defendants considered themselves as innovators and managers of a racial revolution. For more than a century abolitionists, revolutionaries, and imperialists had all agreed in condemning slavery, even in the face of competing theories of racial hierarchy. Germany's leadership rejected this heritage, even though they explicitly understood that their institutions of mass enslavement and annihilation might cost them their lives. At Nuremberg, Fritz Sauckel, Hitler's plenipotentiary for labour mobilization, was prosecuted for managing a recruitment programme which involved

---

[67] B Ferencz *Less Than Slaves: Jewish Forced Labor and the Quest for Compensation* (Harvard University Press Cambridge MA 1979).

[68] Convention to Suppress the Slave Trade (n 60).

the deportation for slave labour of more than five million human beings, 'many of them under terrible conditions of cruelty and suffering'. Sauckel actually rested defence on the grounds that he had personally called Hitler's attention to the fact that their mode of labour recruitment violated international law.[69]

There is little doubt that the return of slavery within Europe itself formed part of a devastating attack on 'civilization's' limits of pre-war international law. Significantly, in the aftermath of the war, slavery was the first violation of human rights listed in the Universal Declaration of 1948.[70] In 1948 the United Nations General Assembly resolved that there would be an increasing need for an international judicial body for the trial of certain crimes under international law. Following many years of negotiation, the Rome Statute of the International Court[71] established such an institution. The International Court of Justice quickly identified protection from slavery as one of two specific examples of obligations ('*erga omnes*—arising out of human rights law')— owed to the international community as a whole.[72]

In the 1990s, another dimension was added to international law on slavery. In most emancipations of New World slavery (the US is the major exception), masters received compensation for the loss of their property. Such compensations might be provided in one of two ways—in labour time or in monetary allotments by the State. Gradual emancipations provided for a period of indentured servitude or 'apprenticeship' for ex-slaves or the free-born children of slaves. Masters might also receive an indemnity from the State for the loss of labour. Even in Haiti the State belatedly agreed to pay compensation to the descendants of French masters who had lost their holdings in the revolutions of 1791–1804.[73]

At the end of the 1990s, European victims of Nazi enslavement, as well as Western prisoners of war and Koreans who were victims of Japanese enslavement, began to demand compensation from private corporations and States. The plaintiffs' claims were intended to supplement international law sanctions first enacted by the Nuremberg tribunals. While State agents committing crimes against humanity fell within the jurisdiction of the International Criminal Court (ICC), bankers who financed the companies that sold barbed wire, manufactured poison gas, or used unpaid slave labour fell outside the ICC jurisdiction. The plaintiffs sought to develop an analogous pattern of legal norms in order to eliminate the possibility of anyone profiting from crimes against humanity. As usual, decisions to settle such claims were probably

---

[69] *Abolition* (n 11) 449.

[70] Universal Declaration of Human Rights(adopted 10 December 1948 UNGA Res 217 A(III) (UDHR) art 4.

[71] Rome Statute of the International Criminal Court (concluded 17 July 1998, entered into force 1 July 2002) 2187 UNTS 90.

[72] *Barcelona Traction, Light and Power Company, Limited (Belgium v Spain) (Second Phase, Judgement)* [1970] ICJ Reports 3 para 34.

[73] SL Engerman *Slavery, Emancipation and Freedom: Comparative Perspectives* (Louisiana State Press Baton Rouge 2007) ch 2.

motivated as much by the power of political sanctions as by the compelling logic of the plaintiff's lawyers. Whether the model of post-Holocaust litigation can be transferred to cases in the period of the transatlantic slave systems or the slave systems of Afro-Asia remains to be seen.[74]

8. CONCLUSION

Over the course of the past five centuries slavery and the slave trade have played a major role in the formation and transformation of international law. Identified in antiquity as a consensual institution of the law of nations, slavery's standing in legal discourse was slowly modified. During four centuries after 1450, some of Europe's metropolises began to identify themselves as lands where the *ius gentium*'s generic verdict on slavery no longer applied. During the same centuries Europeans simultaneously created and maintained vast new empires of slavery in the New World. Juridical scholarship rationalized this dichotomy by developing theories which sanctioned slavery 'beyond the line', while delegitimizing it at home. The American, French, and Haitian revolutions and, above all, the less violent British abolitionist revolution, slowly broke down the geographical, institutional and cultural bases of European imperial slavery. Within a century after the outbreak of the Atlantic revolutions, the empires of slavery had become empires of anti-slavery. In international law anti-slavery was now the gold standard of civilization, a standard that helped to justify collective dependency while it slowly eliminated the status of individual enslavement. In the wake of World War I slavery seemed to be a vanishing institution.

The next great change in the international law of slavery was stimulated by an unanticipated expansion of slavery in the heart of Europe. In the wake of the Second World War, the hierarchy of 'civilization' presumed by 19th-century European expansionists was completely discredited. In both formulation and implementation the equality of individuals theoretically free and equal in rights and obligations had to be paralleled by a world of nations free and equal in rights and sovereignty, both embedded within a consensual international law. The prohibition of slavery remains emblematic of the potential transformations in international law both as inspiration and as caution.

---

[74] B Neuborne 'Holocaust Reparations Litigation: Lessons for the Slavery Reparations Movement' (2003) 58 New York University Annual Survey of American Law 615–22; and SL Engerman 'Apologies, Regrets and Reparations' (2009) 17 European Review 593–610.

Recommended Reading

Bethell, Leslie 'The Mixed Commissions for the Suppression of the Transatlantic Slave Trade in the Nineteenth Century' (1966) 7 Journal of African History 79–93.

Davis, David B *The Problem of Slavery in Western Culture* (Cornell University Press Ithaca Ithaca NY 1966).

Davis, David B *Slavery and Human Progress* (OUP New York 1984).

Drescher, Seymour *From Slavery to Freedom: Comparative Studies in the Rise and Fall of Atlantic Slavery* (New York University Press New York 1999).

Drescher, Seymour *Abolition: A History of Slavery and Antislavery* (CUP New York 2009).

Eltis, David *Economic Growth and the Ending of the Transatlantic Slave Trade* (OUP New York 1987).

Engerman, Stanley L *Slavery, Emancipation and Freedom: Comparative Perspectives* (Louisiana State Press Baton Rouge LA 2007).

Engerman, Stanley L 'Apologies, Regrets and Reparations' (2009) 17 European Review 593–610.

Ferencz, Benjamin B *Less Than Slaves: Jewish Forced Labor and the Quest for Compensation* (Harvard University Press Cambridge MA 1979).

Finkelman, Paul *An Imperfect Union: Slavery, Federalism and Comity* (University of North Carolina Press Chapel Hill NC 1981).

Finkelman, Paul 'The American Suppression of the African Slave Trade: Lessons on Legal Change, Social Policy, and Legislation' (2009) 42 Akron Law Review 433–67.

Finley, Moses I *Ancient Slavery and Modern Ideology* (Penguin Books New York 1983).

Martinez, Jenny S 'Antislavery Courts and the Dawn of International Human Rights Law' (2008) 117 Yale Law Journal 550–641.

Maxwell, John F *Slavery and the Catholic Church* (Barry Rose Chichester 1975).

Miers, Suzanne *Britain and the Ending of the Slave Trade* (Africana Publishing New York New York 1975).

Miers, Suzanne *Slavery in the Twentieth Century* (Altamira Press New York 2003).

Peabody, Sue *'There are No Slaves in France': The Political Culture of Race and Slavery in the Ancien Régime* (OUP New York 1996).

Quirk, Joel and David Richardson 'Anti-slavery, European Identity and International Society: A Macro-historical Perspective' (2009) 7 Journal of Modern European History 68–92.

Redman, Renee C 'The League of Nations and the Right to Be Free From Enslavement: The First Human Right to Be Recognized as Customary International Law' (1994) 70 Chicago-Kent Law Review 759–802.

Rotman, Youval *Byzantine Slavery and the Mediterranean World* (Harvard University Press Cambridge MA 2009).

CHAPTER 38

THE CIVILIZED AND THE UNCIVILIZED

LILIANA OBREGÓN

1. INTRODUCTION

THE word 'civilization,' coined in the 18th century, has a complex history, multiple meanings, and considerable baggage.[1] It has been used to describe a process, destination, benchmark, fact, or an ideal that evaluates the social self-understanding of the 'civilized' in reference to those they considered 'barbarian', 'savage', or 'uncivilized'. Civilization is a key concept to understand the imagined values of 19th-century political communities and their relation to international law.

As with other core 19th-century concepts, civilization was closely related to the idea of progress and the theory that nations advance through different stages of development. The usage of the word 'civilization' spread quickly among learned Europeans who, in relation to other societies, believed they were endowed with an advanced level of social complexity in opposition to 'barbarous' nations, who could possibly acquire civilization if they conformed to certain values, or 'savages', who were condemned to never access it.

---

[1] See B Bowden *The Empire of Civilization: The Evolution of an Imperial Idea* (The University of Chicago Press Chicago 2009).

As a politically efficient concept, the nature and consequences of 'civilization' changed as new 'horizons of expectations' opened up.[2] There was little agreement among those who considered themselves 'civilized', on what were the values or the means to obtain them for an 'uncivilized' society to become 'civilized'. The multiple contents assigned to civilization made it an enduring, ubiquitous, and inescapable concept that burdens the history of international law.[3] Furthermore, international law carries the weight of being pronounced the ultimate product of civilization, making it into an utopian ideal of a transnational organized legal system that would bring progress and peace to the world.

In the 19th century, the adjective 'civilized' and its counter-concept 'uncivilized' made their way into the writings of publicists, judicial decisions, treaties, and institutional documents. The pair described and evaluated peoples, nations, or States in their relation to sovereignty. Applying the civilized/uncivilized to international law simplified the world by dividing it in two. When 'civilized' was used to describe a people, nation or State, it constituted and was constituted by its opposite, the 'uncivilized'. The civilized, those endowed with civilization, were recognized as proper subjects of international law. The uncivilized, those lacking civilization, were left outside of international law.

This labelling had an optimistic and productive side: the possibility of collective progress and improvement through human intellect and work without the interference of nature. The forward looking movement made the possibility of normative consequences acceptable and sustainable.[4] The downside, however, was that those who believed themselves 'civilized' assumed a missionary project which self-legitimized them to enslave, conquer, manage or submit the 'uncivilized' to persistent hierarchical legal, economic, social, and/or political relations.

The dichotomous division of positive and progressive civilized subjects and their negative and regressive contraries denied the possibility of comparison or mutual recognition among them and placed an inherent contradiction to the principle of universal applicability of international law and the equality of nations. These descriptions implied unresolvable and incoherent claims based on a heterogeneity of content ascribed in different localities and times.[5] By excluding the political or social agency of the 'uncivilized', only 'civilized' nations could participate in the project of

---

[2] R Koselleck *Futures Past: On the Semantics of Historical Time* (Columbia University Press New York 2004) at 160.

[3] Brett Bowden's four volume compilation on civilization also demonstrates its centrality to the histories of the humanities and the social sciences. See B Bowden (ed) *Civilization* (4 vols Routledge New York 2009).

[4] J Fisch 'Zivilisation, Kultur' in O Brunner, W Conze, and R Koselleck (eds) *Geschichtliche Grundbegriffe: Historisches Lexikon zur politisch-sozialen Sprache in Deutschland* (Klett-Cotta Stuttgart 1992) vol 7, 679–774.

[5] *Futures Past* (n 2) 156.

international law. Resistance or political action by the 'uncivilized' constituted them as illegal, subversive, barbarian or, at a minimum, marginal.[6]

2. THE 16TH AND 17TH CENTURIES OF CHRISTIANS AND NON-BELIEVING BARBARIANS

A precedent to the 19th century distinction between the civilized and the uncivilized can be found in the 16th- and 17th-century division between Christians and non-Christians. As Europeans conquered and colonized American lands and peoples, new normative questions challenged their Christian vision of law and morality. In his lectures *On Recently Discovered Indians* and *On the Law of War Made by the Spaniards against the Barbarians* Francisco de Vitoria (*c.* 1486–1546) approached the Indians as subjects of theological inquiry and Spanish sovereignty (*potestas*) in his effort to advise the Spanish crown.[7] 'This whole dispute … has arisen', argued Vitoria, 'because of these barbarians in the New World, commonly called Indians, who came under the power of the Spaniards some forty years ago, having been previously unknown to our world.'[8]

Vitoria's judgment of the Indians as barbarian outsiders to the Spanish world is founded on the Aristotelian division between noble, intelligent, virtuous, and god-like Greeks and beastial, mentally inferior, *logos*-lacking babblers who could not speak their language.[9] In ancient Greece, moral and legal order was based on an idea of social and cultural unity among men who should follow primary norms (*prima praecepta*) to obtain a life of happiness (*eudaimonia*), the highest end (*telos*) of all men.[10] Primary norms distinguished between good and evil and ranged from prohibitions of killing, theft, or adultery to behavioural norms such as ways of eating, interacting, or wearing clothes. Barbarians were outsiders with no access to *eudaimonia* because they were thought to be lacking in language and did not build, live in cities, or follow the primary norms.[11]

Like Aristotle, Vitoria's universal legal/moral order (*ius gentium*) was divided in two worlds: a Spanish 'us' of 'our world' and a barbarian or Indian 'them' of the New

---

[6] *Futures Past* (n 2) 158.

[7] A Pagden *The Fall of Natural Man: The American Indian and the Origins of Comparative Ethnology* (3rd edn CUP Cambridge 1990) at 64.

[8] F de Vitoria 'On the American Indians' in A Pagden and J Lawrance (eds) *Vitoria: Political Writings* (CUP Cambrige 1991) 231–92 at 233.

[9] *The Fall of Natural Man* (n 7) 16.

[10] ibid 69.   [11] ibid 94.

World. Both worlds and people were assumed under a Christian universe and a unique normative moral/legal order. For Christians, non-Christians were outsiders who, like the earliest men, behaved violently, in 'uncivil' ways and could not progress because of their idolatry and ignorance of God's laws.[12] Christians, differently from Greeks, however, allowed for baptism as a door to access their world. Once a barbarian was baptized he left his savage life and could live virtuously under God's laws, in order to obtain the *telos* of all Christians: the glory of God.[13]

The Spaniards differentiated themselves from the barbarians in order to distinguish the limits of sovereign rule.[14] Vitoria regarded the Indians as 'not fully unintelligent' since they 'had precise notions of things,' and forms of organization evident in their marriage rituals, family life, laws, and magistrates. However, he argued, they were still barbarians because, they lacked the 'letters, arts, crafts, systematic agriculture, manufacture and other things ... indispensable for human use.'[15] Also, due to an inadequate education and their idolatry, Indians 'were no better than wild beasts' in the art of self-government or in the food they ate. Vitoria concluded that the Spaniards, wiser men, were responsible for providing Indians with a Christian education, baptism, and the administration of their country.[16] Education and conversion did not give Indians equal treatment because they still remained under Spanish *potestas* as subjects of their indoctrination.

3. The Humanistic 18th Century and the Coining of Civilization

In the 18th century, when the word 'civilization' appeared, the concept of the civilized/uncivilized entered legal discourse through the language of the Enlightenment. Christian Wolff (1679–1754) defined civilized nations in his *Jus Gentium* as those who conformed to standards of reason and politeness, cultivated, and perfected intellectual virtues, and trained the mind. Barbarous nations neglected their intellect and followed 'their natural inclinations and aversions'. For Wolff, the Christian individual

---

[12] *The Fall of Natural Man* (n 7) 20–4.

[13] ibid 21.

[14] A Anghie 'Francisco de Vitoria and the Colonial Origins of International Law' in E Darian Smith and P Fitzpatrick (eds) *Laws of the Postcolonial* (The University of Michigan Press Ann Arbor 1999) 89–108.

[15] 'On the American Indians' (n 8) 290.

[16] ibid 290–1; see also Pagden's explanation in *The Fall of Natural Man* (n 7) 79–93.

and the nation had a new *telos:* to be civilized and 'to direct all their efforts to this end'.[17]

Later on, Immanuel Kant (1724–1804) argued in *Perpetual Peace* that 'peoples or nations, regarded as states' could be judged 'like individual men': they were either 'savage' or 'civilized'. Civilized nations had constitutions, they preferred 'rational liberty', 'a legal constraint constituted by themselves' and demanded constitutions from each other to avoid 'mutual injury' and favour their own security. Savage nations, on the other hand, did not want a constitution and remained attached to their 'wild freedom' and 'lawless liberty of … being engaged in incessant conflict with each other'. Civilized nations looked upon uncivilized ones 'with profound contempt' and characterized their condition 'as barbarism, coarseness, and a brutal degradation of humanity'. Kant's *telos* for civilized nations went further than Wolff's: 'a continuously growing state consisting of various nations (*civitas gentium*) which will ultimately include all the nations of the world'. Since Kant recognized that a world State was a utopian goal, he also proposed more feasible alternatives reached through the civilizing process: a league of nations, a federation of free States or alliances that would limit or avoid war.[18]

4. The 19th- and Early 20th-Century Civilizing Mission

The 19th and early 20th centuries epitomized the use of the civilized/uncivilized in its relation to international law, in particular with the doctrine of recognition and the promotion of an implied standard for Europe's 'civilizing mission'.

4.1. The Declaration on the Abolition of the Slave Trade

The 1815 Declaration of the Powers on the Abolition of the Slave Trade was one of the first international instruments to identify nations as civilized: 'the commerce known by the name of "the Slave trade" has been considered by just and enlightened men of all ages, as repugnant to the principles of humanity and universal morality' and 'the

---

[17] C Wolff *Jus Gentium Methodo Scientifica Pertractatum* (Oceana Publications for Carnegie Institution Washington 1964) at 33.

[18] I Kant 'Perpetual Peace' in Hans Reiss (ed) *Kant's Political Writings* (CUP Cambrige 1996); see also the contribution by P Kleingeld 'Immanuel Kant (1724–1804)' in this volume.

public voice, *in all civilized countries*, calls aloud for its prompt suppression'.[19] The declaration regarded 'civilized countries' as both 'Christian powers' and 'European States'. According to the text, 'just and enlightened men of all ages' and 'the public voice in all civilized countries' considered the slave trade—but not necessarily slavery—as repugnant to the principles of humanity and universal morality.[20]

4.2. Recognition of New States

Further into the century, the new American States sought recognition of their independence to participate in the 'community of civilized nations'. A former colony that was not recognized was perceived as a savage or barbarian entity. Thus recognition by European States, especially by the 'mother country,' served two purposes: to avoid recolonization and to allow for commercial treaty-making. The first constitutions of the United States (1787), Haiti (1805), and the former Spanish American colonies (after 1811) were written to demonstrate they were not in a 'savage state of lawlessness' as well as to organize their governments.[21]

The framers of the United States' constitution incorporated the language of the law of nations into the text as a practice of civilization.[22] France recognized the US in 1777, Britain and Netherlands in 1782, Spain, Sweden, and Denmark soon followed. However, US recognition of her American neighbours was complicated by the problem of slavery and the perceived racial composition of the new States.

Indeed, in 1791, half a million slaves revolted in the French colony of Saint Domingue and declared themselves free, initiating a struggle for independence that lasted over a decade of fighting against Spanish, British, and French armies. Soon after the defeat of Napoleon Bonaparte's largest military expedition sent to recover the colony and to reinstate slavery in 1802, the former slaves declared their independence and renamed the territory they controlled as 'Hayti'. At that moment, they became the second independent State of the Americas after the US, but their process of recognition was long deferred.

---

[19] Congress of Vienna 'Déclaration des Puissances sur l'abolition de la Traité des Nègres (8 février 1815)' in *Congrès de Vienne: Acte principal et traités additionnels, édition, complète collationnée sur les documents officiels* (Imprimerie de Gerdès Paris 1874) 119–20 at 119.

[20] On slavery and international law see the contribution by Drescher and Finkelman in this volume.

[21] R Gargarella *The Legal Foundations of Inequality: Constitutionalism in the Americas, 1776–1860* (CUP Cambrige 2010); J Gaffield 'Complexities of Imagining Haiti: A Study of National Constitutions 1801–1807' (2007) 41 Journal of Social History 81–103; DM Golove and DJ Hulsebosch 'A Civilized Nation: The Early American Constitution, the Law of Nations, and the Pursuit of International Recognition' (2010) 85 New York University Law Review 932–1066.

[22] 'A Civilized Nation' (n 21).

The 1804 Haitian declaration of independence and 1805 first constitution inverted the civilized/barbarian labelling: the French were described as the 'barbarians who have bloodied our land for two centuries' while the Haitians were 'a people, free, civilized and independent'. The texts declared 'eternal hatred of France' and portrayed French language, customs, and laws as barbarian interventions, but praised Haitians for abolishing slavery 'forever' and declaring themselves 'black' while prohibiting future property ownership by any 'white' male.

Spanish American leaders admired Haitians for having defeated the strongest European armies, but lived in extreme fear of 'another Haiti' occurring in their territories as the invitations to Simón Bolívar's 1826 Congress of Panama made evident. The congress' purpose was to build regional strength by uniting the new States in hopes of recognition by Spain. The majority of the new States opposed inviting Haiti arguing that it would give her a de facto recognition of statehood, bring negative consequences to the cause of Spanish American independence, show 'considerations of etiquette…reserved for civilized nations' and 'incite a disastrous racial revolution on the continent'.[23] They also did not want to antagonize the United States representatives who opposed Haiti's participation because slavery and the slave trade continued to be essential to the US economy.

France recognized Haiti in 1834, but only in exchange for an agreement made in 1826 for Haiti to pay a 150 million franc indemnity to French plantation and slave owners.[24] The United States recognized Haiti in 1862 after the civil war, and Spanish American States began to recognize Haiti after Brazil in 1865. In 1934, Mexico became the last American State to recognize Haiti.[25]

Spanish American States were concerned with how their status of civilization would affect their recognition and looked to demonstrate it through various means. For example, Simón Bolívar (1783–1830) promoted the unification of principles, forms of government and institutions in hopes that Spain and the other European countries would see it as a proof of internal stability and civilization. Andrés Bello (1781–1865) promoted the teaching and learning of international law, as well as a (Spanish) American literature, grammar and laws to 'complete the civilization' that the Spanish had left unfinished.[26]

[23] Cited in P Verna *Petión y Bolívar: Cuarenta años (1790–1830) de relaciones haitianovenezolanas y su aporte a la emancipación de Hispanoamérica* (Ministerio de Educación—Dirección General Departamento de Publicaciones Caracas 1970).

[24] Haiti defaulted on the first payment and was soon forced to take loans from French banks (and later American and German banks) converting the indemnity into a 'double debt'. It took more than a century for Haiti to pay off the indemnity debt to France.

[25] IM Wallerstein *The Modern World-System* (University of California Press Berkeley 2011) fn 308.

[26] L Obregón 'Construyendo la región americana: Andrés Bello y el Derecho Internacional,' in B González Stephan and J Poblete (eds) *Andrés Bello y los Estudios Latinoamericanos* (IILI University of Pittsburgh 2009) 189–218.

4.3. Civilization Defined

During the second half of the 19th century, international law continued to appear as an image of civilization. In his *Dictionnaire de droit international public et privé* of 1885, Carlos Calvo (1824–1906) defined civilization as:

[T]he state of man in society, in opposition to barbarity. Civilization is the result of the reciprocal action of industry, the arts, the sciences, literature, morals and of religion, in one word, of all that can have an influence over the spirit of man, contribute to exercise the development of his potential, and of the satisfaction of his needs and his well-being in general. *International law is one of the most precious fruits of civilization*: because it has become one of the bases of the organization of societies and therefore an essential element in the harmonic march of humanity.[27]

For Calvo, civilized nations were 'endowed with' civilization because they had 'the polished manners, the customs, the uses that denote a certain moral, political and economic education' and were 'organized on stable and rational basis, on the principles of order, justice and humanity'. As they were 'in opposition to barbarous or savage nations' civilized nations had a mission: 'to promote the education, the guidance, in one word, the civilization of savage peoples, to extend the territory of civilized States more and more, to constitute civilized authorities in the greater name of barbarous regions'. A limit was added, nonetheless: 'civilized nations do not have the right to expel the savage or barbaric races, to destroy them, exterminate their race, or to take away the lands in which they live'.[28]

Late 19th-century Latin American, Japanese, Chinese, Ottoman, and other peripheral lawyers upheld Calvo's definition as they included their States as part of the civilized world but at the same time used the civilizing mission to conquer and control 'noncivilized peoples' in their own States and regions.[29] Peripheral lawyers exceptionally criticized the language of civilization, as did the Japanese lawyer Tsurutaro Senga (1857–1929):

[E]ach religious denomination or philosophical school cherishes a peculiar conception of civilization. When European international law scholars speak about 'civilization' or 'civilized states', they do so likewise from the subjective standpoint of their own *Weltanschauung*.[30]

4.4. The Berlin Act and the Blessings of Civilization

The 19th century ended with the General Act of the Conference at Berlin on West Africa (The Berlin Act) of 1885. That document reflected the colonial discourse of late

---

[27] C Calvo *Dictionnaire de droit international public et privé* (Puttkammer & Muhlbrecht Berlin 1885) vol 1, at 149 (emphasis added).

[28] ibid 148.

[29] A Becker Lorca 'Universal International Law: Nineteenth-Century Histories of Imposition and Appropriation' (2010) 51 Harvard Journal of International Law 475–552 at 497.

[30] Cited in ibid 482.

19th century that structured the relation between the civilized and the uncivilized, despite its multiple ideas of civilization and the lack of a coherent standard. The Berlin Act signers agreed 'to regulate the conditions most favourable to the development of trade and civilization in certain regions of Africa' and

[T]o bind themselves to watch over the preservation of the native tribes, and to care for the improvement of the conditions of their moral and material well-being, and protect and favour all...institutions and undertakings...which aim at instructing the natives and bringing to them the blessings of civilization.[31]

'Certain regions' of Africa were considered free space for occupation due to their status as uncivilized or as land that was 'empty' and not possible to consider a State.[32] By legitimizing occupation as an instrument of the civilizing mission, the Berlin Act promoted European private interests as public ones in the 'scramble' for Africa. The designation of protectorates that would bring the 'blessings of civilization' avoided the burden of full formal administration. The absence of fixed rules of territorial entitlement eliminated the possibility of violating them and negated indigenous pretensions to sovereignty.[33]

4.5. Civilized Nations in the Permanent Court of International Justice's Statute

In 1920, the Council of the League of Nations appointed a committee of jurists to draft the rules and statute of the new Permanent Court of International Justice. Though the statute's article 38—still part of the current ICJ statute—instructed judges to apply the 'general principles of law recognized by civilized nations' to any dispute submitted to it, the committee members displayed different views on civilization and civilized nations but never defined those terms.[34] For the committee's rapporteur, Leon Bourgeois (1851–1925), progress and civilization was the growing interdependence and regulation of political, economic, financial, and social matters as indispensable to the peace and prosperity of each and all.[35]

---

[31] General Act of the Conference at Berlin (signed 26 February 1885) (1885) 165 CTS 485. The Act was signed by the representatives of Great Britain, Austria-Hungary, Belgium, Denmark, France, Germany, Italy, the Netherlands, Portugal, Russia, Spain, Sweden And Norway, Turkey, and the United States.

[32] M Koskenniemi *The Gentle Civilizer of Nations: the Rise and Fall of International Law, 1870–1960* (CUP Cambridge 2002) at 121–7.

[33] J Fisch 'Africa as *Terra Nullius*: The Berlin Conference and International Law' in S Forster, W Mommsen, and R Robinson (eds) *Bismarck, Europe, and Africa: the Berlin Africa Conference 1884–1885 and the onset of partition* (OUP Oxford 1988) 347–75.

[34] League of Nations, Advisory Committee of Jurists *Procès-verbaux of the Committee, June 16th–July 24th 1920, with Annexes* (Van Langenhuysen The Hague 1920).

[35] ibid 9.

He presented international law as the ultimate sign of civilization and the court as its new tool. The court would be the 'judicial power of humanity' and the 'empire of justice' as the 'supreme institution whose decisions must establish the sovereignty of law in all the world'.[36] Speaking on the ruins of four years of war and millions of dead, Bourgeois considered it a 'victory of the soldiers of civilization and of liberty…as conquered peoples have been freed and states have the right to be recognised'. Bourgeois was hopeful of 'humanity as a whole,' the future of international justice, and of a 'universal civilization' no longer divided into 'old' and 'new' worlds.

For the committee's president and Belgian representative, Édouard Descamps (1847–1933), the world was divided into civilized and uncivilized peoples differentiated by their levels of access to law and justice. He proposed that article 38(c) instructs judges to apply the 'rules of international law as recognised by the legal conscience of civilized nations'.[37] The balance of power system for Descamps was unreliable and archaic and thus he saw the committee's role as establishing a coordinated system of international affairs based on principles of justice. International law would be the new system's centre and the heroes would be the 'jurisconsults of authority' who were able to interpret the principles of justice derived from 'the public conscience of civilized nations'. Descamps argued that after a judge had failed to rule based on conventional norms and custom, he must apply general principles of law found in 'the doctrines of publicists carrying authority' as stated by 'the great Chancellor Kent'[38] and the 'legal conscience of civilized peoples' as found in the Martens clause of the second Hague Convention of 1899. He thought his version would limit the arbitrariness of the judge's opinion because 'the fundamental law of justice and injustice—deeply engraved on the heart of every human being—…is given its highest and most authoritative expression in the legal conscience of civilized nations'.[39] He was only opposed by Albert Geouffre De Lapradelle (1871–1955), the representative from France, who agreed that article 38(c) should make reference to 'the general principles of law' but argued that using the term 'civilized nations' was superfluous 'because law implies civilization'.[40]

The role of 'civilized nations' came up again in the discussion on what criteria to adopt for nominating and electing judges. The Spanish jurist, Rafael Altamira (1866–1951), proposed that judges should represent the 'different types of civilization' as

---

[36] ibid 5 and 11.   [37] ibid 306.

[38] Descamps referred to James Kent's argument written a century before '…no civilized nation, that does not arrogantly set all ordinary law and justice at defiance, will venture to disregard the uniform sense of the established writers on international law'. J Kent 'Of the Law of Nations: Lecture 1' in *Commentaries on American Law* (O Halsted New York 1826) vol 1, pt 1, 1–20 at 18.

[39] *Procès-verbaux of the Committee* (n 34) 306–11.   [40] ibid 335.

distinguished by language and the 'different legal systems on the Court'.[41] Altamira's proposal was supported by Descamps who argued that the modification would make the clause much more precise because the 'difference between the various legal systems was based upon the relation between law and the civilization of which it was the reflection…a difference deep(ly) rooted in history'.[42]

For Bourgeois, the Permanent Court's judges should be

[C]hosen not by reason of the state of which they are citizens, but by reason of their personal authority, of their past career, of the respect which attaches to their names known over the whole world. These judges will represent an…international spirit which is the safeguard of [national] interests, within the limits of their legitimacy.[43]

Elihu Root (1845–1937), the US representative, disagreed and insisted that world peace was based on the coexistence of the 'Principal Powers' with other States and that 'from all points of view: population, territory, wealth, trade and commerce, finance, history, race, systems of civilization and jurisprudence, vital interests, regional interests, etc…it was imperative that…the five great Powers be represented on the Court'.[44] Juridical equality of States, for Root, did not coincide with the inequality of practical interests which depended upon the national life of peoples. He argued that his was a 'method of civilization to find the means of conciliating, for a useful end, conflicting political views' like the one made by the United States in 1787 when it created two chambers, one based on the principle of equality of States and the other on population'.[45]

Altamira viewed some of the opinions as containing 'the experience and the psychological sense of some of the great Powers' and thus argued that they should be taken into account because the court's existence depended on their goodwill. Nonetheless, he still thought that the number of the judges should be based on public opinion and the judges' moral qualities, because weaker nations had a greater need that justice be done since law was their only defence. Altamira finally gave in and concluded that, in practice, the powers were 'great' because of their military power, economic development, and their contribution to civilization. The great powers, as they had a more developed civilization, he thought, would have *ipso facto* a larger pool of intellectual men who would represent them on the court, if the simple principle of choosing the best men be followed.[46]

It turns out then, that the PCIJ's committee's discussion was the only international law forum before 1945 where the concept of civilized/uncivilized was interrogated albeit individual perceptions on its meaning differed. But it is only in the second half of the 20th century when academic lawyers began to analyse the meanings, uses, and consequences of the concept of civilization in international legal history.

---

[41] ibid 370.   [42] ibid.   [43] ibid.   [44] ibid.   [45] ibid.   [46] ibid 135.

5. 20TH-CENTURY REFLECTIONS ON THE POWER OF CIVILIZATION

5.1. The Post-war Standard of Civilization

The devastation of two World Wars in the early 20th century brought into question the concepts of civilization and civilized nations. In 1947, the Saudi Arabian delegation protested to the drafting committee of the Universal Declaration of Human Rights that it had 'for the most part taken into consideration only the standards recognized by Western civilization and had ignored more ancient civilizations which were past the experimental stage', and that it was not the committee's task 'to proclaim the superiority of one civilization over all the others or to establish uniform standards for all the countries of the world'.[47]

In his *Der Nomos der Erde im Völkerrecht des Jus Publicum Europaeum* published in 1950, Carl Schmitt (1888–1985) engaged the concept of civilization as a product of the 19th century that eclipsed the view of history.[48] Schmitt claimed that from the 16th to the 20th century,

European international law considered Christian nations to be the creators and representatives of an order applicable to the whole earth....*Civilization* was synonymous with *European* civilization....In this sense Europe was still the center of the earth. With the appearance of the 'New World', Europe became the Old World.[49]

For Schmitt 'the first question in international law was whether the lands of non-Christian, non-European peoples were at such a low stage of civilization that they could become objects of organization by peoples at a higher stage'.[50] As an example, he argued that the question was central to 16th-century Spanish theologians such as Juan Ginés de Sepúlveda (1489–1573) and Francisco de Vitoria, who both agreed with the process of conquest and Christianization but approached the issue of their 'humanity' differently. Sepúlveda used an Aristotelian argument to dispose natives of their human qualities by presupposing a higher humanity of the conqueror and making the Native Americans equal to savages and barbarians. Through this argument Spaniards could obtain legal title for land-appropriation and Indian subjugation.[51] Schmitt wrote that 'it is paradoxical than none other than humanists and humanitarians put forward such inhuman arguments, because the idea of humanity is two-sided and often lends itself to a surprising dialectic'.[52]

---

[47] J Morsink *The Universal Declaration of Human Rights: Origins, Drafting, and Intent* (University of Pennsylvania Press Philadelphia 1999) at 24.

[48] See the contribution by B Fassbender 'Carl Schmitt (1888–1985)' in this volume.

[49] C Schmitt and GL Ulmen *The Nomos of the Earth in the International Law of the Jus Publicum Europaeum* (Telos Press New York 2003) at 86 (original emphasis).

[50] ibid 137.   [51] ibid 103.   [52] ibid.

Vitoria, on the other hand, had a theological and a-historical view on the difference between barbarians and Christians. Schmitt pointed out how Vitoria found the natives barbarous, but still considered them human and thus equal in rights to Christians. Vitoria's main argument in support of conquest and colonization was not about the inhumanity of the natives, wrote Schmitt, but about the legality of a 'just war' when barbarians opposed Spanish rights to free passage, free missions, free propaganda, and free commerce under *ius gentium*. Engaging in a just war 'provided the legal title for occupation and annexation of American territory and subjugation of the indigenous peoples'. Schmitt, however, wrote that Vitoria must be seen in his historical context, as a representative of the Catholic Church and agent of the moral (and legal) authority created for the Crown of Castile's missionary mandate for land appropriation in the New World.[53] 'In reality', wrote Schmitt, 'despite his claim that the Indians are morally inferior, ultimately Vitoria's view of the *conquista* is *altogether positive*. Most significant for him was the fait accompli of Christianization'.[54]

Schmitt had no problem with Sepúlveda or Vitoria's justifications for conquest but rather with later interpretations and uses of their arguments. Sepúlveda's distinction of the conquistadors' humanity became, in 'the humanitarian 18th century' as Schmitt called it, one side of absolute humanity versus the other side of 'the inhuman', or new enemy. 17th- and 18th-century philosophers from Grotius to Wolff developed the scholastic moral doctrine into a more neutral *ius naturale* and *gentium* without distinguishing between believers and non-believers, using Vitoria's Christian/non-Christian discriminatory moral theology for other political goals and intentions.

In the 19th century, argued Schmitt, in deep antithesis to 16th-century thinking, 'the *superhuman* entered history with its hostile twin: the *subhuman*'[55] in a historical mode of thinking that was humanitarian and civilizing, a 'self-conscious arrogance of an idealist philosophy of history' as exemplified by Hegel.[56] Schmitt complained that though 'Vitoria says nothing about the right of a superior civilization or culture, the right of civilized peoples to rule over half-civilized or uncivilized peoples or about "civilization"', his contemporaries revived and misread Vitoria as embedded in a belief in progress and civilization. Since the destruction of the Christian view of history by the Enlightenment in the 18th century, Schmitt argued, the belief in civilization became so widely accepted that it 'has been a decisive concept in European international law'[57] and, along with the belief in 'progress' was 'the main reason for contemporary misunderstanding [of Vitoria]' who was so 'far removed...from such concepts as progress and civilization'.[58]

During the 19th century, Schmitt observed that there was a 'common and unproblematic view of a European civilization' and

---

[53] ibid 111.
[54] ibid 109 (original emphasis).
[55] ibid 104.   [56] ibid 108.   [57] ibid 107.   [58] ibid.

that the concept of *the* international law was a specific *European* international law. That was self-evident on the European continent, especially in Germany. This also was true of such worldwide, universalist concepts such as *humanity, civilization* and *progress*, which determined the general concepts of the theory and vocabulary of diplomats. However, the whole picture thereby was understood to be Eurocentric to the core, since by 'humanity', one understood, above all, *European* humanity. 'Civilization' was self-evidently only *European* civilization and 'progress' was the linear development of *European* civilization.... The great English and French works of this epoch all have a Eurocentric concept of civilization, and distinguish among civilized, semi-civilized and barbarian peoples. But they left this problem in the background... in titling their books *International Law* or *Law of Nations*.[59]

Schmitt pointed out that even in Wheaton's, Calvo's, or Fodéré's textbooks, where the new American States were considered civilized, there was still a common concept of a 'unified European civilization', an unspoken standard presupposed and thought of as a general principle of international law, synonymous with liberal constitutionalism and 'civilization' in the European sense.[60] The belief in civilization and progress declined after the Berlin conference of 1884–85 and until the First World War, when it

[N]o longer could be used to form institutions of international law... Europe was no longer the sacral center of the earth.... The belief in civilization and progress had become nothing more than an ideological facade... in this confusion, the old *nomos* of the earth determined by Europe dissolved.[61]

A few years after Schmitt's *Nomos*, Georg Schwarzenberger (1908–91) reflected on what he called 'the standard of civilization'.[62] But unlike Schmitt, who was a Catholic and supported the Nazi regime, Schwarzenberger was a Jew who had to flee Germany in 1934.[63] Despite their obvious discrepancies, Schwarzenberger confessed to have a great admiration for Schmitt: 'he is not only a "talent", but a real genius, albeit an evil one... Like so many other intelligent people with whom I disagree, he makes me at least think over the reasons why I do so.'[64] Indeed, he disagreed with Schmitt's appraisal that the belief in civilization declined after the Berlin conference and argued that 'the nexus between Civilization and International Law was... a current legal problem of the first order' but in a different way.[64a]

Schwarzenberger was anxious about the 'analytical lawyer's' encounter with the term 'civilized nations' in article 38(c) of the ICJ's statute and the court's interpretation for

[59] ibid 228 (original emphasis).

[60] ibid 228.

[61] ibid 226.

[62] G Schwarzenberger 'The Standard of Civilisation in International Law' (1955) 8 Current Legal Problems 212–34.

[63] LC Green 'Georg Schwarzenberger (1908–1991)' (1992) 86 The American Journal of International Law 341–2.

[64] S Steinle *Völkerrecht und Machtpolitik: Georg Schwarzenberger (1908–1991)* (Nomos Baden-Baden 2002) at 171.

[64a] 'The Standard of Civilisation in International Law' (n 62) 212.

understanding what civilized nations were, preoccupations that 'for generations... have occupied the minds of historians, philosophers and sociologists'.[65] He argued, therefore, that the 'analytical lawyer' had three options: to not give any meaning to the 'embarrassing adjective', to use ad hoc sociological knowledge to explain it, or to become aware of the 'interdependence of all learning', and accept the work of others to clarify the meaning using interdisciplinary tools.[66]

Schwarzenberger tried his own definition of a 'civilized group' as one that had 'acquired a mature apparatus of thought and action and is characterised by the extensive use of rational behaviour patterns'.[67] To define others as 'groups of a rationally less calculable character' was too formal and would not contain the full meaning of the term, though he recognized the existence of 'a plurality and multiplicity of civilizations' but could not accept them as absolutes, for they were 'fragile and relative' and 'contained elements of barbarism'. [68] Schwarzenberger decided it would be egocentric and naïve to identify one particular civilization with 'Civilization' which was, at most, an approximation to an ideal, 'an ever continuing but always precarious effort'. Despite acknowledging the concept's instability, Schwarzenberger concluded that the 'ultimate basis of any civilization is religious and ethical' and is based on principles of agreement, reciprocity and voluntary cooperation. Lesser civilized societies are characterized by their reliance on the exploitation or force of man by man or of one group by another, on crude violence so that democratic States are civilized and totalitarian or authoritarian systems are uncivilized.[69] Schwarzenberger made the distinction between 'savage' groups who had not yet reached any appreciable stage of civilization and 'barbarian' groups that had forsaken civilization, but his anxieties were evident: the Holocaust as his immediate past, the Cold War's bipolar world as his present, and a world nuclear war as the future. [70]

5.2. Three 1984 Books on Civilization and the History of International Law

In 1984, three books discussing the concept of civilization in the history of international law were published: Wilhelm G Grewe's *Epochen der Völkerrechtsgeschichte*,[71] Jörg Fisch's *Die europäische Expansion und das Völkerrecht: Die Auseinandersetzungen um den Status der überseeischen Gebiete vom 15. Jahrhundert bis zur Gegenwart*, and Gerrit Gong's *The Standard of Civilization in International Society*.

---

[65] 'The Standard of Civilisation in International Law' (n 62).   [66] ibid.
[67] ibid.   [68] ibid 296.   [69] ibid 297.   [70] ibid.
[71] Grewe's book was translated by Michael Byers in 2000 as the *Epochs of International Law* with a new epilogue and minor modifications.

Wilhelm Grewe (1911–2000) who in the Third Reich worked for the government-sponsored German Institute for Foreign Policy Research in Berlin, wrote his book as a *Habilitationsschrift* during the Second World War although it was only published in 1984.[72] In the chapter the 'Idea of Civilization and a Universal International Law in a Global State System' Grewe distinguished between 'civilization' in English and French and '*Kultur*' and '*Zivilisation*' in German which, he argued, originated in the German intellectual elite's resistance to portray the First World War as conducted in the name of Western civilization.[73] Grewe understood civilization as an expression of Western European and Anglo-French cultural consciousness 'shaping the European cultural spirit', as superior to others. As a concept closely linked with the intellectual and technical/industrial idea of progress and development, it achieved full precision in the 19th century when it differentiated 'between the action of civilizing and the state of that which is civilized'.[74]

Grewe concluded that 'the equation of the international legal community with the *societé des nations civilisées* in the 19th century was primarily an achievement of British policy and British thinking on the practice and theory of international law'. The requirements for a nation to be considered civilized, according to Grewe's assessment of British policy, was the abolition of the slave trade, the adoption of Christianity and of European social and cultural practices. He cited a passage from Richard Cobden's (1804–1865) work as exemplifying the classic criteria for belonging to the 'civilized world':

Turkey cannot enter into the political system of Europe; for the Turks are not Europeans. During the nearly four centuries that people have been encamped upon the finest soil of the Continent, so far from becoming one of the families of Christendom, they have not adopted one European custom. Their habits are still Oriental, as when they first crossed the Bosphorus. They scrupulously exclude their females from the society of the other sex; they wear the Asiatic dress; sit cross-legged, or loll upon couches, using neither chair nor bed; they shave their heads, retaining their beards; and they use their fingers still, in the place of those civilized substitutes, knives and forks....A printing-press may be said to be unknown in Turkey; or, if one be found at Constantinople, it is in the hands of foreigners. The steam-engine, gas, the mariner's compass, paper money, vaccination, canals, the spinning-jenny, and railroads, are mysteries not yet dreamed about by Ottoman philosophers. Literature and science are so far from finding disciples amongst the Turks, that that people have been renowned as *twice* the destroyers of learning: in the splendid though corrupt remains of Greek literature at Constantinople; and by extinguishing the dawn of experimental philosophy, at the subversion of the Caliphate.[75]

---

[72] B Fassbender 'On Writing the History of International Law in the "Third Reich" and After' (2002) 13 European Journal of International Law 479–512 at 491.

[73] Citing Oswald Spengler's *Decline of the Occident* in G Grewe *The Epochs of International Law* (M Byers trans) (Walter de Gruyter Berlin 2000) at 447.

[74] ibid.

[75] R Cobden *Political Writings* (Wiliam Ridgway London 1867) vol 1, at 270–1, or R Cobden *Russia and the Eastern Question* (John P Jewett & Company Boston 1854) at 86–7.

For Grewe, the spread of Britain's civilization ideology to continental theory culminated in the identification of the European law of nations with the 'common world law of civilized nations'. The Christian European law of nations gradually grew into a global legal order or universal legal system, 'the members of which were...only the "civilized nations"'. The system—deprived of its natural law foundation by the rise of positivism—introduced differentiation through the criterion of civilization and laid the foundation of a new and separate colonial law of nations.[76] With this statement, Grewe opposed Schmitt's view that the international legal order's broadening and transformation began at the end of the 19th century. He denounced Schmitt's work as bad history, 'not in conformity with the historical facts and...unconfirmed by the literature of this period'.[77]

Jörg Fisch, of the post-war generation, wrote on civilization in his 1984 study on European expansion and international law as well as a hundred page essay on the concept of 'Zivilisation' and 'Kultur' for Reinhart Koselleck's Geschichtliche Grundbegriffe.[78] In Expansion, Fisch dedicated two chapters to reject Schmitt's thesis that extra-European colonial space, beyond the line of the Equator, was outside the law, and in a state of perpetual war in contrast to the European sphere of law-abiding States (Jus Publicum Europaeum) where war was contained (Hegung des Krieges) through a European peace by means of an externalization of war to the colonies. The colonies' status of neutrality, Fisch argued, was 'tenable neither empirically nor systematically' because it was the European powers themselves that often declared their legal status in conflicts that arose between them.[79]

For Fisch, European expansion from the 16th to 20th centuries was different from other empire-building processes in world history because it was uniquely grounded in legal and moral justifications among Europeans themselves. Though the legal and moral arguments changed throughout these centuries, one constant theme was the 'teleological view of history as a universalizing process' with a missionary spirit that wanted to shape the world according to its own image. The main tool for European imperial expansion, argued Fisch, was through moral and legal a priori entitlements. From the 16th to the 18th centuries this unilateral entitlement was based on the spread of Christianity. Francisco de Vitoria argued for a universal Christian right of settlement and commerce in pagan territories. In the 18th century, writers such as Wolff, Kant, and de Vattel question the unlimited religion-based unilateral right to occupy territories and govern non-Europeans. During the second half of the 19th century,

---

[76] ibid.   [77] ibid 466.

[78] In a review of the 2004 edition of the Geschichtliche Grundbegriffe Kari Palonen considers Fisch's essay as 'one of the most brilliant and in many respects surprising original pieces of the entire work' K Palonen 'A Train Reading Marathon. Retrospective Remarks on Geschichtliche Grundbegriffe' in H Buchstein (ed) Redescriptions: Yearbook of Political Thought and Conceptual History (Lit Verlag Berlin 2006) vol 10, 160–75 at 162.

[79] J Fisch 'The Role of International Law in the Territorial Expansion of Europe 16th–20th Centuries' (2000) 3 International Center for Comparative Law and Politics Review 4–13.

'civilization' became the new far-reaching claim *a priori* 'consciously or unconsciously…accepted by international lawyers, politicians and the general public in
Europe and in North America'.[80]

Civilization was not a title, explained Fisch, but a belief in a new teleology: 'the modern state was seen both as a product and an agent of modern civilization.… [T]hose
who promoted civilization had more rights than those who were not interested in
it.…In this context "civilization" had the emphatic meaning of "civilized life"'.[81]

On the other hand, civilization was the implicit foundation of a title based on a
doctrine of ownerless sovereignty.[82] Through the Roman law concept of occupation
entitling the appropriation of ownerless objects, a subject of international law could
appropriate the *imperium* rights (the sovereignty) over an uninhabited territory. The
catch was that only 'uncivilized' political communities were subject to *imperium* by
'civilized' European or American States, the ones who decided who was 'uncivilized'
in the first place. Further rights to occupation, showed Fisch, were justified to protect
civilized life as for the perceived risks that civilized (European) nationals ran in
uncivilized territories.

Fisch argued that the belief in civilization or intervention due to 'lack of civilization' and its superior value survived European imperialism and were updated in the
20th century as new claims *a priori* through a just title for intervention with the 'lack
of democracy' argument:

At first the world was destined to become Christian, then it was destined to become civilized,
while now it is destined to become legally…egalitarian, in the sense of the spread of democracy and human rights.[83]

Although Fisch's is the best historically grounded research of the 1984 books, Gerritt
Gong's work is the most cited of the three. One of the last students of Hedley Bull,
author of *The Anarchical Society*, Gong wrote the book as his PhD dissertation. He
made a genealogical account of the 'standard of civilization' as a principle of international law in the 19th century and described how it eventually failed with the two
world wars. Gong surveyed how China, Japan, Siam, Russia, Abyssinia, and the Ottoman empire were expected to conform to a European 'standard of civilization' that
often 'clashed' with their own native standards.[84]

Gong defined the standard first, as 'an expression of the assumptions, tacit and
explicit, used to distinguish those that belong to a particular society from those

---

[80] ibid 9.   [81] ibid 11.   [82] ibid 11.   [83] ibid 5.

[84] Gong's book opens with: 'The confrontation which occurred as Europe expanded into the non-
European world during the 19th and early 20th centuries was not merely political or economic, certainly not only military. It was fundamentally a confrontation of civilizations and their respective
cultural systems. At the heart of this clash were the standards of civilization by which these different
civilizations identified themselves and regulated their international relations.' GW Gong *The Standard of 'Civilization' in International Society* (Clarendon Press Oxford 1984) at 3. This idea was appropriated by SP Huntington for his 1993 essay and 1998 book *The Clash of Civilizations and the Remaking
of World Order*.

that do not' and second, as a general concept 'which determined the domain of international law, and thereby defined the identity and delimited the boundaries of the 'civilized' international society'.[85] Gong argued that the standard was a specific legal principle which developed towards the end of the 19th century. A State was considered civilized if it complied with five requirements that 'reflected the norms of the liberal European civilization which arose to replace, though it remained firmly rooted in, the mores of Christendom'.[86] The five requirements were (1) guarantees for the basic rights of liberty, dignity, property, freedom of travel, commerce, and religion, especially that of foreign nationals; (2) an organized and efficient political bureaucracy with capacity for self-defence; (3) adherence to international law—including the laws of war—and a domestic system of courts, codes, and published laws which guarantee legal justice for foreigners and nationals alike; (4) adequate and permanent diplomatic interchange and communication; and (5) adherence to cultural norms and practices of the 'civilized' international society so that actions like polygamy and slavery that were considered 'uncivilized' were also unacceptable.[87]

The 'civilized', according to Gong, would be 'those who fulfil the requirements of a particular society's standard of civilization', and the uncivilized are those who do not so conform and are left outside of the community as 'not civilized' or possibly 'uncivilized'.[88] Gong believed his standard was applied to individual States and societies as well as to systems of States or international societies of States.

Gong's work has been read in two directions: the first accepts his study as a realist interpretation of international relations which observes a historical normative fact of how States were ordered in a world system and interacted during the 19th century. According to this view, the standard of civilization surged in the 19th century, remained dormant during the Cold War era, and reappeared after the fall of the Berlin Wall in 1989 and again after September 11, 2001. These authors believe that the standard had some negative consequences in the past but is still beneficial and must be updated based on human rights protection or a broader 'membership conditionality' in international organizations that include political, economic, democratic, and good governance criteria.[89]

The second strand of works examine Gong's standard of civilization as the power and use of language and not as an international legal principle or natural rule. Martti Koskenniemi, in *The Gentle Civilizer of Nations*, argued that the standard as such did not exist in the late 19th century:

---

[85]   *The Standard of 'Civilization' in International Society* (n 84).   [86]   ibid.
[87]   ibid.   [88]   ibid.
[89]   J Donnelly 'Human Rights: A New Standard of Civilization?' (1998) 74 International Affairs 1–23; DP Fidler 'Return of the Standard of Civilization, The International Human Rights Law in Practice' (2001) 2 Chicago Journal of International Law 137–57.

No stable standard of civilization emerged to govern entry into the 'community of international law.'...the concept never worked and was never intended to work, as an all-or-nothing litmus test....The existence of a 'standard' was a myth in the sense that there was never anything to gain. Every concession was a matter of negotiation, every status dependent on agreement, *quid pro quo*. But the existence of a *language of a standard* still gave the appearance of fair treatment and regular administration to what was...a conjectural policy....Without such language, it would have been impossible to...explain, let alone to justify, why non-European communities could be subjected to massive colonization....Here was the paradox: if there was no external standard for civilization then everything depended on what Europeans approved. What Europeans approved...depended on the degree to which aspirant communities were ready to play by European rules. But the more eagerly non-Europeans wished to prove that they played by European rules, the more suspect they became.[90]

The aspect of colonization and the usage of the standard by non-Europeans, highlighted by Koskenniemi in this passage, was taken further by Antony Anghie and Brett Bowden, who explore the 'dark side' of the standard and show its negative consequences as the language that allowed for the conquest and colonization of peoples and States by those who thought themselves civilized or at least 'more civilized'.[91] Other scholars have looked at how the concept of civilization was appropriated by non-European lawyers and worked into arguments to further their own national and international law projects.[92]

More recently, Gong has written about the standard and indicated that it 'is not new, nor will it...ever become old. Some standard of civilization will remain a feature of any international society.'[93] While Fisch warns against the uses of new standards of civilization for interventionists purposes in weaker States, Gong argues that standards of human rights, humanitarian law, sustainable development, the environment, international trade, and investment regulations are positive and must be followed for States to be considered 'civilized' by the international community in our modern world. Gong believes that today's international society searches and aspires

[90] M Koskenniemi *The Gentle Civilizer of Nations: the Rise and Fall of International Law, 1870–1960* (CUP Cambridge 2002) at 134–5.

[91] A Anghie *Imperialism, Sovereignty and the Making of International Law* (CUP Cambridge 2005); B Bowden *The Empire of Civilization: The Evolution of an Imperial Idea* (The University of Chicago Press Chicago 2009).

[92] L Obregón 'Completing Civilization: Creole Consciousness and International Law in Nineteenth-Century Latin America' in A Orford (ed) *International Law and its Others* (CUP Cambridge 2006) 247–64; A Becker Lorca 'Universal International Law: Nineteenth-Century Histories of Imposition and Appropriation' (2010) 51 Harvard International Law Journal 475–552; P Singh 'Indian International Law: From a Colonized Apologist to a Subaltern Protagonist' 23 Leiden Journal of International Law 79–103; L Mälksoo 'The History of International Legal Theory in Russia: A Civilizational Dialogue with Europe' (2008) 19 European Journal of International Law 211–32; U Özsu 'A Subject Which Excites the Deepest Interest throughout the Civilized World: The Greek-Turkish Population Exchange and the Craft of Diplomatic Nation-Building' (2011) 24 Leiden Journal of International Law 823–47.

[93] GW Gong 'Standards of Civilization Today' in M Mozaffari (ed) *Globalization and Civilizations* (Routledge London 2002) 77–96 at 94.

for a 'standard of civilization' in order to continue organizing an otherwise anarchical international society and to show a normative path for constant improvement for the future.[94]

6. CONCLUSION

From the 16th century to the early 19th century, the concepts of civilized/uncivilized (and other pairs such as progressive/backward, cultured/barbarian, modern/primitive, white/black) which categorized and stratified peoples, nations or States were key to the language of informal European imperialism. In the late 19th century, the language of civilization transitioned to formal imperialism sustained by international law. Though the legal and moral arguments changed throughout the centuries, the hierarchical description of insiders and outsiders of a legal community, the teleological view, and its missionary spirit are central to understand the history of international law.

In the 16th and 17th centuries, the holistic Christian vision of law and morality was the entitlement for European expansion, as Native Americans entered into the universe of European sovereignty. Indigenous people became liable to management and land appropriation by those who described themselves as being at a higher stage of human evolution because of their religious beliefs and particular forms of social interaction. As barbarians, the indigenous could access Christianity through baptism and the adoption of European cultural and linguistic practices. They then had the possibility of obtaining the individual *telos* of receiving God's glory, but they remained subjects of European indoctrination. Africans also fared a dismal fate, as they were categorized at an even lower stage of human evolution that did not foresee the possibility of progression, and thus allowed the moral and legal justification for their enslavement.

In the 18th century, Enlightenment thought brought forth the concept of the 'human' and its other (the 'inhuman' or 'subhuman') which allowed for an alternative conceptual pair to the previous Christian/non-Christian universal view. The century ended with proposals for the individual human's *telos* to contribute to national civilization and a collective purpose for humanity to reach the unity of all civilized nations through law. Essentially, however, humanity and the law of nations were considered European.

---

[94] GW Gong 'Empires and Civilizations: The Search for Standards Continues' (2010) 12 International Studies Review 144–6.

In the 19th century, civilization became the new *a priori* claim to European expansion based on an accepted way to classify the progress of peoples or States through a range of imagined values. Civilization was a conjectural policy based on contextual variables and a belief in the teleology of the modern State as a product and an agent of modern evolutionary development. In legal terms, those who promoted civilization had rights inherent to their status, entitlement over uninhabited territories or 'uncivilized' political communities. The international legal community was 'the community of civilized nations' and the European law of nations was the common law of civilized nations.

By the end of the 19th century, the civilizing mission was used as an argument in the 'scramble for Africa'. In the interwar period, the idea of civilized nations was institutionalized in article 38 of the PCIJ statute as source for the origins of principles of international law though it was not defined. After the Second World War, several studies acknowledged the relevance of the concept of civilization in the history of international law and began to study the existence of a standard of civilization. Critical authors questioned its continuity or appropriateness as a tool of influence, domination or subordination while others viewed it as a necessary form of universal progress that needed to be updated with current ideas of standards.

In the mid-20th century, as a result of two devastating wars, the term came into crisis. In the context of the decline of Europe's image as 'civilized', the end of the century brought new variables of progress, such as free trade, democracy, and human rights.[95]

To conclude, international law surged in the 19th century as a discipline constituted by the tension in defining its inner and outer limits between the civilized and the uncivilized. The events that mark the dates of international law's historical narrative and origins are defined around these spheres, with the final utopia of international law as the ultimate achievement of civilized progress. To be *in* international law was to be a part of civilization while to be *out* of international law was to be lawless and savage. For many authors of the 19th century and later, reading civilization into international law meant that the moments when there was no international law, or the peoples that did not have it, were barbarous moments or barbarous peoples. The main tenants of international law—the regulation of peace and war—can also be understood as trapped in the dualism of civilized/uncivilized. As a project in expansion, international legal scholars and practitioners built up the chronology of the discipline based on the idea of a normative progress in regulating peace and war constrained by the dichotomy revolving around the limits and conditions of sovereignty. Yet a comprehensive history of the concept of civilization, and its accompanying adjectives civilized/uncivilized in international law has to be written. This overview, taken from a sample of legal scholars' reflections on the topic, hopes to contribute to the debate and open some questions for further research.

---

[95] 'The Role of International Law' (n 79) 6.

RECOMMENDED READING

Anghie, Antony 'Francisco de Vitoria and the Colonial Origins of International Law' in Eve Darian-Smith and Peter Fitzpatrick (eds) *Laws of the Postcolonial (Law, Meaning, and Violence)* (The University of Michigan Press Ann Arbor 1999) 89–107.

Anghie, Anthony *Imperialism, Sovereignty and the Making of International Law* (CUP Cambridge 2005).

Bowden, Brett 'The Colonial Origins of International Law: European Expansion and the Classical Standard of Civilization' (2005) 7 Journal of the History of International Law 1–23.

Bowden, Brett (ed) *Civilization: Critical Concepts in Political Science* (4 vols Routledge New York 2009).

Bowden, Brett *The Empire of Civilization: The Evolution of an Imperial Idea* (The University of Chicago Press Chicago 2009).

Fisch, Jörg *Die europäische Expansion und das Völkerrecht: die Auseinandersetzungen um den Status der überseeischen Gebiete vom 15. Jahrhundert bis zur Gegenwart* (Steiner Verlag Stuttgart 1984).

Fisch, Jörg 'Zivilisation, Kultur' in Otto Brunner, Werner Conze, and Reinhart Koselleck (eds) *Geschichtliche Grundbegriffe: Historisches Lexikon zur politisch-sozialen Sprache in Deutschland* (Klett-Cotta Stuttgart 1992) vol 7, 679–774.

Fisch Jörg 'The Role of International Law in the Territorial Expansion of Europe 16th–20th Centuries' (2000) 3 International Center for Comparative Law and Politics Review 5–15.

Gong, Gerrit W *The Standard of 'Civilization' in International Society* (Clarendon Press Oxford 1984).

Grewe, Wilhelm G *Epochen der Völkerrechtsgeschichte* (Nomos Baden-Baden 1984); *The Epochs of International Law* (M Byers trans) (de Gruyter Berlin 2000).

Koskenniemi, Martti *The Gentle Civilizer of Nations: the Rise and Fall of International Law, 1870–1960* (CUP Cambridge 2002).

Pagden, Anthony *The Fall of Natural Man: The American Indian and the Origins of Comparative Ethnology* (CUP Cambridge 1990).

Schmitt, Carl *Der Nomos der Erde im Völkerrecht des Jus Publicum Europaeum* (Duncker & Humblot Berlin 1950); *The Nomos of the Earth in the International Law of the Jus Publicum Europaeum* (Telos Press New York 2003).

Schwarzenberger, Georg 'The Standard of Civilisation in International Law' (1955) 8 Current Legal Problems 212–34.

PART V

METHODOLOGY AND THEORY

CHAPTER 39

A HISTORY OF INTERNATIONAL LAW HISTORIES

MARTTI KOSKENNIEMI

1. INTRODUCTION

ERNEST NYS (1851–1920), the first professional historian of international law, expressed in his *Les origines du droit international* of 1893 confidence that international law was developing in a beneficial direction. The Hegelian dialectic between the national and the universal would be resolved in favour of the latter. The three great ideas that had dominated world history—progress, freedom, and the 'idea of humanity'—may not immediately lead to a world State, but they did allow the hope that war would soon be extinct as an instrument of politics.[1] Nys began his narrative of the origins of international law with the European renaissance but accepted that there had been international law since the 'Phoenicians' and in fact, his teacher, François Laurent (1810–87), had devoted the first four of his 18-volume *Histoire de droit des gens et des relations internationales* to 'Oriental' empires: Greece, Rome, and early Christianity.[2] For Nys and Laurent, and for the international lawyers who were busy organizing

---

[1] E Nys *Les origines du droit international* (Castaignes Bruxelles 1894) at 404–5.
[2] F Laurent *Histoire du droit des gens et des relations internationales. Tôme Premier: L'Orient* (Durand Paris 1851) Volume 1 (*L'Orient*).

themselves into a profession at the time they wrote, not only was the history of international law really the same as the history of humanity, but 'l'histoire de l'humanité
considerée au point de vue du progrès qu'elle accomplit vers l'unité'.[3] History led
from separation to unity, its intrinsic teleology expressed by and accomplished
through international law.

The cosmopolitan tradition to which these two histories belong frames the ideological context of the establishment in Belgium (where both men acted as professors)
of the *Institut de droit international* in 1873. It drew inspiration from a providential
view of history: even the worst humanitarian disasters pointed to a better future, a
more enlightened, united humanity. They agreed with Immanuel Kant that universal
history had a 'cosmopolitan purpose' that it shared with law: a federation, initially
among free nations, later perhaps among free individuals, would form history's *telos*.[4]
To become an international lawyer would not be to operate a few technical rules
about diplomacy or warfare but to engage with a project for subordinating all the
world under law—a law that would recognize all humans as bearers of rights, citizens
of their nations, organized as secular States, equally participating in a public law governed State-community. This was a project for progress, for a global modernity—the
dream of the entire world one day resembling Europe's idealized image of itself.[5]

One cannot know international law, according to this view, without understanding it as the transformation of humankind's collective experience into a redemptive
future. General histories and opening chapters of textbooks in the 20th century thus
often began like Laurent, with Sumerian city-states or the laws of Manu in ancient
India, followed up by a discussion of the 'international' relations of Greek city-states
as well as an overview of Roman expansion as articulated in Roman law, *ius fetiale*
and *ius gentium*. From observing the dearth of legal arrangements the Middle Ages,
they would move on to the Spanish scholastics of the 16th century, the Protestant
Reformation, and the Peace of Westphalia (1648) as the symbol of the modern States
system, the hidden objective of prior history.[6] Accounts of 'modern' (post-West-

---

[3] F Laurent *Histoire du droit des gens et des relations internationales. Tôme Quatrième—Etudes sur l'histoire de l'humanité* (Durand Paris 1855) at v. Both titles are also included in the second edition of the work, published in Brussels by Méline, in Paris by Librairie internationale 1861–70.

[4] I Kant 'Idea for a Universal History with a Cosmopolitan Purpose' in I Kant *Political Writings* (H Reiss ed and HB Nisbet trans) (CUP Cambridge 1991) especially seventh to ninth propositions, at 47–53; see also M Koskenniemi 'On the Idea and Practice for Universal History with a Cosmopolitan Purpose' in B Puri and H Sievers (eds) *Terror, Peace and Universalism. Essays on the Philosophy of Immanuel Kant* (OUP Oxford 2007) 122–48.

[5] T Skouteris *The Notion of Progress in International Law Discourse* (Springer The Hague 2010).

[6] Thus the long entry on *Völkerrechtsgeschichte* in the Strupp-Schochauer *Wörterbuch* is quite openly teleological: the discussion of Western antiquity and the Middle Ages focuses on the slow emergence of aspects of (modern) statehood, namely entities that are formally independent and equal. Thus the section on the Middle Ages concludes that '[n]och war der Weg zum durchgebildeten souveränen Staat…weit', W Preiser 'Völkerrechtsgeschichte' in K Strupp and HJ Schlochauer *Wörterbuch des Völker-
rechts. Dritter Band* (De Gruyter Berlin 1962) 680–703 at 690; for a very similar discussion, see eg A Wag-
ner *Geschichte des Völkerrechts* (Kohlhammer Stuttgart 1936).

phalian) law would then discuss Emer de Vattel's rejection of the hypothesis of *Civitas Maxima* (1758) before focusing on the consolidation of European diplomacy at the Congress of Vienna 1814–15. Accounts of 19th-century international law would supplement relative peace in Europe and colonial expansion with the way jurists of the period tended to 'exaggerate' the sovereignty of their States, turning to a 'positivism' that neglected international law's natural home in a universal teleology. Nevertheless, late 19th-century institutions such as the Red Cross (1864), the international unions, and the two Hague Peace Conferences (1899, 1907), these accounts would insist, paved the way to the League of Nations and the United Nations, and to the advancement of the discipline's historical project. If the period since the 1960s was one of 'changing structure',[7] this signified the move from statehood to some kind of universal existence—perhaps 'globalization'—that had not yet quite declared its legal form.

Of course, this account is only a sketch, if not a caricature. But it tries to capture something of the kind of teleology that is mediated by 'modern' international law texts to students and professionals. It is part of a larger historical understanding of development as 'progress' that was shared by late 19th-century European elites but that we meet today at institutions of higher learning everywhere. The narrative is expected to inculcate in the members of the professional classes a certain manner of reflecting on the world and on one's historical place in it. Cultural markers such as 'antiquity', 'the Renaissance', or 'globalization' are as much part or it as are technical terms such as 'cannon-shot rule', 'Concert of Europe', or 'humanitarian intervention'. Although all such notions bear the marks of their European origin, they enable lawyers from all over the world to communicate with each other by invoking widely shared historical associations and a normative teleology in which an idealized Europe, coded as 'nationhood', capitalism, 'modernity', or 'rule of law', marks the horizon of their shared imagination.[8]

A full history of international legal histories would require writing a history of international law proper, of its express or implied self-historicizations, the way its institutions embody particular teleologies, its rules turn into precedent or 'crystallize' into customs and become parts of professional vocabularies. This is obviously beyond the scope of this chapter.[9] So I propose to begin with a sketch of forms of historical

---

[7] W Friedmann *The Changing Structure of International Law* (Stevens & Sons London 1964).

[8] The view of an idealized Europe as the indispensable horizon of modern historical consciousness is well presented in D Chakrabarty *Provincializing Europe. Postcolonial Thought and Historical Difference* (Princeton University Press Princeton 2000).

[9] A brief survey of international legal historiography is in A Nussbaum *A Concise History of the Law of Nations* (2nd edn Macmillan New York 1954) at 291–5. Recent discussions of the state of history in the discipline include M Craven 'Introduction: International Law and its Histories' in M Craven, M Fitzmaurice and M Vogiatzi (eds) *Time, History and International Law* (Nijhoff Leiden 2007) 1–25, and R Lesaffer 'International Law and its History: The Study of an Unrequited Love' in ibid 27–41, as well as I Hueck 'The Discipline of the History of International Law' (2001) 3 Journal of the History of International Law 194–217.

consciousness as they emerged from early Christianity to the rise of natural law in the 17th century, and the professional international legal histories of the (long) 19th century (Sections 2–4), followed by an overview of types international legal history in the 20th and 21st centuries (Section 5). Focus will be on the way problems in each type of historiography have inspired alternative historical narratives, illustrating the uses of international law in assisting human communities to imagine their political origins and the manner of their relations with each other.

2. *Ius Gentium* as Historical Law

Roman definitions of *ius gentium* that located the topic within natural law ('what nature teaches to all animals'),[10] entailed the assumption that it had no more of a history than natural history, akin to that of plants or animals. Other Roman jurists, however, addressed *ius gentium* as the positive law that had developed to deal with relations between Romans and foreigners on a universal basis, such as wars, the separation of nations, and commercial and private law institutions that would reflect relatively stable needs of government and commerce everywhere.[11] Throughout the early Christian age, definitions of *ius gentium* oscillated between unchanging natural law and universal (or at least largely shared) institutions of civilized humanity. Bartolus of Saxoferrato frankly stated that the law of nations proceeded in two parts; from natural reason on the one hand (such that promises ought to be kept), and from the customs of the various nations (*usu gentium*) on the other.[12] His distinction between *ius gentium primaevum* and *ius gentium secondarium* was used by many later writers, including Grotius, to distinguish between legal institutions based on 'right reason derived from the will of the gods' and time-bound but still universal 'consensus of all nations'.[13]

Within the *Respublica Christiana,* the historicity of political or legal institutions was always limited by the eschatological view that was politically expressed in the theory of the Four Monarchies (Babylonian, Persian, Greek, and Roman) in the Book of Daniel

[10] *Justinian's Institutes* (P Birks and G McLeod trans and Introduction) (Cornell University Press 1987) lii (37).

[11] 'Ex hoc iure gentium introducta bella, discretae gentis, regna condita, dominia distincta, agris termini positi, aedificia collocata, commercium, emptiones venditiones, locationes conductiones, obligationes institutae: exceptis quibusdam que jure civili introductae sunt' Dig. 1.1.5.

[12] M Scattola *Das Naturrecht vor dem Naturrecht. Zur Geschichte des 'ius naturae' im 16. Jahrhundert* (Niemeyer Tübingen 1999) at 205–7.

[13] Eg H Grotius *Commentary on the Law of Prize and Booty* (MJ von Ittersum ed) (Liberty Fund Indianapolis 2006 [1605–1607]) Prolegomena at 25.

that prophesized the end of the world at the collapse of Rome. This not only prolonged the life of the empire but also hindered the emergence of a historical consciousness that would look beyond the apocalyptic. The medieval mind inserted itself in the history of Roman antiquity with the emperor as its head.[14] This view was only destroyed in the 14th and 15th centuries when humanists such as Machiavelli and his lawyer-friend Guicciardini began to write histories of Rome and of Italy with the intention of depicting change and drawing 'lessons' from the past to present politics.[15]

Humanist historiography entered international law from two directions. A reformist Catholicism in 16th-century Spain used the scholastic frame to take a position on such contemporary issues as expansion in the Indies and the creation of a world-wide net of commercial relations. According to the Genesis, all humans had been created free and equal and shared ownership in common.[16] And yet, princes were claiming absolute rule over their territories and global commerce operated through private property. To accommodate that reality into their Christian ideals, the theologians began to argue that the provision by natural law for common ownership did not actually prohibit its contrary.[17] This allowed them to justify public and private power in terms of a properly historical *ius gentium* that was expressed in a (tacit) agreement by the 'greater part' of the members of community in the course of a long time.[18] In his massive *Tractatus de legibus* (1612) Francisco Suárez[19] explained how diplomacy, professional warfare, and the global networks of trade had been

…[g]radually introduced throughout the world, through a successive process, by means of propagation and mutual imitation among the nations, and without any special and simultaneous compact or consent on the part of all the peoples. For the body of law has such a close relationship to nature and so befits all nations, individually and collectively, that it has grown, almost by a natural process, with the growth of the human race.[20]

---

[14] C Fasolt *The Limits of History* (University of Chicago Press 2005) at 18–20.

[15] N Machiavelli *The Discourses (on Livy)* (B Crick ed) (Penguin Harmondsworth 2003); F Guicciardini *The History of Italy* (S Alexander ed and trans) (Princeton University Press Princeton 1969). The two were cited as examples in A Gentili's description of the qualities that were needed of a good ambassador—a historical sense that would combine with a philosophical spirit. As a further example he would refer to Guicciardini's *History of Italy* that celebrated Lorenzo de Medici's balance of power policy that succeeded in maintained Italy's independence until the end of the 15th century. A Gentili *De Legationibus Libri Tres, Volume Two. The Translation* (GJ Laing trans) (OUP Oxford 1924) at 158, 161.

[16] F de Vitoria *Comentarios a la Secunda secundae de Santo Tomás* (V Beltrán de Heredia ed) (Salamanca 1934/1952) vol III: De justitia Q 62, A 9, at 67; D de Soto *De iustitia et iure libri decem—De la justicia y el derecho en diez libros* (PVD Carro Introduction, PMG Ordonez trans) (Sección Teólogos Juristas Instituto de Estudios Políticos Madrid 1967) book IV Q 3 A 1 (295a–b).

[17] 'Concedimus ergo quod nullius fuit praeceptum quod omnia essent communia, sed solum fuit concessio' Comentarios (n 16) Q 62, A 1, para 20, at 77; for the early canon law origins of this argument, B Tierney 'Permissive Natural Law and Property: Gratian to Kant' (2001) 62 Journal of History of Ideas 384–8.

[18] Comentarios (n 16) Q 62, A 1, fn 23, at 79.

[19] See the contribution by A Brett 'Franciscus de Vitoria (1480–1546) and Francisco Suárez (1548–1617)' in this volume.

[20] F Suárez 'On Law and God the Lawgiver' ['De legibus'] in F Suáréz *Selections from Three Works* (GL Williams trans) (Clarendon Oxford 1944) book II, ch XX, para 1, at 351.

At the same time, in France and the United Provinces, especially within the Protestant camp, an 'elegant jurisprudence' began to stress the historicity of Roman (civil) law and to regard old customs as expressions of a resurgent nationalist (and anti-papist) ideology. Like the Spaniards (whom he greatly admired), the young Hugo Grotius[21] learned to separate a historical *ius gentium* from natural law and, in his mature work of 1625, associated it with the *consensus gentium*, amenable to study by what he called the a posteriori method.[22] Grotius viewed history as a reservoir of edifying examples especially from Greek and Roman antiquity.[23] In this, Grotius' writing resembles that further humanist genre, *raison d'état*, popular especially among counter-reformation intellectuals such as the former Jesuit Giovanni Botero (1544–1617). The point of the latter was to turn Machiavelli on his head—that is to say, by appropriating Machiavelli's arguments to distinguish between 'bad' and 'good' reason of States, the latter being fully compatible with Christian ethics.[24] The *raison d'état* writers, like Grotius in his advocacy for the Dutch East India Company, made sure to argue that providence would guarantee that the good path would in due course coalesce with the more useful one. After all, as Grotius wrote in his brief to support the penetration by the Dutch East India Company (VOC) into the East Indies: 'God Himself by His special favour opened up that part of the world to the Dutch, whose commerce was then on the verge of ruin.'[25]

3. NATURAL-LAW HISTORIES

The problem with natural law had been its ostensibly a-historical character. By contrast, Grotius' follower, the Saxon Samuel Pufendorf[26] understood natural law itself historically, as rational conclusions drawn by human beings who were predominantly

---

[21] See the contribution by P Haggenmacher 'Hugo Grotius (1552–1608)' in this volume.

[22] H Grotius *The Rights of War and Peace* (R Tuck ed) (Liberty Fund Indianapolis 2005) book I The Preliminary Discourse XVIII, at 94.

[23] ibid The Preliminary Discourse XLVII, at 123–4; in addition, see the contribution by K Tuori 'The Reception of Ancient Legal Thought in Early Modern International Law' in this volume.

[24] For overviews, see R Bireley *The Counter-Reformation Prince. Anti-Machiavellianism or Catholic Statecraft in Early Modern Europe* (University of North Carolina Press 1990) and R Descendre *L'état du monde. Giovanni Botero entre la raison d'état et géopolitique* (Droz Genève 2009); on Jesuit reason of state specifically, see H Höpfl *Jesuit Political Thought* (CUP Cambridge 2004) at 84–185.

[25] *Commentary on the Law of Prize and Booty* (n 13) ch XV, 465. Or as he puts it, 'nothing base is truly advantageous, whereas nothing honourable can fail to be expedient by virtue of the very fact that it is honourable' *Commentary on the Law of Prize and Booty* (n 13) ch XV, 463.

[26] See the contribution by K Haakonssen 'Samuel Pufendorf (1632–1694)' in this volume.

motivated by self-interest from their existential situation, that is to say, from their weaknesses; in order to survive, they need to join together.[27] His new theory of sociability, operative already in a state of nature, outlined a historical view of human communities as artificial creations freed from Christian eschatology and Roman law. Pufendorf used that view to reject the allegedly timeless Aristotelian constitutional categories in his 1667 analysis of the status of the Roman-German Empire. The Empire was simply what history had produced in terms of the relationships between its constituent units.[28] In his main work a few years later (*De jure naturae et gentium*, 1672) Pufendorf generalized this view into a theory of modern statehood as an instrument through which self-interested individuals pursued their search for security and welfare.[29] To be successful, they would need to be well aware of the histories of their State and its rivals. It was no accident that Pufendorf himself then entered into the service to courts of Sweden and Prussia in order to produce political histories of both countries. If the law of nations consisted, as Pufendorf assumed, of rational conclusions that humans would make of their existential situation ('office'), then it coalesced with what history taught as wise policy.[30] This became the basis for the 'universal histories' taught by professors of natural law at the new universities at Halle and Göttingen in the course of the 18th century to Europe-wide audiences.[31]

One of them, Johann Jakob Schmauss from Göttingen published in 1751 a nearly 700-page history of European treaties from the 14th to the 18th centuries. He interpreted European history from the perspective of the perpetual French desire for 'universal monarchy' to which others reacted by seeking to uphold the balance of power.[32] It was followed two years later with a three-part critique and construction of natural law. In long quotations from authors from Greek antiquity to the middle of the 18th century, interspersed by his own explanations and critiques, Schmauss narrated the progress of natural-law literature, concentrating on the philosophical contrast between voluntarism and rationalism and on the different understandings of the role 'instinct' played in the law of sociability.[33] For Schmauss, natural law was a 'sys-

---

[27] For a useful account, see P Laurent *Pufendorf et la loi naturelle* (Vrin Paris 1982) at 117–45.

[28] S Pufendorf *The Present State of Germany* (E Bohun and MJ Seidler eds) (Liberty Fund Indianapolis 2007).

[29] S Pufendorf *De jure naturae et gentium, libri octo* (trans as *On the Law of Nature and Nations, in eight books*) (W Oldfather trans) (Oxford Clarendon Press 1934).

[30] A Dufour 'Pufendorfs föderalistisches Denken und die Staatsräsonlehre' in F Palladini and G Hartung (eds) *Samuel Pufendorf und die europäische Frühaufklärung* (Akademie Verlag Berlin 1996) 122.

[31] See especially N Hammerstein *Ius und Historie. Ein Beitrag zur Geschichte des historischen Denkens an deutschen Universitäten im späten 17. und 18. Jahrhundert* (Vandenhoeck & Ruprecht Göttingen 1972).

[32] JJ Schmauss *Einleitung zu der Staats-Wissenschaft I: Die Historie der Balance von Europa, der Barriere der Niederlande* (Göttingen 1751).

[33] JJ Schmauss *Neues System des Rechts der Natur* (Göttingen 1753). The first book is a long history of the subject-matter; the second (*Dubia juris naturae*) a response to certain criticisms of natural law and the third (*Neues Systema des Rechts der Natur*) a sketch of Schmauss' own theory that builds on the origin of natural law in human will that is directed by the intellect to grasping the divinely based rules of sociality.

tem of socialitas' and a thoroughly Protestant science. But although Pufendorf's application of reason to sociability succeeded in developing something like a universal jurisprudence, it still lacked a credible account of obligation. There had to be scientific rules about sociality that intellect would grasp and impose on the will so as to make them binding.[34]

While German lawyers were turning to history at their universities, French writers were using the vocabulary of the *raison d'état* to develop a sociological view of European statehood that sometimes expressed itself in a legal idiom.[35] For example, the *Principes de négociations* published by Abbé de Mably as part of the second edition of his *Droit public de l'Europe fondé sur les traités* (1757) gave an account of European international relations since the Middle Ages in terms of European monarchs' unlimited and irrational 'ambition, avarice and fear'. He developed a theory of European public law as a 'science of negotiations' that would allow everyone to benefit if only all sovereigns paid close attention to their 'fundamental interests'.[36] In learning to do that, it would be useful for statesmen to study past treaties in their context and to gather from this how States had succeeded or failed in these efforts. Like Montesquieu, Mably associated rational government with close attention to the nation's 'real interests'. History would assist as a storehouse of examples of the way European monarchs had let their passions overrule their judgment.

This is the rather static role history plays also in Emer de Vattel's *Droit des gens* (1758) where it would illustrate the operation of rules of reason that would guide princes from their 'passions' towards the rational government of the State with the view of its 'perfectionment'.[37] History was either a literary history of natural-law writings or then examples from past practices that would illustrate passion's dangers and the benefits of cool reason. With the Scottish Enlightenment, and above all with Adam Smith, the natural-law tradition would be accompanied by a theory about the development of all societies in four stages from hunter-gatherers into practitioners of peaceful commerce. But this would turn the school from law to political economy; the benefits of free commerce would achieve what natural lawyers had always desired, the welfare and security of the State.[38]

The 'commercial turn' marked the end of the abstract rationalism of the natural-law tradition. A new generation, represented by Georg Friedrich von Martens, also from

---

[34] ibid 274–6.

[35] See generally, E Thuau *Raison d'état et pensée politique à l'époque de Richelieu* (Albin Michel Paris 1966/2000).

[36] GB de Mably *Principes des négociations pour servir d'introduction au droit public de l'Europe* (M Belissa ed) (Kimé Paris 2001) at 45–50.

[37] E de Vattel *Le droit des gens ou principes de la loi naturelle appliqués à la conduite & aux affaires des nations & des souverains* (London 1758). For Vattel's life and work, see the contribution by E Jouannet 'Emer de Vattel (1714–1767)' in this volume.

[38] I Hont 'The Languages of Sociability and Commerce: Samuel Pufendorf and the Theoretical Foundations of the "Four-Stages" Theory' in I Hont *Jealousy of Trade. International Competition and the Nation-State in Historical Perspective* (Harvard University Press Harvard 2005) 159–84.

Göttingen, vigorously attacked the revolutionary principles of a new *Déclaration de droits des gens* that had been proposed to the National Assembly in Paris as '*leeres Wortgepränge*'.[39] According to Martens, history taught us *Realpolitik*, that even if independence and equality of nations were unobjectionable in their abstract formulation, they were seldom honoured in actual practice. Without consciousness of that history, tragedy would follow.[40] The peoples of the world were simply too different for any universal ('rational') law of nations to emerge. Instead, a practical community among Europeans had grown up from antique origins through the progress of religion, voyages of discovery, and the rise of a system of political hierarchy and equilibrium. The peace of Westphalia and Utrecht had begun 'a new and memorable epoch of positive law of nations'.[41]

[C']est donc dans l'histoire générale et particulier des Etats de l'Europe…qu'on doit puiser l'histoire de l'origine et du progrès du droit des gens conventionnel et coutumier; histoire qui n'a pas encore été traitée avec tout le soin qu'elle merite, quoiqu'on aïe commence à s'en occuper avec success.[42]

In a footnote to that sentence, Martens referred to the first full-scale post-naturalist history of international law by Robert Ward (1795) whose two-volume work had opened with a touching admission by its author that once he had collected all the treaties, cases, and other factual materials, he had to answer the question about their binding force.[43] Although he could see how the practices of Christian nations might become binding to Christians, he found no basis on which to claim that they were binding everywhere. Besides, 'natural law' meant different things to different people so that it was futile and misleading to treat it as a universal category. Only religion could provide certainty; where religions differed, unity was impossible. Accordingly, there must be 'a different law of nations for different parts of the globe'.[44] The first part of Ward's history expounded the theory of its basis in the 'shared morals and shared religion' of particular 'classes of nations' (Chapters I–V) while the second (Chapters VI–XVIII) focused on the law of nations within Christian Europe.[45]

Ward's history of (European) law of nations was a relativist narrative about European progress. It began with the Greeks and the Romans, the ferocious manners of

---

[39] GF von Martens *Einleitung in das positive europäische Völkerrecht auf Verträge und Herkommen gegründet* (Dieterich Göttingen 1796) at ix.

[40] ibid xvi; see further M Koskenniemi 'Into Positivism: Georg Friedrich von Martens (1756–1821) and Modern International Law' (2008) 15 Constellations 198–200.

[41] GF von Martens *Précis du droit des gens moderne de l'Europe fondé sur les traités et l'usage* (Dieterich Göttingen 1801) at 15.

[42] ibid 16, 18.

[43] R Ward *An Enquiry into the Foundation and History of the Law of Nations from the Time of the Greeks and the Romans to the Age of Grotius* (2 vols Butterworth London 1795).

[44] ibid vol 1, xii–xv at xiv.

[45] As Ward stated, among Christians, religion provided 'the only *certain* foundation for that code which is observed by Christian, in other words, by European nations'. *An Enquiry into the Foundation* (n 43) vol 1, at xl, xxxi–xxxiii. For what Ward calls his 'destruction' of the idea of the universality of the law of nations, see especially Chapter II of the work, at 35–119.

the 'Scandinavians', followed by 'the most cruel maxims' and 'bloody and savage customs' of the Middle Ages.[46] But even as the law of nations was unknown and habits were raw, individual rulers (such as Charlemagne) and institutions such as chivalry, feudalism, and Christianity provided civilizing influence—though its peaceful message was often undermined by papal ambition and the unjust treatment of barbarians.[47] More recently, treaties and diplomatic practices had softened the customs of war and even occasionally provided channels for pacific intercourse between 'sets of nations'. These had been articulated as a 'science' first with Grotius, then Pufendorf, Vattel, and the other great jurists, the heroes of Ward's narrative.[48]

4. The Long 19th Century

For Martens and Ward, already, natural law retreated into the position of a background justification for taking pragmatic focus on the practice of (European) States. Somewhat later, Ake Manning's *Commentaries on the Law of Nations* (1839) found the meaning of history in the coming into consciousness of the fact that God wanted humans to be happy and that this meant doing what was most useful.[49] This utility-based law had now been 'acknowledged as binding by the states of Europe and of North America'—sufficient reason for concentrating on what they had done in practice.[50] A full-scale narrative of this type was produced by the American diplomat Henry Wheaton in his Prize Essay to the *Institut de France* of 1839.[51] This was not a literature review but an account of the diplomacy, wars, and peace settlements in Europe, combined with an overview of some of the writings of the principal jurists of each period. No doubt reflecting Wheaton's American background, much attention was given to the law of the sea: prize law, neutrality and contraband, right of visit, and maritime warfare. A discussion of Rousseau's and Bentham's peace plans ended in a resigned acceptance of the paradox that peace appears possible only in the presence of an alliance so strong that would itself become a danger to its weaker members.[52]

---

[46] *An Enquiry into the Foundation* (n 43) vol 1.

[47] Eg ibid vol 2, 111–14, 125–43.

[48] ibid 606–28.

[49] O Manning *Commentaries on the Law of Nations* (S Sweet London 1839) at 58–60.

[50] ibid 76.

[51] H Wheaton *Histoire de progrès de droit des gens depuis la Paix de Westphalie jusqu'au congrès de Vienne* (Brockhaus Leipzig 1841). Although the competition had concerned only progress in the law of nations since Westphalia (showing the central role 1648 already then played in the discipline), Wheaton added to it a part on the earlier period, too, which he continued to expand in later editions. For Wheaton's life and work, see the contribution by LH Liu 'Henry Wheaton (1785–1848)' in this volume.

[52] ibid 258.

Like Martens, Wheaton thought that the French revolutionary wars had illustrated the de facto limits on the independence of nations. His sympathy towards France did not prevent him from seeing in the Vienna arrangement a progressive change, accompanied by the expansion of international law to the North and Central American States and by the renouncement 'by the Mohammedan nations of the Orient' of their violent practices.[53]

German lawyers such as Johann Ludwig Klüber and August Wilhelm Heffter repeated much of this in the opening pages of their widely read textbooks. For both, the history of international law consisted of the treaties and practices of European nations that were parts of European civilization itself, held together by Christianity's cultural and moral power. If the political struggles between European powers often appeared to relegate law into literature, this had not prevented the work of Grotius from becoming a European 'Völker-Codex'.[54] The public law of Europe had emerged from European sources and the behaviour of European nations. It would therefore be unhistorical to apply it in the 'Orient' (with the duly noted exception of Turkey's 1856 acceptance into 'the European community of nations').[55] International law has come to where it now was, wrote Klüber, by the civilization of customs, and the intensive relations between European governments, but also by the influence of academic teaching, the activities of politicians, journalists, scientists, as well as public opinion, assisted by the spread of the freedom of the press.[56]

The two indispensable literary histories of international law in this period were Heinrich Ludwig von Ompteda's *Literatur des gesammten sowohl natürlichen als positiven Völkerrechts* (2 vols 1785) and Carl von Kaltenborn's *Vorläufer des Hugo Grotius auf dem Gebiete des ius naturae et gentium* (1848). Both works associated progress in international law with its development into real 'science' (although they differed in what this meant). Ompteda highlighted an intermediate 'modified-natural' international law as a kind of legal sociology of statehood: without awareness of its existential situation, no nation could progress, and it was the task of law to assist in this.[57] After sketching an ideal presentation of the parts of international law and their relations, he produced a wide-ranging literature review (in 328 paragraphs) of works ranging from histories of learning in general to histories of law and international law,

---

[53] ibid 444–5.

[54] AW Heffter *Das europäische Völkerrecht der Gegenwart* (Schröder Berlin 1867) at 12. Klüber treats the 'literary history' separately from the diplomatic one, and, like the rest, regards Grotius as the founder of the discipline. He is followed up by the standard cast of characters: Zouche, Hobbes, Pufendorf, Wolff, and, as the predominant modern writer, von Martens. Curiously, Vattel is not mentioned by him at all. JL Klüber *Droit des gens moderne de l'Europe* (Aillaud Paris 1831) at 22–7.

[55] ibid 13. Klüber divided in three periods: antiquity; the (middle period) of the popes and the emperor and the modern period, commencing in the late 15th and early 16th century. Unlike Martens and Heffter, Klüber does not mention Westphalia or Utrecht as crucial moments in this story.

[56] ibid 29.

[57] HL von Ompteda *Literatur des gesammten sowohl natürlichen als positiven Völkerrechts* (2 vols Montags Regensburg 1785) at 9–12.

and from general works, collections of treaties, and other official acts, to textbooks, pamphlets, and increasingly more detailed treatments of particular legal institutions and rules. Ompteda appreciated the older works by Oldendorp, Vázquez, and Suárez, and observed that with all his needless displays of learning, Grotius had put the subject on the firm footing of sociability. With Christian Wolff[58] and JJ von Moser, a scientific study of its two elements, natural and positive law, could finally commence.[59]

Kaltenborn's work was inspired by the crisis of natural law that had begun in the late 18th century and to which there seemed to be no end in sight. As he had done in his widely read *Kritik des Völkerrechts*, he accredited this state of things to the absence of methodologically rigorous, systemic and historically conscious treatments of the field. The dual science of natural and international law needed to be understood as an 'organic whole' in which all principles would serve some useful function for the whole body.[60] This had been impossible during the Catholic era when religion had been confused with law and no distinction had been made between natural and positive materials.[61] Even Aquinas' contribution had been 'unclear, incomprehensible and full of jumps and contradictions'.[62] A change was inaugurated only by the writers of the 'reformation period' (roughly 1517–1625).[63] Religious freedom and the freedom of the human person would now be instituted as an autonomous basis for a scientific system of natural and international law.[64] Grotius had done in politics and law what Luther had done for religion: opening the door for the search for freedom in *Rechtsleben*. Altogether, Kaltenborn disparaged the contribution of Catholicism to international law and saw his own work as an effort to make the protestant heritage better known.[65]

But Wheaton and Kaltenborn, Martens, Klüber, and Heffter were lawyers of an old world. After 1848, liberal activists sought increasingly to use the law to influence the course of European modernity. This is the context where, in the aftermath of the Franco-Prussian war (1870–71), a group of lawyers decided to commence the propagation of cosmopolitan ideas and reforms as members of the profession of 'international law' through the establishment of the *Institut de droit international* (1873). It was in this same context where Nys and Laurent identified the history of international law with the progress of humanity itself. Nys had taught legal history

---

[58] See the contribution by K Haakonssen 'Christian Wolff (1679–1754)' in this volume.

[59] Ompteda Literatur (n 57) 171–3.

[60] C von Kaltenborn *Vorläufer des Hugo Grotius auf dem Gebiete des ius naturae et gentium* (2 vols Mayer Leipzig 1848) vol 1, at 27: '…als ein organisch Ganze erscheinen, wovon die einzelnen Doktrinen wesentliche Glieder und nur vollends die Zeitabschnitte in der Entwicklung die Haupttheile und Gliedmassen, Kopf oder Rumpf, Fussgestell, Herz oder Nieren bilden.'

[61] ibid vol 1, 185–90.

[62] ibid vol 1, 43.

[63] ibid vol 1, 24.

[64] ibid vol 1, 49–50.

[65] Thus the second volume of the work is a compilation of quotations from Protestant writers, J Oldendorp, N Heming, and B Winkler. See *Vorläufer* (n 60) vol 1, 231–49 and vol 2.

and jurisprudence at the *Université Libre de Brussel* from 1885 to 1898 and was thereupon appointed to professorship of international law at that same university. His studies include *The Papacy Considered in relation in Relation to International Law* (1879), *Le droit de la guerre et les précurseurs du Grotius* (1884), *Les theories politiques et le droit international en France jusqu'au XVIIIème siècle* (1890), *l'Esclavage noir devant les jurisconsultes et les cours de justice* (1893), and *Le droit international, les principes, les theories, les faits* (3 volumes 1904–6, 1912). Nys also translated into French the works of Jamer Lorimer and John Westlake. Like the other members of the *Institut,* Nys viewed international law as part of Europe's civilizing contribution to the world. With his colleagues he engaged in long debates about the nature of 'Oriental' cultures and about the conditions of their future entry as full subjects of international law. In *L'état indépendant de Congo et le droit international* (1903), he vigorously defended the practices of his King, Léopold II of the Belgians against the malevolent accusations he attributed to commercially motivated interests in Britain.[66]

Les origines du droit international (1893) set down the narrative that legal historians have followed ever since. Nys traced the roots of the discipline to the Roman *ius gentium,* as discussed in civil and canon law from the 12th to the 15th centuries in connection with the jurisdictional disputes between the papacy and the empire. William of Ockham and Marsilius of Padua in the 14th century created 'the programme of the future'—the emergence of independent secular States.[67] International law in part grew out of Christian debates on the just war, in part of inter-sovereign activities in commerce, arbitration, diplomacy, and the uses of the seas. Spanish scholastics were the originators of international law. But it was Grotius who became the 'founder of the science of international law' owing to the way he joined the values of humanism and secularism with definite abandonment of universal empire.[68] Nys also confessed himself an admirer of England's liberties and 'progress' that for him meant civilization, secularism, humanism, and the universal freedom of trade. The greatest obstacles to progress had been papacy and religious warfare. But with humanism and Protestantism the Church had been finally accommodated to the balance of power as the new—beneficial—principle of European order.[69]

Like Nys, Henry Sumner Maine was a professional historian whose brief period in the Whewell Chair in Cambridge was initiated in 1887 by an inaugural lecture where Maine depicted the history of international law in terms of the spread of Roman law all over Europe. As far as the science was concerned, only Grotius and Vattel merited

---

[66] For these debates, see M Koskenniemi *The Gentle Civilizer of Nations. The Rise and Fall of International Law 1870–1960* (CUP Cambridge 2002) at 11–178 and especially at 155–66.

[67] 'Les réformes qu'ils avaient rêvées furent menées à bonne fin; la société laique se dégagea de plus en plus des chaînes dont l'Eglise avait voulu le charger; l'Etat moderne se constitua en dehors et au-dessus des confessions réligieuses'. *Les origines du droit international* (n 1) 42.

[68] ibid 10–12, 401–5.

[69] ibid 164.

mention.[70] 'We may answer pretty confidently that its rapid advance to acceptance by civilised nations was a stage, though a very late stage, in the diffusion of Roman law over Europe.'[71] The result was a law of Christian nations:

[T]hey form together a community of nations united by religion, manners, morals, humanity and science, and united also by the mutual advantages of commercial intercourse, by the habit of forming alliances and treaties with each other, of exchanging ambassadors, and of studying and recognising the same writers and systems of public law.[72]

Like Adam Smith, Maine shared the view that the history of human societies (or of 'progressive societies') had developed through 'stages' from less to increasingly more sophisticated forms, famously 'from status to contact'.[73] The 'savages' of Africa and the 'barbarians' of the Orient (to borrow Lorimer's terminology) manifested forms of life that Europeans had long ago left behind. As Locke had written 'in the beginning, all the world was America'.[74] Maine agreed but was attracted by a geological metaphor that saw the incipient forms of later laws in earlier, more primitive stages. It was the task of legal history, he felt, to examine these primitive forms so as to generalize about the laws of legal development that would be applicable everywhere. Maine's generalizations brought unity to a world that was anxious about the variety of forms of experience that widening international contacts had brought to the notice of European public. The variations could now be explained as different stages in a single, uniform process. Order and hierarchy would be restored with the satisfactory result that the Europeans would find themselves at the top.[75]

Perhaps the best known work on international legal development in this vein was Sir Paul Vinogradoff's series of lectures in Leiden from 1923. Here he sketched a view of five historical types of international law, ranging from the Greek city-states to the Roman *ius gentium,* the law of the *Republica Christiana,* sovereign statehood to contemporary developments pointing to a 'political union' that would be 'wider and more just than that of absolute territorial sovereignty'.[76] In Vinogradoff's matrix, 'collectivistic organization' would become the highest stage of international law.[77]

---

[70]   His indictment of the others was severe: '... it must be confessed that some were superficial, some learned and pedantic, some were wanting in clearness or thought and expression, some were little sensitive to the modifications of moral judgment produced by growing humanity, and some were simply reactionary.' HS Maine *International Law. A Series of Lectures Delivered before the University of Cambridge 1887* (2nd edn Murray London 1915) at 2.

[71]   ibid 16.

[72]   ibid 34.

[73]   HS Maine *Ancient Law* (Dorset Press 1968 [1861]) at 141.

[74]   J Locke *Two Treatises on Government. Second Treatise* (introduction by W Carpenter) (Everyman's London 1984) para 49, at 140.

[75]   See JW Burrow *Evolution and Society* (CUP Cambridge 1966) and *The Gentle Civilizer of Nations* (n 66) 74–6.

[76]   P Vinogradoff 'Historical Types of International Law' (1923) 1 Bibliotheca Visseriana 1–70 at 69.

[77]   ibid 5.

His stages were premised upon a critique, shared with much of inter-war sociology, of the destructiveness of liberal individualism. Not Smith's 'commercial society' but a centrally planned modern bureaucracy would become the ideal of academic intelligentsias.[78]

Vinogradoff's typology expressed a widespread view among international lawyers that the outbreak of the war in 1914 had been caused by excessive emphasis of national sovereignty, an irrational and morally corrupt form of egoism. This, they pointed out, had now become an obvious anachronism. Economics and technology were tying States together into an ever intensifying set of dependencies, prompting a 'move to institutions'.[79] The histories of inter-war international law were overwhelmingly written as prefaces to a call for more integration, more international institutions with an increasingly expanding jurisdiction.

The modernizing ideology behind the League of Nations presupposed that the entire world would develop in the footprints of Europe and that it was the task of international law to assist in this process. The international law profession interpreted this so as to view economics and technology as world-unifying factors. An up-to-date law should facilitate their operation against formal and anachronistic moorings in sovereignty.[80] Only few questioned this. Conservative Germans such as Erich Kaufmann did stress the absence of 'social ideals' from Western law's shallow internationalism. Like Heinrich Triepel, he saw international law as at best a coordinating devise: the deep history of humankind would remain with nation-States. Carl Schmitt wrote these assumptions into his *Nomos der Erde* (1950) that assimilated the enthusiasm for technological and economic progress with Anglo-American imperialism.[81] Soviet jurists, likewise, failed to see in 'bourgeois' international law any historically solid project for the future. If they accepted to deal with the West through it, this was only as a strategic concession; while a completely different teleology would realize itself through class struggle and the impersonal power of productive forces.[82]

But the teleology of Western law was seriously put to question only by decolonization. The enthusiasm with which the non-Western world grasped at its formal sovereignty after 1960 has often been condescendingly dismissed as an expression of the post-colonial elites' lust for power. Nevertheless, the critique of the 'false universality'

---

[78] Eg P Wagner *History and Theory of the Social Sciences* (Sage London 2001) at 7–53.

[79] D Kennedy 'The Move to Institutions' (1987) 8 Cardozo Law Review 841–988.

[80] Eg A Alvarez *La codification du droit international—ses tendences, ses bases* (Pedone Paris 1912) and G Scelle 'Théorie du gouvernement international' (1935) Annuaire de l'institut international de droit public 41–112.

[81] E Kaufmann *Das Wesen des Völkerrechts und die Clausula rebus sic stantibus* (Mohr Tübingen 1911); C Schmitt *Der Nomos der Erde im Völkerrecht des Ius publicum europeaum* (Duncker & Humblot Berlin 1950); for these debates, see *The Gentle Civilizer of Nations* (n 66) 249–65 and 415–37. See also the contribution by B Fassbender 'Carl Schmitt (1888–1973)' in this volume.

[82] For a discussion, see C Miéville *Between Equal Rights. A Marxist Theory of International Law* (Brill Leiden 2005) at 75–289.

of prevailing ideas about universal values or a world community has been invoked sufficiently often in the past fifty years so as to question the narratives of civilization and progress on which Western triumphalism has relied.

5. HISTORIES OF INTERNATIONAL LAW IN THE 20TH AND 21ST CENTURIES

During the first half of the 20th century, much of the history of international law was cut across by a jurisprudential debate on its nature or binding force.[83] Before one could write a history of international law one needed to know what kind of a subject it was. Here a rigorously conceived 'will theory' was confronted by ethically or sociologically inclined views that derived obligation from some universal morality or generalization about human needs. Each came with a particular philosophy of history that projected international law as a reflection of some deeper normative truth about the world—perhaps the 'sovereignty of the state' (on which the will theory largely relied), perhaps some underlying trend towards economic or technological progress, civilization, or humanitarian reason. Historiography became a victim of philosophical conviction: each side could point to aspects of the past that supported its vision as legal history's determining force.

According to the will theory, international law had been, was, and would, in the foreseeable future, be what States wanted it to be. To provide a response to the question, 'what then of its binding force?' the Austrian public lawyer Georg Jellinek developed in the 1880s his massively influential autolimitation view (*Selbstverpflichtungslehre*) that compared international law with constitutional law. Nobody could enforce the constitution against the Parliament, either, without this making the constitution any less real.[84] Others compared it with 'primitive law' that allegedly had no institutional safeguards either but arose from spontaneous custom. Both views implied definite historical perspectives: the constitutional comparison resuscitated the view of international law as external public law and aligned its past with that of (European) *Staatsgewalt*. The primitive law analogy pointed to international law's

---

[83] I have discussed much of this literature in M Koskenniemi *From Apology to Utopia. The Structure of International Legal Argument* (Reissue with a new epilogue CUP Cambridge 2005) at 307–25. The debate was waged with particular intensity in Germany from the last years of the 19th century. For one contemporary overview of the themes, see JL Kunz 'On the Theoretical Basis of the Law of Nations' (1925) 10 Transactions of the Grotius Society 115–41.

[84] G Jellinek *Die rechtliche Natur der Staatenverträge* (Hölder Vienna 1880).

growth towards ever more institutionally complex forms. But there was never any serious study of such analogy so that Hersch Lauterpacht had little difficulty in the 1930s to dismiss it as a superficial attempt to defend the will theory itself. The complex diplomatic and judicial techniques of international law in no way resembled 'primitive law'. The attempt to salvage the will theory (and the theory of sovereignty) by appeal to the 'special character' of international law was simply incoherent: it was not binding because it emerged from some hypothesized 'State will', but because it reflected the needs of an international community.[85]

Lauterpacht was a natural lawyer and an admirer of John Locke and the British tradition of 'liberalism and progress'.[86] In this respect, he was like most other interwar internationalists. For naturalists such as the Viennese Alfred Verdross, access to the law was provided by the Great Books tradition so that the history of international law, too, would have to be conceived as a literary history. In *Die Einheit des rechtlichen Weltbildes*, Verdross argued that 19th-century 'positivism' had broken with the universal ethos of the tradition by creating a wall between domestic and international law. Verdross' objective (which he shared with his teacher Hans Kelsen) was to argue 'sovereignty' into a mere technical competence that had been allocated to the State by an overriding universal moral-legal order, rightly understood as the (implicit) constitution of the world.[87] For him, like for the 16th- and 17th-century naturalists, there was in a sense no history of international law at all—only a history of the slow coming into consciousness of the unity of the law as a reflection of humanity's moral identity. This view turned history into moral progress lessons. In 1932, Cornelius van Vollenhoven saw the principal dynamic in political history constituted of the widening organization of peace and its constant rupture by national egoism and war:

[L]'histoire du droit international équivaut à une épopee, à une lutte grandiose entre deux forces élémentaires. D'un côté on voit un droit de paix, faible au début, mais qui a le besoin de vivre, la volonté de vivre, une foi indéracinable dans sa vocation et son avenir. De l'autre côté on découvre forces pussantes et brutales de la guerre et d'un prétendu droit de guerre.[88]

'Two elementary forces...'. This was literature, of course, but not great literature. Van Vollenhoven narrated the history of international law as a pendulum movement

---

[85] H Lauterpacht *The Function of Law in the International Community* (Clarendon Oxford 1933) at 403–23.

[86] H Lauterpacht *International Law and Human Rights* (Prager New York 1950); H Lauterpacht 'The Grotian Tradition of International Law' (1946) 23 British Yearbook of International Law 1–53; see further M Koskenniemi 'Hersch Lauterpacht 1897–1960' in J Beatson and R Zimmermann (eds) *Jurists Uprooted. German-Speaking Emigré Lawyers in Twentieth-Century Britain* (OUP Oxford 2004) 601–62, and the contribution by IGM Scobbie 'Sir Hersch Lauterpacht (1897–1960)' in this volume.

[87] A Verdross *Die Einheit des rechtlichen Weltbildes auf Grundlage der Völkerrechtsverfassung* (Mohr Tübingen 1923). For Kelsen, see the contribution by B Fassbender 'Hans Kelsen (1881–1973)' in this volume.

[88] C van Vollenhoven *Du droit de paix. De iure pacis* (Nijhoff La Haye 1932) at vii–viii.

between hopes and disappointments about the coming peace.[89] Like so many others, he viewed the League as a promising but fragile step towards the peaceful organization of humankind, still threatened by its members' nationalism. Himself a Dutchman, he was conscious of no irony when he depicted history's great dialectic play itself out in the 1302 war between Philip the Fair and the Flemish peasants, when his examples of evil men came from Spain, or when the ended his book by uplifting sentences from Grotius and William of Orange![90]

Perhaps the best-known post-war international law history, *A Concise History of the Law of Nations* by the German-born Arthur Nussbaum, the first edition of which came out in the United States in 1947, was written in a completely different spirit.[91] Nussbaum regarded anything beyond diplomatic acts, treaties, and case-law as utopian moralism, warning 'against the deflecting influence of ideologies and hope'.[92] He was concerned only to lay out, as clearly and simply as possible, the 'law prevailing among independent states'.[93] The work was free from teleological generalizations or those of 'civilization' of such earlier works as those of van Vollenhoven and merely sought to tell the history of the law of nations 'wie es eigentlich gewesen [ist]'. Like many other refugee intellectuals from Europe, Nussbaum had become a political realist. Meanwhile lawyers on the old continent were facing the future by turning to the past. In his 1962 overview of the 'newest developments', Ulrich Scheuner expressed the largely shared view (especially in post-war Germany) that the unity of the law, based on ethical principles, was now asserting itself despite challenges (as he saw them) from the communist bloc and the newly independent States. In his view, and in the view of many others, 'positivism' and 'Eurocentrism' had now been overcome. Through the institutions of the United Nations international law would now help to set up a universal *Rechtsgemeinschaft*.[94]

International law histories of late 20th century have usually combined accounts of the development of the States system with brief excursions into a well-defined circle of canonical texts. The dominant voice has sounded a sociological register: '*Ubi*

---

[89] In the long period 1492–1780 van Vollenhoven saw no progress at all. Its spokesperson was Vattel whose work '… est tout aussi déstructif d'un droit de paix que ne l'avait été l'oeuvre d'un Pizarre, d'un Cortés, d'un duc d'Albe. Il étale l'autre vice original, celui de vouloir déguiser la mauvaise intention sous les paroles de charité sublime.' *Du droit de paix* (n 88) 99.

[90] Many lawyers were also frustrated by what seemed an endless and inconsequential dispute between the naturalists and the positivists. Thus, for example, de Louter looked for a pragmatic compromise between the positions so starkly juxtaposed in van Vollenhoven. Instead, Louter regarded sovereignty and community like opposite currents of electricity, both necessary for the proper operation of the whole. Naturalism and positivism, the pull to community and the desire of freedom were equally true expressions of the existential state of international law, divided between opposite but equally valuable poles, like human life itself. J de Louter *Le droit international public positif* (2 vols Imprimerie de l'Université Oxford 1920) at 13, 15.

[91] AN Nussbaum *A Concise History of the Law of Nations* (2nd edn Macmillan New York 1954).

[92] ibid x.   [93] ibid ix.

[94] U Scheuner 'Völkerrechtsgeschichte. Neueste Entwicklung (seit 1914)' in *Wörterbuch des Völkerrechts* (n 6) 754–5.

societas, ibi ius'—although just what it means to say that the law 'reflects' anterior social developments has seldom been broached in any depth. Much of this history is geared in a policy-oriented direction as prologue to this or that agenda of reforms. This is intellectually hazardous ground, and the fact that there is not much by way of a historical sociology of international relations renders recourse to the cliché of 'reflection' easily as ideology. Two major currents of contemporary historical writing may be distinguished, both with many variations highlighting some aspects of the past while leaving others necessarily in the shadow.

The first type of history is that where international law appears as wholly enmeshed in the worlds of war and peace, diplomacy, 'development', and the succession of systems of government over the world. In this conception, international law is part of the business of ruling human communities, humanizing State practice, maintaining balance of power, facilitating the movement of ambassadors, or enabling the acquisition of colonies, for example. For this type of 'political history', well-represented in international relations literature, law is usually but a minor aspect of State policy. We meet it during the inter-war period in Alfred Zimmern's characterization of international law as a 'decorous name for the convenience of the Chancelleries' that was at its most useful when it embodied a 'harmonious marriage between law and force'.[95] Zimmern's account of the involvement of international law in the League constituted a powerful prologue to dismissals of the period's hopeless 'idealism'.[96] Later writings of the 'English School' have examined international law as part of the dialectic of 'order' and 'justice', serving useful (though perhaps not essential) 'functions' in the international world.[97] Its role has often been thought to lie in upholding the idea of an 'international society' in the conditions of 'anarchy'.[98]

The difficulty with narratives about international law as a dependent variable of politics lies in the normative frame they project on the past. How far back is it useful to read wars and political relations through legal concepts? Many histories begin with the Sumerians or Assyrians three millennia ago, ancient India and the 'Chinese world'. But as Steiger has queried, is there really much common ground between an instrument in which one party refers to itself as the 'sun' to the others, and the 1969 Vienna Convention on the Law of Treaties?[99] Historians have responded to the charge of anachronism by noting that even if the expression 'international

---

[95] A Zimmern *The League of Nations and the Rule of Law (1918–35)* (Macmillan London 1936) at 94, 95.

[96] ibid 445–6.

[97] H Bull *The Anarchical Society. A Study of Order in World Politics* (Macmillan London 1977) at 127–61, 159.

[98] H Bull 'The Importance of Grotius in the Study of International Relations' in H Bull, B Kingsbury, and A Roberts (eds) *Hugo Grotius and International Relations* (OUP Oxford 1990) 71–5.

[99] H Steiger 'From the International Law of Christianity to the International Law of World Citizen—Reflections on the Formation of the Epochal History of International Law' (2001) 3 Journal of the History of International Law 181–93.

law' may not have been present in those periods, old documents testify to the presence of inter-group relationships that are sufficiently similar to today's interstate relations to allow such generalization. In the same breath, however, it is usually affirmed that a law of the (European) States system is naturally a product of the 15th and 16th centuries and that even if it is only a species of a genus, it still has special importance as 'a lasting legal order', giving permanent form to international relations.[100] The hold of familiar concepts remains strong, and is taken as largely unproblematic.

Periodization, too, remains problematic. This is most evident in the construction of grand 'epochs' reflecting the hegemony of a leading power. Inspired by political realist (perhaps 'Weberian', perhaps 'Marxist', perhaps post-colonial) theory, this approach sees history's driving force in a single determining cause, an 'empire', radiating its influence to all corners of the (legal) world. The leading contemporary *oeuvre* of this type is Wilhelm G Grewe's *Epochen des Völkerrechts* (1984), inspired by Carl Schmitt's notion of *Nomos* and followed in many other works.[101] In their effort to avoid 'utopian' speculation, these authors put forward a 'realist' ethics of cool statecraft, or even a 'political theology' as the appropriate perspective for legal analysis. The fact that realist statecraft never expressly articulated its strong ethical commitments shrouds it in a pretence of neutrality and objectivity that constitutes a powerful incentive for adopting it as a frame for historical study.

Realist history dismisses religions, cultures, and ideologies as well as the autonomy of legal institutions as a mere ideological superstructure underneath which operate determining structures of political, economic, and military power. Thus it remains oblivious to the way structures of (political, economic, military) knowledge are formed and distributed and contribute to the formation of ruling preferences and challenges. Its reliance on unrealistically homogenous 'epochs' ignores that even strong imperial powers rarely have a uniform view of how to sustain their influence; they are internally split—say, between advocates of formal and informal empire—so that counter-hegemonic actors may often operate in relative independence from the centre or play its divisions against each other. This is why post-colonial histories that used to interpret everything about the world as a consequence of imperialism or colonial exploitation have been supplemented by narratives that emphasize the way 'semi-peripheral' actors from Latin America, Japan, Turkey, and China have, from

---

[100] Eg KH Ziegler *Völkerrechtsgeschichte* (Beck Munich 1994) at 4, 12–42; A Truyol y Serra *Histoire de droit international public* (Economica Paris 1995) at 1–3, 5–18; S Laghmani *Histoire du droit des gens. Du jus gentium imperial au jus publicum europaeum* (Pedone Paris 2003) at 7.

[101] WG Grewe *The Epochs of International Law* (M Byers trans) (de Gruyter Berlin 2000). The 'epochal account' has been followed eg in 'Völkerrechtsgeschichte' (n 94). The main inspiration is of course *Der Nomos der Erde* (n 81). I have critiqued Grewe's book in book reviews in (2002) 51 International and Comparative Law Quarterly 746–51 and in (2002) 35 Kritische Justiz 277–81. See also the contribution by O Diggelmann 'The Periodization of the History of International Law' in this volume.

the late 19th century onwards, adopted and adapted international law of European origin so as to further domestic agendas, constrain Europeans, and to transform European legal categories.[102] Rather than examining law by reference to a single centre or origin, these histories aim to grasp it as a platform or a vocabulary that is used by different actors for contradictory purposes.

Realist history also tends to view non-European communities as passive objects of European policy. True, studies have traditionally addressed diplomatic relations in ancient near-Eastern civilizations, the Chinese world and India.[103] But these have been studies of past worlds or perhaps, as Bederman suggests, of the 'intellectual origins' of today's 'mature' international law.[104] The works of Charles H Alexandrowicz, RP Anand, and TO Elias have sought explicit corrections to Eurocentrism by examining legal practices among Asian rulers and treaty relations between African communities even before the entry of the Europeans.[105] To the extent that these studies have been written in the vein of 'they, too, had an international law', they may be objected as once again projecting European categories as universal. The studies in the 1920s by Lindley and Goebel, though very useful and in some of their detailed accounts frankly irreplaceable, were written completely from the perspective of the empire.[106] More recent studies have focused on the encounter with Europe itself, seeking to bring forth a non-European perspective or by highlighting the distortions and

[102] From a very wide collection of recent works, see eg AB Lorca 'Universal International Law: Nineteenth-Century Histories of Imposition and Appropriation' (2010) 51 Harvard International Law Journal 475–552; L Obregón 'Completing Civilization: Creole Consciousness and International Law in Nineteenth-Century Latin America' in A Orford (ed) *International Law and its Others* (CUP Cambridge 2006) 247–64; U Zachmann *Krieg und Ordnungsdenken im völkerrechtlichen Diskurs Japans, 1919–60* (Habilitation thesis Ludwig Maximilians University Munich 2010); see also T Ruskola 'Legal Orientalism' (2002) 101 Michigan Law Review 179–234 and U Özsu 'Agency, Universality, and the Politics of International Legal History' (2010) 51 Harvard International Law Journal 58–72; for a programmatic statement, see eg Y Onuma 'When was the Law of International Society Born? An Inquiry of the History of International Law from an Intercivilizational Perspective' (2000) 2 Journal of the History of the International Law 1–64.

[103] Eg W Preiser *Macht und Norm in der Völkerrechtsgeschichte* (Nomos Baden Baden 1978); DJ Bederman *International Law in Antiquity* (CUP Cambridge 2001); A Altman 'Tracing the Earliest Recorded Conceptions of International Law' (2001) 11 Journal of the History of International Law 125–86 and 333–56.

[104] *International law in Antiquity* (n 103) 1.

[105] CH Alexandrowicz *An Introduction to the History of the Law of Nations in the East Indies (16th, 17th and 18th Centuries)* (Clarendon Oxford 1967); RP Anand *Studies in International Law History: An Asian Perspective* (Nijhoff Leiden 2004); RP Anand 'Maritime Practice in South-East Asia until 1600 and Modern Law of the Sea' in RP Anand (ed) *International Law and the Developing Countries* (Nijhoff Dordrecht 1987) 53–71; RP Anand *Development of Modern International Law and India* (Nomos Baden Baden 2005); TO Elias *Africa and the Development of International Law* (Oceana Leiden 1972).

[106] MF Lindley *The Acquisition And Government Of Backward Territory In International Law: Being A Treatise On The Law And Practice Relating To Colonial Expansion* (London 1926); J Goebel *The Struggle For The Falkland Islands. A Study of Diplomatic History* (Yale University Press New Haven 1927).

ulterior motives of conquerors, the 'false universality' represented by European concepts and practices.[107]

'International law and empire' has now become perhaps the most popular item of international law history. When Jörg Fisch wrote *Die europäische Expansion und das Völkerrecht* in 1984, he was still a path-breaker—even as the overwhelming Anglocentrism of the field has left this basic work relatively unread.[108] The burgeoning literature on the empire that is being produced today remains predominantly focused on the British world-system.[109] Recent writing on European penetration in North America and the Southern hemisphere has focused on the dispossession of the native populations.[110] Regarding the Spanish empire, the works by Luciano Pereña remain largely unknown outside Spain. Though not completely free of imperial apologetics, they are, alongside the 29 volumes of the *Corpus Hispanorum de Pace* (CHP) edited by Pereña, an invaluable (though again, little known) source of materials.[111] In Italy, Luigi Nuzzo has thrown a post-colonial eye on the legal languages of colonization and conquest and new works by Gozzi and Augusti deal with the encounter of non-European world with European law.[112] In Germany, older and newer historical writing covers especially the law and morality of the Spanish conquest, with emphasis often on the writings of the Spanish theologians. But Germany's own colonial period (1880–1919) is still largely untreated from the perspective of international legal his-

[107] The classic here is A Anghie *Imperialism, Sovereignty and the Making of International Law* (CUP Cambridge 2005); see also E Jouannet and H Ruiz-Fabri (eds) *Le droit international et l'impérialisme en Europe et aux Amériques* (Société de droit et de législation comparée Paris 2007). Other shorter works include eg JT Gathii 'Imperialism, Colonialism and International Law' (2007) 54 Buffalo Law Review 1013–66. The many works of works of N Berman may also be classed in this group. See now especially N Berman *Passions et ambivalences: le nationalisme, le colonialisme et le droit international* (A Pedone Paris 2008), also available in English as *Passion and Ambivalence. Colonialism, Nationalism and International Law* (Brill Leiden 2011).

[108] J Fisch *Die europäische Expansion und das Völkerrecht* (Steiner Stuttgart 1984).

[109] Eg C Sylvest 'Our Passion for Legality: International Law and Imperialism in Late Nineteenth-Century Britain' (2008) 34 Review of International Studies 403–23; D Armitage *The Ideological Origin of the British Empire* (CUP Cambridge 2000); K MacMillan *Sovereignty and Possession in the English New World. The Legal Foundations of Empire 1576–1640* (CUP Cambridge 2006); the essays in D Bell (ed) *Victorian Visions of Global Order. Empire and International Relations in Nineteenth-Century Political Thought* (CUP Cambridge 2007) and S Dorsett and I Hunter (eds) *Law and Politics in British Colonial Thought. Transpositions of Empire* (Palgrave-Macmillan London 2010).

[110] For two useful works with a legal angle, concentrating on the dispossession of the Indians, see RA Williams *The American Indian in Western Legal Thought* (OUP Oxford 1990); S Banner *How the Indians Lost their Land. Law and Power on the Frontier* (Harvard University Press Harvard 2005).

[111] For Pereña's own summary, see L Pereña *La idea de justicia en la conquista de América* (Mapfre Madrid 1992). For a very different kind of work exploring international law's uses in Fascist Spain, see I de La Rasilla, 'The Fascist Mimesis in Spanish International Law and its Vitorian Aftermath (1939-1953)' (2012) 14 Journal of the History of International Law 2.

[112] L Nuzzo *Il linguaggio giuridico della conquista. Strategie di controllo nelle Indie spagnole* (Jovene Napoli 2004); G Gozzi *L'Occidente e l'ordine internazionale* (Giappichelli Bologna 2008); E Augusti 'The Ottoman Empire at the Congress of Paris: Between New Declensions and Old Prejudices' in L Back-Varela (ed) *Crossing Legal Cultures* (Meidenbauer Munich 2009) 503–19.

tory. Finally, much of the political and economic history of empire, including novel works in 'world history' is full of legal implications, though rarely treated in a systematic fashion. This applies to accounts of the 'ideologies' of empire as well as on the legal practices sustaining imperial administration.[113]

Histories concentrating on political events and imperial power often do not address the criteria for the choices they make. Nor do they bring out the fact that narration is about 'choice' in the first place. Therefore, a second type of history is needed, one that Nussbaum thought there had been too much of—namely the history of international law as the succession of writings by philosophers, theologians, diplomats, political thinkers, and lawyers that provide the conceptual articulations (and often criticisms) of prevailing practices. The writing of history as the history of doctrines (or of the 'science of international law') is a well-established genre.[114] Most late 18th-and early 19th-century histories were like this but even in the 1990s Truyol y Serra discussed universalist thinkers from Zoroastrian philosophers to the Stoics, and from Grotius to Kant.[115] While these works have sometimes taken a hagiographic attitude towards their protagonists, no naïve views about the exceptional power of individuals need necessarily be entailed. A particular writer may also be interesting as a specimen of a type, and used to illustrate a tendency more widely shared in the relevant period.[116] For example, Ernst Reibstein's 1949 work on the Spanish 16th century jurist Fernando Vázquez de Menchaca has the purpose to examine all the world of pre-Grotian *ius doctrine de la gentium* (but also 18th century natural law) through the work of one influential, though largely forgotten scholar in whose work the naturalist grounding of the law was accomplished in an exemplary way.[117] Likewise, Peter Haggenmacher's 1983 *Grotius et la doctrine de la guerre juste* is much more than merely an account of what Grotius had said about the just war: it is in fact a history of all the key concepts used by Grotius in his works of 1604–6 and 1625, ranging from 'just war' to 'ius gentium' and 'sovereignty', from Roman and canon law to the beginning of the 17th century.[118]

In the 'history of legal thought', mention should be made of the very large literature on the classics of Western political theory that have been important for international law: the Spanish scholastics, Vitoria, Soto and Suárez, the natural lawyers Pufendorf

---

[113] See especially A Pagden *Lords of All the World. Ideologies of Empire in Spain, Britain and France c. 1500–1800* (Yale University Press New Haven 1995); L Benton *Law and Colonial Cultures. Legal Regimes in World History 1450–1900* (CUP Cambridge 2002).

[114] Eg A de Lapradelle *Maîtres et doctrines du droit des gens* (2nd edn Éditions internationales Paris 1950).

[115] A Truyol y Serra *Histoire du droit international public* (Economica Paris 1995).

[116] This is what I attempted to do in *The Gentle Civilizer of Nations* (n 66).

[117] 'Wir finden bei Vasquius zum ersten Mal den literarischen Apparat, mit dem die Naturrechtslehre 150 Jahre lang gearbeitet hat' E Reibstein *Die Anfänge des neueren Natur- und Völkerrechts* (Haupt Bern 1949) at 22.

[118] P Haggenmacher *Grotius et la doctrine de la guerre juste* (Presses universitaires de France Paris 1983).

and Wolff, the philosophers Kant and Hegel, and others. The works vary widely in scope, but sometimes give express attention to the international law aspects of the relevant texts.[119] The contextual histories of early modern political thought by Richard Tuck, Anthony Pagden, Ian Hunter, and Annabel Brett, for example, have significance for the history of international law as well.[120] The same applies to treatments of the Spanish classics not only by Pereña and Truyol y Serra but a number of other Spanish and German authors.[121] There is today a burgeoning literature directed to the history of international 'legal' thought. The oeuvre on Grotius is of course enormous—alongside the definitive work by Haggenmacher mention should be made of Martine Ittersum's discussion of Grotius' role in the justification of Dutch commercial empire.[122] The work on Alberico Gentili is almost as large and increasing attention to (legal) humanism will guarantee continuous interest in him.[123] Emmanuelle Jouannet and Peter Remec have examined aspects of Grotius and Vattel—Jouannet discussing Vattel within the naturalist tradition and, more recently, as the father of a 'welfare-oriented' construction of international law.[124] Marc Bélissa has produced a history of the law of nations among the French *philosophes* and revolutionaries in the late 18th century and expanded that into a discussion of the Napoleonic period.[125] My *Gentle Civilizer* examined the legal thought of mainly continental jurists in the period 1870–1960 and the early part of that period is also covered in Stefano Mannone's

---

[119] Eg S Goyard-Fabre *La construction de la paix—le travail de Sisyphe* (Presses universitaires de France Paris 1994) and A Lejbowicz *Philosophie du droit international. L'impossible capture de l'humanité* (Presses universitaires de France Paris 1999).

[120] R Tuck *The Rights of Peace and War. Political Thought and the International Order from Grotius to Kant* (OUP Oxford 1999); *Lords of All the World* (n 113); I Hunter *Rival Enlightenments. Civil and Metaphysical Philosophy in Early Modern Germany* (CUP Cambridge 2001); A Brett *Liberty, Right and Nature. Individual Rights in Later Scholastic Thought* (CUP Cambridge 1997); A Brett *Changes of State. Nature and the Limits of the City in Early Modern Natural Law* (Princeton University Press Princeton 2011).

[121] A Truyol y Serra *Actualité de la pensée juridique de Francisco de Vitoria* (Brussels 1988). One of the best comprehensive studies on Vitoria, with a large discussion on international law is D Deckers *Gerechtigkeit und Recht. Eine historische Untersuchung der Gerechtigkeitslehre des Francisco de Vitoria* (Universitätsverlag Freiburg 1991) while the leading work on Suárez and international law is J Soder *Francisco Suárez und das Völkerrecht: Grundgedanken zu Staat, Recht und internationale Beziehungen* (Metzner Frankfurt 1973); see further K Seelmann *Theologie und Jurisprudenz an der Schwelle zur Moderne. Die Geburt des neuzeitlichen Naturrechts in der iberischen Spätscholastik* (Nomos Baden-Baden 1997).

[122] M van Ittersum *Profit and Principle. Hugo Grotius, Natural Rights Theories and the Rise of Dutch Power in the East Indies* (Brill Leiden 2006); see also E Wilson *Savage Republic. De Indis of Hugo Grotius, Republicanism and Dutch Hegemony within the Early modern World-System* (Nijhoff Leiden 2008).

[123] See especially D Panizza *Alberico Gentili, Giurista ideologico nell'Inghilterra Elisabettiana* ('La Garangola' Padova 1981); but also eg the essays in B Kingsbury and B Strauman (eds) *The Roman Foundation of the Law of Nations. Alberico Genrtili and the Justice of Empire* (OUP Oxford 2010).

[124] E Jouannet *Emer de Vattel et l'emergence doctrinale du droit international classique* (Pedone Paris 1998) and eg PP Remec *The Position of the Individual in International Law According to Grotius and Vattel* (Martinus Nijhoff The Hague 1960); see now also E Jouannet *Droit international providence. Une histoire de droit international* (Bruylant Brussels 2011).

[125] M Belissa *Fraternité universelle et intérêt national (1713–95). Les cosmopolitiques du droit des gens* (Kimé Paris 1998) and M Belissa *Repenser l'ordre européen 1795–1802* (Kimé Paris 2006).

Potenza e ragione that surveys the efforts by 19th century jurists to develop a 'modern' approach to peace and war.[126]

Many of these works have focused on the contextual, often the 'national' background of their protagonists in open contrast to the earlier fashion of highlighting their quality as 'universal' intellectuals, interesting as originators of present (often progressive) ideas. Where studies by William Butler on the Russian or Truyol y Serra on the Spanish tradition did focus on the context but stressed the 'independence' of their protagonists from it, portraying them as representative of large humanitarian or pacifist ideas,[127] newer histories seek to locate the jurists in their local environments as university professors, diplomats or counsel to governments, having institutional 'projects' of their own. Tony Carty has even tried to attain a psychoanalytical or phenomenological grasp of some of them.[128] General contextual readings of British lawyers in the 19th and 20th century have been made by Casper Sylvest and James Crawford, Mark Janis has written on the 'American tradition' from the founders to the 20th-century while Emmanuelle Jouannet's long essay expounds the history of international law doctrine in 20th-century France.[129] Lauri Mälksoo has written accounts of late 19th- and early 20th-century Baltic international lawyers and Russian international legal theories and similar histories have been written on at least Japanese, Turkish, and Greek international lawyers as well.[130] Many accounts have been written on international law in Germany during the inter-war era, with focus obviously on the Nazi period.[131] Studies on such cen-

---

[126] S Mannone *Potenza e ragione. La scienzia del diritto internazionale nella crisi dell'equilibrio Europeo 1870–1914* (Giuffre Milan 1999).

[127] W Butler *Russia and the Law of Nations in Historical Perspective* (Simmonds & Hill Wildly 2009).

[128] A Carty 'Interwar Theories of International Law: The psychoanalytical or phenomenological Perspectives of Hans Kelsen and Carl Schmitt' (1995) 16 Cardozo Law Review 1235–92.

[129] Eg C Sylvest 'International Law in Nineteenth-Century Britain' (2004) 75 The British Year Book of International Law 9–70; C Sylvest 'The foundations of Victorian International Law' in D Bell (ed) *Victorian Visions of Global Order: Empire and International Relations in Nineteenth-Century Political Thought* (CUP Cambridge 2007) 47–66; J Crawford 'Public International Law in Twentieth-century England' in J Beatson and R Zimmermann (eds) *Jurists Uprooted. German Speaking Émigré Lawyers in Twentieth-century Britain* (OUP Oxford 2004) 681–708; M Janis *The American Tradition in International Law. Great Expectations 1789–1914* (OUP Oxford 2004); E Jouannet 'A Century of French International Law Scholarship' (2009) 61 Maine Law Review 83–132.

[130] L Mälksoo 'The Science of International Law and the Concept of Politics. The Arguments and Lives of the International Law Professors at the University of Dorpat/Iur'ev/Tartu 1855–1985' (2005) 76 British Year Book of International Law 383–502 and L Mälksoo 'The History of International. Legal Theory in Russia: a Civilizational Dialogue with Europe' (2008) 19 European Journal of International Law 211–32. For the interwar Greek internationalist Stelios Seferiades' use of international law as an instrument of 'bourgeois modernization', see T Skouteris, *The Notion of Progress in International Law Discourse* (TMC Asser Press The Hague 2010), 39–92. See further A Becker Lorca, *Mestizo International Law: A Global Intellectual History, 1850–1950* (CUP Cambridge 2013 forthcoming), and the works in note 102 above.

[131] The classic here is DA Vagts 'International Law in the Third Reich' (1990) 84 American Journal of International Law 661–704.

tral European scholars as Lassa Oppenheim and Hersch Lauterpacht have been quite a few—but also James Leslie Brierly has been subjected to discussion.[132] The European Journal of International Law has organized symposia on such international lawyers as Dionisio Anzilotti, Max Huber, Hans Kelsen, Hersch Lauterpacht, Alf Ross, Georges Scelle, and Walther Schücking. But by far the most impressive recent contribution to the history of international law as doctrines and theories and the personal biographies of lawyers is the Max Planck series on the History of International Law that now has studies on Adam Glafey, Erich Kaufmann, Hans Kelsen, Friedrich Liszt, Georg Schwarzenberger, Walther Schücking, Karl Strupp, Helmut Strebel, Hans Wehberg, and a series of accounts of events and problems of particular interests in the German realm.[133] This reflects the very active interest that the German legal community has had to its history.

Yet concentrating on individual writers, national traditions or *Ideengeschichte* leaves untreated the history of 'law' as the development of legal concepts, principles or institutions—or perhaps suggests that those are the creation of particularly brilliant individuals who manipulate the law in their preferred ways. Its reductionism is in a sense diametrically opposed to that of 'epochal' history that leaves no space for any but collective actors. Surely there is (and should be) room for a *Begriffsgeschichte*, or a conceptual history that examines the changes in meaning of legal concepts such as 'sovereignty', 'immunity', 'arbitration', and 'just war' or institutions such as the United Nations, the Red Cross, or Amnesty International. There are many existing histories on international legal institutions, including on the law of the sea by Fulton, Anand, and others, on the laws of war by Neff, on Great Powers by Simpson, and on Peace Treaties by Lesaffer, just to mention some recent English-language works.[134] But these works rarely follow a specific method—not to say anything about adopting a formally 'conceptual history' approach in the vein of Reinhardt Koselleck, for example, that would highlight the polemical character of the vocabularies, the way

[132] On Oppenheim, see eg B Kingsbury 'Legal Positivism as Normative Politics: International Society, Balance of Power and Lassa Oppenheim's 'Positive International Law' (2002) 13 European Journal of International Law 401–35; M Schmoeckel 'The Internationalist as a Scientist: Lassa Oppenheim and his "International Law"' (2000) 11 European Journal of International Law 699–712. See also the contribution by M Schmoeckel 'Lassa Oppenheim (1858–1919)' in this volume. On Brierly, see C Landauer, 'J.L. Brierly and the Modernization of International Law' (1992–93) 25 Vanderbilt Journal of Transnational Law 881–917; on Lauterpacht, see works in note 86 above.

[133] B Fassbender, M Vec, and WG Vitzthum (eds) *Studien zur Geschichte des Völkerrechts* (Nomos Baden-Baden 2001–). For list of publications, see <http://www.nomos-shop.de/reihenpopup.aspx?reihe=254> (26 March 2012).

[134] T Fulton *The Sovereignty of the Sea* (Blackwood London 1911); RP Anand *The Origin and Development of the Law of the Sea* (Kluwer Boston 1982); SC Neff *War and the Law of Nations: A general History* (CUP Cambridge 2008); G Simpson *Great Powers and Outlaw States* (CUP Cambridge 2005); R Lesaffer (ed) *Peace Treaties and International Law in European History* (CUP Cambridge 2004).

the legal concepts and categories receive meaning and applicability in reaction to political developments.[135]

Again, a word of caution is called for here. This type of history cannot be just a history of legal concepts or institutions that travel, as it were, unchanged through time, stable objects for States and their rulers to use or to react to in idiosyncratic ways. This is the manner in which the Alsatian public lawyer Robert Redslob conceived his 1923 history of the four key principles of international law: binding force of treaties, freedom of States, equality of States, and international solidarity. The fate of each principle is surveyed from antiquity through the Middle Ages to the Peace of Westphalia, from the dynastic wars to the French Revolution (1789), and from the Vienna settlement up to the First World War.[136] Even as the development of these principles, Redslob writes, has been neither even nor continuous, in the grand scheme of history, they have still progressed, and, after the German-induced catastrophe that the war was, have been set on a firm footing within the League of Nations: 'une oeuvre architecturale qui relie et consolide les quatre grands principes du droit des gens'.[137] Such an approach takes the present concept or institution as a given and tends to reduce all prior history into the role of its 'primitive' precursor. This would be anachronistic—it would fail to account for the meaning of legal concepts and institutions for the contemporaries for whom each moment is, of course, as modern and as full of meaning as our concepts are for us.

A conceptual history would rather take the legal vocabularies and institutions as open-ended platforms on which contrasting meanings are projected at different periods, each complete in themselves, each devised so as to react to some problem in the surrounding world. Its interest lies in meaning formation ('how does a particular concept receive *this* meaning?') rather than the contents of any stable meaning per se. For this kind of history, legal institutions are constructed constantly anew in polemical confrontations where opposing positions clash against each other: law would be narrated as an aspect of political struggle. A good example of this would be Nathaniel Berman's explorations of the inter-war international law that refer back to the world-views, prejudices, and institutional ambitions of the protagonists whose use of international law cannot be understood without linking it to their often ambivalent political agendas.[138] Nor is history-writing itself free of polemical intentions or effects. We can see this in the on-going debates on the history of human rights. Do rights remain unchanged? And are they historical only to the extent they are present to consciousness? Or are they an effect of 18th-century literary imagination or 20th-century institutional politics?[139] Answers to

---

[135] See R Koselleck, 'The Historical-Political Semantics of Asymmetrical Counterconcepts', in *Futures past. On the Semantics of Historical Time* (Columbia University Press New York 2004), 155–191.

[136] R Redslob *Histoire des grands principes du droit des gens depuis l'Antiquité jusqu'à la veille de la grande guerre* (Rousseau Paris 1923).

[137] ibid 559.

[138] *Passions et ambivalences* (n 107).

[139] For each of the three suggestions, see P Lauren *The Evolution of International Human Rights. Visions Seen* (3rd edn University of Pennsylvania Press Philadelphia 2008); L Hunt *Inventing Human Rights* (Norton New York 2004); S Moyn *The Last Utopia* (Harvard University Press Cambridge MA 2009).

such questions do not only lay out contrasting agendas for historical work but also positions about the political meaning and direction(s) of our present rights vocabulary and policy.

6. Conclusion

The histories of *ius gentium*, natural law, and the law of nations surveyed above, whether from the standpoint of the 14th or the 21st centuries, are situated within a temporal trajectory whose markers come from Europe; they adopt a European horizon of 'progress' and 'modernity'. The rise and globalization of statehood, for example, like the distinctions between 'political' and 'economic' as well as 'private' and 'public' that underlie this history point to specific European experiences and conceptualizations. Even if new approaches to history writing in international law have emerged in which colonialism has become a central theme, it still remains the case that 'Europe rules as the silent referent of historical knowledge'.[140] It is hard to see what could be done with this—apart from encouragement of the study of an increasingly wide field of legal vocabularies, and taking a perspective that would move between the political and the biographical, contextual and the conceptual. What we study as history of international law depends on what we think 'international law' is in the first place; it is only once there is no longer any single hegemonic answer to the latter question, that the histories of international law, too, can be expected to depart from their well-worn paths, and open our eyes to experiences of rule that have hitherto remained in darkness.

Recommended Reading

Anghie, Antony *Imperialism, Sovereignty and the Making of International Law* (CUP Cambridge 2005).
Berman, Nathaniel *Passions et ambivalences: le nationalisme, le colonialisme et le droit international* (Pedone Paris 2008); *Passion and Ambivalence. Nationalism, Colonialism and International Law* (Brill Leiden 2011).
Craven, Matthew, Malgosia Fitzmaurice, and Maria Vogiatzi (eds) *Time, History and International Law* (Nijhoff Leiden 2007).
Fisch, Jörg *Die europäische Expansion und das Völkerrecht* (Steiner Stuttgart 1984).
Gaurier, Dominique *Histoire de droit international. Auteurs, doctrines et développement de l'Antiquité à l'aube de la période contemporaine* (Presses universitaires de Rennes 2005).

[140] Provincializing Europe (n 10) 28.

Gozzi, Gustavo *Diritti e civiltà. Storia e filosofia del diritto internazio*nale (il Mulino Bologna 2010).

Grewe, Wilhelm G *The Epochs of International Law* (M Byers trans) (de Gruyter Berlin 2000).

Haggenmacher, Peter *Grotius et la doctrine de la guerre juste* (Presses universitaires de France Paris 1983).

Jouannet, Emmanuelle *Emer de Vattel et l'emergence doctrinale du droit international classique* (Pedone Paris 1998).

Koskenniemi, Martti *The Gentle Civilizer of Nations. The Rise and Fall of International Law 1870–1960* (CUP Cambridge 2004).

Nussbaum, Arthur *A Concise History of the Law of Nations* (2nd edn Macmillan New York 1954).

Paz, Reut Yael *A Gateway between a Distant God and a Cruel World. The Contribution of Jewish German Scholars to International Law* (Brill Leiden 2012).

Preiser, Wolfgang *Macht und Norm in der Völkerrechtsgeschichte* (Nomos Baden-Baden 1985).

Redslob, Robert *Histoire des grands principes du droit des gens depuis l'Antiquité jusqu'à la veille de la grande guerre* (Rousseau Paris 1923).

CHAPTER 40

DOCTRINE VERSUS STATE PRACTICE

ANTHONY CARTY

1. INTRODUCTION

WHAT the editors had in mind when drafting the subject of 'doctrine versus state practice' as a chapter of Part V of the Handbook on 'Methodology and Theory' was first and foremost the age-old question of how much attention somebody writing the history of international law should devote to doctrine on the one hand (that is, a description of what international legal scholars wrote in the past), and state practice on the other hand. Nussbaum, for instance, addressed that problem in the foreword to his *A Concise History of the Law of Nations,*[1] and so did Grewe in his *Epochen,*[2] claiming that in the past, state practice had been too much neglected. This title could read: 'Doctrine versus state practice in the history writing in international law.' On the other hand, the present title is more open and allows for a broader analysis of the dichotomy beyond historiography—that is, a discussion of how state practice and learned writing influenced each other in the past. The argument that the notion of state practice is an invention of international legal doctrine in the course of the 19th century, while counterintuitive, will be a central feature of this contribution, along-side the equally puzzling way international lawyers react to the inaccessible character

---

[1] A Nussbaum *A Concise History of the Law of Nations* (Macmillan New York 1958) at vii.
[2] WG Grewe *Epochen der Völkerrechtsgeschichte* (Nomos Baden-Baden 1984) at 25.

of that practice. These are very important aspects of several dimensions of the relationship between 'doctrine' (in a wider and in a narrower sense, the latter being the writings of publicists stating their 'own ideas', not pretending to reflect state practice) and 'state practice' as reported in digests, diplomatic correspondence, newspapers, etc. A critical discussion of what we conceive of (or what was conceived of by others) as 'doctrine' and 'state practice', respectively, when we contrast the one with the other, is important to the 'doing' of international legal history.

2. Legal Doctrine and the Creation of State Practice

The distinction is easy enough to make between proposals of writers, for instance, for state conduct, their attempts to describe state practice and the state practice itself. If it is a matter of contrasting the latter two, one can say that, for example, writers describe state practice on the use of force and, alternatively one may simply describe that practice directly, without reference to the opinion of doctrine, although of course one becomes oneself, thereby, an addition to doctrine. Writers may expound a just war theory, while States resort to a practice of unlimited discretion to wage war, or alternatively, States may adhere in practice to a just war theory while authors adopt a strict positivism, interpreting state sovereignty as unrestrained.

Nonetheless, a surprising difficulty can arise when one sets oneself precisely the task of describing what is the state practice itself; this is, when it emerges that there is a real problem with the way the conceptual framework of state practice works out. Consider, for instance, the way that diplomatic history is used to describe the practice of States. Parry says that one cannot construct what is identifiably international law from treaties or diplomatic practice.[3] The great European treaties are part of political history not legal history, never mind law.[4] The series of entries in the *Max Plack Encyclopedia of Public International Law* from Ancient Times to 1918 do precisely that.[5] They appear to fail to recognize what Hoeck and Stolleis regard as the importance of

---

[3] C Parry *The Sources and Evidences of International Law* (Manchester University Press Manchester 1965) at 34–5 and 37–8.

[4] ibid 37–8.

[5] In particular the entries by W Preiser 'History of International Law, Ancient Times to 1648'; S Verosta 'History of International Law, 1648–1815'; and HU Scupin 'History of International Law, 1815 to World War I' in R Wolfrum (ed) *The Max Planck Encyclopedia of Public International Law* (Oxford University Press Oxford 2008) at <www.mpepil.com>. These entries were completed in the 1980s.

the history of the science of international law in itself shaping the agenda of relevant material.[6] While it is perfectly legitimate to decide to treat international law as an appendage of diplomacy, at the very least there is needed some kind of theory of what role international law plays. That would mean understanding how and when it is allowed to come into play.[7] Otherwise there is a crude equation of any treaty with a legal instrument in the sense of the Vienna Convention, etc. As Parry says, the importance of say Vienna 1815, or Paris 1856, 'lies primarily not in their character as examples of the operation of a law-making process… but in their status as politico-military affirmations of a law made largely by other means'.[8] As this great author of the *Consolidated Treaty Series*[9] writes, commenting in particular on Vienna 1815, '[i]f a new age had to be sought, it would be more correct to seek its beginnings in Vattel rather than Vienna'.[10] Concentrating on epochs reflecting the influence of great powers appears an alternative to the apparently tired old conflict between natural law and positivism. It must surely be the case that at least in repositories of state chancelleries and court jurisdictions, there are other sources of law that can be contrasted with doctrine. However, the reality is strangely different. International law chancelleries were only set up in the late 19th century, and many after the First World War.[11] Court cases in turn cover a narrow field of prize, maritime jurisdiction and diplomatic immunity cases.[12]

In fact, the reason international legal history is almost impossible to write is that there is no consensus on what international law is. Even the notion of positive law is not agreed. From Suarez to Bynkershoek to Vattel, there was no concept of general customary law. Hence there was no concept of state practice at all, as we now understand it.[13] There was only the notion of consent, formal or tacit, in which case one could only have a history of international law based on treaties, to which Parry objects.

In the final analysis, what present international lawyers recognize as international law rests in a combination of the Parry-Stolleis picture that the construction of the

---

[6] IJ Hueck 'The Discipline of the History of International Law, New Trends and Methods on the History of International Law' (2001) 3 Journal of the History of International Law 194–217.

[7] Grewe has such a theory, that both writers and practice are an expression of the same Zeitgeist of their Epoch, *Epochen* (n 2). The author broadly agrees with this approach and will come back to it later, when discussing connections between the relationship of the historical school of law and new archival diplomatic history in the 19th century.

[8] Parry's complaint, *The Sources* (n 3) 40.

[9] C Parry (ed) *Consolidated Treaty Series* (Oceana Publications Dobbs Ferry New York 1969–81).

[10] *The Sources* (n 3) 39.

[11] G Marston 'The Evidences of British State Practice in the Field of International Law' in A Carty and G Danilenko (eds) *Perestroika and International Law* (Edinburgh University Press Edinburgh 1990) 27–47 at 40.

[12] A Carty *The Decay of International Law* (Manchester University Press Manchester 1986) at 12, and literature cited therein, particular the work of AM Stuyt and again, *The Sources* (n 3) 23.

[13] P Guggenheim 'Contribution à l'histoire des sources du droit des gens' (1958) 94 Recueil des cours 1–84 provides, in ch 3, 'La coutume', the most erudite and exhaustive account of the development of the concept of custom in international law writing from the late 15th century until the beginning of the 20th century. It is the starting point of research in this area.

discipline comes first in providing the means to recognize what constitutes legally significant state practice. This need not be absolutely the case. Indeed, the author would like to stress that the more the power of the discipline is appreciated, the easier it is to contest the narrowing of the field of historical inquiry which the discipline represents. It is probably this which drives the predominantly German historical tendency[14] to go searching for international legal history among the Assyrians and the rather narrowed Francophone resistance to this on recognizably legal ideological grounds.[15] Indeed, within the history of the discipline itself it may always be possible to recover new parameters for exploring the history of state practice precisely by reverting to a different theory of doctrine. For instance, the natural law school of Grotius, so long as it continues to adhere to the 'just war theory', has a much broader remit to be critical of the conduct of international relations than a strict positivism, which regards 'high politics' as indifferent legally. Conversely, the historical school of legal positivism, itself fairly closely allied to the German school of diplomatic history, is capable of awakening or giving credibility to a much broader range of historical investigations of state practice than classical positivism. The reason is that the historical school approach to customary law treats practice as a narrative of the whole conduct of States and does not just limit itself to registering the treaties which they sign. The field is wide open to a variety of directions of inquiry.

So this chapter endeavours to set up a number of oppositions as heuristic devices to illustrate how doctrine and state practice may play off against one another in the writing of the history of international law, both positively and negatively. The following may be taken as examples which serve to support the Parry–Stolleis thesis about the decisive influence of the discipline (effectively the doctrine) in constructing the practice. The concept of the sovereign State as being above all moral standards and free to do as it pleases unless it chooses to restrict itself, comes from the reconstruction of the Renaissance State from Hobbes onwards. Cassese explains this clearly in his textbook.[16] At the same time, it is possible to insist, as does the German school, that the Treaty of Westphalia incorporated an anti-hierarchical idea of equality in the sense of absence of subordination to either pope or emperor, that is, viewing international legal history as diplomatic history.[17] Nonetheless, the understanding of formal equality of States, as similar to individuals, comes with Vattel, as a form of natural law theory which then became accepted by doctrine as international law in the course of the 19th century, through constant doctrinal repetition, through, for instance,

---

[14] Represented in the entries of the *Max Planck Encyclopedia of Public International Law* on the history of international law.

[15] See eg Robert Kolb's dismissal of ancient India and Chinese contributions to international law as quite simply not conforming to modern Western ideas of law and international law since modern times. R Kolb *Ésquisse d'un droit international public des anciennes cultures, extra-européennes* (Pedone Paris 2010).

[16] A Cassese *International Law* (OUP Oxford 2001) para 16.

[17] 'History of International Law, 1648–1815' (n 5).

Wheaton to Oppenheim.[18] Doctrine develops the idea of equality from the time of Vattel as including the principle of non-intervention and the voluntary character of judicial or arbitral settlement of disputes, that is, the developments within doctrine also shaped the way States were regarded and were equally responsible for the perhaps mistaken belief of international legal doctrine that its own views—for example, of the principle of non-intervention—represented customary international law.

Yet again, the German school of international legal history, while appearing to be determined to get away from doctrine and write history from state practice, is really objecting to a view of the history of international law as a gradual development of limits on state sovereignty, in favour of the view that true historical narrative, of which international legal history is also a part, must take whatever normative attitudes the rulers or managers of independent entities, like nations, peoples, or whatever, actually had in their relations with one another.[19] On this view, 1648 and indeed Europe itself need not be central.[20]

At the same time, the nature of the Vattelian doctrine contrasts effectively with international legal history as diplomacy in another respect, actually making diplomatic legal history more difficult. Hinsley and others (Hedley Bull) say that just as Europe was consolidating into a Christian historical community, he prepared the way for a uni-disciplinary legal formalism, gradually driving international law away from any contact with diplomacy.[21] Indeed, for the legal formalism coming out of Vattel it is difficult to see what interest history can have. Vattelian formalism, as a product of the Enlightenment, is anti-historical. In fact it represents a confidence of an epoch, so that a belief in a mature anarchy among nations prevailed for the whole of the 19th century, the Vattelian period, finally formalized in the clarity of Oppenheim's International Law, the pure statement of positivism.[22] International legal history, in the sense of state practice, if it is to exist at all, can then consist of a Whig-style history of gradually increasing acceptance of regulation, especially in the 19th century.[23] Here, the historical drive need not be very strong, as such histories are of outdated law.

---

[18]   *The Decay of International Law* (n 12) 89–93.

[19]   See especially for this theoretical reflection on the German school, H Steiger 'Universality and Continuity in International Public Law?' in T Marauhn and H Steiger (eds) *Universality and Continuity in International Law* (Eleven International Publishing The Hague 2011) 13–44 at 14.

[20]   Steiger still criticizes Eurocentrism within the German school, particularly *Epochen* (n 2) 40. Such criticism is being given no weight in this chapter since European perspectives on the discipline are still absolutely dominant worldwide, A Carty and F Lone 'Some New Haven International Law Reflections on China, India and Their Various Territorial Disputes' (2011) 19 Asia Pacific Law Review 93–111.

[21]   FH Hinsley *Power and the Pursuit of Peace, Theory and Practice in the History of relations Between States* (CUP Cambridge 1967) and also H Butterfield and M Wight (eds) *Diplomatic Investigations, Essays in the Theory of International Politics* (Harvard University Press Cambridge MA 1968).

[22]   See above all B Kingsbury 'Legal Positivism as Normative Politics: International Society, Balance of Power and Lassa Oppenheim's Legal Positivism' (2002) 13 European Journal of International Law 401–37.

[23]   See especially the contribution of 'History of International Law, 1815 to the First World War' (n 5).

However, there is a fundamental aspect of the story of the history of doctrine and practice that gives the advantage to doctrine. The doctrine of state practice as the ground of general custom is a product of the historical school of law; in other words, a construction of the discipline or science of international law. There is no comprehensive history of the concept of customary international law. Part of the reason is probably that natural law thinking dominated the discipline until the 19th century. Paul Guggenheim, a Swiss French scholar, provides the most complete overview of custom between the 15th and the 19th centuries in 1958.[24] The concept of custom first came out of the Roman law and canon law traditions, says Guggenheim, where custom was a tacit legislation of the people. Francisco Suarez, a 16th-century Spanish Jesuit theologian and specialist in Roman and canon law, presented custom as a positive *ius gentium* (law of peoples), an expression of the tacit will of the peoples of the world. Although it was subordinate to natural law, it still had a valid and independent place. In *De Legibus* (Of Laws), especially in books II and VII, Suarez carves out a space for *ius gentium* including a general customary law of peoples; regarded as radical at the time because Suarez was arguing that not all law came directly by God or from a God-given reason.[25] Tierney also explains that Suarez was assimilating custom to legislation, as the will of the community.[26]

Indeed, as Guggenheim argues, even an early 18th-century international lawyer such as Cornelius van Bynkershoek, who was known as a positivist (in the sense that he thought positive law more important than natural law) still persisted in the view that custom was a form of tacit convention. He wrote his views down in *De foro legatorum, or the Jurisdiction over Ambassadors*. Van Bynkershoek asserts, especially clearly in chapter XIX, that the law of nations is nothing but tacit agreement, a presumption which can always be barred by an express wish, because there is no international law other than what is based on the tacit agreement of voluntary participants.[27]

Guggenheim does explain how in the course of the 19th-century, international lawyers came to believe that all law rested ultimately on custom in the different sense that the practices and usages of communities, including the international community, preceded the gradual growth of the conviction that these practices were binding as law. However, Ago explains more explicitly the break this represents from the older Roman and canonist traditions. The latter always saw custom as a product of conscious will. Yet, says Ago, it is the essence of the modern idea of customary international law

[24] 'Contribution à l'histoire' (n 13).

[25] F Suarez *Selections from Three Works* in JB Scott (ed) *The Classics of International Law* (Carnegie Institution Washington DC 1917).

[26] B Tierney 'Vitoria and Suarez on ius gentium, Natural Law, and Custom' in A Perreau-Saussine and JB Murphy (eds) *The Nature of Customary Law: Legal, Historical, and Philosophical Perspectives* (CUP Cambridge 2007) 101–24.

[27] C van Bynkershoek *De foro legatorum, or the Jurisdiction over Ambassadors* in JB Scott (ed) *The Classics of International Law* (Clarendon Press London 1946).

that it distinguishes a conscious will to create law from a growing consciousness that laws have simply grown up spontaneously out of state practice, so that States gradually become aware of them through reflection on the outcomes of their practice. Ago argues that the distinguishing feature of custom is precisely that as spontaneous law, it is found by inductive inference from the types of claims States make against one another, rather than by evidence of States adhering to a tacit law-making form.[28]

It is remarkable that the doctrine is first most clearly expressed by von Kaltenborn in 1847, but then, in Guggenheim's view, becomes incorporated into international legal science with Alfonse Rivier towards the end of the 19th century. This view was incorporated into mainstream international law doctrine through Oppenheim's acceptance of it, he taking it from Rivier's German colleague von Holtzendorff.[29] Even more remarkably, Koskenniemi says that such a way of thinking of custom was only authoritatively accepted in mainstream international law jurisprudence in the *North Sea Continental Shelf Case* of 1969.[30]

It is suggested that there is an additional aspect of the historical school of law which has not been sufficiently appreciated. It has considerable implications both for the rewriting of the history of international law and for the continuing political significance of customary international law. Kaltenborn's work must be seen in the context of the rise of nationalism, in the first case, German nationalism, after 1815. This was the context in which historical and legal studies were tied together. History was being revalued after the Enlightenment. This is attributable to one simple cause: the belief that only from the 'internal' or personal experience of a subject could any indication be gathered as to what that subject could or should do or be expected to do. The increased 'scientific' study of history was tied to this belief.[31] In the early 19th century the place of philosophy in providing a rational account of man was replaced by history. The new emphasis on historical change and the insistence upon a new precision of documentation were the expression of a desire to see the past from the inside, to relive experience through the eyes of those whom one is studying.[32] The most outstanding historian of the time, Leopold Ranke, could apply this perspective to international relations since the 'documents' which were becoming available were the archives of 'princes and prelates'.[33] At the same time, it was not merely the impor-

---

[28] R Ago 'Science juridique et droit international' in (1956) 90 Recueil des cours 851–958. In ch 5, Ago distinguishes the canonist, legislative tradition of custom from contemporary customary law.

[29] See further *The Decay of International Law* (n 12) 34–6.

[30] M Koskenniemi 'History of International Law since World War II' in *The Max Planck Encyclopedia* (n 5) para 31.

[31] A Carty 'International Law as a Science (The Place of Doctrine in the History of its Sources)' (1980) 18 Indian Yearbook of International Affairs 128–60 at 140 and for what follows in the text subsequently, at 140–1.

[32] In particular see A Marwick *The Nature of History* (Macmillan London 1970) at 35; see also H Butterfield *Man on His Past* (CUP Cambridge 1969) at 103.

[33] *The Nature of History* (n 32) 37–8.

tance of empathy in the researcher, whether jurist or historian which transformed his role. Compared to his counterpart of the Enlightenment, in the search for the normative, it was precisely the nation-state which was becoming the source of 'Enlightenment'. The political State was central to human development. Ranke would have it that States were unique individuals, that they were thoughts of God, who had chosen to express the idea of mankind in various peoples. If there had been only one possibility for the State then only universal monarchy would be reasonable.[34] So for Savigny also the essential role of the jurist/historian was not to legislate but to gather together the elements of custom. It is only by reflection upon historical experience that we can come to a knowledge of our time.[35]

So the Historical School of Law and the Rankean theory of history writing are tied together. They combined two elements which have shaped the consciousness of international lawyers. Firstly, they revalued the actual behaviour of state nations or nation-states as powers themselves of moral significance in history. It is not the simple doings of princes but the life spirit of nations which makes history meaningful and that has to be grasped as accurately as possible. At the same time, this task has to be undertaken as scientifically as possible, through proper archival research, which allows one to understand the very heart of the mentalities, intentions of the nation-states, a hermeneutic of international relations by its nature normative. This is language which is by no accident very similar to that of Steiger, who wishes to justify the open-minded study of all the history of 'peoples-states' from the perspectives which they had of the normative, regardless of time or place.[36]

3. THE DOCTRINAL CREATION OF A STATE PRACTICE, WHICH DOCTRINE CANNOT DECIPHER

It is this historical drive, just described, which explains the continued paramount authority of general customary law as evidenced in the practice of States. Indeed, the movement of the German school to rewrite the histories of international law, too burdened with a history of doctrine and legal ideas, has the same motivation. Nonetheless, it produces a paradoxical situation, at the present time, in any attempt to understand the history of international law as a history of the practice of States. That

---

[34] H Kohn *The Mind of Germany* (Macmillan London 1960) at 59–60.
[35] J Droz *Le romantisme allemand et l'état* (Payot Paris 1966) at 217–19, also quoting Savigny.
[36] 'Universality and Continuity' (n 19).

practice is bound to be significant because it is bound up with the history of human beings in their life among the communities of nations. However, these communities are secretive towards one another.

Back in 1949, the Secretariat of the United Nations submitted a more than 100-page memorandum to the International Law Commission, in the context of an obligation by that body to report to the UN General Assembly on ways and means to make the evidence of customary law more available. The Secretariat's 1949 memorandum, in its conclusions, recognized very well that providing official declarations as documents without what it recognizes as contextualizing 'background materials', renders the documents of imperfect value. The Secretariat outlined four possible categories for organizing the digests: topically, chronologically, by country, and by categories of evidence; for example, national law, judicial decisions.[37] However, the final report of the International Law Commission 1950 simply did not take the matter further, merely recommending to States and the Secretariat to make collections of categories of evidence, as defined above. It excused itself by saying there was little that could be done to persuade governments to stimulate the production of more of their practice, that is, the essential 'background documents'. This would be too arduous.[38] Therefore, the International Law Commission in 1950 declared that there was no reasonable prospect of States making available to one another the archival material necessary to construct a picture of customary law.

This has lead to a division in how to assemble what is taken to be customary law. Following Council of Europe Guidelines many national yearbooks of international law produce copious statements by their politicians as to what their country regards as international law.[39] Together with national court decisions, legislation, participation in international organizations—replete with numerous more statements by politicians—doctrine has plenty to tidy up and systematize in digests. There is a voluntarism in this approach. International law is what States say it is, in their public statements, not only because one cannot know what States are really thinking, but also because such statements are closest to expressions of 'will'.

However, there is a minority academic opinion which is more challenging in calling for what is really a Rankean view of the practice of States. In the 1960s Parry argues that full historical background is necessary to understand evidence of *opinion iuris* in the practice of States. Rejecting the conclusions of the Council of Europe, he said that leaving out 'background materials' rendered official documents difficult to evaluate as to meaning and impact. There is no sound reason to accept declared intentions or

[37] International Law Commission 'Ways and Means of Making the Evidence of Customary International Law more Readily Available: Preparatory Work within the Purview of Article 24 of the Statute of the International Law Commission' (12 April–9 June 1949) A/CN.4/6 and Corr.1.

[38] International Law Commission 'Report of the International Law Commission on the Work of its 2nd Session' (5 June–29 July 1950) UN Doc A/CN.4/34, 367–74 at 373.

[39] Council of Europe 'Model Plan for the Classification of Documents Concerning State Practice in the Field of Public International Law' (adopted 28 June 1968) Resolution 68(17).

attitudes of state officials as a reliable indicator of the real intentions that explain the meaning of actions. States are essentially communities, and the processes whereby they form intentions and execute them are evidenced by many different materials which show the different stages of development of actions.[40] Parry in the 1960s and 1970s undertook the publication of a *British Digest of International Law,* managing a total of six volumes before he died in 1982, each about 800 pages, probably remaining the definitive method of compiling complete historical pictures of legal incidents in a chronological narrative over long periods. One such example concerned issues of aliens, that is, asylum seekers and extradition cases.[41] These surveys of official and unofficial British documents explain practice in the half a century before 1914, for example, the treatment of foreign political dissidents.

The representational skills of the jurist working on such materials, in Parry's case, put international law writing about practice on par with credible history writing. In his case, the assumption is not challenged, that States, as communities, have intentions, some of which are legally relevant, which can be understood in narrative form, provided sufficient rigour in skills of representation exists. However, as can be seen in Parry's case, the representation will not be contemporary. So the work will really be history of international law, while at the same time explaining the evolution of customary international law in a particular State's practice.

History and law have come together in Guggenheim's and Ago's historical explanation of the development of the modern international law concept of general custom through the 19th-century German historical school. Their assumption is that a pattern of consciousness or awareness of States has to be traced continuously from the past to the present, making historical narrative an integral part of legal evolution. Yet it is precisely the closure of contemporary archives of States, already noted by the International Law Commission, which makes the exercise of searching for general custom through state practice problematic, thereby problematizing the whole idea of general customary international law, as now understood to be the practice of States, evidencing a conviction as to what is law.

In other words, the representational function of doctrine comes up against the *sécret de l'état*, in particular of the modern, liberal, democratic State, supposedly governed by the rule of law. It is Allott who has highlighted the difficulty repeatedly since the publication of *Eunomia*. The attempt to represent what Aron has called the 'Cold Monsters' of the State is bound to bring a historically guided hermeneutic, archival approach to state practice into bitter conflict with the State in attempting to penetrate

---

[40] *The Sources* (n 3) 67–8. The problems of gathering evidence of practice in the sense of when and with what effect legal advice is called upon, directed to other states and produces a response, is described exhaustively through the chapter 'Custom or the Practice of States'. These problems are indistinguishable from historiographical problems: how to construct what Steiger has called the narrative which reveals the normative perspectives of the actors.

[41] C Parry *British Digest of International Law* (Stevens and Sons London 1965) vol 6, pt 6 (The Individual in International Law, Aliens and Extradition 1860–1914) at xxxvii and 852.

its practice. In Allott's words, the modern State evacuates the active presence of reason, faith, conscience, and personal responsibility in a legal system whose subjects are not subjective subjects of the system but law-making and law-recognizing, law-applying, and law-enforcing robots. Allott attributes this disaster to what he calls a post-Vattelian era whereby predominantly Western, supposedly liberal democratic, politicians justify their participation in the international system on the ground of some theory of the representation of the people, whereas international affairs remain largely beyond the purview of national electorates, even of intellectual elites. The explosion of international organizations and courts still takes place in the context of the absence of an international public.[42]

Nonetheless, history of state practice, which actually grasps the true legal significance of events, while not comprehensively feasible, is certainly doable on occasions and these occasions can set the standard for what is really the goal to attain. For instance in the 2nd edition of the first volume of *International Law* in 1911 Oppenheim, the arch or classical, positivist, described the absorption of Korea into Japan as having occurred voluntarily as a result of a Treaty. In the same sentence, Oppenheim described this form of territory transfer or state recreation as voluntary subjugation. The subsequently released historical record shows that Britain agreed with Japan under a secret clause of a renewed Anglo-Japanese treaty in 1905, that Japan could use—and did use—whatever coercion was necessary to compel Korea's becoming part of Japan. The record shows the Japanese Korean treaties were induced with physical coercion against Korean officials. At the same time Oppenheim represents in the second volume of his work, in 1912, that Japan's occupation of Korea during the Russian–Japanese war was necessitated by the inability of Korea to defend itself against Russian encroachment. Japan's action was an intervention in Japan's own vital interests, to liberate Korea from Russian occupation. If this representation by a doctrinal writer is both legally and historically incorrect, it is only in the sense that he does not have access to the decision-making process through access to the diplomatic archives.[43] Indeed the UK's 50- and 30-year rules, with respect to document release, while probably the most liberal in the world, condemn doctrine to a truncated historical role in representing state practice.

This revaluation of state practice, paradoxically, does not mean that the practice of States begins only where doctrine has constructed the concept in the course of the 19th century. It means that the whole history of nations can be explored to see what it reveals of human consciousness of law. At the same time, while the romantic, internal, hermeneutical approach to normativity is unsympathetic to the abstract, transcendent moralizing of natural law, it by no means excludes the idea that practice can

---

[42] P Allott *Eunomia: New Order for a New World* (OUP Oxford 1990) at 239–52.

[43] A Carty 'The Japanese Seizure of Korea from the Perspective of the United Kingdom National Archive, 1904–10' (2001/2002) 10 Asian Yearbook of International Law 3–24 and all the references cited therein, particularly to the works of Oppenheim.

be qualitatively judged as good or bad. This underlay Wharton's view of American adherence to customary international law, as expressed in his *Digest*. To search for the legal conscience of States and nations means that one can distinguish conscience from its absence. One does this through historical analysis, while exercising a judgment the same as the natural lawyer does, when determining which conduct is genuinely normative and to be followed. This is clear in the example given by Parry from Wharton's *Digest* of US state practice to explain the doctrine of the incorporation of general customary law into American law.[44] It is interesting that Parry criticizes Wharton as being predominantly interested, in compiling his digest, not in evidence of the conduct of the United States as a source of law, but as evidence of the writings of peculiarly well-qualified (American) publicists, that is, a number of distinguished Secretaries of State.[45] He goes on to note Wharton's view that their opinions have established a jurisprudence for the civilized world. This jurisprudence, quoting Wharton, 'as is the case with all true law whose continued existence depends on its responsiveness to popular conscience and need, adapts itself, in its own instinctive evolution, to the contingencies of each social and political juncture that occurs'.[46] Again, the historical and the normative combine.

This is where also one can return to Allott's critique. His critique is historical and deplores that democratization of the international order has not accompanied the democratization of the national order, the reason for *sécret de l'état*. It might be possible to try to argue theoretically, following Jürgen Habermas's theories of the public space, for a wider public discourse in which the international lawyer could participate effectively in the normative argument both preceding the actions taken by States, and reflection upon those actions afterwards, actions which eventually become international legal practice.[47] Perhaps the original idea behind the Institute of International Law at its foundation in 1873, was that international lawyers could effectively participate in an international legal discourse along with leaders of world opinion inside as well as outside States. However, this belies the continuing, for Allott, Vattelian structure of inter-state relations. The individual doctrinal writer has no international status other than that accorded to him by his/her own State, and remains marginal to great issues of international affairs.

Hence it might be more sound, in trying to ground effectively representational functions for doctrine, to explore more systematically the difficulties underlying the absence of authority for a doctrine that purports to rest upon some normative legal philosophy such as natural law. Yet it is precisely here that one must say it is only the

---

[44] C Parry 'The Practice of States' (1958–59) 44 Transactions of the Grotius Society 145–86 at 145, quoting from F Wharton *A Digest of the International Law of the United States* (2nd edn Government Printing Office Washington 1887) at 149–50.

[45] ibid 151.   [46] ibid 152.

[47] This idea is explored in the author's critique of general customary law in A Carty *Philosophy of International Law* (Edinburgh University Press Edinburgh 2007) at 51–9 and for what follows in the text.

science of international legal history—positivist in its craving for sources and hermeneutic in its understanding of them—that can explain the loss of a critical role for doctrine. Historically at least one strand of doctrine, the natural law as distinct from the positivist approach, was supposed to offer a transcendent standard against which the practice of States can actually be judged as nugatory. Whether one uses the contemporary technical terms 'null and void' to describe the effects of this doctrinal activity, it does definitely claim that there is a human responsibility to resist and disregard offending state practice.

Strangely, a primary obstacle in the way of a natural law-style doctrine comes from within the liberal, democratic paradigm of law and not just from the theory of positivism which denies any transcendent source for legal obligation. The view appears to be shared by almost everyone, that the metaphysics underlying natural law has vanished. For liberal democratic theory, law is what the States' representatives decide following agreed constitutional procedures, and if they have not spoken, there is simply no law. The most vital distinction is then between *lex lata* and *de lege feranda*. International constitutionalists imagine that the 'way forward' internationally is to reproduce agreed law making procedures at the global level, when these are clearly consented to by the international community.

However, it is precisely a challenging of the contemporary doctrinal frames for the practice of States, especially the official ones designated by the Council of Europe and through a completely fresh interaction with alternative theoretical constructions of modern international history (from the 16th to the 21st century), that is, intellectual frames and constructions entirely beyond the contemporary discipline of and doctrine of international law, which can afford the international lawyer the opportunity to engage once again much more profoundly with the historical significance of the actual practice of States. Then the international lawyer may find a way to re-establish the once close relationship between a critical natural law theory and a judgment of the quality of state practice in the light of a normative standard—itself not necessarily easily distinguishable from the historical-positivist search for the presence or absence of legal conscience in the actual practice of States. What this necessitates is a leap outside the usual confines of the international law discipline itself, that is, doctrine in the narrower sense, into a wider intellectual work which is engaging as much with actual state practice as the German School (including the authors of the *Max Planck Encyclopedia* and also Steiger, Grewe, and Nussbaum), could want.

This venture into the history of ideas or intellectual systems is precisely not a concentration upon the history of international legal doctrine, but virtually the opposite. It is a search for alternative intellectual frames which allow one to bring to life the true normative experience of modern peoples, nations, and States in their relations to one another—a life that has become elided from view by a desiccated form of historical legal positivism in its approach to state practice. In fact this is the very sentiment which drives the German School to deplore both the exclusive concentration on history of international law as history of ideas and, alternatively, the peculiarly

Western history of international law as it has developed since the modern construction of the State and the Westphalia Peace of 1648. The difficulty remains that the firm, orthodox holding to the doctrinal view of customary international law is not going to change overnight as a consequence of these attempts at new theoretical reflections. Despite the inaccessibility of the materials needed to judge the practice of States and despite the fact that this is largely attributable to the secretive structure of international relations, it is still possible to look to new frames for understanding the present development of this international structure with a view to drawing once again on the more critical, independent aspects of the international law tradition to challenge it.

4. ALTERNATIVE INTELLECTUAL FRAMES FOR AN UNDERSTANDING OF STATE PRACTICE: FROM LIBERAL DESIRE TO INTERNATIONAL ADMINISTRATIVE LAW

Richard Ned Lebow's *A Cultural History of International Relations* provides a typology of cultural representations of world society in historical perspective, which offers an ideological or structural explanation of the phenomenon of liberal democracy as the political theory for, and systematic representation of, appetite.[48] However, there are two other human motives or drives which help to understand conduct; the drive for honour and the drive away from fear.[49] Liberalism views the human drive of appetite positively and imagines peaceful, productive worlds in which material well-being is a dominant value. Liberals imagine their theories are descriptions of societies that already exist or are coming into being, with proponents of globalization predicting a worldwide triumph of liberal democratic trading States. Its starting point is a fundamentally welfare-oriented, consumerist, and therefore politically postmodern, privately interested, even apolitical 'individual' described by Cooper in the *Breaking of Nations*.[50] Persons may nominally be the best judges of their own interest, but the invisible hand of collective egotism is what ensures public survival. Beyond that there is no formally acknowledged interest in power politics, not to mention aggressive wars of conquest. There is no further need for a critique of human conduct by

---

[48] RN Lebow *A Cultural History of International Relations* (CUP Cambridge 2008) at 72–6.
[49] ibid 61–72 and 88–93.
[50] R Cooper *The Breaking of Nations: Order and Chaos in the Twenty-First Century* (Atlantic Books London 2003) at 62.

reference to a transcendent standard of 'right reason'. This function for doctrine will be lost in the face of the tasks of the management of the welfare, economic machine, the administration of 'things', necessary for the pacification of human appetites.

To return to Allott's metaphors of the State, it is out of the robotic machine of the State of the Enlightenment, that are due to 'pop' the laws, rules, and minor ordinances which will ensure the general prosperity.[51] International society needs to be managed skilfully, which may explain the appropriateness of the emergence of international administrative law as a governing concept to describe the phenomena of contemporary world, not simply state practice.[52] Indeed, Koskenniemi appears to be arguing that the development of a natural law foundation to international law became lost in the intricacies of economic management at the point when Adam Smith abandoned natural jurisprudence for political economy.[53] His complaint is that international law as a dream of the gentle civilizers of nations comes to an end in about 1960, with the triumph of European Law and the assignment of the Frenchman international lawyer Paul Reuters to Brussels. This is another way of saying that international law is about a functionalist management of socio-economic frictions among States, rather than a search for the meaning of their narrative in the onward march of their historical destinies.[54]

The difficulty for 'mainstream' international law is that such a frame for the description of state behaviour is incompatible with the idealist 'mish-mash' of democratic and/or popular nationalism which underlies the confidence that nation-states have a legal conviction which reveals itself in the narrative of their conduct towards one another. One is much closer to the State as a management company accommodating the desires of its otherwise apolitical members. An international administrative law for international civil servants might be 'the practice' supported by a doctrinal school devoted to the political economy of regulation. After resisting Hobbsean nihilism for centuries, international law is finally disposed of by the logic of shopping malls and beach holidays.

This is precisely the conclusion of Michel Foucault. Foucault elaborates very precisely in his *Security, Territory and Population*,[55] on what the managerial State, driven by a welfare motivated *raison d'état*, would mean for international law. Foucault offers three paradigms of social order in *Security, Territory and Population*, which are also tied to his understanding of the nature and usefulness of objective knowledge in

---

[51] P Allott 'International Law and the International Hofmafia: Towards a Sociology of Diplomacy' in W Benedek et al (eds) *Development and Developing International and European Law* (Peter Lang Berlin 1999) 3–19.

[52] See the Global Administrative Law Project <http://iilj.org/GAL/> (16 February 2012).

[53] M Koskenniemi 'The Advantages of Treaties: International Law in the Enlightenment' (2009) 13 Edinburgh Law Review 27–67.

[54] M Koskenniemi *The Gentle Civilizer of Nations: The Rise and Fall of International Law 1870–1960* (CUP Cambridge 2002).

[55] M Foucault *Security, Territory, Population Lectures at the Collège de France 1977–78* (Palgrave Macmillan Basingstoke 2009).

modernity, that is, post-Descartes. He distinguishes three types of order: the legal-juridical, the disciplinary, and the security apparatus. The legal-juridical system works by laying down a law and then a punishment for whoever breaks it. In this case what is not prohibited is permitted. This suggests the rule of law, and basic rights or privileges of the individual. Foucault appears to situate such legal thinking in early modernity; the 16th to 18th century. However, already by the 18th century we have, secondly, a disciplinary regime working as a supplement to the legal-juridical system. The potential culprit/transgressor appears outside the binary opposition of obedience-disobedience. That is to say, outside the legislative act which sets the law and the juridical act which may punish or has punished the culprit/transgressor, there are adjacent, detective, medical, and psychological techniques which fall within the domain of diagnosis and possible transformation of individuals. The apparatus of security cuts across the other two approaches to social order. The security apparatus was not at all about the suspension of law in the face of danger, but instead about the management of populations according to their natural logic, so as to facilitate circulation in a world of inevitably open frontiers among States. This apparatus inserts the phenomenon, or problem to be managed (for example, epidemic, criminality, famine), within a series of probable events.[56]

This apparatus actually calculates freedom of the individual into the equation of development, not simply in the legal sense that some things are forbidden and the rest permitted, but in the sense that there is a combination of spontaneous energy encouraged by *laissez faire,* and a partially directional management of the population. The fundamental point is that, in the final analysis, one is not dealing with a series of individuals making up a people, but with a population as a mass, a natural, material entity with its own natural logic to be managed, to be protected, above all, from famine, epidemics, and whatever other danger which could decimate it. How to achieve these goals was a matter of management, fine-tuned handling. The uncertain is not dangerous. It is natural, but the criterion for the security apparatus is the appropriateness of the judgment of risk and cost. The multiplicity of individuals is no longer what matters but instead, the population, as an object management. As Foucault puts it:

The reactions of power to this phenomenon are inserted into a calculation of cost. Finally, instead of a binary division between the permitted and the prohibited, one establishes an average considered as optimal on the one hand, and, on the other, a bandwidth of the acceptable that must not be exceeded.[57]

What is essential, for Foucault, in the organization of modern societies is that the task of politics is not simply the imposition of a set of laws imposed by God, nor a

---

[56] The scheme is explained in the first lecture, especially ibid 5–8. It is important to appreciate that each successive regime does not replace the other—which is what makes it difficult, perhaps, for the international lawyer to realize that while his particular forms of law continue, they are not dominant, or finally significant.

[57] ibid 6.

disciplinary regime to deal with the innate wickedness of men. Instead, a security apparatus works within reality by getting the components of reality to work in relation to one another, through a series of analyses. The apparatus of security was superior to that of rights.[58] Foucault concludes:

> ... I think the population no longer appears as a collection of subjects of right, as a collection of subject wills who must obey the sovereign's will through the intermediary of regulations, laws, edicts and so on. It will be considered as a set of processes to be managed at the level and on the basis of what is natural in these processes.[59]

What regime of international law and order did this apparatus of security envisage? Around the old and familiar concept of *raison d'état,* Foucault can see no hope for any international, normative order. The concept of *raison d'état* does not yield to any positive, moral, natural, and divine laws because they are stronger, but merely integrates them into its own game of necessity—the State is for and only for itself.[60] The knowledge that a prince must have is not of the laws but of things, of statistics, of the elements that make up the forces and resources that characterize his State at a given moment, a State beyond which there is nothing for which it exists, such as individual salvation, world peace, or a final empire.[61]

Foucault, paradoxically for mainstream international lawyers, thought international law did exist—at least a *ius gentium* binding monarchs—until 1648, when it was abolished. This is for the same reason that the apparatus of security eventually trumps the legal and disciplinary regimes. The fundamental unit of the international system is the self-generating dynamic of the State and the threat of disequilibrium and imbalance which it represents. In the medieval period, war could be a question of right, because princes could quarrel about inheritances and rules of marriage and family. After 1648 wars were fought as wars of State. No juridical reason was needed, even if one might be provided. Purely diplomatic reason was enough; that the balance is in danger and needs to be reestablished. The boundaries of Europe in 1648 were not fixed, as of right, but having regard to this balance of forces. Not according to old rights of inheritance, or even rights of conquest, but in terms of physical principles, it would be decided how an inter-state balance could be established with the most likely prospect of the greatest possible stability.[62]

It was accepted that States were, as spontaneous forces, in permanent competition and rivalry with one another, necessitating a permanently armed peace and vigilant diplomacy. There had to be a permanent negotiation of balance to compromise the dynamics of independent apparatuses of security, although Foucault does not actually use that expression to cover the balance of forces.[63] Foucault only mentions this in a sentence, but the only relation of Europe with the rest of the world was commercial utilization, domination, or exploitation.[64]

---

[58] ibid 47–9.   [59] ibid 70.   [60] ibid 262.   [61] ibid 260 and 274.
[62] ibid 300–2.   [63] ibid 303.   [64] ibid 298.

So, effectively, Foucault concludes that *raison d'état* means a total moral vacuum among States, which exist, indefinitely and without any legitimate foundation or starting point, simply to maintain themselves. As such, this inter-state system is static. It can only perpetuate itself and cannot become anything else, such as a world-state or final empire, in a Christian eschatological sense. Human rights, the rule of law, and democracy have not been replaced as either a first-order or second-order regime of law or discipline, but their existence is permanently precarious. International law is still there, but the complex reality in which it functions means it is virtually always open to suspension.

So, there is not a series of successive elements, the appearance of the new causing the earlier ones to disappear. There is not the legal age, the disciplinary age, and then the age of security. Mechanisms of security do not replace disciplinary mechanisms, which would have replaced juridico-legal mechanisms. In reality you have a series of complex edifices in which, of course, the techniques themselves change and are perfected, or anyway become more complicated, but in which what above all changes is the dominant characteristic, or more exactly, the system of correlation between juridico-legal mechanisms, disciplinary mechanisms, and mechanisms of security.[65]

5. An Intellectual Framing of State Practice which Reintroduces the use of Right Reason

It would be possible to reintroduce a classical natural law role for doctrine if it was possible to find any chink in the structuralist straitjacket presented so far by Lebow and Foucault. It would be necessary to show that there was some place in the contemporary practice of States, as they understand it, for individual choice and responsibility, a capacity to shape events constructively according to some measure or standard of reasonableness. In fact Lebow contrasts appetite societies, such as the liberal, democratic West, primarily with 'spirit societies' where the primary motivation is esteem, both self esteem and esteem which one has won from others, society, etc., according to agreed rules. This drive for self-worth is at least as strong as appetite and often takes over when the former is in some measure satisfied.[66] It is obviously the case that the liberal West is in fact beset with frightening economic and financial

---

[65] ibid 8.
[66] *A Cultural Theory of International Relations* (n 48) 61 ff.

instability, whilst imagining itself beset by the spectre of Islamic militants and terrorism.

Lebow recognizes that what appears strange is that the liberal paradigm of state interest for individual welfare appears to offer no ballast to resist the tendency to fear which the precariousness of an international society, without any overriding author-ity, repeatedly engenders. This is due to the competition which is the main form of contact among States. It is because liberalism does not acknowledge that appetite, like spirit-based societies, has its roots in human motivation, ultimately individual even if inherently socially contagious. Of human motivation Lebow says that:

Spirit and appetite based worlds are inherently unstable. They are intensely competitive, which encourages actors to violate the rules by which honor or wealth is attained. When enough actors do this, those who continue to obey the rules are likely to be seriously handi-capped.[67] ... The difficulty of appeasing the spirit or appetite, or of effectively discriminating among competing appetites, sooner or later propels both kinds of people and regimes down the road to tyranny. Tyranny is initially attractive because the tyrant is unconstrained by laws. In reality, the tyrant is a true slave because he is ruled by his passions and is not in any way his own master.[68]

Of course fear is the other face of tyranny. Fear is a negative emotion essentially deriv-ative, marking an anticipated loss of goods, such as self-esteem and the esteem of others, and, of course, wealth.[69] As the fear grows the counter-measures for protec-tion become self-defeating and intensify the sense of danger. The search for security in this more usual sense of the word—not Foucault's—knows no bounds and spreads fear in the community, whether national or international. This is because the final root of this derivative emotion is always the 'unrestrained' drive for either appetite or the spirit of honour, or both together. This lack of restraint will be a failure of leader-ship by elites, although it may be accompanied by a revolt by the less advantaged who consider that the rules for acquisition of wealth and honour are not being met.[70]

It is the place of reason to exercise restraint on the pursuit of honour and appetite, by which Lebow means *phronēsis*, not an instrumental reason—David Hume's slave of the passions—but a capacity to reformulate behaviour on the basis of reflection. This goes beyond a simple feedback to make conduct more effective, to a learning about one's environment and how it works, to an appreciation that the ability to sat-isfy appetite and spirit rests on a robust society. That, in turn, rests upon affection and the role of close relationships in self-actualizing, where meaningful cooperation becomes possible. This is all drawn from Aristotle, Socrates, and Plato. The funda-mental difficulty leading to the breakdown of orders, for Aristotle, is the parochial pursuit of factional goals, leading others to fear exclusion from the ability to satisfy their goals. For Socrates dialogue is the surest means of making us recognize the parochial and limited range of our goals. For Plato, *eros* can be educated by reason

---

[67] ibid 82.   [68] ibid 83.   [69] ibid 88 ff.   [70] ibid 83–6.

and directed towards the good and the beautiful and even the kind wisdom concerned with ordering of States and societies.[71]

After setting out this normative framework, Lebow illustrates it with the whole sweep of Western history, including some of East Asia in the last 100 years. While international diplomacy virtually always has appetite trumped by the spirit in pursuit of honour, the high point of this tendency was the period 1660 to 1789. Of course the significance of this period is that it is precisely when legal historians are agreed that whatever influence the Grotius tradition of international law doctrine had, it was then. While the State was all the time increasingly consolidated as an institution, it was still visibly directed by sovereign individuals, above all Louis XIV, Peter I of Russia, and Frederick II, all of whom sought and obtained the title of 'Great'. Lebow's argument would not be at all that these rulers studiously read and followed Grotius' maxims. Rather it is that the primary problem they all represented was a lack of restraint in the pursuit of glory, after a period—the Wars of Religion—where public consciousness was especially aware of the absence of all constraints. The function of a classical ethic of reason—right reason—was then not to ensure a balance of power—an unstable concept in an atmosphere of fear—but to restore and maintain a moral balance, an equilibrium in the mentality of the elites of Europe. While wars would frequently have dynastic pretexts, historians are agreed that dynasties usually restrained an ultimate destructiveness in conflict.[72]

6. A LEBOW-STYLE CLASSICAL GREEK FRAMING OF STATE PRACTICE IN THE AGE OF ABSOLUTISM

It is Lebow's argument that the Age of Absolutism was only the clearest example of the need for reason to balance appetite and the craving for honour. The present just as much resembles the past in the craving for status, honour, or rank. Therefore the Grotian project remains the most apposite for the opposition of doctrine and state practice. However, before proceeding to elaborate upon this vital point, it might be helpful to explore more closely doctrine and state practice in the Age of Absolutism. Drawing on the contribution of Lucien Bély in a collective volume *Histoire de la diplomatie française*[73] it is possible to see how such abstract concepts as the following

---

[71] ibid 76–82.   [72] ibid 262–304. From Sun King to Revolution.

[73] L Bély 'Les temps modernes (1515–1789)' in F Autrand et al *Histoire de la diplomatie française* (Perrin Paris 2005) vol 1, 253–400.

of right reason would work out in Bély's contrast between the policies of Richelieu and Mazarin on the one hand, and those of Louis XIV on the other. Bély argues that it is possible to see measure and reason in Richelieu's policies. It was only as an intellectual with a clear capacity to present reasonable and coherent aims and projects that he could persuade Louis XIII and an equally sceptical French opinion to follow him. Steering a course between the Catholic camp in France and the fear of the consequences for France of a joint Habsburg dominance in the Empire and in the Lowlands, he endeavoured, in Bély's view, to play the role of the protector of ancient German, Dutch, and Italian liberties, while driving towards a scheme of collective security in Europe. Richelieu increased and consolidated French territory, but there was no scheme of hegemony and no project to keep Germany weak and divided. A *raison d'état* was imbued with right reason, a prudent reflection on actual conditions.

In contrast, Bély's portrait of Louis XIV is extremely critical—the title of the section of the 'Temps modernes' dealing with him being, 'aggression at the service of grandeur'. Louis XIV clearly stated that his goal was to impose his dominance in Europe, as the first of Christian kings, and Christians being first in the world, that made him first in the world. First the invasion of the Netherlands (United Provinces) and then especially the invasion of the Palatinate united the Dutch, Austrians, many Germans, the Spanish, and the English against his clearly hegemonial ambitions. Louis XIV's lawyers played their part in resurrecting old dynastic and feudal territorial claims. Indeed at Westphalia and Utrecht there were more than a hundred lawyers, but for instance, the Austrians countered Louis XIV's lawyers' argument as a façade to claim a universal monarchy. The cruelty of his armies, in defiance of Grotius' new admonitions, was designed to strike terror in the face of his power, but merely reinforced opposition to him. Bély concludes that France did consolidate its frontiers in Alsace and on the borders with the Spanish and then Austrian Netherlands. The War of the Spanish Succession did put a final end to fears of Habsburg encirclement. The renunciations of dynastic succession demanded at Utrecht had been common practice in French Bourbon marriages with Spanish and Austrian Habsburgs and were, in Bély's view, superfluous. Nonetheless Louis XIV's lack of restraint ruined France.

The lesson of the reign of Louis XIV was that there had to be a reasonable connection between legal claims and how they were seen by others. The central problem of international law and relations—not a particular concern of diplomatic historians—was then the reasonable reliance upon legal right and its reasonable pursuit. All else will provoke extensive reactions from other countries. As they perceive legal claims to be part of a grand hegemonic strategy and the manner of their pursuit to be a war of terror against populations, other countries form effective alliances making it impossible for the overreaching individual prince to achieve any goals. At the death of Louis XIV France was bankrupt and greatly diminished in status from how he had been handed it by Richelieu and Mazarin.

7. LEGAL DOCTRINE AS A CRITIQUE OF STATE PRACTICE BY THE STANDARD OF RIGHT REASON IN THE AGE OF ABSOLUTISM

It is important to understand the various strengths and weaknesses of Grotius without idolizing or rejecting him. Also it is important to understand precisely what is meant by saying that Grotius is clearly attuned to the Age of Absolutism. Jouannet has raised the question whether there could be said to be any international law that would require States at least partially to adapt their conduct to it during the 17th century. She thinks there was not. Hers is, indeed, one part of an argument that, even as a history of international law as doctrine, there is no continuity in the history of international law from the 16th to the 18th century. Instead, she quotes Richelieu as himself citing Machiavelli, that it is not dishonourable to break the conventions by which one has tied the nation. She claims no one continued to speak like that in the 18th century, because there was a legal conscience of a fundamental rule of international law, *pacta sunt servanda*.[74]

However, in making a case for international law doctrine, the test is only whether that doctrine is itself intellectually strong, given the intellectual foundations of both the doctrine and one's understanding of the nature of the state practice. Whether a figure such as Grotius accurately described state practice or whether statesmen listened to him is not the point. The point is whether he framed the nature of the decisions they made in the context of the types of dilemmas which he offered to resolve. This he did do, and as Lebow shows, the need for such decisions and the types of dilemmas they pose continue to be much the same.

Grotius wrote his major work by the 1620s while Richelieu was beginning his second and long mandate. They had only one meeting. Richelieu had insisted upon the diplomatic precedence of ambassadors from Catholic monarchs and as a result Grotius refused to be received at court as the ambassador of Sweden. Richelieu asked for him to be recalled and ways were found to go around Grotius. So Grotius took no part in the development of the crucial French–Swedish diplomatic relations of the late 1620s onwards. This may be judged as a great failure of Grotius and there appears to be nothing in his work about the detail of the contentions between France, Sweden, the German princes, and the Spanish and Austrian Habsburgs. His work on just war and right to property, etc. is abstract and based on Roman law. Bély says that the Austrian Habsburgs and the Spaniards were determined in the 1620s to reverse the Protestant Reformation in Germany and dislodge Protestant princes, replacing them with Catholics. Until 1629 this was successful. At the same time, the Spanish Habsburgs

---

[74] E Jouannet 'Vattel ou le droit des dens des modernes' in Y Sandoz (ed) *Emer de Vattel's 'Law of Nations'* (Bruylant Brussels 2010) 5–16 at 14.

endeavoured once again to defeat the Dutch Revolt. France and Sweden had a common interest in not allowing victories which would have assured a huge Habsburg predominance in Europe, possibly an absolute State emerging from the Holy Roman Empire and a Spanish predominance on France's north-east frontier.

Under Richelieu, Mazarin, after 1642 and further under Louis XIV after 1661, there were lawyers and pamphleteers officially assigned to engage in arguments about feudal vassalage and allegiances on France's eastern frontier and going into the Holy Roman Empire, which went back to the time of the empire of Charlemagne and appeared to be planning to resurrect it. Equally there was scope for elaborate legal argument about the rights of the German princes under the law of the Holy Roman Empire. Whether these legal arguments were in some sense to be judged as sound does not appear in Grotius' work, and not in the histories of international law in the *Max Planck Encyclopedia*. They are considered at length by such French historians as Cornette in his *Le roi de guerre, essai sur la souveraineté dans la France du grande siècle*.[75]

However, the lawyers and pamphleteers on both sides in the Thirty Years War draw a distinction between justifying pretexts of legal arguments and real underlying motives, a distinction which Grotius also does take up as a distinction of interest. While Grotius says, in unhelpfully abstract terms, that war is just if it is undertaken to defend a property right which has been usurped, he goes on to impose upon this abstract framework of an essentially private law notion of property taken from Roman law, the idea that force or war should only be used to defend a credible legal right. In other words, a dimension of judgment arises. Grotius still considers it possible to distinguish a reasonable or credible assertion of a right from an unreasonable assertion and prosecution of a right, the very issue which stimulated Bély's reflections on the difference between Richelieu and Louis XIV. It also reflects the distinction Lebow makes between a restrained and an unrestrained search for prestige and/or wealth in the sense here, of material power.

Grotius' standard is vague because it involves an exercise of judgment in the light of concrete circumstances. In the exercise of judgment about concrete and therefore immensely complex facts, doctrine has still, as much as in the 17th century, a task to fulfil. Of course now, as in Grotius' time, neither doctrine nor the international judiciary will have access to all the necessary information to make the best judgment. However, Parry himself stressed that, however inaccessible the national archives, most of the general outlines of a nation's foreign policy becomes known relatively soon—witness the sequels to the Anglo-American invasion of Iraq.

The continuing relevance of Grotius—it has to be stressed as the archetypal symbol of the primacy of international legal doctrine over state practice in the whole of the international law tradition—lies in his reiteration of the classical Greek standard

---

[75] J Cornette *Le roi de guerre, essai sur la souveraineté dans la France du grande siècle* (Payot Paris 2000).

of reasonable conduct, in terms similar to Lebow's. That is, Lebow helps to show both the sense of Grotius' intentions and his continuing relevance. I think this is especially clear in chapters 22 and 23 of book II of *The Law of War and Peace.*[76] Grotius distinguishes the openly presented so-called justifying reasons from real underlying motives of statesmen. Reason can appear to provide a coherent argument for war, but the underlying motive is still a desire for riches, glory, and empire. Right reason should be able to balance arguments and this is a matter of the exercise of a quality of judgment which should be free of ambition as from envy. Grotius believes that an impartial reason can judge the merits of arguments; for instance, Dante's arguments for the universal jurisdiction of the emperor as tending to be in the interests of mankind. Grotius finds Dante's arguments unconvincing and that the advantages are outweighed by the inconveniences. Convenience of empire is, in any case, not a right of empire, which can only be drawn from consent, the true origin of all right of government. At the very beginning of his chapter 22, Grotius identifies the war of Alexander against the Persian Darius as one which used the pretext of injuries formerly done to the Greeks, whereas Alexander's real motive was the desire for the glory of empire. These are very remote historical examples of intellectual systems and state practice. However, it would have been obvious to his readers how they could be applied to constructions of universal monarchy or attempts at global hegemony in his own time and after.

8. Conclusion

History of international law shows that the very idea of state practice is a construction of doctrine, a confidence in a customary legal order of the normative attitudes and practices which peoples have as to how their relations be conducted. This confidence of 19th-century nationalism and democracy renders natural law critique of state practice redundant. However, the distrust that nations have of one another prevents the disclosure of state intentions and true underlying state practices, thereby rendering uncertain the very concept of state practice. Doctrine persists pragmatically with unscientific constructions of this practice, as does international jurisprudence.

---

[76] Among the innumerable editions of Grotius the one used here is the reprint from the Law Book Exchange, H Grotius *The Rights of War and Peace, in Three Books* (J Barbeyrac ed) (Innis and Manby London 1738, Law Book Exchange Clark New Jersey 2004). The abstract discussion of the right to go to war to defend property is in ch I, book II, while the discussion of pretexts and justified reasons comes later in chs 22 and 23.

Intellectually framing of the history of state conduct, from outside the discipline (cultural history/Lebow and discourse theory/Foucault) invites an alternative critique of state practice as global administration of appetites and desires of mass populations of individuals. Foucault explains that such management requires regimes of security, which do not abolish international law but ensure its secondary status and liability to irregular suspension. At the same time, Lebow exposes the tendency of appetite towards lack of restraint, slipping over into fear as individuals anticipate losing out. This is the occasion for Lebow to reintroduce classical reason as *phronēsis*. Here, once again, Grotius and the natural law tradition of transcendent critique can find their place in restraining and guiding modern 'princes' in all their forms.

RECOMMENDED READING

Carty, Anthony 'International Law as a Science (The Place of Doctrine in the History of its Sources)' (1980) 18 Indian Yearbook of International Affairs 128–60.

Carty, Anthony 'The Practice of International Law' in David Armstrong (ed) *Routledge Handbook of International Law* (London: Routledge 2009) 81–100.

Foucault, Michel *Security, Territory, Population: Lectures at the Collège de France 1977–1978* (Palgrave Macmillan Basingstoke 2009).

Guggenheim, Paul 'Contribution à l'histoire des sources du droit des gens' (1958) 94 Recueil des cours 1–84.

Hueck, Ingo J 'The Discipline of the History of International Law' (2001) 3 Journal of the History of International Law 194–217.

Marston, Geoffrey 'The Evidences of British State Practice in the Field of International Law' in Anthony Carty and Gennady Danilenko (eds) *Perestroika and International Law* (Edinburgh University Press Edinburgh 1990) 27–47.

Parry, Clive 'The Practice of States' (1958–59) 44 Transactions of the Grotius Society 145–86.

Parry, Clive *The Sources and Evidences of International Law* (Manchester University Press Manchester 1965).

Tierney, Brian 'Vitoria and Suarez on *ius gentium*, Natural Law, and Custom' in Amanda Perreau-Saussine and James B Murphy (eds) *The Nature of Customary Law: Legal, Historical, and Philosophical Perspectives* (CUP Cambridge 2007) 101–24.

CHAPTER 41

....

THE PERIODIZATION
OF THE HISTORY OF
INTERNATIONAL LAW

....

OLIVER DIGGELMANN

1. INTRODUCTION

....

1.1. Historiography of International Law and Periodization

The division of historical time into periods is indispensable for any historiographical work. Historical facts cannot be identified without referring to a time frame with a more or less determinable beginning and end. Periods make historical facts 'thinkable', as the Polish historian Krzysztof Pomian said.[1] This chapter explores the significance of the question of periodization in historiography of international law.

Literally, the term 'peri-hodos'—of which the notions 'period' and 'periodization' are derived—means 'the way around' in ancient Greek. From antiquity to the 18th century, the idea that history follows a cyclical and predetermined course played an important and often dominant role. History was imagined as a constant repetition of destined events which could not be altered by human will—like a turning wheel. Contemporary use of the term 'period' no longer connotes the

---

[1] K Pomian *L'ordre du temps* (Gallimard Paris 1984) at 162.

original meaning.[2] It has become a synonym for a certain span along the axis of historical time.

Periodization decisions can be made explicitly or implicitly. If someone analyses, for example, the question of 'Egyptian Responses to the Palestine Problem in the Interwar Period',[3] he operates explicitly with a well-established period. The beginning and end of the relevant time frame are clear and need no further explanation. If someone analyses, however, the topic 'Self-determination and Secession under International Law',[4] the relevant time frame is not specified. Nevertheless, it does exist. It results from the overlap of those time spans during which a right to self-determination, including a right to secession, is recognized, and during which international law exists.

The formation of 'new', formerly unknown periods is an essential part of historiographical innovation. New periodizations aim to provide new insights. They shed different light on historical facts, not only on newly discovered ones but also on supposedly well-known facts. They reorganize historiographical knowledge. It makes a difference, for example, whether we regard the establishment of the United Nations Organization as the beginning of the 'era of the UN' or as an important event in the 'era of modern international law'. It also makes a difference whether we regard the present as part of 'the era of the United Nations' or of the 'post-Cold War era'.

A good example is provided by the well-known book *The Gentle Civilizer of Nations* by the Finnish international lawyer Martti Koskenniemi.[5] The author's intention was to shed new light on the history of international law. He chose the subtitle 'The Rise and Fall of International Law 1870–1960', which was somewhat surprising with respect to the periodization employed. The study analysed the development of a sensitivity towards international affairs. By operating with the period '1870–1960', it challenged predominant views of the history of international law.[6] It challenged, for example, views connected with the established distinction between the period of 'classical international law' and 'modern international law'. Koskenniemi's periodization suggests an interpretation of historical facts, which differs fundamentally from the typical 'narration of progress' in mainstream scholarship.[7]

---

[2] For the development of the notion 'period' cf M Kranz 'Periode, Periodisierung' in J Ritter and K Gründer (eds) *Historisches Wörterbuch der Philosophie* (Schwabe und Co Basel 1989) vol 7, 259–62.

[3] J Jankowski 'Egyptian Responses to the Palestine Problem in the Interwar Period' (1980) 12 International Journal of Middle East Studies 1–38.

[4] VP Nanda 'Self-determination and Secession under International Law: Validity of Claims to Secede' (2001) 29 Denver Journal of International Law and Policy 305–26.

[5] M Koskenniemi *The Gentle Civilizer of Nations. The Rise and Fall of International Law 1870–1960* (CUP Cambridge 2002).

[6] For a more detailed analysis cf GRB Galindo 'Martti Koskenniemi and the Historiographical Turn in International Law' (2005) 16 European Journal of International Law 539–59 at 552–3.

[7] For the role of 'narrations of progress' in historiography of international law cf Section 2.5.

The significance of the question treated here contrasts significantly with the attention paid to it in historiography of international law. There hardly exist any ambitious theoretical contributions to the topic and its far-reaching implications at all. In historiography of international law, defining periods is considered as something one 'does' and not as something one theorizes about. Consequently, this brings up the critical observation that historiography of international law is not fully aware of what it does whenever periodization decisions are not considered.

There might be two main reasons for such an omission. It is likely, on the one hand, that as a theoretical topic, periodization does not offer great promise. The question might seem 'too theoretical' for a legal discipline and is therefore left to historians. On the other hand, not engaging with the issue of periodization might also be connected with widely shared negative attitudes towards 'world history' and 'grand narratives'. The basic idea underlying such scepticism is that it is simply not possible to speak about large time spans in any meaningful way.[8] 'Grand narratives' or 'master narratives'—which necessarily make use of 'master periodizations'—are suspected by many of being ideological or even naïve. A classical example is Arnold J Toynbee's *A Study of History* which was written in the 1930s and contained—in 5,500 pages—an interpretation of the whole world history as a history of civilizations.

1.2. Interests and Values

Periods are not facts. They are concepts helpful for organizing our knowledge, based on a choice of facts which are considered as 'relevant' by an author in the light of the necessity to envelop historical time by some structure. Periods are interpretations of facts, not the facts themselves. Challenging established periods means challenging established interpretations of history.[9] Well-established periods such as 'the Age of Enlightenment' or 'the era of the League of Nations' may have reached a kind of quasi-objective status in practice. It does not alter, however, their purely interpretive character. The fact that periods are only intellectual devices leads some authors to think that there is no such thing as periods or epochs at all.[10] Others—who do not want to go that far—regard periods, metaphorically speaking, as 'grids' we lay over the reality and which help us to organize our knowledge. The German historian Johann Gustav Droysen looked for a metaphor to describe them, given that they are

---

[8] J Osterhammel 'Über die Periodisierung der neueren Geschichte' (2006) 10 Berlin-Brandenburgische Akademie der Wissenschaften. Berichte und Abhandlungen 45–64 at 46.

[9] In general historiography, the periodization-concept of the 'longue durée' (long term) by the French Annales School is an illustrative example. Cf F Braudel 'La longue durée' (1958) 13 Annales d'histoire économique et sociale 725–53.

[10] KH Stierle 'Renaissance—Die Entstehung eines Epochenbegriffs aus dem Geist des 19. Jahrhunderts' in R Herzog and R Koselleck (eds) *Epochenschwelle und Epochenbewusstsein* (Wilhelm Fink München 1987) 453–92 at 453.

no objective reality but nevertheless necessary constructions to understand it. He wrote that in history there are no epochs as there are no lines on the Equator and on the meridian circles; epochs are concepts of thought which are attributed to empirical reality and which serve the aim of grasping it better.[11] How one defines periods is to a large extent a matter of discretion. Even if we admit—to speak with Hans-Georg Gadamer—that in history there exist something like experiences of discontinuity,[12] there is no guidance how to define periods. Which criteria are meaningful? Should the demarcation of a new period actually begin with the appearance of something distinctly new or not before the new, in fact, becomes the dominating factor in its own right? Should we consider such a 'point of no return' as decisive?

Periodization decisions are influenced mainly by two factors. First, there is the historian's inclination to work with established periods if the research topic admits so. A lot of research is conducted within a temporal framework of established periods. In each historiographical discipline there are standard or 'conventional' period-izations available which belong to its basic vocabulary.[13] They can be employed with-out further explanation. The inclination to employ them for reasons of research economy evidently produces a certain conservative element. The second factor is one's personal values. Our values influence our cognitive interests. In this sense, peri-odizations are subjective.[14] Whether one is more interested in 'international stability' or in 'international justice'—whatever the differences may be in detail—in the last instance depends on one's values, which shape our cognitive interests. They structure our perception of the time dimension and determine what the historian is interested in and which facts he chooses to omit.

The so-called socialist theory of international law, for example, which played a role in 20th-century doctrine, was mainly interested in class conflicts. It looked at the his-tory of international law 'through the lens' of class struggles and expected gradual progress for the working class and, finally, its victory. From the socialist perspective, the Bolshevist Revolution has the status of a turning point of history in general and also of the history of international law. A radical variant claimed that there was no history of international law before the Bolshevist Revolution at all.[15] More moderate authors suggested that there was indeed one but which was only 'primitive' in nature. Also, in their view, the Bolshevist Revolution marked the 'beginning' of the history of international law in the proper sense. Periodization decisions structure the 'lens'

---

[11] JG Droysen *Texte zur Geschichtstheorie* (Vandenhoek & Ruprecht Göttingen 1972) at 20.

[12] HG Gadamer *Wahrheit und Methode* (Mohr Tübingen 1986) at 142.

[13] Section 2.1 of this chapter deals with the question of 'conventional periodizations' in the historiog-raphy of international law.

[14] F Graus 'Epochenbewusstsein—Epochenillusion' in *Epochenschwelle und Epochenbewusstsein* (n 10) 531–3 at 532.

[15] O Boutkevitch 'Les origines et l'évolution du droit international selon l'historiographie soviétique' (2004) 6 Journal of the History of International Law 187–207 at 187.

through which we regard the history of international law and thereby reproduce our view of the world.

Illustrative examples are also provided by authors of the 'Third World Approach' to international law. If an author is interested in the question of imperial domination and wants to tell the history of international law 'from an African perspective', he will have to work with completely different periods than socialist authors or authors from Western countries who are interested in the history of specific institutions of the modern State system. From an African perspective, it is plausible to distinguish, for example, the periods 'ancient and pre-Medieval Africa', 'indigenous African States', 'beginnings of European trade', and 'the period of colonial rule'.[16] There is an inescapable dilemma. Periods should, on the one hand, be 'right' and 'true', but, on the other hand, any diligent intellectual has to admit the unavoidable subjectivity of his periodization decisions.

2. Fundamental Questions

2.1. Core of Conventional Periodizations

In historiography of international law a number of 'conventional' periods or periodizations exist. For the purpose of this chapter, I call those time spans 'conventional' that belong to the basic time-vocabulary of the discipline and have a more or less determinable beginning and end. Conventional periodizations can be used without further explanation as they are immediately comprehensible. They facilitate the organization of one's knowledge. Their privileged status is owed to the fact that they have proved meaningful as time frames for historiographical work in a relatively large number of instances.

Which periods belong to this category? The most important conventional periods in historiography of international law are also conventional periods in general historiography. In the first place, the tripartite division of history into ancient, medieval, and modern history has to be mentioned. This was introduced by Christophorus Cellarius (1634–1707).[17] The three periods equally belong to the standard time-vocabulary in historiography of international law and provide its primary temporal structure. Further periodizations developed in general historiography, which have an almost similar status are, for example, 'the Age of Enlightenment', 'the 19th century', and 'the 20th century'.

---

[16] TO Elias *Africa and the Development of International Law* (AW Sijthoff Leiden 1972).
[17] C Cellarius *Historia universalis in antiquam et medii aevi ac novam divisa* (Jena 1704–8).

Several periods developed in the disciplines of international law and international relations are also 'conventional' in the sense described above. The following ones need to be pointed out here in particular: the periods of 'classical international law' and 'modern international law', the period between the Peace of Westphalia and the Napoleonic Wars ('the French age'), the period between the Congress of Vienna and the First World War ('the British age'), and the period between the First and the Second World Wars ('the era of the League of Nations' or the 'inter-war period'). These three mentioned periods are often designated with cyphers (1648–1815, 1815–1914, and 1919–1939).[18] They have the same basic structure. They begin with a peace conference after a great war and they end with the breakdown of an international order.[19]

Conventional periods impose a kind of 'burden of justification' on those who want to depart from them. An author who intends to write, for example, on the topic 'slave trade and international law between 1700 and 1800' will have to justify his periodization. He will most probably expect his approach to generate criticism with respect to the scientific character of his undertaking if he cannot give convincing reasons for the time frame he chooses. In *The Gentle Civilizer of Nations*, Martti Koskenniemi had to justify why he wanted to operate with the period '*1870–1960*'. He did so by pointing to empirical facts to explain why the time frame he introduced, which was considered 'new', provided a meaningful time frame in his view for the particular research undertaking. The creation of 'new' periods does not extinguish old ones. Conventional periods remain present as background time-structures even if we depart from them. We refer to them explicitly or implicitly when we justify the 'new' ones.

2.2. Periods as Units

To some extent, periods are imagined as 'coherent' time units. We imagine that the facts included in them 'belong together'.[20] We speak of a 'spirit' of an age or *Zeitgeist*—the successor of Montesquieu's *esprit du siècle*—or of a specific cultural consciousness which gives the period its particular character.[21] However, any periodization is inherently problematic as any period is an abstraction from the historical process.[22]

---

[18]   For critical reflections on these periodizations cf H Steiger 'From the International Law of Christianity to the International Law of the World Citizen—Reflections on the Formation of the Epochs of the History of International Law' (2001) 3 Journal of the History of International Law 180–93.

[19]   For criticism of periodizations emphasizing historical turning points see IJ Hueck 'The Discipline of the History of International Law' (2001) 3 Journal of the History of International Law 194–217 at 197.

[20]   R Koselleck 'Das achtzehnte Jahrhundert als Beginn der Neuzeit' in *Epochenschwelle und Epochen-bewusstsein* (n 10) 269–82 at 278.

[21]   On the questions connected with descriptions of ages and power structures, cf M Gamper and P Schnyder (eds) *Kollektive Gespenster. Die Masse, der Zeitgeist und andere unfassbare Körper* (Rombach Freiburg im Breisgau 2006).

[22]   M Mandelbaum *The Problem of Historical Knowledge* (Harper and Rowe New York 1967) at 312.

There is no 'general idea' underlying them, they have no 'meaning'. This does certainly not exclude that some of the facts included in them indeed belong together materially. Contemporaneity, however, does not provide material coherence per se. It is a purely formal criterion. Some facts included in a period regularly do not fit together with the rest. It is inevitable that periodizations always appear as inadequate to some extent.[23] Periods are by their nature over-inclusive. They over-unite for the purpose of facilitating intellectual orientation. The bigger a time span, the more over-inclusive it is.

A well-known practice in historiography of international law provides a good example. There exists a common practice to distinguish between the 'practice' and the 'theory' of a period. Studies and book chapters on the inter-war period, for example, regularly contain sections on both topics. However, many important theoretical contributions of the inter-war period rather 'belong' to the extreme experience of the First World War in a material sense. Theoretical writings of the period were in many respects 'reactions' to the war, attempts to regain lost orientation. They were initially not intended as attempts to describe the reality of their time. Given these considerations, it cannot surprise that 'theory' often makes the impression of being somewhat detached from the reality of its time. Theory is always more than an appendix to a particular epoch. It often deals simultaneously with the past, the present and the future. This makes it difficult if not impossible to attribute it to a precise era. The optimistic spirit of George Scelle's writings of the 1930s, for example, openly contrasts with the reality of these years. It cannot be understood properly if it is just read as a theory to describe Scelle's time. Therefore, it is questionable whether periodizations including theory and practice make sense at all.[24]

Periods also tend to overemphasize discontinuities. This is one of the most important problems of periodization. By cutting the time axis into pieces, periodization tends to give preferences to discontinuity over continuity. Introducing a new period primarily provides reasons why a specific time span should be regarded as a 'unit' and be treated separately. This mechanism emphasizes discontinuity, such as the differences between what took place 'before' and 'after' the period under scrutiny. In contrast, continuity receives little attention. The problem can be mitigated to some extent if we speak of a 'threshold between epochs' instead of a 'change of periods' as the notion 'threshold' signals sensitivity for the question discussed here. Nevertheless, by its nature, periodization risks disrupting continuous developments—as subtle as it may be.[25] The cultural historian Jakob Burckhardt complained bitterly about this problem. He called it one of the biggest problems of his discipline as periodizations disrupt long-term continuity and cut history into seemingly discretionary

---

[23] 'Das achtzehnte Jahrhundert als Beginn der Neuzeit' (n 20) at 269.

[24] 'The Discipline of the History of International Law' (n 19) at 198.

[25] On the question of continuities cf S Kadelbach 'Wandel und Kontinuitäten des Völkerrechts und seiner Theorie' (1997) Beiheft 71 Archiv für Rechts- und Sozialphilosophie 178–93.

pieces—just for the sake of making the massive substance of events somehow man-
ageable.[26] General historiography—and also historiography of international law—
struggle with the same fundamental problem. The distinction between the *ancien
régime* and the French Revolution, for example, blurs the fact that there was an
impressive continuity with respect to the leading classes.[27] The distinction between
the periods of 'classical' and 'modern' international law—to return to our discipline—desensitizes the fact that in Europe there was a long tradition of dwelling over
mechanisms to maintain peace and to minimize the costs of wars. There certainly
were important changes after the First World War, but there was also—beneath the
surface—much continuity.

An illustrative example is also provided by Wilhelm Grewe's well-known periodization concept.[28] In his opus magnum, Grewe distinguishes several hegemonic
periods: the age of Spanish, French, English, etc. domination. He calls each period
after the respective hegemonic power. The concept has some evident advantages: it
highlights the great influence of hegemonic powers on the fundamental rules and the
culture of an era. French culture and language, for example, exercised strong influence on the international order in the 17th and 18th centuries when France was the
dominating power. It shaped the culture of international diplomacy in particular.
Grewe's concept, however, disrupts many continuities. Many fundamental rules of
the late 17th and 18th centuries had developed over time and they did not alter fundamentally when France became the hegemonic power. They also continued to exist in
the subsequent era of British domination in many respects. Grewe's periodization is
not at all sensitive for the fact that the European monarchies were anchored in a long-
lasting common political, cultural, and spiritual tradition.

2.3. The 'First' Period

When did the history of international law 'begin'? Which was the 'first' period? There
is evidently no objective 'right' answer to this—admittedly not very new—question.
The period we consider 'the first' depends on the 'concept of international law' we
employ which provides the criteria for our search. In the last instance it depends on
the cognitive interests and values which influence what we mean by 'international
law'. The answer is always a relative one. If we are interested, for example, in the history of the international law of sovereign territorial States, it is plausible to assume

---

[26] J Burckhardt *Die Cultur der Renaissance in Italien. Ein Versuch* (Schweighausersche Verlagsbuchhandlung Basel 1860) at 1–2.

[27] 'Das achtzehnte Jahrhundert als Beginn der Neuzeit' (n 20) at 272.

[28] For a survey of the authors who adopted Grewe's concept of periodization, cf 'The Discipline of the
History of International Law' (n 19) at 196; on the background and the ideas underlying Grewe's work cf
B Fassbender 'Stories of War and Peace. On Writing the History of International Law in the "Third Reich"
and After' (2002) 13 European Journal of International Law 479–512.

the 'beginning' at some point in the late Middle Age or in the early Modern Age. The nucleus of the modern state system developed in the late Middle Age. If we are interested, however, in the history of legal and quasi-legal relations between relatively independent political entities, the answer is different. Wolfgang Preiser, for example, employed three criteria in his search—'inter-state intercourse', 'relative independence of the States', and 'consciousness of legal obligation'—and came to the conclusion that the first international legal system were the rules of the state system of the Near East between 1450 and 1200 BC.[29] Antonio Truyol y Serra used the criterion 'treaty'. He regards the year 3010 BC as the date of birth of international law as then the first treaty was concluded in ancient Mesopotamia.[30]

The question about the 'beginning' of the history of international law is evidently connected to the question about its Eurocentricity. A few remarks may suffice here. Eurocentrism is primarily a question of cognitive interests and subjective values which are also reflected, of course, in periodizations. Eurocentric periodization is a manifestation of Eurocentric cognitive interests. If an author is interested in the expansion of the European international law across the globe, he is likely to write a 'European' history of international law with corresponding periodizations. His perspective predetermines his periodization decisions. If an author is interested, however, in 'Africa's contribution to international law'—to come back to the aforementioned example—the relevant periods could be 'ancient Africa', the era of the 'indigenous African States', etc.[31] Authors may suggest narrating the history of international law for each cultural area separately, that is, for the Mediterranean area, the region of the Near East, for the area of the Arabian caliphat, for India's state system, and the region of East Asia, etc.[32] Each of these areas has its own view of the history of international law and accordingly also, its own 'beginning' and periodization.

2.4. The 'Last' Period

The 'last' period also poses particular challenges. The thorny question is whether the present—which has no determinable end—can be part of a historical period in the sense of meaningful periodization. Historical experience is constituted by 'before' and 'after'.[33] Some authors regard the 'now' as too unspecific to be part of a historical epoch. Periodization requires distance, and history has many examples

---

[29] W Preiser 'Die Epochen der antiken Völkerrechtsgeschichte' (1956) 11 JuristenZeitung 737–44.
[30] A Truyol y Serra *Histoire du droit international public* (Economia Paris 1995) at 5.
[31] *Africa and the Development of International Law* (n 16) 3–33.
[32] S Verosta 'Regionen und Perioden der Geschichte des Völkerrechts' (1979) 30 Österreichische Zeitschrift für Öffentliches Recht und Völkerrecht 1–21; S Verosta 'Die Geschichte des Völkerrechts' in A Verdross *Völkerrecht* (Springer Wien 1964) 31–62.
[33] R Koselleck *Vergangene Zukunft* (Suhrkamp Frankfurt am Main 1989) at 145.

in which the assessment of a time by its contemporaries was not shared by later generations. What might appear as singular to contemporaries—atrocities of war, unexpected atmospheric changes in international relations—is not necessarily singular in a historiographical sense. What might appear as a 'revolution' to contemporaries must not be a revolution in a more ambitious sense. We do not know yet, for example, whether the 'cultural revolution of 1968' will sometime in the future be regarded as a threshold to a new period of social history. It is possible that many aspects will be regarded by future generations as momentary phenomena. The fact that the contemporaries are convinced about the revolutionary character of their time is not per se conclusive. Of course, the events of those years were turning points in the biographies of many of them and made the 'before' seem as something coherent and completed. We do not know enough of the future to contextualize the present adequately. In some instances whole generations were convinced of the singularity of their time. This was the case, for example, in the 14th century when Black Death was considered as an indication for the arrival of the Last Judgment. Posterity, however, adopted a different view. There are no witnesses of changes of epochs. The threshold to a new epoch—the German philosopher Hans Blumenberg wrote—is an 'invisible border'.[34]

In 1914, for example, it was impossible for contemporaries to recognize the coherence of events. They led to the War and finally to a new world order.[35] Contemporaries could hardly imagine which developments were triggered by seemingly unconnected events. They influenced the whole course of the 20th century and changed many of the most important rules of international law. The invisible character of boundaries of epochs needs particular emphasis. Nowadays we speak relatively easily of 'new epochs' and 'historical moments'. The extremely rapid change of the visible world and its constant acceleration permanently reminds us that the old is incessantly replaced by the new.

Historiography of international law is insecure, for example, with respect to the significance of the end of the Cold War. Should it be regarded as the threshold to a new epoch? Or is the present still part of the era which began in 1945 with the Conference of San Francisco or even in 1919 when the partial ban on the use of force was agreed upon? After the fall of the Iron Curtain, there was a strong inclination in the discipline of international law to assume the beginning of a new period. Many regarded the changed atmosphere—the end of the struggle between the two incompatible ideologies—as a clear indication for the beginning of a new era. Many tended to think that the cosmopolitan project which was interrupted by the emergence of the totalitarian ideologies, the Second World War, and the rise of the Iron Curtain could be taken up again.[36] Heinhard Steiger, for example, called the present the period

---

[34] H Blumenberg *Aspekte der Epochenschwelle* (Suhrkamp Frankfurt am Main 1976) at 20.
[35] *Vergangene Zukunft* (n 33) 145.
[36] M Koskenniemi 'Why History of International Law?' (2004) 4 Rechtsgeschichte 61–6 at 63.

of transition to 'an international law of world citizens'.[37] Antonio Cassese argued that the end of the division of the world into three blocks was the decisive step into a new era with only one superpower which leads the Western countries and acts as the world's policeman.[38] The main arguments of those who proclaimed the beginning of a new and more promising period consisted of the far more active role of the UN Security Council, the expansion of human rights instruments, and the emergence of new actors such as the NGOs.

These were evidently important changes. But is this enough to assume the beginning of a new period in a historiographical sense? What about other—confusing—facts such as the unauthorized attacks of NATO against former Yugoslavia, and of the United States and its allies against Iraq? It is not difficult to denounce these wars as flagrant violations of the most fundamental rules of international law. The attacks are difficult to reconcile with the predominantly optimistic view of the time since 1989. Some authors adopt the opposite view: they regard these wars as a threshold to a new and rather dark age in which the ban on the use of force is dead and the most powerful claim a right to overrule the UN Charter.[39] And what about the attacks of 11 September 2001? We cannot assess whether they will be considered as the beginning of an era of asymmetrical wars between States and terrorists, or as merely momentary acts of violence. Any periodization of the present is—metaphorically speaking—skating on thin ice.

2.5. Narrations of Progress

The question of periodization touches also upon questions of philosophy of history. Should the sequence of the periods—regarded in its entirety—reflect a 'general pattern' in the history of international law? Is international law developing in a certain direction which should become manifest in the periods we employ? There are four possibilities for answering the question. The first is to deny it. If history is a contingent process, one can argue, each period is a separate unit. Accordingly, there is no regularity or pattern. One can also answer in an affirmative way and assume a general development towards progress or decline. One can explain the history of international law as a 'narrative of progress' or as a 'narrative of decline'. A fourth possibility is to argue that the history of international law follows a 'cyclical' pattern.

---

[37] 'From the International Law of Christianity' (n 18) 183.

[38] A Cassese *International Law* (OUP Oxford 2005) at 44.

[39] N Paech 'Epochenwechsel im Völkerrecht? Über die Auswirkungen der jüngsten Kriege auf das UNO-Friedenssystem' (2004) 43 Aus Politik und Zeitgeschichte 21–9 at 24.

In the discipline of international law there is a remarkable inclination towards 'narrations of progress'. I am tempted to speak of a relatively wide consensus that 'the present'—despite its shortcomings—should be understood as a higher stage of evolution than 'the past' and that the history of international law should be told accordingly. This tendency towards narrations of progress is manifest, for example, in the discipline's standard vocabulary. The aforementioned distinction of the history of international law in the two periods of 'classical international law' and 'modern international law' is telling. By employing the notion 'modern' to characterize the more recent period, the previous becomes implicitly the 'pre-modern' one—even if it is called 'classical' which sounds somewhat nobler. There is evidently a close connection between the semantics associated with modernity and the idea of progress. Similar considerations apply to the trend since the mid-1990s to describe important contemporary developments as part of a 'constitutionalization process'.[40] By regarding the present as the 'period of constitutionalization', the past automatically becomes the 'pre-constitutional period'. Here too, it is evident that the vocabulary of constitutionalism is connected to the idea of progress. Some historians of international law make their adherence to narrations of progress even explicit. The American Douglas M Johnston, for example, distinguishes the two main periods 'out of the mists' and 'into clear view'.[41] He argues that humanity is capable of learning from the past.[42] Most authors are less explicit. The tone, however, is often similar. Even in 'difficult times', there is a remarkable inclination to present the history of international law as a narrative of progress. The Dutch Cornelis van Vollenhoven, for example, divided the past and the present in 1932 into the epochs 'period of supremacy of war', 'period of war and peace', and 'period of supremacy of peace'.[43]

Why is there such an inclination? Several factors play a role. They create, in their entirety, a remarkable 'discipline optimism' which is also reflected in the periodization decisions. The first factor is the habit of the discipline to regard the ongoing and even accelerated expansion of international law—its intrusion into fields which formerly belonged to the *domaine reservé* of the States—as a sign of progress. It is interpreted as an indication that state egotism loses ground and that collective interests of the world community are becoming more important. Another important factor is the discipline's interests in its own importance. A successful history of international law is also a successful history of the discipline of international law. International lawyers want to be part of a great civilizing project. They

---

[40] Cf eg B Fassbender *The United Nations Charter as the Constitution of the International Community* (Martinus Nijhoff Leiden 2009); J Klabbers, A Peters, and G Ulfstein (eds) *The Constitutionalization of International Law* (OUP Oxford 2009).

[41] DM Johnston *The Historical Foundations of World Order. The Tower and the Arena* (Martinus Nijhoff Leiden 2008) at 143–319 and 321–772.

[42] Explicitly ibid (n 41) xvii.

[43] C van Vollenhoven *Du droit de paix. De jure pacis* (Martinus Nijhoff The Hague 1932).

are consciously or unconsciously guided by the frightening idea that there is simply no alternative to international law's success. Narrations of progress immunize the discipline to some extent against challenges of its relevance: they have a consoling effect. The third factor is the long tradition of narrations of progress in Western culture in general. It is in its core a heritage of the philosophy of history of the 18th and 19th centuries which combined belief in rationality and spiritual relicts of the Christian tradition.[44] Influential philosophies of history which can be considered as decidedly optimistic are, for example, Hegel's philosophy, Marx' historical materialism, and Comte's distinction between a theological, metaphysical, and scientific period.

2.6. Denomination of Periods

The last topic to be discussed here concerns the question of the denomination of the periods. Should they be colourful and 'strong', or noncommital and 'weak'? Strong denominations aim to catch the 'spirit' of an era as precisely as possible. They point directly to its 'core' or 'essence' by highlighting a key trait. Denominations such as 'the Spanish age' or 'the era of the Twenty-Years Crisis'[45] are strong. Strong denominations often operate with the term 'epoch' in order to emphasize the singularity of the respective time span and the relevance of the key trait; the notion has a noble ring and lets the period appear as a quasi-objective time unit. Weak denominations, on the other hand, are intended to remain vague or neutral. They do not 'characterize' the period and avoid prejudices about the facts included therein. They abstain from ambitious abstractions. Denominations such as 'the late Middle Age' and 'antiquity' are examples of colourless denominations. Similarly, a denomination such as 'the period between 1815 and 1914' can be called weak. Precise dates in periodizations are mostly meant as symbols for changes of epochs and should not be understood literally.[46]

The advantages and disadvantages of both concepts have to be balanced. Strong denominations make it easier to see the 'big picture'. They facilitate intellectual orientation in unknown territory by providing interpretive schemes. The essence of a period labelled 'the Spanish age' seems more or less clear. Strong denominations provide fast insights and thereby support the organization of one's knowledge. The disadvantage, however, is that they tend to develop an independent dynamic in their own right. They often depart from the facts which had originally provided the period with its name.[47] Strong denominations are not open to ambiguities and

---

[44] *Vergangene Zukunft* (n 33) 33.
[45] Named after the classical work by EH Carr *The Twenty Years Crisis* (Macmillan London 1939).
[46] 'Das achtzehnte Jahrhundert als Beginn der Neuzeit' (n 20) 269.
[47] 'Renaissance' (n 10) 453.

multifaceted phenomena and elevate a particular aspect of a period to become the representative of the whole. Any denomination which is understood too literally becomes an obstacle to a proper understanding. Weak denominations have the advantage that they facilitate unprejudiced historiographical work. They are less ideological and more open to ambiguities and continuities. However, they do not provide the same *prima facie*-orientation as strong ones do. They are not as effective as 'compasses' in unknown territories. The cultural historian Johan Huizinga recommended weak denominations.[48] He found those denominations the most helpful in practical work, the colourless and unambitious character of which is evident at first sight.[49]

3. Conclusion

The question of periodization belongs to the most fundamental and most underestimated questions of historiography of international law. Periods are more than working tools as which they are often regarded in practice. Periodizations are part of our interpretation of the world and connected to our interests and values. Our socialization and our interests decide in which aspects of the past we are interested in. Periodizations reflect these interests: periodization of the past is therefore always also contemporary history. Attempts to establish new periods are attempts to reshape the present by changing the view of the past and to write a new genealogy of the contemporary world. Periodizations say as much about those who create them as about those who lived in the past. Metaphorically speaking, periodizations always have two masters—the knowledge of the past and the self-perception of the society of the historian which asks about its origins and its own role in history.[50]

Recommended Reading

Craven, Matthew, Malgosia Fitzmaurice, and Maria Vogiatzi (eds) *Time, History and International Law* (Martinus Nijhoff Leiden 2007).

---

[48] J Huizinga *Wege der Kulturgeschichte,* (Drei Masken Verlag München 1930) at 76.

[49] Interestingly, Huizinga did not always take his own recommendation seriously: J Huizinga *The Autumn of the Middle Ages* (E Arnold & Co London 1924); original Dutch title: *Herfsttij der middeleeuwen.*

[50] K Schreiner 'Diversitas Temporum' in *Epochenschwelle und Epochenbewusstsein* (n 10) 381–428 at 383.

Grewe, Wilhelm G *Epochen der Völkerrechtsgeschichte* (Nomos Baden-Baden 1984).

Herzog, Reinhart and Reinhart Koselleck (eds) *Epochenschwelle und Epochenbewusstsein* (Wilhelm Fink München 1987).

Hueck, Ingo J 'The Discipline of the History of International Law. New Trends and Methods on the History of International Law' (2001) 3 Journal of the History of International Law 194–217.

Huizinga, Johan *Wege der Kulturgeschichte* (Drei Masken Verlag München 1930).

Kadelbach, Stefan 'Wandel und Kontinuitäten des Völkerrechts und seiner Theorie' (1997) Beiheft 71 Archiv für Rechts- und Sozialphilosophie 178–93.

Koselleck, Reinhart *Vergangene Zukunft. Zur Semantik geschichtlicher Zeiten* (Suhrkamp Frankfurt am Main 1989).

Koskenniemi, Martti 'Why History of International Law?' (2004) 4 Rechtsgeschichte 61–6.

Onuma, Yasuaki 'When Was the Law of International Society Born? An Inquiry of the History of International Law from an Intercivilizational Perspective' (2000) 2 Journal of the History of International Law 1–66.

Osterhammel, Jürgen 'Über die Periodisierung der neueren Geschichte' (2006) 10 Berichte und Abhandlungen der Berlin-Brandenburgischen Akademie der Wissenschaften 45–64.

Paech, Norman 'Epochenwechsel im Völkerrecht? Über die Auswirkungen der jüngsten Kriege auf das UNO-Friedenssystem' (2004) 43 Aus Politik und Zeitgeschichte 21–9.

Preiser, Wolfgang 'Die Epochen der antiken Völkerrechtsgeschichte' (1956) 11 JuristenZeitung 737–44.

Steiger, Heinhard 'Probleme der Völkerrechtsgeschichte' (1987) 26 Der Staat 103–26.

Steiger, Heinhard 'From the International Law of Christianity to the International Law of the World Citizen—Reflections on the Formation of the Epochs of the History of International Law' (2001) 3 Journal of the History of International Law 180–93.

Teschke, Benno *The Myth of 1648. Class, Geopolitics and the Making of Modern International Relations* (Verso London 2003).

Van der Pot, Johan Hendrik Jacob *Sinndeutung und Periodisierung der Geschichte. Eine systematische Übersicht der Theorien und Auffassungen* (Brill Leiden 1999).

Verosta, Stephan 'Regionen und Perioden der Geschichte des Völkerrechts' (1979) 30 Österreichische Zeitschrift für Öffentliches Recht und Völkerrecht 1–21.

CHAPTER 42

THE RECEPTION OF ANCIENT LEGAL THOUGHT IN EARLY MODERN INTERNATIONAL LAW

KAIUS TUORI[*]

1. INTRODUCTION

DURING the early modern humanistic revival of legal science, scholars sought material and inspiration from classical, mostly Roman, sources. Because generally the reception of law or the transfer of elements of one legal culture to another involves changes in the transferred elements as well as the recipient culture, this reception of ancient law was a complex affair in which not only the content of ancient law but also its cultural prestige were employed to further the agenda of the scholars who utilized it. Furthermore, the transferred law, in the way legal transplants operate, was transformed as well.[1]

[*] The author wishes to thank Dr Benjamin Straumann and the editors for their comments.

[1] The reception of Roman law from the Middle Ages onwards in Europe is the most influential example of the reception and use of ancient law. It has been studied extensively, see eg P Stein *Roman Law*

The purpose of this chapter is to explore the reception of ancient law and legal thinking by early modern scholarship on international law,[2] by authors like Alberico Gentili (1552–1608) and Hugo Grotius (1583–1645),[3] who were mainly responsible for the first stage of the reception, and later scholars like Samuel Pufendorf (1632–1694), Cornelius van Bynkershoek (1673–1743), and Christian Wolff (1679–1754).[4]

The issue at hand contains numerous preliminary controversies in need of clarification. The foremost of the issues is whether or not there existed an international law in antiquity which would have been the object of reception in the early modern era. The ancient traditions of international law naturally encompassed much more than the products of the Greco-Roman world,[5] but their later influence has been

in European History (CUP Cambridge 1999); F Wieacker *A History of Private Law in Europe* (OUP Oxford 1995); JQ Whitman *The Legacy of Roman Law in the German Romantic Era* (Princeton University Press Princeton 1990); P Koschaker *Europa und das römisches Recht* (4th edn Beck München 1966).

 [2] R Lesaffer 'Roman Law and the Early Historiography of International Law: Ward, Wheaton, Hosack and Walker' in T Marauhn and H Steiger (eds) *Universality and Continuity in International Law* (Eleven International Publishing The Hague 2011) 149–84; B Straumann *Hugo Grotius und die Antike* (Nomos Baden-Baden 2007); L Winkel 'The Peace Treaties of Westphalia as an Instance of the Reception of Roman Law' in R Lesaffer (ed) *Peace Treaties and International Law in European History* (CUP Cambridge 2004) 222–40; A Nussbaum 'The Significance of Roman Law in the History of International Law'(1952) 100 University of Pennsylvania Law Review 678–87; H Lauterpacht *Private Law Sources and Analogies of International Law* (Longmans, Green and Co London 1927).

 [3] A Gentili *The Wars of the Romans: A Critical Edition and Translation of* De armis romanis (D Lupher trans, B Kingsbury and B Straumann eds) (OUP New York 2010); B Straumann and B Kingsbury (eds) *The Roman Foundations of the Law of Nations: Alberico Gentili and the Justice of Empire* (OUP New York 2010); K Tuori 'Alberico Gentili and the Criticism of Expansion in the Roman Empire. The Invader's Remorse' (2009) 11 Journal of the History of International Law 205–19; D Panizza 'Political Theory and Jurisprudence in Gentili's De iure belli' (2005) 15 International Law and Justice Working Paper; D Panizza *Alberico Gentili, giurista ideologo nell'Inghilterra elisabettiana* (La Garangola Padova 1981); Centro Internazionale Studi Gentiliani, *Alberico Gentili e la dottrina della guerra giusta nella prospettiva di oggi. Atti del Convegno, III Giornata Gentiliana, 17 Settembre 1988* (Giuffré Milano 1991); Centro Internazionale Studi Gentiliani, *Il diritto della guerra e della pace di Alberico Gentili. Atti del Convegno, IV Giornata Gentiliana, 21 Settembre 1991* (Giuffré Milano 1995); GHJ Van der Molen *Alberico Gentili and the Development of International Law* (Leyde 1968); *Hugo Grotius und die Antike* (n 2); F Mühlegger *Hugo Grotius: Ein christlicher Humanist in politischer Verantwortung* (Walter de Gruyter Berlin 2007); CA Stumpf *The Grotian Theology of International Law* (Walter de Gruyter Berlin 2006); R Tuck *The Rights of War and Peace: Political Thought and the International Order from Grotius to Kant* (OUP Oxford 1999); DJ Bederman 'Reception of the Classical Tradition in International Law: Grotius' *De jure belli ac pacis*' (1996) 10 Emory International Law Review 1–50; Y Ōnuma (ed) *A Normative Approach to War: Peace, War, and Justice in Hugo Grotius* (Clarendon Press Oxford 1993); B Kingsbury, H Bull, and A Roberts, *Hugo Grotius and International Relations* (OUP New York 1990); H Vreeland *Hugo Grotius* (Rothman Littleton 1986); C Gellinek *Hugo Grotius* (Twayne Publishers Boston 1983); E Dumbould *The Life and Legal Writings of Hugo Grotius* (University of Oklahoma Press Norman 1969); C van Vollenhoven *The Framework of De iure belli ac pacis* (Noord-Hollandische Uitgeversmaatschappij Amsterdam 1931); WSM Knight *The Life and Works of Hugo Grotius* (Sweet and Maxwell London 1925).

 [4] *The Rights of War and Peace* (n 3); D Hüning (ed) *Naturrecht und Staatstheorie bei Samuel Pufendorf* (Nomos Baden-Baden 2009); A Kinji *Cornelius van Bynkershoek: His Role in the History of International Law* (Kluwer Hague 1998).

 [5] DJ Bederman *International Law in Antiquity* (CUP Cambridge 2001) at 16–47; A Altman 'Tracing the Earliest Recorded Concepts of International Law—The Early Dynastic Period in Southern Mesopotamia'

limited. Greek and Biblical sources were extensively used by scholars in the early modern period, but their impact was less extensive than the influence of Roman law. While the influence of the Greek tradition of international law as manifested in concepts like treaties between sovereign States has seldom been questioned, the same cannot be said of the Roman legal tradition. Though the strong general influence of the Roman legal tradition in the early modern era—be it in general on the European legal traditions, or specifically in the scholarship on international law—is not in doubt, whether or not there was a Roman tradition of international law is debatable.[6] However, within the scholarship on, for example, Stoic influence in international law, strict distinctions between traditions, be they Greek or Roman, are not necessary.[7]

The Romans divided law into *ius civile* and *ius gentium*, in which the first pertained to the citizens of Rome, while the second was law applied to the peregrines in Roman courts. Thus the Roman *ius gentium* was not international law in the current sense but mostly substantive Roman law applied and developed by Roman magistrates with some characteristics resembling private international law.[8] The actual law between nations was originally covered by the Roman law of warfare, the *ius belli* and *ius fetiale*, which governed the relationship between Rome and its allies and enemies.

Two main interpretations have been made of the impact of Roman law in modern international law. The first is that there was a Roman tradition of international law and that there is continuity from the Roman to the modern tradition. The second, currently more widely accepted interpretation is that the ancient Roman legal tradition that was received and influenced the development of international law in the early modern period was the Roman private law tradition. Naturally, whether there are lines of continuity depends also on the definition of international law.[9]

(2004) 6 Journal of the History of International Law 153–72; A Altman 'Tracing the Earliest Recorded Concepts of International Law—(2) The Old Akkadian and Ur III Periods in Mesopotamia' (2005) 7 Journal of the History of International Law 115–36.

[6] C Baldus 'Vestigia pacis. The Roman Peace Treaty: Structure or Event?' in *Roman Law and the Early Historiography of International Law* (n 2) 103–46 at 107–13; K-H Ziegler 'The Influence of Medieval Roman Law' in *Roman Law and the Early Historiography of International Law* (n 2) 147–61; N Grotkamp *Völkerrecht im Prinzipat* (Nomos Baden-Baden 2009); K-H Ziegler 'Zum Völkerrecht in der römischen Antike' in *Iurisprudentia universalis: Festschrift für Theo Mayer-Maly* (Böhlau Köln 2002) 933–44; *International Law in Antiquity* (n 5); C Phillipson *The International Law and Custom of Ancient Greece and Rome* (Macmillan London 1911).

[7] HW Blom and LC Winkel (eds) *Grotius and the Stoa* (Van Gorcum Assen 2004); M von Albrecht 'Fides und Völkerrecht von Livius bis Hugo Grotius' in *Livius, Werke und Rezeption, Festschrift für Erich Burck* (CH Beck München 1983) 295–9; W Preiser 'Die Philosophie der Stoa in ihrer Bedeutung für das moderne Völkerrecht' (1949–50) 38 Archiv für Rechts- und Sozialphilosophie 364–70.

[8] Gaius *Institutiones* 1.1.

[9] *Roman Law and the Early Historiography of International Law* (n 2) 2–5. According to Lesaffer, supporting the non-continuity are *inter alia International Law in Antiquity* (n 5) 4–6 'Significance of Roman Law' (n 2) 681; WG Grewe *The Epochs of International Law* (M Byers trans) (Walter de Gruyter Berlin

The reuse of ancient law in the early modern era was a product of a number of cultural, political, and social factors. The period was defined by religious polarization and the reduction of the intellectual authority of the church. It has been claimed that, for example, Grotius utilized Roman law to develop a denominationally neutral alternative to Christian ethics as a foundation of natural law.[10] There was also a widespread idealization of classical antiquity, classicism, which manifested itself in legal scholarship in the conviction of the superiority of Roman legal science and its use as an example for contemporary jurisprudence.[11]

This chapter will first explore the general influence of classical culture in the emerging international law scholarship. The first issue is the development of the concept of *ius gentium* in the Roman legal tradition and its transformation into the concept of international law as currently understood from Roman sources and early modern scholarship. The second question is the use of the classical cultural and literary tradition. The cultural prestige of classics was significant and the utilization of the classical literature in education was extensive. How much did this lead to the reception of ancient practices and ancient law?

A selection of examples of ancient law transplants and their transformation will be followed through some of the classical works of early modern international law.[12] The selection of three cases reflecting ancient public international law and three cases showing the transfer of private law conceptions is quite arbitrary and aims only to provide glimpses of a very wide and under-studied field. Many interesting themes are left for future research to tackle.

Of the six practical examples of the transmission of ancient law to early modern international law, the first three are of the more traditional law of nations, while the following three are uses of the Roman private law analogies in international law. How were the Roman conceptions of a just war, the sanctity of envoys, and the freedom of the high seas received in the early modern doctrine of international law? How were analogies from Roman private law such as *pacta sunt servanda*, *terra nullius* and *uti possidetis* utilized to create new rules for the changing circumstances of the early modern era? In all of the examples, it is interesting to follow how the rules established through such reception are retained even after references to the ancient precedents are no longer made.

2000) at 9, while W Preiser *Die Völkerrechtsgeschichte* (Franz Steiner Wiesbaden 1964) and K-H Ziegler 'Die römische Gründlagen des europäischen Völkerrechts' (1972) 4 Ius Commune 1–27 are supporters of the continuity.

[10] B Straumann 'Is Modern Liberty Ancient?' (2009) 27 Law and History Review 55–85 at 61; B Straumann '"Ancient Caesarian Lawyers" in a State of Nature: Roman Tradition and Natural Rights in Hugo Grotius' *De iure praedae*' (2006) 34 Political Theory 328–50.

[11] K Tuori *Ancient Roman Lawyers and Modern Legal Ideals* (Klostermann Frankfurt 2007).

[12] The references to early modern scholarship will be in a double format. Where available, a page reference is made to the currently most commonly available English translation, the *Classics of International Law* series (which is also available in many online databases such as HeinOnline), after which a book, chapter, subchapter reference is made to find the corresponding passage in the original Latin.

2. FROM ROMAN TO EARLY MODERN
IUS GENTIUM

2.1. Gaius and the Digest

Already in the Roman sources one may see the transformation of the concept of *ius gentium* from the original Roman understanding of substantive law applied to peregrines to a meaning closer to the idea of the law of nations.[13] Marcus Tullius Cicero (106–43 BC) outlines the division between *ius civile* and *ius gentium* as two overlapping spheres, with the law of nations deriving from nature and the civil law from human society.[14] Although Cicero's conceptions of *ius gentium* and natural law are by no means clear, *ius gentium* is defined as part of unwritten law common to all people.[15]

Gaius' textbook of Roman law, written in the mid-2nd century AD gives a similar definition, but with greater detail:

All peoples who are governed by laws and customs use law which is partly theirs alone and partly shared by all mankind. The law which each people makes for itself is special to itself. It is called 'state law', the law peculiar to that state. But the law which natural reason makes for all mankind is applied in the same way everywhere. It is called 'the law of all peoples' because it is common to every nation. The law of the Roman people is also partly its own and partly common to all mankind. Which parts are which we will explain below.[16]

Gaius' idea of *ius gentium* may be described as very cosmopolitan,[17] while his near contemporary Aulus Gellius also juxtaposes *ius gentium* with natural law.[18]

Ulpian, a jurist writing in the early 3rd century, added natural law as the third component to Cicero's and Gaius' bipartition:

---

[13] 'The Peace Treaties of Westphalia' (n 2) 225; M Kaser *Ius gentium* (Böhlau Köln 1993).

[14] Cicero *De officiis* 3.17.69: 'itaque maiores aliud ius gentium, aliud ius civile esse voluerunt, quod civile, non idem continuo gentium, quod autem gentium, idem civile esse debet.' See also Cicero *De officiis* 3.5.23: 'natura, id est iure gentium'.

[15] Cicero *Tusculanae disputationes* 1.13.30: 'omni autem in re consensio omnium gentium lex naturae putanda est'; Cicero *De partitione oratoria* 37.130: 'Atque haec communia sunt naturae atque legis, sed propria legis et ea quae scripta sunt et ea quae sine litteris aut gentium iure aut maiorum more retinentur.'

[16] Gaius *Institutiones* 1.1: 'Omnes populi, qui legibus et moribus reguntur, partim suo proprio, partim communi omnium hominum iure utuntur: Nam quod quisque populus ipse sibi ius constituit, id ipsius proprium est vocaturque ius civile, quasi ius proprium civitatis; quod vero naturalis ratio inter omnes homines constituit, id apud omnes populos peraeque custoditur vocaturque ius gentium, quasi quo iure omnes gentes utuntur. Populus itaque Romanus partim suo proprio, partim communi omnium hominum iure utitur. Quae singula qualia sint, suis locis proponemus.' Gaius *The Institutes of Gaius* (WM Gordon and OF Robinson trans) (Duckworth London 1988) at 19.

[17] 'The Peace Treaties of Westphalia' (n 2) 225.

[18] A Gellius *Noctes Atticae* 6.3.45: 'quae non iure naturae aut iure gentium fieri prohibentur'.

Private law is tripartite, being derived from principles of *jus naturale, jus gentium*, or *jus civile. Jus gentium*, the law of nations, is that which all human peoples observe. That it is not co-extensive with natural law can be grasped easily, since this latter is common to all animals whereas *jus gentium* is common only to human beings among themselves.[19]

Ulpian specifically names slavery and manumissions as institutions of *ius gentium*,[20] while civil law overlaps with both natural law and *ius gentium* but is special to the Roman people.[21] The Constitutio Antoniniana of AD 212 had in theory made all the inhabitants of the Roman empire citizens, effectively making the old division between *ius civile* and *ius gentium* redundant except in cases involving peregrines outside the empire.

Hermogenian, a jurist in the late 3rd century, gives a very different definition of *ius gentium* in a passage wedged between Ulpian's passages in the Digest:

As a consequence of this *ius gentium*, wars were introduced, nations differentiated, kingdoms founded, properties individuated, estate boundaries settled, buildings put up, and commerce established, including contracts of buying and selling and letting and hiring (except for certain contractual elements established through *jus civile*).[22]

It is possible that this radically different definition is a result of a fundamental change in the understanding of *ius gentium*, but it is also conceivable that it is an extension of earlier practice and that the quotation does not preserve the whole idea. The use of *ius gentium* in the sense of rules applying between nations may be found in the Roman historical literature already in Livy. In legal writings, the second-century AD author Pomponius called the rules regarding envoys *ius gentium*, in accordance with the modern usage.[23]

The new interpretation of *ius gentium* caught on and towards Late Antiquity its definition as the law between nations becomes dominant. Isidore of Seville's (560–636) definition of *ius gentium* is again a heterogeneous list of things that most nations have in common:

The law of nations (*ius gentium*) concerns the occupation of territory, building, fortification, wards, captivities, enslavements, the rights of return, treaties of peace, truces, the pledge not

---

[19] Digest 1.1.1.2: 'Privatum ius tripertitum est: collectum etenim est ex naturalibus praeceptis aut gentium aut civilibus. 4. Ius gentium est, quo gentes humanae utuntur. Quod a naturali recedere facile intellegere licet, quia illud omnibus animalibus, hoc solis hominibus inter se commune sit.' For the English translation, see *The Digest of Justinian* (GEM de Ste Croix trans, A Watson ed) (University of Pennsylvania Press Philadelphia 1985) at 1.

[20] Digest 1.1.4.

[21] Digest 1.1.6: 'Ius civile est, quod neque in totum a naturali vel gentium recedit nec per omnia ei servit: itaque cum aliquid addimus vel detrahimus iuri communi, ius proprium, id est civile efficimus.'

[22] Digest 1.1.5: 'Ex hoc iure gentium introducta bella, discretae gentes, regna condita, dominia distincta, agris termini positi, aedificia collocata, commercium, emptiones venditiones, locationes conductiones, obligationes institutae: exceptis quibusdam quae iure civili introductae sunt.' For the English translation see *Digest of Justinian* (n 19) 2.

[23] Digest 50.7.18(17).

to molest embassies, the prohibition of marriages between different races. And it is called the 'law of nations' because nearly all nations (*gentes*) use it.[24]

The important change in Isidore in contrast to Ulpian is that *ius gentium* is no longer the usages of all nations, but that of almost all nations.[25] Also, contracts between individuals, which were included in Hermogenian's definition, were left out. Ulpian's definition reflected the Stoic ideals of universality and equality, whereas Isidore paves the way for what is the realistic and limited interpretation of *ius gentium* as the practice of civilized nations.

2.2. Medieval Transformations of *Ius Gentium*

It was Isidore's definition that was adopted into church doctrine in the Middle Ages. The *Decretum Gratiani* borrowed extensively from Isidore in its definition of human and natural laws and even incorporated the definition of *ius gentium* in a slightly altered form.[26] Thus Isidore's definition became part of the *Corpus Iuris Canonici*. The fact that Isidore's definition was adopted took place for reasons that are unclear but probably include textual transmission because Late Antique sources were as a rule better known during the Middle Ages.

Aquinas began as well with Isidore's definition, but categorized *ius gentium* under natural law, because natural law was common to all humans whereas *ius gentium* was common only to most nations.[27] Here Aquinas combines Isidore with Cicero, another medieval favourite, as well as with Ulpian.

2.3. *Ius Gentium* in the Early Modern Understanding

The early modern period is marked by two traditions of interpretation, the medieval Scholastic tradition and the new humanistic school of thought, which favoured clas-

---

[24] Isidore of Seville *Etymologiae* 5.6: 'Quid sit ius gentium. Ius gentium est sedium occupatio, aedificatio, munitio, bella, captivitates, servitutes, postliminia, foedera pacis, indutiae, legatorum non violandorum religio, conubia inter alienigenas prohibita. Et inde ius gentium, quia eo iure omnes fere gentes utuntur.' Isidore of Seville *The Etymologies of Isidore of Seville* (SA Barney et al trans, eds) (CUP Cambridge 2006) at 118.

[25] 'The Peace Treaties of Westphalia' (n 2) 226.

[26] *Decretum Gratiani*, Distinctio 1, *c.* 9: 'Quid sit ius gentium. [Isidor. eod. *c.* 6.] Ius gentium est sedium occupatio, edificatio, munitio, bella, captiuitates, seruitutes, postliminia, federa pacis, induciae, legatorum non uiolandorum religio, conubia inter alienigenas prohibita. § 1. Hoc inde ius gentium appellatur, quia eo iure omnes fere gentes utuntur.'

[27] Aquinas *Summa Theologica* 2.1.95.4: 'Videtur quod inconvenienter Isidorus divisionem legum humanarum ponat, sive iuris humani. Sub hoc enim iure comprehendit ius gentium, quod ideo sic nominatur, ut ipse dicit, quia eo omnes fere gentes utuntur. Sed sicut ipse dicit, ius naturale est quod est

sical over Late Antique sources.[28] Vitoria's conception of *ius gentium* has been described as an intermediary stage between natural law and positive law. It was not dependent on municipal law on its validity, but was based on reason and the common conviction of all peoples.[29] Although it is questionable whether Vitoria made a paradigmatic shift from Gaius' international private law to international interstate law, the conscious ambiguity allowed a wide interpretation that encompassed as subjects both States and people within States.[30]

Gentili, starting from the antiquarian position, first pays lip service to the laws of the fetiales, which governed Roman conduct on international treaties, war and peace, and embassies. He then notes that these existed during the earlier period of the Roman State and fetial law all but disappeared during the empire. Thus the search for the sources of the law of nations should be directed elsewhere, and here Gentili traces the definitions of *ius gentium* from the Digest to Baldus, Doneau, Ambrose, St Jerome, and so on. While he recognizes that the common agreement of all nations is the starting point of the law of nations, there is a deeper root than that; namely the innate sense of justice, the instinctive natural desire for justice. As manifestations and sources of this natural justice, sources like the law of Justinian or the Bible are sources of the law of nations. However, it is the community of peoples and its customs which are the most important.[31]

Grotius defined the law of nations as law that gained its validity from the will of all nations or of many nations. The latter limitation Grotius justified with the claim that there was little law outside the law of nature which would apply to literally all nations. The content of the law of nations may be found in the description of the unbroken custom by expert scholars of history.[32]

Winkel claims that the change in the definition of *ius gentium* was fundamental in the reception of Roman private law concepts in the early international law.

---

commune omnium nationum. Ergo ius gentium non continetur sub iure positivo humano, sed magis sub iure naturali. Distinguitur tamen a lege naturali, maxime ab eo quod est omnibus animalibus communis.'

[28] *The Roman Foundations of the Law of Nations* (n 3) 1–18.

[29] F de Vitoria 'Relectio de Indis' (JB Scott trans) in JB Scott (ed) *The Spanish Origin of International Law* (Clarendon Press Oxford 1934) Appendix A, at xxxvi (3.1); A Pagden and J Lawrance 'Introduction' in A Pagden and J Lawrance (eds) *Francisco de Vitoria, Political Writings* (CUP Cambridge) xv–xvi.

[30] For an overview of the discussion, see R Lesaffer 'The Grotian Tradition Revisited: Change and Continuity in the History of International Law' (2002) 73 British Year Book of International Law 103–39 at 124.

[31] A Gentili *De jure belli* (JC Rolfe trans) in JB Scott (ed) *The Classics of International Law* (Clarendon Press Oxford 1933) vol 2, at 5, 8, 10–11 (book 1, ch 1 pt 5, 10–11, 14–17); B Straumann 'The corpus iuris as a Source of Law Between Sovereigns in Alberico Gentili's Thought' in *The Roman Foundations of the Law of Nations* (n 3) 101–23.

[32] H Grotius *De jure belli ac pacis libri tres* (FW Kelsey trans) in JB Scott (ed) *The Classics of International Law* (Clarendon Press Oxford 1925) vol 2, at 44 (book 1, ch 1, pt 14).

The influence of Grotius and of the Westphalian peace treaties is crucial in this transformation, which is parallel to the general reception of Roman law in legal scholarship.[33]

Earlier, Nussbaum had traced the evolution of the concept of *ius gentium* from Roman municipal law to international law (in itself a term coined only by Bentham in 1789) to Suarez and Hobbes, in which the first would have distinguished two meanings of *ius gentium,* universal law and international law, whilst the latter used *ius gentium* exclusively for international relations.[34]

The decline of the importance of a classical pedigree is evident in the nascent natural law scholarship. Pufendorf questioned the existence of a law of nations separate from natural law. While he acknowledges that there was a Roman *ius gentium* which dealt with the rights of non-citizens in Rome, the law of nations which applies between peoples and nations is only a segment of natural law.[35]

Along with the traditions of natural law scholarship, Wolff dispensed with the niceties of presenting a lineage from the classical tradition and refers only to Grotius and himself. He divided *ius gentium* into four kinds: voluntary, that is, law which arises from universal consensus; stipulative, or law deriving from pacts between nations; customary, or law based on long usage; and, finally, positive law originating from the will of nations.[36]

3. The use of the Classical Tradition in Early Modern International Law Scholarship

3.1. Gentili

The omnipresence of the classical world in early modern scholarship on international law is a fact easily established by a simple look at any of the works of the major scholars of the era.[37] For example, a passage in Gentili's *De jure belli* on religion

---

[33] 'The Peace Treaties of Westphalia' (n 2) 237.

[34] 'Significance of Roman Law' (n 2) 682.

[35] S Pufendorf *De jure naturae et gentium libri octo* (CH Oldfather and WA Oldfather trans) in JB Scott (ed) *The Classics of International Law* (Clarendon Press Oxford 1934) at 226–7 (book 2, ch 3, 23).

[36] C Wolff *Jus gentium methodo scientifica pertractatum* (JH Drake trans) in JB Scott (ed) *The Classics of International Law* (Clarendon Press Oxford 1934) vol 2, at 17–19 (paras 22–6).

[37] See the contribution by M Scattola 'Alberico Gentili (1552–1608)' in this volume.

invokes medieval historical figures Dagobert and the Frisians and Charles the Great and the Saracens, but inexplicably moves to Biblical Judith and Holofernes in the next sentence, to ancient history's Cambyses in the following, then to Antiochus, and finally to the Roman Emperor Elagabalus.[38] For Gentili, the ancient world was a storehouse of examples of human conduct and even though Biblical and more contemporary examples abound, the Greek and especially Roman examples are closest to his heart. For example, when he writes how barbarians may be treated more harshly in war than civilized peoples, the Roman example of crushing the barbarians while winning the civilized over with kindness is mentioned first and only corroborated with Ambrose reminding how Moses had spared not one of the Midianites.[39]

Though not a classicist like many of his scholastic contemporaries, Gentili used the corpus of classical literature extensively and usually quoted their opinions with approval. Unlike some later scholars such as Grotius, Gentili eagerly compared ancient and modern policies and courses of action. For example, on the thorny issue of whether a ruler may resort to war to maintain religion among his subjects, Gentili starts down the road of Biblical, Greek, and Roman examples, but dispenses with them early on and gets to the issue regarding Luther and his followers. Though Roman examples are repeatedly cited in favour of religious tolerance and harmony, the argument is aimed at contemporaries. Here the Roman world is mentioned both for its tolerance and intolerance, as is the Turkish realm and Austria.[40] In his *De armis romanis* Gentili addresses the issue of Roman examples and exemplarity for the international law and demonstrates how classical material may be used to argue both sides of an issue.[41]

3.2. Grotius

Grotius' familiarity with the classical literature was profound. An astute classical philologist, he published translations, commentaries, and other works on *inter alia* Lucan, Plutarch, Euripides, Tacitus, and Seneca.[42] Even though posterity remembers him as a legal scholar, he wrote theological treatises, historical works, poetry, political tracts as well as several collections of letters. How this immense knowledge is put to use varies tremendously from text to text and subject matter. For example, when discussing the obligations of kings, he refers to Vásquez and Suarez on the division between the actions of a king as a king and the actions of a king as a normal person, whereas in the next chapter, when he discusses how the king is bound by the law of

---

[38] De Jure Belli (n 31) 340 (book 3, ch 11, pt 555).
[39] ibid (n 31) 293 (book 3, ch 2, pt 478).
[40] ibid (n 31) 42–8 (book 1, ch 10, pt 66–78).
[41] *The Wars of the Romans* (n 3); 'Alberico Gentili and the Criticism of Expansion' (n 3).
[42] See the contribution by P Haggenmacher 'Hugo Grotius (1583–1645)' in this volume.

nature and not municipal law, the references are to Justinian's *Digest* and the *Code* and Baldus' commentary on them.[43] Then again, in *De jure belli ac pacis* numerous chapters are specifically devoted to how an issue is dealt with in Hebraic law or Roman law.

Besides Grotius' background as a humanist lawyer, Straumann separates four reasons for Grotius' use of the Roman law tradition. First, Grotius wanted to provide a secular, denominationally neutral natural law not based on Biblical tradition. Second, Roman law had developed a ready doctrine for the freedom of the seas. Third, Roman sources tended to support imperialism, which could be used to justify Dutch expansion. Finally, there were advanced contract law remedies in the Roman *ius gentium* which were not limited to Roman citizens. Grotius' theory of subjective natural rights was thus fundamentally founded on the Roman tradition, not on medieval scholars.[44] Grotius was of course not limited to using the Roman tradition; his usage was more instrumental in that he always sought support for his constructions wherever he could find it.[45]

3.3. Pufendorf and Wolff

Pufendorf's reliance on the classical world is strong yet not as pervasive as in the case of Gentili or Grotius.[46] Classical literature continues to supply most of the examples and *bon mots*, but the theoretical framework is that of early modern legal and philosophical scholarship. For example, the theory that all men are naturally equal is supported by statements by ancient authors like Statius, Seneca, Vergil, Cicero, Diodorus Siculus, Quintilian, and Euripides, but the argument itself is aimed at Thomas Hobbes and Michel de Montaigne.[47]

Wolff's relationship to the classical world is very different from the earlier authors as is evident from the almost complete lack of references to classical sources and materials.[48] For example, in the *Jus gentium* almost the only use of classical material is a description of the Roman practice of declaring war.[49] It has been argued that while Gentili and Grotius relied extensively on Roman jurists not as authoritative figures but as evidence, the main figures of the natural law school, Wolff and Vattel, were not familiar in Roman law, which led to its waning influence in international law.[50]

---

[43] *De jure belli ac pacis libri tres* (n 32) 383 (book 2, ch 14, pt 5–6); R Tuck *Philosophy and Government* (CUP Cambridge 1993) at 155.

[44] 'Is Modern Liberty Ancient?' (n 10) 59–60, 62–3.

[45] 'Reception of the Classical Tradition in International Law' (n 3) 4, 29.

[46] See the contribution by K Haakonssen 'Samuel Pufendorf (1632–1694)' in this volume.

[47] *De jure naturae et gentium libri octo* (n 35) 330–2 (book 3, ch 2, pt 1–2).

[48] See the contribution by K Haakonssen 'Christian Wolff (1679–1754)' in this volume.

[49] *Jus gentium methodo scientifica pertractatum* (n 36) 365 (para 707).

[50] 'Significance of Roman Law' (n 2) 686.

4. Law of Nations: Just War, Sanctity of Envoys, and the Freedom of the High Seas

4.1. Just War

The clearest description of the Roman just war (*bellum iustum*) tradition may be found in Cicero's account of the *ius fetiale*. The procedure was formulated like a trial in court, in which the Romans first presented their demands (*rerum repetitio*) in which the injuries suffered by the Romans and their claims to reparations were presented to the opposing side. A *denuntiatio*, or notification of the possibility of war, was issued thirty days later, followed by an *indictio*, a declaration of war. It should be noted that the historical accuracy of the procedure is controversial and it was used only during the Early Republic.[51]

Elsewhere, Cicero frequently defends self-help and self-defence as lawful, right, and just. In *Pro Milone* he famously justifies self-defence as self-preservation when other remedies are not available.[52] In the *Digest of Justinian*, Florentinus maintains that *ius gentium* gives the right to defend against injury with violence.[53]

In the medieval and Scholastic tradition, one of the key issues was whether a Christian could partake in war and under what conditions could a war be justified. The latter issue, when war was justified, was also a prime consideration for Vitoria and other Spanish writers of the period.[54] The theme of a just war was also a central preoccupation in early modern scholarship.

Gentili's eclectic collection of sources makes it quite difficult to deduce whether he is actually following any particular precedent when describing the preconditions of a just war, which he divides into divine, natural, and human reasons. For example, regarding the question whether religion may be a cause for a just war, Gentili cites the almost unanimous approval of ancient and contemporary authorities as well as the continuing practice of waging war on religious grounds, but finally takes a swift turn towards religious tolerance. Gentili claims that while it is lawful to wage war against those who disturb the public peace within the State, to wage war against people in

---

[51] Cicero *De officiis* 1.36; Cicero *De re publica* 2.31, 3.35; Livy 1.32.5–14. See 'Is Modern Liberty Ancient?' (n 10) 349 on the debates. Recently, Ando has argued that the *ius fetiale* was an Augustan construction, see C Ando 'Empire and the Laws of War: A Roman Archaeology' in *The Roman Foundations of the Law of Nations* (n 3) 30–52.

[52] Cicero *Pro Milone* s 10.

[53] Dig 1.1.3: 'ut uim atque iniuriam propulsemus: nam iure hoc euenit, ut quod quisque ob tutelam corporis sui fecerit, iure fecisse existimetur, et cum inter nos cognitionem quandam natura constituit, consequens est hominem homini insidiari nefas esse.'

[54] *Spanish Origin of International Law* (n 29) 200–1; JD Tooke *The Just War in Aquinas and Grotius* (SPCK London 1965); JA Fernández-Santamaria *The State, War and Peace: Spanish Political Thought in the Renaissance 1516–1559* (CUP Cambridge 1977).

other countries whose religious practices or way of living is no imminent threat to you is in no case just.[55]

Gentili employs a similar line of reasoning with regards to pre-emptive strikes, following the line of argument of Roman private law which demanded a just cause for fear and allowed a suitable precaution to be taken, if such was present. Someone may not be punished for just the desire to do harm, but for Romans the imminent danger of someone both possessing the will and the means to do harm justified action, as in the case of Caesar acting against Ariovistus in Gaul when the latter had gained too much strength.[56] In *De armis romanis*, Gentili operates within the Roman tradition of a just war, both attacking and defending the actions of the Romans by using the contradictory Roman sources that defend and criticize imperial expansion.[57]

Grotius proceeds in *De iure belli ac pacis* first to prove that war is permissible under certain circumstances under the law of nature and the law of nations. Only in book II does he treat the just causes of war: the defence of self, property, of what is owed out of contract, and what is owed out of delict. Here, Grotius follows at length the Roman argumentation, because the Romans took great pains in examining the just causes for war. Quoting Livy, he mentions that the Romans thought that their wars were victorious only as long as they were just. However, Grotius also mentions the contrary Roman tradition of criticism of the slaughter and cruelty of wars as a contradiction of the aim of society to limit murder, as formulated by Seneca. Grotius compares the just causes for war to the just causes for a lawsuit: defence, obtaining what is owed and inflicting punishment. Thus he identifies the just causes of war with the *iniuriae* of Roman private law. He refers also to the Roman tradition of fetial law and its practice of *rerum repetitio*, the demands that were made before hostilities commenced. Contrary to the claims of Gentili, Grotius would rather prohibit than allow a pre-emptive strike against a would-be attacker. Here Grotius, though he refers to the same Roman and Greek sources, lays more weight on medieval and early modern authors to produce an opposite interpretation.[58]

When Grotius deals later with the unjust causes for war, a special mention is reserved on one unjust cause, namely of the title of universal empire claimed by the Church. The refutation of the claim of universal empire is backed with purely theological arguments.[59]

---

[55] *De Jure Belli* (n 31) 40 (book 1, ch 9, p 66).

[56] ibid (n 31) 62–6 (book 1, ch 14, p 99–107).

[57] 'Alberico Gentili and the Criticism of Expansion' (n 3); *The Wars of the Romans* (n 3). The Spanish had employed a similar double use of the Roman tradition in the debates over the justification of colonial expansion, see D Lupher *Romans in a New World* (University of Michigan Press Ann Arbor 2003).

[58] *De jure belli ac pacis libri tres* (n 32) 169–75 (book 2, ch 1, pt 1–5); 'Is Modern Liberty Ancient?' (n 10) 338–41; *Just War in Aquinas and Grotius* (n 54) 195–230.

[59] *De jure belli ac pacis libri tres* (n 32) 553–4 (book 2, ch 22, pt 14).

The use of classical precedents and lines of argumentation diminishes with later authors, as does the preoccupation with the issue of a just war. For example, Bynkershoek does not consider the question of a just war at all.[60] His book on war goes straight to the point of whether a declaration of war is needed and what kind of actions are permitted in war. The answer to the first question is that it would be nice, as the Romans did issue such declarations, but not necessary, and to the second question the answer was that every act of force is lawful in war, even though the Romans preferred not to use fraud.[61]

However, the substantive doctrine continues without dramatic changes. Pufendorf claimed that whilst war must be the last resort, one may use force against an attacker and to force the payment of something owed.[62] Wolff's concept of a just cause for war is defined as a response to a wrong done or anticipated.[63]

4.2. Sanctity of Envoys

The Classical Roman jurist Pomponius clearly expressed the concept of the sanctity of ambassadors:

If someone strikes an ambassador of the enemy, he is regarded as having acted against the law of nations, because ambassadors are regarded as sacred.[64]

Pomponius further quotes Quintus Mucius in that whoever strikes an ambassador should be surrendered to the enemy.

In his book on embassies, Gentili notes how the sanctity of envoys was underlined by both Greeks and Romans with examples ranging from Cicero to the Roman jurists presented. However, when the general principle is applied in practice, a more nuanced picture appears and it bears less similarity to the blanket statements presented by ancient authors. Thus spurious embassies, embassies sent by brigands, and other exceptions to the rule are discussed extensively, while the whole argumentation is based on classical sources.[65]

---

[60] See the contribution by K Akashi 'Cornelius van Bynkershoek (1673–1743)' in this volume.

[61] C Bynkershoek, *Quaestionum juris publici libri duo* (T Frank trans) in JB Scott (ed) *The Classics of International Law* (Clarendon Press Oxford 1930) at 15–20 (book 1, chs 1–2).

[62] *De jure naturae et gentium libri octo* (n 35) 386 (book 3, ch 4,6).

[63] *Jus gentium methodo scientifica pertractatum* (n 36) 314–15 (para 617).

[64] Dig 50.7.18(17): 'Si quis legatum hostium pulsasset, contra ius gentium id commissum esse existimatur, quia sancti habentur legati. Et ideo si, cum legati apud nos essent gentis alicuius, bellum cum eis indictum sit, responsum est liberos eos manere: id enim iuri gentium convenit esse. Itaque eum, qui legatum pulsasset, Quintus Mucius dedi hostibus, quorum erant legati, solitus est respondere.' For the English translation see M Crawford in *Digest of Justinian* (n 19). Similarly on the protection of ambassadors and the punishment of violators, Ulpian Digest 48.6.7.

[65] A Gentili *De legationibus libri tres* (OUP New York 1924) 57–8 (book 2, ch 1).

Grotius wrote how the sanctity of envoys was already held to be an inviolable rule of the law of nations among the Romans. Quoting the opinions of Pomponius (Dig 50.7.18) and Ulpian (Dig 48.6.7) from the *Digest of Justinian*, and other examples from Roman historians of the classical period and late Antiquity, Grotius holds that the ancients were nearly unanimous on the sanctity of ambassadors. The rights of ambassadors, as demonstrated by the practice of the ancients, included the right to be admitted and not to be harmed. Of the ancient examples, only in cases where there was an intense hatred or dislike of the people sending ambassadors were these rights not honoured.[66]

Bynkershoek acknowledged the theoretical rights of ambassadors sent by sovereign powers, but notes that such rights were commonly violated; for example, during the Dutch war of independence from Spain. While the Dutch claimed that Spain had violated the sanctity of ambassadors by murdering their envoys, Bynkershoek maintained that actually the Spanish were fully within their rights in killing them because they represented not a sovereign power but a group of rebels. Even the Romans had acted similarly.[67]

Wolff also stoutly defends the sanctity of ambassadors and their immunity from all kinds of violations. This sanctity is for Wolff not a result of a conscious decision or some classical precedent but rather the law of all nations derived from God himself.[68]

4.3. Freedom of the High Seas

One of the important issues for early modern international law scholars was the freedom of the seas. The medieval legal doctrine, confirmed by papal bulls, was clearly against the idea of the freedom of the seas. Both Gentili and Grotius used Roman law doctrine (*Institutes of Justinian* 1.1) to argue that no one could claim exclusive rights or ownership to the sea, and such arguments were then used in diplomatic correspondence of Britain with Spain, and the Dutch with the Portuguese government.[69]

Grotius argues that ownership of the seas would require exclusive possession and such ownership is impossible because nobody can occupy the sea. Furthermore, one may not claim exclusive rights to something that is by its nature not exclusive. Grotius' convoluted definition of non-exclusive is that if something, while serving someone, may serve someone else without limiting the use of the first one, is by nature not to be held exclusively. As Roman jurists stated, such things are by nature common.[70]

---

[66] *De jure belli ac pacis libri tres* (n 32) 438–41 (book 2, ch 18, pt 1–3)
[67] *Quaestionum juris publici libri duo* (n 61) 156–7 (book 2, ch 3).
[68] *Jus gentium methodo scientifica pertractatum* (n 36) 539 (para 1065).
[69] See 'Significance of Roman Law' (n 2) 683–4.
[70] H Grotius *The Freedom of the Seas* (OUP New York 1916) at 26–7 (ch 5); Digest 7.4.13 and 41.1.14.

5. Roman Private Law Analogies

5.1. *Pacta Sunt Servanda*

Though *pacta sunt servanda* is one of the most famous phrases of the Roman law tradition, the expression itself is not Roman but was coined by Grotius. Despite the fact that consensual contracts of Roman law, for example, the contract of sale (*emptio venditio*), were free of forms, they had to meet the legal definition in order to be enforceable.[71] It has been claimed that the roots of the doctrine in international law should be sought from the Canon law tradition which was also a universally accepted and applied system of law in Europe prior to the Reformation.[72]

On the obligations arising from promises, Grotius follows the arguments of Roman jurists in that contractual obligations should be honoured. The central component in the argument is the concept of good faith, which holds that one should keep one's promises to one another. Thus even the Roman jurist Paul maintains that the law of nations demands that if one has promised to pay then one ought to pay, there arising a moral obligation to pay.[73] Never mind that Paul was actually referring to Roman substantive law, after Grotius, *pacta sunt servanda* was accepted as a basic rule of natural law.[74]

Lesaffer has claimed that the European order after 1660 and the rise of sovereign powers could only function if the rule of *pacta sunt servanda* was commonly accepted as the basis of the validity of treaties. They were seen as belonging to natural law and enforceable by force if necessary and to transcend the will of the States themselves.[75] Pufendorf even goes so far as to claim that if someone intentionally fails to fulfil a legally binding pact that is a just cause for war.[76]

Bynkershoek notes that honouring contracts belongs to the realm of civil law and is dependent on good faith, but his classical references are not to Roman jurists. He claims that all agree that good faith would require that international treaties should be followed, but quotes Seneca in noting that good faith is rarely observed when it is not expedient. States are not legally bound by treaties and their observance of treaties depends on whether or not it is against the interests of the State. There is an ethical obligation, but no legally enforceable one.[77]

---

[71] D Johnston *Roman Law in Context* (CUP Cambridge 1999) at 77–84.

[72] R Lesaffer 'The Medieval Canon Law of Contract and Early Modern Treaty Law' (2000) 2 Journal of the History of International Law 178–98.

[73] *De jure belli ac pacis libri tres* (n 32) 329 (book 2, ch 11,1,4).

[74] 'Medieval Canon Law' (n 72) 181–2.

[75] 'Grotian Tradition Revisited' (n 30) 131.

[76] *De jure naturae et gentium libri octo* (n 35) 441 (book 3, ch 7,9).

[77] *Quaestionum juris publici libri duo* (n 61) 190–1 (book 2, ch 10).

Though Wolff again makes no mention of classical precedents, he holds that the good faith of treaties is sacred. Thus the inviolability of treaties and the inviolability of good faith may not be separated.[78]

5.2. *Terra Nullius*

Roman law demanded that a thing acquired by occupation be *res nullius*, that is, not somebody else's property.[79] Ownership of such a thing could be acquired by capturing it; for instance, it might refer to wild animals. However, should such an animal escape, or, to quote one of the issues troubling Roman jurists, the bees not return to their hive, any ownership gained by capture would be lost. The same rule would apply to booty: things captured from the enemy become our property by occupation and should we lose them we also lose ownership over them.[80] The doctrine was adopted in international law under the name *terra nullius*,[81] though in practice the adopted form was more an analogy and reinterpretation of the Roman doctrine, used with other elements as a part of imperial policies of legitimating possession.[82]

Although the property or other rights of peoples following different religions were not always fully recognized, to say the least, Vitoria supported the claim of Aquinas that religious matters have no bearing on the title of ownership or sovereignty. Aquinas stated that even infidels are the masters of their own property and relieving them of it would be theft.[83] Thus in the case of the Spanish expansion in America, relieving the natives of their possessions could not be legal.[84]

Grotius notes that Roman jurists held that according to the law of nations one could only acquire property by occupation (*occupatio*) if it belonged to no one. In the *De jure belli ac pacis*, the discussion on the matter of ownerless things related mostly to wild animals, alluvial deposits forming new islands, and old islands disappearing by inundation, which was of course a matter of some importance in the Netherlands.[85] However, the matter was a tad more pressing in the *Mare liberum*, where the

---

[78] *Jus gentium methodo scientifica pertractatum* (n 36) 282 (para 550).

[79] See also the contributions by D Khan 'Territory and Boundaries' and by M Craven 'Colonization and Domination' in this volume.

[80] Gaius 2.66–9, similarly Digest 41.2.1.1 and 41.1.5.7: 'Item quae ex hostibus capiuntur, iure gentium statim capientium fiunt'; Digest 41.1.1.1 on the rules deriving from *ius gentium*.

[81] R Lesaffer 'Argument from Roman Law in Current International Law: Occupation and Acquisitive Prescription' (2005) 16 The European Journal of International Law 25–58 at 45. B Straumann criticizes in 'Is Modern Liberty Ancient?' (n 10) 78 Lesaffer's view of Roman law not accepting occupation as a mode of acquisition as too limited.

[82] L Benton and B Straumann 'Acquiring Empire by Law: From Roman Doctrine to Early Modern European Practice' (2010) 28 Law and History Review 1–38.

[83] 'Relectio de Indis' (n 29) v–ix, xi (s 1, sub-ss 4–7, 19); Summa Theologica 2.2. q 10, a 12.

[84] 'Acquiring Empire by Law' (n 82) 22–3 *et passim*.

[85] *De jure belli ac pacis libri tres* (n 32) 296–296 (book 2, ch 8, 1).

issue was the ownership of indigenous lands outside Europe. Following Roman law doctrine, Grotius claimed that the Portuguese could be owners by discovery only if the territories were *res nullius*. Since Portugal could neither claim to be the first to discover the new territories nor that they had possession of them, then their claims for exclusive rights by sovereignty were unfounded.[86]

Another widely circulated theory was that of original common property, which claimed that there were no ownerless things but only things in which ownership had not been individualized. For example, Pufendorf rejects Hobbes' theory of first occupation and claims that there was an original common ownership.[87] But regarding the occupation of uninhabited lands, the occupation may only extend to as much land as the occupants may use and defend. Should someone claim an entire island which would support an untold number of inhabitants based on very limited use, this claim would be invalid.[88]

Wolff followed the doctrine of *res nullius* of ownership following from occupation, but notes that it would follow from the will of the nation whether ownership was created. He mentions that the Romans had made a specific law regarding the presumption favouring occupation, but the presumption is also natural and thus in accordance to natural law. The right of occupation of uninhabited lands belongs to all nations indiscriminately. Here Wolff again refers to the Roman practice of establishing colonies.[89] Typical of natural law scholarship, Wolff has a habit of mentioning that institutions originating from Roman law such as *usucapio* belong to natural law.[90]

5.3. *Uti Possidetis*

The origins of the *uti possidetis* doctrine are to be found in the Roman law *interdictum uti possidetis*, which was part of *ius civile*.[91] It was a legal remedy available to Roman citizens against disturbance in possession before and during court proceedings in which the use of force against the current possession was forbidden.[92]

The international law doctrine of *uti possidetis* was only formulated during the early 17th century, and it has been claimed that the peace treaties of Westphalia were the first to cite the doctrine in State practice. Grotius maintained that rights to immovable property taken in war require firm possession, meaning that the area is

---

[86] *Freedom of the Seas* (n 70) 13 (ch 2); *Philosophy and Government* (n 43) 176–9.

[87] *De jure naturae et gentium libri octo* (n 35) 338 (book 3, ch 2,5).

[88] ibid 386 (book 4, ch 6,3–4).

[89] *Jus gentium methodo scientifica pertractatum* (n 36) 142–3, 147–8 (paras 280, 291).

[90] ibid 184–5 (paras 358).

[91] See also the contributions by D Khan 'Territory and Boundaries' and by M Craven 'Colonization and Domination' in this volume.

[92] Gaius 4.160: 'uti nunc possidetis, qui minus ita possideatis, vim fieri veto' 'The Peace Treaties of Westphalia' (n 2) 229–30.

fortified in such a way that a credible defence is possible. [93] In one of the peace treaties of Westphalia, the Treaty of Münster between Spain and the Dutch Republic, the principle of *uti possidetis* was explicitly adopted for the demarcation of territories between the parties. Each side would remain effectively in possession and enjoyment of the territory they held at the time.[94]

Pufendorf mentions that Roman law includes property rights to things acquired from an enemy by occupancy, the *res nullius* rule. However, he notes that ownership of things taken from their owners in war acquires full validity only when claims to them are renounced when making peace.[95]

Bynkershoek confirms the doctrine of *uti possidetis* and follows the opinion of Paul in the *Digest* (Dig 41.2.3) on the extent of the possession: if a part is occupied then the whole is also occupied if that is the intention of the captor, even though Celsus (Dig 41.2.18.4) disagrees.[96]

Again, making no references to classical material, Wolff defends the ownership and sovereignty of nations in that no nation may expel another from the territory it occupies. The law of nations protects the rights and ownership of nations as well as individuals.[97]

6. Conclusion

The reception of ancient international law in the early modern era was part of a general reception of ancient, mostly Roman, law in the period. Like the reception of ancient law in general, there were various reasons for this reception: classical precedents were invoked to utilize the cultural prestige of the ancient world and guidance was sought from the technical rules of Roman private law which was perceived to have almost universal validity.

What was received was not necessarily the rules of ancient international law but the rules of Roman private law adapted to the context of international law. It is currently a matter of some debate whether there actually was a Roman system of international law in the first place. Because early modern scholarship used, for example,

---

[93] *De jure belli ac pacis libri tres* (n 32) 667 (book 3, ch 6,4).
[94] 'The Peace Treaties of Westphalia' (n 2) 230–1.
[95] *De jure naturae et gentium libri octo* (n 35) 584–5 (book 4, ch 4,14).
[96] *Quaestionum juris publici libri duo* (n 61) 44–5 (book 1, ch 6).
[97] *Jus gentium methodo scientifica pertractatum* (n 36) 144 (para 282).

Greek philosophical theories on natural law extensively, the actual relevance of the issue of the existence of ancient international law is slight.

This chapter examined ancient influences on early modern international law through several viewpoints: first, the transformation of the concept of *ius gentium* and, second, the use of the classical literary tradition as examples and context, and, finally, through six examples, the transmission of ancient Roman legal rules to the early modern doctrine of international law.

Ius gentium was originally a concept of Roman substantive law, that is, the law that was applied to peregrines or resident non-citizens. During the imperial period, the extension of citizenship made this interpretation redundant and *ius gentium* was increasingly understood as the law between nations. This interpretation, while it had been present, albeit marginally, even in the 1st century AD, gained prominence in late antiquity, from which it was picked up by medieval canon law scholarship. Antiquarian early modern legal scholarship returned to classical sources, but retained the view that *ius gentium* was law that was accepted by most nations and sources to it could be found everywhere from the Bible to the *Code of Justinian*. This conception was changed only by its justification by the nascent natural law scholarship, which kept the rules while dispensing with the classical references.

The use of the classical literary tradition in early modern scholarship was both extensive and eclectic. Gentili and Grotius were intimately familiar with ancient history and literature and used them as a storehouse of examples with which to illustrate and justify rules and interpretations. They clearly recognized that the expressed rules of Roman law only convey half the story and thus they quote ancient historians and philosophers to shed light on ancient practice. Classical examples were practical because they were free of the baggage that religious material had during a time of extreme controversy among the Christian churches. The examples also gave ample support for the endeavours of trading empires such as freedom of trade, imperialism and expansion. However, classical examples also gave support for the criticism of empire.

The reception of the Roman law doctrine of international law was followed through three examples: a just war, the sanctity of envoys, and the freedom of the high seas. The Roman conception of a just war was a complicated affair, but subsequent scholarship mostly adopted the right to self-defence. This right was interpreted widely where need arose, for example when justifying military expansion, and narrowly where needed, for example, denying the right to attack nations who professed a different faith. The sanctity of envoys was a clear rule of Roman law that was confirmed in several instances. It was adopted by early modern scholars, who proceeded to develop a number of exceptions to the general rule. Although the freedom of the seas was for the Romans a rule of private law, it was interpreted as a rule of sovereignty or the lack of it over the high seas, and helped to overturn the long-standing doctrine to the contrary.

The reinterpretation of Roman private law analogies to the new international law doctrine was explored in three examples: the *pacta sunt servanda* rule, the concept of *terra nullius,* and the *uti possidetis* doctrine. *Pacta sunt servanda*, a principle that a contract was generally valid and enforceable, was not a rule of classical Roman law, which demanded that contracts had to meet a number of definitions to be enforceable. Grotius adopted another Roman concept, good faith, and claimed that contractual obligations should be honoured because of the presence of a moral obligation. The Roman law rule of *res nullius,* which stated that one gained ownership to an ownerless thing through occupation, was transformed in international law to the rule of *terra nullius.* The idea of *terra nullius* was used both to support claims to sovereignty to discovered lands during the period of European expansion and conversely to deny sovereignty because of existing indigenous title. The case of *uti possidetis* was a more creative adaptation because the original rule was part of the *ius civile*, the law applicable only to Roman citizens. During the early modern period, both Grotius in scholarship and the emerging State practice led to the interpretation that after armed conflict, concrete possession became the rule of demarcation between parties.

In most of the cases of the adoption of Roman legal rules, the trend has been that only the first generation of receivers such as Gentili and Grotius referred to the sources of the rule in ancient law. Later scholars showed a diminishing interest in the origins of the doctrine and referred mostly to the first generation of scholars.

Recommended Reading

Bederman, David J 'Reception of the Classical Tradition in International Law: Grotius' *De jure belli ac pacis*' (1996) 10 Emory International Law Review 1–50.

Benton, Lauren and Benjamin Straumann 'Acquiring Empire by Law: From Roman Doctrine to Early Modern European Practice' (2010) 28 Law and History Review 1–38.

Lauterpacht, Hersch *Private Law Sources and Analogies of International Law* (Longmans, Green and Co. London 1927).

R Lesaffer 'Roman Law and the Early Historiography of International Law: Ward, Wheaton, Hosack and Walker' in T Marauhn and H Steiger (eds) *Universality and Continuity in International Law* (Eleven International Publishing The Hague 2011).

Nussbaum, Arthur 'The Significance of Roman Law in the History of International Law' (1952) 100 University of Pennsylvania Law Review 678–87.

Straumann, Benjamin '"Ancient Caesarian Lawyers" in a State of Nature: Roman Tradition and Natural Rights in Hugo Grotius's De iure praedae' (2006) 34 Political Theory 328–50.

Straumann, Benjamin *Hugo Grotius und die Antike* (Nomos Baden-Baden 2007).

Straumann, Benjamin and Benedict Kingsbury (eds) *The Roman Foundations of the Law of Nations: Alberico Gentili and the Justice of Empire* (OUP New York 2010).

Winkel, Laurens 'Les origines antiques de l'appetitus societatis de Grotius' (2000) 68 Legal History Review 393–403.

Winkel, Laurens 'The Peace Treaties of Westphalia as an Instance of the Reception of Roman Law' in Randall Lesaffer (ed) *Peace Treaties and International Law in European History* (CUP Cambridge 2004) 222–40.

CHAPTER 43

EUROCENTRISM IN THE HISTORY OF INTERNATIONAL LAW

ARNULF BECKER LORCA

1. INTRODUCTION

HISTORIANS of international law, before embarking on the task of writing, face a number of choices regarding the definition of their subject: is the history of international law a history of rules, or legal ideas, is it about sovereign states or international lawyers? Given that international law involves rules, States, lawyers, and sovereigns interacting across the globe, there is another methodological choice that the historian faces: should a history of international law be written from a Western point of view, from the standpoint of the centre of the international world? Or should a historical narrative consider also international law in the peripheries of the world?

Traditionally, the history of international law has been deeply Eurocentric.[1] Centred in the West mainstream histories have defined borders: from Grotius to

---

[1] Martti Koskenniemi has recently described the Eurocentric nature of the history of international law: 'Europe served as the origin, engine and *telos* of historical knowledge.' M Koskenniemi 'Histories of International Law: Dealing with Eurocentrism' (2011) 19 Rechtsgeschichte 152–76 at 158.

Lauterpacht, from the Thirty Years War, to the World Wars, from the Treaty of West-phalia, to the League of Nations and the United Nations.[2] But what is the problem with Eurocentrism?

Most international lawyers consider, for instance, the Treaty of Westphalia of 1648 to have been the foundational moment that defined international law's central *prob-lématique* as that of governing the interaction between autonomous sovereigns. International lawyers writing history thus have to explain, for example, the emer-gence of the European inter-state system simply because the Treaty of Westphalia was concluded in Münster and Osnabrück. This history is Eurocentric. It recounts a story from a Western standpoint. But this is not a problem as such, for writing history always entails the production of a perspective from which to include and interpret relevant material and exclude material that is regarded irrelevant to explain the past.

However, there is a problem if a Eurocentric perspective generates a distortion in the historical narrative. A distortion that overemphasizes the centrality of Western contexts of practice—including authors, ideas, and events—and underemphasizes the practice of international law outside the West.[3] Identifying a Eurocentric distor-tion is difficult. It requires constructing a non-Eurocentric reading of international law's origin and development that diverges from conventional narratives. At the same time, as a plausible reading of the past, a divergent narrative also converges and over-laps with the Western history of international law.

A history of international law centred in the West can be narrow, dull, and ethno-centric. Although only if this historical narrative acquires political relevance, if it is understood to perform an ideological function—universalizing and legitimizing the particular Western standpoint—can international lawyers devote energy to produce a divergent narrative and reveal a Eurocentric distortion. This chapter explores two moments in the intellectual history of international law in which some, mostly non-Western, international lawyers, have dealt with the problem of Eurocentrism by producing divergent narratives exposing a distortion in conventional histories of international law.

First, between roughly the 1950s and the 1980s, the claim that international law had an exclusive European nature and origin was questioned by international lawyers writing histories showing the universal nature and plural origins of international law. Second, between roughly the 1980s and the 2000s, conventional histories with a strong narrative of progress asserting international law's promotion of goals such as

---

[2] Among others, German historian Wolfgang Preiser, in a book where he sets out to study the history of non-Western legal orders, states: 'Up to now, the history of international law has been predominantly preoccupied with the law that in the European world developed into an interstate order, and that from there has, since the beginning of modern times, expanded over the world.' W Preiser *Frühe völkerrechtliche Ordnungen der außereuropäischen Welt: Ein Beitrag zur Geschichte des Völkerrechts* (F. Steiner, Wiesbaden 1976) at 7. Non-European international legal orders are only considered relevant if they came into con-tact with the European world. ibid 8.

[3] For the idea of Eurocentrism as a distortion, see S Amin *Eurocentrism* (Monthly Review Press New York 1989) at vi–viii.

peace, trade, and human rights, were questioned by scholars showing a link between international law and colonialism.

2. A SHORT INTELLECTUAL HISTORY OF INTERNATIONAL LAW AND THE RISE OF EUROCENTRISM

The rise of the problem of Eurocentrism in the history of international law presupposes the geographic universality of international law. Only if international law has a universal scope of validity, only if there are Western and non-Western contexts of practice, can the question regarding the geopolitical standpoint from which to centre a historical narrative become relevant. If, on the other hand, the Western nature of international law circumscribes its history within the Western world, we may describe this type of history as ethnocentric or parochial rather than Eurocentric, in the sense that it fails to recognize the existence of other regional inter-state regimes beyond the West. Thus, historians of international law routinely face questions that are crucial for recognizing the rise of Eurocentrism. When and how did the contemporary international legal order, an order with a global scope of validity, become universal? Is Europe the place where contemporary international law originated?

Historians who understand international law to be a system of legal rules governing the interaction between relatively autonomous and equal entities, have explored international law before modern times, both inside and outside the West, and in some instances have included interactions between Western and non-Western polities.[4] When, and if, these authors decided to examine the historical roots of modern international law, they generally supplement the definition of international law as rules with ideas about a more developed rule-of-law system, about secularism, or about the commitment to fairness and formal equality.

Most historians believe that international law, as law governing inter-state relations under formal equality, was first European and that it then globalized. During the 19th century, some non-European polities were admitted to the international

---

[4] Historians of international law have identified a number of legal regimes, which between approximately the 5th century BCE and the 19th century have governed interactions between semi-autonomous polities in different regions of the world. Among others see *Frühe völkerrechtliche Ordnungen* (n 2) and D Bederman *International Law in Antiquity* (CUP Cambridge 2001).

community, understood as a family of 'civilized' nations. During the 1960s, decolonization transformed international law into a global order governing an inclusive international community. After decolonization, a transnational profession emerged, including non-Western internationalists who could make use of international law, engage in the discipline's central debates, and produce academic writings, among these, histories of international law.

Many aspects of the abovementioned narrative, which establishes a clear trajectory from a European to a universal international law, became contested when international lawyers from newly independent nations irrupted into the international scene. In 1961, for example, JJG Syatauw, a young scholar from Indonesia who would later become a renowned international lawyer, disputed the European nature of international law. Syatauw criticized jurists who insist that modern international law 'was conceived in the state practice of European nations of the 16th and 17th centuries and that Asian nations could not possibly have contributed', for historians have regarded this idea as a 'colossal distortion'.[5]

As international law expanded, locating the geopolitical standpoint from which to narrate its history became a relevant question. But the problem of Eurocentrism emerged only in the 1960s with the 'universalization' of the discipline of international law, when non-Western lawyers like Syatauw exposed a historical distortion and offered a divergent narrative that—discontent with 'a Europe-centric point of view'—looks at the history of international law 'through Asian eyes'.[6]

Histories of international law had been certainly written before the 1960s and before international law became universal. One may expect histories of international law, which began to appear at the end of the 18th century, to have been naturally centred within the West, for they explored the past of a regional, namely European, legal order. For example, the *History of the Law of Peoples* (1764) by the German scholar Friedrich Karl Moser, or the *History of the Law of Nations* (1795) by the English scholar Robert Ward were in fact histories of European law.[7] But later on, others like Belgian François Laurent, following an encyclopaedic approach, were less interested in establishing the specific role of the European tradition than in giving an account of the history of humanity as a whole, including the non-Western world.[8]

---

[5] JJG Syatauw *Some Newly Established Asian States and the Development of International Law* (Martinus Nijhoff The Hague 1961) at 29–30.

[6] Moreover Syatauw asks his hypothetical jurist: 'How much direct connection is there between these historical errors and modern international law?' The answer is: 'Very much indeed.' ibid 29.

[7] Eg 'When we speak of the Law of Nations, we mean only the Nations of our own Set, that is, of Europe' R Ward *An Enquiry into the Foundation and History of the Law of Nations in Europe, from the Time of the Greeks and Romans, to the Age of Grotius* (Butterworth London 1795) at 162 (original emphasis). FC von Moser *Beyträge zu dem Staats und Völker-Recht und der Geschichte* (JC Gebhard Franckfurt 1764).

[8] Laurent's history was published in various volumes, the first dedicated to the 'Orient' F Laurent *Histoire du droit des gens et des relations internationales L'Orient* (Durand Paris 1851).

It is only much later, when non-European States began to be admitted to the international community as sovereigns, that the question about historical origins emerged clearly. Overemphasizing Western contexts of practice to produce a Eurocentric history is a fairly recent practice. Only late in the 19th century, Belgian international lawyer Ernst Nys affirmed the European origin of international law, an idea that crystallized at the beginning of the 20th century, for instance, in Oppenheim's *International Law, A Treatise* 1905. Before that, the idea of an exclusive European origin was, for example, neither present in Bluntschli who recognizes the beginnings of the law of people, among others, in the old civilized peoples of Asia, nor in Holtzendorff who locates the beginnings of the history of the world, coinciding with the establishment of inter-state relations, in the Orient.[9]

Eurocentric histories appeared at the time when some non-European states were admitted into the international community and when some members of non-Western elites had become professional lawyers-diplomats. A first generation of non-Western international lawyers wrote textbooks (including historical introductions) and general histories of international law, but they did not produce divergent narratives exposing a Eurocentric distortion. Rather than challenging the conventional narrative about the Western origin of international law, authors like Argentinean Carlos Calvo and Estonian/Russian Fedor Martens included their nations as part of the familiar European history of international law. I have elsewhere shown how non-Western international lawyers appropriated classical international law. Writing a history in which the Russian Empire or Latin American nations appeared in a Western history of international law was part of the effort to show that these states had met the standard of civilization and that they belonged within the family of civilized nations.[10]

During the first decades of the 20th century, a new generation of internationalists from non-European States that had been admitted to the international community realized that classical international law conferred much less autonomy and equality than they had anticipated. Rejecting their predecessor's strategy of internalizing classical international law they advocated for the dissolution of the standard of civilization and the coexistence of regional legal orders within a modern and cosmopolitan international law.[11] The approach to historical writing followed by these non-Western lawyers changed. For example, Alejandro Alvarez, a Chilean legal scholar, ICJ judge and the most vocal advocate of regional particularism, defended

[9] E Nys *Les origines du droit international* (Castaigne Bruxelle 1894); L Oppenheim *International Law, A Treatise* (2 vols 1st edn Longmans Green London 1905); JC Bluntschli *Das moderne Völkerrecht der civilisirten Staten* (CH Beck Nördlingen 1872) at 12 ff; Franz Holtzendorff *Handbuch des Völkerrechts: Auf Grundlage europäischer Staatspraxis* (Habel Berlin 1885) 157–392.

[10] See A Becker Lorca 'Universal International Law: Nineteenth Century Histories of Imposition and Appropriation' (2010) 51 Harvard Journal of International Law 475–552 and A Becker Lorca *Mestizo International Law: A Global Intellectual History 1850–1950* (CUP Cambridge 2012).

[11] I develop this argument in A Becker Lorca 'Sovereignty beyond the West. The End of Classical International Law' (2011) 13 Journal of the History of International Law 7–73 and *Mestizo International Law* (n 10).

the idea of a 'Latin American international law' in part through a historical narrative about the region's distinctiveness.[12] Histories of Chinese, Japanese, Indian, Islamic, or Latin American international law were not written to become part of the universal history of international law and thus were not intended to correct the conventional Western history. Foregrounding cultural, political, or religious particularities, these histories supported distinctive and to some extent diverging regional international legal orders.[13]

This regionalist trend in the intellectual history of international law faded away after the Second World War, because on the one hand, it became identified with Nazi, fascist, and nationalist doctrines of international law. On the other hand, striving to reconstruct the international legal order after the Great War, international lawyers, throughout the Western and non-Western world, rediscovered the universal language of international rules and rights and rejected the regionalism of the inter-war period. Now that international law was again considered a universal language with a global scope of validity, the question of the standpoint from where to write history remerged. But now that the international legal profession had become more transnational, the problem of Eurocentrism emerged for the first time as a disciplinary debate between Western and non-Western international lawyers.

3. CHALLENGING THE WESTERN ORIGIN AND NATURE OF INTERNATIONAL LAW, 1950s–1980s

The first problem Eurocentrism imposes on the writing of history, namely, the distortion produced when overemphasizing Western contexts of practice to assert the Western origin and nature of international law, was exposed by histories written from a 'universal' standpoint. The disciplinary controversy that emerged in the 1950s over the origin and nature of international law reflected the deep transformations the international legal order experienced during the first half of the 20th century.

---

[12] A Alvarez *Le droit international américain, son fondement, sa nature, d'après l'histoire diplomatique des états du Nouveau Monde et leur vie politique et économique* (Pédone Paris 1910).

[13] See eg P Bandyopadhyay *International Law and Custom in Ancient India* (University Press Calcutta 1920); SV Viṣvanātha *International Law in Ancient India* (Longmans Bombay 1925); M Khadduri 'Islam and the Modern Law of Nations' (1956) 50 American Journal of International Law 358–72; N Armanazi *L'Islam et le droit international* (Picart Paris 1929); T Ch'eng 'International Law in Early China 1122–249 B.C.' (1927) 11 Chinese Social and Political Science Review 38–55 and 251–70 at 44; S Takahashi 'Le droit international dans l'histoire du Japon' (1901) 3 Revue de Droit International et de Legislation Comparée 188–201.

The principle of self-determination, which had irrupted into the international arena at the end of the First World War, but failed to be applied in favour of most non-Western peoples subjected to either colonial rule or unequal treatment, reappeared, after the Second World War, as a right detached from the standard of civilization and complemented by a formal—rather than substantive—doctrine of recognition.[14] These changes signified a radical transformation of international law, from an order recognizing realms of sovereign equality and realms of inequality, to an inclusive order governing relations between sovereign nations. Decolonization, now supported by international law, brought not only new independent States into the international community, but also a new generation of non-Western lawyers eager to participate in an increasingly transnational profession and to contribute to the construction of a more just international order.[15] These transformations changed both the meaning and significance of the history of international law as well as the goals and interests pursued by the international lawyer writing history.

For most European lawyers, writing history became a vehicle to reaffirm international law's Western nature, a way to avoid losing control over, and at times critique, the expansion of international law. Conversely, non-Western lawyers believed that writing inclusive histories would seal the admission of their nations into the international community. A history including non-Western international legal orders became the type of history required by a universal international law.

3.1. Finding a European Origin after the Universalization of International Law

European international lawyers represented the expansion of international law as a quantitative change involving an increase of the States that had been admitted to the international community. Affirming the quantitative character of the expansion allowed European scholars to claim that regardless of the admission of non-Western nations, international law remained firmly entrenched in Western civilization.[16] A historical narrative about Western origins became central to the claim of the Western nature of international law. Oppenheim's *International Law, A Treatise*, one of the

---

[14] *Mestizo International Law* (n 10).

[15] Eg 'the challenges of the time requires [international law] to show itself capable of adaptation and expansion, in order to enable it to fulfil its destiny.' TO Elias 'Expanding Frontiers of Public International Law' in W Jenks (ed) *International Law in a Changing World* (Oceana New York 1963) 97–104 at 103.

[16] Wilhelm G Grewe eg argues that in spite of the expansion, international law remained at its essential core an order of Western Christianity. WG Grewe 'Vom europäischen zum universellen Völkerrecht' (1982) 42 Zeitschrift für ausländisches öffentliches Recht und Völkerrecht 449–79; see in general WG Grewe *Epochen der Völkerrechtsgeschichte* (Nomos Baden-Baden 1988) ch 2, pt 4, at 541 ff.

most influential treatises in the English-speaking world, for example, opens the first 1905 edition with a definition of international law, adding immediately in the paragraph that follows that in its origin, international law is 'essentially a product of Christian civilisation'.[17]

Oppenheim received the conventional wisdom of the 19th century that took the standard of civilization as the doctrine determining membership in the Family of Nations.[18] In the later editions, we see new nations being admitted, the standard of civilization being eroded, and international law becoming universal.[19] But the Western origin is continuously reaffirmed: 'International Law as a law between sovereign and equal States based on the common consent of these States is a product of Christian civilisation, and may be said to be hardly four hundred years old'.[20]

Defending international law's Western origin was not a monopoly of conservative outliers like Carl Schmitt, who considered international law to have been born out of the European inter-state system. Schmitt was only unique in that rather than voicing the claim of European origin to defend the Western nature of an international law turned universal, he bitterly resented that universalization entailed not simply a geographical expansion, but the radical transformation of the *Ius Publicum Europaeum*, into the 'spaceless universalism' of a liberal international legal order that no longer differentiated between Western and non-Western States.[21] Conversely, a committed internationalist of the stature of Dutch international lawyer and legal historian JHW Verzijl, for example, claimed international law to be an exclusive product of the 'European mind'.[22] A universal international law, according to Verzijl, continued to be Western not only because of its origin, but also because the absence of any substantive non-Western contribution to its development.[23] This was the commonsensical mid-20th century view, shared by Western international lawyers

[17] *International Law, A Treatise* (n 9) vol 1 at 2.

[18] ibid 31.

[19] In the 7th edition, prepared by Hersch Lauterpacht in 1948, the treatise affirms that '[r]eligion and the controversial test of degree of civilization have ceased to be, as such, a condition of recognition of the membership of the "Family of Nations".' L Oppenheim *International Law, A Treatise* (7th edn Longmans Green London 1948) vol 1, at 47.

[20] *International Law, A Treatise* (n 9) (1st edn) vol 1, 48; this phrase survived many editions: *International Law, A Treatise* (n 19) (7th edn) vol 1, 68

[21] C Schmitt 'Die Auflösung der europäischen Ordnung im "International Law" (1890–1939)' in C Schmitt (ed) *Staat, Großraum, Nomos. Arbeiten aus den Jahren 1916–1969* (Duncker & Humblot Berlin 1995) 372–87; and generally C Schmitt *Der Nomos der Erde im Völkerrecht des Jus Publicum Europaeum: Im Völkerrecht des Jus Publicum Europaeum* (Duncker & Humblot Berlin 1988) at 111–86.

[22] '[T]he actual body of international law…is not only the product of the conscious activity of the European mind, but has also drawn its vital essence from a common source of European beliefs, and in both of these aspects it is mainly of Western European origin.' JHW Verzijl *International Law in Historical Perspective* (Sijthoff Leyden 1968) at 435–6.

[23] '[N]o extra-European nation made any essential contribution [to the development of modern international law]…resemblances…are fortuitous…' ibid 446.

ranging from the conservative, to the liberal internationalist, and the follower of sociological jurisprudence.[24]

The expansion of international law became for many Western international lawyers a source of apprehension.[25] After the admission of non-Western nations, the privileged position bestowed upon Western sovereigns could be lost (Schmitt), international law's content could be diluted (Stone, Verzijl), and the international order's capacity to harmonize differences between States that share a common cultural substratum could be undermined (Visscher, Jennings).[26] Writing a historical narrative centred in the West was one of Western lawyers' defence mechanisms. Non-Western internationalists, on the other hand, understood the universalization of international law to be a hard-fought victory that had to be secured, in part through a historical narrative challenging the centrality of the West.[27]

3.2. Disputing the European Origin to Universalize International Law

Well aware of the importance that the writing of history had acquired, Indian scholar RP Anand, a prominent figure in the Third World Approaches to International Law (TWAIL) movement, offered a forthright critique of Eurocentrism. In an article published in 1983, Anand displays the central insights he and other scholars had advocated over more than two decades to challenge conventional histories of international law.[28] Anand starts out arguing that law grows slowly to meet the needs of the community that it governs. Fulfilling the 'essential needs of men organized in

---

[24] Stone, an advocate of sociological jurisprudence, believed that the expansion of international law brought 'a continuous dilution of its content, as it is reinterpreted for the benefit of newcomers'. J Stone *Quest for Survival: The Role of Law and Foreign Policy* (Harvard University Press Cambridge 1961) at 88.

[25] A Verdross thought that it is dangerous that new States that never belonged to the Christian-European culture represent legal attitudes that diverge from the Western concept of law. A Verdross *Völkerrecht* (Springer Wien 1950) at 39ff.

[26] C de Visscher believed that the expansion of international law weakened the unity of the international community. C de Visscher *Théories et réalités en droit international public* (Pedone Paris 1953) at 182; RY Jennings 'Universal International Law in a Multicultural World' in M Bos and I Brownlie (eds) *Liber amicorum for the Rt. Hon. Lord Wilberforce* (Clarendon Press Oxford 1987) 39–51 at 40–1.

[27] Eg 'For the newly independent states, sovereignty is the hard won prize of their long struggle for emancipation' G Abi-Saab 'The Newly Independent States and the Rules of International Law' (1962) 8 Howard Law Journal 95–121 at 103.

[28] In this article Anand explicitly uses the term Eurocentrism to refer to the reduction of international law's scope of application during the transition from the laws of people based on natural law to an international law based on positivism and the standard of civilization. RP Anand 'The Influence of History on the Literature of International Law' in RStJ MacDonald and DM Johnston (eds) *The Structure and Process of International Law: Essays in Legal Philosophy, Doctrine, and Theory* (Martinus Nijhoff The Hague 1983) 341–80 at 352.

separate communities', international law provides stability. In addition to organic historical growth, Anand believes that law emerges out of the struggle between conflicting demands for change. Law is flexible, it adapts to new challenges, and it reflects people's struggles to 'obtain principles of law for the achievement of ever-growing purposes'.[29] On the basis of the double nature of law, as a force securing stability and striving for change, Anand discovers a universal history of international law beyond the West and determines the direction of international law's historical development towards a more just and inclusive legal order.

On the one hand, pointing out that interactions between a particular group of sovereigns does not explain the origin of international law, but rather the necessity to give stability and predictability to these interactions, Anand describes international law as a universal phenomenon. Each time one can recognize autonomous political organizations regulated by legal rules, one can retrieve a universal history stretching far back in time and in many directions: 'There is little doubt that in some form or another, rules of inter-state conduct or what we now call international law can be traced to some of the most ancient civilizations, like China, India, Egypt and Assyria'.[30]

Conventional history's first vice is, as a result, to believe that international law is exclusively Western. Anand states this idea choosing a form of wording that reads like a direct (though not acknowledged) answer to Oppenheim's treatise:

It is not...correct to assume that international law has developed only during the last four or five hundred years and only in Europe, or that Christian civilization has enjoyed a monopoly in regard to prescription of rules to govern inter-state conduct.[31]

Anand was well aware of the conventional view affirming that non-Western international orders were not legal, since they were pre-modern orderings enmeshed in a religious world view, and that they did not influence the modern European inter-state system. A Western law of peoples based on Christian theology and natural law—Anand mentions in passing—was no more secular than any of the coexisting non-European inter-state orders. Anand then directly disputes the idea of international law's pure European origin.

Before Western colonial expansion, before the emergence of a world order with Europe at its centre—Anand insists—the European inter-state system was a regional order, coexisting and in some cases interacting with other regional orders. For example, between the 16th and the 18th centuries, inter-state relations between Europe and Asia were regulated by laws that were understood to have universal applicability and that recognized equality. These legal interactions are important not just because they show that basic principles of international law, such as freedom of the seas and diplomatic immunity, had validity beyond the West, but also because they

---

[29] ibid 341–2. Anand is aware of bringing Savigny and Jhering together.
[30] ibid 342.   [31] ibid.

influenced the Western legal tradition. Anand is emphatic: 'the influence of Asian maritime practices and freedoms of navigation and trade, on Grotius and even other "founders" of European international law, has been generally ignored by jurists'.[32]

Anand's 1983 article exemplifies the divergences between Western and non-Westerns histories. Anand uncovers a Eurocentric distortion affecting two of the central claims advanced by Western authors: that international law is a uniquely Western phenomenon, and that international law developed without significant non-Western influences, that it has pure European origins. Anand's article shows also how the Eurocentric distortion is revealed through the construction of two alternative historical narratives: universal histories of international law and histories of international law's plural origins.

3.2.1. *Universal Histories of International Law*

In 1972, before becoming a judge and later president of the ICJ, Nigerian scholar Taslim Olawale Elias published *Africa and the Development of International Law*. Elias opens his book as follows: 'If we are to grasp something of the significance of Africa in current international affairs, we must begin with a brief account of the role which different parts of the so-called Dark Continent played since recorded history in their internal as well as external relations'.[33]

Elias traces this history far back to ancient times. Beginning with Carthage and mentioning Herodotus' account of the 'silent trade' between Carthaginians and a Northern African tribe comes as no surprise, for this is a story that highlights the universal nature of international law: wherever there are interactions between autonomous polities, there are rules governing and making these interactions safe and predictable.[34] Elias uses Carthage to 'africanize' the conventional narrative about origins because Carthage already has a place in history.[35] Bringing Africa back into international law's historical map reveals a forgotten inter-state practice. Trade routes going northwards, from Western African goldfields across the Sahara and to the Mediterranean Sea, connected various empires and kingdoms. Trade in luxuries was followed by more complex commercial and diplomatic exchanges between medieval African sovereigns, such

---

[32] ibid 347 quoting Alexandrowicz's work.

[33] TO Elias *Africa and the Development of International Law* (2nd edn Martinus Nijhoff Dordrecht 1988) at 3; on the work of TO Elias see also the contribution by JT Gathii 'Africa in the History of International Law' in this volume.

[34] 'Silent trade' is described as follows: Carthaginians would arrive to African shores, leave goods on the beach and send a smoke signal; locals would inspect the goods and leave a pile of gold in exchange and retrieve; Carthaginians would take the gold and leave if satisfied, otherwise the operation would be repeated until reaching agreement on the exchange. Whereas *International Law, A Treatise* (n 9) vol 1, 49 invokes ancient Greece to underscore the idea that common interests and aims bind States together in a community governed by law, *Africa and the Development of International Law* (n 33) invokes ancient Africa.

[35] See eg K Strupp *Urkunden zur Geschichte des Völkerrechts* (Perthes Gotha 1911) (starting the collection with a treaty between Rome and Cartage); for a contemporary example, S Neff 'A Short History of International Law' in M Evans (ed) *International Law* (3rd edn OUP Oxford 2009).

as Ghana, the Mali Empire, or the kingdom of Songhai, and between them and European and Asian merchants and sovereigns.[36]

A history written on the basis of the universality of international law rediscovers the histories of 'silent trade', the histories of non-Western empires and kingdoms interacting through law. Yet, as European scholars had pointed out, if the existence of functionally equivalent inter-state orders beyond the West does not alter the fact of the European nature of its doctrinal apparatus, the Western nature of international law remains intact. African scholars, however, retrieved a universal history to uncover not only 'silent trade,' but also a 'silent contribution' to the doctrinal development of international law. Even though the encounter between European and African peoples transformed international law, this doctrinal transformation –Ghanaian scholar AK Mesah-Brown points out– was 'Euro-centered,' it did not recognize any African contribution: 'Africa did not produce any Suarez, Grotius or Zouche.'[37] Regardless of this Eurocentrism, Mesah-Brown reaffirms Africa's silent contribution:

To say that African did not contributed actively or personally towards the development of the doctrine of the law of nations does not preclude the consideration that the indigenous policies within the continent, whatever their phases of development, had some knowledge of, or ever practised in the spirit of, some law governing interstate relations, which was strikingly similar to, if not identical with, the law governing interstate relations in Europe.[38]

Mesah-Brown thus sees Africa's place in the history of international law not to be reduced to having had rules governing interactions between sovereigns, but its historical contribution lies 'in the state practices which were aimed at the promotion of peaceful interstate relations'. While the Western tradition had given too much relevance to sovereignty, the African tradition could help to rebalance international law'.[39]

Although 'international law-in-the-books' was of European creation—Mensah-Brown continues—'international law-in-action' on which the former depends, emerged from both European and African State practice, practices that to a great extent were the same, and therefore facilitated, much later but before the colonial period, striving Euro-African relations.[40]

Elias, for instance, concludes the historical review at the beginning of his book with a list of inter-state relations extending beyond the continent, including not only treaties—'alliances of attack and defence between the Kings of Ghana and

---

[36] *Africa and the Development of International Law* (n 33) 15.

[37] AK Mesah-Brown 'Notes on International Law and Pre-colonial History of Modern Ghana' in K Mensah-Brown (ed) *African International Legal History* (UN Institute for Training and Research New York 1975) 107–24 at 109.

[38] ibid.

[39] ibid. See also *Africa and the Development of International Law* (n 33) 45 and *Some Newly Established Asian States* (n 5).

[40] This State practice included law of war rules, limited right of conquest, right of passage, rules of admission and treatment of aliens, rules regulating treaty making and alliances. See 'Notes on International Law' (n 37) 109 and 123.

Mali and that of Morocco over the centuries'—and diplomatic exchanges—
'between the King of Portugal and of Benin...and Congo in the 15th century', and
between 'African courts and those of Spain, Egypt and most of Asia'. But he also
includes legal scholars. Elias refers to Ibn Battuta, an Islamic legal scholar from
Morocco who during his world adventures reached Delhi in 1333 and was appointed
Qadi.[41]

These examples of inter-state practice support Elias' central conclusion that 'a universal body of principles of African customary law' existed, a body of laws 'not essentially dissimilar to the broad principles of European law'.[42]

This is however not a history book. Beyond the historical introduction, Elias' book
reads instead as a textbook covering a variety of international law themes from an
African perspective. Reviewing international law's non-European history to demonstrate the universality of certain elements of both non-European as well as European
international legal orders was brought into play with the purpose of reforming an
international law perceived to be Eurocentric even after decolonization. Producing a
historical narrative dating back to pre-colonial Africa gave new African States an
independent history, and offered new international lawyers from Africa a position
from which to critique international law in their own right: 'The way is thus clear for
the emergent States of Africa today to be willing and ready to enter into new international relationships with other States, without feeling too much like strangers in the
international community'.[43]

Not feeling like strangers would allow Africans to break away from the 'narrow
limits set for it by the older few,' in the direction of an international law 'based on a
wider consensus,' based on the 'principal legal systems and cultures of the world'.[44]
This is the central difference between Elias and someone like Wolfgang Preiser, one of
the few European historians who had concluded that European international law was
a regional order coexisting with several other international legal orders developing
independently from each other.[45] Elias' historical survey is followed by a call for
greater Third World participation, to contribute to the growth of international law,
both in 'quantity and quality'. In relation to the former, to make room for new States,
Elias for example supports enlarging membership of UN bodies such as the Security
Council and ECOSOC, and praises the selection of ICJ judges from Africa and Asia.
Furthermore, to tackle the special needs and aspirations of the new members, Elias
advocates widening the scope and function of existing UN organs as well as establishing new UN organs (like UNDP). In relation to a qualitative transformation, He

---

[41] *Africa and the Development of International Law* (n 33) 5 and 42.
[42] ibid 43.
[43] ibid 45.
[44] ibid 33.
[45] *Frühe völkerrechtliche Ordnungen* (n 2) see conclusions, esp 184.

recounts the efforts to redefine the content of the prohibition to use force, to include under 'force', economic, and political pressures, and concludes: 'The Third World and the Soviet bloc say "Yes," but the Western bloc say "No".'[46]

Universal histories created a discursive platform from which to justify a selective inclusion and exclusion of what was believed to be part of universal international law, in both the European and non-Western traditions: self-determination, yes; the standard of civilization, no.[47] Writing universal histories became a way to legislate, for example, a way to dispute the validity of customary rules that had emerged without the consent of newly independent States.[48]

However, some international lawyers, especially non-Western scholars of the generation that followed the first TWAIL movement, were highly critical of the project of finding universal histories. Yasuaki Onuma, for example, described these as 'we too had international law' histories, which fell into the trap of Western universalism.[49] But the universal histories reviewed here did not express a conceptual or ideological commitment to Western universality. As Indian scholar BS Chimni has suggested, writing universal histories was part of 'an effort to produce universal international law'.[50] Joseph-Marie Bipoun-Woum from Cameroon, for example, produced a historical narrative that reclaims an African juridical consciousness to argue that general international law should be adjusted according to the demands imposed by a regional African international law.[51]

Works recovering histories of international law in different regions of Africa, China, or India proliferated between the 1950s and the 1980s. After independence, during the 1950s, Indian international lawyers began to produce work that first showed the existence of international law in ancient India and then leapt into independent India's use of international law and contribution to its development. Joseph

---

[46] *Africa and the Development of International Law* (n 33) 56 and 58 ff.

[47] Abi-Saab eg directly examines the attitudes of newly independent States towards the rules of international law and 'if existing rules of international law meet the needs of the newly independent states' because the question about their legal personality in pre-colonial times has been demonstrated. 'The Newly Independent States' (n 27) 97.

[48] Eg GI Tunkin *Theory of International Law* (W Butler trans) (Harvard University Press Cambridge 1974) at 28–9 and 123–33; T Wang 'The Third World and International Law' in *The Structure and Process of International Law* (n 28) 955; SP Sinha 'Perspective of the Newly Independent States on the Binding Quality of International Law' (1965) 14 The International and Comparative Law Quarterly 121–31 at 128; and generally RP Anand *New States and International Law* (Vikas Delhi 1972).

[49] Y Onuma 'When Was the Law of International Society Born?—An Inquiry of the History of International Law from an Intercivilizational Perspective' (2000) 2 Journal of the History of International Law 1–66 at 61.

[50] BS Chimni 'The Past, Present and Future of International Law: A Critical Third World Approach' (2007) 8 Melbourne Journal of International Law 499–516 at 502.

[51] J-M Bipoun-Woum *Le droit international africain: Problèmes généraux, règlement des conflits* (Librairie générale de droit et de jurisprudence Paris 1970) at 47, 57, and 132 ff.

Chacko's exploration of India's ancient past, for instance, is followed by a survey of the application of international law by Indian courts after independence.[52]

In the 1960s, Syatauw, for example, clarifies in the historical section of his book that before colonialism, Asian States had 'such degree of international organization and external relations that they were–*in fact*–considered states and treated accordingly by their contemporary world'.[53] Then, in the conclusions, Syatauw argues that after decolonization Asian States have contributed to the development of international law, especially in the fields of decolonization, self-determination, neutralism, and peaceful coexistence.[54] By the 1970s, this mode of writing the history of international law outside Europe by connecting the pre-colonial past with the post-colonial present had become a very common genre among those in the non-Western world who had become professional international lawyers and were beginning to occupy prominent positions in the profession's international circles.

In addition to Elias, one might recall other scholars who later became ICJ judges, like Singh, Ranjeva, and Wang. Nagendra Singh, an Indian scholar, member of the International Law Commission and later appointed judge and President of the ICJ, published a history of international law in ancient India.[55] A young Raymond Ranjeva, a scholar from Madagascar, argues in 1972 that before colonization, the Malagasy Monarchy had achieved statehood and had established international legal relations with European and Indian sovereigns. International relations lasted until the 19th century. Interrupted by colonialism, the history of international law resumed after decolonization.[56] Finally, well into the 1980s, when Wang Tieya, the most prominent Chinese international lawyer of the People's Republic, then unknown to Western readers, was invited for the first time to a conference in the West, he chose as the theme for his debut at The Hague: 'China and International Law, a Historical Perspective'.[57]

3.2.2. *International Law's Plural Histories*

One of the objectives behind writing universal histories was to uncover functional equivalences between international legal orders across the globe. Another goal was, on the basis of these equivalences, to discover concrete interactions between sovereigns from Africa, Asia, and Europe. After finding treaties between European and

---

[52] CJ Chacko 'India's Contribution to the Field of International Law Concepts' (1958) 93 Recueil des Cours de l'Académie de Droit International de La Haye 117–222; Chacko concludes the historical survey affirming the universal character of international law.

[53] See *Some Newly Established Asian States* (n 5) 49 (original emphasis).

[54] ibid 234–7.

[55] N Singh *India and International Law* (Chand Delhi 1973).

[56] R Ranjeva 'The Malagasy Monarchy and International Law' in *African International Legal History* (n 37) 125–35.

[57] T Wang 'China and International Law, a Historical Perspective' in TMC Asser Instituut (ed) *International Law and the Grotian Heritage* (TMC Asser Instituut The Hague 1985) 260–4.

non-European sovereigns, specifically rules in treaties recognizing formal equality between both parties, it was only a small step further to argue that international law had plural origins, and furthermore, that some principles of law had non-Western origins. Anand, for example, reminding that at a time when the Roman and Rhodesian freedom of the sea had been long forgotten and denied in Europe, Grotius, one of the alleged founding fathers of international law, rediscovered this principle while looking into the freedom of navigation in the Indian Ocean, which was governed not only by rules of customary law, but also by rules that had been codified in the Codes of Macassar and Malacca of the 13th century.[58]

Although in its own time less relevant than writing universal histories, showing international law's plural origins has now become topical when re-appropriated by contemporary scholarship to affirm the hybrid character of European international law itself—revealing thus a different and persisting Eurocentric distortion.[59] The very rich but relatively under-explored work of Polish scholar CH Alexandrowicz has been at the centre of this line of inquiry. Alexandrowicz not only pursued a universal history—showing that South Asian powers governed their interactions based on a tradition that compared to the European was 'more ancient than their own and in no way inferior to notions of European civilization'—but also showed that between the 16th and 18th centuries, interactions between East Indian and European sovereigns developed in relative equal footing. The series of treaties governing this relationship reflected mutually agreed principles of inter-state dealings, which not only shaped the content of the Law of Nations, but also shaped international law's doctrinal outlook, influencing the intellectual legacy of what is conventionally believed to be a purely European tradition.[60]

Western historians have not only neglected these interactions and the influence they exerted on international law. Alexandrowicz points out: 'The orthodox eurocentric view…is that most of the Afro-Asian countries joined the Family of Nations as full and equal members only recently, anyhow, not before World War I.'[61]

But also, Western historians have vigorously rejected Alexandrowicz's effort to historicize the selfsame notion of an exclusively European law of nations. In particular, they have ignored the claim that before the 19th century, international law developed through the legal interactions between European and non-European sovereigns. According to Alexandrowicz, it was only during the course of the 19th century, when international law shifted from natural law into positivism, that European international lawyers reconceived international law as exclusively European.[62] If the standard

---

[58] 'The Influence of History' (n 28) 347.   [59] See Section 5.

[60] CH Alexandrowicz *An Introduction to the History of the Law of Nations in the East Indies: (16th, 17th and 18th Centuries)* (Clarendon Press Oxford 1967). Remember that Oppenheim, for example, had declared that there was no constant intercourse between 'Christian and Buddhistic' States (n 9) 30.

[61] CH Alexandrowicz 'The Afro-Asian World and the Law of Nations (Historical Aspects)' (1968) 123 Recueil des Cours de l'Académie de Droit International de La Haye 117–214 at 121.

[62] *An Introduction to the History* (n 60) 9–10 and 237.

of civilization reduced international law to Europe, showing pre-existing legal interactions beyond Europe and recognizing the shift from naturalism to positivism, allows Alexandrowicz to explain the contraction of international law's scope as a result of a confrontation between European and Afro-Asian orders, rather than as a result of an inherently Western contribution, a confrontation in which Western sovereigns prevailed by force.

4. Exposing the Dark Sides: Histories of International Law in the Non-Western World, 1980s–2000s

This last aspect of Alexandrowicz's work—the confrontation between the Western and non-Western world—gained centrality for the generation of non-Western scholars who appeared in the 1980s and 1990s. Writing history, for the first TWAIL generation—a generation that faced the challenge of becoming international lawyers in a rather hostile professional environment, for whom acquiring sovereignty and self-determination were hard-fought victories—was not only a way to deal with the trauma of colonialism by carving out an independent position within the international legal tradition, but also a first step in a legal argument to either demand changes or utterly reject some of the rules of international law under which newly independent States would be governed. To a second generation of TWAIL academics, colonialism seemed too distant, imperialism too close, while memories of the struggle for self-determination had faded away.

Closer to the non-Western international law scholar of the 1980s and 1990s were the perceived limitations that international law's formal autonomy and equality offered to States in the periphery, limitations that prevented post-colonial States from bringing substantive improvement to the lives of peoples in the Third World.[63] If international law was now seen as an obstacle rather than as a vehicle for the emancipation of the Third World, writing history became one of the ways to support this claim.[64]

---

[63] A Anghie and BS Chimni 'Third World Approaches to International Law and Individual Responsibility in Internal Conflicts' (2003) 2 Chinese Journal of International Law 77–103 at 84; TWAIL scholars, Chimini complains, did not pursue a post-colonial critique of the State. 'The Past, Present and Future of International Law' (n 50) 504.

[64] Chimni eg notes that the recent revival of historical studies in international law may be part of either an hegemonic project, serving the functional need to generate a common understanding of the past, which promotes and projects capitalist globalization into the future; or an emancipatory project,

At the same time, Western international lawyers invoked the demise of the Third World movement as a reaffirmation of the historical progress of international law. After the Third World and the Soviet bloc relinquished their divergent positions, Western lawyers welcomed their integration into an international community that regained universality and into an international law that reassumed its pattern of progress: from a law preoccupied with inter-state coexistence, towards a law of cooperation advancing the values and interests of the international community writ large.[65] A renewed international law was thought to have regained relevance in a globalized world, it also faced the fragmentation of its classical structure, by the proliferation of special bodies responding to a variety of functional needs—protecting trade, human rights, the environment, democracy, development. Western scholars found unity in a renewed Western universalism.[66]

Writing history offered scholars the opportunity to expose the relationship between international law and colonialism, between Western sovereignty and Western imperialism, between the promotion of human rights, international trade or development, and new forms of subordination.[67] Histories exposing the dark sides of international law served as a cautionary tale against the optimistic universalism of both the first generation TWAIL scholar who defended international law's emancipatory potential and the Western lawyer who believed in the progress of an international legal tradition that had left behind its colonial legacies to embrace universal values. Those initiating this scholarship were not lawyers but historians of international relations. Published in 1984, Gerrit Gong's history of the emergence of the standard of civilization proved highly influential.[68]

Gong's work opened a research agenda soon followed by international lawyers interested in reinvigorating TWAIL studies. Gong showed that the encounter between Western and non-Western peoples brought about a clash over different standards of civilization, and that throughout this encounter, Western lawyers constructed the

---

preventing global capitalism's worst effects by producing histories that come to terms with the dark past of international law. 'The Past, Present and Future of International Law' (n 50) 512–13.

[65]   The literature is immense, since this was the most common way, during the 1990s and early 2000s, to reposition international law in world politics. For a rendering of this trajectory in a history work, see M-H Renaut *Histoire du droit international public* (Ellipses Paris 2007); for an account of the recurrence of the narrative of progress, see T Skouteris *The Notion of Progress in International Law Discourse* (Asser The Hague 2009).

[66]   The literature on globalization and fragmentation is also enormous. For an example of a contemporary Eurocentric invocation of universality see A Bogdandy and S Dellavalle 'Universalism and Particularism as Paradigms of International Law' (2008) 3 Institute for International Law and Justice Working Papers 1–57.

[67]   M Koskenniemi 'Why History of International Law Today?' (2004) 4 Rechtsgeschichte 61–6 at 65.

[68]   G Gong *The Standard of Civilization in International Society* (Clarendon Press Oxford 1984) In addition to Gong, also in 1984, Jörg Fisch published the most comprehensive history of the expansion of international law, only less influential because of the hegemony of the English language, see J Fisch *Die europäische Expansion und das Völkerrecht: Die Auseinandersetzungen um den Status der überseeischen Gebiete vom 15. Jahrhundert bis zur Gegenwart* (Steiner Stuttgart 1984).

standard of civilization according to which non-European States would be admitted to the Western international community.[69] For the new generation of TWAIL scholars, exploring the history of the encounter between the European and non-European world became—as Anghie and Chimni put it—a central quest. This meant

understand[ing] the extent to which the doctrines of international law had been created through the colonial encounter. It was principally through colonial expansion that international law achieved one of its defining characteristics: universality. Thus the doctrines used for the purpose of assimilating the non-European world into this 'universal' system the fundamental concept of sovereignty and even the concept of law itself—were inevitably shaped by the relationships of power and subordination inherent in the colonial relationship.[70]

Exposing the relationship between international law and non-Western subjugation, revealed a particular Eurocentric distortion in the narrative of progress present in conventional, liberal-internationalist histories. Progress is sustained on the basis of a Western standpoint that allows to establish a pattern of development: from the use of force in European inter-state relations to the proscription of force, from States as the only international legal entity to the irruption of the individual protected by international human rights.[71] Overemphasizing progress disavows the role of Western international law in producing colonialism, imperialism and the subjugation of the non-Western world.[72]

TWAIL scholars not only established a historical link between international law and the subjugation of non-Western peoples, but also asserted the trans-historical character of this interrelation.[73] Antony Anghie's *Imperialism, Sovereignty and the Making of International Law*, one of the most influential works of its generation, discovered a deep structure.[74] There are aspects of international law—Angie argues—that repeat themselves throughout history: the 'dynamic of difference' and the rhetoric of the 'civilizing mission'. International law, on the one hand, constructs a cultural difference, an unbridgeable gap between: the Spanish and the Indigenous (16th-century naturalism), the civilized and the uncivilized (19th-century positivism),[75] the developed and the developing (20th-century pragmatism),

---

[69] *The Standard of Civilization* (n 68) and G Gong 'China's Entry into International Society' in H Bull and A Watson (eds) *The Expansion of International Society* (Clarendon Press Oxford 1984) 171–83.

[70] 'Third World Approaches to International Law' (n 63) 84.

[71] To take just one example: A Cassese *International Law* (2nd edn OUP Oxford 2005) at 30–45.

[72] Downplaying colonialism is not only present in histories with a narrative of progress but also in histories written from the standpoint of political realism. The translation of Grewe's work was important to generate a TWAIL reaction against this type of Eurocentrism. In Grewe's 800 pages long history, decolonization is mentioned in one page: *Epochen der Völkerrechtsgeschichte* (n 16) 759–60.

[73] 'TWAIL...sees international law in terms of its history of complicity with colonialism, a complicity that continues now in various ways with the phenomenon of neocolonialism, the identifiable and systematic pattern whereby the North seeks to assert and maintain its economic, military and political superiority'. 'Third World Approaches to International Law' (n 63) 96.

[74] A Anghie *Imperialism, Sovereignty and the Making of International Law* (CUP Cambridge 2007).

[75] Cf the contribution by L Obregón 'The Civilized and the Uncivilized' in this volume.

the civilized and the barbaric/terrorist (today). Then, on the other hand, international law gets mobilized by the civilizing mission that attempts to bridge the gap, respectively: by recognizing Indian possession of universal reason thus making them subjects of rights and duties, by civilizing the uncivilized, by promoting well-being and self-government, by humanizing through war in self-defence.[76] But bridging the gap proves impossible, for the target is constantly displaced and the cultural dichotomy reasserted. The deep structure surfaces in what Angie believes to be the most disturbing of his findings, in whatever period: *'imperialism is a constant'*.[77]

5. Conclusion: Global Histories of International Law and the Problem of Eurocentrism Today

It is hard to overstate the impact Anghie's work has had on international law scholarship. International lawyers, writing on various topics ranging from international human rights to international trade, from development assistance to legal theory and the laws of war, have generally become more aware about the colonial origins of their own fields of expertise and more cautious about international law's emancipatory potential. Second-generation TWAIL scholars' awareness about the connections between international law and colonialism/neo-colonialism has conferred on their work a strong historical dimension. Post-colonial histories of international law have become today one of the most dynamic and interesting areas of research.[78] In this new context, where the relation between international law and the subjugation of the non-Western world seems difficult to ignore, has the history of international law finally overcome the problem of Eurocentrism?

For better or worse, gone are the times when European lawyers would openly attack non-Western international lawyers' efforts to rewrite the history of

---

[76] ibid 6, 29, 37, and 311–15.

[77] ibid 315 (original emphasis).

[78] Among others see N Berman *Passion and Ambivalence: Colonialism, Nationalism, and International Law* (Brill Leiden 2011); M Craven *The Decolonization of International Law. State Succession and the Law of Treaties* (OUP Oxford 2007); E Jouannet and H Ruiz Fabri *Impérialisme et droit international en Europe et aux États-Unis: Mondialisation et fragmentation du droit* (Société de législation comparée Paris 2007); S Pahuja *Decolonising International Law Development, Economic Growth and the Politics of Universality* (CUP Cambridge 2007).

international law. Today, the presence of Eurocentric distortions in the history of international law will depend on the type of history predominating in academic writing. In spite of the intellectual status enjoyed by second-generation TWAIL scholars, the historical introduction of most international law textbooks, and thus arguably the teaching of international law, has not departed from the narrative of progress common in liberal-internationalist histories. However, realist histories, in which international law evolves according to the interests of the world's Western hegemonic powers, have seen a revival after the translation in 2000 of Wilhelm Grewe's *Epochen der Völkerrechtsgeschichte*. Today, post-colonial, liberal-internationalist, and realist histories of international law coexist, each bringing a different Eurocentric distortion when overemphasizing Western contexts of practice.

While liberal-internationalist histories no longer sustain the exclusively Western origin and nature of international law (they may even insert passages on non-Western legal orders in ancient history within a narrative of progress as universalization), they persistently ignore international law's involvement in colonialism and imperialism. Overlooking these connections not only obscures international law's dark past, but also distorts the more recent history of decolonization and the globalization of international law. These appear as either concessions or necessary steps in the universalization of international law, rather than as conquests in which non-Western lawyers used and appropriated international legal arguments in their struggle for self-determination, in a struggle that transformed international law.

In a history narrated from a Western standpoint, the voice, interests, victories, and defeats of non-Western international lawyers are absent. Most intriguing, both realist and post-colonial histories of international law treat non-Western contexts of practice as peripheral. Realist and post-colonial historians believe that international law is a superstructure determined by power. Accordingly, the great Western powers have developed international law to legitimize and stabilize an order that universalizes their self-interest. While the realist looks at a sequence of Western sovereigns that have become the international system's central hegemonic power, in order to see how that power controls the nature and development of international law, the post-colonial historian looks at this same succession to find the different but constant modes through which sovereignty is reasserted in the West and excluded in the non-Western world. Finding international law's transhistorical structure of domination has been particularly onerous on the post-colonial historian. Although post-colonial histories have set out to retrieve the history of international law in the non-Western world, structuralism has created a blind spot regarding counter-hegemonic uses of international law by non-Western actors.

Post-colonial historians opened rich avenues of research beyond the narrative of progress imposed by liberal-internationalism. But a deep structuralism has given post-colonial studies a puzzlingly ahistorical flavour. After post-colonial histories, where to go next? I suggest three different trends followed by contemporary historians who are aware of potential Eurocentric—liberal-internationalist, realist, and post-colonial—distortions.[79]

First, historians of international relations have written histories in which international law both reflects the interests of powerful Western sovereigns and enables weaker actors to resist by appealing to the universal language of rights. The most relevant work of this type is Jörg Fisch's history of the role of international law in the European expansion.[80] Fisch presents the relation between Europe's expansion through direct conquest or indirect domination and the development of legal forms reflecting the subordination of non-Western nations. Yet within this general trend, Fisch shows not only international law providing legitimacy to the colonial enterprise, resolving disputes between Western sovereigns with competing claims in relation to overseas territories, but also Western sovereigns accepting subordinate positions in relation to non-Western polities that were too powerful, too distant, or not significant enough to be dominated. Along with a more nuanced picture of the role of law in international politics, a history of international law in the non-Western world emerges, a history showing more than the domination of the non-Western world.

Second, the publication of *The Gentle Civilizer of Nations* by Martti Koskenniemi represented a turning point in the writing of history by legal scholars.[81] Turning international lawyers into the main protagonists, Koskenniemi's history of international law as intellectual history showed a way to move beyond both realist and post-colonial structuralism, as well as beyond liberal histories of ideas committed to a narrative of progress. Koskenniemi offers an account of the rise and fall of internationalist 'sensibilities,' that is, the 'attitudes and preconceptions about matters international' shared by international lawyers, which although, as Koskenniemi himself warns, centred in the West, proved extremely appealing to legal historians interested in moving beyond Eurocentrism.

Reconstructing the cosmopolitan sensibilities and political projects of mainstream international lawyers, Koskenniemi's history contains passages where international lawyers seem not just inventive and politically engaged but also successful in giving institutional form to the liberal internationalist project. At the same time, the narrative shows international lawyers' professional failures and the final demise of the liberal internationalist sensibility, as well as the profession's darkest passages, its support of imperialism, and the civilizing mission. This history, showing the relative autonomy

---

[79] Asking a similar question, Koskenniemi sketches four strategies to deal with Eurocentrism: (1) 'careful demonstrations of the colonial origins of an international legal rule or institution'; (2) 'focusing on the encounter between European and the new world as an important, even foundational moment of the discipline itself'; (3) looking at the 'hybridization of the legal concepts as they travel from the colonial metropolis to the colonies; (4) 'exoticize (provincialize) Europe and European laws'. 'Histories of International Law' (n 1) 170–5.

[80] *Die europäische Expansion und das Völkerrecht* (n 68).

[81] M Koskenniemi *The Gentle Civilizer of Nations. The Rise and Fall of International Law 1870–1960* (CUP Cambridge 2002).

of the international legal discourse, its capacity to shape the interests and international agendas of Western States, showing how this discourse has been channelled towards projects of domination and emancipation, opened up the field for new histories foregrounding the interactions and tensions between actors at the centres and peripheries of the world.

Third, following the turn to intellectual history, a number of legal scholars have been exploring the dynamics between centre and periphery as a heuristic to retrieve the history of international law in its global rather than simply Western dimensions. This latest trend, which one may describe as global histories of international law, has had the special series on 'International Law in the Periphery', edited by Fleur Johns, Thomas Skouteris, and Wouter Werner for the Leiden Journal of International Law, as one of its main driving forces. Already in its fourth special issue, a significant body of work has coalesced. Some have reconstructed the history of international law in the periphery itself, as a site not only of domination, but also resistance. Others have looked at the periphery in its relation to the centre, retrieving forgotten or silenced contributions to the global tradition.[82]

The disciplinary controversies reviewed in this chapter have transformed the history of international law into a lively field of inquiry. Disagreement regarding the Western nature and origin of international law and regarding the relationship between international law and colonialism have brought into the foreground the conflicting standpoints from which history is written. But claims about pure origins and histories based on a narrative of progress obscuring international law's dark past still abound. The field is lively because these controversies have not been settled. And to the extent that Eurocentric histories reflect international law's hegemonic face, and to the extent that divergent narratives exploit the opportunities for resistance, these debates cannot be settled.

Recommended Reading

Anand, Ram P 'The Influence of History on the Literature of International Law' in Ronald St J Macdonald and Douglas M Johnston (eds) *The Structure and Process of International Law: Essays in Legal Philosophy, Doctrine, and Theory* (Martinus Nijhoff The Hague 1983) 341–80.
Gathii, James T 'International Law and Eurocentricity' (1998) 9 European Journal of International Law 184–211.

---

[82] See various authors in The Periphery Series: 'Alejandro Álvarez' (2006) 19 Leiden Journal of International Law 875 ff; 'Taslim Olawale Elias' (2008) 21 Leiden Journal of International Law 289 ff; 'India and International Law' (2010) 23 Leiden Journal of International Law 1 ff; 'The League of Nations and the Construction of the Periphery' (2011) 24 Leiden Journal of International Law 797 ff.

Johns, Fleur, Thomas Skouteris, and Wouter Werner (eds) 'Editors' Introduction: Alejandro Álvarez and the Launch of the Periphery Series' (2006) 19 Leiden Journal of International Law 875–7.

Johns, Fleur, Thomas Skouteris, and Wouter Werner (eds) 'Editors' Introduction: Taslim Olawale Elias in The Periphery Series' (2008) 21 Leiden Journal of International Law 289–90.

Johns, Fleur, Thomas Skouteris, and Wouter Werner (eds) 'Editors' Introduction: India and International Law in The Periphery Series' (2010) 23 Leiden Journal of International Law 1–3.

Johns, Fleur, Thomas Skouteris, and Wouter Werner (eds) 'The League of Nations and the Construction of the Periphery. Introduction, (2011) 24 Leiden Journal of International Law 797–8.

Koskenniemi, Martti 'Histories of International Law: Dealing with Eurocentrism' (2011) 19 Rechtsgeschichte 152–76.

CHAPTER 44

IDENTIFYING REGIONS IN THE HISTORY OF INTERNATIONAL LAW

ANTONY ANGHIE

1. INTRODUCTION

THE topic of 'regionalism' and its relationship with international law has now acquired a particular and considerable significance. Contemporary scholars have argued that the emergence of regional organizations and the legal systems and institutions associated with them may result in the fragmentation of international law[1]—or, somewhat contrastingly, that it is through regional organizations that international law may actually achieve some sort of reality and effective enforcement.[2] The idea of 'regional international law' acts as a complex bridge between the sovereign State and international law: on the one hand—as in the case of regional trade agreements—it

---

[1] For exploration of this theme see International Law Commission 'Report of the International Law Commission of its 57th Session' (2 May–3 June and 11 July–5 August 2005) UN Doc A/60/10, ch XI, 204–25 (Fragmentation of International Law: Difficulties Arising from the Diversification and Expansion of International Law).

[2] See AM Slaughter and WB White 'The Future of International Law is Domestic (or, the European Way of Law)' (2006) 47 Harvard International Law Journal 327–52.

represents a desirable progress away from a narrow preoccupation on the nation-State towards a more international system. On the other, it represents a threat to the aspiration of creating a universal system of international law, precisely because its success could result in the fragmentation of international law. This dual, ambivalent character of regionalism animates a great deal of contemporary scholarship. Further, scholars have also been suggesting that something like 'comparative' international[3] law may be emerging: a study of international human rights law, for instance, would be incomplete without a close examination of the jurisprudence of regional institutions such as the Inter-American Court of Human Rights, the European Court of Human Rights, and the African Commission of Human Rights. The myriad questions raised by these developments are a particular product of the unique character of international law and institutions at the beginnings of this millennium. But the question also arises as to how what we may broadly and provisionally term the problem of 'regions' has been understood in different periods of the history of international law. Inevitably, the issue of 'regions', whatever its commonplace meaning—Herodotus after all set about the task of examining the different customs that governed different societies—has been conceptualized in different ways according to the jurisprudence of the period, and the perception of what were the major issues confronting the discipline.

The concept of a region most basically suggests a geographical entity; 'Europe' or 'Asia' or 'Africa', for instance. However, the immediate problem confronting any attempt to base a history of international law on the concept of regions is suggested by Norman Davies when he examines the evolution of the idea of 'Europe' and the many different meanings associated with that term.[4] The term 'Third World' is sometimes equated with a geography, with 'Southern States'; but what each concept attempts to capture, however inadequately, is a political, economic, and social experience—hardship, impoverishment, under-development, imperialism—and to equate it with a geographic region. The construction of a particular region, then, is not simply a question of geography—which in any event, of course, has its own complexities; it is a political and ideological construct, and it is only by examining the particular context in which the terminology of regions is employed that we may understand its significance and use. While several of the major international law societies in the world are organized on a regional basis—the European Society of International Law and the Asian Society of International Law, for instance—the question of whether there is a distinctly 'European' or 'Asian' approach to international law occasions much soul searching and few clear answers.

Despite all the obvious difficulties associated with the concept of regions, however, it does play a useful and sometimes indispensable role when used in an appropriately

---

[3] A Roberts 'Comparative International Law? The Role of National Courts in Creating and Enforcing International Law' (2011) 60 International and Comparative Law Quarterly 57–92.

[4] N Davies *Europe: A History* (OUP Oxford 1996) at 7–16.

qualified and contextualized way, to enable an analysis and exploration of some of the fundamental features of the history and character of international law.

2. The Concept of Regional Law

The idea that particular regions develop a set of rules or practices that enable the various entities that are members of that regional grouping to interact with each other on an ongoing basis is powerful, commonplace, and enduring. Many of the most venerable and classical works of history are animated by an understanding that, whatever the internecine struggles dividing them, the Greek city-states formed an entity quite distinct from the Persians.[5] It is in many ways an extension of the idea that each community or society is unique in terms of its customs and traditions, political systems, and social institutions. Given this broad assumption, questions inevitably arise as to how these regional systems relate to international law—since international law is, almost by definition, universal, binding on all regions regardless of their unique characteristics, just as it is binding on all States, whatever their own legal systems.

It is common in many textbooks of international law that commence with a short history of the discipline to acknowledge that regional systems of what might be termed 'international law' had existed among the Greek city-states, and in ancient China and India among other places, before then asserting that modern international law began in Europe.[6] It appears historically valid to assume that, whatever the other differences separating them, all people in a similar geographical region or proximity must engage with each other and develop a common culture, a shared history that somehow creates a distinctive legal regime. Divisions, even wars, within different entities within these regions do not undermine this thesis; rather, such events may even affirm and solidify the sense of belonging to a region, and result in the formulation of particular institutions or doctrines to deal with the ongoing tensions between such entities. The question of 'regional' international law then, appears in even the most cursory and introductory histories of international law.

Another approach to 'regions' focuses on the areas covered by particular political entities. This is the approach taken by Stephan Verosta, whose important historical

---

[5] Further, conflicts between regional customs and understandings can lead to dire consequences: 'The Asiatics, according to the Persians, took the seizure of women lightly enough, but not so the Greeks: the Greeks merely on account of a girl from Sparta, raised a big army, invaded Asia and destroyed the empire of Priam.' Herodotus *The Histories* (A de Sélincourt trans) (revised edn 2003 Penguin Books 1954) at 4.

[6] See eg P Malanczuk *Akehurst's Introduction to Modern International Law* (7th edn Routledge New York 1997) at 1–32.

work examines the relationship between the Roman and Persian Empires, and the doctrines developed between the two empires to manage interaction between them.[7] Verosta argues that these doctrines have endured in various ways and that versions of them may be found in modern international law. Many ancient and medieval political systems involved relations between entities which had very different capacities and power—ranging from empires to vassal States to tribes.[8] As a consequence, a complex, differentiated, and variegated system of norms and obligations developed among these different entities. Nevertheless, it can be argued that these entities developed rules regarding diplomatic relations, treaties, the conduct of war, and religious tolerance.

The idea that international law is essentially European in character, that it is in effect a *jus publicum Europaeum,* is powerful and enduring, and has been an almost invariable starting point of histories of modern international law.[9] Nevertheless, in his survey of the history of international law, Preiser points to the fact that non-European developments of international law are excluded from the consideration of many traditional histories of international law. This arises from the premise of many of these histories that international law begins with Grotius and/or the modern sovereign State.[10] In arguing against such a Eurocentric approach to the writing of the history of international law, Preiser asserted that even if one focused on Europe, one could not properly understand intellectual developments within Europe without examining the way in which ideas originating outside Europe had affected this tradition. Secondly, any truly 'universal' history of international law would seek to include the forms of regional international law that emerged in ancient China or ancient South and South-East Asia. As such, Preiser urged an examination of 'independently developed, functional international legal orders which helped influence the legal character of their respective eras'.[11]

Thus, the first and second edition of the *Encyclopedia of Public International Law* contains articles by several distinguished scholars such as Nagendra Singh on international law in South Asia and South-East Asia, Taslim O Elias on African International

---

[7] S Verosta 'International Law in Europe and Western Asia Between 100 and 650 AD' (1964-III) 113 Recueil des cours 485–651.

[8] See S Hamamoto 'International Law: Regional Developments: East Asia' in R Wolfrum (ed) *The Max Planck Encyclopedia of International Law* (OUP Oxford 2011) at <www.mpepil.com>, and DA Desierto 'Regional Developments: South and South-East Asia' in ibid

[9] Cf the contribution by A Becker Llorca 'The Problem of Eurocentrism in the History of International Law' in this volume.

[10] W Preiser 'History of the Law of Nations: Basic Questions and Principles' in R Bernhardt (ed) *Encyclopedia of Public International Law* (2nd edn Elsevier North-Holland 1995) vol 2, at 127.

[11] *History of the Law of Nations* (n 10) 129. Preiser also makes it clear that such an undertaking would not in any way undermine the uncontestable achievement of Europe: the European achievement is 'secure for all time by reason of the fact that European international law developed into world international law'.

Law, and Shigeki Miyazaki on East Asia.[12] As discussed subsequently, the concept of 'regions' is connected in a complex manner with the concept of 'civilizations', which has perhaps played a more prominent role in histories of international law.[13] This is also suggested by the fact that the entry by Ahmed El-Kosheri is titled 'History of the Law of Nations Regional Developments: Islam'.[14]

The particular analytic or heuristic framework in which the question of regions has been located in the history of international law requires a closer examination of what is meant by the term 'the history of international law'. It is hardly controversial to assert that the issue of how international law should be written has been the subject of ongoing and, in recent times, lively debate[15]—whether, for instance, it should focus on State practice, or the extant theories and jurisprudence of international law.[16] Preiser, in his survey of the historiography of international law his article in the *Encyclopedia of Public International Law,* refers to the problems arising from the failures of early historians of the discipline to satisfactorily combine an account of international relations with international legal issues and the theories of international jurists. Historians of the discipline, Preiser noted, offered legal theory, 'the schools of thought in international law which followed, one upon the other'.[17] What might be termed the 'problem of regions' in international law would have featured very differently in the thinking of the great scholars of international law whose work provide the subject of such historians (a distinction may be made between the works of jurists such as Vitoria, Grotius, and Vattel, and the scholars who wrote about them as self-conscious historians of the discipline; the first such historian identified by Preiser is Robert Ward).[18]

Despite this, few jurists or international legal historians—as discussed below—have systematically attempted to identify the specific and unique problems and questions arising from this broad and somewhat unexamined concept, and the

---

[12] 'History of the Law of Nations regional Developments' in *Encyclopedia of Public International Law* (n 10) vol 2: N Singh 'South and South-East Asia' (ibid 824–39); TO Elias 'Africa' (ibid 793–802); S Miyazaki 'Far East' (ibid 802–9).

[13] For a far reaching analysis of international law based on the concept of 'civilizations' see O Yasuaki *A Transcivilizational Perspective on International Law* (Martinus Nijhoff Publishers Leiden 2010); also the contribution by L Obregón 'The Civilized and the Uncivilized' in this volume.

[14] A El-Kosheri 'History of the Law of Nations regional Developments: Islam' in *Encyclopedia of Public International Law* (2nd edn Elsevier North-Holland 1995) vol 2, 809–18.

[15] See for instance, M Craven and M Fitzmaurice *Time History and International Law* (Martinus Nijhoff Leiden 2007); I de la Rasilla del Moral 'International Law in the Historical Present Tense' (2009) 22 Leiden Journal of International Law 629–49; GRB Galindo 'Martti Koskenniemi and the Historiographical Turn in International Law' (2005) 16 European Journal of International Law 539–59.

[16] This is the problem Grewe attempts to address: '[I]t is important to recognize and demarcate the close connection between legal theory and State practice, and to comprehend that both are forms of expression of the same power, which characterize the political style of an epoch just as much as its principles of social, economic and legal organisation.' WG Grewe *The Epochs of International Law* (Walter de Gruyter Berlin 2000) at 6.

[17] *History of the Law of Nations* (n 10) 126.

[18] R Ward *An Enquiry into the Foundation and History of the Law of Nations in Europe and from the Time of the Greeks and Romans to the Age of Grotius* (A Strahan and W Woodfall London 1795).

accompanying analytic framework that it generates. The question remains open as to whether the idea of regions which seems fundamental to international law—given the premise that every region develops its own form of law—has featured significantly in the writing of the history of international law. What indeed are, what might be provisionally called, the problems of regions in international law? This chapter attempts to address some of these issues. I do so, first, by providing a broad, chronological overview of the jurisprudence of international law since its early modern beginnings in the 16th century, and by then considering the ways in which authors such as Wilhelm Grewe and Carl Schmitt who self-consciously set about the task of writing histories of international law, approached these issues in their own surveys of the jurisprudence and State practice of the time. A related question is the complex issue of the relationship between 'regions' and 'civilization' or 'culture'.

In the second half of this chapter I point to a different approach to the issue of 'regions' in international law—an approach that focuses on issues of space and geography. If governance is intimately related to the conceptualization and management of space, then it would be useful to understand how international law deals with these questions. Carl Schmitt's work is helpful in identifying some of the issues raised by the relationship among space, sovereignty, and international law, and how this relationship has changed over time.

3. Regions and the Early-modern Beginnings of International Law

Most eminent histories of international law attempt to combine an examination of the theories of international law, such as those propounded by thinkers such as Hugo Grotius, with an explication and assessment of contemporaneous State practice.[19] Inevitably, the two approaches are linked in various ways, as State practice itself acquires a different significance depending on the extant jurisprudence, and as a jurists were anxious to provide theories of law that accorded with the immediate and pressing needs of their time. Grotius was not only a great jurist, but equally importantly, the legal adviser to the Dutch East India Company.[20]

---

[19] As Grewe argues, for instance, '[I]t is important to recognise and demarcate the close connection between legal theory and State practice, and to comprehend that both are forms of expression of the same power, which characterize the political style of an epoch just as much as its principles of social, economic and legal organization.' *The Epochs* (n 16) 6.

[20] The extent of this involvement has been studied in detail by M van Ittersum 'The Long Goodbye: Hugo Grotius' Justification of Dutch Expansion Overseas, 1615–1645' (2010) 36 History of European Ideas 386–411.

While acknowledging these complexities, I will focus here on the writings of some of the great jurists of the 16th and 17th centuries. For scholars such as Francisco de Vitoria, who, while inhabiting polity in which spiritual authority, the Pope, wielded enormous power, firmly adhered to the natural law tradition—even while accepting the existence of categories such as 'man made law' or 'human law'—the issue of regions is not a major theoretical problem because all peoples were governed by a universal natural law.[21] This natural law may have turned out, on inspection, to have been simply an idealized embodiment of the mores of Catholic Spain. But the larger point remains; that the customs and practices of other, foreign peoples, such as the Indians of the New World that Vitoria examines, are not in and of themselves of interest to Vitoria—except to the extent that they fail to comply with the prescriptions of natural law.

Grotius—whose early work in particular was heavily influenced by Vitoria—similarly operates on the assumption that natural law is universal. As recent scholars have argued, however, it is clear that the universal rules of natural law have to be implemented in different ways in different regions of the world. Thus, within Europe, the right to go to war in self-defence was monopolized by the sovereign State. In the East Indies, however, where no common political system existed, the natural right to go to war in self-defence devolved to individuals—and, as it so happens, corporations such as the Dutch East India Company, striving to protect its rights not only against the oriental peoples and rulers they encountered, but against other depredating European powers such as the Portuguese.[22] As Edward Keene has argued Grotius distinguishes broadly between two broad spheres of law, law as it applied within European States, and a separate law that applied between European and non-European entities.[23] While this broad distinction may suggest something comparable to what contemporary scholars might recognize as 'the problem of regions', the difference between the European and non-European worlds was conceptualized more in terms of a difference of culture or civilization, rather than a difference of regions. Inevitably, the relationship between 'regions' and 'culture' is a very complex one: we might conceptualize the problem of regions as being a problem, essentially, of the management of space, whereas the problem of civilizations has to do with the management of cultural difference.

With the gradual shift in international legal jurisprudence to positivism, European positivist scholars such as John Westlake developed a clearer sense of regions—even if regions were understood principally in terms of the problem of culture.[24] Thus, European jurists distinguished between 'civilized States' that enjoyed a form

---

[21] F de Vitoria *De Indis et De iure belli relectiones* (E Nys ed, JP Bate trans) (Carnegie Institute Washington, DC 1917).

[22] I Porras 'Constructing the International Law in the East Indies' (2005–6) 31 Brooklyn Journal of International Law 741–804; R Tuck *The Rights of War and Peace* (OUP Oxford 1999).

[23] E Keene *Beyond the Anarchical Society* (CUP Cambridge 2002).

[24] J Westlake *Chapter on the Principles of International Law* (CUP Cambridge 1894).

of civilization different from that of Europe, and were therefore excluded from the European family of nations—examples cited included States such as China—whereas peoples living in other regions such as Africa and the Pacific were denounced as primitive and backward, with no recognition given to the complex societies that had developed in these places. The focus on 'civilization' and on related concepts such as 'society' was driven in many ways by Darwinian ideas about progress and the evolution of societies.[25] Different techniques were used to account for the acquisition of European sovereignty over non-European peoples. In the case of Australia, for instance, 'discovery' was posited as the basis of British title over the continent; the Aboriginal peoples of Australia, who had inhabited the land for thousands of years, were not regarded as 'people'.[26] In the case of Africa and Asia, as the work of Charles Henry Alexandrowicz reveals, European States claimed to acquire sovereignty through a combination of means including through conquest, and by way of cession—the 'unequal treaties' that European States and non-European States entered into.[27]

By the beginning of the 20th century, then, an international law originating in Europe had become universal, and in so doing, had extinguished all potentially competing regional systems of order—whether these were conceived of as regional systems based on Chinese power and its attendant Confucian values, or the systems that existed in Africa or in South and South East Asia. For many European scholars such as Jan Hendrik Willem Verzijl these developments represented the logical 'triumph' of Europe.[28] This was the history of the relationship between European international law and 'regions' that was traditionally presented by many of the most prominent scholars of the discipline such as Verzijl and Arthur Nussbaum in his short history of the discipline. The focus of these histories was very much on what might be termed the issue of culture and civilization rather than 'regions'. Indeed, 'regions' assumed some sort of significance within these histories principally as a rough approximation for civilizations.

While European international law had established itself as 'universal', the gradual emergence of the United States as a world power was recognized as presenting a new set of issues relating to 'regional international law'. The United States had formulated the Monroe doctrine in 1823. Under this doctrine, broadly, the US claimed that it would regard any European interference or intervention in the affairs of the Americas as an act of war. By the time of the League of Nations, the existence of something akin to a regional international law was explicitly recognized in a regime, the most

---

[25] See in this volume, for an extended analysis, 'The Civilized and the Uncivilized' (n 13).

[26] See the discussion of these issues in MF Lindley *The Acquisition and Government of Backward Territory in International Law* (Longmans, Green and Co London 1926).

[27] CH Alexandrowicz *The European-African Confrontation: A Study in Treaty Making* (AW Sitjhoff Leiden 1973); CH Alexandrowicz *An Introduction to the History and Law of Nations in the East Indies* (Clarendon Oxford 1967)

[28] JHW Verzijl *International Law in Historical Perspective* (AW Sijthoff Leiden 1968) vol 1.

ambitious up to its time, that purported to be universal. Article 21 of the League of Nations Covenant asserted that 'regional understandings like the Monroe doctrine' would remain unaffected by the principles outlined in the League Covenant with regard to the maintenance of peace.[29] As commentators at the time were quick to point out, the implicit endorsement of something like a regional variation raised a number of issues. For instance, it was unclear as to what constituted a 'regional understanding', who articulated the nature of the understanding, and what the limits were of any such understandings with regard to the League.[30] All these discussions suggested both an acknowledgement of the significance of regional developments for international law and a shifting approach towards the relationship between these developments and the broader body of purportedly 'universal' international law. They also indicate the problem of how 'regions' were to be conceptualized. However, with the outbreak of the Second World War, these questions were given less prominence than the broader question of how international law and institutions could create an effective system of international government. Article 53 of the UN Charter, which explicitly brings regional organizations under the control of the Security Council, addressed this issue.

Another major development in the 'problem of regions' was represented by the important work of the great Chilean jurist, Alejandro Alvarez. His pioneering article, 'Latin American International Law',[31] published in 1909 in the American Journal of International Law provides an outline of how regional international law may be conceptualized, how it emerges, and how it relates to the 'universal' international law propounded by Europe. Alvarez is clear to demonstrate that Latin America borrowed from both the United States and Europe. In its public law, the United States as a recently independent nation was a model; in the case of private law Europe, and especially France, provided the model. As Alvarez notes, Latin American States were 'exposed to the direct influence of Europe, as they were of the same civilization and connected with the Old World by powerful bonds of culture and commerce'.[32]

While recognizing that Latin American States were diverse, Alvarez argued that geographical factors, shared historical experiences, and political solidarity united them. In particular, they were united in resisting the dangers of European intervention, they understood that they experienced unique problems, and they sought to further their unity and resolve their conflicts in a manner compatible with their own traditions, customs, and needs.[33]

---

[29] League of Nations Covenant (signed 28 June 1919, entered into force 10 January 1920) 225 CTS 195, art 21.

[30] GG Wilson 'Regional Understandings' (1933) 27 The American Journal of International Law 310–11.

[31] A Alvarez 'Latin America and International Law' (1909) 3 American Journal of International Law 269–353.

[32] ibid 273.

[33] See eg ibid 270.

Alvarez asserts a distinctive approach to international law in that he presents regionalism as having a dual relationship with European international law, from which Latin America received its earliest inspiration. In emphasizing the European elements of Latin American international law, Alvarez was essentially and strategically asserting that Latin America was indeed 'civilized' and thus properly belonged to the Family of Nations.[34] At the same time, however, Latin American international law was in many respects unique and was seeking to depart from the strictures of European international law. For Alvarez, an appreciation of Latin American international law, and its own distinctive character, could enrich international law.[35] Seen from a broader perspective, the timing of this article raises interesting issues. By 1909, European international law had triumphantly expanded beyond its original confines to become universally applicable. In so doing, it had overcome and replaced all the previous 'regional systems' that had existed in East Asia, Africa, and South Asia. It is in precisely this period, however, that Alvarez questions this primacy by pointing to the novel phenomenon of a regional system that had been a product of Europe and which was now transcending, if not challenging, the original source. The implications of this approach are disconcerting because of the suggestion that the universality of international law was in question. The Monroe doctrine, analysed by Alvarez, and cited by him as an element of Latin America distinctiveness, became a prominent issue around which the issue of regions was debated in the post-war period.[36]

4. CONCEPTUALIZING REGIONS—THE THIRD WORLD RESPONSE

The history of international law, until relatively recent times, has been written by scholars from the 'developed countries', the successors of the imperial powers of the West. Once Third World States acquired sovereignty, however, scholars who were sympathetic to the concerns of developing countries provided very different

---

[34] Many 'semi-peripheral jurists' as Arnulf Becker terms them in his important work, that is, jurists from States such as Chile, Argentina, Turkey and Japan, adopted the strategy of internalizing and reformulating the 'standard of civilization' that was so crucial to determining the legal status of a particular society. See A Becker 'Universal International Law: Nineteenth Century Histories of Imposition and Appropriation' (2010) 51 Harvard International Law Journal 475–552.

[35] For a detailed study of the controversies arising from Alvarez's claims about a distinctive Latin-American international law, and the background to these claims, see the contribution by J Esquirol 'Latin America' in this volume.

[36] 'Latin America and International Law' (n 31) 275.

approaches to the history of international law. For scholars such as Ram P Anand,[37] Taslim O Elias,[38] Charles Henry Alexandrowicz and their colleagues, the history of international law needed to be rewritten in order to appreciate better the systems of law that appeared to operate in non-European areas such as Africa and Asia. Many of the essays and book chapters produced at this time deal with 'regions' and their connection with international law. For example, Taslim Elias' chapter in the *Encyclopedia of International Law* is titled 'History of the Law of Nations Regional Developments: Africa'.[39] Nevertheless, an examination of the contents of the chapter reveals that the concept of a 'region'—Africa—is a given, and what is presented is a history of the relations between various African societies and kingdoms, the advent of imperialism, and then, decolonization. Nagendra Singh's chapter on 'History of the Law of Nations Regional Developments: South and South-East Asia'[40] suggests the ways in which some of the fundamental concepts of Indian civilization—deriving from Buddhism and Hinduism, for instance—shaped the principles of inter-state relations, and extended out to influence the larger regions of South and South-East Asia. Singh further points out that, even in the Vedic period from 4000 BC to 1000 BC, different political entities had emerged in northern India; they were understood to possess different statuses based on the power they exercised. Importantly, however, they developed principles that governed relations among them. The work of scholars such as Kautilya[41] in his treatise on statecraft provides accounts of such relations.[42] Further, religiously inspired works—the Code of Manu, the Ramayana, and the Mahabharata—all provided principles of conduct that could be extended to deal with inter-state relations, which related, for instance, to what might now be termed 'the laws of treaties' and 'the laws of war'. The concept of *dharma* or law was crucial to an understanding of the principles guiding inter-state behaviour at this time.

Singh's work, like that of another eminent international lawyer, Ram P Anand, is in many ways animated by the concerns of the period in which it was written. For this generation of Third World international law scholars, historical analysis was important to demonstrate that South Asia and India more particularly were not 'strangers' to some of the basic principles and doctrines of international law. Thus, detailed studies were made to demonstrate that the rules of inter-state relations that were found in ancient India were comparable to so called modern and Western doctrines relating, for instance, to the laws of war, the law of treaties, State respon-

---

[37] See eg RP Anand *Development of Modern International Law and India* (Indian Society of International Law New Delhi 2005).

[38] TO Elias *Africa and the Development of International Law* (AW Sijthoff Leiden 1972).

[39] Cf 'Africa' (n 12)

[40] 'South and South-East Asia' (n 12).

[41] Kautilya *The Arthashastra* (LN Rangarajan ed, rearranged, and trans) (Penguin Classics India 1992).

[42] *History of the Law of Nations* (n 40) 825–6.

sibility and the status of ambassadors.[43] The developing country scholars of the 1960 and 1970s were attempting to write the histories of their own regions in part because international lawyers, almost by definition, would have to focus on a 'region' in order to articulate such a proto-history of international law, as it is only if different political entities within a region interacted with each other that some claim could be made that a transnational, inter-national system existed, and that the principles governing such a system could be seen as an early example of inter-national law.[44] Needless to say, the writing of history is an inherently political act. It is hard to avoid the conclusion that much of this scholarship was driven by an intention to contest the views of many Western scholars at the time, who were fear-ful that the entry of non-European States would undermine, if not destroy the system of international law that was ineluctably and inescapably Western—the fur-ther implication being that the non-European world could not adapt to a European based system of law. What is clear from a survey this literature, however, is that even the concept of 'regional international law' is presented in terms of several broad themes: first, how the politics and civilizations of a region—the concept of 'region' is generally treated as a given rather than problematized in any way—gave rise to certain principles that governed relations among entities in those regions; secondly, how European expansion affected that region and resulted in its colonization; and finally, how the entities of that region emerged as new States as a consequence of self-determination and decolonization. To the extent that the major theoretical concerns of these histories of regions can be identified, they had to do with the nature of the principles that governed relations among regional entities, the reli-gious, and civilizational sources of these principles, and the relationship between these principles and contemporary international law.

5. REGIONS AND GEOPOLITICS: INTERNATIONAL LAW AND THE MANAGEMENT OF SPACE

Another approach to the issue of 'regions' in international law is to focus less on the idea of regions as a political construct and more on their geographic dimension—to conceptualize regions in their original spatial terms rather than as a crude proxy for

[43] See also CJ Chacko 'India's Contribution to the Field of International Law Concepts' (1958) 93 Recueil des cours 117–221.

[44] As Singh puts it, '[i]f the conditions necessary for the origin and development of international law are examined, it will be found that first, there must be the existence of separate political units.' *History of the Law of Nations* (n 40) 825.

political or civilizational entities.[45] The control and management and regulation of space were of crucial significance to governance and statecraft even prior to the emergence of the modern State, as a survey of manuals of warfare and histories of conflict would suggest.

Several of the most crucial concerns of international law are geographically based. The modern idea of statehood is inherently connected with the concept of bounded territory. Territory is the foundation of the State. More broadly, numerous significant events in international law focus on demarcation. Thus Pope Alexander VI's edict of 1493 granted the Spanish rights to the newly discovered lands of the New World;[46] the Treaty of Tordesillas in 1494,[47] between Spain and Portugal,[48] divided non-European lands between these two powers, with Spain claiming rights in the Americas, and Portugal rights in the East Indies. These divisions, inevitably contested by States that were not party to these treaties, attempted to prevent future disputes between great powers.

Geography provides a vital mode of defence; and international relations scholars and strategists from Sun Tzu[49] to Halford Mackinder[50] have focused on this reality in their analysis of conflict and Great Power politics. Further, the idea of 'natural frontiers', for instance, has preoccupied scholars dealing with territorial disputes and international legal approaches to nationalism and ethnic conflict. As Robert Redslob observes, natural frontiers refer to boundaries which offer advantages by the geographical structure and the resources of the circumscribed country. To have natural frontiers is to possess a territory, which gives facilities of defence against an invasion, and which, on the other hand, is an important source of economic subsistence.[51]

This idea of 'natural frontiers' has resulted in a tension between what might be described a 'geographical frontiers' and 'political frontiers'. The fact that a State's security is perceived to require control or influence over areas which are not within its sovereignty has resulted in the formation of 'buffer zones' and 'spheres of influence'. Disputes over control of the seas has been another issue of ongoing importance to international law. Scholars ranging from Grotius to Alfred Thayer Mahan[52] and beyond have been preoccupied with the question of control over the sea.

---

[45] Cf the contribution by D-E Khan 'Territory and Boundaries' in this volume.

[46] See *The Epochs* (n 16) 233.

[47] Treaty of Tordesillas (signed 7 June 1494) reprinted in WG Grewe (ed) *Fontes Historiae Iuris Gentium: Sources Relating to the History of the Law of Nations* (De Gruyter Berlin 1988) vol 2, 110–16.

[48] *The Epochs* (n 16) 234.

[49] Sun Tzu *The Art of War* (5th century BC) (J Minford ed and trans) (Penguin Classics New York 2002).

[50] HJ Mackinder 'The Geographical Pivot of History' (1904) 21 The Geographical Journal 421–37.

[51] R Redslob 'The Problem of Nationalities' (1932) 17 Grotius Society Proceedings 21–34 at 21.

[52] AT Mahan *The Influence of Sea Power on History, 1660–1783* (Little, Brown, and Co Boston 1860).

If we interpret the issue of regions to be the control and management of space, then it is clear that this question is a central preoccupation of international law, as so many areas of the first importance to the discipline—the concept of territorial sovereignty itself, the law relating to the settlement of territorial disputes, the law of the sea, and indeed, the evolving law of outer space, all deal with this central issue, and the major works that deal with these subjects can be seen as addressing the problem of regions. It is inevitable and unsurprising, then, that international law has established numerous doctrines to deal with the regulation of space; that territorial disputes have generated an enormous jurisprudence; that entire treaties, conventions and dispute resolution mechanisms are devoted to the issues relating to sovereignty and rights over space. Clearly, then, histories of international law that systematically examine the different doctrines used in international law to deal with these issues are of major importance. It is notable, furthermore, that geographic explanations—which have been used to account for issues such as poverty and unequal development—are now once again becoming prominent, as witnessed by the work of Ian Morris[53] and John Darwin.[54] Given the clear importance of the management of space for international relations, the question arises as to how general histories of international law have dealt with this subject.

Of all the major historians of international law, it is perhaps Carl Schmitt who focuses most closely and explicitly on space, and who analyses both State practice and all the prominent thinkers of the discipline in terms of how they addressed the issue of space. Schmitt recognizes the management of space to be the central preoccupation of international relations. Every *nomos* of the earth addresses the fundamental issue of spatial ordering:

This is the sense in which the nomos of the earth is spoken of here. Every new age and every new epoch in the co-existence of peoples, empires, and countries, of rulers and power formations of every sort, is founded on new spatial divisions, new enclosures, and new spatial orders of the earth.[55]

What is powerful and striking about Schmitt's account is his attempt to demonstrate that all law emerges from the appropriation of land: 'In every case, land-appropriation, both internally and externally, is the primary legal title that underlies all subsequent law.'[56] The appropriation of land precedes the private/public distinction, private property itself; it is radical title.[57] Schmitt traces the idea of

---

[53] I Morris *Why the West Rules—for Now* (McClelland & Stewart Ltd Toronto 2010).

[54] J Darwin *After Tamerlane: The Rise and Fall of Global Empires 1400–2000* (Bloomsbury Publishing London 2009).

[55] C Schmitt *The Nomos of the Earth in the International Law of the Jus Publicum Europaeum* (Telos Press Publishing New York 2003) at 79; B Fassbender 'Carl Schmitt (1888–1985)' in this volume.

[56] ibid 46. Interestingly, Schmitt, cites Kant as being in agreement (referring to Kant's *Philosophy of Law* in this regard).

[57] ibid 47.

the fundamental importance of land appropriation in the writings of Giambattista Vico, Immanuel Kant, and John Locke. But his own and original contribution to this debate is his claim that the question of war was intimately and inseparably linked to the issue of land appropriation, and that what was achieved by the *Jus Publicum Europaeum* was a bracketing of war with regard to land appropriation.[58] The governing and indispensable element of the *nomos* that Schmitt celebrated with such eloquence was the division of the earth into two spheres—the European and non-European spheres. The availability of 'free land' in the non-European world was fundamental to this spatial division of the world and the bracketing of war that followed.[59] Schmitt calmly made the stunning assertion that non-European territories were 'free land' that could be appropriated by European powers. Together with this system is the idea that while the terrestrial world was spatially divided in this way, the sea remained free. The significance of scholars such as Grotius—who was not greatly esteemed by Schmitt, it seems—was his work on 'The Free Sea'.

The crucial issues of war and peace were in turn based on this elemental distinction. Schmitt argued that different concepts of 'enemy, war, and plunder' were generated by these divisions.[60] Indeed, the 'bracketing of war' that is such an essential aspect of his jurisprudence 'pertained only to European land wars among States, pursued on European soil or on soil having the same status'.[61] By this he refers to 'a rationalization, humanization and legalization—a bracketing—of war' achieved through this spatial division.[62]

The spatial order of Europe that is the subject of Schmitt's admiration and, indeed, nostalgia, was based on a specific structure of power that was managed by the Great Powers of Europe.[63] However, the system was sufficiently flexible to allow for the emergences of new Great Powers—such as the as the United States and even Japan after its defeat of Russia. For Schmitt,

the recognition of a Great Power was the most important legal institution of international law with respect to land appropriation. It signified the right to participate in European conferences and negotiations, which was fundamental for this reality of European interstate international law.[64]

---

[58] The core of this *nomos* lay in the division of European soil into State territories with firm borders, which immediately initiated an important distinction, namely that this soil of recognized European States and their land had a special territorial status in international law. It was distinguished from the 'free soil' of non-European princes and peoples open for European land appropriations. ibid 148.

[59] 'Vast seemingly endless free spaces made possible and viable the internal law of an interstate European order.' ibid 183.

[60] ibid 184.

[61] ibid 184.

[62] ibid 100.

[63] 'The earlier European conferences demonstrated that the interstate international law of Europe was grounded in a comprehensive Eurocentric spatial order, which, in common consultations and resolutions, had developed its methods and forms for all significant territorial changes and had given the concept of an equilibrium beneficial meaning.' ibid 190.

[64] ibid 191.

This was the basic framework, one powerfully based on concepts of space and territory that Schmitt used to analyse major international events. Thus the Berlin Conference of 1885 was simultaneously the apogee and perigee of this system. It was a classical European conference in that it was intent on land appropriation and the carving up in a peaceful manner of another, different continent that was awaiting appropriation; the creation of a set of procedures to enable this was an indispensable part of this process. And yet, for Schmitt, the confusion about the status of non-European lands as a result of the uncertain characterization of the legal status of the Congo[65] and the ambiguous involvement of the United States suggested disturbing trends, the breakdown of the system he espoused.

For Schmitt, the emergence of the United States resulted in a disruption of this spatial system and thereby introduces 'a new concept of war into world history'.[66] The United States, for Schmitt, rather than accepting its new status and the accompanying rules of spatial order—which it could itself now participate in applying and managing—undermined the system with an alternative system of order. Referring to the Monroe doctrine, Schmitt argued that '[t]he line of a Western hemisphere already contained a polemical challenge to the specific European concept of a global spatial order.'[67] For Schmitt, the system collapsed with the League of Nations, when 'the European order dissolved into spaceless universalism, and no new order took its place'.[68] The League created a system of law based on an unreal universality '[t]he dissolution into general universality simultaneously spelled the destruction of the traditional global order of the earth.'[69]

Schmitt's arguments, however controversial and disconcerting—if not completely bizarre—demand some attention because they contain many original insights, and because they treated the issue of space and regions profoundly seriously. Schmitt's sweeping and in many ways disturbing vision raises a number of complex questions. What are the crucial elements of his jurisprudence, and how do the different elements of his jurisprudential structure connect together? How does the division of the world into sovereign European spheres and free (to appropriate) non-European spheres result in the bracketing of war? How does this system operate and evolve? How should we now think of Schmitt's work if approached in terms of the ideas of geography and space?[70]

The European *res publicae* for Schmitt embodied a 'concrete order'. In this regard Schmitt was like many of the writers discussed earlier in his belief that a particular region, Europe, had developed a system of international law that was somehow more authentic and effective because it was based on a shared history and values. It

---

[65] Schmitt argued that Belgium, through skilful diplomacy and sleight of hand, acquired sovereignty over the Congo without regard to the established scheme of European public order—without the permission granted by Great Powers and instead, relying on the doctrine of 'effective occupation'. ibid 223–5.

[66] ibid 100.   [67] ibid 191.   [68] ibid 192.   [69] ibid 227.

[70] For an illuminating set of essays that focuses on this aspect of Schmitt's work, see S Legg (ed) *Spatiality, Sovereignty and Carl Schmitt: Geographies of the Nomos* (Routledge London 2011).

is clear that Schmitt was vehemently opposed to a 'universalistic' international law. For Schmitt, it would appear, a 'concrete order' is an order that is created by a specific community of States that share a common culture and consciousness and which, most importantly, manifests this unity by adopting a shared set of principles regarding space.[71] For Schmitt, then, the idea of 'international law' somewhat paradoxically is specific to a continent or more particularly a real and shared culture. The League of Nations therefore is disastrous as it lacks such an underlying common culture or community—it has no regional basis—and because it correspondingly fails to articulate a coherent, concrete 'spatial order'. The League was a 'disorganized mass of more than 50 heterogeneous states, lacking any spatial or spiritual consciousness of what they once had in common'.[72] It is understandable then, that despite their completely different approaches to the Monroe doctrine, Schmitt complimented Alvarez for his understanding of the importance of a regional international law as being the only possibility, a specifically American international law.[73]

Many of Schmitt's arguments bear a striking resemblance to the arguments made by post-colonial and Third World scholars regarding the character and geopolitics of international law. Schmitt is unerring and unrelenting in basically asserting that the European system of international law and relations, indeed, European order itself, was based on the endless appropriation of non-European lands and peoples against whom war could be waged without any limits or restrictions. International law is based on a fundamental distinction between European and non-European States, for instance, and the appropriation of the non-European world was crucial to the well-being and very existence of Europe. Schmitt is quite breathtaking in his simple assumption that conquest and exploitation are unavoidable features of any political system, and that the non-European lands were simply available for appropriation. It is startling to note, for instance, that Schmitt's principle criticism of the Monroe doctrine appears to be, in substance, that it prevented European appropriation of lands in the Western hemisphere. Schmitt, however, laments the collapse of this order whereas the Third World critique was intent on illuminating and denouncing its very existence.

Schmitt is telling in his analysis of why the League of Nations was a failure in terms of its inability to establish a 'spatial order' for the earth—a problem that could be attributed to many different factors. The principle of 'nationalities' asserted by Wilson's espousal of self-determination, for instance, disrupted the idea that territorial issues could be simply decided by the great powers; the ambivalence of the United States—both a powerful presence within the system and yet outside it—compounded the problem. But Schmitt never gives any sense of

---

[71] What this dissolution heralded was the collapse of a 'concrete order, above all a spatial order, by a true community of European princely houses, states and nations'. *Nomos of the Earth* (n 55) 233–4.
[72] ibid 234.   [73] ibid 229.

how the system that he so ardently champions collapsed with such horrifying results: he does point to the beginning of the disintegration of the European system—which corresponded with the Berlin conference and its dual character, as both an affirmation of the system—the European powers were meeting to allocate 'free lands' in the non-European world and a process which led to its undermining, through the peculiar manner in which Belgium acquired rights over the Congo, and the beginning of the US practice that was to appear in a far more significant form in the Paris deliberations of 1919, of being both present and absent in major international negotiations. However, there is no clear link drawn between such events and the conflagration of the First World War.[74] Whatever the many criticisms that can be made of Schmitt's work, for the purposes of this chapter he is crucial for his assertion that the management of space is the central task of any particular order and for writing a history of international law that is based on this premise. His work is also noteworthy for the suggestion that a key aspect of any civilization is its conceptualization and management of space—key because so many other issues such as war and peace and integrally related to it.

6. REGIONS AND FUTURE HISTORIES OF INTERNATIONAL LAW

A renewed interest in the history of international law is now taking place—and it is an interest that has engaged not only international lawyers, but political theorists and scientists, historians, and philosophers. History, by its very nature, is more preoccupied with questions of time rather than space, the developments of events and civilizations and empires and ideas over particular periods. However, it is clear that international law is unavoidably concerned with question of sovereignty, power, governance and empire, and none of these issues can be addressed without some conceptualization of space. Suggestively, for Foucault, the term 'region' is a 'fiscal, administrative, military notion'.[75] As the prominent colonial administrator, Lord Curzon put it, referring to another geographical term '[f]rontiers are indeed the razor's edge on which hang suspended the modern issues of war and peace, of

---

[74]   There is a hint that Belgium, once again, deviated from the proper rules of the European system by denouncing the Germans who had just invaded their territory in violation of numerous treaties as being engaged in an 'unjust war'. ibid 259.

[75]   M Foucault 'Questions on Geography' in J Crampton and S Elden (eds) *Space, Knowledge and Power: Foucault and Geography* (C Gordon trans) (Ashgate Hampshire 2007) 173–82 at 176.

life or death of nations',[76] in other words, the central concerns of international law.

Recent important works have attempted to provide histories of the relationship between international law and geography. Thus Lauren Benton has written an illuminating history of the way in which European empires developed complex versions of sovereignty to deal with different geo-political realities. These empires seldom established one clear model of sovereignty over the territories and areas they controlled; rather, '[e]ven in the most paradigmatic cases, an empire's spaces were politically fragmented; legally differentiated; and encased in irregular, porous, and sometimes undefined borders'.[77] Different and intricate regimes had to be devised to enable empires to control sea routes, mountainous regions, and estuaries, and the character of these regimes is the subject of Benton's important work.

The relationship between international law and geography is also a central theme in Tayyab Mahmud's work on the Durand line separating Afghanistan and Pakistan and splitting the Pashtun people. As Mahmud argues, '[n]ineteenth century constructs of international law, geography, geopolitics and the frontier, fashioned in the age of empire, were interwoven in the enabling frame that made the drawing of colonial borders like the Durand line possible.'[78] The work of scholars such as Benton and Mahmud's provide models of the relationships between geography and international law, and how these issues may be explored.

The study of international law and geopolitics implicates, then, a whole series of questions that have been, historically, of the first importance to international law. Simply, borders and regions that have been dictated by external political imperatives and instantiated into international law rarely produce happy outcomes to the actual inhabitants. There is a vast literature on questions of ethnicity and borders. The works of anthropologists such as Thongchai Winichakul[79] and James Scott,[80] who deal in different ways with issues of nationhood, governance, and territory, may offer other important insights into the relationships between geography and law. Globalization, further has profoundly affected conceptualizations of space—commerce is

---

[76] GN Curzon *Frontiers: The Romanses Lectures, 1907* (Clarendon Press Gloucestershire 1907, repr Elibron Classics New York 2006) at 7; cited in Mahmud 'Colonial Cartographies, Postcolonial Borders, and Enduring Failures of International Law: The Unending Wars Along the Afghanistan-Pakistan Frontier' (2010) 36 Brooklyn Journal of International Law 1–74. Curzon was one of the notable viceroys of India.

[77] L Benton *A Search for Sovereignty: Law and Geography in European Empires, 1460–1900* (CUP Cambridge 2010).

[78] T Mahmud 'Colonial Cartographies, the Postcolonial Borders, and Enduring Failures of International Law: the Unending War Along the Afghanistan-Pakistan Frontier' (2010) 36 Brooklyn Journal of International Law 1–74.

[79] T Winichakul *Siam Mapped: A History of the Geo-Body of A Nation* (University of Hawai'i Press Honolulu 1994) at 2.

[80] JC Scott *The Art of Not Being Governed: An Anarchist History of Upland Southeast Asia* (Yale University New Haven 2009).

conceived of as 'spaceless', ideas of 'political belonging' and 'the nation-State' have been transformed—and this raises additional important issues whose genealogies remain to be traced by scholars of international law.

7. Conclusions

Any attempt to discuss 'regional international law' is confronted by the difficulty that a 'region' may be defined in numerous ways, depending on geographical, political, and ideological criteria. Nevertheless, the idea that particular regions have developed a unique international law has persisted in the writing of histories of international law. If anything, the significance of 'regional international law' has increased in recent times as a result of the emergence of regional entities with carefully defined memberships, and corresponding adjudicatory systems. Such developments raise the question, once again, of the relationship between 'regional' international law and universal international law. This chapter has suggested that further research into the relationship between international law and regions—understood as the management of space—may provide important insights into the history and nature of international law.

Recommended Reading

Alexandrowicz, Charles H *An Introduction to the History and Law of Nations in the East Indies* (Clarendon Oxford 1967).

Alvarez, Alejandro 'Latin America and International Law' (1909) 3 American Journal of International Law 269–353.

Anand, Ram P *Development of Modern International Law and India* (Indian Society of International Law New Delhi 2005).

Benton, Lauren *A Search for Sovereignty: Law and Geography in European Empires, 1460–1900* (CUP Cambridge 2010).

Elias, Taslim O *Africa and the Development of International Law* (AW Sijthoff Leiden 1972).

Grewe, Wilhelm G *The Epochs of International Law* (Walter de Gruyter Berlin 2000).

Legg, Stephen (ed) *Spatiality, Sovereignty and Carl Schmitt: Geographies of the Nomos* (Routledge London 2011).

Preiser, Wolfgang 'History of the Law of Nations: Basic Questions and Principles' in Rudolph Bernhardt (ed) *Encyclopedia of Public International Law* (Elsevier North-Holland 1995) vol 2, 716–21.

Schmitt, Carl *The Nomos of the Earth in the International Law of the Jus Publicum Europaeum* (Telos Press Publishing New York 2003) at 79.

Singh, Nagendra 'History of the Law of Nations: South and South-East Asia' in Rudolph Bern-
    hardt (ed) *Encyclopedia of Public International Law* (Elsevier North-Holland 1995) vol 2,
    824–39.
Slaughter, Anne-Marie and William Burke-White 'The Future of International Law is Domes-
    tic (or, the European Way of Law)' (2006) 47 Harvard International Law Journal 327–52.
Verosta, Stephan 'International Law in Europe and Western Asia Between 100 and 650 AD'
    (1964) 113 Recueil des cours 485–651.

PART VI

PEOPLE IN PORTRAIT

CHAPTER 45

MUHAMMAD AL-SHAYBĀNĪ (749/50–805)

MASHOOD A BADERIN

1. INTRODUCTION

CONTRARY to the popular view in Western legal scholarship, which often refers to the 16th/17th-century Dutch jurist, Hugo Grotius (1583–1645), as the 'father of international law', Islamic legal scholarship identifies Muhammad al-Shaybānī as having preceded Hugo Grotius by some eight centuries with the compilation and systemization of the rules of Islamic international law under a specialized subject area of Islamic law termed *al-Siyar*, which covers the laws of war and peace according to the *Shariʿah*. Reviewing one of al-Shaybānī's main works on the subject in 1827, Joseph Freiherr von Hammer-Purgstall, a 18th/19th-century Austrian diplomat and pioneer orientalist, described him as the Hugo Grotius of the Muslims.[1] In a more recent work, Christopher Weeramantry, a former judge and Vice-President of the International Court of Justice, identified al-Shaybānī as the author of the most detailed early treatise on

---

[1] IG Hülsemann (ed) *Jahrbücher der Literatur* (Carl Gerold Wien 1827) vol 40, at 48 cited in M Khadduri *The Islamic Law of Nations: Shaybani's Siyar* (Johns Hopkins Press Baltimore 1966) at 56; see also generally H Kruse 'The Foundation of Islamic International Jurisprudence: Muhammad al-Shaybani: The Grotius of the Muslims' (1955) 3 Journal of the Pakistan Historical Society 231–67.

international law,[2] observing that *al-Siyar* was a precursor for the development of modern international law and that Hugo Grotius' work on international law might have been influenced by earlier Islamic scholarship, including the works of al-Shaybānī, on the subject.[3] This, arguably, makes al-Shaybānī the 'grandfather of international law'.[4] He was a great 8th/9th-century Islamic law jurist and the most acclaimed contributor of his time to the systemization of the rules of international law from an Islamic legal perspective. His writings on the subject continue to influence Islamic legal thinking and scholarship on international law up to modern times. Also his juristic works continue to serve as primary jurisprudential authority of the Hanafi School and influenced some important jurisprudential work of the Mālikī School, two schools of law followed in a large part of the Muslim world today.

2. His Life and Legal Training

His full names were Abū Abd Allah Muhammad ibn al-Hasan ibn Farqad al-Shaybānī. He was born between 749 to 750 AD in Wasit, a military and commercial city of medieval Iraq established by the Umayyad Governor of Iraq, al-Hajjāj ibn Yūsuf al-Thaqafī, in 702 AD as a military base and administrative centre between Basra and Kufa. His father, who was a soldier, had migrated from their hometown in Damascus to Iraq towards the end of the Umayyad Dynasty to settle in Wasit. Al-Shaybāni, however, grew up in Kufa where he first studied under one of the four eponyms of the Sunnī Schools of Islamic law, Imām Abū Hanīfah al-Nuʿmān. After the death of Abū Hanifah, he continued his study under his senior student colleague, Abū Yūsuf, and also attended the study circles of other leading scholars of his time in Kufa. He and Abū Yūsuf are acknowledged to have played leading roles in the development of the Hanafī School of Islamic law. He eventually moved to the Hijāz, where he also studied under Imām Mālik ibn Anas, the eponym of the Mālikī School of Islamic law.

Al-Shaybānī taught Islamic jurisprudence in Kufa from the early age of 20, and Imām al-Shāfiʼī, the eponym of the Shāfiʼī School of Islamic law, was one of his students. He was eventually appointed as a judge in one of the provinces of Iraq by the Abassid Caliph, Harūn al-Rashīd, and he provided advice to the Caliph on different

---

[2] CG Weeramantry *Islamic Jurisprudence: An International Perspective* (Macmillan Hampshire 1988) at 132.

[3] ibid 149–58.

[4] It must be noted that the characterization of Grotius as 'father of international law' is largely being given up in more recent international law literature.

matters of State, including those relating to international law.[5] Through studying and engaging with the most leading scholars and jurists of his time, al-Shaybānī acquired thorough training in legal reasoning. He mastered both the traditionalist and rationalist approaches to Islamic law prevailing in his time through studying under both Imām Abū Hanīfah and Imām Mālik.

3. HIS SCHOLARSHIP AND CONTRIBUTION TO INTERNATIONAL LAW

Similar to other aspects of Islamic law, the rules of *al-Siyar* are derived from the Qur'an, the Prophet's practices (the *Sunnah*), and relevant practices of the earliest Muslim Caliphs, so al-Shaybānī was neither the founder nor the first Islamic jurist to write on the subject of Islamic international law. While his teacher, Abū Hanīfah, is considered as the first to compose an independent work on the subject,[6] al-Shaybānī is, however, acknowledged as the most prolific jurist of his time who wrote extensively on the subject in a systematic way, but often citing the views of his teacher Abū Hanīfah and that of his senior/teacher Abū Yūsuf in his work. Khadduri has observed that al-Shaybānī's contribution is invaluable, 'for he was the first to consolidate all the legal materials relevant to the subject and to provide the most detailed and thorough study of it'.[7]

He wrote many books covering different aspects of Islamic jurisprudence, and dealt with issues relating to international law in many of his works, such as *Kitāb al-Asl* (The Basic Book [of Jurisprudence]) also known as *al-Mabsūt* (The Comprehensive), *Kitāb al-Jāmi' al-Saghīr* (The Shorter Compilation [on Jurisprudence]), and *Kitāb al-Jāmi' al-Kabīr* (The Longer Compilation [on Jurisprudence]). He devoted two books exclusively to the subject of international law; namely, *Kitāb al-Siyar al-Saghīr* (The Shorter Book on International Law) and *Kitāb al-Siyar al-Kabīr* (The Longer Book on International Law). Both were written in the 8th century. The latter was written in response to a critic of the former by another leading jurist of *al-Siyar* at the time, Abd al-Rahmān al-Awzā'ī,[8] and is considered as al-Shaybānī's *magnum opus* on the subject.

---

[5] MZ al-Kawthari *Bulūgh al-Amānī fī Sirah al-Imām Muhammad ibn al-Hasan al-Shaybānī* (Authoritative Biography of Imām Muhammad ibn al-Hasan al-Shaybānī) (Maktabah Dār al-Hidāyah Cairo 1985) at 53–4.

[6] Early Islamic sources record that Abū Hanīfah composed an earlier treatise titled *Kitāb al-Siyar*.

[7] The Islamic Law of Nations (n 1) 56.

[8] M Sarakhsi *Sharh al-Siyar al-Kabīr* (Commentary on the Longer Book on International Law) (S Munajjid ed) (Matba'ah Sharikah al I'lānāt al-Sharqiyyah Cairo 1971) at 3.

While al-Shaybānī's works on *al-Siyar* principally systematized the rules of conduct in war and peacetime that the Muslim realm (*Dār al-Islām*) must uphold in its relationship with the non-Muslim realm (*Dār al-Harb*), it nevertheless covered many of the issues of modern international law, such as treaties, territorial jurisdiction, nature, kinds, and conduct of war, peaceful relations, diplomatic relations, and neutrality rules. For example, he established in his writings that there can be permanent treaty relationships between Muslim and non-Muslim States and that there should be no misappropriation, treachery, mutilation of the dead, and killing of children during warfare. In a recent article on the history of international law, Lesaffer observed notably that, 'the precursors of Grotius and Westphalia need to be studied sincerely if we are ever to understand the formation of this law of nations', and that Grotius' 'main source of inspiration remains a blank spot on the historical map'[9] of international law. There is no doubt that al-Shaybānī and his works on *al-Siyar* should form part of that study for a full understanding of his immense contribution to the formation of international law as a jurist that preceded Hugo Grotius by some eight centuries in that field.

Recommended Reading

al-Ghunaimi, Muhammad T *The Muslim Conception of International Law and the Western Approach* (Martinus Nijhoff Publishers Hague 1968).

al-Kawthari, Muhammad *Zāhid Bulūgh al-Amānī fi Sīrah al-Imām Muhammad ibn al-Hasan al-Shaybāni* (Authoritative Biography of Imām Muhammad ibn al-Hasan al-Shaybānī) (Maktabah Dār al-Hidāyah Cairo 1985).

al-Shaybani, Muhammad *Kitāb al-Siyar al-Kabīr* (The Longer Book on International Law) (Salah al-Din al Munajjid ed) (Matba'ah Sharikah al I'lānāt al-Sharqiyyah Cairo 1971).

al-Shaybani, Muhammad *Kitāb al-Siyar al-Saghīr* (The Shorter Book on International Law) (Muhammad Sarakhsi ed) (Dār al-Ma'rifah Beirut 1985).

al-Shaybani, Muhammad *The Shorter Book on Muslim International Law* (Mahmood A Gazi trans) (Adam New Delhi 2004).

al-Shaybani, Muhammad *Kitāb al-Asl; al-M'arūf bi al-Mabsūt* (The Basic Book [of Jurisprudence] known as The Comprehensive) (Al-Afghāni Abū al-Wafā' ed) (Matba'ah Idārah al-Qur'ān Karachi nd.

Bsoul, Labeeb A *International Treaties (Mu'āhadāt) in Islam: Theory and Practice in the Light of Islamic International Law (Siyar) According to Orthodox Schools* (University Press of America Maryland 2008).

Hamidullah, Muhammad 'Muhammad Al-Shaybani, A Contemporary of Charlemagne: The Greatest Jurist of the Time (8th Century CE)' (1969) 57 The Islamic Review and Arab Affairs 5–7.

---

[9] R Lesaffer 'International Law and Its History: The Story of an Unrequited Love' in M Craven et al (eds) *Time, History and International Law* (Martinus Nijhoff Leiden 2007) 27–42 at 40.

Hamidullah, Muhammad *The Muslim Conduct of State* (7th edn Muhammad Ashraf Lahore 1977).

Kelsay, John 'Al-Shaybani and the Islamic Law of War' (2003) 2 Journal of Military Ethics 63–75.

Khadduri, Majid (ed) *The Islamic Law of Nations: Shaybani's Siyar* (Johns Hopkins Baltimore 1966).

Kruse, Hans 'Al-Shaybani on International Instruments' (1953) 1 Journal of Pakistan Historical Society 90–100.

Kruse, Hans 'The Foundations of Islamic International Jurisprudence: Muhammad al-Shaybani: The Grotius of the Muslims' (1955) 3 Journal of Pakistan Historical Society 231–67.

Sarakhsi, Muhammad *Sharh al-Siyar al-Kabīr* (Commentary on the Longer Book on International Law) (S Munajjid ed) (Matba'ah Sharikah al I'lānāt al-Sharqiyyah Cairo 1971).

Weeramantry, Christopher *Islamic Jurisprudence: An International Perspective* (Macmillan Hampshire 1988).

CHAPTER 46

FRANCISCO DE VITORIA (1483–1546) AND FRANCISCO SUÁREZ (1548–1617)

ANNABEL BRETT

1. INTRODUCTION

FRANCISCO de Vitoria (1483–1546) and Francisco Suárez (1548–1617) are today's best-known members of the major 16th- and 17th-century intellectual movement known as the 'School of Salamanca' or the 'second scholastic'. Both were by profession theologians, not lawyers (although Suárez had studied canon law), and both spent most of their lives in a university milieu.[1] A large part of their intellectual endeavour was dedicated to the renewal and systematization of Catholic theology, especially moral theology, as part of the Counter-Reformation Church's effort to restore Catholicism both intellectually and politically in the wake of the Reformation. Both worked within

---

[1] For details of Vitoria's biography, see JB Plans *La escuela de Salamanca* (Biblioteca de Autores Cristianos Madrid 2000) at 313–98; for Suárez, J Soder *Francisco Suárez und das Völkerrecht. Grundgedanken zu Staat, Recht und internationalen Beziehungen* (Metzner Frankfurt 1973) at 15–47; M Kremer *Den Frieden verantworten. Politische Ethik bei Francisco Suárez (1548–1617)* (Kohlhammer Stuttgart 2008) at 23–32.

the heritage of the natural law theology of Thomas Aquinas, mediated through other strands of the scholastic tradition, bending and shaping Thomist teachings to answer questions that the original had not posed. This work was done primarily through university lecturing, in dialogue and often polemic with other past and contemporary scholars. However, it would be a mistake to think that their work was narrowly academic. The first generation of the School of Salamanca was heavily involved in the question of the theological legitimacy of Crown policy, both in the Indies and at the Council of Trent.[2] The Society of Jesus, to which Suárez belonged, was equally politically involved; Suárez himself was called upon to defend Catholic consciences against James VI/I in the English Oath of Allegiance controversy.[3] Their work upon their intellectual heritage was done in the context of these wider concerns, although it cannot always be reduced to them: theirs are works of enormous complexity and sophistication in which the question of intentionality is not always easily answered.

2. Francisco de Vitoria

Vitoria addressed the question of the *ius gentium* both in his regular lectures on Aquinas' *Summa theologiae* and in the occasional *relectiones* given at the end of his lecture courses. In his commentary on the *Secunda secundae*, dating from 1534–37, he engaged directly with Aquinas' positioning of the *ius gentium* as a kind of natural, as opposed to positive, law, consisting in natural reason.[4] Here, Vitoria moved away from the Thomist position to make the *ius gentium* a kind of positive law, based on inter-human agreement.[5] The universal character of that agreement meant that it retained a close proximity to natural law, both in being a result of natural reasoning processes and in functioning to protect the operation of natural law. Nevertheless, it had a human source in 'the consensus of all peoples and nations' or 'of the whole world',[6] two

---

[2] See ARD Pagden *The Fall of Natural Man. The American Indians and the Origins of Comparative Ethnology* (CUP Cambridge 1980) ch 1.

[3] See H Höpfl *Jesuit Political Thought. The Society of Jesus and the State, c. 1540–1630* (CUP Cambridge 2004).

[4] T Aquinas *Summa theologiae* (Forzani Rome 1894) 2ª2ae, question 57, art 2. By contrast, in the *Prima secundae*, Aquinas had seen the *ius gentium* as a kind of 'human law' as opposed to natural law, though still differing from civil law by its direct derivation from the principles of natural law or natural reason. Ibid 1ª2ae, question 95, art 4.

[5] F de Vitoria *Comentarios a la Secunda secundae de Santo Tomás* (VB de Heredia ed) (Apartado 17 Salamanca 1934) vol III, question 57 art 3, nn 1–5. See the discussion in D Deckers *Gerechtigkeit und Recht. Eine historisch-kritische Untersuchung der Gerechtigkeitslehre des Francisco de Vitoria (1483–1546)* (Herder Freiburg 1992) at 358–65.

[6] *Comentarios a la Secunda secundae* (n 5) vol III, question 57, art 3, nn 4 and 5.

locutions between which Vitoria evidently saw no conflict but which require some explanation. In his early *Relectio de potestate civili* of 1528, Vitoria spoke of this legislator of the *ius gentium* as 'the whole world, which is in a sense [*quasi*] a commonwealth',[7] thus apparently underlining the analogy between the *ius gentium* and civil law as types of positive rather than natural law. The *quasi* is important, however. Vitoria did not think of the whole world as one commonwealth like the particular commonwealths of France or Spain. If it were, a universal emperor, a *dominus mundi*, would be a possibility. But in the later *Relectio de Indis* of 1539, Vitoria expressly denied this: there neither is nor can be any universal civil jurisdiction spanning all peoples, and consequently no universal civil law.[8] In this work, the universal law of nations figures as a *ius inter gentes*, replacing the *ius inter homines* of the Roman law. By rewording the definition in this way, Vitoria was clear that the *ius gentium* was not a law that governs individuals in the first instance, but this does not mean that he saw it as a law between commonwealths or 'States' either.[9] On the contrary, he simultaneously underlined its close proximity to, if not identity with, natural law. This does not necessarily entail a contradiction between the *De Indis* and the earlier pronouncements. Rather, the *ius gentium* is part of an essentially temporal narrative of the separation of peoples 'within' a natural pan-human community, a narrative that is different from that of the founding of commonwealths.[10] This is why Vitoria can both affirm that the *ius gentium* is the product of all the nations or of the whole world, and can move easily between its positive and its natural character.

Vitoria worked within this framework to stabilize a position on the legitimacy of the Spanish conquest of the Indies. As we have seen, he denied universal imperial jurisdiction as a legitimizing framework, and he did the same for universal papal jurisdiction.[11] The Indians had true *dominium* both in the sense of jurisdiction and in the sense of property, and such *dominium* was not taken away by their lack of Christian faith, nor by some putative argument that they were irrational.[12] However, just like European commonwealths, their commonwealths were situated within the broader 'society of the human race', and therefore their actions were subject to its

---

[7]   F de Vitoria *De potestate civili* ('On Civil Power') in ARD Pagden and J Lawrance (eds) *Francisco de Vitoria. Political Writings* (CUP Cambridge 1992) question 3, art 4, para 21, at 40.

[8]   F de Vitoria *Relectio de Indis* ('On the American Indians') in *Political Writings* (n 7) question 2, art 1, para 25, at 257–8.

[9]   See the discussion of this contested passage in HG Justenhoven *Francisco de Vitoria zu Krieg und Frieden* (Bachem Köln 1991) at 64–71; P Haggenmacher *Grotius et la guerre juste* (Presses Universitaires de France Paris 1983) at 313–25 and 334–41; S Langalla *Teologia e legge naturale. Studi sulle lezioni di Francisco de Vitoria* (Glauco Brigati Genova 2007) at 178–89.

[10]   I have attempted to sketch this narrative in A Brett *Changes of State. Nature and the Limits of the City in Early Modern Natural Law* (Princeton University Press Princeton 2011) at 196–8. For the importance of temporality in late medieval and early modern conceptions of the *ius gentium*, see *Grotius et la guerre juste* (n 9) 326 and 343.

[11]   *Relectio de Indis* (n 8) question 2, art 2, para 27, at 259–61.

[12]   See the discussion in B Tierney *The Idea of Natural Rights* (Emory Atlanta Georgia 1997) ch 11.

norms. Vitoria listed a series of just titles of conquest based on an Indian violation of the *ius gentium*, the first and most controversial of which is the *ius communicandi*, the right of inter-human communication or sharing.[13] The *ius communicandi* is the necessary complement of the division of the human race into separate nations, which would otherwise tear its unity apart. Its scope is huge, including the right to travel freely in another's territory, the right to appropriate any 'unoccupied' goods therein, the right to inter-marriage, and to the acquisition of citizenship.[14] If the Indians violate this right, for example by forbidding the Spaniards entry, then war is justified. Vitoria hedged this conclusion around with several caveats, recognizing that Indians have just cause to be fearful of the Spaniards and holding that their actions must be judged in the light of this fact, rather than immediately interpreted as unjustified aggression.[15] Nor did he allow conquest on the sole grounds that certain practices were against the law of nature.[16] Nevertheless, Vitoria's juridical universalism combined with the particularity of its application to the Indians undoubtedly operated to open their commonwealths to European invasion.[17]

3. Francisco Suárez

Francisco Suárez addressed the question of the *ius gentium* in the course of his massive treatise *On the Laws and God the Lawgiver* of 1612.[18] In this work, he developed Vitoria's position in the commentary on the *Secunda secundae*, by now endorsed by the Dominican Domingo de Soto and Suárez' fellow-Jesuit Luis de Molina as well, that the *ius gentium* was positive rather than natural law. It cannot be, as Aquinas had suggested in the *Prima secundae* of his *Summa theologiae*, a series of conclusions from the principles of natural reason or natural law, because anything that necessarily follows from natural reason or natural law is effectively already contained within that law. Suárez thus broke the link between the *ius gentium* and natural reason that Vitoria had striven to protect. The *ius gentium* as a separate domain of law is based

---

[13] *Relectio de Indis* (n 8) question 3, art 1, at 278–84.

[14] See the discussion in G Cavallar *The Rights of Strangers. Theories of International Hospitality, the Global Community, and Political Justice since Vitoria* (Ashgate Aldershot 2002) ch 2.

[15] *Relectio de Indis* (n 8) question 3, art 1, at 282.

[16] F de Vitoria *Relectio de temperantia* ('On dietary laws, or self-restraint') question 1, art 5 in *Political Writings* (n 7) 225–6.

[17] As argued forcefully in A Anghie *Imperialism, Sovereignty and the Making of International Law* (CUP Cambridge 2002) ch 1.

[18] F Suárez *De legibus ac Deo legislatore* (L Pereña ed) (CSIC Madrid 1971–81) book II, chs 17 and 19.

not on natural reason but on customary usage, and is thus positive and not natural.[19] Suárez was also concerned to argue, in a way that Vitoria had not, that it was indeed a domain of 'law', responding to the challenge of his fellow-Jesuit Gabriel Vázquez that the *ius gentium* is simply a series of rights (the right to declare war, the right to trade, etc.), with the normativity of the exercise of such rights springing not from any law of nations but from the law of nature. From this perspective, the only international norm was the law of nature. Suárez vehemently denied this position; the *ius gentium* is a series of international norms, not just rights.[20]

If so, and if the norms are based on custom, then whose custom counts as generating international law? Here Suárez made a crucial distinction. There are customs that are shared across all commonwealths, such as buying and selling. These had traditionally been placed under the *ius gentium* in the Roman law.[21] Suárez denied this; they are norms in all nations, certainly, thus generating a kind of cross-nation normativity (one might expect to buy and sell in Spain in much the same way as in France), but they are not properly norms between nations. They are a *ius intra gentes*. The *ius gentium* properly speaking, however, is a *ius inter gentes*, a law between separate commonwealths.[22] It is the customs that govern the behaviour of States, for example, that the injured State has a right to punish through war the injuring State, that truly constitute the law of nations. Thus Suárez might be thought to have taken a significant step down the road to a truly positive international law.[23] However, two caveats need to be made. One is that Suárez retains, in some sense, the proximity of these norms to natural reason: negotiating delicately with the position of Aquinas, he allowed, for example, that although the nations might have adopted some other position on the right to wage war (the appointment of third-party arbitration), the current custom is more in accordance with nature.[24] Secondly, Suárez grounded the necessity for such international norms not on the utility of States but on the fundamental unity of the entire human race; commonwealths are separate, but they are still part of a broader human society, which has needs of interaction that prevent the free play of state activity and bring it under a common legal framework. This aspect of his thought has much in common with that of Vitoria. However, in contrast to Vitoria, Suárez made the *gentes* understood as commonwealths or States the individual members of this broader community, and it is their practice that makes the *ius gentium*, losing the fluidity between 'the whole world' and 'all the nations' that marks

---

[19] ibid ch 17, nn 8–9; see the discussion in *Francisco Suárez und das Völkerrecht* (n 1) 163–87; B Tierney 'Vitoria and Suárez on *ius gentium*, Natural law, and Custom' in A Perreau-Saussine and J Murphy (eds) *The nature of customary law* (CUP Cambridge 2007) 101–24.

[20] See the discussion in JP Doyle 'Francisco Suárez and the law of nations' in MW Janis and C Evans (eds) *Religion and international law* (Nijhoff The Hague-London 1999) 103–20; *Den Frieden verantworten* (n 1) 127–30; *Francisco Suárez und das Völkerrecht* (n 1) 199–203.

[21] Hermogenianus D.1.1.5.

[22] *De legibus* (n 18) book II, ch 19, n 8.

[23] *Francisco Suárez und das Völkerrecht* (n 1) 213.

[24] *De legibus* (n 18) book II, ch 19, nn 3 and 8.

the thought of Vitoria.[25] Thus Suárez' distinction between the *ius intra gentes* and the *ius inter gentes* marked a significant innovation within the theoretical construction of the law of nations, while at the same time his thought was conditioned by a human universalism and a proximity to natural reason that bound it firmly to that of his predecessors.

RECOMMENDED READING

Anghie, Antony *Imperialism, Sovereignty and the Making of International Law* (CUP Cambridge 2002).

Bunge, Kirstin, Anselm Spindler, and Andreas Wagner (eds) *Die Normativität des Rechts bei Francisco de Vitoria—The Normativity of Law According to Francisco de Vitoria* (Frommann Holzboog Stuttgart-Bad Canstatt 2011).

Deckers, Daniel *Gerechtigkeit und Recht. Eine historisch-kritische Untersuchung der Gerechtigkeitslehre des Francisco de Vitoria (1483–1546)* (Herder Freiburg 1992).

Doyle, John P *Collected Studies on Francisco Suárez SJ (1548–1617)* (Victor Salas ed) (Leuven University Press Leuven 2011).

Haggenmacher, Peter *Grotius et la guerre juste* (Presses Universitaires de France Paris 1983).

Justenhoven, Heinz G *Francisco de Vitoria zu Krieg und Frieden* (Bachem Köln 1991).

Kremer, Markus *Den Frieden verantworten. Politische Ethik bei Francisco Suárez (1548–1617)* (Kohlhammer Stuttgart 2008).

Soder, Josef Francisco *Suárez und das Völkerrecht. Grundgedanken zur Staat, Recht und internationalen Beziehungen* (Metzner Frankfurt am Main 1973).

Tierney, Brian *The Idea of Natural Rights: Studies on Natural Rights, Natural Law and Church Law, 1150–1625* (Scholars Press Atlanta Georgia 1997).

---

[25] ibid book II, ch 19, n 9; and see the discussion in *Francisco Suárez und das Völkerrecht* (n 1) 220–48 and 67–70 (contrast with the Jesuit Juan de Salas).

CHAPTER 47

ALBERICO GENTILI (1552–1608)

MERIO SCATTOLA

1. LIFE AND TEACHING

ALBERICO Gentili was born in 1552 in San Ginesio in the Papal States, and after studying civil law in Perugia, he lived as city attorney in that town. Suspected of heresy, he fled in 1579 to the Holy Roman Empire and settled in 1580 in London, starting a new career as attorney. Here he was introduced to Robert Dudley, and under his protection he began teaching in 1581 at St John College in Oxford, where he was appointed regius professor in 1587.

In Oxford, Alberico Gentili wrote a large number of works, which can be divided in four main groups. The first group comprises treatises on topics of the civil law, such as his collection of ten academic dissertations, his commentary on the title of the *Codex* about magicians, and his commentary on the title *On Meaning of Words*. All these works followed and defended the *mos Italicus* learned in Perugia. Gentili dedicated a second group of writings to the law of nations. He began in this field with the *Three Books on Embassies* (1585), which were also concerned with the case of Bernardino de Mendoza (*c.* 1540–1604), the Spanish ambassador expelled in 1584 for having being involved in a plot against Elizabeth I. In 1589, after the attack of the *Armada invincible*, Gentili published three dissertations on the law of war that he resumed in 1598 in his major work, the *Three Books on the Law of War*. He completed the discussion on this topic in 1599 with his *Two Books on the Roman Armies*, where he defended the assumption that the ancient Romans always fought just wars.

Writings of a third kind dealt with issues pertaining to political theology, as they considered the duty of the king who had to mediate a transcendent order into a human commonwealth.[1] Gentili gave a first assertion of the royal power in the disputation *On the Prince*, included within the ten disputations published in 1587.[2] He expanded his argument in 1605 in the *Three Royal Disputations*, where he explained that the king had an absolute power, that the three kingdoms of Britain could be legitimately united, and that the subjects had no right to resist the power of the English king. On the issue of the resistance to a legitimate king, he published a series of ten disputations commenting two titles of the *Codex Iustinianus*. With these political writings, Gentili took position in favour of James I and his programme of a Eusebian monarchy, against both the Presbyterian idea of a compact and the Catholic theory of an indirect power of the pope, and entered into a large polemical stream which dominated the European discussion in the early 17th century.

The fourth group of works comprises a large number of writings dedicated to various questions of legal erudition. Gentili wrote on the books of the legal collections, on the language of the Roman law, on the names of historical periods, on the morality of the actors, and on Biblical issues.

He held the chair in Oxford until the end of his life, but from 1590 he was also active at the Court of Admiralty in London, which applied continental civil law. From 1605 to 1608 he served as official attorney of the Spanish embassy and from this experience wrote his third great work on law of nations, the *Two Books of Spanish Attorneyship*, published posthumously in 1613.

2. Gentili and the History of International Law

During his life Gentili was not as famous as his younger brother Scipione and was quickly forgotten after his death. He was rediscovered in 1874 by Thomas Erskine Holland (1835–1926), who provided a new edition of the *Law of War*. Since then he has been regarded as a 'father of the international law', although this is probably better expressed as a 'father of the law of nations'. As opposed to the modern understanding of an international law established through rational agreement between free and independent states,[3] Gentili regarded the law of nations as a form of private law,

---

[1] M Scattola *Teologia politica* (Il Mulino Bologna 2007).
[2] A Gentili *Disputationum decas prima* (Excudebat Iohannes Wolfius London 1587) at 34.
[3] A Verdross *Völkerrecht* (Springer Wien 1955) at 34–9.

which comprised those common rules used by people of different nations, and applied also between commonwealths. Secondly, it referred to a natural or divine order expressed in a set of innate ideas. Thirdly, it operated with ontologically independent rules, which could be interpreted only in topological argumentation. In this sense Gentili was part of a legal tradition that stretched back to ancient and medieval jurisprudence and theology, reached its highest point with Hugo Grotius (1583–1645) and was then replaced, totally or partly, by the modern teaching of natural law. Nevertheless during the 16th century arose the necessity of identifying a set of rules within this comprehensive law of nations pertaining only to commonwealth, that is, a 'public' law of nations beside the 'private' one. This project was already underway, begun by the Scholastic theologians in Salamanca, who had identified some specific problems in the relationships among nations and developed a particular literary form in order to transmit their teaching.

This theological tradition of 'public' law of nations had two main faults in the eyes of Gentili. First of all, it was developed from materials of the Catholic tradition, which could not fit a kingdom fighting on one side against the papacy and Spain, and on the other side against Presbyterians and Puritans. Secondly, it was produced by a theological scholarship which had its own agenda of questions and answers, its own authorities, and its own codes and media, as in early modern times political and juridical discussions were performed within clear detached communities of discourse.[4]

Gentili was to build an extensive doctrine about the 'public' law of nations by means of the legal tradition. Actually, the topic of war was well known in late medieval jurisprudence, which had produced a number of treatises on this subject gathered together in the great legal collections of the 16th century. But this literature treated single parts or actors and could not depict war in all its aspects. Also, Roman jurisprudence presented various rules of war in the *Corpus iuris*, and finally, a large number of observations could be made simply by the scrutiny of ancient historiography, which showed the Romans at war in practice and offered a basis for a comprehensive doctrine, as was developed some decades later by Hugo Grotius.

Gentili based his 'public' law of nation upon these three traditions, but he did not propose a 'systematic' theory since he lacked an epistemic unitary point of view, such as was developed later on within modern natural law. He organized his law of nations as a collection of main questions, unified within a topical distribution and not dependent on a single principle. Thus he treated law of embassy as a *speculum legati*, he discussed law of war in a triadic scheme that roughly followed the development of a conflict, and he presented the law of sea through an independent scheme based on legal practice.

[4]　M Scattola *Krieg des Wissens—Wissen des Krieges* (Unipress Padova 2006) at 36–50.

3. GENTILI AND THE DOCTRINE OF WAR

Already in early dissertations, Gentili clearly stated his intention to construct a political doctrine with arguments of the juridical tradition. The second dissertation on the royal power clarifies at the beginning that this topic is going to be treated using the rules of Roman law, omitting all philosophical arguments,[5] especially those of John Case, Gentili's colleague in Oxford, who taught Aristotelian politics and defended opposite views.

Even more explicit are the opening pages of the *Three Books on the Law of War*. Here Gentili claims that all philosophers have completely ignored the topic of war because they sought the good life within a single commonwealth, and did not explain the rights and duties among enemies. These writings presume the existence of a greater community, the society of the whole mankind,[6] which was thinkable only when European societies, living according to Roman or common law, came into direct touch with a number of nations living according to different customs. What law could regulate both European and extra-European countries? A kernel in the civil law ought to exist that was valid both for European and non European populations. Gentili solved this problem answering that it is possible that some rules, although they appear to us as universal und eternal, have been forgotten to some extent.[7] So the same law exists that rules over the whole world, explicitly or implicitly.

The ancient Romans had a complete science of this law. They applied it when they dealt with foreigners and enemies, and they preserved it in the *Libri fetiales*. Unfortunately this knowledge disappeared since the end of the republic, and only Justinian saved some isolated pieces of it. The lawyers today can reconstruct such a lost law, preserved in the Roman jurisprudence and testified in the histories, applying those legal first ideas to historical materials, and so they can establish a new version of the old 'public' law of nations.[8]

On these premises Gentili offered in the *Three Books on the Law of War* a collection of all the arguments gathered by the legal tradition. He insisted on the principle that war is always an action of justice; he defined war as 'a just conflict with public armed forces',[9] and stressed the three concepts of 'armed', 'public', and 'just'.

Justice of war is explained through the four Aristotelian causes, which supply the pattern for the whole treatise. Chapters 1–6 of the first book describe the prince as the efficient cause, whereas the remaining chapters 7–25 show the material cause, that is, the reasons of fighting a war. The second book is dedicated to the

---

[5] *Disputationum decas prima* (n 2) 32.
[6] Gentili *De iure belli libri tres* (Antonius Hanau 1612) book I, ch 1, at 2.
[7] ibid 8–10.   [8] ibid 4.   [9] ibid ch 2, at 17.

formal cause, or the right way of making war, and the third book explains its final cause, its conclusion, and the following peace.[10] Particular attention is paid to the reasons for waging war, which must always be suggested by true justice. Only defence can be a true reason of war, and it can be thought both as a reaction against an unjust attack or as claim of a right that was unjustly taken away or refused.[11] Religion can in this sense never be a just cause of war, and divine wars were possible only in ancient time, when God governed over His people and spoke directly to them. Nevertheless religion can be invoked by a king against his subjects when they dissent from the public cult and rebel against the legitimate magistrate, because the power to determine the religion of a country pertains only to the king.[12]

RECOMMENDED READING

Gentili, Alberico *De iuris interpretibus dialogi sex* (Wolfius London 1582).

Gentili, Alberico *Lectionum et epistolarum, quae ad ius civile pertinent, libri IV* (Wolfius London 1583–84).

Gentili, Alberico *De legationibus libri tres* (Vautrollerius London 1585).

Gentili, Alberico *Disputationum decas prima* (Wolfius London 1587).

Gentili, Alberico *De iure belli libri tres* (1st edn 1598, Antonius Hanau 1612).

Gentili, Alberico *De armis Romanis Libri duo* (Antonius Hanau 1599).

Gentili, Alberico *Ad titulum Codicis De maleficiis et mathematicis et ceteris similibus commentarius* (Antonius Hanau 1604).

Gentili, Alberico *Regales disputationes tres: I. De potestate regis absoluta; II. De unione regnorum Britanniae; III. De vi civium in regem semper iniusta* (Vautrollerius London 1605).

Gentili, Alberico *In titulos Codicis Si quis Imperatori maledixerit, Ad legem Juliam maiestatis disputationes decem* (Antonius Hanau 1607).

Gentili, Alberico *Hispanicae advocationis libri duo* (Antonius Hanau 1613).

Gentili, Alberico *In titulum Digestorum De verborum significatione commentarius* (Aubrius Hanau 1614).

Benedictis, Angela de 'Gentili, Alberico' in Mario Caravale (ed) *Dizionario biografico degli italiani* (Istituto dell'Enciclopedia italiana Roma 1999) vol 53, at 245–51.

Haggenmacher, Peter 'Grotius and Gentili. A Reassessment of Thomas E. Holland's Inaugural Lecture' in Hedley Bull, Benedict Kingsbury, and Adam Roberts (eds) *Hugo Grotius and International Relations* (Clarendon Press Oxford 1990) 133–76.

Minnucci, Giovanni *Alberico Gentili tra mos Italicus e mos Gallicus. L'inedito commentario Ad legem Iuliam de adulteriis* (Monduzzi Bologna 2002).

Molen, Gezina van der *Alberico Gentili and the Development of International Law: His Life, Work and Times* (2nd edn Sijthoff Leyden 1968).

---

[10] ibid ch 7, at 55–6.   [11] ibid ch 5, at 45.   [12] ibid ch 10, at 66–78.

Panizza, Diego (ed) *Alberico Gentili. Politica e religione nell'età delle guerre di religione* (Giuffrè Milano 2002).

Scattola, Merio '*Scientia Iuris* and *Ius Naturae*. The Jurisprudence of the Holy Roman Empire in the Seventeenth and Eighteenth Centuries' in Damiano Canale, Paolo Grossi, and Hasso Hofmann (eds) *A Treatise of Legal Philosophy and General Jurisprudence* (Dordrecht Springer 2009) vol 9 (*A History of the Philosophy of Law in the Civil Law World, 1600–1900*) 1–41.

CHAPTER 48

HUGO GROTIUS
(1583–1645)

PETER HAGGENMACHER

GROTIUS is nowadays essentially remembered as a jurist, particularly in legal and political philosophy, and above all in international law. In his own century he enjoyed much wider fame, not only for his position with regard to religious controversies, but more generally as an outstanding citizen of the Republic of Letters. Richelieu, despite heartily disliking him, still declared him one of the three greatest humanists of his age, a judgment amply borne out by his vast corpus of works spreading well beyond law into various fields such as classical philology, historiography, and theology.

His life can roughly be divided into three periods: his youth as a precocious classicist, lawyer, and rising politician in his native Holland, until his brutal fall—with his mentor Oldenbarnevelt—and condemnation to life imprisonment (1583–1618); his exile, first in Paris (1621–31) and later, after an unsuccessful attempt to regain his country, in Hamburg (1632–34); and finally his ambassadorship for Sweden at the French court (1635–45).

The work on which his posthumous reputation is mainly founded was written in Paris soon after his escape from Loevestein Castle and published in 1625. Entitled *De iure belli ac pacis* (On the Law of War and Peace), it earned him the long-standing title of 'father of international law'. While this exclusive paternity has been challenged on behalf of other presumable genitors, it remains widely accepted that the treatise played a decisive part in the emergence of international law as a separate legal discipline. Its author's crucial contribution is usually perceived in his specifically modern conception of natural law, freed from the theological shackles of the scholastics who had lost their credit with the breakdown of medieval Christendom; this offered a neutral ground on which the struggling confessional parties could agree and find their way back to peace in the midst of the Thirty Years' War: Grotius' system was thus to serve as a theoretical blueprint for the so-called Westphalian order supposed to have been set up soon after his demise. Yet this piously nurtured foundational myth, which smacks of 19th-century hero worship and anticlericalism, is hardly borne out by the text of Grotius' masterpiece. Neither does it propound a new 'secular' conception of natural law, nor is it really a system of international law.

Grotius had no intention of ousting God from his legal cosmos, any more than the Spanish scholastics had done. His definition of natural law is basically in line with Suarez' conception.[1] If he declares it 'valid to some degree even if God did not exist',[2] it is only by way of hypothesis in order to stress its intrinsic validity, which makes it immutable even in the eyes of God. But God remains the ultimate legitimizing authority as the creator of the universe: having endowed man with a rational and sociable nature, he cannot but recognize the basic values it entails, and sanction by his command the rules which necessarily flow therefrom. Grotius' point was to put beyond doubt the existence of an unwritten law inherent in human nature and hence binding on the whole of mankind, apart from any positive enactment, be it human or divine. Here lies the gist of his famous diatribe against Carneades and other 'realists' who would reject as a pure illusion the very idea of such a universal natural law, since all law for them follows not justice but mere utility at the hands of the powers that be.[3]

For all this, Grotius does not dismiss utility as a basis of law, but he confines it to positive law, which draws its validity not from nature but from some legislative will. Apart from civil (that is, municipal) law, such is the case of the law of nations inasmuch as it springs from the free consent of nations. Grotius was the first scholar, with Suarez, to redefine the Roman *ius gentium* as a properly international law (instead of being merely the common municipal law it had traditionally been). For both authors, however, it obliges individuals rather than States as such and, instead of forming by itself a complete system, it rather consists of specific rules and institutions which complement the very general principles of the law of nature. Only in conjunction, as *ius naturae et gentium*, could they both make up something akin to international law as we know it, and this is indeed the subtitle of Grotius' *magnum opus*. It remains to be seen whether by its features and general spirit the work can be considered as a treatise of international law.

At first sight the title would suggest an affirmative answer, although one would rather expect peace to have precedence over war. Yet the word order is in fact quite

---

[1] H Grotius *De iure belli ac pacis* (1625) I, I, X.
[2] ibid Prolegomena, at 11.
[3] ibid Prolegomena, at 3–27.

revealing, for Grotius' title (of Ciceronian descent) has to be read, not in the light of classical international law which was yet to emerge, but of the old established discipline of the law of war, of which the treatise constitutes the ultimate culmination. The *ius belli* forms its essential theme; the *ius pacis* figures in it merely as a set of rules to end war.

Grotius' central purpose was to ascertain the existence of a higher legal order governing war as to its beginning, its conduct, and conclusion. The overall structure of his treatise corresponds to the scholastic just war theory. Grotius had already delved into the relevant materials two decades earlier as a young lawyer in a substantial dissertation written in defence of a prize case involving the Dutch East India Company. Hence the title, *De iure praedae*, of that first inquiry into the law of war, which, except for one chapter published in 1609 under the celebrated title *Mare liberum*, remained unknown until its discovery in 1864. The treatise he published twenty years later drew heavily on this remarkable piece of advocacy and scholarship. Grotius once again took up and further developed the idea which lies at the heart of the just war theory, admitting recourse to armed force only as a means of last resort to sanction a wrong when ordinary legal remedies are not available. 'Where judgments cease, war begins', was his basic axiom,[4] war taking the place of an action at law in the absence of a competent jurisdiction. The major problem was to determine the lawful causes of action. One of Grotius' foremost concerns was to draw a neat line between legal grounds proper and merely prudential or utilitarian motives for making war. He therefore built up an entire body of substantive law in book II, which makes up about half of the whole work. It is presented as a comprehensive system of subjective rights supposed to inhere in human beings as such, which is why any person of whatever condition is potentially entitled to enforce them in case of violation.

While the immediate function of this system of rights was thus to indicate exhaustively and infallibly what could be legally valid grounds for war, Grotius attached a wider significance to it,[5] and this is why it could be exploited by his successors in several directions, private law above all, but also constitutional and criminal law, and of course international law. Not least, even modern human rights law finds in it one of its roots. Yet, fraught as it is with potentialities, Grotius' treatise still remains essentially a generalized theory of just war. Rather than calling it an international law (as is clearly the case, a quarter of century later, with Zouche's *Ius feciale sive ius inter gentes*), one might therefore label it a law applying to extra-national conflicts. This assessment, which merely tries to capture the genuine spirit of the work, detracts nothing from what undoubtedly is one of the most important legal monuments of the past millennium.

[4] ibid II, I, II, 1.
[5] ibid Prolegomena, at 30–1.

Recommended Reading

Grotius, Hugo *De jure belli ac pacis libri tres, in quibus jus naturae et gentium, item juris publici praecipua explicantur* (Three Books on the Law of War and Peace, Wherein Are Explained, the Law of Nature and Nations, and the Principal Points Relating to Government) in JB Scott (ed) *The Classics of International Law* (2 vols Clarendon Press Oxford, Humphrey Milford London 1913–25) .

Grotius, Hugo *De iure praedae commentarius* (Commentary on the Law of Prize and Booty) (2 vols Clarendon Press Oxford and Geoffrey Cumberledge London 1950).

Bull, Hedley, Benedict Kingsbury, and Adam Roberts (eds) *Hugo Grotius and International Relations* (Clarendon Press Oxford 1990).

Dufour, Alfred, Peter Haggenmacher, and Jiří Toman (eds) *Grotius et l'ordre juridique international: Travaux du colloque Hugo Grotius, Genève 10–11 novembre 1983* (Payot Lausanne 1985).

Edwards, Charles S *Hugo Grotius, The Miracle of Holland: A Study of Political and Legal Thought* (Nelson Hall Chicago 1981).

Foisneau, Luc (ed) *Politique, droit et théologie chez Bodin, Grotius et Hobbes* (Editions Kimé Paris 1997).

Haggenmacher, Peter *Grotius et la doctrine de la guerre juste* (Presses Universitaires de France Paris 1983).

Haggenmacher, Peter 'La paix dans la pensée de Grotius' in Lucien Bély and Isabelle Rochefort (eds) *L'Europe des traités de Westphalie: Esprit de la diplomatie et diplomatie de l'esprit* (Presses Universitaires de France Paris 2000) 67–79.

Remec, Peter P *The Position of the Individual in International Law according to Grotius and Vattel* (Nijhoff The Hague 1960).

Straumann, Benjamin *Hugo Grotius und die Antike: Römisches Recht und römische Ethik im frühneuzeitlichen Naturrecht* (Nomos Baden-Baden 2007).

CHAPTER 49

SAMUEL PUFENDORF
(1632–1694)

KNUD HAAKONSSEN

SAMUEL Pufendorf (1632–94) was born in Saxony and educated in Leipzig and Jena, where he was taught by Erhard Weigel, who was also Leibniz's teacher. In 1660, he was appointed professor of philology and the law of nations at Heidelberg, but was soon (1668) sought for the new Swedish University of Lund as professor of the law of nature and nations. In 1677 Pufendorf was called to Stockholm as Swedish historiographer royal. Finally, in 1688 he heeded a call to the corresponding position for Brandenburg-Prussia.

Pufendorf was, in his own time and well into the 18th century, one of the most well-known philosophers, easily comparable to John Locke in fame and influence.[1] His political and legal theory was in the genre known as natural law, but it is important to note that this label had distinctly different connotations from those of today. It was not a coherent or uniform set of doctrines; rather, it was a broad practical language that was used by widely differing philosophical theories. Because of its utilization of a common stock of legal and political materials, much of it derived from Roman law and its commentary literature, it offered the appearance of a certain coherence. The pioneer in this eclectic effort was the great humanist scholar Hugo Grotius, and its main defining point was that its practitioners saw him as the founder. However, it was

---

[1] The best brief overview is M Seidler 'Pufendorf's Moral and Political Philosophy' in EN Zalta (ed) *The Stanford Encyclopedia of Philosophy* (2010) at <http://plato.stanford.edu/>.

above all Pufendorf's major treatise, *The Law of Nature and Nations* (1672), and its textbook abbreviation, *On the Duty of Man and Citizen* (1673), that shaped natural law, so that it became both a philosophical and juridical teaching subject that was adopted across Europe and beyond as part of educational, legal, and institutional modernization.[2]

The first thing to note about Pufendorf's theory of the law of nations is that it shares Hobbes's idea that this law is nothing but the law of nature applied to the State. And the first thing to note about Pufendorf's conception of the law of nature is that it has virtually nothing to do with the notions of natural law that are common in the 21st century. Pufendorf's natural law is not a substantial *Grundnorm* that is founded upon one or another form of transcendent authority, and which provides a comprehensive normative content by means of which moral rules and positive law can be measured. The law of nature is certainly conceived as God's command, but both this status itself and the actual content of the law are matters of empirical observation and inference from such observation.

In Pufendorf's Lutheran view, humanity cannot have access to the divine mind, except through the observable actions of that mind, and these observations include as a central point the overwhelming dependence of humanity upon its ability and willingness to live socially. If we in our imagination dismiss all social relations, we find a natural being that exhibits a complete discrepancy between the species' needs and ambitions, and the means of fulfilling these, but which also has the capacity to appreciate that the resulting disorder would make the inclusion of humanity in the creation a piece of divine senselessness. With nature, including human nature, as empirical evidence of the divine intention, even the poorest understanding will see the point of being sociable. When we notice the overwhelming power of a Creator who has such intentions, we have reason to expect repercussions for non-compliance. This combination of understanding of (1) reasons for actions by reference to the goods of life, and (2) the enforceability of compliance, is what Pufendorf understands by obligation.[3]

The content of natural law is simply that we must live socially, but what this means is entirely dependent upon our particular circumstances and our responses thereto. Social life arises from human choices or acts of will individually and collectively; by adopting rules, strictures, distinctions, institutions and the like, we transform natural human beings into a wide variety of social personae characterized by their offices. In Pufendorf's language, we impose 'moral entities' upon 'natural entities'. The types of such offices can be established in general terms, and much of Pufendorf's major natural law writing is devoted to this task, but specific offices are determined by the given

---

[2] See K Haakonssen 'Natural Law' in J Skorupski (ed) *Routledge Companion to Ethics* (Routledge London 2010) 76–87.

[3] K Haakonssen 'Natural law and Personhood: Samuel Pufendorf on Social Explanation' (Max Weber Lecture Series No 2010/06) at <http://cadmus.eui.eu/handle/1814/14934> (accessed on 26 January 2012).

social situation, which is the subject of history. And Pufendorf was as much a historian as a natural lawyer.

The most important means for self-interested, needy humanity to live sociably is the State, and this 'moral entity', the composite person of the State, which Pufendorf accounts for in contractual terms, is analogous to the natural person. The idea of the State as an artificial person with an identity distinct from human persons, including those in authority, who 'carry' it, is one of Pufendorf's major contributions.[4] In serving the self-interest of their members, States are in a state of nature and have to regulate their self-interest among each other by the basic rule of sociability and what this rule implies. This is the law of nations, of which those parts that apply to nations simply as such are 'absolute', for example, the ban on needless war; while other rules are 'hypothetical', presupposing the existence of some sort of relations between States, for example, the conduct of war, the sending of embassies, etc. Both types of law derive their obligation from the need for sociability, that is, peace. The extent of hypothetical laws depends upon the circumstances of given states and times. However, it is clear that for Pufendorf, the law of nations proper provides for only the most elementary universal moral order, because human needs and interests are overwhelmingly particular in their expression, and must be satisfied with regard to the specific social and political context. Accordingly, the so-called voluntary or positive law of nations that is created purely by the legislation of individual States and by particular agreements between States is not law proper. Alongside a regard for the universal but minimal demands of the law of nature/nations, any person—natural or composite—must therefore have the skill of recognizing the true interest of the persona in question and to balance these two types of consideration against each other. The universal duty to sociability imposed by the law of nature and nations requires that we look after our particular interests; in order to take care of our interests, we have to heed the duty of the law. Pufendorf's theoretical works on the law of nature and nations and his major histories are inherently connected.[5]

The State as a composite person with its own duties and rights is only an effective means of sociability if these duties and rights take precedence over those of its constituent members: it must have supreme (unrivalled) sovereignty (which may be either absolute or limited, depending on circumstances). Sovereignty thus entails territorial supremacy, an idea that led Pufendorf to discern sovereignty not only in European States, but also in American tribes. At the same time, the law of nature and nations by defining the task of the State, peace, limited it from other tasks, specifically any responsibility for the spiritual life of its members.

---

[4] D Boucher 'Pufendorf and the Person of the State' in D Boucher (ed) *Political Theories of International Relations* (OUP New York 1998) 223–54.

[5] See editorial introduction in S Pufendorf *An Introduction to the History of the Principal Kingdoms and States of Europe* (M Seidler ed, J Crull trans) (Liberty Fund Indianapolis 2011).

This suite of concepts, the State's personhood, its supreme sovereignty, its territoriality, its duty to the law of nations as a minimal universal order within which to pursue its shifting self-interests, constitutes the theoretical core of Pufendorf's contribution. Viewed historically, it was his attempt to deal with the situation of Europe in the wake of the Peace of Westphalia, not least that of the German Empire.

Recommended Reading

Pufendorf, Samuel, *De officio hominis civis juxta legem naturalem: Libri duo* (1682) in JB Scott (ed) *The Classics of International Law* (2 vols OUP New York 1927).

Pufendorf, Samuel *De jure naturae et gentium libri octo* (1688) in JB Scott (ed) *The Classics of International Law* (2 vols Clarendon Press Oxford 1931).

Pufendorf, Samuel *An Introduction to the History of the Principal Kingdoms and States of Europe* (Michael Seidler ed, Jodocus Crull trans) (Liberty Fund Indianapolis 2011).

Pufendorf, Samuel *On the Duty of Man and Citizen* (James Tully ed, Michael Silverthorne trans) (CUP Cambridge 1991).

Pufendorf, Samuel *Gesammelte Werke* (Wilhelm Schmidt-Biggemann ed) (Akademie Verlag Berlin 1996).

Boucher, David *Political Theories of International Relations* (OUP Oxford 1998).

Hunter, Ian *Rival Enlightenments: Civil and Metaphysical Philosophy in Early Modern Germany* (CUP Cambridge 2001).

Kingsbury, Benedict and Benjamin Straumann 'State of Nature versus Commercial Sociability as the Basis of International Law: Reflections on the Roman Foundations and Current Interpretations of the International Political and Legal Thought of Grotius, Hobbes and Pufendorf' in Samantha Besson and John Tasioulas (eds) *The Philosophy of International Law* (OUP New York 2010) ch 1, 33–51.

CHAPTER 50

CHRISTIAN WOLFF
(1679–1754)

KNUD HAAKONSSEN

CHRISTIAN Wolff (1679–1754) was educated in Jena and Leipzig, where he taught until he was called to be professor of philosophy in the new University of Halle (1707), which he was forced by the Prussian king to leave in 1723. After seventeen years as professor in Marburg, he was recalled to Halle by Frederick the Great. He was by then the most influential philosopher in the German-speaking world and had considerable influence in the wider Enlightenment world. Wolff was the great systematizer of all areas of knowledge, moving from 'logic', or general theory of knowledge, through theoretical philosophy (ontology, cosmology, empirical and rational psychology, and natural theology), to practical philosophy (ethics, natural law, law of nations, politics, economics). His original formulation of the system in German was revised and extended in Latin for the wider European audience.[1] The following sketch is based upon the *Ius naturae, methodo scientifica pertractatum* (1740–48), *Jus gentium, methodo scientific pertractatum* (1750),[2] and *Grundsätze des Natur- und Völckerrechts* (1754).

---

[1] For Wolff's collected works in German and in Latin, see C Wolff *Gesammelte Werke* (J École ed) (Olms Hildesheim 1962) Abteilung I: *Deutsche Schriften* 24 vols; Abteilung II: *Lateinische Schriften* 38 vols.

[2] C Wolff *Jus gentium, methodo scientifica pertractatum* (1764) in JB Scott (ed) *The Classics of International Law* (2 vols Oxford Clarendon Press 1934).

Like most of the early-modern natural lawyers, Christian Wolff extended his idea of natural law to apply also to nations, although according to him, the two are not identical. The natural law theory in question was essentially neo-scholastic, positing a teleological vision of human life, individual as well as collective, according to which humanity's natural destiny was perfectibility, in sharp contrast to Pufendorf's willed sociability. Perfectibility was understood as a composite of the realization of our natural abilities in harmony with ourselves and others, and the happiness that arises from the rational understanding that each particular instance of perfection is part of the general design of perfect happiness in the creation. The driving force in the pursuit of perfection is rational insight into this human condition and its place in the overall system of nature as designed by the divinity. Our moral freedom to be obliged by natural law simply consists in this rational understanding; only intellectual deficiency or irrational (passionate) willfulness will make us un-free and incapable of obligation. The core of Wolff's theory is this strongly intellectualist account of perfection, happiness, moral freedom, and obligation to the law of nature that at one and the same time describes and prescribes the way to our natural goal.

Each individual has a natural inalienable right to pursue perfection according to personal insight; this right is entailed in the natural duty to seek such perfection. However, the insight may include a preference for not exercising the natural right and instead rely on the insight of some other person(s). The former situation is the 'original state' of natural liberty; the latter condition is an adventitious state, that is, a condition with relations of governance. When an adventitious state is the best means of maximizing perfection and happiness, natural law prescribes that people exercise their natural liberty to give up the future exercise of that liberty. This is Wolff's basic idea of the contract as the foundation of all governance. The point of it is not a genetic, quasi-historical justification, it is a conceptual clarification: relations of governance 'mean' that those who govern are judges of the perfectibility of the collective. This judgment as well as the 'original' motives for the contract may be good, bad or indifferent, like all other actual judgments.

The basic adventitious society is pre-political, consisting of private property relations and familial and feudal organizations. The major step beyond this is civil society, which is conceived as a contractual relationship, not between individuals as in the adventitious society, but between groups, such as households and (feudal) estates, represented by their heads. The justification also of this kind of society is to find the most effective means of perfectibility, and to this end Wolff formulates in considerable detail the idea of a total welfare and security State.

While civil society, or the State, historically speaking was the highest form of social organization in the service of perfectibility, Wolff saw the full implication of his natural law theory to be a universal society that encompassed humanity as a whole. He called it *civitas maxima*, the greatest society. It is the basic natural law of perfectibility that ties all forms of human life together, from family society, through feudal and corporate institutions, to civil society and the greatest society of humanity in general.

In its natural potential, or ideally, this entire system of the moral creation is perfectly well ordered, so that all instances of the pursuit of 'perfection *cum* happiness' by individuals or collectives play some role in bringing about total happiness, or beatitude. Such relations are in other words logically necessary, according to Wolff. Objectively speaking, there is always one right way of acting; in conflicts, one party or the other is in the right. However, in reality, each individual person or specific society is subject to historical contingency, arising from ignorance and passion. So one thing is the social relations that are 'necessary' according to natural law, another the actual contracts that individuals have entered into, wisely or unwisely, but creating the historical societies in which natural law now has to be honoured. This is important for the law of nations.

Civil societies deal with their historically given limitations through the creation of positive law that adheres as closely as possible to the obligatory natural law. Analogously, the universal society, *societas maxima*, tries to meet its historically given circumstances by the 'voluntary *ius gentium*', which cleaves to the 'necessary *ius gentium*' as closely as it can. The latter is the law of nature as it applies to relations between the world's civil societies. In addition to the necessary and the voluntary *ius gentium*, Wolff operates with the *ius gentium* that arises from contracts between civil societies and from custom, but he considers the voluntary *ius gentium* the more important. The universal society does not and cannot have an actual sovereign, since it consists of sovereign civil societies, but the voluntary *ius gentium* exists 'as if' given by a sovereign. This sovereign is constituted by contracts between civil sovereigns that are implied by the necessary *ius gentium*, and the *societas maxima* is therefore a direct democracy. However, since the civil societies of the world cannot literally convene to make law, the voluntary *ius gentium* must be taken to be that which is 'approved by the more civilized nations'. In a further analogy with civil society, *civitas maxima*'s sovereignty implies that it has a ruler, *rector*, to whom the sovereignty is transferred. Both *societas maxima*, its sovereignty and its *rector,* are legal fictions, fictions entailed by the law of nature when this is extended to apply in a world with civil societies, and the basic duty imposed by this law is that of keeping up these fictions, that is, to make them effective in the real world.

Each civil society is in itself a legal fiction, a juridical person characterized by its sovereignty, understood as freedom to choose for itself. In this regard, all civil societies are equal; without sovereignty, no civil society. Consequently, each sovereignty's opinion of the justice of its actions must be considered to be of equal status. So although in international disputes there is, of necessity, an objective right and wrong according to the necessary *ius gentium*, by the voluntary *ius gentium,* both (or all) parties to any dispute are just. However, in the 'exercise' of these rights sovereign societies are bound by the necessary *ius gentium*, so that, for example, the killing of non-combatants and plunder cannot be allowed as part of the voluntary *ius gentium* (though it may have become part of de facto custom). In this sense, the necessary *ius gentium* 'limits' the voluntary *ius gentium*.

RECOMMENDED READING

Wolff, Christian *Jus gentium, methodo scientifica pertractatum* (1764) in JB Scott (ed) *The Classics of International Law* (2 vols Clarendon Press Oxford 1934).

Wolff, Christian *Gesammelte Werke* (J École ed) (Olms Hildesheim 1962) Abteilung I: *Deutsche Schriften* 24 vols; Abteilung II: *Lateinische Schriften* 38 vols.

Cavallar, Georg *The Rights of Strangers: Theories of International Hospitality, the Global Community, and Political Justice since Vitoria* (Ashgate Aldershot 2002) 208–21.

Haakonssen, Knud 'German Natural Law' in Mark Goldie and Robert Wokler (eds) *Cambridge History of Eighteenth-Century Political Thought* (CUP Cambridge 2006) 251–90.

Onuf, Nicholas G *The Republican Legacy in International Thought* (CUP Cambridge 1998) 60–70.

CHAPTER 51

CORNELIUS VAN BYNKERSHOEK (1673–1743)

KINJI AKASHI

1. LIFE AND WORK

CORNELIUS van Bynkershoek (1673–1743) was a son of a respectable middle-class family in Middelburg, the capital city of the Dutch province of Zeeland. Having completed his secondary education in his birthplace, he entered the University of Franeker (shut in 1816) in Friesland where he first studied theology and then law. In 1694 he obtained doctoral degree (*doctor iuris utriusque*) under the guidance of, *inter alia*, Ulrich Huber who then enjoyed a European reputation. Having completed his study at Franeker (and having endured the death of his beloved mother), van Bynkershoek settled himself at The Hague, the seat of the highest court of the Dutch provinces of Holland, Zeeland, and West Friesland. During the first decade at The Hague he worked as a lawyer, then, in 1704, he was appointed a judge of the court and in 1724 its president. His presidency continued until he passed away in 1743.

Besides his practice as a lawyer and a judge, van Bynkershoek wrote a number of treatises and smaller essays on law, especially Roman law and Dutch law. Compared to these two fields of law, his writing dealing with the issues of international law (*ius gentium*) is somewhat limited, and his principal works in the field are as follows: *De dominio maris dissertatio* (Dissertation on the Dominion of the Sea),[1] *De foro legatorum tam in causa civili, quam criminali liber singularis* (Single Book on the Jurisdiction over Ambassadors in Both Civil and Criminal Cases),[2] and *Quaestionum juris public libri duo* (Two Books on Questions of Public Law).[3] The first work deals with the question of the dominion of the seas, 'which has been the cause of more than one war'.[4] Besides the argument on the origin of ownership and the citation of the precedents concerning the subject matter, van Bynkershoek postulates that 'the territorial authority ends where the power of weapons ends'.[5] The same view is reiterated in *QJP*, namely '*imperium terrae finiri, ubi finitur armorum potestas*'.[6] This formulation has been called the 'cannon shot rule', which has been evaluated as a theory providing the basis for defining the outer limit of the 'territorial sea'. It should, however, be pointed out that what van Bynkershoek proposed is not the breadth of the maritime belt, but the extent to which the terrestrial authority reaches. It is unclear in his argument whether or not his theory is based on the premise that a fortress or battery really ought to exist on the shore. The second work, beginning with the origin and titles of envoys, discusses the issues on the jurisdiction over ambassadors quite extensively. While the inspiration for publishing this book apparently derived from an actual case, the questions pertaining to ambassadors, the author himself considered, had been the most debated in public law in his days.[7] The third work is composed of two 'books'. Although its title may suggests that this volume explores the questions of public law in general, the first 'book' concerns itself with the laws of war, and the second miscellaneous issues on public law.

2. EVALUATION

When the writers of textbooks on the history of international law evaluate the contribution of van Bynkershoek to its development, in addition to his contribution to each of the fields with which he dealt, they usually mention his methodology. It has

---

[1] *De dominio maris dissertatio* (Apud Joannem Kerckhem Leiden1702) (hereinafter *DMD*).
[2] *De foro legatorum tam in causa civili, quam criminali liber singularis* (Apud Joannem Kerckhem Leiden) 1721) (hereinafter *DFL*).
[3] *Quaestionum juris public libri duo* (Apud Joannem Kerckhem Leiden1737) (hereinafter *QJP*).
[4] 'Ad lectorem' in DMD (n 1).
[5] '*potestatem terrae finiri, ubi finitur armorum vis*' DMD (n 1) ch ii.
[6] QJP (n 3) book I, ch viii; see also book II, ch xxi.
[7] 'Ad lectorem' in DFL (n 2).

generally been maintained that he was a leading figure of the positivist school in international jurisprudence, based on the trilateral categorization of the methodological tendencies: Naturalist, 'Grotian', and positivist. It is true that he cites many precedents and examples ('state practice') for proving the existence of legal rules and judging legality of given cases. This distinct characteristic of his methodology may support his traditional reputation as a positivist. Yet it soon becomes obvious that such precedents and examples are only secondary sources for his argumentation when we read his writings in detail. In order to re-examine his methodology, we will focus on two aspects: the concept of 'international law' (*ius gentium*) and the importance of 'reason' (*ratio*) in his theory. As regards the former, van Bynkershoek (unlike Grotius, Pufendorf, Wolff, de Vattel, etc. who deserve to be called 'system-builders') does not allocate any specific chapter or section for the exposition of his own definition or concept of international law. In *DMD*, only limited mention is made. In *DFL* and *QJP*, he refers to it in scattered sentences and passages. It is, nonetheless, possible to extrapolate his understanding from these types of references, and observe the 'mutation' among the three works which may be evaluated as a 'development' of his concept from the first work to the last. *DMD* is a rudimentary work in regard to the concept of international law, and in *DFL*, the author seems to have established his own concept, the essential part of which is passed on to *QJP*. The core concept of international law based on the passages in *DFL* is as follows: international law is tacit agreement presented in custom (*consuetudo*) and custom is composed of reason and usage (*usus*). A similar idea is retained in *QJP* in that van Bynkershoek referred to 'international law deriving from tacit and presumed agreements produced by reason and usage'.[8] Hence his concept of international law may, with only minimal inconsistency, be defined as follows: international law is both tacit agreement and custom which should be supported by reason and usage, and the contents of tacit agreement and those of custom should be regarded as identical. These formulae and references reveal the importance of reason, namely the second aspect, as one of the bases of international law. The author, indeed, wrote 'thus, there are two bases, namely reason and usage'.[9] Yet, his argumentation should be understood differently, since from his concept of international law, 'perpetual usage' is substantially equivalent to 'custom observed among divergent peoples who are *sui juris*', and the custom that 'solid and vigorous reason has persuaded them, and we call it *jus gentium*'.[10] In short, perpetual usage is custom and when custom is persuaded by reason, it shall be named international law. Hence, 'persuasion by reason' is a prerequisite for custom to be recognized as international law. The importance of reason is observable when we look into the relation between reason and treaties (*pacta gentium*). In his discussion concerning the doctrine of 'enemy ships, enemy goods', van Bynkershoek first recites treaties

---

[8]   QJP (n 3) book III, ch x.
[9]   '*Duo igitur ejus quasi fulcra sunt, ratio & usus*' DFL (n 2) ch iii.
[10]   'Dedicatio' in DFL (n 2).

endorsing the doctrine and suddenly rejects the legal effect of the treaties by declaring, 'it will by no means be possible to defend this kind of law according to reason'.[11] Hence, when treaties collide with reason, he always recognizes the superiority of the latter over the former. Thus both van Bynkershoek's concept of international law and reliance on reason in legal arguments cast doubt on his reputation as a positivist. Yet we ought not impeach the generally accepted evaluation. Rather, it should be pointed out that even van Bynkershoek, a greatly experienced practising lawyer and judge, showed no hesitation in invoking 'reason'. This suggests the persistent existence of a factor which cannot be compatible with a truly positivistic method in international law.

Recommended Reading

Bynkershoek, Cornelius van *De dominio maris dissertatio* (Apud Joannem van Kerckhem Leiden 1702).

Bynkershoek, Cornelius van *De foro legatorum tam in causa civili, quam criminali liber singularis* (Apud Joannem van Kerckhem Leiden 1721).

Bynkershoek, Cornelius van *Quaestionum juris public libri duo* (Apud Joannem van Kerckhem Leiden 1737).

Akashi, Kinji *Cornelius van Bynkershoek: His Role in the History of International Law* (Kluwer Law International The Hague 1998).

Delpech, Joseph 'Bynkershoek' in Joseph Barthélemy et al (eds) *Les fondateurs du droit international* (V Giard & E Brière Paris 1904) 385–446.

Oudendijk, Johanna K *Status and Extent of Adjacent Waters* (Sijthoff Leiden 1970).

Phillipson, Coleman 'Cornelius van Bynkershoek' in John Macdonell and Edward Manson (eds) *Great Jurists of the World* (John Murray London 1913) 390–416.

Reibstein, Ernst 'Von Grotius zu Bynkershoek' (1953) 4 Archiv des Völkerrechts 1–29.

Star Numan, Oncko W *Cornelis van Bynkershoek, Zijn Leven en Zijne Geschriften* (Cornelis van Bynkershoek, His Life and His Writings) (Hazenberg Leiden 1869).

---

[11] '*Ex ratione utique ejusmodi jus defendi non poterit*' QJP (n 3) book I, ch xiii.

CHAPTER 52

JEAN-JACQUES ROUSSEAU (1712–1778)

GEORG CAVALLAR

ROUSSEAU, born in Geneva in June 1712 and spending most of his life in France, had a turbulent life which can be divided into three parts: his 'apprentice' years end in 1749 with his 'illumination' on his way to Vincennes; the years of maturity (1750–64), which were marked by his major publications, among them the three *Discourses*, *Émile*, and *The Social Contract*; and finally the years of decline up to his death in 1778.[1]

Rousseau's writings on international law and international relations fall into the second period. In 1756, he moved to a cottage called the Hermitage at Montmorency, and the following five years proved to be the most creative of his life. There he also prepared extracts from the work of the Abbé de Saint-Pierre, an idealistic reformer of the early 18th century, subsequently published as *Extrait du projet de Paix Perpétuelle de Monsieur L'Abbé de Saint-Pierre* (1761) and *Jugement sur la Paix Perpétuelle* (1782). *Abstract* and *Judgement* are Rousseau's most succinct statements on international law, but there are also scattered passages in the fragment 'The State of War' (first published in 1896), the *Discourse on Political Economy* (1755), *The Social Contract* (1762), and *Considerations on the Government of Poland* (finished in 1771). Rousseau never managed to write the planned book on the *Principles of the Right of War*.[2]

---

[1] N Dent *Rousseau* (Routledge London 2005) 18 f.

[2] JJ Rousseau 'Of the Social Contract' in JJ Rousseau *The Social Contract and Other Later Political Writings* (V Gourevitch ed) (CUP Cambridge 1997) 39–152 at 40; in the French standard edition JJ Rousseau *Oeuvres complètes* (Éditions Gallimard Paris 1964) vol III (*Du contrat social, écrits politiques*) at 116, 349 and 431; see O Asbach 'Staatsrecht und Völkerrecht bei Jean-Jacques Rousseau' in R Brandt and K Herb (eds) *Jean-Jacques Rousseau. Vom Gesellschaftsvertrag oder Prinzipien des Staatsrechts* (Akademie

According to a widespread interpretation, Rousseau was a profoundly anti-cosmopolitan pessimist who believed that European international society should end, and that 'moral regeneration in the face of the state of war' was impossible.[3] It is more plausible, however, to see Rousseau's project as encompassing two elements, 'the diagnosis of human and social ills', and 'an attempt to find their remedy'.[4]

I start with the diagnosis. Rousseau claimed that the law of nations was not based on or identical with natural law, but a human creation.[5] The *droit public d'Europe*, in particular, 'has never been passed or sanctioned by common agreement. It is not based upon any general principles. It varies incessantly from time to time and from place to place'.[6] It was an illusion since the deficient 'natural' (that is, particular) law had not (yet) been replaced by true rational law. International relations (the relations among independent States) were necessarily a state of war, since there was neither sovereign authority nor 'common agreement'. While Rousseau rejected Hobbes' hypothesis of the war of all against all as a natural order of things, he saw it as the result of a historical process culminating in the establishment of States, which made the lives of citizens even more miserable than before. Historical developments, States themselves (and not human nature) create wars. 'It is the relation between things and not between men that constitutes war... War is then not a relationship between one man and another, but a relationship between one State and another'.[7] Rousseau offered a structural interpretation of Hobbes' state-of-nature hypothesis: the plurality of States with their individual wills, and a lack of common legislation, executive, and jurisdiction, made the state of war inevitable.

Verlag Berlin 2000) 241–69 at 241; F Cheneval *Philosophie in weltbürgerlicher Bedeutung. Über die Entstehung und die philosophischen Grundlagen des supranationalen und kosmopolitischen Denkens der Moderne* (Schwabe Basel 2002) at 365 f and 390.

[3] DP Fidler 'Desperately Clinging to Grotian and Kantian Sheep: Rousseau's Attempted Escape from the State of War' in I Clark and IB Neumann (eds) *Classical Theories of International Relations* (Macmillan Press Houndmills 1996) 120–41 at 131.

[4] *Rousseau* (n 1) 80. Much of the following is based on the interpretations of *Philosophie in weltbürgerlicher Bedeutung* (n 2) and 'Staatsrecht und Völkerrecht' (n 2); M Köhler 'Einleitung zu Rousseaus Friedensschriften' in JJ Rousseau *Friedensschriften* (Felix Meiner Hamburg 2009) ix–lxxix; JF Thibault 'Les relations internationales et la crise de la pensée politique moderne selon Jean-Jacques Rousseau' (2006) 37 Etudes Internationales—Quebec 205–22; and M Forschner 'Jean-Jacques Rousseau über Krieg und Frieden' in M Kremer and HR Reuter (eds) *Macht und Moral—Politisches Denken im 17. und 18. Jahrhundert* (Kohlhammer Stuttgart 2007) 306–20; see also S Goyard-Fabre *La construction de la paix, ou le travail de Sisyphe* (Vrin Paris 1994); and F Ramel and JP Joubert *Rousseau et les relations internationales* (Harmattan Montréal 2000).

[5] JJ Rousseau 'Discourse on the Origin and the Foundations of Inequality Among Men' in JJ Rousseau *The Discourses and Other Early Political Writings* (V Gourevitch ed) (CUP Cambridge 1997) 113–222 at 174; *Oeuvres complètes* (n 2) 178.

[6] JJ Rousseau 'Abstract and "Judgment" of the Abbé de Saint-Pierre's Project for Perpetual Peace' in E Aksu (ed) *Early Notions of Global Governance* (University of Wales Press Cardiff 2008) 95–131 at 100; *Oeuvres complètes* (n 2) 568 f.

[7] 'Of the Social Contract' (n 2) 46; *Oeuvres complètes* (n 2) 357; see JJ Rousseau 'The State of War' in *The Social Contract* (n 2) 162–76 at 166; *Oeuvres complètes* (n 2) 169, 601, and 605.

Rousseau did not stop with this diagnosis, which usually assigns him to the camp of realists. He tried to offer a remedy: namely, a form of international social contract which should form the basis of a true international society. His remedy came in two versions: the confederation of small republics and a European federation of States. The former was necessary since small republics were in jeopardy, and the domestic social contract had to be supplemented.[8] The second model was a European federation of States. In the 'Abstract', Rousseau argued that Europe was a specific form of cultural, legal, and political community, due to, among others, Christianity, the Roman legal tradition, and the balance-of-power system. However, since they did not recognize an 'earthly superior', the European powers were 'strictly in a state of war'.[9] In order to turn Europe 'into an authentic confederation', the States had to form a 'permanent Congress', submit to arbitration and the coercive powers of the federation, and cede their external sovereignty.[10]

Rousseau eyed these two remedies with profound scepticism. First, he did not see the historical conditions as ideal (to put it mildly). The '*Judgment*' offers a ferocious criticism of 18th-century absolutism, of its bellicose tendencies abroad and of the willingness to suppress and exploit citizens at home. Thus a European federation is neither realistic (princes do not want peace, but aggrandizement) nor desirable (the federation would increase domestic exploitation). Secondly, as far as the federation of small republics is concerned, Rousseau seemed to argue that it would amount to a dissolution of the social contract, which was not legitimate, since popular sovereignty was inalienable and indivisible. Representation became the key problem of an international organization.[11] In the end, Rousseau seemed to advocate the autarky and independence of republics, and their citizens' love of country and republican patriotism (rather than full-blown nationalism).[12]

Finally, Rousseau squarely faced the problem of realization of an international organization. On the one hand, Rousseau the realist saw the use of violence as unavoidable, perhaps even as 'historically inevitable'. Rousseau the moralist, on the other hand, realized that 'peace through force' was morally highly dubious and self-contradictory.[13]

According to Jean-François Thibault, Rousseau's reflections on international relations brought the 'contradictions' and the 'deadlock' of modern political thought to the fore.[14] Rousseau the revolutionary launched an all-out attack on the law of nations

---

[8] 'Of the Social Contract' (n 2) 115 f; *Oeuvres complètes* (n 2) 431; 'Staatsrecht und Völkerrecht' (n 2) 242 f and 261–6; *Philosophie in weltbürgerlicher Bedeutung* (n 2) 378–83.

[9] 'Abstract' (n 6) 100; *Oeuvres complètes* (n 2) 572.

[10] ibid 106 f; *Oeuvres complètes* (n 2) 573.

[11] 'Of the Social Contract' (n 2) 57; *Oeuvres complètes* (n 2) 369; 'Staatsrecht und Völkerrecht' (n 2) 262; *Philosophie in weltbürgerlicher Bedeutung* (n 2) 381–6; 'Einleitung zu Rousseaus Friedensschriften' (n 4) lvi f and lx f.

[12] G Cavallar 'Educating Émile: Jean-Jacques Rousseau on Cosmopolitanism' (2012) 17(4) European Legacy 485–99.

[13] 'Abstract' (n 6) 131; *Oeuvres complètes* (n 2) 599 f.

[14] 'Les relations internationales' (n 4) 217 and 221.

and the *droit public d'Europe*, and here he was even more radical than Hobbes or Pufendorf. Rousseau the rationalist hoped to lay the foundations of a more authentic law between States. His emphasis on normative individualism and on legal freedom (rather than security) marked the breakthrough in the development of cosmopolitan contractualism.[15]

RECOMMENDED READING

Rousseau, Jean-Jacques 'Of the Social Contract' in Victor Gourevitch (ed) *The Social Contract and Other Later Political Writings* (CUP Cambridge 1997) 39–152.

Rousseau, Jean-Jacques 'The State of War' in Victor Gourevitch (ed) *The Social Contract and other later political writings* (CUP Cambridge 1997) 162–76.

Rousseau, Jean-Jacques 'Abstract and "Judgment" of the Abbé de Saint-Pierre's Project for Perpetual Peace' in Eşref Aksu (ed) *Early Notions of Global Governance* (University of Wales Press Cardiff 2008) 95–131.

Asbach, Olaf 'Staatsrecht und Völkerrecht bei Jean-Jacques Rousseau' in Reinhard Brandt and Karlfriedrich Herb (eds) *Jean-Jacques Rousseau. Vom Gesellschaftsvertrag oder Prinzipien des Staatsrechts* (Akademie Verlag Berlin 2000) 241–69.

Carter, Christine J *Rousseau and the Problem of War* (Garland New York 1987).

Cavallar, Georg ' "La société générale du genre humain": Rousseau on Cosmopolitanism, International Relations, and Republican Patriotism' in Paschalis M Kitromilides (ed) *From Republican Polity to National Community* (Voltaire Foundation Oxford 2003) 89–109.

Cavallar, Georg *Imperfect Cosmopolis: Studies in the History of International Legal Theory and Cosmopolitan Ideas* (University of Wales Press Cardiff 2011).

Cheneval, Francis *Philosophie in weltbürgerlicher Bedeutung. Über die Entstehung und die philosophischen Grundlagen des supranationalen und kosmopolitischen Denkens der Moderne* (Schwabe Basel 2002) 351–99.

Fidler, David P and Stanley Hoffmann (eds) *Rousseau on International Relations* (Clarendon Press Oxford 1991).

Köhler, Michael 'Einleitung zu Rousseaus Friedensschriften' in Jean-Jacques Rousseau *Friedensschriften* (Felix Meiner Hamburg 2009) ix–lxxix.

Ramel, Fréderic and Jean-Paul Joubert *Rousseau et les relations internationales* (Harmattan Montréal 2000).

Roosevelt, Grace G *Reading Rousseau in the Nuclear Age* (Temple University Press Philadelphia 1990).

Roosevelt, Grace G 'Rousseau versus Rawls on International Relations' (2006) 5 European Journal of Political Theory 301–20.

Thibault, Jean François 'Les relations internationales et la crise de la pensée politique moderne selon Jean-Jacques Rousseau' (2006) 37 Etudes Internationales—Quebec 205–22.

---

[15] *Philosophie in weltbürgerlicher Bedeutung* (n 2) 351, 369 f and 391; 'Einleitung zu Rousseaus' (n 4) XXII; and G Cavallar *The Rights of Strangers: Theories of International Hospitality, the Global Community, and Political Justice since Vitoria* (Ashgate Aldershot 2002) at 284–305.

CHAPTER 53

EMER DE VATTEL
(1714–1767)

EMMANUELLE JOUANNET

EMER de Vattel (1714–1767), was born on 25 April 1714 in the province of Neuchâtel, the son of protestant refugees.[1] In 1758, he published *The Law of Nations or the Principles of Natural Law Applied to the Conduct and to the Affairs of Nations and of Sovereigns.*[2] The work enjoyed considerable success, much to the amazement of the author himself. As a result, he was immediately summoned to Dresden by Augustus III who offered him employment as a diplomat, a position to which he had long aspired. From its first publication, Vattel's *Law of Nations* attracted widespread interest. Numerous editions and translations followed, and its influence reached across the Channel to England and from there to the United States, where the book soon became a reference manual in American universities. From the 18th to the beginning of the 20th century, his authority on the subject of international law remained unrivalled.

The immense and enduring acclaim enjoyed by *The Law of Nations* should come as no surprise. Vattel was the first to have described the law of nations as a set of rules

---

[1] For a comprehensive biography of Vattel's life see E Beguelin *En souvenir de Vattel, 1714–1767* (P Attinger Neuchâtel 1929).

[2] E de Vattel *Le droit des gens ou principes de la loi naturelle appliqués à la conduite et aux affaires des nations et des souverains* (Journal Helvétique Neuchâtel 1758; reprint Carnegie Institution of Washington Washington 1916). This is Vattel's best known work and the only one which is dedicated exclusively to the law of nations. The book was first published in 1758 under the supervision of the author in Neuchâtel and 1,200 copies were printed by *Journal Helvétique*. The title page also indicates London, no doubt as a tribute to England.

governing the conduct of sovereign States both in times of peace and in times of war. In other words, he was the man who defined the paradigm of international law that was to hold sway over the following two centuries. There are three fundamental aspects of his *Law of Nations* that should be highlighted in this context.

To begin with, on all issues relating to the law of nations, Vattel moved away from the interpersonal concept espoused by his predecessors, and in its place applied a strictly inter-state perspective where the law of nations is specifically the law governing relations between States. A number of decisive consequences derive from this position. First, he relegates the individual to the internal sphere of the State, thus denying him the status of subject under the law of nations. Second, Vattel went considerably further than Wolff in defending the principle that international society, for whom the law of nations represents the legal order, is truly a society of sovereign, equal, and independent States. Furthermore, by virtue of their sovereign will, only States have the capacity of determining the applicability of international rights and obligations.[3] Finally, he established the legal constructs for classical international law which would be relied on by jurists and politicians for centuries, revolving as they all did around the principle of the sovereign State as the subject of international law: the law of treaties, diplomatic relations, the law of neutrality, the *ius ad bellum*, the humanization of *ius in bello*, and the right of responsibility.

Secondly, Vattel unreservedly recognized the existence of a duality of norms governing the conduct of sovereign States: the norms imposed by natural law and those imposed by the positive law of nations.[4] Here he took up one of the most decisive contributions of his mentor Wolff, and highlights three aspects of the law of nations, the *voluntary*, the *conventional*, and the *customary*, in addition to the natural law of nations. Although by doing so he opened the door to State voluntarism in international law, it would be doing him an injustice to consider him the 'prince of positivists', which was the description bestowed upon him by George Scelle.[5] He remained a proponent of the school of natural law, subordinating the positive law of nations to the natural law of nations.[6]

Thirdly, Vattel theorized about a law of nations that is both 'liberal and pluralist'[7] and which is very much in line with the state of European society at the time of the

---

[3] *Le droit des gens* (n 2) Preliminaries, at 22 and III, XII, at 163–4.

[4] ibid Preliminaries, para 27, at 15.

[5] G Scelle *Manuel élémentaire de droit international public* (2nd edn Domat-Montchrestien Paris 1948) at 44.

[6] This was realized by the primacy of the voluntary law of nations, the external and perfect rights which have primacy over the internal natural law of nations and customary and conventional law. In reality, the voluntary law of nations is natural law. *Le droit des gens* (n 2) Preface, at xx ff and Preliminaries, at 4 ff. See on this point E Jouannet *Emer de Vattel et l'émergence doctrinale du droit international classique* (A Pedone Paris 1996) at 155 ff.

[7] We refer here to the very pertinent distinctions made by Gerry Simpson in G Simpson *Great Powers and Outlaw States: Unequal Sovereign in the International Legal Order* (CUP London 2004) at 76 ff.

Enlightenment and with the pluralism of this 'anarchical society' which Hedley Bull[8] describes so well. It responds to the need to provide a number of small and medium-sized States with the tools to manage their relations at a time when the old feudal or imperial structures were in decline. This was also a time when Europe had begun to emerge from the horrifying wars of religion and needed to find a way of managing relations between States that now had different religions and different subjective concepts of what constitutes a 'good life'. Now Vattel's liberal and pluralist law of nations was perfectly well suited to this situation since its underlying principles are the principle of neutrality or tolerance vis-à-vis the political regime, the customs and the religion of each State. Vattel's *Law of Nations* upheld the principle of the pluralism of States as well as their sovereign freedom to choose their system of government and religion; the principle of sovereign freedom; and finally the principle of equality between States, regardless of their size or strength.[9] The basic tenet is quite simple and represents a perfect summary of a system of individual freedoms: the exercise of the rights and duties asserted by each State is limited only by the sovereign rights and duties other States are entitled to enjoy. A liberal system of law defining relations between nations, possessing a distinct and sovereign legal personality that treat each other as equals and are independent of one another, was established in order to meet a twofold objective. Internally, it aims to ensure the freedom of each State to do whatever it wishes on its own territory, and externally, it aims to limit the hegemonic impulses of a State, the Pope, or the Emperor vis-à-vis any other State.

In fact, Vattel's *Law of Nations* was far more complex. Its purpose was to establish the eudaimonic notion of well-being which the author considered absolutely essential and which he believed would contribute to the happiness and perfectibility of nations. To that end, he believed it necessary to impose upon them internal legal obligations.[10] Vattel's *Law of Nations* is thus not so much a liberal law as a liberal-providentialist law which seeks at one and the same time to ensure the respect of the individual freedoms of the State, and to promote the happiness and well-being its people.[11] This does of course raise a number of difficulties, since the principle of the liberal State and pluralism in the sovereign choices of States with regard to the good life and the political system stands in contradiction with the eudaimonic purpose posited on the implementation of a particular notion of a political system, happiness, and perfectibility. Since States could find themselves caught between contradictory requirements derived from different purposes, Vattel had to determine a ranking order, and to claim that the liberal should prevail over the providentialist approach. He succeeded to such a degree that the 'providentialist' purpose was soon cast aside

---

[8] H Bull *The Anarchical Society: A Study of Order in World Politics* (3rd edn Pallgrave Macmillan Basingstoke 2002).

[9] *Le droit des gens* (n 2) Preliminaries, at 9 and I, II, at 22 ff.

[10] ibid I, II, at 23–4.

[11] Cf E Jouannet *Le droit international libéral-providence. Une histoire du droit international* (Bruylant Brussels 2011).

by other practitioners and theorists of international law who considered it both inef-fective and inoperative in law.[12]

It is thus not surprising that Vattel's *Law of Nations* has remained the seminal work for so long. The jurist from Neuchâtel provided Europe's sovereigns as well as legal practitioners with their first standard textbook on international law, and he did so in a manner that allowed them to satisfy their desire for both sovereign independence and security.

Recommended Reading

Guggenheim, Paul *Emer de Vattel et l'étude des relations internationales en Suisse* (Georg et Cie Genève 1956).

Jouannet, Emmanuelle *Emer de Vattel et l'émergence doctrinale du droit international classique* (A Pedone Paris 1993).

Jouannet, Emmanuelle *The Liberal-Welfarist Law of Nations: A History of International Law* (Christopher Sutcliffe trans) (CUP Cambridge 2012).

Sandoz, Yves (ed) *Réflexions sur l'impact, le rayonnement et l'actualité du droit des gens d'Emer de Vattel* (Bruylant Bruxelles 2010).

[12] Cf *Le droit international libéral-providence* (n 11).

CHAPTER 54

IMMANUEL KANT (1724–1804)

PAULINE KLEINGELD

IMMANUEL Kant has decisively shaped debates in Western philosophy on a broad range of subjects, including ethics, political philosophy, and philosophy of law. His contributions to the field of international law include most famously his advocacy of a league of nations, his claim that 'republican' States tend not to start a war, and his defence of what he termed 'cosmopolitan law'. His precise position on these issues remains a subject of dispute, however, as does the overall consistency of his published views.

1. BRIEF BIOGRAPHY

Kant was born in 1724 in Königsberg, East Prussia, where he spent almost his entire life. He first worked as a private tutor, then as a university instructor lecturing on topics such as philosophy, mathematics, and the natural sciences. He published several books in philosophy and in science, and in 1770 he accepted the University of Königsberg chair in logic and metaphysics. After a decade in which he published hardly anything at all, he published his ground-breaking work on metaphysics and epistemology, the *Critique of Pure Reason* (1781). He subsequently published two famous works in moral theory, *Groundwork for the Metaphysics of Morals* (1785) and the *Critique of Practical Reason* (1788), and developed his aesthetic theory and philosophy of biology in his *Critique of Judgment* (1790). Although he had broached issues of international law already in his 1784 essay, 'Idea for a Universal History from a Cosmopolitan Perspective', he did not elaborate his political philosophy and legal theory fully until the decade following the French Revolution. Especially noteworthy here are 'On the Common Saying: This May Be True in Theory, but It Does Not Hold in Practice' (1793), *Toward Perpetual Peace: A Philosophical Sketch* (1795), and the *Metaphysics of Morals* (1797). He died in 1804 after several years of dementia.

2. Kant's Importance in the History Of International Law

Kant's importance for the history of international law is connected with the following three essential elements of his views on the subject. First, Kant argued that there is an essential connection between the internal constitution of a State and its external tendency towards peace. He claimed that despots easily declare war because they can use their subjects at will, but that 'republican' States, in which the citizens can vote via their representatives on whether to go to war, would hesitate to start a war because the citizens themselves would bear the burdens of warfare. Ever since Michael Doyle found empirical confirmation for this thesis when narrowed to the claim that (in modern parlance) liberal or democratic States do not wage war 'against each other', the claim has been the subject of much empirical research and theoretical debate, and it has even been used as a basis for US foreign policy.[1]

Second, Kant's advocacy of a league of nations has often been credited with influencing historical developments in the direction of the League of Nations and the United Nations. Kant defended a normative theory of international law according to which States ought to join a peace-promoting league. This league should not aim to interfere with the internal affairs of member States, but promote peace through

---

[1] This more restricted version of Kant's claim is known as the 'Democratic Peace Thesis' or the thesis of 'Liberal Peace'. See the essays collected in MW Doyle *Liberal Peace: Selected Essays* (Routledge London 2011).

mediation, arbitration, and joint defence against outside attacks. Kant was fiercely anti-realist, but he argued that it was also in the best interest of States to form a league. Neither the League of Nations nor the United Nations fully matches Kant's ideal (if only because standing armies were not abolished), but they certainly realize it to a considerable degree.

Third, more recently, there has been increasing attention for Kant's concept of cosmopolitan law. This regulates the interaction between States and foreigners (whether individuals such as refugees or traders, or collective agents such as non-state peoples or businesses). Because Kant defined international law strictly as governing the interactions among States, he considered cosmopolitan law to be a separate part of public law; the rights he mentions as part of it are currently subsumed under international law.

In current debates, relatively little attention is devoted to the topics that Kant discusses in the sections on international law in the *Metaphysics of Morals*, such as the restricted right of States to go to war, the right of the State to use its subjects in wars against other States, the justified means of self-defence, and so on.

3. Current Research Debates

Within Kant scholarship and the Kantian tradition, there are conflicting interpretations of Kant's international political theory and equally conflicting assessments of its cogency. Especially pronounced are the disagreements over Kant's position on whether international law should become public coercive law. Some claim that Kant regarded coercive international law as necessary, while most claim, by contrast, that he was strongly opposed to it. The root of these disagreements is Kant's claim that reason demands a worldwide federation with coercive powers, but that international law mandates a voluntary league because States do not 'want' to join such a strong federation.[2] This last assertion is often read as an inconsistent capitulation to what is 'realistic', and many authors argue that Kant should instead have argued for the formation of a federative world State. I have argued instead that Kant's defence of the league is motivated by his insistence on the importance of the self-determination of peoples (who should not be coerced into a federation if they do not want to join one).[3] In the latter case, Kant's defence of the league as a matter of international law

---

[2] I Kant 'Toward Perpetual Peace' and other Writings on Politics, Peace, and History (P Kleingeld ed, DL Colclasure trans) (Yale University Press New Haven 2006) 8: 357.

[3] See P Kleingeld *Kant and Cosmopolitanism: The Philosophical Ideal of World Citizenship* (CUP Cambridge 2012).

is consistent with his expressed hope that republics will, in time, voluntarily transform the loose league or 'congress' of States into a federation with coercive powers.

Kant's insistence on the self-determination of peoples (in the political, not nationalist sense of 'peoples') has led to the objection that his theory of international law and its Kantian successors, such as Rawls' *Law of Peoples*, wrongly give priority to the interests of States, at the expense of those of individuals. In the eyes of the 'cosmopolitan' critics, a theory of global justice requires identifying principles of justice to govern humanity at large instead of principles that merely govern the interactions among States. Similarly, critics have argued that Kant's strong advocacy of peoples' right to self-determination makes it almost impossible to justify humanitarian intervention. Kant and Kantians may reply that there certainly are demanding duties of assistance towards those in foreign States who suffer from poverty, injustice, or both, but that assistance should be given in a way that is compatible with the principle of the self-determination of peoples.

There is more consensus about the details of Kant's conception of cosmopolitan law. Kant limits it to the 'right to hospitality', which, contrary to what the term seems to imply, is not a right to be a guest, but a right to present oneself to a foreign individual or State without being treated with hostility. Those visited have a right to refuse further contact or entry into their territory, on condition that this does not cause the visitors' demise. Cosmopolitan law thus includes the right of non-refoulement and the prohibition of annexing the territory of non-state peoples as colonies. One difficulty raised by Kant's view is the question of the possibility of the enforcement of cosmopolitan law, because he hardly addresses this issue. In all likelihood, the answer to this question has to be found in Kant's argument that the approximation of perpetual peace depends upon the approximate realization of public law in 'all three' areas (constitutional, international, and cosmopolitan law).[4] Once States become republics, they will tend toward peace and join an international federation, which in turn provides these republics with security and stability. The federation and its members may include the provisions of cosmopolitan law in their laws. Even though cosmopolitan law would then be asymmetrically dependent upon the institutions demanded by constitutional law and international law, this would provide a way to implement it.

RECOMMENDED READING

Kant, Immanuel '*Toward Perpetual Peace*' *and other Writings on Politics, Peace, and History* (Pauline Kleingeld (ed) David L Colclasure trans with essays by Jeremy Waldron, Michael W Doyle and Allen W Wood) (Yale University Press New Haven 2006).

Bohman, James and Matthias Lutz-Bachmann (eds) *Perpetual Peace: Essays on Kant's Cosmopolitan Ideal* (MIT Press Cambridge MA 1997).

---

[4] *Toward Perpetual Peace* (n 2) 8: 349; *Metaphysics of Morals* (n 2) 6: 311.

Brown, Garrett W *Grounding Cosmopolitanism: From Kant to the Idea of a Cosmopolitan Constitution* (Edinburgh University Press Edinburgh 2009).

Byrd, Sharon B and Joachim Hruschka *Kant's Doctrine of Right: A Commentary* (CUP Cambridge 2010).

Caranti, Luigi (ed) *Kant's Perpetual Peace: New Interpretive Essays* (Luiss University Press Rome 2006).

Cavallar, Georg *Kant and the Theory and Practice of International Right* (University of Wales Press Cardiff 1999).

Franceschet, Antonio *Kant and Liberal Internationalism* (Palgrave Macmillan New York 2002).

Höffe, Otfried *Kant's Cosmopolitan Theory of Law and Peace* (Alexandra Newton trans) (CUP Cambridge 2006).

Kleingeld, Pauline *Kant and Cosmopolitanism: The Philosophical Ideal of World Citizenship* (CUP Cambridge 2012).

Tesón, Fernando 'The Kantian Theory of International Law' (1991) 92 Columbia Law Review 53–102.

CHAPTER 55

GEORG WILHELM FRIEDRICH HEGEL (1770–1831)

ARMIN VON BOGDANDY AND SERGIO DELLAVALLE

GEORG Wilhelm Friedrich Hegel is generally considered one of the thinkers who conceptually shaped the transition from the understanding of international order of the enlightenment era to the romantic, anti-universalistic view that characterized a great part of the 19th century. Having left behind the Kantian vision which saw the establishment of peace as the main content of international law, Hegel would have endorsed—at least according to this interpretation—the opposite theory of international relations based on the self-affirmation of the nation as well as of an international law of little normative relevance.

If we group the lawyers and philosophers who have elaborated the most important theories on international law around two main paradigms—'universalism' as the approach which considers a normative order of peace feasible even beyond the borders of the single State, and 'particularism', claiming that order is possible exclusively within the individual polities, whereas between them only a limitation of disorder is achievable—then Hegel would be a (if not *the*) champion of the latter. However, if we analyse Hegel's works in more depth, things turn out to be less evident than widely assumed, and the philosopher transforms himself into probably the first thinker who blazed a possible path beyond the sheer universalism-particularism dichotomy.

1 INTERNATIONAL LAW AS 'EXTERNAL STATE LAW'

Within his political and legal philosophy, Hegel pays comparatively little attention to international law and relations. To their presentation are dedicated, indeed, only twenty rather short paragraphs of his *Philosophy of Right* (1820/1821), from §321 up to and including §340. Furthermore, we have the transcription of many lectures held by Hegel on political and legal philosophy, some of them predating the publication of the *Philosophy of Right*, others following it. Except for marginal differences, the presentation of international law in the lectures coincides with the contents of the book's chapters. More than other parts of his philosophy, Hegel's theory of international law therefore seems to be unequivocal, raising no significant philosophical and philological debates on what he 'really' meant. Nevertheless, this may prove to be a shallow impression.

The fundamental element of Hegel's theory of international law is the centrality of State sovereignty. This can be better understood if we consider the pre-eminent role of the State according to his view of law and politics. It is well-known that Hegel's philosophical system raises the ambitious claim of providing an all-round interpretation of the natural and human world as well as of the knowledge that we have of it. In his understanding, all things that we experience as well as all our thoughts, are expressions of the 'idea'. The highest expression of the 'idea' is located by Hegel in the 'spirit' (*Geist*)—a term that in his philosophy describes the properly *human* dimension of experience, ranging from mental processes to social and political life, as well as from art and religion to philosophy. The *internal* articulation of the 'spirit' has three levels, the first of which is the individual mind—or 'subjective spirit'—and the third is the domain of the 'pure' culture, that is, the 'absolute spirit' as the realm of art, religion, and philosophy. Social life, politics, and law—and therefore international law and relations—belong to the second level, the 'objective spirit'. Here the *Geist* is thought to realize itself in the world of human interactions. And here Hegel situates the State as the most perfect realization of the 'spirit' in the 'objective' world, that is, in the world of social and political interactions.

Although being the highest concretization of the *Geist* in the objective world, the State is nevertheless affected by a significant deficit. As an alienation of the 'idea' in the material world, it is forced to lose that self-evident unity that characterizes the 'pure' expressions of the 'idea', such as, for instance, philosophical thinking. As a phenomenon of the real world the State is therefore *plural*: we do not have 'one State', but necessarily many of them, often conflicting with each other. Furthermore, just as the 'universal subjectivity' becomes concrete in the shape of the plurality of individuals, so are States as mundane concretizations of the *Geist* themselves individualities, and like any individual is a *holon* based on self-control and on the distinction from the 'other', so every State seeks its payoffs and acts as a sovereign. The theory of the State as a 'sovereign individuality' has three consequences: first, as the most accomplished expression of the *Geist* on earth, it can legitimately curb the rights of the individuals for the sake of the common good; second, the supreme competence in the field of foreign policy is assigned to the institutional representative of the individuality of the State, namely to the monarch; third, every State individuality is a closed institutional structure, opposed in principle to any other State individuality. Hegel's world is therefore, analogously to how Carl Schmitt put it a century later, a 'pluriverse', not a 'universe'.

Building on these premises, Hegel's understanding of international relations can only be based on conflict, with war as an ever-concrete possibility. Hegel rejects the idea of 'just war', since in his eyes the reasons to wage war never have a normative—be it moral or legal—content, but are always rooted in the selfish interests of the individual State. Coherently, he also rejects the hypothesis of a *super partes* arbitration because every single State is always the supreme authority in its own matters. As a consequence, international law is of weak normative relevance: insofar as States are unlimited sovereigns, their agreements always depend on the free will of each of them and no moral or political authority of a supra-state institution will urge it to comply with the law. In Hegel's words, international law is only an 'ought' which, faced with the reality of the world, is doomed to pitiless failure.

2 AGAINST UNIVERSALISM—AND PARTICULARISM AS WELL

Trying now to situate Hegel's conception of international law within the dichotomy between particularism and universalism, what first comes to the fore is his rejection of any idea of a 'universal' order as realized by legal norms or political agreements. Hegel's dismissal of classic universalism, in particular as it was developed in the peace projects of the enlightenment, becomes evident in his criticism of Kant and the proposal for perpetual peace, considered a mere chimera.

While Hegel is surely not a supporter of universalism, he can however hardly be seen as a 'particularist' either. Three main differences distinguish him from the exponents of romantic and nationalistic particularism, which developed at the dawn of the 19th century. First, in his understanding war is not the highest manifestation of the existential self-affirmation of the nation, but rather—with an approach shared by many authors in the aftermath of the French Revolution—a kind of healthy wind that shakes up the status quo bringing fresh air to backward-oriented societies. Second, international law may be characterized by a weak normativity, but it has nevertheless a significant function, which 'true' particularists generally deny; namely, it guarantees the mutual recognition between States. Third, the idea of a universal international order is indeed present in Hegel's view, yet it is not realized in the law that organizes the relations among States, but is accomplished in 'world history'. In other words, the setting of international relations reveals an underlying rational and universal structure, yet this is not implemented by legal norms and political procedures, but by the 'cunning of reason' of historic fate.

Concluding, provided that Hegel is indubitably not a universalist, he is not a typical exponent of the 19th-century's romantic-particularistic idea of international (dis)order either. Rather, his philosophy paves the way for a conception that overcomes the dichotomy by incorporating the most fruitful elements of both approaches. Indeed, he maintains the centrality of individual States, which is denied by many universalists, rejecting their largely unfeasible vision of the *civitas maxima* or the 'world republic'. On the other hand, the international world is according to Hegel not the realm of disorder, although the supra-state order is guaranteed only at a level beyond the law. The central theoretical element for Hegel's construction of political order is his concept of *Geist*: conceiving human interaction within a multilevel and— at least potentially—inter-subjective setting, it allows reconciling in a single structure, at different levels, elements that were seen as contradictory, such as individual States and the idea of a supra-state order. Admittedly, this powerful vision remains a nascent potentiality in Hegel's works: in particular, it is not really convincing why the conciliating aim of the *Geist* should be unrealizable in the legal and political world, thus relegating supra-state order to the realm of historic *facta bruta*. This seems to be in Hegel's view a question of principle rather than a matter of coherently deduced and proved argumentation. Nevertheless, the seed for overcoming the particularism/ universalism dichotomy was sown—for fruits to be harvested many decades later.

Recommended Reading

Hegel, Georg WF *Vorlesungen über Rechtsphilosophie 1818–1831* (Karl-Heinz Ilting ed) (Frommann-Holzboog Stuttgart-Bad Cannstatt 1974).

Hegel, Georg WF *Vorlesungen über Naturrecht und Staatswissenschaft 1817/18: Mit Nachträgen aus den Vorlesungen 1818/19* (Claudia Becker et al eds) (Meiner Hamburg 1983).

Hegel, Georg WF *Grundlinien der Philosophie des Rechts* (1st edn In der Nikolaischen Buchhandlung 1820; Meiner Hamburg 2009); *Philosophy of Right* (Clarendon Press Oxford 1967).

Arndt, Andreas (ed) *Zwischen Konfrontation und Integration* (Akademie Berlin 2007).

Avineri, Shlomo *Hegel's Theory of the Modern State* (CUP Cambridge 1972).

Hicks, Steven V *International Law and the Possibility of a Just World Order* (Rodopi Amsterdam 1999).

Jaeschke, Walter 'Vom Völkerrecht zum Völkerrecht' (2008) 56 Deutsche Zeitschrift für Philosophie 277–98.

Peperzak, Adriaan 'Hegel contra Hegel in His Philosophy of Right' (1994) 32 Journal of the History of Philosophy 241–63.

Siep, Ludwig 'Das Recht als Ziel der Geschichte' in Christel Fricke, Peter König, and Thomas Petersen (eds) *Das Recht der Vernunft: Kant und Hegel über Denken, Erkennen und Handeln* (Frommann-Holzboog Stuttgart-Bad Cannstatt 1995) 355–79.

Smith, Steven B 'Hegel's Views on War, the State and International Relations' (1983) 77 The American Political Science Review 624–32.

CHAPTER 56

HENRY WHEATON
(1785–1848)

LYDIA H LIU

1. Introduction

Henry Wheaton emerged as an authoritative figure in international law with the publication of *Elements of International Law* in 1836. Within a couple of decades after the first edition, this book began to eclipse major competing works and was adopted as the foremost modern text of international law in the diplomatic establishments of the United States, Britain, France, and other European countries. Wheaton's impact on the 19th century is often said to be comparable to that of Emer de Vattel in the 18th century or that of Hugo Grotius in the 17th century. Indeed, the extraordinary influences of Elements of International Law reverberated beyond the West—through translation and foreign legation channels—in Asia, Latin America, and other peripheries of the imperial world order.

2. Wheaton's Life and Career

Henry Wheaton was born in Providence, Rhode Island on 27 November 1785. He graduated from Brown University in 1802 and was admitted to the Rhode Island Bar at the age of 19. After two years studying in Europe, he returned to practise law in Providence (1807–12) and in New York (1812–27). Wheaton was appointed a justice of the Marine Court of New York from 1815–19, and served as the third reporter of the United States Supreme Court in 1816–27. In 1825, he aided in the revision of the laws of the state of New York. His chief contribution to American jurisprudence in this period lies in a number of important publications, including *Digest of the Law of Maritime Captures* (1815) and 12 volumes of *Supreme Court Reports* from 1816–27.[1]

In 1827, Wheaton was appointed *chargé d'affaires* to Denmark by President John Quincy Adams. He then served as the US minister to the Court of Berlin from 1837–46. Wheaton's diplomatic service and his broad learning allowed him to communicate regularly with the leading legal scholars, writers, and philosophers of Europe and Britain such as Johann Ludwig Klüber, Alexander von Humbolt, Sir William Scott, James Mackintosh, and Jeremy Bentham.

Wheaton was the first North American lawyer and diplomat to devote his attention to a systematic study of international law and to make a significant contribution to the development of that field. From its early inception, public international law has been subjected to numerous criticisms for its perceived failure to enforce law or put an end to wars among nations. These criticisms have tended to overlook a distinction between the legal efficacy of international law in its stated goals and the discursive or political power of its texts in historical practices. If it can be shown that while international law is less than effective in regulating and resolving international conflicts, this does not alter the fact that a body of printed texts known as 'international law' has proliferated globally in recent history and become inextricably entangled with world historical processes. Wheaton seemed to grasp the discursive function of international law in diplomatic practices very well but his intellectual ambitions extended well beyond the legal dimensions of public international law. This is clearly indicated by the companion volume he composed in French, *Histoire des progrès du droit des gens en Europe*, and published in 1841,[2] and his subsequent revisions and posthumous editions of *Elements of International Law,* all of which suggest how the discursive power of his writing answered the historical exigencies of his own time and those of the next several generations and beyond.

---

[1] C Joyce 'The Rise of the Supreme Court Reporter: An Institutional Perspective on Marshall Court Ascendancy' (1985) 83 Michigan Law Review 1291–391; and ML Cohen and SH O'Connor *A Guide to the Early Reports of the Supreme Court of the United States* (Fred B Rothman & Co Littleton CO 1995) at 35–59.

[2] The English translation of *Histoire des progrès du droit des gens en Europe* was published in 1845. It incorporates substantial addition to the French version and is entitled *History of the Law of Nations in Europe and America from the Earliest Times to the Treaty of Washington, 1842.*

3. ELEMENTS OF INTERNATIONAL LAW

This book, first published under the title *Elements of International Law: With a Sketch of the History of the Science* in 1836, was not only Wheaton's most important work but also the first English-language treatise on international law. The 1846 French version—known as the third edition—incorporated substantial revisions and amplifications. Numerous editions, reprints, and translations appeared after the author's death.

Wheaton regards public international law as an 'imperfect' positive law both 'on account of the indeterminateness of its precepts, and because it lacks that solid basis on which rests the positive law of every particular nation, the political power of the State and a judicial authority competent to enforce the law'. He does not, however, fully endorse Austin's denial of international law as positive law, for he quickly adds that 'the progress of civilization, founded on Christianity, has gradually conducted us to observe a law analogous to this in our intercourse with all the nations of the globe, whatever may be their religious faith, and without reciprocity on their part'.[3] The universalism of international law and its efficacy are thus grounded in the progress of civilization peculiar to Christendom. Contrary to the universalism of Grotius—whom Wheaton cites copiously—which extended the rights and duties of *ius gentium* to nations outside of the West, Wheaton determines that

[t]he law of nations, or international law, as understood among civilized Christian nations, may be defined as consisting of those rules of conduct which reason deduces, as consonant to justice, from the nature of society existing among independent nations; with such definitions and modifications as may be established by general consent.[4]

If the international law of civilized Christian nations of Europe and America is fundamentally different from that which governs the foreign relations of non-Western nations, does it abdicate its own universal validity? Wheaton's answer is no, for he regards the progress of (Christian) civilization as the only source of universalism. For the non-universal character of particular European and American international law will, with the passage of time, become universal with the progress and spread of Christianity and its civilization, and this will force the 'barbarous' and 'semi-civilized' nations of Asia and Africa to accept the truth of international law. Wheaton's resolute rejection of reciprocity—a 19th-century sensibility—would have seemed foreign to the pioneer of *jus gentium*, Grotius. By turning international law into a historical imperative, *Elements of International Law* shifts the ground of the universal, and cannot but justify the colonial expansion and imperialism of the European powers.

---

[3] H Wheaton *Elements of International Law* (RH Dana ed) (8th edn Clarendon Press Oxford 1866) at 21–2.

[4] ibid 23.

It is reasonable to infer that Wheaton proposed Christianity as the moral guarantor of the efficacy of international law in order to respond to Austin's criticism.[5] There are, however, other reasons for him to take the position he did that are more historically compelling than the debate within the legal field. Numerous revisions and editions of *Elements of International Law* suggest that Wheaton kept abreast with the events and conquests that were unfolding at the time, and that these developments in turn contributed to his reworking of the universalism of international law as a historical process. In the third edition (1846), he cites the treaty signed between the five European powers and the Ottoman Empire on the 13 July 1841[6] to argue that '[t]he more recent intercourse between the Christian nations in Europe and America and the Mohammedan and Pagan nations of Asia and Africa indicates a disposition, on the part of the latter, to renounce their peculiar international usages and adopt those of Christendom.'[7] In its dealings with the Christian States of Europe, the Ottoman Empire was brought 'within the pale of the public law of former', and the rights of legation were now recognized by Turkey, Persia, Egypt, and the States of Barbary, etc.[8] Wheaton's revised editions of *Elements of International Law* grew with accumulated new cases and treaty arrangements so as to illustrate the universal validity of international law.

Following Wheaton's death in 1848, many new editions of the book began to appear.[9] *Elements of International Law* garnered so much worldwide recognition in the latter half of the 19th century that it turned into a normative instrument in the fashioning of modern international relations. Richard Henry Dana brought out the eighth English edition of *Elements of International Law* in 1866, and this edition served as the definitive text in the *Classics of International Law* series issued by the Clarendon Press in 1936.

RECOMMENDED READING

Wheaton, Henry *History of the Law of Nations in Europe and America: From the Earliest Times to the Treaty of Washington, 1942* (Gould, Banks & Co New York 1845).

[5] This is Mark Weston Janis' argument in MW Janis *The American Tradition of International Law: Great Expectations 1789–1914* (Clarendon Press Oxford 2004) at 48.

[6] Treaty between Austria, France, Great Britain, Prussia, Russia, and Turkey respecting the Straits of the Dardanelles and Bosphorus (signed 13 July 1841) (1841) 92 CTS 7.

[7] *Elements of International Law* (n 3) 21.

[8] ibid 21–2.

[9] On the classical Chinese translation in 1864 called the *Wanguo gongfa*, see the contribution of S Kawashima 'China' in this volume. For a discussion of how Wheaton's text, instead of Vattel's, was promoted in China by the American de legation in Beijing and translated by Christian missionary WAP Martin, see LH Liu *The Clash of Empires: The Invention of China in Modern World Making* (Harvard University Press Cambridge MA 2004) at 108–39.

Wheaton, Henry *Elements of International Law* (RH Dana ed) (8th edn Clarendon Press Oxford 1866).

Baker, Elizabeth F *Henry Wheaton 1785–1848* (University of Pennsylvania Press Philadelphia PA 1937).

Gong, Gerrit W *The Standard of 'Civilization' in International Society* (Clarendon Press Oxford 1984).

Janis, Mark W *The American Tradition of International Law: Great Expectations 1789–1914* (Clarendon Press Oxford 2004).

Kennedy, David 'International Law and the Nineteenth Century: History of an Illusion' (1997) 17 Quinnipiac Law Review 99–138.

Liu, Lydia H *The Clash of Empires: The Invention of China in Modern World Making* (Harvard University Press Cambridge MA 2004).

CHAPTER 57

FRANCIS LIEBER
(1798–1872)

SILJA VÖNEKY

1. LIFE

1.1. Biography

The German-born Francis (originally *Franz*) Lieber referred to himself as a 'philosophic historian' and was not only one of the most important American jurists of his time but also a political philosopher, political scientist, and publicist.[1] His significant impact on the development of international law and humanization of the laws of war contributed to his universal appreciation; this is evident in the 21st century even more than during his lifetime.

Lieber was born in Berlin on 18 March 1798.[2] He left Europe as a young man for North America where he died in New York on 2 October 1872. To understand the life and work of Lieber, it is necessary to separate the two phases of his life: the formative years of boyhood and young adulthood in Europe, and his later life in North America which was characterized by a remarkable productivity and academic career.

---

[1] B Röben *Johann Caspar Bluntschli, Francis Lieber und das moderne Völkerrecht 1861–1881* (Nomos Baden-Baden 2003) at 85.

[2] ibid 15.

His childhood was overshadowed by the Napoleonic Wars. Deeply disturbed by seeing Napoleon's troops enter Berlin,[3] he joined the Prussian Army at only 16 and took part in the Battle of Waterloo in 1815, where he was seriously injured. It was the personal experience of the cruelties of war and detention which was the reason for his later lifelong struggle to humanize the laws of war.[4] Because of his political activities with the aim of uniting Germany, he was imprisoned in Berlin and denied admission to all universities of Prussia.[5] He finally started his academic studies in 1820 at the more liberal University of Jena, graduating in the same year with a dissertation in mathematics. After further but unfinished academic studies,[6] Lieber fought in the Greek War of Independence in 1821. Back in Berlin in 1823 he was persecuted and detained again. In 1826, Lieber fled from the repressive Prussia to London. He finally left Europe in 1827 and emigrated to Boston to promulgate the leading idea and passion of his life: a life of civil freedom and liberty.[7]

His academic career started in 1835, when he became professor of history and political economics at South Carolina College. In 1860 he was appointed professor of political economy, political science, and history at Columbia College, New York, and was co-founder of the associated law school.[8] During the American Civil War, he also worked as legal advisor of the United States in questions of the laws of war.[9] Lieber esteemed North America as a 'fortunate country, whose happiness is founded on its liberty'.[10]

1.2. Publications

Although he had already published articles in Germany, Lieber's decisive publications were written and edited after his emigration to North America: he became editor and founder of the *Encyclopedia Americana* (1829–33) and wrote, *inter alia, A Manual of Political Ethics* (1838–39).[11] Lieber never published a book on public

---

[3] ibid.

[4] ibid 16 with further references.

[5] F Freidel *Francis Lieber, Nineteenth-Century Liberal* (Lawbook Exchange New Jersey 2003).

[6] ibid 29.

[7] F Lieber *The Ancient and the Modern Teacher of Politics* (Board of Trustees of Columbia College New York 1859) at 34.

[8] Ibid 293; *Johann Caspar Bluntschli* (n 1) 32.

[9] For an overview see *Johann Caspar Bluntschli* (n 1) 33 ff.

[10] F Lieber (ed) *Encyclopaedia Americana* (Mussey & Co Boston 1830) vol 1, at vii; *Johann Caspar Bluntschli* (n 1) 20; *Francis Lieber* (n 5) 105 ff.

[11] Other important publications include *On Legal and Political Hermeneutics* (CC Little and J Brown Boston 1838); *Laws of Property: Essays on Property and Labor, as connected with Natural Law and the Constitution of Society* (Harper New York 1842); and *On Civil Liberty and Self Government* (R Bentley London 1853).

international law,[12] but since 1862 he was in close correspondence with all relevant international legal experts of his time, including Wilhelm August Heffter (1796–1880) and Johann Caspar Bluntschli (1808–81).[13] Moreover, he drafted his most influential contribution concerning the development of international law: the *Instructions for the Government of Armies of the United States in the Field* (1863).

2. Main Work: The Lieber Code

On behalf of US President Lincoln, Lieber prepared the General Order No 100 containing the *Instructions for the Government of the Armies of the United States in the Field* of 24 April 1863.[14] It has since become known as the Lieber Code. The Code regulates martial law, public and private property of an enemy, the treatment of deserters, prisoners of war, hostages, and partisans, armistices, insurrections, civil wars, and rebellions. The Code was adopted by the United States to inform the military personnel of the armed forces of the Union during the American Civil War (1861–65) about the rules of the laws of war. Hence the Code was an internal non-binding code of conduct and the first national manual on the laws of armed conflict.[15]

However, it would be imprecise to say that the Code is a codification of the laws of war of 1863. Lieber himself stated in a letter to a colleague:

[Y]ou...know that nothing of the kind exists in any language. I had no guide, no groundwork, no text-book....Usage, history, reason, and conscientiousness, a sincere love of truth, justice and civilization have been my guides.[16]

Being a military manual, the Code is not a source of international law but provides evidence of State practice and of the United States' *opinio iuris* regarding the laws of land warfare at that time. In fact, the Code laid down rules which were partly customary law of war of the time and, as a military manual, demonstrated the will of the United States to bring those rules into effect. The Code also strongly influenced the

---

[12] *Johann Caspar Bluntschli* (n 1) 38.

[13] ibid 69 ff. It was Lieber who gave JC Bluntschli the impulse to write his famous book *Das moderne Völkerrecht der civilisirten Staten als Rechtsbuch dargestellt* (CH Beck'sche Buchhandlung Nördlingen 1868); see *Johann Caspar Bluntschli* (n 1) 1.

[14] See the Introduction of the Lieber Code.

[15] See *Francis Lieber* (n 5) 334 ff; T Meron 'Francis Lieber's Code and Principles of Humanity' (1998) 36 Columbia Journal of Transnational Law 269–82 at 269 and 280; R Hartigan *Lieber's Code and the Law of War* (Precedent Publishing Chicago 1983) at 2.

[16] Quoted in *Lieber's Code and the Law of War* (n 15) 10.

further codification and development of the laws of war and the adoption of similar manuals by other States.[17]

Despite having been drafted a century ago, the Code still embodies the modern or 'civilized' laws of war and codified legal limitations of the right to harm the enemy during a war that are still valid today.[18] A striking example is the principle of limitation: only militarily necessary damages are allowed according to Lieber's concept of public war. This stands in sharp contrast to all the then-popular theories of total war.[19]

Another example is the principle of individual criminal responsibility for war crimes. The Code stipulated that an individual was criminally responsible if the laws of war were not obeyed. Even the defence of superior order was not recognized by the Code. Yet, for a conviction, certain procedural rights and the principle of proportionality had to be observed according to the Code.

Further evidence that the Code is the nucleus of the modern laws of war is the first explicit prohibition of torture to extort confessions,[20] the duty to protect cultural property, and rules that are decisive for today's understanding of the status of a prisoner of war.[21]

It was the achievement of Lieber and his Code to systematize all rules applicable during land warfare and effectively incorporated the aim to humanize them: he was the catalysing force for the development of modern humanitarian law.

RECOMMENDED READING

Lieber, Francis *A Manual of Political Ethics* (2 vols CC Little and J Brown Boston 1838/1839).

Lieber, Francis *On Civil Liberty and Self-Government* (2 vols R Bentley London 1853).

Lieber, Francis 'Instructions for the Government of Armies of the United States in the Field' in Dietrich Schindler and Jiří Toman (eds) *The Laws of Armed Conflicts* (4th edn Nijhoff Leiden 2004) 3–20.

Carnahan, Burrus M 'Lincoln, Lieber and the Laws of War: The Origins and Limits of the Principle of Military Necessity' (1998) 92 American Journal of International Law 213–31.

[17] The Code was the model for the 1864 Geneva Convention, the 1868 Declaration of St Petersburg, and the 1874 Brussels International Declaration on the Laws of War which was never adopted but influenced the 1899 Hague Rules of Land Warfare; see Lieber's Code and the Law of War (n 15) 23.

[18] The notion used in Das moderne Völkerrecht der civilisirten Staten (n 13) 34 ff.

[19] For details see S Vöneky 'Der Lieber Code und die Wurzeln des modernen Kriegsvölkerrechts' (2002) 62 Zeitschrift für ausländisches öffentliches Recht und Völkerrecht 423–60 at 425.

[20] D Kretzmer 'Prohibition of Torture' in R Wolfrum (ed) *Max Planck Encyclopedia of Public International Law* (OUP Oxford 2008) at <www.mpepil.com>.

[21] RM Chesney 'Prisoners of War' in R Wolfrum (ed) *Max Planck Encyclopedia of Public International Law* (OUP Oxford 2008) at <www.mpepil.com>.

Freidel, Frank *Francis Lieber, Nineteenth-Century Liberal* (Lawbook Exchange New Jersey 2003).

Hartigan, Richard S *Lieber's Code and the Law of War* (Precedent Publishing Chicago 1983).

Mack, Charles R and Henry H Lesesne (eds) *Francis Lieber and the Culture of the Mind* (University of South Carolina Press Columbia 2005).

Meron, Theodor 'Francis Lieber's Code and Principles of Humanity' (1998) 36 Columbia Journal of Transnational Law 269–82.

Röben, Betsy *Johann Caspar Bluntschli, Francis Lieber und das moderne Völkerrecht 1861–1881* (Nomos Baden-Baden 2003).

Root, Elihu 'Francis Lieber' (1913) 7 American Journal of International Law 453–69.

Vöneky, Silja 'Der Lieber Code und die Wurzeln des modernen Kriegsvölkerrechts' (2002) 62 Zeitschrift für ausländisches öffentliches Recht und Völkerrecht 423–60.

CHAPTER 58

BERTHA VON SUTTNER (1843–1914)

SIMONE PETER

1. Bertha von Suttner

THE Austrian writer Bertha von Suttner was one of the leading figures of the late 19th-century peace movement. Her novel *Die Waffen nieder!* (*Lay Down Your Arms!*) was published 1889 and was soon translated into major European languages.[1] In 1891, she founded and presided over the Austrian Society for Peace (*Österreichische Gesellschaft der Friedensfreunde*). In 1876, she met the Swedish inventor of dynamite, Alfred Nobel, with whom she maintained an extensive correspondence. It is now well known that she had significant influence on Nobel's decision to include in his will a prize to be distributed 'to the person who shall have done the most or the best work for fraternity between nations, for the abolition or reduction of standing armies and for the holding and promotion of peace congresses.'[2] To the surprise of all contemporary observers, Bertha von Suttner had been passed over four times by the Norwegian Nobel Committee by the time she was awarded the Peace Laureate in 1905. She died on 21 June 1914, just a few days before the Austrian prince's assassination in Sarajevo.

---

[1] B von Suttner *Lay Down Your Arms!* (T Holmes trans) (Longmans Green London 1892).
[2] Full text of Alfred Nobel's Will in an official English translation at <http://www.nobelprize.org/alfred_nobel/will/will-full.html> (22 December 2011).

2. Early Life

Baroness Bertha von Suttner was born Bertha Felicita Sophia Countess Kinsky von Chinič und Tettnau on 9 June 1843 in Prague, daughter of a high noble Royal and Imperial Field Marshal and Chamberlain who died before her birth. Bertha's mother Sophie Körner preferred to spend her time in the fashionable spas and casinos of the epoch. Despite the busy social life of contemporary aristocracy, Bertha got an unusually good education and was taught French and English. In 1873, she joined the household of Baron Karl von Suttner as a governess, where she fell in love with the son, Arthur Gunaccar Freiherr von Suttner. The relationship was deemed inappropriate, so Bertha had to leave the household. She applied for a position as a personal secretary to Alfred Nobel in Paris. She married Arthur Suttner in 1876, leaving Vienna to live with him in the Caucasus for the next nine years. They made their living as writers and teachers. She wrote several books, among them *Inventarium einer Seele* (*Inventory of a Soul*) (1883)[3] and *Das Maschinenalter: Zukunftsvorlesungen über unsere Zeit* (*The Age of Machines: Future Lectures About Our Age*, 1889). Both books revealed a commitment to the idea of human progress. The scientific and philosophical issues that were addressed in those books required her to use pen names in order to hide her gender.[4]

3. The International Peace Movement

Bertha learned about the existence of the International Peace and Arbitration Association founded by Hodgson Pratt in London in 1880. When she discovered that such an organization existed, she was 'electrified' by the news that 'the idea of justice between nations, the struggle to do away with war, had assumed form and life'.[5] She aimed at bringing the ideas of the peace movement to a broader public when she published the novel *Die Waffen nieder!* (*Lay Down Your Arms!*) in 1889. The book is regarded as a novel of purpose. It tells the story of the aristocratic heroine Martha von Tilling who faces the horrors of war several times. Martha develops from a naïve young girl, admiring the glamour of uniforms and military virtues, into a strong

---

[3] B Oulot (B von Suttner) *Inventarium einer Seele* (4th edn Pierson Dresden 1904).

[4] B von Suttner *Memoirs of Bertha von Suttner: The Records of an Eventful Life* (authorized translation) (Ginn & Co Boston and London 1910) vol 1, at 275.

[5] ibid 287.

opponent of war. The novel combines dialogues with impressive realistic descriptions of contemporary battlefields. In 1891, Leo Tolstoy wrote to Bertha von Suttner: 'The abolition of slavery was preceded by the famous book of a woman, Mrs Beecher Stowe; God grant that the abolition of war may follow upon yours'.[6] Among its readers were Max Huber who was so 'deeply moved' by the novel that 'he vowed to dedicate his life to serving world peace',[7] and probably also Tsar Nikolas II who convened the first international peace conference in The Hague in 1899.[8] In 1892, the catchy title of the book was adopted for a monthly periodical whose editor Bertha von Suttner was until 1899. It was co-founded with the publisher Alfred Herman Fried who became the editor of its successor *Die Friedens-Warte: Zeitschrift für zwischenstaatliche Organisation* (now the Journal of International Peace and Organization) in 1899. Both periodicals were important channels for Bertha von Suttner's ideas which appeared monthly as *Randglossen zur Zeitgeschichte*.[9]

The peace movement of the late 19th century was split into many different organizations, some of them created by Bertha von Suttner. By the turn of the century, she was the leading figure in the organized international peace movement, being influential and yet powerless. Accordingly, her salon became one of the most important social *lieu de rencontre* at The Hague's first peace conference in 1899, but she had no access to the negotiations and was deeply disappointed by the non-committal results of the conference. In the years to come, lecture tours and networking activities brought her to Monaco (1903), to the US (1904 and 1912), Germany (1905), Sweden and Norway (1906), where the Nobel Peace Prize was finally awarded to the woman who had been its most important initiator.

4. Peace and Law

Bertha von Suttner's attitude towards international law reflects the 19th century optimism of liberal internationalism, characterized by its belief in rational thought and its advocacy for international cooperation within international institutions.[10] She was influenced by contemporary Darwinism and considered

---

[6] Tolstoy in a letter to von Suttner (22 October 1891) found in ibid 343.

[7] D Schindler 'Max Huber—His Life' (2007) 18 European Journal of International Law 81–95 at 83; on Huber see the portrait by Oliver Diggelmann, in this volume.

[8] *Memoirs* (n 4) vol 2, 193.

[9] B von Suttner *Der Kampf um die Vermeidung des Weltkriegs: Randglossen aus zwei Jahrzehnten zu den Zeitereignissen vor der Katastrophe* (Erich Fried ed) (2 vols Orell Füssli Zürich 1917).

[10] M Koskenniemi *The Gentle Civilizer of Nations* (CUP Cambridge 2002).

human progress as a continuous process of civilization. Strongly opposed to the nationalist militarism of her time, she relentlessly pointed out that peace, and not war, belonged to the higher level of evolution. She was convinced that the century witnessed 'a gradual extermination of the tribes that wage war by peaceful nations', aspiring towards 'a union of world interests growing into a closer and closer brotherhood'.[11] To her, law was a sign of progress, bringing peoples and nations to a higher level of civilization where arbitral tribunals were established to avoid war. In *Das Maschinenalter* (*The Age of Machines*), she affirmed her strong conviction that law would replace violence one day by referring to the ambiguity of the German term *Gewalt*, which means both violence and power: '*Gestern: Gewalt als Recht. Morgen: Recht als Gewalt*' (Yesterday: violence as law. Tomorrow: law as power).[12] Although those passages stress the importance of international law in general, she was strenuously opposed to all contemporary attempts to codify international humanitarian law specifically. She insisted that she was not interested in the 'question of the humanization of war' but in the 'codification of peace'.[13]

In sum, Bertha von Suttner was one of the leading 'populist pacifists'[14] of the late 19th and early 20th centuries. She was a talented propagandist whose aristocratic social background helped her to get access to the circles of power and influence, although she was often ridiculed and mocked for being utopian and naïve. Nevertheless, she convinced the inventor of war's most important agent to establish a prize— dedicated to war's most important adversaries.

RECOMMENDED READING

Suttner, Bertha von *Der Kampf um die Vermeidung des Weltkriegs: Randglossen aus zwei Jahrzehnten zu den Zeitereignissen vor der Katastrophe* (Erich Fried ed) (2 vols Orell Füssli Zürich 1917).

Suttner, Bertha von *Lay down your Arms!* (T Holmes trans) (Longmans Green London 1892).

Suttner, Bertha von *Memoirs of Bertha von Suttner: The Records of an Eventful Life* (authorized trans) (2 vols Ginn & Co Boston and London 1910).

Abrams, Irwin 'Bertha von Suttner and the Nobel Peace Prize' (1962) 22 Journal of Central European Affairs 286–307.

---

[11] *Inventarium* (n 3); the English translation of the quote is taken from B Hamann *Bertha von Suttner: A Life for Peace* (A Dubsky trans) (Syracuse University Press Syracuse NY 1996) at 41.

[12] Jemand (B von Suttner) *Das Maschinenalter: Zukunftsvorlesungen über unsere Zeit* (2nd edn Verlags-Magazin Zürich 1889) at 292.

[13] *Memoirs* (n 4) vol 2, at 278.

[14] RP Alford 'The Nobel Effect: Nobel Peace Prize Laureates as International Norm Entrepreneurs' (2008) 49 Virginia Journal of International Law 61–134 at 68 ff.

Alford, Roger P 'The Nobel Effect: Nobel Peace Prize Laureates as International Norm Entrepreneurs' (2008) 49 Virginia Journal of International Law 61–134.

Biedermann, Edelgard (ed) *Chère baronne et amie, cher monsieur et ami. Der Briefwechsel zwischen Alfred Nobel und Bertha von Suttner* (Georg Olms Hildesheim 2001).

Hamann, Brigitte *Bertha von Suttner: A* Life for Peace (Ann Dubsky trans) (Syracuse University Press Syracuse NY 1996).

CHAPTER 59

FRIEDRICH FROMHOLD VON MARTENS (FYODOR FYODOROVICH MARTENS) (1845–1909)

LAURI MÄLKSOO

1. LIFE AND WORK

FYODOR Fyodorovich Martens (also known as Friedrich Fromhold von Martens, 1845–1909) was the foremost Russian international lawyer of the Tsarist period. As professor of international law at St Petersburg University, he authored a number of influential texts on international law that were translated in a number of foreign languages. His most significant work was the first comprehensive Russian textbook on international law, *Contemporary International Law of Civilized Nations* (1882–83). Moreover, in 1874–1909, at the request of the Russian Ministry of Foreign Affairs, Martens edited a 15-volume series of treaties, *Recueil des traités et conventions, conclus par Russie avec les états étrangers*. Martens was also a frequent contributor to the leading international law journal of his time, *Revue de droit international et de législation comparée.* The sheer volume and influence of the scholarly output of Martens is impressive and already secures him a lasting place in the history of international law.

Yet Martens also led another life: that of a diplomat in the service of the Ministry of Foreign Affairs of Russia. Perhaps his fame was due particularly to the fact that he was able to combine the two careers, academic and diplomatic, in a single lifetime, being simultaneously a leading expert/writer in the field of international law *and* a legal-diplomatic voice of the Russian Empire. He played a major role in the first Hague Peace Conference of 1899 which was convened at the initiative of Russia. At the conference, Martens managed to solve a deadlock between major European powers and smaller States concerning the issue of the right to military resistance of the citizens of countries under military occupation. Thus, the 'Martens clause' was born, a stipulation in the preamble to the second Hague Convention of 1899 (Laws and Customs of War on Land). The Martens clause states the following:

Until a more complete code of the laws of war is issued, the High Contracting Parties think it right to declare that in cases not included in the Regulations adopted by them, populations and belligerents remain under the protection and empire of the principles of international law, as they result from the usages established between civilised nations, from the laws of humanity and the requirements of the public conscience.

The Martens clause remains part of international humanitarian law to this day and has been referred to in the jurisprudence of the International Court of Justice.[1]

The 1899 conference in The Hague also adopted the Convention on the Peaceful Settlement of International Disputes and established the Permanent Chamber of the International Court of Arbitration. The institution of international commissions of enquiry was created and received its baptism of fire when the Hull incident involving Russia and Britain occurred in 1904.

Martens also acted as arbitrator in a number of high-profile cases of his time, especially the Anglo-Venezuelan Arbitration (1899). The latter arbitration became controversial because half a century later, an American lawyer who was involved in the arbitration (the US sided with Venezuela in the dispute) argued that Martens as the presiding arbitrator had struck a deal with the arbiters appointed by Britain and effectively presented the American arbiters with an ultimatum to accept his (pro-British) solution or face an even harsher defeat.

In 1905, Martens was member of the Russian delegation in the Russo-Japanese peace conference in Portsmouth, New Hampshire. At the second Hague Peace Conference of 1907, Martens was a head of committee and contributed significantly to the

---

[1] Legality of the Threat or Use of Nuclear Weapons (Advisory Opinion) (1996) 35 ILM 814. See especially the state submissions and dissenting opinions.

diplomatic preparation of the conference. He was considered as candidate for the Nobel Peace Prize but did not receive it.

2. APPRAISAL

There exist conflicting views on Martens' legacy. One can distinguish between critical-dismissive (Nussbaum), defensive-patriotic (Pustogarov), and romantic-national (Kross) approaches. The core of Arthur Nussbaum's (1877–1964) criticism was that, in Tsarist Russia, Martens the scholar did not have the kind of independence that his contemporary scholars in Western Europe enjoyed.[2] Regardless of whether Martens received direct orders from the Foreign Ministry, to Nussbaum, he was first of all the State's spokesperson rather than an independent expert of international law.

Vladimir Pustogarov's (1920–99) biography of Martens signified a turn in Russian international law scholarship. Pustogarov points out that during the Soviet period, the official attitude towards Martens was negative.[3] Even in 2009, Sergey Bakhin of St Petersburg University writes that he was asked by a distinguished Russian international law colleague: 'Why suddenly so much of Martens? Haven't we started over-emphasizing his role in Russia'[4]

These intra-Russian debates have less to do with Martens than with Russia's fluctuating relationship with Europe. Being a non-ethnic Russian by birth and representing the Germanized culture of Russia's Baltic provinces, Martens represented a distinctively European voice in Russia's international law—to the extent that we can ask whether he represented Russia in Europe or, rather, Europe in Russia. The title chosen for the 2000 English translation of Pustogarov's work is quite revealing: *Our Martens*. This emphasizes Russia's desired unity with (rather than the Soviet-era isolation from) the rest of Europe. Yet in order to play up Martens' significance, Pustogarov played down some justified criticisms that Martens received not only from abroad but also from his contemporaries in Russia. Whilst during the Soviet period, Martens was 'bad' (as a Tsar's man and imperialist), now he had to be 'good'.

[2] A Nussbaum 'Frederic de Martens. Representative Tsarist Writer on International Law' (1952) 22 Nordisk Tidsskrift International Ret (Acta Scandinavia juris gentium) 51–66 at 60.

[3] VV Pustogarov *Our Martens: FF Martens, International Lawyer and Architect of Peace* (WE Butler trans, ed) (Kluwer Law International The Hague 2000) at 3–4.

[4] SV Bakhin 'Paradoks professora Martensa' (The Paradox of Professor Martens) (2009) Russian Yearbook of International Law (Neva Saint Petersburg) 35–53 at 37.

Jaan Kross (1920–2007), the Estonian novelist whose own career as an international law scholar at Tartu ended with his arrest and deportation to Siberia in 1946, published a novel entitled *Professor Martens' Departure* in 1984. Based on parish registers kept in Estonia, Kross claims that Martens had ethnic Estonian roots. When writing his novel, Kross did not have access to Martens' actual diaries (1883–1909) which are now kept in the Archive on the Foreign Policy of the Russian Empire in Moscow.[5]

Martens' diaries reveal the less appealing aspects of his international success. Combining professorial and ministerial careers was not just glamour. Martens was very concerned about imperial Russia's present and future; his political identity was that of an (increasingly disappointed) imperial man. While Kross's novel suggests that after such a successful career Martens might have felt fulfilled, the diaries sadly reveal that, in reality, Martens was intensely frustrated that his career had come to an end. (He wanted an ambassadorial post in The Hague or in southern Europe.) It seems that at the end of his life, Martens was indeed considered a professor rather than a diplomat. For example, when going to the Portsmouth peace negotiations with the Japanese, Martens was insulted when his Russian colleagues-diplomats demonstratively addressed him as (only) 'professor'.[6]

Martens' fantasy stream of thought as imagined by Kross raises the most important question about any international lawyer: the ethics of the profession. What is the price of success? Who uses whom more, the State the international lawyer, or vice versa? In his diaries, Martens was extremely critical of the Tsar, the Russian government, and his colleagues at the Russian Ministry of Foreign Affairs. ('Poor, poor Russia', is a frequent plaint).[7] He often felt more understood and appreciated abroad than at home, where he had started to perceive the 'glass ceiling'. Yet he also seems to have forgotten that his fame would not have been possible without the opportunities he enjoyed by representing Russia. The opportunities that the sovereign gave, it could easily take away. Notwithstanding his world renown, to those in power, Martens was just a talented lawyer, not a sovereign. On 26 March 1907, Martens declared in his diary with some bitterness that his personal independence was most important for him and he would not allow anyone to become his censor.

Thus, the story of the outstanding international lawyer FF Martens represents the inherent tension of being an 'independent' international law expert and 'dependent' State representative at the same time. The pact required in order to combine the two roles may turn out to be a Faustian one.

---

[5] Arkhiv Vneshnei Politiki Rossiiskoi Imperii (AVPRI) (Russian: Archive of Foreign Policy of the Russian Empire), Fond No 340, opis' No 787, delo 1–10.

[6] Diary entries of 9 July 1905, 22 July 1905, 29 July 1905, and 28 November 1908.

[7] Diary entries of 27 January 1906 and 2 April 1906.

RECOMMENDED READING

Martens, Fyodor F *Sovremennoe mezhdunarodnoe pravo tsivilizovannykh narodov* (Contemporary International Law of Civilised Nations) (2 vols Zertsalo Moscow 2008).

Bakhin, Sergey V 'Paradoks professora Martensa' (2009) Russian Yearbook of International Law (Neva Saint Petersburg) 35–53.

Kross, Jaan *Professor Martens' Departure* (Anselm Hollo trans) (New Press, New York City 1994).

Mälksoo, Lauri 'The Liberal Imperialism of Friedrich (Fyodor) Martens (1845–1909)' in Hélène Ruiz Fabri, Emanuelle Jouannet and Vincent Tomkiewicz (eds) *Select Proceedings of the European Society of International Law* (Hart Publishing Oxford 2006) vol 1, 173–180.

Nussbaum, Arthur 'Frederic de Martens: Representative Tsarist Writer on International Law' (1952) 22 Nordisk Tidsskrift International Ret (Acta Scandinavia juris gentium) 51–66.

Pustogarov, Vladimir V *Our Martens: F.F. Martens, International Lawyer and Architect of Peace* (William E Butler trans, ed) (Kluwer Law International The Hague 2000).

CHAPTER 60

LASSA OPPENHEIM
(1858–1919)

MATHIAS SCHMOECKEL

LASSA Oppenheim (his birth name was Lahsa) was born in Windecken near Frank-furt-am-Main in 1858 as son of a Jewish horse trader. His father acquired considerable wealth, which enabled his family to move to Frankfurt and to live off private means. Lassa received an excellent education. In 1878 he started studying law in Göttingen, where he studied Roman law with Rudolph von Jhering. He took courses in psychol-ogy with Wilhelm Wundt, and in metaphysics with Hermann Lotze. In Berlin he attended the classes of Julius Baron, Heinrich Brunner, Georg Beseler, and the great historian Heinrich von Treitschke. At Heidelberg he studied international law with Caspar Bluntschli. The supervisor of his doctoral dissertation was the commercial lawyer Heinrich Thöl, the theses was submitted in Göttingen in 1881.

Afterwards he chose Karl Binding as his mentor in order to start an academic career in criminal law. Yet Oppenheim's study took place in Freiburg in 1885 as Baden was among the most liberal parts of Germany concerning the attitude towards Jews. However, even there it was difficult for a practising Jew to obtain a chair. In 1889 Oppenheim was appointed Extraordinarius (non-tenured professor) in Freiburg. He published five books and various articles on criminal law in this time. But in spite of his expectations he was not promoted to a full professorship. For this reason he moved to Basel in 1892 where he was appointed full professor a year later.

In 1895 Oppenheim left Switzerland and went to London. British relatives, liberal inclinations, financial independence, and perhaps a propensity for the British way of life may have induced him to take this unusual step, but the main motivation remains a mystery. With this decision, he abandoned not only his professorship in Basel but also his career as a criminal lawyer, because the knowledge he had gathered in that field in Germany and Switzerland was not applicable to the British common law system. Unlike other immigrants, he did not come to England in order to find a job. but he developed an interest in international law and started teaching, first at night schools, and later at the London School of Economics. He was naturalized in 1900 and called himself Lassa Francis Lawrence Oppenheim. In 1902 he married Elizabeth Alexandra, a daughter of Lieutenant-Colonel Phineas Cowan, and in 1904 their only daughter was born.

After his naturalization, Oppenheim began his connection with the Foreign Office in London. The Office started to borrow books from Oppenheim's extensive library, and later asked him to give legal advice on international legal matters, especially after the publication of his textbook on international law in 1905[1]. Having been recommended by John Westlake, who considered Oppenheim's positivism useful for the modernization of British legal science, he was appointed Whewell Professor of international law at Cambridge University in 1908. He held that chair until his death in October 1919.

His treatise was an immediate success. As its author, Oppenheim gained a worldwide reputation. Destined to be read by a wider audience, and not only by lawyers, it was to be both exhaustive and impartial. For this reason it did not explain the author's methods. Oppenheim hinted at his methodology only in other publications. His basic assumptions can only be understood in the light of his previous German writings. And yet everybody noticed, and the critics praised, his new systematic approach. To Oppenheim, (international) law consisted only in what practice accepted as law. Accordingly, only treaty law and custom could be regarded as proper sources of law, whereas doctrine and court decisions were only means to recognize the law, thus playing only a subsidiary role.

In displaying all the opinions of legal writers about the issues presented in his textbook, and by aiming at fairness and truthfulness, Oppenheim tried to convince the reader of the impartiality and objectivity of his statements. He thus hoped to help peoples and States to know and obey the law, to prevent disputes and to foster peace. The increasing number of international treaties helped him to believe in a constant 'constitutionalization' of international law.

To strengthen the educational goal of his treatise, Oppenheim presented five 'lessons' derived from the history of international law. These 'morals' were intended as advice to the reader, references to common sense, and as clues for understanding the transformation of the law. Instead of a mere deduction of rules, Oppenheim hoped to propagate a common legal sense (not far apart from Jhering's 'Rechtsgefühl') and thus to prevent international violence. According to these five morals,

---

[1] L Oppenheim *International Law: A Treatise* (2 vols Longman, Green & Co London 1905).

- international law needed an equilibrium among the Great Powers in order to subsist;
- international law should be in accordance with the interests of States (including their economic interests) in order to prosper;
- the forces of nationalism were too strong to be stopped;
- international law would need due time to ripen, thus the establishment of the Permanent Court of Arbitration was a welcome step towards the codification of international law; and
- the development of international law further depended on the standard of public morality.

These assumptions clearly make the treatise appear as a product of the finale of the classical epoch of international law. As in the 19th century, the world was governed by the Great Powers, and only civilization hindered mere force to rule. In order to establish an enduring order, law has to be in accordance with the interests of its subjects. In later articles, published after the First World War, Oppenheim welcomed the League of Nations as a new parliament of States, and as an important step towards the establishment of a world constitution. Yet he stressed the necessity for enlisting all major States, so that the League would not become a club of the victorious. But it became increasingly difficult to adopt positions in international law that were equally acceptable to all countries. The growing tension between Germany and the United Kingdom during the First World War forced Oppenheim already in 1916 to distance himself publicly from German politics.

In the golden age of textbooks, such books were translated and read in other countries; they thus aimed at a unified understanding of international law. Oppenheim's textbook was appreciated and quoted in all countries. It therefore can be regarded as the last important textbook in the tradition of classical international law.

The long-lasting fame of this book is mainly due to subsequent editions. Gradually, Oppenheim's *International Law* became *Oppenheim's International Law*. The author was able to write important parts of the third edition of his treatise in 1920–21, but that edition had to be completed by his student Ronald Roxburgh (1889–1981). Oppenheim bequeathed some money to secure a publication of following editions, but the publisher was also very interested to keep the best-selling book alive. In 1926–28 it was (Lord) Arthur Duncan McNair (1885–1975), Oppenheim's successor in Cambridge, who prepared the next edition. The fifth (1935) and subsequent editions until the eighth (1955) were edited by Sir Hersch Lauterpacht (1897–1960). Sir Robert Jennings (1913–2004) was yet another holder of the Whewell chair who, together with Sir Arthur Watts, published a ninth edition in 1992–96. Roxburgh, McNair, and Lauterpacht not only kept the book up-to-date but also adopted an even more British standpoint. McNair, for instance, added a new 'moral' of international law according to which the progress of international law is connected with the victory of democracy over autocracy. This was clearly a British reaction to the First World War, and hardly compatible with Oppenheim's conviction of the necessity of a balance of power. Lauterpacht included another lesson of international law, emphasizing that in international relations, international lawyers must play a more important role than diplomats in order to defend the law against a practice of unprincipled bargaining. In the fifth edition, Lauterpacht even criticized rigid positivism—obviously referring to Oppenheim—which, he held, no longer was in accordance with contemporary international law. To Lauterpacht, the prevailing approach to international law was represented by what he called the Grotian school; in other words, his own natural law approach. Thus the text changed considerably from each edition to the next.

The impact of *Oppenheim's International Law* can be proven by the number of citations in the decisions of international courts. The work ranks clearly among the most cited treatises of international law. From the fourth edition onwards this success was less attributable to Oppenheim but rather to McNair and, especially, Hersch Lauterpacht. It appears from the courts' decisions that the editions for which Lauterpacht was responsible were regarded as a highly reliable depiction and analysis of the respective current legal issues. Lauterpacht's editions gained an authority unmatched by any other textbook of the time. Many young scholars from other countries studied in Cambridge and learned international law with *Oppenheim's International Law*. To that extent, the worldwide influence of this textbook is also due to the dominant position of the Cambridge school of international law in the 20th century. The work became one of the most successful treatises of international law in the 20th century, and in that sense a classic of international law.

RECOMMENDED READING

Oppenheim, Lassa *International Law: A Treatise* (2 vols Longman, Green & Co London 1905).

Faulenbach, Florian *Bedeutung und Funktion der Doktrin in der Rechtsprechung der Internationalen Gerichtshöfe* (Peter Lang Frankfurt aM 2010).

Kingsbury, Benedict 'Legal Positivism as Normative Politics: International Society, Balance of Power and Lassa Oppenheim's Positive International Law' (2002) 13 European Journal of International Law 401–36.

Perreau-Saussine, Amanda 'A Case Study of Jurisprudence as Source of International Law: Oppenheim's Influence' in Matthew CR Craven, Malgosia Fitzmaurice, and Maria Vogiatzi (eds) *Time, History, and International Law* (Brill Leiden 2007) 91–117 at 98 and 104.

Reisman, W. Michael 'Lassa Oppenheim's Nine Lives' (1994) 19 Yale Journal of International Law 255–80.

Schmoeckel, Mathias 'Lassa Oppenheim (1858–1919)' in Jack Beatson and Reinhard Zimmermann (eds) *Jurists Uprooted: German-speaking émigré Lawyers in Twentieth-century Britain* (OUP Oxford 2004) 583–99.

Schmoeckel, Mathias 'Lassa Oppenheim and his Reaction to World War I' in Randall Lesaffer (ed) *Peace Treaties and International Law in European History. From the Late Middle Ages to World War One* (CUP Cambridge 2004) 270–88.

Schmoeckel, Mathias 'The Story of a Success: Lassa Oppenheim and his "International Law"' in Michael Stolleis and Masaharu Yanagihara (eds) *East Asian and European Perspectives on International Law* (Nomos Baden-Baden 2004) 57–138.

CHAPTER 61

MAX HUBER
(1874–1960)

OLIVER DIGGELMANN

1. INTRODUCTION

THE Swiss lawyer Max Huber was a sociologically oriented theorist of international law as well as a judge and President of the Permanent Court of International Justice. He is also known as an international arbitrator, particularly in the *Island of Palmas Case*, as a member of the Aaland Commission of the League of Nations, and as president of the International Committee of the Red Cross during the Second World War. His most important theoretical work is a longer essay published in 1910 that is usually cited under the title of the 1928 reprint *Die soziologischen Grundlagen des Völkerrechts* (The Sociological Foundations of International Law).[1]

---

[1] M Huber 'Beiträge zur Kenntnis der soziologischen Grundlagen des Völkerrechts und der Staatengesellschaft' (1910) 4 Jahrbuch des öffentlichen Rechts 56–134, reprinted in 1928 as *Die soziologischen Grundlagen des Völkerrechts* (Verlag Dr Walther Rothschild Berlin-Grunewald 1928). The following citations refer to the reprint.

2. ACADEMIC LIFE AND PUBLIC FUNCTIONS

After completing his legal education in Lausanne and Berlin with a dissertation on the problem of State succession, Huber became a professor of international law, constitutional law, and canon law in Zurich in 1902. He was, at the age of 33, a member of the Swiss delegation to the Hague Peace Conference. He was disappointed with the realities of international power politics and particularly with the modest results in the field of pacific dispute settlement, where he had proposed what is now known as the 'optional clause' of article 36 (2) of the Statute of the International Court of Justice.[2] His essay of 1910 on the sociological foundations of international law, which pioneered the sub-discipline of 'sociology of international law', reflects this experience. The essay also expresses hope, however, that internationalist movements such as pacifism, which inspired the Conference, might contribute to a developed international consciousness, which he deemed highly necessary.

After the First World War, Huber took on several important public functions. As a member of the so-called Commission of Jurists of the League of Nations in the *Aaland Case* in 1920, he greatly influenced the commission's report, a milestone in the development of the principle of self-determination of peoples. There are remarkable connections between Huber's theoretical positions and the then surprising findings of the Commission.[3] After stepping down from his academic position in Zurich, he became a judge at the Permanent Court of International Justice, where he presided from 1925 to 1927. His casting vote as President in the *Lotus Case* (1927), commonly regarded as the main authority for the principle *in dubio pro libertate* in international law, and his dissenting opinion in the *Wimbledon Case* (1923), which he drafted jointly with his colleague and friend Dionisio Anzilotti, were his most important contributions to the Court's jurisprudence.[4]

Huber's name also became synonymous with the arbitral decision in the *Island of Palmas Case* (1928), one of the most influential arbitral decisions ever.[5] The award

---

[2] D Schindler 'Max Huber—His Life' (2007) 18 European Journal of International Law 81–95 at 88.

[3] League of Nations 'Report of the International Committee of Jurists Entrusted by the Council of the League of Nations with the Task of Giving an Advisory Opinion upon the Legal Aspects of the Aaland Islands Question' in Official Journal of the League of Nations, Special Supplement No 3 October 1920; O Diggelmann 'The Aaland Case and the Sociological Approach to International Law' (2007) 18 European Journal of International Law 135–43.

[4] O Spiermann 'Max Huber at the Permanent Court of International Justice' (2007) European Journal of International Law 115–33.

[5] DE Khan 'Max Huber as Arbitrator: The Palmas (Miangas) Case and Other Arbitrations' (2007) 18 European Journal of International Law 145–70.

fleshed out the principles of territorial ownership and elaborated on the notion of inter-temporal law. As a sole arbitrator, Huber had contributed some years earlier to the development of the principles guiding State responsibility with his decision in the *British Claims in the Spanish Zone of Morocco Arbitration* (1923–25). The case dealt, *inter alia*, with the question of internationally wrongful acts of territory owners.

From 1928 to 1946, Huber acted as President of the International Committee of the Red Cross.[6] The organization was awarded the Noble Peace Price in 1944; it did not escape, however, subsequent criticism for not having protested vigorously enough against the extermination of the Jewish people.

3. CONCEPT OF INTERNATIONAL LAW

3.1. State and State Society

The concept of international law and international relations set out by Huber in 1910 combines realistic with idealistic elements.[7] Huber considers, in line with pre-First World War doctrine, States as the sole international actors and subjects of international law. Nations and nation states are in his view communities in the sense of Ferdinand Tönnies; they are built on a strong and natural sense of belonging and thereby 'naturally given units'. States develop out of the wish of nations to organize themselves politically.

In contrast, the international society is a society of naturally egotistic participants. It is characterized by a tendency of its members to expand, and peace is fragile. Huber insists, however, that the degree of state egotism is variable.[8] It is here that idealist thought enters his concept. The degree varies mainly according to the individual's attitude towards the State (*Staatsbewusstsein*), and exaggerated state egotism is the result of reckless mass suggestions by powerful classes. Huber's view is influenced on one hand by Gustave Le Bon's theory of the crowd, and on the other by elements of Marxist thought.

---

[6] Y Sandoz 'Max Huber and the Red Cross' (2007) 18 European Journal of International Law 191–7.

[7] For a concise summary of Huber's concept see J Delbrück 'Max Huber's Sociological Approach to International Law Revisited' (2007) 18 European Journal of International Law 97–113.

[8] *Soziologischen Grundlagen* (n 1) 73–4.

3.2. Binding Force of International Law

Huber criticizes positivist doctrine for deriving the binding force of international law in an overly simplistic manner from consensus. In his view, consensus theories cannot explain why States can withdraw from some international agreements while at the same time being permanently bound by others. To solve this problem, he suggests distinguishing the question of the binding force of international law in general from that of concrete norms.[9] He makes a distinction between 'collective' and 'particular' interests of States and claims that the legally binding nature of international law in general depends on the existence of a collective interest in its binding character. Concrete norms become 'law' when they are covered by these collective interests.

Collective interests are, however, not naturally given facts. They result from specific circumstances that deserve closer analysis. Collective interests in binding international law typically develop when no State is capable of imposing its will on the other States and when there is a balance of power among the great powers. The latter are, in Huber's view, informal 'representatives' of the State society.[10]

International law in Huber's concept is pure power-based law. It therefore tends to emancipate itself from the social reality less than municipal law but adapts itself constantly to changing circumstances.[11] Later in his life, Huber felt uneasy with this position and moved away from his strictly power-oriented concept of law.

3.3. International Integration

One of the most interesting parts of Huber's essay is devoted to the question of international integration.[12] In his view, integration results either from hegemony or from solidarity. As there was in this period no clear hegemonic power, integration could only be promoted by strengthening solidarity. Huber the liberal considers international trade as key to promoting bonds of solidarity between the States.[13] He refers to the then very influential sociological theory of Herbert Spencer, and sees a direct correlation between the growth of population ('densification') inside States and the growth of international solidarity based on increasing interests in international trade.

The second factor in promoting international solidarity is transnational movements. Huber acknowledges the important role of movements such as socialism and pacifism in changing the way people think.

---

[9] ibid 52–3.   [10] ibid 53.   [11] ibid 8–10.   [12] ibid 53.   [13] ibid 61.

4. CONCLUSION

Huber was the first theorist of international law to analyse the influence of socio-psychological factors on the development of international law and the maintenance of peace. He recognized the crucial role of transnational movements and elaborated a theory of the legally binding character of international law. Elements of his writing were further developed by Dietrich Schindler Sr in his lecture at the Hague Academy in 1933 entitled *Contribution à l'étude des facteurs sociologiques et psychologiques du droit international*, which became a classic text of 20th-century international legal theory.

Huber, who devoted only a relatively small part of his life to academic work, did not found a school of thought, strictly speaking. Nevertheless he influenced international lawyers of later generations such as Dietrich Schindler Jr and Daniel Thürer. Huber may, as the Dutch international lawyer Jan Klabbers put it, be considered a founding father of the science of international law.[14]

RECOMMENDED READING

Huber, Max 'Beiträge zur Kenntnis der soziologischen Grundlagen des Völkerrechts und der Staatengesellschaft' (1910) 4 Jahrbuch des öffentlichen Rechts 56–134, reprinted as: *Die soziologischen Grundlagen des Völkerrechts* (Verlag Dr Walter Rothschild Berlin-Grunewald 1928).

Huber, Max *Die Staatensuccession—Völkerrechtliche und staatsrechtliche Praxis* (Duncker & Humblot Leipzig 1998).

Delbrück, Jost 'Max Huber's Sociological Approach to International Law Revisited' (2007) 18 European Journal of International Law 97–113.

Diggelmann, Oliver *Anfänge der Völkerrechtssoziologie—Die Völkerrechtskonzeptionen von Max Huber und Georges Scelle im Vergleich* (Schulthess Zurich 2000).

Diggelmann, Oliver 'The Aaland Case and the Sociological Approach to International Law' (2007) 18 European Journal of International Law 135–43.

Khan, Daniel-Erasmus 'Max Huber as Arbitrator: The Palmas (Miangas) Case and Other Arbitrations' (2007) 18 European Journal of International Law 145–70.

Klabbers, Jan 'The Sociological Jurisprudence of Max Huber: An Introduction' (1992) 43 Austrian Journal of International Law 197–213.

Sandoz, Yves 'Max Huber and the Red Cross' (2007) 18 European Journal of International Law 171–97.

---

[14] J Klabbers 'The Sociological Jurisprudence of Max Huber: An Introduction' (1992) 43 Austrian Journal of International Law 197–213 at 197.

Schindler, Dietrich Jr 'Max Huber—His Life' (2007) 18 European Journal of International Law 81–95.

Spiermann, Ole 'Judge Max Huber at the Permanent Court of International Justice' (2007) 18 European Journal of International Law 115–33.

Thürer, Daniel 'Max Huber: A Portrait in Outline' (2007) 18 European Journal of International Law (2007) 69–80.

CHAPTER 62

GEORGES SCELLE (1878–1961)

OLIVER DIGGELMANN

1. INTRODUCTION

GEORGES Scelle was a French theorist of international law and a member of the International Law Commission of the United Nations. He advocated a radically anthropocentric theory of international law called 'methodological individualism', which focuses on actions and responsibilities of individuals and aims to demystify the State. His main work, *Précis de droit des gens*, and several other writings mainly of the 1930s contrast positive international law with 'objective law', which consists of the rules he deems required by social reality.[1] Well-known elements of his theory are his concept of *dédoublement fonctionnel* (role splitting) and his reflections on 'international constitutional law'.

2. ACADEMIC LIFE AND PUBLIC FUNCTIONS

When Scelle took up his legal studies in Paris in 1897, France was divided into a state-loyal and state-sceptical camp over the Dreyfus Affair.[2] Scelle belonged to the latter,

---

[1] G Scelle *Précis de droit des gens* (2 vols Sirey Paris 1932; 1934).
[2] A detailed biography and a thorough analysis of the political and intellectual background of Scelle's theory can be found in A Wüst *Das völkerrechtliche Werk von Georges Scelle im Frankreich der Zwischenkriegszeit* (Nomos Baden-Baden 2007) at 53–64.

and distrust of the powerful became the overarching theme of his intellectual and political life. His voluminous doctoral thesis on the Spanish slave trade from the 16th to the 18th century, which was published in 1906, dealt with legal as well as with economic aspects of the topic.[3] From 1908 to 1912, he took on short-term academic positions in Sofia, Dijon, and Lille, and in 1912, he joined the faculty in Dijon, where he stayed for two decades. From 1914 to 1918, he served in the French army, mainly as a legal expert.

After the First World War, Scelle started to intervene much more often in public debate. He criticized, for example, the French occupation of the Ruhr area in 1923 fiercely, and he ran the considerable risk of not being appointed full professor. In 1924, he was a member of the French delegation to the League of Nations, and between 1924 and 1925, he served in the cabinet of the French Minister of Labour. When the Ministry of Education wanted to appoint him lecturer at the Paris Law Faculty in 1925, right-wing students organized a strike that led to a closure of the faculty for several weeks. Even the French parliament had to deal with the *affaire Scelle*, which ended with his return to Dijon.[4]

Scelle became full professor in Dijon in 1927, where he concentrated on the elaboration of his theory. He built it on ideas that were largely already contained in an essay published in 1923.[5] In 1933, he was elected member of the Paris Law Faculty, where he stayed until his retirement in 1948. From 1948 to 1960, he was a member—and temporarily the president—of the International Law Commission of the United Nations.

3. Concept of International Law

3.1. Objective and Positive Law

Scelle's theory is essentially a normative counter-model to positive international law. He calls the benchmark for assessing positive law 'objective law', a term he borrows from the French constitutional lawyer Léon Duguit. 'Objective law' consists of the rules that correspond with essential social needs. It is therefore of 'biological origin', as it reflects the living conditions of man.

---

[3] G Scelle *La traite négrière aux Indes de Castilles—Contrats et traités d'assiento* (2 vols Larose & Tenin Paris 1906).

[4] M Koskenniemi *The Gentle Civilizer of Nations—The Rise and Fall of International Law 1870–1960* (CUP Cambridge 2001) at 316–17.

[5] G Scelle 'Essai de systématique du droit international—Plan d'un cours de droit international' (1923) 30 Revue Générale de Droit International Public 116–42.

The term 'competence' is a key element in Scelle's theory. Objective law requires not absolute, abstract rights, which are detached from the prevailing circumstances, but specific 'competences' of individuals adapted to concrete contexts.[6] Competences are exercised by individuals, not by abstract units such as States which in Scelle's view are fictions of positive law, devised for practical purposes.

Objective law in the sense described exists in any society: in national and international, private and public societies. There is a unity of law in the sense that objective law is always of the same 'biological origin'. This unity is the background against which Scelle adheres to a radically monistic concept of international law that denies essential differences between international and domestic law.

Positive law—that is, the rules which are legally binding in the conventional sense—is a 'translation' of objective law into 'sanctioned competences'. The translation can be made correctly or incorrectly as, for example, when there is not enough information available or when legal consciousness is underdeveloped. The result of incorrect translations is in Scelle's terms 'anti-social' or 'anti-juridical' law. The concept of sovereignty is in his view an example of anti-social positive law.[7] Scelle analyses the translation of objective into positive law in detail. He calls the process, which in his understanding is a strictly scientific process, 'legal technique'. Politics is merely an element in this process which should be as precise as possible.

The crucial question about Scelle's theory is, of course, which rules one may call objective law: which are required by 'social necessity'? The criteria seem vague and lend themselves to being occupied by one's political convictions. Scelle is a consequent leftwinger: he regards those rules as socially necessary that correspond with the requirements of solidarity.

3.2. International Law and 'Role Splitting'

In Scelle's view, there is in the international sphere a constant increase in the number of societies. He considers not only the creation of public societies such as the League of Nations as relevant, but also that of private societies. He mentions, for example, the international movement of workers and the Catholic Church.[8] The increasing number of societies is mainly the result of the increasing division of labour across borders. This leads, according to Scelle, to a progressive form of solidarity, to interdependence based on cooperation. In contrast, solidarity on the grounds of similarity, which is another form of solidarity, is in his view an archaic phenomenon. He takes

---

[6] G Scelle 'Règles Générales du droit de la paix' (1933) 46 Recueil des cours 331–703.
[7] *Précis* (n 1) vol 1, at 78–81.
[8] ibid vii.

the distinction between the two forms of solidarity from the sociological theory of Emile Durkheim who was then very influential in France.

Scelle considers the translation of objective into positive law in the international sphere as particularly cumbersome. The main reason is the under-developed institutional framework in which it occurs. The process often leads to antisocial law, as, for example, when decisions that affect other States are taken unilaterally. With a view to solving this problem, Scelle develops his well-known concept of *dédoublement fonctionnel* ('role splitting') to assure 'correct' translations.[9] This concept claims in essence that State governments are required by objective law to act in the international sphere not only as representatives of their States, but also of the concerned international societies that lack own representatives.

What is the relationship between the objective laws of the several societies? Many of them overlap so that the problem of collisions of norms arises. Scelle's answer is clear cut: more inclusive societies are always superior to less inclusive ones, and their law is superior to the law of the latter. There is a strict hierarchy between the legal systems, and international law is always superior to domestic law, as its social substratum is more inclusive. The highest legal system is the law of the most inclusive society, the world society. Scelle calls the elemental legal rules of this society 'international constitutional law'.[10]

4. Conclusion

Scelle's radically anti-voluntaristic and anti-positivist concept did not found a school of thought named after him. The main reason may be that his concept was only capable to a limited degree of describing a reality in which States continue to play the key role. Nevertheless Scelle's thought, and in particular his well-developed sense of the shortcomings of positive law, influenced a series of 20th-century French authors such as René-Jean Dupuy, Charles Rousseau, and Georges Burdeau.

Scelle's theory has gained the reputation of a 'modern' approach to international law. It deserves this label, despite its under-theorized notion of law, insofar as it was in line with the 'mega-trend' of the increasingly important role of the individual in international law. The theory is also sensitive to the important question of collisions

---

[9] A Cassese 'Remarks on Scelle's Theory of "Role Splitting" (dédoublement fonctionnel) in International Law' (1990) 1 European Journal of International Law 210–31.

[10] G Scelle 'Le droit constitutionnel international' in J Duquesne (ed) *Mélanges R. Carré de Malberg* (Librairie du Recueil Sirey Paris 1933) 501–16.

of legal systems, though Scelle's answer is simplistic. Scelle's reflections on 'international constitutional law' became particularly popular at the end of the last century when the search for hierarchical elements in international law intensified in the era of globalization.

Recommended Reading

Scelle, Georges 'Essai de systématique du droit international—Plan d'un cours de droit international' (1923) 30 Revue Générale de Droit International Public 116–42.

Scelle, Georges *Précis de droit des gens* (2 vols Sirey Paris 1932; 1934).

Scelle, Georges *Générales du droit de la paix* (1933) 46 Recueil des cours 331–703.

Scelle, Georges 'Théorie du gouvernement international' (1935) Annuaire de l'Institut International de Droit Public 41–112.

Cassese, Antonio 'Remarks on Scelle's Theory of "Role Splitting" (dédoublement fonctionnel) in International Law' (1990) 1 European Journal of International Law 210–31.

Diggelmann, Oliver *Anfänge der Völkerrechtssoziologie—Die Völkerrechtskonzeptionen von Max Huber und Georges Scelle im Vergleich* (Schulthess Zurich 2000).

Dupuy, René-Jean 'Images de Georges Scelle' (1990) 1 European Journal of International Law 235–40.

Koskenniemi, Martti *The Gentle Civilizer of Nations—The Rise and Fall of International Law 1870–1960* (CUP Cambridge 2001) at 327–38.

Tanca, Antonio 'Georges Scelle (1878–1961): Biographical Note with Bibliography' (1990) 1 European Journal of International Law 165–74.

Thierry, Hubert 'The Thought of Georges Scelle' (1990) 1 European Journal of International Law 193–209.

Wüst, Anja *Das völkerrechtliche Werk von Georges Scelle im Frankreich der Zwischenkriegszeit* (Nomos Baden-Baden 2007).

CHAPTER 63

HANS KELSEN
(1881–1973)

BARDO FASSBENDER

Hans Kelsen (1881–1973) is one of the most significant legal scholars of the 20th century. His work has been studied wherever legal theory is studied. It has been particularly influential in Europe and Latin America. Kelsen will be first and foremost remembered as a theorist and philosopher who renewed legal positivism and found new answers to the fundamental question of how law is to be constructed and understood. He gained a worldwide reputation for his 'pure theory of law' (*Reine Rechtslehre*)—a view of law 'purified of all political ideology and all elements of natural sciences',[1] and encompassing the whole body of law, private and public, national and international. He insisted, as Hedley Bull put it, that 'legal issues should be separated from other normative issues, and that law is a distinct science that should not be confused with morals, sociology, or politics', however important those may be for understanding the role of law in society.[2]

---

[1] H Kelsen *Reine Rechtslehre. Einleitung in die rechtswissenschaftliche Problematik* (Franz Deuticke Leipzig 1934) iii; translation: *Introduction to the Problems of Legal Theory* (B Litschewski Paulson and SL Paulson trans) (Clarendon Oxford 1992). A second, completely revised and considerably enlarged edition was published in 1960 (Deuticke Wien); translation: *Pure Theory of Law* (Max Knight trans) (University of California Press Berkeley 1967). See also H Kelsen *General Theory of Law and State* (Harvard University Press Cambridge MA 1945).

[2] H Bull 'Kelsen and International Law' in R Tur and W Twining (eds) *Essays on Kelsen* (Clarendon Oxford 1986) 321–36 at 331.

Kelsen was one of only a few scholars who systematically paid regard to international law in the framework of a general theory of law. In addition, a substantial part of his work of the 1930s and 1940s was devoted to the then-pressing problems of international law, in particular the maintenance of international peace through international organization(s) and international courts.[3] In many ways, Kelsen's ideas and view on international law proved prescient, anticipating a world characterized by a network of ever closer and more intense and reliable international relations.

Kelsen was born in Prague and raised in Vienna.[4] He studied law at the University of Vienna and obtained his doctoral degree in 1906. After a one-year-long internship with the Viennese courts he went to Heidelberg to write his *Habilitationsschrift* about 'central problems of constitutional doctrine as developed from the theory of the legal rule'.[5] In 1911, he became a *Privatdozent* in Vienna for constitutional law and jurisprudence. A year later he married Margarethe (Grete) Bondi (1890–1973). At the time of the First World War, when he did his military service in the government and the judiciary, he wrote his first book on an issue of international law: *The Problem of Sovereignty and the Theory of International Law.*[6] That very issue would be on his mind all through his life. In the book's subtitle, Kelsen's famous notion of the 'pure theory of law' appeared for the first time. In 1919, Kelsen contributed to the drafting of the new Austrian republican constitution promulgated in 1920. Following his proposals, a constitutional court was established, independent of the ordinary courts, and with an exclusive competence to review laws adopted by parliament with regard to their constitutionality, which served as a model for similar courts, especially in Europe. Kelsen was appointed as a judge of that court for life. Having obtained a chair in constitutional law and administrative law in 1919, Kelsen taught in Vienna until 1930 when he accepted an offer from the University of Cologne. His decision to leave Vienna was induced by serious verbal assaults from Catholic and anti-Semitic circles and by his removal from the Constitutional Court as a consequence of a constitutional amendment. In Cologne, Kelsen taught international law and legal philosophy.

---

[3] For an analysis of Kelsen's work in international law, see A Rub *Hans Kelsens Völkerrechtslehre* (Schulthess Zürich 1995); J von Bernstorff *The Public International Law Theory of Hans Kelsen: Believing in Universal Law* (CUP Cambridge 2010).

[4] The only Kelsen biography is still RA Métall *Hans Kelsen: Leben und Werk* (Deuticke Wien 1969) (with a list of Kelsen's publications at 122–55; a supplement to that list was published in A Merkl et al (eds) *Festschrift für Hans Kelsen zum 90. Geburtstag* (Deuticke Wien 1971) at 325–26). See also H Kelsen 'Autobiographie (1947)' in H Kelsen *Werke* (M Jestaedt ed) (Mohr Siebeck Tübingen 2007) vol 1, 29–91. The same book includes photographs of Kelsen and his family at 109–32. To listen to Kelsen's farewell lecture of 1952 'What is Justice?', visit the UC Berkeley's website 'Graduate Council Lectures' at <grad.berkeley.edu/lectures/> (5 March 2012).

[5] H Kelsen *Hauptprobleme der Staatsrechtslehre, entwickelt aus der Lehre vom Rechtssatze* (JCB Mohr Tübingen 1911).

[6] H Kelsen *Das Problem der Souveränität und die Theorie des Völkerrechts. Beitrag zu einer reinen Rechtslehre* (JCB Mohr Tübingen 1920).

In 1933, after Hitler had come to power, Kelsen was dismissed from his chair as a prominent defender of parliamentary democracy and because of his Jewish descent.[7] The only colleague not signing a petition of the Cologne law faculty on his behalf was Carl Schmitt, whose appointment Kelsen had supported in spite of fundamental scientific and political differences of opinion. Kelsen went to Geneva where he taught until 1940 at the *Institut universitaire des hautes études internationales.*[8] In 1936, Kelsen was appointed professor at the (German) University of Prague.[9] He wanted to combine his work there with that in Geneva. But once more anti-Semitic and National Socialist circles turned against him. Under the most difficult circumstances Kelsen could only teach in Prague for three semesters (winter 1936–37, summer 1937, and winter 1937–38).[10] In June 1940, Kelsen and his wife left Geneva for the United States. In 1941, Kelsen delivered the Oliver Wendell Holmes Lectures at Harvard Law School about 'Law and Peace in International Relations'.[11] His hope to get a permanent position at Harvard, which in 1933 had awarded him an honorary doctorate, was not realized. From the spring of 1942 onward, he taught international law and jurisprudence at the political science department of the University of California at Berkeley, first as a visiting professor, then as a lecturer (1943–45), and finally as a full professor. In his autobiography, he wrote somewhat sadly: 'With my pure theory of law, I'd better fit in with a law school. But American law schools do not have a particular interest in an academic theory of law.'[12] He retired in 1951 and died in 1973 in California, only three months after his wife who had shared his life for more than sixty years. His last monograph, a general theory of (legal, moral, and logic) norms, was published posthumously in 1979.[13]

Before Kelsen came to Cologne in 1930, he had dealt with international law mainly in the context of constructive problems, in particular the notion of state sovereignty, the relationship between domestic law and international law, and the problem of sanctions.[14] It was in Cologne, where he had to teach international law in the first place, that he began studying 'positive' international law. From now on, international law was the only field of law current problems of which he addressed in his

---

[7] For details, see O Lepsius 'Hans Kelsen und der Nationalsozialismus' in R Walter, W Ogris and T Olechowski (eds) *Hans Kelsen: Leben—Werk—Wirksamkeit* (Manz Wien 2009) 271–87.

[8] Cf N Bersier Ladavac *Hans Kelsen à Genève (1933–1940)* (Thémis Genève 1996).

[9] In 1882, the Charles-Ferdinand University (*Universitas Carolo Ferdinandea*) had been divided into a German and a Czech university. In 1920, the Czech university was named Charles University.

[10] Cf J Osterkamp 'Hans Kelsen in der Tschechoslowakei' in *Hans Kelsen* (n 7) 305–18.

[11] H Kelsen *Law and Peace in International Relations: The Oliver Wendell Holmes Lectures, 1940–41* (Harvard University Press Cambridge MA 1948).

[12] 'Autobiographie' (n 4) 90.

[13] H Kelsen *Allgemeine Theorie der Normen* (K Ringhofer and R Walter eds) (Manz Wien 1979).

[14] *Das Problem der Souveränität* (n 6); H Kelsen 'Les rapports de système entre le droit interne et le droit international public' (1926) 14 Recueil des cours 227–331; H Kelsen 'Théorie générale du droit international public—Problèmes choisis' (1932) 42 Recueil des cours 117–351; H Kelsen 'Unrecht und Unrechtsfolge im Völkerrecht' (1932) 12 Zeitschrift für öffentliches Recht 481–608.

publications. His work now turned to the League of Nations and the Peace Treaties of 1919–20 (Versailles, Saint Germain, Sèvres), the international judiciary, and the problem of disarmament.[15] Understandably, the focus of his work on international law increased during his Geneva years. In a book of 1939, a precursor of his later commentary of the United Nations Charter, he criticized the many mistakes which in his view had been made in the drafting of the Covenant of the League, and suggested improvements.[16] During the Second World War, Kelsen almost naturally moved on to projecting a new world organization to replace the League of Nations. Another issue attracting his attention at that time was the responsibility of individuals for war crimes.[17] Here again a topical practical problem (how to deal with Germany's and Japan's political and military leadership after the war) raised a 'larger' and more fundamental question—that of the place of the individual in the international legal order, and of the duties of the individual directly imposed by international law. In the spring of 1945, Kelsen was appointed advisor to the United Nations War Crimes Commission. He was not consulted in the process of drafting the UN Charter either before or during the San Francisco Conference.

Beginning in 1944, Kelsen devoted a row of articles to the new United Nations Organisation and its Charter (dealing with issues like the functions of the UN, sanctions under the Charter, or the organization and procedure of the Security Council), and established himself as a leading exegete of the new Charter law. His studies led to his impressive work *The Law of the United Nations: A Critical Analysis of Its Fundamental Problems*,[18] published in 1950 with the help of Georg Schwarzenberger and his London Institute of World Affairs. Faithful to his theory of law, Kelsen wrote in the book's preface:

This book is a juristic—not a political—approach to the problems of the United Nations. It deals with the law of the Organisation, not with its actual or desired role in the international play of powers. Separation of law from politics in the presentation of national or international problems is possible in so far as law is not an end in itself, but a means or…a specific social technique for the achievement of ends determined by politics.[19]

Kelsen described his primary task as examining whether the Charter was 'consistent in itself', or 'unambiguous'. It does not come as a surprise that the result of this

---

[15]   See B Fassbender 'Hans Kelsen und die Vereinten Nationen' in PM Dupuy et al (eds) *Common Values in International Law: Essays in Honour of Christian Tomuschat* (NP Engel Kehl 2006) 763–84 at 765–7.

[16]   H Kelsen *Legal Technique in International Law: A Textual Critique of the League Covenant* (Geneva Research Centre Geneva 1939).

[17]   H Kelsen *Peace through Law* (The University of North Carolina Press Chapel Hill 1944) at 69–124 ('Peace guaranteed by individual responsibility for violations of international law').

[18]   H Kelsen *The Law of the United Nations: A Critical Analysis of Its Fundamental Problems* (Stevens & Sons London and FA Praeger New York 1950). In 1951, Kelsen added a supplement *Recent Trends in the Law of the United Nations*. See also Kelsen's later monographic work, based on lectures at the US Naval War College in 1953–54, *Collective Security under International Law* (US Government Printing Office Washington 1957).

[19]   ibid xiii.

examination was negative. The author regretted 'the general tendency which prevailed in drafting the Charter—the predominance of the political over the legal approach'.[20] Kelsen summarized his work on a theory and the general principles of international law in a treatise published in 1952.[21]

Kelsen's work has had a strong impact on international law in the decades following the Second World War. It was continued and developed by his students Adolf Merkl, Alfred Verdross, Leo Gross, Alf Ross, and Josef L Kunz.[22] But beyond this, and perhaps more importantly, Kelsen influenced the post-war science of international law in consequence of a peculiar amalgam of his legal theory and his political goals (a peaceful world governed by law) in the minds of his readers, a mélange which stands in marked contrast to his postulate of a strict separation of law and politics. Kelsen's demystification of the State paved the way for a recognition of an international legal personality of non-state actors, especially individuals, and their ensuing responsibility for violations of international law. His monistic proposition that domestic law and international law are not 'intrinsically different' in character (as claimed by the then dominant dualist theory) but that they both regulate human behaviour facilitated the expansion of international law into all areas of human life. Today, many scholars of international law understand sovereignty in the way Kelsen defined it in 1944: as 'the legal authority of the States under the authority of international law'.[23] Another example of a theory of Kelsen's (borrowed from Adolf Merkl)[24] which has been widely accepted is the notion of the *Stufenbau des Rechts* (law as a set of steps), according to which the municipal law of a State represents nothing but one of many steps of a universal legal order. As such, it does not have a different quality than local or provincial law ('below' the level of the State), or the law of associations or confederations of States ('above' that level).[25] Furthermore, in many respects today's 'international community school' in international law draws on Kelsen's legacy which is also one of the roots of the idea of a 'constitutionalization' of international law. Kelsen's strong interest in the UN Charter in his writings after 1945 raised awareness of

---

[20] ibid 735.

[21] H Kelsen *Principles of International Law* (Rinehart New York 1952; 2nd edn RW Tucker Holt ed Rinehart and Winston New York 1966).

[22] For writings of Verdross and Merkl in the field of international law, see HR Klecatsky, R Marcic, and H Schambeck (eds) *Die Wiener rechtstheoretische Schule—Schriften von Hans Kelsen, Adolf Merkl, Alfred Verdross* (Europa Verlag Wien and Pustet Salzburg 1968, 2nd edn Franz Steiner Stuttgart and Verlag Österreich Wien 2010) vol 2, pt 4. For short biographies of Gross, Ross, and Kunz, see R Walter, C Jabloner, and K Zeleny (eds) *Der Kreis um Hans Kelsen—Die Anfangsjahre der Reinen Rechtslehre* (Manz Wien 2008) at 115–33, 243–59, and 409–43.

[23] H Kelsen 'The Principle of Sovereign Equality of States as a Basis for International Organisation' (1944) 53 Yale Law Journal 207–20 at 208.

[24] See M Borowski 'Die Lehre vom Stufenbau des Rechts nach Adolf Julius Merkl' in SL Paulson and M Stolleis (eds) *Hans Kelsen* (Mohr Siebeck Tübingen 2005) 122–59.

[25] See H Kelsen 'Souveränität, völkerrechtliche' in K Strupp (ed) *Wörterbuch des Völkerrechts und der Diplomatie* (de Gruyter Berlin 1925) vol 2, 554–9 at 554.

the eminent importance of that constitutional document as a foundation of the post-war international legal order.

In a photo taken on his 90th birthday in October 1971,[26] less than two years before his death, Kelsen looks a bit tired but content. He had done what he could do to foster a world order which he tentatively had described in his 1952 farewell lecture at Berkeley in the following words: 'I cannot say what justice is, the absolute justice for which mankind is longing. I must acquiesce in a relative justice and I can only say what justice is to me.…."My" justice, then, is the justice of freedom, the justice of peace, the justice of democracy—the justice of tolerance.'[27]

RECOMMENDED READING

Bernstorff, Jochen von *The Public International Law Theory of Hans Kelsen: Believing in Universal Law* (CUP Cambridge 2010).

Bull, Hedley 'Hans Kelsen and International Law' in Richard Tur and William Twining (eds) *Essays on Kelsen* (Clarendon Press Oxford 1986) 321–36.

Rub, Alfred *Hans Kelsens Völkerrechtslehre: Versuch einer Würdigung* (Schulthess Zürich 1995).

[26] Reproduced in *Werke* (n 4) at 132.

[27] H Kelsen 'What is Justice?' in H Kelsen *What is Justice? Justice, Law, and Politics in the Mirror of Science: Collected Essays* (University of California Press Berkeley 1957) 1–24 at 24.

CHAPTER 64

··

CARL SCHMITT
(1888–1985)

··

BARDO FASSBENDER

CARL Schmitt (1888–1985) was one of the most influential German legal scholars and political theorists of the 20th century. While the focus of his work was constitutional law, legal theory, and philosophy, he also had a strong influence on the jurisprudence of international law, perhaps less so via those of his writings mainly devoted to issues of international law than because of the impact of his general ideas and concepts, such as the distinction of friend and foe, the state of exception, the juxtaposition of legitimacy and legality, or the Hobbesian nexus between protection and obedience. In past decades, Schmitt's thinking has fascinated lawyers and philosophers far beyond German-speaking countries and Europe.[1] This was no least because of his style, which was more literary than is usually encountered in legal writing, and for this he was noticed in wider intellectual and artistic circles, especially in the era of the Weimar Republic. Schmitt is a divisive and polarizing thinker who has been admired and praised by some, and sharply criticized and even condemned by others. A matter of particular controversy was his role in the Third Reich.

It is not easy to say why his 'thought has meant so much and so many seemingly contradictory things to so many'.[2] One answer may be that although a number of

---

[1] Cf PC Caldwell 'Controversies over Carl Schmitt: A Review of Recent Literature' (2005) 77 Journal of Modern History 357–87. For a bibliography of Schmitt's works, including translations and secondary literature, see A de Benoist *Carl Schmitt: Internationale Bibliographie der Primär- und Sekundärliteratur* (Ares Graz 2010).

[2] JW Müller *A Dangerous Mind: Carl Schmitt in Post-War European Thought* (Yale University Press New Haven 2003) at 2.

fundamental beliefs and ideas pervade his work, most of his publications before 1945 were reactions to concrete situations and problems. Further, Schmitt 'was a thinker during a time of transition—and a thinker *of* the transition, in particular the transition from a European to a post-European age'.[3] As such, he could and did not aspire to systematic coherence but instead to intellectual stimulation and provocation. In addition, he preferred not to write meticulously researched articles. He wanted to say the unexpected.

Carl Schmitt was born in 1888 in Plettenberg, a small Catholic village in Westphalia, which at the time was one of the Western provinces of Prussia.[4] He studied law in Berlin, Munich, and Strasbourg where he obtained his legal doctorate in 1910 with a dissertation on a subject of criminal law. Six years later, also in Strasbourg, he submitted his *Habilitationsschrift* on 'The Worth of the State and the Importance of the Individual' and received the venia legendi for constitutional law and theory, administrative law, and international law. In 1919, Schmitt became a tenured lecturer (*Dozent*) in public law at the *Handelshochschule* (school of commerce) in Munich. In 1921, he gained his first chair at the University of Greifswald. Only a year later, he transferred to Bonn, the second largest and academically much more renowned Prussian university. It was during his years in Bonn that Schmitt earned his reputation as a leading constitutional lawyer of the Weimar Republic. In 1927, he published the first version of *Der Begriff des Politischen* (The Notion of the Political),[5] a pivotal text about the character of the political community and the State, and a year later his *Verfassungslehre*,[6] a theory of constitutional law centered on the German Constitution of 1919. To many, the latter book remained his most important work. In Bonn Schmitt also emerged as a Catholic thinker.[7] In 1928, he left Bonn for the *Handelshochschule* in Berlin, an institution of higher education founded in 1903 by Berlin trade and industry. In the fall of 1932, he accepted an offer by the University of Cologne. By the time he began teaching there in the summer of 1933, Hitler had come to power. In early 1933, Schmitt decided to approve the National Socialist takeover (which in 1932 he had actively tried to prevent by counselling the von Papen Government on the possibility

[3] ibid 245.

[4] For details of Schmitt's life and an overview of his work, see R Mehring *Carl Schmitt: Aufstieg und Fall—Eine Biographie* (CH Beck München 2009); JW Bendersky *Carl Schmitt: Theorist for the Reich* (Princeton University Press Princeton 1983); and P Noack *Carl Schmitt: Eine Biographie* (Propyläen Berlin 1993); see also *A Dangerous Mind* (n 2) 15–47.

[5] C Schmitt 'Der Begriff des Politischen' (1927) 58 Archiv für Sozialwissenschaft und Sozialpolitik 1–33. Later and amended editions appeared in 1932 (Duncker & Humblot Berlin) and 1933 (Hanseatische Verlagsanstalt Hamburg). Schmitt republished the 1932 version with additional chapters in 1963 (Duncker & Humblot Berlin). Translation: *The Concept of the Political* (G Schwab trans) (The University of Chicago Press Chicago 2007).

[6] C Schmitt *Verfassungslehre* (Duncker & Humblot München 1928); translation: *Constitutional Theory* (J Seitzer ed and trans) (Duke University Press Durham 2008).

[7] See, in particular, C Schmitt *Römischer Katholizismus und politische Form* (Jakob Hegner Hellerau 1923, 2nd edn Theatiner-Verlag München 1925); translation: *Roman Catholicism and Political Form* (GL Ulmen trans) (Greenwood Press Westport CT 1996).

of an indefinite dissolution of the Reichstag and measures to be taken against the Communist as well as the National Socialist Party), and to exploit the opportunities made possible by the new situation, both in terms of his influence as a political and legal thinker and his future career. He was 'underestimating the dynamism and revolutionary nature of the movement he was trying to serve and for which he was attempting to construct a legal framework'.[8] In April 1933 he joined the National Socialist Party; in July he was appointed member of the Prussian State Council by Göring in his capacity as Prime Minister of Prussia; in September he was offered a newly created chair in public law at the University of Berlin which he promptly accepted. After three-and-a-half years of intense support of National Socialist rule and ideology, including its anti-Semitic hatred, and a steep rise in the party organizations in the field of legal affairs and education, Schmitt was brought down in late 1936 by Himmler's SS which regarded him as an opportunist who lacked true National Socialist conviction and did not support the supremacy of the party over the State. He lost his party positions but not his chair which he retained until the end of the Second World War. In September 1945, he was arrested and, for more than a year, confined in US 'Civilian Detentions Camps' in Berlin. In March 1947, he was transferred as a possible defendant to Nuremberg where he was interrogated by the Assistant US Chief Counsel Robert Kempner. After his release in May 1947 he returned to his native Plettenberg to live there until his death in 1985. As opposed to the majority of law professors who had supported Hitler, Schmitt was not given a chance to teach again at a German university. However, he lectured in private circles, often invited by former students, and abroad (in particular in Spain), was visited by younger academics who cherished his knowledge, charm, and wit, and maintained an extensive correspondence.[9]

In 1940, Schmitt published a collection of articles which had appeared in law journals and newspapers since 1923 as *Positionen und Begriffe im Kampf mit Weimar, Geneva, Versailles*—'Positions and Notions in the Fight against Weimar, Genf and Versailles'.[10] The title expresses his philosophy. Like most German international lawyers of the time, he denounced the League of Nations as an imperialist instrument of Great Britain and France, designed to give the unjust 'Dictat of Versailles' the appearance of law, and to perpetuate the defeat of Germany. But more clearly than others he realized the consequences of a construction of the League as an 'ecumenical world order', and of the Covenant as 'higher' universal international law, for classical inter-state law and the idea of national autonomy. To Schmitt, pacifism

---

[8] *Carl Schmitt: Theorist for the Reich* (n 4) 210.

[9] See D van Laak *Gespräche in der Sicherheit des Schweigens: Carl Schmitt in der politischen Geistesgeschichte der frühen Bundesrepublik* (Akademie Verlag Berlin 1993).

[10] Hanseatische Verlagsanstalt Hamburg 1940, repr Duncker & Humblot Berlin 1988. For a new, annotated edition of Schmitt's writings on questions of international law (excluding the writings on the *Grossraum*), see C Schmitt *Frieden oder Pazifismus? Arbeiten zum Völkerrecht und zur internationalen Politik 1924–1978* (G Maschke ed) (Duncker & Humblot Berlin 2005).

was a dangerous and untruthful ideology because it depreciated classical inter-state war (which he saw as a necessary form of conflict between political communities), gave the Western powers controlling the League a cutting edge by cloaking their wars as 'police actions' executed in the name of humanity, and radicalized warfare by de-legitimizing the enemy and precluding the status of neutrality. Inter-state war, as a circumscribed and regulated form of political violence, was replaced by a total international civil war. To Schmitt, the entire construction of international law depended on how war was understood and defined. The most important writings of the 1920s and 1930s elaborating this belief are *Der Begriff des Politischen* and *Die Wendung zum diskriminierenden Kriegsbegriff* (The Turn to a Discriminating Notion of War) of 1938,[11] the latter being a critique of Scelle's and Lauterpacht's writings.

After the Second World War, Schmitt continued these studies in his short 'Theory of the Partisan' of 1963 which he labelled a (new) 'remark about the notion of the political'. In his introduction, he recalled the 'classical law of war' as a law characterized by clear distinctions between war and peace, combatants and non-combatants, the enemy and the criminal. 'War is conducted by a state against another state, as a war of regular armies and between sovereign holders of a *jus belli* who respect each other as enemies and do not disparage each other as criminals, so that it is possible to make peace'.[12] Against this background, he outlined the modern history of the partisan, as the epitome of the irregular fighter, from the Spanish guerilla war against the French Army (1808–13), to the wars in Indochina (1946–54), and Algeria (1954–62). 'The modern partisan', Schmitt observed, 'expects from his enemy neither justice nor mercy. He has turned away from the conventional enemy-ship of the tamed and hedged war and placed himself in the sphere of a different and real hostility which escalates through terror and anti-terror into extermination.'[13]

Beginning in 1939, Schmitt's publications focused on the themes of hegemony, the *Reich, Raum* (space), and *Grossraum* (grand space). Based on a lecture delivered at Kiel University on 1 April 1939—that is after the 'Anschluss' of Austria (1938) and the invasion of Czechoslovakia (March 1939) but before the German attack on Poland on 1 September 1939—he published the article *Völkerrechtliche Gross-raumordnung mit Interventionsverbot für raumfremde Mächte*.[14] Referring to the

---

[11] Duncker & Humblot München 1938, 2nd edn Duncker & Humblot Berlin 1988, reprinted in *Frieden oder Pazifismus?* (n 10) 518–66.

[12] C Schmitt *Theorie des Partisanen: Zwischenbemerkung zum Begriff des Politischen* (Duncker & Humblot Berlin 1963) at 16; translation: *Theory of the Partisan* (GL Ulmen trans) (Telos New York 2007).

[13] *Theorie des Partisanen* (n 12) 17.

[14] Deutscher Rechtsverlag Berlin and Wien 1939, 4th amended edn 1941 (repr Duncker & Humblot Berlin 1991). For an annotated edition of the 4th edition, see C Schmitt *Staat, Grossraum, Nomos: Arbeiten aus den Jahren 1916–1969* (G Maschke ed) (Duncker & Humblot Berlin 1995) 269–371.

American Monroe Doctrine as the 'original precedent' of the *Grossraum* principle in international law, he asserted the existence, and demanded the recognition, of a Central and Eastern European *Grossraum* controlled and protected by the German *Reich* in which foreign powers may not intervene. Instead of States, *Reiche* are said to be the new building blocks of international law. It is characteristic of Schmitt's writings that the exact consequences of this *Grossraum* idea, such as the legal status of the individual States and nations within the *Grossraum* or the importance of ethnical distinctions, are not spelled out. The State was not discarded but defended as a necessary 'element of order'. Unlike other and more radical international lawyers in Nazi Germany, Schmitt did not suggest the construction of international law as a system of relations between biologically and racially defined groups only ('völkisches Völkerrecht').[15]

Although in the years of the war Schmitt gave many lectures on the *Grossraum* topos, his research increasingly turned to historical subjects like the antagonism of land and sea, or land-based and maritime powers, in the development of international law.[16] His studies led to his book *Der Nomos der Erde im Völkerrecht des Jus Publicum Europaeum*[17] of 1950 in which Schmitt told an unconventional story of the rise and fall of the 'inter-state era of international law' (for him, the time between the 16th and the end of the 19th century). The book is a collection of essays grouped in the three parts: 'The Appropriation of the New World', 'The Jus Publicum Europaeum', and 'The Question of a New Nomos of the Earth'. Its main issue is the connection and correlation of law and territory, the dependence of any legal order on a concrete terrestrial existence ('Recht als Einheit von Ordnung und Ortung'). In the preface, Schmitt wrote: 'The former, Eurocentric order of international law is perishing today. With it, the old nomos of the earth is vanishing which had emerged from the fairytale-like and unexpected discovery of a New World, an unrepeatable historical event'. In the 1963 edition of *Der Begriff des Politischen*, Schmitt declared the 'epoch of the State' to be ending. In the final analysis, his work was driven by the question of what this supposed dissolution of the state, and of the legal notions both defining it and produced by it, means for constitutional and international law.

If Schmitt was an opportunist in the first years of Hitler's regime, he swam against the tide for most of his life before and after. Especially after 1945, he refused to make any concession to the *Zeitgeist* that dominated politics and legal science. He was fight-

[15] See DF Vagts 'International Law in the Third Reich' (1990) 84 American Journal of International Law 661–704 at 689.

[16] C Schmitt *Land und Meer: Eine weltgeschichtliche Betrachtung* (Reclam Leipzig 1942).

[17] Greven Verlag Köln 1950; repr Duncker & Humblot Berlin 1974; translation: *The Nomos of the Earth in the International Law of the Jus Publicum Europaeum* (GL Ulmen trans) (Telos New York 2003).

ing a lost cause, and he knew it. Schmitt can be read as an antidote to an overdose of liberal optimistic internationalism.

Recommended Reading

Bendersky, Joseph W *Carl Schmitt: Theorist for the Reich* (Princeton University Press Princeton, New Jersey 1983).

Hooker, William *Carl Schmitt's International Thought: Order and Orientation* (CUP Cambridge 2009).

Koskenniemi, Martti 'International Law as Political Theology: How to Read *Nomos der Erde*?' (2004) 11 Constellations 492–511.

Schwab, George *The Challenge of the Exception: An Introduction to the Political Ideas of Carl Schmitt between 1921 and 1936* (Duncker & Humblot Berlin 1970, Greenwood Press Westport 1989).

CHAPTER 65

HERSCH LAUTERPACHT (1897–1960)

IAIN SCOBBIE

HERSCH Lauterpacht was born on 16 August 1897 in Żółkiew in Eastern Galicia, part of the Austro-Hungarian Empire which reverted to Poland in 1919.[1] He died in London on 8 May 1960.

Between 1916 and 1917 he studied law at the University of Lemberg (Lwów), and from 1919 at the University of Vienna, graduating Doctor Jur in 1921, before being awarded a doctorate in political science in 1922 for a dissertation examining the League mandate system.[2] Hans Kelsen stated that Lauterpacht 'was one of my best students when I was teaching General Theory of State and Austrian Constitutional Law at the Law School of the University of Vienna'.[3]

In 1923, Lauterpacht entered the London School of Economics (LSE) as a research student, supervised by Arnold McNair who became a close friend. He gained an LLD

---

[1] E Lauterpacht *The Life of Hersch Lauterpacht* (CUP Cambridge 2010) at 17–18. Apart from his monographs, Lauterpacht's papers, published and unpublished, are compiled in E Lauterpacht (ed) *International Law: Being the Collected Papers of Hersch Lauterpacht* (5 vols CUP Cambridge 1970–2004).

[2] An English translation entitled 'The Mandate under International Law in the Covenant of the League of Nations', appears in *Collected Papers of Hersch Lauterpacht* (n 1), vol 3 (1977), 29–84.

[3] See RH Graveson and RY Jenninngs 'Tributes to Sir Hersch Lauterpacht (From Professor Hans Kelsen)' (1961) International and Comparative Law Quarterly 1–17 at 2–3; republished in (1997) 8 European Journal of International Law 309–12 at 309–10.

in 1925 for his dissertation, subsequently published as *Private Law Sources and Analogies of International Law* (1927). He became a member of the academic staff at the LSE, and published *The Function of Law in the International Community* (1933), which has been described as 'the most important English-language book on international law in the twentieth century'.[4] In 1937, Lauterpacht was appointed to the Whewell Chair of International Law at the University of Cambridge.

During the Second World War, Lauterpacht undertook two extensive trips to the United States, principally to lecture, but he also met Robert Jackson, then US Attorney-General. Lauterpacht proposed to Jackson that the trial of the major war criminals at Nuremberg adopt a tripartite structure, proceeding on the basis of allegations of crimes against peace, war crimes, and crimes against humanity. He suggested this last term as an alternative to 'atrocities', which Jackson wished to avoid.[5] Lauterpacht contributed substantially to the work of the British prosecution team at Nuremberg.[6]

In 1948, at the request of the UN Secretariat's Division of Codification, Lauterpacht proposed a list of topics to be codified by the International Law Commission (ILC), which it largely adopted.[7] He was appointed to the ILC in 1952, but resigned following his election to the International Court of Justice in 1954. Until his death in 1960, Lauterpacht participated in nine cases and advisory opinions. In most, he delivered individual opinions in accordance with his view that the role of the international judge is to develop the law. His last major work, *The Development of International Law by the International Court*, was published in 1958.

Lauterpacht's vision of international society was founded on the rule of law or, as Koskenniemi puts it, that 'international lawyers, in particular international judges, should rule the world'.[8] Lauterpacht's conception of the rule of law demonstrates the influence of his teacher, Kelsen, because of the centrality it accords to the notion that legal rules are abstract and only resolve into individual legal relations through judicial decision or the agreement of the parties:[9] thus, for Lauterpacht,

---

[4] M Koskenniemi 'The Function of Law in the International Community: 75 Years After' (2008) 79 British Yearbook of International Law 353–66 at 366.

[5] See *Life of Hersch Lauterpacht* (n 1) 272; M Koskenniemi 'Hersch Lauterpacht and the Development of International Criminal Law' (2004) 2 Journal of International Criminal Justice 810–25 at 811 and 814; W Schabas 'International Criminal Jurisdictions: Nuremberg to the Hague. Group Discussion' in J Crawford and M Young (eds) *The Function of Law in the International Community: An Anniversary Symposium* (Cambridge 2008), Proceedings of the 25th Anniversary Conference of the Lauterpacht Centre for International Law, at 2, at <www.lcil.cam.ac.uk/25th_anniversary/book.php> (accessed on 27 June 2012).

[6] See *Life of Hersch Lauterpacht* (n 1) 273–8; and 'Development of International Criminal Law' (n 5) 821–2.

[7] *Life of Hersch Lauterpacht* (n 1) 303–4; the proposed list of topics is reprinted in *Collected Papers of Hersch Lauterpacht* (1975) vol 1 (n 1) 445–530.

[8] 'Function of Law' (n 4) 366.

[9] See 'Kelsen's Pure Science of Law' reprinted in *Collected Papers of Hersch Lauterpacht* (1975) vol 2 (n 1) 404–30 at 410–11.

'judicial activity is essentially the last link in the chain of the crystallization of the rule of law'.[10] Despite Kelsen's influence, Lauterpacht was not a rigid positivist, as a thread of natural law runs through and unifies his work. He argued that the demands of morality moderate a strict positivist understanding of all forms of law,[11] and particularly of international law as it 'frequently lags behind morals to an extent unknown to the law obtaining within the State'.[12] For Lauterpacht, the individual was 'the ultimate unit of all law',[13] and that 'the State ... has no justification and no valid claim to obedience except as an instrument for securing the welfare of the individual human being'.[14]

Lauterpacht's concern for the individual bore practical fruit. In 1942, he was invited by the American Jewish Committee to write a monograph on the international law of human rights. This encompassed not only an enumeration of substantive human rights, but also the means for their international enforcement.[15] Published in 1945, around the time the UN Charter was being drafted, *An International Bill of the Rights of Man* was 'the first ever book on the subject'.[16] In 1947, Lauterpacht delivered lectures at the Hague Academy of International Law on the protection of human rights,[17] and was appointed as rapporteur to the International Law Association's committee on human rights. The Association adopted his report at its annual meeting in 1948. Simpson argues that the institutional structure contained in the European Convention of Human Rights was partially derived from Lauterpacht's work.[18]

Lauterpacht synthesized continental European and common law approaches to international law. Koskenniemi comments that the *Function of Law* 'could only have been written from the inside of the German tradition',[19] while Kammerhofer has noted that Lauterpacht's initial Austrian perspective was modified by pragmatism, probably prompted by McNair.[20] Indeed, when McNair was editor of *Oppenheim's*

---

[10] H Lauterpacht *The Function of Law in the International Community* (Clarendon Press Oxford 1933) at 102.

[11] See further I Scobbie 'The Theorist as Judge: Hersch Lauterpacht's Conception of the International Judicial Function' (1997) 8 European Journal of International Law 264–98 at 266–9. Apart from *The Function of Law in the International Community*, Lauterpacht's most important publication expressing his adherence to natural law is 'The Grotian Tradition in International Law' reprinted in *Collected Papers of Hersch Lauterpacht* (1975) vol 2 (n 1) 307–65.

[12] *The Function of Law* (n 10) vii.

[13] 'Grotian Tradition' (n 11) 336; see 333–9 generally.

[14] H Lauterpacht *International Law and Human Rights* (Praeger London 1950) at 80.

[15] *Life of Hersch Lauterpacht* (n 1) 251; see Chapter 8 generally.

[16] AWB Simpson 'Hersch Lauterpacht and the Genesis of the Age of Human Rights' (2004) 120 Law Quarterly Review 49–80 at 55; see also *Life of Hersch Lauterpacht* (n 1) 3.

[17] H Lauterpacht 'The International Protection of Human Rights' (1947-I) 70 Recueil des cours 5–108.

[18] 'Genesis of the Age of Human Rights' (n 16) 77; see 70–7 generally.

[19] *Function of Law* (n 4) 356.

[20] J Kammerhofer 'The Lauterpacht Tradition and its Successors: Towards Theory? Group Discussion' in *Anniversary Symposium* (n 5) at 2.

International Law, he engaged Lauterpacht as an assistant.[21] Lauterpacht subsequently edited it himself despite disagreeing with the extreme positivist method embodied in *Oppenheim's International Law.* Further, Lauterpacht and McNair jointly founded the *Annual Digest and Reports of Public International Law Cases* (subsequently the *International Law Reports*).[22] No doubt these experiences inculcated common law method into Lauterpacht's understanding of international law.

Nevertheless, at times Lauterpacht's 'foreign-ness', and commitment to human rights, engendered opposition within the British establishment. In 1946, Eric Beckett, then Legal Adviser to the Foreign Office, opposed Lauterpacht's nomination as the British representative to the UN Human Rights Commission:

> I think that Professor Lauterpacht would be a very bad candidate...It would be disastrous, I think, to make him a delegate. Professor Lauterpacht, though a distinguished and industrious international lawyer, is, when all is said and done, a Jew recently come from Vienna. Emphatically, I think that the representative of [the British government] on human rights must be a very English Englishman imbued throughout his life and hereditary to the real meaning of human rights as we understand this in this country.[23]

In 1946, Lauterpacht had been in Britain for twenty-three years, and naturalized for fifteen. Similarly, when he was being considered for nomination to the International Court, his views on human rights were again regarded apprehensively, with opposition coming from one official on the basis that the nominee should 'both be and be seen to be thoroughly British' which Lauterpacht was not 'either by birth, by name or by education'.[24] On that occasion, however, prejudice did not prevail.

Fifty years after his death, why does Lauterpacht have such an enduring legacy when other jurists of his generation no longer command the attention they once received?

This is due to the academic legacy of his writings and their vision of world order, the methodological and intellectual perspectives they embody. There is also his practical legacy, arising from his involvement in the Nuremberg trial; his groundbreaking work on human rights; his identification of the foundational issues of international law which required clarification by the ILC; and the influence of his judicial opinions. With Lauterpacht, however, it is false to separate the practical and the academic. At the heart of the invisible academy of international lawyers for decades, he endeavoured in all his work to put his theoretical vision into practice.

---

[21] *Life of Hersch Lauterpacht* (n 1) 49 and 51.
[22] *Life of Hersch Lauterpacht* (n 1) 50 and 67–70.
[23] Quoted in 'Genesis of the Age of Human Rights' (n 16) 64; and in *Life of Hersch Lauterpacht* (n 1) 258.
[24] *Life of Hersch Lauterpacht* (n 1) 376; see 375–7.

Recommended Reading

Lauterpacht, Hersch *The Function of Law in the International Community* (Clarendon Press Oxford 1933; OUP Oxford 2011).

Lauterpacht, Hersch (ed) *International Law: Being the Collected Papers of Hersch Lauterpacht* (5 vols CUP Cambridge 1970–2004).

Carty, Anthony 'Hersch Lauterpacht: A Powerful Eastern European Figure' (2007) 7 Baltic Yearbook of International Law 1–28.

Friedmann, Wolfgang G 'Sir Hersch Lauterpacht and the International Court' (1959) 45 Virginia Law Review 407–13.

Koskeniemmi, Martti 'Lauterpacht: The Victorian Tradition in International Law' (1997) 8 European Journal of International Law 216–63.

Koskeniemmi, Martti 'Hersch Lauterpacht (1897–1960)' in Jack Beatson and Reinhard Zimmermann (eds) *Jurists Uprooted: German-speaking Emigré Lawyers in Twentieth–century Britain* (OUP Oxford 2004).

Scobbie, Iain 'The Theorist as Judge: Hersch Lauterpacht's Conception of the International Judicial Function' (1997) 8 European Journal of International Law 264–98.

Simpson, AWB 'Hersch Lauterpacht and the Genesis of the Age of Human Rights' (2004) 120 Law Quarterly Review 49–80

Vrdoljak, Ana F 'Human Rights and Genocide: The Work of Lauterpacht and Lemkin in Modern International Law', (2009) 20 European Journal of International Law 1163–94.

INDEX

IL = international law